C0-APZ-949

Sander's List of

ORCHID HYBRIDS

ADDENDUM

1971–1975

containing the

Names and Parentage of all
ORCHID HYBRIDS

registered from 1st January 1971 to 31st December 1975

Compiled and Listed in
Tabular Alphabetical Form by

THE ROYAL HORTICULTURAL
SOCIETY

as

International Authority for the Registration of Orchid Hybrids

Sole Publishers
© THE ROYAL HORTICULTURAL SOCIETY
Vincent Square, London, SW1P 2PE

ISBN 0 900629 851

Printed in Great Britain at
The Spottiswoode Ballantyne Press
by William Clowes and Sons, Limited,
London, Colchester and Beccles

CONTENTS

THE REGISTRATION OF ORCHID HYBRIDS

In 1895 Messrs. Sander & Sons, Orchid Growers, of St. Albans, England, instituted a system for the registration of orchid hybrids and in due course published in 1906 the first issue of *Sander's List of Orchid Hybrids*. At intervals of subsequent years several volumes of addenda have been published and orchid hybridists throughout the world remain greatly indebted to the Sander Family for the initiative taken in providing a most valuable service.

Owing to the great increase in the number of hybridists in recent years which had in turn led to a correspondingly large increase in the work of registration, Messrs David Sander's Orchids Ltd., expressed a desire to be relieved of the work. At the third World Orchid Conference in London, in May, 1960, it was recommended and subsequently agreed that The Royal Horticultural Society should assume the duties of International Registration Authority for Orchid Hybrids, in accordance with the provisions of the International Code of Nomenclature for Cultivated Plants.

These duties were taken over by The Royal Horticultural Society with effect from January 1st, 1961, and in accordance with the obligations accepted as *International Registration Authority*, the Society has agreed to publish, from time to time, a list of all registrations accepted after December 31st, 1960. In order to maintain continuity, the title *Sander's List of Orchid Hybrids* is retained.

Anyone who wishes to register an orchid hybrid should do so with the Registrar of Orchid Hybrids, The Royal Horticultural Society, Vincent Square, London SW1P 2PE, using a form which may be obtained from the Registrar. The fee for each registration is printed on the current form.

A form is also available for the convenience of applicants who wish to have a written record of permission-to-register, from the originator of the cross. (See *Handbook on Orchid Nomenclature and Registration*, Second Edition (1976), Part VIII, para 6 (c) on pages 78–9). This form, which can be obtained from the Registrar, on request, **should be retained by the applicant after completion by the originator.**

INTRODUCTION

In 1972 the Royal Horticultural Society, as International Registration Authority for Orchid Hybrids, reviewed the pattern upon which Addenda to *Sander's List of Orchid Hybrids* were published, and concluded that it would be better in all ways if Addenda were published every five years as part of the permanent record rather than to publish (as was done in the 1961–70 period, for example) two interim Addenda of three years each which, four years later, became superseded by an integrated 10-year work. The Society now has pleasure in presenting the first five-year Addendum published under the revised policy, covering registrations during the period 1st January 1971 to 31st December 1975 inclusive.

The 'One-Table' format, first introduced in the 1946–60 volumes and also used in 1961–70, is continued as before. This volume lists the names, parents (and grandparents), registrants, originators and dates of approximately 7000 new grexes (man-made hybrids) registered in the period it concerns. They are contained within 248 genera appearing in registration use herein; these consist of 183 hybrid-genera (of which 61 are new to registration in this five-year period) and 65 naturally occurring genera (of which 9 are new to registration in the same period).

HANDBOOK ON ORCHID NOMENCLATURE AND REGISTRATION

This is the first Addendum whose period of registration commenced after the first publication (in 1969) of the international *Handbook on Orchid Nomenclature and Registration* and whose registrations have fallen wholly under the rules and procedures published therein. These procedures etc. are modified from time to time, and the major changes are published by notice in the monthly lists of new hybrids in the *Orchid Review*; moreover the lists of names in certain special categories contained in the Handbook are subject to frequent additions etc., especially as new hybrid-genera enter registration. The consequent need for an updated Handbook has resulted in the publication at the end of 1976 of a much revised Second Edition, following and based on the approval of a complete re-draft, subject to certain modifications, by the International Orchid Commission (IOC) meeting at the 8th World Orchid Conference in Frankfurt in 1975. Since almost all the sections of the Handbook have bearing, to some degree, upon the registration of orchid hybrids (and exclusively so in the cases of Parts IV and VIII) its acquisition for reference and study by all those who breed and register orchids cannot be too highly recommended; its relevance to the contents of this Addendum makes this special reference to it not merely appropriate but almost essential. Wherever the expression 'the Handbook' is mentioned hereinafter, it is the *Second* Edition (1976) of the *Handbook on Orchid Nomenclature and Registration* that is referred to. It is available from the Royal Horticultural Society in London, England, and from the American Orchid Society in Cambridge, Massachusetts, USA.

SOME COMMENTS UPON THE CONTENTS OF THIS ADDENDUM

The **List of Genera** and the **List of Generic Combinations** constituting hybrid-genera have, in this volume, been integrated into a single 'one-table' list (pp. xi to xxi) on principles similar to those used in the main list of hybrids. The format and layout, including typography, are identical to those used in the Handbook and as explained in the preamble to Part IV thereof; the content of the list herein is confined to those genera appearing in registration use in this Addendum.

The **List of Registrants and Originators** (pp. xxii to l) has its own preamble with explanatory notes on the contents of the list which it is hoped may clarify points which have been raised in the past.

The **List of Corrigenda to Earlier Volumes** (pp. li to lxvii) is extremely important (as have been its predecessors) inasmuch as the implementation of such corrigenda is essential so that users of all volumes may have an updated view of the Register as it existed at the time this Addendum went to press. Many of the corrigenda are no more than minor orthographic corrections resulting from past errors or omissions in printing or proofreading; others, however, reflect changes of principle or in the taxonomic status of parent species resulting from new information or from reclassifications adopted for the purpose of hybrid registration. It cannot be too highly stressed, nevertheless, that such reclassifications of parent species are adopted for registration use only with great reserve and following the fullest consideration, in each individual case, of the implications and consequences of such changes in the Register as a whole. Where it is felt that the adoption of such changes for horticultural purposes would cause needless excess confusion (for example where considerable use already exists of the species concerned as a parent in past registration under its earlier classification or name) then the changes are not adopted for registration purposes; and where this results in the continuing use of a species name no longer *botanically* 'correct', such name is treated as a 'horticultural equivalent' for registration use. A whole section of the Handbook (Part VI) is devoted to an explanation of this principle, together with a list of the cases involved as at its date of going to press.

In the **List of Hybrids** constituting the main text of this Addendum certain conventions are used and some comments upon these follow:

ORIGINATORS:

Where the originator of a grex is other than the registrant, the name of the originator, where known, is given in parentheses following the year of registration; where unknown, it is so stated.

SYN./SEE:

Where two or more names are referred to as being in competition for the same taxon, then —

(i) names following the abbreviation **syn**. are treated as synonyms for horticultural purposes and are no longer accepted as parental names for future registrations. The appropriate symbols against such names, however, may indicate where they had earlier been accepted in such use in past volumes, even where subsequently published corrigenda have eliminated such past use.

(ii) names following the word **see** are treated as correct names for horticultural (including registration) purposes and are accepted as parental names for future registrations.

The foregoing all holds good irrespective of whether the acceptable name is botanically correct or whether it is a 'horticultural equivalent' adopted for, or continued in, registration use under the principles earlier described in this Introduction. However, where the acceptable name for registration is *other than* the botanically correct name then explanatory notes are added to the text to state the position. In these explanatory notes the expression 'botanically correct name' means (unless the context indicates otherwise) the correct name in the majority opinion of practising botanists at the time their opinions were solicited with a view to stabilising the name to be recommended for future horticultural use, including registration use as a parent name; the expression 'horticulturally recommended name' means a name adopted for continuing use in grex registration as a parent when this is *other than* the botanically correct name as defined above. This may be abbreviated as 'hort. rec.' where space is limited.

SYMBOLS AND ABBREVIATIONS

A key to symbols and general abbreviations appearing in the main text is given at the beginning of that text on page 1. Abbreviations in the epithets of hybrids have been strictly avoided in the main (bold type) entries at the left-hand margin; however, for space economy common abbreviations of such words as Memoria (Mem.), Saint (St.), Doctor (Dr.), Mount (Mt.), etc. may appear in names cited as *parents* in such entries and also in 'secondary' entries (i.e. resulting crosses in ordinary roman typeface set out below a main entry). The abbreviated forms of *generic* names in the main text (likewise necessary for space economy) are those standardised recommended abbreviations given in the List of Genera on pp. xi to xxi. Where *no* generic name or its abbreviation immediately precedes a specific or grex epithet in any entry, then the generic name appearing as a centralised heading immediately above on the same page is implied.

NATURAL HYBRIDS

The typographic principles used in the listing of natural hybrids are the same as in the previous Addendum (1961–1970) — see p. vi, para. 2 of that volume. There is a minor alteration in their layout in this volume in that the two typographic forms of each such epithet are bracketed together to show the common parentage in the centre of the page and, on the right, the respective status of 'Nat. hyb.' and either 'hort.' (indicating garden origin) or the name of the registrant and date (in cases where the cross has also been actually registered as a man-made hybrid). In some special cases additional explanatory notes are given whose purpose is self-evident. This is to follow the nomenclatural principles relating to the treatment of natural hybrids and their man-made equivalents as set out in the Handbook on pp. 5 and 6.

SOME COMMENTS UPON ALPHABETICAL SEQUENCE

Superficially it would seem sufficient to say that the lists in this volume are arranged alphabetically. However, what truly constitutes alphabetical sequence depends upon what is being arranged; if it is *single words* the rules are few, but if it is *groups of words* there is more than one system available. The following are the rules and systems used in this Addendum:

(1) **As applied to single words:**

Any abbreviations used for space economy in special places are treated, for alphabetical sequence, as the word is spelt in full and not (necessarily) in sequence of the abbreviations *per se*. This applies to standard abbreviations of generic names, abbreviations of words like Memoria (Mem.) etc. as listed above, and to words and names which commence with Mc... which are all treated alphabetically as if they were written Mac.. . . Exceptionally the abbreviation 'Mrs.' is treated as a full word for alphabetical sequence and not as spelt out 'Mistress' in full. Hyphens, apostrophes and diacritic signs such as diaereses, accents, umlauts, etc. are disregarded for alphabetical sequence.

(2) **As applied to groups of words:**
Two slightly different systems are used for (a) the List of Registrants and (b) the List of Hybrids, as follows:—

(a) **The List of Registrants etc.** The first word of the name (usually the registrant's surname or family name) is placed in its normal alphabetical sequence having regard to (1) above. Where more than one registrant's name has the same first word, then they are next placed in order of the following word or initial; and then the next, and so on. Thus Bates, W. J. would precede Bateson, which would precede Bateson, A. F. and so on; Tan Ming Ho would precede Tan, P. B., which would precede Tang Ah Seng, which would precede Tang Choo Ai, etc. Code abbreviations (for registrants' names) which consist solely of initials or groups of initials are placed, in their own alphabetical order, at the beginning of the first letter concerned, and are frequently cross-referred to under the full name later in the list. Thus under this system alphabetical sequence is **word by word** or **initial by initial**.

(b) **The List of Hybrids**. In the list of *plant* names, where a grex epithet consists of two or more words (or even initials in the case of some older hybrids brought forward as current parents) the whole epithet is treated for alphabetical sequence as if it were **one continuous entity and not word by word**. Under such system the epithet Gold Beauty would precede all epithets of which the first word was Golden . . . which would precede such epithets as Gold Field, Gold Flight, etc. In any list of crosses derived from, and listed under, a particular parent (the 'index-parent') the crosses are first listed where the *second* parent is of the *same* genus as the index-parent (and *no* generic abbreviation precedes either the second parent or the resulting grex epithet); such crosses are in the alphabetical sequence of the second parent according to the 'continuous entity' system explained above. These entries are then followed by crosses (if any) where the second parent is of a genus *different* from that of the index-parent; in such crosses the generic abbreviation of the second parent *is* stated, and their alphabetical sequence is firstly by the generic *name* of the second parent and secondly by the specific/grex epithet of the second parent according to the 'continuous entity' system explained above. The *resulting* grex name (following the = sign) in any of these 'secondary' entries has no bearing whatever upon alphabetical sequence.

SOME PERSONAL COMMENTS AND THANKS BY THE REGISTRAR

I would like to extend my personal thanks to all those whose valuable advice and help, freely given, have contributed much to the work of hybrid registration over the past five years and to the preparation of this Addendum. These include all members of the Orchid Registration Advisory Committee of the Royal Horticultural Society, among whom I must especially mention Mr Peter F. Hunt whose continuous help to registration work during the whole of the five-year period in providing advice upon botanical matters, and upon horticultural decisions related to them, has been a great tower of strength. In the preparation of this Addendum I have been further assisted by Peter, his wife Doreen and my own dear wife Hilary, who have all given countless voluntary hours to proof-reading and correction for which I cannot express too highly my appreciation; whatever errors may still obtain, there would have been many more without their tremendous help.

To these names I must add those of Messrs D. A. Bishop, J. R. Fisher and A. R. Koester, and of Mrs K. Yocom — all of USA — who especially have done so much by drawing attention to errors in past volumes to enable me to publish corrections; to these and any others who have made such contributions my thanks are also expressed.

Finally I must not neglect to mention, and to record appreciation of, the work carried out by my predecessor as Registrar, Mrs Marjorie Wreford, during the first year of this five-year period. To Marjorie I offer my thanks for the ease with which her records and systems enabled me to assume her mantle of responsibility from early in 1972. There can be little higher ambition in this work than to hope to maintain the very high standards she set over many years, both for the Royal Horticultural Society (from 1961) and earlier for the late Mr David Sander who, and whose family before him, laid the major foundations for the orchid hybrid Register as we have it today. As Marjorie knew and wrote herself in the Introduction to the 1961–70 Addendum, in any work of this nature and length some errors are almost inevitable, however much checking and re-checking is done. I, too, know that there will be errors in *this* volume, despite all efforts to exclude them; I hope that I shall continue to receive the help of any who find them and who let me know so that corrections may, where appropriate, be published in due course.

Jack Greatwood
Registrar

January 1977

ALPHABETICAL ONE-TABLE LIST OF GENERA AND INTERGENERIC COMBINATIONS

(with parentage, where applicable, and standard abbreviations)

(NB. This list contains the names and intergeneric combinations of only those genera which appear (either as such or as component of a hybrid genus so appearing) **in registration use in this Addendum.**)

AËRANGIS (Aërgs.) = Natural genus
× Angraecum = Angrangis
AËRANTHES (Aërth.) = Natural genus
× Angraecum = Angranthes
AËRIDACHNIS (Aërdns.) = **Aërides** × **Arachnis**
AËRIDES (Aër.) = Natural genus
× Arachnis = Aëridachnis
× Arachnis × Ascocentrum × Vanda = Lewisara
× Arachnis × Renanthera = Lymanara
× Arachnis × Rhynchostylis = Sagarikara
× Arachnis × Trichoglottis = Paulsenara
× Arachnis × Vanda = Burkillara
× Ascocentrum = Aëridocentrum
× Ascocentrum × Renanthera × Vanda = Robinara
× Ascocentrum × Vanda = Christieara
× Doritis = Aëriditis
× Luisia = Aëridisia
× Neofinetia × Vanda = Vandofinides
× Renanthera = Renades
× Renanthera × Rhynchostylis = Chewara
× Renanthera × Vanda = Nobleara
× Rhynchostylis = Rhynchorides
× Vanda = Aëridovanda
× Vanda × Vandopsis = Maccoyara
× Vandopsis = Vandopsides
AËRIDISIA (Aërsa.) = **Aërides** × **Luisia**
AËRIDITIS (Aërdts.) = **Aërides** × **Doritis**
AËRIDOCENTRUM (Aërctm.) = **Aërides** × **Ascocentrum**
AËRIDOVANDA (Aërdv.) = **Aërides** × **Vanda**
AGANISIA (Agn.) = Natural genus
× Batemannia × Otostylis × Zygosepalum = Downsara
ALICEARA (Alcra.) = **Brassia** × **Miltonia** × **Oncidium**
ALLENARA (Alna.) = **Cattleya** × **Diacrium** × **Epidendrum** × **Laelia**
ANGRAECUM (Angcm.) = Natural genus
× Aërangis = Angrangis
× Aëranthes = Angranthes
× Cyrtorchis = Angraeorchis
ANGRAEORCHIS (Angchs.) = **Angraecum** × **Cyrtorchis**
ANGRANGIS (Angrs.) = **Aërangis** × **Angraecum**
ANGRANTHES (Angth.) = **Aëranthes** × **Angraecum**
ANGULOA (Ang.) = Natural genus
× Lycaste = Angulocaste
ANGULOCASTE (Angcst.) = **Anguloa** × **Lycaste**
ARACHNIS (Arach.) = Natural genus
× Aërides = Aëridachnis
× Aërides × Ascocentrum × Vanda = Lewisara
× Aërides × Renanthera = Lymanara
× Aërides × Rhynchostylis = Sagarikara
× Aërides × Trichoglottis = Paulsenara
× Aërides × Vanda = Burkillara
× Ascocentrum × Renanthera × Vanda = Yusofara
× Ascocentrum × Rhynchostylis × Vanda = Bovornara
× Ascocentrum × Vanda = Mokara
× Ascoglossum = Arachnoglossum
× Phalaenopsis × Vanda = Trevorara
× Renanthera = Aranthera
× Renanthera × Vanda = Holttumara
× Renanthera × Vandopsis = Limara
× Rhynchostylis = Arachnostylis
× Vanda = Aranda
× Vanda × Vandopsis = Leeara
× Vandopsis = Vandachnis
ARACHNOGLOSSUM (Arngm.) = **Arachnis** × **Ascoglossum**

ARACHNOSTYLIS (Arnst.) = **Arachnis × Rhynchostylis**
ARANDA (Aranda) = **Arachnis × Vanda**
ARANTHERA (Arnth.) = **Arachnis × Renanthera**
ASCANDOPSIS (Ascdps.) = **Ascocentrum × Vandopsis**
ASCOCENDA (Ascda.) = **Ascocentrum × Vanda**
ASCOCENTRUM (Asctm.) = Natural genus
× Aërides = Aëridocentrum
× Aërides × Arachnis × Vanda = Lewisara
× Aërides × Renanthera × Vanda = Robinara
× Aërides × Vanda = Christieara
× Arachnis × Renanthera × Vanda = Yusofara
× Arachnis × Rhynchostylis × Vanda = Bovornara
× Arachnis × Vanda = Mokara
× Ascoglossum × Renanthera × Vanda = Shigeuraara
× Doritis = Doricentrum
× Doritis × Phalaenopsis = Beardara
× Doritis × Phalaenopsis × Vanda = Vandewegheara
× Doritis × Vanda = Ascovandoritis
× Gastrochilus × Vanda = Eastonara
× Luisia × Neofinetia = Luascotia
× Luisia × Vanda = Debruyneara
× Neofinetia = Ascofinetia
× Neofinetia × Renanthera = Rosakirschara
× Neofinetia × Vanda = Nakamotoara
× Pelatantheria = Pelacentrum
× Phalaenopsis = Asconopsis
× Phalaenopsis × Renanthera × Vanda = Stamariaara
× Phalaenopsis × Vanda = Devereuxara
× Renanthera = Renancentrum
× Renanthera × Rhynchostylis = Komkrisara
× Renanthera × Vanda = Kagawara
× Rhynchostylis = Rhynchocentrum
× Rhynchostylis × Vanda = Vascostylis
× Trichoglottis × Vanda = Fujioara
× Vanda = Ascocenda
× Vanda × Vandopsis = Wilkinsara
× Vandopsis = Ascandopsis
ASCOFINETIA (Ascf.) = **Ascocentrum × Neofinetia**
ASCOGLOSSUM (Ascgm.) = Natural genus
× Arachnis = Arachnoglossum
× Ascocentrum × Renanthera × Vanda = Shigeuraara
× Renanthera = Renanthoglossum
ASCONOPSIS (Ascps.) = **Ascocentrum × Phalaenopsis**
ASCOVANDORITIS (Asvts.) = **Ascocentrum × Doritis × Vanda**
ASPASIA (Asp.) = Natural genus
× Brassia = Brapasia
× Brassia × Miltonia = Forgetara
× Cochlioda × Odontoglossum = Lagerara
× Miltonia = Milpasia
× Odontoglossum = Aspoglossum
× Oncidium = Aspasium
ASPASIUM (Aspsm.) = **Aspasia × Oncidium**
ASPOGLOSSUM (Aspgm.) = **Aspasia × Odontoglossum**

BARBOSAARA (Bbra.) = **Cochlioda × Gomesa × Odontoglossum × Oncidium**
BATEMANNIA (Btmna.) = Natural genus
× Aganisia × Otostylis × Zygosepalum = Downsara
× Otostylis = Bateostylis
× Otostylis × Zygosepalum = Palmerara
BATEOSTYLIS (Btst.) = **Batemannia × Otostylis**
BEALLARA (Bllra.) = **Brassia × Cochlioda × Miltonia × Odontoglossum**
BEARDARA (Bdra.) = **Ascocentrum × Doritis × Phalaenopsis**
BOVORNARA (Bov.) = **Arachnis × Ascocentrum × Rhynchostylis × Vanda**
BRADEARA (Brade.) = **Comparettia × Gomesa × Rodriguezia**
BRAPASIA (Brap.) = **Brassia × Aspasia**
BRASSAVOLA (B.) = Natural genus
× Cattleya = Brassocattleya
× Cattleya × Epidendrum = Vaughnara
× Cattleya × Epidendrum × Laelia = Yamadara
× Cattleya × Epidendrum × Laelia × Sophronitis = Rothara
× Cattleya × Laelia = Brassolaeliocattleya
× Cattleya × Laelia × Schomburgkia = Recchara
× Cattleya × Laelia × Sophronitis = Potinara

Brassavola *(continued)*
× Cattleya × Sophronitis = Rolfeara
× Epidendrum = Brassoepidendrum
× Laelia = Brassolaelia
× Laelia × Sophronitis = Lowara
× Schomburgkia = Schombavola
× Sophronitis = Brassophronitis
BRASSIA (Brs.) = Natural genus
× Aspasia = Brapasia
× Aspasia × Miltonia = Forgetara
× Cochlioda × Miltonia × Odontoglossum = Beallara
× Cochlioda × Miltonia × Odontoglossum × Oncidium = Goodaleara
× Miltonia = Miltassia
× Miltonia × Odontoglossum = Degarmoara
× Miltonia × Oncidium = Aliceara
× Odontoglossum = Odontobrassia
× Oncidium = Brassidium
BRASSIDIUM (Brsdm.) = Brassia × Oncidium
BRASSOCATTLEYA (Bc.) = Brassavola × Cattleya
BRASSOEPIDENDRUM (Bepi.) = Brassavola × Epidendrum
BRASSOLAELIA (Bl.) = Brassavola × Laelia
BRASSOLAELIOCATTLEYA (Blc.) = Brassavola × Cattleya × Laelia
BRASSOPHRONITIS (Bnts.) = Brassavola × Sophronitis
BROUGHTONIA (Bro.) = Natural genus
× Cattleya = Cattleytonia
× Cattleya × Diacrium = Brownara
× Cattleya × Laelia = Laeliocatonia
× Cattleyopsis = Cattleyopsistonia
× Cattleyopsis × Diacrium = Nashara
× Diacrium = Diabroughtonia
× Epidendrum = Epitonia
× Laelia = Laelonia
× Laelia × Laeliopsis = Jimenezara
× Laeliopsis = Lioponia
× Laeliopsis × Schomburgkia = Hildaara
BROWNARA (Bwna.) = Broughtonia × Cattleya × Diacrium
BURKILLARA (Burk.) = Aërides × Arachnis × Vanda
BURRAGEARA (Burr.) = Cochlioda × Miltonia × Odontoglossum × Oncidium

CATANOCHES (Ctnchs.) = Catasetum × Cycnoches
CATASETUM (Ctsm.) = Natural genus
× Cycnoches = Catanoches
CATTLEYA (C.) = Natural genus
× Brassavola = Brassocattleya
× Brassavola × Epidendrum = Vaughnara
× Brassavola × Epidendrum × Laelia = Yamadara
× Brassavola × Epidendrum × Laelia × Sophronitis = Rothara
× Brassavola × Laelia = Brassolaeliocattleya
× Brassavola × Laelia × Schomburgkia = Recchara
× Brassavola × Laelia × Sophronitis = Potinara
× Brassavola × Sophronitis = Rolfeara
× Broughtonia = Cattleytonia
× Broughtonia × Diacrium = Brownara
× Broughtonia × Laelia = Laeliocatonia
× Diacrium = Diacattleya
× Diacrium × Epidendrum × Laelia = Allenara
× Epidendrum = Epicattleya
× Epidendrum × Laelia = Epilaeliocattleya
× Epidendrum × Laelia × Schomburgkia = Northenara
× Epidendrum × Sophronitis = Stacyara
× Laelia = Laeliocattleya
× Laelia × Schomburgkia × Sophronitis = Herbertara
× Laelia × Sophronitis = Sophrolaeliocattleya
× Schomburgkia = Schombocattleya
× Sophronitis = Sophrocattleya
CATTLEYOPSIS (Ctps.) = Natural genus
× Broughtonia = Cattleyopsistonia
× Broughtonia × Diacrium = Nashara
CATTLEYOPSISTONIA (Ctpsta.) = Broughtonia × Cattleyopsis
CATTLEYTONIA (Ctna.) = Broughtonia × Cattleya
CHEWARA (Chew.) = Aërides × Renanthera × Rhynchostylis
CHRISTIEARA (Chtra.) = Aërides × Ascocentrum × Vanda
CIRRHOPETALUM (Cirr.) = Natural genus

COCHELLA (**Chla**).) = **Cochleanthes** × **Mendoncella**
COCHLEANTHES (**Cnths.**) = Natural genus

× Mendoncella	= Cochella

COCHLIODA (**Cda.**) = Natural genus

× Aspasia × Odontoglossum	= Lagerara
× Brassia × Miltonia × Odontoglossum	= Beallara
× Brassia × Miltonia × Odontoglossum × Oncidium	= Goodaleara
× Gomesa × Odontoglossum × Oncidium	= Barbosaara
× Miltonia × Odontoglossum	= Vuylstekeara
× Miltonia × Odontoglossum × Oncidium	= Burrageara
× Odontoglossum	= Odontioda
× Odontoglossum × Oncidium	= Wilsonara
× Oncidium	= Oncidioda

COLMANARA (**Colm.**) = **Miltonia** × **Odontoglossum** × **Oncidium**
COMPARETTIA (**Comp.**) = Natural genus

× Gomesa × Rodriguezia	= Bradeara
× Odontoglossum	= Odontorettia
× Oncidium	= Oncidettia
× Oncidium × Rodriguezia	= Warneara
× Rodriguezia	= Rodrettia

CYCNOCHES (**Cyc.**) = Natural genus

× Catasetum	= Catanoches

CYMBIDIUM (**Cym.**) = Natural genus
CYRTORCHIS (**Cyrtcs.**) = Natural genus

× Angraecum	= Angraeorchis

DEBRUYNEARA (**Dbra.**) = **Ascocentrum** × **Luisia** × **Vanda**
DEGARMOARA (**Dgmra.**) = **Brassia** × **Miltonia** × **Odontoglossum**
DENDROBIUM (**Den.**) = Natural genus
DEVEREUXARA (**Dvra.**) = **Ascocentrum** × **Phalaenopsis** × **Vanda**
DIABROUGHTONIA (**Diab.**) = **Broughtonia** × **Diacrium**
DIACATTLEYA (**Diaca.**) = **Cattleya** × **Diacrium**
DIACRIUM (**Diacm.**) = Natural genus

× Broughtonia	= Diabroughtonia
× Broughtonia × Cattleya	= Brownara
× Broughtonia × Cattleyopsis	= Nashara
× Cattleya	= Diacattleya
× Cattleya × Epidendrum × Laelia	= Allenara
× Epidendrum	= Epidiacrium

DILLONARA (**Dill.**) = **Epidendrum** × **Laelia** × **Schomburgkia**
DORICENTRUM (**Dctm.**) = **Ascocentrum** × **Doritis**
DORIELLA (**Drlla.**) = **Doritis** × **Kingiella**
DORIFINETIA (**Dfta.**) = **Doritis** × **Neofinetia**
DORITAENOPSIS (**Dtps.**) = **Doritis** × **Phalaenopsis**
DORITIS (**Dor.**) = Natural genus

× Aërides	= Aëriditis
× Ascocentrum	= Doricentrum
× Ascocentrum × Phalaenopsis	= Beardara
× Ascocentrum × Phalaenopsis × Vanda	= Vandewegheara
× Ascocentrum × Vanda	= Ascovandoritis
× Kingiella	= Doriella
× Neofinetia	= Dorifinetia
× Phalaenopsis	= Doritaenopsis
× Phalaenopsis × Vanda	= Hagerara
× Phalaenopsis × Vandopsis	= Hausermannara
× Renanthera	= Dorthera

DORTHERA (**Dtha.**) = **Doritis** × **Renanthera**
DOWNSARA (**Dwsa.**) = **Aganisia** × **Batemannia** × **Otostylis** × **Zygosepalum**

EASTONARA (**Eas.**) = **Ascocentrum** × **Gastrochilus** × **Vanda**
EPICATTLEYA (**Epc.**) = **Cattleya** × **Epidendrum**
EPIDELLA (**Epdla.**) = **Epidendrum** × **Nageliella**
EPIDENDRUM (**Epi.**) = Natural genus

× Brassavola	= Brassoepidendrum
× Brassavola × Cattleya	= Vaughnara
× Brassavola × Cattleya × Laelia	= Yamadara
× Brassavola × Cattleya × Laelia × Sophronitis	= Rothara
× Broughtonia	= Epitonia
× Cattleya	= Epicattleya
× Cattleya × Diacrium × Laelia	= Allenara
× Cattleya × Laelia	= Epilaeliocattleya
× Cattleya × Laelia × Schomburgkia	= Northenara
× Cattleya × Sophronitis	= Stacyara

Epidendrum (*continued*)

× Diacrium = Epidiacrium
× Laelia = Epilaelia
× Laelia × Schomburgkia = Dillonara
× Laelia × Sophronitis = Stanfieldara
× Nageliella = Epidella
× Schomburgkia = Schomboepidendrum
× Sophronitis = Epiphronitis

EPIDIACRIUM (Epdcm.) = Diacrium × Epidendrum
EPILAELIA (Epl.) = Epidendrum × Laelia
EPILAELIOCATTLEYA (Eplc.) = Cattleya × Epidendrum × Laelia
EPIPHRONITIS (Ephs.) = Epidendrum × Sophronitis
EPITONIA (Eptn.) = Broughtonia × Epidendrum

FORGETARA (Fgtra.) = Aspasia × Brassia × Miltonia
FUJIOARA (Fjo.) = Ascocentrum × Trichoglottis × Vanda

GASTROCHILUS (Gchls.) = Natural genus
× Ascocentrum × Vanda = Eastonara
× Sarcochilus = Gastrosarcochilus

GASTROSARCOCHILUS (Gsarco.) = Gastrochilus × Sarcochilus
GOFFARA (Gfa.) = Luisia × Rhynchostylis × Vanda
GOMESA (Gom.) = Natural genus
× Cochlioda × Odontoglossum × Oncidium = Barbosaara
× Comparettia × Rodriguezia = Bradeara
× Oncidium = Oncidesa

GOODALEARA (Gdlra.) = Brassia × Cochlioda × Miltonia × Odontoglossum × Oncidium

HAGERARA (Hgra.) = Doritis × Phalaenopsis × Vanda
HAUSERMANNARA (Haus.) = Doritis × Phalaenopsis × Vandopsis
HAWAIIARA (Haw.) = Renanthera × Vanda × Vandopsis
HERBERTARA (Hbtr.) = Cattleya × Laelia × Schomburgkia × Sophronitis
HILDAARA (Hdra.) = Broughtonia × Laeliopsis × Schomburgkia
HOLTTUMARA (Holtt.) = Arachnis × Renanthera × Vanda
HUEYLIHARA (Hylra.) = Neofinetia × Renanthera × Rhynchostylis

IONOCIDIUM (Incdm.) = Ionopsis × Oncidium
IONOPSIS (Inps.) = Natural genus
× Oncidium = Ionocidium
× Rodriguezia = Rodriopsis

JIMENEZARA (Jmzra.) = Broughtonia × Laelia × Laeliopsis
JOANNARA (Jnna.) = Renanthera × Rhynchostylis × Vanda

KAGAWARA (Kgw.) = Ascocentrum × Renanthera × Vanda
KINGIELLA (King.) = Natural genus
× Doritis = Doriella
× Phalaenopsis = Phaliella

KOMKRISARA (Kom.) = Ascocentrum × Renanthera × Rhynchostylis

LAELIA (L.) = Natural genus
× Brassavola = Brassolaelia
× Brassavola × Cattleya = Brassolaeliocattleya
× Brassavola × Cattleya × Epidendrum = Yamadara
× Brassavola × Cattleya × Epidendrum × Sophronitis = Rothara
× Brassavola × Cattleya × Schomburgkia = Recchara
× Brassavola × Cattleya × Sophronitis = Potinara
× Brassavola × Sophronitis = Lowara
× Broughtonia = Laelonia
× Broughtonia × Cattleya = Laeliocatonia
× Broughtonia × Laeliopsis = Jimenezara
× Cattleya = Laeliocattleya
× Cattleya × Diacrium × Epidendrum = Allenara
× Cattleya × Epidendrum = Epilaeliocattleya
× Cattleya × Epidendrum × Schomburgkia = Northenara
× Cattleya × Schomburgkia × Sophronitis = Herbertara
× Cattleya × Sophronitis = Sophrolaeliocattleya
× Epidendrum = Epilaelia
× Epidendrum × Schomburgkia = Dillonara
× Epidendrum × Sophronitis = Stanfieldara
× Leptotes = Leptolaelia
× Schomburgkia = Schombolaelia
× Sophronitis = Sophrolaelia

LAELIOCATONIA (Lctna.) = Broughtonia × Cattleya × Laelia
LAELIOCATTLEYA (Lc.) = Cattleya × Laelia

LAELIOPSIS (**Lps.**) = Natural genus
× Broughtonia = Lioponia
× Broughtonia × Laelia = Jimenezara
× Broughtonia × Schomburgkia = Hildaara
LAELONIA (Lna.) = Broughtonia × Laelia
LAGERARA (Lgra.) = Aspasia × Cochlioda × Odontoglossum
LEEARA (Leeara) = Arachnis × Vanda × Vandopsis
LEOCHILUS (**Lchs.**) = Natural genus
× Oncidium = Leocidium
LEOCIDIUM (Lcdm.) = Leochilus × Oncidium
LEPANTHES (**Lths.**) = Natural genus
LEPTOLAELIA (Lptl.) = Laelia × Leptotes
LEPTOTES (**Lpt.**) = Natural genus
× Laelia = Leptolaelia
LEWISARA (Lwsra.) = Aërides × Arachnis × Ascocentrum × Vanda
LIMARA (Lim.) = Arachnis × Renanthera × Vandopsis
LIOPONIA (Lpna.) = Broughtonia × Laeliopsis
LOWARA (Low.) = Brassavola × Laelia × Sophronitis
LUASCOTIA (Lscta.) = Ascocentrum × Luisia × Neofinetia
LUINETIA (Lnta.) = Luisia × Neofinetia
LUINOPSIS (Lnps.) = Luisia × Phalaenopsis
LUISANDA (Lsnd.) = Luisia × Vanda
LUISIA (**Lsa.**) = Natural genus
× Aërides = Aëridisia
× Ascocentrum × Neofinetia = Luascotia
× Ascocentrum × Vanda = Debruyneara
× Neofinetia = Luinetia
× Phalaenopsis = Luinopsis
× Pomatocalpa = Pomatisia
× Rhynchostylis × Vanda = Goffara
× Vanda = Luisanda
LUTHERARA (Luth.) = Phalaenopsis × Renanthera × Rhynchostylis
LYCASTE (**Lyc.**) = Natural genus
× Anguloa = Angulocaste
× Maxillaria = Maxillacaste
LYMANARA (Lymra.) = Aërides × Arachnis × Renanthera

MACCOYARA (Mcyra.) = Aërides × Vanda × Vandopsis
MACRADENIA (**Mcdn.**) = Natural genus
× Oncidium = Oncidenia
MASDEVALLIA (**Masd.**) = Natural genus
MAXILLACASTE (Mxcst.) = Lycaste × Maxillaria
MAXILLARIA (**Max.**) = Natural genus
× Lycaste = Maxillacaste
MENDONCELLA (**Mdcla.**) = Natural genus
× Cochleanthes = Cochella
MILPASIA (Mpsa.) = Aspasia × Miltonia
MILTASSIA (Mtssa.) = Brassia × Miltonia
MILTONIA (**Milt.**) = Natural genus
× Aspasia = Milpasia
× Aspasia × Brassia = Forgetara
× Brassia = Miltassia
× Brassia × Cochlioda × Odontoglossum = Beallara
× Brassia × Cochlioda × Odontoglossum × Oncidium = Goodaleara
× Brassia × Odontoglossum = Degarmoara
× Brassia × Oncidium = Aliceara
× Cochlioda × Odontoglossum = Vuylstekeara
× Cochlioda × Odontoglossum × Oncidium = Burrageara
× Odontoglossum = Odontonia
× Odontoglossum × Oncidium = Colmanara
× Oncidium = Miltonidium
MILTONIDIUM (Mtdm.) = Miltonia × Oncidium
MOIRARA (Moir.) = Phalaenopsis × Renanthera × Vanda
MOKARA (Mkra.) = Arachnis × Ascocentrum × Vanda

NAGELIELLA (**Ngl.**) = Natural genus
× Epidendrum = Epidella
NAKAMOTOARA (Nak.) = Ascocentrum × Neofinetia × Vanda
NASHARA (Nash.) = Broughtonia × Cattleyopsis × Diacrium
NEOFINETIA (**Neof.**) = Natural genus
× Aërides × Vanda = Vandofinides
× Ascocentrum = Ascofinetia

Neofinetia (*continued*)

× Ascocentrum × Luisia	= Luascotia
× Ascocentrum × Renanthera	= Rosakirschara
× Ascocentrum × Vanda	= Nakamotoara
× Doritis	= Dorifinetia
× Luisia	= Luinetia
× Phalaenopsis	= Phalanetia
× Renanthera	= Renanetia
× Renanthera × Rhynchostylis	= Hueylihara
× Vanda	= Vandofinetia

NOBLEARA (Nlra.) = **Aërides** × **Renanthera** × **Vanda**
NORTHENARA (Nrna.) = **Cattleya** × **Epidendrum** × **Laelia** × **Schomburgkia**

ODONTIODA (Oda.) = **Cochlioda** × **Odontoglossum**
ODONTOBRASSIA (Odbrs.) = **Brassia** × **Odontoglossum**
ODONTOCIDIUM (Odcdm.) = **Odontoglossum** × **Oncidium**
ODONTOGLOSSUM (Odm.) = Natural genus

× Aspasia	= Aspoglossum
× Aspasia × Cochlioda	= Lagerara
× Brassia	= Odontobrassia
× Brassia × Cochlioda × Miltonia	= Beallara
× Brassia × Cochlioda × Miltonia × Oncidium	= Goodaleara
× Brassia × Miltonia	= Degarmoara
× Cochlioda	= Odontioda
× Cochlioda × Gomesa × Oncidium	= Barbosaara
× Cochlioda × Miltonia	= Vuylstekeara
× Cochlioda × Miltonia × Oncidium	= Burrageara
× Cochlioda × Oncidium	= Wilsonara
× Comparettia	= Odontorettia
× Miltonia	= Odontonia
× Miltonia × Oncidium	= Colmanara
× Oncidium	= Odontocidium
× Rodriguezia	= Rodriglossum

ODONTONIA (Odtna.) = **Miltonia** × **Odontoglossum**
ODONTORETTIA (Odrta.) = **Comparettia** × **Odontoglossum**
ONCIDENIA (Oncna.) = **Macradenia** × **Oncidium**
ONCIDESA (Oncsa.) = **Gomesa** × **Oncidium**
ONCIDETTIA (Onctta.) = **Comparettia** × **Oncidium**
ONCIDIODA (Oncda.) = **Cochlioda** × **Oncidium**
ONCIDIUM (Onc.) = Natural genus

× Aspasia	= Aspasium
× Brassia	= Brassidium
× Brassia × Cochlioda × Miltonia × Odontoglossum	= Goodaleara
× Brassia × Miltonia	= Aliceara
× Cochlioda	= Oncidioda
× Cochlioda × Gomesa × Odontoglossum	= Barbosaara
× Cochlioda × Miltonia × Odontoglossum	= Burrageara
× Cochlioda × Odontoglossum	= Wilsonara
× Comparettia	= Oncidettia
× Comparettia × Rodriguezia	= Warneara
× Gomesa	= Oncidesa
× Ionopsis	= Ionocidium
× Leochilus	= Leocidium
× Macradenia	= Oncidenia
× Miltonia	= Miltonidium
× Miltonia × Odontoglossum	= Colmanara
× Odontoglossum	= Odontocidium
× Rodriguezia	= Rodricidium
× Trichocentrum	= Trichocidium

OPSISANDA (Opsis.) = **Vanda** × **Vandopsis**
OPSISTYLIS (Opst.) = **Rhynchostylis** × **Vandopsis**
OTOSTYLIS (Otst.) = Natural genus

× Aganisia × Batemannia × Zygosepalum	= Downsara
× Batemannia	= Bateostylis
× Batemannia × Zygosepalum	= Palmerara

PALMERARA (Plmra.) = **Batemannia** × **Otostylis** × **Zygosepalum**
PAPHIOPEDILUM (Paph.) = Natural genus
PARACHILUS (Prcls.) = **Parasarcochilus** × **Sarcochilus**
PARASARCOCHILUS (Psarco.) = Natural genus

× Sarcochilus	= Parachilus

PAULSENARA (Plsra.) = **Aërides** × **Arachnis** × **Trichoglottis**
PELACENTRUM (Plctm.) = **Ascocentrum** × **Pelatantheria**

PELATANTHERIA (Pthia.) = Natural genus
× Ascocentrum = Pelacentrum
PHALAENOPSIS (Phal.) = Natural genus
× Arachnis × Vanda = Trevorara
× Ascocentrum = Asconopsis
× Ascocentrum × Doritis = Beardara
× Ascocentrum × Doritis × Vanda = Vandewegheara
× Ascocentrum × Renanthera × Vanda = Stamariaara
× Ascocentrum × Vanda = Devereuxara
× Doritis = Doritaenopsis
× Doritis × Vanda = Hagerara
× Doritis × Vandopsis = Hausermannara
× Kingiella = Phaliella
× Luisia = Luinopsis
× Neofinetia = Phalanetia
× Renanthera = Renanthopsis
× Renanthera × Rhynchostylis = Lutherara
× Renanthera × Vanda = Moirara
× Vanda = Vandaenopsis
PHALANETIA (Phnta.) = Neofinetia × Phalaenopsis
PHALIELLA (Phlla.) = Kingiella × Phalaenopsis
PHRAGMIPEDIUM (Phrag.) = Natural genus
POMATISIA (Pmtsa.) = Luisia × Pomatocalpa
POMATOCALPA (Pmcpa.) = Natural genus
× Luisia = Pomatisia
POTINARA (Pot.) = Brassavola × Cattleya × Laelia × Sophronitis

RECCHARA (Recc.) = Brassavola × Cattleya × Laelia × Schomburgkia
RENADES (Rdns.) = Aërides × Renanthera
RENAGLOTTIS (Rngl.) = Renanthera × Trichoglottis
RENANCENTRUM (Rnctm.) = Ascocentrum × Renanthera
RENANETIA (Rnet.) = Neofinetia × Renanthera
RENANOPSIS (Rnps.) = Rananthera × Vandopsis
RENANSTYLIS (Rnst.) = Renanthera × Rhynchostylis
RENANTANDA (Rntda.) = Renanthera × Vanda
RENANTHERA (Ren.) = Natural genus
× Aërides = Renades
× Aërides × Arachnis = Lymanara
× Aërides × Ascocentrum × Vanda = Robinara
× Aërides × Rhynchostylis = Chewara
× Aërides × Vanda = Nobleara
× Arachnis = Aranthera
× Arachnis × Ascocentrum × Vanda = Yusofara
× Arachnis × Vanda = Holttumara
× Arachnis × Vandopsis = Limara
× Ascocentrum = Renancentrum
× Ascocentrum × Ascoglossum × Vanda = Shigeuraara
× Ascocentrum × Neofinetia = Rosakirschara
× Ascocentrum × Phalaenopsis × Vanda = Stamariaara
× Ascocentrum × Rhynchostylis = Komkrisara
× Ascocentrum × Vanda = Kagawara
× Ascoglossum = Renanthoglossum
× Doritis = Dorthera
× Neofinetia = Renanetia
× Neofinetia × Rhynchostylis = Hueylihara
× Phalaenopsis = Renanthopsis
× Phalaenopsis × Rhynchostylis = Lutherara
× Phalaenopsis × Vanda = Moirara
× Rhynchostylis = Renanstylis
× Rhynchostylis × Vanda = Joannara
× Rhynchostylis × Vandopsis = Yoneoara
× Trichoglottis = Renaglottis
× Vanda = Renantanda
× Vanda × Vandopsis = Hawaiiara
× Vandopsis = Renanopsis
RENANTHOGLOSSUM (Rngm.) = Ascoglossum × Renanthera
RENANTHOPSIS (Rnthps.) = Phalaenopsis × Renanthera
RHYNCHOCENTRUM (Rhctm.) = Ascocentrum × Rhynchostylis
RHYNCHORIDES (Rhrds.) = Aërides × Rhynchostylis
RHYNCHOSTYLIS (Rhy.) = Natural genus
× Aërides = Rhynchorides
× Aërides × Arachnis = Sagarikara
× Aërides × Renanthera = Chewara

Rhynchostylis *(continued)*

× Arachnis	= Arachnostylis
× Arachnis × Ascocentrum × Vanda	= Bovornara
× Ascocentrum	= Rhynchocentrum
× Ascocentrum × Renanthera	= Komkrisara
× Ascocentrum × Vanda	= Vascostylis
× Luisia × Vanda	= Goffara
× Neofinetia × Renanthera	= Hueylihara
× Phalaenopsis × Renanthera	= Lutherara
× Renanthera	= Renanstylis
× Renanthera × Vanda	= Joannara
× Renanthera × Vandopsis	= Yoneoara
× Sarcochilus	= Sartylis
× Vanda	= Rhynchovanda
× Vandopsis	= Opsistylis

RHYNCHOVANDA (Rhv.) = Rhynchostylis × Vanda
ROBINARA (Rbnra.) = Aërides × Ascocentrum × Renanthera × Vanda
RODRETTIA (Rdtta.) = Comparettia × Rodriguezia
RODRICIDIUM (Rdcm.) = Oncidium × Rodriguezia
RODRIGLOSSUM (Rdgm.) = Odontoglossum × Rodriguezia
RODRIGUEZIA (Rdza.) = Natural genus

× Comparettia	= Rodrettia
× Comparettia × Gomesa	= Bradeara
× Comparettia × Oncidium	= Warneara
× Ionopsis	= Rodriopsis
× Odontoglossum	= Rodriglossum
× Oncidium	= Rodricidium

RODRIOPSIS (Rodps.) = Ionopsis × Rodriguezia
ROLFEARA (Rolf.) = Brassavola × Cattleya × Sophronitis
ROSAKIRSCHARA (Rskra.) = Ascocentrum × Neofinetia × Renanthera
ROTHARA (Roth.) = Brassavola × Cattleya × Epidendrum × Laelia × Sophronitis

SAGARIKARA (Sgka.) = Aërides × Arachnis × Rhynchostylis
SARCOCHILUS (Sarco.) = Natural genus

× Gastrochilus	= Gastrosarcochilus
× Parasarcochilus	= Parachilus
× Rhynchostylis	= Sartylis

SARTYLIS (Srts.) = Rhynchostylis × Sarcochilus
SCHOMBAVOLA (Smbv.) = Brassavola × Schomburgkia
SCHOMBOCATTLEYA (Smbc.) = Cattleya × Schomburgkia
SCHOMBOEPIDENDRUM (Smbep.) = Epidendrum × Schomburgkia
SCHOMBOLAELIA (Smbl.) = Laelia × Schomburgkia
SCHOMBURGKIA (Schom.) = Natural genus

× Brassavola	= Schombavola
× Brassavola × Cattleya × Laelia	= Recchara
× Broughtonia × Laeliopsis	= Hildaara
× Cattleya	= Schombocattleya
× Cattleya × Epidendrum × Laelia	= Northenara
× Cattleya × Laelia × Sophronitis	= Herbertara
× Epidendrum	= Schomboepidendrum
× Epidendrum × Laelia	= Dillonara
× Laelia	= Schombolaelia

SHIGEURAARA (Shgra.) = Ascocentrum × Ascoglossum × Renanthera × Vanda
SOPHROCATTLEYA (Sc.) = Cattleya × Sophronitis
SOPHROLAELIA (Sl.) = Laelia × Sophronitis
SOPHROLAELIOCATTLEYA (Slc.) = Cattleya × Laelia × Sophronitis
SOPHRONITIS (Soph.) = Natural genus

× Brassavola	= Brassophronitis
× Brassavola × Cattleya	= Rolfeara
× Brassavola × Cattleya × Epidendrum × Laelia	= Rothara
× Brassavola × Cattleya × Laelia	= Potinara
× Brassavola × Laelia	= Lowara
× Cattleya	= Sophrocattleya
× Cattleya × Epidendrum	= Stacyara
× Cattleya × Laelia	= Sophrolaeliocattleya
× Cattleya × Laelia × Schomburgkia	= Herbertara
× Epidendrum	= Epiphronitis
× Epidendrum × Laelia	= Stanfieldara
× Laelia	= Sophrolaelia

STACYARA (Stac.) = Cattleya × Epidendrum × Sophronitis
STAMARIAARA (Stmra.) = Ascocentrum × Phalaenopsis × Renanthera × Vanda
STANFIELDARA (Sfdra.) = Epidendrum × Laelia × Sophronitis

TREVORARA (**Trev.**) = **Arachnis** × **Phalaenopsis** × **Vanda**
TRICHOCENTRUM (**Trctm.**) = Natural genus
× Oncidium = Trichocidium
TRICHOCIDIUM (**Trcdm.**) = **Oncidium** × **Trichocentrum**
TRICHOGLOTTIS (**Trgl.**) = Natural genus
× Aërides × Arachnis = Paulsenara
× Ascocentrum × Vanda = Fujioara
× Renanthera = Renaglottis
× Vanda = Trichovanda
TRICHOVANDA (**Trcv.**) = **Trichoglottis** × **Vanda**

VANDA (**V.**) = Natural genus
× Aërides = Aëridovanda
× Aërides × Arachnis = Burkillara
× Aërides × Arachnis × Ascocentrum = Lewisara
× Aërides × Ascocentrum = Christieara
× Aërides × Ascocentrum × Renanthera = Robinara
× Aërides × Neofinetia = Vandofinides
× Aërides × Renanthera = Nobleara
× Aërides × Vandopsis = Maccoyara
× Arachnis = Aranda
× Arachnis × Ascocentrum = Mokara
× Arachnis × Ascocentrum × Renanthera = Yusofara
× Arachnis × Ascocentrum × Rhynchostylis = Bovornara
× Arachnis × Phalaenopsis = Trevorara
× Arachnis × Renanthera = Holttumara
× Arachnis × Vandopsis = Leeara
× Ascocentrum = Ascocenda
× Ascocentrum × Ascoglossum × Renanthera = Shigeuraara
× Ascocentrum × Doritis = Ascovandoritis
× Ascocentrum × Doritis × Phalaenopsis = Vandewegheara
× Ascocentrum × Gastrochilus = Eastonara
× Ascocentrum × Luisia = Debruyneara
× Ascocentrum × Neofinetia = Nakamotoara
× Ascocentrum × Phalaenopsis = Devereuxara
× Ascocentrum × Phalaenopsis × Renanthera = Stamariaara
× Ascocentrum × Renanthera = Kagawara
× Ascocentrum × Rhynchostylis = Vascostylis
× Ascocentrum × Trichoglottis = Fujioara
× Ascocentrum × Vandopsis = Wilkinsara
× Doritis × Phalaenopsis = Hagerara
× Luisia = Luisanda
× Luisia × Rhynchostylis = Goffara
× Neofinetia = Vandofinetia
× Phalaenopsis = Vandaenopsis
× Phalaenopsis × Renanthera = Moirara
× Renanthera = Renantanda
× Renanthera × Rhynchostylis = Joannara
× Renanthera × Vandopsis = Hawaiiara
× Rhynchostylis = Rhynchovanda
× Trichoglottis = Trichovanda
× Vandopsis = Opsisanda
VANDACHNIS (**Vchns.**) = **Arachnis** × **Vandopsis**
VANDAENOPSIS (**Vdnps.**) = **Phalaenopsis** × **Vanda**
VANDEWEGHEARA (**Vwga.**) = **Ascocentrum** × **Doritis** × **Phalaenopsis** × **Vanda**
VANDOFINETIA (**Vf.**) = **Neofinetia** × **Vanda**
VANDOFINIDES (**Vfds.**) = **Aërides** × **Neofinetia** × **Vanda**
VANDOPSIDES (**Vdpsd.**) = **Aërides** × **Vandopsis**
VANDOPSIS (**Vdps.**) = Natural genus
× Aërides = Vandopsides
× Aërides × Vanda = Maccoyara
× Arachnis = Vandachnis
× Arachnis × Renanthera = Limara
× Arachnis × Vanda = Leeara
× Ascocentrum = Ascandopsis
× Ascocentrum × Vanda = Wilkinsara
× Doritis × Phalaenopsis = Hausermannara
× Renanthera = Renanopsis
× Renanthera × Rhynchostylis = Yoneoara
× Renanthera × Vanda = Hawaiiara
× Rhynchostylis = Opsistylis
× Vanda = Opsisanda
VASCOSTYLIS (**Vasco.**) = **Ascocentrum** × **Rhynchostylis** × **Vanda**

VAUGHNARA (Vnra.) = **Brassavola × Cattleya × Epidendrum**
VUYLSTEKEARA (Vuyl.) = **Cochlioda × Miltonia × Odontoglossum**

WARNEARA (Wnra.) = **Comparettia × Oncidium × Rodriguezia**
WILKINSARA (Wknsra.) = **Ascocentrum × Vanda × Vandopsis**
WILSONARA (Wils.) = **Cochlioda × Odontoglossum × Oncidium**

YAMADARA (Yam.) = **Brassavola × Cattleya × Epidendrum × Laelia**
YONEOARA (Ynra.) = **Renanthera × Rhynchostylis × Vandopsis**
YUSOFARA (Ysfra.) = **Arachnis × Ascocentrum × Renanthera × Vanda**

ZYGOPETALUM (Z.) = Natural genus
ZYGOSEPALUM (Zspm.) = Natural genus
× Aganisia × Batemannia × Otostylis = Downsara
× Batemannia × Otostylis = Palmerara

Key-list to the Names and Addresses of Registrants and Originators Listed in this Addendum

(arranged alphabetically according to their code abbreviations in the main text)

It will be appreciated that this list must include the names of many registrants and originators who are deceased, or firms etc. who have gone out of business or organisations which have ceased to exist. This is because many grexes which appear as *parents* under the One-Table layout (and whose registrants etc. are also stated) were themselves first registered very many years ago. No attempt is made to indicate such cases specially since the position is continuously changing and no such indications could ever be complete.

All addresses given are the latest addresses notified to the International Registration Authority at the time of going to press, or the last addresses known in the case of deceased, etc. registrants or originators. Where the names of countries etc. have changed they have been updated. It should be noted that the addresses of some clubs or societies may often change with periodic appointment of new officers. The following abbreviations are used in addresses in this list:

BC —British Columbia
Blvd.—Boulevard
Cr. —Crescent
E. —East
Dr. —Drive
GB. —Great Britain
Hwy.—Highway
La. —Lane
N. —North
N.E. —North East
N.S. —Negri Sembilan
NSW—New South Wales
N.W.—North West
Pl. —Place
Pk. —Park
Qld. —Queensland
Rd. —Road
Rt. —Route
SA —South Australia
S. Af.—South Africa
S.E. —South East
So. —South
SP —São Paulo
Sq. —Square
St. —Street (or Saint, according to context)
Str. —Strasse
S.W. —South West
USA —United States of America
Vic. —Victoria
W. —West
W.A. —Western Australia

Official postal abbreviations of all State-names of USA are used; also many commonly used abbreviations of county of state names in other countries, as well as postal zip-codes or postcodes where known.

A. . . . . H. G. Alexander Ltd., Larchwood, 59 Newbridge Hill, Bath, Avon, GB.
A. & B. . . . . Armstrong & Brown, Orchidhurst, Liptraps Lane, Tunbridge Wells, Kent TN2 3BX, GB.
A.C.O.C. . . . . Australian Cymbidium Orchid Co., 175 Tooronga Rd., Perry Hills, Sydney, NSW, Australia.
A. & M. . . . . Alberts & Merkel Bros. Inc., P.O. Box 537, 2210 So. Federal Hwy., Boynton Beach, FL 33425, USA.
A. & R. . . . . Armacost & Royston (of Santa Barbara) Inc., 3376 Foothill Rd., P.O. Box 385, Carpinteria, CA 93013, USA.
Abbott . . . . Miss Nancy Ann Abbott, 401 El Cerrito Ave., Hillsborough, CA, USA.
Abe, Y. . . . . 2007 10th Ave., Honolulu, HI, USA.
Abel . . . . Hazel Abel, 1659 16th Ave., San Francisco, CA 94122, USA.
Aberconway . . . . . . Henry, The Lord Aberconway, C.B.E., V.M.H., Bodnant, Tal-y-Cafn, North Wales, GB.
Adam . . . . Adam Orchids, c/o 8 Adam Road, Singapore 11.
Adam, Mrs. P. . . . . . The Shooting Lodge, Georges Farm, Crookham Common, Newbury, Berks., GB.
Adamson . . . . J. B. Adamson, Townsley Grove, Daggers Hall Lane, Blackpool, Lancs., GB.
Adelaide . . . . Adelaide Orchids, Briardale Rd., O'Halloran Hill, SA 5158, Australia.
Ah Lai . . . . 13B, Gali Batu, Singapore 23.
Ai . . . . David C. Ai, P.O. Box 1559, 2727a Kapiolani Blvd., Honolulu, HI 96802, USA.
Aimrasamee . . . . . . Sanga Aimrasamee, Prommart Nursery, 107–111 Rajamulka Rd., Chiengmai, Thailand.
Ainsworth . . . . Mrs. A. G. Ainsworth, Oak Forest, Rt. 2, Gonzales, TX 78629, USA.
Aisaka . . . . Francis F. Aisaka, 99-540 Kahilinai Pl., Aiea, HI 96701, USA.
Akranithi . . . . C. Akranithi, c/o RHS of Thailand (q.v.).
Alberts . . . . Albert A. Alberts, 2645 California St., Apt. 101, Mountain View, CA 94040, USA.
Allan, H. L. . . . . . . Dr. Harry L. Allan, 715 Lake Maggiore Blvd. S., St. Petersburg, FL 33705, USA.; and at 432 3rd North St., St. Petersburg, FL 33701, USA.
A'Logann . . . . Charles A'Logann, 220 Indio Dr., So. San Francisco, CA 94080, USA.
A'Logann Labs. . . . . . A'Logann Laboratories, 220 Indio Dr., So. San Francisco, CA 94080, USA.
Alphonso, A. G. . . . . . Director Botanic Gardens, 51 Greenleaf Place, Singapore 10.
Allyn . . . . Mrs. Dorothy Allyn, 26120 Hurlingham Rd., Beachwood, OH 44122, USA.
Alsagoff . . . . Syed Yusof Alsagoff, 4 Lakme St., Singapore, 16.
Altenburg . . . . Rolf Altenburg, Caixa Postal 501, 24.000 Niterói, RJ, Brazil.
Anderson, V. & M. . . . . Vern & Mary Anderson, 2024 Rockefeller Rd., Wickliffe, OH 44092, USA.
Anderson, W. T. . . . . . Mr. & Mrs. W. T. Anderson, 29 Latchford St., Pimlico, Townsville, Qld., Australia.
Andrade . . . . Joseph Andrade, 3845 Owena Dr., Honolulu, Hawaii, USA.
Andrew, C. K. . . . . . Butts Cottage, Plush, Dorset, GB.
Andrew Orchids . . . . . Keith Andrew Orchids Ltd., Plush, Dorchester, Dorset, GB.

Angleton	James Angleton, 4814 North 33rd Rd., Arlington, VA 22207, USA.
Aoki	Robert H. Aoki, 99-121 Kihewa Pl., Honolulu, HI 96701, USA.
Aotaki, Larry	467 Aki Street, Lahainaa, Maui, HI 96761, USA.
Aow Boon Kee	176 Jalan Bukit Tuan Sheikh, Port Dickson, Negri Sembilan, W. Malaysia.
Arai	Kiyohiko Arai, 35-8, 1-chome, Bunkyo-ku, Tokyo, Japan.
Arblaster, George	Hill Crest Orchids, 50 Sheffield Rd., Killamarsh, Sheffield, Yorks. S31 8EA, GB.
Arhontes, J.	Dr. John Arhontes, 4139 Cadiz Ct., Fremont, CA, USA.
Ariza Julia	(see Julia)
Armour	Alf Armour, Church St., Tinaroo Falls, N. Qld., Australia.
Arnold, J. Y.	3 South Lake Trail, Palm Beach, FL, USA.
Arnold, J. Y., Sr.	3 South Lake Trail, Palm Beach, FL, USA.
Arnold, J. Y. III	245 Dunbar Rd., Palm Beach, FL 33480, USA.
Aronson	Mrs. Jo Aronson, 100 Acres, Bixby Hill Rd., Arcade, NY, USA.
Arvida	Arvida Orchid Co., Miami, FL, USA.
Asdornithee	Chaveng Asdornithee, 117 Yannawa, Bangkok, Thailand.
Askin	F. R. Askin, 152 Moxham Ave., Wellington, 3, New Zealand.
Atherton	F. C. Atherton, Honolulu, HI, USA.
Atkinson	Charles E. Atkinson, 3336 Market St., San Francisco, CA, USA.
Augustyniak	Jan Augustyniak, 5230 S.W. 99th Ave., Miami, FL 33165, USA.
Australian Cymbidium Orchid Co.	(see A.C.O.C.)
Ayers	Jasper R. Ayers, 156 Zils Rd., Watsonville, CA 95076, USA.
Azienda Florentia	(see Florentia)
B.	Black & Flory Ltd., Orchid Nursery, Slough, Bucks. SLB 63Y, GB.
B. & W.	Bowers & Wigelsworth, 4 Bradbury Hills Rd., Bradbury, CA, USA.
B.G.S. Orchids	(Mr. H. K. Lau), 12 Soi Nomchitr, Nares Rd., Sypha, Bangkok, Thailand.
Bachman	Dr. & Mrs. Rowland Bachman, Alrow Farm, R. D. 2, Allentown, PA 18103, USA.
Bachner	Martin Bachner, Chester Hills Orchids, R.D. 2, 962 Catfish La., Pottstown, PA 19464, USA.
Baer	Allen Baer, 14 Fawnwood Dr., St. Louis, MO 63128, USA.
Baggeler	Harald Baggeler, 507 Bergisch Gladbach, Amselweg 28, Germany.
Baitson	John Baitson, 10 Chapel Close, Thornhill, Dewsbury, Yorks. WF12 0DL, GB.
Bakar, S. A.	Syed Aboo Bakar Idid, 4 Lakme St., Singapore, 16.
Baker	Harvey A. Baker, 143 Santa Cruz Rd., Arcadia, CA, USA.
Baker, G. R.	Gary R. Baker, Rt. 2, Box 519, Vashon, WA 98070, USA.
Baker, John	3310 S.W. Huber St., Portland, OR 97219, USA.
Baker, R.	Mr. & Mrs. Robert Baker, 9848 Bird Rd., Miami, FL, USA.
Baker, W. L.	Dr. W. L. Baker, Powderworks Rd., Elanora Heights, NSW 2101, Australia.
Baldwin	G. E. Baldwin Inc., 307 Rockland Dr. & Grand St., P.O. Box 398, Mamaroneck, NY, USA.
Bance	Mrs. S. L. Bance, 11968 Bombardier Ave., Norwalk, CA 90650, USA.
Bangkrabue	Bangkrabue Nursery, 15 Klahom's La., Bangkrabue, Bangkok, Thailand.
Bangyikhun	Bangyikhun Nursery, c/o RHS of Thailand (q.v.).
Banka	F. W. Banka, 4101 Bayshore Blvd. N.E., St. Petersburg, FL 33703, USA.
Banluesin	Narong Banluesin, 63 Soi Nian-u-tis, Huay Khwang, Bangkok, Thailand.
Bannochie	Mrs. Iris Bannochie, Andromeda, Bathsheba, St. Joseph, Barbados, West Indies.
Baramee	Chaiya Baramee, Nakorn Sawan, Thailand.
Barlow	A. H. Barlow, Oaklands, Kersal, Manchester, Lancs., GB.
Barnett	Mr. & Mrs. P. G. Barnett, 442 Fullerton Ave., Newport Beach, CA 92660, USA.
Barron	John S. Barron, 5720 Woodburn Dr., Knoxville, TN 37919, USA.
Basson	Dr. C. H. Basson, 65 Forest Dr., Pinelands, C.P., S. Af.
Bates, M. J.	Bates Orchids, 7911 U.S. 301, Ellenton, FL 33532, USA.
Bates Orchids	(see M. J. Bates)
Bath	J. Reynolds Bath, P.O. Box 7477, Alexandria, LA 71301, USA.
Battle	Kenneth Battle, 1615 Bowles Ave., Fenton, MO 63026, USA.
Beall	The Beall Co. (formerly Beall Greenhouse Co.), P.O. Box 467, Vashon, WA 98070, USA.
Bean	Robert Bean, Robert Bean Orchid Nursery, 10136 Foothill Blvd., San Fernando, CA, USA.
Beard	Charles L. Beard, 3330 N. Flagler Dr., West Palm Beach, FL 33407, USA.
Beaumont, C. F.	Claire F. Beaumont, 7940 S.W. 97th Terrace, Miami, FL 33156, USA.
Beckenbach	Dr. J. R. Beckenbach, 2126 N.W. 11th Ave., Gainesville, FL 32601, USA.
Bedford	R. B. Bedford, 37 Alan Ave., Seaforth, NSW 2092, Australia.
Bee Lian	Bee Lian Orchid Nursery, 15 SS3/48 University Garden, Sg. Way/Subang, Selangor, Malaysia.
Behiels	R. Behiels, Belgium.
Bell, A. J.	Athol James Bell, 2 Thomas St., Cronulla, NSW 2230, Australia.
Bell, F. A.	Fred A. Bell, 14 Rowley St., Brighton le Sands, Sydney, NSW, Australia.
Bell, J. E.	James E. Bell, 4372 Highland Ave., San Diego, CA 92115, USA.
Bell, S.	Selwyn G. S. Bell, 87 Woolooware Rd., Cronulla, NSW 2230, Australia.
Bell, S. P.	12 Bolton St., Cairns, Qld. 4870, Australia.

Benis	Norton Benis, 16198 N.E. 9th Ct., North Miami Beach, FL, USA.
Bergman, F. J.	c/o Rayridge Orchids (see Rayridge).
Berliner, Dr. B. C.	Dr. Benjamin C. Berliner, 40 Duncaster, Bloomfield, CT 06002, USA.
Berman	John D. Berman, 18 Sanderstead Ave., London SW2 1SG, GB.
Berne, Judge	Judge F. W. Berne, Telopea St., Mount Colah, Sydney, NSW, Australia.
Bernhart, Herbert	Rosentr. 17, D-4802 Halle, Germany.
Berry, W. G.	Middleshaw, Shaw Hill, Whittle-le-Woods, Chorley, Lancs., GB.
Berryman	Robert C. Berryman, 636-59th St., West Palm Beach, FL 33407, USA.
Bert	E. Bert, Bois Colombes, 92-Hauts-de-Seine, France.
Bertram	Edward G. Bertram, S75 W14463 Pilgrim Dr., Hales Corners, WI 53130, USA.
Bertsch	Walter Bertsch, 315 E. 70th St., New York, NY 10021, USA.
Betts	Bob Betts, Bob Betts Orchids, 2225 Hoskins Dr., Houston, TX 77080, USA.
Beville	John B. Beville, Beville's Greenhouses, 818 Clairemont, Fort Worth, TX 76103, USA.
Bhimayothin	Thospol Bhimayothin, 56 Soi Mek Sawasdi, Toongmahamek, Bangkok, Thailand.
Bianchi	I. W. Bianchi, Jr., Box B, East Patchogue, Long Island, NY 11772, USA.
Bibus	Paul L. Bibus, 102 48th St. W., Bradenton, FL 33505, USA.
Bingham	A. J. Bingham, 5300 12th Ave., Sacramento, CA 95820, USA.
Bingham, F. O.	Frasier O. Bingham, 2440 S.W. 23rd Terrace, Miami, FL, USA.
Birk	Lance A. Birk, 1721 Las Canoas Rd., Santa Barbara, CA 93105, USA.
Bishop	David A. Bishop, 3105 Loyola La., Austin, TX 78723, USA.
B'kok. Gdng. Supplies	(Mr. H. K. Lau), Bangkok Gardening Supplies, 12 Soi Nomchitr, Nares Rd., Syphya, Bangkok, Thailand.
Black & Flory, Ltd.	(see B.)
Black, George	Ash Trees, Burford Rd., Brize Norton, Oxon., GB.
Blackmore, J. D.	John D. Blackmore, 4302 Britanny Rd., Orlando, FL, USA.
Blaumann	Alfredo Blaumann, Los Palos Grandes, Calle 7, No. 1, Dt. Sucre, Estado Miranda, Venezuela.
Blauvelt	120 N.W. 42nd St., Fort Lauderdale, FL 33309, USA.
Bleu	(no other data recorded)
Bloom's Nursery	1329 N.E. 7th Ave., Fort Lauderdale, FL 33304, USA.
Blue, David	David B. Blue Jr., 4114 S. Zunis Ave., Tulsa, OK 74101, USA.
Blue Grass	Blue Grass Orchids, Winchester Rd., Rt. 4, Lexington, KY, USA.
Bolt	Alvin L. Bolt, 325 Fieldcrest Dr., Nashville, TN 37211, USA.
Bond, Alfred	23 Mary St., Parkside, Ayr, N. Qld., Australia.
Bonniewood	Bonniewood Orchids Inc., 14248 Des Moines Way S., Seattle, WA, USA.
Boonphyoong	Sanga Boonphyoong, c/o R.H.S. of Thailand (q.v.).
Boonyakachana	Sathian Boonyakachana, Bangkok, Thailand.
Borg	Dr. Frejvid Borg, Nådendal, Finland.
Borissow	R. Borissow, The Mews, Angley Park, Cranbrook, Kent.
Bosco	Charles Bosco & Partners, Riverview Orchids, East Liverpool, OH, USA.
Bowers	Arno H. Bowers, 3 Deodar La., Bradbury Estates, Duarte, CA, USA.
Bowers & Wigelsworth	(see B. & W.)
Bowman	Mrs. Alexander Bowman, P.O. Box 7211, Hilo, HI, USA.
Boyd, A.	Al Boyd, P.O. Box 247, Pine Mountain, GA 31822, USA.
Boyd, Gene	819 E. Valencia Ave., Burbank, CA 91501, USA.
Boyd, H.	Henry Boyd, 109 Holterman St., Crows Nest, NSW 2065, Australia.
Boyd, Mrs. W. H.	Mrs. William H. Boyd (Louise Boyd), 951 N.E. 25th Ave., Pompano Beach, FL 33062, USA.
Boyle	Mrs. Edward L. Boyle, 5474 Pinellas Park, FL 33561, USA.
Bracey	B. O. Bracey & Co., 544 Emerald Bay, Laguna Beach, CA 92651, USA.
Braemar	Braemar Orchids (Richard V. Bean), P.O. Box 3056, Santa Barbara, CA, USA.
Braga	A. J. Braga, 10 Binjai Rise, Singapore 21.
Bramblett	Orgel C. Bramblett, 18950 S.W. 136th St., Miami, FL 33157, USA.
Branch	C. A. Branch, East Lea, Warnham, Sussex, GB.
Braverman	Tom A. Braverman, 4550 Sheridan Ave., Miami Beach, FL 33140, USA.
Breckinridge	Breckinridge Orchids (Mr. Mark Rose), Rt. 1, Box 212, Folsom, LA 70437, USA.
Brice	Herman Brice, 11205 S.W. 93rd St., Miami, FL 33168, USA.
Brighton Farms	Linwood, NJ, USA.
Briscoe, R. J.	450 San Bernando Ave., Newport Beach, CA 92660, USA.
Bristol Zoological Society	(see Zool. Soc. Bristol)
Bromilow	H. J. Bromilow, Rann Lea, Rainhill, Lancs., GB.
Brooks	Dr. & Mrs. H. K. Brooks, 2119 N.E. 16th Terrace, Gainesville, FL 32601, USA.
Brookville	Brookville Orchids, Suite 609, 366 Madison Ave., New York, NY, USA.
Brough	Harry W. Brough, 338 Morgan Pl., Vista, CA 92083, USA.
Broughton	Major The Hon. H. R. Broughton, South Walsham Hall, Norwich, Norfolk, GB.
Brown, G. J. A.	12 Buck Stone Green, Alwoodley Park, Leeds, Yorks. LS17 5HA, GB.
Brown, Glen	342 N. Patton Ave., Stockton, CA 95205, USA.
Brown, J. O.	3420 Doreen Ct., Lakeland, FL 33801, USA.
Brown, Mrs. T.	Mrs. Thomas Brown (Janet Brown), 4601 Linwood Dr., West Bloomfield, MI 48033, USA.
Brown, W. E.	William Eric Brown, Mount Pleasant, 99 Ermin St., Blunsdon, Swindon, Wilts. SN2 4AA, GB.
Browne	Fred L. Browne, 817 Novelda Rd., Alhambra, CA, USA.

Bruce	Keith Bruce, 31 Glen Ebor Ave., Blackburn, Vic. 3130, Australia.
Brummitt, A. R.	Arthur R. Brummitt, Broughton Rd., Banbury, Oxon., GB.
Brummitt, L. W.	30 Bloxham Road, Banbury, Oxon., GB.
Bryant, A. R.	Alvin Richard Bryant, 18 Kangaroo Point Rd., Sylvania, NSW 2224, Australia.
Bryant & Gillson	A. R. Bryant & F. A. Gillson (c/o A. R. Bryant—q.v.).
Bull	W. Bull & Sons, Kings Rd., Chelsea, London, GB.
Bumroongsoonthorn	Lok Bumroongsoonthorn, 144/6 Bangparkok, Lardburana, Bangkok, Thailand.
Bun	Dr. P. S. Bun (Bun Pak Sun), 8 Narooma Rd., Singapore, 11.
Bundt	C. L. Bundt, 15 Djalan Muchtarluthfi, Makassar, Sulawesi, Indonesia.
Bunyavibul	Priyabhan Bunyavibul, 20 Soi Ratapan, Makasan, Bangkok, Thailand.
Burgeff	Prof. Dr. H. Burgeff, Wurzburg, Klinikstrasse 5, Germany.
Burgun	Charles W. Burgun, 1027 Ave. Hermosa, West Palm Beach, FL 33405, USA.
Burke, W. D.	109 W. Laila Ct., West Melbourne, FL 32901, USA.
Burkhalter	James C. Burkhalter, Box 462, Deland, FL 32720, USA.
Burleigh Pk.	Burleigh Park Orchid Nursery, De Coursey St., Mundingburra, Townsville, Qld., Australia.
Burnett	Harry Burnett, 1845 17th St. N.W., Winter Haven, FL 33880, USA.
Burnham	Burnham Nurseries Ltd., Kingsteignton, Newton Abbot, Devon, GB.
Burns, W. T.	William T. Burns, M.D., Orchids, 807 Ritchie St., Prince Rupert, BC, Canada.
Burstow	W. J. Burstow, The Old Quarry, Lucastes Ave., Haywards Heath, Sussex, GB.
Burton, A. F.	Adin F. Burton, 11130 N.W. 58th Ave., Hialeah, FL 33012, USA.
Burton's	Burton's Orchids (c/o Burton, A. F.—q.v.).
Bush	Stephen S. Bush, 573 Buckeye St., Vacaville, CA 95688, USA.
Butler, I. A.	30 Boundary Rd., Wahroonga, NSW, Australia.
C.	Charlesworth & Co. Ltd., 47 Lewes Rd., Haywards Heath, Sussex, GB.
C.C.	Charlesworth & Co. (Division of McBeans Orchids Ltd.) Cooksbridge, Sussex, GB.
C. & D.	R. P. Calmette & L. E. Drumm, 296 Bronwod Ave., Los Angeles, CA 90049, USA.
C. & H.	Carter & Holmes Orchids, P.O. Box 668, Newberry, SC 29108, USA.
Calmette & Drumm	(see C. & D.)
Cameron, R. C.	Robert C. Cameron, 13734 Weddington St., Van Nuys, CA, USA.
Cameron, T. W. F.	Dr. T. W. F. Cameron, 102 Ashford Rd., Iver Heath, Bucks., GB.
Campbell	D. N. Campbell, 26 Kahibah Rd., Waratah, NSW 2298, Australia.
Cannons	W. G. Cannons, Wayside Nursery, Fenhill Fd., Macquarie, NSW 2444, Australia.
Cardosa	Arnold J. Cardosa, 946 Hygeia St., Encinitas, CA 92024, USA.
Carlson	Elwood J. Carlson, West Coast Orchids, 4905 Cherryvale Ave., Soquel, CA 95073, USA.
Carlson, J. T.	Jon Tyler Carlson, 118 Wesley St., Capitola, CA 95010, USA.
Carlton	Carlton's Orchids, 542 So. Granados, Solana Beach, CA 92075, USA.
Carmichael	Paul W. Carmichael, P.O. Box 3212, Naples, FL 33940, USA.
Carnosa Plants	The Cedar Orchid Nursery, Wash Lane, South Mimms, Herts., GB.
Carpentier	Mrs. E. Carpentier, 4691 Via Roblada, Hope Ranch Pk., Santa Barbara, CA, USA.
Carter	(see C. & H.)
Carter, Dr. W.	Dr. Walter Carter, 3234 Woodland Drive, Honolulu, HI, USA.
Casa Luna	Casa Luna Orchids, Star Rt. 1, Box 219A, Beaufort, SC 29902, USA.
Casamajor	Robert Casamajor, 395 East Green St., Pasadena, CA, USA.
Casey	Eugene A. Casey, 932 Crest Dr., Encinitas, CA 92024, USA.
Cassella	Gerry Cassella, 39 Pitt Ave., Staten Island, NY 10314, USA.
Cavaco	T. Cavaco, 244A Kihapai St., Honolulu, HI 96734, USA.
Cavaco, A. S.	244A Kihapai St., Kailua, HI 96734, USA.
Cecil Park Orchids	Mulgoa Rd., Cecil Pk., NSW, Australia.
Chaisiri	Chuang Chaisiri, 30 Soi Sailom 1, Paholyothin Rd., Bangkok, Thailand.
Chaisomboon	Longwa Chaisomboon, 403/9 Bangkunsri, Bangkoknoi, Dhonburi, Thailand.
Chamberlain	The Right Hon. J. Chamberlain, Highbury, Moor Green, Birmingham, GB.
Chambers	J. C. Chambers, R.D. 3, Forrest Dr., Lloyd Harbor, Huntington, NY 11743, USA.
Champion	Phillips K. Champion, M.D., 930 Harman Ave., Dayton, OH 45419, USA.
Chan	Patrick Chan, Civil Engineering Dept., Harbour Board, Singapore 9.
Chan, George	George C. C. Chan, 41 Belmont Rd., Singapore, 10.
Chandler	C. H. Chandler, High Warren, Theydon Mount, Epping, Essex, GB.
Chandramonthol, P.	Poch Chandramonthol, c/o RHS of Thailand (q.v.).
Chang, A. C.	Alex. C. Chang, 1718 Kealia Dr., Honolulu, HI 96817, USA.
Chang Chao-Tang	Long Life Orchids, 5, 229 La., Ming-Chuan Rd., Taichung, Taiwan.
Chang, C. W.	1758 Pauls Dr., Honolulu, HI, USA.
Chang, W. A.	Wilbur A. Chang, 45-111-C William Henry Rd., Kaneohe, HI 96744, USA.
Chantramontol	Pote Chantramontol, c/o RHS of Thailand (q.v.).
Chanyakomol	Phot Chanyakomol, 13/24 Soi Somboon Vatana 1, Suthisarn Rd., Bangkok, Thailand.
Cha-om	Seng Cha-om, c/o RHS of Thailand (q.v.).
Chapman	George Chapman, 148 Cameron St., South Ayr, Ald. 4807, Australia.
Charanasri	Uthai Charanasri, Horticulture Dept., Kasetsart University, Bangkok, Thailand.
Charlesworth & Co. (Div. of McBeans)	(see C.C.)
Charlesworth & Co. Ltd	(see C.)
Charoen	Wilas Tan Charoen, c/o RHS of Thailand (q.v.).

Charoen-ngam . . . . . Sangiem Charoen-ngam, c/o Prof. R. Sagarik (see Sagarik).
Chartniyom . . . . . . Suchart Chartniyom, c/o RHS of Thailand (q.v.).
Charungraksa . . . . . . (see Raksa)
Charusorn . . . . Patrapara Charusorn, 9 Sukumvit 36, Bangkok, Thailand.
Chase . . . . Chase Gardens, Rt. 2, Eugene, OR, USA.
Chassaing . . . . M. Chassaing, Jardinier-en-chef, Chateau de Ferrieres-en-Brie, S. & M., France.
Chavalit . . . . Dr. Sommart Chavalit, 27 Sukumvit Soi 47, Sukumvit Rd., Bangkok, Thailand.
Cheah Kheng Cheong . . c/o Perak River Hydro, Malim Nawar, Perak, Malaysia.
Cheang Kok Choy . . . . Botanic Gardens, Penang, Malaysia.
Chen . . . . Aston L. Chen, 141 Princess St., Kingston, Jamaica, West Indies.
Cheok Jiak Kim . . . . . 11 How Sun Ave., off Paya Lebar Rd., Singapore 19.
Cheong Chee Yon . . . . 11 Jalan Trus, J.B., Johore, W. Malaysia.
Cheong Pak Yik . . . . . 1 Lorong Putri "F" (Rd. No. 5/9 "F"), Petaling Jaya, Selangor, Malaysia.
Cheong, S. S. H. . . . . . Steven S. H. Cheong, No. 33 Jalan 14/59, P.O. Box 40, Petaling Jaya, Selangor, Malaysia.
Chester Hills . . . . . . Chester Hills Orchids (Martin Bachner), R.D. 2, Catfish Lane, Pottstown, PA 19464, USA.
Chevalier . . . . C. A. Chevalier, Tjiboenoetweg 6, Bandoeng, Java, Indonesia.
Cheu Ming Shuan . . . . c/o Chalor Thongsuphan (see Thongsuphan).
Chew Peng Kah . . . . . 29 Jalan Kuching, Canning Garden, Ipoh, Perak, Malaysia.
Chew Wong . . . . . . 1134 Koko Head Ave., Honolulu, HI, USA.
Chia Kay Heng . . . . . 21 Jalan Korma, Singapore, 11.
Chick . . . . B. Chick, Wade St., Muwillumbah, NSW, Australia.
Chin Jiunn Shie . . . . . 768 Chung Cheng Rd., Miao-Li, Taiwan.
Chin Sheng Li . . . . . . 15 Nei-Wei Rd., Kao-Hsiung, Taiwan.
Chindavanic . . . . . . Phor Chindavanic, c/o Chalor Thongsuphan (see Thongsuphan).
Ching, Jack . . . . Jack D. S. Ching, P.O. Box 567, Waianae, Oahu, HI 96792, USA.
Ching, Mrs. Jack . . . . . P.O. Box 567, Waianae, Oahu, HI 96792, USA.
Chit . . . . Prachark, c/o RHS of Thailand (q.v.).
Chitpimolwat . . . . . . Chaiwat Chitpimolwat, 186 Suranai Rd., Nakornratsema, Thailand.
Chitswang . . . . Chitswang Nursery, 100 Charoenprated Rd., Chiengmai, Thailand.
Cholburi Ny. . . . . . . Cholburi Nursery, Cholburi, Thailand.
Cholet . . . . Pierre Cholet et Cie., Ste. Ame, Chateau d/Achtendries, Ghent, Belgium.
Cholratanakul . . . . . Prasert Cholratanakul, 844/31 Sukumvit Rd., Cholburi, Thailand.
Chomtongdee . . . . . . Suchart Chomtongdee, c/o RHS of Thailand (q.v.).
Chong, A. J. S. . . . . . Andrew J. S. Chong, 743 Makaleka St., Honolulu, HI, USA.
Chong Beng Tiat . . . . Telecoms. Dept., Alor Star, Kedah, Malaysia.
Chong Chok Chye . . . . 30 Linden Dr., Raffles Pk., Singapore, 11.
Chong Orchids . . . . . Salak South Gardens, Kuala Lumpur, Malaysia.
Chong, Peter . . . . . . Peter Y. C. Chong, 1071 Lanui Pl., Honolulu, HI, USA.
Choo Cheng Choong . . . Dr. Choo Cheng Choong, M.B., B.S., 191 Jalan Ampang, P.O. Box 478, Kuala Lumpur, Malaysia
Choo Kok Thye . . . . . Mrs. Choo Kok Thye, 146 Ampang Rd., Kuala Lumpur, Malaysia.
Choo Yeok Koon . . . . 45-D, Jalan Saksama, Singapore, 17.
Chorsatayadham . . . . Pleng Chorsatayadham, c/o RHS of Thailand (q.v.).
Chow . . . . Mrs. S. E. Chow, 158 Ampang Rd., Kuala Lumpur, Malaysia.
Chow Ah Wing . . . . . 5 First Ave., Singapore, 10.
Chow Cheng . . . . . . Chow Cheng Orchids, 194 Litoh St., Taichung, Taiwan.
Chow, Donald . . . . . Donald Y. W. Chow, 1660 Paula Dr., Honolulu, HI, USA.
Chow Yee Wah . . . . . 1130 Hot Spring Rd., Setapak, Kuala Lumpur, Malaysia.
Choy . . . . Clifford K. Choy, 1317B Ahiahi St., Honolulu 17, HI, USA.
Christ . . . . J. H. Christ, 1134 Arrowhead Rd., Pebble Beach, CA 93953, USA.
Christie . . . . Miss Welda F. Christie, 10001 S.W. 68th St., Miami, FL 33143, USA.
Chua Swee Cheng . . . . 121 Jalan Ampang, Kuala Lumpur, Malaysia.
Chuanyen . . . . Swang Chuanyen, Somthawil Orchid Farm, 84/1 Bangpai, Pasicharern, Bangkok, Thailand.
Chuanyen, P. . . . . . . Miss Praneet Chuanyen, Somthawil Orchid Farm, 84/1 Bangpai, Pasicharern, Bangkok, Thailand.
Chun, Edith . . . . . . Edith J. Chun, 6 Jalan Kampong Chantek, Singapore 21.
Chung-Chweng Chen . . Dr. Chung-Chweng Chen, 212 Liteh St., Taichung, Taiwan.
Chunhopakorn . . . . . Wichien Chunhopakorn, 11 Sapanku, Thung Maya Mek, Yannava, Bangkok, Thailand.
Church . . . . Mr. & Mrs. F. J. Church, Orchid by Church, Rt. 1, Box 310, Delray Beach, FL 33444, USA.
Ciesinski . . . . Ronald R. Ciensinski, 22030 Harmon, Taylor, MI 48180, USA.
Clarelen . . . . Clarelen Orchids (C. K. Schubert), Fox Bluff, Waunakee, WI, USA.
Clarke, Astor . . . . . 121-A Plantation Ct. E., Temple Terrace, FL 33617, USA.
Coastal Gdns. . . . . . Coastal Gardens, 137 Tropical La., Corpus Christi, TX 78408, USA.
Cobbs' . . . . Cobbs' Orchids Inc., 780 La Buena Tierra, Santa Barbara, CA 93105, USA.
Cochran . . . . A. N. Cochran, 817 S.W. 20th St., Fort Lauderdale, FL 33315, USA.
Cole, I. . . . . Mrs. Ita Cole, 76 Dresden St., Heidelberg N. 23, Vic., Australia.
Cole, Jack . . . . Jack L. Cole, P.O. Box 224, Signal Mountain, TN 37377, USA.
Coleman . . . . W. R. Coleman, 23 Grafton St., Cairns, N. Qld., Australia.
Coll . . . . Mrs. Carmen A. Coll, 4 Grosvenor Cr., Durban North, Natal, S/Af.

Collett	Lt. Cmdr. A. F. Collett, The Yew Tree, Lydart, Monmouth, Gwent, GB.
Colman	Sir Jeremiah Colman, Bt., Gatton Park, Reigate, Surrey, GB.
Cone	James O. Cone, Rt. 3, Box 555G, Valrico, FL 33594, USA.
Conklin	Lloyd D. Conklin, Kahuku, Oahu, HI, USA.
Cooke	Sir William Cooke, Wyld Court, Hampstead Norris, Newbury, Berks., GB.
Cooke, F. J.	Mrs. Freda Jane Cooke, Aber Artro Hall, Llanbedr, Conwy, Gwynedd, N. Wales, GB.
Cookson, C.	Clive Cookson, Nether Warden, Hexham, Northumberland, GB.
Cookson, N. C.	Norman C. Cookson, Oakwood, Wylam-on-Tyne, Northumberland, GB.
Cooper, Padriac	15745 Morrison St., Encino, CA 91316, USA.
Corban	Assid K. Corban, M. A. Corban Orchids, 312 Great N. Rd., Henderson, Auckland, New Zealand.
Corbett	R. Corbett, 16 Jalan Enam, Housing Trust, Kampar Rd., Ipoh, Perak, Malaysia.
Cornejo	Antonio Cornejo, Ave. Coyoacan 959, Colonia del Vallo, Mexico City, Mexico.
Correa	Eduardo Correa, Avenida Andrés Bello, Urb. Los Palos Grandes, Edif. Vista Hermosa, Apto. 17, Caracas, Venezuela.
Cosanka	Fred Cosanka, 773 Springfield Ave., Summit, NJ, USA.
Cotton	Mrs. Gloria Cotton, "Stripes Hill", Warwick Rd., Knowle, Solihull, West Midlands B93 0DT, GB.
Cowan	Cowan & Co., Old Southgate, London N.14, GB.
Cowart	J. Kimzie Cowart, 2101 Lake Dr., Cocoa, FL 32922, USA.
Cowden	Dan Cowden Orchids, 2615 W. 183rd St., Redondo Beach, CA 90278, USA.
Cox's	Mrs. Thomas J. Cox, Cox's Orchids, 820 Cedros Ave., Solana Beach, CA, USA.
Coyle	Richard D. Coyle, 154 Didge Ave., East Haven, CT, USA.
Craig, Mrs. Valya	First Ave., Sutherland, NSW 2232, Australia.
Craig, Robert	Robert W. Craig, 9302 E. de Adelina St., Rosemead, CA 91770, USA.
Craig's	Craig's Cyps., 9302 de Adelina St., Rosemead, CA 91770, USA.
Crawford	Mr. & Mrs. Donald Crawford, 3509 Mayer Dr., Murrysville, PA 15668, USA.
Crawshay	de Barri Crawshay, Rosefield, Sevenoaks, Kent, GB.
Crestwood	Crestwood Orchids, 420 Fairmount Rd., Signal Mountain, TN 37377, USA.
Creve Coeur	Creve Coeur Orchids, 12 Graesner Acres, Creve Coeur, MO 63141, USA.
Crocker, G	Gene Crocker, Box 3404, Concord, NC 28025, USA.
Crombleholme	Revd. J. Crombleholme, St. Marys, Clayton-le-Moors, Accrington, Lancs., GB.
Crookshank	J. Crookshank Sr., 34 Rhode Ave., St. Augustine, FL 32084, USA.
Crothers	Herbert W. Crothers, 425 Hillside Terrace, Vista, CA 92083, USA.
Cryder	R. W. Cryder, 20 Top Pl., Salinas, CA 93901, USA.
Cummins, J. A.	Honolulu, HI, USA.
Cummins, T. P.	821 18th Ave., Honolulu, HI, USA.
Cummins, W.	Wood K. Cummins, 5384 Kalanianaole Highway, Honolulu, HI, USA.
Cunliffe	(no other data recorded)
Curson	N. W. Curson, 2246 96th Ave., Oakland, CA, USA.
Curry	C. C. Curry, 3929 Fontainbleu Dr., P.O. Box 22581, Tampa, FL 33622, USA.
Cussons	A. T. Cussons, Oaklands, Vine St., Kersal, Manchester, Lancs., GB.
C.Y. Nursery	458/1 Sukumvit Rd., North Samrong, Samuthprakarn, Thailand.
D.	Dorset Orchids Ltd., Plush, Dorchester, Dorset, GB.
D.S.O.	David Sander's Orchids, Lavender Cottage, Wallcrouch, Wadhurst, Sussex, GB.
Dale, A. E.	Tarvin Hall, Tarvin, Chester, GB.
Dallemagne	A. Dallemagne, Rambouillet, 78-Yvlines, France.
Dane	Ernest B. Dane, Roughwood, Chestnut Hill, MA, USA.
Darunee	Darunee Orchid, c/o RHS of Thailand (q.v.).
Darwen	W. H. Darwen, 33 Meadowlands Road, Peakhurst, Sydney, NSW 2210, Australia.
Das	Dick Das Orchids, 2121 Das Way, Orlando, FL 32808, USA.
Daubón, V.	Vasco Daubón, Ponce de Leon Ave. 1510, Santurce, PR 00909, USA.
David Sander's Orchids	(see D.S.O.)
Day, Clark, Jr.	Orchids, 19311 So. Bloomfield Ave., Cerritos, CA 90701, USA.
Day, Lambert	222 So. Anita Ave., West Los Angeles, CA 90049, USA.
de Bruyne	V. C. de Bruyne, 7 Jalan Limau Kasturi, Bangsar Pk., Kuala Lumpur, Malaysia.
De Garmo	Lloyd R. De Garmo, 8555 Rose St., Bellflower, CA 90706, USA.
de Jong	G. A. de Jong, Rijswijk (Z-H.), Netherlands.
de Lacy	Jack de Lacy, 9 Avenell Rd., Bayswater, W. Australia 6053, Australia.
de Paula	Renato de Paula, Rua das Camelias 271, Blo. Horizonte (30.000), Minas Gerais, Brazil.
De 'Quincey	R. De 'Quincey, The Vern, Marden, Hereford, GB.
de Rothschild, Lionel	(see L. de R.)
de Saram	Ernest de Saram, Charmaine, Galagedera, Sri Lanka.
Dean, Nancy	Mrs. Nancy Louise Dean, 2444 McGregor Blvd., Fort Myers, FL 33901, USA.
Dean, R.	Robert Dean, 816 E. Washington St., Greencastle, IN 46135, USA.
Dean, R. J.	Raymond John Dean, 17 Raym Rd., Kenthurst, NSW 2157, Australia.
Dechjun	Ithipol Dechjun, c/o Prof. R. Sagarik (see Sagarik).
Deearom	Tanu Deearom, Chonburi, Thailand.
Deechai	Lt. Amnuay Deechai, 36/3 Prapathone, Nakornprathom, Thailand.
Degenhardt	Richard K. Degenhardt, P.O. Box 7497, Ashville, NC, USA.
Dejdhana, Charoon Sakul	(see Sakuldejdhana)

Dell Park	Dell Park Nurseries (B. L. Schroder), Englefield Green, Egham, Surrey, GB.
Denny	Richard Denny, c/o RHS of Thailand (q.v.).
Dewey	Lynn M. Dewey, 40 N. Tropical Trail, Merritt Island, FL 32952, USA.
Dickey	Dan Dickey, 15071 Valley Vista, Sherman Oaks, CA 91403, USA.
Dickinson, C. E.	Rear Adm. C. E. Dickinson, USN. Retd., 110 Quien Sabe, P.O. Box 307, Carmel Valley, CA 93924, USA.
Dickinson, Mrs. D. V. . .	Mrs. Doreen V. Dickinson, 56 Highfield Rd. South, Chorley, Lancs., GB.
Diggelman	Walter R. Diggelman, 2356 Tiffin Rd., Oakland, CA, USA.
Dittmer	(no other data recorded)
Dixon, E. W.	Mrs. E. W. Dixon, Ronaele Farms, Elkins Pk., PA, USA.
Dixon, F. E.	Mr. & Mrs. F. E. Dixon, Ronaele Manor, Elkins Pk., PA, USA.
D'Lin	D'Lin Orchids (Don Lindabury), 1019 W. 10th, Topeka, KS 66604, USA.
Doan	James Doan, 789 Moreno Ave., Palo Alto, CA, USA.
Dobkin	Irene Dobkin, P.O. Box 175, Huntington Beach, CA 92648, USA.
Dodge	Douglas S. Dodge, Bow Wow Rd., Sheffield, MA 01257, USA.
Doering	Richard Doering, Caixa Postal 11305, São Paulo, Capital, 0,1000, Brazil.
Doerslaer	Franz van Doerslaer, de ten Ryen, Gontrode, Belgium.
Doi, T.	(no other data recorded)
Donnelly	(no other data recorded)
Donning	Stafford Donning, 15 Dorincourt, Talbot Rd., Birkenhead, Merseyside, GB.
Dorp	L. V. Dorp, 7885 S.W. 132nd St., Miami, FL, USA.
Dorset Orchids Ltd. . . .	(see D.)
Dos Pueblos	Dos Pueblos Orchid Co., P.O. Box 158, Goleta, CA 93017, USA.
Dos Pueblos Pty.	Dos Pueblos Pty. Ltd., Dee Why, NSW, Australia.
Doubrava	Charles Doubrava, 125 E. 41st St., Hialeah, FL 33012, USA.
Dugger	R. B. Dugger, 762 N. Granados, Solana Beach, CA 92075, USA.
Duke Farms	Somerville, NJ, USA.
Duncan, I. L.	Dr. Ian Lovell Duncan, 102 1st Ave., Five Dock, NSW 2046, Australia.
Dunhill	Richard Dunhill, "Five Diamonds", Nightingales La., Chalfont St. Giles, Bucks., GB.
Dunkelberger	John A. Dunkelberger, R.D. 1, Centre Hall, PA 16828, USA.
Dunn	Dr. Seymour Dunn, 707 St. Andrews Rd., Hollywood, FL 33021, USA.
Dunning	Lionel S. Dunning, Orchidella, Peover La., Chelford, Macclesfield, Cheshire, GB.
du Pont, W. K.	Mrs. W. K. du Pont, Wilmington, DE, USA.
Duruty	Gregor A. Duruty, 9 Valleton Ave., Maraval, Trinidad, West Indies.
Duveen	Mrs. Geoffrey Duveen, Broadway, Limpsfield, Surrey, GB.
Earl, H. W.	Herbert W. Earl, P.O. Box 466, Deming, NM 88030, USA.
Easton	Andrew W. Easton, Box 10092, 183 Bar M Dr., Eugene, OR 97401, USA.
Eastwood	Revd. H. Quarmby Eastwood, 8 Roumania Dr., Llandudno, Gwynedd, N. Wales, GB.
Ecret	Carl Ecret, 160 E. Orange St., Lake Alfred, FL 33850, USA.
Edelbrock	H. H. Edelbrock, M.D., 5200 Alta Canyada Rd., La Canada, CA 91011, USA.
E. de R.	Edmund de Rothschild, Exbury, Southampton, Hants, GB.
Edin. Bot. Gdns.	Edinburgh Botanical Gardens, Edinburgh, Scotland, GB.
Edris	Col. G. L. Edris, Mu Mu Beach, Maravu Estate, Savu Savu, Fiji.
Edwards Orchids	(William J. Edwards), Rt. 1, Box 622, West Aurora Rd., Eau Gallie, FL 32935, USA.
E. F. G. Orchids	E. F. G. Orchids Inc., 2N134 Addison Rd., Addison, IL 60101, USA.
Eikarat	Sawat Eikarat, c/o RHS of Thailand (q.v.).
Elenewski	Elenewski Bros., Trenton, NJ, USA.
Elle	Artur Elle, Orchideen Farm, 3101 Hambühren 1, Bahnhofsweg, Germany.
Elle & Co,.	Artur Elle & Co., Orchideen-Farm, 3101 Hambühren 1, Bahnhofsweg, Germany.
Elliott, R. J.	56 Belmont Ave., Cockfosters, Barnet, Herts. EN4 9LA, GB.
Elmhurst	Elmhurst Flower Growers Inc., 2N134 Addison Rd., Addison, IL 60101, USA.
Elsner	Willi Elsner, 4441 Wettringen, Konigsbergerstr. 9, Germany.
Enomoto, T.	Todashi Enomoto, Waipahu, Oahu, HI, USA.
Enright	Enright Nursery Co. (Austin Enright), 3011 Capitola Rd., Santa Cruz, CA, USA.
Er Cheng Meng	37 Kolam Rumput Track, Singapore 18.
Ernst	Robert Ernst, 12401 Helena St., Los Angeles, CA 90049, USA.
Escobar, C. A.	Carmen A. Escobar, 45 Valley Rd., Cubao, Quezon City 3001, Philippines.
Escobar, J.	Juan Escobar, 45 Valley Rd., Cubao, Quezon City 3001, Philippines.
Euprayoonwong	Prapin Euprayoonwong, World Florist, Phaholyothin Rd., Bangkok, Thailand.
Eureka Orchid Gdn. . . .	Eureka Orchid Garden, 15850 S.W. 184th St., Miami, FL, USA.
Everett Everett Nurs. }	(no other data recorded)
Everglades	Everglades Orchids, P.O. Box 652, Belle Glade, FL 33430, USA.
Ewe Boon Lee	23 Lorong Aman, Alor Atah, Kedah, Malaysia.
Ewing, J.	John Ewing Orchids, P.O. Box 613, Chatsworth, CA 91311, USA.
Exbury	Exbury Gardens Ltd., Exbury, Southampton, Hants, GB.
Ezzy	John Lloyd Ezzy, 5 Corella Rd., Kirrawee, NSW 2232, Australia.
F.	Le Long Fond (formerly Flandria), 117 Chaussée de Bruxelles, 1310 La Hulpe, Belgium.
Fairburn	David C. Fairburn, 2440 Fairway Dr., Vero Beach, FL 32960, USA.
Faitel	Robert T. Faitel, 18686 Horace St., Northridge, CA, USA.

Fanchaly . . . . Helen Fanchaly, 26424 Cranage Dr., Olmstead Falls, OR, USA.
Fantastic Gdns. . . . . . Fantastic Gardens (W. M. Billing), 9550 S.W. 67th Ave., Miami, FL 33156, USA.
Farnes . . . . S. Farnes, Ashcroft, London Rd., East Grinstead, Sussex, GB.
Feairheller . . . . Dr. & Mrs. Stephen H. Feairheller, 7807 Linden Rd., Wyndmoor, PA 19118, USA.
Fehlandt . . . . Dr. Philip R. Fehlandt, 2715 N. 29th St., Tacoma, WA 98407, USA.
Fennell . . . . Fennell Orchid Co., Inc., 26715 S.W. 157th Ave., Homestead, FL 33030, USA.
Ferguson, A. . . . . . . Alicia Ferguson, c/o Fred A. Stewart Inc. (see Stewart Inc.).
Fernando . . . . Dr. Henry E. Fernando, "Halipolani", Handessa, Sri Lanka.
Ferreira . . . . Mrs. Flora Ferreira, 1020 14th Ave., Honolulu, HI, USA.
Ferrer . . . . Dr. H. P. Ferrer, 30 Brookside Rd., Sale, Cheshire, GB.
Fetherston . . . . John Peter Fetherston, 18 Barker Rd., Strathfield, NSW 2135, Australia.
Fetzer . . . . Ludwig A. Fetzer, 2029 Old York Rd., Hartsville, Bucks County, PA 18974, USA.
Field, R. M. . . . . . . Roy Milton Field, 4018 Whittier Blvd., Los Angeles, CA 90023, USA.
Fields Orchids . . . . . (Roy K. Fields), 196 N.W. 91st St., Miami, FL 33150, USA.
Fields, R. K. . . . . . . c/o Fields Orchids (q.v.).
Fields, Roy . . . . (see R. K. Fields)
Fischer, Ted . . . . . . 319 Sylvan Dr., Goleta, CA 93017, USA.
Fisher, John T. . . . . . Priestgate, East Markham, Newark, Notts., GB.
Fitch . . . . Charles Marden Fitch, 1120 Cove Rd., Mamaroneck, NY 10543, USA.
Florentia . . . . Azienda Florentia (G. Frua), via Privata Scoglio 8, San Remo, Italy.
Flowers, H. M. . . . . . H. Marugame Flowers, 45-228B-5 William Henry Rd., Kaneohe, HI 96744, USA.
Flynn, Elliott . . . . . . 3417 Gray Court, Tampa, FL 33609, USA.
Foo Hok Lee . . . . . . (H. L. Foo), 63 Gopeng Rd., Ipoh, Perak, Malaysia.
Ford, Virgil . . . . 820-A Corcoran Ave., Santa Cruz, CA 95340, USA.
Fordyce . . . . Frank Fordyce, c/o Rod McLellan Co. (q.v.).
Fort Caroline . . . . . . Fort Caroline Orchids Inc., 13142 Fort Caroline Rd., Jacksonville, FL 32225, USA.
Foster . . . . (see Foster Bot. Gdn.)
Foster Bot. Gdn. . . . . . Foster Botanic Gardens, 1520 Nuuanu Ave., Honolulu, HI, USA.
Foster Gdns. . . . . . . (see Foster Bot. Gdn.)
Foster's, Rex . . . . . . Rex Foster's Orchids, 2645 Massachusetts Ave., P.O. Box 458, Lemon Grove, CA 92045, USA.
Foulds . . . . Mrs. M. B. Foulds, "Lynton", 54 Gresham Rd., Hall Green, Birmingham, GB.
Fouquette . . . . Charles R. Fouquette, Fouquette Orchids, 9349 Burning Tree Way, Santee, CA 92071, USA.
Fouraker . . . . Stanley R. Fouraker, 2572 Pineridge Rd., Jacksonville, FL 32207, USA.
Fournier . . . . (no other data recorded)
Fowler . . . . J. Gurney Fowler, Brackenhurst, Pembury, Kent, GB.
Fowler, June . . . . . . Mrs. June Fowler, 6343 Western Way, Lake Worth, FL 33460, USA.
Fox, Mrs. H. W. . . . . . Mrs. Harrison W. Fox, 3230 Walnut St. N.W., St. Petersburg, FL 33204, USA.
Fox Orchids . . . . . . Fox Orchids Inc., 6615 W. Markham, Little Rock, AR 72205, USA.
Frackowiak . . . . Engelbert Frackowiak, School House Rd., Gwynedd Valley, PA 19437, USA.
Francis, Kay . . . . . . Mrs. Kay Francis, 637 Vista Ave., Pasadena, CA 91105, USA.
Freed . . . . Arthur Freed Orchids Inc., 5731 Bonsall Dr., Malibu, CA 90265, USA.
Frese . . . . Mrs. Renate Frese, 5038 Hahnwald Post, Rodenkirchen bei Köln, Im Hasengarten 27, Germany.
Fresh . . . . Mr. & Mrs. J. L. Fresh, 8777 SW 76th St., Miami, FL 33143, USA.
Freund . . . . Neal E. Freund, 5916 Wassman Rd., Knoxville, TN 37912, USA.
Friedel . . . . Vince Friedel, 4160 S.W. 53rd Ave., Davie, FL 33314, USA.
Friend . . . . Robert G. M. Friend, 7 Trentwood Park, Avalon Beach, NSW 2107, Australia.
Frua, G. . . . . (see Florentia)
Fuchs Jr. . . . . Fred J. Fuchs Jr., Fuchs Orchids, Box 1113, Naranja, FL 33390, USA.
Fuchs Sr., F. . . . . . . Fred J. Fuchs Sr., 28100 S.W. 182nd Ave., Homestead, FL 33030, USA.
Fuchs, R. F. . . . . . . Robert F. Fuchs, 286 Old Dixie Hwy., Homestead, FL 33030, USA.
Fugedy . . . . John L. Fugedy, P.O. Box 462, Rogers, AR 72756, USA.
Fuglerk . . . . Swudi Fuglerk, 710 Sriyarn Soi 1, Narkornchaisri Rd., Bangkok, Thailand.
Fujimoto . . . . Harold N. Fujimoto, Box 32, Honomu, HI, USA.
Fuji Nurs. . . . . Fuji Nurseries, P.O. Box 43, Kurashiki, Japan.
Fujinaga, Y. . . . . . . Mrs. Yasu Fujinaga, 3039a Waipuna Rise, Honolulu, HI, USA.
Fujino . . . . Robert T. Fujino, 3423 Maunalea Ave., Honolulu, HI, USA.
Fujio . . . . Richard T. Fujio, 3161 Papala St., Honolulu, HI 96822, USA.
Fujio, K. . . . . Kengo Fujio, Hara, Hatsukaichi Cho, Saikigun, Hiroshima-ken, Japan.
Fujiwara, Dr. T. . . . . . Dr. & Mrs. Thomas Fujiwara, 2649 Huapala St., Honolulu, HI 96822, USA.
Fujiwara, Mrs. T. F. . . . Mrs. Thomas F. Fujiwara, 2649 Huapala St., Honolulu, HI 96822, USA.
Fukudo . . . . Mitsuyoshi Fukudo, 1411 Mamalu St., Honolulu, HI, USA.
Fukuhara . . . . Yoshiharu Fukuhara, 7-4 Zushi, 6-chome, Zushi-shi, Kanagawa-ken, 249, Japan.
Fukumura . . . . T. Fukumura, Box 339, Kahului, Maui, HI, USA.
Fukumura, G. M. . . . . George M. Fukumura, 277 Pohakulani St., Hilo, HI 96720, USA.
Fukumura, R. T. . . . . . 49 E. Kauai St., Kahului, Maui, HI 96732, USA.
Fukumura Orchids . . . . R. T. Fukumura Orchids, 49 E. Kauai St., Kahului, Maui, HI 96732, USA.
Fukunaga . . . . Tom Fukunaga, 1659 Liholiho St., Honolulu, HI, USA.
Funston . . . . Wilbur H. Funston, P.O. Box 1633, Huntsville, AL 35807, USA.
Furrow . . . . J. W. Furrow, Furrow & Co. Inc., P.O. Box 1256, Oklahoma City, OK 73101, USA.

Furst	John N. Furst, M.D., 1120 S.W. Stopp Pl., Corvallis, OR 97330, USA.
Furumizo	Henry K. Furumizo, 403 Oahu St., Kahului, Maui, HI 96732, USA.
Fyfe	Clyde Fyfe, "Onika", Australian Dock, Palm Beach, FL 33480, USA.
G. & S.	Gallup & Stribling Orchids Inc., 3450 N. Via Real, Carpinteria, CA 93013, USA.
G. & S. Int.	Gallup & Stribling International, 3450 N. Via Real, Carpinteria, CA 93013, USA.
G. Orchids	Ampung Muang, Chonburi, Thailand.
Gaar	Mrs. Kermit A. Gaar (Franceil F. Gaar), 911 Monrovia St., Shreveport, LA 71106, USA.
Gaine	Brian Gaine, 6395 S.W. 96th St., Miami, FL 33156, USA.
Galaxy Gdns.	Galaxy Gardens (W. P. Corley), 351 Schoen St. S.E., Atlanta 15, GA, USA.
Gallup & Stribling	(see G. & S.)
Gallup & Stribling International	(see G. & S. Int.)
Gamble	Franklin W. Gamble, 62 Shell Rd., Alto Mill Valley, CA, USA.
Gardiner, J. H.	J. H. Gardiner Jr., 1614 Overlook Rd., Orlando, FL, USA.
Gardner	C. D. Gardner, 35030 Buena Mesa, Calimesa, CA, USA.
Gardner, Carlton	P.O. Box 122, Bonsall, CA 92003, USA.
Gardner, R. N.	Richard N. Gardner, Jr., 948 Sproul Rd., Bryn Mawr, PA 19010, USA.
Garth	Eric Garth, Sunvalley Nursery, 63/1 Kundasale, Sri Lanka.
Gauda	H. Gauda, Orchids, Kokusai Nursery Co. Ltd. 1-10 Taishido, 2-chome, Setagaya-ku, Tokyo, Japan.
Gavelek	J. A. Gavelek, 2800 S.W. 18th St., Miami, FL 33145, USA.
Gem Nursery	172 Moulmein Rd., Singapore 11.
Gemenis	Dr. C. M. Gemenis, 695 Anzac Parade, Maroubra 2035, Australia.
Gera	Raymond M. Gera, 535 Seminole Dr., Eau Gallie, FL, USA.
Gerard	Catherine Jean Gerard, 178 National Ave., Loftus, NSW 2232, Australia.
Gerbig	Howard A. Gerbig, 935 S.W. 7th Ave., Fairbault, MN 55021, USA.
Gesatis	Mr. & Mrs. Ben Gesatis, Gesatis Greenhouses, 7949 S.E. Glencoe Rd., Portland, OR, USA.
Gesler	Ross W. Gesler, 16411 Arrow Blvd., Fontana, CA 92335, USA.
Gesmaris	V. Gesmaris, c/o RHS of Thailand (q.v.).
Giatgong	Dr. Piya Giatgong, 592/1 Klong Chugpra, Talingchan, Thonburi, Thailand.
Gibson, A. R.	c/o W. C. Ross Ltd., Frederick St., Port of Spain, Trinidad, West Indies.
Gibson, R. A.	Cmdr. R. A. Gibson, 6303 Thumper St., Jacksonville, FL 32210, USA.
Giles, G. Giles, L.	(see Wondabah)
Glasgow, E.	Earl Glasgow, 2172 Magnolia, Sarasola, FL, USA.
Gleneyrie	Gleneyrie Orchids, Southfield, MI, USA.
Gnanasuntharam	P. Gnanasuntharam, Technical Teachers Training College, 4¼ Mile, Cheras Rd., Kuala Lumpur, Malaysia.
Goddard	C. R. Goddard, M.D., 37 Willow Oak Rd. W., Hilton Head Island, SC 29928, USA.
Goff	Marvin Edwin Goff, 15910 N.W. 44th Ct., Opa Locka, FL 33054, USA.
Goff, E. K.	Mrs. Eva K. Goff, 15910 N.W. 44th Ct., Opa Locka, FL 33054, USA.
Goh Gin Hwa	998N Sembawang Rd., Singapore, 27.
Goo	Lum Goo, 582 M. Rd., Damon Tract, Honolulu, HI, USA.
Goodchild	Norman John Goodchild, 6 Braye Cr., Garden Suburbs, Kotara, Newcastle, NSW 2288, Australia.
Gore	R. H. Gore Orchids, Box 211, 1611 S.W. 9th Ave., Fort Lauderdale, FL 33315, USA.
Goshima	Hachizaemon Goshima, 382 Higashi Koiso, Oiso-machi, Nakagun, Kanagawa-ku, Japan.
Gotoh, K.	Kenkichi Gotoh, Yotsuyasakamachi 22, Shinjuku, Tokyo, Japan.
Goudie	Noel Goudie, 56 Yamba Rd., Como West, Sydney, NSW 2226, Australia.
Goulton	J. H. Goulton (no address recorded).
Gowling, W. & A.	W. R. & A. J. Gowling, Lot 5D, States Rd., Hackham, SA 5163, Australia.
Graf, H.	Henry Graf, P.O. Box 68033, Caracas, 106, Venezuela.
Graham	E. Marvin Graham, 137 Alma St., Watsonville, CA 95076, USA.
Gratiot	M. le Docteur Jean Gratiot, Ferté-sous-Jouarre, S. & M., France.
Gratrix	S. Gratrix, West Point, Whalley Range, Manchester, GB.
Gratrix, Mrs.	Mrs. S. Gratrix, West Point, Whalley Range, Manchester, GB.
Graves	Willard E. Graves, 2743 Kelton Ave., Los Angeles, CA 90064, USA.
Green, Ted	340 Halemaumau Pl., Honolulu, HI 96821, USA.
Greendyke	Dr. R. M. Greendyke, 152 W. Jefferson Rd., Pittsford, NY 14534, USA.
Greene, R. O.	Robert O. Greene, 8744 Ralph St., Rosemead, CA 91770, USA.
Greenoaks	(Mrs. E. W. Menninger) Greenoaks, 1030 Old Ranch Rd., Arcadia, CA 91006, USA.
Grezaffi	Joe Grezaffi III, 620 Acacia Ave., Melbourne, FL 32901, USA.
Griffiths	K. J. Griffiths, Jilltana Orchids, 1003 Richard Ave., Kannapolis, NC 29081, USA.
Gripp	Paul Gripp, Santa Barbara Orchid Estate (see Santa Barbara).
Grittiya	Grittiya Orchid, c/o RHS of Thailand (q.v.).
Grodske	Mr. & Mrs. Donald W. Grodske, 16717 Devonshire St., Granada Hills, CA, USA.
Grogan	(no other data known)
Gronwall	Frank A. Gronwall, P.O. Box 6, Kihi Kihi, New Zealand.
Gubler	Gubler Orchids, 9441 E. Broadway, Temple City, CA 91780, USA.

Gunderson	Morris R. Gunderson, 8932 Costello Ave., Panorama City, CA 91402, USA.
Gunzenhauser	E. Gunzenhauser, Orchideenkulturen, 4460 Gelterkinden, Switzerland.
Guthrie Jr.	John B. Guthrie Jr., 2857 S.W. 13th Ct., Fort Lauderdale, FL 33312, USA.
Gutierrez	J. L. Gutierrez Jr., 4235 S.W. 98th Ct., Miami, FL 33165, USA.
Guttin	(no other data recorded)
H.	Lt. Col. Sir George Holford, C.I.E., K.C.V.O., Westonbirt, Tetbury, Glos., GB.
Habanananda	Nang Chad Habanananda, Bangkok, Thailand.
Haber	Wolfgang Haber, 805 Fresing, W. Germany.
Hack	E. R. Hack, R.F.D. 1, Box 989, Sequim, WA 98322, USA.
Hackett	John Joseph Hackett, 1513 Wiley St., Hollywood, FL, USA.
Hagan	Charles E. Hagan, 1744 W. Las Olas Blvd., Fort Lauderdale, FL 33312, USA.
Hager	Herb Hager Orchids, 30th Capitola Rd., Box 544, Santa Cruz, CA 95060, USA.
Hall, Richard	Richard W. R. Hall, 25 Ruskin Row, Avalon Beach, Sydney, NSW, Australia.
Hall, Roy K.	9962 Greenfield Dr., Dallas, TX 75238, USA.
Hall, W. K.	W. Knowlton Hall, 1314 Glenn Ave., Augusta, GA 30904, USA.
Hamilton, R. M.	Robert M. Hamilton, 921 Beckwith Rd., Richmond, BC, V6X 1V7, Canada.
Hanaoka	Masoa Hanaoka, 7088 Niumalu Loop, Honolulu, HI 96825, USA.
Hanbury	Fred J. Hanbury, Brockhurst, East Grinstead, Sussex, GB.
Hancock	Clarence W. Hancock, 483 Cuesta Dr., Los Altos, CA 94022, USA.
Hands, G.	Geoffrey Hands, 7 Featherston Rd., Streetly, Sutton Coldfield, W. Midlands, GB.
Hanes	John W. Hanes, Hanes Orchids, 6264 N. Bion Ave., San Gabriel, CA 91775, USA.
Hankey	W. Barnard Hankey, Dorset Orchids Ltd., Plush, Dorchester, Dorset, GB.
Hansen	Knud Hansen, 560 W. Woodbury Rd., Altadena, CA, USA.
Hansen, J. E.	Jerry E. Hansen, 1270 N. Main St., East Peoria, IL 61611, USA.
Hanson, H. C.	Mrs. Hazel Catherine Hanson, 429 Ellerslie-Panmure Hwy., Panmure, Auckland, 6, New Zealand.
Harben	Guy P. Harben, Colbury House, Totton, Southampton, GB.
Harding	A. H. Harding, Labu Estate, Labu, Negri Sembilan, Malaysia.
Hark	Fritz Hark, 478 Lippstadt i/w, Schmales Feld 35, Germany.
Harnpongtham, Mrs. R.	Mrs.Rachadaporn Harnpongtham, 224/1 Suksawas Rd., Bangpakok, Bangkok, Thailand.
Harnpongtham, S.	Suchuit Harnpongtham, 224/1 Suksawas Rd., Bangpakok, Bangkok, Thailand.
Harris, B. F.	21 Park Ave., Walnut Creek, CA 94595, USA.
Harris, F. L.	Florence L. Harris, 21 Park Ave., Walnut Creek, CA 94595, USA.
Harrison	Alwyn Harrison, Risdene, Sharnbrook, Bedford, GB.
Hartson	Merritt O. Hartson, Steffeny Rd., Randallstown, MD 21133, USA.
Harvest	James J. Harvest, 1456 Leilani St., Honolulu, HI, USA.
Hashimoto, E. Y.	P.O. Box 212, Hakalau, HI, USA.
Hassall	Hassall & Co., Southgate, London, N., GB.
Hattori	Yoshitoshi Hattori, 12 Tanaka-Higashi-Hinokuchi-cho, Sakyo-ku, Kyoto-shi, Kyoto-fu, Japan.
Hausermann	Hausermann's Orchids Inc., Box 363, Elmhurst, IL 60126, USA.
Haw. Mt. O.	Hawaii Mountain Orchids Inc., P.O. Box 934, Hilo, HI 96720, USA.
Hawaii Mountain Orchids	(see Haw. Mt. O.)
Hawaii V. N.	Hawaii Vanda Nursery, 10/11 Young Building, Hilo, HI, USA.
Hawkins	Hobbie L. Hawkins, P.O. Box 903, 9406 Okeechobee Rd., West Palm Beach, FL 33406, USA.
Hawley	Ronald M. Hawley, 156 Stanford Ave., Mill Valley, CA 94941, USA.
Haynes, Elroy	Elroy D. Haynes, 2910 Oahu Ave., Honolulu, HI 96822, USA.
Heaner	Mrs. M. R. Heaner, 701 State National Building, 412 Main St., Houston, TX 77002, USA.
Heaton	J. J. Heaton, Dahmoy, New St., Farsley, Leeds, GB.
Hecht	H. A. Hecht, Gray Summit Orchids, 12 N. Graeser Rd., Creve Coeur, MO, USA.
Hecker	Grayce Hecker Orchids, 2525 W. Charleston Rd., Las Vegas, NV, USA.
Helton	Odie Helton, 2735 Wayside La., Springfield, OR 97477, USA.
Hennis	Wilhelm Hennis, Orchideen-Kultur, Hildesheim, Gr. Venedig 4, (Hann.), Germany.
Henry, Tom	Tom Henry Pty. Ltd., 25 Ruskin La., Avalon Beach, NSW 2107, Australia.
Herman, D. E.	c/o Trymwood Orchids, 2500 Rockdell St., La Crescenta, CA 91214, USA.
Hernlund	Kermit Hernlund, P.O. Box 775, Hilo, HI 96720, USA.
Hernlund, M.	Mary Hernlund, c/o Hawaii Mountain Orchids (see Haw. Mt. O.); also 1911 Kalananeole Ave., Apt. 307, Hilo, HI 96720, USA.
Hershy	William Hershy, 4 Midfarm Rd., Rockville Center, Long Island, NY 11570, USA.
Hesse	Henry M. Hesse, 45135 Naoku St., Kaneohe, HI 96744, USA.
Hew Nurseries	Old Airport Rd., Kuala Lumpur, Malaysia.
Hewlett	Dr. Amoit Hewlett, Star Rt. 1, Box 219A, Beaufort, SC 29902, USA.
Hey	Mr. & Mrs. G. L. Hey, 162 Old Bedford Rd., Luton, Beds., GB.
Hiatt	Glen H. Hiatt, Los Angeles State & County Arboretum, 301 N. Baldwin Ave., P.O. Box 688, Arcadia, CA, USA.
Hieda	Eichi Hieda, 4015 Palua Pl., Honolulu, HI, USA.
Hiew Kim Sang	22 Perak Rd., Kuala Lumpur, Malaysia.
Hiews'	Hiews' Nurseries, 76 Jalan Weld., Kuala Lumpur, Malaysia.

Higa	Mildred Higa, 5012 Kilauea Ave., Honolulu, HI 96816, USA.
Higuchi	Mrs. Yoshiko Higuchi, 85-810 Farrington Hwy., Waianae, HI, USA.
Hill, Daniel M.	Hill's Orchid Laboratory, 605 East Granada Ct., P.O. Box 1184, Ontario, CA 91762, USA.
Hill, H. A.	Howard A. Hill, 1649 W. Cypress, Redlands, CA 92373, USA.
Hiranburana	Dr. Arom Hiranburana, 77 Soi Chompol, Ladpraw Rd., Bangkok, Thailand.
Hirano	Albert Hirano, 1307 University Ave., Honolulu, HI, USA.
Hirisatja	Uthai Hirisatja, c/o RHS of Thailand (q.v.).
Hironaka	Hajime Hironaka, 2204 Dale St., Honolulu, HI 96814, USA.
Hirose	Hirose Nurseries, 46 Josephine La., Hilo, HI, USA.
Hirotsee	James T. Hirotsee, P.O. Box 357, Wailuku, Maui, HI 96793, USA.
Hisazaki	Dr. Takahiro Hisazaki, 5-101 Sakurayama-cho, Show-ku, Nagoya, Japan.
Ho, A. C.	611 Duncan Dr., Kaneohe, HI, USA.
Ho, Herbert	537 Kipaka Pl., Kailua, HI 96734, USA.
Ho Kean Keat	4548 Jalan Kampong Paya, Butterworth, Malaysia.
Ho King	17 Ettrick Terrace, Singapore, 15.
Ho, Philip	Philip T. S. Ho, 1020 Valley View Dr., Honolulu, Oahu, HI 96819, USA.
Hoadley	Peter Hoadley, St. Andrew's Terrace, Port of Spain, Trinidad, West Indies.
Hofsommer	Dr. & Mrs. Armin C. Hofsommer, 1122 Castle Way, Menlo Pk., CA 94025, USA.
Holford, Lt. Col. Sir George	(see H.)
Holguin, L.	Leo Holguin, c/o Armacost & Royston Inc. (see A. & R.).
Holland	Mrs. Frank L. Holland, Regency Apt., Winter Haven, FL, USA.
Holland, Frank	Frank L. Holland, Regency Apt., Winter Haven, FL, USA.
Holm, B.	D-4293 Dingden, Lankern Nr. 56, Germany.
Holvichai	Mrs. Vipa Holvichai, c/o Siam Society of Plant Culture, 933 Mahachai Rd., Bangkok, Thailand.
Homosassa	Homosassa Springs Orchids, P.O. Box 8, Homosassa Springs, FL 32647, USA.
Hon San	309J Rasah Rd., Seremban, N.S., W. Malaysia.
Hong Kok Hoo	734 Jalan 17/32, Petaling Jaya, Malaysia.
Hong-Sie Chen / Hong Sih Chen	Hong-Sie Chen (formerly known as Hong Sih Chen), 212 Liteh St., Taichung, Taiwan.
Honwichai	Phiew Honwichai, c/o RHS of Thailand (q.v.).
Hoornaert	Firme Louis Hoornaert, Orchid Growers & Exporters, St. Nicholas W., Belgium.
Hornvichai	Piew Hornvichai, c/o Prof. R. Sagarik (see Sagarik).
Hopson	Oliver W. Hopson, 8015 Mivorna Way, Fair Oaks, CA 95628, USA.
Horridge	Capt. W. Horridge, M.C., Boltholt House, Bury, Lancs., GB.
Hoshino	Dr. Francis Hoshino, 2079 Iholina, Honolulu, HI, USA.
Hoshino, F. Y.	Francis Y. Hoshino (and Mrs. F. Y. Hoshino), 1902d Aleo Pl., Honolulu, HI 95822, USA.
Hothfield	Lt. Col. The Lord Hothfield and The Lady Hothfield, Castle Hill, Englefield Green, Egham, Surrey, GB.
Houston	Mrs. Stephanie Houston, 2051 Laura La., West Palm Beach, FL, USA.
How Yee Peng	91 Nemesu Ave., Singapore, 20.
Howard, Nell	Mrs. Nell Howard, 13708 Cordary Ave., Hawthorne, CA, USA.
Howe	Don Howe, Rt. 3, Atlanta, TX 75551, USA.
Howell	Oscar F. Howell, 2950 Holly Rd., Fort Myers, FL 33901, USA.
Hoyt	Gordon M. Hoyt, Seattle Heights, WA 98063, USA.
Hozaki	James Hozaki, 155 West Papa Ave., Kahului, Maui, HI 96732, USA.
Hubbard	Edward E. Hubbard, 256 Tring Rd., Aylesbury, Bucks., GB.
Hudson	Mordecai Hudson, 94-144 Mokukaua St., Waipahu, HI 96797, USA.
Hueylih Jane	(no other data recorded)
Hughes	Sir Harrison T. Hughes, Eddington House, Hungerford, Berks., GB.
Hughes, J. F.	J. Frank Hughes, 480 Eureka Canyon Rd., Watsonville, CA 95076, USA.
Hughes, Frank	(see Hughes, J. F.)
Hughes, W. L.	William Leonard Hughes, Lot 3, Jones Ave., Primbee, NSW 2504, Australia.
Hung Ung Young	Hung Ung Young Nursery, 1143a 7th Ave., Honolulu, HI, USA.
Hunnewell	Walter Hunnewell, 863 Washington St., Wellesley, MA 02181, USA.
Hurtt	Lawrence Hurtt Jr., 6915 Forest Hill Dr., St. Louis, MO 63121, USA.
Hutchison	Renton Hutchison, 1818 Waianuenue Ave., Hilo, HI 96720, USA.

Ichijyo	Shigeaki Ichijyo, 6-7 Onagamachi, Hiroshima, Japan.
Ikeda	Narikatsu Ikeda, Japan Horticulture Co. Ltd., Oiso, Kanagawa-ken, Japan.
Ilgenfritz	Margaret M. Ilgenfritz Orchids, P.O. Box 665, 62 E. Elm Ave., Monroe, MI 48161, USA.
Ilsley	Philip Ilsley, P.O. Box 69695, West Branch, Los Angeles, CA 90060, USA.
Ilsley Orchids	12835 Mulholland Dr., Beverly Hills, CA, USA.
Inada	Yoshihiro Inada, 1918 Higashibun, Utazo-cho, Ayauta-gun, Kagawa-ken 769-02, Japan.
Ingram	C. L. Ingram, Elstead House, Godalming, Surrey, GB.
Inouye, Y.	Yoshito Inouye, 673 Akoakoa St., Kailua, HI 96734, USA.
Intachote	Boonchu Intachote, 67/8 Khunpithuk, Damnersadouk, Ratchaburi, Thailand.
Introini	Mrs. Elsie Introini, 319 Point San Pedro Rd., San Rafael, CA, USA.

Ireland . . . . Mrs. H. B. Ireland (Mary Bea Ireland), 146 Coronada Circle, Santa Barbara, CA 93108, USA.
Irving . . . . Mr. & Mrs. Jack Irving, Rt. 2, Box 100, Tavares, FL 32778, USA.
Ishikawa . . . . Masatoshi Ishikawa, 1505 Tamura, Hiratsuka-shi, Kanagawa-ken, Japan.
Itagaki . . . . Genzo Itagaki, 1718A Mikahala Way, Honolulu, HI 96816, USA.
Ito, H. . . . . Henry Ito, 274 Makua St., Wailuku, Maui, HI 96793, USA.
Itoh . . . . Masaaki Itoh, 35, 2-chome Hagiyama-cho, Mijuho-ku, Nagoya City, Aichi-Prefecture, Japan.
Iwanaga, E. . . . . Ernest T. Iwanaga, 2614 Waiomao Rd., Honolulu, HI 96816, USA.
Iwanaga, Mrs. E. . . . . 2614 Waiomao Rd., Honolulu, HI 96816, USA.
Iwasaki, G. . . . . George Iwasaki, Kalanianaoto Hwy., Honolulu, HI, USA.

J. & L. . . . . J. & L. Orchids (Lee B. Kuhn), 20 Sherwood Rd., Easton, CT 06612, USA.
J. & S. . . . . Jones & Scully Inc., 2200 N.W. 33rd Ave., Miami, FL 33142, USA.
Jackson, A. . . . . Andrew Jackson, 250 East 11th St., Hialeah, FL, USA.
Jackson, D. C. . . . . . . Legal Adviser's Chambers, Johure Bahru, Malaysia.
Jaderstrom . . . . Hilma R. Jaderstrom, 570 Uluhala St., Kailua, HI 96734, USA.
Jain . . . . Alok P. Jain, c/o Orchid Society of Thailand, GPO Box 953, Bangkok, Thailand.
Jalavicharana . . . . . . Kahn Jalavicharana, Dept. of Agriculture, Bangkok, Thailand.
Jalichan, D. . . . . . . Damkerng Jalichan, 339/1 Soi Rajaprarob, Makasan, Bangkok, Thailand.
James, I. D. . . . . No. 2 R. D., Hamilton, New Zealand.
Janes . . . . Mr. & Mrs. P. D. Janes, 46 Woodlands La., Shirley, Solihull, West Midlands, GB.
Jansen . . . . Anthony Samuel Jansen, c/o Shell Eastern Petroleum (Pte) Ltd., Pulau Bukom, Singapore.
Jarzab . . . . Edwin W. Jarzab, 5307 W. Oakdale Dr., Oaklawn, IL 60453, USA.
Jay, J. M. . . . . Joe Ming Jay, 912 17th Ave., Honolulu, HI, USA.
Jayaratna . . . . Anong Jayaratna, c/o RHS of Thailand (q.v.).
Jeals . . . . Jeals Nurseries (Fernhill) Ltd., Fernhill Rd., Horley, Surrey, GB.
Jeal . . . . Wilfred J. Jeal, 4171 W. 190th St., Torrance, CA, USA.
Jelinek . . . . Roy Jelinek, 71 Pine Island Rd., Fort Myers, FL, USA.
Jenkins . . . . Harry J. Jenkins, 14 Bay St., Beauty Point, NSW, Australia.
Jensen . . . . N. M. Jensen, Duke's Edge, Woldingham, Surrey, GB.
Jesup . . . . Mr. & Mrs. H. P. Jesup, 183 Fox Den Rd., Bristol, CT 07010, USA.
Jesurún . . . . Abraham Jesurún, Calle Los Alpes, Quinta Gloria, Urb. Prados del Este, Caracas, Venezuela.
Jiranuvat . . . . Police Lt. Col. Swang Jiranuvat, c/o C. Thongsuphan (see Thongsuphan).
Jitra . . . . Mrs. Jitra, c/o RHS of Thailand (q.v.).
Joaquim . . . . Miss Agnes Joaquim (no other data recorded).
Johnson, F. . . . . Frank Johnson, Nash Farm, Scaynes Hill, Haywards Heath, Sussex, GB.
Johnson, Loren . . . . . J. & L. Tropicals, 4734 Cogswell Rd., El Monte, CA 91732, USA.
Johnston, D. W. . . . . . 19931 Lorne St., Reseda, CA, USA.
Johnston, P. W. . . . . . P. Worrall Johnston Sr., 103 Westgate Dr., Westgate Farms, Wilmington, DE 19808, USA.
Johnstone, Jo . . . . . . Mrs. Jo Johnstone, Cross St., R.D.2, Hammondsport, NY 14840, USA.
Jolibois . . . . (no other data recorded)
Jones & Scully Inc. . . . . (see J. & S.)
Jones, Mrs. Ethel . . . . Maui Meadows, Kihea, Maui, HI 96733, USA.
Jones, J. E. . . . . (see under Limberlost)
Jordahn . . . . A. C. Jordahn, Box 292, Coconut Grove, Miami 33, FL, USA.
Joseph . . . . Albert Joseph, 1774B Palola Ave., Honolulu, HI, USA.
Jost, R. P. . . . . Richard P. Jost, 143 Ackerman Ave., Clifton, NJ 07011, USA.
Jost & Rumrill . . . . . . 143 Ackerman Ave., Clifton, NJ 07011, USA.
Juanita Nurs. . . . . . . Juanita Nursery, La Boheme Ave., Caringbah, Sydney, NSW, Australia.
Juanyen . . . . (see Chuanyen)
Juergens . . . . Fritz Juergens, D-4905 Spenge 3, Am. Katzenholz 8, Germany.
Julia . . . . Luis Ariza Julia, Puerto Plata, Republic Dominicana, West Indies.
Jupp, V. & N. . . . . . . V. F. & N. C. Jupp, Riverdene Nurseries, P.O. Box 1, East Gresford, NSW 2491, Australia.

K. . . . . A. K. Keeling & Son, Westgate Hill, Bradford, Yorks, GB.
Kaewkamnerd . . . . . . Mano Kaewkamnerd, Chiengmai, Thailand.
Kaga . . . . Mrs. Chiyo Kaga, Tenozan, Ohyamazaki-mura, Otagi-gun, Kyoto-fu, Japan.
Kagawa, H. . . . . Hiroshi Kagawa, 348 Maluniu Ave., Kailua, HI 95734, USA.
Kagawa, Dr. K. . . . . . 111 Bishop St., Honolulu, HI 96813, USA.
Kagawa, S. . . . . Dr. Shinso Kagawa, 3215 Kaohinani Dr., Honolulu, HI, USA.
Kako, Koichi . . . . . . Koichi Kako, 26 Miyanowaki, Kagiya-cho, Toaki City, Aichi, Japan.
Kamemoto, K. . . . . . . Kazuo Kamemoto, 3380 E. Manoa Rd., Honolulu, HI 96822, USA.
Kam In Chong . . . . . . Mrs. Kam In Chong, 286 Beach Walk, Honolulu, HI, USA.
Kammerer . . . . William Kammerer, Townsend Hill Rd., Townsend, MA 01469, USA.
Kamol . . . . Mr. Kamol, c/o RHS of Thailand (q.v.).
Kamolparawat . . . . . . Sam Rit Kamolparawat, 261 Trok Talad Noi, Charoen Krung Rd., Bangkok, Thailand.
Kanemitsu . . . . Hisaji Kanemitsu, 166 Alae St., Hilo, HI, USA.

Kanemitsu, Mrs. H.	166 Alae St., Hilo, HI, USA.
Kanayama	Richard K. Kanayama, 45-155 Awele Pl., Kaneohe, HI 96744, USA.
Kaneshiro	Stanley Kaneshiro, 3418B McCorriston St., Honolulu, HI 96815, USA.
Kanniah	M. Kanniah, Education Office, Seremban, Negri Sembilan, Malaysia.
Kanpai	Chit Kanpai, 7/2 Soi Vatana Vong, Makasan, Bangkok 4, Thailand.
Kantajaraniti	Kriengkrai Kantajaraniti, c/o RHS of Thailand (q.v.).
Karaket	Mongkol Krisna Karaket, c/o RHS of Thailand (q.v.).
Karasawa	Kohji Karasawa, 458 Aono-machi, Nara-shi, Nara-ken, Japan.
Kareboon	Miss Kareboon, c/o RHS of Thailand (q.v.).
Karleen	Philip E. Karleen, M.D., 4605 Opal Cliff Dr., Santa Cruz, CA 95062, USA.
Karthaus	A. C. Karthaus, Potsdam, Germany.
Kasem	Kasem Orchids, 107/29 Soi Mansin 4, Prarama 6 Rd., Bangkok, Thailand.
Kasetsart Univ.	Kasetsart University, Horticulture Dept., Bangkok 9, Thailand.
Kasky	Dan A. Kasky, 249 23rd. St., Brooklyn 15, NY, USA.
Kasten	Al. Kasten, 1601 Binney Dr., Fort Pierce, FL 33450, USA.
Kato	Tadanobu Kato, 88 Ueda-machi, Oura, Nagasaki City, Japan.
Katsuura	Katsuura Shoyoen Orchid Co. Ltd., (Takayoshi Katsuura), 4-6-20 Kitakasugaoka, Ibaraki City, Osaka 567, Japan.
Kavanagh	Mrs. Irene Nellie Kavanagh, 47 May Rd., Dee Why, NSW, Australia.
Kawabata	Ray Kawabata, 45-547 Nakumanu Pl., Kaneohe, HI 96744, USA.
Kawamoto, H. N.	Henry N. Kawamoto, 159 Hualalai St., Hilo, HI, USA.
Kayima	K. Kayima (no other data recorded).
Kazumura, T.	145 N. Judd St., Honolulu, HI 96817, USA.
Keen	James H. Keen, 2618 Cayuga Rd., Dartmouth Woods, Wilmington, DE 19810, USA.
Keesa-nga	Amnuay Keesa-nga, 46/3 Prapoothabat, Saraburi, Thailand.
Kehr	A. B. Kehr, 1414 Highland Ave., Abington, PA, USA.
Keith	Mervyn James Keith, 26 Gorari St., Idalia Estate, Townsville, Qld., Australia
Keller	Austil Keller, 3709 Round Top Dr., Honolulu, HI 96822, USA.
Kelley, M.	Mrs. Myra Kelley, 133 Kamarin St., Manly, Qld. 4179, Australia.
Kellogg, C. S.	C. S. Kellogg, M.D., 6800 Chapman Field Dr., Miami, FL 33156, USA.
Kelly	Warren R. Kelly, 11295 S.W. 93rd St., Miami, FL 33156, USA.
Kembla	Kembla Orchids, 116 Farmborough Rd., Unanderra, NSW, Australia.
Kenny	Vicharti Kenny, 112 Samsennai Dusit, Bangkok, Thailand.
Kensington	Kensington Orchids Inc. (E. McPeak), 3301 Plyer's Mill Rd., Kensington, MD 20795, USA.
Kern	Frank R. Kern, 547 Naples St., San Francisco, CA 94112, USA.
Kersey	B. B. Kersey, 6901 S.W. 97th Ave., Miami, FL 33143, USA.
Kesamarit	Vilas Kesamarit, c/o RHS of Thailand (q.v.).
Keyes, C. & I.	Carl & Imogene Keyes, 1260 Orchid Dr., Santa Barbara, CA 93111, USA.
Keyes	Mr. & Mrs. C. F. Keyes, 906 E. Valencia Ave., Burbank, CA 95101, USA.
Khadaroo	A. Majeed Khadaroo, 3 Ave. Bernardin de St. Pierre, Quatre Bornes, Mauritius.
Khempunya	Major Prakong Khempunya, 315 Rajavithi Rd., Tungpayathai, Bangkok, Thailand.
Khoo Boo Hin	45 Swettenham Rd., Taipeng, Perak, Malaysia.
Khoo Kay Ann	Sunmist Orchids, 281-D Arumugam Rd., Singapore 14.
Khunawat	Pol. Capt. Nares Khunawat, 403/4 Garansanitvong Rd., Bangplad, Bangkok, Thailand.
Kido	C. Kido, 3420 Pehu St., Honolulu, HI 96816, USA.
Kiesewetter	(see Kwr.)
Kihara	T. Kihara, 1805 Fernandez St., Honolulu, HI, USA.
Kikuchi	James Kikuchi, Wailuku, Maui, HI 96793, USA.
Kikuchi, J.	James Kikuchi, 640 Waikanaloa St., Honolulu, HI 96821, USA.
Kimhorn	Sim Kimhorn, Ministere de l'Interieur, Bureau de la Pacification, Phnom-Penh, Cambodia.
Kimkris	(see Komkris)
Kimura	Dr. Motoo Kimura, c/o National Institute of Genetics, Mishima-shi, Shizuoka-ken, Japan.
Kindlmann	Mrs. Marcia Kindlmann, 75 Woodland Dr., Northford, CT 06472, USA.
King	Tom H. King, 2508 Tower Life Building, San Antonio 5, TX, USA.
King, Lois D.	8570 S.W. 27th Terrace, Miami 55, FL, USA.
King, Owen	Owen King, M.D., 1361 Keene Rd., Clearwater, FL 33516, USA.
Kirch	Wm. Kirch Orchids Ltd., 2630 Waiomao Rd., Honolulu, HI 96816, USA. (Originator's rights (as to permission to register) formally assigned to Michael H. Kirch and Dianna M. Kirch, c/o Sea God Nurs. (q.v.).)
Kirkwood	Thos. C. Kirkwood, Richmond Highlands, Washington, USA.
Kirsch, O.	Oscar Kirsch, 47-039 Okana Pl., Kaneohe, HI 96744, USA.
Kirsch, R. B.	Rose B. Kirsch, 47-039 Okana Pl., Kaneohe, HI 96744, USA.
Knowles	Mrs. Marg Knowles, 480 Allen Dr., Merritt Island, FL 32952, USA.
Knowlton, H. A.	H. A. Knowlton, M.D., 901 Swann Ave., Tampa 6, FL, USA.
Koch, Hans	Dipl.-Gartenbauinspektor, D-4750 Unna/Westf., Massenerstr. 37, Germany.
Kock	Winston E. Kock, 903 Oakdale Rd., Barton Hills, Ann Arbor, MI 48105, USA.
Kodama	Kodama Orchid Nursery, 1034 Kam IV Rd., Honolulu, HI 96819, USA; also 86-379 Lualualei Homestead Rd., Waianae, HI 96792, USA.
Kodama, B.	Ben Kodama, Kodama Orchid Nursery (see Kodama).

Koesomboon	Praphant Koesomboon, 50/20 Paholyothin Rd., Bangkhen, Bangkok, Thailand.
Koh Keng Hoe	Koh Keng Hoe Orchid Nursery, 45 Kovan Rd., Singapore 19; also 8 Adam Rd., Singapore 11.
Kojima	Hiroshi Kojima, Ewa, Oahu, HI, USA.
Kojima, K.	Kazumasa Kojima, 161 Okanminami, Arimastu-cho, Midori-ku, Nagoya, Japan.
Kolopaking	Atmo Kolopaking (Liem Khe Wie), Djl. Pungkurargo No. 1, Lawang, East Java, Indonesia.
Komiyama	Arthur T. Komiyama, 712 Kuniwai La., Honolulu, HI, USA.
Komkris	Prof. Thiem Komkris, c/o Prof. R. Sagarik (see Sagarik).
Kondo, E. S.	Esther S. Kondo, 350A Ulupaina, Kailua, Oahu, HI, USA.
Kone	Mrs. Kenneth Kone, 5571 N.E. 26th Ave., Fort Lauderdale, FL 33308, USA.
Kongthana	Thongchai Kongthana, c/o RHS of Thailand (q.v.).
Kono, T.	Takumi Kono, 227 Kaumana Dr., Hilo, HI 96720, USA.
Kosel	Richard Kosel, 8600 S.W. 124th St., Miami, FL 33156, USA.
Kranji	Kranji Orchids Ltd., 250-E Stagmont Ring, Singapore 25.
Kratzer	Gordon L. Kratzer, 12606 Arliss Dr., Lakewood, OH 44107, USA.
Krieger	Kuno Krieger, Egge 65, D-5804 Herdecke/Ruhr, Germany.
Kuansuwan	Artorn Kuansuwan, 124/1 Terdthai Rd., Taladplu, Bangkok, 6, Thailand.
Kubo	Haruhito Kubo, 11-4 Hyogo-machi, Takamatsu City, Kagawa-ken, Japan.
Kugust	Karl Kugust, 36 Standish Rd., Valley Stream 5, NY, USA.
Kuhn	L. B. Kuhn, 20 Sherwood Rd., Easton, CT 06612, USA.
Kullama	Pol. Lt. Col. Wanich Kullama, P.O. Box 953, Bangkok, Thailand.
Kuni	Yoshimasa Kuni, 222 Nishi Orchiai-cho, Itchome, Shinjuku-ku, Tokyo, Japan.
Kushima	Harold M. Kushima, 91-707 Makule Rd., Ewa Beach, Oahu, HI 96706, USA.
Kwr.	Ralph R. Kiesewetter, 223 I. U. Willetts Rd., Albertson, NY 11507, USA.
L.	Stuart Low (Benenden) Ltd. Stuart Low Co. Stuart Low Orchids } Jarvis Brook, Crowborough, Sussex, GB.
L. de R.	Lionel de Rothschild, Exbury, Southampton, Hants, GB.
L. & H.	Lager & Hurrell, Summit, NJ, USA.
L. & W.	J. Lambert & H. Wight, 21 Soldiers Point Dr., Norah's Head, NSW 2263, Australia.
Laddaland	Laddaland Co. Ltd., Huey Kaew Rd., Chiengmai, Thailand.
Ladhaphitoon	Harn Ladhaphitoon, c/o RHS of Thailand (q.v.).
Lager	(see L. & H.)
Laksanaphuk	Dr. Prayat Laksanaphuk, 33 Sthavimol La., Rajprarop Rd., Bangkok, Thailand.
Lambeau	Firmin Lambeau, Villa Volgelsang, Brussels, Belgium.
Lambert, J. & Wight, H. .	(see L. & W.)
Landamar	Landamar Orchids, 7430 Balboa Blvd., Van Nuys, CA 91406, USA.
Larrabee	Daniel Larrabee, Everglades Greenhouse, P.O. Box 336, Naples, FL, USA.
Larrabee, Mrs. W. E. . . .	5545 Cathedral Oaks, Santa Barbara, CA 93111, USA.
Larry's	Larry's Orchid Nursery, (L. Suzuki), 70 E. Hawaii St., Kahului, Maui, HI 96732, USA.
Lau	Margaret L. Lau, 1000 Iolani St., Hilo, HI, USA.
Lau, H. K.	Bangkok Gardening Supplies, 12 Soi Nomchitr, Nares Rd., Syphya, Bangkok, Thailand.
Laurent	Mrs. S. Laurent, 14 & 15 Leotaud Lands, Arima, Trinidad, West Indies.
Lawrence	Sir Trevor Lawrence, Bt., Burford Lodge, Dorking, Surrey, GB.
Lawrence, E. F.	3835 Kroy Way, Sacramento, CA, USA.
Lawrence, H.	Harry Z. Lawrence, 6214 Meadow Rd., Dallas 30, TX, USA.
Lawson	H. P. Lawson and Miss Helen Lawson, Lynbrook, Knaphill, Surrey, GB.
Laycock	J. Laycock, Nunes Building, Malacca St., Singapore.
Lazaroo	Mrs. I. Lazaroo, 40 Blandford Dr., Singapore 19.
Lazetera	Mrs. Josephine Lazetera, 1651 E. Campbell Ave., San Jose, CA 95125, USA.
Le Long Fond	(see F.)
LeBuff	Mr. & Mrs. Leban LeBuff, 6024 Kelly Rd., Naples, FL 33940, USA.
Lecoufle, Marcel	5 Rue de Paris, 94470 Boissy-Saint-Leger, France.
Lee, Gordon	3308 Party Dr., Honolulu, HI 96822, USA.
Lee, K. C.	20 Kampong Pandan Rd., Kuala Lumpur, Malaysia.
Lee Kim Hong	339 Thomson Rd., Singapore 11.
Lee, W. R.	Plumpton Hall, Heywood, Lancs., GB.
Leelasiri	Nateera Leelasiri, 99/6 Ladpraw Rd., Bangkok, Thailand.
Lemförder Orch.	Lemförder Orchideenzucht, Erika Reuter, 2844 Lemförde, Germany.
Lenavat	Phairot Lenavat, 376 Sathupradit Rd., Yanawa, Bangkok, Thailand.
Lenette	Lenette Inc., 923 S. Main St., Kannapolis, NC 28081, USA.
LeNobel	James N. LeNobel, LeNobel Orchids, 1140 River Rd., Richmond, BC, Canada.
Lenz	Lee W. Lenz, 1500 N. College, Claremont, CA 91711, USA.
Leon	Sir H. S. Leon, Bt., and Lady Leon, Bletchley Park, Milton Keynes, Bucks., G.B.
Lerchenmuller	J. Lerchenmuller (no other data recorded).
Levensdale	Levensdale Orchid Nursery, 43 Alexandra St., North Ward, Townsville, Qld., Australia.
Leverett, G.	G. Leverett & Co., Moorabbui, Vic., Australia.
Levi	Robert D. Levi, 156 Stanford Ave., Mill Valley, CA 94941, USA.

Levin	Ruth Levin, 926 Topaz St., New Orleans, LA 70124, USA.
Lewis, Mrs. Gracia	3 Chatsworth Park, Singapore 10.
Li Chin-sheng	15 Nei-Wei Rd., Kao-Hsiung, Taiwan.
Liebman	Dr. Howard Liebman, 316 Crane Blvd., Los Angeles, CA 90065, USA.
Liem Khe Wie	(see also Kolopaking)—Simanis Orchids, Djalan Pungkurargo No. 1, Lawang, E. Java, Indonesia.
Lim, Charles	Greenfields Orchid Nursery, Jalan Hussan Abas, Telok Bahang, Penang, W. Malaysia.
Lim Chooi Seng	c/o 3 Gentle Rd., Singapore.
Lim, David	42 Club St., Singapore 1.
Lim Jet Thien	7489-C Mayfair Garden, Klebang Besar, Malacca, W. Malaysia.
Lim, K. C.	Lim Kean Chye, 32 Kelawei Rd., Penang, W. Malaysia.
Lim Kim Yoo	814/7-8 Thadingdaeng Rd., Klong-sarn, Dhonburi, Thailand.
Lim Ming Kwai	284 Upper Paya Lebar Rd., Singapore 19.
Lim, Rodney	57 Woo Mun Chew Rd., Singapore 16.
Lim Sim Pang	17 Oei Tiong Ham Park, Singapore.
Lim Soon Khim	609-C Balik Pulau Rd., Ayer Itam, Penang, W. Malaysia.
Lim Swee Aun	Dr. Lim Swee Aun, J.P., 74 Kota Rd., Taiping, Perak, Malaysia.
Lim Swee Aun, Mrs.	74 Kota Rd., Taiping, Perak, Malaysia.
Lim Swee Guan	1171 Lucky Garden, Jalan Rasah, Seremban, N.S., W. Malaysia.
Lim Teik Ee	87 Cantonment, Penang, W. Malaysia.
Limberlost	Limberlost Nursery (J. E. Jones), P. O. Freshwater, Cairns, N. Qld., Australia.
Lim-im	Lt. Col. Chaiya Lim-im, 143 Toongsonghong, Bangkhen, Thailand.
Lind	Frank J. Lind, Pascak Rd., Westwood, NJ 07675, USA.
Linden	(no other data recorded)
Lines	Lines Orchids Inc., Taft Highway, Signal Mountain, TN 37377, USA.
Lipanda	Lipanda Orchids, The Vandas, Sidbury, Bridgnorth, Salop, WV16 6PY, GB.
Lista, Peter	P.O. Box 242, Orangefield, TX 77639, USA.
Little, F. E.	Florence E. Little, 1601 Conrad Sauer Dr., Houston, TX 77043, USA.
Little, Mrs. J. P.	Mrs. Jack P. Little, 1601 Conrad Sauer Dr., Houston, TX 77043, USA.
Little, Ken	c/o Trade Winds Orchids Inc., 23100 S.W. 192nd Ave., Homestead, FL 33030, USA.
Llewelyn	(no other data recorded)
Lockhart	W. L. Lockhart, 511 43rd St., West Palm Beach, FL 33407, USA.
Lodge	H. J. Lodge, 100 Spring Rd., Thornlie, W.A., Australia.
Loha-udom	Mangkorn Loha-udom, 40/59 Sawaisuvan La., Bangsue, Dusit, Bangkok, Thailand.
Loke Che Sung	74 Coronation Rd., Singapore 10.
Loke Luen She	Loke Orchid Garden, 89 Jalan Terbang Lama, Kuala Lumpur, Malaysia.
Long, H. L.	Mrs. H. L. Long, 1375 Twin Palm Dr., Fort Myers, FL 33901, USA.
Lonya	Somjin Kiew Lonya, c/o RHS of Thailand (q.v.).
Loo, Edward	3646 Waokanaka St., Honolulu, HI 96817, USA.
Lorenzen	Mrs. Ruby Lorenzen, 231 McMullin St., San Antonio 10, TX, USA.
Lorpongpanich	Suwat Lorpongpanich, 218/1 Soi Sasana, Klong Papa, Bangkok, Thailand.
Los Padres	Los Padres Orchid Co. (Forrest & Emily Fowler), 2940 Valencia Dr., Santa Barbara, CA 93105, USA.
Louboonmee	Amnuey Louboonmee, 5 Soi Prommit, Sukumvit 39, Bangkok, Thailand.
Low	(see L.)
Low Kee Sing	22 Huddington Ave., Singapore 19.
Lui	Harry H. W. Lui, 2017 Oswald St., Honolulu, HI 96816, USA.
Lum Chin Orchids	Lum Chin Orchid Nursery, Road 7, Happy Garden, off Old Kuchai Rd., Kuala Lumpur, Malaysia.
Lum Choon	Lum Choon Orchids, Happy Garden, 4½ M.S. Jalan Klang, Kuala Lumpur, Malaysia.
Luth	Alf. H. Luth, 77 Thomas St., Waverley, NSW, Australia.
Luxen	John J. Luxen, 11735 S.W. 196th Terrace, Miami, FL 33177, USA.
M.	McBeans Orchids Ltd., Cooksbridge, Sussex, GB.
M. & H.	Mansell & Hatcher Ltd., Cragg Wood Nurseries, Rawdon, Leeds, Yorks. LS19 6LQ. GB.
M.O.N.	Malayan Orchid Nursery, 10 Glasgow Rd., Singapore 19.
M. & Sch.	McBeans Orchids Ltd. (see M.) and H. W. B. Schroder (see Schroder).
McAdam	Robin McAdam, 24 Ewart Park, Singapore 10.
McAllister	Mrs. Decker McAllister, 700 Eucalyptus Ave., Hillsborough, CA 94010, USA.
McBeans Orchids Ltd.	(see M.)
McBroom, W. T.	Mr. & Mrs. W. T. McBroom, 10203 S.W. 67th Ave., Miami, FL 33156, USA.
McClain	J. F. McClain, McClain's Orchid Range, 6237 Blanding Blvd., Jacksonville, FL 32210, USA.
McCoy	Mrs. Lester McCoy, 3735 Diamond Head Rd., Honolulu, HI, USA.
McCreery	M. E. McCreery, 4231 Marina Dr., Santa Barbara, CA 93105, USA.
McDade	Clint McDade, P.O. Box 7, Semmes, AL 36575, USA.
McDade, N.	Mrs. & Mrs. Neil McDade, 690 Highland Pk. Dr., Nashville, TN 37205, USA.
McDade, R. C.	Ruth Cline McDade, Box 2842, Maryville, TN 37801, USA.
McDonald	Dr. H. E. T. McDonald, 54 Duke St., Kingston, Jamaica, West Indies.
McElderry	Robert E. McElderry, 224 Clarendon Rd., Burlingame, CA 94010, USA.

McFarlane . . . . K. J. McFarlane, 26 Goodwin St., Edgehill, Cairns, N. Qld., Australia.
MacGregor . . . . Lt. Comdr. M. F. MacGregor, RNVR., Cardney, Dunkeld, Perthshire, Scotland, GB.
Machle . . . . Dr. W. Machle, Boca Raton, FL, USA.
McKechnie . . . . Dr. J. K. McKechnie, 23 Kings Ave., Westville, Natal, South Africa.
MacKenzie . . . . George MacKenzie, Istana Gardens, Johore Bahru, Malaysia.
McKenzie, J. S. . . . . . Dr. John S. McKenzie, P.O. Box 877, Lake Placid, FL 33852, USA.
McKenzie, L. M. . . . . . Lars Morgan McKenzie, 49 Scarborough Rd., Redcliffe, Qld. 4020, Australia.
McKeral . . . . McKeral's Orchids (John McKeral), 1801 Hypoluxo Rd., Lake Worth, FL 33462, USA.
Mackinney's . . . . . . Mackinney's Nursery, 87 Turton St., Sunnybank, Qld., Australia.
McLaren . . . . The Honble. Henry D. McLaren, Bodnant, Tal-y-cafn, North Wales, GB.
McLaughlin . . . . . . Laurence L. McLaughlin, 1518 7th Ave., San Francisco, CA 94122, USA.
McLellan, E. W. . . . . . E. W. McLellan Co., Box 111, Mount Eden, CA 94557, USA.
McLellan Co., Rod . . . . 1450 El Camino Real, So. San Francisco, CA 94080, USA.
McLeod . . . . Ray McLeod, 29701 Baden Pl., Malibu, CA 90265, USA.
McNally . . . . William E. McNally, 2407 W. 228th St., Torrance, CA 90501, USA.
McPeak . . . . Edgar M. McPeak, M.D., 3133 Connecticut Ave., Washington, DC 20008, USA.
MacPherson . . . . . . K. A. MacPherson, P.O. Box 51, Proserpine, Qld., Australia.
McQuerry . . . . Jack W. McQuerry, 5700 Salerno Rd. W., Jacksonville, FL 32210, USA.
Madhyamachandra . . . Chavee Madhyamachandra, 1815/58 Soi wat Ruag, Bang Bam Ru, Bangkoknoi, Dhonburi, Thailand.
Maggi Ponti . . . . . . Pier Franco Maggi Ponti, Ca 'Delle Orchidee, Bordighera, Italy.
Magin . . . . Arthur J. Magin, 33B Sydenham Ave., St. Anns, Trinidad, West Indies.
Mailamai . . . . Sarwarng Mailamai, 1/12 Nakornchaisri, Nakorn Prathom, Thailand.
MAJ Orchids . . . . . . (Marvin Ragan), 126 Wild Orchid La., Orange Pk., FL 32073, USA.
Mak Chin On . . . . . . 74N Track 13, Pouggol Rd., Singapore 19.
Malayan Orchid Nursery . (see M.O.N.)
Manda . . . . Edward A. Manda & Son Inc., 737 Northfield Ave., West Orange, NJ, USA.
Maneetarn . . . . Swasdi Maneetarn, c/o Chitswang Nursery (see Chitswang).
Mangkiatkul . . . . . . Pong Mangkiatkul, c/o RHS of Thailand (q.v.).
Mann . . . . Max Mann, Kastanienwall 19, 492 Lemgo, Germany.
Manor Orchids . . . . . 970 E. Social Row Rd., Dayton, OH 45459, USA.
Mansell & Hatcher Ltd. . . (see M. & H.)
Manske . . . . Dr. R. H. Manske, 27 Chadwick Ave., Guelph, Ontario, Canada.
Marabella . . . . Peter J. Marabella, 5715 West Airport Blvd., Houston, TX 77035, USA.
Marion, Mrs. H. . . . . . Mrs. Howard Marion, 580 Terry Pl., Merritt Island, FL 32950, USA.
Markell . . . . Mrs. Elliott R. Markell, Spring Hollow Rd., Far Hills, NJ, USA.
Marlborough . . . . . . His Grace the Duke of Marlborouh, Blenheim Palace, Oxon, GB.
Maron . . . . C. Maron et Fils, Brunoy, 91-Essonne, France.
Marquit . . . . Syvil Marquit, 1290 N.E. 82nd St., Miami Shores, FL 33138, USA.
Marr . . . . H. J. Marr, The Cottage, Panfield, Braintree, Essex, GB.
Marriott . . . . Sir Charles Marriott, Down House, Blandford, Dorset, GB.
Marsden . . . . John Marsden, 64 Whirlow La., Sheffield 11, Yorks, GB.
Marsh, O. G. . . . . . . Oren G. Marsh, 9275 S.W. 44th St., Miami, FL 33165, USA.
Marshall, E. C. . . . . . Ernest C. Marshall Jr., Marshall Orchids, P.O. Box 303, Plymouth, FL 32768, USA.
Marshall Orchids . . . . (Ernest C. Marshall), P.O. Box 303, Plymouth, FL 32768, USA.
Marshall, W. H. . . . . . William H. Marshall, 3904 Bardstown Rd., Louisville, KY 40218, USA.
Martin, Dr. J. G. . . . . 1019 Evergreen Hill Rd., Dallas, TX 75208, USA.
Martinelli, A. F. . . . . . Avenida D. Pedro 295, Santo André, São Paulo, Brazil.
Martino . . . . Mrs. F. C. Martino, 7902 N. Blvd., Tampa, FL 33604, USA.
Marugame . . . . H. Marugame Flowers, 45-228B-5 Wm. Henry Rd., Kaneohe, HI 96744, USA.
Marugami . . . . Harry R. Marugami, 358 Halupania St., Kailua, HI 96734, USA.
Mason, Noble . . . . . . Noble L. Mason, 5225 S.W. 91st Ave., Miami, FL, USA.
Matatics . . . . Mrs. Stephen J. Matatics, 1825N.E., 27th Dr., Fort Lauderdale, FL 33306, USA.
Matsumoto . . . . Roy Matsumoto, 1317 Hala Dr., Honolulu, HI 96817, USA.
Matsuo, C. M. . . . . . . (no other data recorded)
Matthews, M. C. . . . . . Mrs. M. C. Matthews, P.O. Box 996, Yucca Valley, CA 92284, USA.
Mead . . . . T. L. Mead, Ovieda, FL, USA.
Measures, R. H. . . . . . Camberwell, London, GB.
Measures, R. I. . . . . . Camberwell, London, GB.
Melchet . . . . (no other data recorded)
Mercer . . . . Frank Mercer, "Clovelly", Steyning, Sussex, GB.
Mercier, P. . . . . Paula M. Mercier, 6281 Quiet Pl., Lake Worth, FL 33463, USA.
Meredith . . . . York Meredith, Willandra Orchid Co., Little Willandra Rd., Dee Why, Sydney, NSW, Australia.
Meredith, R. K. . . . . . Rodney K. Meredith, 7624 Prescott Way, Sacramento, CA 95823, USA.
Merlo . . . . Lewis M. Merlo, 65 Spring La., Tiburon, CA 94920, USA.
Merriman . . . . Alan J. Merriman, 8 Selby Pl., Blacktown, NSW 2148, Australia.
Mese . . . . Jack Mese, 41 N.E. 109th St., Miami, FL 33161, USA.
Messick . . . . Mrs. Walter Messick, Hixson, TN, USA.
Mid-Florida Orch. . . . . Mid-Florida Orchids Inc., P.O. Box 1031, 703 S. Vineland Rd., Winter Garden, FL 32787, USA.
Midkiff . . . . Kenneth F. Midkiff, 412 East Cliff St., Solana Beach, CA 92075, USA.

Miles, A. E.	Arthur E. Miles, Woodcliffe Lake, NJ, USA.
Miles, Wm. A.	William A. Miles, 624 Woodley Dr., Maitland, FL 32751, USA.
Milindasuta	Phrinya Milindasuta, 796/4 Bangkolam, Tannawa, Bangkok, Thailand.
Miller, Clay	Miller Gardens, 5874 Cove Dr., Orlando, FL 32809, USA.
Miller Coll.	Miller Collection (Paul Miller), 2532 Nabal St., Escondido, CA 92025, USA.
Miller, E. W.	3755-36 Vista Compana North, Oceanside, CA 92054, USA.
Miller, John F.	4313 Niagara Ave., San Diego, CA 92107, USA.
Miller, John H.	2021 Margie La., Anaheim, CA 92802, USA.
Miller, L.	Ryecroft, 22 Dudsbury Rd., Wimborne, Dorset, GB.
Miller, M. W.	M. Wayne Miller, 1611 29th Ave. West, Seattle, WA 98199, USA.
Miller, Paul	Paul F. Miller, 29821 W. Baden Pl., Malibu, CA, USA.
Miller, T.	Ted Miller, 2001 Normandy Rd., Kannapolis, NC 28081, USA.
Millington	Frank R. Millington, P.O. Box 1585 Thousand Oaks, CA 91360, USA.
Minne	Dr. S. L. Minne, Box 207 Pietersburg, South Africa.
Miskimens	J. H. Miskimens, Miskimens Orchids, 13420 Borden Ave., Sylmar, CA 91342, USA.
Missouri Botanical Gardens	(see Mo. Bot. Gdn.)
Mitterer	Mrs. Joseph Mitterer, 13981 Silver Palm Dr., Goulds, FL 33170, USA.
Miura	Jiro Miura, Miura Mericlone Ltd., Suge 2489, Tama-ku, Kawasaki, Kanagawa, Japan.
Miwa, G. B.	217B Judd St., Honolulu, HI 96817, USA.
Miyamoto	Masatoshi Miyamoto (M. Miyamoto Orchids), 85-576-A Waianae Valley Rd., Waianae, HI 96792, USA.
Miyamoto, K.	Dr. Kazuo Miyamoto, 1225 Nehoa St., Honolulu, HI, USA.
Miyao	Masaya Miyao, 545 Iwalani St., Hilo, HI 96720, USA.
Miyata	Norman S. Miyata, 3851 Leahi Ave., Honolulu, HI, USA.
Mizuta, Mrs. J.	Mrs. Jiuichi Mizuta, 1325c Kalani, Honolulu, HI, USA.
Mizuta, R. K.	Richard K. Mizuta, 2881 Booth Rd., Honolulu, HI 96813, USA.
Mo. Bot. Gdn.	Missouri Botanical Garden, 2315 Tower Grove, St. Louis, MO 63110, USA.
Moffett, V.	Virginia Moffett, 2853 Ontario Rd. N.W., Apt. 209, Washington, DC 20009, USA.
Moir, W. W. G.	W. W. Goodale Moir, 3311 Kahawalu Dr., Honolulu, HI 96817, USA.
Mok, B. P.	9H Asia Insurance Building, Singapore.
Mok, C. Y.	189-A Blk. 23A, Queens Close, Singapore 3.
Moore	G. F. Moore, Chardwar, Bourton-on-the-Water, Cheltenham, Glos., GB.
Moore, H. B.	Dr. H. B. Moore, 307 Alesio Ave., Coral Gables, FL, USA.
Moore, L. E.	Louise E. Moore (Mrs. Franklin Moore), 671 S.W. Elm Tree La., Boca Raton, FL 33432, USA.
Moore, M.	Mrs. Marjory Moore, Duckyls, East Grinstead, Sussex, GB.
Moore, Miss	(no other data recorded)
Moran	George Moran, Orchids of Los Osos, 1614 Sage Ave., Los Osos, CA 93402, USA.
Morgenstern	K. D. Morgenstern, 50 Buttermere Court, Boundary Rd., London NW8 6NS, GB.
Morioka, To	Toichi Morioka Orchids, 1233 Ekaha Ave., Honolulu, HI 96816, USA.
Morita	Charles Morita, 842 20th Ave., Honolulu, HI, USA.
Moriyama	Tsuguo Moriyama, 17-47 Sodegahama, Hiratsuka City, Kanagawa-prefecture, Japan.
Morley	Harold Morley, 1421 Kehaulani St., Lanikai, Oahu, HI, USA.
Morrison, Dr. D.	Dr. Donald Morrison Jr., P.O. Box 12054, Gainesville, FL 32601, USA.
Moulson	John Moulson, Bradford, Yorks. G.B.
Muir	W. B. Muir, Box 43, Ayr, Qld., Australia.
Muktamara	(see Muttamara)
Muller, L. C.	Louis C. Muller, 91 San Felipe Ave., San Francisco, CA 94127, USA.
Munich Bot. Gdns.	Munich Botanical Gardens, Munich, Germany.
Munz	Emil Munz, Grossgartneri, Waiblingen, Germany.
Murakami	Takashi Murakami, Box 27, Papaaloa, HI 96780, USA.
Muroki	Kiyomi Muroki, Kalawai Dr., Wailuku, Maui, HI 96793, USA.
Muse	Brooks M. Muse, 3187 SW 26th St., Miami, FL, USA.
Muse's	Muse's Orchids, Route 2, Box 1616, Orchid Dr., Haines City, FL 33844, USA.
Muttamara	Capt. Chumpol Muttamara, c/o RHS of Thailand (q.v.).
Nagai	Toshiyuki Nagai, 3-288-6 Sakura Machi, Kagagmihara-shi, Gifu-ken, Japan.
Nagano	Dr. & Mrs. Yoshio Nagano, Orchids, 261 Eifukucho, Suginami, Japan.
Nagel	R. F. Nagel, 9323 Lincoln Dr., St. Louis, MO 63127, USA.
Nagrok	(no other data recorded)
Nakamoto, W. K.	Wallace K. Nakamoto, 3244A Woodlawn Dr., Honolulu, HI 96822, USA.
Napasab	Yongyuth Napasab, c/o RHS of Thailand (q.v.).
Narattrugsa	Prasert Narattrugsa, c/o RHS of Thailand (q.v.).
Naugle	Mr. & Mrs. John H. Naugle, P.O. Box 977, Brandon, FL 33511, USA.
Nelson, J.	Julius L. Nelson, 10535 Santa Susanna Ave., Chatsworth, CA 91311, USA.
Netzer	Jurgen Netzer, 68 Mannheim-Neuostheim, Germany.
Neville Orchids	Neville Orchids Ltd., Baltonsborough, Glastonbury, Somerset BA6 8QG, GB.
Nevins	A. R. Nevins, 413 Mulgrave Rd., Cairns, N. Qld., Australia.
Ng Hoe Hai	c/o Ooi Leng Sun Orchid Nursery (see Ooi Leng Sun).
Ng & Tan	Ng Peng Wah & Tan Aun Phaik, 392 Chor Sin Kheng Rd., Penang, Malaysia.
Ngam, Sangiem Charoen	(see Charoen-ngam)
Niamnuamtham	N. Niamnuamtham, c/o RHS of Thailand (q.v.).

Nicholson	R. E. Nicholson, 225 Avenue K. N.E., Winter Haven, FL 33850, USA.
Nielson, Holm	A. Holm Nielsen, Dyrlaege, Ystrup 4174, Denmark.
Nielsen, W.	Walter Nielsen, Elbren Nurseries, 663 Idlewild Circle, Birmingham, AL 35205, USA.
Nirei, M.	Masaru Nirei, 271 Moni La., Wailuku, Maui, HI, USA.
Nishiguchi	Hitoshi Nishoguchi, P.O. Box 202, Pahala, HI 96777, USA.
Nishimoto	William A. Nishimoto, 45-622 Uhilehua St., Kaneohe, Oahu, HI 96744, USA.
Nishimura, Dr. H.	10–11 Young Building, Hilo, HI, USA.
Nishimura, I.	Isao Nishimura, 276 Takegawa, Meiwa-cho, Taki-gun, Mie-ken, Japan.
Nitta	Hideichi Nitta, 4118 Ahakeo Pl., Honolulu, HI, USA.
Nitta, H. K.	Harold Kazuto Nitta, 2165 Kauhana St., Honolulu, HI 96816, USA.
Noa, John	41-668 Bell St., Waimanalo, Oahu, HI 96795, USA.
Noa, J. K.	3394 Waialae Ave., Honolulu, HI, USA.
Noble, N. E.	Noel Edgar Noble, 25 Barron Rd., Birkdale, Brisbane, Qld. 4159, Australia.
Noda, S.	Mr. & Mrs. Steere Noda, 549 Kiholo St., Honolulu, HI 96821, USA.
Nonaka	Takashi Nonata, Papaiko, HI, USA.
Normoyle	William L. Normoyle, P.O. Box 571, Paho, HI 96778, USA.
Norrsell	Bertil Norrsell, 29010 Tollarp, Sweden.
Norwood	Samuel L. Norwood Jr., 7112 Schouest St., Metairie, LA 70003, USA.
Nuuanu O. G.	Nuuanu Orchid Garden, 4 Puukane Pl., Kailua, HI, USA.
O. Sp. Sp.	Orchid Species Specialities (W. J. Rybaczyk), 3853 Michillinda Dr., Pasadena, CA 91107, USA.
Oakley	W. K. Oakley, P.O. Box 53b, Port Neches, TX 77651, USA.
O'Brien	Henry G. O'Brien, 341 N.E. 197th Ave., Portland OR 97230, USA.
Ochikubo	Kazutomo Ochikubo (no address recorded).
O'Dell	William H. O'Dell, 11371 S.W. 186th St., Miami, FL 33157, USA.
Off	George Off & Sons, Waldor Orchids, 744 Shore Rd., Linwood, NJ 08221, USA.
Ogawa	Takeji Ogawa, 592 Kilauea Ave., Hilo, HI 96720, USA.
Ogawa Orchids, T.	1454 Kilauea Ave., Hilo, HI 96720, USA.
Ohba	Suguru Ohba, 227 Yoshigiwa, Hiratsuka, Kanagawa, Japan.
Oka, K.	Kaoru Oka, 1346 Wilhelmina Rise, Honolulu, HI 96816, USA.
Oka, Robt.	Robert M. Oka, 5680 Opihi St., Honolulu, HI 96821, USA.
Oka, Teruo	Teruo Oka, 99-825 Aliipoe Dr., Aiea, Oahu, HI 96701, USA.
Okubo	Richard & Ted Okubu, 1211 Kalama St., Honolulu, HI, USA.
Ong Aye Ho	69 Jalan SS 1/38, Petaling Jaya, Selangor, Malaysia.
Ong Soon Kim	General Hospital, Singapore.
Ong Thye Thiew	6 Meyer Chambers, Singapore, 1.
Ono	Hajime Ono, 326 Iliwai Dr., Wahiawa, Oahu, HI 96786, USA.
Ooi Boon Huat	1 Jalan Lumpur, Alor Star, Kedah, Malaysia.
Ooi Leng Sun	Ooi Leng Sun Orchid Nursery, 873 Sungei Dua, Province Wellesley, Penang, Malaysia.
Ooi Teng Kwee	(no other data recorded)
O/Oshtemo	Orchids from Oshtemo, 6641 W. Michigan Ave., Oshtemo, MI 49077, USA.
Opoix	O. Opoix, aux Jardins du Luxembourg, Paris, France.
Orban	Louis Orban, 412 Leyden Ave., Bordentown, NJ 08505, USA.
Orchid House, The	(Norris H. Powell) The Orchid House, 1699 Sage Ave., Los Osos, CA 93402, USA.
Orchid Pacifica	5850 Heleola St., Honolulu, HI 96821, USA.
Orchid Research	Orchid Research Co., Altadena, CA, USA.
Orchid Species Specialities	(see O. Sp. Sp.)
Orchid, W. P.	(see W. P. Orchid)
Orchids from Oshtemo	(see O/Oshtemo; also Oshtemo).
Orchids unLtd.	627 So. Pearl St., Tacoma, WA 98465, USA.
Orchidwood	Orchidwood Inc., 830 Pelhandle Ave., New Rochelle, NY, USA.
Orear	Mrs. J. H. Orear, 914 Blossom Way, Hayward, CA 94541, USA.
Ornest	Mrs. Barbara Ornest, Miami, FL, USA.
Orq. Catarinense	Orquidearío Catarinense (see Seidel).
Osgood	W. Vernon Osgood, Osgood Orchids, 2009 Burton Ave., Orange, TX 77630, USA.
Oshtemo	Orchids from Oshtemo, 6641 W. Michigan Ave., Oshtemo, MI 49077, USA.
Osment	Mr. & Mrs. William Osment, 2435 Cleveland St., Hollywood, FL 33020, USA.
Ospina	Mariano Ospina H., Apartado Aereo 4725, Medelin, Colombia.
Ostbo	Endre Ostbo (no other data recorded).
Ota, K.	Koji Ota, 8-35 Kawara-machi, 2-chome, Takamatsu-shi, Kagawa-ken, Japan.
Otaguro	Wallace H. Otaguro, 3018 Puhala Rise, Honolulu, HI 96822, USA.
Otake	Harry Otake, 45-270A Puaae Rd., Kaneohe, HI 96744, USA.
Ottens	Frau Charlotte Ottens, 636 Bad Homburg, Promenade 151, Germany.
Oumae	Walter Oumae, 4212 Juanui St., Honolulu, HI 96816, USA.
Owens Orchids	P.O. Box 365, Pisgah Forest, NC 28768, USA.
Ozaki	Earl T. Ozaki, 3319 Pakanu St., Honolulu, HI 96822, USA.
Ozawa	Hiromasa Ozawa, Ryoke 681-1 Urawa City, Saitana-ken, Japan.
Ozzella	J. Ozzella Orchids, Hawthorne, CA, USA.
Ozzella, J.	Joe Ozzella, 14326 Cordary Ave., Hawthorne, CA, USA.

P. & C.	Porter & Cambourn, 14 Henderson St., Eastwood, NSW, Australia.
Pabst	Rudolf Pabst, 440 Pullman Rd., Hillsborough, CA 94010, USA.
Page	L. G. Page, 66 Teignmouth Rd., London W.2, GB.
Paireepairit	Paiboon Paireepairit, 49/47 Soi Thanpooying Phahol, Ngarmwongwan Rd., Bangkok, 9, Thailand.
Pallister	Ronald E. Pallister, 4201 Berger Ave., St. Louis, MO 63109, USA.
Palm Orchids	c/o RHS of Thailand (q.v.).
Palmer, Raymond	Riverway Rd., Corcorite/Tumpuna Rd., 1¼ Mile Post, c/o Arima P.O., Trinidad, West Indies.
Pamonbut	San Pamonbut, c/o RHS of Thailand (q.v.).
Panchasarp	Verachai Panchasarp, c/o Prof. R. Sagarik (see Sagarik).
Panczak	Rolf Panczak, D-2116 Hanstedt 1, Seevstr. 11, Germany.
Pang Keng How	Bernard Pang Keng How, 47th M.S. Johore Bahru, Ayer Hitam Rd., Simpang Rengam, Johore, W. Malaysia.
Panjup	Arvoot Panjup, 8/1 Ngarm Wong Warn Rd., Lad Yao, Bangkhen, Bangkok, Thailand.
Pantapa	Mjr. Genl. Pradit Pantapa, c/o Laddaland (q.v.).
Panthong	La-ong Panthong, Lopburi, Thailand.
Paripoonanonda	Prasan Paripoonanonda, 16/3 Soi Prachavitee, Krungdheb-Nontaburi Rd., Taopoon, Bangkok, Thailand.
Park	Carey E. Park, 1328 Grandview Rd., Vista, CA 92803, USA.
Parmentier	Parmentier's Roses, Bayport, Long Island, NY, USA.
Patamakom	Col. Sawai Patamakom, Bangkok, Thailand.
Paterson	Robert Paterson, Stonehurst, Ardingly, Sussex, GB.
Patterson, E. F.	Mr. & Mrs. E. F. Patterson, 1504 Cornwall La., Virginia Beach, VA 23454, USA.
Patterson, H.	H. Patterson & Sons, Orchidhaven, 332 East Main St., Bergenfield, NJ 07621, USA.
Pattison	Mrs. Nedra Pattison, 4023 West Alabama, Houston, TX 77027, USA.
Paul, H.	Helmut Paul, SR Box C-18-G, Keaau, HI 96749, USA.
Paul, M.	Michael A. M. Paul, Emmastraat 14, Aalsmeer, Netherlands.
Pauwels	T. Pauwels & Cie, Meirelbeke, Ghent, Belgium.
Payne, G. H.	George H. Payne, 3728 N.W. 36th St., Oklahoma City, OK 73112, USA.
Pechpaisit	C. Varat Pechpaisit, 1142/3 Pichai Cross, Nakornchaisri Rd., Dusit, Bangkok, Thailand.
Pedlar	Mrs. E. Pedlar, "Merriemeade", 6 Compass Hill, Taunton, Somerset, GB.
Peeters	A. A. Peeters, Laeken, Brussels, Belgium.
Peh Eng Kee & Peh Eng Khim	4 Jalan Jambu Batu, Singapore 21.
Pelc	Larry L. Pelc, Rt. 1, Bel-air, Inverness, FL 32650, USA.
Pelc, K. L.	Kenneth L. Pelc, Rt. 2, Box 162B, Inverness, FL 32650, USA.
Pelot	John C. Pelot, Pelots Orchids, 1812 Glengary St., Sarasota, FL 33579, USA.
Pengboonma	Somsik Pengboonma, 201/6 Bang Krasor, Nonthaburi, Thailand.
Perera, H. E.	Dr. Henry E. Perera, Trincomalee St., Kandy, Sri Lanka.
Perlstein	E. Philip Perlstein, P.O. Box 257, Honolulu, HI, USA.
Perreira	Robert J. Perreira, 45-722 Puohala St., Kaneohe, HI 96744, USA.
Perry	Mrs. Rona G. Perry, 1623 Alapai St., Honolulu, HI, USA.
Perry, Stevens	T. O. Stevens Perry, Hartland, West Byfleet, Weybridge, Surrey, GB.
Petch Aporn	Petch Aporn Orchids, 202 Panitchalearn Rd., Petchaburi, Thailand.
Peterson Bros.	Peterson Bros. Inc., 646 Romero Canyon Rd., Santa Barbara, CA 93103, USA.
Phairot's	Phairot's Orchids, 376 Sathupradit Rd., Yanawa, Bangkok, Thailand.
Phalaenoptimists	The Phalaenoptimists, 1224E Idlewild, Tampa, FL, USA.
Phatanodom	Charoenrat Phatanodom, 51 Artnarong Rd., Bangkok, Thailand.
Phenphaisit	Chavaratana Phenphaisit, 1128 Trok Siyaek Phichai, Nakorn Chaisri Rd., Bangkok, Thailand.
Phillips, C. J.	The Glebe, Sevenoaks, Kent, GB.
Phimpong	Miss Phimpong, c/o RHS of Thailand (q.v.).
Phit	Thong Phit, c/o RHS of Thailand (q.v.).
Phong-aksorn	Chaivat Phong Aksorn, Pra Bhuda-aksorn, Saraburi, Thailand.
Phoon Yoon Seng	No. 1 Jalan Kurnia, Singapore 19.
Phooncharoen	Nopdol Phooncharoen, c/o RHS of Thailand (q.v.).
Phornprapha	Prinya Phornprapha, 142 Sukumvit 16, Bangkok, Thailand.
Phunthonglor	Somporn Phunthonglor, c/o Prof. R. Sagarik (see Sagarik).
Pickell	Mrs. Edmund Pickell, 2750 S.E. 9th St., Pompano Beach, FL 33062, USA.
Pierson	A. N. Pierson Inc., Cromwell, CT, USA.
Pimental	Charles Pimental, 1309 Konia St., Honolulu, HI, USA.
Pinchess	E. S. Pinchess, "Stretton Poplars", Hinckley, Leics., GB.
Pinkepank	Heinz M. Pinkepank, 334 Wolfenbüttel, Rossitenweg 10, Germany.
Pinneri, D.	Dorothy L. Pinneri, 4918 Lennox Blvd., Inglewood, CA, USA.
Pinvatanapruk	Udom Pinvatanapruk, c/o RHS of Thailand (q.v.).
Pinwathanapurg	Udom Pinwathanapurg, Udom Orchid, Ramintra Rd., Bangkapi, Bangkok, Thailand.
Pisalsithivat	Somkiat Pisalsithivat, 29/2 Bangmod, Bangkhuntian, Bangkok, Thailand.
Piswong	Mrs. Piswong, c/o RHS of Thailand (q.v.).
Pitt	H. T. Pitt, Rosslyn, Stamford Hill, London N., GB.
Pitta	Joseph J. Pitta, 141 Dahill Rd., Brooklyn, NY 11218, USA.

Pitta, M.	Mary Pitta, 141 Dahill Rd., Brooklyn, NY 11218, USA.
Piyasena	J. M. Piyasena, 3/1 Gregory's Rd., Colombo 7, Sri Lanka.
Plaxico	Charles M. Plaxico, Rt. 1, Brentwood, TN 37027, USA.
Plewka	Donald F. Plewka, 4343 Causeway Dr., Rt. 1, Lowell, MI 49331, USA.
Ploypanich	Tong Tame Ploypanich, 19 Sukhumvit 24, Bangkok, Thailand.
Polacheck	Lucille Polacheck, 9863 Stearns Ave., Oakland, CA 94605, USA.
Pongplab	Chamnium Pongplab, c/o 30/71 Suthisarn Rd., Bangkok, 4, Thailand.
Pongprayoon	Col. Chai Prongprayoon, 33 Soi Santisuk, Pichai Rd., Bangkok, Thailand.
Porlick, Mrs. R.	Mrs. Robert A. Porlick, 1822 S.W. 62nd Pl., Miami, FL 33155, USA.
Potisuk	Kovit Potisuk, 24/19 Ladyao, Bangkhen, Bangkok, Thailand.
Powell, N.	Norris Powell, The Orchid House, 699 Sage Ave., San Luis Obispo, CA 93402, USA.
Powers, M. E.	Maurice E. Powers, 1408 Mitchell, Olympia, WA 98506, USA.
Prachak	Prachak Orchids, c/o RHS of Thailand (q.v.).
Praet	(no other data recorded)
Prague Bot. Gdns.	Prague Botanical Gardens, Prague, Czechoslovakia.
Praimanee	Pheun Praimanee, 82/106 Prachacheun Rd., Bangkhen, Bangkok, Thailand.
Pramwuet	Yoh Pramwuet, Laddaland Co. Ltd. (see Laddaland).
Prayoonrat	B. Prayoonrat, c/o RHS of Thailand (q.v.).
Prayoonratana	Bovorn Prayoonratana, 37 Sukhumvit 101, Punnavithai 12, Bangkok, Thailand.
Price	Mr. & Mrs. Louis Price, 1120 Cassett Ave., Jacksonville, FL 32205, USA.
Proebstle	A. J. Proebstle, Box 266, Brazoria, TX 77422, USA.
Prombutra	Pote Prombutra, Bangpra Agric. College, Sriracha, Cholburi, Thailand.
Prommart Ny.	Prommart Nursery, 107-109-111 Rajamulka Rd., Chiengmai, Thailand.
Proypanich	Thongterm Proypanich, c/o RHS of Thailand (q.v.).
Pung	Col. William S. C. Pung, 3709 Pahoa Ave., Honolulu, HI, USA.
Pung Par Dist	Sampast Pung Par Dist, 315 Sukothai Rd., Bangkok, Thailand.
Quyn	B. St. H. Quyn, No. 7 Ambagahapara Housing Scheme, Boralesgamuwa, Sri Lanka.
R. B. G. Peradeniya	Royal Botanic Garden, Peradeniya, Sri Lanka.
R.C.K.	Rotary Club of Kandy, Queens Hotel, Kandy, Sri Lanka.
RHS of Thailand	The Royal Horticultural Society of Thailand, 30/71 Suthisanvinichai Rd., Bangkok, 4, Thailand.
Raasch	Gilbert L. Raasch, 3481 Milton St., Pasadena 10, CA, USA.
Rabago	Mercedes Rabago, 99/1019 Aiea Heights Dr., Aiea, Oahu, HI, USA.
Radcliffe, G.	George Radcliffe, 3309 Salak So., Kuala Lumpur, Malaysia.
Ragan	Marvin Ragan, Rt. 1, Box 346A, Orange Pk., FL 32073, USA.
Rainbow	Rainbow Orchids, 2806 S.W. 69th Ave., Miami, FL, USA.
Rakpaiboonsombat, P.	Mrs. Prajuab Rakpaiboonsombat, 30/71 Suthisanvinichai Rd., Bangkok, Thailand.
Rakpaiboonsombat, S.	(see Rakpaibulsombat, S.)
Rakpaiboonsombat, T.	(see Rakpaibulsombat, T.)
Rakpaibulsombat, S.	Somsak Rakpaibulsombat, 30/71 Suthisarn Rd., Bangkok, Thailand.
Rakpaibulsombat, T.	Thonglor Rakpaibulsombat, 30/71 Suthisarn Rd., Bangkok, Thailand.
Raksa	Jarung Raksa, c/o RHS of Thailand (q.v.).
Ramos	Mercedes Seng Ramos, Rua Santa Cruz 195, Caixa Postal 724, Campinas, São Paulo, Brazil.
Ramu	A. Ramu, 3 Central Miranda, Sydney, NSW 3228, Australia.
Rands	Ray Rands, 15322 Mulholland Dr., Los Angeles, CA 90024, USA.
Rapella	Rapella Orchid Co., 13518 Yukon Ave., Hawthorne, CA, USA.
Ratana	Suvat Roong Ruang Ratana, R. R. Ratana Orchids, 218/1 Soi Sassana, Bangkok, Thailand.
Ratananda	Perm Ratananda, 40 Soi Attavimol, Rashaprarop Rd., Bangkok, Thailand.
Ratanapeanchai	Chitti Ratanapeanchai, 111/3 Bangkae, Pechakasem Rd., Bangkok, Thailand.
Ratanavaraka	Major Chamniem Ratanavaraka, c/o RHS of Thailand (q.v.).
Ratcliffe	R. & E. Ratcliffe (Orchids) Ltd., Downland Nurseries, Chilton Didcot, Oxon OX11 0RT, GB.
Rayola	Guy Rayola, 65 Glenchester Dr., Long Beach 5, CA, USA.
Rayridge	Rayridge Orchids (F. J. Bergman), 9401 E. 103rd St., Kansas City, MO 64134, USA.
Recker-Koch	Herr'n. Recker-Koch (Hans Koch), Gartenbau-Ingenieur Hans Koch, 475 Unna, Massenerstr. 37, Germany.
Redlinger	Joe Redlinger, 9236 S.W. 57th Ave., Miami, FL 33156, USA.
Reed, Mrs. D. D.	Mrs. Douglas D. Reed, 668 N.E. 72nd St., Miami, FL 33138, USA.
Regnier	A. Regnier, Fontenay sous Bois, 94 Val-de-Marne, France.
Rehfield	Jerry Rehfield, 27603 Eldena Dr., San Pedro, CA 90732, USA.
Reid	Harry V. Reid & Harry Reid Jr., Rt. 1, Box 43, Lugoff, SC 29078, USA.
Reinikka	Merle A. Reinikka, 3407 S.E. 120th St., Portland, Oregon, 97266, USA.
Reimer	Ron Reimer, 2696 Montrose Pl., Santa Barbara, CA 93105, USA.
Repasky	Albert A. Repasky, 313 Bond St., Hampton, VA 23666, USA.
Reyes	Mrs. Katherine Reyes, 21 E. Papa Ave., Kahalui, Maui, HI 96732, USA.
Rice	Dick Rice, Aiea Heights, Honolulu, HI, USA.
Richards	G. T. Richards, 217-645 Fort St., Victoria, BC, Canada.
Richardson, Don	Greentree, Manhasset, NY, USA.

Richella	Richella Orchids (R. & S. Mizuta), 2881 Booth Rd., Honolulu, HI 96813, USA.
Richmond Floral	Richmond Floral Co. Inc., 169 Arthur Kill Rd., Staten Island, NY 10306, USA.
Richmond, W.	Mrs. William H. Richmond, Rt. 3, 1155 Idlewild Ave., Sarasola, FL 33580, USA.
Richter	Walter Richter, c/o German Orchid Society, Siesmeyerstr. 61, 6000 Frankfurt/Main, Germany.
Rickards	R. W. Rickards, Usk Priory, Usk, Gwent, Wales, GB.
Rideout	Norman Rideout, 32 Branksome Wood Rd., Bournemouth, Dorset, GB.
Ridgeway	Ridgeway Orchid Gardens, (G. W. Thomas), 2467 Ridgeway Dr., National City, CA 92050, USA.
Ridley	H. N. Ridley (no other data recorded).
Rietkerk	Ray Rietkerk, 269 E. 21st St., Upland, CA, USA.
Riewthong	P. Riewthong, c/o RHS of Thailand (q.v.).
Rikel, J.	Glendale, CA, USA.
Riley, L. C.	Leo C. Riley, 3644 Bartlett Dr., Corpus Christi, TX 78408, USA.
Rinaman, Mrs. Kay	254 Park Ave., San Carlos, CA 94070, USA.
Riopelle	Mr. & Mrs. James H. Riopelle, 3631 S.E. Roswell St., Portland, OR 97202, USA.
Risch	George Risch, 127 W. 85th St., Kansas City, MO 64114, USA.
Ritter, Thomas	P.O. Box 1027, 101 Kreuger St., Orlando, FL 32809, USA.
Rivermont	Rivermont Orchids, P.O. Box 67, Signal Mountain, TN, USA.
Rivermont of Bangkok	Bangkok, Thailand.
Riverview	Riverview Orchids Inc., Anderson Blvd., East Liverpool, OH 43920, USA.
Rives	Joe E. Rives, 10300 S.W. 60th St., Miami, FL 33147, USA.
Roberts, Nell	Miss Nell C. Roberts, 927 Audubon La., Lake Charles, LA 70601, USA.
Robertson	John B. Robertson, 45 Lubnaig Rd., Glasgow, S.3, Scotland, GB.
Robinson	T. Robinson, Littlepark Farm, Brimpton, Reading, Berks., GB.
Roccaforte	Michael Roccaforte, 414 Naples St., San Francisco, CA 94112, USA.
Rodillas	Charles Rodillas, 59 Kamana St., Hilo, HI 96720, USA.
Rodrigues	Manuela Rodrigues, Hale Pua Okika, P.O. Box J, Wailuku, Maui, HI 96793, USA.
Roehl	(see Röhl)
Röhl	Adolf Röhl, D-4771, Paradiese over Soest, Germany.
Rojanadara	W. Rojanadara, c/o RHS of Thailand (q.v.).
Rojanavicha	Thanat Rojanavicha, 788 Soi Pra Deo 1, Yannawa, Bangkok, Thailand.
Rojanavichai, Tanad	407/5 Soi Pradu 1, Yannawa, Bangkok, Thailand.
Rojanavichai, Thongbai	407/5 Soi Pradu 1, Yannawa, Bangkok, Thailand.
Röllke	Gerd Röllke, D-4800 Bielefeld 14, Von Möller Str. 25c, Germany.
Romanoff	William Romanoff, Canterbury, CT, USA.
Rooks	R. D. Rooks, 1217 Boston Ave., Fort Pierce, FL 33450, USA.
Rootstein	E. Rootstein, New York City, NY, USA.
Rope	Robert W. Rope, 5808 Harrington Dr., Orlando, FL 32808, USA.
Rose, C. R.	Mr. & Mrs. C. R. Rose, 49 Violet St., Wynnum Heights, Brisbane, Qld. 4178, Australia.
Rose, Mark	(see Breckinridge)
Rosen	Dr. Warren L. Rosen, 7030 Birch St., New Orleans, LA 70118, USA.
Rosjanavichai, Mrs. T.	Mrs. Tongbai Rosjanavichai, Soi Pradu 1, Yannawa, Bangkok, Thailand.
Ross	Frank J. Ross, 10682 Newport Ave., Rt. 1, Santa Ana, CA, USA.
Rotary Club of Kandy	(see R.C.K.)
Rotchanai	Boonsong Rotchanai, c/o RHS of Thailand (q.v.).
Roth	Mr. & Mrs. Richard H. Roth, 5221 N.E. 17th Ave., Fort Lauderdale, FL 33308, USA.
Roth, J. A.	Mrs. Jo Ann Roth, 811 N.W. 37th St., Fort Lauderdale, FL 33309, USA.
Rothwell	(no other data recorded)
Rowland, A. N.	25 All Saints Rd., Weston-super-Mare, Avon, GB.
Royal Botanic Garden	(see R.B.G. . . .)
Royal E. L.	Edward L. Royal, 800 Lido Nord, Lido Isle, Newport Beach, CA, USA.
Royden	Royden Orchids, Perks La., Prestwood, Great Missenden, Bucks., GB.
Royal Horticultural Society of Thailand	(see RHS of Thailand)
Ruben	Ruben In Orchids (R. Sauleda), 12500 S.W. 46th St., Miami, FL 33165, USA.
Rubens, R. H.	Richard H. Rubens, 2113 Kenilworth Ave., Wilmette, IL 60091, USA.
Rujirawongse	Madame Chuli Rujirawongse, c/o RHS of Thailand (q.v.).
Rujirawongse, P.	Pravit Rujirawongse, c/o RHS of Thailand (q.v.).
Rumrill	James E. Rumrill, 7 Redding Pl., Towaco, NJ 07082, USA.
Russell, C. A.	Clarence A. Russell, P.O. Box 61307, Houston, TX 77061, USA.
Russell, J. E.	Mrs. John Russell, 42 Puiwa Rd., Honolulu, HI, USA.
Russell, J. P.	2416 Ferdinand Ave., Honolulu, HI, USA.
Ryerson	Daniel Ryerson, P.O. Box 805, Homestead, FL 33030, USA.
Ryerson Orchids	18320 S.W. 294th St., Homestead, FL 33030, USA.
Ryerson, M.	Mrs. Marion Ryerson, 18320 S.W. 294th St., Homestead, FL 33030, USA.
S.	(Formerly) Sanders (St. Albans) Ltd., Royal Orchid Nurseries, St. Albans, Herts., GB. (later) D. F. Sander, Lavender Cottage, Wallcrouch, Wadhurst, Sussex, GB.
S.A.	L. Sherman Adams Co., Benvenue St., Wellesley, MA, USA.
S.B.G.	Singapore Botanic Gardens, Cluny Road, Singapore, 10.
S.E.O.	South East Orchids, 12/4 Mou 4, Sumkumvit Rd., Chonburi, Thailand.

S.F.E.S.	Sembawang Field Experimental Station, Republic of Singapore (Primary Production Dept.—Agricultural Section), 10½ m.s. Sembawang Rd., Singapore 26.
Saenswang	Swas Saenswang, c/o Prof. R. Sagarik (see Sagarik).
Saeng Udom	Dr. Chairoj Saeng Udom, Faculty of Medicine, Cheingmai University, Chiengmai, Thailand.
Sagarik	Prof. Rapee Sagarik, 38 Paholyothin Rd., P.O. Box 953, Bangkhen, Bangkok, Thailand.
Sagawa	Dr. Yoneo Sagawa, Ph.D., Lyon Arboretum, University of Hawaii, 3860 Manoa Rd., Honolulu, HI 96822, USA.
Sahanawin	Suriya Sahanawin, 16/127 Sooksant Village, Paholyothin Rd., Bangkok, Thailand.
Sainsbury	Sir Robert and Lady Sainsbury, The Old Vicarage, Bucklebury, Reading, Berks., GB.
St. Quintin	W. H. St. Quintin, Sacmpton Hall, Rillington, Malton, N. Yorks, GB.
Sakamoto	Sueo Sakamoto, 265 Elelupe Rd., Honolulu, HI, USA.
Sakdi Sri	Sakdi Sri Nursery Orchids, G.P.O. Box 510, 35 Sucharit 1 La., Dusit, Rama V. St., Bangkok, Thailand.
Sakell	Harry Sakell, Box 161, Georgia Tavern Rd., Farmingdale, NJ 07727, USA.
Sakuldejtana	Charoon Sakuldejtana, 219 Sukumvit Rd., Bansuan Amphur Muang, Cholburi, Thailand.
Salyaphongse	Silp Salyaphongse, 1/94 Kaset Silp, Klong Po, Utradit, Thailand.
Samachai	Sombat Samachai, 67/8 Samnern Sadouk, Rashburi, Thailand.
Sander et Fils	St. André, Bruges, Belgium; also includes Sanders Orchids (England) Ltd., Hempstead Rd., Watford, Herts., GB.
Sanders, T. M.	12502 Prospect Ave., Santa Ana, CA, USA.
Sanders, W. J.	William J. Sanders, 19339 Strathern St., Reseda, CA 91335, USA.
Sandy	G. J. Sandy, "Goodwood Cottage", 98 Haywards Rd., Haywards Heath, Sussex, GB.
Sanimthong	Supote Sanimthong, 72 Pongsuriya Rd., Tharab Muang, Phetburi, Thailand.
Santa Barbara	Santa Barbara Orchid Estate (Paul Gripp), 1250 Orchid Dr., Santa Barbara, CA 93111, USA.
Santa Cruz	Santa Cruz Tropical Gardens, 1220 41st Ave., Santa Cruz, CA, USA.
Santos	Geraldo Maheiros Santos, Alameda Ipé Branco 597, Belo Horizonte (30.000), Minas Gerais, Brazil.
Saporita	Richard D. Saporita, 245 Alpine Rd., West Palm Beach, FL 33405, USA.
Sasso	L. Sasso, 8 Sherwin St., Henley, NSW, Australia.
Satirasut / Sathirasut	Amnuay Satirasut, c/o RHS of Thailand (q.v.).
Satori	Mrs. Marita Satori, Ap. 3532, Caracas, Venezuela.
Saucier	Don Saucier, 4621 Clearlake Dr., Metairie, LA 70002, USA.
Sauleda	(see Ruben)
Scanes	S. G. Scanes, Flat No. 1, Bronshill Rd., Torquay, Devon, GB.
Scardefield	Henry T. Scardefield Jr., 28 Bayview Rd., Box 415, Beacon, NY 12508, USA.
Schaffner	Dr. Carl P. Schaffner, 10 Young's Rd., Trenton, NJ 08619, USA.
Schloat	Don T. Schloat, 837 Barsby St., Vista, CA 92083, USA.
Schmidt, Gloria	99-526 Kaulainahee Pl., Aiea, HI 96701, USA.
Schmidt-Mumm	Helmuth Schmidt-Mumm, Ap. aéreo 3737, Bogotá, Columbia.
Schmitt, H.	Harold Schmitt, 1601 Kramer La., Austin, TX 78758, USA.
Schneider	Dr. Max Schneider, 111 N. Bayview, Fairhope, AL 36532, USA.
Schöttler	Bodo Schöttler, 584 Schwerte Bergstr. 8, Schwerter Orchideen-Zucht, Germany.
Schroder	H. W. B. Schroder, The Dell Park, Englefield Green, Egham, Surrey, GB.
Schroder, B. L.	(see Dell Park)
Schulstad	Mr. & Mrs. Donald Schulstad, 2301 Bendlow Trail, Tampa, FL 33609, USA.
Schultz	Mrs. Marion I. Schultz, 400 Kiaora St., Miami, FL 33133, USA.
Scott	Harold D. Scott, 1617 Fones Rd., Box 43, Olympia, WA 98501, USA.
Scriven	B. J. Scriven, 7 Osanna St., Daisy Hill, Qld. 4128, Australia.
Sea God Nurs.	Sea God Nurseries (Raymond Burr), P.O. Box 8575, Universal City, CA 91608, USA.
Seidel	Alvim Seidel, Orquideario Catarinense, P.O. Box 1, Corupa, Robert Seidel St. 1981, Santa Catarina, Brazil.
Seidel, Alfred	6361 Niddatal-Kaichen, Altenstadter Str. 20, Germany.
Seidel, Gart.	Gartenbaubetrieb Seidel, 6361 Niddatal-Kaichen, Altenstadter Str. 20, Germany.
Seidel, K.	Karl Seidel, 6361 Niddatal-Kaichen, Altenstadter Str. 20, Germany.
Seidel, R.	Rose Seidel, 10619 N.E. 10th Ct., Miami, FL 33138, USA.
Sekimura	Mrs. Kizu Sekimura, 1464 Kinoole St., Hilo, HI, USA.
Sell	Dr. Wendell B. Sell, 16063 Royal Oak Rd., Encino, CA 91316, USA.
Sellon, D. R.	Dennis R. Sellon, 7921 S.E. Clackmans Rd., Milwaukee, OR 97222, USA.
Sellon, R. A.	Ronald A. Sellon, 7921 S.E. Clackmans Rd., Milwaukee, OR 97222, USA.
Semachai	Sombat Semachai, 67/8 Khunpitthuk, Damnernsadouk, Ratchaburi, Thailand.
Sembawang Field Experimental Station	(see S.F.E.S.)
Seminole Gdns.	Seminole Gardens, P.O. Box 462, Deland, FL, USA.
Seng Heng	Seng Heng Orchid Nursery, 208 Thomson Rd., Singapore 11.
Senghas	Dr. K. Senghas, Botanischer Garten der Universitat, 69 Heidelberg, Hofmeisterweg 4, Germany.
Senior	Evan Senior, 25 Stack House, Ebury Sq., London SW1 9JS, GB.
Sermsuwan	Anurak Sermsuwan, c/o RHS of Thailand (q.v.).

Severin	Henry J. Severin, Severin Acres, 22570 Jan Juan Rd., Cupertino, CA 95014, USA.
Shaban, W. J.	William Jay Shaban, 2910 N. Spaulding Ave., Chicago, IL 60618, USA.
Shackleton	(no other data recorded)
Shaffer's	Shaffer's Tropical Gardens, 1220 41st Ave., Capitola, CA 95010, USA.
Shaffer, Dale	Dale Shaffer Orchids, 1101 Lincoln Rd., Miami Beach, FL, USA.
Shave	W. C. Shave, 7480 S.W. 126th St., Miami, FL, USA.
Shaw, R.	Shingley Beach, 13 Faust St., Proserpine, Qld., Australia.
Shepler	Jeff H. Shepler, Rt. 2, Box 318, Leander, TX, USA.
Sherman	Sherman Orchid Gardens, Grand Ave. & Gladstone, Glendora, CA, USA.
Sherman Adams Co.	(see S.A.)
Shibuya	Takeshi Shibuya, P.O. Box 76, Wailuku, Maui, HI, USA.
Shigaki	Neil K. Shigaki, 2415 Kini Pl., Honolulu, HI 96819, USA.
Shikuma	Jiro Shikuma, 3505 Akaka Pl., Honolulu, HI 96822, USA.
Shimadzu	Capt. H. H. Prince T. Shimadzu, M.V.O., Sodegasaki, Ebaragun, Tokyo, Japan.
Shimamoto	T. Shimamoto, Wailuku, Maui, HI, USA.
Shipman	Herbert Shipman, Keaau, Hilo, HI, USA.
Shirai	Raymond S. Shirai, 2512 Kapiolani Blvd., Honolulu, HI 96814, USA.
Sideris	Dr. C. P. Sideris, 2533 Malama Way, Honolulu, HI, USA.
Sieff	The Lord Sieff, Lane End Cottage, Brimpton Common, Reading, Berks., GB.
Siegwart	Siegwart & Slotter, Jessup, MD, USA.
Sierke	W. H. Sierke, 1101 Sutton Ave., Mobile, AL 36601, USA.
Silpaprasert	Vichit Silpaprasert, 256 Soi Chokchai 1, Park-Klong, Ampur Pasi Charoen, Bangkok, Thailand.
Silva, W.	Waldemar Silva, P.O. Box 323, Campinas, Estado do Rio, Brazil.
Simanton	Mrs. W. A. Simanton, 405 West Lake Summit Dr., Winter Haven, FL 33880, USA.
Simpson, C.	Colin Simpson, 15 Joyce St., East Ipswich, Qld. 4305, Australia.
Singapore Botanic Gardens	(see S.B.G.)
Singapore Orchids	(see S'pore Orchids)
Sinsook	Thavee Sakdi Sinsook, c/o RHS of Thailand (q.v.).
Siriphab	Mrs. Chalad Siriphab, Photisan School, Nakhorn Swan, Thailand.
Siriswadi	Mrs. P. Siriswadi, c/o RHS of Thailand (q.v.).
Siriyakorn	Kasam Siriyakorn, c/o RHS of Thailand (q.v.).
Siu	Larry Siu, 2127 Houghtailing Rd., Honolulu, HI, USA.
Skinner	Wilfred James Skinner, 94 Namly Ave., Singapore 10.
Sladden	Charles Sladden, Orchidophile, Bois de Breux, Liege, Belgium.
Slade	G. Hermon Slade, 15/104 Darley Rd., Manly, NSW 2095, Australia.
Slattery	Frank Slattery, 12 Eddystone Rd., Bexley, NSW, Australia.
Slocum	Charles P. Slocum, P.O. Box 805, Homestead, FL, USA.
Small	Earl J. Small Orchids Inc., 6901 49th St., Pinellas Park, FL 33565, USA.
Smith, Brian	20 Tanyard Rd., Quarmby, Huddersfield, Yorks., GB.
Smith, Mrs. Paul L.	1732 Union Ctr-Maine Hwy., Endicott, NY 13760, USA.
Smith, Robt.	Robert T. Smith, 396 Forest Ave., Maysville, Kentucky 41056, USA.
Smith, W. L.	8645 S.W. 126th Terrace, Miami, FL 33156, USA.
Smithers	Sir Peter Smithers, Colebrook House, Winchester, Hants, GB.
Sng Choo Eng	106 Highland Rd., Singapore 19.
Snimthong	Subhot Snimthong, c/o RHS of Thailand (q.v.).
Snyder Bros	Plainfield, NJ, USA.
Snyder, C. H.	C. Harrison Snyder, 326 Garden Rd., Harahan, LA 70123, USA.
Soebsanguan	(see Suebsanguan)
Soh Kim Kang	723 Havelock Rd., Singapore 3.
Sokoloski	Audrey Sokoloski, 1606 Ville-Maura La., Hazelwood, MO 63042, USA.
Somboonpol	Savasdi Somboonpol, 37/6 Nongklaem, Bangkok, Thailand.
Somboonpol, Sawang	37/1 Laksong Nongkham, Bangkok, Thailand.
Sombuntham	Chaiyot Sombuntham, C.Y. Nursery, 458/1 Sukumvit Rd., North Samrong, Samutprakarn, Thailand.
Song Ear	75 Kaewfa La., Bangkok, Thailand.
Song Sae Eah	c/o RHS of Thailand (q.v.).
Song Saw Eiaw	c/o RHS of Thailand (q.v.).
Songer	N. N. Songer, 1960 S.W. 23rd. Terrace, Miami, FL, USA.
Soo Kwong Man	P.O. Box 383, Sandakan, Sabah, Malaysia.
Soonthonwana	T. Soonthonwana, c/o RHS of Thailand (q.v.).
Sophonsiri	Treekul Sophonsiri, 468 Charoen Nakorn Rd., Dhonburi, Bangkok, Thailand.
Sorayama	Fusao Sorayama, 69 East Kauai St., Kahului, Maui, HI 96732, USA.
South East Orchids	(see S.E.O.)
Sparks	W. H. Sparks, 2425 Lake Sue Dr., Orlando, FL 32803, USA.
Sparrow	G. M. Sparrow, "Shawlands", Potten End, Berkhamsted, Herts., GB.
Spencer	Murray Spencer, 1014 Pima Ave., West Covina, CA 91790, USA.
Spencer, R. W.	Ralph W. Spencer, 2620 Via Rivera, Palos Verdes Estates, CA 90274, USA.
S'pore Orchids	Singapore Orchids (Pte.) Ltd., 2 Swettenham Rd., Singapore 10.
Srisangkaew	Mrs. Aimorn Srisangkaew, 25/1 Soi Sapan Noppakaew, Klong Prapa, Bangsue, Bangkok, Thailand.
Sta Maria	Noel Sta Maria, 129 Serangoon Garden Way, Singapore 19.

Stacy	John E. Stacy, 76 Sherburn Circle, Weston, MA 02193, USA.
Stage	Harry H. Stage, Rt. 2, Box 298, Coos Bay, OR 97420, USA.
Stamme	Frank A. Stamme, 2738 N.W. 29th St., Miami, FL, USA.
Stampley	Mrs. Walter J. Stampley, 1575 Diana Blvd., Merritt Island, FL 32952, USA.
Starke, H. R.	Mr. & Mrs. Howard R. Starke, 320 Wailupe Circle, Honolulu, HI 96821, USA.
Starke, L. E.	Mr. & Mrs. Lesley E. Starke, 708 N. Grandview, Fullerton, CA 92632, USA.
Starke & Son	William H. Starke & Son Inc., Jarretown Rd., Jarretown, PA 19025, USA.
Starke, W. H.	William H. Starke, Green Meadows, Jarretown, PA 19025, USA.
Steen	William H. Steen, 335 McCormick St., Shreveport, LA 71104, USA.
Steindorf	R. A. Steindorf, 1240 W. Latimer Ave., Campbell, CA 95008, USA.
Stem	Richard K. Stem, 1210 Knob Ave., New Albany, IN 47150, USA.
Stephens	Harry S. Stephens, 1004 Beck Building, Shreveport, LA, USA.
Stevenson	F. L. Stevenson, 3201 Parkridge Cr., Chamblee, GA 30005, USA.
Stewart Inc.	Fred A. Stewart Inc., P.O. Box 307, San Gabriel, CA 91778, USA.
Stirling	Dr. William Stirling, O.B.E., Whatcroft Hall, Northwich, Cheshire, GB.
Stoddard	Guy R. Stoddard, M.D., 4 La Gorce Circle, Miami Beach 41, FL, USA.
Stoops	Chester W. Stoops, 304 Stimson St., Orlando, FL 32809, USA.
Stott	Dr. D. A. Stott, 252 Malden Rd., New Malden, Surrey, GB.
Strann	Mel Strann, 8644 Jellico Ave., Northridge, CA 91324, USA.
Strauss	R. Strauss, Stonehurst, Ardingly, Haywards Heath, Sussex, GB.
Street	H. V. Street, 6771 S.W. 106th St., Miami, FL 33156, USA.
Suddhipaca	Chob Suddhipaca, 12 Tharmvichai Rd., Nakorn Swan, Thailand.
Suebsaguan	(see Suebsanguan)
Suebsanguan	Pol. Col. Somsakdi Suebsanguan, c/o RHS of Thailand (q.v.).
Sugihara	Sadao Sugihara, 759 Kalanikoa St., Hilo, HI 96720, USA.
Sugimoto	Shigemi Sugimoto, 34 Umemoto-cho, Date-machi, Usu-gun, Hokkaido, Japan.
Sugiyama	Akira Sugiyama, 101 3-chome, Omiyamae, Suginami-ku, Tokyo, Japan.
Sukontasup	Major Suvicha Sukontasup, 159/5 Squad 4, Municipal La. 12, Samutprakan, Thailand.
Sukonth'sithi	Seri Sukonth'sithi, c/o RHS of Thailand (q.v.).
Suling	Tidarma Suling, Jln. Cipinang-Cempedak 1/57, Jatinegara, Jakarta, Indonesia.
Sullivan	Mr. & Mrs. S. J. Sullivan, 9319 Gothic Ave., Sepulveda, CA 91343, USA.
Sulyaphongse	Silp Sulyaphongse, 1/94 Kasetsilp, Klong Po, Utaradit, Thailand.
Sulyapong	Silp Sulyapong, 1/94 Kasetsilp, Klong Po, Utaradit, Thailand.
Sumner, G. W.	George W. Sumner, 178 Dowsett Ave., Honolulu, HI, USA.
Sumner, R. D.	Mrs. R. D. Sumner, 80 Via de la Reina, Merritt Island, FL 32952, USA.
Sumner, Vic	12608 Browning Court, Colton, CA, USA.
Sunkakul, P.	Mrs. Pimporn Sunkakul, c/o RHS of Thailand (q.v.).
Sunkakul, T.	Flight Sgt. Thavil Sunkakul, c/o RHS of Thailand (q.v.).
Sunthonwan	Thananchai Sunthonwan, c/o RHS of Thailand (q.v.).
Supachadiwong	T. Supachadiwong, 1186 Petburi Rd., Bangkok, Thailand.
Suphatamakit	Pahnuwit Suphatamakit, Famui Orchid, 102/11 Ronachai 2, Sethasiri Rd., Phayathai, Bangkok, Thailand.
Suppachatwong	Thumrong Suppachatwong, 499/17 Rachatave Sq., Bangkok, Thailand.
Suravallop	Samai Suravallop, c/o RHS of Thailand (q.v.).
Sutherland	Sutherland Shire Orchid Society, c/o Mrs. K. Wilson, 34 Coral Rd., Cronulla, NSW, Australia.
Sutton	T. Sutton, 748 Templeton, Daly City, CA, USA.
Suyama	Earl M. Suyama, 204 Kapiolani St., Hilo, HI 96720, USA.
Suzuki, L.	Lawrence Suzuki, 70 E. Hawaii St., Kahului, Maui, HI 96732, USA.
Suzuki, N.	Noboru Suzuki, Ave. Pres. Vargas 62, Caixa Postal 143, Dracena, São Paulo, Brazil.
Swangaroon	Thwach Swangaroon, 1988/2 Parkpreo, Saraburi, Thailand.
Swartz, M. T.	Mark T. Swartz Jr., 287 Chipman Rd., Easton, PA 18042, USA.
Swearingen	Cdr. R. W. Swearingen, Fernandez Juncos Station, Santurce, Puerto Rico, West Indies.
Szmant	Mrs. Harry Szmant, 21900 E. Valley Woods Dr., Birmingham, MI 48010, USA.
T.M.A.	T.M.A. Orchids, 61/63 High st., Singapore 6.
T. Orchids	30/71 Suthisarn Rd., Bangkok, Thailand.
Tagawa	H. M. Tagawa, 1508 Pualele Pl., Honolulu, HI 96816, USA.
Takafuji	S. Takafuji, 2900 Nuuanu Ave., Honolulu, HI, USA.
Takagi	Tatsuya Takagi, Araebisu, Nishinomiya City, Hyogo-ken, Japan.
Takahashi	Toshikazu Takahashi, 6-chome, 23-24 Funabashi, Setagaya-ku, Tokyo, Japan.
Takakura	Francis Takakura (Takakura Orchids), P.O. Box 240, 221 Baldwin Ave., Paia, Maui, HI 96779, USA.
Takakura, Mrs. T.	Mrs. Tami Takakura, 221 Baldwin Ave., Paia, Maui, HI 96779, USA.
Takase	Richard Y. Takase, 166 Kaliko Dr., Wahiawa, HI 96786, USA.
Takatsuka	Takatsuka Orchids, 601-2 Kawairi, Okayama City, Japan.
Takeda, C.	Mr. & Mrs. Chobei Takeda, 1736-2 Tezaki, Sumiyoshi-cho, Higashimada-ku, Kobe, Japan; also c/o Takeda Pharmaceutical Industries Ltd., 27 Doshomachi 2-chrome, Higashi-ku, Osaka, Japan.
Takeda, S.	Mrs. Shigeko Takeda, Tezaki, Mikage-cho, Higash-Nadaku, Kobe, Japan.
Takemoto	Isao Takemoto, 2212 Hunnewell Pl., Honolulu, HI 96822, USA.

Takeya . . . . Yukio Takeya, 400 Laulani Dr., Hilo, HI, USA.
Takiguchi . . . . Thomas Takiguchi, 94-538 Manager's Dr., Waipahu, HI 96797, USA.
Tam Kam Weng . . . . . No. 7 R. Murah, Rompin, Via Gemmas, Negri Sembilan, W. Malaysia.
Tan . . . . Tan Hoon Siang, 22a–23a South Canal Rd., Singapore 1.
Tan, Andrew . . . . . . 8-A Jalan Balakong, Pekan Cheras, Kajang, Selangor, Malaysia.
Tan Chee Seng . . . . . Malayan Green House, 118 Orchard Road, Singapore.
Tan Geat Leng . . . . . 6 Bournemouth Rd., Singapore 15.
Tan Gim Hoon . . . . . 632 East Coast Rd., Singapore.
Tan Hoon Siang . . . . . (see Tan).
Tan Kit Mun . . . . . . 75 Dutches Rd., Singapore 10.
Tan, M. K. . . . . Dr. M. K. Tan, 18 Lengkongan Jenjarom, 2½ Mile Klang Rd., Opp. Taman Saputch, Kuala Lumpur, Malaysia.
Tan Nai Hee . . . . . . 34 Chee Hoon Ave., Singapore 11.
Tanabe . . . . Edward M. Tanabe, 110 Kulana St., Hilo, HI 96720, USA.
Tanaka, B. . . . . B. Tanaka Orchid Nursery, 1528 Dillingham Blvd., Honolulu, HI, USA.
Tanaka, F. . . . . Francis Tanaka, 99-845 Aiea Heights Dr., Aiea, HI 96701, USA.
Tanaka, M. T. . . . . . . Masame T. Tanaka, c/o Earl Suyama (see Suyama).
Tanaka, R. . . . . Richard Tanaka Nursery, 99 W. Kahopea St., Hilo, HI, USA.
Tancharoen . . . . . . Wilas Tancharoen, 101/5 Pikul La., Sathorn Rd., Bangkok, Thailand.
Tancharoen, P. . . . . . Mrs. Piswong Tancharoen, 101/5 Pikul La., Sathorn Rd., Bangkok, Thailand.
Tancig . . . . W. J. Tancig, Apt. 7M East, 40 N. Tower Rd., Oakbrook, IL 60521, USA.
Tang, M. S. . . . . Mengchew Sae Tang, Petchaburi, Thailand.
Tang Tee Heng . . . . . 1945 Kulim Rd., Bukit Mertajam, Prov. Wellesley, Penang, Malaysia.
Tani . . . . Goro Tani, 10/11 Young Buildings, Hilo, HI, USA.
Tanimoto . . . . Ralph Tanimoto, 1848 10th Ave., Honolulu, HI, USA.
Tanmukayakul . . . . . Nai Pravit Tanmukayakul, c/o RHS of Thailand (q.v.).
Taratikun . . . . Songlap Taratikun, 13 Charter Bank La., Selom, Bangkok, Thailand.
Tatichalearn . . . . . . Prakop Tatichalearn, c/o RHS of Thailand (q.v.).
Tatiyawanitkul . . . . . Chaikit Tatiyawanitkul, 148/4 Ladpraw, Bangkapi, Bangkok, Thailand.
Tavares . . . . Mrs. A. Richard Tavares, 25 Colonial Hills Parkway, St. Louis, MO, USA.
Tavivatana . . . . Prasern Tavivatana, 45/3 Soi Siri, Ramaindra Rd., Bangkok, Thailand.
Tayama . . . . Tayama Greenhouses Inc., 710 Riquesa St., Encinitas, CA, USA.
Tellio . . . . Jack Tellio, 45-651 Keneke St., Kaneohe, HI, USA.
Teo Boon Hian . . . . . Teo Boon Hian & Co., 6 Berrima Rd., Singapore 11; also 85 Dunearn Rd., Singapore 11.
Teo Koon Hong . . . . . 324 Adam Rd., Singapore 11.
Teoh Chee Keat . . . . . 25 Burmah Cr., Penang, Malaysia.
Teoh Eng Soon . . . . . Dr. Teoh Eng Soon, 435 Shaw Centre, Scotts Rd., Singapore 9.
Teoh Phaik Khuan . . . . 435 Shaw Centre, Scotts Rd., Singapore 9.
Teoh Seng Aun . . . . . 91 Jalan Chan Siew Teong, Tanjong Bungah, Penang, Malaysia.
Teoline . . . . Teoline Orchids (Teo Boon Hian & Co.), 85 Dunearn Rd., Singapore 11.
Terry . . . . Mrs. M. Terry, Saffron Court, 24 Mead Rd., Livermead, Torquay, Devon TQ2 6TF, GB.
Tew . . . . John H. Tew, 1212 Ulupuni St., Kailua, HI 96844, USA.
Tewtong . . . . Dej Tewtong, 4-029 Mueng Thong Nives, Tung Song Hong, Bangkhen, Bangkok, Thailand.
Thaichai . . . . Suthep Thaichai, 8 Soi S. Kiatchai 1, Pracharaj, Bampen Rd., Houykwang, Bangkok, Thailand.
Thaisrisuthi . . . . Mrs. Bamring Thaisrisuthi, 101 Pechakasem Rd., Thonburi, Thailand.
Tham Tuck Onn . . . . . 26 Barker Rd., Singapore 11.
Thamaragsa . . . . . . Mano Thamaragsa, Laddaland Co. Ltd. (see Laddaland).
Thamungraksut . . . . . S. Thamungraksut, c/o RHS of Thailand (q.v.).
Thanasuwat . . . . . . Dr. Prija Thanasuwat, 16 Soi 61 Sukumwit Rd., Bangkok, Thailand.
Thancitt . . . . Sawang Thancitt, 876/16 Soi Saraphi 3, Charoenrat Rd., Bangkok, Thailand.
Tharp, A. G. . . . . . . Dr. A. G. Tharp, 4132 Lomina Ave., Lakewood, CA 90713, USA.
Thayer . . . . Eugene Thayer, Lancaster, MA, USA.
Thephasdin . . . . Jarungruk Thephasdin, Na Ayuthaya, 61 Kakumvit 3, Klongtue, Prakanong, Bangkok, Thailand.
Thephasdin, O. . . . . . Obhas Thephasdin, Na Ayuthaya, 61 Kakumvit 3, Klongtue, Prakanong, Bangkok, Thailand.
Thiagarajan . . . . . . S. Thiagarajan, 19 Brighton Cr., Singapore 19.
Thiansiri . . . . Chinda Thiansiri, 152 Soi Udomsuk, Dusit, Bangkok, Thailand.
Thitapitchaya . . . . . . Vichai Thitapitchaya, c/o RHS of Thailand (q.v.).
Thomas, J. W. . . . . . . Dr. J. W. Thomas, 7250 Arbutus Pl., West Vancouver, BC, Canada.
Thomas, Lyle . . . . . . Col. Lyle Thomas, 103A Worthington St., Hickam A.F.B., Honolulu, HI, USA.
Thomas, R. K. . . . . . . Rolla K. Thomas, 2626 Anuenue Ave., Honolulu, HI, USA.
Thomdel . . . . Thomdel Collection, c/o Rex J. Van Delden 984 S. Oakland Ave., Pasadena, CA 91106, USA; and c/o Hans Thommen, 202 Lehenmattstrasse, Basel 4000, Switzerland.
Thompson . . . . W. Thompson, Walton Grange, Stone, Staffs., GB.
Thompson, A. M. . . . . A. Malcolm Thompson, 5425 Myrtle Ave., Long Beach, CA 90805, USA.
Thomson, G. M. . . . . Highlands South Drive, St. Georges Hill, Weybridge, Surrey, GB.

Thong	Col. S. C. Thong, 8 Pulasan Rd., Singapore 15.
Thong, N. P. R.	Nai Prachak Riew Thong, c/o RHS of Thailand (q.v.).
Thongsuphan	Chalor Thongsuphan, c/o The Thai Insurance Co. Ltd., 933 Mahachai Rd., Bangkok, Thailand.
Thornton Labs.	Thornton Laboratories Inc., 1145 E. Cass St., Tampa, FL 33601, USA.
Thornton, Fredk. L.	Frederick L. Thornton, 4225 45th St., Lot 1-9, West Palm Beach, FL 33407, USA.
Thornton's	Thornton's Orchids (Fred L. Thornton), 3200 N. Military Trail, West Palm Beach, FL 33409, USA.
Thwaites	Mr. & Mrs. R. G. Thwaites, Chessington, Streatham, London, S.W.16, GB.
Tie	Vincent Tie, 48 Meranti Rd., Singapore 15.
Tiew	Jinhui Sae Tiew, 504 Kose Rd., Nakorn Sawan, Thailand.
Timmons	Claude W. Timmons (Voo Doo Orchids), 1340 Jewel Box Ave., Naples, FL 33940, USA.
Tipawasdi	Prakob Tipawasdi, c/o RHS of Thailand (q.v.).
Tiraprateep	Boonroje Tiraprateep, 1882 Soi Pra-mae Maree, Trokchand, Yannawa, Bangkok, Thailand.
Tjiauw	Dr. The Bing Tjiauw, 77 Cairnhill Circle, Singapore 9.
Toffler	Jerry Toffler, 6815 Maynada Ave., Coral Gables, FL 33146, USA.
Toh Chin Soo	2093 Jalan Sir Chulan, Ipoh, Perak, W. Malaysia.
Toh-Chirakul	Praneet Toh-Chirakul, c/o RHS of Thailand (q.v.).
Toh Chor Soon	c/o Messrs. Behn Meyer & Co., Kuala Lumpur, Malaysia.
Tokugawa	Kuninari Tokugawa, 1215 Migawa-cho, Mito-shi, Ibaraki Pref., Tokyo, Japan.
Tokyo Bot. Gdns.	Tokyo Botanic Gardens, Tokyo, Japan.
Tom, D.	Daniel Tom, 1126 3rd Ave., Honolulu, HI 96816, USA.
Tomita	Nobuteru Tomita, 45-150 Hinapu St., Kaneohe, HI 96744, USA.
Tomiyasu	T. Tomiyasu, 3449 Hardesty St., Honolulu, HI, USA.
Tompkins	Frederick E. Tompkins, 105 Delaplane Ave., Delaplane Manor, Newark, DE 19711, USA.
Tomlinson	David R. Tomlinson, M.D., 40 Pinewoods Ave., Troy, NY 12180, USA.
Tonganant	Major Anant Tonganant, 80 Lad Prao Rd., Bangkapi, Bangkok, Thailand.
Tongdee	Pol. Lt. Col. Prayuth Tongdee, 1702 Soi Bu Nga, Krungdheb-Nonburi Rd., Bangsue, Bangkok, Thailand.
Tonkin	William John Tonkin, 119 Saint Albans Rd., Berkeley, CA 94708, USA.
Toogood	George D. Toogood, 13 Sturgess St., Townsville, Qld., Australia.
Toy	Toy's Orchids, 454 East Olive St., Gardena, CA, USA.
Toy, Louie Y.	c/o Toy's Orchids (see Toy).
Toy, Genevieve	c/oToy's Orchids (see Toy).
Toyama, Y.	Yuzo Toyama, 1349-1 Hiramatsu-cho, Hamamatsu-shi, Shizuoka-ken, Japan.
Toyota	Wakami Toyota, 1293 Fuseishi-machi, Takamatsu-shi, Kagawa-ken, Japan.
Trade Winds	Trade Winds Orchids Inc., (Ken Little), 23100 S.W. 192nd Ave., Homestead, FL 33030, USA.
Trevor	E. S. Trevor, New Labu Group Estates, Nilai, Negri Sembilan, Malaysia.
Triswasdi	Pol. Mjr. D. Triswasdi, c/o RHS of Thailand (q.v.).
Trout	Mrs. T. J. Trout, 5980 S.W. 79th St., Miami, FL, USA.
Trymwood	Trymwood Orchids, (Donald E. Herman), 2500 Rockdell St., La Crescenta, CA 91214, USA.
Tsubaki	Yoshiharu Tsubaki, Aipuni St., Hilo, HI 96720, USA.
Tsukagoshi	Masao Tsukagoshi, 798 Ohma, Kohnosu-shi, Saitama-ken, Japan.
Tsukamoto	Mrs. Edward Tsukamoto, 1312 Kaumualii St., Honolulu, HI, USA.
Tsunoda	I. Tsunoda, Heiwa Mura, Aichi Pref., Japan.
Tubtimtep	B. Tubtimtep, 237/2 Rajvitee Rd., Bangkok, Thailand.
Tubtimtepya	Boonchok Tubtimtepya, c/o RHS of Thailand (q.v.).
Tucker, Tom	Box 687, Hendry Creek Dr., Fort Myers, FL 33901, USA.
Tunprayoon	Supoge Tunprayoon, 238/50 Soi Rojanamit, Jaransanitwong Rd., Bang-or, Bangkok, Thailand.
Turner, R. C.	Robert C. Turner, 915 So. Highland, Bloomington, IN 47401, USA.
Twins Teo	7 Moonbeam View, Singapore 10.
U. of H.	University of Hawaii, Horticulture Dept., Honolulu, HI 96822, USA.
Uathawikul	Dr. Phaibul Uathawikul, 197/32 Soi Sup-prasert, Samyaek Thapra, Petchkasem Rd., Bangkok, Thailand.
Uedoi	Robert Uedoi, 4592 Kalanianaole Hwy., Honolulu, HI, USA.
Uehara	Wallace Uehara, 98-140 Honomanu St., Aiea, Honolulu, HI, USA.
Ueno	S. Ueno, Makiki Heights, Honolulu, HI, USA.
Ueprayoonvong	Prapin Ueprayoonvong, 115 Trok Wat Umphawan, Siyek Rojawat, Dusit, Bangkok, Thailand.
Umaki	Roy H. Umaki, 1638 Ruth Pl., Honolulu, HI, USA.
Universal	Universal Orchid Co., 780 La Buena Tierra, Santa Barbara, CA 93105, USA.
University of Hawaii	(see U. of H.)
Upton, W. T.	71 Wesley St., Eleanora Heights, NSW 2101, Australia.
Urmston	Joseph W. Urmston, 1415 Wilson Ave., San Marino, CA, USA.
Urpía	Hernani Urpía, Caixa Postal 798, Salvador, Bahia, Brazil.

V.	Maison Henri Vacherot-Lecoufle, La Tuilerie, Boissy-St. Leger, 94 Val de Marne, France.
V. & L., Pff.	Les Petiti-fils et fils de Vacherot & Lecoufle, La Tuilerie, B.P. 8, 94470 Boissy-St. Leger, France.
Vacherot, Maurice	31 Rue de Valenton, Boissy-St. Leger, 94 Val de Marne, France.
Vagner	Richard E. Vagner, P.O. Box 607, Windermere, FL 32786, USA.
Vajrabhaya	T. Vajrabhaya, c/o RHS of Thailand (q.v.).
Vallemar	Vallemar Gardens, Highway 1, Pacifica, CA, USA.
Valley Orchids	Valley Orchids Pty. Ltd., Pimpala Rd., Reynella, S. Australia 5161, Australia.
Valmayor	Helen L. Valmayor, University of Philippines at Los Baños, Philippines.
van Brero	J. van Brero, Tjipaganti, Java, Indonesia.
Van Delden	Rex Van Delden, c/o Fred A. Stewart Inc. (see Stewart Inc.).
van Deventer	W. van Deventer (no other data recorded).
Van Houtte	Messieurs Louis Van Houtte Père, La Pinte, Ghent, Belgium.
Vande Weghe	Jerome R. Vande Weghe, P.O. Box 1123, Hobe Sound, FL 33455, USA.
Vandeveer	William P. Vandeveer, 490 Riqueza St., Encinitas, CA 92024, USA.
Vandyke	Dr. R. Vandyke, R.M.B. 12, Campbelltown Rd., Ingleburn, NSW 2565, Australia.
Vardhanabhuti	Dr. Sman Vardhanabhuti, 906 Ngam-wong-warn Rd., Nondhaburi, Thailand.
Vatanamas	Yen Veera Vatanamas (see Weerawathanamas).
Vaughn	Lewis C. Vaughn, 6000 So. Olive Ave., West Palm Beach, FL 33402, USA.
Veerabhongs	Kiti Veerabhongs, 584 Soi Taksin 8, Charurnnakorn Rd., Bangkok, Thailand.
Veeravatanamat	(see Weerawathanamas)
Veitch	J. Veitch & Sons, Slough, Bucks, GB.
Veravatanamat, Y.	(see Weerawathanamas)
Verboonen	Jorge Luiz Joao Verboonen, Rua Fernandes, Vieira 390, Petropolis, RJ, Brazil.
Vichiencharoen	Bangkok, Thailand.
Vichitr	C. I. Vichitr, Vichitr Orchids, 359 Soi King Charn, Tung Wat Don, Yannawa, Bangkok, Thailand.
Vickers	Gordon T. Vickers, 3740 Bessent Rd., Jacksonville, FL 32218, USA.
Vidulich	John N. Vidulich, 1318 Malgren Ave., San Pedro, CA 90732, USA.
Vincke	Gustave Vincke, 105 Chaussée d'Ostende, Bruges, Belgium.
Vipar	Vipar Orchid Co., c/o RHS of Thailand (q.v.).
Voelker	E. J. Voelker, 1620 23rd St., Manhattan Beach, CA 90266, USA.
von Drateln	Herman von Drateln, Mexico City, Mexico.
von Paulsen	Capt. & Mrs. C. von Paulsen, Fiddlers Green, Rt. 1, Box 256, Goulds, FL 33170, USA.
von Paulsen, B.	Betty von Paulsen, Fiddlers Green, Rt. 1, Box 256, Goulds, FL 33170, USA.
Voo Doo Orchids	(Claude W. Timmons), 1150 E. Tamiami Trail, Naples, FL 33940, USA.
Vöth	Walter Vöth, Haydngasse 29/9, A-2340 Modling, Germany.
Vyeda	Joseph L. Vyeda, 675 Lakeview Rd., Watsonville, CA 95076, USA.

Waddell	A. Waddell, 305 Ross River Rd., Aitkenvale, Townsville, Qld., Australia.
Wagner, R. O.	Dr. & Mrs. Ralph O. Wagner, 5451 Masonic Ave., Oakland, CA 94618, USA.
Wakasugi	Wakasugi Orchids, P.O. Box 1004, Miami, FL 33156, USA.
Wakasugi, G.	George Wakasugi, 9100 S.W. 115 Terrace, Miami, FL 33156, USA.
Wakulich	Dolores Wakulich, 698 W. 43rd Pl., Hialeah, FL 33012, USA.
Waldor Orchids	George Off & Sons (see Off).
Wallace	Dr. Jack Wallace, West Covina, CA, USA.
Wallar	J. Lloyd Wallar, Suite 308, 3650 South, Lakewood, CA 90712, USA.
Wallbrunn	Dr. Henry M. Wallbrunn, 7016 20th Pl., Gainesville, FL 32601, USA; also College of Arts & Sciences, Dept. of Zoology, Univ. of Florida, Gainesville, FL 32601, USA.
Ward, J. M.	John M. Ward, 280 Bleecker St., New York City, NY 10014, USA.
Ward, R. E.	6206 St. Andrews Circle, Fort Myers, FL 33901, USA.
Warne, J. Milton	260 Jack Lane, Honolulu, HI 96817, USA.
Warne, R. E.	Robert E. Warne, 4 Puukani Pl., Kailua, HI, USA.
Warner	D. Warner, 19 Kembla St., Arncliffe, Sydney, NSW, Australia.
Warren	Edgar E. Warren, 3 Martin La., Englewood, CO 80110, USA.
Waskow	Marie H. Waskow, 405 Wilson La., Windsor, CA 95492, USA.
Watanabe	Masayoshi Watanabe, 70 Higashi Oizumi-machi, Nerima-ku, Tokyo, Japan.
Watanabe, T.	Teizo Watanabe, 16-8 1-chome, Nagaoka, Fukuoka, Japan.
Watanarojrueng	Nimit Watanarojrueng, 2314 Chompol Rd., Nakornrajsima, Thailand.
Watford	Mrs. Jean Watford, 115 Alexandra St., Bardon, Brisbane, Qld., Australia.
Watford, K.	Kevin Watford, 115 Alexandra St., Bardon, Brisbane, Qld., Australia.
Watson, M.	86 Ross River Rd., Mundingburra, Townsville, N. Qld., Australia.
Watson, R. G.	Raymond George Watson, 12 Pollock St., Balmoral, Brisbane, Qld. 4171, Australia.
Watson, R. L.	Richard L. Watson, 2711 Beech St., Bakersfield, CA 93301, USA.
Wavrin	Marquis de Wavrin, Chateau de Somerghem, Ghent, Belgium.
Webb, H.	Mrs. Helen Webb, Box 1809, 321 Palm Trail, Delray Beach, FL 33444, USA.
Wechsawarn	Col. Prasit Wechsawarn, 40 Soi Intemara, 29 Suthisarn Rd., Bangkok, Thailand.
Wee Sian Hee	1249 P.W.D. Qrs., Jalan Changkat, Petaling Jaya, Malaysia.
Weeki Wachee	Weeki Wachee Orchid Gardens Inc., Rt. 4, Box 551, Brooksville, FL, USA.
Weeks	Miss Josephine Weeks, Orchid Nursery, 127 J. Ruis St., San Juan, Rizal, Philippines.

Weerasekera	Dhanapala Weerasekera, Weerakoon Mawatha, Hokandara Rd., Talawatugoda, Sri Lanka.
Weerawathanamas	Yen Weerawathanamas, 95 Samyaksapra, Jaransanithwong Rd., Bangkokyai, Bangkok, Thailand.
Wellesley	F. Wellesley, Westfield, Woking, Surrey, GB.
Wenzel	Ewaldo Wenzel, Orquideario Rioclarense, Rio Claro, SP, Brazil.
West, G. C.	Gene C. West, 13142 Fort Caroline Rd., Jacksonville, FL 32225, USA.
West, Mrs. J.	Mrs. J. S. West, Ashlands Cottage, Church Rd., Combe Down, Bath, Avon, GB.
Westenberger	Westenberger Orchid Co., 10150 Foothill Blvd., San Fernando, CA 91342, USA.
Whisenant	Kenneth M. Whisenant, P.O. Box 629, Montgomery, TX 77356, USA.
White, D. B.	Durward B. White Jr., 217 Ivanhoe Dr., Sherwood Estates, Titusville, FL 32780, USA.
White, Harold	421 S.W. 70th Ave., Pembroke Pines, FL 33023, USA.
White, J. R.	J. Rae White, North Hiawatha Dr., Crystal River, FL 32629, USA.
White, W. E.	Dr. William E. White, 529 Hillyer High Rd., Anniston, AL 36201, USA.
White, William F.	2004 53rd Ave., Bradenton, FL 33507, USA.
White, Mrs. W. F.	2004 53rd Ave., Bradenton, FL 33507, USA.
Whitebrook	Mrs. Carol S. Whitebrook, 145 South Hibiscus Dr., Hibiscus Island, Miami Beach, FL 33139, USA.
Whitesell	Mrs. Henry C. Whitesell, 12051 Walsingham Rd., Largo, FL 33540, USA.
Whitlow	Carson E. Whitlow, 3821 36th St., Des Moines, IA 50310, USA.
Whitton	(no other data recorded)
Wichmann	H. Wichmann Orchids, Celle, Bahnhofstrasse 34, Germany.
Wiggins	F. A. Wiggins, 115 Chamberlayne Rd., Kensal Rise, London N.W.10, GB.
Wilcox, E. C.	1336 Michillinda Ave., Arcadia, CA 91006, USA.
Wilfret	Dr. Gary Wilfret, 208 65th St., Ct. N.W., Bradenton, FL 33505, USA.
Wilkins	Wilkins Orchids (Mrs. James B. Wilkins), 21905 S.W. 157th Ave., Goulds, FL 33170, USA.
Wilkins, C. C. P.	Frogpool, Stockleigh Pomeroy, Crediton, Devon, GB.
Willandra	Willandra Orchid Co., (York Meredith), Little Willandra Rd., Dee Why, Newcastle, Sydney, NSW, Australia.
Williams, Ellen	Miss Ellen Williams, Honolulu, HI, USA.
Williams, F. H.	Frank Henry Williams, 5 Frank St., Maryborough, Qld. 4650, Australia.
Williams, H. G.	Harry G. Williams, 112 Lake Gatlin Rd., Orlando, FL 32806, USA.
Williamson, L. H.	535 Lamont Ave., San Antonio 9, TX, USA.
Williamson, R. J.	Orchidglen Nursery, 25 Ayr St., Morningside, Qld. 4170, Australia.
Wilson, John E.	2865 Sheffield Rd., San Marino, CA 91108, USA.
Wilson, J. J.	(no other data recorded)
Wilson, Mrs. L.	Lillian B. Wilson (Mrs. Frank L. Wilson), 500 S.E. 18th Court, Fort Lauderdale, FL 33316, USA.
Wilson, W. W.	Dr. & Mrs. William W. Wilson, 239 Old Gulph Rd., Wynnewood, PA 19096, USA.
Wimber, D. E.	Biology Dept., Univ. of Oregon, Eugene, OR 06311, USA.
Winter, H.	Hermann Winter, Lankern 53, 4293 Dingden, Germany.
Withers	Withers Orchid Village, 745 E. 8th La., Hialeah, FL 33010, USA.
Withner	Prof. Carl L. Withner, Biology Dept., Brooklyn College, Brooklyn, NY 11210, USA.
Wittaya	Tammy Wittaya, 27 Soi Sailom, Paholyothin Rd., Bangkok, Thailand.
Wolter	Paul Wolter, Magdeburg, Germany.
Wondabah	Wondabah Orchids Pty. Ltd., 724 Pennant Hills Rd., Carlingford, NSW, Australia.
Wong	Wong Orchid Nursery, 77 Dunearn Rd., Singapore 11.
Wong Chong Kew	c/o Lady Templer Hospital, P.O. Box 569, Jalan Cheras, Kuala Lumpur, Malaysia.
Wong, Edward	99-007 Kealakaha Dr., Aiea, Oahu, HI 96701, USA.
Wong Hi Yet	c/o P.O. Box 61, Kota Kinabalu, Sabah, E. Malaysia.
Wong Leong Fatt	3 Cowdray Ave., Singapore; also 200 Telok Bahang, Penang, Malaysia.
Wong Loong Fatt	17 Taman Berjaya, Penang, Malaysia.
Wong Weng Hoong	14 Lorong 47D, Petaling Jaya, Selangor, Malaysia.
Wong Yin Khom	c/o P.O. Box 61, Kota Kinabalu, Sabah, E. Malaysia.
Wong Yoot Gnoh	Madam Wong Yoot Gnoh, 11 Jalan Besi, Penang, Malaysia.
Woo, C. T.	28 Happy Ave. E., Singapore 13.
Wood, Bernie	59 Claremont Ave., Long Beach 3, CA, USA.
Wood, M. W.	Great Bardfield Hall, Great Bardfield, Braintree, Essex, GB.
Woodlawn	Woodlawn Nursery, 3023 Wapipuna Rise, Honolulu, HI, USA.
Wooldridge	Cecil C. Wooldridge, 15972 Holly Dr., Fontana, CA 92335, USA.
Woolnough	Lloyd Woolnough, 8 Rimmington St., Artarmon, Sydney, NSW 2064, Australia.
Worsley	T. Worsley, Carter Pl., Haslingden, Lancs., GB.
Worsley, H.	(no other data recorded)
W. P. Orchid	101/5 Soi Pikul, Satorn Rd., Bangkok, Thailand.
Wray	S. G. Wray, 509 Carrington Rd., RD 1, New Plymouth, New Zealand.
Wright	Blue Grass Orchids, Winchester Pike, R.D.F., 4 Lexington, KY, USA.
Wright, G. A.	127 South 170th St., Seattle, WA 98148, USA.
Wright, H. D.	Harold D. Wright Nursery, P.O. Box 7557, Mountain Brook Branch, Birmingham 13, AL, USA.
Wright, S.	Waldeck, Soke Rd., Silchester, Reading, Berks., GB.
Wulfert	Karl Wulfert, 4780 Lippstadt, Tannenweg 5, Germany.

Wyld Court	Wyld Court Orchids, Hampstead Norris, Newbury, Berks. RG16 0TN, GB.
Yaemboonchoo	Col. Praphorn Yaemboonchoo, 220/3 Paholyothin Rd., Bangkok, Thailand.
Yagi	Ralph S. Yagi Orchids, 330 Naholo Circle, Kahului, Maui, HI 96732, USA.
Yahiro, R.	2045 9th Ave., Honolulu, HI 96816, USA.
Yahiro, T.	Tomii Yahiro, Waipahu, Oahu, HI, USA.
Yamada, G.	George Yamada, 99-620 Haaes Pl., Aiea, HI, USA.
Yamada, M.	Rev. Masao Yamada, 436 Kainalu Dr., Kailua, HI 96734, USA.
Yamamoto	H. Yamamoto, 3473 Akaka Pl., Honolulu, HI, USA.
Yamamoto, Hiroyuki . . .	557 Kitahata, Motoyamacho, Higashinada-ku, Kobe 658, Japan.
Yamamoto, J.	Jiro Yamamoto, 220 Hamano, Okayama City, Japan.
Yamaoka	Kentaro Yamaoka, Hachizuka 3-7-11, Ikeda, Osaka, Japan.
Yamaoka, T.	Toshio Yamaoka, 216 W. Niihau St., Kahului, Maui, HI 96732, USA.
Yamato-Noen	Yamato-Noen Orchids Ltd., Yamamoto, Takarazuka, Japan.
Yamboonchoo	Praphon Yamboonchoo, 297 N. Nakorn Rajasima Rd., Bangkok, Thailand.
Yamockul	Pravit Yamockul, 525-241 Soi Watdan Samrong, Samutprakarn, Bangkok, Thailand.
Yanagihara	Matsuo Yanagihara, 1319 E. Yanonalli St., Santa Barbara, CA 93103, USA.
Yap	E. C. Yap, 21 South Canal Rd., 2nd Floor, Singapore 1.
Yap, K. F.	Yap Kim Fatt, 61 Sian Tuan Ave., Singapore 21.
Yap, Leo	71 Olona St., Hilo, HI 96720, USA.
Yap Wee Chee	27 Pudu St., Kuala Lumpur, Selangor, Malaysia; also 10 Jalan Pisang, 3¾ ml. Klang Rd., Kuala Lumpur, Selangor, Malaysia.
Yasuda	Joseph Yasuda, 5536 Haleola St., Honolulu, HI 96821, USA.
Yee, R.	Ronald Yee, 725 Piikoi St., Honolulu, HI, USA.
Yen Orchid	95 Sam-Yae Thapra, Jarunsanitwongse Rd., Bangkok, Thailand.
Yeoh, Dr.	Dr. Yeoh Bok Choon, S.M.J., M.B.E., 7 Julan Scudai, Johore Bahru, Malaysia.
Yin	J. C. Y. Yin, 2058 St. Louis Dr., Honolulu, HI, USA.
Yip Sum Wah	House No. 12, Road 12, Petaling Jaya, Kuala Lumpur, Malaysia.
Yocom	Kenneth Hay Yocom, 660 Bollard Pl., Naples, FL 33940, USA.
Yokohama Nursery . . .	Yokohama Ueki Nursery Ltd., 11 Yamamoto-machi, Yokohama, Japan.
Yonezawa	Koichi Yonezawa, Jyonan, Tabuse-machi, Kumake-gun, Yamaguchi-ken, Japan.
Yong Swee Kee	194 Joo Chiat Terrace, Singapore 15.
Yoon Pooi-Kong	Dr. Yoon Pooi-Kong, c/o The Rubber Research Inst. of Malaysia, 260 Jalan Ampang, P.O. Box 150, Kuala Lumpur 01-02, W. Malaysia.
York	Duncan York, Rt. 1, Box 462, Canby, OR 97013, USA.
Yoshida	Dorothy Yoshida, 2244B Nuuanu Ave., Honolulu, HI 96817, USA.
Yoshimura	Masayuki Yoshimura, 3238 Kaunaoa St., Honolulu, HI, USA.
You Nan Chang	207-1 Chung-Shan Rd., Fong Yuan Cheng, Taichung Hsien, Taiwan.
Young, E. E.	Eric E. Young, 42 King St., St., St. Helier, Jersey, Channel Islands, GB.
Young, F. S.	R.D. 3, Hamilton, New Zealand.
Young, H. Y.	676 Hakaka St., Honolulu, HI 96815, USA.
Young, J. A.	Jacolyn A. Young, 7668 Lytle St., Sacramento, CA 95832, USA.
Youngkin	Dr. C. K. Youngkin, 101 Osceola Rd., Belleair, Clearwater, FL 33516, USA.
Yuill	John W. Yuill, 1118 W. 126th St., Los Angeles, CA, USA.
Yuktanonda	Cherdkiat Yuktanonda, 390/20 Sooi Thaparung, Sumrong, Samuthprakorn, Thailand.
Zain	b. Md. Idris Zain, 1025 Jalan Yusof, Ipoh, Malaysia.
Zeramby	Mrs. Sunny Zeramby, 5442 Walton St., Long Beach, CA 90815, USA.
Zinski	John Zinski, 322 Vandeveer Rd., Somerville, NJ, USA.
Zool. Soc. Bristol	Bristol, Clifton & West of England Zoological Society, Clifton, Bristol, Avon, GB.
Zuck	Theodore T. Zuck, M.D., 4468 Via Allegre, Hope Ranch Pk., Santa Barbara, CA 93110, USA.

CORRIGENDA TO EARLIER VOLUMES
OF SANDER'S LISTS OF ORCHID HYBRIDS
(MAIN WORK 1854-1945; ONE-TABLE LIST 1946-1960, Vols. 1 and 2; and ADDENDUM 1961-1970)

Note: This list of corrigenda *supplements* the lists of corrigenda to earlier volumes (a) published as a separate Corrigendum by David Sander's Orchids Ltd. in 1961 and (b) published on pp. lvi to lxiv of the 1961-1970 Addendum. It is a collation of all corrigenda to earlier volumes as published in the *Orchid Review* from March 1972 to January 1977 inclusive.

The main list hereunder is arranged volume by volume in chronological order, and by page sequence within each volume. The main list is preceded by some **general corrections** which apply to more than one volume; the paged list for each individual volume is, where necessary, preceded by certain **special corrigenda** which relate to more than one page in that particular volume.

GENERAL CORRECTIONS

1. The following corrections result from parent misidentifications discovered and notified subsequent to the publications concerned. Key to abbreviations used below is as follows: 46/60 = Volume 1 of Sander's List of Orchid Hybrids 1946-1960; 61/70 = Addendum 1961-1970 to Sander's List of Orchid Hybrids:—

(A) The parent Oncidium sylvestre should read Oncidium velutinum in the following six hybrids where indicated:—

Oncidium Andros (61/70 p. 428; also pp. 428, 440, 441).
Oncidium Anna Rosa (46/60 p. 569; also pp. 573, 574, 574: 61/70 p. 428).
Oncidium Henri Christophe (61/70 p. 432; also pp. 432, 440, 441).
Oncidium Hispaniola (46/60 p. 571; also pp. 570, 574, 574).
Oncidium La Romana (61/70 p. 434; also pp. 440, 441, 441).
Oncidium Petionville (61/70 p. 437; also pp. 432, 440, 441).

(B) The parent Oncidium sylvestre should read Oncidium scandens in the following two hybrids where indicated:—

Oncidium Petite Pink (61/70 p. 437; also pp. 439, 441. NB: the parental entry under **sylvestre** on p. 440, which would have had to be deleted, was in any case omitted by error in original printing).
Oncidium Saint Louis (61/70 p. 439; also pp. 431, 439, 440).

(C) The parent Oncidium guibertianum should read Oncidium lemonianum in the following three hybrids where indicated:—

Oncidium La Vega (61/70 p. 434; also pp. 431, 431, 434).
Oncidium San Jose (61/70 p. 439; also pp. 431, 434, 440).
Oncidium Sosua (61/70 p. 439; also pp. 431, 432, 434).

In all cases above, the page numbers following the word "also" in the course of each correction represent the pages on which corrections, deletions or insertions will need also to be made under the *parental* entries of the hybrid concerned; that is to say, under the *incorrect* parent name, under the parent name *as corrected*, and under the *second* (*unaltered*) parent name.

(D) The following consequential point also arises from the foregoing corrigenda:—

When considered in conjunction with the deletion (see paged corrections 61/70 p. 440 below) of the entry, under Oncidium **sylvestre**, of × variegatum = Jeremie, the implementation of the corrigenda above leaves *no* crosses in registration under the species *Oncidium sylvestre* (46/60 p. 574 and 61/70 p. 440); similarly it leaves no crosses in registration under the species *Oncidium guibertianum* (61/70 p. 431). Therefore both *sylvestre* and *guibertianum* may be deleted from those places; both exist as good species but will not show as bred from in registration up to 1970 inclusive.

2. The species commonly known by the name *Oncidium intermedium*, and bred from and recorded as a parent in registration under that name for 20 hybrids registered between 1943 and 1970, is in fact the species now correctly called *Oncidium desertorum* Nash ex Withner, and is not *Oncidium intermedium* Bertero (1826), whose existence or true identity is in doubt (See Amer. Orch. Soc. Bull. 38: 309-312, 1967 for full data). Therefore wherever the name *Oncidium intermedium* occurs as a parent in published orchid registration lists as indicated below, it should be corrected to read *Oncidium desertorum*. Such corrections produce no conflict with other crosses from *Oncidium desertorum* already published as such in registration.

The twenty hybrids concerned as published in the Sander's Lists of Orchid Hybrids 1854-1945, 1946-1960 Vol. 1, and Addendum 1961-1970 are listed below; in each case the parent *Oncidium intermedium* should be corrected to read *Oncidium desertorum* wherever it occurs in the lists shown, including the correction, deletion, or insertion, as appropriate, under the second (unaltered) *parent* name, the incorrect *parent* name, and the *parent* name as corrected:—

Oncidettia	Ecuador	(1961-1970)
Oncidium	Barahona	(1961-1970)
,,	Canary	(1854-1945)
,,	Constanza	(1961-1970)
,,	El Seibo	(1961-1970)
Oncidium	Golden Gem	(1961-1970)
,,	Grand Bahama	(1961-1970)
,,	Haitian Gold	(1961-1970)
,,	Jarabacoa	(1961-1970)
,,	La Citadelle	(1961-1970)

Oncidium Mirebalais	(1961-1970)	Oncidium Sunshine	(1946-1960 Vol. 1)
,, Pastel	(1946-1960 Vol. 1 and 1961-1970)	,, Tiny Tim	(1946-1960 Vol. 1 and 1961-1970)
		,, Waikiki Sunset	(1946-1960 Vol. 1 and 1961-1970)
,, Pink Dancer	(1961-1970)	Rodricidium Bora Bora	(1961-1970)
,, Samana Bay	(1961-1970)	,, Calypso	(1946-1960 Vol. 1)
,, Sunrise	(1946-1960 Vol. 1)		

Consequential corrections:

Sander's List of Orchid Hybrids 1854-1945, Table II, p. 291: **intermedium** should read **intermedium** (see *desertorum* — Nash ex Withner; not *intermedium* Bertero 1826).

Sander's One-Table List of Orchid Hybrids 1946-1960, Vol. 1, p. 571: **intermedium*** should read **intermedium*** (see *desertorum** — Nash ex Withner; not *intermedium* Bertero 1826).

Sander's List of Orchid Hybrids, Addendum 1961-1970:

p. 430: **desertorum** should read **desertorum***† (syn. *intermedium* auctt. not *intermedium* Bertero 1826).

p. 432: **intermedium***† should read **intermedium***† auctt. (see *desertorum**† — Nash ex Withner, including vars. *alborubrum*, *album* and *aureorubrum*; not *intermedium* Bertero 1826).

3. *Wherever* the name Sophronitis grandiflora appears as a parent in Sander's List of Orchid Hybrids 1854-1945 and in Sander's One-Table List of Orchid Hybrids 1946-1960 Vol. 2, it should be corrected to read Sophronitis coccinea (syn. *grandiflora*). (N.B. This general correction is *supplementary* to the individual corrections appearing on pages lviii to lxi of the 1961-1970 Addendum to Sander's List of Orchid Hybrids, which covered the appropriate corrections to earlier volumes only under the entry of the name *Sophronitis grandiflora* as such. It is felt that the consequent corrections elsewhere — i.e. under the names of listed progeny, and under the names of the second parents of such progeny — should be explicit and not merely implicit.)

SANDER'S LIST OF ORCHID HYBRIDS (1854-1945)

Special Corrigenda:

1. The earlier and correct name for *Paphiopedilum victoria-mariae* is *Paphiopedilum victoria-regina*. The following corrections are therefore necessary in this volume:
   Table II p. 173: **victoria-mariae** (originally spelt in this volume as **Victoria-Marie**) should read **victoria-regina** (syn. *victoria-mariae*); similarly wherever it occurs in all consequential entries in Table I (under its listed progeny) and in Table II (under the second-listed parent of each of such progeny).
2. Table II, p. 93: **Parishii Sanderae** should read **parishii**; similarly wherever it occurs in Table I (under its listed progeny) and in Table II (under the second-listed parent of each of such progeny).
3. Table II, p. 107: **Beeckmannii** should read **Beeckmanii**; similarly wherever else Beeckmanii is mis-spelled in Table I and Table II entries as a parent of its progeny listed here. It is to be noted, however, that the grex epithets of its progeny remain as originally spelled in Table I, even where they end in "... mannii" (i.e. Aesmannii, Hera-Beeckmannii and Curtmannii all retain the "... nn ...."; Luxmanii and Archmanii, however, were originally spelled with one "n" and so remain).

List of Registrants Abbreviations:

Against Ri: H. I. H. Price Ri (etc.) should read H. I. H. Prince Ri (etc.).
After L. O. Co.: insert Longhé . . . France (no other data recorded).
After Mead: insert Mercer . . . Frank Mercer, Clovelly, Steyning, Sussex.
Summer . . . George W. Summer (etc.) should read Sumner . . . George W. Sumner (etc.).
After Burkinshaw: insert Burstow . . . W. J. Burstow, The Old Quarry, Lucastes Ave., Haywards Heath, Sussex.

List of Generic Abbreviations:

Insert Gastrochilus . . . . Gchls.
Insert Mendoncella . . . . Mdcla.
Insert Zygocella . . . . Zcla.

Alphabetical List of Generic Parents:

Insert Mendoncella × Zygopetalum = Zygocella
Insert Zygopetalum × Mendoncella = Zygocella

Table I

Page

3, Balzar (etc.): this entry is out of order; it should follow Balmoral (same page).
5: Galatee should read Galatée.
6, below Helena: insert Heloise (Mrs. J. Leemann × C. Adula); (registrant and date unknown).
8, below Mars: insert Marthe Gratiot (parentage unknown) — Gratiot (date unknown).
9: delete Planter etc. (this is *Brassolaeliocattleya* — see re-insertion p. 20 corrigendum below).
12, BRASSOEPIDENDRUM: insert Cuco (Epi. cochleatum × B. cucullata) — Mead 1902.
13: Atalante should read Atalanta.
20, below Pink Pearl: insert Planter (Muriel × C. Prince John) — Hughes 1933.
20, below Queen Enid: insert Queen Eva (Bc. British Queen × Lc. Eva Baldwin); (registrant and date unknown).
21: Simonee should read Simone.
29, below Charlesworthii: insert Charlotte (hyb. ign.).
29, below Chula Vista: insert Cicely (Antiope × Rhoda); (registrant and date unknown).
30, Crashleyi: add (see Mary Gratrix).
38, parent of Linchmere: Charlotee should read Charlotte.

Page

39, Mary Gratrix: add (syn. Crashleyi); also parent Harrisoniana should read loddigesii (syn. harrisoniana).
44, parent of Pua Liilii: Harrisoniana should read loddigesii (syn. harrisoniana).
57, below Gammieianum: insert Gandavensis (syn. Viceroy) (Gottianum × Venus) — C. de H. 1935.
66: Tenderden should read Tenterden.
69: Albacord should read Albacored.
70: Amum Ra should read Amun Ra.
71, parent of Anson: Chrysotoxum should read Chrysostom.
72: Armette should read Armetta.
73, parent of Audacity: Mme. Albert Ferrier should read Mme. Albert Fevrier.
74, registrant of Banbury: Brummitt should read A. R. Brummitt.
74, Basildon: add (see Broadway II); also delete parentage, registrant and date.
74-77: registrant Brummitt should read L. W. Brummitt for each of the following hybrids: Balscote, Barton, Beckley, Benson, Bibury, Bicester, Bladon, Bledington, Bletchley, Blockley, Bloxham, Bodicote, Brackley, Bradden, Brailes, Braunston, Brill, Broadway II, Buckingham II, Buckland, Burford, Byfield.
75: Bandigo should read Bendigo; parentage should read Bronzino × Niobe.
76, below Boreas: insert Borwick (Conference × Perseus); (registrant and date unknown).
76: Bracyanum should read Braceyanum.
77, Broadway II: add (syn. Basildon).
80, parent of Charles Puddle: Chrysostom should read Chrysotoxum.
81, below Cheviot: insert Chevy Chase (Cappamagna × Crusader); (registrant and date unknown).
81, below Chorltonii: insert Chorltonville (Pyramus × Shogun); (registrant and date unknown).
82, parent of Colense: Cymatodes beechense should read Cymatodes (Beechense).
84: Cymatodes beechense should read Cymatodes (Beechense). (NB: 'Beechense' is a cultivar of Cymatodes.)
84: Cyreniaca should read Cyrenaica.
85: Denester should read Denesta.
87, Eclipse: parentage should read Calypso × stonei.
88, parentage of Edithiae: col. 1 add (syn. Rowena); col. 2 delete syn. Rowena and substitute (bellatulum × chamberlainianum); insert registrant and date — C. 1902.
88, parent of Elizabethiae: Lawreeanum should read lawrenceanum.
89, parent of Ernest Read: William Matthews should read William Mathews.
90, below Eurydice: insert Eurydina (Eurybiades × Idina); (registrant and date unknown).
90: Evalyne Naylor should read Evelyne Naylor.
91: Fieldmarshal should read Field Marshal.
93: Gardwood should read Garswood.
93, parent of Garvin: Chrysostom should read Garostom.
95: Greyii should read Greyi.
96: Guildo should read Guido.
96, parent of Gwendolin: Ethel M. du Bourlay should read Ethel M. du Boulay.
99, Ianthe: delete parentage and substitute — see Williamsianum (1882).
101, below John Tipping: insert Joiceyi (barbatum × Selligerum); (registrant and date unknown).
101, below J. S. Cannington: insert J. T. Barker (San-Actaeus × Shogun); (registrant and date unknown).
101: J. Gurney-Fowler should read J. Gurney Fowler (i.e. delete the hyphen).
103, parent of Lambourn: Phulbiades should read Alciphu (syn. Phulbiades).
104: Lemani Ducis should read Lemanii Ducis; parent Curtmanii should read Curtmannii.
105, below Longwoodense Lord Ossulston: insert Loot (Earl of Tankerville × Waterloo); (registrant and date unknown).
105, below Loot (as above): insert Lord Allenby (Baron Harefield × Gaston Bultel); (registrant and date unknown).
105, parent of Louryanum: Germaine Opoix should read Ashburtoniae.
105: Lowegranianum should read Lowegrenianum.
105, below Lucidum: insert Lucile Williams (Everest × Lemanii Ducis); (registrant and date unknown).
108: Marshall Haig should read Marshal Haig.
109, parent of Mawlaik: Malaya should read Malaga.
109, parent of May Day: Maimona should read Maimoa.
109: May Fair should read Mayfair.
109, below Melchet Superb: insert Meldrum (Hyb. ign.).
109: Mellactus should read Mellactis.
110, below Mermaid: insert Mermaid II (San-Actaeus × Troilus); (registrant and date unknown).
111, parent of Mindoro: Meekon should read Mekong.
111, parent of Misantla: Chrysotoxum should read Chrysostom.
116, registrant of Norina: N. should read M.
117, registrant of Osyanum: Longhe should read Longhé.
122, Redrush: parentage should read Red Admiral × Windrush.
123: Rossi should read Rossii.
123, Rowena: delete parentage and substitute — see Edithiae (1902).
124, below St. Alban: insert St. Azrael (Azrael × Lord St. Vincent); (registrant and date unknown).
124, registrant of Salus: Measures should read R. I. Measures.
124: Sanderiano-superbeins should read Sanderiano-superbiens.
125, parent of Scarsam: Masters-villosum should read Mastersio-villosum.
125, registrant of Saron: Measures should read R. I. Measures.
126: Shipwavae should read Shipwayae.
127: Stephen should read Stephan.

Page

129: Tappermoor should read Teppermoor; also correct its position to below Tennyson, same page.
130, Titan: delete parentage and substitute (see Hestia — 1919).
131: Van Dyck should read Vandyck.
134, above Williamsonianum: insert Williamsianum (syn. Ianthe) (Harrisianum × venustum) — 1882; (registrant unknown).
135: Yadia should read Yadie.
137, parent of Caesar: Schroderianum should read phalaenopsis (syn. schroderanum).
139, parent of Leeanum: Schroderianum should read phalaenopsis (syn. schroderanum).
141, parent of Wilhelm Stuber: Schroderianum should read phalaenopsis (syn. schroderanum).
142, parent of Epicattleya Figaro: falcatum should read parkinsonianum (syn. falcatum).
143: delete entry for Epidendrum Cuco (transferred to Brassoepidendrum — see p. 12 corrigendum above).
144, parent of Epilaelia Whitei: falcatum should read parkinsonianum (syn. falcatum).
144: insert generic heading **GASTROCHILUS**; thereunder insert bellino-bigibbus / Bellino-bigibbus } (bellinus × bigibbus) { Nat. hyb. / hort.
145, Laelia Pilcheri: add registrant and date — Dominy 1868.
155: De Loris Ziegfield should read De Loris Ziegfeld.
172, below Miss Gilberta Blount: insert Miss Faith H. Hanbury (L. Cinnabrosa × Canhamiana) Hanbury 1928.
182, parent of S. J. Bracey: Thebes should read C. Thebes.
188, parent of Lycaste Arthuriana, Ebor and Gratrixiae: plana should read macrophylla (syn. plana).
188, parent of Lycaste Brugensis: gigantea should read longipetala (syn. gigantea).
189: Masdevallia Frasero-ludibunda should read Fraseri-ludibunda; parent ludibunda should read estradae (syn. ludibunda).
198: Carail should read Corail.
205, parent of Red Flame: Lambeauianum should read Lambeauiana.
205, Orthia: out of order — should follow Ornata, p. 204.
221, below Isolene: insert Isolene-Olympia (Isolene × Olympia) . . . V. 1929 (C.).
223, below Lemispum: insert Lemonianum (Hyb. ign.) pre-1944; (registrant unknown).
223, below Lemonianum (as above): insert L'Empereur (Hyb. ign.) pre-1919; (registrant unknown).
239, parent of Oncidium Gardneri and Wheatleyanum: dasytyle should read dasystyle.
240, parent of Phaius Ashworthianus: maculatus should read flavus (syn. maculatus).
240, parent of Phaius Maculato-grandifolius: maculatus should read flavus (syn. maculatus).
240, parent of Phaius Opoixii: delete parentage and substitute (see Owenianus).
240, Phaius Owenianus: add (syn. Opoixii); parent bicolor (Oweniae) should read wallichii (syn. bicolor).
240, parent of Phalaenopsis Adrian: Grand Conde should read Grand Condé.
241: Grande Conde should read Grand Condé.
241, parent of Gyp: Algers should read Alger; also delete full stop after Gyp in col. 1.
242, parent of Raritan: Grande Conde should read Grand Condé.
243, parent of Promenaea Colmaniana: citrina should read xanthina (syn. citrina).
244: delete **SACCOLABIUM** and the entry thereunder (transferred to Gastrochilus — see corrigendum p. 144 above).
250: langleyense should read Langleyensis.
250, below Miami: insert Mikado (Prince Hirohito × C. Empress Frederick) Schroder 1927.
258: insert generic heading **ZYGOCELLA**; thereunder insert the following entries transferred from Zygopetalum (see below):—
Leucochilum (Mdcla. burkei × Z. mackayi) . . . Veitch 1892
Max-Jorisii (Mdcla. jorisiana × maxillare) . . . R. I. Measures 1904
258: delete entry for Zygopetalum Leucochilum }
258: delete entry for Zygopetalum Max-Jorisi } (transferred to Zygocella — see above).

Table II

2, BRASSAVOLA digbyana: × Dowiana should read × C. dowiana (= Bc. Mrs. J. Leemann).
2, under BRASSAVOLA cucullata: insert × Epi. cochleatum = Bepi. Cuco.
3, BRASSAVOLA nodosa × C. bowringiana: = B. Makai should read = Bc. Makai.
4, British Queen × Blc. Blenheim King: = Blc. Daytona should read = Blc.Datoma (not Blc. Daytoma as published in an earlier corrigendum).
4, Cliftonii × C. Schroderae: = Grand Monarque should read = Grande Monarque.
4, Cliftonii × C. Dominiana: = G. V. Llewellyn should read = G. V. Llewelyn.
5, Digbyano-Mossiae × C. Rex: = Lotos should read = Lotus.
6, Gatton Lily × C. Cowaniae: = Maid should read = Maud.
6, Grande Monarque × C. Mossiae: = Sab Blas should read = San Blas.
6, Grande Monarque: × Lc. Andreana = Blc. Andrenarque should read × Lc. Audrena = Blc. Audrenarque.
6, Heatonensis × L. tenebrosa: = Blc. Brigette Horsey should read = Blc. Brigette Horney.
7, Madame Charles Maron × C. Ballantineana: = Balzer should read = Balzar.
10, Mrs. J. Leemann × Slc. Dorila: = Pot. Princess Shimadzu should read = Pot. Prince Shimadzu.
10, Mrs. Joseph Manda × Lc. Mrs. Medo: = Blc. Nemanda should read = Blc. Memanda.
10: delete Muriel and entry thereunder (This is *Blc* to which entry is transferred — see p. 15 corrigendum below).
10, Nestor × C. Dinah: = Dinestar should read = Dinestor.
10, Pallas × Lc. Soulange: = Blc. Seus should read = Blc. Zeus.
10, Penelope × C. Santa Monica: = La Graciosa should read = La Gracia.
10, Princess Patricia × C. Belgica: = Galates should read = Galatée.
11, Rosita × C. Tityus: = Geo Wood should read = George Ward.

Page
11, Sindoro × C. Trimos: = Valerie should read = Valeria.
11, Sofrano × Lc. Luminosa: = Blc. Zanta should read = Blc. Zante.
15, under Muriel: insert × C. Prince John = Planter.
18, CATTLEYA Acis × Iris: = Kathleen Scot should read = Katherine Scott.
20, Angelina × Gaston Bultel: = Janice T. Tanaka should read = Janice Tanaka.
20, Antiope × Dowiana: = Hedga should read = Helga.
20, Ariel × maxima: = Princess Helena Victoria should read = Princess Helen Victoria.
21, Armstrongiae × intricata: = venustra should read = Venusta.
21, Ballantineana × Elizabeth Prentiss: = George A. Terhune should read = George A. Terhume.
21, Ballantineana × Lueddemanniana: = Colodor should read = Coloder.
21, Ballantineana × Madame C(harles) Maron: = Bc. Balzer should read = Bc. Balzar.
22, Beryl × Blc. Antoinette: = Blc. Ellen Willmott should read = Blc. Ellen Willmot.
26, Dinah × Bc. Pallas: = Albana should read = Abana.
27, Dominiana × Bc. Cliftonii: = G. V. Llewellyn should read = G. V. Llewelyn.
31: **Edithae** should read **Edithiae**.
31, Elizabeth Prentiss × Ballantineana: = George A. Terhune should read = George A. Terhume.
32, under Empress Frederick: insert × Slc. Prince Hirohito = Slc. Mikado.
33, Enid × Lc. Coronis: = Enaeus should read = Enoeus.
37, Gaston Bultel × Angelina: = Janice T. Tanaka should read = Janice Tanaka.
38, granulosa: × Harrisoniana should read × loddigesii (syn. harrisoniana) (= Mary Gratrix).
38, granulosa × loddigesii: = Crashleyi should read = Mary Gratrix (syn. Crashleyi).
41, Harrisoniana: delete × Triumphans = Pua Liilii.
43, intermedia: × Epid. falcatum should read × E. parkinsonianum (syn. falcatum) (= Ec. Figaro).
44, Iris × Acis: = Katherine Scot should read = Katherine Scott.
48, Loddigesii × granulosa: = Crashleyi should read = Mary Gratrix (syn. Crashleyi).
49, under Loddigesii: insert × Triumphans = Pua Liilii.
55, Mossiae: × Grande Monarque should read × Bc. Grande Monarque (= Bc. San Blas).
61, Prince John: × Bc. Muriel = Bc. Planter should read × Blc. Muriel = Blc. Planter.
62: **R. Cadwaladar** should read **R. Cadwalader**.
62, R. Cadwalader × Lc. Princess Margaret: = De Louis Ziegfeld should read = De Loris Ziegfeld.
63, Rhoda × Antiope: = Ciceley should read = Cicely.
64, Santa Monica × Bc. Penelope: = La Graciosa should read = La Gracia.
71, Trimos × Bc. Sindoro: = Valerie should read = Valeria.
71, Triumphans: × Harrisoniana should read × loddigesii (syn. harrisoniana) (= Pua Liilii).
99, Actaeus × Golden Dawn: = Achaeon should read = Achaean.
99, under Actaeus: insert × Golden Glory = Glorita.
100, above Aeson: insert **Adrift**; under Adrift insert × Sebastian Cabot = Boat.
100, under Alberis: delete × Makeda = Illogan (correctly Illogen; fully entered in 1946/1960 work, Vol. 1).
100, under Alcibiades: insert × charlesworthii × Alciworthii.
101, under Alciphu: delete × Euryostom = Madge Le Gros; insert × Atlantis × Buckie; insert × Festivity = Lambourn.
102, at foot of Col. 1: insert **Amarah**; under Amarah insert the following — × F. C. Puddle = Dainty; × Radina = Radamar; × Vestalia = Yellow Underwing.
103, argus × Oenanthum: = Madame Josci Descombes should read = Madame Josee Descombes.
103, argus × superbiens: = Eustacenum should read = Eustaceanum.
104, Atlantis × Clarion: = Broadway should read = Broadway II.
105, Aure-Euryades × Cappamagna: = Parana should read = Pavana.
105, aureum: × Curtmanii should read × Curtmannii (= Madame Henon).
106, barbatum × concolor: = Tesselatum should read = Tessellatum.
107, beechense: add (see Cymatodes); delete × Columbus = Colense (as transferred to Cymatodes p. 119 below).
107, bellatulum × chamberlainianum: = Rowena should read = Edithiae (syn. Rowena).
109, Bordube × Gwen Hannen: = Mai-moa should read = Maimoa.
109, boxalli × venustum: = pavonianum should read = Pavoninum.
110, callosum: × William Matthews should read × William Mathews (= Ernest Read).
111, Cappamagna × Aure-Euryades: = Parana should read = Pavana.
111, Cardinal Mercier × Dixon Thorpe: = Thotmes should read = Thothmes.
113, chamberlainianum × bellatulum: = Rowena should read = Edithiae (syn. Rowena).
113, chamberlainianum × spiceranum: = Deedmanianum should read = Deedmannianum.
113, chamberlainianum × villosum: = Madiottianum should read = Madiotianum.
114, charlesworthii × villosum: = Wrigleyii should read = Wrigleyi.
116, Chrysotoxum × Beeckmanii: = hortonensis should read = Hortonense.
117, ciliolare × niveum: = Aylingi should read = Aylingii.
117, Clarion × Atlantis: = Broadway should read = Broadway II.
117, Columbus: × beechense should read × Cymatodes (syn. beechense) (= Colense).
118, concolor × lawrenceanum: = Concolawre should read = Conco-lawre.
119, Crusader × Our Prince: = Royal Scot should read = Royal Scott.
119, under Cymatodes: insert × Columbus = Colense.
121, Dixon Thorpe × Cardinal Mercier: = Thotmes should read = Thothmes.
122, Draco × Hera: = Sadie should read = Yadie.
123, Elaine × Hancar: = Christobel should read = Christabel.
124: **Ethel M. du Bourlay** should read **Ethel M. du Boulay**.
124, Etta × Lady Phulmoni: = May Fair should read = Mayfair.

Page

125, exul × mastersianum: = Masterso-exul should read = Mastersio-exul.
126, Festivity: × Phulbiades should read × Alciphu (= Lambourn).
128, under Germaine Opoix: insert × Beeckmanii = Mrs. de Lazlo.
129, under glaucophyllum: insert × rothschildianum = Vanguard.
130, Golden Dawn × Actaeus: = Achaeon should read = Achaean.
130, Golden Emblem × Wellesley: = Amber should read = Amber II.
130, above Golden Moon: insert **Golden Glory**; under Golden Glory insert × Actaeus = Glorita.
131, above gratrixianum: insert **Gratrixiae**; under Gratrixiae insert × viridissimum = Lewis Knudsen.
131, under gratrixianum: delete × viridissimum = Lewis Knudsen.
132: **Gretel** should read **Gretal**.
132, Gwen Hannen × Bordube: = Mai-moa should read = Maimoa.
132, Gwen Hannen: × Ethel M. du Bourlay should read × Ethel M. du Boulay (= Gwendolin).
133, Hancar × Elaine: = Christobel should read = Christabel.
133, Harrisianum × Christine: = Christobel should read = Cristobel.
133, Harrisianum × venustum: = Ianthe should read Williamsianum (syn. Ianthe).
137, insigne: × Lowi should read × lowii (= Rossii).
141, Lady Phulmoni × Etta: = May Fair should read = Mayfair.
142, Leander × Olympus: = Olympia II should read = Olympia.
143, lawrenceanum × parishii: = Elizabethae should read = Elizabethiae.
145, lowii × stonei: = Mercatelli should read = Mercatelii.
146: delete Maimona; entries thereunder to be integrated alphabetically with those under Maimoa (same page).
146, Manela: × Meekon should read × Mekong (= Mindoro).
147, Marlpit: × Monvik = Mimbu should read × Monavik = Minbu.
147: **Masters-villosum** should read **Mastersio-villosum**.
148, Mayfair: this name is correct here but is incorrectly printed as × May Fair in its breeding under — Alston (p. 102); Brita (p. 109); Lady Phulmoni (p. 141); Memphis (p. 150); and Thias (p. 170), where it should read × Mayfair in each case.
148: **Meekon** should read **Mekong**.
148, Memoria F. M. Ogilvie × Beeckmanii: = Cog should read = Gog. (N.B. *Paphiopedilum* Cog is a quite separate and distinct grex (Garibaldi × Gurkley) registered in 1969.)
150, Merlene: delete × Alcibiades = Mavis.
150: insert **Merlin**; under Merlin insert × Alcibiades = Mavis.
151, Monavik × Marlpit: = Mimbu should read = Minbu.
153, Mrs. William Mostyn × Leander: = Catiline should read = Catilene.
156, niveum × philippinense: = Vipani should read = Vipanii.
157, Noel Hardy: × Maimona should read × Maimoa (= May Day).
157, Oenanthum × argus: = Madame Josci Descombes should read = Madame Josee Descombes.
158, Olympus × Leander: = Olympia II should read = Olympia.
158, Our Prince × Crusader: = Royal Scot should read = Royal Scott.
158, Pallida × Troilus: = Kilum should read = Kilium.
158, parishii × lawrenceanum: = Elizabethae should read = Elizabethiae.
160, Phulbiades: add (see Alciphu); delete entry thereunder, which is transferred to Alciphu (see corrig. p. 101).
162, Radina: × Amaran should read × Amarah (= Radamar).
164, San-Actaeus × Troilus: = Mermaid should read = Mermaid II.
165, Scarab: × nitens-villosum should read × Mastersio-villosum (= Scarsam).
166, Shogun: × Masters-villosum should read × Mastersio-villosum (= Strongitharm).
167, stonei × lowii: = Mercatellii should read = Mercatelii.
170, Thompsonii: × Mem. Jerninghamae = Sir Wm. Chance should read × Mem. Jerninghamiae = Sir William Chance.
172, Troilus × Pallida: = Kilum should read = Kilium.
172, Troilus × San-Actaeus: = Mermaid should read = Mermaid II.
172, Vandyck: this spelling and form is correct, but in the Table I entries of its progeny listed here, and in their Table II entries under the second parents listed here, Vandyck is variously printed as Van Dyck (6 places) and Vandyke (2 places). It should consistently read Vandyck.
172, venustum × Harrisianum: = Ianthe should read = Williamsianum (syn. Ianthe).
173, virens × dayanum: = Petrii should read = Petri.
174, above Wellesleyae: insert **Wellesley**; under Wellesley insert × Golden Emblem = Amber II.
174, under Wellesleyae: delete × Golden Emblem = Amber.
175: **William Matthews** should read **William Mathews**.
178, lasianthera: × schroderanum (as inserted per earlier corrigendum) should read × phalaenopsis (syn. schroderanum) (= Wilhelm Stuber).
180, under phalaenopsis: insert × lasianthera = Wilhelm Stuber.
180, under phalaenopsis: insert × stratiotes = Caesar.
180, under phalaenopsis: insert × violaceo-flavens = Indonesia (syn. Arcuatum).
180, under schroderanum: delete × lasianthera = Wilhelm Stuber.
180, under schroderanum: delete × stratiotes = Caesar.
180, under schroderanum: delete × violaceo-flavens = Indonesia (Arcuatum).
181, stratiotes: × schroderianum should read × phalaenopsis (syn. schroderanum) (= Caesar).
182, Dendrobium violaceo-flavens: × schroderianum should read × phalaenopsis (syn. schroderanum) (= Indonesia).
183, cochleatum: × cucullatum = Cuco should read × B. cucullata = Bepi. Cuco.

Page

183, cucullatum: add (see *Brassavola cucullata*); also delete entry thereunder (transferred per p. 2 corrig. to *Brassavola cucullata*, which is the correct name).

183, falcatum: add (see *parkinsonianum*); also delete entries thereunder (transferred to *parkinsonianum* as per corrig. below).

183, parkinsonianum: add (syn. *falcatum*); insert thereunder the following additional entries transferred from falcatum — × C. intermedia = Ec. Figaro; × L. cinnabarina = El. Whitei.

184: insert generic heading **GASTROCHILUS**: insert thereunder the following entries: **bellinus** × bigibbus = bellino-bigibbus; **bigibbus** × bellinus = bellino-bigibbus.

185, cinnabarina: × E. falcatum should read × E. parkinsonianum (syn. falcatum) (= El. Whitei).

186, under Cinnabrosa: insert × Lc. Canhamiana = Lc. Miss Faith Hanbury.

186, under cowanii: × Dominiana should read × Lc. Dominiana (= Lc. Tigris).

191, above Laeliocattleya Althea: insert **Altesse**; under Altesse insert × C. Enid = Alten.

193: **Audreana** should read **Audrena**; likewise in all consequential entries in Table I of its progeny listed here and in Table II under the second parents of such progeny.

196, under Canhamiana: insert × L. Cinnabrosa = Lc. Miss Faith Hanbury.

215, Myra: × Slc. Althea should read × Slc. Althaea (= Slc. Myra).

224: **Trivenhoe** should read **Trivanhoe**.

226, Lycaste Balliae: × plana should read × macrophylla (syn. plana) (= Arthuriana).

226, Lycaste gigantea: add (see *longipetala*); delete entry thereunder (transferred to *longipetala* as per p. 227 corrig. below).

227, Lycaste lanipes: × plana should read × macrophylla (syn. plana) (= Ebor).

227, Lycaste lawrenceana: × plana should read × macrophylla (syn. plana) (= Gratrixiae).

227, above Lycaste macrobulbon: insert **longipetala** (syn. *gigantea*); thereunder insert × skinneri = Brugensis.

227, Lycaste macrophylla: add (syn. *plana*); also insert thereunder all entries transferred from under plana, as below.

227, Lycaste plana: add (see *macrophylla*); also delete all entries thereunder (transferred to under *macrophylla*, as above).

227, Lycaste skinneri: × gigantea should read × longipetala (syn. gigantea) (= Brugensis).

227, Masdevallia estradae: add (syn. *ludibunda*); also insert thereunder × fraseri = Fraseri-ludibunda.

228: insert generic heading **MENDONCELLA**; under Mendoncella insert the following entries:
burkei (syn. *Zygopetalum burkei*) × Z. mackayi = Zcla. Leucochilum
jorisiana (syn. *Zygopetalum jorisianum*) × Z. maxillare = Zcla. Max-Jorisii

228, Masdevallia fraseri: × ludibunda should read × estradae (syn. ludibunda) (= Fraseri-ludibunda).

228, Masdevallia ludibunda: add (see *estradae*); also delete entry thereunder, as transferred to *estradae* per corrigendum above.

268, under Isolene: insert × Olympia = Isolene-Olympia.

274, under Olympia: insert × Isolene = Isolene-Olympia.

291, crispum: × dasytyle should read × dasystyle (= Wheatleyanum).

291: **dasytyle** should read **dasystyle**.

291, forbesii: × dasytyle should read × dasystyle (= Gardneri).

292, Phaius bicolor: add (see *wallichii*); also delete entry thereunder.

292, above Phaius grandifolius: insert **flavus** (syn. *maculatus*): add thereunder the following entries transferred from under *maculatus*, as per corrig. p. 293 below) —
× grandifolius = Maculato-grandifolius; × wallichii = Ashworthianus.

292, Phaius grandifolius: × maculatus should read × flavus (syn. maculatus) (= Maculato-grandifolius).

292, Phaius humblotii: delete × bicolor = Owenianus.

292, Phaius humblotii × wallichii: = Opoixii should read = Owenianus (syn. Opoixii).

293, Phaius maculatus: add (see *flavus*); also delete entries thereunder.

293, Phaius wallichii × humblotii: = Opoixii should read = Owenianus (syn. Opoixii).

293, Phaius wallichii: × maculatus should read × flavus (syn. maculatus) (= Ashworthianus).

293, Phalaenopsis Confirmation × Grand Condé: = Sappho should read = Sapho.

294, Grand Condé × Confirmation: = Sappho should read = Sapho.

296, Promenaea citrina: add (see *xanthina*); also delete entry thereunder, transferred to *xanthina*, as below.

296, Promenaea xanthina: add (syn. *citrina*); also insert the following entry thereunder (transferred from under *citrina* as above) —× Crawshayana = Colmaniana.

297: delete **SACCOLABIUM** and the entries thereunder (transferred to *Gastrochilus* as per corrig. p. 184 above).

300, Sophrolaeliocattleya: **Althea** should read **Althaea**.

300, Sophrolaeliocattleya Dorila × Bc. Mrs. J. Leemann: = Pot. Princess Shimadzu should read = Pot. Prince Shimadzu.

302, under Prince Hirohito: insert × C. Empress Frederick = Mikado.

307, Zygopetalum burkei: add (see *Mendoncella burkei*); also delete entry thereunder.

308, Zygopetalum jorisianum: add (see *Mendoncella jorisiana*); also delete entry thereunder.

SANDER'S ONE-TABLE LIST OF ORCHID HYBRIDS (1946-1960) Volume 1

List of Registrants Abbreviations:

Page

x, Burstow: add name and address . . . W. J. Burstow, The Old Quarry, Lucastes Ave., Haywards Heath, Sussex, GB.

xv, Mercer: add name and address . . . Frank Mercer, Clovelly, Steyning, Sussex, GB.

xv: insert Moore, M. . . . Mrs. Majory Moore, Duckylls, East Grinstead, Sussex, GB.

xvii: insert Roy. Gdns. . . . The Royal Gardens, Windsor, Berkshire, GB.

xx: insert Young, H. U. . . . (see Hung Ung Young).

List of Hybrids:

Page

316, AUTUMN TINTS: insert × parishii = Prelude.

323-371: the parent parishii sanderae should read parishii in each of the following seven *Cymbidium* hybrids — Cetus, Dryad, Elfin, Garnet, Jasper, Martin and Seamew.

350, registrant of Margot: Baillon should read Ballion.

358, above PARK LANE: insert **parishii*** . . . **species**: under parishii insert × Autumn Tints = Prelude.

362, above PRESIDENT WILSON: insert **PRELUDE (parishii × Autumn Tints)** . . . **A. & R. 1953**.

374, registrant of STOURBRIDGE: M. should read M. & H.

381, ACTAEUS BIANCA: delete parentage and substitute (syn. Actaeus); also crosses under Actaeus Bianca to be transferred to and integrated alphabetically with those under ACTAEUS; ('Bianca' is a cultivar of Actaeus).

382, ALBERIS × Makeda: = Illogan should read = Illogen.

383: **ALIESEUM** should read **ALIESCUM**.

384: **AMARAH** should read **AMARAH***.

386, parent of ANSON: Chrysotoxum should read Chrysostom.

386, parent of ARCHMANII: Beeckmannii should read Beeckmanii.

390-414: registrant Brummitt should read L. W. Brummitt for each of the following hybrids: BALDOCK, BAMFORD, BANSTEAD, BARMOUTH, BARNSLEY, BARNSTAPLE, BATLEY, BIBURY, BINTON, BISLEY, BLAKESLEY, BLEDLOW, BLETCHLEY, BLOCKLEY, BOVINGTON, BLISWORTH, BOWDEN, BRAEMAR, BRAILES, BRIDLINGTON, BRILL, BRINKLOW, BROADWAY II, BROMSGROVE, BUCKNELL, BUSHEY, BUXTON, BYFIELD, DORIS BRUMMITT.

391, parent of BARBOURN: Barbarossa should read Barbarrosa.

393, parent of BETTY BRACEY: Actaeus Bianca should read Actaeus.

399, CARANDRA: insert registrant and date — **L. 1946**.

412, DIANA BROUGHTON: × Actaeus Bianca should read × Actaeus (= Dianthus).

412, parent of DIANTHUS: Actaeus Bianca should read Actaeus.

428, parentage of GREATHEART: should read Chatwode × Commander Howard Wethey.

430, GWENPUR: × Actaeus Bianca should read × Actaeus (= Betty Bracey).

432, parent of HELLAS: Desdemonia should read Desdemona.

437, J. M. BLACK × Theseus: = Roxana should read = Roxana II.

440, parent of LAMBOURN: Phulbiades should read Alciphu (syn. Phulbiades).

441, parent of LEMANII DUCIS: Curtmanii should read Curtmannii.

446, MAKEDA × Alberis: = Illogan should read = Illogen.

461, PAPILLON: insert registrant — **L.**

467, parentage of REDRUSH: should read Red Admiral × Windrush.

470: **ROXANA** should read **ROXANA II** (N.B. the grex epithet Roxana was registered for another *Paphiopedilum* cross in 1929).

475, parent of SOSSMOSS: Actaeus Bianca should read Actaeus.

476, above SUMELAINE: insert **SUMDEL (delenatii × Sumurun)** . . . **S. 1953**.

479, THESEUS × J. M. Black: = Roxana should read = Roxana II.

479, parent of THIAS: Beeckmannii should read Beeckmanii.

481: **TRIGOL** should read **TRIGAL**.

483, above VILLOTRA: insert **VILLOSMUND (villosum × Osmund)** . . . **Stirling 1953**.

484, WENDBOURN: × Barbarossa should read × Barbarrosa (= Barbourn).

487, date of YOKOHAMA: 194- should read 1956.

488, registrant of ALE ALE KAI: P. Yahiro should read R. Yahiro.

490, registrant of ANDREW PERSSON: Persson should read Slade.

493, CAESAR: add (syn. E. P. Boyle); also parent schroderianum (syn. phalaenopsis) should read phalaenopsis (syn. schroderanum).

496, dicuphum: × schroderianum should read × phalaenopsis (syn. schroderanum) (= White Gem).

497, E. P. BOYLE: add (see Caesar).

503, parent of INDONESIA: schroderianum should read phalaenopsis (syn. schroderanum); registrant and date should read van Brero 1930.

518, date of PEARL: 195 should read 1959.

518, under phalaenopsis: insert × dicuphum = White Gem.

518, phalaenopsis × stratiotes: = E. P. Boyle should read = Caesar (syn. E. P. Boyle).

520, parent of ROSE MARIE: lepinorum should read leporinum.

522, under schroderianum: delete × dicuphum = White Gem.

523, stratiotes × phalaenopsis: = E. P. Boyle should read = Caesar (syn. E. P. Boyle).

529, parent of WHITE GEM: schroderianum var. album should read phalaenopsis (syn. schroderanum).

530, parent of Lycaste BRUGENSIS: gigantea should read longipetala (syn. gigantea).

531: **ARMANDA** should read **ARMANDA***.

532: **CLAIRE FELL** should read **CLAIRE PELL**.

534, MARIETTA ARMACOST (see Esperance) × Telka: = Claire Fell should read = Claire Pell.

537, TELKA × Esperance (syn. Marietta Armacost): = Claire Fell should read = Claire Pell.

548, ASCANIA: × lemonianum should read × Lemonianum (= Gilda).

554, parent of GILDA: lemonianum should read Lemonianum.

554, GLEDHOW: × Red Skin should read × Redskin (= Melissa Jane).

556, parent of IDALAN: Red Skin should read Redskin.

557: **lemonianum** . . . **species** should read **Lemonianum (hyb. ign.)** . . . — **pre-1944**.

558, parent of MELISSA JANE: Red Skin should read Redskin.

563: **RED SKIN** should read **REDSKIN**.

Page
563, ROBIN HOOD: × Red Skin should read × Redskin.
571: **jamaica** should read **JAMAICA**; also registrant and date should read W. W. G. Moir 1956.

SANDER'S ONE-TABLE LIST OF ORCHID HYBRIDS (1946-1960) Volume 2

List of Abbreviations of Registrants:

Page
xi: insert Aldridge . . . William Aldridge, Benson, Oxon, GB.
xiii: insert Doi, T. . . . (address unrecorded).
xiv: Fuchs Jr. should read Fuchs Jr. / Fuch's Orchids
xvi, against Lancaster: A. H. Lancaster etc. should read Charles H. Lankester, O.B.E., Las Concavas, Cartago, Costa Rica.
xvii: insert Matsuo, C. M. . . . (address unrecorded).
xxii: insert Yamaoka, K. ... Kentaro Yamaoka, Hachizuka 3-7-11, Ikeda, Osaka, Japan.

List of Hybrids:

579, AËRIDES: virens should read odorata (syn. *virens*).
579, parent of Aëridovanda BLUE JADE: Aër. virens should read Aër. odorata (syn. virens).
599, parent of OLIVE D. WATT: Leemaniae should read Mrs. J. Leemann (syn. Leemanniae).
605, VISCOUNT TODA: parentage should read Ilene × C. Rhoda.
607, APPARITION: registrant and date should read L. 1949.
612, parent of CONNIE WALLAR: Bc. Leemanniae should read Bc. Mrs. J. Leemann (syn. Leemanniae).
614, above DONALUCCA: insert **DOCTOR STERLING V. MEAD (Lc. Sargon × Muriel)** . . . **Siegwart 1950**.
644, Note to **CATTLEYA** heading: add following supplementary Note: "For revised position as from 1961 see Introduction to 1961/1970 Addendum, page vii."
645, ALCILETEN × eldorado: = Schneewitchen should read = Schneewittchen II.
655, BOW BELLS: × White Bell should read × White Belle (= Mem. Paul T. Yamada).
667, eldorado × Alcileten: = Schneewittchen should read = Schneewittchen II.
674, parent of FRITZ RESS: Altica should read Celtica.
678, under guttata: insert × Nigrella = New Era.
680, harrisoniae: × L. regnellii should read × lundii (syn. regnellii) (= Lc. Alvim Seidel).
680, under harrisoniae: delete × Lc. Bonanza = Lc. Clustery (see transfer to *loddigesii* p. 692 below).
686, JOSE MARTI: after name of registrant add date 1959.
689, under labiata: insert × Lc. Mary Rose = Lc. Cheyita.
691, after leopoldii: (syn. guttata*) should read (see guttata*).
691, under leopoldii: delete × Nigrella = New Era (as transferred to *guttata* — see p. 678 corrig. above).
692, under loddigesii: insert × Lc. Bonanza = Lc. Clustery.
698, parent of MEM. PAUL T. YAMADA: White Bell should read White Belle.
704, parent of NEW ERA: leopoldii should read guttata (syn. leopoldii).
705, NIGRELLA: × leopoldii should read × guttata (syn. leopoldii) (= New Era).
712, parent of PUA LIILII: harrisoniae should read loddigesii (syn. harrisoniana).
713, date of REDTOP MOUNTAIN: 195- should read 1959.
713, REMY CHOLLET × Lc. Bonanza: = Lc. Vallecholet should read = Lc. Vallechollet.
716: **SCHNEEWITTCHEN** should read **SCHNEEWITTCHEN II**.
733, Cycnoches aureum: add (see *egertonianum*) and transfer entry thereunder to under *egertonianum* as per corrig. below.
733, Cycnoches dianae: × aureum should read × egertonianum (syn. aureum) (= Hawaiian Lei).
733, Cycnoches: insert **egertonianum** (syn. *aureum*); insert entry thereunder — × dianae = Hawaiian Lei.
733, Cycnoches HAWAIIAN LEI (as inserted per corrig. in Addendum 1961/70 p. lxii): parentage etc. should read — egertonianum (syn. aureum) × dianae . . . W. W. G. Moir 1961.
740, at foot of page: insert **grandiflora***; thereunder insert the entry — × Laeliopsis domingensis = Liaopsis Lilac (as transferred from *Laelia speciosa* per corrig. p. 741 below; *L. grandiflora* is the horticulturally recommended name for *L. speciosa*).
741, above PACAVIA: insert lundii (syn. *regnellii*); insert thereunder the entry — × C. harrisoniae = Lc. Alvim Seidel (as transferred from *regnellii* per corrig. below).
741, regnellii: add (see *lundii*); also delete entry thereunder (transferred to *lundii* as above).
741, speciosa: add (see *grandiflora*); also delete entry thereunder (transferred to *grandiflora* as above).
745: **ALTESSE** should read **ALTESSE***.
745, parent of ALVIM SEIDEL: L. regnelii should read L. lundii (syn. regnellii).
752, BLANCHETTE × Edith Dorpe: = Niobe should read = Niobe II.
753, parent of BONANZA: Prospector should read C. Prospector.
753, BONANZA: × C. harrisoniae should read × C. loddigesii (= Lc. Clustery).
756: **CANDERA** should read **CANDORA**; also transfer to correct alphabetical position above CANDOUR same page.
759, parent of CHANTECLER: C. Embress Frederick should read C. Empress Frederick.
760, originator of CHOTON: (K. Yamaoko) should read (K. Yamaoka).
761, parent of CLUSTERY: C. harrisoniae should read C. loddigesii (syn. harrisoniae).
770, EDITH DORPE × Blanchette: = Niobe should read = Niobe II.

Page
771, under ELISSA: insert × Momus = Momel.
774, below EWA: insert **EWELME (Princess Juliana × Princess Margaret) . . . Aldridge 1955.**
791, INVICTA × Modasa: = Newick should read = Newick II.
811, MODASA × Invicta: = Newick should read = Newick II.
811, below MOLOSS: insert **MOMEL (Momus × Elissa) . . . S. Tharp 1954.**
811, under MOMUS: insert × Elissa = Momel.
815: **NEWICK** should read **NEWICK II.**
816: **NIOBE** should read **NIOBE II.**
823, under PRINCESS JULIANA: insert × Princess Margaret = Ewelme.
824, under PRINCESS MARGARET: insert × Princess Juliana = Ewelme.
830, RUDGWICK × Santa Claus: = Shipley should read = Shipley II.
833, SANTA CLAUS × Rudgwick: = Shipley should read = Shipley II.
835: **SHIPLEY** should read **SHIPLEY II.**
836, parent of S. J. BRACEY: Thebes should read C. Thebes.
836, S. J. BRACEY: × Bc. Leemanniae should read × Bc. Mrs. J. Leemann (= Blc. Connie Wallar).
846: **VALLECHOLET** should read **VALLECHOLLET.**
852, Laeliopsis domingensis: × L. speciosa should read × L. grandiflora (syn. speciosa) (= Liaopsis Lilac).
852, parent of Liaopsis LILAC: L. speciosa should read L. grandiflora (syn. speciosa).
854, amphitrite: × Grande Condé should read × Grand Condé (= Conditrite).
858, parent of CONDITRITE: Grand Conde should read Grand Condé.
860, date of ELDORA: 194- should read 1957.
863, parent of GRANART: Grande Conde should read Grand Condé.
863: GRANDE CONDE should read GRAND CONDÉ.
878, stuartiana: × Grande Conde should read × Grand Condé (= Granart).
881, date of WHITE MONARCH: 195 should read 1960.
883, DOROTHY L. ADAIR: after name of registrant add date 1960.
902: **D. S. SENONAYAKE** should read **D. S. SENANAYAKE.**
902, registrant of ELLEN NOA: Noa should read J. K. Noa.
903, FRANK SCUDDER: × Aërides virens should read × Aërides odorata (syn. virens) (= Aëridovanda Blue Jade).
909, registrant of LESTER McCOY: Cummins should read J. A. Cummins.
911, MAURICE RESTREPO × sanderana: = Yang Yuet Lim should read = Yuet Yeng Lim.
911, MEM. TADAICHI DOI: registrant and originator should read C. M. Matsuo (T. Doi).
916, sanderana × Maurice Restrepo: = Yong Yuet Lim should read = Yuet Yeng Lim.
916, sanderana: × Denisonica should read × Denizonica (= Dennisand).

SANDER'S LIST OF ORCHID HYBRIDS — ADDENDUM 1961-1970

Special Corrigenda:

1. The earlier and correct name for *Cymbidium hoosai* is *Cymbidium sinense*. Since no conflict exists between their respective registered crosses, the following corrections are to be effected to past registrations as recorded in the 1961/70 Addendum:—
   (a) correct the parent name hoosai to read sinense (syn. hoosai) in each of the following Cymbidium hybrids:— Bizen (p. 154); China Doll (p. 159); Dusk (p. 167); Fido (p. 172); Ken (p. 184); Kitten (p. 185); Loho (p. 187); Peppermint (p. 201); Red Star (p. 206); Skyrocket (p. 214); Soho (p. 215); Toots (p. 220). Also make similar corrections to the corresponding entry under the second parent of each hybrid listed above.
   (b) page 179, hoosai: add (see *sinense*); also transfer all the entries under *hoosai* to be listed under *sinense* (p. 214) in alphabetical integration with those already listed under *sinense*.
   (c) page 214, sinense: add (syn. *hoosai*).
2. The following general orthographic correction is to be effected to the name Laeliocattleya Jose Dias Castro wherever it appears in this volume: add acute accent (′) to the terminal e of Jose, to read José; that is to say—
   (a) under its own entry on p. 345.
   (b) wherever it occurs as a parent in the entry of each of its progeny listed on p. 345.
   (c) wherever it occurs under the entry of each second parent of its progeny listed on p. 345.
3. The earlier and correct name for *Oncidium retemeyeranum* is *Oncidium lindenii*. The following corrections are to be effected to past registrations recorded in the 1961/70 Addendum:—
   (a) correct the parent name retemeyeranum to read lindenii (syn. retemeyeranum) in each of the following Oncidium hybrids:— Anne Louise McLaughlin (p. 428); Kumblebee (p. 433); Randall McLaughlin (p. 438). Also make similar corrections to the corresponding entry under the second parent of each of these three hybrids.
   (b) page 434, above LINSTEAD: insert lindenii (syn. *retemeyeranum*); thereunder insert all the entries previously listed under *retemeyeranum*.
   (c) page 438, retemeyeranum: add (see *lindenii*): delete all entries thereunder (transferred to under lindenii as inserted p. 434 per corrig. above).
4. The intergeneric orchid name *Sarcorhiza* was discovered to be so similar to *Sarcorrhiza*, a name earlier given to a genus outside the Orchidaceae, that it must be regarded as a later homonym and therefore unacceptable. The orchid intergeneric *Sarcorhiza* (*Rhinerrhiza* × *Sarcochilus*) has therefore been re-named *Rhinochilus* (recommended abbreviation *Rhincs.*). Consequential corrections to the 1961/70 Addendum appear in detailed corrigenda below.

List of Genera:

Page
x, below RHINERRHIZA: insert RHINOCHILUS (Rhincs.) = Rhinerrhiza × Sarcochilus.
xi: delete SARCORHIZA etc.

List of Generic Parents:

Page

xvii, Rhinerrhiza × Sarcochilus (and reverse entry same page): = Sarcorhiza should read = Rhinochilus.

List of Registrants and Originators:

xix, at end of page: insert Arblaster, George . . . Hill Crest Orchids, 50 Sheffield Rd., Killamarsh, Sheffield, Yorks. S31 8EA, GB.

xx: insert Archer . . . H. C. Archer, P.O. Box 422, Gosford, NSW 2250, Australia.

xxii: insert Bryant & Gillson . . . c/o A. R. Bryant (q.v.).

xxii, against Borg: Dr. Trejvid Borg should read Dr. Frejvid Borg.

xxii: insert Bruce . . . Keith Bruce, 31 Glen Ebor Ave., Blackburn, Victoria, Australia.

xxiii: insert C. & D. . . . R. P. Calmette & L. E. Drumm, 296 Bronwood Ave., Los Angeles, CA 90049, USA.

xxiii, Burstow: add name and address . . . W. J. Burstow, The Old Quarry, Lucastes Ave., Haywards Heath, Sussex, GB.

xxiii: insert Cavaco . . . (see Cavaco, T.).

xxiv, Chandler: add . . . C. H. Chandler, High Warren, Theydon Mount, Epping, Essex, GB.

xxiv: insert Chen, C. M. . . . 5-A Chancery Hill Rd., Singapore.

xxiv: insert Chen, Dr. T. S. . . . c/o Teang Seng Hospital, 63 Hsing Yung St., Chia-Yi, Taiwan.

xxv: Cookson, N. C. should read Cookson
Cookson, N. C.

xxvii: du Pont, W. K. should read du Pont
du Pont, W. K.

xxvii: insert Doi, T. . . . (address unrecorded).

xxviii, Edwards, H. M.: add address . . . P.O. Box 708, Marandellas, Rhodesia.

xxviii: insert Everett
Everett Nurs. . . . (address unrecorded).

xxviii, Fairburn: add address . . . 2440 Fairway Dr., Vero Beach, FL 32960, USA.

xxix, below Fosnaugh: insert Foster . . . (see Foster Gdns.)

xxix: Fujinaga, Y. should read Fujinaga
Fujinaga, Y.

xxxii: insert Hall, Richard . . . Richard W. R. Hall, 25 Ruskin Row, Avalon Beach, Sydney, NSW, Australia.

xxxiv: Iwanaga, E. should read Iwanaga
Iwanaga, E.

xxxiv, Ishikawa: add name and address . . . Masatoshi Ishikawa, 1505 Tamura, Hiratsuka-shi, Kanagawa-ken, Japan.

xxxv: insert Jayaratna . . . Anong Jayaratna, c/o The Thai Insurance Co. Ltd., 933 Mahachai Rd., Bangkok, Thailand.

xxxv, above Johnston, C. L.: insert Johnston . . . (see Johnston, D. W.).

xxxv: insert Jost, R. P. . . . Richard P. Jost, 143 Ackerman Ave., Clifton, NJ. 07011, USA.

xxxv: insert Kagawa, Dr. K. . . . 1111 Bishop St., Honolulu, HI 96813, USA.

xxxvi: insert Kanayama . . . Richard K. Kanayama, 45-115 Awele Pl., Kaneohe, HI 96744, USA.

xxxvi: insert Katsuura . . . Katsuura Shoyoen Orchid Co., 2908-2 Yamada-Ogawa, Ibaraki City, Osaka, Japan.

xxxvi: Kimkris etc. should read Komkris . . . Professor Thiem Komkris etc. . . . ; also transfer to correct alphabetical position on p. xxxvii.

xxxvii, below Konishi: insert Kono . . . (see Kono, T.).

xxxvii, Kojima, K.: address should read 161 Arimatsu-cho, Midori-ku, Nagoya, Japan.

xxxvii, against Lancaster: A. H. Lancaster etc. should read Charles H. Lankester, O.B.E., Las Concavas, Cartago, Costa Rica.

xxxviii, Lawson: add name and address . . . H. P. Lawson & Miss Helen Lawson, Lynbrook, Knaphill, Surrey, GB.

xxxviii: insert Leverett, G. . . . G. Leverett & Co., Moorabbui, Victoria, Australia.

xxxix: insert Lista . . . Peter E. Lista, P.O. Box 242, Orangefield, TX 77639, USA.

xxxix: insert Lovas . . . J. Lovas, R.D.1., Old Dover Rd., Morris Plains, NJ, USA.

xxxix, immediately above Machle: insert Mac/Mc . . . For names starting Mac . . . or Mc. . . see following My. . . (on pp. xli and xlii).

xl: insert Matsuo, C. M. . . . (address unrecorded).

xl, against Mercer: add . . . Frank Mercer, Clovelly, Steyning, Sussex, GB.

xl: Miles, A. E. should read Miles
Miles, A. E.

xli: after Montgomery, G. F.: insert Moore . . . G. F. Moore, Chardwar, Bourton-on-the-Water, Cheltenham, Glos., GB.

xlii, McLeod: add . . . Ray McLeod, 29701 Baden Pl., Malibu, CA 90265, USA.

xlii, Nagano: Mr. & Mrs. Hoshio Nagano (etc.) should read Dr. & Mrs. Yoshio Nagano (etc.).

xlii, below Nakagawa: insert Nakamoto
Nakamoto, W. . . . (see Nakamoto, W. K.).

xlii: Nakayama Bros. should read Nakayama
Nakayama Bros.

xlii: insert Nelson, J. . . . Julius L. Nelson, 10535 Santa Susanna Ave., Chatsworth, CA 91311, USA.

xliv, below Patmayodhin: insert Patterson
Patterson & Sons . . . (see Patterson, H.).

xlv: insert Pinchess . . . E. E. Pinchess, "Stretton Poplars", Hinckley, Leics., GB.

xlv: Raybridge should read Rayridge; also at end of address (Dr. J. Bergman) should read (F. J. Bergman).

xlv: insert Reed, Mrs. D. D. . . . Mrs. Douglas D. Reed, 668 N.E. 72nd St., Miami, FL 33138, USA.

Page

xlvi: Robago etc. should read Rabago . . . Mrs. Mercedes Rabago (etc.); also transfer entry to correct alphabetical position following Raasch on p. xlv.

xlvi: Royal, E. L. should read Royal
Royal, E. L.

xlvi: insert Royden . . . Royden Orchids, Perks La., Prestwood, Great Missenden, Bucks., GB.

xlvi: insert Roy. Gdns. . . . The Royal Gardens, Windsor, Berks., GB.

xlvi: insert Rujirawongse . . . Mme. Chuli Rujirawongse, c/o The Thai Insurance Co. Ltd., 933 Mahachai Rd., Bangkok, Thailand.

xlvii: insert Scaynes . . . R. G. Scaynes, Flat No. 1., Bronshill Rd., Torquay, Devon, GB.

xlviii: insert Shay . . . Weston W. Shay, 141 N. Barrington Ave., Los Angeles, CA 90049, USA.

xlviii: insert Shoyoen . . . (see Katsuura Shoyoen Orchid Co.).

xlix: insert Sparrow . . . G. M. Sparrow, "Shawlands", Potten End., Berkhamsted, Herts., GB.

xlix: Stewart Inc. should read Stewart
Stewart, F. A.
Stewart Inc.

xlix: insert Sunthonwan . . . Thananchai Sunthonwan, c/o The Thai Insurance Co. Ltd., 933 Mahachai Rd., Bangkok, Thailand.

l, below Takase: insert Takeda . . . (see Takeda, S.).

l: insert Tan Gim Hoon . . . 632 East Coast Rd., Singapore.

l: insert Tan Kit Mun . . . 75 Dutches Rd., Singapore 10.

li: Thomas, Lyle should read Thomas, L. S.
Thomas, Lyle

li: insert Thomson, G. M. . . . Highlands, South Dr., St. George's Hill, Weybridge, Surrey, GB.

lii: insert Vandeveer . . . Wm. P. Vandeveer, 490 Riqueza St., Encinitas, CA 92024, USA.

liii: insert Whitton . . . (no other data recorded).

liii, below Willersdorf: insert Williams . . . (see Williams, Ellen).

liii: insert Wimber, D. E. . . . Biology Dept., Univ. of Oregon, Eugene, OR 06311, USA.

liv: insert Yanagihara . . . Matsuo Yanagihara, 1319 E. Yanonalli St., Santa Barbara, CA 93103, USA.

List of Corrigenda:

lxii, re. p. 873, PINOCCHIO: add 'also on pp. 875 and 881.'

lxiv, final entry re. p. 920: The correction itself contains the following orthographic error: VANDA YUET LENG LIM should have read VANDA YUET YENG LIM

List of Hybrids:

2: **multiflora** should read **multiflora***.

6: **ISHBEL** should read **ISHBEL†**.

6, under ISHBEL: delete × V. Poepoe = Aranda Lynn Kong.

8, against HILDA GALISTAN: delete (syn. Lucy Laycock); also parent V. tricolor should read V. suavis. (N.B. Although the name *Vanda suavis* is no longer accepted as a parental name in *new* grex registrations — being treated in such cases as conspecific with *Vanda tricolor* as per Introduction to 1961/70 Addendum p. vii — it must nevertheless still be recorded as the parental name in the cases of certain hybrids so registered in the *past* which fall within the category covered by the provisions on pp. 59/60 of the Handbook on Orchid Nomenclature and Registration, 2nd. Edition (1976), Part VI preamble, System of Presentation (1)(d).)

9: delete LYNN KONG etc. (this was a later synonym of *Aranda* Wong Mook Kwi (1959) and its publication in the Orchid Review list of Dec. 1968 was later cancelled in the list of April 1969).

9, against LUCY LAYCOCK: delete (syn. Hilda Galistan).

12, GOLD BUTTONS × V. Charm: = Saboh should read = Sabah.

14, registrant of PENSOM: Kimkris should read Komkris.

14, parent of PISWONG: Diana Ogawa should read Diane Ogawa.

14: **SABOH** should read **SABAH**.

14, parent of SEECHANG: V. Diana Ogawa should read V. Diane Ogawa.

17, Aspasia epidendroides: × marshallianum should read × Onc. marshallianum (= Aspsm. My Darlings).

32, APPARITION: registrant and date should read L. 1949.

36, CINNAMON PEAK × Zanget: = Hazell Dell should read = Hazel Dell.

36, parent of CONNIE WALLAR: Bc. Leemanniae should read Bc. Mrs. J. Leemann (syn. Bc. Leemanniae).

42, registrant of GLORIA SCHMIDT: Schmidt should read Gloria Schmidt.

45: **HAZELL DELL** should read **HAZEL DELL**.

46: **HERMAN LEEBL** should read **HERMAN LOEBL**.

47, above JAMES HAUSERMANN: insert **JAKO (Lc. Orange Ann × Ojai)** . . . **Rod McLellan Co. 1967**.

49, KAPIOLANI BEAUTY × C. Bertii: = Herman Leebl should read = Herman Loebl.

50: **KONG URAI-GOLD** should read **KONG-URAI GOLD**.

53, registrant of MARY BETH HANCOCK: McBroom should read W. T. McBroom.

69, registrant of YACHIYO: Otaguro should read Kido.

69, ZANGET × Cinnamon Peak: = Hazell Dell should read = Hazel Dell.

70, registrant of Brassophronitis EDNA: Shaw should read C. S. Shaw.

70, Broughtonia sanguinea × Epi. bifidum: = Starlight should read = Spotlight; also transfer to correct alphabetical position (following × Diab. Alice Hart = Diab. Newcastle).

71, Catasetum: **pileatum** should read **pileatum***; also **warscewiczii** should read **warscewiczii†**.

Page

77: the entry of BATALINII should read — **batalinii / BATALINII** bicolor × intermedia **Nat. hyb. / S. 1892**

(NB. the entries *under* BATALINII are not altered by this correction which is merely to indicate the status of this hybrid as both a natural hybrid and a registered grex.)

77: BERTII × Blc. Kapiolani Beauty: = Herman Leebl should read = Herman Loebl.
93, above EUGENE HAUSERMANN: insert **EUCHONIANA** (see Henrietta Japhet†).
95, parent of FRITZ RESS: Altica should read Celtica.
99, against guttata: (syn. leopoldii†) should read (syn. leopoldii*†).
101, against HENRIETTA JAPHET†: insert (syn. Euchoniana).
102: HYBRIDA*† should read HYBRIDA*.
103, INTERTEXTA JULIETTIAE (see Intertexta): add explanatory note in parentheses — (Intertexta 'Juliettiae' is in fact a true albino cultivar of the grex *Cattleya* Intertexta produced from a particular raising — viz. *C. mossiae* var. *wagneri* × *C. warneri* var. *alba*. Nomenclaturally, however, it falls within the grex *C.* Intertexta, which is the grex name to represent the progeny from crossing *any* variety or cultivar of *C. mossiae* with *any* variety or cultivar of *C. warneri*).
105: delete entry for Cattleya JAKO (this is a *Brassolaeliocattleya*, as inserted per corrig. p. 47 above).
106, JOSE MARTI: after name of registrant von Paulsen add date 1959.
109, against leopoldii: (see guttata†) should read (see guttata*†).
109, parent of LILLIAN WHITE: Mrs. Gratrix should read Lillian Stewart.
112, against lucieniana and LUCIENIANA: (see Hybrida*†) should read (see Hybrida*).
118, below MIRELLE TOOGOOD: insert **MISSIONARY RIDGE (Bow Bells × Intermediette) Rivermont 1966**.
124, PATRICIA LINES × Celia: = Patricia Lines should read = Celia Lines.
124, against PATROCINII and PATROCINII GAUDII: (see Hybrida*†) should read (see Hybrida*).
127, date of REDTOP MOUNTAIN: 195- should read 1959.
129, R.(owena) PROWE: delete × Schom. lyonsii = Smbc. Ala Makane; (Smbc. Ala Makane is a different cross and is correct in all entries).
137, UNDINE: × Lc. Marina should read × Lc. Mariner (= Lc. Blue Diamond).
138: **velutina**† should read **velutina***†.
143, against Cochlioda sanguinea: (syn. *Symphoglossum sanguinae*) should read (syn. *Symphoglossum sanguineum*).
144, Comparettia falcata × Rdza. teuscheri: = Rdtta. Henry Teuscheri should read = Rdtta. Henry Teuscher.
145, ADELMA × Alexanderi: = Nicholas Den should read = Nicolas Den.
145, date of AIRKHAN: 1969 should read 1964.
146, ALEXANDERI: × Princess Maria should read × Princesse Maria (= Marialex).
147-210: in each of the following Cymbidiums the name of registrant Arblaster should read George Arblaster — Andrew Arblaster (p. 147); Anna Baldry (p. 148); Darren Arblaster and Deborah Banks (p. 164); Erica Gallatly (p. 170); Jean Arblaster (p. 181); Lilian Arblaster (p. 186); Ruth Keefe (p. 210).
148, ANN GREEN: × John Bowers should read × John Blowers (= Me-No).
149, date of ATLANTES: 1957 should read 1927.
150, BABYLON × Etta Barlow: = Pink Monmouth should read = Pink Momouth.
150, under BABYLON: insert × Fair Pearl = Jester.
151, BALKIS × Coningsbyanum: = John Freemont should read = John Fremont.
151, BALKIS: × Marian Lenfesty should read × Marian Lenfestey (= Bobbin Head).
151, under BALKIS: insert × Mirella = George Brandt.
153, BEXLEY AURORA: parentage should read Baltic × Lucy.
153, BEXLEY RADIANCE: after registrant and date insert name of originator (Lovas).
154, parent of BOBBIN HEAD: Marian Lenfesty should read Marian Lenfestey.
154, BOMBADIER: after registrant and date insert name of originator (C. K. Andrew).
154, date of BIRKA: 1970 should read 1969.
155, registrant of BRENTWOOD: Weber should read Paul Weber.
155, date of BURNHAM: 1964 should read 1942.
157, date of CAROLYN ETHEL: 1969 should read 1964.
159: **CHINCILLA** should read **CHINCHILLA**.
160, CHRISTMAS BEAUTY: × Pacific Beauty should read × Pacific Pearl (= Isle).
161, CLYDE LANDERS × pumilum: = Fairy Range should read = Fairy Rouge.
162, CONINGSBYANUM × Balkis: = John Freemont should read = John Fremont.
162, date of CREAMGREEN: 1968 should read 1967.
164, registrant of DAWN ANGELA: D. should read B.
164, registrant of DECEMBER: Stewart Inc. should read Sherman.
164, originator of DENISE RUTH: (C. R. Barrow) should read (Barrow).
166, DORCHESTER × pumilum: = Java should read = Jana.
167: entries for **DR. LLOYD HAWKINSON** and **DR. PAUL VEAZEY** to be transferred to their correct alphabetical position on p. 165 (following **DOCTOR BENJAMIN KORTS**).
167, registrant of DRIKSON: Fujio Nurs. should read Fuji Nurs.
167, parent of DRYAD: parishii sanderae should read parishii.
168, date of EARLY LEMON: 1970 should read 1963.
169: **EL PASSO** should read **EL PASEO**.
169: **EMMA MENNIGER** should read **EMMA MENNINGER**.
171, under ETTA BARLOW: delete × Jungle Queen = Ann Burns (Ann Burns is a different cross and is correct in all entries).
173, FLAVIAN × Vieux Rose: = Henry Dickenson should read = Henny Dickenson.
173, date of FORT AUGUSTUS: 1970 should read 1969.

Page
173: **FLANK SLATTERY** should read **FRANK SLATTERY**.
174, parent of GARNET: parishii sanderae should read parishii.
176, GRANODOS: delete entry; this is a superfluous and incorrect repeat of GRANADOS, qv. p. 175, which is correct.
176, registrant of GREEN KNIGHT: Lee Grande should read Le Grande.
178, HAWK MOTH: × Con Amone should read × Con Amore (= Yuko).
179, date of HIGHLAND PEAK: 1970 should read 1969.
180, IRISH PEARL × Ramboda: = Iribod should read = Iriboda.
181: **JAVA** should read **JANA**; also transfer to correct position above JANE GRADY, same page.
182, date of JET: 1967 should read 1968.
182, registrant of JILBOA: E. de B. should read E. L. de R.
183, date of JOY SANDER: 1942 should read 1924.
184, KAREN CAMERON × Balkis: = Brigette Whellan should read = Brigette Wellan.
184, KHYBER PASS: × Shokei Pass should read × Shokei (= Ningio Pass).
184, date of KING EVELAKE: 1960 should read 1969.
185, KURUN: × Charmont should read × Charmant (= Caprice).
185, KURUN × Redwood: = Realite should read = Realité.
186, date of LEGONAIRE: 1966 should read 1968.
187, LOUIS SANDER: × Rio Perfection should read × Rio-Perfection (= Yosemite).
189, parent of MALEK: Carroll should read Caroll.
190: **MARY GOSS JACOBSON** should read **MARY GOSS JACOBSEN**.
192, parent of MILANO: Solano should read Solana.
194, parent of MOPSA: Mem. P. W. Jenssen should read Mem. P. W. Janssen.
195, registrant of NANCY THOMSON: Thomson should read G. M. Thomson.
196, registrant of NINGIO PASS: Fujio Nurs. should read Fuji Nurs.
196: **nivio-marginatum** should read **niveo-marginatum**.
197, registrant of OISOKE: Fujio should read K. Fujio.
199, PARACEL: × Pari should read × Peri (= Seville).
199, PASTORAL × Balkis: = Sprindrift should read = Spindrift.
199, parent of PATARAK: Joan of Ark should read Joan of Arc.
200, date of PATRICIA REYNOLDS: 1969 should read 1964.
200, PEARL × Remus: = Gilham's Birch should read = Gilhams Birch.
203, PRINCE CHARLES × Hawtescens: = Ballethie should read = Ballathie.
203, PROFITA: × Marion Lenfestey should read × Marian Lenfestey (= Kyeena).
204, pumilum × Alderman: = Rem Imp should read = Red Imp.
204, pumilum: × Carroll should read × Caroll (= Malek).
204, pumilum × devonianum: = Miss Muffit should read = Miss Muffet.
204, pumilum × Dorchester: = Java should read = Jana.
204, date of PUNITA: 1964 should read 1961.
205: **REALITE** should read **REALITÉ**.
206, under REGENTS PARK: insert × Flare = Park Lights.
206, under REGENT STREET: delete × Flare = Park Lights.
206, RED IMP: after name of registrant insert name of originator (Ireland).
206, REDWOOD × Kurun: = Realite should read = Realité.
207, RHODA: × Ortolon should read × Ortolan (= Rhodalon).
207, parent of RHODALON: Ortolon should read Ortolan.
207, RIO RITA: × Stawbury Fair should read × Strawberry Fair (= Urax).
208, under ROSANNA: insert × Finetta = Annetta.
211, registrant of SAN DIEGO: Vandeever should read Vandeveer.
211, SAN MIGUEL: × Solano should read × Solana (= Milano).
214, parent of SIR GALAHAD: Brandogras should read Brandogas.
215, registrant of SOHO: Yamamato-Noen should read Yamato-Noen.
215: **SOLANO** should read **SOLANA**.
215, parent of SONATA: Carol should read Caroll.
220, TWELFTH NIGHT: × Solano should read × Solana (= Wintertime).
222, VIEUX ROSE: × San Rita should read × Sanrita (= Glencoe).
222, registrant of WESTERN ROSE: Borrison should read Borrisow.
222, under WESTERN ROSE: insert × Fred Stewart = Doug Lanceley.
223, parent of WINTERTIME: Solano should read Solana.
224, date of YIN CHEE: 1969 should read 1964.
226, registrant of ALE ALE KAI: P. Yahiro should read R. Yahiro.
227, registrant and originator of ALICE CHONG: P. Y. C. Chong (Chang) should read Peter Chong (A. C. Chang).
228, ANDREW PERSSON: insert name of registrant — Slade.
229, registrant of AURORA HEART: Yamamoto should read J. Yamamoto.
231, **bifalce** should read **bifalce**†.
231, registrant of BONNIE: Kamemoto should read K. Kamemoto.
233, parent of CASSIOPE: monile should read moniliforme.
233, registrant of CHARLES TANAKA: Tanaka should read R. Tanaka.
234, registrant of CIRCE: Oka should read K. Oka.
234, registrant of CLAIRE: Kamemoto should read K. Kamemoto.
237: **DEE LYN** should read **DEE LYNN**.

Page
242, parent of GOLD CREST: Lillian Ozumo should read Lillian Izumo.
243: **HALA WA BEAUTY** should read **HALAWA BEAUTY**.
245, registrant and date of INDONESIA: Tjipeganti should read van Brero 1930.
246, parent of ISAMI DOI: Jaqueline Thomas should read Jaquelyn Thomas.
246, JANICE TANAKA: × Mary Trouse should read × Mary Trowse (= Mary Gold).
247, parent of JOEJAY: Mary Neal should read May Neal; also registrant Jay should read J. M. Jay.
249: **KATHERYN TERRY** should read **KATHERYNE TERRY**.
256, registrant of both MANOA and MANOA GOLD: Kamemoto should read K. Kamemoto.
257, parent of MARGARET JOAN FELL: Paleface should read Pale Face.
257, parent of MARY GOLD: Mary Trouse should read Mary Trowse.
260, registrant of MEM. WALTER SOULÉ: Fukumura should read R. T. Fukumura.
261, against monile: syn moniliforme should read (see *moniliforme*); also delete entry thereunder, transferred to *moniliforme* as per corrig. below.
261, against moniliforme: see monile should read (syn. *monile*. Whilst *monile* is the botanically correct name, *moniliforme* is retained as the horticulturally recommended name for registration purposes).
261, under moniliforme: insert × Royal Sovereign = Winter Star (as transferred from under *monile* per corrig. above).
263, registrant of OBOROZUKI: Yamamoto should read J. Yamamoto.
264, registrant of PAKANU: Kamemoto should read K. Kamemoto.
266, registrant of PERMER, PERMISSKO and PERMOS: Yamamoto should read J. Yamamoto.
266, originator of PERMOS: H. Yamamoto should read Hiroyuki Yamamoto.
266, phalaenopsis: × Paleface should read × Pale Face (= Margaret Joan Fell).
269, parent of ROSE MARIE: lepinorum should read leporinum.
273, registrant of SPELLBOUND: Kamemoto should read K. Kamemoto.
276, originator of THEODORE TAKIGUCHI: (Enomoto) should read (T. Enomoto).
280, above WONG-KIEW YOONG: insert **WINTER STAR (Royal Sovereign × moniliforme)** . . . **Gauda 1968**.
289, parent of Epicattleya SUSAN NAOMI: C. Ravel should read C. Revel.
292, above fragrans: insert **falcatum*** (see *parkinsonianum**).
292, against parkinsonianum: add (syn. *falcatum**).
296, Epidiacrium: BICO MIYO should read BICO MOYO.
301, parent of Laelia AL SCIURBA: speciosa should read grandiflora (syn. speciosa).
302, above grandis: insert **grandiflora***† . . . **species**; also insert thereunder the following entries — × grandis = Al Sciurba; × Lc. Issy = Lc. Jill Gaspar.
302, grandis: × speciosa should read × grandiflora (syn. speciosa) (= Al Sciurba).
302, ICARUS × Slc. Anzac: = Lc. Icaruzac should read = Slc. Icaruzac.
303: **lundii** (syn. **regnellii**) should read **lundii**† (syn. *regnellii*†).
303, above rubescens: insert **regnellii**† (see *lundii*†).
303, against speciosa: add (see *grandiflora**†, which is the horticulturally recommended name retained for registration purposes); also delete the entries thereunder, as transferred to under *grandiflora* as inserted per corrig. p. 302 above.
305: **AIDA** should read **AÏDA**.
306: **ALTESSE**† should read **ALTESSE***†.
306: **ALTEN** should read **ALTEN**†.
307, ANN HARDY and entries thereunder: transfer to correct alphabetical position above ANNICE ROCHLIN (same page).
308: **ARABIAN NIGHT** should read **ARABIAN NIGHTS**.
311: **BESS WHALDON** should read **BESS WALDON**.
312, parent of BLUE DIAMOND: Marina should read Mariner.
312, parent of BONANZA: Prospector should read C. Prospector.
314, parent of BUENA FLORA: Polanaise should read Polonaise.
315, CANHAMIANA × Snowdrift: = Bess Whaldon should read = Bess Waldon.
320: **CALORAMA** should read **COLORAMA**.
321, under CROWBOROUGH: delete × Slc. Sunburst = Slc. Pixie Fire.
321, under CROWBOROUGH SUNSHINE: insert × Slc. Sunburst = Slc. Pixie Fire.
326, ELEGANS: the *first* entry of this epithet (where shown as a natural hybrid) should read **elegans** (i.e. wholly lower case).
336, GOVERNOR GORE: × Vallecholet should read × Vallechollet (= Howard Anderson).
341, parent of HOWARD ANDERSON: Vallecholet should read Vallechollet.
343, ISHTAR × Pot. Belgravia: = Pot. Ewal do Wenzel should read = Pot. Welson Gasparini.
343, ISSY: × L. speciosa should read × L. grandiflora (syn. speciosa) (= Jill Gaspar).
344, parent of JILL GASPAR: L. speciosa should read L. grandiflora (syn. speciosa).
345, registrant of JOAN MATTHEWS: Matthews should read M. C. Matthews.
353, above MACK GENTRY: insert **McCORMICK PHOENIX (Harold J. Patterson × Margate)** . . . **Hausermann 1967**.
355, under MARINA: delete × C. Undine = Blue Diamond.
355, under MARINER: insert × C. Undine = Blue Diamond.
359: the entries for MEME BEETHAM and MEMLING are out of correct alphabetical position and should be transferred to immediately above MEM. ALBERT HEINECKE on p. 357. (N.B. for purposes of alphabetical listing, abbreviated forms of words such as St. (Saint), Dr. (Doctor), Mem. (Memoria) etc. are to be treated as if they were written in full.)
363, NIGRESCENT × Margate: = Judeth Lynn Hausermann should read = Lynn Hausermann.
372, registrant of RED WARRIOR: McKenzie should read J. S. McKenzie.

Page

375: all entries from SAINT-EXUPERY to ST.-LOUIS inclusive are out of correct alphabetical position and should be transferred to immediately above SALLY SANDER (same page).

378, parent of S. J. BRACEY: Thebes should read C. Thebes.

379, SNOWDRIFT × Canhamiana: = Bess Whaldon should read = Bess Waldon.

386: **VALLECHOLET** should read **VALLECHOLLET**.

391, parent of Lycaste ARTHURIANA: plana should read macrophylla (syn. plana).

391, parent of Lycaste BRUGENSIS: gigantea should read longipetala (syn. gigantea).

392, against LUCIANII: hort. should now read Sparrow 1972.

396, CANTAB: after date add name of originator (C. Cookson).

397, date of EMOTION: 1962 should read 1945.

399, ISIS: after date add name of originator (C. Cookson).

399: **LANIKEA** should read **LANIKAI**.

400, MINAS GERAIS × Victoria: = Lanikea should read = Lanikai.

402, parent of SUMAS: Lynnewood should read Lynnwood.

403, YALE: after date add name of originator (C. Cookson).

404, under Miltonidium KILAUEA: delete × Brs. Coronet = Alcra. Pacesetter.

404, above MAI TAI: insert **LUSTRE (Onc. powellii × Milt. warscewiczii) . . . W. W. G. Moir 1958**; thereunder insert entry × Brs. Coronet = Alcra. Pacesetter.

406, Odontioda ANTON: parentage should read Ann Dore × Odm. Halton.

407, CARMINE × Onc. leucochilum: = Wils. Jean De Pont should read = Wils. Jean Du Pont.

419, above GOLDHURST: insert **GOLDEN RANSOM (Yukon Harbor × Golden Butterfly) . . . Beall 1967**.

419, HALTON: × Red Skin should read × Redskin (= Relton).

420, MANPEROR × Pescalo: = Orpesco should read = Orpesca.

422, PESCALO × Manperor: = Orpesco should read = Orpesca.

423: **RED SKIN** should read **REDSKIN**.

423, parent of RELTON: Red Skin should read Redskin.

431: **GARDNERI†** should read **GARDNERI*†**.

431, below FROME: insert **furcyense** (see Jeremie p. 433) (**variegatum × scandens**) **Nat. hyb. 1969**.

432, under haitiense: insert × quadrilobum = Osmentii.

433, parent of JEREMIE: sylvestre should read scandens; also add the following note against Jeremie — (Note: this cross was also later described in 1969 as a natural hybrid *Onc.* × *furcyense*. Future crosses from either *furcyense* or Jeremie will be listed under Jeremie).

433, against JACMEL: add (see Lavender Lady) and delete parentage, registrant and date (the parentage of Jacmel should have read *pulchellum* × *scandens*, not *pulchellum* × *velutinum*. The error was discovered by the registrant of Jacmel only after *pulchellum* × *scandens* had meantime been registered as Lavender Lady).

433, parent of KURON: variegatum should read Sultane.

434, against LAVENDER LADY: add (syn. Jacmel).

436: **osmentii** . . . **species** should read **osmentii (quadrilobum × haitiense) Nat. hyb.**
OSMENTII (quadrilobum × haitiense) hort.

436: transfer from under osmentii to under OSMENTII the entry × Claremont = Eaton Hall.

438, under pulchellum: delete × velutinum = Jacmel.

438, under quadrilobum: insert × haitiense = Osmentii.

439, under scandens: insert × variegatum × Jeremie.

439, parent of SAN JUAN: leoboldii should read leiboldii.

440, under sylvestre: delete × variegatum = Jeremie.

441, variegatum: × sylvestre should read × scandens (= Jeremie).

441, velutinum should read velutinum† (resulting from General Corrections 1 (A)).

441, under velutinum: delete × pulchellum = Jacmel.

444, parent of ANNA PAVLOVA: Sumurum should read Sumurun.

444, parent of ALMA GAVAERT: lawrencianum should read lawrenceanum.

447, registrant of BEAUTÉ: Dale should read A. E. Dale.

447, BELL RINGER × Blagrose: = Bell Ringer should read = Bellrose.

449, registrant of BRAILES: Brummitt should read L. W. Brummitt.

452, CHILTON × Moreton Bay: = Chiltonbay should read = Chilton Bay.

452: **CHILTONBAY** should read **CHILTON BAY**.

453: **concolor** should read **concolor***.

457, registrant of DORIS BRUMMITT: Brummitt should read L. W. Brummitt.

459: fairieanum† should read fairieanum*†.

464, GREATHEART: parentage should read Chatwode × Commander Howard Wethey.

466, parent of HELLAS: Desdemonia should read Desdemona.

471, parent of LEMANII DUCIS: Curtmanii should read Curtmannii.

477, MORETON BAY × Chilton: = Chiltonbay should read = Chilton Bay.

480, registrant of PERSEUS: Lee should read W. R. Lee.

483, REDRUSH: parentage should read Red Admiral × Windrush.

484: **RHODORE** should read **RHODORA**.

484, ROBIN I. HALL × Radley: = Rhodore should read = Rhodora.

490, parent of THIAS: Beeckmannii should read Beeckmanii.

492, WENDBOURN: × Cardinal Mercia should read × Cardinal Mercier (= Tadorna).

497, registrant of ANNE CAVACO: Cavaco should read A. A. Cavaco.

509: **DOTTY ROW** should read **DOTTIE ROW**.

510, date of ELDORA: 194- should read 1957.

Page

511, equestris × sumatrana: = Hanauma should read = Equitrana.

517: **GRANDE CONDE** should read **GRAND CONDÉ**.

527: **LITTTLE LADY** should read **LITTLE LADY**.

530, MAHININ: × Grande Conde should read × Grand Condé (= Starglow).

530, above MANBRIATA: insert **MAMIE MOSER (Ramona × schillerana) . . . H. Tanaka 1964**.

531, parent of MARGARET BEAN: Altedena should read Altadena.

533, above MEM. EMIL RICHTER: insert **MEM. ELVA HAMRIC (Dawn Mist × Calpine) . . . Ted Fischer 1969**.

533: delete entry for MARY MOSER (should read MAMIE MOSER — q.v. p. 530 above).

535, registrant and date of MRS. J. H. VEITCH: Rivermont 1958 should read Veitch — .

536, parent of OCTORINE LIM: Grande Conde should read Grand Condé.

544, under R. H. MONTGOMERY: delete × Irma Rath = Charles Louis Williams.

544, under RICHARD SHAFFER: insert × Irma Rath = Charles Louis Williams.

547, RUBY WELLS: × Grande Conde should read × Grand Condé (= Octorine Lim).

548, SATIN ROUGE: after the date add name of originator (Frank Hughes).

549, schillerana × Ramona: = Mary Moser should read = Mamie Moser.

552, parent of STARGLOW: Grande Conde should read Grand Condé.

552, above STAR OF HANOVER: insert **STAR OF FLORIDA (Princess Kaiulani × Ambotrana) . . . Fredk. L. Thornton 1967**.

553, registrant of SUNNY: Lewis should read Mrs. Gracia Lewis.

561, Phalandopsis MILENA JOST: after the date add name of originator (R. P. Jost).

576, Rhinerrhiza divitiflora × Sarco. fitzgeraldii: = Srza. Rona should read = Rhincs. Rona.

576, Rhinerrhiza divitiflora × Sarco. hartmanii: = Srza. Dorothy should read = Rhincs. Dorothy.

577, under Rhynchostylis coelestis: delete × V. luzonica = Rhv. Galaxy.

577, under Rhynchostylis gigantea: insert × V. luzonica = Rhv. Galaxy.

580, Sarcochilus fitzgeraldii × Rhin. divitiflora: = Srza. Rona should read = Rhincs. Rona.

580, Sarcochilus hartmanii × Rhin. divitiflora: = Srza. Dorothy should read = Rhincs. Dorothy.

580, Sarconopsis: MARQUARIE SUNSET should read MACQUARIE SUNSET.

580: generic heading SARCORHIZA should read RHINOCHILUS; also transfer it and entries thereunder to the appropriate alphabetical position on page 576 (immediately after *Rhinerrhiza* and its entries).

583, under Schomburgkia undulata: × Schom. undulata should read × Slc. Salamander (= Hbtr. Danny).

588, ESTELLA JEWELL × Jewel Box: = Gipsy Jewels should read = Gypsy Jewels.

589: **GIPSY JEWELS** should read **GYPSY JEWELS**; also transfer to new alphabetical position as corrected.

589, HELEN VELIZ: parentage should read Rainbow Hill × Sc. Eleanor; date should read 1960.

589, JEWEL BOX: × Estella Jewel should read × Estella Jewell (= Gypsy Jewels).

592, PEARL SPENCER: registrant should read Genevieve Toy; originator should read (Louie Y. Toy).

593, parent of PIXIE FIRE: Lc. Crowborough should read Lc. Crowborough Sunshine.

595, SUNBURST: × Lc. Crowborough should read × Lc. Crowborough Sunshine (= Pixie Fire).

602, CHARM × Ascda. Gold Buttons: = Saboh should read = Sabah.

603, registrant of DAWN NISHIMURA: Nishimura should read Dr. H. Nishimura.

605, registrant of ELLEN NOA: Noa should read J. K. Noa.

606, FRANK CROOK: × Tay Chay Yan should read × Tan Chay Yan (= Madame Poon Wah).

608, date of HAWAIIAN BLUE: 1970 should read 1959.

613, registrant of LAUREL YAP: Yap should read Leo Yap.

613, registrant of LESTER McCOY: Cummins should read J. A. Cummins.

616, MEM. TADAICHI DOI: registrant and originator should read C. M. Matsuo (T. Doi).

620, under POEPOE: delete Arach. Ishbel = Aranda Lynn Kong.

620, parent of PRACHARK CHIT: Jean Rothsand should read Joan Rothsand.

625, registrant of TELLEE: Reed should read Mrs. D. D. Reed.

LIST OF ORCHID HYBRIDS

1971-1975

The following is the key to symbols and abbreviations used in the text:

*	= crosses also listed in Main Work (1854-1945).
†	= crosses also listed in Vols. I and II. (1946-1960).
‡	= crosses also listed in Addendum (1961-1970).
h. ign.	= hybrid ignotus — parentage unknown.
nat. hyb.	= natural hybrid.
q.v.	= quod vide — which see.
syn.	= synonymous.
hort.	= of garden origin.

ACACALLIS

cyanea (see *Aganisia cyanea*) — **species**

AËRANGIS

fastuosa — **species**

× Angcm. philippinense	= Angrs. Snow Nymph		

AËRANTHES

arachnites — **species**

× Angcm. Veitchii	= Angth. Coquí		

ramosus‡ — **species**

× Angcm. magdalenae	= Angth. Lomarlynn		

AËRIDACHNIS

BOGOR‡ — **Arach. hookerana × Aër. odorata** — **M. Yamada 1967**

× Ascda. Blue Boy	= Lwsra. Chittivan	× V. Poepoe	= Burk. Coy Maiden
× Rhy. gigantea	= Sgka. Siam	× V. Rothschildiana	= Burk. Tidarma Suling
× V. Blue Fantasy	= Burk. Fancy Free	× V. sanderana	= Burk. Sanderling
× V. Dawn Nishimura	= Burk. Ong Thye Chiew		

COLOMBIA — **Aër. odorata × Arach. maingayi** — **von Paulsen 1972 (Originator unknown)**

× Trgl. fasciata	= Plsra. Medellin		

ELIZABETH HOWIE — **Arach. Ishbel × Aër. lawrenceae** — **C. C. P. Wilkins 1974**

MANDAI — **Arach. hookerana × Aër. augustiana** — **S'pore Orchids 1963**

× Ren. Brookie Chandler	= Lymra. Frankfurt Fireworks	× V. tricolor	= Burk. August Rose

ROSY DAWN — **Arach. hookerana × Aër. lawrenceae** — **S'pore Orchids 1965**

× Ren. storiei	= Lymra. Mandai Grace	× V. Poepoe	= Burk. Fancy Flight

SPRING SONG — **Arach. hookerana × Aër. jarckiana** — **S'pore Orchids 1974 (Mrs. Gracia Lewis)**

AËRIDES

affine* (see *multiflora**‡) — **species**

AMY EDE — **lawrenceae × jarckiana** — **S'pore Orchids 1972 (Mrs. Gracia Lewis)**

ballantineana (see *odorata*†‡) — **species**

BANGKOK — **multiflora × falcata** — **Laksanaphuk 1974**

cornuta (see *odorata*†‡) — **species**

crassifolia*†‡ — **species**

× fieldingii	= Dottie's Delight	× Rhy. gigantea	= Rhrds. Korat
× jarckiana	= Valmayor	× V. Beebe Sumner	= Aerav. Sumalee
× Ascda. Meda Arnold	= Chtra. Chula	× V. denisoniana	= Aërdv. Pranin
× Ren. coccinea	= Rnds. Mem. John Donnelly		

DOTTIE'S DELIGHT — **crassifolia × fieldingii** — **Fresh 1975**

falcata†‡ — **species**

× flabellata	= Kanchana	× Asctm. miniatum	= Aërctm. Champatong
× multiflora	= Bangkok	× V. brunnea	= Aërdv. Suebsanguan
× odorata	= Pussadi	× V. denisoniana	= Aërdv. Photisan
× Ascda. Medasand	= Chtra. Thai	× V. Onomea	= Aërdv. Permmit
× Ascda. Yip Sum Wah	= Chtra. Nam-Oi		

fieldingii†‡ — **species**

× crassifolia	= Dottie's Delight	× Dor. pulcherrima	= Aërdts. Hermon Slade
× Ascda. Meda Arnold	= Chtra. Mem. Raymond Mercier		

flabellata‡ — **species**

× falcata	= Kanchana	× V. denisoniana	= Aërdv. Vieng Ping
× odorata	= Sukho	× V. Eisenhower	= Aërdv. Bronze Triumph
× Ascda. Meda Arnold	= Chtra. Bangkok	× V. Mem. Madame Pranerm	= Aërdv. Natee Gold
× Ascda. Medasand	= Chtra. Tha Yang	× V. Rothschildiana	= Aërdv. Wittaya
× Ascda. Yip Sum Wah	= Chtra. Bangpra	× V. Sarojini	= Aërdv. Rungsit
× Rhy. coelestis	= Rhrds. Thai Noi		

flavida (see *odorata*†‡) — **species**

godefroyana (see *multiflora**‡) — **species**

houlletiana — **species**

× Ren. storiei	= Rnds. Houlstoria

japonica*‡ — **species**

(This is retained as the horticulturally recommended name for registration purposes even though reclassified by some botanists as *Sedirea japonica.*)

× Dor. pulcherrima	= Aërdts. Mem. Arthur Freed	× Lsa. teres	= Aërsa. Rumrill

jarckiana†‡ — **species**

× crassifolia	= Valmayor	× V. coerulea	= Aërdv. Blue Chips
× lawrenceae	= Amy Ede	× V. Diane Ogawa	= Aërdv. Deechai
× Arach. hookerana	= Aërdns. Spring Song	× V. Rothschildiana	= Aërdv. Siam Orchids
× Ascda. Meda Arnold	= Chtra. Virginia Braga		

KANCHANA — **flabellata × falcata** — **Suebsanguan 1973**

lawrenceae†‡ — **species**

× jarckiana	= Amy Ede	× V. Hilo Blue	= Aërdv. Moonface
× odorata	= Punchinello	× V. Josephine van Brero	= Aërdv. Aristocrat
× Arach. Ishbel	= Aërdns. Elizabeth Howie	× V. Manisaki	= Aërdv. Janice Choo
× Ascda. Yip Sum Wah	= Chtra. Ruth Murai	× V. Monacensis	= Aërdv. Stanley Smith

lobbii (see *multiflora**‡) — **species**

AËRIDES

mitrata‡ **species**

(This is retained as the horticulturally recommended name for registration purposes, even though this species has been reclassified by some botanists as *Seidenfadenia mitrata.*)

× Ascda. Tan Chai Beng = Chtra. Pink Glory
× Asctm. curvifolium = Aërctm. Cholratana
× Vf. Premier = Vfds. Rumrill

multiflora*‡ **species**

(syn. *affine**; *godefroyana*; *lobbii*; *rosea*; *veitchii*)

× falcata = Bangkok
× Lsa. teres = Aërsa. Towaco
× Ren. Brookie Chandler = Rnds. Rosette
× Ren. Tom Thumb = Rnds. Eva Jean
× Rhy. coelestis = Rhrds. Cholratanakul
× V. Onomea = Aërdv. Gaine
× V. Rothschildiana = Aërdv. Suraprabha

nobile (see *odorata†‡*) **species**

odorata†‡ **species**

(syn. *ballantineana*; *cornuta*; *flavida*; *nobile*; *reichenbachii*; *rohaniana*; *sanderae*; *suavissima*; *virens†*)

× falcata = Pussadi
× flabellata = Sukho
× lawrenceae = Punchinello
× Arach. maingayi = Aërdns. Colombia
× Ascda. Meda Arnold = Chtra. Changchenkit
× Asctm. miniatum = Aërctm. Chet Yod
× Ren. Brookie Chandler = Rnds. Summer Light
× Ren. Tom Thumb = Rnds. Honeymoon
× V. Bill Sutton = Aërdv. Kalya
× V. Sandamo = Aërdv. Hideichi Nitta

PUNCHINELLO	**odorata × lawrenceae**	**S'pore Orchids 1972 (Mrs. Gracia Lewis)**
PUSSADI	**falcata × odorata**	**Paireepairit 1974**
quinquevulnerum†‡	**species**	

× Ren. Brookie Chandler = Rnds. Spring Joy

reichenbachii (see *odorata†‡*)	**species**	
rohaniana (see *odorata†‡*)	**species**	
rosea (see *multiflora*‡*)	**species**	
sanderae (see *odorata†‡*)	**species**	
suavissima (see *odorata†‡*)	**species**	
SUKHO	**odorata × flabellata**	**Ladhaphitoon 1975 (Bangkrabue)**
VALMAYOR	**jarckiana × crassifolia**	**Sagarik 1974**
veitchii (see *multiflora*‡*)	**species**	
virens† (see *odorata†‡*)	**species**	

AËRIDISIA

RUMRILL	**Aër. japonica × Lsa. teres**	**Rumrill 1974**
TOWACO	**Aër. multiflora × Lsa. teres**	**Rumrill 1975**

AËRIDITIS

HERMON SLADE	**Dor. pulcherrima × Aër. fieldingii**	**W. W. G. Moir 1973**
MEMORIA ARTHUR FREED	**Dor. pulcherrima × Aër. japonica**	**Freed 1975**

AËRIDOCENTRUM

CHAMPATONG	**Aër. falcata × Asctm. miniatum**	**Paireepairit 1973**
CHET YOD	**Aër. odorata × Asctm. miniatum**	**Laddaland 1975 (Pramwuet)**
CHOLRATANA	**Aër. mitrata × Asctm. curvifolium**	**Cholratanakul 1971**
LUKE NOK	**Aër. flabellata × Asctm. curvifolium**	**Yaemboonchoo 1966**

× Ascda. Yip Sum Wah = Chtra. Sum Nok
× V. Josephine van Brero = Chtra. Malibu Gold

AËRIDOVANDA

ARISTOCRAT	V. Josephine van Brero × Aër. lawrenceae	S'pore Orchids 1973
BLUE CHIPS	Aër. jarckiana × V. coerulea	Crestwood 1973
BRONZE TRIUMPH	V. Eisenhower × Aër. flabellata	Perreira 1974
DEECHAI	Aër. jarckiana × V. Diane Ogawa	Deechai 1974 (T. Orchids)
GAINE	Aër. multiflora × V. Onomea	Gaine 1974 (Originator unknown)
HIDEICHI NITTA	V. Sandamo × Aër. odorata	H. K. Nitta 1972
JANICE CHOO	Aër. lawrenceae × V. Manisaki	Choo Yeok Koon 1972
KALYA	V. Bill Sutton × Aër. odorata	Sagarik 1972
MOONFACE	Aër. lawrenceae × V. Hilo Blue	S'pore Orchids 1972
NATEE GOLD	V. Mem. Madame Pranerm × Aër. flabellata	Leelasiri 1973
PERMMIT	Aër. falcata × V. Onomea	Bunyavibul 1974
PHOTISAN	Aër. falcata × V. denisoniana	Siriphab 1971
PRANIN	V. denisoniana × Aër. crassifolia	Suebsanguan 1974
RUNGSIT	V. Sarojini × Aër. flabellata	Suphatamakit 1972
SIAM ORCHIDS	Aër. jarckiana × V. Rothschildiana	T. Orchids 1973 (T. Rakpaibulsombat)
STANLEY SMITH	V. Monacensis × Aër. lawrenceae	O. Kirsch 1974
SUEBSANGUAN	V. brunnea × Aër. falcata	Suebsanguan 1974
SUMALEE	Aër. crassifolia × V. Beebe Sumner	Yen Orchid 1975
SURAPRABHA	Aër. multiflora × V. Rothschildiana	Laksanaphuk 1973
VIENG PING	Aër. flabellata × V. denisoniana	Suddhipaca 1973
WITTAYA	V. Rothschildiana × Aër. flabellata	Wittaya 1972 (Suphatamakit)

AGANISIA

cyanea (syn. *Acacallis cyanea*) — species
× Plmra. Raymond Palmer = Dwsa. Psythenis

ALICEARA

BANDEIRA	Mtssa. Harry Dunn × Mtdm. Lee Hirsch	W. W. G. Moir 1973
CHIYO	Mtssa. Bold × Mtdm. Cleopatra	W. W. G. Moir 1973
DON RICHARDSON	Mtssa. Cartagena × Mtdm. Carioca	W. W. G. Moir 1973
MAURY ISLAND	Mtssa. Vino × Onc. marshallianum	Beall 1975
MONTE CRISTO	Mtssa. Cartagena × Onc. varicosum	Beall 1973
PACESETTER	Brsdm. Coronet × Mtdm. Lustre	E. Iwanaga 1964
× Onc. varicosum = Palolo		
PALOLO	Pacesetter × Onc. varicosum	W. W. G. Moir 1974 (E. Iwanaga)
SURPRISE CREEK	Mtssa. Charles M. Fitch × Onc. varicosum	Beall 1974

ALLENARA

OCEAN SPRAY	Eplc. Envy × Diacm. bicornutum	W. W. G. Moir 1975

ANGRAECUM

ALABASTER	eburneum × Veitchii	O. Kirsch 1960
× eburneum = Christmas Star		
CHRISTMAS STAR	Alabaster × eburneum	Kirch 1975

ANGRAECUM

CRESTWOOD	**Veitchii × sesquipedale**	**Crestwood 1973**
eburneum*†	**species**	
× Alabaster	= Christmas Star	
eichleranum	**species**	
× Cyrtcs. arcuata	= Angchs. Mad	
magdalenae	**species**	
× Aërth. ramosus	= Angth. Lomarlynn	
philippinense	**species**	
× Aërgs. fastuosa	= Angrs. Snow Nymph	
sesquipedale*‡	**species**	
× Veitchii	= Crestwood	
Veitchii†	**eburneum × sesquipedale**	**Veitch 1899**
× sesquipedale	= Crestwood	
× Aërth. arachnites	= Angth. Coquí	

ANGRAEORCHIS

MAD	**Angcm. eichleranum × Cyrtcs. arcuata**	**Rumrill 1974**

ANGRANGIS

SNOW NYMPH	**Aërgs. fastuosa × Angcm. philippinense**	**Fort Caroline 1972**

ANGRANTHES

COQUÍ	**Aërth. arachnites × Angcm. Veitchii**	**E. F. Patterson 1975**
LOMARLYNN	**Angcm. magdalenae × Aërth. ramosus**	**Ilgenfritz 1975 (Ciesinski)**

ANGULOA

ruckeri*	**species**	
× Lyc. lasioglossa	= Angcst. Mildred Zaiman	

ANGULOCASTE

APOLLO†‡	**Ang. clowesii × Lyc. Imschootiana**	**Cooke 1952**
× Lyc. xytriophora	= Gemini	
GEMINI	**Lyc. xytriophora × Apollo**	**Wyld Court 1972**
GEORGIUS REX	**Ang. cliftonii × Lyc. Imschootiana**	**Colman 1937**
× Lyc. macrophylla	= Mem. Abbott Robinson	
HIGHLAND PEAK	**Olympus × Lyc. Sunrise**	**M. 1973**
JUPITER	**Lyc. Balliae × Apollo**	**Wyld Court 1962**
× Lyc. macrobulbon	= Scorpio	
MEMORIA ABBOTT ROBINSON	**Georgius Rex × Lyc. macrophylla**	**Dr. B. C. Berliner 1975**
MILDRED ZAIMAN	Ang. ruckeri × Lyc. lasioglossa	**Dr. B. C. Berliner 1975**
OLYMPUS	**Apollo × Lyc. Sunrise**	**Wyld Court 1959**
× Lyc. Sunrise	= Highland Peak	

ANGULOCASTE

SCORPIO | **Jupiter × Lyc. macrobulbon** | **Wyld Court 1972**

ARACHNANTHE

cathcartii (see *ARACHNIS cathcartii*) **species**

ARACHNIS

alba* (see *hookerana**†‡) **species**

breviscapa†‡ **species**

× Ishbel	= Capabel	× Ren. storiei	= Arnth. Mandai Clarion

CAPABEL | **Ishbel × breviscapa** | **S'pore Orchids 1973**

cathcartii **species**

(This is retained as the horticulturally recommended name for registration purposes, even though *Esmeralda cathcartii* is the botanically correct name for this species. Also syn. *Arachnanthe cathcartii.*)

× Ren. Brookie Chandler	= Arnth. Sauleda	× V. Rothschildiana	= Aranda Primi
× Ren. imschootiana	= Arnth. Ruben		

flos-aëris*†‡ (syn. *moschifera**) **species**

× Rnps. Lena Rowold	= Lim. Mandai Majesty	× V. Rothschildiana	= Aranda Mem. Lilian Garth
× V. Harvest Time	= Aranda Toh Chong Boon	× V. tessellata	= Aranda Bussaracum

hookerana*†‡ **species**

(syn. *alba**; syn. *Renanthera hookerana*)

× Aër. jarckiana	= Aërdns. Spring Song	× Ascda. Navy Blue	= Mkra. Viroonchan Blue
× Ascda. Buddy Choo	= Mkra. Bovorn	× Ascda. Wilas	= Mkra. Winnie Ling
× Ascda. Coppertone	= Mkra. Madame Yip Khew-Ying	× Ascda. Yip Sum Wah	= Mkra. Ena Ling
		× V. Dawn Nishimura	= Aranda Noorah Alsagoff
× Ascda. Habananda	= Mkra. Kelvin	× V. Diane Ogawa	= Aranda Suharto
× Ascda. Koh Man	= Mkra. Yoon Weng-Low	× V. Laurel Yap	= Aranda Anne Khoo
× Ascda. Mangkiatkul	= Mkra. Viroonchan	× V. Thananchai	= Aranda Adilah
× Ascda. Meda Arnold	= Mkra. Sally Lim	× Vasco. Blue Fairy	= Bov. Bovorn Beauty
× Ascda. Medasand	= Mkra. Sayan		

ISHBEL‡ | **maingayi × hookerana** | **S.B.G. 1940**

× breviscapa	= Capabel	× Ren. matutina	= Arnth. Alice Fuss
× Aër. lawrenceae	= Aërdns. Elizabeth Howie	× Ren. philippinensis	= Arnth. Yee Peng
× Ascda. Wilas	= Mkra. Lim Sin Kiaw	× V. Cooperi	= Aranda Easter Joy
× Ascda. Yip Sum Wah	= Mkra. Harriet Lim	× V. Hilo Blue	= Aranda Johore Beauty
× Ascgm. calopterum	= Arngm. Calobel	× V. Onomea	= Aranda Blue Star

MAGGIE OEI†‡ | **hookerana × flos-aëris** | **Laycock 1940**

× Ascda. Meda Arnold	= Mkra. Magmeda	× V. bensonii	= Aranda Sansai
× Ascda. Yip Sum Wah	= Mkra. Dear Heart	× V. brunnea	= Aranda Sulyaphongse
× Ren. isosepala	= Arnth. Ubol	× V. Dawn Nishimura	= Aranda Neo Hoe Kiat
× Ren. philippinensis	= Arnth. Tanewan	× V. merrillii	= Aranda Merry Maggie
× Rhy. coelestis	= Arnst. Choompoo	× V. Rose Davis	= Aranda Er Cheng Meng
× V. Beebe Sumner	= Aranda Phuket	× Vdps. parishii	= Vchns. Somthawil

maingayi*† **species**

× Aër. odorata	= Aërdns. Colombia		

MAROON MAGGIE | **Maggie Oei × flos-aëris** | **Pestana 1956**

× V. Dawn Nishimura	= Aranda Ang Hee Seng	× V. Yukum Braga	= Aranda Yeok Koon

moschifera* (see *flos-aëris**†‡) **species**

ARACHNOGLOSSUM

CALOBEL	Arach. Ishbel × Ascgm. calopterum	S'pore Orchids 1972

ARACHNOSTYLIS

CHOOMPOO	Arach. Maggie Oei × Rhy. coelestis	Chuanyen 1975

ARANDA

ADILAH	Arach. hookerana × V. Thananchai		Alsagoff 1975
ANG HEE SENG	Arach. Maroon Maggie × V. Dawn Nishimura		Mak Chin On 1975 (Alsagoff)
ANNE KHOO	Arach. hookerana × V. Laurel Yap		Ng & Tan 1973 (Ho Kean Keat)
BEACH BELLE	Golden Sands × V. Hilo Blue		S'pore Orchids 1973
BINTANG	Arach. hookerana × V. Tatzeri		S.B.G. 1965
× V. Piha Moon	= Lovely Bird		
BLUE STAR	Arach. Ishbel × V. Onomea		Cheong Chee Yon 1973 (Chong Chok Chye)
BUSSARACUM	Arach. flos-aëris × V. tessellata		Chuanyen 1975 (Sagarik)
CHIA SHUI KENG	Nancy × V. insignis		Bun 1965 (Seng Heng)
× Arnth. Beatrice Ng	= Holtt. Andromeda	× V. Patricia Lee	= Nicole Kong
× V. merrillii	= Iris Bannochie	× Vdps. lissochiloides	= Leeara Mem. Jean Black
DANNY BOY	Lucy Laycock × V. Gilbert Triboulet		Palm Orchids 1973
DE ZON SINGAPURA	Lucy Laycock × V. Piha Moon		Cheong Chee Yon 1973 (Chong Chok Chye)
EASTER JOY	Arach. Ishbel × V. Cooperi		S'pore Orchids 1973
ER CHENG MENG	Arach. Maggie Oei × V. Rose Davis		Er Cheng Meng 1975
GOLDEN SANDS	Arach. hookerana × V. insignis		S'pore Orchids 1964
× V. Hilo Blue	= Beach Belle		
HILDA GALISTAN†‡	Arach. hookerana × V. suavis		S.B.G. 194-
× V. Fair Queen	= Sweet Honey		
HOW YEE PENG	Tay Theng Suan × V. Dawn Nishimura		How Yee Peng 1975
IRIS BANNOCHIE	Chia Shui Keng × V. merrillii		George Black 1973
JOHORE BEAUTY	Arach. Ishbel × V. Hilo Blue		Cheong Chee Yon 1973
LEE YORK SIM	Tay Theng Suan × V. tessellata		How Yee Peng 1975
LILY CHONG‡	Arach. Ishbel × V. sanderana		Chong Chok Chye 1961 (S.B.G.)
× Ascda. Yee Peng	= Mkra. Monique	× V. Honolulu	= Tan Seng Beng
× V. Alicia Ono	= Singapura	× V. Rothschildiana	= Mas
× V. Dawn Nishimura	= Wong Bee Yeok	× V. Takeji Ogawa	= Yeap Hong Ghee
LOVELY BIRD	Bintang × V. Piha Moon		Cheong Chee Yon 1973 (Chong Chok Chye)
LUCY LAYCOCK‡	Arach. hookerana × V. tricolor		Laycock 195-
× Ascda. Medasand	= Mkra. Soon Khim	× V. Piha Moon	= De Zon Singapura
× V. Gilbert Triboulet	= Danny Boy	× Vdps. lissochiloides	= Leeara Lissom Lucy
MAS	Lily Chong × V. Rothschildiana		Cheong Chee Yon 1973 (Chong Chok Chye)
MEMORIA LILIAN GARTH	Arach. flos-aëris × V. Rothschildiana		Garth 1973

ARANDA

MERRY MAGGIE	Arach. Maggie Oei × V. merrillii	S'pore Orchids 1972 (Mrs. Gracia Lewis)
NAOMI	Ruby Pestana × V. sanderana	Fernando 1974
NEO HOE KIAT	Arach. Maggie Oei × V. Dawn Nishimura	How Yee Peng 1975
NICOLE KONG	Chia Shui Keng × V. Patricia Lee	George Black 1975
NOORAH ALSAGOFF	Arach. hookerana × V. Dawn Nishimura	Alsagoff 1972 (Kranji)
PHUKET	V. Beebe Sumner × Arach. Maggie Oei	Weerawathanamas 1975
PRIMI	Arach. cathcartii × V. Rothschildiana	Ruben 1972
QUEEN OF PURPLES‡	Arach. hookerana × V. coerulea	van Brero 1940
× Phal. Sulochana	= Trev. Wong Sew Lan	
RUBY PESTANA	Arach. flos-aëris × V. coerulea	S.B.G. 1951
× V. sanderana	= Naomi	
SANSAI	Arach. Maggie Oei × V. bensonii	Tewtong 1974 (Kaewkamnerd)
SINGAPURA	Lily Chong × V. Alicia Ono	Cheong Chee Yon 1972 (Chong Chok Chye)
SUHARTO	V. Diane Ogawa × Arach. hookerana	Cheang Kok Choy 1974 (Ooi Leng Sun)
SULYAPHONGSE	Arach. Maggie Oei × V. brunnea	Sulyaphongse 1975
SWEET HONEY	Hilda Galistan × V. Fair Queen	Cheong Chee Yon 1973 (Chong Chok Chye)
TAN SENG BENG	Lily Chong × V. Honolulu	Cheong Chee Yon 1972 (Chong Chok Chye)
TAY THENG SUAN	Arach. Ishbel × V. Ernest Fujinaga	How Yee Peng 1964 (Tan Chee Seng)
× V. Dawn Nishimura	= How Yee Peng | × V. tessellata	= Lee York Sim
TOH CHONG BOON	V. Harvest Time × Arach. flos-aëris	Toh Chor Soon 1971
WONG BEE YEOK	Lily Chong × V. Dawn Nishimura	Mak Chin On 1975 (Alsagoff)
YEAP HONG GHEE	Lily Chong × V. Takeji Ogawa	Cheong Chee Yon 1972 (Chong Chok Chye)
YEOK KOON	Arach. Maroon Maggie × V. Yukum Braga	Choo Yeok Koon 1972

ARANTHERA

ALICE FUSS	Arach. Ishbel × Ren. matutina	S'pore Orchids 1972
ANNE BLACK‡	Arach. Maggie Oei × Ren. coccinea	S.B.G. 1957
× Ascda. Meda Arnold	= Ysfra. Nong	
BEATRICE NG	Ren. storiei × Arach. Ishbel	Koh Keng Hoe 1961
× Aranda Chia Shui Keng	= Holtt. Andromeda	
BLOODSHOT	Arach. Ishbel × Ren. coccinea	S.B.G. 1957
× V. limbata	= Holtt. Patricia Postlethwaite	
LILLEPUT	Arach. hookerana × Ren. elongata	S.B.G. —
× Ren. Brookie Chandler	= Lillibrook | × V. tricolor	= Holtt. Bright Eyes
LILLIBROOK	Lilleput × Ren. Brookie Chandler	S'pore Orchids 1973
MANDAI CLARION	Ren. storiei × Arach. breviscapa	S'pore Orchids 1975
RUBEN	Ren. imschootiana × Arach. cathcartii	Ruben 1972

ARANTHERA

Name	Parentage	Registrant
SAULEDA	Ren. Brookie Chandler × Arach. cathcartii	Ruben 1972
TANEWAN	Arach. Maggie Oei × Ren. philippinensis	Laddaland 1975 (Thamaragsa)
UBOL	Arach. Maggie Oei × Ren. isosepala	Koesomboon 1973 (Sagarik)
YEE PENG	Arach. Ishbel × Ren. philippinensis	How Yee Peng 1972 (S.B.G.)

ASCANDOPSIS

Name	Parentage	Registrant
SCARLET FLAME	Vdps. parishii × Asctm. curvifolium	Crestwood 1975

ASCOCENDA

Name	Parentage	Registrant
AGNES KAGAWA	Meda Arnold × V. Judy Miyamoto	H. Kagawa 1972 (Tew)
AHUIMANU	V. Pauahi × Ophelia	O. Kirsch 1975
ALICIA ONO	V. Takeji Ogawa × Asctm. curvifolium	Ono 1972
ALOK JAIN	Medasand × Meda Arnold	Jain 1972 (Rakpaiboonsombat)
ANJOMEA	V. Onomea × Anjo Mitterer	Ruben 1974
ANJO MITTERER	V. Frank Crook × Meda Arnold	Mitterer 1969
× V. Onomea	= Anjomea	
ANN	V. Lenavat × Mangkiatkul	S.E.O. 1975
ARIBARG	Medasand × V. Thananchai	Chantramontol 1973 (Bhimayothin)
ARIES	V. Gillian Trevor × Meda Arnold	Wilkins 1973
AROONSRI BEAUTY	Yip Sum Wah × Asctm. curvifolium	Song Sae Eiaw 1970
× V. Rothschildiana	= Silpaprasert	
ASOKE	Ooi Boon Huat × Tan Chai Beng	Supachadiwong 1975
ATHIT-UTHAI	V. Tubtimtepya × Asctm. curvifolium	Hirisatja 1972
AURORA	V. Low Kee Sing × Asctm. curvifolium	R. E. Ward 1974 (Voo Doo Orchids)
AUTUMN JOY	Meda Arnold × Charm	W. K. Nakamoto 1965
× Red Gem	= Jocla	
× Yip Sum Wah	= Red Buttons	
AYER ITAM BEAUTY	V. Sathaprudit × Piswong	Lim Soon Khim 1975
BANGKOK GOLD	Ophelia × Asctm. Sagarik Gold	Sagarik 1972
BANG PLA SROI	Medasand × Wilas	Sakuldejtana 1973
BANG SAAI	Medasand × Yip Sum Wah	Sakuldejtana 1973
BARBARA FREED SALTZMAN	Meda Arnold × Malibu Oneohtwo	Freed 1975
BILL FOX	V. Rothschildiana × Asctm. aurantiacum	Mrs H. W. Fox 1975 (Takemoto)
BLUE BOY‡	Meda Arnold × V. coerulea	Ono 1967 (W. K. Nakamoto)
× Meda Arnold	= Melanie Ono	
× Aërdns. Bogor	= Lwsra. Chittivan	
× Rhy. gigantea	= Vasco. Karavek	
× V. Bonnie Blue Fukumura	= Lorene Beauty	
× V. Royal Blue	= Harry Blauvelt	
× V. Sarojini	= Fermilliana Calma	
BLUE HEAVEN	V. Hilo Blue × Meda Arnold	R. K. Mizuta 1969
× Elieen Beauty	= Cosmo Pink	
BONANZA	V. Pukele × Meda Arnold	Sorayama 1970
× V. coerulea	= Leontine Ho	
× V. sanderana	= Hong Kok Hoo	

ASCOCENDA

Name	Parentage	Registrant
BUDDY CHOO	**Yip Sum Wah × V. sanderana**	**Choo Cheng Choong 1970**
× Arach. hookerana	= Mkra. Bovorn	
× V. Lenavat	= Toh Chin Soo	
× V. Thananchai	= Kasetsilp	
BUSADEE	**V. Satta × Meda Arnold**	**Thamungraksut 1975 (Suphatamakit)**
BUSARAPORN	**Mangkiatkul × V. Sinard**	**Sinsook 1974 (Chavalit)**
CAPRICORN	**V. Eisenhower × Meda Arnold**	**Wilkins 1972 (Rodillas)**
CAPTAIN CHOR	**V. Joan Rothsand × Asctm. curvifolium**	**Yaemboonchoo 1972**
× V. Thananchai	= Yellow Captain	
CARNIVAL	**V. tessellata × Asctm. curvifolium**	**J. & S. 1971**
CAROLAINE	**V. Emma van Deventer × Mem. Choo Laikeun**	**Wong Loong Fatt 1974**
CHAISIRI	**V. denisoniana × Asctm. miniatum**	**Chaisiri 1975**
CHAIYOT	**V. Josephine van Brero × Yip Sum Wah**	**Sombuntham 1973**
CHAO KHUN YARN	**V. Charlesworthii × Yip Sum Wah**	**C. Y. Nursery 1974**
CHARM‡	**V. pumila × Portia Doolittle**	**M. Yamada 1960**
× James Furumizo	= Sunburst	
CHING MOOK CHOON	**V. Emma van Deventer × Meda Arnold**	**Wong Loong Fatt 1974**
CHOLBURI	**V. Lumpini × Meda Arnold**	**Napasab 1973**
× V. Lenavat	= Thai Ruby	
CHOLNAPHA	**Mangkiatkul × V. Diane Ogawa**	**Thitapitchaya 1973 (Chavalit)**
CHOMNARD	V. sanderana × Tan Chai Beng	**Song Sae Eah 1973**
CHOM YONG	**V. Pikul × Red Gem**	**W. P. Orchid 1971**
CHRIS MILES	**V. Frank Crook × Ophelia**	**Wm. A. Miles 1970 (Miyamoto)**
× V. Rothschildiana	= Rio's Sapphire	
CHRISTINE ANG	**V. sanderana × Erika Reuter**	Teo Boon Hian 1974
CHUM LONG	**V. Mary Fermin × Asctm. curvifolium**	**T. Orchids 1975**
CHUMPOL	**V. Kapiolani × Meda Arnold**	Muktamara 1972
CONSTANCE DE BRUYNE	**Yip Sum Wah × V. helvola**	**de Bruyne 1975**
COPPERTONE	**V. sanderana × Red Gem**	**Wilkins 1969**
× Arach. hookerana	= Mkra. Madame Yip Khew-Ying	
CORLIS TAKAHASHI	**Elieen Beauty × Yip Sum Wah**	**Ono 1974**
COSMO PINK	**Elieen Beauty × Blue Heaven**	**R. K. Mizuta 1975**
DAENG SIAM	**V. Sinard × Elieen Beauty**	Cholburi Ny. 1974
DAINTY MAID‡	**V. Hilo Blue × Asctm. curvifolium**	**R. K. Mizuta 1966**
× Yip Sum Wah	= Eugene Hamamoto	
DAISY MAY	**V. Tubtimtepya × Meda Arnold**	**Fresh 1971**
DARAKAM	**Tan Chai Beng × V. Thananchai**	**Kongthana 1973 (Sunthonwan)**
DARCEY STARR	**V. Eisenhower × Asctm. curvifolium**	**J. Arhontes 1971 (L. Aotaki)**
× Asctm. miniatum	= Wimwawan	
× V. Jennie Hashimoto	= Phrapinit	
× V. Ohuohu	= Pakawadee	
DARUNEE	**V. Pukele × Yip Sum Wah**	**Kanpai 1973**

ASCOCENDA

DAWN FUKUMURA	Tan Chai Beng × V. Kalama Maui	G. M. Fukumura 1975 (R. T. Fukamura)
DECHJUN	V. Rose Davis × Yip Sum Wah	Dechjun 1973
DITTAGONE	V. lamellata × Yip Sum Wah	Laddaland 1975 (Pantapa)
DJAJA	V. Lenavat × Meda Arnold	Lenavat 1974
DOCTOR SHINSO KAGAWA	V. Judy Miyamoto × Elieen Beauty	R. K. Mizuta 1971
DOCTOR SWART	Tan Chai Beng × Yip Sum Wah	Kullama 1975 (Originator unknown)
DONG TARN	Medasand × Elieen Beauty	Sakuldejtana 1973
DUANG PORN	V. Thananchai × Yip Sum Wah	Siriyakorn 1973
EISEN BEAUTY	V. Eisenhower × Elieen Beauty	Ono 1973
ELIEEN BEAUTY‡	Meda Arnold × Asctm. curvifolium	W. K. Nakamoto 1965

× Blue Heaven = Cosmo Pink
× Meda Arnold = Lorene
× Medasand = Dong Tarn
× Ophelia = Julian Aherrera
× Yip Sum Wah = Corlis Takahashi
× Rhy. coelestis = Vasco. Dreamy Blue
× V. bensonii = Maneetarn
× V. coerulescens = Louise Boyd
× V. Diane Ogawa = Polly Adams
× V. Eisenhower = Eisen Beauty
× V. Judy Miyamoto = Dr. Shinso Kagawa
× V. Kathy Olyphant = Lois Kashiwada
× V. Kapiolani = Paratee
× V. Pukele = Weeravan
× V. Sinard = Daeng Siam
× V. Thananchai = Impossible Star

ELLA FREED	V. Onomea × Asctm. miniatum	Freed 1973 (Originator unknown)
ERIKA REUTER	V. sanderana × Asctm. curvifolium	Woodlawn 1968 (E. Iwanaga)

× Ophelia = Golden Gem
× Yip Sum Wah = Stephanie Chun
× Asctm. curvifolium = Tou Dang
× V. coerulea = Navy Blue
× V. Princess Blue = Pramote
× V. sanderana = Christine Ang
× V. Sarojini = Jessie May
× V. Thananchai = Royal Flight

EUGENE HAMAMOTO	Yip Sum Wah × Dainty Maid	R. K. Mizuta 1971
FERMILLIANA CALMA	V. Sarojini × Blue Boy	Ono 1975
FLAMBEAU	Yip Sum Wah × V. tessellata	S'pore Orchids 1972 (Mrs. Gracia Lewis)
FLORA YAP	V. Frank Crook × Yip Sum Wah	T. Rakpaibulsombat 1974
FLORIDA SUNSET	V. Jeffrey × Asctm. curvifolium	Ruben 1971
GISELE MARTIN	V. Mabelmae Kamahele × Yip Sum Wah	R. K. Mizuta 1973
GOLDEN GEM	Erika Reuter × Ophelia	R. K. Mizuta 1973
GOLDEN GLOW	Medasand × Asctm. miniatum	P. Rujirawongse 1973
GOODHOPE	V. Onomea × Mem. Choo Laikeun	Ng Hoe Hai 1975 (Wong Leong Fatt)
GOULDS GLOW	V. Laurel Yap × Sunkist	Wilkins 1974
GRACE CALLARD	V. Patricia Low × Yip Sum Wah	H. Kagawa 1975
GRACIOUS LADY	V. Mary Catherine Bowman × Meda Arnold	Jaderstrom 1975 (Tew)
GUO CHIA LONG	V. Mem. Madame Pranerm × Yip Sum Wah	Kamolparawat 1970 (Patamakom)

× V. Thananchai = Udomsuk

HAAD RAVAI	V. Mem. Madame Pranerm × Medasand	Vipar 1974

× Ren. storiei = Kgw. Mem. Thep Satree

HABANANANDA‡	V. Gertrude Miyamoto × Asctm. curvifolium	Habanananda 1960

× Arach. hookerana = Mkra. Kelvin

HAM REILLY	V. Yellowstone × Asctm. curvifolium	Church 1974
HAPPY BEAUTY	V. sanderana × Mem. Choo Laikeun	Lum Chin Orchids 1974

ASCOCENDA

Name	Parentage	Registrant
HARRY BLAUVELT	**V. Royal Blue × Blue Boy**	**Mrs. W. H. Boyd 1972 (Richella)**
HAWAIIAN BLUE	**V. Harriet Miyao × Meda Arnold**	**R. K. Mizuta 1971**
HAWAIIAN DELIGHT	**V. Diane Ogawa × Yip Sum Wah**	**Perreira 1971**
HAWAIIAN MONARCH	**Yip Sum Wah × V. Keoni Noa**	**Perreira 1973**
HEAH HOCK HENG	**V. Josephine van Brero × Hilo Rose**	**How Yee Peng 1975**
HILO BELLE	**V. Laurel Yap × Meda Arnold**	**Miyao 1972**
HILO ROSE	**V. Hilo Queen × Meda Arnold**	**Miyao 1971**
× V. Josephine van Brero	= Heah Hock Heng	
HILO SUNSET	**V. Hilo Queen × Ophelia**	**Miyao 1972**
HOLLIS YAP	**V. Laurel Yap × Tropicana**	**Leo Yap 1973**
HONG KOK HOO	**Bonanza × V. sanderana**	**Hong Kok Hoo 1975**
HONOR FIRST	**V. Susan Lynn × Asctm. curvifolium**	**Vipar 1971**
HONWICHAI	**Meda Arnold × V. Joan Rothsand**	**Honwichai 1968**
× Ren. storiei	= Kgw. Kanith	
× V. Pranerm Violet	= Ponpen	
× V. Rothschildiana	= Ruby Belle	
× Vdps. parishii	= Wknsra. Samphan	
HUGO FREED	**V. Soo Hor Weng × Asctm. curvifolium**	**Freed 1973 (Originator unknown)**
HUMDINGER	**V. Princess Blue × Meda Arnold**	**Wilkins 1975**
ILIWAI	**V. Takeji Ogawa × Meda Arnold**	**Ono 1973**
IMPOSSIBLE STAR	**V. Thananchai × Elieen Beauty**	**Grittiya 1974**
ITTHIPOL	**Tan Chai Beng × V. Wongse**	**Dechjun 1974**
JAMES FURUMIZO	**V. Green Gold × Meda Arnold**	**Furumizo 1969**
× Charm	= Sunburst	
JESSIE MAY	**Erika Reuter × V. Sarojini**	**Teo Boon Hian 1974**
JIM LIM	**V. bensonii × Meda Arnold**	**Ratananda 1971**
JOANNA ONO	**V. Jeffrey × Meda Arnold**	**Ono 1973**
JOCLA	**Autumn Joy × Red Gem**	**Ono 1973**
JULIAN AHERRERA	**Ophelia × Elieen Beauty**	**Ono 1973**
KANOKWON	**Tropicana × V. Boonchoke**	**Pamonbut 1974 (Kenny)**
KAREN BEAUTY	**V. Jeffrey × Elieen Beauty**	**Ono 1969**
× Asctm. curvifolium	= Venerose Calma	
KAREN CODLING	V. Josephine van Brero × Mem. Choo Laikeun	**Charles Lim 1974 (Wong Loong Fatt)**
KAREN McCLOSKEY	**V. Takeji Ogawa × Yip Sum Wah**	**Ono 1974**
KAREN ONO	**Yip Sum Wah × V. coerulea**	**Ono 1972**
KASETSART BEAUTY	**V. Rothschildiana × Asctm. Sagarik Gold**	**Sagarik 1972**
KASETSILP	**Buddy Choo × V. Thananchai**	**Sulyaphongse 1975**
KATHLEEN KAGAWA	**V. Leslie H. Kagawa × Asctm. curvifolium**	**H. Kagawa 1975**
KATHY ERNE	**V. Jean Fukudo × Asctm. curvifolium**	**Muse's 1971**
KAY YOSHIDA	**V. Joyce Lynne Chong × Ophelia**	**Ono 1973**
KAZUTO NITTA	**V. Trisher × Meda Arnold**	**H. K. Nitta 1972**
KHEM THAI	**V. Thai × Asctm. curvifolium**	**Laksanapbuk 1973**
KITIGA	V. Aurawan × Meda Arnold	**Kongthana 1973 (Karaket)**
KITIVAL	**V. brunnea × Asctm. miniatum**	**Veerabhongs 1975**
KOH MAN‡	**V. Manila × Asctm. curvifolium**	**Yap Wee Chee 1965 (Shimamoto)**
× Arach. hookerana	= Mkra. Yoon Weng-Low	
× V. Pukele	= Susan Mae	
KORB FAH	**V. Eisenhower × Yip Sum Wah**	**Vipar 1971**

ASCOCENDA

KRISTI NAKATSU	**Ophelia × V. Nancy Rodillas**	**Rodillas 1974**
LADAVAN	**V. Prachark Chit × Asctm. curvifolium**	**W. P. Orchid 1974**
LADY ARUNEE	**Mangkiatkul × V. Hilo Queen**	**Chavalit 1973**
LADY BOONKUA	**V. Onomea × Meda Arnold**	**Vipar 1969**

× V. Thananchai = Swangaroon

LADY FAY	**V. Mary Foster × Meda Arnold**	**Muttamara 1973**
LAIKEUN	**Ophelia × V. Rothschildiana**	**Chua Swee Cheng 1966 (M. Nirei)**

× Ophelia = Pung Par Dist | × Vasco. Susan = Vasco. Kiat Silp
× V. Thananchai = Pasana

LANI BIRD	**Red Gem × Meda Arnold**	**R. K. Mizuta 1966**

× Yip Sum Wah = Rickie Torress | × V. Eisenhower = Paradise Queen

LANI GIRL	**V. Lynne Sugihara × Asctm. curvifolium**	**S. Noda 1972**
LAUREEN ONO	V. Ellen Noa × Portia Doolittle	**Ono 1972**
LEE YOKE SUM	**V. Mem. Frieda Hantober × Red Gem**	**Tam Kam Weng 1975**
LENG	**V. James Toogood × Yip Sum Wah**	**T. Orchids 1972 (S. Rakpaiboonsombat)**
LEONTINE HO	**Bonanza × V. coerulea**	**Chantramontol 1974**
LIEUTENANT CHOR	**V. James Toogood × Meda Arnold**	**Yaemboonchoo 1972**
LIL	**V. Oscar M. Kirsch × Tropicana**	**H. V. Street 1972**
LIM KIM YOO	**Medasand × V. tessellata**	**Lim Kim Yoo 1975**
LINDA CALMA	**Meda Arnold × Yooko Murata**	**Ono 1975**
LITTLE PASHA	V. Emma van Deventer × Yip Sum Wah	**R. K. Mizuta 1973**
LOIS KASHIWADA	**V. Kathy Olyphant × Elieen Beauty**	**Ono 1973**
LOLLIPOP	**V. Patricia Low × Meda Arnold**	**Wilkins 1973**
LORENE	**Elieen Beauty × Meda Arnold**	**Ono 1972**
LORENE BEAUTY	**Blue Boy × V. Bonnie Blue Fukumura**	**Ono 1974**
LOUISE BOYD	V. coerulescens × Elieen Beauty	**Mrs. W. H. Boyd 1975 (Mrs. H. W. Fox)**
LUK JEAP	**Yip Sum Wah × V. Kapiolani**	**Sakuldejtana 1972**
LULU	**V. Colorful × Meda Arnold**	**Wilkins 1973**
LULUKIST	**V. Honolulu × Sunkist**	**Ruben 1975**
MADAME KENNY	**Yip Sum Wah × V. Boonchoke**	**Kenny 1973**
MADAME NOK	**V. Hilo Blue × Yip Sum Wah**	**Rakpaiboonsombat 1971**
MADAME VANIDA	**V. Eisensander × Yip Sum Wah**	**Vipar Orchids 1972**
MAEKLONG	**V. Varavan × Tan Chai Beng**	**Lim-im 1975**
MAJOR CHAMNIEN	**V. Hilo Charm × Yip Sum Wah**	**Ratanavaraka 1973 (Chindavanic)**
MAJOR CHOR	**V. James Toogood × Asctm. curvifolium**	**Yaemboonchoo 1967**

× Asctm. curvifolium = Navaratana

MALIBU ONEOHTWO	**V. Sandamo × Ophelia**	**Freed 1974 (originator unknown)**

× Meda Arnold = Barbara Freed Saltzman

MALINI	**Medasand × V. Boonchoke**	**Kenny 1974**
MANEETARN	**V. bensonii × Elieen Beauty**	**Chitswang 1975 (Maneetarn)**
MANGKIATKUL	**V. Jennie Hashimoto × Meda Arnold**	**Mangkiatkul 1968 (Phenphaisit)**

× Arach. hookerana = Mkra. Viroonchan | × V. Lenavat = Ann
× V. Diane Ogawa = Cholnapha | × V. Rothschildiana = Thidaratana
× V. Hilo Queen = Lady Arunee | × V. Sinard = Busaraporn

ASCOCENDA

MARLENE SUNDERMIER	**V. Eve × Tropicana**	**Garth 1973**
MARY STRANN	**Meda Arnold × V. Kathy Olyphant**	**A. & M. 1973 (Strann)**
MAUI GOLD	**V. Eisenhower × Asctm. miniatum**	**A. G. Tharp 1973 (R. T. Fukumura)**
MAUI KAIMANA	**V. Kalama Maui × Yip Sum Wah**	**R. T. Fukumura 1975**
MEDA ARNOLD‡	**Asctm. curvifolium × V. Rothschildiana**	**Sideris 1950**

× Blue Boy	= Melanie Ono
× Elieen Beauty	= Lorene
× Malibu Oneohtwo	= Barbara Freed Saltzman
× Medasand	= Alok Jain
× Mem. Choo Laikeun	= Yoon Weng-Low
× Mem. Jim Wilkins	= Rio's Sangria
× Sunkist	= Medakist
× Yooko Murata	= Linda Calma
× Aër. crassifolia	= Chtra. Chula
× Aër. fieldingii	= Chtra. Mem. Raymond Mercier
× Aër. flabellata	= Chtra. Bangkok
× Aër. jarckiana	= Chtra. Virginia Braga
× Aër. odorata	= Chtra. Changchenkit
× Arach. hookerana	= Mkra. Sally Lim
× Arach. Maggie Oei	= Mkra. Magmeda
× Arnth. Anne Black	= Ysfra. Nong
× Asctm. miniatum	= Pralor
× Dtps. Mem. Clarence Schubert	= Vwga. Jerry Vande Weghe
× Phal. stuartiana	= Dvra. Ella Freed
× Phal. Zada	= Dvra. Marjorie Wreford
× Rnds. Red Jewel	= Rbnra. Kosher Red
× Rntda. Lyn Andrade	= Kgw. Yuthayong Beauty
× Ren. imschootiana	= Kgw. Red Lava
× Ren. philippinensis	= Kgw. June
× Rnthps. Moon Walk	= Stmra. Noel
× Rhv. Bangkok Sky	= Vasco. Tukta
× Rhv. Galen Kanayama	= Vasco. Janice Kanayama
× Rhv. Sagarik Wine	= Vasco. Prasarn
× Rhv. Wong Yoke Sim	= Vasco. Apricot Gleam
× Trgl. brachiata	= Fjo. Gem
× V. Aurawan	= Kitiga
× V. bensonii	= Jim Lim
× V. Boonchoke	= Ring Lyman
× V. Colorful	= Lulu
× V. denisoniana	= Tavivat
× V. Eisenhower	= Capricorn
× V. Eisensander	= Mittaparb Rama
× V. Emma van Deventer	= Ching Mook Choon
× V. Gillian Trevor	= Aries
× V. Haihai	= Ooi Boon Huat
× V. Harriet Miyao	= Hawaiian Blue
× V. Hilo Queen	= Hilo Rose
× V. Honolii	= Sunny Day
× V. Hukilau	= Teoline Fiery
× V. James Toogood	= Lieutenant Chor
× V. Jeffrey	= Joanna Ono
× V. Judy Miyamoto	= Agnes Kagawa
× V. Kalama Maui	= Mildred Furumizo
× V. Kapiolani	= Chumpol
× V. Kathy Olyphant	= Mary Strann
× V. Laurel Yap	= Hilo Belle
× V. Lenavat	= Djaja
× V. Lumpini	= Cholburi
× V. Mary Catherine Bowman	= Gracious Lady
× V. Mary Foster	= Lady Fay
× V. Nancy Rodillas	= Teoline Festival
× V. Patricia Low	= Lollipop
× V. Piha Moon	= Teoline Blaze
× V. Princess Blue	= Humdinger
× V. Sandamo	= Ronald Nitta
× V. Satta	= Busadee
× V. Sue Saito	= Mitsy Shinsato
× V. Takeji Ogawa	= Iliwai
× V. Teoline Rosieglow	= Teoline Celebration
× V. Thananchai	= Took-Ta
× V. Trisher	= Kazuto Nitta
× V. Tubtimtepya	= Daisy May
× V. Winifred Kurihara	= Mem. Jutaro Nitta
× V. Wongse	= Teoline Apron
× Vasco. Blue Fairy	= Vasco. Mem. Arthur Freed

MEDAKIST	**Meda Arnold × Sunkist**	**Ruben 1974**
MEDASAND‡	**V. sanderana × Meda Arnold**	**M. Yamada 1967**

× Elieen Beauty	= Dong Tarn
× Meda Arnold	= Alok Jain
× Seechang	= Seethai
× Tan Chai Beng	= Panchasarp
× Wilas	= Bang Pla Sroi
× Yip Sum Wah	= Bang Saai
× Aër. falcata	= Chtra. Thai
× Aër. flabellata	= Chtra. Tha Yang
× Arach. hookerana	= Mkra. Sayan
× Aranda Lucy Laycock	= Mkra. Soon Khim
× Asctm. miniatum	= Golden Glow
× Ren. storiei	= Kgw. Teo Boon Hian
× V. Aurawan	= Ployphommas
× V. bensonii	= Sam Muang
× V. Boonchoke	= Malini
× V. coerulea	= Rakpaibulsombat
× V. denisoniana	= Nibha
× V. Diane Ogawa	= Suthisan
× V. Frank Crook	= Prayoon
× V. Hilo Queen	= Mem. Verawan
× V. Jennie Hashimoto	= South East Star
× V. Lenavat	= Phairot
× V. Mem. Madame Pranerm	= Haad Ravai
× V. Rose Davis	= Morakot
× V. Rothschildiana	= Queen Florist
× V. sanderana	= Thonglor
× V. Satta	= Panthong
× V. Sinard	= Vilawan
× V. tessellata	= Lim Kim Yoo
× V. Thananchai	= Aribarg
× Vdps. parishii	= Wknsra. Thanasuwat

MELANIE ONO	**Meda Arnold × Blue Boy**	**Ono 1972**

ASCOCENDA

MEMORIA ARTHUR FREED	**V. cristata × Yip Sum Wah**	**Freed 1975 (Originator unknown)**
MEMORIA CHOO LAIKEUN‡	**V. Tita Marks × Asctm. curvifolium**	**Chua Swee Chang 1965 (R. T. Fukumura)**

× Meda Arnold	= Yoon Weng-Low	× V. Onomea	= Goodhope
× V. Emma van Deventer	= Carolaine	× V. sanderana	= Happy Beauty
× V. Josephine van Brero	= Karen Codling		

MEMORIA JIM WILKINS	**V. Jennie Hashimoto × Asctm. curvifolium**	**Wilkins 1969**

× Meda Arnold	= Rio's Sangria	× V. Rothschildiana	= Spellbound
× Gchls. monticolus	= Eas. Advancement		

MEMORIA JUTARO NITTA	**V. Winifred Kurihara × Meda Arnold**	**H. K. Nitta 1973**
MEMORIA LOVELL GARTH	**V. tessellata × Tropicana**	**Garth 1973**
MEMORIA VERAWAN	**Medasand × V. Hilo Queen**	**Chavalit 1974**
MEMORIA VIVIAN FUSE	**V. Mary Catherine Bowman × Yip Sum Wah**	**R. K. Mizuta 1972**
MERRILL SUM WAH	**V. merrillii × Yip Sum Wah**	**Otaguro 1972**
MIAMI	**V. Honolii × Asctm. curvifolium**	**Ruben 1971**
MILDRED FURUMIZO	**V. Kalama Maui × Meda Arnold**	**H. Furumizo 1971**
MITSY SHINSATO	**V. Sue Saito × Meda Arnold**	**H. Kagawa 1975**
MITTAPARB RAMA	**V. Eisensander × Meda Arnold**	**Vipar 1971**
MONIQUE	**Ophelia × Asctm. miniatum**	**H. Kagawa 1975**
MORAKOT	**Medasand × V. Rose Davis**	**Cholburi Ny 1974**
NAVARATANA	**Major Chor × Asctm. curvifolium**	**Thongsuphan 1973**
NAVY BLUE	**Erika Reuter × V. coerulea**	**Hirisatja 1972**

× Arach. hookerana	= Mkra. Viroonchan Blue

NIBHA	**Medasand × V. denisoniana**	**Denny 1973**
NICKY NG	**V. lamellata × Red Gem**	**Thong 1973**
NO KA OI	**V. Denizonica × Ophelia**	**M. Nirei 1971**
NONGKHAM	**V. Jennie Hashimoto × Priyavadee**	**Sawang Somboonpol 1975**
NOPARAT	**Sagarik × V. sanderana**	**Sulyapong 1974 (Sagarik)**
ONE BLUE	**V. Charlesworthii × Ophelia**	**Sawang Somboonpol 1974**
ONOKIST	**Sunkist × V. Onomea**	**Ruben 1974**
OOI BOON HUAT	**V. Haihai × Meda Arnold**	**Ng & Tan 1971 (Fukumura Orchids)**

× Tan Chai Beng	= Asoke

OPHELIA	**V. Bill Sutton × Asctm. curvifolium**	**O. Kirsch 1960**

× Elieen Beauty	= Julian Aherrera	× V. denisoniana	= Philoden
× Erika Reuter	= Golden Gem	× V. Denizonica	= No Ka Oi
× Laikeun	= Pung Par Dist	× V. Fair Queen	= Palm Beach Maid
× Yip Sum Wah	= Rose Charm	× V. Hilo Queen	= Hilo Sunset
× Asctm. miniatum	= Monique	× V. Joyce Lynne Chong	= Kay Yoshida
× Asctm. Sagarik Gold	= Bangkok Gold	× V. Marguerite Rice	= Palm Beach Delight
× Dor. pulcherrima	= Asvts. John Miller	× V. Mem. Frieda Hantober	= To Soon
× Lsa. jonesii	= Dbra. Victoria de Bruyne	× V. Nancy Rodillas	= Kristi Nakatsu
× Phal. serpentilingua	= Dvra. Susanne Mary Coutts	× V. Ohuohu	= Palm Beach Holiday
× Ren. imschootiana	= Kgw. Red Elf	× V. Pauahi	= Ahuimanu
× Rngm. Red Delight	= Shgra. Tangerine Beauty	× V. Pukele	= Pata
× Rnthps. Amy Russell	= Stmra. Rayna	× V. Sandamo	= Malibu Oneohtwo
× Rhy. coelestis	= Vasco. Mem. Charles Blauvelt	× V. teres	= Peacock Flower
× V. Charlesworthii	= One Blue	× V. Thananchai	= Teoline Bewitch
		× Vasco. Susan	= Vasco. Bangkok Ball

PACALARANN	**V. Patricia Lee × Asctm. curvifolium**	**C. S. Kellogg 1972 (Wakasugi)**
PAIDEE MADEE	**Tan Chai Beng × V. James Harding**	**Muttamara 1974**

ASCOCENDA

PALM BEACH DELIGHT	V. Marguerite Rice × Ophelia	Thornton's 1975
PALM BEACH HOLIDAY	V. Ohuohu × Ophelia	Thornton's 1975
PALM BEACH MAID	V. Fair Queen × Ophelia	Thornton's 1975
PANTHONG	Medasand × V. Satta	Sakuldejtana 1974
PAKAWADEE	Darcey Starr × V. Ohuohu	Bunyavibul 1974
PANCHASARP	Medasand × Tan Chai Beng	Panchasarp 1973 (Kenny)
PARADISE QUEEN	V. Eisenhower × Lani Bird	Perreira 1973
PARATEE	V. Kapiolani × Elieen Beauty	Chorsatayadham 1974 (Chavalit)
PASANA	Laikeun × V. Thananchai	Sulyapong 1974 (Sagarik)
PATA	V. Pukele × Ophelia	Wee Sian Hee 1972 (Chow Yee Wah)
PEACOCK FLOWER	Ophelia × V. teres	Fort Caroline 1973 (Wallbrunn)
PEARLY	Ophelia × Asctm. curvifolium	Ono 1969

× V. Mem. Tadaichi Doi = Ruth Levin

PEGGY FOO	V. Bonnie Blue Fukumura × Asctm. curvifolium	Foo Hock Lee 1970 (R. T. Fukumura)

× Ren. philippinensis = Kgw. Madame Yip Khew-Ying

× V. sanderana = Tan Chin Heong

PENSOM	V. Waipuna × Asctm. curvifolium	Komkris 1969

× V. coerulea = Tud Tou

PHAIROT	V. Lenavat × Medasand	Lenavat 1972
PHILODEN	Ophelia × V. denisoniana	S'pore Orchids 1972
PHRAPINIT	V. Jennie Hashimoto × Darcey Starr	Suebsanguan 1974
PICHARN	V. Tan Chin Tuan × Yip Sum Wah	Prayoonratana 1975
PIM SIRI	V. Jennie Hashimoto × Tan Chai Beng	Napasab 1973
PINK DOLL	V. Bill Sutton × Yip Sum Wah	R. T. Fukumura 1974
PISWONG	V. Diane Ogawa × Meda Arnold	P. Tancharoen 1969

× V. Sathupradit = Ayer Itam Beauty

PIYADA	V. parviflora × Asctm. curvifolium	Laddaland 1975 (Pantapa)
PLOYPHOMMAS	V. Aurawan × Medasand	T. Orchids 1975
POLLY ADAMS	Elieen Beauty × V. Diane Ogawa	Perreira 1971
PONG	V. Rothschildiana × Asctm. miniatum	Mangkiatkul 1971
PONPEN	V. Pranerm Violet × Honwichai	Siriyakorn 1974
PORTIA DOOLITTLE†‡	Asctm. curvifolium × V. lamellata	Sideris 1949

× V. Ellen Noa = Laureen Ono

PRACHIT GOLD	V. Tubtimtepya × Asctm. miniatum	Praimanee 1972
PRADIT	V. laotica × Yip Sum Wah	Laddaland 1975 (Pantapa)
PRALOR	Meda Arnold × Asctm. miniatum	Milindasuta 1973
PRAMOTE	V. Princess Blue × Erika Reuter	T. Orchids 1975
PRAYOON	V. Frank Crook × Medasand	T. Orchids 1975
PRIMA BELLE	Tan Chai Beng × V. Rothschildiana	Vipar 1975
PRIYAVADEE	V. Rothschildiana × Red Gem	Bunyavibul 1971

× Ren. storiei = Kgw. Doungdee
× Rhv. Wong Yoke Sim = Vasco. Jairak

× V. Jennie Hashimoto = Nongkham

ASCOCENDA

PUANG LADA	**V. Sivanart Palm × Yip Sum Wah**	**Kuansuwan 1975 (C. Y. Nursery)**
PUDTAN	**Tan Chai Beng × V. coerulea**	**Chavalit 1974**
PUNG PAR DIST	**Ophelia × Laikeun**	**Pung Par Dist 1973 (Sagarik)**
QUEEN FLORIST	**Medasand × V. Rothschildiana**	**P. Rakpaiboonsombat 1972 (T. Rakpaiboonsombat)**
RAKPAIBULSOMBAT	**Medasand × V. coerulea**	**T. Orchids 1974**
RAM INDRA	**V. Tubtimtepya × Yip Sum Wah**	**Pinvatanapruk 1972 (Praimanee)**
RAPEEPAT	**Tropicana × Asctm. curvifolium**	**Rojanadara 1972 (W. A. Chang)**
RED BUTTONS	**Autumn Joy × Yip Sum Wah**	**R. T. Fukumura 1974**
RED GEM‡	**V. merrillii × Asctm. curvifolium**	**E. Iwanaga 1962**
× Autumn Joy	= Jocla	
× Ren. Brookie Chandler	= Kgw. Shumoon Abdulali	
× Rhv. Bangkok Sky	= Vasco. Pranee	
× V. Eisenhower	= Robert Berryman	
× V. Josephine van Brero	= Yeap Eng Sim	
× V. lamellata	= Nicky Ng	
× V. Mem. Frieda Hantober	= Lee Yoke Sum	
× V. Pikul	= Chom Yong	
× V. Rothschildiana	= Priyavadee	
× Vdps. parishii	= Wknsra. Gemini	
RED GLOW	V. Trimerrill × Asctm. curvifolium	**Ruben 1971**
REDLAND	**V. Fair Queen × Red Gem**	**Wilkins 1969**
× Rose Seidel	= Redrose	
REDROSE	**Redland × Rose Seidel**	**Ruben 1975**
RICKIE TORRESS	**Yip Sum Wah × Lani Bird**	**M. Nirei 1972**
RING LYMAN	**V. Boonchoke × Meda Arnold**	**Chartniyom 1974 (Kenny)**
RIO'S SANGRIA	**Meda Arnold × Mem. Jim Wilkins**	**Ruben 1974**
RIO'S SAPPHIRE	**Chris Miles × V. Rothschildiana**	**Ruben 1974**
ROBERT BERRYMAN	**V. Eisenhower × Red Gem**	**Berryman 1972**
RONALD NITTA	**V. Sandamo × Meda Arnold**	**H. K. Nitta 1973**
ROSE CHARM	**Yip Sum Wah × Ophelia**	**R. T. Fukumura 1974**
ROSE SEIDEL	**V. Frank Crook × Asctm. curvifolium**	**Mitterer 1969**
× Redland	= Redrose	
ROTHKIST	**V. Rothschildiana × Sunkist**	**Ruben 1974**
ROYAL FLIGHT	**V. Thananchai × Erika Reuter**	**Grittiya 1974**
RUBY BELLE	Honwichai × V. Rothschildiana	**Vipar 1975**
RUMRILL	**V. cristata × Asctm. curvifolium**	**Rumrill 1973**
RUTH LEVIN	**V. Mem. Tadaichi Doi × Pearly**	**Levin 1975 (S. Noda)**
RUTH SHAVE	**V. Eisensander × Ophelia**	**Shave 1967**
× V. Tom Ritter	= Tammy Wakasugi	
SAGARIK	**V. sanderana × Asctm. miniatum**	**Sagarik 1966**
× V. sanderana	= Noparat	
SAGARIK SHINE	**V. Onomea × Asctm. Sagarik Gold**	**Siriyakorn 1974**
SAM ANG	**V. B.P. Mok × Yip Sum Wah**	**Sombuntham 1972**
SAM MUANG	**V. bensonii × Medasand**	Prommart Ny. 1975 **(Aimrasamee)**
SANDKIST	**V. sanderana × Sunkist**	**Ruben 1974**
SANTISUK	**V. Karen Ono × Yip Sum Wah**	**Napasab 1973**
SARA	**Asctm. curvifolium × V. coerulea**	**Chindavanic 1973 (Suravallop)**

ASCOCENDA

SARASIRI	**V. bensonii × Asctm. curvifolium**	**Paireepairit 1974**
SAUVANEE	**V. Jennie Hashimoto × Yip Sum Wah**	**Hirisatja 1972 (Kesamarit)**
SAVITA	**Tan Chai Beng × V. Diane Ogawa**	**Chavalit 1974**
SEECHANG	**V. Diane Ogawa × Red Gem**	**Sakuldejtana 1969 (W. P. Orchid)**

× Medasand	= Seethai	× V. sanderana	= Sethtee
× Ren. storiei	= Kgw. Viroonchan Ruby	× V. Thananchai	= Seelom
× V. Rothschildiana	= Seedee		

SEEDEE	**V. Rothschildiana × Seechang**	**Lenavat 1974**
SEELOM	**V. Thananchai × Seechang**	**Satirasut 1975**
SEETHAI	**Medasand × Seechang**	**Lenavat 1974**
SETHTEE	**V. sanderana × Seechang**	Cholburi Ny. 1974
SILPAPRASERT	**V. Rothschildiana × Aroonsri Beauty**	**Silpaprasert 1974 (Song Sae Eiaw)**
SISOM	**V. Nancy Rodillas × Asctm. curvifolium**	**Lenavat 1971**
SOUTH EAST LIGHT	V. Thananchai × Wilas	**S.E.O. 1973**
SOUTH EAST STAR	**V. Jennie Hashimoto × Medasand**	**S.E.O. 1973**
SPELLBOUND	V. Rothschildiana × Mem. Jim Wilkins	**Wilkins 1974 (Mitterer)**
SRISUPA	**Sunkist × V. coerulea**	**Deearom 1973 (Sagarik)**
STEERE NODA	**V. Sandamo × Asctm. curvifolium**	**S. Noda 1972**
STEPHANIE CHUN	**Erika Reuter × Yip Sum Wah**	**Perreira 1971**
STEPHEN SNG	**V. Hilo Blue × Ophelia**	**Sng Choo Eng 1969**

× Mkra. Magmeda	= Mkra. Oil

STHAPORN	**V. Lenavat × Yip Sum Wah**	**Song Sae Eiaw 1973**
SUNBURST	**Charm × James Furumizo**	**Perreira 1974**
SUNEE	**Sunkist × V. Thananchai**	**Chantramontol 1973**
SUNFUN	Sunkist × Asctm. curvifolium	**Ruben 1974**
SUNKIST	**V. sanderana × Ophelia**	**Takakura 1966**

× Meda Arnold	= Medakist	× V. Laurel Yap	= Goulds Glow
× Asctm. curvifolium	= Sunfun	× V. Onomea	= Onokist
× Ren. imschootiana	= Kgw. Nell Carlson	× V. Rothschildiana	= Rothkist
× V. coerulea	= Srisupa	× V. sanderana	= Sandkist
× V. denisoniana	= Theptong	× V. Thananchai	= Sunee
× V. Honolulu	= Lulukist	× V. Trimerrill	= Trikist

SUNNY DAY	**V. Honolii × Meda Arnold**	**Vipar 1972**
SUSAN MAE	**Koh Man × V. Pukele**	**H. Kagawa 1975**
SUTHISAN	Medasand × V. Diane Ogawa	**Rakpaiboonsombat 1971**
SWANGAROON	**V. Thananchai × Lady Boonkua**	**Swangaroon 1974 (Pinwathanapurg)**
TAMMY WAKASUGI	**Ruth Shave × V. Tom Ritter**	**G. Wakasugi 1972**
TAN CHAI BENG‡	**Meda Arnold × V. Rothschildiana**	**Tan Nai Hee 1965 (Takakura)**

× Medasand	= Panchasarp	× V. Karen Ono	= Vuthichai
× Ooi Boon Huat	= Asoke	× V. Laurel Yap	= Wasana
× Yip Sum Wah	= Doctor Swart	× V. Lenavat	= Yachitr
× Aër. mitrata	= Chtra. Pink Glory	× V. Onomea	= Venus
× Rhv. Wong Yoke Sim	= Vasco. Blue Kahili	× V. Rothschildiana	= Prima Belle
× V. coerulea	= Pudtan	× V. sanderana	= Chomnard
× V. Diane Ogawa	= Savita	× V. Thananchai	= Darakam
× V. James Harding	= Paidee Madee	× V. Varavan	= Maeklong
× V. Jennie Hashimoto	= Pim Siri	× V. Wongse	= Itthipol
× V. Kalama Maui	= Dawn Fukumura	× Vasco. Blue Fairy	= Vasco. Kled Kaew

ASCOCENDA

TAN CHIN HEONG	**V. sanderana × Peggy Foo**	**Andrew Tan 1973**
TARATIKUN	**Tropicana × V. Jennie Hashimoto**	**Taratikun 1972 (Song Ear)**
TAVIVAT	**Meda Arnold × V. denisoniana**	**Tavivatana 1974**
TEOLINE APRON	**Meda Arnold × V. Wongse**	**Teo Boon Hian 1974**
TEOLINE BEWITCH	**Ophelia × V. Thananchai**	**Teo Boon Hian 1974**
TEOLINE BLAZE	**V. Piha Moon × Meda Arnold**	**Teo Boon Hian 1974**
TEOLINE CELEBRATION	**Meda Arnold × V. Teoline Rosieglow**	**Teo Boon Hian 1974**
TEOLINE FESTIVAL	**Meda Arnold × V. Nancy Rodillas**	**Teo Boon Hian 1974**
TEOLINE FIERY	**Meda. Arnold × V. Hukilau**	**Teo Boon Hian 1974**
TEOLINE WORTH	V. Waipuna × Yip Sum Wah	**Teo Boon Hian 1974**
THAI RUBY	**V. Lenavat × Cholburi**	**Lenavat 1974**
THEPTONG	**Sunkist × V. denisoniana**	**O. Thephasdin 1975**
THIDARATANA	**V. Rothschildiana × Mangkiatkul**	**Riewthong 1974**
THONGLOR	**Medasand × V. sanderana**	**T. Rakpaiboonsombat 1971**
TINY BUBBLE	**V. Bonnie Blue Fukumura × Yip Sum Wah**	**R. T. Fukumura 1975**
TINY JUNE	**V. Mary Foster × Asctm. curvifolium**	**Muttamara 1973**
TOH CHIN SOO	**Buddy Choo × V. Lenavat**	**Toh Chin Soo 1975 (Choo Cheng Choong)**
TOOK-TA	**V. Thananchai × Meda Arnold**	**Napasab 1973**
TO SOON	**V. Mem. Frieda Hantober × Ophelia**	**J. & S. 1975 (Toh Chor Soon)**
TOU DANG	**Erika Reuter × Asctm. curvifolium**	**Grittiya 1974**
TRIKIST	**V. Trimerrill × Sunkist**	**Ruben 1975**
TROPICANA	**V. Betsy Sumner × Asctm. curvifolium**	**Sorayama 1966**

× Asctm. curvifolium	= Rapeepat	× V. Laurel Yap	= Hollis Yap
× V. Boonchoke	= Kanokwon	× V. Oscar M. Kirsch	= Lil
× V. Eve	= Marlene Sundermier	× V. tessellata	= Mem. Lovell Garth
× V. Jennie Hashimoto	= Taratikun		

TUD TOU	**Pensom × V. coerulea**	**Laddaland 1975 (Pantapa)**
UDOMSUK	**V. Thananchai × Guo Chia Long**	**S.E.O. 1974**
VENEROSE CALMA	**Karen Beauty × Asctm. curvifolium**	**Ono 1975**
VENUS	**V. Onomea × Tan Chai Beng**	**Phooncharoen 1974 (Kantajaraniti)**
VILAWAN	**V. Sinard × Medasand**	**Chavalit 1974**
VIOLET YAP	**V. Laurel Yap × Asctm. curvifolium**	**Leo Yap 1972**
VUTHICHAI	**V. Karen Ono × Tan Chai Beng**	**Napasab 1973**
WACHARIN	**Yip Sum Wah × Asctm. Sagarik Gold**	**Chuanyen 1975**
WASANA	**V. Laurel Yap × Tan Chai Beng**	**Kullama 1975 (Originator unknown)**
WEERAVAN	V. Pukele × Elieen Beauty	**Kanpai 1973**
WILAS	**V. Diane Ogawa × Asctm. curvifolium**	**Charoen 1968**

× Medasand	= Bang Pla Sroi	× Arach. Ishbel	= Mkra. Lim Sin Kiaw
× Arach. hookerana	= Mkra. Winnie Ling	× V. Thananchai	= South East Light

WIMWAWAN	**Asctm. miniatum × Darcey Starr**	**Suebsanguan 1974**
WINIFRED HAMAMOTO	**V. Winifred Kurihara × Asctm. curvifolium**	**H. K. Nitta 1974**
YACHITR	**V. Lenavat × Tan Chai Beng**	**Song Sae Eiaw 1973**
YEAP ENG SIM	**V. Josephine van Brero × Red Gem**	**Andrew Tan 1973**
YEE PENG	**Yip Sum Wah × V. Dawn Nishimura**	**Soh Kim Kang 1970**

× Aranda Lily Chong	= Mkra. Monique

YELLOW CAPTAIN	**Captain Chor × V. Thananchai**	**Grittiya 1974**

ASCOCENDA

YIP SUM WAH‡ — **V. Pukele × Asctm. curvifolium** — **Yip Sum Wah 1965 (Fukumura)**

× Autumn Joy = Red Buttons
× Dainty Maid = Eugene Hamamoto
× Elieen Beauty = Corlis Takahashi
× Erika Reuter = Stephanie Chun
× Lani Bird = Rickie Torress
× Medasand = Bang Saai
× Ophelia = Rose Charm
× Tan Chai Beng = Doctor Swart
× Aër. falcata = Chtra. Nam-Oi
× Aër. flabellata = Chtra. Bangpra
× Aër. lawrenceae = Chtra. Ruth Murai
× Aërctm. Luke Nok = Chtra. Sum Nok
× Arach. hookerana = Mkra. Ena Ling
× Arach. Ishbel = Mkra. Harriet Lim
× Arach. Maggie Oei = Mkra. Dear Heart
× Asctm. Sagarik Gold = Wacharin
× Ren. John Tew = Kgw. Inferno
× Ren. philippinensis = Kgw. Yoon Weng-Low
× Ren. storiei = Kgw. Boon Rubb
× Rhv. Bangkok Sky = Vasco. Somboonpol
× Rhv. Blue Angel = Vasco. Bluebird
× Rhv. Busakorn = Vasco. Chitswang
× V. Bill Sutton = Pink Doll
× V. Bonnie Blue Fukumura = Tiny Bubble
× V. Boonchoke = Madame Kenny
× V. B.P. Mok = Sam Ang
× V. Charlesworthii = Chao Khun Yarn
× V. coerulea = Karen Ono
× V. cristata = Mem. Arthur Freed
× V. Diane Ogawa = Hawaiian Delight
× V. Eisenhower = Korb Fah
× V. Eisensander = Madame Vanida
× V. Emma van Deventer = Little Pasha
× V. Frank Crook = Flora Yap
× V. helvola = Constance de Bruyne
× V. Hilo Blue = Madame Nok
× V. Hilo Charm = Major Chamnien
× V. James Toogood = Leng
× V. Jennie Hashimoto = Sauvanee
× V. Josephine van Brero = Chaiyot
× V. Kalama Maui = Maui Kaimana
× V. Kapiolani = Luk Jeap
× V. Karen Ono = Santisuk
× V. Keoni Noa = Hawaiian Monarch
× V. lamellata = Dittagone
× V. laotica = Pradit
× V. Lenavat = Sthaporn
× V. Mabelmae Kamahele = Gisele Martin
× V. Mary Catherine Bowman = Mem. Vivian Fuse
× V. merrillii = Merrill Sum Wah
× V. Patricia Low = Grace Callard
× V. Pukele = Darunee
× V. Rose Davis = Dechjun
× V. Sivanart Palm = Puang Lada
× V. Takeji Ogawa = Karen McCloskey
× V. Tan Chin Tuan = Picharn
× V. tessellata = Flambeau
× V. Thananchai = Duang Porn
× V. Tubtimtepya = Ram Indra
× V. Waipuna = Teoline Worth
× Vdps. parishii = Wknsra. Lopburi
× Vasco. Blue Fairy = Vasco. Asdornithee
× Vasco. Susan = Vasco. Flirtasia

YOOKO MURATA — **V. Takeji Ogawa × Elieen Beauty** — **Ono 1970**

× Meda Arnold = Linda Calma

YOON WENG-LOW — **Meda Arnold × Mem. Choo Laikeun** — **Yoon Pooi-Kong 1974 (Cheah Keng Cheong)**

ASCOCENTRUM

ampullaceum‡ — **species**

× miniatum = Mona Church
× Rhctm. Sagarik = Rhctm. Bamrung

aurantiacum — **species**

× V. Rothschildiana = Ascda. Bill Fox

curvifolium†‡ — **species**

× Aër. mitrata = Aërctm. Cholratana
× Ascda. Erika Reuter = Ascda. Tou Dang
× Ascda. Karen Beauty = Ascda. Venerose Calma
× Ascda. Major Chor = Ascda. Navaratana
× Ascda. Sunkist = Ascda. Sunfun
× Ascda. Tropicana = Ascda. Rapeepat
× Rnst. Queen Emma = Kom. Thonburi
× Rhctm. Sagarik = Rhctm. Siriporn
× V. bensonii = Ascda. Sarasiri
× V. coerulea = Ascda. Sara
× V. cristata = Ascda. Rumrill
× V. Eisenhower = Ascda. Darcey Starr
× V. Honolii = Ascda. Miami
× V. Jean Fukudo = Ascda. Kathy Erne
× V. Jeffrey = Ascda. Florida Sunset
× V. Joan Rothsand = Ascda. Captain Chor
× V. Laurel Yap = Ascda. Violet Yap
× V. Leslie H. Kagawa = Ascda. Kathleen Kagawa
× V. Low Kee Sing = Ascda. Aurora
× V. Lynne Sugihara = Ascda. Lani Girl
× V. Mary Fermin = Ascda. Chum Long
× V. Mary Foster = Ascda. Tiny June
× V. Nancy Rodillas = Ascda. Sisom
× V. parviflora = Ascda. Piyada
× V. Patricia Lee = Ascda. Pacalarann
× V. Prachark Chit = Ascda. Ladavan
× V. Sandamo = Ascda. Steere Noda
× V. Soo Hor Weng = Ascda. Hugo Freed
× V. Susan Lynn = Ascda. Honor First
× V. Takeji Ogawa = Ascda. Alicia Ono

ASCOCENTRUM

curvifolium†‡ (*continued*)

× V. tessellata	= Ascda. Carnival	× V. Winifred Kurihara	= Ascda. Winifred Hamamoto
× V. Thai	= Ascda. Khem Thai	× V. Yellowstone	= Ascda. Ham Reilly
× V. Trimerrill	= Ascda. Red Glow	× Vdps. parishii	= Ascdps. Scarlet Flame
× V. Tubtimtepya	= Ascda. Athit-Uthai		

miniatum†‡ — **species**

× ampullaceum	= Mona Church	× Rhctm. Sagarik	= Rhctm. Bangkae
× Aër. falcata	= Aërctm. Champatong	× Rhy. coelestis	= Rhctm. Ladda Gold
× Aër. odorata	= Aërctm. Chet Yod	× Rhy. gigantea	= Rhctm. Bumroongsoonthorn
× Ascda. Darcey Starr	= Ascda. Wimwawan	× Rhv. Bangkok Sky	= Vasco. Nutmeg Dolly
× Ascda. Meda Arnold	= Ascda. Pralor	× V. brunnea	= Ascda. Kitival
× Ascda. Medasand	= Ascda. Golden Glow	× V. denisoniana	= Ascda. Chaisiri
× Ascda. Ophelia	= Ascda. Monique	× V. Eisenhower	= Ascda. Maui Gold
× Dtps. Mem. Clarence Schubert	= Bdra. Melrose	× V. Onomea	= Ascda. Ella Freed
× Dor. pulcherrima	= Dctm. Pulcherrimin	× V. Rothschildiana	= Ascda. Pong
× Ren. storiei	= Rnctm. Voravut	× V. Tubtimtepya	= Ascda. Prachit Gold

MONA CHURCH	**miniatum × ampullaceum**	**Church 1972**
SAGARIK GOLD	**miniatum × curvifolium**	**Sagarik 1966**

× Ascda. Ophelia	= Ascda. Bangkok Gold	× Rhy. coelestis	= Rhctm. Petchburi Gold
× Ascda. Yip Sum Wah	= Ascda. Wacharin	× V. Onomea	= Ascda. Sagarik Shine
× Pthia. ctenoglossa	= Plctm. Suebsanguan	× V. Rothschildiana	= Ascda. Kasetsart Beauty
× Phal. equestris	= Ascps. Vivacious Vixen		

ASCOFINETIA

PEACHES‡	**Neof. falcata × Asctm. curvifolium**	**E. Iwanaga 1962**

× Lsa. teres	= Lscta. Rumrill	× Ren. monachica	= Rskra. Liliput

ASCOGLOSSUM

calopterum‡ — **species**

× Arach. Ishbel	= Arngm. Calobel	× Ren. monachica	= Rngm. Rumrill

ASCONOPSIS

FEETZ CORNWELL	**Irene Dobkin × Phal. lueddemanniana**	**Wallbrunn 1974**
IRENE DOBKIN	**Phal. Doris × Asctm. miniatum**	**Fredk. L. Thornton 1968**

× Phal. Dos Pueblos	= Rayna Wallbrunn	× Phal. lueddemanniana	= Feetz Cornwell
× Phal. Lady Doreen	= Sirena		

RAYNA WALLBRUNN	**Irene Dobkin × Phal. Dos Pueblos**	**Wallbrunn 1973**
SIRENA	**Irene Dobkin × Phal. Lady Doreen**	**R. K. Mizuta 1974**
VIVACIOUS VIXEN	**Phal. equestris × Asctm. Sagarik Gold**	**Perreira 1974**

ASCOVANDORITIS

JOHN MILLER	**Dor. pulcherrima × Ascda. Ophelia**	**Thornton's 1972 (Fredk. L. Thornton)**

ASPASIA

epidendroides†‡ — **species**

× Brs. lawrenceana	= Brap. Tiger Star	× Odm. Yellowstone Basin	= Aspgm. Copper Butte
× Odm. Grand Tetons	= Aspgm. Coyote Rocks	× Onc. forbesii	= Aspsm. Cherry-Pie

ASPASIA

lunata‡		**species**	
× Onc. papilio	= Aspsm. Rio Luna	|	
principissa*‡		**species**	
× Oda. Taw	= Lgra. Printaw	|	× Odm. Peggy Richardson = Aspgm. Peggy Richardson
variegata‡		**species**	
× Milt. regnellii	= Mpsa. Buff Ball	|	

ASPASIUM

CHERRY-PIE	**Asp. epidendroides × Onc. forbesii**	**Osment 1973**
RIO LUNA	**Onc. papilio × Asp. lunata**	**Ruben 1974**

ASPOGLOSSUM

COPPER BUTTE	**Asp. epidendroides × Odm. Yellowstone Basin**	**Beall 1973**
COYOTE ROCKS	**Asp. epidendroides × Odm. Grand Tetons**	**Beall 1973**
PEGGY RICHARDSON	**Asp. principissa × Odm. Peggy Richardson**	**Scardefield 1973**

BARBOSAARA

JOÃO RODRIGUES	**Wils. Insignis × Gom. recurva**	**W. W. G. Moir 1974**

BATEOSTYLIS

SILVER STAR	**Btmna. colleyi × Ost. brachystalix**	**George Black 1967**
× Zspm. labiosum	= Plmra. Raymond Palmer |	

BEALLARA

CARNIVAL	Mtssa. Vino × Oda. Apricot Meadows	**W. W. G. Moir 1975**
TAHOMA GLACIER	**Mtssa. Cartagena × Oda. Alaskan Sunset**	**Beall 1970 (W. W. G. Moir)**
× Onc. Elegance	= Gdlra. Stella Mizuta |	

BEARDARA

CHARLES BEARD	**Dtps. Red Coral × Asctm. miniatum**	**Beard 1970**
× Phal. Amber Sands	= Gertrude Beard |	
GERTRUDE BEARD	Phal. Amber Sands × Charles Beard	**Beard 1974**
MELROSE	**Dtps. Mem. Clarence Schubert × Asctm. miniatum**	**Hausermann 1973**

BOVORNARA

BOVORN BEAUTY	**Arach. hookerana × Vasco. Blue Fairy**	**Prayoonratana 1975**

BRADEARA

BRASIL	**Rdtta. Henry Teuscher × Gom. recurva**	**W. W. G. Moir 1973**

BRAPASIA

SERENE — **Asp. principissa × Brs. gireoudiana** — **W. W. G. Moir 1959**

× Milt. Fortaleza	= Fgtra. Mexico		

TIGER STAR — **Asp. epidendroides × Brs. lawrenceana** — **Withner 1974**

BRASSAVOLA

amazonica‡ (see *martiana‡*) — **species**

ARISTOCRAT — **glauca × digbyana** — **Roccaforte 1973 (Kern)**

cordata†‡ — **species**

(This is retained as the horticulturally recommended name for registration purposes, even though *subulifolia* is the botanically correct name for this species.)

× C. aurantiaca	= Bc. Elise White	× L. milleri	= Bl. Cordy Miller
× Epi. pabstii	= Bepi. Surprise		

cucullata*†‡ — **species**

× Epi. conopseum	= Bepi. Mini-Cu		

digbyana*†‡ — **species**

(This is retained as the horticulturally recommended name for registration purposes, even though *Rhyncholaelia digbyana* is the botanically correct name for this species.)

× glauca	= Aristocrat	× Blc. Spring and Summer	= Blc. Pennsylvania Spring
× nodosa	= Jimminey Cricket	× Blc. Zanturano	= Blc. Gloria Shouse
× perrinii	= Gerry Cassella	× C. Brabantiae	= Bc. Ellen Stampley
× Blc. Envy	= Blc. New England Spring	× C. Fulvescens	= Bc. Vivian Moore
× Blc. Golden Galleon	= Blc. Cristobel Kathleen Kock	× C. King George	= Bc. Marie Collette
		× C. maxima	= Bc. Terepaima
× Blc. Goldmine	= Blc. Mem. Walter Brown	× Lc. Elstead Gem	= Blc. Catnip
× Blc. Green Giant	= Blc. Vermonts Green Mountains	× Lc. Lagoon	= Blc. Trio
		× Lc. Lee Langford	= Blc. Sally Staggs
× Blc. Lester McDonald	= Blc. Mystic Mariner	× Schom. superbiens	= Smbv. Dipsy Doodle

fragrans* — **species**

× Slc. Anzac	= Pot. Little Suzie		

GERRY CASSELLA — **perrinii × digbyana** — **Withner 1972**

glauca*†‡ — **species**

(This is retained as the horticulturally recommended name for registration purposes, even though *Rhyncholaelia glauca* is the botanically correct name for this species.)

× digbyana	= Aristocrat	× C. Okami	= Bc. Glaucamora
× Bc. Déesse	= Bc. Memory Lane	× Epi. pseudepidendrum	= Bepi. Peggy Ann
× Blc. Nanette	= Blc. Laura Vandorn Schneider	× Lc. Antonica Fredrick	= Blc. Lothlorien
		× Lc. Gleneyrie	= Blc. Avon Kotae
× C. luteola	= Bc. Don Morrison	× Soph. coccinea	= Bnts. Claire Beaumont

JIMMINEY CRICKET — **nodosa × digbyana** — **Stewart Inc. 1974**

martiana‡ (syn. *amazonica‡*; syn. *multiflora*) — **species**

× C. forbesii	= Bc. Max Schneider		

multiflora (see *martiana‡*) — **species**

nodosa*†‡ — **species**

× digbyana	= Jimminey Cricket	× C. percivaliana	= Bc. Karin Lomer
× Blc. Dark Waters	= Blc. Merlin	× Epi. bifidum	= Bepi. Bifidosa
× Blc. Golden Slippers	= Blc. Gohl Lee	× Epi. plicatum	= Bepi. Plidosa
× Blc. Jane Helton	= Blc. Rio's Polka Dot	× Epi. pseudepidendrum	= Bepi. Pseudosa
× C. Claire Dreier	= Bc. Tara Rajcoomar	× Epi. radiatum	= Bepi. Moon Mist
× C. gaskelliana	= Bc. Little Sulema	× L. harpophylla	= Bl. Harposa
× C. Leona Bloom	= Bc. Mem. Harry Grimes	× Lc. Antonica Fredrick	= Blc. Binnie Foster
× C. luteola	= Bc. Sea Mist	× Lc. Golden Spring	= Blc. Rio's Spring
× C. North Star	= Bc. Pelleas	× Lc. Helen Mizuta	= Blc. Joan Bramwell

BRASSAVOLA

nodosa*†‡ (*continued*)

× Lc. Lee Langford	= Blc. Enigma Variations	× Lc. Zada Fields	= Blc. Naples Night
× Lc. Lorraine Shirai	= Blc. Keowee	× Sl. Betty Jean Scott	= Low. Peter Whyte
× Lc. Mem. Maria Miranda	= Blc. Mem. Josefa Martinez	× Slc. Anzac	= Pot. Melisande

perrinii*‡ **species**

× digbyana	= Gerry Cassella	× C. labiata	= Bc. Perula
× C. Christina Waglay	= Bc. Snow Waltz	× C. schillerana	= Bc. Candy Star
× C. forbesii	= Bc. Brazil		

subulifolia (see *cordata*†‡) **species**

BRASSIA

antherotes‡ **species**

× Odm. wyattianum = Odbrs. Inca

caudata†‡ **species**

× Onc. sphacelatum = Brsdm. Moonbeam

gireoudiana†‡ **species**

× Milt. Crimson Crest	= Mtssa. Jet Setter	× Onc. chrysornis	= Brsdm. Golden Delicious

lawrenceana* **species**

× Asp. epidendroides = Brap. Tiger Star

longissima†‡ **species**

× Onc. maculatum	= Brsdm. Fiesta	× Onc. wentworthianum	= Brsdm. Gilded Urchin

maculata†‡ **species**

× Milt. spectabilis	= Mtssa Fort George Beauty	× Onc. pulchellum	= Brsdm. Lady in Red
		× Onc. splendidum	= Brsdm. Mayan Dancer

REX **verrucosa × gireoudiana** **W. W. G. Moir 1964**

× Milt. Cogniauxiae	= Mtssa. Copan	× Milt. Minas Gerais	= Mtssa. Olmec
× Milt. Ka Moi	= Mtssa. Bill Burke		

BRASSIDIUM

ALOHA	**Gemini × Onc. forbesii**	**Ciesinski 1975 (W. W. G. Moir)**
FIESTA	**Onc. maculatum × Brs. longissima**	**Rumrill 1973 (Jost & Rumrill)**
GEMINI	**Brs. gireoudiana × Onc. crispum**	**W. W. G. Moir 1965**

× Onc. forbesii = Aloha

GILDED URCHIN	**Brs. longissima × Onc. wentworthianum**	**Rod McLellan Co. 1971**
GOLDEN DELICIOUS	**Brs. gireoudiana × Onc. chrysornis**	**Beall 1973 (W. W. G. Moir)**
LADY IN RED	**Brs. maculata × Onc. pulchellum**	**W. W. G. Moir 1973**
MAYAN DANCER	**Brs. maculata × Onc. splendidum**	**W. W. G. Moir 1971**
MOONBEAM	**Onc. sphacelatum × Brs. caudata**	**Crestwood 1974**

BRASSOCATTLEYA

ALBION*†‡	**Thorntonii × C. trianaei**		**L. 1921**
× Blc. Glorious	= Blc. Comet Kohoutek		
ALIZÉ	**C. Marie-José × Liesbeth Hacke**		**F. 1972**
ALOOWA	**C. Empress Bells × Mount Anderson**		**Bonniewood 1971**
ANDRÉ GUTTIN*†	Digbyano-trianaei × C. Hardyana		**Guttin 1928**
× L. anceps	= Blc. Charles Hagan		
ANN LATHAM	**Mount Hood × Evelyn Zuck**		**O. Kirsch 1973**
ANN SLADDEN†‡	**Digbyano-mossiae × C. Souv. de Louis Sander**		**Sladden 1946**
× C. Catherine Patterson	= Felice Dickson		
ANTON	**Antwerp × Cliftonii**		**Katsuura 1968**
× Lc. Bonanza	= Blc. Bonton		
BARQUISIMETO	Languedoc × C. lueddemanniana		**J. & S. 1975**
BELLTRAYNE	**Marie Marie × C. Bow Bells**		**A. J. Bell 1974**
BERANEE	**C. Rita Renee × Berangere**		**Stewart Inc. 1972**
BERANGERE	**Déesse × C. Hardyana**		**Pff. V. & L. 1958**
× Déesse × C. Dubiosa	= Feria = Heart's Desire	× C. Rita Renee	= Beranee
BILL WORSLEY	**B. nodosa × C. aurantiaca**		**Fouraker 1965 (Fort Caroline)**
× Blc. Limelight × Lc. Antonica Fredrick	= Blc. Galadriel = Blc. Merry	× Lc. Fiery × Lc. Red Empress	= Blc. Magic = Blc. Empress Worsley
BRAZIL	**B. perrinii × C. forbesii**		**Withner 1972 (Originator unknown)**
× L. grandis	= Blc. Day And Night		
CALDARELLO	**Henrietta × C. bowringiana**		**Pff. V. & L. 1971**
CALYPSO	**B. digbyana × C. bicolor**		**H. 1908**
× Blc. Fortune	= Blc. Calypso Singer	× L. Zip	= Blc. Calyzip
CANDY STAR	**B. perrinii × C. schillerana**		**Limberlost 1971**
CHARLOTTE AMALIE	C. Estelle × Déesse		**J. & S. 1974**
CHESTY PULLER	**Déesse × C. Empress Bells**		**Stewart Inc. 1974 (A. & R.)**
C. H. LANKESTER†	**C. Snow White × B. digbyana**		**B. 1951**
× C. Bow Bells	= Enid Oppenheim		
CONFIDENCE	**Languedoc × C. Joyce Hannington**		**Pff. V. & L. 1974**
CORNELIUS‡	**C. Rembrandt × Hartland**		**M. Yamada 1960**
× Lc. Valor	= Blc. Brandon	× Smbl. Maunalani	= Recc. Dr. Harry Arnold
COTTON CANDY	**Mount Anderson × Mount Hood**		**J. & S. 1974**
DAFFODIL†‡	**B. glauca × C. aurantiaca**		**Fennell 1949**
× Blc. Kathy Krugman × Blc. Malvern × Blc. Mellowglow × C. Varuna × Epc. Lily Moody	= Blc. Parakeet = Blc. Malodil = Blc. Ann Kientzy = Mem. Leighton Long = Vnra. Ressie Toy	× Lc. Adolph Hecker × Lc. Antonica Fredrick × Lc. Flirtie × Lc. Pixie Gold × Soph. coccinea	= Blc. Renee Nicolson = Blc. Voo Doo = Blc. Lorrito = Blc. Daffy Pixie = Rolf. Little Mountain
DÉESSE†‡	**Ferriéres × C. Lamartine**		**V. 1947**
× Berangere × B. glauca × Blc. Fortune	= Feria = Memory Lane = Blc. Fortunes Smile	× Blc. Harlequin × Blc. Jane Helton × Blc. Luis H. Yanes	= Blc. Jane Paton = Blc. Linden Lime = Blc. Nuuanu Dawn

DÉESSE†‡ (*continued*)

× Blc. Normoma	= Blc. Norméesse	× C. trianaei	= Tridees
× Blc. Tiara	= Blc. Steven Holguin	× C. Tribells	= Faithful Star
× C. Bertie DeMartini	= Palais de Glace	× Lc. Blue Boy	= Blc. Rosemary Hayden
× C. Empress Bells	= Chesty Puller	× Lc. Bonanza	= Blc. Cherry Paradise
× C. Estelle	= Charlotte Amalie	× Lc. Dolores Hoyt	= Blc. Cheeri-Lee
× C. Mount Shasta	= Minnie Bath	× Lc. Fedora	= Blc. Meditation
× C. Night Watch	= Reflection Lake	× Lc. Hertha	= Blc. Hertéesse
× C. Old Whitey	= Princess Teresa	× Pot. Lemon Tree	= Pot. Golden Sands
× C. Princess Bells	= Prachuab	× Slc. Brandywine	= Pot. Cherry Blossom
× C. Suavior	= Marasri		

DIGBYANO-MOSSIAE*† **B. digbyana × C. mossiae** **Veitch 1889**
(syn. Veitchii†)

× C. Trithena = Marenore

DOCTOR A. KOSKY†‡ **Tova × C. labiata** **Ozzella 1948**

× Lc. Joseph Hampton = Blc. Morris Gunderson | × Lc. Laurie Lynn = Blc. Stanton Berman

DOCTOR STEPHEN GIBBS **C. Daniel Ryerson × Hartland** **W. L. Smith 1971**
DON MORRISON **B. glauca × C. luteola** **D. Morrison 1971**
DORIS† **Mme. Charles Maron × C. Lord Rothschild** **B. 1915**

× Lc. Bonanza = Blc. Dorbon

DOROTHY MARCUS **Mount Hood × Joya** **O. Kirsch 1972**
EAGLE‡ **Hartland × C. Belgica** **Gore 1954**

× Blc. Molflora = Blc. Jack Hatfield

EAST DEAN **British Queen × C. Leda** **L. 1950**

× C. Nigritian = Mem. Bill Kerns

ELISE WHITE **C. aurantiaca × B. cordata** **W. E. White 1974**
(Originator unknown)
ELLEN STAMPLEY **C. Brabantiae × B. digbyana** **Stampley 1972**
(Dewey)
EMILY TERUKO **C. Edithiae × Sonia** **Mrs. H. Kanemitsu 1972**
(Kanemitsu)
ENID OPPENHEIM C. H. Lankester × C. Bow Bells **B. 1971**
ESTO GILLETT **C. Gay Bells × Mount Hood** **M. J. Bates 1975**
EVELYN ZUCK‡ **Sonia × C. Brussels** **Zuck 1956**
(O. Kirsch)

× Mount Hood	= Ann Latham	× C. Rembrandt	= Remelyn
× Blc. Norman's Bay	= Blc. Pigeon Bay	× L. purpurata	= Blc. Romania Woolley

FAITHFUL STAR **Déesse × C. Tribells** **J. & S. 1974**
FELICE DICKSON **Bc. Ann Sladden × C. Catherine Patterson** **Goff 1973**
(A. Jackson)
FERIA **Déesse × Berangere** **Pff. V. & L. 1974**
FERRIÈRES‡ **B. digbyana × C. Dionysius** **Chassaing 1942**

× C. Joyce Hannington = Mae Campbell | × C. Mlle. Louise Pauwels = Folies Bergeres

FOLIES BERGERES **Ferrières × C. Mlle. Louise Pauwels** **Pff. V. & L. 1975**
FOULARD **Pastoral × C. Idettae** **F. 1972**
GLADYS CHAPMAN **C. Cooksonii × Olna** **Chapman 1974**
(Originator unknown)
GLAUCAMORA **B. glauca × C. Okami** **O. Kirsch 1972**
GOLDEN SUNSHINE **Daffodil × C. aurantiaca** **W. W. G. Moir 1969**

× Sl. Psyche = Pot. Managua

GRANPRAE — **Praetii × C. granulosa** — **Stewart Inc. 1975 (Rehfield)**

GREEN DAWN — **B. glauca × C. granulosa** — **O. Kirsch 1962**

× C. schillerana = Green Star
× Lc. Gladys Millner = Blc. Kaena
× Lc. Rosa Kirsch = Blc. Kalakoa

GREEN MEADOW — **Olympic Meadows × Mount Hood** — **A. & R. 1973**
GREEN STAR — **Green Dawn × C. schillerana** — **Dewey 1971**
GREEN SURREY — C. forbesii × Praetii — **Edelbrock 1972**
GROGANIAE — **B. digbyana × C. loddigesii** — **Grogan —**

× C. dowiana = Saturday Special

HARRY RUBENS — **Mount Hood × Hartland** — **R. H. Rubens 1975**
HARTLAND*†‡ — **Hannibal × C. Leda** — **L. 1933**

× Mount Hood = Harry Rubens
× Blc. Wake Island = Blc. My Pride
× C. Daniel Ryerson = Doctor Stephen Gibbs
× C. Portia = Portland
× Lc. California = Blc. Hartcal
× Lc. Elizabeth Off = Blc. Cherokee Chief
× Lc. Hurricane = Blc. Lara
× Lc. José Dias Castro = Blc. Helena Tricca
× Lc. Nigrescent = Blc. Rio Tampa
× Lc. Twinkle Star = Blc. Starland
× Slc. Naomi Kerns = Pot. Grindal Shoals

HEART'S DESIRE — **C. Dubiosa × Berangere** — **Stewart Inc. 1973**
HEATHER CAMPBELL — **Mount Hood × C. White Swan** — **A. & R. 1973**
HEATONENSIS*†‡ — **B. digbyana × C. Hardyana** — **C. 1902**

× Blc. Mem. Crispin Rosales = Blc. Heaton Rosales
× Lc. Mem. Maggie Hood = Blc. Florence Lockhart

HELENA DOERING — **Marthe Gratiot × C. Odalisque** — **Doering 1974**
HENRIETTA* — **Mantinariae × C. amabilis** — **V. 1927**

× C. bowringiana = Caldarello

HERB MOSLEY — **C. Karae Lyn Sugiyama × North Columbia** — **Warren 1975**
HULA GIRL‡ — **Mrs. J. Leemann × C. Delphin** — **R. E. Warne 1945**

× Lc. Sunburn = Blc. Sunny Sands

IMPERIAL NOBILIOR — **C. walkerana × Imperialis** — **J. & S. 1971**
IMPERIALIS*†‡ — **Cliftonii × C. mossiae** — **Cunliffe 1918**

× C. walkerana = Imperial Nobilior

JOYA — **C. Joyce Hannington × Talahina** — **M. Yamada 1962**

× Mount Hood = Dorothy Marcus

JUNE BENNETT — **Swan Mountain × C. Charlotte Sell** — **M. J. Bates 1975**
KARIN LOMER — **C. percivaliana × B. nodosa** — **H. Graf 1974 (Blaumann)**

LANGUEDOC‡ — **Déesse × C. Mem. Rosemary** — **Pff. V. & L. 1956**

× C. Joyce Hannington = Confidence
× C. lueddemanniana = Barquisimeto

LEEMANNIAE (see Mrs. J. Leemann*†‡)
LIESBETH HACKE† — **Sindoro × C. Woltersiana** — **F. 1936**

× C. Marie-José = Alizé

LIM THENG HIN — **C. Bow Bells × B. digbyana** — **Ng & Tan 1957 (M. & H.)**

× C. Bob Betts = Oriel Nevins

LINDA BERG — **Mount St. Helens × C. Empress Bells** — **Bonniewood 1971**
LITTLE SULEMA — **B. nodosa × C. gaskelliana** — **Raymond Palmer 1975**
MAE CAMPBELL — **C. Joyce Hannington × Ferrières** — **Pelc 1972**

MAIACA — **Maikai × C. aurantiaca** — **Voo Doo Orchids 1974**

MAIKAI — **B. nodosa × C. bowringiana** — **Hirose 1944**

× C. aurantiaca	= Maiaca	× Lc. Ronselensis	= Blc. Royal Harbor

MARASRI — **Déesse × C. Suavior** — **Boonphyoong 1972**

× Blc. Acapana	= Blc. Chaweevan

MARENORE — **Digbyano-mossiae × C. Trithena** — M. T. Swartz 1972 (Bachman)

MARIE COLLETTE — **C. King George × B. digbyana** — **W. L. Smith 1971 (Ryerson)**

MARIE MARIE*†‡ — **Ilene × C. Clotho** — **F. E. Dixon 1931**

× C. Bow Bells	= Belltrayne

MARS*†‡ — **Mrs. J. Leemann × C. Maggie Raphael** — **A. & B. 1915**

× Blc. Golden Galleon	= Blc. Kim Ann Bauer

MARTHE GRATIOT — **(parentage unknown)** — **Gratiot —**

× C. Odalisque	= Helena Doering

MAUNA PUHALA — **Seafoam × C. Princess Bells** — **Otaguro 1971**

MAX SCHNEIDER — **C. forbesii × B. martiana** — **Schneider 1975 (M. J. Bates)**

MEMORIA BILL KERNS — **East Dean × C. Nigritian** — **R. Nevins 1972**

MEMORIA HARRY GRIMES — **B. nodosa × C. Leona Bloom** — **Church 1975**

MEMORIA JOHN DICKINSON — **C. Bow Bells × Mount Hood** — **C. E. Dickinson 1973 (Hoyt)**

MEMORIA LEIGHTON LONG — **Daffodil × C. Varuna** — **H. L. Long 1972**

MEMORY LANE — **Déesse × B. glauca** — **Crothers 1975**

MINNIE BATH — **Déesse × C. Mount Shasta** — **Bath 1974 (A. & R.)**

MOON MISS — **C. Myron A. Hofer × Mount Hood** — **Rod McLellan Co. 1971**

MOUNT ANDERSON‡ — **C. Bow Bells × Déesse** — **Beall 1962**

× Mount Hood	= Cotton Candy	× Lc. Congo	= Blc. Congo Mountain
× C. Empress Bells	= Aloowa	× Lc. Magadha	= Blc. Floradora
× Lc. Bonanza	= Blc. Teng		

MOUNT HOOD‡ — **Déesse × C. Claris** — **Beall 1962**

× Evelyn Zuck	= Ann Latham	× C. Gay Bells	= Esto Gillett
× Hartland	= Harry Rubens	× C. General Patton	= Pink Cloud
× Joya	= Dorothy Marcus	× C. Myron A. Hofer	= Moon Miss
× Mount Anderson	= Cotton Candy	× C. White Swan	= Heather Campbell
× Olympic Meadows	= Green Meadow	× Lc. Amber Glow	= Blc. Sunwapta Peak
× Blc. Green-heart	= Blc. Martha McAllister	× Lc. Bonanza	= Blc. Cannes Festival
× Blc. Nacouchee	= Blc. Lingerie	× Lc. Excellency	= Blc. Brilliant Wings
× Blc. Norman's Bay	= Blc. Granite Bay	× Lc. Walter Slagle	= Blc. Beauford Fisher
× C. Bow Bells	= Mem. John Dickinson	× Lc. Yolo	= Blc. Yolo Hood
× C. Estelle	= Trudy Baker		

MOUNT JUNEAU — **Déesse × C. Mount Baker** — **Beall 1963**

× Lc. Resolution Mountain	= Blc. Redoubt Mountain

MOUNT SAINT HELENS‡ — **Déesse × C. Helen Durfee** — **Beall 1962**

× C. amethystoglossa	= Yachats	× C. Empress Bells	= Linda Berg

MRS. J. LEEMANN*†‡ — **B. digbyana × C. dowiana** — **Maron 1902**
(syn. Leemanniae)

× Pot. Dorothy L. Adair	= Pot. Memoria Arthur Armbrister

BRASSOCATTLEYA

NORTH COLUMBIA — **Cliftonville × C. Prospector** — **Bracey 1952**
× C. Karae Lyn Sugiyama = Herb Mosley

OLNA†‡ — **Digbyano-mossiae × C. Hassallii** — **C. 1934**
× C. Cooksonii = Gladys Chapman

OLYMPIC MEADOWS — **Déesse × C. guttata** — **Beall 1966**
× Mount Hood = Green Meadow | × Blc. Rain Forest = Blc. Moss Creek Gorge

ORIEL NEVINS — **Lim Theng Hin × C. Bob Betts** — **R. Nevins 1973 (McFarlane)**

PALAIS DE GLACE — **Déesse × C. Bertie DeMartini** — **Rod McLellan Co. 1975**

PASTORAL‡ — **C. Mlle. Louise Pauwels × Déesse** — **Altenburg 1961**
× C. Idettae = Foulard | × Lc. Paradisio = Blc. Oswaldo Paulino Santos

PATRICIA PORTIA — **C. Portia × Princess Patricia** — **Gauda 1974**

PELLEAS — **B. nodosa × C. North Star** — **Voo Doo Orchids 1974**

PERULA — **B. perrinii × C. labiata** — **Withner 1973**

PINK CLOUD — **C. General Patton × Mount Hood** — **Casa Luna 1973 (Beall)**

PLUTO* — **B. digbyana × C. granulosa** — **H. 1907**
× Blc. Moonglow = Blc. Limestone

PORTLAND — **C. Portia × Hartland** — **G. H. Payne 1972 (Ozzella)**

PRACHUAB — **C. Princess Bells × Déesse** — **T. Orchids 1975**

PRAETII‡ — B. digbyana × C. guttata — **Praet 1904**
× C. forbesii = Green Surrey | × C. granulosa = Granprae

PRINCESS PATRICIA*†‡ — **Cliftonii × C. Enid** — **C. 1919**
× C. Portia = Patricia Portia

PRINCESS TERESA — **Déesse × C. Old Whitey** — **Barnett 1974 (A. & R.)**

REFLECTION LAKE — **C. Night Watch × Déesse** — **Beall 1973**
× Pot. Hidden Peak = Pot. Hidden Chasm

REMELYN — **C. Rembrandt × Evelyn Zuck** — **W. W. G. Moir 1971**

SATURDAY SPECIAL — **C. dowiana × Groganiae** — **Stevenson 1973**

SEAFOAM†‡ — **Albion × C. Cooksonii** — **L. 1941**
× C. Estelle = Seastelle | × Lc. Blanchflava = Blc. Yellow Sea
× C. Princess Bells = Mauna Puhala

SEA MIST — **B. nodosa × C. luteola** — **Rod McLellan Co. 1975**

SEASTELLE — **Seafoam × C. Estelle** — **Kensington 1973**

S. M. DAMON†‡ — **B. digbyana × C. Mrs. Edward Roehrs** — Miyamoto 1946
× Blc. Samoset = Blc. Emily Simmons

SNOW WALTZ — **C. Christina Waglay × B. perrinii** — **Rod McLellan Co. 1972**

SONIA*†‡ — **B. digbyana × C. Hesta** — **C. 1934**
× C. Edithiae = Emily Teruko

SPECIOSA*†‡ — **Digbyano-mendelii × C. schroderae** — **Maron 1908**
× Slc. Anzac = Pot. Specizac

STAR RUBY — **B. nodosa × C. Batalinii** — **W. W. G. Moir 1965**
× Lc. Carrie Estelle = Blc. Star Topaz

SWAN MOUNTAIN — **Mount Hood × C. Francis T. C. Au** — **Beall 1969**
× C. Charlotte Sell = June Bennett

BRASSOCATTLEYA

TAQUIN‡	**Ferrières × C. Odalisque**		**V. 1949**
× Lc. Princess	= Blc. Opal Wilde		
TARA RAJCOOMAR	**B. nodosa × C. Claire Dreier**		**Raymond Palmer 1975**
TEREPAIMA	**C. maxima × B. digbyana**		**Jesurún 1972**
THALIE	**Déesse × C. Odalisque**		**V. 1955**
× Lc. Gaillard	= Blc. Georges Morel		
THE GLOBE*†‡	**Cliftonii × C. trianaei**		**A. & B. 1924**
× Blc. Norman's Bay	= Blc. Globe Bay		
TRIDEES	**Deésse × C. trianaei**		**Stewart Inc. 1975**
TRUDY BAKER	**Mount Hood × C. Estelle**		**John Baker 1971**
VEITCHII† (see Digbyano-mossiae*†)			
VIVIAN MOORE	**C. Fulvescens × B. digbyana**		**Robt. Smith 1973**
WHITE BALL‡	**Bruges × C. George Eastman**		**Chung-Chweng Chen 1960**
× Blc. Yellow Peril	= Blc. Yellow Ball		
YACHATS	**C. amethystoglossa × Mount St. Helens**		**Bonniewood 1971**

BRASSOEPIDENDRUM

BIFIDOSA	**B. nodosa × Epi. bifidum**	**Osment 1972**
MINI-CU	**Epi. conopseum × B. cucullata**	**Rumrill 1975 (Jost & Rumrill)**
MOON MIST	**B. nodosa × Epi. radiatum**	**Osment 1972**
PEGGY ANN	**Epi. pseudepidendrum × B. glauca**	**Kosel 1971**
PLIDOSA	**B. nodosa × Epi. plicatum**	**J. M. Ward 1974 (Voo Doo Orchids)**
PSEUDOSA	**B. nodosa × Epi. pseudepidendrum**	**Voo Doo Orchids 1974**
SURPRISE	**B. cordata × Epi. pabstii**	**Rumrill 1974**

BRASSOLAELIA

CORDY MILLER	**B. cordata × L. milleri**		**W. W. G. Moir 1971**
HARPOSA	**B. nodosa × L. harpophylla**		**Voo Doo Orchids 1974**
ILIMA	**B. glauca × L. Firefly**		**W. W. G. Moir 1962**
× Lc. Little Sunbeam	= Blc. Mokihana		
SEA URCHIN	**L. anceps × B. glauca**		**Rod McLellan Co. 1964**
× C. forbesii	= Blc. Ativa	× C. R.(owena) Prowe	= Blc. Ocean Spray

BRASSOLAELIOCATTLEYA

ACAPANA‡	**Lc. Grandee × Green-heart**		**Bracey 1961**
× Citron Pass	= Elysian Fields	× Lc. Amber Glow	= Jitra
× Gold Coast	= Fulton Rice Miller	× Lc. Edgard van Belle	= Aspen Inlet
× Malworth	= Belle Stewart	× Lc. Waianae Sunset	= Mount Garibaldi
× Nanette	= Helen Huntington	× Pot. Gordon Siu	= Pot. Troublesome Creek
× Bc. Marasri	= Chaweevan	× Pot. Spanish Banks	= Pot. Mem. Grace Sokolowski
× C. aurantiaca	= Gaiety		
× C. Iris	= Ed O'Neal	× Pot. Sunset Bay	= Pot. Ruben's Sunset
× C. Nellie Roberts	= Margie Dickie		
ACCLAIM	**Xanthette × Malvern**		**Rod McLellan Co. 1975**
ACHILLES SHOAL	**Herons Ghyll × C. Bow Bells**		**Beall 1965**
× Zanget	= Mem. Darrel Cole		
AFRICAN QUEEN	**Helen Morita × Joyance**		**Stewart Inc. 1973**

BRASSOLAELIOCATTLEYA

AGNES HAYNES	**Lc. Lollypop × Agnes McWilliams**	**J. Milton Warne 1972**
AGNES McWILLIAMS*†‡	**Bl. Helen × C. Leda**	**Duke Farms 1935**
× Lc. Lollypop	= Agnes Haynes	
ALICE MULLER‡	**Lc. Lee Langford × Ojai**	**Toy 1955**
× Shining Harvest	= Norma Bee	
ALLISON MELINDA WALLAR	**Connie Wallar × Helen Morita**	**Spencer 1975** (Wallar)
ALMA KEE	**Lc. Alma × Cheah Bean-Kee**	**Miyamoto 1975**
AMANDA GIBSON·	**Zeecrabbe × C. Sudan**	**Coastal Gdns. 1964**
× Lc. Mrs. Medo	= Dream Queen	
AMENITY	**Lc. Mercia × Rising Sun**	**Rod McLellan Co. 1973**
AMERICAN FRONTIER	**Painted Desert × Bobby Ward**	**Stewart Inc. 1974**
AMERICAN HERITAGE	**Golden Slippers × Fortune**	**Stewart Inc. 1974**
AMY WAKASUGI	**Lc. Bonanza × Herons Ghyll**	**Wakasugi 1966**
× Lc. Bonanza	= Fall Splendor	
ANGELA STARKE	**Pastel × C. Ruth M. Johnston**	**H. R. Starke 1973 (Yasuda)**
ANN	**Caligula × Lc. Cassandra**	**A. 1940**
× Lc. Irene Finney	= Terrie	
ANN FORTUNE	**Lc. Ann Follis × Fortune**	**Stewart Inc. 1975**
ANN KIENTZY	**Bc. Daffodil × Mellowglow**	**Pallister 1974**
ANTOINETTE*†	**Bl. Helen × C. Portia**	**Colman 1917**
× C. Porcia	= Christine Barfield	
APERTIF	**Sundust × Pacific Gold**	**Rod McLellan Co. 1975 (Originator unknown)**
APRICA*†‡	**The Baroness × Lc. Ixion**	**C. 1927**
× Lc. Mem. Albert Heinecke	= Oro Rico	
ARMIDA†‡	**Ophelia × Bc. Mrs. John Netherway**	**C. 1943**
× Golden Queen	= Dr. Kinji Hisazaki	
× Lc. Twinkle Star	= Twilight Time	
ART BANTA	**Momercia × Lc. Manila**	**Rod McLellan Co. 1971**
ASHIYA	**Lc. Balkis × Nai Thong Leng**	**Miyamoto 1966**
× Norman's Bay	= Margaret Way	
ASPEN INLET	**Acapana × Lc. Edgard van Belle**	**Beall 1973**
ATIVA	**Bl. Sea Urchin × C. forbesii**	**Gerbig 1973**
AUTUMN GHYLL	**Lc. Autumn Symphony × Herons Ghyll**	**Muse's 1971**
AUTUMN GLORY	Summer Shades × Lc. Gatton Glory	**Rod McLellan Co. 1972**
AUTUMN GLOW	**Jane Helton × C. bicolor**	**Lines 1965**
× C. bicolor	= Green Goddess	
AVON KOTAE	**Lc. Gleneyrie × B. glauca**	**Fort Caroline 1973 (O/Oshtemo)**
AZTEC PRINCESS	**Lc. Morro Rock × Herons Ghyll**	**A. & R. 1966**
× Lucky Strike	= Pis-Vimol	
× C. Dark Emperor	= Black Mesa	
BABY DOLL	**Pastel × Pearl Harbor**	**A. & R. 1959**
× C. Esbetts	= Nickie Holguin	
BARBARA O'BRIEN	**Camilla × Edith McLeod**	**O'Brien 1972**
BEACON MOUNTAIN	**C. Interglossa × Coronet Bay**	**Beall 1975**

BRASSOLAELIOCATTLEYA

BEARPAW MOUNTAIN — C. Okami × Coronet Bay — Beall 1975
BEAUFORD FISHER — Lc. Walter Slagle × Bc. Mount Hood — Rod McLellan Co. 1971
BELLE STEWART — Acapana × Malworth — J. & S. 1973
BENIN BRONZE — Camilla × Xanthedo — Jeals 1967

× Otomayim = Sun Trail

BETTY BORER — Jane Helton × Lc. Charlesworthii — Fort Caroline 1973
BETTY MIDKIFF — C. Elizabeth Anderson × Norman's Bay — Midkiff 1975
BETTY MOE‡ — L. cinnabarina × Green-heart — Fouraker 1959 (Bracey)

× Lc. Gladys Millner = Winnie The Pooh

BIG CANARY PEAKS — Lc. Flavius × Klondike Belle — Beall 1975
BILLYE — Polka Dot × Lc. Lorraine Shirai — Irving 1971 (Small)

BISCAYNE SKIES — Mem. Ruth Gessner × Lc. Blue Boy — Fields Orchids 1972
BINNIE FOSTER — B. nodosa × Lc. Antonica Fredrick — Church 1975
BIT-OF-GOLD — Lc. Rojo × Bouton D'Or — Wilkins 1975
BLACK MESA — Aztec Princess × C. Dark Emperor — A. & R. 1973
BLANCHE CARTER — Lc. Integrity × Norman's Bay — A. & R. 1961

× Lc. Cuesta = Kona Reef

BLANCHE OKAMOTO†‡ — Lc. Canberra × Nanette — Kodama 1952

× Goldenette	= Dawn Song	× Llewellyn	= Lleblanche
× Jane Helton	= Sahara Sand		

BOBBYDON — Lc. Medon × Bobby Ward — R. K. Meredith 1973 (Hopson)

BOBBY WARD — Joyance × Lc. Grandee — A. & R. 1964

× Fortune	= Royal Fortune	× Painted Desert	= American Frontier
× Gold City	= Gold Wood	× Lc. Medon	= Bobbydon
× Golden Galleon	= Norma Briscoe	× Lc. Western Sunset	= Corcoran Sunset
× Joyance	= Copper Hill		

BOLD RULER — James Hausermann × Lc. George Baldwin — Hausermann 1975
BOMERCIA — Momercia × Lc. Bonanza — Stewart Inc. 1972
BONDARK — Lc. Bonanza × Dark Waters — Altenburg 1972
BONITA — Yellow Imp × C. aurantiaca — Voo Doo Orchids 1974
BONNIE WARREN — Lc. Charlie Stem × Mem. Crispin Rosales — Warren 1974
BONTON — Bc. Anton × Lc. Bonanza — Katsuura 1973
BOUTON D'OR — C. Wolteriana × Buttercup — Small 1968

× C. aurantiaca	= Gold Bug	× Lc. Red Gold	= Debba-Doo
× Lc. Pixie Gold	= Yellow Buttons	× Lc. Rojo	= Bit-of-Gold

BRANDON — Bc. Cornelius × Lc. Valor — Naugle 1975
BRILLIANT WINGS — Lc. Excellency × Bc. Mount Hood — A. & R. 1973
BRITESIDE — Lc. Western Sunset × Setting Sun — Rod McLellan Co. 1973
BRYCE CANYON — Nacost × Patricia Purves — A. & R. 1973
BULLION GOLD — C. Balu × Mellowglow — Lenette 1974 (Rivermont)

BUTTERCUP‡ — Primate × Golden Myth — Rivermont 1961

× Glorious	= Green Apple	× Nanette	= Neil McDade
× Golden Galleon	= Road to Mandalay	× Setting Sun	= Oleo
× Goldmine	= Will Bates	× C. mendelii	= Ruth Cline McDade
× Honeybee	= Honeycup	× L. milleri	= California Sunset
× Iliad	= Mem. Amelia Bertsch	× Lc. Amber Glow	= Dandy Lion
× Missy	= Mary Crocker	× Lc. Thurderniana	= Donna Gillis

BRASSOLAELIOCATTLEYA

Name	Parentage	Registrant
CALDRON	Lc. Western Sunset × Mamie Fouraker	Rod McLellan Co. 1974 (Fordyce)
CALIFORNIA FANTASY	Lc. Dormaniana × Golden Slippers	Pabst 1975
CALIFORNIA SPECIAL	Mamie Fouraker × Painted Desert	Crothers 1973
CALIFORNIA SUNSET	Buttercup × L. milleri	Spencer 1973
CALYPSO SINGER	Bc. Calypso × Fortune	Stewart Inc. 1974
CALYZIP	L. Zip × Bc. Calypso	Stewart Inc. 1975
CAMILLA‡	Zamilla × Capella	Jeal 1956
× Edith McLeod = Barbara O'Brien		
CANARI*†	Joan × C. Empress Frederick	F. 1931
× Lc. Bergamote = Zafaran	× Lc. Mem. Albert Heinecke = Yap Eng Hoe	
CANDEE	Lc. Laurie Lynn × Molflora	Rivermont 1971
CANNES FESTIVAL	Lc. Bonanza × Bc. Mount Hood	Katsuura 1973
CARLY HAUSERMANN	Fleur de Lys × Lc. Bruno Alberts	Hauserman 1965
× Lc. Nelly Corradi = Gale Nigro		
CARMEN CESTERO	Sunflame × Lc. Bonanza	W. S. Murray 1965 (Hoyt)
× Lc. Nigrescent = Ruby Watanabe		
CARMEN JIMINEZ‡	C. General Pulteney × The Baroness	Fields Orchids 1957
× Golden Myth = Golden Beach		
CAROL BOUDEMAN	Sunkist × C. Iris	Fort Caroline 1973 (Wallbrunn)
CATNIP	Lc. Elstead Gem × B. digbyana	Pabst 1975
CHARLES HAGAN	Bc. André Guttin × L. anceps	Hagan 1973
CHAWEEVAN	Bc. Marasri × Acapana	Boonphyoong 1972
CHEAH BEAN-KEE	Lc. Los Angeles × Norman's Bay	Ng. & Tan 1964 (Kirch)
× Lc. Alma = Alma Kee		
CHEERI-LEE	Bc. Déesse × Lc. Dolores Hoyt	R. Shaw 1972 (Juanita Nurs.)
CHEROKEE CHIEF	Lc. Elizabeth Off. × Bc. Hartland	Crestwood 1974
CHERRY PARADISE	Lc. Bonanza × Bc. Déesse	Katsuura 1975
CHIC JARDINE	Lc. Issy × Mem. Crispin Rosales	George Black 1974
CHIEF JOSEPH†‡	Bc. Durga × Lc. Mrs. Medo	A. & R. 1942
× C. Priscilla Ward = War Eagle		
CHIEF OSCEOLA	Lc. Cassandra × Norman's Bay	Fort Caroline 1972 (Crookshank)
CHINESE JADE	C. guttata × Greenwich	Stewart Inc. 1973
CHRISTINE BARFIELD	C. Porcia × Antoinette	Coastal Gdns. 1973
CHUNG-CHWENG CHEN	Kuo Kuang × Norman's Bay	Hong-Sie Chen 1975 (Chung-Chweng Chen)
CINDITA	Lc. Luminosa × Gladys Lines	Ruben 1974
CINNAMON PEAK‡	Lc. Kuakini × Ojai	Beall 1955
× Epi. gracile = Yam. Midnight Magenta		
CIRCUS	Lc. Golden Gate × Blanche Okamoto	Rod McLellan Co. 1964
× Malvern = Gold of Old × Midas Copper = Verinice	× Lc. Edgard van Belle = Circus Belle × Slc. Anzac = Pot. Rouge	
CIRCUS BELLE	Circus × Lc. Edgard van Belle	Rod McLellan Co. 1973

BRASSOLAELIOCATTLEYA

CITRON PASS | **Pimola × Green Grotto** | **Beall 1966**

× Acapana = Elysian Fields
× C. Fulvescens = Enchanted Valley
× Lc. Mem. Albert Heinecke = Sunset Gorge

C. K. AI | **C. Ashlands × Wake Island** | **Ai 1958 (Miyamoto)**

× C. elongata = Eau Gallie

CLARA HELENA KIENZLE | **C. percivaliana × Mèrimée** | **Doering 1974**
COLONIAL JEWEL | **Lc. Wheal Rose × Jewel Higdon** | **Rivermont 1971**
COLOR EQUATION | **Lc. Colorama × Iliad** | **Kay Francis 1973**
COMET KOHOUTEK | **Bc. Albion × Glorious** | **Bishop 1974 (Originator unknown)**
CONGO MOUNTAIN | **Lc. Congo × Bc. Mount Anderson** | **Rod McLellan Co. 1974**
CONNIE WALLAR‡ | **Bc. Mrs. J. Leemann × Lc. S. J. Bracey** | **Ozzella 1956**

× Helen Morita = Allison Melinda Wallar

CONQUISTADOR | **Golden Galleon × Golden Slippers** | **Trymwood 1974**
CONSTANT SPRING | **Envy × C. bicolor** | **Stewart Inc. 1975**
COPPER HILL | **Joyance × Bobby Ward** | **A. & R. 1975**
CORCORAN SUNSET | **Bobby Ward × Lc. Western Sunset** | **Rod McLellan Co. 1973 (Virgil Ford)**
CORONET BAY | **Bc. Déesse × Lc. Battle of Britain** | **Beall 1967**

× C. Interglossa = Beacon Mountain
× C. Okami = Bearpaw Mountain
× Lc. Excellency = Mystic Whaler
× Lc. Peggy Huffman = Mount John Jay

COSMIC GALE | **Mellowglow × C. intermedia** | **Kay Francis 1973**
CRATER LAKE | **Lc. Mariner × Victoria** | **Beall 1973**
CRISTOBEL KATHLEEN KOCK | **Golden Galleon × B. digbyana** | **Kock 1973 (Stewart Inc.)**
CROWDERS MOUNTAIN | **Ruth Cline McDade × L. Gold Star** | **Lenette 1974**
CROWN JEWEL | **Lc. Ennerdale × Norman's Bay** | **Abbott 1960**

× Winston Hoshino = Winston's Jewel

CROWN PRINCE AKIHITO‡ | **Lc. Helen Mizuta × Ishford** | **Otaguro 1960 (Miyamoto)**

× C. Crown Princess Michiko = Hirono-Miya Naruhito
× Lc. Cabazon = Yoshie Evelyn Sawai
× Lc. Dorothy Fried = Whiskey Girl
× Lc. Lenn Follett = Sadao Yamamoto
× Slc. Tropic Dawn = Pot. Ayano-Miya Fumihito

CUTLER BAY | **Norman's Bay × Lc. George Cutler** | **Rod McLellan Co. 1974**
DAFFY PIXIE | **Lc. Pixie Gold × Bc. Daffodil** | **Muse's 1971**
DAHROS | **Lc. Dahlia × Mem. Crispin Rosales** | **Katsuura 1973**
DANA THOMAS | **Lc. Lorraine Shirai × Gold Coast** | **Fields Orchids 1974**
DANDY LION | **Lc. Amber Glow × Buttercup** | **Wallbrunn 1972**
DANNY KALEIKINI | **Golden Queen × C. O'brieniana** | **Hershy 1975 (Originator unknown)**

× Sheila Scarlet = Manoa Valley

DARK PRINCE | **Lc. Princess Margaret × Dark Waters** | **Altenburg 1971**
DARK SMOKE | **Lc. Dark Eyes × Dark Waters** | **Altenburg 1971**
DARK WATERS‡ | **Norman's Bay × C. Nigritian** | **Abbott 1960**

× Nymph Bay = Tansei
× B. nodosa = Merlin
× C. loddigesii = Herb Jones
× Lc. Bonanza = Bondark
× Lc. Dark Eyes = Dark Smoke
× Lc. Fort Lauderdale = Takanao Seki
× Lc. Princess Margaret = Dark Prince
× Pot. Lafayette Nery = Pot. Tutomu Suzuki

BRASSOLAELIOCATTLEYA

DAVID CHRISTIAN HELBLING	Herons Ghyll × C. Antigo	Mrs. W. H. Boyd 1973 (Blauvelt)
DAWN SONG	Blanche Okamoto × Goldenette	Rod McLellan Co. 1975
DAY AND NIGHT	Bc. Brazil × L. grandis	Withner 1972
DAYSTAR	Lc. Orange Ann × Pacific Gold	Rod McLellan Co. 1973
DEANA	Keopulani × Polynesian	J. Milton Warne 1975 (Gordon Lee)
DEBBA-DOO	Lc. Red Gold × Bouton D'Or	Wilkins 1973 (H. Brice)
DESTINY	Xanthette × Primate	Stewart Inc. 1968

× Golden Galleon = Golden Destiny

DEW DROP	Gola × Golden Slippers	Rex Foster's 1975
DIANACITA	Ranger Six × C. Little Angel	Crothers 1973
DIANE KATHERINE SAULEDA	Jane Helton × Green-heart	Ruben 1972
DIANE SOO HOO	C. loddigesii × Norman's Bay	Miyao 1972
DIATOM	Lc. Yellowlake × Jane Helton	Rod McLellan Co. 1975
DINDISIO	Dinsmore × Lc. Paradisio	J. & S. 1971
DINH THUY YEN	Lc. Lorraine Shirai × Jewel-Glo	J. & S. 1974
DINSMORE‡	Lc. Schroderae × Blc. h. ign.	J. & S. 1964

× Golden Beach = Primrose Beauty
× C. Brabantiae = Lisa Marie
× Lc. Paradisio = Dindisio

DISTINCTION	Momercia × Lc. Grub Stake	Rod McLellan Co. 1971
DOCTOR CHEN	Mem. Crispin Rosales × C. Sedlescombe	Hong-Sie Chen 1975 (Chung-Chweng Chen)
DOCTOR KINJI HISAZAKI	Armida × Golden Queen	Hisazaki 1971
DONNA GILLIS	Lc. Thurderniana × Buttercup	Wallbrunn 1971
DORBON	Bc. Doris × Lc. Bonanza	Miskimens 1973
DORCILLE LITTLE	Norman's Bay × Lc. Lee Langford	Trade Winds 1972
DORIS AILEEN	Malvern × Nugget	Manske 1973
DOROTHY HARRISON	Jewel Higdon × C. Nigritian	J. S. McKenzie 1975
DREAM QUEEN	Amanda Gibson × Lc. Mrs. Medo	Bishop 1974
DUSK	Canari × Lc. Floralies	F. 1956

× C. Dupreana = Menure
× Lc. President de Brouwer = Paonneau

EAU GALLIE	C. K. Ai × C. elongata	Edwards Orchids 1971
EDITH McLEOD‡	Lc. S. J. Bracey × Aprica	A. & R. 1963 (R. McLeod)

× Camilla = Barbara O'Brien

ED O'NEAL	Acapana × C. Iris	Mrs. Wm. Boyd 1971 (Gamble)
EDWIN CHONG‡	Dawn Angela × Lc. Princess Margaret	Yin 1953 (Kwr.)

× C. guttata = Evelyn
× Lc. Mem. Albert Heinecke = Northern Lights
× Lc. Suzanne Fullerton = Sweet Sue

ELINETTE	Lc. Elinor × Xanthette	Stewart Inc. 1973
ELIZABETH CALDWELL	Nanette × C. Sunrise Chalet	Casa Luna 1975
ELYSIAN FIELDS	Acapana × Citron Pass	Beall 1973
EMERALD MEADOW‡	Green Grotto × C. bicolor	Beall 1966

× Lc. Alma Wichmann = Table Mountain
× Lc. Rainbow Inlets = Fern Grotto
× Lc. Seminole Sunset = Paradise Caves

BRASSOLAELIOCATTLEYA

EMILY SIMMONS	Samoset × Bc. S. M. Damon	C. & H. 1971 (T. Kazumura)
EMPRESS RANGE	C. Old Whitey × Ranger Six	A. & R. 1973
EMPRESS WORSLEY	Bc. Bill Worsley × Lc. Red Empress	Voo Doo Orchids 1974
ENCHANTED VALLEY	Citron Pass × C. Fulvescens	Beall 1973
ENGRAVED	Lc. Mem. Albert Heinecke × Zeecrabbe	Rod McLellan Co. 1974 (Fordyce)
ENIGMA VARIATIONS	B. nodosa × Lc. Lee Langford	Fort Caroline 1972
ENVY	Kong-Urai Gold × Golden Galleon	Stewart Inc. 1969
× B. digbyana	= New England Spring	× C. bicolor = Constant Spring
ERMINE‡	Aurea × C. Amabilis	F. 1935
× Morning Sun	= Sunlit Morn	× C. Wolteriana = Goulds Gold
ESMERALDA	Holiday Gem × Lester McDonald	Ruben 1975
ESTHER SCHABER	Pimola × C. Bob Betts	Sea God Nurs. 1975
ETTA K. KINLEY‡	Dawn Angela × Lc. Windermere	Rivermont 1958
× Lc. Areca	= Kinare	
EUNICE HELEN	C. Fulvescens × Nanette	Limberlost 1972
EVA PATTERSON†	Bc. Eileen × Lc. Aphrodite	H. Patterson 1943
× Lc. Bonanza	= Norma Kumiko Heen	
EVE	Lc. Miriam Marks × J. H. Robinson	Senior 1973 (Sieff)
EVELYN	C. guttata × Edwin Chong	Harold White 1975
EWART McDONALD	Norman's Bay × Lc. Vallandina	McDonald 1960 (M. & H.)
× C. intermedia	= Rojanadara	
FALL FESTIVAL	Lc. Dewsbury × Mem. Crispin Rosales	Rod McLellan Co. 1975 (Spencer)
FALL SPLENDOR	Amy Wakasugi × Lc. Bonanza	Lenette 1974
FAYE MIYAMOTO	Lc. Amber Glow × Lleblanche	Miyamoto 1975
FERN GROTTO	Emerald Meadow × Lc. Rainbow Inlets	Beall 1973
FIRST ADVENTURE	Golden Galleon × Mem. Crispin Rosales	D. E. Herman 1971
FIRST NIGHTER‡	Dawn Angela × Lc. Hyperion	Rivermont 1954
× Lc. Bonanza	= Ivan Coll	
FLEUR DE LYS‡	Lc. Helen Wilmer × Bc. Imperialis	Rivermont 1954
× C. Hardyana	= Purple Glory	
FLO	Lc. Curtis Hansard × Rising Sun	Homosassa 1975 (J. R. White)
FLO FLEECE	Lc. Florence Machle × Golden Fleece	Yocom 1975 (Originator unknown)
× Sc. Cleopatra	= Pot. Susan Wanner	
FLORADORA	Lc. Magadha × Bc. Mount Anderson	Stewart Inc. 1972
FLORENCE DICKINSON	Lc. Walter Slagle × Norman's Bay	C. E. Dickinson 1975 (B. Kodama)
FLORENCE LOCKHART	Bc. Heatonensis × Lc. Mem. Maggie Hood	Lockhart 1971
FORMOSAN GOLD	Lc. Lorraine Shirai × Spun Gold	Chow Cheng 1975
FORTUNE‡	Lc. Mem. Albert Heinecke × Xanthette	Stewart Inc. 1963
× Bobby Ward	= Royal Fortune	× Joyance = Gold Country
× Glorious Gold	= Golden Fortune	× Sheer Melody = Golden Shower
× Golden Slippers	= American Heritage	× Zanget = Halloween Canyon

FORTUNE‡ *(continued)*

× Bc. Calypso	= Calypso Singer	× Lc. Lee Langford	= Marita
× Bc. Déesse	= Fortunes Smile	× Lc. Mem. Albert Heinecke	= Thunder Mountain
× C. aclandiae	= Lost Treasure	× Lc. Odessa	= Gold Range
× C. dowiana	= Nguyen Thi Mai-Anh	× Pot. Gordon Siu	= Pot. Spice Islands
× C. guttata	= Tropical Market	× Schom. thomsoniana	= Recc. Zamboanga
× L. Zip	= Saracen	× Slc. Fort Caroline	= Pot. Canyon Sands
× Lc. Alma Wichmann	= Klondike Creek		
× Lc. Ann Follis	= Ann Fortune		

FORTUNES SMILE	**Bc. Déesse × Fortune**	**Stewart Inc. 1975**
FRANCES CAMPBELL DeGEAR	**Lc. Lydia Hubbell × Pacific Gold**	**Rod McLellan Co. 1974**
FRANCES MILES	**Richard Nixon × Lc. Mem. Albert Heinecke**	**Wm. A. Miles 1971 (Hoyt)**
FRANCIS Y. HOSHINO‡	**Lc. S. J. Bracey × Dennis Nishida**	Mrs. F. Y. Hoshino 1961
× Lc. Lee Langford	= Harriett Kawakami	
FRANK TATSUMURA†‡	**Lc. Cabazon × Bc. Hartland**	**Shirai 1953 (Tatsumura)**
× Lc. Rosa Kirsch	= Waikane	
FREDA COOKE	**Nigiana × Lc. Kathleen Jeal**	**F. J. Cooke 1972 (Jeals)**
FREDERICK SCHMIDT	**Gloria Schmidt × Sunset Bay**	Gloria Schmidt 1974 **(Kodama)**
FRED STEWART	**Mem. Crispin Rosales × Norman's Bay**	**Stewart Inc. 1966**
× C. bowringiana	= Gina Stewart	
FULTON RICE MILLER	**Acapana × Gold Coast**	**Mrs. W. H. Boyd 1973 (Blauvelt)**
FULVANO	**C. Fulvescens × Zanturano**	**Rivermont 1970**
× Jewel Higdon	= Rivermont's Gold	
GAIETY	**Acapana × C. aurantiaca**	**Thornton's 1975**
GALADRIEL	**Bc. Bill Worsley × Limelight**	**Voo Doo Orchids 1974**
GALE NIGRO	**Carly Hausermann × Lc. Nelly Corradi**	**Elmhurst 1971**
GALWAY BAY	**Mem. Helen Brown × Modjeska**	**McNally 1974**
GAMBOL ON GREEN	**Lc. Matilija × Lester McDonald**	**Stewart Inc. 1975**
GENE McKENZIE	Lc. Antonica Fredrick × Jewel Higdon	**J. S. McKenzie 1972**
GEORGE RISCH	**Lc. Dorothy Fried × Mem. Crispin Rosales**	**Rayridge 1974 (Risch)**
GEORGES MOREL	**Lc. Gaillard × Bc. Thalie**	**Marcel Lecoufle 1974**
GILD	**Pacific Gold × Goldenette**	**Rod McLellan Co. 1973**
GINA STEWART	**C. bowringiana × Fred Stewart**	**Stewart Inc. 1974**
GLADYS LINES‡	**Jane Helton × Malvern**	**Lines 1958**
× C. Fulvescens	= Mem. Arthur Pancoast	× Lc. Luminosa = Cindita
GLOBE BAY	**Bc. The Globe × Norman's Bay**	**J. & S. 1971**
GLO HELIN	**Mellow Vista × Lc. Orange Gem**	**Kay Francis 1974**
GLORIA SCHMIDT	**Blanche Okamoto × Ophelosa**	**Gloria Schmidt 1968 (Kodama)**
× Sunset Bay	= Frederick Schmidt	
GLORIA SHOUSE	**Zanturano × B. digbyana**	**Coastal Gdns. 1974**
GLORIOUS†‡	**C. Solario × Zanturano**	**McDade 1951**
× Buttercup	= Green Apple	× Bc. Albion = Comet Kohoutek
× Mountelia	= Highland Fling	

BRASSOLAELIOCATTLEYA

GLORIOUS GOLD‡ — **Jane Helton × Glorious** — **Rivermont 1961**
× Fortune = Golden Fortune | × Goldenette = Imperial Nugget

GLOZAN — **Glorious × Zanturano** — **Rivermont 1962**
× Lc. Lee Langford = Zanleeglo

GOHL LEE — **Golden Slippers × B. nodosa** — **Stewart Inc. 1974**
GOLA — **Lc. Golden Gate × Pimola** — **Rex Foster's 1975 (Originator unknown)**
× Golden Slippers = Dew Drop

GOLD BUG — **Bouton D'Or × C. aurantiaca** — **Wilkins 1974**
GOLD CITY — **Lc. Gatton Glory × Malvern** — **Sermsuwan 1968 (A. & R.)**
× Bobby Ward = Gold Wood | × Lc. Brilliant Orange = Sun Crest

GOLD COAST — **Lc. Derrynane × Malvern** — **Trade Winds 1962**
× Acapana = Fulton Rice Miller | × Lc. Lorraine Shirai = Dana Thomas

GOLD COUNTRY — **Fortune × Joyance** — **Stewart Inc. 1972**
GOLD DUNE — **Lc. S. J. Bracey × Malvern** — **Rod McLellan Co. 1974**
GOLDEN BEACH — **Carmen Jiminez × Golden Myth** — **Fields Orchids 1973**
× Dinsmore = Primrose Beauty

GOLDEN DESTINY — **Golden Galleon × Destiny** — **Stewart Inc. 1975**
GOLDEN DISCOVERY — **Pacific Gold × Golden Spires** — **Rod McLellan Co. 1973**
GOLDEN DOME‡ — **Golden Crown × Xanthea** — **C. 1946**
× Lc. Mem. Albert Heinecke = Penn State | × Slc. Vallezac = Pot. Heidi Gubler

GOLDEN DREAM — **Jane Helton × Lc. Golden Charm** — **Stewart Inc. 1964**
× Golden Slippers = Peking Gold

GOLDENETTE‡ — **Jaunette × Goldenthea** — **Jeal 1956**
× Blanche Okamoto = Dawn Song | × Pacific Gold = Gild
× Glorious Gold = Imperial Nugget | × Lc. S. J. Bracey = Golden Lyre
× Otomayim = Meadow Sun

GOLDEN FLEECE — **Heliolata × Golden Crown** — **Schroder 1952**
× Lc. Florence Machle = Flo Fleece

GOLDEN FOREST — **Lc. Amber Glow × Jane Helton** — **Crestwood 1973**
GOLDEN FORTUNE — **Glorious Gold × Fortune** — **Spencer 1975**
GOLDEN GALLEON‡ — **Xanthette × Camilla** — **Clark Day Jr. 1962**
× Bobby Ward = Norma Briscoe | × Bc. Mars = Kim Ann Bauer
× Buttercup = Road to Mandalay | × C. bicolor = Indian Treasure
× Destiny = Golden Destiny | × C. General Patton = Kaliope
× Golden Slippers = Conquistador | × Low. Spitfire = Pot. Tiger Tears
× Mem. Crispin Rosales = First Adventure | × Pot. Medea = Pot. Wanda Mayo
× B. digbyana = Cristobel Kathleen Kock

GOLDEN GIFFORD — **Robert Gifford × Golden Queen** — **Miyamoto 1975**
× Hanako M. Miyamoto = Helen Pastushin

GOLDEN GLADES — **Malvern × Tiara** — **Thornton's 1959 (Gore)**
× Kong-Urai Gold = King's Gold

GOLDEN HUE — **Lc. Lydia Hubbell × Setting Sun** — **Rod McLellan Co. 1975**
GOLDEN LLEWELLYN‡ — **Llewellyn × Nugget** — **Kodama 1966**
× Setting Sun = National Gold | × Lc. Ann Follis = Heavenly Valley

BRASSOLAELIOCATTLEYA

GOLDEN LYRE — **Goldenette × Lc. S. J. Bracey** — **Rod McLellan Co. 1975**

GOLDEN MYTH†‡ — **Mithra × Lc. Golden Gleam** — **McDade 1949**

× Carmen Jiminez	= Golden Beach	× Lc. Elinor	= Lemon Lass
× C. General Patton	= Patton Myth	× Lc. Lydia Hubbell	= Primrose Path

GOLDEN QUEEN*†‡ — **Golden Crown × C. Miguelito** — **Paterson 1928**

× Armida	= Dr. Kinji Hisazaki	× C. O'brieniana	= Danny Kaleikini
× Robert Gifford	= Golden Gifford		

GOLDEN REWARD — **Summer Shades × Lc. Pacific Sun** — **Rod McLellan Co. 1971**

GOLDEN SHOWER — **Sheer Melody × Fortune** — **Stewart Inc. 1972 (J. Rikel)**

GOLDEN SLIPPERS — **Helen Morita × Golden Galleon** — **Stewart Inc. 1967**

× Fortune	= American Heritage	× Xanthette	= William Stewart
× Gola	= Dew Drop	× Yellow Jewell	= Joanna Dawn
× Golden Dream	= Peking Gold	× B. nodosa	= Gohl Lee
× Golden Galleon	= Conquistador	× C. bicolor	= Yorktown
× Jane Helton	= Pirates Quest	× Lc. Dormaniana	= California Fantasy
× Malworth	= Malworth Slippers	× Lc. Faith Dee Fanchaly	= Mount Mitchell
× Primate	= Trojan Gold	× Pot. Gordon Siu	= Pot. Siu Slippers

GOLDEN SPIRES — **Lc. Orange Beauty × Alice Muller** — **Rod McLellan Co. 1966**

× Pacific Gold	= Golden Discovery	× Slc. Paprika	= Pot. Treasure Glow

GOLDEN SUCCESS — **Jane Helton × Helen Morita** — **Rod McLellan Co. 1973 (Fordyce)**

GOLDFIELD‡ — **Lc. Golden Gate × Golden Myth** — **Rod McLellan Co. 1963**

× Otomayim	= John Smithson	× Slc. Anzac	= Pot. Spicey
× Lc. Copperwick	= Impression		

GOLDMINE‡ — **Safran × Jane Helton** — **Rivermont 1958**

× Buttercup	= Will Bates	× B. digbyana	= Mem. Walter Brown

GOLD OF OLD — **Circus × Malvern** — **Rod McLellan Co. 1974**

GOLD RANGE — **Lc. Odessa × Fortune** — **Beall 1975**

GOLD TORCH — **Summer Shades × Lc. Mary Jo Nelson** — **Rod McLellan Co. 1974**

GOLD WOOD — **Bobby Ward × Gold City** — **Rod McLellan Co. 1974**

GOLDWORTH — **Lc. Charlesworthii × Kong-Urai Gold** — **Redlinger 1971**

GOULDS GLORY — **Goulds Gold × Orange Glory** — **Wilkins 1975**

GOULDS GOLD — **Ermine × C. Wolteriana** — **Wilkins 1971**

× Orange Glory	= Goulds Glory		

GRANITE BAY — **Bc. Mount Hood × Norman's Bay** — **Rod McLellan Co. 1974**

GRAYBACK MOUNTAIN — **Lc. Mem. Albert Heinecke × Lonesome Cove** — **Beall 1975**

GREEN APPLE — **Glorious × Buttercup** — **Furrow 1971**

GREEN BELLE — **Green-heart × Lc. Edgard van Belle** — **Ruben 1974**

GREEN EMPIRE — **Lester McDonald × Lc. Mem. Albert Heinecke** — **Beall 1973**

GREEN GIANT‡ — **C. guttata × Xanthette** — **Gamble 1962**

× B. digbyana	= Vermonts Green Mountains	× C. guttata	= Green Gremlin

GREEN GODDESS — **Autumn Glow × C. bicolor** — **Lenette 1974**

GREEN GREMLIN — **Green Giant × C. guttata** — **Stewart Inc. 1972**

GREEN-HEART†‡ — **Bc. Heatonensis × Lc. Condrey** — **Bracey 1954 (S.)**

× Holiday Gem	= Mint Julep	× Lc. Edgard van Belle	= Green Belle
× Jane Helton	= Diane Katherine Sauleda	× Lc. Mem. Albert Heinecke	= Leslie Hoffman
× Lester McDonald	= Ruben's Verde		
× Bc. Mount Hood	= Martha McAllister		

BRASSOLAELIOCATTLEYA

Name	Parentage	Registrant
GREEN JEWEL	Lc. Kencolor × Lester McDonald	Rod McLellan Co. 1972
GREEN MOUNT	Pimola × C. Karae Lyn Sugiyama	McAllister 1975
GREENSTONE CANYON	Rain Forest × Zanget	Beall 1975
GREENWICH	Lc. Ann Follis × Lester McDonald	Rod McLellan Co. 1968

× C. guttata = Chinese Jade

Name	Parentage	Registrant
GUAYMAS	Helen Morita × Lc. Pirate King	Stewart Inc. 1973
HALLOWEEN CANYON	Fortune × Zanget	Beall 1975
HANAKO M. MIYAMOTO	Lc. Grandee × Nanette	Miyamoto 1954 (Goo)

× Golden Gifford = Helen Pastushin | × Lc. Edgar Omura = Hanako Omura

Name	Parentage	Registrant
HANAKO OMURA	Lc. Edgar Omura × Hanako M. Miyamoto	Miyamoto 1975

× Lc. Terry Wayne = Neal Blaisdell

Name	Parentage	Registrant
HANGOVER	Mary Battle × Lc. Elizabeth Off	Battle 1975
HARLEQUIN	Lc. Mem. Albert Heinecke × Nugget	Bracey 1960

× Mem. Crispin Rosales = Mem. Frank Holland | × Bc. Déesse = Jane Paton

Name	Parentage	Registrant
HARRIETT KAWAKAMI	Francis Y. Hoshino × Lc. Lee Langford	Otaguro 1974
HARTCAL	Bc. Hartland × Lc. California	Kensington 1973
HAZEL DELL	Zanget × Cinnamon Peak	Beall 1967

× Slc. Brandywine = Pot. War Dance

Name	Parentage	Registrant
HEADLINER	Momercia × C. Metapan	Rod McLellan Co. 1974
HEART PEAKS	Lc. Purple Heart × Mem. Crispin Rosales	Beall 1975
HEATON ROSALES	Bc. Heatonensis × Mem. Crispin Rosales	Otaguro 1973
HEAVENLY VALLEY	Lc. Ann Follis × Golden Llewellyn	Rod McLellan 1971
HELENA TRICCA	Bc. Hartland × Lc. José Dias Castro	N. Suzuki 1971
HELEN HUNTINGTON	Nanette × Acapana	Kensington 1974 (Bracey)
HELEN MORITA‡	Gillian × Consul Greig	Morita 1953 (Kwr)

× Connie Wallar = Allison Melinda Wallar | × Joyance = African Queen
× Jane Helton = Golden Success | × Lc. Pirate King = Guaymas

Name	Parentage	Registrant
HELEN PASTUSHIN	Hanako M. Miyamoto × Golden Gifford	Miyamoto 1975
HERB JONES	C. loddigesii × Dark Waters	Limberlost 1972
HERONS ENCHANTMENT	Lc. Land of Enchantment × Herons Ghyll	J. & S. 1975 (Stoddard)
HERONS GHYLL‡	Norman's Bay × Lc. Ishtar	L. 1955

× C. Antigo = David Christian Helbling | × Lc. Edgard van Belle = Herons van Belle
× C. Nigrella = Mem. Oliver Coffee | × Lc. Ibbie = Heron's Nest
× Lc. Adolph Hecker = Sandy Robinson | × Lc. Land of Enchantment = Herons Enchantment
× Lc. Autumn Symphony = Autumn Ghyll | × Lc. Manila = Manila Ghyll

Name	Parentage	Registrant
HERON'S NEST	Herons Ghyll × Lc. Ibbie	J. & S. 1974 (Stoddard)
HERONS VAN BELLE	Lc. Edgard van Belle × Herons Ghyll	McAllister 1974
HERTÉESSE	Lc. Hertha × Bc. Déesse	Wondabah 1974
HIEI	C. Akebono × Jahorco	Hattori 1975
HIGHLAND FLING	Glorious × Mountelia	Crothers 1974
HILO GLORY	Norman's Bay × Kapiolani Beauty	M.Miyao 1971
HIRONO-MIYA NARUHITO	C. Crown Princess Michiko × Crown Prince Akihito	Otaguro 1971

BRASSOLAELIOCATTLEYA

HISAYO HIRONAKA Naomi M. Yahiro × Lc. S. J. Bracey Hironaka 1973

HOFSOMMER'S GOLD Lc. Ken Battle × Mellowglow Hofsommer 1973 (Battle)

HOLIDAY GEM Pimola × Lc. Elstead Gem L. E. Starke 1966 (Bracey)

× Green-heart = Mint Julep
× Lester McDonald = Esmeralda
× Lc. Peggy Huffman = Ruben's Gem

HONEYBEE Lc. G. S. Ball × Mellowglow Rivermont 1963

× Buttercup = Honeycup

HONEYCUP Honeybee × Buttercup Furrow 1971

HOWARD'S LUCK C. Porcia × Norman's Bay H. R. Starke 1974

ILIAD†‡ Bc. Digbyano-trianaei × Lc. Orange Blossom A. & R. 1937

× Buttercup = Mem. Amelia Bertsch
× Midas Charm = Mem. Dorothy Bertsch
× Lc. Colorama = Color Equation
× Lc. Lorraine Shirai = Virgin Gold

IMPERIAL NUGGET Glorious Gold × Goldenette Rod McLellan Co. 1975 (Spencer)

IMPRESSION Lc. Copperwick × Goldfield Rod McLellan Co. 1975

INCANDESCENT Lc. Bonanza × Magenta Intense Rod McLellan Co. 1973

INDIAN TREASURE C. bicolor × Golden Galleon Stewart Inc. 1972

IRON CAP MOUNTAIN Norman's Bay × Lc. Zada Fields Beall 1973

IROQUOIS TRAIL Lc. Lee Langford × Pamela Farrell Beall 1975

ISABEL BAY C. Isabel Sander × Norman's Bay Kodama 1968

× Mem. Crispin Rosales = Kaoru Fujikawa

IVAN COLL Lc. Bonanza × First Nighter Coll 1974

JACK HATFIELD Molflora × Bc. Eagle Fort Caroline 1973

JAHORCO Heather Queen × C. Alexandra T. Kazumura 1950

× C. Akebono = Hiei

JAMES HAUSERMANN‡ Edwin Chong × Lc. Harold J. Patterson Hausermann 1965

× Lc. George Baldwin = Bold Ruler
× Lc. Irene Finney = Mem. Grant Eichler

JANE FLEMING Mem. Crispin Rosales × Lc. Adolph Hecker Nicolson 1971

JANE HELTON†‡ Dorothy Drury-Lowe × Xanthea McDade 1950

× Blanche Okamoto = Sahara Sand
× Golden Slippers = Pirates Quest
× Green-heart = Diane Katherine Sauleda
× Helen Morita = Golden Success
× Jewel Higdon = Rio's Jewel
× Lester McDonald = Solimar
× Maude Montgomery = Mont Jane
× Mellowglow = Laura McCall
× Nugget = Nuggeton
× B. nodosa = Rio's Polka Dot
× Bc. Déesse = Linden Lime
× C. Chamberlainiana = Kenji Onodera
× C. Nigrella = Jungle Jane
× Lc. Amber Glow = Golden Forest
× Lc. Canberra Glow = Yoshiko Asato
× Lc. Charlesworthii = Betty Borer
× Lc. Doubloon = Nuuanu Sunshine
× Lc. Summerland Girl = Jane Summerland
× Lc. Yellowlake = Diatom
× Pot. Gordon Siu = Pot. Esther Costa
× Pot. Sunset Bay = Pot. Cumberland Sunset
× Slc. Kao Hsiung = Pot. Jacquie Awana
× Slc. Rainbow Hill = Pot. Irene Brouard

JANE PATON Bc. Déesse × Harlequin A. & R. 1975

JANE RUSSELL‡ Bc. Hartland × Lc. Balkis Chew Wong 1958 (Miyamoto)

× Slc. Anzac = Pot. Precious

JANE SHEROUSE Jewel-Glo × Lc. Antonica Fredrick Fields Orchids 1973

JANE SUMMERLAND Lc. Summerland Girl × Jane Helton J. & S. 1974

JANICE WATSON Ranger Six × C. Bob Betts R. G. Watson 1972 (Originator unknown)

BRASSOLAELIOCATTLEYA

Grex	Parentage	Registrant
JEWEL-GLO‡	**Jewel Higdon × Mellowglow**	**Fields Orchids 1964**
× Lc. Antonica Fredrick = Jane Sherouse	× Lc. Lorraine Shirai = Dinh Thuy Yen	
JEWEL HIGDON‡	**Jane Helton × Zanturano**	**Lines 1957**
× Fulvano = Rivermont's Gold	× Lc. Anne Walker = Yellow Jewell	
× Jane Helton = Rio's Jewel	× Lc. Antonica Fredrick = Gene McKenzie	
× C. Nigritian = Dorothy Harrison	× Lc. Maggie Hurst = Jewelled Gold	
× C. Pittiana = Laura-Jane	× Lc. Wheal Rose = Colonial Jewel	
× Lc. Amber Glow = Warren Wever		
JEWELLED GOLD	**Lc. Maggie Hurst × Jewel Higdon**	**J. S. McKenzie 1972**
J. H. ROBINSON	**Bc. Delius × Lc. Elissa**	**Sieff 1953**
× Lc. Miriam Marks = Eve		
JITRA	**Lc. Amber Glow × Acapana**	**Jitra 1974 (Boonphyoong)**
JOAN BRAMWELL	**B. nodosa × Lc. Helen Mizuta**	**Raymond Palmer 1975**
JOANNA DAWN	**Yellow Jewell × Golden Slippers**	Lenette 1974 **(T. Miller)**
JOHN BEVILLE	**Norman's Bay × Lc. Walter Winchell**	**Beville 1967**
× Lc. Irene Finney = Lisa Irene		
JOHN SMITHSON	**Goldfield × Otomayim**	**Rod McLellan Co. 1971**
JOYANCE†‡	**Ojai × Lc. S. J. Bracey**	**A. & R. 1948**
× Bobby Ward = Copper Hill	× Lc. Canberra = Road To Rio	
× Fortune = Gold Country	× Lc. Mem. Albert Heinecke = Sumatra Safari	
× Helen Morita = African Queen		
× Mary Beth Hancock = Mary Joy		
JUNE MOORE‡	**Nugget × Lc. Aconcagua**	**B. 1963**
× C. Nerto = San Remo		
JUNGLE JANE	**C. Nigrella × Jane Helton**	**Kensington 1973**
JUNGLE RIVER	**Lc. Lagoon × Xanthette**	**Stewart Inc. 1974**
KAENA	**Lc. Gladys Millner × Bc. Green Dawn**	**O. Kirsch 1972**
KAHAOPEA BEAUTY	**Herons Ghyll × C. General Patton**	**R. Tanaka 1964**
× Norman's Bay = Miki Miyajima	× Lc. S. J. Bracey = Yuka Miyajima	
KALAKOA	**Bc. Green Dawn × Lc. Rosa Kirsch**	**O. Kirsch 1972**
KALIOPE	**C. General Patton × Golden Galleon**	**Rex Foster's 1973 (Fordyce)**
KAORU FUJIKAWA	**Isabel Bay × Mem. Crispin Rosales**	**Otaguro 1975**
KAPIOLANI BEAUTY‡	**C. Bow Bells × Norman's Bay**	**Suyama 1960**
× Norman's Bay = Hilo Glory		
KATHY KRUGMAN†‡	**Mithra × Irma**	**H. Patterson 1952**
× Bc. Daffodil = Parakeet		
KAY HERON	**Lc. Edgard van Belle × Otomayim**	**Rod McLellan Co. 1972**
KELLY BROOKS	**L. tenebrosa × Orange Glory**	**Fort Caroline 1971** (Oshtemo)
KELLY WILLIAMS	**Sylvia Reilly × Lester McDonald**	**H. G. Williams 1972**
KENJI ONODERA	**C. Chamberlainiana × Jane Helton**	**Otaguro 1974**
KEOPULANI	**Bc. Hartland × Lc. Lady May**	**Kodama 1945**
× Polynesian = Deana		
KEOWEE	**Lc. Lorraine Shirai × B. nodosa**	**C. & H. 1975 (Small)**

BRASSOLAELIOCATTLEYA

KIM ANN BAUER	Bc. Mars × Golden Galleon	Stewart Inc. 1974
KIMBERLEY ANN ROCCAFORTE	Pacific Gold × Lester McDonald	Roccaforte 1972
KINARE	Etta K. Kinley × Lc. Areca	Kensington 1973
KING'S GOLD	Golden Glades × Kong-Urai Gold	Redlinger 1971
KLONDIKE BELLE‡	Bc. Mount St. Helens × Lc. Golden Concolor	Beall 1966
× Lc. Flavius	= Big Canary Peaks	
KLONDIKE CREEK	Lc. Alma Wichmann × Fortune	Beall 1972
KOHOUTEK	Lc. Western Sunset × Otomayim	Rod McLellan Co. 1974
KOINABA	Lc. Sacramento × Norman's Bay	Gauda 1973
KONA REEF	Blanche Carter × Lc. Cuesta	Edelbrock 1974
KONG-URAI GOLD‡	Zanturano × Malvern	Rivermont of Bangkok 1957
× Golden Glades	= King's Gold	
× Lc. Charlesworthii	= Goldworth	
× Lc. Fedora	= Pimas Crown	
× Lc. Mem. Maggie Hood	= Yellow Butterfly	
KRISTIN	Lc. Lorraine Shirai × Nanette	Voo Doo Orchids 1974
KUO KUANG	Galatea × Lc. Hyperion	Li Chin-sheng 1959
× Norman's Bay	= Chung-Chweng Chen	
LANDSCAPE‡	Chief Joseph × Myophia	Miyamoto 1953
× Pot. Gordon Siu	= Pot. Emiko Togashi	
LARA	Bc. Hartland × Lc. Hurricane	V. Daubón 1972
LAURA-JANE	Jewel Higdon × C. Pittiana	Schneider 1975 (Originator unknown)
LAURA McCALL	Jane Helton × Mellowglow	Fields Orchids 1973
LAURA VANDORN SCHNEIDER	Nanette × B. glauca	Schneider 1975 (Rivermont)
LEILA	Bc. Mrs. J. Leemann × Lc. Senate	L. 1932
× Slc. Radians	= Pot. Darlene	
LEMON LASS	Lc. Elinor × Golden Myth	Stewart Inc. 1974
LEMON LIGHT	Nugget × Lc. Grandee	Voelker 1972
LEONIE MACKAY	C. Yertala × Nanette	Limberlost 1972
LESLIE HOFFMAN	Lc. Mem. Albert Heinecke × Green-heart	Stewart Inc. 1972
LESTER McDONALD‡	Lc. Ann Follis × B. digbyana	Rod McLellan Co. 1963
× Green-heart	= Ruben's Verde	
× Holiday Gem	= Esmeralda	
× Jane Helton	= Solimar	
× Pacific Gold	= Kimberley Ann Roccaforte	
× Rain Forest	= Shamrock Dome	
× Sylvia Reilly	= Kelly Williams	
× B. digbyana	= Mystic Mariner	
× Lc. Kencolor	= Green Jewel	
× Lc. Matilija	= Gambol on Green	
× Lc. Mem. Albert Heinecke	= Green Empire	
LIMELIGHT‡	Zanturano × Morning Sun	Rivermont 1956
× Bc. Bill Worsley	= Galadriel	
LIMESTONE	Bc. Pluto × Moonglow	Robt. Smith 1973
LINDEN LIME	Jane Helton × Bc. Déesse	A. & R. 1975
LINGERIE	Nacouchee × Bc. Mount Hood	Rod McLellan Co. 1973
LISA IRENE	Lc. Irene Finney × John Beville	Hausermann 1973
LISA MARIE	Dinsmore × C. Brabantiae	Fort Caroline 1974 (Brooks)
LITTLE BOY BLUE	Mem. Ruth Gessner × L. rupestris	Fields Orchids 1973
LITTLE MEADOW MOUNTAIN	Rain Forest × Lc. Elstead Gem	Beall 1975
LLEBLANCHE	Llewellyn × Blanche Okamoto	Miyamoto 1975
× Lc. Amber Glow	= Faye Miyamoto	

BRASSOLAELIOCATTLEYA

LLEWELLYN†‡ — **Bc. Minerva × Lc. Mrs. Medo** — **Manda 1937**

× Blanche Okamoto = Lleblanche

LONESOME COVE — **Bc. Déesse × Lc. Kuakini** — **Beall 1967**

× Lc. Mem. Albert Heinecke = Grayback Mountain

LORRAINE MALWORTH — **Lc. Lorraine Shirai × Malworth** — **J. & S. 1971**

LORRITO — **Lc. Flirtie × Bc. Daffodil** — **J. M. Ward 1974 (Voo Doo Orchids)**

LOST TREASURE — **Fortune × C. aclandiae** — **Rex Foster's 1973**

LOTHLORIEN — **Lc. Antonica Fredrick × B. glauca** — **Voo Doo Orchids 1974**

LOUIS PALACIO — Norman's Bay × Lc. Momus — Dobkin 1971 (Bracey)

LO YING — **C. Sedlescombe × Norman's Bay** — **Hong-Sie Chen 1975 (Chung-Chweng Chen)**

LUCKY‡ — **Lc. Tegucigalpa × Wendell Hoshino** — **Kodama 1955 (Miyamoto)**

× Lc. Bonanza = Lucky Bonanza

LUCKY BONANZA — **Lucky × Lc. Bonanza** — **Otaguro 1973**

LUCKY STRIKE — **Mem. Crispin Rosales × Lc. Bonanza** — **T. M. Sanders 1966**

× Aztec Princess = Pis-Vimol
× Pamela Farrell = Phinijsikakarn

LUIS H. YANES — **Bc. Hula Girl × Lc. Copper Charm** — **J. Milton Warne 1961**

× Bc. Déesse = Nuuanu Dawn
× C. Enid = Nuuanu Fancy

LYDA BELL HOWE — **Molflora × Lc. Land of Enchantment** — **Howe 1974**

MAGENTA INTENSE — **Lc. Cuesta × Momercia** — **Rod McLellan Co. 1965**

× Lc. Bonanza = Incandescent

MAGIC — **Lc. Fiery × Bc. Bill Worsley** — **Voo Doo Orchids 1974**

MAKAHA GLOLIGHT — **Nancy Wittorf × Lc. Waianae Sunset** — **A. G. Tharp 1972 (Miyamoto)**

MALIBU GEM — **C. Horace × Pamela Farrell** — **Freed 1973**

MALODIL — **Malvern × Bc. Daffodil** — **Kosel 1971**

MALRICK — **Lc. Antonica Fredrick × Malvern** — **Fields Orchids 1973**

MALU — **Malvern × Ubangi** — J. S. McKenzie 1972

MALVERN†‡ — **The Baroness × Lc. Canberra** — **B. 1943**

× Circus = Gold of Old
× Nugget = Doris Aileen
× Ubangi = Malu
× Xanthette = Acclaim
× Bc. Daffodil = Malodil
× Lc. Antonica Fredrick = Malrick
× Lc. Lee Langford = Orange Gold
× Lc. S. J. Bracey = Gold Dune
× Slc. Emberglow = Pot. Gold Piece
× Slc. Hermes = Pot. Tabo
× Slc. Ramona = Pot. Hicee

MALWORTH‡ — **Lc. Charlesworthii × Malvern** — **J. & S. 1963**

× Acapana = Belle Stewart
× Golden Slippers = Malworth Slippers
× Lc. Lorraine Shirai = Lorraine Malworth
× Slc. Naomi Kerns = Pot. Clown

MALWORTH SLIPPERS — **Golden Slippers × Malworth** — **J. & S. 1975**

MAMIE FOURAKER — **Lc. Grandee × Primate** — **Fouraker 1959 (Bracey)**

× Painted Desert = California Special
× Lc. Orange Gem = Samarkand
× Lc. Western Sunset = Caldron

MANATEE GOLD — **Sunflame × Tiara** — **Mrs. W. F. White 1975 (William F. White)**

× Soph. coccinea = Pot. Mem. Bill White

BRASSOLAELIOCATTLEYA

MANDARIN BAY	Lc. Orange Charm × Rising Sun	Rod McLellan Co. 1973
MANILA GHYLL	Herons Ghyll × Lc. Manila	Hisazaki 1972
MANOA VALLEY	Danny Kaleikini × Sheila Scarlet	Hershy 1975 (Originator unknown)
MARGARET WAY	Ashiya × Norman's Bay	N. Tomita 1972 (Miyamoto)
MARGIE DICKIE	Acapana × C. Nellie Roberts	George Black 1973
MARIGOLD MEADOWS	Sylvia Reilly × Lc. Western Sunset	Beall 1973
MARION MORELAND	Wake Island × C. Yertala	Limberlost 1974
MARION RYERSON†‡	Bc. Hartland × Lc. Linnaeus T. Savage	Fields Orchids 1950
× C. trianaei	= Zelma Long Frazer	
MARITA	Lc. Lee Langford × Fortune	H. Graf 1974 (Stewart Inc.)
MARJORIE FREY‡	Lc. Rembrandt × Wake Island	Komiyama 1957 (Kodama)
× Smbc. Perfection	= Recc. Eglon Scott	
× Slc. Anzac	= Pot. Ruth Rettig	
MARK ZEUG	Mem. Bill Fouraker × Lc. Bonanza	Otaguro 1973
MARTHA McALLISTER	Bc. Mount Hood × Green-heart	McAllister 1973
MARY BATTLE	Norman's Bay × Lc. Molly Tyler	Creve Coeur 1964
× Lc. Elizabeth Off	= Hangover	
MARY BETH HANCOCK	Helmsman × Nugget	W. T. McBroom 1964 (Bracey)
× Joyance	= Mary Joy	
MARY CROCKER	Missy × Buttercup	G. Crocker 1972 (Small)
MARY ISLAND	Wake Island × Lc. Mary Rose	Rayridge 1974
MARY JOY	Joyance × Mary Beth Hancock	Padriac Cooper 1974 (L. Holguin)
MARY M. DAMON	Llewellyn × C. Triumphans	Miyamoto 1948
× Walter Abe	= Mary Shipman	
MARY SHIPMAN	Mary M. Damon × Walter Abe	Hernlund 1972 (Miyamoto)
MASAYUKI ECHIGO	Lc. Kilauea Iki × Mem. Crispin Rosales	Otaguro 1973
MATRIARCH‡	Wake Island × C. Tityus	Miyamoto 1953
× Lc. Twinkle Star	= Twinkle Mater	
MAUDE MONTGOMERY	Truffautiana × C. dowiana	McPeak 1957
× Jane Helton	= Mont Jane	
MAURICE GUSMAN	C. Pearl Harbor × Nacouchee	J. & S. 1974
MEADOW SUN	Otomayim × Goldenette	Rod McLellan Co. 1974
MEDELLIN	Natoma × Lc. Lomita Park	Rod McLellan Co. 1972
MEDITATION	Bc. Déesse × Lc. Fedora	Nishimoto 1974
MELLOWGLOW‡	Golden Myth × Lc. Prince Smilax	Rivermont 1958
× Jane Helton	= Laura McCall	
× Bc. Daffodil	= Ann Kientzy	
× C. Balu	= Bullion Gold	
× C. intermedia	= Cosmic Gale	
× Lc. Ken Battle	= Hofsommer's Gold	
× Lc. Mem. Albert Heinecke	= San Juan Sunset	
× Pot. Red Lava	= Pot. Lava Glow	
× Soph. coccinea	= Pot. Sundance	
MELLOW VISTA	Mellowglow × C. George Asder	Kay Francis 1966
× Lc. Orange Gem	= Glo Helin	

BRASSOLAELIOCATTLEYA

MEMORIA AMELIA BERTSCH	Iliad × Buttercup	Bertsch 1972
MEMORIA ARTHUR FREED	Pamela Farrell × Norman's Bay	Freed 1975
MEMORIA ARTHUR PANCOAST	Gladys Lines × C. Fulvescens	A. Boyd 1973
MEMORIA BENIAMINO GIGLI	Lc. José Dias Castro × Norman's Bay	Altenburg 1971
MEMORIA BILL FOURAKER‡	Lc. Atlantis × Norman's Bay	Fouraker 1961 (Bracey)

× Lc. Bonanza	= Mark Zeug	× Lc. Quadroon	= Rose Chiyoko Kakazu

MEMORIA CRISPIN ROSALES‡	Lc. Bonanza × Norman's Bay	Bracey 1959

× Golden Galleon	= First Adventure	× Lc. Ennerdale	= Mem. Henry Morikubo
× Harlequin	= Mem. Frank Holland	× Lc. George MacDonell	= Robert Kamiyama
× Isabel Bay	= Kaoru Fujikawa	× Lc. Hyperion	= Toshikazu Takahashi
× Bc. Heatonensis	= Heaton Rosales	× Lc. Issy	= Chic Jardine
× C. Chamberlainiana	= Summer Festival	× Lc. Kilauea Iki	= Masayuki Echigo
× C. Horace	= Tribute	× Lc. Maria Ozzella	= Ruby Mesa
× C. Peetersii	= Spencer Beauty	× Lc. Purple Heart	= Heart Peaks
× C. Redgatta	= Pu'ula'ula	× Lc. Twinkle Star	= Twinkle Rosales
× C. Redtop Mountain	= Naniwa	× Lc. Yukiko Hironaka	= Mem. Giichi Otaguro
× C. Sedlescombe	= Doctor Chen	× Lc. Yvette Ann	= Rounder
× Lc. Adolph Hecker	= Jane Fleming	× Slc. Anzac	= Pot. Yuriko Hananoki
× Lc. Charlie Stem	= Bonnie Warren	× Slc. Estella Jewell	= Pot. Florence Brady
× Lc. Dahlia	= Dahros	× Slc. Marion Black	= Pot. Evening Glow
× Lc. Dee Dee	= Mem. Richard Black	× Slc. Pearl Spencer	= Pot. Sunny's Favorite
× Lc. Dewsbury	= Fall Festival	× Slc. Vallezac	= Pot. Vallespin
× Lc. Dorothy Fried	= George Risch		

MEMORIA DARREL COLE	Zanget × Achilles Shoal	I. Cole 1972 (Beall)
MEMORIA DOROTHY BERTSCH	Iliad × Midas Charm	Bertsch 1972
MEMORIA FLOSSIE GUNTER	Royal Nan × C. Bow Bells	Lenette 1974
MEMORIA FRANK HOLLAND	Harlequin × Mem. Crispin Rosales	Holland 1971 (Frank Holland)
MEMORIA GIICHI OTAGURO	Mem. Crispin Rosales × Lc. Yukiko Hironaka	Otaguro 1973
MEMORIA GRANT EICHLER	James Hausermann × Lc. Irene Finney	Hausermann 1974
MEMORIA HELEN BROWN	Xanthette × Lc. Ann Follis	Stewart Inc. 1967

× Modjeska	= Galway Bay

MEMORIA HENRY MORIKUBO	Mem. Crispin Rosales × Lc. Ennerdale	Otaguro 1973
MEMORIA JOSEFA MARTINEZ	Lc. Mem. Maria Miranda × B. nodosa	Ruben 1975
MEMORIA KEVIN WATFORD	Mernia × Lc. Ashgrove	J. Watford 1972 (K. Watford)
MEMORIA MARGARET KOSEL	C. Porcia × Osiris	Kosel 1973
MEMORIA OLIVER COFFEE	C. Nigrella × Herons Ghyll	Trade Winds 1972
MEMORIA RALPH PLACENTIA	Lc. Mem. Albert Heinecke × Norman's Bay	Stewart Inc. 1973
MEMORIA RICHARD BLACK	Mem. Crispin Rosales × Lc. Dee Dee	George Black 1973
MEMORIA ROSELYN REISMAN	Norman's Bay × Lc. Elizabeth Off	Lines 1967

× Pot. Yamockul	= Pot. Marie Pallister

MEMORIA ROY GARRITY	Norman's Bay × Lc. Buccaneer	Rod McLellan Co. 1972
MEMORIA RUTH GESSNER	C. Phillips × Dinsmore	Fields Orchids 1964

× L. rupestris	= Little Boy Blue	× Lc. Blue Boy	= Biscayne Skies

BRASSOLAELIOCATTLEYA

MEMORIA WALTER BROWN — Goldmine × B. digbyana — Coastal Gdns. 1973

MENA DE GARCIA — C. Penang × Norman's Bay — Jesurún 1973

MENE — Green-heart × Golden Myth — Bracey 1961
× Slc. Anzac = Pot. Menezac

MENURE — Dusk × C. Dupreana — F. 1972

MÈRIMÉE† — Bc. Sindorossiama × Lc. Claude Monet — V. 1939
× C. percivaliana = Clara Helena Kienzle

MERLIN — B. nodosa × Dark Waters — Voo Doo Orchids 1974

MERNIA — Mercia × Lc. Ivernia — C. 1940
× Lc. Ashgrove = Mem. Kevin Watford

MERRY — Lc. Antonica Fredrick × Bc. Bill Worsley — Voo Doo Orchids 1974

MICHELLE ORBAN — C. Rembrandt × Yasuko Tachibana — Orban 1975 (Miyamoto)

MIDAS†‡ — The Baroness × Lc. Mrs. Medo — L. 1931
× Lc. Choton = Midaton

MIDAS CHARM — Midas × Lc. Golden Charm — Rod McLellan Co. 1962
× Iliad = Mem. Dorothy Bertsch | × Lc. Ethel D. Giddings = Shirley Raps

MIDAS COPPER — Lc. Copperopolis × Golden Myth — Rod McLellan Co. 1964
× Circus = Verinice | × Summer Shades = Midas Touch

MIDAS TOUCH — Summer Shades × Midas Copper — Rod McLellan Co. 1973

MIDATON — Midas × Lc. Choton — Chin Jiunn Shie 1975 (Chin Sheng Li)
× Ruth Witbeck = Ruth Mao-Li

MIDENETTE†‡ — Zante × Lc. Mrs. Medo — S.A. 1941
× Lc. Haroldiana = Mildred Tucker

MIKI MIYAJIMA — Kahaopea Beauty × Norman's Bay — M. T. Tanaka 1972

MILDRED TUCKER — Midenette × Lc. Haroldiana — Sullivan 1973

MINT JULEP — Holiday Gem × Green-heart — Ruben 1973

MISSY — Golden Myth × Wolteriana — Small 1962
× Buttercup = Mary Crocker

MODJESKA‡ — Nugget × Green-heart — Bracey 1956
× Mem. Helen Brown = Galway Bay

MOKIHANA — Lc. Little Sunbeam × Bl. Ilima — O. Kirsch 1972

MOLFLORA†‡ — Bc. Florence × Lc. Molly Tyler — E. W. Dixon 1939
× Bc. Eagle = Jack Hatfield | × Lc. Laurie Lynn = Candee
× Lc. Land of Enchantment = Lyda Bell Howe | × Lc. South Esk = Molly Esk
| × Slc. Anzac = Pot. Jack Weaver

MOLLY ESK — Lc. South Esk × Molflora — Furrow 1971

MOMERCIA†‡ — Mercia × Lc. Momus — C. 1939
× C. Metapan = Headliner | × Lc. Lomita Park = Spring Acres
× Lc. Bonanza = Bomercia | × Lc. Manila = Art Banta
× Lc. Grub Stake = Distinction

MOONGLOW‡ — C. Araca × Golden Myth — Rivermont 1956
× Bc. Pluto = Limestone

MONT JANE — Maude Montgomery × Jane Helton — Kensington 1974

BRASSOLAELIOCATTLEYA

Name	Parentage	Registrant
MOON HALO	**Lc. New World × Xanthette**	**Rod McLellan Co. 1975**
MORNING SUN†‡	**The Baroness × C. Enid**	**L. 1937**

× Ermine	= Sunlit Morn	× Lc. Robertsoniae	= Sun-Son
× C. Mrs. Frederick Knollys	= Mrs. Sun		

Name	Parentage	Registrant
MORRIS GUNDERSON	**Bc. Dr. A. Kosky × Lc. Joseph Hampton**	**Gunderson 1973**
MOSS CREEK GORGE	**Rain Forest × Bc. Olympic Meadows**	**Beall 1975**
MOUNTELIA†	**Ophelia × Lc. Evelyn Mountain**	**C. 1949**

× Glorious	= Highland Fling

Name	Parentage	Registrant
MOUNT GARIBALDI	**Acapana × Lc. Waianae Sunset**	**Beall 1975**
MOUNT JOHN JAY	**Coronet Bay × Lc. Peggy Huffman**	**Beall 1975**
MOUNT LOGAN	**C. Fulvescens × Pimola**	**Beall 1975**
MOUNT MITCHELL	**Lc. Faith Dee Fanchaly × Golden Slippers**	**Lenette 1974**
MRS. SUN	**Morning Sun × C. Mrs. Frederick Knollys**	**Kensington 1973**
MY PRIDE	**Bc. Hartland × Wake Island**	**Rayridge 1975 (F. J. Bergman)**
MYSTIC MARINER	**Lester McDonald × B. digbyana**	**Stewart Inc. 1974**
MYSTIC WHALER	**Lc. Excellency × Coronet Bay**	**Beall 1973**
NACOST‡	**Nacouchee × Lc. Mem. Walter Armacost**	**A. & R. 1960**

× Patricia Purves	= Bryce Canyon

Name	Parentage	Registrant
NACOUCHEE†‡	**Headon × C. Estelle**	**A. & R. 1952**

× Bc. Mount Hood	= Lingerie	× Lc. Steb Teal	= North Wind
× C. Peanuts	= Pink Ornament	× Slc. Helen Veliz	= Pot. Metal Creek
× C. Pearl Harbor	= Maurice Gusman		

Name	Parentage	Registrant
NANCY WITTORF	**C. Thebes × Norman's Bay**	**Dr. K. Kagawa 1968 (Miyamoto)**

× Lc. Waianae Sunset	= Makaha Glolight

Name	Parentage	Registrant
NANETTE*†‡	**Everest × C. Annette**	**L. 1932**

× Acapana	= Helen Huntington	× C. Fulvescens	= Eunice Helen
× Buttercup	= Neil McDade	× C. Sunrise Chalet	= Elizabeth Caldwell
× B. glauca	= Laura Vandorn Schneider	× C. Yertala	= Leonie Mackay
× C. Barbara Arrowsmith	= Pat Marshall	× Lc. Lorraine Shirai	= Kristin

Name	Parentage	Registrant
NANIWA	**C. Redtop Mountain × Mem. Crispin Rosales**	**Katsuura 1973**
NANKEEN GOLD	**Lc. Marie Stocking × Nugget**	**Crothers 1973**
NAOMI M. YAHIRO	**Norman's Bay × Lc. S. J. Bracey**	**T. Yahiro 1960 (Tagawa)**

× Lc. S. J. Bracey	= Hisayo Hironaka

Name	Parentage	Registrant
NAPLES NIGHT	**B. nodosa × Lc. Zada Fields**	**Voo Doo Orchids 1974**
NATIONAL GOLD	**Golden Llewellyn × Setting Sun**	**Rod McLellan Co. 1975**
NATOMA	**Lc. Mamie Eisenhower × Momercia**	**Rod McLellan Co. 1961**

× Lc. Lomita Park	= Medellin

Name	Parentage	Registrant
NEAL BLAISDELL	**Hanako Omura × Lc. Terry Wayne**	**Miyamoto 1975**
NEIL McDADE	**Nanette × Buttercup**	**Lenette 1974 (Rivermont)**
NEW ENGLAND SPRING	**Envy × B. digbyana**	**Stewart Inc. 1974**
NGUYEN THI MAI-ANH	**Fortune × C. dowiana**	**Stewart Inc. 1974**
NICKIE HOLGUIN	**Baby Doll × C. Esbetts**	**A. & R. 1975**

BRASSOLAELIOCATTLEYA

NIGIANA†‡	**Lc. Mossiana × Nigon**	**Jeal 1955 (C)**

× Lc. Kathleen Jeal = Freda Cooke

NORMA BEE	**Shining Harvest × Alice Muller**	**Briscoe 1971 (Genevieve Toy)**
NORMA BRISCOE	**Golden Galleon × Bobby Ward**	**Clark Day Jr. 1975**
NORMA KUMIKO HEEN	**Eva Patterson × Lc. Bonanza**	**Otaguro 1973**
NORMANI	**Norman's Bay × C. Niger**	**Pff. V. & L. 1975**
NORMAN'S BAY†‡	**Bc. Hartland × Lc. Ishtar**	**L. 1946**

× Ashiya = Margaret Way
× Kahaopea Beauty = Miki Miyajima
× Kapiolani Beauty = Hilo Glory
× Kuo Kuang = Chung-Chweng Chen
× Pamela Farrell = Mem. Arthur Freed
× Sassacus = Ryoshin Okano
× Bc. Evelyn Zuck = Pigeon Bay
× Bc. Mount Hood = Granite Bay
× Bc. The Globe = Globe Bay
× C. Akebono = Norman's Dawn
× C. Elizabeth Anderson = Betty Midkiff
× C. loddigesii = Diane Soo Hoo
× C. Nellie Roberts = Tan Loh Teck
× C. Niger = Normani
× C. Penang = Mena de Garcia
× C. Porcia = Howard's Luck
× C. Sedlescombe = Lo Ying
× Lc. Buccaneer = Mem. Roy Garrity
× Lc. Cassandra = Chief Osceola
× Lc. Crowborough Sunshine = Sunshine Bay
× Lc. Excellency = Tom Tom
× Lc. Fort Lauderdale = Nubia Nicoli Cabral
× Lc. George Cutler = Cutler Bay
× Lc. José Dias Castro = Mem. Beniamino Gigli
× Lc. Lee Langford = Dorcille Little
× Lc. Lenn Follett = Tomoko Kubo
× Lc. Mem. Albert Heinecke = Mem. Ralph Placentia
× Lc. Momus = Louis Palacio
× Lc. Nigrescent = Paul Shodo Yempuku
× Lc. Sacramento = Koinaba
× Lc. Security Gate = Norman's Gate
× Lc. Waianae Sunset = War Chant
× Lc. Walter Slagle = Florence Dickinson
× Lc. Zada Fields = Iron Cap Mountain
× Pot. Gordon Siu = Pot. Norman's Glory
× Sc. Cleopatra = Pot. Cleo Bay
× Slc. Helen Veliz = Pot. Scott Holguin
× Slc. Naomi Kerns = Pot. Peter Haynes
× Slc. Persian Garden = Pot. Persian Bay

NORMAN'S DAWN	**C. Akebono × Norman's Bay**	**Otaguro 1972**
NORMAN'S GATE	**Lc. Security Gate × Norman's Bay**	**E. F. Patterson 1973**
NORMÉESSE	**Normoma × Bc. Déesse**	**Wondabah 1974**
NORMOMA	**Norman's Bay × Lc. Titymoma**	**Wondabah 1964**

× Bc. Déesse = Norméesse

NORTELA	**C. Tela × Norman's Bay**	**J. & S. 1965**

× Lc. Fort Lauderdale = Shinsei

NORTHERN LIGHTS	**Lc. Mem. Albert Heinecke × Edwin Chong**	**Rex Foster's 1973 (Fordyce)**
NORTH WIND	**Nacouchee × Lc. Steb Teal**	**Miskimens 1973**
NUGGET†‡	**Palmyre × Lc. Luminosa**	**S. 1941**

× Jane Helton = Nuggeton
× Malvern = Doris Aileen
× Lc. Grandee = Lemon Light
× Lc. Marie Stocking = Nankeen Gold

NUGGETON	**Jane Helton × Nugget**	**Rayridge 1975**
NUUANU DAWN	**Luis H. Yanes × Bc. Déesse**	**J. Milton Warne 1973**
NUUANU FANCY	**Luis H. Yanes × C. Enid**	**J. Milton Warne 1971**
NUUANU SUNSHINE	**Lc. Doubloon × Jane Helton**	**J. Milton Warne 1975**
NUBIA NICOLI CABRAL	**Norman's Bay × Lc. Fort Lauderdale**	**N. Suzuki 1971**
NYMPH BAY	**Bc. Nymphe × Norman's Bay**	**Altenburg 1963**

× Dark Waters = Tansei

OCEAN SPRAY	**Bl. Sea Urchin × C. R.(owena) Prowe**	**W. W. G. Moir 1971**
OLEO	**Setting Sun × Buttercup**	**Rod McLellan Co. 1975 (Spencer)**

BRASSOLAELIOCATTLEYA

OLIVE WRIGHT	**Xanthedo × Rebecca Sieff**	**S. Wright 1973 (Sieff)**
OPAL WILDE	**Lc. Princess × Bc. Taquin**	**Pelc 1972**
ORANGE GOLD	**Malvern × Lc. Lee Langford**	**Reimer 1973**
ORANGE GLORY‡	**Bc. Heatonensis × Lc. Elinor**	**A. 1928**

× Goulds Gold	= Goulds Glory	× C. Nellie Roberts	= Sheila Scarlet
× C. Barney Aronson	= Tiffany Renee Colborne	× L. tenebrosa	= Kelly Brooks

ORANGE SHERBET‡	**Lc. Orange Beauty × Bc. Diadem**	**Rod McLellan Co. 1962**

× Epi. guatemalense	= Yam. Offbeat

ORIENTAL GEM	**Mem. Crispin Rosales × Coed**	**Kushima 1968**

× Slc. Mossiabella	= Pot. Esperanza dela Cruz

ORO RICO	**Aprica × Lc. Mem. Albert Heinecke**	**A. & R. 1973 (R. McLeod)**
OSIRIS‡	**Lc. Princess Ishtar × Bc. Princess Patricia**	**Raasch 1954**

× C. Porcia	= Mem. Margaret Kosel	× Pot. Hugo Porto	= Pot. Palmetto

OSWALDO PAULINO SANTOS	**Bc. Pastoral × Lc. Paradisio**	**N. Suzuki 1975**
OTANGO	**Lc. Wendy Tayler × Otomayim**	**Rod McLellan Co. 1974**
OTOMAYIM	**Lc. S. J. Bracey × Llewellyn**	**Rod McLellan Co. 1969 (Miyamoto)**

× Benin Bronze	= Sun Trail	× C. Tethys	= Syto
× Goldenette	= Meadow Sun	× Lc. Edgard van Belle	= Kay Heron
× Goldfield	= John Smithson	× Lc. Wendy Tayler	= Otango
× Setting Sun	= Solo Sun	× Lc. Western Sunset	= Kohoutek
× Xanthette	= Sale O'Gold		

PACEMAKER	**Lc. Western Sunset × Xanthette**	**Rod McLellan Co. 1973**
PACIFIC CORONET	**Pacific Gold × L. Coronet**	**Rod McLellan Co. 1973**
PACIFIC GOLD‡	**Lc. Pacific Sun × Golden Myth**	**Rod McLellan Co. 1963**

× Goldenette	= Gild	× L. Coronet	= Pacific Coronet
× Golden Spires	= Golden Discovery	× Lc. Edgard van Belle	= Vanci
× Lester McDonald	= Kimberley Ann Roccaforte	× Lc. Lydia Hubbell	= Frances Campbell DeGear
× Rising Sun	= Stellar Gold	× Lc. Orange Ann	= Daystar
× Sundust	= Apertif	× Slc. Anzac	= Pot. Pacific Warrior

PAINTED DESERT‡	**Kathy Krugman × Midenette**	**Jeal 1955**

× Bobby Ward	= American Frontier	× C. aurantiaca	= Poppy Trail
× Mamie Fouraker	= California Special	× C. velutina	= Sunrise Serenade

PAMELA FARRELL	**Norman's Bay × Herons Ghyll**	**A. & R. 1961**

× Lucky Strike	= Phinijsikakarn	× Lc. Amber Glow	= Port Sherry
× Norman's Bay	= Mem. Arthur Freed	× Lc. Lee Langford	= Iroquois Trail
× C. Horace	= Malibu Gem		

PAONNEAU	**Lc. President de Brouwer × Dusk**	**F. 1972**
PARADISE CAVES	**Emerald Meadow × Lc. Seminole Sunset**	**Beall 1972**
PARADOR	**Simoun × Lc. Edgard van Belle**	**Pff. V. & L. 1973**
PARAKEET	**Kathy Krugman × Bc. Daffodil**	**Whitebrook 1974 (Voo Doo Orchids)**
PASTEL†‡	**Queen of the Belgians × C. Estelle**	**A. & R. 1950**

× C. Ruth M. Johnston	= Angela Starke

BRASSOLAELIOCATTLEYA

PAT MARSHALL	**C. Barbara Arrowsmith × Nanette**	**W. H. Marshall 1972**
PATRICIA PURVES‡	**Norman's Bay × Bc. Hartland**	**A. & R. 1961**

× Nacost = Bryce Canyon

PATRICK MIZUTA‡	**Wake Island × J. K. Lilly**	**Miyamoto 1954**

× Lc. Summerland Girl = Somthawil

PATTON MYTH	**C. General Patton × Golden Myth**	**Kensington 1973**
PAUL SHODO YEMPUKU	**Norman's Bay × Lc. Nigrescent**	**Otaguro 1973**
PEKING GOLD	**Golden Dream × Golden Slippers**	**Rod McLellan Co. 1973 (Fordyce)**
PENN STATE	**Golden Dome × Lc. Mem. Albert Heinecke**	**Gubler 1974**
PENNSYLVANIA SPRING	**Spring and Summer × B. digbyana**	**Stewart Inc. 1975 (Rehfield)**
PERKO McALLISTER	**Pimola × Lc. Ann Follis**	**McAllister 1972**
PHINIJSIKAKARN	**Pamela Farrell × Lucky Strike**	**Tipawasdi 1973 (Chindanavic)**
PIGEON BAY	**Bc. Evelyn Zuck × Norman's Bay**	**O. Kirsch 1971**
PIMAS CROWN	**Kong-Urai Gold × Lc. Fedora**	**Rod McLellan Co. 1973 (Spencer)**
PIMOLA‡	**C. granulosa × Ojai**	**Abbott 1957**

× C. Bob Betts = Esther Schaber
× C. Fulvescens = Mount Logan
× C. Karae Lyn Sugiyama = Green Mount
× Lc. Ann Follis = Perko McAllister
× Lc. Edgard van Belle = Splash Belle
× Lc. Golden Gate = Gola

PINEY PATTERSON	**Lc. David Lozoya × Herons Ghyll**	**E. F. Patterson 1970 (R. K. Fields)**

× C. Tango = Summer Tango
× Pot. Rebecca Merkel = Pot. Bicentennial

PINKIE‡	**C. Bow Bells × Nanette**	**Bracey 1960**

× Lc. Pirate King = Whitney Lawler

PINK ORNAMENT	**C. Peanuts × Nacouchee**	**Rod McLellan Co. 1972**
PIRATES QUEST	**Jane Helton × Golden Slippers**	**Rod McLellan Co. 1974 (Fordyce)**
PIS-VIMOL	**Aztec Princess × Lucky Strike**	**Chindanavic 1975**
POLKA DOT	**B. nodosa × Lc. Autumn Yellow**	**Small 1962**

× Lc. Lorraine Shirai = Billye

POLYNESIAN	**Wake Island × Lc. Mira**	**J. Milton Warne 1962**

× Keopulani = Deana

POPPY TRAIL	**C. aurantiaca × Painted Desert**	**Crothers 1971**
PORT SHERRY	**Pamela Farrell × Lc. Amber Glow**	**Fields Orchids 1972**
PRIMATE†‡	**Primrose × Bc. Heatonensis**	**S. 1941**

× Golden Slippers = Trojan Gold
× Pot. Florence Powell = Pot. Soraya

PRIMROSE BEAUTY	**Dinsmore × Golden Beach**	**Fields Orchids 1973**
PRIMROSE PATH	**Lc. Lydia Hubbell × Golden Myth**	**Rod McLellan Co. 1973**
PURPLE GLORY	**Fleur de Lys × C. Hardyana**	**Mrs. W. F. White 1975 (William F. White)**
PU'ULA'ULA	**C. Redgatta × Mem. Crispin Rosales**	**Otaguro 1973**
RAIN FOREST	**Lc. Kencolor × Pimola**	**Beall 1965**

× Lester McDonald = Shamrock Dome
× Zanget = Greenstone Canyon
× Bc. Olympic Meadows = Moss Creek Gorge
× Lc. Elstead Gem = Little Meadow Mountain

RAMPART RIDGE	**Zanget × Lc. Waianae Sunset**	**Beall 1973**

BRASSOLAELIOCATTLEYA

RANGER SIX‡ Nacouchee × C. Empress Bells A. & R. 1964

× C. Bob Betts = Janice Watson
× C. Empress Bells = Six Bells
× C. Little Angel = Dianacita
× C. Old Whitey = Empress Range

REBECCA BULL C. Luegeae × Robert Gifford F. H. Williams 1974 (Originator unknown)

REBECCA SIEFF‡ Bikan × Lc. Canberra Sieff 1953

× Xanthedo = Olive Wright

REDOUBT MOUNTAIN Bc. Mount Juneau × Lc. Resolution Mountain Beall 1975
RED OWL MOUNTAIN Secret Cove × Lc. Fires of Spring Beall 1974
RENEE NICOLSON Lc. Adolph Hecker × Bc. Daffodil Nicolson 1971
RICHARD NIXON‡ Malvern × C. Bow Bells Rivermont 1960

× L. Coronet = Ruby Lantern
× Lc. Mem. Albert Heinecke = Frances Miles

RIO'S JEWEL Jewel Higdon × Jane Helton Ruben 1974
RIO'S POLKA DOT Jane Helton × B. nodosa Ruben 1975
RIO'S SPRING Lc. Golden Spring × B. nodosa Ruben 1974
RIO TAMPA Lc. Nigrescent × Bc. Hartland Ruben 1975
RISING SUN Meru × Lc. Orange Beauty Rod McLellan Co. 1965

× Pacific Gold = Stellar Gold
× Lc. Curtis Hansard = Flo
× Lc. Mercia = Amenity
× Lc. Orange Charm = Mandarin Bay
× Lc. Pacific Sun = Sunshine Meadow

RIVERMONT'S GOLD Jewel Higdon × Fulvano Lenette 1975 (Rivermont)

ROAD TO MANDALAY Golden Galleon × Buttercup Crothers 1971
ROAD TO RIO Lc. Canberra × Joyance Stewart Inc. 1974
ROBERT GIFFORD‡ Golden Queen × Nugget Tomiyasu 1958 (Miyamoto)

× Golden Queen = Golden Gifford
× C. Luegeae = Rebecca Bull

ROBERT KAMIYAMA Lc. George MacDonell × Mem. Crispin Rosales Otaguro 1974
ROJANADARA Ewart McDonald × C. intermedia Rojanadara 1975
ROMANIA WOOLLEY Bc. Evelyn Zuck × L. purpurata O. Kirsch 1972
ROSE CHIYOKO KAKAZU Lc. Quadroon × Mem. Bill Fouraker Otaguro 1974
ROSEMARY HAYDEN Bc. Déesse × Lc. Blue Boy Heaner 1973 (Beall)

ROUNDER Mem. Crispin Rosales × Lc. Yvette Ann Rex Foster's 1973 (Fordyce)

ROYAL FORTUNE Fortune × Bobby Ward Stewart Inc. 1974
ROYAL HARBOR Lc. Ronselensis × Bc. Maikai Voo Doo Orchids 1974
ROYAL NAN C. Empress Bells × Nanette Rivermont 1965

× C. Bow Bells = Mem. Flossie Gunter

RUBEN'S GEM Holiday Gem × Lc. Peggy Huffman Ruben 1974
RUBEN'S VERDE Green-heart × Lester McDonald Ruben 1974
RUBY LANTERN L. Coronet × Richard Nixon Crothers 1973
RUBY MESA Lc. Maria Ozzella × Mem. Crispin Rosales Rod McLellan Co. 1975 (Spencer)

RUBY WATANABE Carmen Cestero × Lc. Nigrescent Otaguro 1973
RUSTY ZEIGLER Lc. Golden Ray × Xanthedo Robt. Smith 1971 (Ryerson)

RUTH CLINE McDADE Buttercup × C. mendelii Lenette 1974 (Rivermont)

× L. Gold Star = Crowders Mountain

BRASSOLAELIOCATTLEYA

RUTH MAO-LI	**Midaton × Ruth Witbeck**	**Chin Jiunn Shie 1975**
RUTH WITBECK	**Mountelia × Jane Helton**	**Gore 1958**
× Midaton × Sc. Cleopatra	= Ruth Mao-Li = Pot. Sunray	× Slc. Langleyensis = Pot. Margaret Sadoyama
RYOSHIN OKANO	**Sassacus × Norman's Bay**	**Otaguro 1973**
SADAO YAMAMOTO	**Crown Prince Akihito × Lc. Lenn Follett**	**Otaguro 1973**
SAHARA SAND	**Blanche Okamoto × Jane Helton**	**Rod McLellan Co. 1975**
SALE O'GOLD	**Otomayim × Xanthette**	**Rod McLellan Co. 1975**
SALLY STAGGS	**Lc. Lee Langford × B. digbyana**	**Fort Caroline 1972**
SAMARKAND	**Lc. Orange Gem × Mamie Fouraker**	**Crothers 1971**
SAMOSET†‡	**Bc. Ilene × Lc. Lucy Marcelene**	**A. & R. 1942**
× Bc. S. M. Damon	= Emily Simmons	
SANDY ROBINSON	Lc. Adolph Hecker × Herons Ghyll	**J. O. Brown 1971** **(Originator unknown)**
SAN JUAN SUNSET	**Lc. Mem. Albert Heinecke × Mellowglow**	**Beall 1973**
SAN REMO	**C. Nerto × June Moore**	**Altenburg 1971**
SARACEN	**Fortune × L. Zip**	**Stewart Inc. 1974**
SASSACUS	**King Emperor × C. Remy Chollet**	**A. & R. 1944**
× Norman's Bay	= Ryoshin Okano	
SECRET COVE	**Ryersonwood × Lc. Bonanza**	**Beall 1967**
× Lc. Fires of Spring	= Red Owl Mountain	
SETTING SUN	**Lc. Pacific Sun × Blanche Okamoto**	**Rod McLellan Co. 1963**
× Buttercup × Golden Llewellyn × Otomayim	= Oleo = National Gold = Solo Sun	× Lc. Lydia Hubbell = Golden Hue × Lc. Western Sunset = Briteside × Slc. Brandywine = Pot. Edith Hancock
SHAMROCK DOME	**Rain Forest × Lester McDonald**	**Beall 1975**
SHEER MELODY	Helen Morita × Xanthette	**Stewart Inc. 1965**
× Fortune	= Golden Shower	
SHEILA SCARLET	**Orange Glory × C. Nellie Roberts**	**Hershy 1975** **(Originator unknown)**
× Danny Kaleikini	= Manoa Valley	
SHINING HARVEST†	**Morning Sun × Consul Greig**	**Rivermont 1953**
× Alice Muller	= Norma Bee	
SHINSEI	**Nortela × Lc. Fort Lauderdale**	**N. Suzuki 1972**
SHIRLEY RAPS	**Midas Charm × Lc. Ethel D. Giddings**	Bertsch 1972
SIMOUN†‡	**Costes × C. Princess Royal**	**V. 1943**
× Lc. Edgard van Belle	= Parador	
SIX BELLS	**Ranger Six × C. Empress Bells**	**Casey 1972**
SOLIMAR	**Jane Helton × Lester McDonald**	**Ruben 1975**
SOLO SUN	**Setting Sun × Otomayim**	**Rod McLellan Co. 1974**
SOMTHAWIL	**Lc. Summerland Girl × Patrick Mizuta**	**Chuanyen 1975**
SPENCER BEAUTY	**C. Peetersii × Mem. Crispin Rosales**	**Stewart Inc. 1974** **(Spencer)**
SPLASH BELLE	**Pimola × Lc. Edgard van Belle**	**McAllister 1975**
SPRING ACRES	**Momercia × Lc. Lomita Park**	**Rod McLellan Co. 1975**
SPRING AND SUMMER	**Lc. Cinnamon Stick × Xanthette**	**Stewart Inc. 1968**
× B. digbyana	= Pennsylvania Spring	
SPUN GOLD	**Brocade × Malvern**	**Rivermont 1961**
× Lc. Lorraine Shirai	= Formosan Gold	

BRASSOLAELIOCATTLEYA

Name	Parentage	Registrant
STANTON BERMAN	Bc. Dr. A. Kosky × Lc. Laurie Lynn	Gunderson 1971
STARLAND	Lc. Twinkle Star × Bc. Hartland	J. & S. 1971
STAR TOPAZ	Lc. Carrie Estelle × Bc. Star Ruby	W. W. G. Moir 1973
STELLAR GOLD	Pacific Gold × Rising Sun	Rod McLellan Co. 1975
STEVEN HOLGUIN	Bc. Déesse × Tiara	A. & R. 1975
SUMATRA SAFARI	Lc. Mem. Albert Heinecke × Joyance	Stewart Inc. 1974
SUMMER FESTIVAL	C. Chamberlainiana × Mem. Crispin Rosales	Katsuura 1973
SUMMER SHADES‡	Lc. S. J. Bracey × Blanche Okamoto	Rod McLellan & Co. 1964

× Midas Copper = Midas Touch | × Lc. Mary Jo Nelson = Gold Torch
× Lc. Gatton Glory = Autumn Glory | × Lc. Pacific Sun = Golden Reward
× Lc. Lee Langford = Titian Queen

Name	Parentage	Registrant
SUMMER TANGO	Piney Patterson × C. Tango	Lenette 1974
SUN CREST	Gold City × Lc. Brilliant Orange	Rod McLellan Co. 1975
SUNDUST	Golden Myth × Lc. Golden Charm	Rod McLellan Co. 1965

× Pacific Gold = Apertif

Name	Parentage	Registrant
SUNFLAME‡	Priapus × Lc. Sunburst	C. 1948

× Tiara = Manatee Gold

Name	Parentage	Registrant
SUNKIST‡	Lc. Lucida × Green-heart	Spencer 1958 (Bracey)

× C. Iris = Carol Boudeman | × Epi. gracile = Yam. Hawk's Nest

Name	Parentage	Registrant
SUNLIT MORN	Ermine × Morning Sun	Muse's 1971
SUNNY SANDS	Lc. Sunburn × Bc. Hula Girl	J. Milton Warne 1975
SUNRISE SERENADE	Painted Desert × C. velutina	Crothers 1973
SUNSET BAY	Llewellyn × Lc. Waianae Sunset	Matsumoto 1968 (Miyamoto)

× Gloria Schmidt = Frederick Schmidt

Name	Parentage	Registrant
SUNSET GORGE	Lc. Mem. Albert Heinecke × Citron Pass	Beall 1973
SUNSHINE BAY	Lc. Crowborough Sunshine × Norman's Bay	Crothers 1973
SUNSHINE MEADOW	Lc. Pacific Sun × Rising Sun	Rod McLellan Co. 1975
SUNSHINE NARROWS	Zanget × Lc. Sunburn	Beall 1973
SUN-SON	Morning Sun × Lc. Robertsoniae	Kensington 1973
SUN TRAIL	Benin Bronze × Otomayim	Rod McLellan Co. 1974
SUNWAPTA PEAK	Bc. Mount Hood × Lc. Amber Glow	Beall 1975
SWEET SUE	Edwin Chong × Lc. Suzanne Fullerton	L. E. Moore 1972
SYLVIA REILLY‡	Lc. Lorraine Shirai × Xanthedo	Waddell 1962 (Limberlost)

× Lester McDonald = Kelly Williams | × Pot. Tapestry Peak = Pot. Haystack Mountains
× Lc. Western Sunset = Marigold Meadows | × Slc. Anzac = Pot. Barbara Wichmann

Name	Parentage	Registrant
SYTO	C. Tethys × Otomayim	Rod McLellan Co. 1975
TABLE MOUNTAIN	Lc. Alma Wichmann × Emerald Meadow	Beall 1975
TAKANAO SEKI	Lc. Fort Lauderdale × Dark Waters	Suzuki 1971
TAN LOH TECK	C. Nellie Roberts × Norman's Bay	Ng & Tan 1971
TANSEI	Nymph Bay × Dark Waters	Suzuki 1971
TENG	Lc. Bonanza × Bc. Mount Anderson	Katsuura 1973
TERRIE	Lc. Irene Finney × Ann	Hausermann 1974
TERRI HOOVER	Wake Island × Lc. Brazoria	Coastal Gdns. 1971
THUNDER MOUNTAIN	Lc. Mem. Albert Heinecke × Fortune	Beall 1975
TIARA†‡	Palmyre × Lc. Nugget	S. 1946

× Sunflame = Manatee Gold | × Bc. Déesse = Steven Holguin

BRASSOLAELIOCATTLEYA

TIFFANY RENEE COLBORNE	C. Barney Aronson × Orange Glory	Tompkins 1975
TITIAN QUEEN	Summer Shades × Lc. Lee Langford	Rod McLellan Co. 1975
TOMOKO KUBO	Norman's Bay × Lc. Lenn Follett	Otaguro 1973
TOM TOM	Norman's Bay × Lc. Excellency	Stewart Inc. 1972
TOSHIKAZU TAKAHASHI	Mem. Crispin Rosales × Lc. Hyperion	Takahashi 1973
TRIBUTE	Mem. Crispin Rosales × C. Horace	Trymwood 1974
TRIO	Lc. Lagoon × B. digbyana	Stewart Inc. 1973
TROJAN GOLD	Golden Slippers × Primate	Crothers 1974
TROPICAL MARKET	C. guttata × Fortune	Stewart Inc. 1974 (J. Rikel)
TWILIGHT TIME	Armida × Lc. Twinkle Star	Rod McLellan Co. 1975 (Spencer)
TWINKLE MATER	Matriarch × Lc. Twinkle Star	McAllister 1975
TWINKLE ROSALES	Lc. Twinkle Star × Mem. Crispin Rosales	Gauda 1973
UBANGI‡	Lc. Golden Lustre × Myophia	Rivermont 1962
× Malvern	= Malu	
VANCI	Lc. Edgard van Belle × Pacific Gold	Rod McLellan Co. 1975
VERINICE	Circus × Midas Copper	Rod McLellan Co. 1972
VERMONTS GREEN MOUNTAINS	Green Giant × B. digbyana	Stewart Inc. 1975 (Rehfield)
VICTORIA‡	Antoinette × C. Portia	Colman 1929
× Lc. Mariner	= Crater Lake	
VIRGIN GOLD	Iliad × Lc. Lorraine Shirai	J. & S. 1974
VOO DOO	Bc. Daffodil × Lc. Antonica Fredrick	Voo Doo Orchids 1974
WAIKANE	Lc. Rosa Kirsch × Frank Tatsumura	O. Kirsch 1971
WAIKIKI SUNSET	Walter Abe × Waianae Sunset	Matsumoto 1966 (Miyamoto)
× Slc. Naomi Kerns	= Pot. Mem. Seichi Iwasaki	
WAKE ISLAND†‡	Agnes McWilliams × C. Reseda	R. E. Warne 1945
× Bc. Hartland	= My Pride	× Lc. Brazoria = Terri Hoover
× C. Yertala	= Marion Moreland	× Lc. Mary Rose = Mary Island
WALTER ABE‡	Llewellyn × Lc. Kaumana	B. Tanaka 1954 (Abe)
× Mary M. Damon	= Mary Shipman	× Lc. Amber Glow = Walter's Glow
WALTER'S GLOW	Walter Abe × Lc. Amber Glow	Miyamoto 1975
WAR CHANT	Norman's Bay × Lc. Waianae Sunset	Goddard 1973 (Kirch)
WAR EAGLE	C. Priscilla Ward × Chief Joseph	W. W. Wilson 1973
WARREN WEVER	Jewel Higdon × Lc. Amber Glow	Pickell 1975 (Rivermont)
WHISKEY GIRL	Lc. Dorothy Fried × Crown Prince Akihito	D. Tom 1972
WHITNEY LAWLER	Pinkie × Lc. Pirate King	Gubler 1971
WILL BATES	Goldmine × Buttercup	Furrow 1972
WILLIAM STEWART	Xanthette × Golden Slippers	Stewart Inc. 1973
WINNIE THE POOH	Lc. Gladys Millner × Betty Moe	Fort Caroline 1973
WINSTON HOSHINO‡	Lc. S. J. Bracey × Wendell Hoshino	F. Y. Hoshino 1952
× Crown Jewel	= Winston's Jewel	
WINSTON'S JEWEL	Winston Hoshino × Crown Jewel	Miyamoto 1975
XANTHEDO†‡	Xanthea × Lc. Mrs. Medo	C. 1939
× Rebecca Sieff	= Olive Wright	× Lc. Golden Ray = Rusty Zeigler

BRASSOLAELIOCATTLEYA

XANTHETTE†‡ — **Midenette × Xanthedo** — **S.A. 1948**

× Golden Slippers = William Stewart
× Malvern = Acclaim
× Otomayim = Sale O'Gold
× Lc. Elinor = Elinette
× Lc. Lagoon = Jungle River
× Lc. New World = Moon Halo
× Lc. Western Sunset = Pacemaker

YAP ENG HOE — **Lc. Mem. Albert Heinecke × Canari** — **Stewart Inc. 1971**

YASUKO TACHIBANA — **Norman's Bay × Lc. Mysedo** — **Choy 1961 (Fujino)**

× C. Rembrandt = Michelle Orban

YELLOW BALL — **Bc. White Ball × Yellow Peril** — **You Nan Chang 1975**

YELLOW BUTTERFLY — **Kong-Urai Gold × Lc. Mem. Maggie Hood** — **Beard 1971**

YELLOW BUTTONS — **Lc. Pixie Gold × Bouton D'Or** — **Wilkins 1973**

YELLOW IMP — **Bc. Daffodil × Lc. Neon** — **Clarelen 1958**

× C. aurantiaca = Bonita

YELLOW JEWELL — **Jewel Higdon × Lc. Anne Walker** — **Lenette 1974 (Rivermont)**

× Golden Slippers = Joanna Dawn

YELLOW PERIL — **The Baroness × Lc. Odessa** — **Abbott 1960**

× Bc. White Ball = Yellow Ball

YOLO HOOD — **Bc. Mount Hood × Lc. Yolo** — **McAllister 1975**

YORKTOWN — **C. bicolor × Golden Slippers** — **Stewart Inc. 1974**

YELLOW SEA — **Lc. Blanchflava × Bc. Seafoam** — **Lenette 1974 (Rivermont)**

YOSHIE EVELYN SAWAI — **Crown Prince Akihito × Lc. Cabazon** — **Otaguro 1972**

YOSHIKO ASATO — **Lc. Canberra Glow × Jane Helton** — **Otaguro 1973**

YUKA MIYAJIMA — **Kahaopea Beauty × Lc. S. J. Bracey** — **M. T. Tanaka 1972**

ZAFARAN — **Lc. Bergamote × Canari** — **F. 1972**

ZANGET‡ — **Zanturano × Nugget** — **Stamme 1963**

× Achilles Shoal = Mem. Darrel Cole
× Fortune = Halloween Canyon
× Rain Forest = Greenstone Canyon
× Lc. Sunburn = Sunshine Narrows
× Lc. Waianae Sunset = Rampart Ridge

ZANLEEGLO — Glozan × Lc. Lee Langford — **Rod McLellan Co. 1975 (Spencer)**

ZANTURANO†‡ — **Tucurano × Zante** — **C. 1943**

× B. digbyana = Gloria Shouse

ZEECRABBE†‡ — **Bc. Vilmoriniana × Lc. Abyssinia** — **S. 1946**

× Lc. Mem. Albert Heinecke = Engraved

ZELMA LONG FRAZER — **C. trianaei × Marion Ryerson** — **Gaar 1972 (Ryerson)**

BRASSOPHRONITIS

CLAIRE BEAUMONT — **Soph. coccinea × B. glauca** — C. F. Beaumont 1972

BROUGHTONIA

sanguinea†‡ — **species**

× C. Bactia = Ctna. Summer Dream
× C. Phyllis Hetfeld = Ctna. Summer Madness
× C. Picturata = Ctna. Summer Laughter
× C. violacea = Ctna. Ultra-violent
× C. Wolteriana = Ctna. Little Treasure

BROUGHTONIA

sanguinea†‡ *(continued)*

× Ctps. Libertad	= Ctpsta. Jamacuba	× Epi. stamfordianum	= Eptn. Bohio
× Ctna. Keith Roth	= Ctna. Jamaica Red	× Eptn. Alice Pancoast	= Eptn. Fort Lauderdale
× Ctna. Rosy Jewel	= Ctna. Alina Froelich	× Lna. Ruby	= Lna. Jim Bloom
× Epi. mariae	= Eptn. Calypso		

BROWNARA

ROBERT	**Diab. Alice Hart × C. O'brieniana**	**W. W. G. Moir 1973**

BURKILLARA

AUGUST ROSE	**Aërdns. Mandai × V. tricolor**	**S'pore Orchids 1971**
COY MAIDEN	**Aërdns. Bogor × V. Poepoe**	**S'pore Orchids 1971**
FANCY FLIGHT	**Aërdns. Rosy Dawn × V. Poepoe**	**S'pore Orchids 1973**
FANCY FREE	**Aërdns. Bogor × V. Blue Fantasy**	**S'pore Orchids 1972 (Mrs. Gracia Lewis)**
ONG THYE CHIEW	**Aërdns. Bogor × V. Dawn Nishimura**	**How Yee Peng 1975**
SANDERLING	**Aërdns. Bogor × V.** sanderana	**S'pore Orchids 1972**
TIDARMA SULING	**Aërdns. Bogor × V. Rothschildiana**	**Suling 1975**

BURRAGEARA

AKALA	**Mtdm. Hapahaole × Oda. Apricot Meadows**	W. W. G. Moir 1971
SAMBU RIVER	**Mtdm. Aztec Gold × Oda. Isabella**	W. W. G. Moir 1974
SANGUINE	**Mtdm. Cleopatra × Vuyl. Sunset Bay**	W. W. G. Moir 1972

CATANOCHES

REBECCA NORTHEN	**Ctsm. roseum × Cyc. chlorochilon**	**Furrow 1973**

CATASETUM

DELIGHTFUL	**roseum × pileatum**	**Furrow 1973**
expansum	**species**	

× pileatum = Orchidglade

fimbriatum	**species**	

× trulla = Francis Nelson

FRANCIS NELSON	**trulla × fimbriatum**	**Allyn 1974 (Beall)**
GRACE DUNN‡	**warscewiczii × roseum**	**W. W. G. Moir 1959**

× roseum = Rebecca Northen

MARY SPENCER	**trulla × pileatum**	**R. W. Spencer 1974**
ORCHIDGLADE	**pileatum × expansum**	**J. & S. 1974**
pileatum‡	**species**	

× expansum	= Orchidglade	× roseum	= Delightful
× platyglossum	= Platypil	× trulla	= Mary Spencer

platyglossum‡	**species**	

× pileatum = Platypil

PLATYPIL	**platyglossum × pileatum**	**R. W. Spencer 1974**

CATASETUM

REBECCA NORTHEN	**Grace Dunn × roseum**		**W. W. G. Moir 1971**
roseum†	**species**		
× Grace Dunn	= Rebecca Northen	× Cyc. chlorochilon	= Ctnchs. Rebecca Northen
× pileatum	= Delightful		
trulla	**species**		
× fimbriatum	= Francis Nelson	× pileatum	= Mary Spencer

CATTLEYA

ABE KEHR	**Albania × Bob Betts**		**Kehr 1960**
× Bow Bells	= Classique		
aclandiae*†‡	**species**		
× aurantiaca	= Robin Colleen	× Lc. Antonica Fredrick	= Lc. Leigh Ann Blackmore
× luteola	= Small World	× Sl. Psyche	= Slc. Precious Stones
× Blc. Fortune	= Blc. Lost Treasure		
× Epi. atropurpureum	= Epc. Aroma Grande		
ADABETT	**Bob Betts × Yvonne Adair**		**Kensington 1973**
ADRIA CARITA OSIA	**Morne Le Blanc × Rivermont Imperial**		**Rod McLellan Co. 1972**
AFFECTION†‡	**White Bell × Swan**		**Rivermont 1955**
× Intermediette	= Erica Antoinette	× The Friendly Third	= Virginia Bonner
AGE OF SAIL	**Silver Lining × The Friendly Third**		**Stewart Inc. 1974**
AKEBONO†‡	**labiata × Fabiata**		**S. Takeda 1952**
× Blc. Jahorco	= Blc. Hiei	× Blc. Norman's Bay	= Blc. Norman's Dawn
ALBATROSS†‡	**Mlle. Louise Pauwels × Vanir**		**Rivermont 1956**
× Celė Markell	= Dream of Summer	× Epi. mariae	= Epc. Green Marie
ALICE PEARCE‡	**mossiae × Princess Royal**		**H. Patterson 1952**
× Lc. Lucie Hausermann	= Lc. Lupe		
ALICE SHIRAI†‡	**Bow Bells × Snow Song**		**Shirai 1951**
× luteola	= Suzanne Snyder		
ALLIE CALHOUN	**Myron A. Hofer × Henrietta Japhet**		**M. J. Bates 1973**
ALLYN STAR	**Highburiensis × Catherine Digwood**		**V. & N. Jupp 1975**
ALWYNII†‡	**Amabilis × Enid**		**Harrison 1911**
× Eileen Patterson	= Dark Memory		
amethystoglossa*†‡	**species**		
× Cotton Belle	= Rowena Baer	× Bc. Mount St. Helens	= Bc. Yachats
× Enid	= Chewelah	× Lc. El Cerrito	= Lc. Little Ben
× Guatemalensis	= Dale Edward		
AMY WARREN	**Ballet Girl × Karae Lyn Sugiyama**		**Warren 1975**
ANGEL BELLS‡	**Empress Bells × Little Angel**		**Rivermont 1960**
× Princess Bells	= Rio's Princess	× Lc. Queen Kate	= Lc. Murielle Larrabee
ANGELWALKER	**Little Angel × walkerana**		**J. & S. 1969**
× Claesiana	= Circassian Beauty	× White Blossom	= Snow Jewels
× intermedia	= Cherry Chip	× Epc. Ruben's Gold	= Epc. Mem. Florence Poole
× Margaret Stewart	= Margaret Angel		
ANGEL WINGS	**Henrietta Japhet × Morne Le Blanc**		**Rod McLellan Co. 1972**

ANN ALBERTS†‡ — **Edithiae × Souvenir de Louis Sander** — **A. & M. 1946**

× Little Angel = Joan Tennant

ANNE LYDIE — **Little Angel × Suavior** — **Rosen 1972**

ANN MISTY — **Elizabeth Ann Thedford × Misty** — **A. & R. 1973**

ANN WARREN — **Myron A. Hofer × Ballet Girl** — **Warren 1974**

ANTIGO‡ — **Fabulous × granulosa** — **Clarelen 1950**

× Blc. Herons Ghyll = Blc. David Christian Helbling

ARDENTISSIMA*†‡ — **Fabia × Peetersii** — **S. 1925**

× Lc. David Lozoya = Lc. Davitissima
× Lc. Lee Langford = Lc. Burma Queen
× Lc. Mem. Albert Heinecke = Lc. Pride of Texas

ARDMORE†‡ — **Enid × mossiae** — **S. A. 1938**

× Bess Truman = Mem. Lillian Kallman

ARIEL*†‡ — **bowringiana × gaskelliana** — **Colman 1915**

× gaskelliana = Chilean Lakes
× Portia = Summer Blue
× Undine = Persian Blue
× warneri = Caribbean Skies

ATHENA† — **mossiae × ?** — **T. Young —**

× mossiae = Mossena
× trianaei = Trithena
× Lc. Georgette = Lc. Gena

AUDITOR†‡ — **loddigesii × Mrs. Gratrix** — **Hughes 1937**

× Petite = Monte Sano

AULD ACQUAINTANCE — **Little Angel × General Patton** — **Slocum 1966**

× Karae Lyn Sugiyama = Bering Glacier

aurantiaca*†‡ — **species**

× aclandiae = Robin Colleen
× Baby Jane = Viola Sanjume
× Barbara Billingsley = Virginia Greenwood
× dowiana = Rubencito
× Dubiosa = Joe Santoro
× Edithiae = Edith Aurum
× luteola = Helen Jarzab
× Marion Patterson = Florida Dawn
× Melodboa = Blossomwood Elf
× Mrs. Robert Jewell = Lois Rinehart
× schillerana = Duchess of Colima
× Suzanne Hye = Tomoko
× velutina = Charlotte Goddard
× White Blossom = Eleanor Papac
× B. cordata = Bc. Elise White
× Bc. Maikai = Bc. Maiaca
× Blc. Acapana = Blc. Gaiety
× Blc. Bouton D'Or = Blc. Gold Bug
× Blc. Painted Desert = Blc. Poppy Trail
× Blc. Yellow Imp = Blc. Bonita
× Lc. Antonica Fredrick = Lc. Tim's Fire
× Lc. Brilliant Orange = Lc. Oroyum
× Lc. Goldcrest = Lc. Chicanery
× Lc. Hazel Abel = Lc. Betty von Paulsen
× Lc. Mercia = Lc. Snippet
× Lc. Red Gold = Lc. Red Imp
× Lc. Rojo = Lc. Ladybug
× Lc. Tom Braverman = Lc. Donna's Sunset
× Lc. Twinkle Star = Lc. Carolyn Reid
× Slc. Beacon Hill = Slc. Sangre de Dios
× Slc. Brandywine = Slc. Titillate
× Slc. Kao Hsiung = Slc. Alethea
× Slc. Kiaora Red = Slc. Swizzle
× Slc. Lindores = Slc. Thrill

AURANTI-MEDIA — **aurantiaca × intermedia** — **Thayer —**

× Dubiosa = Ruthabell Thompson
× Lc. Ozark = Lc. Kim Miller
× Soph. coccinea = Sc. Ellen Esther Hood

aurea (see *dowiana**†‡) — **species**

AVALANCHE PASS — **Ethel Bishop × Mount Baker** — **Beall 1973**

BABY JANE‡ — **aurantiaca × December Snow** — **Tsukamoto 1950**

× aurantiaca = Viola Sanjume
× Lc. Rosa Kirsch = Lc. Kiliwehi

BABY KAY — **bicolor × luteola** — **Keller 1963**

× guttata = Baby Wintergreen
× Sl. Psyche = Slc. Ginny Champion

BABY WINTERGREEN — **Baby Kay × guttata** — **Pabst 1974**

BACTIA‡ — **bowringiana × guttata** — **Veitch 1901**

× Bro. sanguinea = Ctna. Summer Dream | × Lc. Pacific Sun = Lc. Royal Pacific

BAGLEY ICE FIELDS — **Princess Bells × Little Angel** — **Beall 1967**

× Charlotte Sell = Fluffer Duffer

BALLET GIRL — **Highburiensis × Empress Bells** — **Freed 1964**

× Karae Lyn Sugiyama = Amy Warren | × Myron A. Hofer = Ann Warren

BALU — **Barbara Billingsley × luteola** — **Rivermont 1963**

× Blc. Mellowglow = Blc. Bullion Gold

BAMBI LYNN MARTINI — **Hilda Battle × Flossie Bow** — **Battle 1972**

BARBARA ARROWSMITH — **Suzanne Hye × Empress Bells** — **Levensdale 1967**

× Blc. Nanette = Blc. Pat Marshall

BARBARA BILLINGSLEY†‡ — **Mandanae × trianaei** — **H. Patterson 1946**

× aurantiaca = Virginia Greenwood | × skinneri = Raymond Palmer
× Little Angel = Osa Mae Barton | × Tiffin Bells = Spring Climax

BARBARA DANE*†‡ — **labiata × Phoebe Snow** — **Dane 1932**

× Bow Bells = Cicely Angleton

BARBARA HECHT‡ — **Leah Adis × loddigesii** — **Lines 1960**

× Star Kissed = Doctor Harold Hecht

BARBARA KINNEY — **Charybdis × Gloriette** — **Rod McLellan Co. 1974**

BARBARA KIRCH‡ — **aurantiaca × bowringiana** — **Woodlawn 1952**

× Gloriette = Rodco's Glory | × Slc. Anzac = Slc. Aguilino Piche
× Lc. Kensella = Lc. Tibouchina | × Slc. Firefly = Slc. Orange Psyche
× Lc. Red Gold = Lc. Julia Kersey | × Slc. Sunburst = Slc. Froufrou
× Sc. Cleopatra = Sc. Nubbin

BARBARA SANDER‡ — **loddigesii × Auguste Van Halme** — **D.S.O. 1959 (S.)**

× Highburiensis = Margaret Chapman

BARBARA SPENCER — **Karae Lyn Sugiyama × White Blossom** — **Spencer 1973**

BARNEY ARONSON — **Joyce Hannington × Wedding Day** — **Aronson 1962 (Pierson)**

× Blc. Orange Glory = Blc. Tiffany Renee Colborne

batalinii / **BATALINII‡** — **bicolor × intermedia** — **Nat. hyb.** / **S. 1892**

× Lc. Semaphore = Lc. Keri | × Slc. Naomi Kerns = Slc. Bill's Red

BEE BEAMENT — **intermedia × Louise Georgianna** — **Ross 1955**

× Epi. tampense = Epc. Poopsie

BEN DODSON — **Joyce Hannington × Gertrude Hausermann** — **Mrs. L. Wilson 1975**

BEN NEVIS†‡ — **Alcimeda × Intertexta** — **S. 1935**

× Bob Betts = White Radiance

BERDANE — **Helen P. Dane × Bertha Waters** — **Kensington 1973**

BERING GLACIER — **Auld Acquaintance × Karae Lyn Sugiyama** — **Beall 1975**

CATTLEYA

BERTHA WATERS	**Mina × Snow Song**		**McDade 1946**
× Helen P. Dane	= Berdane		
BERTIE DeMARTINI	**Joyce Hannington × Mission Dolores**		**Rod McLellan Co. 1966**
× Bc. Déesse	= Bc. Palais de Glace		
BERTII*†‡	**loddigesii × labiata**		**Bert 1904**
× Porcia	= Guyana		
BESS TRUMAN‡	**Clotho × Ardmore**		**Lines 1962**
× Ardmore	= Mem. Lillian Kallman	× Jacqueline Kennedy	= President's Lady
BETTY McNAMARA	**High Light × Queen Sirikhit**		**Rod McLellan Co. 1972**
BETTY WEBB	**Claesiana × Mlle. Louise Pauwels**		**Rod McLellan Co. 1975 (Enright)**
BEVERLY O'DELL	**Mary Langford × Earl**		**W. H. Marshall 1973**
bicolor*†‡	**species**		
× Pearl Harbor	= Star of Malibu	× Epi. tampense	= Epc. Joseph Riley
× Porcia	= Bill Crocker	× L. milleri	= Lc. Mrs. Red
× schillerana	= Something Else	× Lc. Antonica Fredrick	= Lc. Hot Chili Pepper
× Blc. Autumn Glow	= Blc. Green Goddess	× Lc. Edgard van Belle	= Lc. Bell O'Bronze
× Blc. Envy	= Blc. Constant Spring	× Lc. Eva	= Lc. Randy Redhot
× Blc. Golden Galleon	= Blc. Indian Treasure	× Lc. Issy	= Lc. San Pablo
× Blc. Golden Slippers	= Blc. Yorktown	× Soph. coccinea	= Sc. Pearlouis
× Epi. dichromum	= Epc. Bichron	× Slc. Indian Springs	= Slc. Hong Kong
BIG SPLASH	**Nutley × intermedia**		**Woodlawn 1968 (Bracey)**
× Lc. Mariner	= Lc. Taco		
BILL CROCKER	**Porcia × bicolor**		**G. Crocker 1974**
BLANCHE	**labiata × maxima**		**Colman 1916**
× L. flava	= Lc. Blanchflava		
BLESS PAT	**luteola × velutina**		**Stevenson 1975**
BLOSSOMWOOD ELF	**Melodboa × aurantiaca**		**Funston 1975**
BLUE JAY	**Undine × Portia**		**Beall 1973**
BOB BETTS†‡	**Bow Bells × mossiae**		**McDade 1950**
× Ben Nevis	= White Radiance	× Yvonne Adair	= Adabett
× Carl Hausermann	= Hausermann's Seafoam	× Bc. Lim Theng Hin	= Bc. Oriel Nevins
× Esbetts	= Tyrone	× Blc. Pimola	= Blc. Esther Schaber
× Etta Price	= Mem. Sig Reimer	× Blc. Ranger Six	= Blc. Janice Watson
× Katherine Walker	= Boberine	× L. anceps	= Lc. Small Talk
× Lorraine Sawtelle	= Tommy Tomita	× L. flava	= Lc. Loony Goon
× Mem. Paul T. Yamada	= Tera Hausermann	× Lc. Aïda	= Lc. Stacey Bull
× Metropolitan	= Marge Bergman	× Lc. Bonanza	= Lc. Bonbetts
× Naka-Nani	= Jane Taura	× Lc. Clifton Down	= Lc. Freda Miskimens
× Queen Sirikhit	= Juthathip	× Lc. Suprême	= Lc. James Bell
× Stanley Fouraker	= Linda Palconit	× Soph. coccinea	= Sc. Rose Pixie
BOBERINE	**Bob Betts × Katherine Walker**		**Kensington 1973**
BONANZA	**Athena × Prospector**		**A. & R. 1949**
× Lc. Harold J. Patterson	= Lc. Hausermann's Melody		
BOW BELLS†‡	**Edithiae × Suzanne Hye**		**B. 1945**
× Abe Kehr	= Classique	× Francis T. C. Au	= Naseema
× Barbara Dane	= Cicely Angleton	× Helen Patterson	= Pete-Bo
× Carlos Gomes	= Julieta MacFadden	× Katherine Walker	= Kay Bells

BOW BELLS†‡ *(continued)*

- × Morne Le Blanc = Eleanor Spicer
- × New Albion = Toshiyasu Miyajima
- × Patrice Munsell = Madame Khadaroo
- × Rahima = Djalil
- × Souv. de Louis Sander = Sweet Liberty
- × Bc. C. H. Lankester = Bc. Enid Oppenheim
- × Bc. Marie Marie = Bc. Belltrayne
- × Bc. Mount Hood = Bc. Mem. John Dickinson
- × Blc. Royal Nan = Blc. Mem. Flossie Gunter
- × Epc. Lime Sherbet = Epc. Mem. Ruth Hoyt
- × Epi. conopseum = Epc. Brian David
- × Lc. Elizabeth Off = Lc. Great Tellico
- × Lc. Eunice = Lc. Mem. Zannie Melton
- × Lc. Ludgate = Lc. Mem. Irwin DeLong
- × Sc. Cleopatra = Sc. Nile Queen
- × Soph. coccinea = Sc. Marionette

bowringiana*†‡ — **species**

- × Chocolate Drop = Chongkolnee
- × Peanuts = Hagoromo
- × Bc. Henrietta = Bc. Caldarello
- × Blc. Fred Stewart = Blc. Gina Stewart
- × Epi. eggersii = Epc. Luis Ariza Julia
- × Epi. gracile = Epc. Charlie Brown
- × Lc. Bowri-albida = Lc. Smile
- × Lc. Princess Cooper = Lc. Mem. Alfredo Urpía
- × Lc. Roitelet = Lc. Alicia
- × Pot. Judy Lynn King = Pot. Betty Watson

BRABANTIAE‡ — **aclandiae × loddigesii** — **Veitch 1863**

- × Confetti = Miz Whiz
- × Mrs. Mahler = Fort Motte
- × B. digbyana = Bc. Ellen Stampley
- × Blc. Dinsmore = Blc. Lisa Marie

BRECKINRIDGE SNOW — **Lucille Small × Bridal Bouquet** — **Breckinridge 1972 (Small)**

BRIDAL BOUQUET‡ — **Henrietta Japhet × Barbara Billingsley** — **Small 1956**

- × Lucille Small = Breckinridge Snow
- × White Clover = Cloud Cap

BRIGADE PIRON — **Fabia × Nigrella** — **S. 1945**

- × Mrs. Mahler = Carnival

BRIGHTON — **Stella Elenewski × Joyce Hannington** — **C. & H. 1973 (Brighton Farms)**

BROWNIAE†‡ — **bowringiana × harrisoniana** — **S. 1904**

- × Suavior = Suabrowniae
- × L. cinnabarina = Lc. Peggy Lynn Grezaffi

CALIFLORA‡ — **mossiae × J. A. Carbone** — **A. & R. 1964 (Chase)**

- × Lc. Irene Finney = Lc. John MacArthur

CARL HAUSERMANN‡ — **Bob Betts × Diane Sato** — **Hausermann 1964**

- × Bob Betts = Hausermann's Seafoam
- × Eugene Hausermann = Robert Schweppe
- × intermedia = White Aries
- × Picasso = Charley Juza
- × Lc. Dee Dee = Lc. Hausermann's Pride

CARIBBEAN SKIES — **Ariel × warneri** — **Stewart Inc. 1974 (Whitlow)**

CARLOS GOMES — **Swan × Dr. Behiels** — **W. Silva 1971**

- × Bow Bells = Julieta MacFadden

CARNIVAL — **Mrs. Mahler × Brigade Piron** — **H. A. Hill 1972**

CATHERINE DIGWOOD‡ — **Lady Veitch × intermedia** — **Toogood 1963 (Dos Pueblos)**

- × Highburiensis = Allyn Star

CATHERINE PATTERSON‡ — **Enid × Mrs. Frederick Knollys** — **H. Patterson 1952**

- × Bc. Ann Sladden = Bc. Felice Dickson
- × Lc. Clara Schriever = Lc. Ruth Williams
- × Lc. Edgar Omura = Lc. Kaguyama
- × Lc. George Woodhams = Lc. Stela Marcia
- × Lc. Mem. Maggie Hood = Lc. Catherine Hood
- × Lc. Pegi Mayne = Lc. Bill Shave

CATTLEYA

CECELIA RHODES — **Rivermont Imperial × Little Angel** — **Tom Tucker 1973**

CELE MARKELL‡ — **Gravesiana × Souv. de Louis Sander** — **Kwr. 1946**

× Albatross = Dream of Summer

CELIA*†‡ — **loddigesii × Lady Veitch** — **Hassall 1920**

× Sl. Gustave Vincke = Slc. Maxine Hudson

CHAMBERLAINIANA*‡ (syn. Taboo) — **dowiana × guttata** — **Veitch 1881**

× Blc. Jane Helton = Blc. Kenji Onodera
× Blc. Mem. Crispin Rosales = Blc. Summer Festival
× Lc. Isotta = Lc. Chamberlain Isotta

CHARLEY JUZA — **Picasso × Carl Hausermann** — **Hausermann 1973**

CHARLOTTE GODDARD — **velutina × aurantiaca** — **Fort Caroline 1973 (Wallbrunn)**

CHARLOTTE SELL — **Hanniwell × New Albion** — **Sell 1969**

× Bagley Ice Fields = Fluffer Duffer
× Roman Silver = Lillian Wallace
× Bc. Swan Mountain = Bc. June Bennett

CHARYBDIS†‡ — **Chelsea × Dinah** — **Orchidwood 1944**

× Gloriette = Barbara Kinney
× Lc. Bonanza = Lc. Mary Kawena Pukui

CHERRY CHIP — **Angelwalker × intermedia** — **J. & S. 1974**

CHEWELAH — **Enid × amethystoglossa** — **Bonniewood 1971**

CHICAGO TODAY — **Carl Hausermann × Elizabeth Carlson** — **Hausermann 1969**

× Picasso = Swingtime

CHILEAN LAKES — **Ariel × gaskelliana** — **Stewart Inc. 1974 (Whitlow)**

CHLOE*‡ — **bicolor × bowringiana** — **Veitch 1896**

× guttata = Doctor Max Schneider

CHOCOLATE DROP — **guttata × aurantiaca** — **Stewart Inc. 1955**

× bowringiana = Chongkolnee
× Slc. Ramona = Slc. Redhead

CHONGKOLNEE — **bowringiana × Chocolate Drop** — **Tavivatana 1973 (Sagarik)**

CHRISTINA WAGLAY‡ — **El Cerrito × Claesiana** — **A. & R. 1962**

× B. perrinii = Bc. Snow Waltz

CHUN YUEH — **Sedlescombe × Enid** — **Li Chin-sheng 1959**

× North Star = Tsukiboshi

CICELY ANGLETON — **Barbara Dane × Bow Bells** — **Angleton 1973**

CIRCASSIAN BEAUTY — **Claesiana × Angelwalker** — **Stewart Inc. 1974**

CITRIFORM — **forbesii × citrina** — **Neville 1971**

citrina*‡ — **species**

(This is retained as the horticulturally recommended name for registration purposes, even though *Encyclia citrina* is the botanically correct name for this species.)

× forbesii = Citriform

CLAEGIGAS — **warscewiczii × Claesiana** — **Stewart Inc. 1973**

claesiana / **CLAESIANA*†‡** — **intermedia × loddigesii** — **Nat. hyb.** / **A. & B. 1916**

× Angelwalker = Circassian Beauty
× Esbetts = Polly Watson
× Mademoiselle Louise Pauwels = Betty Webb

claesiana
CLAESIANA*†‡ *(continued)*

× Mary Bea Ireland	= June Priest	× L. gouldiana	= Lc. Pink Panty
× Mrs. Pitt	= Mem. Dorothy Marie	× L. rubescens	= Lc. Mem. Francis Knaebel
× warscewiczii	= Claegigas		
× Epi. conopseum	= Epc. Joyita	× Lc. Peggy Huffman	= Lc. Peggy Anna

CLAIRE AYAU‡ — **Celia × Snow Song** — **Goo 1948**
× Fleecy Clouds = Summer Dawn

CLAIRE DREIER — **Florence Patterson × Dorothy Mackaill** — **Small 1960**
× B. nodosa = Bc. Tara Rajcoomar

CLARIS†‡ — **Clementine Goldfarb × Eucharis** — **Brookville 1949**
× Sc. Petite Fleur = Sc. Petite Claire

CLARK HERMAN — **Marjorie Hausermann × Fred Cole** — **Elmhurst 1972**
CLASSIQUE — **Abe Kehr × Bow Bells** — **Rod McLellan Co. 1974**
CLAY O'BRIEN — **Claesiana × O'Brieniana** — **Rod McLellan Co. 1964**
× L. rupestris = Lc. Clay O'Pestris

CLEMENTINE GOLDFARB†‡ — **Cybele × Snowdon** — **Orchidwood 1939**
× Joan Manda = Rahima

CLOUD CAP — **Bridal Bouquet × White Clover** — **Crothers 1971**
CONFETTI‡ — **aurantiaca × trianaei** — **L. de. R. 1935**
× Brabantiae = Miz Whiz | × intermedia = Rebel

COOKSONII*†‡ — **Hardyana × trianaei** — **Cookson 1906**
× Bc. Olna = Bc. Gladys Chapman

CORFLAMBO†‡ — **Ardentissima × Jicarillo** — **A. & R. 1946**
× Lc. Princess Margaret = Lc. Summer Sunset | × Lc. Tokyo Rose = Lc. Toflam

CORNDEAN LEE — **Estelle × Undine** — **Kensington 1973**
COTTON BELLE†‡ — **Bobbie Jewell × Minnehaha** — **McDade 1949**
× amethystoglossa = Rowena Baer

CRASHLEYI (see Mary Gratrix*‡)
CRISPETTE (see Highburiensis‡)
CROWN PRINCESS MICHIKO‡ — **Marion Patterson × Bob Betts** — **Otaguro 1960 (Miyamoto)**
× Blc. Crown Prince Akihito = Blc. Hirono-Miya Naruhito

CRYSTAL PALACE — **Dorothy Mackaill × Frost** — **Rod McLellan Co. 1963**
× Sunrise Chalet = Morality

DALE EDWARD — **amethystoglossa × Guatemalensis** — **W. Richmond 1972**
DAMOISEAU‡ — **Fabianid × Ann Sander** — **V. 1953**
× Lc. Harold J. Patterson = Lc. Roseval

DANIEL RYERSON‡ — **Wottho × Remy Chollet** — **H. Patterson 1952**
× Bc. Hartland = Bc. Doctor Stephen Gibbs

DANTE — **Nonoska × dowiana** — **Pff. V. & L. 1960**
× Lc. Saadia = Lc. Georges Coudroux

CATTLEYA

DARK EMPEROR‡ — **Nigritian × Nigrella** — **Gore 1957**

× Hybrida = Muscadine
× Blc. Aztec Princess = Blc. Black Mesa
× Lc. Armaris = Lc. Ganado
× Lc. Mary Weaver = Lc. Mem. Katie Muse
× Lc. Quadroon = Lc. Enoree

DARK MEMORY — **Alwynii × Eileen Patterson** — **Coastal Gdns. 1973**

DARSHELLE ABRAHAM — **R. Prowe × Ruth M. Johnston** — **D. Tom 1971**

DAVID SWEET‡ — **Alice Pearce × aurantiaca** — **Small 1961**

× Lc. Charlesworthii = Lc. Princess Orange

dayana / **DAYANA** — **forbesii × guttata** — **Nat. hyb.** / **W. W. G. Moir 1966**

× Lc. Wine Festival = Lc. Melissa

DECEMBER SNOW†‡ — **Edithiae × trianaei** — **W. K. du Pont 1944**

× Lc. G. S. Ball = Lc. Mike Shaw

DENPA — **Sonia Altenburg × Enid** — **N. Suzuki 1972**

DINAH*†‡ — **Dupreana × Elvina** — **M. 1919**

× Gloriette = Mem. Midori Nakano
× Martha Van Doerslaer = Dindoer
× Lc. Arny Freeman = Lc. Resolution Mountain

DINDOER — **Dinah × Martha Van Doerslaer** — **F. H. Williams 1974 (Originator unknown)**

× Lc. Molly Tyler = Lc. Katreena Howard

DJALIL — **Bow Bells × Rahima** — **Khadaroo 1975 (Riverview)**

DOCTOR BEHIELS‡ — **trianaei × White Empress** — **Behiels 1949**

× Swan = Carlos Gomes

DOCTOR HAROLD HECHT — **Barbara Hecht × Star Kissed** — **Creve Coeur 1973**

DOCTOR MAX SCHNEIDER — **Chloe × guttata** — **Schneider 1975 (Rivermont)**

DOGWOOD HILL — **Mount Baker × intermedia** — **Robt. Smith 1972 (Ryerson Orchids)**

DONNA CRAIG — **Old Whitey × General Patton** — **A. & R. 1975**

DOREBELLE — **White Belle × Dorene** — **Howe 1974 (R. C. McDade)**

DORENE†‡ — **Douai × Irene** — **McDade 1948**

× Tiffin Bells = Vanilla Sundae
× White Belle = Dorebelle

DOROTHY GEILS — **Irene Finney × Picasso** — **Hausermann 1974**

DOS RIOS — **True White × Jose Marti** — **Ruben 1975**

dowiana*†‡ (syn. *aurea*) — **species**

× aurantiaca = Rubencito
× Bc. Groganiae = Bc. Saturday Special
× Blc. Fortune = Blc. Nguyen Thi Mai-Ánh
× L. gloedeniana = Lc. War Dance
× L. grandis = Lc. Helena Baraya
× L. Zip = Lc. Zippity Doodow
× Lc. Michele Hege Lys = Lc. Mem. Gordon Vickers

DREADNOUGHT‡ — **Joyce Hannington × Clementine Goldfarb** — **Pierson 1957**

× Summer Ski Slope = Summer Romance

DREAM OF SUMMER — **Albatross × Cele Markell** — **Coastal Gdns. 1973**

DREAMY WHITE — **Sunrise Chalet × Hoshang** — **Hausermann 1974 (H. Patterson)**

× Princess Bells = Salvadore

DUBIOSA†‡ — **harrisoniae × trianaei** — **Maron 1890**

× aurantiaca = Joe Santoro
× Auranti-media = Ruthabell Thompson
× Empress Bells = Oriental Pearl
× Henrietta Japhet = Mary Williams
× Rita Renee = Dubonnet
× Wolteriana = Wolteriosa
× Bc. Berangere = Bc. Heart's Desire
× Lc. Bonanza = Lc. Best Regards
× Slc. Lindores = Slc. Saucy One

DUBONNET — **Dubiosa × Rita Renee** — **Stewart Inc. 1974**

DUCHESS OF COLIMA — **schillerana × aurantiaca** — **O.Sp.Sp. 1975**

DUPREANA*†‡ — **warneri × warscewiczii** — **Lambeau 1906**

× Hentschelii = Duprishell
× Blc. Dusk = Blc. Menure

DUPRISHELL — **Dupreana × Hentschelii** — **Kensington 1973**

DUSSELDORFEI (see Undine*†‡)

EARL‡ — **Empress Bells × General Patton** — **Suyama 1961**

× Mary Langford = Beverly O'Dell

EDELWEISS‡ — **Althea × Astron** — **S. 1948**

× Edithiae = Limonade

EDGEWOOD PEARL‡ — **Helen P. Dane × Bobbie Jewel** — **H. Patterson 1957 (Elenewski)**

× L. harpophylla = Lc. Beverly Perry

EDISTAR — **Muse's Little Star × Edithiae** — **Muse's 1971**

EDITH AURUM — **Edithiae × aurantiaca** — **Otaguro 1972 (B. Tanaka)**

× Slc. Lindores = Slc. Ohelohelo

EDITHIAE*†‡ — **Suzanne Hye × trianaei** — **Pauwels 1914**

× aurantiaca = Edith Aurum
× Edelweiss = Limonade
× Muse's Little Star = Edistar
× Bc. Sonia = Bc. Emily Teruko
× L. anceps = Lc. Mem. Kurazo Ogata

EDOUARD DARTOIS†‡ — **Empress Frederick × Remy Chollet** — **Sladden 1935**

× trianaei = Tridart

EILEEN PATTERSON‡ — **Catherine Patterson × Ardmore** — **H. Patterson 1964**

× Alwynii = Dark Memory

ELEANORE*†‡ — **Hardyana × warscewiczii** — **Schroder 1918**

× Lc. Jane Froman = Lc. Summer Sand

ELEANOR PAPAC — **White Blossom × aurantiaca** — **Vidulich 1975**

ELEANOR SPICER — **Morne Le Blanc × Bow Bells** — **Rod McLellan Co. 1973**

ELIZABETH ANDERSON — **Pele × Nigritian** — **W. T. Anderson 1967**

× Blc. Norman's Bay = Blc. Betty Midkiff

ELIZABETH ANN THEDFORD‡ — **Bobbie Jewel × Rita Sladden** — **McDade 1951**

× Misty = Ann Misty

ELMER HISLE — **Remy Chollet × Winnietha** — **Rod McLellan Co. 1971**

elongata*‡ — **species**

× violacea = Mary Reed
× Blc. C. K. Ai = Blc. Eau Gallie
× L. milleri = Lc. Cherry Torte

EMPRESS BELLS†‡ — **Bow Bells × Edithiae** — **Suyama 1952 (McDade)**

× Dubiosa = Oriental Pearl
× Esbetts = Empress Betts
× Ethel Savage = Empress Ethel
× Karae Lyn Sugiyama = Snow Dawn
× Meige = Mem. Frank Redman
× Patricia Lines = Melani Beard
× Rahima = Oumel Baneen
× Bc. Déesse = Bc. Chesty Puller
× Bc. Mount Anderson = Bc. Aloowa
× Bc. Mount St. Helens = Bc. Linda Berg
× Blc. Ranger Six = Blc. Six Bells
× Smbc. Harry Dunn = Smbc. Yaquina

EMPRESS BETTS — **Esbetts × Empress Bells** — **A. & R. 1975**

EMPRESS ETHEL — **Empress Bells × Ethel Savage** — **Kensington 1973**

ENID*†‡ — **mossiae × warscewiczii** — **Veitch 1898**

× amethystoglossa = Chewelah
× Sonia Altenburg = Denpa
× Blc. Luis H. Yanes = Blc. Nuuanu Fancy
× Lc. Cantabile = Lc. Clown's Nose
× Lc. Fedora = Lc. Cara Nome
× Lc. Peggy Huffman = Lc. Ermine Robe
× Lc. Whitewings = Lc. Kannapolis

ERICA ANTOINETTE — **Affection × Intermediette** — **Bingham 1973**

ESBETTS‡ — **Bob Betts × Estelle** — **Shibuya 1956 (Fukumura)**

× Bob Betts = Tyrone
× Claesiana = Polly Watson
× Empress Bells = Empress Betts
× General Patton = Silver City
× Helen P. Dane = Voelker Glacier
× Mount Rainier = Helen Parashis
× Old Whitey = Ruth Gee
× Princess Bells = Margaret Makino
× Blc. Baby Doll = Blc. Nickie Holguin
× Lc. Bonanza = Lc. Moochie

ESTELLE†‡ — **Cowaniae × Edithiae** — **Cowan 1931**

× Florence Patterson = Ruth Ellis
× Tomiko Takafuji = New Life
× Undine = Corndean Lee
× Bc. Déesse = Bc. Charlotte Amalie
× Bc. Mount Hood = Bc. Trudy Baker
× Bc. Seafoam = Bc. Seastelle

ESTHER KENNEDY†‡ — **Estelle × Mrs. Robert Stone** — **Ozzella 1950**

× Princess Bells = Lynn Dewey

ETHEL BISHOP†‡ — **Barbara Dane × S. E. Endicott** — **H. Patterson 1945**

× Mount Baker = Avalanche Pass

ETHEL SAVAGE — **Cowaniae × White Empress** — **Siegwart 1952**

× Empress Bells = Empress Ethel

ETTA PRICE‡ — **Edithiae × loddigesii** — **Vallemar 1958**

× Bob Betts = Mem. Sig Reimer

EUCHONIANA (see Henrietta Japhet†‡)

EUGENE HAUSERMANN — **Bob Betts × Elizabeth Carlson** — **Hausermann 1967**

× Carl Hausermann = Robert Schweppe

EVAMAY PATTERSON (see Hoshang‡)

FABIA*†‡ — **dowiana × labiata** — **Veitch 1894**

× Slc. Meuzac = Slc. National City

FABIANEGRA — **Fabianid × Nigrella** — **A. & R. 1975**

FABIANID*†‡ — **Enid × Fabia** — **Marlborough 1916**

× Nigrella = Fabianegra

FABINGIANA‡ — **bowringiana × Fabiata** — **S. Takeda 1952 (Kaga)**

× Slc. Anzac = Slc. Fabinzac

FABULOUS*†‡ — **Fabia × Flame** — **S. 1934**

× Lc. Canhamiana = Lc. Florence Harris

FAIR LADY — **Mount Shasta × Bob Betts** — **Freed 1958**

× gaskelliana = Sierra Summit

FASCELINA — **velutina × Fascelis** — **Wallbrunn 1973**

FASCELIS — **aclandiae × bicolor** — **Veitch 1900**

× velutina = Fascelina
× Lc. Ann Follis = Lc. Seminole Meadows
× Pot. Glowing Beauty = Pot. Stella Maris

FITZ EUGENE DIXON — **Portia × walkerana** — **F. E. Dixon 1922**

× Soph. coccinea = Sc. Retha

FLEECY CLOUDS — **gaskelliana × Ella Sutton** — **McDade 1962**

× Claire Ayau = Summer Dawn
× gaskelliana = Summer Girl
× Harold = Summer Lady
× Little Angel = Summer Wind
× Picturata = Summer Eyes
× Summer Ski Slope = Summer Song
× Wendy Patterson = Summer Surprise

FLORENCE PATTERSON†‡ — **Clementine Goldfarb × Rita Sladden** — **H. Patterson 1948**

× Estelle = Ruth Ellis
× Lc. Brown Derby = Lc. Good Try

FLORIDA DAWN — **Marion Patterson × aurantiaca** — **Fairburn 1974**

FLOSSIE BOW — **Florence Patterson × Bow Bells** — **Rivermont 1963**

× Hilda Battle = Bambi Lynn Martini

FLUFFER DUFFER — **Bagley Ice Fields × Charlotte Sell** — **M. J. Bates 1975**

forbesii*†‡ — **species**

× citrina = Citriform
× Little Angel = Mary Turner Whitney
× rex = Sister John Karen
× B. martiana = Bc. Max Schneider
× B. perrinii = Bc. Brazil
× Bc. Praetii = Bc. Green Surrey
× Bl. Sea Urchin = Blc. Ativa
× Diaca. Pink Glory = Diaca. Meffords Fort
× Epi. atropurpureum = Epc. Florence Burton
× Epi. umbellatum = Epc. Icy Parfait
× Lc. Fiery = Lc. Sparkler

FORT CRONKHITE — **H. B. Turner × Leda** — **Rod McLellan Co. 1954**

× granulosa = Granfort

FORT MOTTE — **Mrs. Mahler × Brabantiae** — **C. & H. 1973**

FRANCIS T. C. AU‡ — **Bow Bells × Swan** — **R. Yee 1953 (Rivermont)**

× Bow Bells = Naseema
× Thomas Flynn = Rubens Ribeiro
× Lc. Colorama = Lc. Platinum Sun

FRED COLE — **Henrietta Japhet × Vesper Bells** — **Jack Cole 1964 (Lines)**

× Gertrude Hausermann = Hank Fischer
× Kazuko Fujii = Melanie
× Marjorie Hausermann = Clark Herman
× O'brieniana = Hausermann's Happiness

FROSTING — **Salinas × Tiffin Bells** — **Rod McLellan Co. 1974**

FULVESCENS*†‡ — **dowiana × forbesii** — **C. 1901**

× Hermosa = Tinaburra Sunset
× B. digbyana = Bc. Vivian Moore
× Blc. Citron Pass = Blc. Enchanted Valley
× Blc. Gladys Lines = Blc. Mem. Arthur Pancoast
× Blc. Nanette = Blc. Eunice Helen
× Blc. Pimola = Blc. Mount Logan
× Sl. Gustave Vincke = Slc. Linda Jones

CATTLEYA

gaskelliana*†‡ — **species**

(This and *C. schroederae* are both treated for registration purposes as specifically distinct from *C. labiata,* though ranked as conspecific therewith by some authorities)

× Ariel = Chilean Lakes | × Ray Park = White Summer
× Fleecy Clouds = Summer Girl | × B. nodosa = Bc. Little Sulema
× Fair Lady = Sierra Summit | × L. Sunol = Lc. Summer Sun
× Quinquecolor = Jennie

GAY BELLS — **Empress Bells × Mission Dolores** — **Rod McLellan Co. 1965**

× Bc. Mount Hood = Bc. Esto Gillett

GENERAL PATTON†‡ — **Bow Bells × Barbara Billingsley** — **Suyama 1952 (McDade)**

× Esbetts = Silver City | × Blc. Golden Galleon = Blc. Kaliope
× granulosa = Patlosa | × Blc. Golden Myth = Blc. Patton Myth
× Old Whitey = Donna Craig | × Slc. Phena = Slc. Shigedonia
× Pascaline = Jean Pallister | × Slc. Ramona = Slc. Yuko Shiono
× Bc. Mount Hood = Bc. Pink Cloud

GENERAL RUSSKY — **Amabilis × dowiana** — **S. 1915**

× Joan Hanniwell = Gloria Tamashiro

GEORGE EASTMAN*†‡ — **Cantuarie × chocoensis** — **L. 1930**

× Soph. coccinea = Sc. Yone Arai

GERIANT — **Fabianid × Remy Chollet** — **A. & R. 1951**

× Lc. F. O. Thompson = Lc. Dorothy Shields

GERRY CASSELLA — **guttata × Little Angel** — **Cassella 1972 (Originator unknown)**

GERTRUDE HAUSERMANN — **Empress Bells × Bow Bells** — **Hausermann 1964**

× Fred Cole = Hank Fischer | × Pearl Harbor = Second Time
× Joyce Hannington = Ben Dodson

GERTRUDE MATTHEWS — **Intermediette × Sunrise Chalet** — **Owens Orchids 1974**

gigas (see warscewiczii*†‡) — **species**

GIGI — **Mount Shasta × Henrietta Japhet** — **Freed 1960**

× loddigesii = Tiuna | × Schom. crispa = Smbc. Urimare
× Epi. Santander = Epc. Chiquita Bonita

GINNY — **Bob Betts × New Albion** — **Sparks 1965**

× Karae Lyn Sugiyama = Ginny Lyn

GINNY LYN — **Ginny × Karae Lyn Sugiyama** — **Marshall Orchids 1975 (Mid-Florida Orch.)**

GLORIA TAMASHIRO — **Joan Hanniwell × General Russky** — **Otaguro 1972**

GLORIETTE*†‡ — **Hardyano-warneri × Tityus** — **Cowan 1928**

× Barbara Kirch = Rodco's Glory | × Dinah = Mem. Midori Nakano
× Charybdis = Barbara Kinney

GRACE DARLING — **Pamela Stewart × Prima Donna** — **Stewart Inc. 1975**

GRANFORT — granulosa × Fort Cronkhite — **Rod McLellan Co. 1975**

× Lc. Ann Follis = Lc. Gwin

GRANIRIS — **granulosa × Iris** — **C. J. Phillips 1903**

× Epi. mariae = Epc. Green Goddess | × Lc. Mem. Maggie Hood = Lc. Pilot Mountain

granulosa*†‡ — **species**

× Fort Cronkhite	= Granfort	× Bc. Praetii	= Bc. Granprae
× General Patton	= Patlosa	× Epi. leucochilum	= Epc. Alfred Blaumann
× luteola	= Margaret Morrison	× L. milleri	= Lc. Alachua
× Mary Gratrix	= Mary Jane Mayfield		

GRETA — **Liu × Hedwig** — **Maggi Ponti 1975**

guatemalensis / GUATEMALENSIS†‡ — **aurantiaca × skinneri** — **Nat. hyb. / hort.**

× amethystoglossa	= Dale Edward	× Lc. Mercia	= Lc. Baby Nuuanu
× Lc. Brilliant Orange	= Lc. Orange Aurea	× Lc. Peggy Huffman	= Lc. Patricia Kelly

guttata*†‡ (syn *leopoldii**†) — **species**

× Baby Kay	= Baby Wintergreen	× Blc. Greenwich	= Blc. Chinese Jade
× Chloe	= Doctor Max Schneider	× L. milleri	= Lc. Jalapa
× Interglossa	= Morningside Splash	× Lc. Derna	= Lc. Debbie Brown
× Little Angel	= Gerry Cassella	× Lc. Evelyn Mountain	= Lc. Sunset Flare
× Patricia Ann	= Phyllis Hetfield	× Lc. George Cutler	= Lc. Anita King
× Prospector	= Little Miss Muffet	× Lc. Lagoon	= Lc. Leafwood Lane
× Trimos	= Sivam	× Schom. thomsoniana	= Smbc. Gee Willikers
× Blc. Edwin Chong	= Blc. Evelyn	× Schom. tibicinis	= Smbc. Billie Pickell
× Blc. Fortune	= Blc. Tropical Market	× Sc. Cleopatra	= Sc. Bonfire
× Blc. Green Giant	= Blc. Green Gremlin	× Sc. Luton Charm	= Sc. Little Bigred

GUYANA — **Bertii × Porcia** — **W. W. G. Moir 1973**
HAGOROMO — **bowringiana × Peanuts** — **Katsuura 1975**
HALLIE ROGERS — **O'brieniana × walkerana** — **Ecret 1975 (Hewlett)**

HANK FISCHER — **Fred Cole × Gertrude Hausermann** — **E. F. G. Orchids 1974**
HANNIWELL‡ — **Joyce Hannington × Bobbie Jewel** — **Fetzer 1953**

× Joan Holloway = Joan Hanniwell

hardyana / HARDYANA*†‡ — **dowiana × warscewiczii** — **Nat. hyb. / hort.**

× Blc. Fleur de Lys	= Blc. Purple Glory	× Lc. South Esk	= Lc. Benjamin Harris
× Lc. Dulzura	= Lc. Dulhard		

HAROLD*†‡ — **gaskelliana × warscewiczii** — **N. C. Cookson 1893**

× Fleecy Clouds = Summer Lady

HAROLD MANEKS — **Jose Marti × Princess Bells** — **Hausermann 1974**
harrisoniae*† (see *loddigesii**†‡) — **species**
harrisoniana* (see *loddigesii**†‡) — **species**
HAUSERMANN'S HAPPINESS — **O'brieniana × Fred Cole** — **Hausermann 1972**
HAUSERMANN'S SEAFOAM — **Bob Betts × Carl Hausermann** — **Hausermann 1972**
HEATHER BRACHER — **intermedia × Margaret Lambert** — **Starke & Son 1975**
HEDWIG — **Paolo Ferko × Omar** — **Maggi Ponti 1955**

× Liu = Greta

HELENE GARCIA — **Henrietta Japhet × aurantiaca** — **J. & S. 1961**

× Lc. Henrietta Gold	= Lc. Garcia's Gold	× Pot. Gordon Siu	= Pot. Petite

HELEN JARZAB — **aurantiaca × luteola** — **Jarzab 1972**
HELEN MILLIKEN — **William B. Olsen × The Friendly Third** — **Lines 1973**
HELEN PARASHIS — **Mount Rainier × Esbetts** — **A. & R. 1975**
HELEN PATTERSON†‡ — **Rita Sladden × Barbara Dane** — **Patterson 1952**

× Bow Bells = Pete-Bo

CATTLEYA

HELEN P. DANE†‡ — **Barbara Dane × Edithiae** — **Dane 1941**

× Bertha Waters = Berdane
× Esbetts = Voelker Glacier
× Scintillation = Sindane

HENRIETTA JAPHET†‡ — **Eucharis × loddigesii** — **McDade 1946**
(syn. Euchoniana)

× Dubiosa = Mary Williams
× Moerae = Moeriet
× Morne Le Blanc = Angel Wings
× Myron A. Hofer = Allie Calhoun
× Epi. obesum = Epc. Hello Dolly
× L. Gold Star = Lc. Henrietta Gold
× Lc. Bonanza = Lc. Bonphet

HENTSCHELII*†‡ — **Dupreana × warscewiczii** — **C. 1919**

× Dupreana = Duprishell

HERMOSA*† — **Cooksonii × Maggie Raphael** — **A. & R. 1934**

× Fulvescens = Tinaburra Sunset

HIDDEN GOLD — **Loddiaca × Rivermont Imperial** — **Stewart Inc. 1974**

HIGHBURIENSIS‡ (syn. Crispette) — **loddigesii × mossiae** — **Chamberlain 1903**

× Barbara Sander = Margaret Chapman
× Catherine Digwood = Allyn Star
× L. flava = Lc. Midnight Street

HIGH LIGHT — **El Cerrito × O'brieniana** — **Rod McLellan Co. 1964**

× Queen Sirikhit = Betty McNamara

HIGH REGARD — **Tomiko Takafugi × Rivermont Imperial** — **Rod McLellan Co. 1971**

HILDA BATTLE — **Hoshang × General Patton** — **Lines 1966**

× Flossie Bow = Bambi Lynn Martini

HORACE†‡ — **trianaei × Woltersiana** — **F. 1938**

× Blc. Mem. Crispin Rosales = Blc. Tribute
× Blc. Pamela Farrell = Blc. Malibu Gem
× Lc. Colorama = Lc. Prism Palette

HOSHANG‡ (syn. Evamay Patterson) — **Intertexta × trianaei** — **A. & R. 1946**

× Sunrise Chalet = Dreamy White

hybrida / **HYBRIDA*‡** — **guttata × loddigesii** — **Nat. hyb.** / **hort.**
(syn. *patrocinii**; *lucieniana*)

× Dark Emperor = Muscadine
× Lc. Barton = Lc. Buffalo Trace

IDETTAE*†‡ — **Edithiae × Virginalis** — **F. 1929**

× mossiae = Platine
× Bc. Pastoral = Bc. Foulard

INTERGLOSSA* — **amethystoglossa × intermedia** — **Thayer 1902**

× guttata = Morningside Splash
× Blc. Coronet Bay = Blc. Beacon Mountain
× Epi. atropurpureum = Epc. Adin Burton
× Lc. Parysatis = Lc. Kindee

intermedia*†‡ — **species**

× Angelwalker = Cherry Chip
× Carl Hausermann = White Aries
× Confetti = Rebel
× Margaret Lambert = Heather Bracher
× Mount Baker = Dogwood Hill
× Okami = Wings of Red
× Blc. Ewart McDonald = Blc. Rojanadara
× Blc. Mellowglow = Blc. Cosmic Gale
× Epc. Purple Glory = Epc. Mayan Rose
× Epi. atropurpureum = Epc. Leon Glicenstein
× Lc. Amber Glow = Lc. Solitude
× Lc. Bonanza = Lc. Adele Goddard
× Lc. Cinnalo = Lc. Color Collage
× Lc. Clara Schriever = Lc. Guadeloupe
× Lc. Colorama = Lc. Mime
× Lc. Queen Kate = Lc. Prince Gordon
× Sc. Chamberlainiana = Sc. Petitpoint Pink
× Sl. Jinn = Slc. Lilliput

CATTLEYA

INTERMEDIETTE†‡ — **Henrietta Japhet × intermedia** — **Rivermont 1955**

- × Affection = Erica Antoinette
- × Margaret Stewart = Wydewood
- × Sunrise Chalet = Gertrude Matthews
- × Epc. Georgia Mariae = Epc. Icecream Frosting
- × Epi. mariae = Epc. Green Chiffon
- × Epi. phoeniceum = Epc. Kay Boyle
- × Epi. plicatum = Epc. Blue Star

IRENE*†‡ — **mossiae × Suzanne Hye** — **Fowler 1914**

- × Lc. Bride's Bouquet = Lc. Louise Alexander

IRENE FINNEY — **Elizabeth Carlson × Erwin Hausermann** — **Hausermann 1969**

- × Picasso = Dorothy Geils

IRGATTA — **Iridescens × elongata** — **Kirch 1968**

- × Lc. Belle of Celle = Lc. William of Woodlawn

IRIS*†‡ — **bicolor × dowiana** — **C. 1901**

- × Marge Bergman = Wings
- × Blc. Acapana = Blc. Ed O'Neal
- × Blc. Sunkist = Blc. Carol Boudeman
- × L. cinnabarina = Lc. Flaemmchen
- × Lc. Bright Night = Lc. Simone Kim-Cuc Bauer
- × Lc. Cloth of Gold = Lc. Mem. Garrison Ainsworth
- × Pot. Red Dawn = Pot. Shawnee Hills
- × Sl. Gratrixiae = Slc. Painted Savage

IVY WATKINS — **Rivermont Imperial × Karae Lyn Sugiyama** — **Sea God Nurs. 1975**

J. A. CARBONE†‡ — **mossiae × Prospector** — **A. & R. 1945**

- × Lc. Frank Lind = Lc. Marti Lind
- × Lc. Sargarno = Lc. Jyla Sheikhi

JACQUELINE KENNEDY — **Enid × Ardmore** — **H. Patterson 1961**

- × Bess Truman = President's Lady
- × Lc. Whitewings = Lc. North Carolina

JAMES DICK — **Mayor Tucker × walkerana** — **Fyfe 1972 (Thornton's)**

JANE TAURA — **Naka-Nani × Bob Betts** — **N. Tomita 1972 (G. Iwasaki)**

JEANNE SICKLER — **Muse's Little Star × Margaret Stewart** — **Mrs. W. H. Boyd 1973 (Blauvelt)**

JEAN PALLISTER — **Pascaline × General Patton** — **Pallister 1971 (Battle)**

JENNIE — **gaskelliana × Quinquecolor** — **Hunnewell 1975**

JOAN HANNIWELL — **Hanniwell × Joan Holloway** — **Otaguro 1972 (H. Patterson)**

- × General Russky = Gloria Tamashiro

JOAN HOLLOWAY‡ — **Edithiae × Belle Jones** — **H. Patterson 1952**

- × Hanniwell = Joan Hanniwell

JOAN MANDA*†‡ — **Suzanne Hye × White Empress** — **Manda 1937**

- × Clementine Goldfarb = Rahima

JOAN OWEN — **Louise Georgianna × Undine** — **Owens Orchids 1974**

JOAN TENNANT — **Ann Alberts × Little Angel** — **A. & M. 1973**

JOE SANTORO — **Dubiosa × aurantiaca** — **Kersey 1971**

JOSE MARTI‡ — **Bob Betts × Bow Bells** — **von Paulsen 1959 (Fields Orchids)**

- × Princess Bells = Harold Maneks
- × True White = Dos Rios

JOYCE ARNEILL — **Myron A. Hofer × Karae Lyn Sugiyama** — **Warren 1974**

JOYCE HANNINGTON†‡ | **Barbara Dane × Snowdon** | **Dane 1945**

× Gertrude Hausermann = Ben Dodson
× Prima Donna = Mildred Faye White
× Stella Elenewski = Brighton
× Bc. Ferrières = Bc. Mae Campbell
× Bc. Languedoc = Bc. Confidence
× Lc. Lorraine Shirai = Lc. Admiral Stokes

JULIETA MacFADDEN | **Carlos Gomes × Bow Bells** | **W. Silva 1971**
JUNE PRIEST | **Claesiana × Mary Bea Ireland** | **A & R. 1973**
JUTHATHIP | **Bob Betts × Queen Sirikhit** | **Lim-im 1972**
KARAE LYN SUGIYAMA‡ | **Joyce Hannington × Edithiae** | **Kwr. 1951**

× Auld Acquaintance = Bering Glacier
× Ballet Girl = Amy Warren
× Empress Bells = Snow Dawn
× Ginny = Ginny Lyn
× Myron A. Hofer = Joyce Arneill
× New Albion = Yaigwavong
× North Star = Sandpiper
× Rivermont Imperial = Ivy Watkins
× White Blossom = Barbara Spencer
× Bc. North Columbia = Bc. Herb Mosley
× Blc. Pimola = Blc. Green Mount
× Lc. Bonanza = Lc. Mary Jean Warren
× Lc. Schillerana = Lc. Kalani Castro

KATHERINE WALKER | **Undine × Joan Manda** | McPeak 1953

× Bob Betts = Boberine
× Bow Bells = Kay Bells

KAY BELLS | **Katherine Walker × Bow Bells** | **Kensington 1973**
KAZUKO FUJII | **Dreadnought × Bob Betts** | **Hausermann 1970**

× Fred Cole = Melanie

KENJI GOTO | **Pua Liilii × Southern Belle** | **Shikuma 1972**
KERCHOVEANA | **granulosa × schillerana** | **Peeters 1900**

× Epi. atropurpureum = Epc. Harald

KING GEORGE*†‡ | **dowiana × Triumphans** | **B. 1915**

× B. digbyana = Bc. Marie Collette

KISSED PINK | **Star Kissed × Siegfried** | **Edelbrock 1973**
KITCHEN DELIGHT | **Ezio Pinza × forbesii** | **Mo. Bot. Gdn. 1958**

× Epi. tampense = Epc. Little O'that

KITTIWAKE†‡ | **Brussels × Luegeae** | **A. & R. 1948**

× Lc. Aconcagua = Lc. Preferment
× Lc. Mem. Maggie Hood = Lc. Ahmad Sheikhi
× Lc. Pegi Mayne = Lc. Persepolis

KIWANDA | **mossiae × skinneri** | **Bonniewood 1971**
labiata*†‡ | **species**

(This is treated for registration purposes as specifically distinct from both *C. gaskelliana* and *C. schroederae*, though the latter are ranked as conspecific with *C. labiata* by some authorities) (syn. *C. lawrenceana*)

× B. perrinii = Bc. Perula
× Epi. vitellinum = Epc. Tell
× Lc. Elizabeth Off = Lc. Avalon
× Lc. Mariner = Lc. Blue Pacific
× Lc. Molly Tyler = Lc. Carolyn Hurtt
× Lc. Parysatis = Lc. Granite Mountain

lawrenceana (see *C. labiata**†‡) | **species**
LEILA ARONSON‡ | **Joyce Hannington × Robert H. Jewell** | **Aronson 1956 (Kwr.)**

× Lc. Crowborough Sunshine = Lc. Siamese Cat

LEONA BLOOM‡ | **loddigesii × Tango** | **A. & M. 1962**

× B. nodosa = Bc. Mem. Harry Grimes
× Epc. Susan Naomi = Epc. Anne Anderson

leopoldii*† (see *guttata**†‡) | **species**
LILLIAN WALLACE | **Roman Silver × Charlotte Sell** | **M. J. Bates 1975**

LIMONADE — **Edelweiss × Edithiae** — **F. 1972**

LINDA PALCONIT — **Stanley Fouraker × Bob Betts** — **D. Tom 1972**

LITTLE ANGEL†‡ — **O'brieniana × loddigesii** — **J. & S. 1959**

- × Ann Alberts = Joan Tennant
- × Barbara Billingsley = Osa Mae Barton
- × Fleecy Clouds = Summer Wind
- × forbesii = Mary Turner Whitney
- × guttata = Gerry Cassella
- × Margaret Hort = Tia Kay Sovereign
- × Rivermont Imperial = Cecelia Rhodes
- × Suavior = Anne Lydie
- × Whistler's Ridge = Summer Ridge
- × Blc. Ranger Six = Dianacita
- × Epi. adenocarpon = Epc. Angela Ragan
- × Lc. Red Empress = Lc. Janet Brown

LITTLE BIT — **luteola × intermedia** — **Small 1962**

- × Epi. atropurpureum = Epc. Moynette

LITTLE MISS MUFFET — **guttata × Prospector** — **Stewart Inc. 1974**

LIU — **Maggie Raphael × Intertexta** — **Maggi Ponti 1955**

- × Hedwig = Greta

LODDIACA‡ — **loddigesii × aurantiaca** — **Stewart Inc. 1962**

- × Rivermont Imperial = Hidden Gold
- × L. flava = Lc. Heidi

loddigesii*†‡ (syn. *harrisoniae**†; *harrisoniana**) — **species**

- × Gigi = Tiuna
- × Pamela Stewart = Snowberry
- × Rivermont Imperial = Silver Flute
- × Wolteriana = Pamela Muse
- × Blc. Dark Waters = Blc. Herb Jones
- × Blc. Norman's Bay = Blc. Diane Soo Hoo
- × Epi. Anza = Epc. Anza Lode
- × Lc. Derrynane = Lc. Midi
- × Lc. Jonáral = Lc. Ballyhoo
- × Lc. Luiz Martinelli = Lc. Leonor Lisbôa Caldas
- × Smbc. Snow White = Smbc. Ding Bat
- × Schom. tibicinis = Smbc. Perfection

LOIS RINEHART — **aurantiaca × Mrs. Robert Jewell** — **Mrs. W. H. Boyd 1972 (Goff)**

LORRAINE SAWTELLE — **Barbara Dane × Clementine Goldfarb** — **H. Patterson 1955**

- × Bob Betts = Tommy Tomita

LOUISE GEORGIANNA†‡ — **intermedia × Souv. de Louis Sander** — **Kwr. 1946**

- × Morne Le Blanc = Morning Snow
- × Star Kissed = Traci Noelle Watson
- × Undine = Joan Owen
- × Epi. ionocentrum = Epc. Doll Baby
- × Epi. plicatum = Epc. Plianna

lucieniana / **LUCIENIANA** (see Hybrida*‡) — **harrisoniana (= loddigesii) × leopoldii (= guttata)** — **Nat. hyb.** / **hort.**

LUCILLE SMALL‡ — **Bow Bells × Dorothy Mackaill** — **Small 1960**

- × Bridal Bouquet = Breckinridge Snow

lueddemanniana*†‡ (syn. *speciosissima*) — **species**

- × Bc. Languedoc = Bc. Barquisimeto

LUEGEAE*†‡ — **dowiana × Enid** — **C. 1910**

- × Blc. Robert Gifford = Blc. Rebecca Bull

luteola*†‡ — **species**

- × aclandiae = Small World
- × Alice Shirai = Suzanne Snyder
- × aurantiaca = Helen Jarzab
- × granulosa = Margaret Morrison
- × velutina = Bless Pat
- × Wendlandiana = Wendeola
- × B. glauca = Bc. Don Morrison
- × B. nodosa = Bc. Sea Mist
- × L. rubescens = Lc. Rubescent Luteus
- × Lc. Adelaide Waltman = Lc. Luteous Gem
- × Lc. Ann Follis = Lc. Cuiseag
- × Lc. Bimur = Lc. Entwood
- × Lc. Blue Boy = Lc. Azure Hill
- × Lc. Orange Gem = Lc. Gemola
- × Lc. Ronselensis = Lc. Pippin
- × Soph. cernua = Sc. Frudo

LYNN DEWEY — **Esther Kennedy × Princess Bells** — **Dewey 1971**

MADAME KHADAROO — **Bow Bells × Patrice Munsell** — **Khadaroo 1975 (Riverview)**

MADELEINE KNOWLTON‡ — **Bow Bells × Joyce Hannington** — **H. A. Knowlton 1954 (Kwr.)**

× Lc. Dee Dee = Lc. Hausermann's Rhapsody

MADEMOISELLE LOUISE PAUWELS*†‡ — **Edithiae × Intertexta** — **F. 1931**

× Claesiana = Betty Webb | × Bc. Ferrières = Bc. Folies Bergeres

MAGBAROLA‡ — **Maggie Bartel × luteola** — **Stevenson 1965 (Small)**

× Epi. tampense = Epc. Little Beginning

MAGGIE RAPHAEL*†‡ — **dowiana × trianaei** — **Leon 1889**

× Lc. Princess Ishtar = Lc. Princess Raphael | × Lc. S. J. Bracey = Lc. Potomac

MARACANGALHA — **Fabia × Nigritian** — **W. Silva 1963**

× Lc. Ella Esk = Lc. Southe Nigra

MARGARET ANGEL — **Margaret Stewart × Angelwalker** — **Stewart Inc. 1974**

MARGARET CHAPMAN — **Highburiensis × Barbara Sander** — **Chapman 1974 (Originator unknown)**

MARGARET HORT — **Breydon × intermedia** — **Toogood 1962 (Dos Pueblos)**

× Little Angel = Tia Kay Sovereign

MARGARET LAMBERT — **Jeanne Patterson × Bob Betts** — **Lines 1958**

× intermedia = Heather Bracher

MARGARET MAKINO — **Esbetts × Princess Bells** — **Otaguro 1974**

MARGARET MORRISON — **granulosa × luteola** — **D. Morrison Jr. 1971**

MARGARET STEWART‡ — **Dorothy Mackaill × loddigesii** — **Stewart Inc. 1957**

× Angelwalker = Margaret Angel | × Epi. gracile = Epc. Anna Kessler
× Intermediette = Wydewood | × L. cinnabarina = Lc. Freshie
× Muse's Little Star = Jeanne Sickler

MARGE BERGMAN — **Bob Betts × Metropolitan** — **Rayridge 1974**

× Iris = Wings

MARIE-JOSÉ†‡ — **Pauwelsii × Woltersiana** — **F. 1938**

× Bc. Liesbeth Hacke = Bc. Alizé

MARION PATTERSON†‡ — **Marion Davies × trianaei** — **H. Patterson 1952**

× aurantiaca = Florida Dawn

MARJORIE HAUSERMANN‡ — **Henrietta Japhet × Ethel Leder** — **Hausermann 1964**

× Fred Cole = Clark Herman

MARTHA VAN DOERSLAER — **Fabia × Gloriette** — **Doerslaer 1946**

× Dinah = Dindoer

MARY BEA IRELAND†‡ — **Celia × Estelle** — **A. & R. 1948**

× Claesiana = June Priest

MARY GRATRIX*‡ (syn. Crashleyi) — **granulosa × loddigesii** — **Gratrix 1897**

× granulosa = Mary Jane Mayfield

MARY JANE MAYFIELD	**Mary Gratrix × granulosa**	**Bishop 1973 (Helton)**
MARY LANGFORD‡	**Estelle × Jean Barrow**	**Bracey 1953**
× Earl	= Beverly O'Dell	
MARY LOU	**O'brieniana × intermedia**	**Freund 1967 (Messick)**
× Lc. Red Gold	= Lc. Jay Jay	
MARY LYNN McKENZIE‡	**Bob Betts × Swan**	**J. S. McKenzie 1958 (Fields Orchids)**
× Lc. Golden Charm	= Lc. Joanne Sullivan	
MARY REED	**elongata × violacea**	**Dewey 1973**
MARY TURNER WHITNEY	**Little Angel × forbesii**	**Casa Luna 1973**
MARY WILLIAMS	**Henrietta Japhet × Dubiosa**	**Sea God Nurs. 1975**
MAUDE KILSBY	**Southern Belle × Claesiana**	**Stewart Inc. 1960**
× Pearl Harbor	= Petite Pearl	
maxima*‡	**species**	
× B. digbyana	= Bc. Terepaima	
MAYOR TUCKER‡	**bowringiana × Juanna**	Mo. Bot. Gdn. 1959
× walkerana	= James Dick	
MEADII	**bowringiana × forbesii**	**Mead 1904**
× Epi. plicatum	= Epc. Vicky	
MEIGE†‡	**Ben Nevis × labiata**	**S. 1946**
× Empress Bells	= Mem. Frank Redman	
MELANI BEARD	**Patricia Lines × Empress Bells**	**Beard 1973**
MELANIE	**Kazuko Fujii × Fred Cole**	**Hausermann 1974**
MELODBOA	**bowringiana × Claesiana**	**Mead —**
× aurantiaca	= Blossomwood Elf	
MELODY†	**Octavia × Suavior**	**L. 1933**
× Slc. Naomi Kerns	= Slc. Cascade	
MEMORIA DOROTHY MARIE	**Mrs. Pitt × Claesiana**	**Gubler 1974**
MEMORIA FRANK REDMAN	**Empress Bells × Meige**	**Bishop 1974 (Originator unknown)**
MEMORIA LILLIAN KALLMAN	Ardmore × Bess Truman	**Lines 1972**
MEMORIA MIDORI NAKANO	**Dinah × Gloriette**	**Hisazaki 1972**
MEMORIA PAUL T. YAMADA†‡	**Bow Bells × White Bell**	**G. Yamada 1954**
× Bob Betts	= Tera Hausermann	
MEMORIA SIG REIMER	**Bob Betts × Etta Price**	**Reimer 1973**
mendelii*†‡	**species**	
× Blc. Buttercup	= Blc. Ruth Cline McDade	
× Lc. Altesse	= Lc. Tom Braverman	
× Lc. Lucien Pauwels	= Lc. Hussard	
METAPAN†	**Moumoss × mossiae**	**H. Patterson 1944**
× Blc. Momercia	= Blc. Headliner	
× Lc. Lomita Park	= Lc. Spring Arrival	
× Lc. Paradisio	= Lc. Spring Tradition	

METROPOLITAN — **mossiae × December Snow** — **McDade 1951**
× Bob Betts = Marge Bergman

MICHAEL SANDER*†‡ — **Enid × Majestic** — **S. 1934**
× Lc. Lee Langford = Lc. Takeshi Doc Yatabe | × Lc. Princess Margaret = Lc. Marsander

MILDRED FAYE WHITE — **Prima Donna × Joyce Hannington** — **D. B. White 1975**
MILTON WARNE — **Hybrida × Suavior** — **R. E. Warne 1965**
× Lc. Jane Warne = Lc. Dorothy Warne

MISTY‡ — **Angelus × loddigesii** — **Clark Day Jr. 1962**
× Elizabeth Ann Thedford = Ann Misty

MIYAKO OCHIKUBO — **Estelle × White Lady** — **Ochikubo 1949**
× Princess Bells = Princess Lynn

MIZ WHIZ — **Brabantiae × Confetti** — **Betts 1974 (Whisenant)**

MLLE. LOUISE PAUWELS*†‡ (see Mademoiselle Louise Pauwels*†‡)
MOERAE — **Bob Betts × labiata** — **Bracey 1961**
× Henrietta Japhet = Moeriet

MOERIET — **Moerae × Henrietta Japhet** — **Katsuura 1973**
MONTE SANO — **Auditor × Petite** — **Funston 1975 (Rivermont)**

MORALITY — **Crystal Palace × Sunrise Chalet** — **Rod McLellan Co. 1971**
MORNE LE BLANC†‡ — **Joan Manda × Edithiae** — **Clarelen 1944**
× Bow Bells = Eleanor Spicer | × Louise Georgianna = Morning Snow
× Henrietta Japhet = Angel Wings | × Rivermont Imperial = Adria Carita Osia

MORNINGSIDE SPLASH — **guttata × Interglossa** — **R. J. Williamson 1974**
MORNING SNOW — **Louise Georgianna × Morne Le Blanc** — **Rod McLellan Co. 1974**
MOSCOMBE — **Mosnor × Sedlescombe** — **Chung-Chweng Chen 1963**
× Lc. Bonanza = Lc. Chiou-Jye Chen | × Slc. Anzac = Slc. Yeong-Huei Chen

MOSSENA — **mossiae × Athena** — **Kensington 1973**
mossiae*†‡ — **species**
× Athena = Mossena
× Idettae = Platine
× skinneri = Kiwanda
× Epi. atropurpureum = Epc. Jesse Ferreira
× Epi. conopseum = Epc. Marion Ruff Sheehan
× L. pumila = Lc. Lorna Dene Whitlow
× Lc. Alten = Lc. Hausermann's Nocturne
× Lc. Blue Boy = Lc. Clear Blue Sky
× Lc. George Cutler = Lc. Spring Reward
× Lc. Georgette = Lc. Chelmo
× Lc. Irene Finney = Lc. Time-Life
× Lc. Mamie Eisenhower = Lc. Frank Mantua
× Lc. Velvet Spring = Lc. Purple Majesty

MOSSMIST — **mossiae × Michaelmas** — **Rod McLellan Co. 1970**
× Lc. Louis Dorp = Lc. Spring Fancy

MOUNT BAKER‡ — **Bow Bells × Henrietta Japhet** — **Beall 1955**
× Ethel Bishop = Avalanche Pass | × intermedia = Dogwood Hill

MOUNT RAINIER†‡ — **Suzanne Hye × Ethel Bishop** — **Beall 1955**
× Esbetts = Helen Parashis

MOUNT SHASTA†‡ — **Bebe White × Estelle** — **A. & R. 1949**
× Bc. Déesse = Bc. Minnie Bath

MRS. FREDERICK KNOLLYS*†‡ **Hardyana × mossiae** **Wellesley 1906**

× Blc. Morning Sun	= Blc. Mrs. Sun	× Lc. St. Helena	= Lc. Rodco's Pleasure

MRS. J. W. WHITELEY* **bowringiana × Hardyana** **S. 1899**

× Lc. Bonanza	= Lc. Mabel Carr Thornton		

MRS. MAHLER*‡ **bicolor × guttata** **R. H. Measures 1901**

× Brabantiae	= Fort Motte	× Lc. Luminosa	= Lc. Lindy Lee
× Brigade Piron	= Carnival	× Slc. Brandywine	= Slc. Castle Mountain
× Epi. plicatum	= Epc. Myriam-de-Vilanova	× Slc. Estella Jewell	= Slc. Fiesta

MRS. PITT*†‡ (syn. Sappho*) **dowiana × harrisoniana** **Hanbury 1913**

× Claesiana	= Mem. Dorothy Marie	× Lc. Mem. Albert Heinecke	= Lc. Priya Rana
× Lc. Gladys Millner	= Lc. Pitcairn	× Slc. Anzac	= Slc. Penza
× Lc. Lee Langford	= Lc. Glowing Amber		

MRS. ROBERT JEWELL† **Maggie Raphael × schröderae** **Kirkwood 1930**

× aurantiaca	= Lois Rinehart		

MUSCADINE **Hybrida × Dark Emperor** **G. Crocker 1972**

MUSE'S LITTLE STAR **Claesiana × Louise Georgianna** **Muse 1963**

× Edithiae	= Edistar	× Pearl Harbor	= Star Harbor
× Margaret Stewart	= Jeanne Sickler		

MYRON A. HOFER‡ **Mission Dolores × Claesiana** **Rod McLellan Co. 1961**

× Ballet Girl	= Ann Warren	× Karae Lyn Sugiyama	= Joyce Arneill
× Henrietta Japhet	= Allie Calhoun	× Bc. Mount Hood	= Bc. Moon Miss

NAKA-NANI **Pearl Harbor × Bob Betts** **G. Iwasaki 1958**

× Bob Betts	= Jane Taura		

NASEEMA **Bow Bells × Francis T. C. Au** **Khadaroo 1974 (Riverview)**

NELLIE ROBERTS†‡ **Bow Bells × dowiana** **B. 1953**

× Portia	= Pierre Trudeau	× Blc. Orange Glory	= Blc. Sheila Scarlet
× Blc. Acapana	= Blc. Margie Dickie	× Lc. Lee Langford	= Lc. MeLing Ho
× Blc. Norman's Bay	= Blc. Tan Loh Teck	× Pot. Lim Theng Hin	= Pot. Tun Abdul Razak

NERTO‡ **Bembridge × Amabilis** **V. 1952**

× Blc. June Moore	= Blc. San Remo		

NEW ALBION‡ **Joyce Hannington × Herbert L. Dillon** **Urmston 1956**

× Bow Bells	= Toshiyasu Miyajima	× Karae Lyn Sugiyama	= Yaigwavong

NEW ERA‡ **guttata × Nigrella** **S. 1951**

× Lc. Rosa Kirsch	= Lc. Manu		

NEW LIFE **Estelle × Tomiko Takafuji** **Rod McLellan Co. 1971**

NIGER‡ **Thora × Fabianid** **V. 1951**

× Blc. Norman's Bay	= Blc. Normani	× Lc. Hernani	= Lc. Gitana
× Lc. Dusky Maid	= Lc. Farandole		

NIGHT WATCH‡ **Tethys × Cargill** **Beall 1963**

× Bc. Déesse	= Bc. Reflection Lake		

NIGRELLA*†‡ — **Fabia × Ypres** — **S. 1934**

× Fabianid = Fabianegra
× Patricia Ann = Ruben
× Blc. Herons Ghyll = Blc. Mem. Oliver Coffee
× Blc. Jane Helton = Blc. Jungle Jane
× Lc. Mysedo = Lc. Janet Fujikawa
× Pot. Medea = Pot. Potomac
× Slc. Anzac = Slc. Primi

NIGRITIAN†‡ — **Fred Sander × Nigrella** — **S. 1945**

× Octave Doin = Tinnie Schmitt
× Rembrandt = Weldon Abell
× Bc. East Dean = Bc. Mem. Bill Kerns
× Blc. Jewel Higdon = Blc. Dorothy Harrison
× Lc. Mem. Buddy Clark = Lc. Lost Weekend
× Lc. Fabiadale = Lc. King Ennerbia
× Lc. Ishtar = Lc. Tia Maria
× Lc. José Dias Castro = Lc. Perle Noir
× Lc. Vallechollet = Lc. Fusilier
× Slc. Canzac = Slc. Fred King

NORTH STAR‡ — **Bow Bells × Helen P. Dane** — **Rivermont 1955**

× Chun Yueh = Tsukiboshi
× Karae Lyn Sugiyama = Sandpiper
× B. nodosa = Bc. Pelleas

NUCLEAR AGE‡ — **bicolor × Arctic Snow** — **Gamble 1962**

× L. Zip = Lc. Nuclear Zip

o'brieniana
O'BRIENIANA*†‡ — **dolosa × loddigesii** — **Nat. hyb. / hort.**

× Fred Cole = Hausermann's Happiness
× walkerana = Hallie Rogers
× Blc. Golden Queen = Blc. Danny Kaleikini
× Diab. Alice Hart = Bwna. Robert

OCTAVE DOIN*†‡ — **dowiana × mendelii** — **Maron 1899**

× Nigritian = Tinnie Schmitt

ODALISQUE†‡ — **Linda × Suzanne Hye** — **V. 1940**

× Bc. Marthe Gratiot = Bc. Helena Doering

OKAMI‡ — **Suavior × warscewiczii** — **Tokyo Bot. Gdns. 1924**

× intermedia = Wings of Red
× Sirido = Sirido Kami
× B. glauca = Bc. Glaucamora
× Blc. Coronet Bay = Blc. Bearpaw Mountain
× L. anceps = Lc. Kamokila
× Lc. Excellency = Lc. Sawtooth Mountain
× Lc. Flirtie = Lc. Flirtatious Okami

OLD WHITEY — **Mount Rainier × Empress Bells** — **A. & R. 1969**

× Esbetts = Ruth Gee
× General Patton = Donna Craig
× Bc. Déesse = Bc. Princess Teresa
× Blc. Ranger Six = Blc. Empress Range

ORIENTAL PEARL — **Dubiosa × Empress Bells** — **Stewart Inc. 1973**

OSA MAE BARTON — **Barbara Billingsley × Little Angel** — **A. & M. 1971**

OUMEL BANEEN — **Empress Bells × Rahima** — **Khadaroo 1975 (Riverview)**

PAMELA MUSE — **Wolteriana × loddigesii** — **Muse's 1971**

PAMELA STEWART†‡ — **Concinnity × White Cloud** — **Stewart Inc. 1951**

× loddigesii = Snowberry
× Prima Donna = Grace Darling

PARTY GIRL — **Nutley × Harold** — **McDade 1952**

× Lc. Summer Sand = Lc. Summer Symphony

PASCALINE — **Ben Nevis × Estelle** — **Doerslaer 1950**

× General Patton = Jean Pallister

PATLOSA — **granulosa × General Patton** — **J. Milton Warne 1971**

PATRICE MUNSELL‡ — **Cowaniae × Irene** — **McDade 1946**

× Bow Bells = Madame Khadaroo

PATRICIA ANN‡ | **bicolor × Leda** | **Jelinek 1958 (Ryerson)**

× guttata	= Phyllis Hetfield	× Nigrella	= Ruben

PATRICIA LINES‡ | **Barbara Billingsley × Bob Betts** | **Lines 1957**

× Empress Bells	= Melani Beard		

patrocinii / PATROCINII* | **leopoldii (= guttata) × loddigesii** | **Nat. hyb. / hort.**

(see Cattleya Hybrida*‡)

PAVLOVA†‡ | **Egret × mossiae** | **A. 1939**

× L. cinnabarina	= Lc. Dorothy Baxter		

PEACE | **Joyce Hannington × Empress Bells** | **G. B. Miwa 1958 (M. Yamada)**

× Lc. Hurricane	= Lc. Bernice Dodson		

PEANUTS | **Porcia × Nellie Roberts** | **Rod McLellan Co. 1964**

× bowringiana	= Hagoromo	× Lc. Bonanza	= Lc. Victor Canavese
× Blc. Nacouchee	= Blc. Pink Ornament	× Lc. Grodske's Gold	= Lc. Patty Lynn Smith

PEARL BELLE | **Southern Belle × Pearl Harbor** | **Rayridge 1974**

PEARL HARBOR†‡ | **Bow Bells × Celia** | **Joseph 1951**

× bicolor	= Star of Malibu	× Princess Bells	= William Carter
× Gertrude Hausermann	= Second Time	× Southern Belle	= Pearl Belle
× Maude Kilsby	= Petite Pearl	× Blc. Nacouchee	= Blc. Maurice Gusman
× Muse's Little Star	= Star Harbor		

PEETERSII*‡ | **Hardyana × labiata** | **Peeters 1902**

× Blc. Mem. Crispin Rosales	= Blc. Spencer Beauty		

PENANG | **Nigrella × bowringiana** | **J. & S. 1963**

× Blc. Norman's Bay	= Blc. Mena de Garcia	× Lc. Adolph Hecker	= Lc. Aquarius
× Epc. Night Hawk	= Epc. Dadeland		

percivaliana*†‡ | **species**

× B. nodosa	= Bc. Karin Lomer	× Lc. Ormesby	= Lc. Carlos Relvas
× Blc. Mèrimée	= Blc. Clara Helena Kienzle	× Sl. Psyche	= Slc. Psychedelic Virgin

PERSIAN BLUE | **Ariel × Undine** | **Beall 1973**

PETE-BO | **Helen Patterson × Bow Bells** | **Kensington 1973**

PETITE | **Celia × warscewiczii** | **Rivermont 1958**

× Auditor	= Monte Sano		

PETITE PEARL | **Maude Kilsby × Pearl Harbor** | **Muse's 1972**

PHYLLIS HETFIELD | **guttata × Patricia Ann** | **M. J. Bates 1973**

× Bro. sanguinea	= Ctna. Summer Madness		

PICASSO | **Elizabeth Carlson × Nancy Gray** | **Hausermann 1967**

× Carl Hausermann	= Charley Juza	× Irene Finney	= Dorothy Geils
× Chicago Today	= Swingtime		

pictùrata / PICTURATA | **guttata × intermedia** | **Nat. hyb. / Veitch 1877**

× Fleecy Clouds	= Summer Eyes	× Bro. sanguinea	= Ctna. Summer Laughter

PIERRE TRUDEAU | **Nellie Roberts × Portia** | **Garth 1971**

CATTLEYA

PITTIANA*†‡ | **dowiana × granulosa** | **Pitt 1902**

× Blc. Jewel Higdon = Blc. Laura-Jane

PLATINE | **Idettae × mossiae** | **F. 1972**

POLLY WATSON | **Claesiana × Esbetts** | **R. L. Watson 1971**

PORCIA†‡ | **Armstrongiae × bowringiana** | **A. 1927**

× Bertii = Guyana
× bicolor = Bill Crocker
× Blc. Antoinette = Blc. Christine Barfield
× Blc. Norman's Bay = Blc. Howard's Luck
× Blc. Osiris = Blc. Mem. Margaret Kosel
× L. anceps = Lc. Stepladder
× Lc. Picardy = Lc. Carmen Escobar

PORTIA*†‡ | **bowringiana × labiata** | **Veitch 1897**

× Ariel = Summer Blue
× Nellie Roberts = Pierre Trudeau
× Undine = Blue Jay
× Bc. Hartland = Bc. Portland
× Bc. Princess Patricia = Bc. Patricia Portia
× Lc. Ishtar = Lc. Ishtia
× Lc. Schillerana = Lc. Babe Bergin
× Sl. Gustave Vincke = Slc. Marie King

PORTISONIAE‡ | **Portia × loddigesii** | **Rod McLellan Co. 1960**

× Lc. Bonanza = Lc. Joe Osorio
× Lc. Guerrero = Lc. Bob's Love
× Lc. Quadroon = Lc. Portrait

PRESIDENT'S LADY | **Jacqueline Kennedy × Bess Truman** | **Rod McLellan Co. 1974**

PRESIDENT WILSON*†‡ | **Fabia × labiata** | **Colman 1916**

× Lc. Lenn Follett = Lc. Mamoru Ogata

PRIMA DONNA‡ | **Bow Bells × Minnehaha** | **Rivermont 1953**

× Joyce Hannington = Mildred Faye White
× Pamela Stewart = Grace Darling

PRINCESS BELLS‡ | **Empress Bells × Bob Betts** | **Kushima 1959**

× Angel Bells = Rio's Princess
× Dreamy White = Salvadore
× Esbetts = Margaret Makino
× Esther Kennedy = Lynn Dewey
× Jose Marti = Harold Maneks
× Miyako Ochikubo = Princess Lynn
× Pearl Harbor = William Carter
× Bc. Déesse = Bc. Prachuab
× Bc. Seafoam = Bc. Mauna Puhala
× Lc. Canhamiana = Lc. Ricke Kaname Fujino
× Sl. Psyche = Slc. Henry Severin

PRINCESS LYNN | **Princess Bells × Miyako Ochikubo** | **Edwards Orchids 1971**

PRISCILLA WARD‡ | **granulosa × forbesii** | **Woodlawn 1954**

× Blc. Chief Joseph = Blc. War Eagle
× Lc. Mem. Masa Matsumoto = Lc. Okana
× Lc. Mercia = Lc. Little Girl

PROSPECTOR†‡ | **Remy Chollet × Santa Monica** | **A. & R. 1937**

× guttata = Little Miss Muffet

PUA LIILII†‡ | **loddigesii × Triumphans** | **Hirose 1944**

× Southern Belle = Kenji Goto

QUEEN SIRIKHIT‡ | **Bow Bells × O'brieniana** | **B. 1958**

× Bob Betts = Juthathip
× High Light = Betty McNamara

QUINQUECOLOR | **aclandiae × forbesii** | **Veitch 1865**

× gaskelliana = Jennie
× Lc. Edmund Rothwell = Lc. Take Five

RAHIMA | **Clementine Goldfarb × Joan Manda** | **Khadaroo 1975 (Riverview)**

× Bow Bells = Djalil
× Empress Bells = Oumel Baneen

RAYMOND PALMER | **skinneri × Barbara Billingsley** | **A. R. Gibson 1971 (R. Palmer)**

CATTLEYA

RAY PARK‡ | **Bow Bells × Pavlova** | **Rod McLellan Co. 1956 (E. W. McLellan)**

× gaskelliana = White Summer

REBEL | **Confetti × intermedia** | **Stevenson 1973**

REDGATTA | **Redtop Mountain × elongata** | **Kirch 1968**

× Blc. Mem. Crispin Rosales = Blc. Pu'ula'ula

REDTOP MOUNTAIN†‡ | **guttata × Princess Royal** | **Beall 1959 (Clarelen)**

× Blc. Mem. Crispin Rosales = Blc. Naniwa

REMBRANDT*†‡ | **elongata × labiata** | **Maron 1901**

× Nigritian = Weldon Abell
× Bc. Evelyn Zuck = Bc. Remelyn
× Blc. Yasuko Tachibana = Blc. Michelle Orban

REMY CHOLLET*†‡ | **Monarch × trianaei** | **S. 1926**

× Winnietha = Elmer Hisle
× Lc. Dahlia = Lc. Dahllet
× Lc. Twinkle Star = Lc. Twinkle Chollet

REVEL‡ | **Rembrandt × velutina** | **Woodlawn 1958**

× Lc. Carrie Estelle = Lc. Carvel

rex*†‡ | **species**

× forbesii = Sister John Karen

RIO'S PRINCESS | **Angel Bells × Princess Bells** | **Ruben 1974**

RITA RENEE‡ | **Edithiae × Brussels** | **Ozzella 1956**

× Dubiosa = Dubonnet
× Bc. Berangere = Bc. Beranee
× L. anceps = Lc. Garden Delight
× Lc. Grub Stake = Lc. Melecio Huerta
× Lc. Mem. Maggie Hood = Lc. Nippon

RIVERMONT IMPERIAL‡ | **Bow Bells × loddigesii** | **Rivermont 1961**

× Karae Lyn Sugiyama = Ivy Watkins
× Little Angel = Cecelia Rhodes
× Loddiaca = Hidden Gold
× loddigesii = Silver Flute
× Morne Le Blanc = Adria Carita Osia
× Ruth Shepherd = White Shepherd
× Tomiko Takafuji = High Regard

ROBERT SCHWEPPE | **Eugene Hausermann × Carl Hausermann** | **Hausermann 1974**

ROBIN COLLEEN | **aclandiae × aurantiaca** | **Rope 1973 (Vagner)**

RODCO'S GLORY | **Barbara Kirch × Gloriette** | **Rod McLellan Co. 1972**

ROMAN SILVER | **Estelle × Empress Bells** | **A. & R. 1963**

× Charlotte Sell = Lillian Wallace

ROWENA BAER | **amethystoglossa × Cotton Belle** | **Baer 1972 (Hecht)**

R.(OWENA) PROWE*†‡ | **intermedia × Suzanne Hye** | **S. 1914**

× Ruth M. Johnston = Darshelle Abraham
× Bl. Sea Urchin = Blc. Ocean Spray

RUBEN | **Patricia Ann × Nigrella** | **Ruben 1972**

RUBENCITO | **dowiana × aurantiaca** | **Ruben 1972**

× Lc. Mem. Maria Miranda = Lc. Doña Josefa

RUBENS RIBEIRO | **Thomas Flynn × Francis T. C. Au** | **Altenburg 1975**

RUTHABELL THOMPSON | **Dubiosa × Auranti-media** | **Fort Caroline 1975**

RUTH ELLIS | **Estelle × Florence Patterson** | **Rod McLellan Co. 1971**

RUTH GEE | **Esbetts × Old Whitey** | **A. & R. 1975**

CATTLEYA

RUTH M. JOHNSTON‡ — **Bob Betts × General Patton** — **D. W. Johnston 1960**

× R. Prowe	= Darshelle Abraham	× Blc. Pastel	= Blc. Angela Starke

RUTH SHEPHERD‡ — **O'brieniana × Brenda** — **Bracey 1961**

× Rivermont Imperial = White Shepherd

SALINAS‡ — **Jeanne Patterson × Dorothy Mackaill** — **Rod McLellan Co. 1959**

× Tiffin Bells = Frosting

SALVADORE — **Dreamy White × Princess Bells** — **Hausermann 1974**

SAND ISLAND — **Manzanita × Redtop Mountain** — **Beall 1967**

× Lc. Zada Fields = Lc. Winyah

SANDPIPER — **North Star × Karae Lyn Sugiyama** — **Fort Caroline 1975**

SAPPHO* (see Mrs. Pitt*†‡)

schillerana*†‡ — **species**

× aurantiaca	= Duchess of Colima	× Epc. Rosita	= Epc. Rosiana
× bicolor	= Something Else	× Epi. Tampico	= Epc. Dorothy Isemonger
× B. perrinii	= Bc. Candy Star	× Schom. thomsoniana	= Smbc. Elegance
× Bc. Green Dawn	= Bc. Green Star		

schroderae*†‡ — **species**

(This and *C. gaskelliana* are both treated for registration purposes as specifically distinct from *C. labiata*, though ranked as conspecific by some authorities.)

× L. milleri = Lc. Ben Bracey

SCINTILLATION†‡ — **Bow Bells × Cowaniae** — **Rivermont 1954**

× Helen P. Dane = Sindane

SEA BREEZE — **warneri × walkerana** — **Stewart Inc. 1972**

SECOND TIME — **Pearl Harbor × Gertrude Hausermann** — **J. & S. 1975 (Stoddard)**

SEDLESCOMBE†‡ — **Annette × Suavior** — **L. 1932**

× Blc. Mem. Crispin Rosales	= Blc. Doctor Chen	× Lc. Bonanza	= Lc. Hong-Sie Chen
× Blc. Norman's Bay	= Blc. Lo Ying	× Lc. Princess Esk	= Lc. Chen's Beauty
		× Slc. Anzac	= Slc. Grace Chen

SIEGFRIED — **Enid × intermedia** — **Karthaus 1909**

× Star Kissed = Kissed Pink

SIERRA SUMMIT — **gaskelliana × Fair Lady** — **D. E. Herman 1971**

SILVER CITY — **Esbetts × General Patton** — **A. & R. 1975**

SILVER FLUTE — **Rivermont Imperial × loddigesii** — **Stewart Inc. 1973**

SILVER LINING‡ — **Dorothy Mackaill × mossiae** — **Rapella 1958**

× The Friendly Third	= Age of Sail	× White Blossom	= Valley Forge

SINDANE — **Helen P. Dane × Scintillation** — **Kensington 1973**

SIRIDO‡ — **Bob Betts × Joyce Hannington** — **W. Silva 1960**

× Okami = Sirido Kami

SIRIDO KAMI — **Sirido × Okami** — **Otaguro 1973**

SISTER JOHN KAREN — **rex × forbesii** — **Burton's 1973 (Originator unknown)**

SIVAM — **Trimos × guttata** — **R. M. Hamilton 1973 (Ryerson)**

CATTLEYA

skinneri*†‡ — **species**

× Barbara Billingsley = Raymond Palmer | × Epi. atropurpureum = Epc. Silvester
× mossiae = Kiwanda | × Lc. Canhamiana = Lc. Florence Dawson

SMALL WORLD — **aclandiae × luteola** — **Rod McLellan Co. 1975**
SNOWBERRY — **Pamela Stewart × loddigesii** — **Stewart Inc. 1972**
SNOW DAWN — **Karae Lyn Sugiyama × Empress Bells** — **McAllister 1975**
SNOW JEWELS — **White Blossom × Angelwalker** — **Stewart Inc. 1975**
SNOW WHITE†‡ — **Eucharis × Mina** — **B. 1942**

× Lc. Bride's Bouquet = Lc. Mem. Ronnie Endsley |

SOHMA*† — **Empress Frederick × mossiae** — **B. 1923**

× Lc. Shenandoah = Lc. Longwood Gardens |

SOMETHING ELSE — **schillerana × bicolor** — **Fort Caroline 1971 (Wallbrunn)**

SONIA ALTENBURG — **Enid × Nerto** — **Altenburg 1963**

× Enid = Denpa |

SOUTHERN BELLE† — **Minnehaha × mossiae** — **McDade 1950**

× Pearl Harbor = Pearl Belle | × L. flava = Lc. Small Paul
× Pua Liilii = Kenji Goto |

SOUVENIR DE LOUIS SANDER†‡ — **Blanchelys × Douai** — **Sladden 1936**

× Bow Bells = Sweet Liberty |

speciosissima (see *lueddemanniana**†‡) — **species**
SPRING CLIMAX — **Tiffin Bells × Barbara Billingsley** — **Rod McLellan Co. 1971**
STANLEY FOURAKER‡ — **Bow Bells × intermedia** — **Fouraker 1957 (Rivermont)**

× Bob Betts = Linda Palconit |

STAR HARBOR — **Pearl Harbor × Muse's Little Star** — **Muse's 1972**
STAR KISSED — **Henrietta Japhet × loddigesii** — **Stewart Inc. 1962**

× Barbara Hecht = Doctor Harold Hecht | × Siegfried = Kissed Pink
× Louise Georgianna = Traci Noelle Watson |

STAR OF MALIBU — **Pearl Harbor × bicolor** — **Sokoloski 1972 (Freed)**

STELLA ELENEWSKI† — **Suzanne Hye × Helen P. Dane** — **H. Patterson 1953 (Elenewski)**

× Joyce Hannington = Brighton |

SUABROWNIAE — **Browniae × Suavior** — **Gauda 1973**
SUAVIOR*†‡ — **intermedia × mendelii** — **Veitch 1887**

× Browniae = Suabrowniae | × Bc. Déesse = Bc. Marasri
× Little Angel = Anne Lydie | × Lc. Irene Finney = Lc. Aqui-Finn

SUDAN‡ — **Ardentissima × Nigritian** — **Bracey 1958**

× Lc. Peggy Huffman = Lc. Theresa Rose |

SUMMER BLUE — **Ariel × Portia** — **Beall 1973**
SUMMER DAWN — **Claire Ayau × Fleecy Clouds** — **Lenette 1974**
SUMMER EYES — **Picturata × Fleecy Clouds** — **Lenette 1974**

CATTLEYA

SUMMER GIRL — **Fleecy Clouds × gaskelliana** — **Lenette 1974**
SUMMER LADY — **Harold × Fleecy Clouds** — **Lenette 1974**
SUMMER RIDGE — **Whistler's Ridge × Little Angel** — **Lenette 1974**
SUMMER ROMANCE — **Summer Ski Slope × Dreadnought** — **Lenette 1974**
SUMMER SKI SLOPE — **Karae Lyn Sugiyama × warneri** — **Beall 1969**

× Dreadnought = Summer Romance | × Fleecy Clouds = Summer Song

SUMMER SONG — **Summer Ski Slope × Fleecy Clouds** — **Lenette 1974**
SUMMER SURPRISE — **Wendy Patterson × Fleecy Clouds** — **Lenette 1974**
SUMMER WIND — **Fleecy Clouds × Little Angel** — **Lenette 1974**
SUNRISE CHALET†‡ — **Henrietta Patterson × mossiae** — **Beall 1954**

× Crystal Palace = Morality | × White Blossom = White Chalet
× Hoshang = Dreamy White | × Blc. Nanette = Blc. Elizabeth Caldwell
× Intermediette = Gertrude Matthews |

superba*† (see *violacea*‡) — **species**
SUZANNE HYE*†‡ — **gaskelliana × mossiae** — **Hye 1906**

× aurantiaca = Tomoko |

SUZANNE SNYDER — **Alice Shirai × luteola** — **C. H. Snyder 1974**
SWAN†‡ — **Edithiae × Mlle. Louise Pauwels** — **F. 1946**

× Dr. Behiels = Carlos Gomes |

SWEET LIBERTY — **Souv. de Louis Sander × Bow Bells** — **Rod McLellan Co. 1971**
SWINGTIME — **Picasso × Chicago Today** — **Hausermann 1975**
TABOO (see Chamberlainiana*‡)
TANGO‡ — **A. J. Ruck × Ruby** — **A. & M. 1955**

× Blc. Piney Patterson = Blc. Summer Tango | × Lc. S. J. Bracey = Lc. Golden Rhapsody
× Lc. Belle of Celle = Lc. Color Plus | × Lc. Summerland Girl = Lc. Dottie Kone
× Lc. Golden Nymph = Lc. Paul Joseph Weber | × Lc. Twinkle Star = Lc. Royal Ruby

TERA HAUSERMANN — **Mem. Paul T. Yamada × Bob Betts** — **Elmhurst 1974**
TETHYS†‡ — **Annie J. Lines × Ardentissima** — **A. & R. 1946**

× Blc. Otomayim = Blc. Syto |

THEBES*†‡ — **Adula × dowiana** — **Fowler 1914**

× Lc. Hassallii = Lc. Joyce Pickell |

THE FRIENDLY THIRD‡ — **Sunrise Chalet × Bob Betts** — **Lines 1961**

× Affection = Virginia Bonner | × William B. Olsen = Helen Milliken
× Silver Lining = Age of Sail |

THETIS†‡ — **Delphin × Titrianae** — **Schroder 1937**

× Lc. Bonanza = Lc. Thebon |

THOMAS FLYNN — **loddigesii × Joyce Hannington** — **Richmond Floral 1966**

× Francis T. C. Au = Rubens Ribeiro |

TIA KAY SOVEREIGN — **Margaret Hort × Little Angel** — **Warren 1975**
TIFFIN BELLS‡ — **White Blossom × Bow Bells** — **Diggelman 1962**

× Barbara Billingsley = Spring Climax | × Salinas = Frosting
× Dorene = Vanilla Sundae |

TINABURRA SUNSET — **Fulvescens × Hermosa** — **Limberlost 1975**
TINNIE SCHMITT — **Octave Doin × Nigritian** — **H. Schmitt 1974**

TITRIANAE*†‡ — **Tityus × trianaei** — **M. 1923**
× Lc. Adina = Lc. Yukiko Hironaka | × Lc. Godiva = Lc. Titriva

TIUNA — **loddigesii × Gigi** — **Jesurún 1971**
TOMIKO TAKAFUJI‡ — **Joyce Hannington × Estelle** — **Takafuji 1954**
× Estelle = New Life | × Rivermont Imperial = High Regard

TOMOKO — **Suzanne Hye × aurantiaca** — **I. Nishimura 1972**
TOMMY TOMITA — **Lorraine Sawtelle × Bob Betts** — **N. Tomita 1972 (G. Iwasaki)**

TOSHIYASU MIYAJIMA — **Bow Bells × New Albion** — **M. T. Tanaka 1972**
TRACI NOELLE WATSON — **Louise Georgianna × Star Kissed** — **Watson 1971**
trianaei*†‡ — **species**
× Athena = Trithena
× Edouard Dartois = Tridart
× Bc. Déesse = Bc. Tridees
× Blc. Marion Ryerson = Blc. Zelma Long Frazer
× Lc. Pink Pearl = Lc. Lourdes Falabella

TRIBELLS‡ — **Bow Bells × trianaei** — **Rivermont 1966**
× Bc. Déesse = Bc. Faithful Star |

TRIDART — **trianaei × Edouard Dartois** — **Altenburg 1971**
TRIMOS*†‡ — **mossiae × trianaei** — **L. —**
× guttata = Sivam |

TRITHENA — **trianaei × Athena** — **M. T. Swartz 1972 (Originator unknown)**
× Bc. Digbyano-mossiae = Bc. Marenore |

TRUE WHITE — **trianaei × Souv. de Louis Sander** — **Gore 1958**
× Jose Marti = Dos Rios |

TSUKIBOSHI — **North Star × Chun Yueh** — **Gauda 1971**
TYRONE — **Bob Betts × Esbetts** — **A. & R. 1975**
UNDINE*†‡ (syn. Dusseldorfei) — **intermedia × mossiae** — **H. 1906**
× Ariel = Persian Blue
× Estelle = Corndean Lee
× Louise Georgianna = Joan Owen
× Portia = Blue Jay

VALLEY FORGE — **Silver Lining × White Blossom** — **Stewart Inc. 1974**
VANILLA SUNDAE — **Dorene × Tiffin Bells** — **J. & S. 1974**
VARUNA†‡ — **Annie J. Lines × Intertexta** — **A. & R. 1945**
× Bc. Daffodil = Bc. Mem. Leighton Long |

velutina*†‡ — **species**
× aurantiaca = Charlotte Goddard
× Fascelis = Fascelina
× luteola = Bless Pat
× Blc. Painted Desert = Blc. Sunrise Serenade
× L. milleri = Lc. Chester Goddard

venosa / **VENOSA‡** — **forbesii × loddigesii** — **Nat. hyb.** / **hort.**
× Lc. Puppet = Lc. Imp of Gold | × Lc. Sunburst = Lc. Rhonda Fisher

CATTLEYA

violacea‡ (syn. *superba**†) — **species**

×	=	×	=
× elongata	= Mary Reed	× Epi. atropurpureum	= Epc. Night Hawk
× Bro. sanguinea	= Ctna. Ultra-violent		

Name	Parentage	Registrant
VIOLA SANJUME	**Baby Jane × aurantiaca**	**Perreira 1975**
VIRGINIA BONNER	**The Friendly Third × Affection**	**Jack Cole 1972 (Lines)**
VIRGINIA GREENWOOD	**Barbara Billingsley × aurantiaca**	**W. L. Smith 1971**
VOELKER GLACIER	**Esbetts × Helen P. Dane**	**Voelker 1973**

walkerana*†‡ — **species**

×	=	×	=
× Mayor Tucker	= James Dick	× Epi. mariae	= Epc. Green Gem
× O'brieniana	= Hallie Rogers	× L. anceps	= Lc. Twilight Song
× warneri	= Sea Breeze	× Lc. Blue Boy	= Lc. Blue Dynasty
× Bc. Imperialis	= Bc. Imperial Nobilior	× Lc. Elegans	= Lc. At Dusk
× Diacm. bicornutum	= Diaca Lin Toy	× Smbc. Snow White	= Smbc. Meringue

warneri*†‡ — **species**

×	=	×	=
× Ariel	= Caribbean Skies	× Lc. Blue Boy	= Lc. Blue Ribbon
× walkerana	= Sea Breeze	× Lc. Princess Margaret	= Lc. Lyndel Worthman
× L. jongheana	= Lc. Jonghewar		

WARPAINT — **Tango × aurantiaca** — **Bloom's Nursery 1967**

× Lc. Red Gold = Lc. Gold Digger

warscewiczii*†‡ (syn. *gigas*) — **species**

× Claesiana = Claegigas

Name	Parentage	Registrant
WELDON ABELL	**Rembrandt × Nigritian**	**Limberlost 1973**
WENDEOLA	**Wendlandiana × luteola**	**Cryder 1974**
WENDLANDIANA*	**bowringiana × warscewiczii**	**Veitch 1894**

× luteola = Wendeola

WENDY PATTERSON — **Helen P. Dane × intermedia** — **H. Patterson 1965**

× Fleecy Clouds = Summer Surprise

WHISTLER'S RIDGE — **Little Angel × Dreadnought** — **Beall 1968**

× Little Angel = Summer Ridge

Name	Parentage	Registrant
WHITE ARIES	**intermedia × Carl Hausermann**	**Hausermann 1972**
WHITE BELLE†‡	**mossiae × White Empress**	**S.A. 1949**

× Dorene = Dorebelle | × Lc. Bride's Bouquet = Lc. White Gull

WHITE BLOSSOM†‡ — **Concinnity × Estelle** — **Ozzella 1950**

×	=	×	=
× Angelwalker	= Snow Jewels	× Silver Lining	= Valley Forge
× aurantiaca	= Eleanor Papac	× Sunrise Chalet	= White Chalet
× Karae Lyn Sugiyama	= Barbara Spencer		

Name	Parentage	Registrant
WHITE CHALET	**Sunrise Chalet × White Blossom**	**A. & R. 1973**
WHITE CLOVER‡	**Snowsprite × Snowfall**	**Bracey 1956**

× Bridal Bouquet = Cloud Cap

Name	Parentage	Registrant
WHITE RADIANCE	**Bob Betts × Ben Nevis**	**Reimer 1972**
WHITE SHEPHERD	**Rivermont Imperial × Ruth Shepherd**	**Stewart Inc. 1974**
WHITE SUMMER	**Ray Park × gaskelliana**	**E. W. McLellan 1973**
WHITE SWAN‡	**Joan Manda × Alaska**	**Kodama 1954 (Kido)**

× Bc. Mount Hood = Bc. Heather Campbell

CATTLEYA

WILLIAM B. OLSEN†‡ — **Edithiae × Ann Faller** — **Patterson 1952**

× The Friendly Third = Helen Milliken

WILLIAM CARTER — **Princess Bells × Pearl Harbor** — **R.C.K. 1974 (Garth)**

WINGS — **Marge Bergman × Iris** — **Rayridge 1975 (F. J. Bergman)**

WINGS OF RED — **Okami × intermedia** — **Coastal Gdns. 1973**

WINNIETHA†‡ — **Clotho × loddigesii** — **de Saram 1940**

× Remy Chollet = Elmer Hisle | × Lc. Lomita Park = Lc. Spring Romance

WOLTERIANA‡ — **aurantiaca × schroderae** — **Wolter 1909**

× Dubiosa = Wolteriosa | × Lc. Antonica Fredrick = Lc. Gimli
× loddigesii = Pamela Muse | × Lc. Rojo = Lc. Loge
× Blc. Ermine = Blc. Goulds Gold | × Slc. Pacific Gem = Slc. Mabel Goerth
× Bro. sanguinea = Ctna. Little Treasure

WOLTERIOSA — **Wolteriana × Dubiosa** — **Muse's 1971**

WOLTERSIANA*† — **Queen Mary × Rajah** — **Pauwels 1923**

× Lc. Hertha = Lc. Hertersiana

WYDEWOOD — **Intermediette × Margaret Stewart** — **Gavelek 1973 (Originator unknown)**

YAIGWAVONG — **New Albion × Karae Lyn Sugiyama** — **Sanimthong 1975 (Daniel M. Hill)**

YERTALA — **Edelweiss × trianaei** — **Limberlost 1963**

× Blc. Nanette = Blc. Leonie Mackay | × Blc. Wake Island = Blc. Marion Moreland

YVONNE ADAIR†‡ — **Clementine Goldfarb × Helen P. Dane** — **H. Patterson 1952**

× Bob Betts = Adabett

CATTLEYOPSIS

LIBERTAD — **ortgiesiana × cubensis** — **Osment 1970**

× Bro. sanguinea = Ctpsta. Jamacuba

CATTLEYOPSISTONIA

JAMACUBA — **Ctps. Libertad × Bro. sanguinea** — **Osment 1974**

LEONA — **Bro. sanguinea × Ctps. ortgiesiana** — **Bloom's Nursery 1966 (W. W. G. Moir)**

× Diab. Newcastle = Nash. George

CATTLEYTONIA

ALINA FROELICH — **Rosy Jewel × Bro. sanguinea** — **Szmant 1973 (Timmons)**

JAMAICA RED — **Bro. sanguinea × Keith Roth** — **W. W. G. Moir 1972**

KEITH ROTH — **C. bicolor × Bro. sanguinea** — **Fields Orchids 1966**

× Bro. sanguinea = Jamaica Red | × Lc. Mattie Shave = Lctna. Roy Fields

LITTLE TREASURE — **C. Wolteriana × Bro. sanguinea** — **Bloom's Nursery 1974**

ROSY JEWEL‡ — **C. bowringiana × Bro. sanguinea** — **W. W. G. Moir 1956**

× Bro. sanguinea = Alina Froelich

SUMMER DREAM — **C. Bactia × Bro. sanguinea** — **Lenette 1974**

CATTLEYTONIA

SUMMER LAUGHTER	C. Picturata × Bro. sanguinea	Lenette 1974
SUMMER MADNESS	C. Phyllis Hetfield × Bro. sanguinea	Lenette 1974
ULTRA-VIOLENT	C. violacea × Bro. sanguinea	Wallbrunn 1973

CAULARTHRON

bicornutum (see *Diacrium bicornutum**†‡) **species**

CHEWARA

RUTH WONG	Rnds. Mahani × Rhy. retusa	Takemoto 1973

CHONDRORHYNCHA

discolor (see *Cochleanthes discolor*†‡) **species**

CHRISTIEARA

BANGKOK	Aër. flabellata × Ascda. Meda Arnold	Laksanaphuk 1973
BANGPRA	Ascda. Yip Sum Wah × Aër. flabellata	Muttamara 1973
CHANGCHENKIT	Aër. odorata × Ascda. Meda Arnold	Saeng Udom 1974
CHULA	Aër. crassifolia × Ascda. Meda Arnold	Laksanaphuk 1973
MALIBU GOLD	V. Josephine van Brero × Aërctm. Luke Nok	Freed 1973 (Originator unknown)
MEMORIA RAYMOND MERCIER	Aër. fieldingii × Ascda. Meda Arnold	P. Mercier 1975 (Originator unknown)
NAM-OI	Aër. falcata × Ascda. Yip Sum Wah	Tavivatana 1974 (Charoen-ngam)
PINK GLORY	Ascda. Tan Chai Beng × Aër. mitrata	Perreira 1973
RUTH MURAI	Aër. lawrenceae × Ascda. Yip Sum Wah	Furumizo 1975
SUM NOK	Ascda. Yip Sum Wah × Aerctm. Luke Nok	Miskimens 1973 (R. K. Mizuta)
THAI	Ascda. Medasand × Aër. falcata	Sombuntham 1973 (Lenavat)
THA YANG	Ascda. Medasand × Aër. flabellata	Suebsanguan 1975
VIRGINIA BRAGA	Aër. jarckiana × Ascda. Meda Arnold	T. Orchids 1974

CIRRHOPETALUM

ornatissimum* **species**
× rothschildianum = Vindobona |

rothschildianum‡ **species**
× ornatissimum = Vindobona |

VINDOBONA	ornatissimum × rothschildianum	Voth 1975

COCHELLA

LITTLE TURTLE	Cnths. discolor × Mdcla. grandiflora	W. W. Wilson 1975

COCHLEANTHES

discolor†‡ **species**
(syn. *Chondrorhyncha discolor*; *Warscewiczella discolor*)
× Mdcla. grandiflora = Chla. Little Turtle

COCHLIODA

noezliana*†‡ **species**
× Oda. Ariitea = Oda. Picasso

sanguinea*‡ **species**
(This is retained as the horticulturally recommended name for registration purposes even though *Symphoglossum sanguineum* is the botanically correct name for this species.)
× Onc. incurvum = Oncda. Robin | × Onc. ornithorhynchum = Oncda. Beatrice Ramirez

COLMANARA

BOGOTA	**Mtdm. Cleopatra × Odm. Mount Baker**	**W. W. G. Moir 1972**
CAUCA VALLEY	**Mtdm. Aztec Gold × Odm. Mount Baker**	**W. W. G. Moir 1974**
DESDAMONA	**Milt. Peru × Odcdm. Carrykylum**	**W. W. G. Moir 1973 (Kirch)**
FERGUSON BEALL	**Milt. Crimson Crest × Odcdm. Tiger Butter**	**W. W. G. Moir 1973**
GOODALE	**Odtna. Debutante × Onc. varicosum**	**Kirch 1969**

× Onc. crispum = Winter Sunshine

HAWAII NEI	**Mtdm. Autumn Glow × Odm. Yukon Harbor**	**W. W. G. Moir 1972**
MARTIN ORENSTEIN	**Sir Jeremiah × Onc. Sultamyre**	**W. W. G. Moir 1973 (E. Iwanaga)**
MOON GOLD	**Mtdm. Aztec Gold × Odm. Yukon Harbor**	**W. W. G. Moir 1973**
MUSTARD POT	**Sir Jeremiah × Onc. orthostates**	**George Black 1973**
PUGET SOUND	**Mtdm. Surprise × Odm. Mount Baker**	**W. W. G. Moir 1973**
PURPLE GEM	**Milt. Cogniauxiae × Odcdm. Dainty**	**George Black 1973**
SHOWER OF GOLD	**Odtna. Debutante × Mtdm. Summer Fantasy**	**Beall 1973**
SIR JEREMIAH	**Odm. bictoniense × Mtdm. Lee Hirsch**	**W. W. G. Moir 1963**

× Onc. orthostates = Mustard Pot | × Onc. Sultamyre = Martin Orenstein

WINTER SUNSHINE	**Goodale × Onc. crispum**	**W. K. Hall 1975**

COMPARETTIA

falcata†‡ **species**
× Odm. bictoniense = Odrta. Violetta

macroplectron‡ **species**
× Odm. bictoniense = Odrta. Dümmerbrand | × Onc. leitzii = Onctta. Ruben's Twinkle
× Onctta. Ecuador = Onctta. Colombia | × Rdcm. Primi = Wnra. Ruben

speciosa‡ **species**
× Odm. bictoniense = Odrta. Mandarine | × Onc. Tiny Tim = Onctta. Sunflake

CYCNOCHES

chlorochilon‡ **species**
(This is treated for registration purposes as specifically distinct from *Cycnoches ventricosum*, though the latter is ranked as a synonym by some authorities.)
× maculatum = Rip-Van-Winkle | × Ctsm. roseum = Ctnchs. Rebecca Northen

CYCNOCHES

maculatum **species**

× chlorochilon = Rip-Van-Winkle

RIP-VAN-WINKLE **maculatum × chlorochilon** **Osment 1975**

CYMBIDIUM

ACAPULCO **Jungfrau × Claudona** **Dos Pueblos 1958**

× Joan of Arc	= Pristine	× Wampum	= April

AIRBORNE† **Capella × Louis Sander** **Cooke 1947**

× Curlew	= Gavotte	× Silvio	= Silvair
× Flare	= Eric Brown	× Vieux Rose	= Patricia Norrie

AIVALER **Balkis × Green Goddess** **Miller Coll. 1971**

ALCOR **simulans × canaliculatum** **Miller Coll. 1971**

ALDWORTH **Romeo × Babylon** **Wyld Court 1972**

ALEXALBAN† **Albania × Alexanderi** **Hanbury 1933**

× Lucense	= Shanida	× Showgirl	= Richard Gardner

ALEXANDERI*†‡ **Eburneo-lowianum × insigne** **H. 1911**

× Baltic	= Trefain	× Thanksgiving	= Via Vista Grande
× lancifolium	= Lancer	× Via Tranquila	= Via Tehachapi

ALISON TREACHER **Oiso × Charles Darwin** **George Arblaster 1971**

ALLEGRETTA **Finetta × Allegro** **Stewart Inc. 1971**

ALLEGRO‡ **Liliana × Ruth Castator** **Stewart Inc. 1962**

× Finetta	= Allegretta	× sinense	= Cottontail

ALNWICK CASTLE‡ **Reginald × Corinth** **L. 1954**

× Apollo	= Springfield	× Durham Castle	= Sleeping Blossom
× Auriga	= Goldenette	× Sleeping Beauty	= Sleeping Queen
× Balkis	= Lady Bird Johnson	× Warona	= Wallacia
× Dorama	= Valley Sheen		

AMBER FLASH†‡ **Coningsbyanum × Louis Sander** **Cooke 1946**

× Babylon	= Pleiades	× Dartmoor	= Pink Flash

AMERICAN BEAUTY **Claudona × Artisan** **Stewart Inc. 1974**

ANDORINHA **Oystercatcher × Swallow** **Wyld Court 1974**

ANDY HAMILTON **Greenwood × Early Bird** **R. M. Hamilton 1974 (Hoyt)**

ANNAN **Camelot × Berwick** **M. 1973**

ANNE ARCHER **Jungfrau × Vieux Rose** **A'Logann 1975**

ANNE BAXTER‡ **Flamingo × Balkis** **Dos Pueblos 1961**

× Balkis	= Valley Anne	× Pearl-Balkis	= Valley Charm
× Etta Barlow	= Valley Scene	× San Miguel	= Valley Haze
× Mary Ann	= Valley Snow	× virescens	= Shunga
× Mazatlan	= Valley Falls		

ANNE HAMILTON **Las Pulgas × Sicily** **R. M. Hamilton 1973 (Rod McLellan Co.)**

ANNE MICHELE **Rio Rita × Shiraz** **A'Logann 1975**

ANN GREEN‡ **Rosanna × Babylon** **Dos Pueblos 1958**

× Cariga	= Antipodes	× Rosinante	= Rosyann
× Hi-Rated	= New Moon	× Saigon	= Philomena Cardosa
× Marquesa Prescott	= Laurel Jean Sakell	× Vintage	= Valley Flare

CYMBIDIUM

ANTIPODES — **Ann Green × Cariga** — **I. D. James 1975**

APOLLO*†‡ — **Curlew × Miranda** — **A. 1932**

× Alnwick Castle = Springfield
× Celadon = Little Mermaid

APRIL — **Wampum × Acapulco** — **Carlton 1972**

ARABY — **Doris × Joan** — **L. 1932**

× Blue River = Earle Dodson

ARALUEN — **President Wilson × Sussex Dawn** — **Tom Henry 1973**

ARCADIAN MELODY — **Irish Melody × Stanley Fouraker** — **Greenoaks 1966**

× Balkis = Valley Symphony
× Cleo Sherman = Cleo's Melody
× Lady Lucy = Via Arcadian Lady
× Mary Ann = Doreen Darwen
× Miracle = Arcadian Sunshine
× Pearl-Easter = Bob Waabel
× Rincon = Via Arcadian Rincon
× Snow Sprite = Arcadian Snow
× Solana Beach = Via Solana
× Sussex Dawn = Via Arcadian Dawn
× Thanksgiving = Via Natividad
× Westholme = Valley Melody

ARCADIAN SNOW — **Arcadian Melody × Snow Sprite** — **Goodchild 1972 (Willandra)**

ARCADIAN SUNSHINE — **Arcadian Melody × Miracle** — **Borg 1973**

ARDINGLY — **Clarissa × Remus** — **Stonehurst 1973**

ARTISAN‡ — **Dorama × Babylon** — **Stewart Inc. 1961**

× Claudona = American Beauty
× Dorama = Margaret Kakis
× George Lycurgas = Toshikazu Takahashi
× Sussex Dawn = Karen Henry

ATLANTES†‡ — **Alexanderi × erythrostylum** — **Hanbury 1927**

× Louis Sander = Eva Borg
× Monsoon = Atlantic Sun

ATLANTIC SUN — **Monsoon × Atlantes** — **G. & S. 1973 (E. W. Miller)**

× Rincon = Via Grandioso
× Sussex Dawn = Via Atlantica
× Verde de Invierno = Via Verde Fresco

atropurpureum — **species**

× ensifolium = Clare Natasha

ATSUKO — **pumilum × Fairy** — **I. Nishimura 1974**

AUREART — **Doris Aurea × Fred Stewart** — **Stewart Inc. 1973**

AURIGA*†‡ — **Alexanderi × Excelsior** — **M. 1923**

× Alnwick Castle = Goldenette
× Jeanne-Marie = Mariga
× Mary Ann = Valley Avilion
× Nicky = Nickalong-Campbell
× Wiena = Wattle Glen

AUTUMN DAY — **erythrostylum × Lucy** — **M. & H. 1975 (M.)**

× Rio Rita = Rio Autumn

AUTUMN KING — **Autumn Leaves × Imperial** — **Borg 1973**

AUTUMN LEAVES — **Kurun × Autumn Tints** — **Sander et Fils 1970**

× Imperial = Autumn King
× Lady Lucy = Lady Autumn
× Rincon = Clear Autumn

AUTUMN SKIES — **Monte Rosa × Early Bird** — **Sander et Fils 1966**

× Louis Sander = Redskies
× Stanley Fouraker = Ruby Skies

BABY LARRY — **Magpie × Lucy** — **Sakell 1974 (H. Patterson)**

× Grand Monarch = Green Fields

CYMBIDIUM

BABYLON†‡ — **Olympus × Pauwelsii** — **A. 1942**

× Amber Flash = Pleiades
× Baltic = Michael Evans
× faberi = Irish Lulabye
× Ispahan = Sasha Berman
× Miracle = Mirahill
× Romeo = Aldworth
× Sugar Palm = Sugar Bush
× Tapestry = Dark Wonder
× Vieux Rose = Rose Park
× Warrah = Lofty
× Wyld Court Swift = Courtier

BALASTES — **Baldur × Lucastes** — **C. 1971**

BALDUR*†‡ — **Alexanderi × Castor** — **A. 1929**

× Lucastes = Balastes

BALKIDARWIN — **Balkis × Charles Darwin** — **Stewart Inc. 1974**

BALKIS*†‡ — **Alexanderi × Rosanna** — **L. de R. 1934**

× Alnwick Castle = Lady Bird Johnson
× Anne Baxter = Valley Anne
× Arcadian Melody = Valley Symphony
× Bernadette = Hattie
× Brissie = Valley Rosetta
× Canara = Wattle Vale
× Charles Darwin = Balkidarwin
× Darjeeling = Kampur
× Defiant = Highland Sunset
× Etta Barlow = Valley King
× Fanfare = Dress Parade
× Giuse = Mem. Milena Sutter
× Green Goddess = Aivaler
× Janine = Valley Imperial
× Joan Luth = Premier
× Jocosity = Valley Joy
× Lunagrad = Reynella
× Mary Ann = Valley Glacier
× Merry Christmas = Christmas Party
× Miraluce = Patchogue
× Ora Lee = Eleni
× Orphan = Chipper Hamilton
× parishii = Belle Glade
× Runnymede = Yellow Prince
× Sheba = Valley Tryst
× Sugar Palm = Sugar Candy
× tigrinum = Tigris
× Twelfth Night = Valley Lake
× Vieux Rose = Royden

BALLIG — **Larne × elegans** — **Andrew Orchids 1975**

BALTIC†‡ — **Midas × Riga** — **Schroder 1950**

× Alexanderi = Trefain
× Babylon = Michael Evans
× Defiant = Selkirk
× Epping = Celtic Oak
× Green Knight = Baltic Knight
× Janora = Mildred Foulds
× Oystercatcher = Shantila
× Parma = Marilyn
× Vale of Kashmir = Kashtic
× Vieux Rose = Baltic Rose
× York Meredith = Fort George

BALTIC KNIGHT — **Baltic × Green Knight** — **F. S. Young 1974**

BALTIC ROSE — **Baltic × Vieux Rose** — **Andrew Orchids 1971 (C. K. Andrew)**

BANFF — **Putana × Lucetta** — **M. 1972**

BARBARA HANCOCK — **Princess Desirée × pumilum** — **A'Logann Labs. 1972**

BARBARA LOVE — **Rosanna × Marquesa Prescott** — **Shaffer's 1973**

BARTOLME FERRELLO‡ — **Dorchester × Babylon** — **Dos Pueblos 1961**

× Sussex = Redford Beauty

BELAIR — **Irish Melody × Etta Barlow** — **Adelaide 1975 (Originator unknown)**

BELLE GLADE — **parishii × Balkis** — **Everglades 1975**

BENWICK — **Sweetheart × Con Amore** — **Miller Coll. 1971**

BERNADETTE†‡ — **Alexanderi × Sheila** — **B. 1942**

× Balkis = Hattie

BERNICE FARRELL‡ — **Adarissa × Miretta** — **Dos Pueblos 1958 (Ireland)**

× Miretta = Elton Gripp

BERWICK‡ — **Cambria × Carisette** — **M. 1970**

× Camelot = Annan
× Clarissa = Coldstream
× Putana = Strathavon

CYMBIDIUM

BETHLEHEM‡	**Frederica × Earlyana**		**Stewart Inc. 1963**
× Dainty	= Victoria Arvanitis	× Rio Rita	= Mary Stortecky
× Earlyana	= Three Wise Men	× Stanley Fouraker	= Early Magic
× Magpie	= Howell		
BETTY OTT‡	**Clarissa × Doris Aurea**		**Gamble 1957 (Everett Nurs.)**
× Putana	= Edith Logan-Home		
BETTY VYEDA	**Fairy Pearl × Cleo Sherman**		**Vyeda 1974 (Hager)**
BIG PINE	**Blue Smoke × Sicily**		**Sherman 1958**
× devonianum	= Bright Eyes	× Mount Everest	= Marcus Aurelius
BIG TREES‡	**Erica Sander × Sherwood Forest**		**Rod McLellan Co. 1958 (E. W. McLellan)**
× Dorama	= Green Fortune	× Miretta	= Green Victory
× Irina	= Green Spirit		
BLUE QUEEN‡	**Queen Mary × Blue Smoke**		**A. & R. 1956**
× Sea Foam	= Gold Rush		
BLUE RIVER	**Beatrice × Blue Smoke**		**Sherman 1954**
× Araby	= Earle Dodson		
BLUE SMOKE†‡	**lowianum × Mirabel**		**Cooke 1946**
× Celadon	= Lunette	× Stanley Fouraker	= Hitoshi Ohno
× Great Day	= Great Smoke		
BOBTAIL	**Chiron × tigrinum**		**Andrew Orchids 1973**
BOB WAABEL	**Pearl-Easter × Arcadian Melody**		**Darwen 1973 (A.C.O.C.)**
BODALEITH	**Inverleith × Ramboda**		**C. 1971**
BODMIN MOOR*†‡	**Alexanderi × Erica Sander**		**S. 1936**
× Eagle	= Eagle Moor		
BOKHARA	**Cinderella × Remus**		**D. 1965**
× Fascination	= Loki		
BRENTWOOD‡	**Midas × Irina**		**Paul Weber 1954 (Carpentier)**
× Dag	= Dagwood	× niveo-marginatum	= Siempre
BRIGHT EYES	**Big Pine × devonianum**		**Rod McLellan Co. 1971**
BRIGHT TOPAZ	**Miretta × Snow Sprite**		**Cotton 1975 (M.)**
BRIGITTE MAIER	**Prince Charles × Joan of Arc**		**A'Logann 1975**
BRISSIE	**Pixie × Lucy**		**F. A. Bell 1950**
× Balkis	= Valley Rosetta		
BROOK STREET	**Mayfair × devonianum**		**Andrew Orchids 1974**
BUD MARCH	**Balkis × Shiraz**		**Dos Pueblos 1967**
× Dorama	= Valley Gold		
BUFFY	**Fairy Wand × Dante**		**Greenoaks 1971**
BUOYANT	**Wood Nymph × Swallow**		**Stewart Inc. 1972**
BUTTONS AND BOWS	**sinense × Stanley Fouraker**		**Stewart Inc. 1973**

CYMBIDIUM

CABERNET	**Promona × Carisona**		**Easton 1974 (Dos Pueblos)**
CAITHNESS	**Western Rose × Sea Gem**		**M. 1972**
CALAO	**Kurun × John Sander**		**Pff. V. & L. 1964**
× Kurun	= Laperrine		
CALDY	**Ramesis × Vieux Rose**		**Andrew Orchids 1972**
CALIFORNIA ROMANCE	**Sweetheart × Mount Everest**		**Rod McLellan Co. 1971**
CALLANDER	**Putana × Miretta**		**M. 1970**
CALLE DEL REY	**King Arthur × Pixie Moor**		**G. & S. 1973**
CALLE LAGUNA	**King Arthur × Fred Stewart**		**G. & S. 1973**
CALLE LOS OLIVOS	**King Arthur × Sussex Dawn**		**G. & S. 1973**
CAMBRIA†‡	**Carisbrook × Ramboda**		**Harben 1948**
× Joan of Arc	= Kim Brady		
CAMDERS	**Karen Cameron × Clyde Landers**		**Borg 1973**
CAMELOT‡	**Dryad × pumilum**		**Paul Miller 1962 (B. & W.)**
× Berwick	= Annan	× Spray	= Camelot Queen
× San Miguel	= Green Prince		
CAMELOT QUEEN	**Camelot × Spray**		**Rod McLellan Co. 1971**
CAMILLA†‡	**Doris × Lowio-grandiflorum**		**Cowan 1925**
× Monsoon	= Green Coral		
canaliculatum‡	**species**		
× finlaysonianum	= Iris Bannochie	× simulans	= Alcor
CANARA	**Auriga × Wyalong**		**Wondabah 1967**
× Balkis	= Wattle Vale		
CANDY ANN RADZINS	**Joan of Arc × Princess Desirée**		**A'Logann Labs. 1972**
CANTERBURY TALES	**King Arthur × Ora Lee**		**Miller Coll. 1972**
CARIGA†‡	**Carlos × Riga**		**M. 1951**
× Ann Green	= Antipodes	× Redwood	= Precocious
× Moonman	= Egmont	× Rusper	= Sunny Dream
× Putana	= Stoneaven	× Seabird	= Maspalomas
× Ramboda	= Mary Yendall		
CARIKHYBER	**Carisona × Khyber Pass**		**Stewart Inc. 1971**
CARISONA†‡	**Carisbrook × Cremona**		**M. 1947**
× Khyber Pass	= Carikhyber	× Promona	= Cabernet
× Marquesa Prescott	= Marquisona		
CAROL-ANA	**Carol Cox × Earlyana**		**Stewart Inc. 1975**
CAROL COX	**Vanguard × Atlantes**		**Cox's 1967 (Sherman)**
× Earlyana	= Carol-Ana		
CARRIE MANSFIELD	**Shiraz × San Miguel**		**Romanoff 1971**
CELADON‡	**pumilum × Ruskin**		**Greenoaks 1962**
× Apollo	= Little Mermaid	× Irish Melody	= Dorothy Ann Wright
× Blue Smoke	= Lunette	× Southborough	= Minette
× chloranthum	= Chloradon		
CELAYA	**Doris Aurea × Stanley Fouraker**		**Stewart Inc. 1971**
CELTIC OAK	**Epping × Baltic**		**Woolnough 1974 (Dos Pueblos Pty.)**

CHAFFINCH†‡ | **Doris × Gottianum** | **S. 1917**
× Stardust = Lagrange

CHARLES DARWIN‡ | **Dorama × Balkis** | **Stewart Inc. 1962**
× Balkis = Balkidarwin
× Desirée A'Logann = Darwinesque
× Early Forest = Farmingdale
× Oiso = Alison Treacher
× Ora Lee = Peggy Richardson

CHER AMI‡ | **Chiron × Curlew** | **Hankey 1948**
× devonianum = Mon Ami

CHIEF JOSEPH | **Ivy Fung × Susa** | **Easton 1975 (Dos Pueblos)**

CHIPPER HAMILTON | **Orphan × Balkis** | **Hamilton 1971 (Rod McLellan Co.)**

CHIRON*†‡ | **Bustard × President Wilson** | **A. & B. 1935**
× devonianum = Corfu
× tigrinum = Bobtail

CHLORADON | **Celadon × chloranthum** | **Greenoaks 1975**

chloranthum | **species**
× Celadon = Chloradon
× erythrostylum = Chlorey
× Korintji = Nancy Carpenter

CHLOREY | **chloranthum × erythrostylum** | **Ireland 1971**
CHOCOLATE GEM | **Mimi × Rincon** | **Greenoaks 1974**
CHRISTINE PEAKE | **Oiso × Pearl-Balkis** | **Arblaster 1971**
CHRISTMAS CAROLS | **Stanley Fouraker × Magpie** | **Stewart Inc. 1971**
CHRISTMAS CLARION | **Rincon × Peetie** | **Los Padres 1974**
CHRISTMAS GREEN‡ | **Bimbo × Sicily** | **Sherman 1958**
× Fred Stewart = Mem. William Flynn
× Twelfth Night = Xmas Night

CHRISTMAS PARTY | **Merry Christmas × Balkis** | **Peterson Bros. 1972**

CHRISTMAS RADIANCE‡ | **Rio Rita × erythrostylum** | **M. 1967**
× Lucy Moor = Shetland Isles

CLARE NATASHA | **ensifolium × atropurpureum** | **Sainsbury 1975 (George Black)**

CLARENDON | **Sweetheart × Radak** | **Adelaide 1975 (Paul Miller)**

CLARET‡ | **Clarissa × Atlantes** | **Sherman 1961**
× Louis Sander = Consistent Pink

CLARIANCE | **King Arthur × Radak** | **Miller Coll. 1971**
CLARINDA | **Claudona × Rincon** | **Wyld Court 1974**
CLARISSA†‡ | **Carisbrook × Rio Rita** | **M. 1948**
× Berwick = Coldstream
× Putana = Invergarry
× Remus = Ardingly
× Sunrise = Tamatea
× Touchstone = Miniatures Delight

CLAUBODA | **Claudona × Ramboda** | **M. 1963**
× Mary Ann = Highland Giant

CLAUDONA†‡ | **Claudette × Cremona** | **M. 1946**
× Artisan = American Beauty
× Dorama = Valley Pasture
× Fred Stewart = Yankee Whaler
× Rincon = Clarinda
× Sleeping Beauty = Sleeping Spring
× Sussex Dawn = Valley Green

CYMBIDIUM

CLEAR AUTUMN	**Autumn Leaves × Rincon**	**Borg 1973**
CLEO SHERMAN‡	**Alexanderi × Babylon**	**Sherman 1956**

× Arcadian Melody = Cleo's Melody
× Dainty = Lee Setsko Boyar
× Fairy Pearl = Betty Vyeda
× Fanfare = Utopia
× Fred Stewart = Valley Prince
× Mary Ann = Ludwig Fetzer
× Pacific Pearl = Pearly Shells
× Pearl-Balkis = Marie Fetzer
× Rosanna = Warminster
× Sea Foam = Inez Magan

CLEO'S MELODY	**Arcadian Melody × Cleo Sherman**	**R. J. Dean 1974 (Meredith)**
CLERGERIE	**Kurun × Magpie**	**Pff. V. & L. 1975**
CLYDE LANDERS‡	**Spartan Queen × Carisona**	**Dos Pueblos 1963**

× Karen Cameron = Camders
× Swallow = Congier

COLDSTREAM	**Clarissa × Berwick**	**M. 1973**
CON AMORE‡	**Liliana × Parsifal**	**Stewart Inc. 1962**

× Sweetheart = Benwick

CONGIER	**Clyde Landers × Swallow**	**Borg 1973**
CONQUISTADOR	**George Lycurgas × Priam**	**Stewart Inc. 1971**
CONSISTENT PINK	**Claret × Louis Sander**	**Rod McLellan Co. 1971**
CORAL SEA‡	**Swallow × Babylon**	**Stewart Inc. 1956**

× Mem. Francis Cobb = Mem. Susan Urban
× Suva = Suva Sea

CORFU	**Chiron × devonianum**	**Andrew Orchids 1973**
CORONADO‡	**Shina Black × Miretta**	**Dos Pueblos 1957**

× Miretta = Green Champ

COTTONTAIL	**sinense × Allegro**	**Stewart Inc. 1973**
COURTIER	**Wyld Court Swift × Babylon**	**A. & B. 1974**
CRACKER JACK	**Ivy Fung × Robin**	**Santa Barbara 1974**
CURLEW*†	**Alexanderi × Butterfly**	**H. 1922**

× Airborne = Gavotte

DAG	**Esmeralda × pumilum**	**Ireland 1964**

× Brentwood = Dagwood

DAGWOOD	**Dag × Brentwood**	**Pabst 1974**
DAINLEY	**Dainty × Stanley Fouraker**	**Stewart Inc. 1973**
DAINTY‡	**Luminous × Lyoth**	**A. & R. 1955**

× Bethlehem = Victoria Arvanitis
× Cleo Sherman = Lee Setsko Boyar
× Stanley Fouraker = Dainley

DAKARA	**Rutana × Sensation**	**Wondabah 1971**
DALNSPIDAL	**Darjeeling × Nicky**	**MacGregor 1971 (D.)**
DANTE*†‡	**Bullfinch × Goosander**	**A. 1932**

× Fairy Wand = Buffy

DARJEELING‡	**Blue Smoke × Rosette**	**Stewart Inc. 1954**

× Balkis = Kampur
× Nicky = Dalnspidal

DARK WONDER	**Babylon × Tapestry**	**Rod McLellan Co. 1971**
DARTMOOR‡	**Adonis × Bodmin Moor**	**S. 1948**

× Amber Flash = Pink Flash

DARWINESQUE	**Charles Darwin × Desirée A'Logann**	**Stewart Inc. 1975**

DASU | **Sussex Moor × Ramboda** | **C. 1971 (Ratcliffe)**

DAUGHTER LAUREL | **Stanley Fouraker × Prince Charles** | **Sakell 1971**

dayanum*‡ (syn. *simonsianum*) | **species**

× elegans	= Elsimon		

DEFIANT | **Pixie × Challenge** | **H. 1955**

× Balkis	= Highland Sunset	× Vieux Rose	= Sparkle
× Baltic	= Selkirk		

DESIRÉE A'LOGANN‡ | **Balkis × Babylon** | **A'Logann 1956**

× Charles Darwin	= Darwinesque	× Shina Black	= Kathy Landry
× Sanrita	= Polka Time	× Sweetheart	= Teri Garr

devonianum*‡ | **species**

× Big Pine	= Bright Eyes	× Park Lights	= Devon Park
× Cher Ami	= Mon Ami	× sinense	= Minnehaha
× Chiron	= Corfu	× Sussex Dawn	= Maribelle
× Mayfair	= Brook Street	× Woodalda	= Devon Wood

DEVON PARK | **Park Lights × devonianum** | **McKechnie 1973 (Andrew Orchids)**

DEVON WOOD | **Woodalda × devonianum** | **Andrew Orchids 1974**

DIANA*†‡ | **Eburneo-lowianum × Pauwelsii** | **Hassall 1916**

× Stanley Fouraker	= Huntress		

DILAS | **Sunstroke × Flycatcher** | **Andrew Orchids 1972 (De'Quincey)**

DOLORES HOYT | **King Arthur × Endre Ostbo** | **Hoyt 1972**

DONALD WILSON | **Khyber Pass × Vieux Rose** | **Easton 1975**

DONEGAL | **Larne × Parma** | **M. & H. 1975**

DORAMA‡ | **Dorchester × President Wilson** | **M. 1950**

× Alnwick Castle	= Valley Sheen	× Pearl-Balkis	= Valley Topaz
× Artisan	= Margaret Kakis	× Peri	= Hidden Promise
× Big Trees	= Green Fortune	× Pixie Dawn	= Via Arroyo
× Bud March	= Valley Gold	× Rusper	= Rodco's Creation
× Claudona	= Valley Pasture	× Shiraz	= Valley Gem
× Grandly	= Valley Field	× Snow Sprite	= Valley Sapphire
× Green Spring	= Via Cajon Verde	× Southborough	= Valley Opal
× Janet	= Janora	× Sussex Moor	= Dorama Moor
× Lunagrad	= Flagstaff Hill	× Wyanga	= Gwen Sternbeck
× Nila	= Shanthi		

DORAMA MOOR | **Sussex Moor × Dorama** | **Goodchild 1972 (Meredith)**

DORCHESTER*† | **Alexanderi × Tityus** | **A. & B. 1932**

× Durham Castle	= Tarun	× Mary Ann	= Valley Eden
× Joan of Arc	= Valley Nymph	× Mem. Walter Kavanagh	= Kitty White
× Marian Lenfestey	= Nariel		

DOREEN DARWEN | **Arcadian Melody × Mary Ann** | **Darwen 1972 (A.C.O.C.)**

DORILOW | **Pumilow × Doris Aurea** | **Andrew Orchids 1974**

DORIS AUREA†‡ | **Chiron × Lysander** | **B. 1942**

× Fred Stewart	= Aureart	× Stanley Fouraker	= Celaya
× Pumilow	= Dorilow		

DOROTHY ANN WRIGHT | **Celadon × Irish Melody** | **Greenoaks 1975**

DOWNS DELIGHT | **Janine × Sussex Dawn** | **Valley Orchids 1973 (Vandyke)**

× Siram = Valley Delight
× Sleeping Beauty = Sleeping Promise

DREAMLAND | **Miretta × Mount Everest** | **Peterson Bros. 1972**

DRESS PARADE | **Balkis × Fanfare** | **Peterson Bros. 1972**

DUNEBA | **Profita × Regency** | **Wondabah 1971**

DURHAM CASTLE‡ | **Ruth × Plover** | **L. 1954**

× Alnwick Castle = Sleeping Blossom
× Dorchester = Tarun
× Early Bird = Shining Mountain
× Ramesis = Sleeping Gold
× San Miguel = Sleeping Girl
× Sleeping Glow = Sleeping Delight
× Sleeping Monarch = Sleeping Castle
× Warella = Weipa

EAGLE*†‡ | **Alexanderi × Gottianum** | **S. 1922**

× Bodmin Moor = Eagle Moor
× Pearly Queen = Queagle

EAGLE MOOR | **Bodmin Moor × Eagle** | **C. 1971**

EARLE DODSON | **Blue River × Araby** | **Hamilton 1971 (Originator unknown)**

EARLYANA‡ | **Early Bird × Louisiana** | **Stewart Inc. 1962**

× Bethlehem = Three Wise Men
× Carol Cox = Carol-Ana
× Lunagrad = Luana
× Lustrous = Valley Premiere
× Shiraz = Tanunda
× Stanley Fouraker = Valley Mayflower

EARLY BIRD†‡ | **Edward Marshall × erythrostylum** | **S. 1946**

× Durham Castle = Shining Mountain
× Greenwood = Andy Hamilton

EARLY CALL | **Rincon × Glasgow** | **Los Padres 1974**

EARLY FOREST‡ | **Redwood × Lucy** | **Rod McLellan Co. 1964**

× Charles Darwin = Farmingdale
× Fanfare = Kauri Forest

EARLY MAGIC | **Bethlehem × Stanley Fouraker** | **Stewart Inc. 1971**

EARLY SPRING | **Fred Stewart × Frederica** | **Sakell 1971**

EBURNEO-LOWIANUM*†‡ | **eburneum × lowianum** | **Veitch 1889**

× virescens = Wakaba

EDINBURGH | **Sea Gem × Lucense** | **M. 1973**

EDITH LOGAN-HOME | **Putana × Betty Ott** | **George Arblaster 1973**

EDZELL*†‡ | **Ceres × Lysander** | **B. 1936**

× Putana = Skye

EGMONT | **Moonman × Cariga** | **Wray 1975 (Originator unknown)**

ELEGANCE | **Esmeralda × President Wilson** | **M. 1950**

× Sussex Dawn = Highland Valley

elegans*‡ | **species**

× dayanum = Elsimon
× Larne = Ballig
× Redwood = Elwood

ELENI | **Balkis × Ora Lee** | **Sakell 1975 (Universal)**

ELFRIDA BERMAN | **Susan Berman × Rosanna** | **Berman 1973 (Stonehurst)**

ELLA BULSTRODE | **Oiso × Mary Yendall** | George Arblaster 1971

ELSIMON | **elegans × dayanum** | **Andrew Orchids 1974**

ELTON GRIPP	**Miretta × Bernice Farrell**		**Santa Barbara 1975**
ELWOOD	**elegans × Redwood**		**Andrew Orchids 1974**
EMBER GLEAM	**Mimi × insigne**		**Greenoaks 1975**
EMBERS	**Fairy Wand × Rio Rita**		**Greenoaks 1975**
EMMELINE	**Grand Monarch × Pearl**		**Santa Barbara 1963 (Carpentier)**
× Monsoon	= Noel Green	× Verde Grande	= Grand Em
× Stanley Fouraker	= Melody Fair		
ENDRE OSTBO	**Esmeralda × Europa**		**Hoyt 1959 (Ostbo)**
× King Arthur	= Dolores Hoyt		
ENID HAUPT†‡	**Diana × Francis Barbour**		**Baldwin 1948**
× Liliana	= Mellow Brown	× Peetie	= Mellow Yellow
× Miretta	= Green Chance		
ENSENADA	**Irina × Mazatlan**		**Carlton 1972**
ensifolium†‡	**species**		
× atropurpureum	= Clare Natasha	× Vieux Rose	= Happy Talk
EPPING	**Sussex Dawn × Eider**		**Chandler 1963 (A. & B.)**
× Baltic	= Celtic Oak		
ERIC BROWN	**Airborne × Flare**		**W. E. Brown 1971 (M.)**
erythrostylum*†‡	**species**		
× chloranthum	= Chlorey	× Stanley Fouraker	= Pioneer
× Lucy	= Autumn Day		
ESMERALDA*†‡	**lowianum × Venus**		**M. 1937**
× suave	= Evonne		
ETTA BARLOW‡	**Rosanna × Balkis**		**Dos Pueblos 1958**
× Anne Baxter	= Valley Scene	× Lunagrad	= Susan Hughes
× Balkis	= Valley King	× Miretta	= Green Reward
× Fred Stewart	= Valley Progress	× Nila	= Sweet Patience
× Green Spring	= Via El Dorado	× Pearl-Balkis	= Valley Sunset
× Irish Melody	= Belair	× Vieux Rose	= Janet Marion
EVA	**Evelyn × Rosefieldense**		**M. 1937**
× Stanley Fouraker	= Great Waltz		
EVA BORG	**Louis Sander × Atlantes**		**Borg 1973**
EVONNE	**Esmeralda × suave**		**Cannons 1973**
faberi	**species**		
× Babylon	= Irish Lulabye	× Fifi	= Fad
FAD	**Fifi × faberi**		**Ireland 1972**
FAIR GREEN	**pumilum × Fanfare**		**Stewart Inc. 1974**
FAIR PROMISE	**Vieux Rose × Mary Ann**		**Dell Park 1974**
FAIRWAY PARK	**Bodmin Moor × Constance Flory**		**A. & B. 1957**
× Liliana	= Margaret Tate		
FAIRY*	**erythrostylum × Gottianum**		**S. 1922**
× pumilum	= Atsuko		

CYMBIDIUM

FAIRY PEARL	**Pearl × Mayfair**	**MacGregor 1955 (Farnes)**

× Cleo Sherman	= Betty Vyeda		

FAIRY WAND‡	**pumilum × Princess Maria**	**Greenoaks 1956**

× Dante	= Buffy	× Rincon	= Rincon Fairy
× Firewheel	= Fire Wand	× Rio Rita	= Embers
× insigne	= Fleurette	× Rosanna	= Rose Wand

FANFARE‡	**Verde Grande × Mount Everest**	**Braemar 1965**

× Balkis	= Dress Parade	× pumilum	= Fair Green
× Cleo Sherman	= Utopia	× San Miguel	= Voice of Spring
× Early Forest	= Kauri Forest	× Swallow	= Melody Lane
× Parma	= Kelly Green	× Wood Nymph	= Tidbit

FARMINGDALE	**Early Forest × Charles Darwin**	**Sakell 1971**
FASCINATION‡	**Joyful × Constance Flory**	**A. & B. 1954**

× Bokhara	= Loki	× Plush	= Orquil
× Flare	= Felicitas	× Susan Berman	= General Lord Norrie
× Paracel	= Redcliffe	× Suva	= Fassuva
× Piccadilly	= Firesprite		

FASSUVA	**Suva × Fascination**	**Stewart Inc. 1973**
FELICITAS	**Flare × Fascination**	**Dell Park 1973**
FIFI	**madidum × Argonaut**	**Ireland 1964**

× faberi	= Fad		

FINETTA†‡	**Lyoth × Susette**	**L. 1942**

× Allegro	= Allegretta		

finlaysonianum*†‡	**species**	

× canaliculatum	= Iris Bannochie	× Pauwelsii	= Freshie
× madidum	= Francis Hunte		

FIRESPRITE	**Fascination × Piccadilly**	**Mrs. J. West 1973 (Andrew Orchids)**
FIRE WAND	**Fairy Wand × Firewheel**	**Greenoaks 1971**
FIREWHEEL‡	**Doris Aurea × Rio Rita**	**Greenoaks 1961**

× Fairy Wand	= Fire Wand	× pumilum	= Red Jewel
× Miretta	= Joanna Camilla		

FLAGSTAFF HILL	**Dorama × Lunagrad**	**Adelaide 1975**
FLAMINGO*†‡	**Alexanderi × Merlin**	**H. 1925**

× Snow Goose	= Snow Bunting		

FLARE†‡	**Edzell × Rio Rita**	**Hothfield 1946**

× Airborne	= Eric Brown	× O'Grady	= Little Redhead
× Fascination	= Felicitas	× Rio Rita	= Lily Brown
× Mimi	= Red Flare		

FLEURETTE	**Fairy Wand × insigne**	**Greenoaks 1971**
FLYCATCHER†‡	**Alexanderi × Delphine**	**Cooke 1946**

× Rio Rita	= Rubicon	× Sunstroke	= Dilas
× Sugar Palm	= Sugar Bird		

FORT GEORGE	**Baltic × York Meredith**	**M. 1972**
FRANCIS HUNTE	**madidum × finlaysonianum**	**George Black 1973**
FREDERICA*†‡	**Hanburyanum × Schlegelii**	**M. 1935**

× Fred Stewart	= Early Spring	× Redwood	= Rodco's Emerald

FRED STEWART‡	**Early Bird × Balkis**	**Stewart Inc. 1964**

× Christmas Green	= Mem. William Flynn	× Pearl-Easter	= Valley Mist
× Claudona	= Yankee Whaler	× Rampur	= Valley View
× Cleo Sherman	= Valley Prince	× Rincon	= Via Rincon
× Doris Aurea	= Aureart	× Rio Rita	= Via Rubra
× Etta Barlow	= Valley Progress	× San Miguel	= Valley Limelight
× Frederica	= Early Spring	× Sheba	= Valley Heights
× Heathrow	= Via Invierno	× Shiraz	= Valley Hope
× Janine	= Valley Xmas	× Showgirl	= Showart
× Joan of Arc	= Ron Junod	× Solana Beach	= Via Costa
× King Arthur	= Calle Laguna	× Stanley Fouraker	= Winter Fair
× Liliana	= Star of India	× Sussex	= Poplan
× Marquesa Prescott	= Gladys Vincent	× Sussex Dawn	= Via San Gabriel
× Mary Ann	= Valley Promise	× Thanksgiving	= Via Barranca
× New Horizon	= Frosted Pearl	× Twelfth Night	= Valley Dream
× Pearl-Balkis	= Valley Pearl		

FRESHIE	**Pauwelsii × finlaysonianum**	**Fresh 1972**
FROSTED PEARL	**New Horizon × Fred Stewart**	**Stewart Inc. 1971**
GAVOTTE	**Curlew × Airborne**	**Wyld Court 1972**
GENERAL LORD NORRIE	**Susan Berman × Fascination**	**Berman 1974**
GEORGE LYCURGAS‡	**Maya × Apollo**	**H. N. Kawamoto 1953 (Stewart Inc.)**

× Artisan	= Toshikazu Takahashi	× Priam	= Conquistador
× Joan of Arc	= Pasadena Beautiful	× Sussex Moor	= Lycurgas Moor
× Korintji	= Lycurintji	× Woodalda	= Lemon Grove

GIBSON GIRL	**Louis Sander × Tapestry**	**Rod McLellan Co. 1972**
GIUSE	**Princesse Astrid × Narciso Rapuzzi**	**Maggi Ponti 1967**

× Balkis = Mem. Milena Sutter

GLADYS VINCENT	**Marquesa Prescott × Fred Stewart**	**Sakell 1974**
GLASGOW*†‡	**Alexanderi × Eburneo-lowianum**	**Whitton 1922**

× Rincon = Early Call

GLOIRE DELL PARK	**Magna Charta × Ormoulu**	**Dell Park 1973**
GOBLIN	**devonianum × Nicky**	**D. 1963 (Ratcliffe)**

× Harem = Yashmak

goeringii (see *virescens*‡)	**species**	
GOLDEN BEAUTY	**Vale of Kashmir × Irish Melody**	**C. J. Sandy 1971**
GOLDENETTE	**Alnwick Castle × Auriga**	**Wondabah 1971**
GOLDEN SUNSET	**San Miguel × Rincon**	**Cobbs' 1969**

× Solana Beach = Via del Sol

GOLDEN WEDDING	**Swallow × Woodalda**	**Stewart Inc. 1971**
GOLD RUSH	**Blue Queen × Sea Foam**	**Stewart Inc. 1971**
GRACILLAKER	**gracillimum × Stanley Fouraker**	**Stewart Inc. 1974**
gracillimum‡	**species**	

× Stanley Fouraker = Gracillaker

GRAND EM	**Verde Grande × Emmeline**	**Sakell 1971**
GRANDLY‡	**Grand Monarch × Sicily**	**Santa Barbara 1963 (Carpentier)**

× Dorama	= Valley Field	× Pearl-Easter	= Grand Parade
× Pearl-Balkis	= Valley Grand		

CYMBIDIUM

GRAND MONARCH*†‡ — grandiflorum × Wiganianum — M. 1931
× Baby Larry = Green Fields | × Wyanga = Sleeping Monarch

GRAND PARADE — Grandly × Pearl-Easter — Mrs. Valya Craig 1971 (Santa Barbara)

GREAT DAY‡ — Balkis × Swallow — Stewart Inc. 1958
× Blue Smoke = Great Smoke | × Peach Bloom = Mary Ann LaCauza
× Nila = Rinconada |

GREAT SMOKE — Great Day × Blue Smoke — Stewart Inc. 1971
GREAT WALTZ — Eva × Stanley Fouraker — Miura 1973 (Santa Barbara)

GREEN CHAMP — Miretta × Coronado — Rod McLellan Co. 1971
GREEN CHANCE — Miretta × Enid Haupt — Rod McLellan Co. 1972
GREEN CORAL — Camilla × Monsoon — Peterson Bros. 1972
GREEN ELF — Woodhamsianum × pumilum — Greenoaks 1972
GREEN FIELDS — Baby Larry × Grand Monarch — Sakell 1974
GREEN FORTUNE — Big Trees × Dorama — Rod McLellan Co. 1972
GREEN GODDESS — O'Grady × Miretta — Freed 1961
× Balkis = Aivaler | × Nam Khan = High Sierra

GREEN KNIGHT — Claudona × Miretta — Le Grande 1962 (M)
× Baltic = Baltic Knight | × Hi-Rated = Rae James

GREEN MOUNTAIN — Vale of Kashmir × Sicily — Le Nobel 1975 (Dos Pueblos)

GREEN NYMPH — Mandarin × Eider — A. & B. 1965
× Wyanga = Kathie Lovell |

GREEN PRINCE — Camelot × San Miguel — Rod McLellan Co. 1971
GREEN REWARD — Miretta × Etta Barlow — Rod McLellan Co. 1971
GREENRIDGE — Southborough × Nicky — Wondabah 1974
GREEN SPIRIT — Big Trees × Irina — Rod McLellan Co. 1971
GREEN SPRING — Miretta × Green Stream — G. & S. 1969
× Dorama = Via Cajon Verde | × Joan of Arc = Via Arco Verde
× Etta Barlow = Via El Dorado | × Pink Momouth = Via Verde Limon
× Hope Ranch = Via Rancho Verde | × Raquel Abril = Via Abril Verde

GREENSTONE — Wyanga × Sussex Dawn — Easton 1975
GREEN VICTORY — Miretta × Big Trees — Rod McLellan Co. 1971
GREEN WINGS — Sherwood Forest × Lucy — Rod McLellan Co. 1964
× Peach Bloom = Tralee | × Sweetheart = Winter's Fantasy

GREENWOOD‡ — Frederica × Sicily — Hoyt 1962 (Everett)
× Early Bird = Andy Hamilton | × madidum = Little Nugget

GREEN WORLD — Monsoon × Redwood — Rod McLellan Co. 1972
GUELDA*†‡ — Coningsbyanum × Doris — M. 1933
× Rincon = Rinda |

GWEN STERNBECK — Wyanga × Dorama — Henry Boyd 1971
HAPPY TALK — ensifolium × Vieux Rose — Andrew Orchids 1975
HAREM — Darjeeling × Ramesis — D. 1966
× Goblin = Yashmak |

HARRYS ARC — **Mem. Francis Cobb × Joan of Arc** — **Sakell 1971**

HATHOR† — **Cormorant × Wheatear** — **A. 1932**
× Irish Pearl = Irithor

HATTIE — **Balkis × Bernadette** — **R. O. Greene 1973**
HEATHROW†‡ — **Claudette × Erica Sander** — **S. 1948**
× Fred Stewart = Via Invierno

HIDDEN PROMISE — **Peri × Dorama** — **Rod McLellan Co. 1972**
HIGHLAND GIANT — **Clauboda × Mary Ann** — **M. 1971**
HIGHLAND GLOW — **Mary Ann × Nile** — **M. 1971**
HIGHLAND ROSE — **Vieux Rose × Ngaire** — **M. 1971**
HIGHLAND SNOW — **Mary Ann × Sussex Moor** — **M. 1971**
HIGHLAND SUNSET — **Defiant × Balkis** — **M. 1971**
HIGHLAND VALLEY — **Elegance × Sussex Dawn** — **M. 1971**
HIGH SIERRA — **Green Goddess × Nam Khan** — **Santa Barbara 1975 (Originator unknown)**

HI-RATED — **Swallow × Etta Barlow** — **Graves 1966**
× Ann Green = New Moon | × Shiraz = Moongold
× Green Knight = Rae James

HITOSHI OHNO — **Blue Smoke × Stanley Fouraker** — **H. Ohno 1974**
HONEST GREEN — **Miretta × Vesper** — **Rod McLellan Co. 1972**
hoosai‡ (see *sinense*‡) — **species**
HOOSAILUM — **pumilum × sinense** — **Ireland 1972**
HOPE RANCH — **Shiraz × Etta Barlow** — **G. & S. 1969 (McCreery)**
× Green Spring = Via Rancho Verde | × Pixie Dawn = Via Laguna Blanca

HOWELL — **Magpie × Bethlehem** — **Sakell 1971**
HUNTRESS — **Diana × Stanley Fouraker** — **Stewart Inc. 1971**
IAN DUNCAN — **Wyanga × San Miguel** — **Henry Boyd 1971**
IDA SIEGEL — **Joan of Arc × lowianum** — **Liebman 1973**
IMPERIAL — **Emperor × Lilian Sander** — **S. 1947**
× Autumn Leaves = Autumn King

INEZ MAGAN — **Sea Foam × Cleo Sherman** — **Sakell 1975**
insigne*†‡ — **species**
× Fairy Wand = Fleurette | × Mimi = Ember Gleam

INVERGARRY — **Putana × Clarissa** — **M. 1972**
INVERLEITH* — **Coningsbyanum × lowianum** — **Edin. Bot. Gdns. 1926**
× Ramboda = Bodaleith

iridifolium (see *madidum*‡) — **species**
IRINA†‡ — **Adastra × Adelma** — **A. 1943**
× Big Trees = Green Spirit | × Mazatlan = Ensenada

IRIS BANNOCHIE — **finlaysonianum × canaliculatum** — **George Black 1973**
IRISH LUCY — **Lucy × Irish Melody** — **Greenoaks 1974**
IRISH LULABYE — **faberi × Babylon** — **Everglades 1971 (Rod McLellan Co.)**

IRISH MELODY‡ — **Jason × Martin** — **L. de R. 1941**
× Celadon = Dorothy Ann Wright | × Mazatlan = Sea Melody
× Etta Barlow = Belair | × Vale of Kashmir = Golden Beauty
× Lucy = Irish Lucy

IRISH PEARL†‡ — **Esmeralda × Pearl** — **Hankey 1943**
× Hathor = Irithor | × Midabel = Midapearl

IRITHOR — **Irish Pearl × Hathor** — **C. 1971**

ISPAHAN†‡ — **Lowio-grandiflorum × Rosanna** — **L. de R. 1941**
× Babylon = Sasha Berman |

IVY FUNG — **Mary Pinchess × Carisona** — **Dos Pueblos 1967**
× Robin = Cracker Jack | × Susa = Chief Joseph

JACK FROST — **Showgirl × Stanley Fouraker** — **Greenoaks 1974**

JANE MOULTON — **Oiso × Mary Ann** — **George Arblaster 1972**

JANET — **Alexanderi × Dorothy** — **Schroder 1934**
× Dorama = Janora | × Ormoulu = Meliona

JANET MARION — **Vieux Rose × Etta Barlow** — **Dell Park 1974**

JANETTE†‡ — **Alexanderi × Joy Sander** — **M. 1935**
× Nile = Sylvadell |

JANINE‡ — **Albania × Schlegelii** — **M. 1935**
× Balkis = Valley Imperial | × Stanley Fouraker = Valley Dawn
× Fred Stewart = Valley Xmas | × Sussex Dawn = Downs Delight
× Pearl-Balkis = Valley Empress | × Twelfth Night = Valley Star

JANORA — **Janet × Dorama** — **Foulds 1972**
(Originator unknown)
× Baltic = Mildred Foulds |

JEANNE-MARIE‡ — **Elfin × Gold Mohur** — **Hoonaert 1964**
× Auriga = Mariga |

JENNIFER LYNN — **erythrostylum × Eburneo-lowianum** — **Greenoaks 1964**
(Greenoaks & Lambert Day)
× Stanley Fouraker = Jenny Lind |

JENNY LIND — **Jennifer Lynn × Stanley Fouraker** — **Greenoaks 1971**

JISSY MUPP — **Wood Nymph × pumilum** — **V. & N. Jupp 1973**

JOAN LUTH — **Magog × Charm** — **Luth 1953**
× Balkis = Premier | × pumilum = John Ezzy

JOANNA CAMILLA — **Firewheel × Miretta** — **Mrs. P. Adam 1974**
(Sieff)

JOAN OF ARC†‡ — **Alexanderi × Balkis** — **A. 1943**
× Acapulco = Pristine | × lowianum = Ida Siegel
× Cambria = Kim Brady | × Mem. Francis Cobb = Harrys Arc
× Dorchester = Valley Nymph | × Prince Charles = Brigitte Maier
× Fred Stewart = Ron Junod | × Princess Desirée = Candy Ann Radzins
× George Lycurgas = Pasadena Beautiful | × Reginetta = Via Rosario
× Green Spring = Via Arco Verde | × Suva = Pride of Carousel
× Karen Cameron = Teddi Sutton |

JOCOSITY† — **Curlew × Lowio-grandiflorum** — **A. & R. 1943**
× Balkis = Valley Joy |

JOHN BERMAN — **Susan Berman × Mayfair** — **Berman 1972**
(Stonehurst)

JOHN EZZY — **Joan Luth × pumilum** — **Sutherland 1971**

JUNGFRAU*†‡ — **Alexanderi × Eagle** — **A. 1933**
× Vieux Rose = Anne Archer |

CYMBIDIUM

KALANG	**Lustrous × Henry Davis**	**Wondabah 1967**

× Westholme = Wilton

KAMPUR	**Darjeeling × Balkis**	**Andrew Orchids 1972**
KAREN CAMERON‡	**Balkis × Nam Khan**	**A'Logann 1956**

× Clyde Landers = Camders | × Rangi = Karen Rose
× Joan of Arc = Teddi Sutton | × Redstart = Karex

KAREN HENRY	**Artisan × Sussex Dawn**	**Tom Henry 1973**
KAREN ROSE	**Karen Cameron × Rangi**	**Borg 1973**
KAREX	**Karen Cameron × Redstart**	**Borg 1973**
KASHETTA	**Miretta × Vale of Kashmir**	**M. & H. 1975**
KASHTIC	**Baltic × Vale of Kashmir**	**M. & H. 1975**
KATHIE LOVELL	**Green Nymph × Wyanga**	**I. L. Duncan 1974 (Tom Henry)**
KATHY LANDRY	**Desirée A'Logann × Shina Black**	**A'Logann 1972**
KAURI FOREST	**Fanfare × Early Forest**	**Easton 1975**
KELLY GREEN	**Parma × Fanfare**	**Peterson Bros. 1972**
KELPIE	**Larne × pumilum**	**Andrew Orchids 1975**
KHYBER PASS‡	**Profita × Carisona**	**Stewart Inc. 1956**

× Carisona = Carikhyber | × Spartan Queen = Red Baron
× Louis Sander = Pink Sensation | × Vieux Rose = Donald Wilson

KIM BRADY	**Cambria × Joan of Arc**	**A'Logann 1972**
KING ARTHUR‡	**Sweetheart × Nila**	**Paul Miller 1963 (B. & W.)**

× Endre Ostbo = Dolores Hoyt | × Pixie Moor = Calle del Rey
× Fred Stewart = Calle Laguna | × Radak = Clariance
× madidum = Sunshine Falls | × Showgirl = Myponga
× Ora Lee = Canterbury Tales | × Sussex Dawn = Calle Los Olivos

KITTY WHITE	**Mem. Walter Kavanagh × Dorchester**	**Henry Boyd 1971**
KLUCA	**Lucastes × Sedgewick**	**C. 1971**
KORINTJI‡	**ensifolium × Rangoon**	**Stewart Inc. 1963**

× chloranthum = Nancy Carpenter | × George Lycurgas = Lycurintji

KURANDA	**madidum × suave**	**Greenoaks 1972**
KURUN‡	**Cornette × Stardust**	**V. 1953**

× Calao = Laperrine | × Miretta = Mirun
× Magpie = Clergerie | × Stanley Fouraker = Snooks

LADY AUTUMN	**Lady Lucy × Autumn Leaves**	**Borg 1973**
LADY BIRD JOHNSON	**Balkis × Alnwick Castle**	**Bianchi 1971**
LADY LUCY‡	**Dresden Lady × Lucy**	**Carlton 1959**

× Arcadian Melody = Via Arcadian Lady | × Autumn Leaves = Lady Autumn

LAGRANGE	**Stardust × Chaffinch**	**Pff. V. & L. 1973**
LANCER	**lancifolium × Alexanderi**	**Scarcefield 1973**
lancifolium	**species**	

× Alexanderi = Lancer

LAPERRINE	**Kurun × Calao**	**Pff. V. & L. 1975**
LARNE	**Irish Mist × Nicky**	**D. 1965**

× elegans = Ballig | × pumilum = Kelpie
× Parma = Donegal

CYMBIDIUM

LAS PULGAS — **Studley × Princess Elizabeth** — **Rod McLellan Co. 1958 (E. W. McLellan)**

× Sicily = Anne Hamilton

LAUREL JEAN SAKELL — **Ann Green × Marquesa Prescott** — **Sakell 1971**

LEE SETSKO BOYAR — **Cleo Sherman × Dainty** — **Stewart Inc. 1974**

LEGAYE — **Stanley Fouraker × Rampur** — **Kembla 1972 (Cecil Park Orchids)**

LEMON GROVE — **Woodalda × George Lycurgas** — **Stewart Inc. 1974**

LERWICK — **Putana × Sussex Moor** — **M. 1971**

LILA — **Stanley Fouraker × Babylon** — **Greenoaks 1968**

× Pearl-Balkis = Valley Brook
× Pearl-Easter = Valley Easter
× Sylvania = Valley Sylvan

LILIANA†‡ — **Lilian Sander × Louisiana** — **S. 1946**

× Enid Haupt = Mellow Brown
× Fairway Park = Margaret Tate
× Fred Stewart = Star of India
× Marquesas = Rombout
× Paracel = Paralil
× Stanley Fouraker = Lilianley

LILIANLEY — **Liliana × Stanley Fouraker** — **Stewart Inc. 1973**

LILY BROWN — **Rio Rita × Flare** — **W. E. Brown 1974 (A. & B.)**

LINDA ANN — **pumilum × Plover** — **Schulstad 1973 (Ireland)**

LITTLE MERMAID — **Celadon × Apollo** — **Greenoaks 1975**

LITTLE NUGGET — **madidum × Greenwood** — **Greenoaks 1974**

LITTLE REDHEAD — **O'Grady × Flare** — **Freed 1971**

× Sweetheart = Moriah

LOFTY — **Warrah × Babylon** — **Easton 1975 (Dos Pueblos Pty.)**

LOKI — **Bokhara × Fascination** — **Mrs. J. West 1973 (Andrew Orchids)**

LOUIS SANDER*†‡ — **Alexanderi × Ceres** — **S. 1924**

× Atlantes = Eva Borg
× Autumn Skies = Redskies
× Claret = Consistent Pink
× Khyber Pass = Pink Sensation
× Prince Charles = Mem. James Sakell
× Tapestry = Gibson Girl
× Vieux Rose = Tyra Borg

lowianum*†‡ — **species**

× Joan of Arc = Ida Siegel

LUANA — **Lunagrad × Earlyana** — **W. & A. Gowling 1975**

LUCASTES*†‡ — **grandiflorum × Warbler** — **Burstow 1928**

× Baldur = Balastes
× Sedgewick = Kluca

LUCENSE‡ — **Lucy × Moirense** — **M. 1952**

× Alexalban = Shanida
× Sea Gem = Edinburgh

LUCETTA — **Lucense × Miretta** — **M. 1965**

× Putana = Banff.

LUCY†‡ — **Doris × Lucastes** — **M. 1935**

× erythrostylum = Autumn Day
× Irish Melody = Irish Lucy
× madidum = Madelene Madsen
× Magpie = Baby Larry
× Putana = Mollie Logan-Home
× Westholme = Nell Potts

CYMBIDIUM

LUCY MOOR‡ — **Bodmin Moor × Lucy** — **M. 1955**

× Christmas Radiance = Shetland Isles

LUDWIG FETZER — **Mary Ann × Cleo Sherman** — **Fetzer 1971**
LUMINYA — **Lunagrad × Sirius** — **W. & A. Gowling 1975**
LUNAGRAD — **Miracle × San Miguel** — **Graves 1967**

× Balkis = Reynella
× Dorama = Flagstaff Hill
× Earlyana = Luana
× Etta Barlow = Susan Hughes
× Sirius = Luminya
× Wakakusa = Walu

LUNETTE — **Celadon × Blue Smoke** — **Greenoaks 1974**
LUSTROUS†‡ — **Louisiana × Sunrise** — **S. 1947**

× Earlyana = Valley Premiere

LYCURGAS MOOR — Sussex Moor × George Lycurgas — **Stewart Inc. 1973**
LYCURINTJI — **Korintji × George Lycurgas** — **Stewart Inc. 1974**
LYOTH*†‡ — **Ceres × insigne** — **C. 1928**

× Marquesa Prescott = Taffy

LYSANDER*†‡ — **Lady Colman × President Wilson** — **B. 1931**

× Shiraz = Schiehallion

MADELENE MADSEN — **madidum × Lucy** — **Greenoaks 1972**
madidum‡ (syn. *iridifolium*) — **species**

× Greenwood = Little Nugget
× finlaysonianum = Francis Hunte
× King Arthur = Sunshine Falls
× Lucy = Madelene Madsen
× suave = Kuranda

MAGNA CHARTA — **Runnymede × Flare** — **Schroder 1961**

× Ormoulu = Gloire Dell Park

MAGPIE†‡ h. ign. — **? × ?**

× Bethlehem = Howell
× Kurun = Clergerie
× Lucy = Baby Larry
× Marquesas = Stratford
× Rio Rita = Winter Pink Ice
× San Miguel = Patricia Lea
× Stanley Fouraker = Christmas Carols

MARCUS AURELIUS — **Big Pine × Mount Everest** — **Rod McLellan Co. 1972**
MARGARET KAKIS — **Artisan × Dorama** — **Sakell 1974**
MARGARET TATE — **Liliana × Fairway Park** — **I. L. Duncan 1974 (Tom Henry)**

MARIAN LENFESTEY‡ — **Flamingo × Babylon** — **Dos Pueblos 1961**

× Dorchester = Nariel
× Sheba = Valley Glow

MARIBELLE — **Sussex Dawn × devonianum** — **A. & B. 1973**
MARIE FETZER — **Cleo Sherman × Pearl-Balkis** — **Fetzer 1973**
MARIGA — **Jeanne-Marie × Auriga** — **Borg 1973**
MARILYN — **Baltic × Parma** — **A. & B. 1973**
MARQUESA PRESCOTT — **Louis Sander × Babylon** — **Braemar 1962**

× Ann Green = Laurel Jean Sakell
× Carisona = Marquisona
× Fred Stewart = Gladys Vincent
× Lyoth = Taffy
× Rosanna = Barbara Love
× Swallow = Swalita

MARQUESAS — **Coningsbyanum × Eagle** — **Stewart Inc. 1961**

× Liliana = Rombout
× Magpie = Stratford
× Martin = Wolcott

MARQUISONA — **Marquesa Prescott × Carisona** — **Borg 1973**

CYMBIDIUM

MARTHA DAENIKER — **Swallow × Vieux Rose** — **Strauss 1971 (Stonehurst)**

MARTIN*† — **Lowio-grandiflorum × parishii** — **H. 1920**

× Marquesas = Wolcott

MARY ANN‡ — **Pearl-Easter × Rosanna** — **Coyle 1960 (M.)**

× Anne Baxter = Valley Snow
× Arcadian Melody = Doreen Darwen
× Auriga = Valley Avilion
× Balkis = Valley Glacier
× Clauboda = Highland Giant
× Cleo Sherman = Ludwig Fetzer
× Dorchester = Valley Eden
× Fred Stewart = Valley Promise
× Nicky = Nicky Ann
× Nile = Highland Glow
× Oiso = Jane Moulton
× San Miguel = Sally Alexandra
× Sleeping Beauty = Valley Dew
× Sleeping Glow = Valley Wine
× Southborough = Noarlunga
× Stanley Fouraker = Valley Stream
× Sussex Dawn = Valley Conquest
× Sussex Moor = Highland Snow
× Twelfth Night = Valley Sweetheart
× Vieux Rose = Fair Promise

MARY ANN LaCAUZA — **Great Day × Peach Bloom** — **Rod McLellan Co. 1973**

MARY STORTECKY — **Bethlehem × Rio Rita** — **Sakell 1974**

MARY YENDALL — **Cariga × Ramboda** — **George Arblaster 1971**

× Oiso = Ella Bulstrode

MASPALOMAS — **Seabird × Cariga** — **Dell Park 1973**

MATANA‡ — **Claudette × Ramboda** — **M. 1951**

× Stanley Fouraker = True Delight

MAYFAIR†‡ — **Edzell × Olympus** — **B. 1942**

× devonianum = Brook Street
× Susan Berman = John Berman

MAZATLAN‡ — **Nam Khan × Alexanderi** — **Dos Pueblos 1958**

× Anne Baxter = Valley Falls
× Irina = Ensenada
× Irish Melody = Sea Melody
× Sussex Dawn = Mem. Frank Taylor
× Swallow = Patrician

MELIONA — **Janet × Ormoulu** — **T. W. F. Cameron 1972 (Dell Park)**

MELLOW BROWN — **Liliana × Enid Haupt** — **Rod McLellan Co. 1971**

MELLOW YELLOW — **Peetie × Enid Haupt** — **Easton 1975 (Dos Pueblos)**

MELODY FAIR — **Emmeline × Stanley Fouraker** — **Muira 1973 (Santa Barbara)**

MELODY LANE — **Swallow × Fanfare** — **Peterson Bros. 1972**

MEMORIA FRANCIS COBB — **Balkis × Louis Sander** — **Braemar 1963 (Shaffer's)**

× Coral Sea = Mem. Susan Urban
× Joan of Arc = Harrys Arc

MEMORIA FRANK TAYLOR — **Sussex Dawn × Mazatlan** — **L. & W. 1975**

MEMORIA JAMES SAKELL — **Louis Sander × Prince Charles** — **Sakell 1971**

MEMORIA MILENA SUTTER — **Giuse × Balkis** — **Maggi Ponti 1975**

MEMORIA SUSAN URBAN — **Coral Sea × Mem. Francis Cobb** — **Sakell 1971**

MEMORIA WALTER KAVANAGH‡ — **Castor × Olympus** — **Kavanagh 1964 (L.)**

× Dorchester = Kitty White

MEMORIA WILLIAM FLYNN — **Christmas Green × Fred Stewart** — **Sakell 1974**

MERRY CHRISTMAS — **Rio Rita × Claret** — **Peterson Bros. 1968**

× Balkis = Christmas Party

CYMBIDIUM

MICHAEL EVANS — **Baltic × Babylon** — **Wyld Court 1975**

MIDABEL‡ — **Midas × Mirabel** — **M. 1953**

× Irish Pearl = Midapearl

MIDAPEARL — **Irish Pearl × Midabel** — **C. 1971**

MIGUEL MOOR — **San Miguel × Pixie** — **Stewart Inc. 1975 (E. W. Miller)**

MILDRED FOULDS — **Janora × Baltic** — **Foulds 1972**

MIMI — **pumilum × Doris Aurea** — **Greenoaks 1961**

× Flare = Red Flare
× insigne = Ember Gleam
× Rincon = Chocolate Gem

MINETTE — **Celadon × Southborough** — **Greenoaks 1971**

MINIATURES DELIGHT — **Touchstone × Clarissa** — **Strauss 1972**

MINNEHAHA — **sinense × devonianum** — **Wyld Court 1972**

MIRACLE‡ — **Ramboda × Miretta** — **Freed 1956**

× Arcadian Melody = Arcadian Sunshine
× Babylon = Mirahill

MIRAHILL — **Miracle × Babylon** — **H. C. Hanson 1972 (Graves)**

MIRALUCE — **Miretta × Lucy** — **M. 1965**

× Balkis = Patchogue

MIRETTA†‡ — **Claudette × Mirabel** — **M. 1946**

× Bernice Farrell = Elton Gripp
× Big Trees = Green Victory
× Coronado = Green Champ
× Enid Haupt = Green Chance
× Etta Barlow = Green Reward
× Firewheel = Joanna Camilla
× Kurun = Mirun
× Mount Everest = Dreamland
× Putana = Callander
× Snow Sprite = Bright Topaz
× Vale of Kashmir = Kashetta
× Vesper = Honest Green
× Western Rose = Western Highlands

MIRUN — **Kurun × Miretta** — **Pff. V. & L. 1974**

MOLLIE LOGAN-HOME — **Putana × Lucy** — **George Arblaster 1973**

MON AMI — **Cher Ami × devonianum** — **Andrew Orchids 1974**

MONSOON‡ — **Lucy × Sicily** — **Stewart Inc. 1956**

× Atlantes = Atlantic Sun
× Camilla = Green Coral
× Emmeline = Noel Green
× Redwood = Green World

MOONGOLD — **Hi-Rated × Shiraz** — **I. D. James 1975**

MOONMAN — **Rosette × Rosanna** — **Parmentier 1969**

× Cariga = Egmont

MORIAH — **Sweetheart × Little Redhead** — **Miller Coll. 1972**

MOUNT EVEREST‡ — **Apollo × Adarissa** — **Parmentier 1953**

× Big Pine = Marcus Aurelius
× Miretta = Dreamland
× San Miguel = Pleasant Surprise
× Sweetheart = California Romance

MUSITA‡ — **Remus × Profita** — **A. & B. 1961**

× Vieux Rose = Phyllis Friedlander

MYPONGA — **King Arthur × Showgirl** — **Adelaide 1975 (Paul Miller)**

NAM KHAN†‡ — **Pauwelsii × Rosanna** — **L. de R. 1941**

× Green Goddess = High Sierra

NANCY CARPENTER — **Korintji × chloranthum** — **Everglades 1974**

NARIEL — **Dorchester × Marian Lenfestey** — **Wondabah 1971**

CYMBIDIUM

Name	Parentage	Registrant
NELL POTTS	**Lucy × Westholme**	**I. L. Duncan 1974 (W. L. Baker)**
NEW HORIZON‡	**Fleur de Lys × Celeste**	**Stewart Inc. 1960**
× Fred Stewart	= Frosted Pearl	
NEW MOON	**Hi-Rated × Ann Green**	**I. D. James 1975**
NGAIRE‡	**Clarissa × Rio Rita**	**M. 1959**
× Vieux Rose	= Highland Rose	
NICKALONG-CAMPBELL	**Nicky × Auriga**	**Campbell 1973 (Wondabah)**
NICKY‡	**Erica Sander × Radak**	**Sieff 1954 (Ratcliffe)**
× Auriga	= Nickalong-Campbell	
× Darjeeling	= Dalnspidal	
× Mary Ann	= Nicky Ann	
× Southborough	= Greenridge	
NICKY ANN	**Nicky × Mary Ann**	**Goudie 1971 (Dos Pueblos)**
NILA‡	**Esmeralda × Irina**	**Carpentier 1954**
× Dorama	= Shanthi	
× Etta Barlow	= Sweet Patience	
× Great Day	= Rinconada	
NILE‡	**Baltic × Ramesio**	**Schroder 1957**
× Janette	= Sylvadell	
× Mary Ann	= Highland Glow	
niveo-marginatum†‡	**species**	
× Brentwood	= Siempre	
NOARLUNGA	**Southborough × Mary Ann**	**Adelaide 1975**
NOEL GREEN	**Monsoon × Emmeline**	**Sakell 1971**
NYANDA	**Sensation × Prince Charles**	**Wondabah 1971**
O'GRADY‡	**Adelma × Thora**	**E. de R. 1947**
× Flare	= Little Redhead	
O'HALLORAN HILL	**Pelleas × Sensation**	**Adelaide 1975**
OISO‡	**pumilum × hyb. ign.**	**Ikeda 1956**
× Charles Darwin	= Alison Treacher	
× Mary Ann	= Jane Moulton	
× Mary Yendall	= Ella Bulstrode	
× Pearl-Balkis	= Christine Peake	
ORA LEE‡	**Conejo × Mount Everest**	**Braemar 1966**
× Balkis	= Eleni	
× Charles Darwin	= Peggy Richardson	
× King Arthur	= Canterbury Tales	
ORMOULU‡	**Pearl Beryl × Baltic**	**Schroder 1957**
× Janet	= Meliona	
× Magna Charta	= Gloire Dell Park	
ORPHAN‡	**Doris Aurea × Bensons**	**Rod McLellan Co. 1955 (E. W. McLellan)**
× Balkis	= Chipper Hamilton	
ORQUIL	**Plush × Fascination**	**Mrs. J. West 1973 (Andrew Orchids)**
OVATION	**Sussex Dawn × Parma**	**A. & B. 1973**
OYSTERCATCHER‡	**Dabchick × Pearl**	**Cooke 1952**
× Baltic	= Shantila	
× Swallow	= Andorinha	

CYMBIDIUM

PACIFIC PEARL‡ — **Sicily × Pearl** — **Sherman 1956**

× Cleo Sherman = Pearly Shells
× Swallow = South Pacific

PARACANO — **Paracel × Volcano** — **Stewart Inc. 1973**

PARACEL‡ — **Mildred Hunter × Clarissa** — **Stewart Inc. 1954**

× Fascination = Redcliffe
× Liliana = Paralil
× Princess Desirée = Robyn Hilton
× sinense = Peter Piper
× Volcano = Paracano
× Voodoo = Satsuma Beauty

PARALIL — **Paracel × Liliana** — **Rod McLellan Co. 1972**

parishii*† — **species**

× Balkis = Belle Glade

PARK LIGHTS — **Flare × Regents Park** — **Andrew Orchids 1967**

× devonianum = Devon Park

PARMA — **Parakeet × Miretta** — **Exbury 1963**

× Baltic = Marilyn
× Fanfare = Kelly Green
× Larne = Donegal
× Sussex Dawn = Ovation

PASADENA BEAUTIFUL — **Joan of Arc × George Lycurgas** — **Stewart Inc. 1975**

PATCHOGUE — **Balkis × Miraluce** — **Bianchi 1973**

PATRICIA LEA — **Magpie × San Miguel** — **Romanoff 1971**

PATRICIAN — **Swallow × Mazatlan** — **Carlton's 1971**

PATRICIA NORRIE — **Airborne × Vieux Rose** — **Wyld Court 1974**

PAUL MILLER — **Showgirl × Sylvia Miller** — **Adelaide 1975 (Paul Miller)**

PAUWELSII*†‡ — **insigne × lowianum** — **Pauwels 1911**

× finlaysonianum = Freshie
× Rhoda = Susan Berman

PEACH BLOOM — **Miretta × Babylon** — **Rod McLellan Co. 1962 (Ireland)**

× Great Day = Mary Ann LaCauza
× Green Wings = Tralee

PEARL-BALKIS — **Pearl-Easter × Balkis** — **M. 1962**

× Anne Baxter = Valley Charm
× Cleo Sherman = Marie Fetzer
× Dorama = Valley Topaz
× Etta Barlow = Valley Sunset
× Fred Stewart = Valley Pearl
× Grandly = Valley Grand
× Janine = Valley Empress
× Lila = Valley Brook
× Oiso = Christine Peake
× San Miguel = Valley Shamrock
× Sylvania = Valley Sonnett

PEARLBEL‡ — **Pearl × Mirabel** — **M. 1952**

× Ranjita = Skomer

PEARL-EASTER†‡ — **Pearl × Dorchester** — **M. 1951**

× Arcadian Melody = Bob Waabel
× Fred Stewart = Valley Mist
× Grandly = Grand Parade
× Lila = Valley Easter
× San Miguel = Valley Emerald
× Sussex Dawn = Valley Meadow
× Sylvania = Valley Paradise
× York Meredith = Valley York

PEARLY QUEEN‡ — **Pearl × Susette** — **C. 1956**

× Eagle = Queagle
× Rio Rita = Queen Rita

PEARLY SHELLS — **Cleo Sherman × Pacific Pearl** — **Peterson Bros. 1972**

PEETIE — **Sicily × San Miguel** — **Sherman 1963**

× Enid Haupt = Mellow Yellow
× Rincon = Christmas Clarion

PEGGY RICHARDSON — **Ora Lee × Charles Darwin** — **Sakell 1974**

Name	Parentage	Registrant
PEKOE	**Swallow × suavissimum**	**Andrew Orchids 1975 (C. K. Andrew)**
PELLEAS	**Sweetheart × Claucis**	**Paul Miller 1962 (B. & W.)**
× Sensation	= O'Halloran Hill	
PERI*†‡	**Pauwelsii × President Wilson**	**S. 1927**
× Dorama	= Hidden Promise	
PETER PIPER	sinense × Paracel	**Stewart Inc. 1973**
PHILOMENA CARDOSA	**Saigon × Ann Green**	**Stewart Inc. 1971 (Cardosa)**
PHYLLIS FRIEDLANDER	**Musita × Vieux Rose**	**A. & B. 1973**
PICCADILLY‡	**Pearl × Picardy**	**Hankey 1948**
× Fascination	= Firesprite	
PINK CHAMPAGNE	**Rosinante × Rincon**	**Easton 1974 (Dos Pueblos)**
PINK FLASH	**Dartmoor × Amber Flash**	**Wyld Court 1972**
PINK ICE	Vieux Rose × Snow Sprite	**Lady Hothfield 1971**
PINK MOMOUTH	**Babylon × Etta Barlow**	**Cobbs' 1969**
× Green Spring	= Via Verde Limon	× Rincon = Via Constelado
× Pixie Dawn	= Via de Madrugada	
PINK PRINCESS	**Charmion × Dryad**	**G. & S. 1970**
× Rio Rita	= Princess Rita	
PINK SENSATION	**Khyber Pass × Louis Sander**	**Rod McLellan Co. 1971**
PIONEER	**erythrostylum × Stanley Fouraker**	**Greenoaks 1974**
PIXIE*†‡	**Ceres × Landrail**	**M. 1933**
× San Miguel	= Miguel Moor	
PIXIE DAWN	**Pixie Moor × Sussex Dawn**	**G. & S. 1969**
× Dorama	= Via Arroyo	× Pink Momouth = Via de Madrugada
× Hope Ranch	= Via Laguna Blanca	
PIXIE MOOR‡	**Pixie × Bodmin Moor**	**M. 1956**
× King Arthur	= Calle del Rey	× Raquel Abril = Via Raquel
PLEASANT SURPRISE	**Mount Everest × San Miguel**	**Stewart Inc. 1971**
PLEIADES	**Amber Flash × Babylon**	**Wyld Court 1972**
PLOVER*†‡	**Lowio-grandiflorum × Pauwelsii**	**H. 1925**
× pumilum	= Linda Ann	
PLUSH‡	**Regents Park × Cinderella**	**D. 1963**
× Fascination	= Orquil	
POLKA TIME	Sanrita × Desirée A'Logann	**Rod McLellan Co. 1972**
POPLAN	**Sussex × Fred Stewart**	**Stewart Inc. 1973**
PRECOCIOUS	**Cariga × Redwood**	**Rod McLellan Co. 1971**
PREMIER	**Balkis × Joan Luth**	**A. J. Bell 1973**
PRESIDENT WILSON*†‡	**Alexanderi × lowianum**	**S. 1917**
× Sussex Dawn	= Araluen	
PRIAM*†‡	**Ceres × President Wilson**	**S. 1930**
× George Lycurgas	= Conquistador	

PRIDE OF CAROUSEL — **Suva × Joan of Arc** — **de Lacy 1973 (Stewart Inc.)**

PRINCE CHARLES†‡ — **Balkis × Pauwelsii** — **B. 1949**

× Joan of Arc = Brigitte Maier
× Louis Sander = Mem. James Sakell
× Sensation = Nyanda
× Stanley Fouraker = Daughter Laurel

PRINCESS DESIRÉE‡ — **Babylon × Prince Charles** — **A'Logann 1959**

× Joan of Arc = Candy Ann Radzins
× Paracel = Robyn Hilton
× pumilum = Barbara Hancock

PRINCESS RITA — **Rio Rita × Pink Princess** — **G. & S. 1973**

PRISTINE — **Acapulco × Joan of Arc** — **Carlton's 1971**

PROFITA†‡ — **Profusion × Rio Rita** — **M. 1950**

× Regency = Duneba

PROMONA†‡ — **Cremona × Profusion** — **M. 1943**

× Carisona = Cabernet

PUMILOW — **lowianum × pumilum** — **Andrew Orchids 1967 (C. K. Andrew)**

× Doris Aurea = Dorilow

pumilum*†‡ — **species**

× Fairy = Atsuko
× Fanfare = Fair Green
× Firewheel = Red Jewel
× Joan Luth = John Ezzy
× Larne = Kelpie
× Plover = Linda Ann
× Princess Desirée = Barbara Hancock
× sinense = Hoosailum
× Sleeping Beauty = Sarah Jean
× Suva = Suvalum
× Woodhamsianum = Green Elf
× Wood Nymph = Jissy Mupp

PUTANA — **Rutana × pumilum** — **M. 1966**

× Berwick = Strathavon
× Betty Ott = Edith Logan-Home
× Cariga = Stoneaven
× Clarissa = Invergarry
× Edzell = Skye
× Lucetta = Banff
× Lucy = Mollie Logan-Home
× Miretta = Callander
× Sussex Moor = Lerwick

QUEAGLE — **Pearly Queen × Eagle** — **C. 1971**

QUEEN RITA — **Pearly Queen × Rio Rita** — **C. 1971**

RADAK‡ — **Claudette × Pearl** — **M. 1943**

× King Arthur = Clariance
× Sweetheart = Clarendon

RAE JAMES — **Green Knight × Hi-Rated** — **I. D. James 1975**

RAMBODA†‡ — **Pearl × Venus** — **M. 1937**

× Cariga = Mary Yendall
× Inverleith = Bodaleith
× Sussex Moor = Dasu

RAMESIS†‡ — **Midas × Ramboda** — **Schroder 1950**

× Durham Castle = Sleeping Gold
× Sleeping Beauty = Sleeping Lamb
× Vieux Rose = Caldy

RAMPUR‡ — **Ramboda × Lucy** — **M. 1956**

× Fred Stewart = Valley View
× Sleeping Beauty = Sleeping Valley
× Stanley Fouraker = Legaye

RANGI†‡ — **Olive × Ruanda** — **M. 1949**

× Karen Cameron = Karen Rose

RANJITA — **Darjeeling × Claudona** — **D. 1963**

× Pearlbel = Skomer
× Vieux Rose = Ranrose

CYMBIDIUM

Grex	Parentage	Registrant
RANROSE	**Ranjita × Vieux Rose**	**Andrew Orchids 1973**
RAQUEL ABRIL	**Joan of Arc × Dorama**	**G. & S. 1968**

× Green Spring = Via Abril Verde
× Pixie Moor = Via Raquel
× Verde de Invierno = Via Jalisco

Grex	Parentage	Registrant
RED BARON	**Spartan Queen × Khyber Pass**	**I. D. James 1975**
RED BIRD	**Vintage × Rio Rita**	**Shaffer's 1971**
REDCLIFFE	**Fascination × Paracel**	**Adelaide 1975 (Originator unknown)**
RED FLARE	**Mimi × Flare**	**Greenoaks 1972**
REDFORD BEAUTY	**Sussex × Bartolme Ferrello**	**Stewart Inc. 1975**
RED JEWEL	**pumilum × Firewheel**	**Greenoaks 1975**
REDSKIES	**Louis Sander × Autumn Skies**	**Borg 1973**
REDSTART*†‡	**Dryad × Pauwelsii**	**H. 1920**

× Karen Cameron = Karex

REDWOOD†‡ — **Chesham × erythrostylum** — **Rod McLellan Co. (E. W. McLellan)**

× Cariga = Precocious
× elegans = Elwood
× Frederica = Rodco's Emerald
× Monsoon = Green World
× Westholme = Sagami

REGENCY‡ — **Remus × Mayfair** — **A. & B. 1959**

× Profita = Duneba

REGINETTA — **Reginald × Finetta** — **G. & S. 1969**

× Joan of Arc = Via Rosario

REMUS†‡ — **Regulus × Joyful** — **Schroder 193–**

× Clarissa = Ardingly
× Snow Sprite = Snow Knight

Grex	Parentage	Registrant
REYNELLA	**Balkis × Lunagrad**	**Adelaide 1975**
RHODA†‡	**Flamingo × Pauwelsii**	**A. 1932**

× Pauwelsii = Susan Berman

Grex	Parentage	Registrant
RICHARD GARDNER	**Showgirl × Alexalban**	**R. N. Gardner 1974**
RINCON‡	**Pearl × Windsor**	**Carlton 1957**

× Arcadian Melody = Via Arcadian Rincon
× Atlantic Sun = Via Grandioso
× Autumn Leaves = Clear Autumn
× Claudona = Clarinda
× Fairy Wand = Rincon Fairy
× Fred Stewart = Via Rincon
× Glasgow = Early Call
× Guelda = Rinda
× Mimi = Chocolate Gem
× Peetie = Christmas Clarion
× Pink Momouth = Via Constelado
× Rosinante = Pink Champagne
× Solana Beach = Via del Playa
× Sussex Dawn = Via Ruborosa
× Twelfth Night = Shortest Day

Grex	Parentage	Registrant
RINCONADA	**Great Day × Nila**	**Los Padres 1975**
RINCON FAIRY	**Fairy Wand × Rincon**	**Greenoaks 1975**
RINDA	**Guelda × Rincon**	**Borg 1973**
RIO AUTUMN	**Autumn Day × Rio Rita**	**M. & H. 1975**
RIO RITA*†‡	**Pearl × Ruby**	**M. 1937**

× Autumn Day = Rio Autumn
× Bethlehem = Mary Stortecky
× Fairy Wand = Embers
× Flare = Lily Brown
× Flycatcher = Rubicon
× Fred Stewart = Via Rubra
× Magpie = Winter Pink Ice
× Pearly Queen = Queen Rita
× Pink Princess = Princess Rita
× Shiraz = Anne Michele
× Vintage = Red Bird
× Woodland = Welsh Song

ROBIN — **Khyber Pass × Doris Aurea** — **Rod McLellan Co. 1963**

× Ivy Fung = Cracker Jack

Name	Parentage	Registrant
ROBYN HILTON	**Paracel × Princess Desirée**	**A'Logann Labs. 1975**
RODCO'S CREATION	**Rusper × Dorama**	**Rod McLellan Co. 1972**
RODCO'S EMERALD	**Redwood × Frederica**	**Rod McLellan Co. 1972**
ROMANTICA	**Sirius × San Miguel**	**Pff. V. & L. 1974**
ROMBOUT	**Marquesas × Liliana**	**Scardefield 1971**
ROMEO†‡	**grandiflorum × Pearl**	**M. 1943**

× Babylon = Aldworth

Name	Parentage	Registrant
RON JUNOD	**Fred Stewart × Joan of Arc**	**Sakell 1974**
ROSANNA*†‡	**Alexanderi × Kittiwake**	**A. 1927**

× Cleo Sherman = Warminster
× Fairy Wand = Rose Wand
× Marquesa Prescott = Barbara Love
× Ruskin = Rusland
× Susan Berman = Elfrida Berman

Name	Parentage	Registrant
ROSE PARK	**Babylon × Vieux Rose**	**Borg 1973**
ROSE WAND	**Fairy Wand × Rosanna**	**Greenoaks 1975**
ROSINANTE‡	**Abona × Dante**	**E. de R. 1950**

× Ann Green = Rosyann
× Rincon = Pink Champagne

Name	Parentage	Registrant
ROSYANN	**Ann Green × Rosinante**	**Borg 1973**
ROYDEN	**Balkis × Vieux Rose**	**Royden 1972**
RUBICON	**Flycatcher × Rio Rita**	**Wyld Court 1972**
RUBY SKIES	**Stanley Fouraker × Autumn Skies**	**Borg 1973**
RUNNYMEDE‡	**Babylon × Roxana**	**Hothfield 1949**

× Balkis = Yellow Prince

Name	Parentage	Registrant
RUSKIN†‡	**Ceres × Pearl**	**M. 1938**

× Rosanna = Rusland

Name	Parentage	Registrant
RUSLAND	**Rosanna × Ruskin**	**Andrew Orchids 1972**
RUSPER†‡	**Pearl × Veronique**	**M. 1940**

× Cariga = Sunny Dream
× Dorama = Rodco's Creation

Name	Parentage	Registrant
RUTANA†‡	**Coningsbyanum × Pearl**	**M. 1947**

× Sensation = Dakara

Name	Parentage	Registrant
SAGAMI	**Redwood × Westholme**	**Ohba 1972**
SAIGON†‡	**Peregrine × Carisona**	**Stewart Inc. 1954**

× Ann Green = Philomena Cardosa

Name	Parentage	Registrant
SALLY ALEXANDRA	**Mary Ann × San Miguel**	**Romanoff 1971**
SAN MIGUEL‡	**Doris Aurea × Sicily**	**Dos Pueblos 1957**

× Anne Baxter = Valley Haze
× Camelot = Green Prince
× Durham Castle = Sleeping Girl
× Fanfare = Voice of Spring
× Fred Stewart = Limelight
× Magpie = Patricia Lea
× Mary Ann = Sally Alexandra
× Mount Everest = Pleasant Surprise
× Pearl-Balkis = Valley Shamrock
× Pearl-Easter = Valley Emerald
× Pixie = Miguel Moor
× Shiraz = Carrie Mansfield
× Sirius = Romantica
× Sleeping Beauty = Sleeping Lake
× Stanley Fouraker = Valley Song
× Sussex Dawn = Zumma Boyd
× Thanksgiving = Via Miguel
× Wyanga = Ian Duncan

Name	Parentage	Registrant
SANRITA†‡	**Louis Sander × Rio Rita**	**M. 1950**

× Desirée A'Logann = Polka Time
× Sweetheart = Sweet San

Name	Parentage	Registrant
SARAH JEAN	**pumilum × Sleeping Beauty**	**Valley Orchids 1973 (Vandyke)**
SASHA BERMAN	**Ispahan × Babylon**	**Berman 1974 (Stonehurst)**

CYMBIDIUM

SATSUMA BEAUTY	**Paracel × Voodoo**		**Rod McLellan Co. 1972**
SCHIEHALLION	**Shiraz × Lysander**		**MacGregor 1971 (D.)**
SEABIRD‡	**Baltic × Parakeet**		**Schroder 1961**
× Cariga	= Maspalomas	× Snow Sprite	= Seasprite
SEA FOAM‡	**Apollo × Blue Smoke**		**A. & R. 1953**
× Blue Queen	= Gold Rush	× Cleo Sherman	= Inez Magan
SEA GEM	**Miretta × Baltic**		**M. 1967**
× Lucense	= Edinburgh	× Western Rose	= Caithness
SEA MELODY	**Irish Melody × Mazatlan**		**Vandeveer 1973**
SEASPRITE	**Seabird × Snow Sprite**		**John T. Fisher 1973 (Dell Park)**
SEDGEWICK†	**Magali Sander × Pauwelsii**		**Burstow 1935**
× Lucastes	= Kluca		
SELKIRK	**Baltic × Defiant**		**M. 1973**
SENSATION‡	**Spartan Queen × Fascination**		**Wondabah 1961**
× Pelleas	= O'Halloran Hill	× Sussex Pearl	= Winegrove
× Prince Charles	= Nyanda	× Westholme	= Terama
× Rutana	= Dakara	× Whyba	= Winevale
SHANIDA	**Lucense × Alexalban**		**Andrew Orchids 1974**
SHANTHI	**Dorama × Nila**		**Carlton Gardner 1975**
SHANTILA	**Oystercatcher × Baltic**		**Wyld Court 1972**
SHEBA‡	**Vieux Rose × Nam Khan**		**A. & B. 1966**
× Balkis	= Valley Tryst	× Snow Sprite	= Valley Sprite
× Fred Stewart	= Valley Heights	× Twelfth Night	= Valley Flower
× Marian Lenfestey	= Valley Glow		
SHETLAND ISLES	**Lucy Moor × Christmas Radiance**		**M. 1973**
SHINA BLACK†‡	**Curlew × Edzell**		**B. 1942**
× Desirée A'Logann	= Kathy Landry		
SHINING MOUNTAIN	**Early Bird × Durham Castle**		**Beall 1972**
SHIRAZ†‡	**Shirley × Alexanderi**		**M. 1954**
× Dorama	= Valley Gem	× Lysander	= Schiehallion
× Earlyana	= Tanunda	× Rio Rita	= Anne Michele
× Fred Stewart	= Valley Hope	× San Miguel	= Carrie Mansfield
× Hi-Rated	= Moongold	× Stanley Fouraker	= Valley River
SHORTEST DAY	**Rincon × Twelfth Night**		**Ridgeway 1973**
SHOWART	**Showgirl × Fred Stewart**		**Warner 1975 (Originator unknown)**
SHOWGIRL‡	**Sweetheart × Alexanderi**		**Baker 1962 (Bowers)**
× Alexalban	= Richard Gardner	× Stanley Fouraker	= Jack Frost
× Fred Stewart	= Showart	× Sylvia Miller	= Paul Miller
× King Arthur	= Myponga		
SHUNGA	**Anne Baxter × virescens**		**T. Watanabe 1974 (Kato)**
SICILY†‡	**Baldur × Grand Monarch**		**A. & R. 1943**
× Las Pulgas	= Anne Hamilton	× Vale of Kashmir	= Green Mountain

SIEMPRE — **niveo-marginatum × Brentwood** — **Rod McLellan Co. 1973 (Ireland)**

SILVAIR — **Silvio × Airborne** — **Wyld Court 1972**

SILVIO — **Louis Sander × Capric** — **Cooke 1951**

× Airborne = Silvair

simonsianum (see *dayanum**‡) — **species**

simulans‡ — **species**

× canaliculatum = Alcor

sinense‡ (syn. *hoosai‡*) — **species**

× Allegro = Cottontail
× devonianum = Minnehaha
× Paracel = Peter Piper
× pumilum = Hoosailum
× Stanley Fouraker = Buttons and Bows

SIRAM — **Rampur × Sirius** — **A. R. Bryant 1970**

× Downs Delight = Valley Delight

SIRIUS‡ — **Wylan × Lucy** — **P. & C. 1958**

× Lunagrad = Luminya
× San Miguel = Romantica

SKOMER — **Ranjita × Pearlbel** — **Andrew Orchids 1972**

SKYE — **Putana × Edzell** — **M. 1971**

SLEEPING BEAUTY‡ — **Sussex Dawn × Durham Castle** — **A. R. Bryant 1970 (Bryant & Gillson)**

× Alnwick Castle = Sleeping Queen
× Claudona = Sleeping Spring
× Downs Delight = Sleeping Promise
× Mary Ann = Valley Dew
× pumilum = Sarah Jean
× Ramesis = Sleeping Lamb
× Rampur = Sleeping Valley
× San Miguel = Sleeping Lake
× Sleeping Glow = Sleeping Dream
× Sleeping Monarch = Sleeping Giant
× Sussex Dawn = Sleeping Dawn
× Wyanga = Sleeping Nymph

SLEEPING BLOSSOM — **Alnwick Castle × Durham Castle** — **Valley Orchids 1973 (Vandyke)**

SLEEPING CASTLE — **Durham Castle × Sleeping Monarch** — **Valley Orchids 1974 (Vandyke)**

SLEEPING DAWN — **Sleeping Beauty × Sussex Dawn** — **Valley Orchids 1973 (Vandyke)**

SLEEPING DELIGHT — **Sleeping Glow × Durham Castle** — **Valley Orchids 1973 (Vandyke)**

SLEEPING DREAM — **Sleeping Beauty × Sleeping Glow** — **Valley Orchids 1973 (Vandyke)**

SLEEPING GIANT — **Sleeping Beauty × Sleeping Monarch** — **Valley Orchids 1974 (Vandyke)**

SLEEPING GIRL — **Durham Castle × San Miguel** — **Valley Orchids 1973 (Vandyke)**

SLEEPING GLOW — **Durham Castle × Wondah** — **A. R. Bryant 1970**

× Durham Castle = Sleeping Delight
× Mary Ann = Valley Wine
× Sleeping Beauty = Sleeping Dream

SLEEPING GOLD — **Durham Castle × Ramesis** — **Valley Orchids 1974 (Vandyke)**

SLEEPING LAKE — **Sleeping Beauty × San Miguel** — **Valley Orchids 1973 (Vandyke)**

SLEEPING LAMB — Sleeping Beauty × Ramesis — **Valley Orchids 1973 (Vandyke)**

SLEEPING MONARCH — **Wyanga × Grand Monarch** — **Valley Orchids 1974 (Originator unknown)**

× Durham Castle = Sleeping Castle
× Sleeping Beauty = Sleeping Giant

CYMBIDIUM

SLEEPING NYMPH	**Sleeping Beauty × Wyanga**	**Valley Orchids 1973 (Vandyke)**
SLEEPING PROMISE	**Downs Delight × Sleeping Beauty**	**Valley Orchids 1973 (Vandyke)**
SLEEPING QUEEN	**Alnwick Castle × Sleeping Beauty**	**Valley Orchids 1973 (Vandyke)**
SLEEPING SPRING	**Claudona × Sleeping Beauty**	**Valley Orchids 1973 (Vandyke)**
SLEEPING VALLEY	**Sleeping Beauty × Rampur**	**Valley Orchids 1973 (Vandyke)**
SNOOKS	**Kurun × Stanley Fouraker**	**Merriman 1974**
SNOW BUNTING	**Flamingo × Snow Goose**	**Wyld Court 1972**
SNOW GOOSE	**Jungfrau × Flamingo**	**Wyld Court 1956 (Cooke)**

× Flamingo	= Snow Bunting		

SNOW KNIGHT	**Remus × Snow Sprite**	**Hothfield 1974**
SNOW SPRITE‡	**Pearl-Easter × Alexanderi**	**Clark Day Jr. 1961 (M.)**

× Arcadian Melody	= Arcadian Snow	× Sheba	= Valley Sprite
× Dorama	= Valley Sapphire	× Sussex Dawn	= Valley Gnome
× Miretta	= Bright Topaz	× Vieux Rose	= Pink Ice
× Remus	= Snow Knight	× virescens	= Viresprite
× Seabird	= Seasprite		

SOLANA BEACH	**Rincon × Atlantes**	**Cobbs' 1969**

× Arcadian Melody	= Via Solana	× Sussex Dawn	= Via Nogales
× Fred Stewart	= Via Costa	× Thanksgiving	= Via Vista
× Golden Sunset	= Via del Sol	× Winter Solstice	= Via del Soledad
× Rincon	= Via del Playa		

SOUTHBOROUGH‡	**Lowio-grandiflorum × Enchantress**	**A. & B. 1954**

× Celadon	= Minette	× Mary Ann	= Noarlunga
× Dorama	= Valley Opal	× Nicky	= Greenridge

SOUTH PACIFIC	**Swallow × Pacific Pearl**	**Peterson Bros. 1972**
SPARKLE	**Vieux Rose × Defiant**	**M. 1971 (Hothfield)**
SPARTAN QUEEN†‡	**Regina × Sparta**	**S. 1946**

× Khyber Pass	= Red Baron		

SPRAY‡	**Egret × Studley**	**Rod McLellan Co. 1969**

× Camelot	= Camelot Queen		

SPRINGFIELD	**Alnwick Castle × Apollo**	**Andrew Orchids 1972**
STANLEY FOURAKER‡	**Alexanderi × Early Bird**	**Stewart Inc. 1958**

× Autumn Skies	= Ruby Skies	× Kurun	= Snooks
× Bethlehem	= Early Magic	× Liliana	= Lilianley
× Blue Smoke	= Hitoshi Ohno	× Magpie	= Christmas Carols
× Dainty	= Dainley	× Mary Ann	= Valley Stream
× Diana	= Huntress	× Matana	= True Delight
× Doris Aurea	= Celaya	× Prince Charles	= Daughter Laurel
× Earlyana	= Valley Mayflower	× Rampur	= Legaye
× Emmeline	= Melody Fair	× San Miguel	= Valley Song
× erythrostylum	= Pioneer	× Shiraz	= Valley River
× Eva	= Great Waltz	× Showgirl	= Jack Frost
× Fred Stewart	= Winter Fair	× sinense	= Buttons and Bows
× gracillimum	= Gracillaker	× Suva	= Suvaley
× Janine	= Valley Dawn	× Sylvania	= Valley Nightingale
× Jennifer Lynn	= Jenny Lind	× York Meredith	= Valley Falcon

STARDUST†‡ | **Doris × Margot** | **Cholet 1946**

× Chaffinch = Lagrange

STAR OF INDIA | **Liliana × Fred Stewart** | **Stewart Inc. 1972**
STONEAVEN | **Putana × Cariga** | **M. 1972**
STRATFORD | **Marquesas × Magpie** | **Scardefield 1971**
STRATHAVON | **Putana × Berwick** | **M. 1971**
suave‡ | **species**

× Esmeralda = Evonne
× madidum = Kuranda

suavissimum | **species**

× Swallow = Pekoe

SUGAR BIRD | **Sugar Palm × Flycatcher** | **Wyld Court 1972**
SUGAR BUSH | **Sugar Palm × Babylon** | **Wyld Court 1972**
SUGAR CANDY | **Sugar Palm × Balkis** | **Wyld Court 1972**
SUGAR PALM† | **Godwit × Louis Sander** | **Cooke 1946**

× Babylon = Sugar Bush
× Balkis = Sugar Candy
× Flycatcher = Sugar Bird

SUNNY DREAM | **Rusper × Cariga** | **Rod McLellan Co. 1972**
SUNRISE†‡ | **Ceres × Swallow** | **S. 1931**

× Clarissa = Tamatea

SUNSHINE FALLS | **King Arthur × madidum** | **Stewart Inc. 1972**
SUNSTROKE‡ | **Dabchick × Louis Sander** | **Cooke 1951**

× Flycatcher = Dilas

SUSA‡ | **Susette × Sussex** | **M. 1950**

× Ivy Fung = Chief Joseph

SUSAN BERMAN | **Pauwelsii × Rhoda** | **Berman 1972 (Stonehurst)**

× Fascination = General Lord Norrie
× Mayfair = John Berman
× Rosanna = Elfrida Berman

SUSAN HUGHES | **Etta Barlow × Lunagrad** | **W. L. Hughes 1974 (W. L. Baker)**

SUSSEX†‡ | **Landrail × Profusion** | **M. 1940**

× Bartolme Ferrello = Redford Beauty
× Fred Stewart = Poplan

SUSSEX DAWN‡ | **Sussex × Ramboda** | **M. 1955**

× Arcadian Melody = Via Arcadian Dawn
× Artisan = Karen Henry
× Atlantic Sun = Via Atlantica
× Claudona = Valley Green
× devonianum = Maribelle
× Elegance = Highland Valley
× Fred Stewart = Via San Gabriel
× Janine = Downs Delight
× King Arthur = Calle Los Olivos
× Mary Ann = Valley Conquest
× Mazatlan = Mem. Frank Taylor
× Parma = Ovation
× Pearl-Easter = Valley Meadow
× President Wilson = Araluen
× Rincon = Via Ruborosa
× San Miguel = Zumma Boyd
× Sleeping Beauty = Sleeping Dawn
× Snow Sprite = Valley Gnome
× Solana Beach = Via Nogales
× Thanksgiving = Via Noviembre
× Wyanga = Greenstone

SUSSEX MOOR‡ | **Sussex × Bodmin Moor** | **M. 1953**

× Dorama = Dorama Moor
× George Lycurgas = Lycurgas Moor
× Mary Ann = Highland Snow
× Putana = Lerwick
× Ramboda = Dasu

SUSSEX PEARL‡ | **Sussex × Pearl** | **M. 1954**

× Sensation = Winegrove

CYMBIDIUM

SUVA‡	**Volcano × Saigon**	**Stewart Inc. 1963**

× Coral Sea	= Suva Sea	× pumilum	= Suvalum
× Fascination	= Fassuva	× Stanley Fouraker	= Suvaley
× Joan of Arc	= Pride of Carousel		

SUVALEY	**Suva × Stanley Fouraker**	**Stewart Inc. 1973**
SUVALUM	**Suva × pumilum**	**Stewart Inc. 1972**
SUVA SEA	**Suva × Coral Sea**	**Stewart Inc. 1971**
SWALITA	**Marquesa Prescott × Swallow**	**Borg 1973**
SWALLOW*†‡	**Alexanderi × Pauwelsii**	**S. 1916**

× Clyde Landers	= Congier	× Pacific Pearl	= South Pacific
× Fanfare	= Melody Lane	× suavissimum	= Pekoe
× Marquesa Prescott	= Swalita	× Vieux Rose	= Martha Daeniker
× Mazatlan	= Patrician	× Woodalda	= Golden Wedding
× Oystercatcher	= Andorinha	× Wood Nymph	= Buoyant

SWEETHEART‡	**pumilum × Alexanderi**	**Bowers 1955**

× Con Amore	= Benwick	× Mount Everest	= California Romance
× Desirée A'Logann	= Teri Garr	× Radak	= Clarendon
× Green Wings	= Winter's Fantasy	× Sanrita	= Sweet San
× Little Redhead	= Moriah		

SWEET PATIENCE	**Etta Barlow × Nila**	**Universal 1971**
SWEET SAN	**Sweetheart × Sanrita**	**Rod McLellan Co. 1972**
SYLVADELL	**Janette × Nile**	**A. & B. 1973**
SYLVANIA	**Early Bird × Sheba**	**A. R. Bryant 1970**

× Lila	= Valley Sylvan	× Pearl-Easter	= Valley Paradise
× Pearl-Balkis	= Valley Sonnett	× Stanley Fouraker	= Valley Nightingale

SYLVIA MILLER	**Mary Pinchess × Sussex**	**Dos Pueblos 1968**

× Showgirl	= Paul Miller		

TAFFY	**Lyoth × Marquesa Prescott**	**Peterson Bros. 1972**
TAMATEA	**Sunrise × Clarissa**	**Easton 1974 (Moulson)**
TANUNDA	**Earlyana × Shiraz**	**Adelaide 1975 (Originator unknown)**
TAPESTRY	**Khyber Pass × Voodoo**	**Rod McLellan Co. 1963**

× Babylon	= Dark Wonder	× Louis Sander	= Gibson Girl

TARUN	**Dorchester × Durham Castle**	**Wondabah 1971**
TEDDI SUTTON	**Karen Cameron × Joan of Arc**	**Sutton 1975 (A'Logann Labs.)**
TERAMA	**Westholme × Sensation**	**Wondabah 1971**
TERI GARR	**Sweetheart × Desirée A'Logann**	**A'Logann 1975**
THANKSGIVING	**Doris Aurea × Monsoon**	**G. & S. 1969**

× Alexanderi	= Via Vista Grande	× San Miguel	= Via Miguel
× Arcadian Melody	= Via Natividad	× Solana Beach	= Via Vista
× Fred Stewart	= Via Barranca	× Sussex Dawn	= Via Noviembre

THREE WISE MEN	**Bethlehem × Earlyana**	**Stewart Inc. 1973**
TIDBIT	**Wood Nymph × Fanfare**	**Stewart Inc. 1973**
tigrinum*†‡	**species**	

× Balkis	= Tigris	× Chiron	= Bobtail

TIGRIS	**Balkis × tigrinum**	**Borg 1973**
TOSHIKAZU TAKAHASHI	**George Lycurgas × Artisan**	**T. Takahashi 1971**

CYMBIDIUM

Name	Parentage	Registrant
TOUCHSTONE	**devonianum × Mission Bay**	**Ratcliffe 1962**
× Clarissa	= Miniatures Delight	
TRALEE	**Green Wings × Peach Bloom**	**Rod McLellan Co. 1972**
TREFAIN	**Baltic × Alexanderi**	**Andrew Orchids 1972**
TRUE DELIGHT	**Matana × Stanley Fouraker**	**Stewart Inc. 1971**
TWELFTH NIGHT‡	**Charmant × Stanley Fouraker**	**Greenoaks 1966**
× Balkis	= Valley Lake	
× Christmas Green	= Xmas Night	
× Fred Stewart	= Valley Dream	
× Janine	= Valley Star	
× Mary Ann	= Valley Sweetheart	
× Rincon	= Shortest Day	
× Sheba	= Valley Flower	
TYRA BORG	**Louis Sander × Vieux Rose**	**Borg 1973**
UTOPIA	**Cleo Sherman × Fanfare**	**Peterson Bros. 1972**
VALE OF KASHMIR‡	**Blue Smoke × Claudona**	**Stewart Inc. 1955**
× Baltic	= Kashtic	
× Irish Melody	= Golden Beauty	
× Miretta	= Kashetta	
× Sicily	= Green Mountain	
VALLEY ANNE	**Anne Baxter × Balkis**	**Valley Orchids 1974 (Vandyke)**
VALLEY AVILION	**Mary Ann × Auriga**	**Valley Orchids 1974 (Vandyke)**
VALLEY BROOK	**Lila × Pearl-Balkis**	**Valley Orchids 1974 (Vandyke)**
VALLEY CHARM	**Anne Baxter × Pearl-Balkis**	**Valley Orchids 1974 (Vandyke)**
VALLEY CONQUEST	**Mary Ann × Sussex Dawn**	**Valley Orchids 1973 (Vandyke)**
VALLEY DAWN	**Stanley Fouraker × Janine**	**Valley Orchids 1973 (Vandyke)**
VALLEY DELIGHT	**Siram × Downs Delight**	**Valley Orchids 1974 (Vandyke)**
VALLEY DEW	**Sleeping Beauty × Mary Ann**	**Valley Orchids 1973 (Vandyke)**
VALLEY DREAM	**Fred Stewart × Twelfth Night**	**Valley Orchids 1973 (Vandyke)**
VALLEY EASTER	**Lila × Pearl-Easter**	**Valley Orchids 1974 (Vandyke)**
VALLEY EDEN	**Dorchester × Mary Ann**	**Valley Orchids 1974 (Vandyke)**
VALLEY EMERALD	**Pearl-Easter × San Miguel**	**Valley Orchids 1973 (Vandyke)**
VALLEY EMPRESS	**Pearl-Balkis × Janine**	**Valley Orchids 1974 (Vandyke)**
VALLEY FALCON	**Stanley Fouraker × York Meredith**	**Valley Orchids 1974 (Vandyke)**
VALLEY FALLS	**Mazatlan × Anne Baxter**	**Valley Orchids 1973 (Vandyke)**
VALLEY FIELD	**Grandly × Dorama**	**Valley Orchids 1974 (Vandyke)**
VALLEY FLARE	**Ann Green × Vintage**	**Valley Orchids 1973 (Vandyke)**
VALLEY FLOWER	**Twelfth Night × Sheba**	**Valley Orchids 1973 (Vandyke)**

CYMBIDIUM

VALLEY GEM	Dorama × Shiraz	Valley Orchids 1973 (Vandyke)
VALLEY GLACIER	Balkis × Mary Ann	Valley Orchids 1973 (Vandyke)
VALLEY GLOW	Sheba × Marian Lenfestey	Valley Orchids 1973 (Vandyke)
VALLEY GNOME	Sussex Dawn × Snow Sprite	Valley Orchids 1973 (Vandyke)
VALLEY GOLD	Dorama × Bud March	Valley Orchids 1973 (Vandyke)
VALLEY GRAND	Grandly × Pearl-Balkis	Valley Orchids 1974 (Vandyke)
VALLEY GREEN	Claudona × Sussex Dawn	Valley Orchids 1973 (Vandyke)
VALLEY HAZE	Anne Baxter × San Miguel	Valley Orchids 1973 (Vandyke)
VALLEY HEIGHTS	Fred Stewart × Sheba	Valley Orchids 1973 (Vandyke)
VALLEY HOPE	Fred Stewart × Shiraz	Valley Orchids 1973 (Vandyke)
VALLEY IMPERIAL	Janine × Balkis	Valley Orchids 1973 (Vandyke)
VALLEY JOY	Jocosity × Balkis	Valley Orchids 1974 (Vandyke)
VALLEY KING	Balkis × Etta Barlow	Valley Orchids 1973 (Vandyke)
VALLEY LAKE	Balkis × Twelfth Night	Valley Orchids 1973 (Vandyke)
VALLEY LIMELIGHT	Fred Stewart × San Miguel	Valley Orchids 1973 (Vandyke)
VALLEY MAYFLOWER	Stanley Fouraker × Earlyana	Valley Orchids 1973 (Vandyke)
VALLEY MEADOW	Pearl-Easter × Sussex Dawn	Valley Orchids 1973 (Vandyke)
VALLEY MELODY	Arcadian Melody × Westholme	Valley Orchids 1974 (Vandyke)
VALLEY MIST	Pearl-Easter × Fred Stewart	Valley Orchids 1973 (Vandyke)
VALLEY NIGHTINGALE	Stanley Fouraker × Sylvania	Valley Orchids 1974 (Vandyke)
VALLEY NYMPH	Joan of Arc × Dorchester	Valley Orchids 1973 (Vandyke)
VALLEY OPAL	Southborough × Dorama	Valley Orchids 1974 (Vandyke)
VALLEY PARADISE	Pearl-Easter × Sylvania	Valley Orchids 1974 (Vandyke)
VALLEY PASTURE	Dorama × Claudona	Valley Orchids 1973 (Vandyke)
VALLEY PEARL	Fred Stewart × Pearl-Balkis	Valley Orchids 1973 (Vandyke)
VALLEY PREMIERE	Lustrous × Earlyana	Valley Orchids 1973 (Vandyke)
VALLEY PRINCE	Fred Stewart × Cleo Sherman	Valley Orchids 1973 (Vandyke)

VALLEY PROGRESS	**Fred Stewart × Etta Barlow**	**Valley Orchids 1973 (Vandyke)**
VALLEY PROMISE	**Fred Stewart × Mary Ann**	**Valley Orchids 1973 (Vandyke)**
VALLEY RIVER	**Stanley Fouraker × Shiraz**	**Valley Orchids 1973 (Vandyke)**
VALLEY ROSETTA	**Balkis × Brissie**	**Valley Orchids 1974 (Vandyke)**
VALLEY SAPPHIRE	**Snow Sprite × Dorama**	**Valley Orchids 1974 (Vandyke)**
VALLEY SCENE	**Etta Barlow × Anne Baxter**	**Valley Orchids 1973 (Vandyke)**
VALLEY SHAMROCK	**San Miguel × Pearl-Balkis**	**Valley Orchids 1974 (Vandyke)**
VALLEY SHEEN	**Dorama × Alnwick Castle**	**Valley Orchids 1973 (Vandyke)**
VALLEY SNOW	**Anne Baxter × Mary Ann**	**Valley Orchids 1973 (Vandyke)**
VALLEY SONG	**Stanley Fouraker × San Miguel**	**Valley Orchids 1973 (Vandyke)**
VALLEY SONNETT	**Pearl-Balkis × Sylvania**	**Valley Orchids 1974 (Vandyke)**
VALLEY SPRITE	**Snow Sprite × Sheba**	**Valley Orchids 1974 (Vandyke)**
VALLEY STAR	**Twelfth Night × Janine**	**Valley Orchids 1973 (Vandyke)**
VALLEY STREAM	**Mary Ann × Stanley Fouraker**	**Valley Orchids 1973 (Vandyke)**
VALLEY SUNSET	**Etta Barlow × Pearl-Balkis**	**Valley Orchids 1974 (Vandyke)**
VALLEY SWEETHEART	**Twelfth Night × Mary Ann**	**Valley Orchids 1973 (Vandyke)**
VALLEY SYLVAN	**Lila × Sylvania**	**Valley Orchids 1974 (Vandyke)**
VALLEY SYMPHONY	**Balkis × Arcadian Melody**	**Valley Orchids 1973 (Vandyke)**
VALLEY TOPAZ	**Dorama × Pearl-Balkis**	**Valley Orchids 1974 (Vandyke)**
VALLEY TRYST	**Balkis × Sheba**	**Valley Orchids 1973 (Vandyke)**
VALLEY VIEW	**Fred Stewart × Rampur**	**Valley Orchids 1973 (Vandyke)**
VALLEY WINE	**Sleeping Glow × Mary Ann**	**Valley Orchids 1973 (Vandyke)**
VALLEY XMAS	**Fred Stewart × Janine**	**Valley Orchids 1973 (Vandyke)**
VALLEY YORK	Pearl-Easter × York Meredith	**Valley Orchids 1974 (Vandyke)**
VERDE DE INVIERNO	**Lucense × Sussex Dawn**	**G. & S. 1970**

× Atlantic Sun = Via Verde Fresco | × Raquel Abril = Via Jalisco

VERDE GRANDE‡	**Sicily × Paulette**	**Braemar 1960 (Carpentier)**

× Emmeline = Grand Em |

VESPER	**Erica Sander × Venus**	**S. 1937**

× Miretta = Honest Green

VIA ABRIL VERDE	**Raquel Abril × Green Spring**	**G. & S. 1973**
VIA ARCADIAN DAWN	**Arcadian Melody × Sussex Dawn**	**G. & S. 1973**
VIA ARCADIAN LADY	**Lady Lucy × Arcadian Melody**	**G. & S. 1973**
VIA ARCADIAN RINCON	**Arcadian Melody × Rincon**	**G. & S. 1973**
VIA ARCO VERDE	**Joan of Arc × Green Spring**	**G. & S. 1973**
VIA ARROYO	**Pixie Dawn × Dorama**	**G. & S. 1973**
VIA ATLANTICA	**Sussex Dawn × Atlantic Sun**	**G. & S. 1973**
VIA BARRANCA	**Fred Stewart × Thanksgiving**	**G. & S. 1973**
VIA CAJON VERDE	**Dorama × Green Spring**	**G. & S. 1973**
VIA CONSTELADO	**Rincon × Pink Momouth**	**G. & S. 1973**
VIA COSTA	**Solana Beach × Fred Stewart**	**G. & S. 1973**
VIA DEL PLAYA	**Solana Beach × Rincon**	**G. & S. 1973**
VIA DEL SOL	**Golden Sunset × Solana Beach**	**G. & S. 1973**
VIA DEL SOLEDAD	**Solana Beach × Winter Solstice**	**G. & S. 1973**
VIA DE MADRUGADA	**Pixie Dawn × Pink Momouth**	**G. & S. 1973**
VIA EL DORADO	**Green Spring × Etta Barlow**	**G. & S. 1972**
VIA GRANDIOSO	**Rincon × Atlantic Sun**	**G. & S. 1973**
VIA INVIERNO	**Fred Stewart × Heathrow**	**G. & S. 1973**
VIA JALISCO	**Verde de Invierno × Raquel Abril**	**G. & S. 1973**
VIA LAGUNA BLANCA	**Pixie Dawn × Hope Ranch**	**G. & S. 1973**
VIA MIGUEL	**Thanksgiving × San Miguel**	**G. & S. 1973**
VIA NATIVIDAD	**Arcadian Melody × Thanksgiving**	**G. & S. 1973**
VIA NOGALES	**Solana Beach × Sussex Dawn**	**G. & S. 1973**
VIA NOVIEMBRE	**Sussex Dawn × Thanksgiving**	**G. & S. 1973**
VIA RANCHO VERDE	**Green Spring × Hope Ranch**	**G. & S. 1973**
VIA RAQUEL	**Raquel Abril × Pixie Moor**	**G. & S. 1973**
VIA ROSARIO	**Joan of Arc × Reginetta**	**G. & S. 1973**
VIA RINCON	**Fred Stewart × Rincon**	**G. & S. 1973**
VIA RUBOROSA	**Rincon × Sussex Dawn**	**G. & S. 1973**
VIA RUBRA	**Fred Stewart × Rio Rita**	**G. & S. 1973**
VIA SAN GABRIEL	**Sussex Dawn × Fred Stewart**	**G. & S. 1973**
VIA SOLANA	**Solana Beach × Arcadian Melody**	**G. & S. 1973**
VIA TAHOE VISTA	**Via Tranquila × Winter Solstice**	**G. & S. 1973**
VIA TEHACHAPI	**Via Tranquila × Alexanderi**	**G. & S. 1973**
VIA TRANQUILA	**Guelwood × Sussex Dawn**	**G. & S. 1970**

× Alexanderi = Via Tehachapi
× Winter Solstice = Via Tahoe Vista

VIA VERDE FRESCO	**Verde de Invierno × Atlantic Sun**	**G. & S. 1973**
VIA VERDE LIMON	**Green Spring × Pink Momouth**	**G. & S. 1973**
VIA VISTA	**Thanksgiving × Solana Beach**	**G. & S. 1973**
VIA VISTA GRANDE	**Thanksgiving × Alexanderi**	**G. & S. 1973**
VICTORIA ARVANITIS	**Bethlehem × Dainty**	**Sakell 1974**
VIEUX ROSE‡	**Babylon × Rio Rita**	**Hothfield 1949**

× Airborne = Patricia Norrie
× Babylon = Rose Park
× Balkis = Royden
× Baltic = Baltic Rose
× Defiant = Sparkle
× ensifolium = Happy Talk
× Etta Barlow = Janet Marion
× Jungfrau = Anne Archer
× Khyber Pass = Donald Wilson
× Louis Sander = Tyra Borg
× Mary Ann = Fair Promise
× Musita = Phyllis Friedlander
× Ngaire = Highland Rose
× Ramesis = Caldy
× Ranjita = Ranrose
× Snow Sprite = Pink Ice
× Swallow = Martha Daeniker
× Voodoo = Voodoo Park

VINTAGE‡ **Spartan Queen × Ceres** **Sherman 1956**

× Ann Green = Valley Flare | × Rio Rita = Red Bird

virescens‡ **species**

(This is retained as the horticulturally recommended name for registration purposes, even though *Cymbidium goeringii* is the botanically correct name for this species.)

× Anne Baxter = Shunga | × Snow Sprite = Viresprite
× Eburneo-lowianum = Wakaba

VIRESPRITE **virescens × Snow Sprite** **Stewart Inc. 1971**
VOICE OF SPRING **Fanfare × San Miguel** **Stewart Inc. 1972**
VOLCANO‡ **Spartan Queen × Doris Aurea** **Sherman 1957**

× Paracel = Paracano

VOODOO‡ **Clarissa × Auribrook** **Sherman 1957**

× Paracel = Satsuma Beauty | × Vieux Rose = Voodoo Park

VOODOO PARK **Voodoo × Vieux Rose** **Borg 1973**
WAKABA **virescens × Eburneo-lowianum** **Katsuura 1973**
WAKAKUSA **Eburneo-lowianum × pumilum** **Katsuura 1968**

× Lunagrad = Walu

WALLACIA **Warona × Alnwick Castle** **Wondabah 1974**
WALU **Lunagrad × Wakakusa** **Katsuura 1973**
WAMPUM **Irina × Apollo** **Dos Pueblos 1963**

× Acapulco = April

WARELLA **Lustrous × Sirius** **Wondabah 1964**

× Durham Castle = Weipa | × Westholme = Westmark

WARMINSTER **Cleo Sherman × Rosanna** **Fetzer 1973**
WARONA‡ **Sussex × Remus** **Wondabah 1961**

× Alnwick Castle = Wallacia

WARRAH **Sussex × Spartan Queen** **Wondabah 1964**

× Babylon = Lofty

WATTLE GLEN **Wiena × Auriga** **Wondabah 1974**
WATTLE VALE **Balkis × Canara** **Wondabah 1974**
WEIPA **Warella × Durham Castle** **Wondabah 1974**
WELSH SONG **Woodland × Rio Rita** **Rod McLellan Co. 1971**
WESTERN HIGHLANDS **Miretta × Western Rose** **M. 1971**
WESTERN ROSE‡ **Alexanderi × Vieux Rose** **Borissow 1965 (M. & Sch.)**

× Miretta = Western Highlands | × Sea Gem = Caithness

WESTHOLME‡ **Lustrous × Wylan** **Wondabah 1962**

× Arcadian Melody = Valley Melody | × Redwood = Sagami
× Kalang = Wilton | × Sensation = Terama
× Lucy = Nell Potts | × Warella = Westmark

WESTMARK **Warella × Westholme** **Wondabah 1974**
WHYBA‡ **Spartan Queen × Remus** **Wondabah 1961**

× Sensation = Winevale

WIENA **Sirius × Alnwick Castle** **Wondabah 1964**

× Auriga = Wattle Glen | × Wyalong = Wyel

CYMBIDIUM

WILTON	**Westholme × Kalang**	**Wondabah 1974**
WINEGROVE	**Sussex Pearl × Sensation**	**Wondabah 1974**
WINEVALE	**Whyba × Sensation**	**Wondabah 1974**
WINTER FAIR	**Fred Stewart × Stanley Fouraker**	**Stewart Inc. 1971**
WINTER'S FANTASY	**Sweetheart × Green Wings**	**Rod McLellan Co. 1972**
WINTER PINK ICE	**Magpie × Rio Rita**	**Sakell 1974**
WINTER SOLSTICE	**Early Bird × Mary Ann**	**G. & S. 1969 (Romanoff)**

× Solana Beach	= Via del Soledad	× Via Tranquila	= Via Tahoe Vista

WOLCOTT	**Marquesas × Martin**	**Scardefield 1971**
WOODALDA‡	**Woodhamsianum × Esmeralda**	**Stewart Inc. 1957**

× devonianum	= Devon Wood	× Swallow	= Golden Wedding
× George Lycurgas	= Lemon Grove		

WOODHAMSIANUM*†‡	**Eburneo-lowianum × lowianum**	**A. & B. 1907**

× pumilum	= Green Elf		

WOODLAND	**Redwood × Orphan**	**Rod McLellan Co. 1962**

× Rio Rita	= Welsh Song		

WOOD NYMPH‡	**Sea Foam × tigrinum**	**Stewart Inc. 1961**

× Fanfare	= Tidbit	× Swallow	= Buoyant
× pumilum	= Jissy Mupp		

WYALONG‡	**Sussex × Profita**	**Wondabah 1961**

× Wiena	= Wyel		

WYANGA	**Ramboda × Sirius**	**Wondabah 1964**

× Dorama	= Gwen Sternbeck	× San Miguel	= Ian Duncan
× Grand Monarch	= Sleeping Monarch	× Sleeping Beauty	= Sleeping Nymph
× Green Nymph	= Kathie Lovell	× Sussex Dawn	= Greenstone

WYEL	**Wiena × Wyalong**	**Wondabah 1974**
WYLD COURT SWIFT	**Alexanderi × Godwit**	**Cooke 1939**

× Babylon	= Courtier		

XMAS NIGHT	**Christmas Green × Twelfth Night**	**Ridgeway 1973**
YANKEE WHALER	**Claudona × Fred Stewart**	**Stewart Inc. 1973**
YASHMAK	**Goblin × Harem**	**Andrew Orchids 1973**
YELLOW PRINCE	**Balkis × Runnymede**	**Borg 1973**
YORK MEREDITH‡	**Sanrita × Miretta**	**M. 1962 (Judge Berne)**

× Baltic	= Fort George	× Stanley Fouraker	= Valley Falcon
× Pearl-Easter	= Valley York		

ZUMMA BOYD	**San Miguel × Sussex Dawn**	**Henry Boyd 1971**

CYRTOCHILUM

macranthum (see *Oncidium macranthum**†‡) **species**

CYRTORCHIS

arcuata **species**

× Angcm. eichleranum	= Angchs. Mad		

DEBRUYNEARA

VICTORIA DE BRUYNE | **Ascda. Ophelia × Lsa. jonesii** | **de Bruyne 1972 (Hew Nurseries)**

DEGARMOARA

ADMIRALTY ISLANDS | **Mtssa. Charles M. Fitch × Odm. Jackie Gleason** | **Beall 1972**
ORCUS ISLAND | **Mtssa. Charles M. Fitch × Odm. Mount Baker** | **Beall 1974**

DENDROBIUM

ACHARA | **phalaenopsis × formosum** | **Thaichai 1975**

adae | **species**

× falcorostrum = Leonie Jane

affine‡ | **species**

× Louisae = Ham Sarjana
× veratrifolium = Sidabutar

AGNUS‡ | **Gatton Belle × Mont Blanc** | **J. Yamamoto 1968 (Yamaoka)**

× Gatton Beau = Gatton Prince
× Gatton Belle = Agnusbelle

AGNUSBELLE | **Agnus × Gatton Belle** | **J. Yamamoto 1973 (Yamaoka)**

× Ainsworthii = Pinocchio
× Kobayashi = Berimont
× Sagimony = Hatuyuki
× Sagimusume = Yukimusume

AHIAHI | **Joejay × Gold Flush** | **T. Kazumura 1972**

AILING | **Ainsmerlin × Permos** | **J. Yamamoto 1968**

× Akatuki = Gion
× Charm Blossom = Melody of Spring
× Glorious Rainbow = Fujimusume
× Orion = Sao Paulo
× Red Star = Christmas Chime

AINA HAINA†‡ | **Helen Bromley × Shibata** | **Miyamoto 1952**

× Cathy-Jan = Alison Yoshida
× Shibata = Nuuanu

AINSMERLIN‡ | **Ainsworthii × Merlin** | **J. Yamamoto 1968**

× Valamissko = Charm Blossom

AINSWORTHII*†‡ | **aureum × nobile** | **Ainsworth 1874**

× Agnusbelle = Pinocchio

AKANE | **Seto × Asahi** | **Takatsuka 1975**

AKATUKI | **Permos × Konan** | **J. Yamamoto 1970**

× Ailing = Gion
× Charm Star = Hope
× Glorious Rainbow = Malones
× Minori = Odeon
× Perning = Peace
× Red Star = Damsel

AKEMI‡ | **Lois Anderson × Jaquelyn Thomas** | **Takiguchi 1967**

× Dale Takiguchi = Chieko
× Darcie Mikami = Phyllis Chong
× Yoshie = Doreen Eto

ALE ALE KAI‡ | **Lady Hamilton × Top Hat** | **R. Yahiro 1958 (Fukumura)**

× Maui Beauty = Kamerunga Beauty

ALI BABA | **Sanders Crimson × Shibata** | **C. W. Chang 1953 (Mrs. J. Mizuta)**

× May Neal = Mailamai

DENDROBIUM

ALICE CHONG‡ | **May Neal × stratiotes** | **Peter Chong 1954 (A. C. Chang)**

× Aries Gold = Maemae
× Bronze Queen = Alice Queen
× Liholiho = Yellow Stone
× Rose Chong = Ooi Guat Im
× taurinum = Ching Chee

ALICE LIM | **gouldii × Lady Hamilton** | **Lim Sim Pang 1964**

× Euroka Beauty = Indira Ghandi

ALICE QUEEN | **Alice Chong × Bronze Queen** | **T. Kazumura 1972**

ALICE SPALDING†‡ | **tokai × undulatum** | **Ueno 1950**

× Jaquelyn Thomas = Ng Eng Cheow

ALISON YOSHIDA | **Aina Haina × Cathy-Jan** | **Yoshida 1972**

ALLAN NOBLE | Fort Allan × Fort Noble | **C. 1971**

ALLYN GEM | **Jaquelyn Thomas × compactum** | **V. & N. Jupp 1973**

ALMA CHONG | **Darcie Mikami × Tomie** | **Takiguchi 1975**

ALPENGLOW | **Princess Sharon × undulatum** | **Teruo Oka 1973**

ALTHEA HAUSERMANN | **Tim Tam × Dorado** | **Hausermann 1968**

× Hickam Deb = Amy Hausermann
× Marten Hausermann = Eric Stromsland

ALWYN HILL | **Tangold × johannis** | **McFarlane 1973**

AMERICAN BEAUTY‡ | **Anouk × Lady Hamilton** | **Kushima 1957**

× Betty Hecht = Damnern Sadouk
× Dale Takiguchi = Nell Hoadley
× Garden = Hawaiian Glory
× Khaw Yeong Hong = Scarlet Flame
× Margie Thomas = Pirates Moon

AMIN | **ostrinoglossum × schulleri** | **Alsagoff 1971**

× Kit Mun = Monawen

AMY HAUSERMANN | **Althea Hausermann × Hickam Deb** | **Hausermann 1975**

ANDEMOS | **Valademos × Anne Marie** | **J. Yamamoto 1975**

× Glorious Rainbow = Olympia

ANDREW PERSSON | **speciosum × falcorostrum** | **Slade 1960**

× delicatum = Tom Jupp

ANGEL FLOWER | **Permos × Regalsohma** | **J. Yamamoto 1968**

× Anne Marie = Angel Marie
× Dream = Yuzuki
× Evening Glow = Anglow
× Geory = Cinderella
× Glorious Rainbow = Momozono
× Konan = Console
× Oborozuki = Milky Way
× Orion = Lucky Lady

ANGEL MARIE | **Anne Marie × Angel Flower** | **J. Yamamoto 1975**

ANGEL WINGS | **Happiness × Sagimony** | **J. Yamamoto 1974**

ANGLOW | **Angel Flower × Evening Glow** | **J. Yamamoto 1974**

× Red Star = White Pony

ANITA | **Louisiae × phalaenopsis** | **de Saram 1940**

× macrophyllum = Meta Sari Mustika

ANNA BIBUS | **Doreen × phalaenopsis** | **Bibus 1973 (M. J. Bates)**

ANNE MARIE‡ | **Montrose × Winifred Fortescue** | **Wichmann 1963**

× Angel Flower = Angel Marie
× nobile = Dancing Waters
× Red Star = Baron
× Valademos = Andemos

DENDROBIUM

ANN NEWTON | **Salak × vestigiiferum** | **Alfred Bond 1971 (MacPherson)**

ANN SCHNEIDER | **Concert × bigibbum** | **Schneider 1975 (Originator unknown)**

ANOCHA | **Pikul × May Neal** | **Lonya 1974**

ANOM | **Mildred Kazumura × schulleri** | **Alsagoff 1964**

× Meala = Menom

anosmum (see *superbum**†‡)

(*anosmum* is botanically correct but *superbum* is retained as the horticulturally recommended name of this species for registration purposes.)

ANOUK†‡ | **Pompadour × phalaenopsis** | **V. 1950**

× Dunhill = Lakmini | × Roadrunner = Barbara Ann Bishop

antennatum (see *d'albertisii**†‡) | **species**

ANTHONY JANSEN | **Mei Lin × Peggy Shaw** | **Jansen 1972**

APPROVAL | **Impact × Ultimatum** | **McFarlane 1975**

ARCUATUM (see Indonesia†‡) | **phalaenopsis × violaceo-flavens** | **Tjipeganti —**

ARIES GOLD‡ | **Goldenhill × aries** | **T. Kazumura 1966**

× Alice Chong = Maemae | × May Neal = Hinano

ASAHI | **Kibi × Impara Beauty** | **Takatsuka 1971**

× Seto = Akane

ATAKIT | **Gold Flush × Lynne Kitsuki** | **Lonya 1973**

ATSUSHI | **Troy Mikami × phalaenopsis** | **Takiguchi 1974**

AURORA HEART‡ | **Thwaitesiae × Taketane** | **J. Yamamoto 1969**

× Misstomopink = Hatuharu | × Orion = Shinonome

× Oborozuki = Bright Star

AUTUMN LACE | **strebloceras × canaliculatum** | **Wilfret 1973**

BAJA | **Nandi × Roberta** | **K. Oka 1972**

BANGKHEN‡ | **stratiotes × Anouk** | **Jalavicharana 1950**

× Caesar = Somthawil | × schulleri = Haruko

BANGKOK YELLOW | **C. K. Ai × pulchellum** | **Proypanich 1974**

BARBARA ANN BISHOP | **Roadrunner × Anouk** | **Bishop 1973 (Kirch)**

× Carole Curry = Dava Wava | × Hickam Deb = Princess April

× compactum = Little April | × phalaenopsis = Motor Mouth

BARBARA CARTLAND | **Winifred Jackson × Euroka Beauty** | **Garth 1975**

BARBARA JARDINE | **Lily Doo × Hickam Deb** | **George Black 1974**

BARON | **Anne Marie × Red Star** | **J. Yamamoto 1975**

BARRY FUJIMOTO | **Princess Sharon × Jaq-Hawaii** | **Terus Oka 1975**

BARTELSIANUM* | **Rolfeae × Wiganiae** | **Colman 1908**

× Murrhiniacum = Mhairi Robertson

BEACH GIRL†‡ | **Pauline × schulleri** | **G. B. Miwa 1950**

× Cheong Chee Yon = Lakran | × schulleri = Sunny

BEE LIAN BEAUTY | **Chao Phya River × Lady Hamilton** | **Bee Lian 1975**

bellatulum | **species**

× Isabel Sander = White Ibis

BELLFLOWER | **Hawaii × Shibata** | **Miyamoto 1953**

× ionoglossum = Wei-lin

DENDROBIUM

BENI — **Miss Hawaii × Little Hawaii** — **Matsumoto 1967**

× May Neal = Lipstick May

BERIMONT — **Agnusbelle × Kobayashi** — **J. Yamamoto 1973**

× Sagimusume = Mount Fuji

BERTHA WEISENBACH — **Umphorn × Lady Fay** — **Matatics 1972 (G. Wakasugi)**

× Tammy Wakasugi = Stephen Matatics

BETTER TIMES — **Elmer Hausermann × Margie Thomas** — **Hausermann 1975**

BETTY HECHT‡ — **Ewa × Fair Lady** — **Tomiyasu 1965**

× American Beauty = Damnern Sadouk
× Bonnie = Sandy Ahu
× compactum = Pearl Yagi
× gouldii = Dana Tamashiro
× Juddhill = Hearthrob
× Margie Thomas = Sandra Kurakake
× Mem. Walter Soulé = Sari-Janine

BETTY HO — **Misty Green × Maynouk** — **Philip Ho 1975 (Miyamoto)**

bifalce†‡ — **species**

× undulatum = Gold Stripe

bigibbum*†‡ — **species**

× Calvin Morioka = Bo-Peep
× Chios = Toni Ahu
× Concert = Ann Schneider
× Lady Paul = Redcliffe Beauty
× Little Profusion = Vivian Snider
× New Horizon = Jon

BILLIE WILSON — **Dee Lynn × Helen Fukumura** — **H. L. Allan 1974**

BIZEN — **Evening Glow × Glorious Rainbow** — **J. Yamamoto 1971**

× Marimos = Yayoifuji

BLACK LIGHT — **Dorado × Margie Thomas** — **J. & S. 1971**

× Hickam Deb = Mem. George Ozment

BLACK MOON — **Maui Beauty × Lady Charm** — **Limberlost 1969**

× phalaenopsis = Noel's Compact
× Sybil Jones = Noel's Ultimate

BLACK MOUNTAIN‡ — **Agnes Ann × Anouk** — **Limberlost 1961**

× Lunar Eclipse = Midnight Magic

BLANCHE AISAKA — **Blue Jay × gouldii** — **Aisaka 1974 (Teruo Oka)**

BLAZE — **Dark Crown × Steven Ai** — **K. Oka 1973**

BLUE BEAUTY‡ — **Moanalua × gouldii** — **Matsumoto 1961**

× Phyllis = Fiona Dunlop

BLUE BONNET‡ — **May Neal × Mountain Haze** — **G. B. Miwa 1955**

× ionoglossum = Blue Pacific

BLUECOLOR — **toftii × Verigrant** — **Limberlost 1963**

× Kam Heights = Blue Hills
× williamsianum = Royal Snow

BLUE HILLS — **Kam Heights × Bluecolor** — **Limberlost 1973**

BLUE JAY‡ — **Louisiae × toftii** — **Kodama 1955**

× canaliculatum = Wee Willie
× compactum = Kimi Itagaki
× gouldii = Blanche Aisaka
× Tenmujin = Kalanai

DENDROBIUM

BLUE PACIFIC | **Blue Bonnet × ionoglossum** | **Perreira 1973**

BLUE TORO | **Taurus × undulatum** | **Limberlost 1970**

× canaliculatum = Chocolate Twist | × stratiotes = Sepik Blue

BOBBIE AISAKA | **Linda × Valley Gold** | **Aisaka 1975 (Teruo Oka)**

BODHI KAEW | **Valley King × Jaq-Hawaii** | **Chanyakomol 1973**

BODHI NGERN | **Lim Chong Min × Jaq-Hawaii** | **Chanyakomol 1973**

BONE GOLD | **Salak × Russell Heads** | **Limberlost 1973**

BONNIE‡ | **Lady Fay × Vera Patterson** | **K. Kamemoto 1968 (K. Oka)**

× Betty Hecht = Sandy Ahu | × Margie Thomas = Patricia Ward
× Helen Oka = Deann Oi

BOONCHU | **Manichote × Damnern Sadouk** | **Intachote 1975**

BOONROJE | **Louis Bleriot × Ethel Kawamoto** | **Tiraprateep 1973 (Somboonpol)**

BO-PEEP | **Calvin Morioka × bigibbum** | **Teruo Oka 1973**

BOUGAINVILLE BEAUTY | **Pauline × ostrinoglossum** | **Limberlost 1971**

BRENDA MOWE | **Prince Akihito × ionoglossum** | **K. F. Yap 1975**

BRIGHT EYES | **White Gem × Margaret Joan Fell** | **Coleman 1974**

BRIGHT STAR | **Aurora Heart × Oborozuki** | **J. Yamamoto 1974**

BRINSLY QUYN | **Pompadour × Joyce Weerasekera** | **Quyn 1972**

bromfieldii (see undulatum*†‡) | **species**

BRONZE QUEEN†‡ | **Aloha × schulleri** | **G. B. Miwa 1950**

× Alice Chong = Alice Queen | × Moonbeam = Florence Sukita
× Liholiho = Kanealii | × Nanette Leilani Todd = Ilima

BROWN DERBY†‡ | **Jaquelyn Thomas × schulleri** | **Miwa 1955**

× gouldii = Monaraine | × Paula Ann = Lobburi
× Liholiho = Kamoi

BUDDY SHEPLER‡ | **Helen Fukumura × Annemieke** | **Shepler 1962 (Sagarik)**

× Cheong Chee Yon = Lakmal | × Purple Wings = Lakbima
× Hoon Cheong San = Lakliya

BUSABA | **Bangkok Star × Malee-Kanya** | **Panjup 1968**

× Lady Charm = Srisomboon

CAESAR†‡ (syn. E. P. Boyle) | **phalaenopsis × stratiotes** | **Nagrok —**

× Bangkhen = Somthawil | × Pale Face = Tinaroo Falls
× Hula Girl = Loo Meow Lan | × Tengku Abdul Rahman = Mandai Cheer
× Jean Tan = Pearl See-Thoe

CALVIN MORIOKA‡ | **superbiens × veratrifolium** | **To. Morioka 1953 (Miyamoto)**

× bigibbum = Bo-Peep

canaliculatum†‡ | **species**

× Blue Jay = Wee Willie | × Midnight = Purple Charm
× Blue Toro = Chocolate Twist | × New Horizon = Little Lulu
× compactum = Mini Pearl | × Princess Sharon = Jisoo Sanjume
× Goldenhill = Goldkin | × strebloceras = Autumn Lace
× Hawaii = Mini Charm | × Walter Oumae = Pearly Snow
× Joyce Uehara = Mariner's Gold

CANARY GOLD | **Verninha × Gold Flush** | **Limberlost 1973**

DENDROBIUM

CAPE BEDFORD — **Salak × johannis** — **Limberlost 1975**

CARL LUDWIG BUNDT — **ionoglossum × lasianthera** — **Wallbrunn 1968 (Bundt)**

× williamsianum = Howard Harting

CARMEN — **Marimos × Utopia** — **J. Yamamoto 1974**

CAROL ANN‡ — **Lester McCoy × gouldii** — **To. Morioka 1956**

× Sunset Hill = Nicole De Verteuil

CAROLE CURRY — **Mary Katherine × Lady Fay** — **Curry 1964**

× Barbara Ann Bishop = Dava Wava
× Hickam Deb = Kam Au
× Lady Hay = Lady Carole

CASSIOPE*‡ — **moniliforme × nobile** — **N. C. Cookson 1890**

× Lady Colman = King Lake
× Pinocchio = Fubuki

CATHY — **Sunset × undulatum** — **A. C. Chang 1957**

× Janice Tanaka = Cathy-Jan

CATHY-JAN — **Cathy × Janice Tanaka** — **Yoshida 1972 (A. C. Chang)**

× Aina Haina = Alison Yoshida
× Shibata = Frances Walter

CHANG AH SONG — **Olive × Salome** — **Chong Beng Tiat 1971 (Ooi Leng Sun)**

CHAO PHYA RIVER — **Kasetsart × Malee-Kanya** — **Panjup 1967**

× Elaine = Mollisa
× Hawaiian Beauty = Surisi
× Lady Charm = New Bangkok
× Lady Hamilton = Bee Lian Beauty
× Louis Bleriot = Yaowamal
× Malee-Kanya = Diamond King's

CHARAL MABE — **Haunani Gay Ho × Linda** — **Aoki 1972 (Miyamoto)**

CHARLES TANAKA†‡ — **May Neal × Ruth Thomas** — **R. Tanaka 1954**

× Liholiho = Golden Giant

CHARM BLOSSOM — **Ainsmerlin × Valamissko** — **J. Yamamoto 1971**

× Ailing = Melody of Spring

CHARM STAR — **Permos × Permissko** — **J. Yamamoto 1970**

× Akatuki = Hope
× Glorious Rainbow = Yamato
× Myojo = Sunshine

CHEONG CHEE YON — **Cheong Fook Sum × Queen Emma** — **Cheong Chee Yon 1970**

× Beach Girl = Lakran
× Buddy Shepler = Lakmal
× Cheryl Cummins = Lakmalwatta
× Jaquelyn Concert = Dunhill
× Lim Tar Fang = Gordy's Girl
× Ng Eng Cheow = Lakmutha

CHEONG FOOK SUM — **Maui Beauty × Buddy Shepler** — **Cheong Chee Yon 1970 (Koh Keng Hoe)**

× Dan O'Brien = Johore Beauty

CHERRY GLOW — **Konan × Glorious Rainbow** — **J. Yamamoto 1971**

CHERYL CUMMINS — **Pompadour × gouldii** — **T. P. Cummins 1953 (McCoy)**

× Cheong Chee Yon = Lakmalwatta
× compactum = Little Profusion

CHERYL ITAGAKI — **Kimi Itagaki × ionoglossum** — **Itagaki 1975 (K. Oka)**

DENDROBIUM

Grex	Parentage	Registrant
CHEW POH KHIM	Merza Le × Mercedes Rabago	Chew Peng Kah 1971 (R. T. Fukumura)
CHIC	Valley King × violaceo-flavens	R. K. Mizuta 1973
CHIEKO	Dale Takiguchi × Akemi	Takiguchi 1973
CHINA LILY	formosum × draconis	H. L. Allan 1974
CHING CHEE	Alice Chong × taurinum	Edith Chun 1972
CHIOS	Gail Kurakake × undulatum	Aoki 1970 (K. Oka)

× bigibbum = Toni Ahu

Grex	Parentage	Registrant
CHO-CHO SAN	Maui Beauty × Mary Katherine	Y. Inouye 1968

× Maui Beauty = Donald Ira Wijewrdene

Grex	Parentage	Registrant
CHOCOLATE GOLD	Prince Akihito × Taurus	Limberlost 1973
CHOCOLATE TWIST	Blue Toro × canaliculatum	Limberlost 1971
CHRISTINE HARADA	Teri Higa × Kathleen Naomi Kagawa	Teruo Oka 1974
CHRISTMAS CHIME	Ailing × Red Star	J. Yamamoto 1974
chrysotoxum*†‡	species	

× phalaenopsis = Korat

Grex	Parentage	Registrant
CINDERELLA	Geory × Angel Flower	J. Yamamoto 1974
C. K. AI	May Neal × Hula Girl	Ai 1956 (Kodama)

× pulchellum = Bangkok Yellow

Grex	Parentage	Registrant
CLAIRE	Bonnie × American Beauty	K. Kamemoto 1968 (K. Oka)

× Lady Hamilton = Purple Beauty
× Shirley Suzuki = Mitchell Sado
× Steven Ai = Kathryn Itagaki
× Vera Patterson = Paul Suzuki

Grex	Parentage	Registrant
CLARA BUNDT†	Ale Ale Kai × Pompadour	Bundt 1964

× Latimodjong = Malino

Grex	Parentage	Registrant
CLARICE FUJIMOTO	Linda × Joyce Uehara	Teruo Oka 1973
COLIN SIMPSON	Maui Beauty × Frank Simpson	C. Simpson 1973
compactum‡	species	

× Barbara Ann Bishop = Little April
× Betty Hecht = Pearl Yagi
× Blue Jay = Kimi Itagaki
× canaliculatum = Mini Pearl
× Cheryl Cummins = Little Profusion
× Concert = Keiki Belle
× Diamond Head Beauty = Little Diamond
× Elaine = Sueo Sakamoto
× Hickam Deb = First Love
× Jaquelyn Thomas = Allyn Gem
× Lady Hamilton = Midnight Prince
× minax = Minapac

Grex	Parentage	Registrant
CONCERT†‡	Orchidwood × Alice Spalding	Miyamoto 1953

× bigibbum = Ann Schneider
× compactum = Keiki Belle
× Liholiho = Garnet Beauty
× Little Eliza = Tammy Rita

Grex	Parentage	Registrant
CONCERTO	Jaquelyn Concert × Pupukea Beauty	Kushima 1975
CONSOLE	Konan × Angel Flower	J. Yamamoto 1975
CONSTANCE†‡	undulatum × lasianthera	Laycock 1940

× Noor Aishah = Evelyn Foo

Grex	Parentage	Registrant
CONTEMPO	Helen Oka × Juddhill	Teruo Oka 1973
COOL WATERS	Lowana Bicolor × Margaret Joan Fell	Limberlost 1975
COPPERFIELD	Fiftieth State × undulatum	McFarlane 1973

DENDROBIUM

CRIMSON BELLE **Cleopatra × Lady Diamond** **Kushima 1964**
× Maui Charm = Crimson Charm

CRIMSON BOW **Crimson Charm × Mercedes Rabago** **Kushima 1975**
CRIMSON CHARM **Crimson Belle × Maui Charm** **Kushima 1973**
× Mercedes Rabago = Crimson Bow

CRYSTAL CASCADES **Pale Face × Silver Gull** **Limberlost 1969**
× Pale Face = Sand Cay

CUPID **Shiranami × Sagimony** **J. Yamamoto 1972**
d'albertisii*†‡ **species**
(This is retained as the horticulturally recommended name for registration purposes, even though *Dendrobium antennatum* is the botanically correct name for this species.)
× Jaquelyn Thomas = Uniwai Profusion

DALE TAKIGUCHI‡ **Valley King × Theodore Takiguchi** **Takiguchi 1964**
× Akemi = Chieko
× American Beauty = Nell Hoadley
× phalaenopsis = Jason Yamashita
× Theodore Takiguchi = Mieko Uehara
× Tomie = Sean Oshiro

dalhousieanum*† (see *pulchellum*†‡) **species**
DALLIANCE **Alice Noda × Queensland** **S'pore Orchids 1966**
× phalaenopsis = Fond Lover

DAMNERN SADOUK **Betty Hecht × American Beauty** **Samachai 1973 (Chaisomboon)**
× Manichote = Boonchu

DAMSEL **Akatuki × Red Star** **J. Yamamoto 1975**
DANA TAMASHIRO **Betty Hecht × gouldii** **Teruo Oka 1974**
DANCING WATERS **Anne Marie × nobile** **V. & N. Jupp 1975**
DAN O'BRIEN **Manoa Gold × schulleri** **W. H. Nakamoto 1965 (Kayima)**
× Cheong Fook Sum = Johore Beauty

DARCIE MIKAMI **Theodore Takiguchi × Akemi** **Takiguchi 1970**
× Akemi = Phyllis Chong
× Tomie = Alma Chong

DARK CROWN **Purple Crown × Maui Beauty** **McFarlane 1970**
× Steven Ai = Blaze

DARK VICTORY†‡ **Pompadour × undulatum** **Conklin 1951**
× Glenn Young = Kahului Red

DAVA WAVA **Carole Curry × Barbara Ann Bishop** **Bishop 1975**
DEANN OI **Helen Oka × Bonnie** **Robt. Oka 1975 (K. Oka)**
× Steven Ai = Hisako Oka

DEBI DEBRA **Lim Chong Min × Drake Kubo** **Shigaki 1975**
DEE LYNN **Lady Hamilton × Hickam Deb** **Whitesell 1964**
× Dorado = Kathy Rooks
× Helen Fukumura = Billie Wilson
× Hickam Deb = James Dick
× Minapac = Minalynn

delicatum‡ **species**
× Andrew Persson = Tom Jupp
× gracillimum = Sun Sprite
× tetragonum = Ku-Ring-Gai

densiflorum (see *thyrsiflorum**) — **species**

DHONBURI — **Indonesia × May Neal** — **Boonphyoong 1956**

× May Neal = Sukontha

DIAMOND HEAD BEAUTY†‡ — **bigibbum × Sanders Crimson** — **McCoy 1951**

× compactum = Little Diamond

DIAMOND KING'S — **Chao Phya River × Malee-Kanya** — **A. Panjup 1971**

DIMBULAH — **Malee-Kanya × Lady Fay** — **Limberlost 1971**

discolor (see *undulatum**†‡) — **species**

DONALD IRA WIJEWRDENE — **Cho-Cho San × Maui Beauty** — **Garth 1975**

DORADO‡ — **Khaw Yeong Hong × Margie Thomas** — **Fields Orchids 1965**

× Dee Lynn = Kathy Rooks | × Margie Thomas = Black Light
× Hickam Deb = Dorado Deb

DORADO DEB — **Dorado × Hickam Deb** — **Fields Orchids 1973**

DOREEN‡ — **Theodore Takiguchi × phalaenopsis** — **Takiguchi 1961**

× phalaenopsis = Anna Bibus | × Valley King = Soh Sew Eng

DOREEN ETO — **Yoshie × Akemi** — **Takiguchi 1975**

DOROTHY JOYCE — **Princess Sharon × Tenmujin** — **Shigaki 1974 (K. Oka)**

DOROTHY OKA — **Princess Sharon × Jaquelyn Concert** — **Teruo Oka 1975**

draconis†‡ — **species**

× formosum = China Lily

DRAKE KUBO — **Theodore Takiguchi × Lois Anderson** — **Takiguchi 1970**

× Lim Chong Min = Debi Debra

DREAM — **Fiona × Ijyuin** — **J. Yamamoto 1970**

× Angel Flower = Yuzuki | × Golden Wave = Orange Blossom
× Golden Eagle = Golden Blossom

DUANG TAWAN — **Sangsuriya × Siamese Pretty** — **Madhyamachandra 1973**

DUNHILL — **Jaquelyn Concert × Cheong Chee Yon** — **Dunhill 1973 (Koh Keng Hoe)**

× Anouk = Lakmini | × Irene Cheong = Lakravi

DUO‡ — **Gatton Monarch × nobile** — **Sander et Fils 1958**

× nobile = Happy Red

DUSKY GOLD — **Ismail Trengganu × schulleri** — **S.F.E.S. 1975**

DZEMAL BIJEDIC — **Tumphal × ostrinoglossum** — **S.B.G. 1973**

EDDY DJAYA REMADJA — **Meta Sari Mustika × superbum** — **Kolopaking 1975**

EDITH HOWELL — **Margie Thomas × Lila Gera** — **Howell 1972**

EDSA LOO — **Surprise × Forty Niner** — **Edward Loo 1975 (Perreira)**

EDWIN OKA — **Princess Sharon × gouldii** — **Teruo Oka 1973**

EDYTHE PUNG‡ — **schulleri × Caesar** — **Pung 1954 (G. B. Miwa)**

× Fiftieth State Beauty = Esther Zane Shigaki

EILEEN FOO — **Nanae × Jaquelyn Concert** — **Koh Keng Hoe 1973**

ELAINE‡ — **Maui Beauty × Shangri-La** — **Muroki 1961 (Fukumura)**

× Chao Phya River = Mollisa | × compactum = Sueo Sakamoto

ELAINE‡ *(continued)*

× Helen Oka	= Shirley Suzuki	× Shelli	= Yuriko
× Hickam Deb	= Midnight Dream	× Theodore Takiguchi	= Tunku Irinah
× Shelley Maurine Thomas	= West Indian	× Vera Patterson	= Lawrence Suzuki

ELIZABETH — **Mustard × Noor Aishah** — **S. B. G. 1972**

ELLEN TAKIGUCHI‡ — **Charlotte Matsuda × Lady Hamilton** — **Takiguchi 1957 (Otake)**

× Monika Renfro	= Roadrunner	× Rose Yoshida	= Misako

ELLI KARSTEN — **Sunrise × Hercules** — **Robertson 1973**

ELMER HAUSERMANN — **Tim Tam × Margie Thomas** — **Hausermann 1969**

× Margie Thomas	= Better Times

ELVES — **Glonmery × Madoromi** — **J. Yamamoto 1971**

ENGLAN BLUE — **Hirakawa × phalaenopsis** — **Lim Swee Aun 1960 (Kirch)**

× Yellow Curls	= Kiril Siebert

E. P. BOYLE(see Caesar†‡)

ERIC STROMSLAND — **Althea Hausermann × Marten Hausermann** — **Hausermann 1973**

ERIKA REUTER — **Golden Wave × Winifred Fortescue** — **Fennell 1974**

ESTHER ZANE SHIGAKI — **Edythe Pung × Fiftieth State Beauty** — **Shigaki 1972 (Matsumoto)**

ETHEL KAWAMOTO†‡ — **Shibata × undulatum** — **Miyamoto 1952**

× Louis Bleriot	= Boonroje

EUROKA BEAUTY — **Anouk × Maui Beauty** — **Limberlost 1968**

× Alice Lim	= Indira Ghandi	× Winifred Jackson	= Barbara Cartland
× Maui Beauty	= Mem. Paul Harris		

EVELYN FOO — **Constance × Noor Aishah** — **Koh Keng Hoe 1973**

EVENING GLOW — **Nobirose × Valadeva** — **J. Yamamoto 1971**

× Angel Flower	= Anglow	× Oborozuki	= Oriental Paradise
× Glorious Rainbow	= Bizen	× Orion	= Reimei
× Permos	= Perning		

falcorostrum†‡ — **species**

× adae	= Leonie Jane	× tetragonum	= Star of Gold
× fleckeri	= Peter		

farmeri*‡ — **species**

× Theodore Takiguchi	= Khempunhya	× thyrsiflorum	= farmeri-thyrsiflorum (nat. hyb.) / Farmeri-thyrsiflorum (Reg'd. grex)

farmeri-thyrsiflorum / **FARMERI-THYRSIFLORUM** — **farmeri × thyrsiflorum** — **Nat. hyb.** / **Cannons 1973**

FAYE‡ — **Robbie Camp × Shibata** — **Kodama 1954 (Miyamoto)**

× Maui Beauty	= Manichote

FIERY GOLD — **Ismail Trengganu × Guadalcanal** — **S.F.E.S. 1975**

FIFTIETH STATE‡ — **New Guinea × phalaenopsis** — **Cavaco 1959 (McCoy)**

× strebloceras	= Flair	× undulatum	= Copperfield

DENDROBIUM

FIFTIETH STATE BEAUTY — **Edythe Pung × Sunset Beauty** — **Matsumoto 1967**
× Edythe Pung = Esther Zane Shigaki | × Mini Girl = Summit Gold

FIONA DUNLOP — **Phyllis × Blue Beauty** — **Lazaroo 1972 (S.B.G.)**

FIRE BALL — **Tenmujin × Vera Patterson** — **J. Hirotsu 1971**
FIRST LOVE — **Hickam Deb × compactum** — **Bishop 1974**
FLAIR — **strebloceras × Fiftieth State** — **McFarlane 1975**
FLAREPATH — **Princess Sharon × ionoglossum** — **Teruo Oka 1973**
fleckeri‡ — **species**
× falcorostrum = Peter |

FLORENCE SUKITA — **Moonbeam × Bronze Queen** — **Perreira 1975**
FOND LOVER — **Dalliance × phalaenopsis** — **S'pore Orchids 1971**
formosum*†‡ — **species**
× draconis = China Lily | × Snowdrift = Snow Queen
× Mermaid = Prapoothabat | × superbiens = Mem. Professor Knudson
× phalaenopsis = Achara |
× Siamese Pretty = Kitiporn |

FORT ALLAN — **Bridge of Allan × Winifred Fortescue** — **C. 1961**
× Fort Noble = Allan Noble |

FORT NOBLE — **nobile × Winifred Fortescue** — **C. 1959**
× Fort Allan = Allan Noble | × Perfection = Tammany

FORTY NINER† — **Evening Star × nobile** — **G. B. Miwa 1949**
× Surprise = Edsa Loo |

FRANCES WALTER — **Cathy-Jan × Shibata** — **Yoshida 1972**
FRANK SIMPSON — **Helen Fukumura × Lady Hay** — **C. Simpson 1973 (Originator unknown)**
× Maui Beauty = Colin Simpson |

FUANG FAH — **Lily Doo × phalaenopsis** — **Proypanich 1974**
FUBUKI — **Cassiope × Pinocchio** — **J. Yamamoto 1975**
FUJIMUSUME — **Ailing × Glorious Rainbow** — **J. Yamamoto 1972**
× Glorious Rainbow = Polestar |

GARDEN — **Lady Constance × Louis Bleriot** — **Miyamoto 1953**
× American Beauty = Hawaiian Glory |

GARNET BEAUTY — **Concert × Liholiho** — **Perreira 1973**
GATTON BEAU‡ — **Alpha × Chessingtonense** — **Colman 1924**
× Agnus = Gatton Prince |

GATTON BELLE*‡ — **Alpha × Wiganianum** — **Colman 1924**
× Agnus = Agnusbelle |

GATTON PRINCE — **Agnus × Gatton Beau** — **Yonezawa 1975**
× Melanodiscus = Zuiko | × Mont Blanc = White King

GAZELLE — **Louisae × ostrinoglossum** — **Limberlost 1971**
GEOFFREY — **Khaw Yeong Hong × Anouk** — **George Black 1966**
× Hickam Deb = Lady Lisa |

GEORY — **Lady Colman × Permos** — **J. Yamamoto 1974**
× Angel Flower = Cinderella |

DENDROBIUM

GION — **Ailing × Akatuki** — **J. Yamamoto 1975**

GLACE — **Lady Colman × Thwaitesiae** — **J. Yamamoto 1968 (K. Gotoh)**

× Ise = Isuzugawa
× Thwaitesiae = Golden Dream

GLENN YOUNG — **442nd Infantry × gouldii** — **Hung Ung Young 1953**

× Dark Victory = Kahului Red

GLONMERY — **Mary Caine × Permos** — **J. Yamamoto 1969**

× Madoromi = Elves

GLORIOUS RAINBOW — **Permos × Valademos** — **J. Yamamoto 1968**

× Ailing = Fujimusume
× Akatuki = Malones
× Andemos = Olympia
× Angel Flower = Momozono
× Charm Star = Yamato
× Evening Glow = Bizen
× Fujimusume = Polestar
× Konan = Cherry Glow
× Oborozuki = Otohime
× Orion = Utopia
× Permissko = Red Fairy
× Red Star = Spring Wind
× Zakimos = Myojo

GOH GIN HUA — **Valley King × Liholiho** — **Goh Gin Hwa 1975**

GOLD CREST — **Lillian Izumo × Alice Chong** — **K. Oka 1966**

× Liholiho = Nandi

GOLDEN BELL — **Mary Trowse × May Neal** — **T. Kazumura 1965**

× Golden Queen = Noel

GOLDEN BLAZE — **Prince Akihito × May Neal** — **Perreira 1972 (A. S. Cavaco)**

GOLDEN BLOSSOM — **Golden Eagle × Dream** — **J. Yamamoto 1971**

GOLDEN BOY — **Alice Chong × schulleri** — **T. Kazumura 1968**

× Green Hornet = Lime Twist

GOLDEN DERBY — **Brown Derby × Gold Flush** — **T. Kazumura 1967**

× Sunset Glow = Peter Hoadley

GOLDEN DREAM — **Glace × Thwaitesiae** — **Yonezawa 1975**

GOLDEN EAGLE — **Mont Blanc × Golden Wave** — **J. Yamamoto 1971**

× Dream = Golden Blossom

GOLDEN GIANT — **Charles Tanaka × Liholiho** — **Perreira 1974**

GOLDENHILL‡ — **May Neal × schulleri** — **T. Kazumura 1965**

× canaliculatum = Goldkin
× Gold Flush = Maile

GOLDEN PIXIE — **Alice Chong × canaliculatum** — **R. K. Mizuta 1968**

× Haunani Gay Ho = Pixie Nani

GOLDEN PRINCE — **Prince Akihito × Manoa Gold** — **R. K. Mizuta 1968**

× Lihowaii = Shigaki Neil

GOLDEN QUEEN‡ — **Rose Chong × Bronze Queen** — **T. Kazumura 1967**

× Golden Bell = Noel

GOLDEN TALISMAN‡ — **Blumenau × Variabilis** — **Altenburg 1969**

× Oborozuki = Hambühren Gold

GOLDEN WAVE — **Mont Blanc × Thwaitesiae** — **J. Yamamoto 1968**

× Dream = Orange Blossom
× Mont Blanc = Golden Eagle
× Winifred Fortescue = Erika Reuter

GOLD FLUSH†‡ | **Shibata × May Neal** | **Woodlawn 1954**

× Goldenhill	= Maile	× Verninha	= Canary Gold
× Joejay	= Ahiahi	× violaceo-flavens	= Violaceoflush
× Lynne Kitsuki	= Atakit		

goldiei (see superbiens*†‡)

GOLDKIN | **Goldenhill × canaliculatum** | **Perreira 1975**

GOLD STRIPE | **bifalce × undulatum** | **Limberlost 1973**

GORDY'S GIRL | **Lim Tar Fang × Cheong Chee Yon** | **Kratzer 1975 (Koh Keng Hoe)**

gouldii†‡ | **species**

(syn. *lineale*; *Den gouldii* and *Den. veratrifolium* are treated for registration purposes as specifically distinct from each other, though ranked as conspecific by some authorities.)

× Betty Hecht	= Dana Tamashiro	× Helen Oka	= Kellie Tamashiro
× Blue Jay	= Blanche Aisaka	× Princess Sharon	= Edwin Oka
× Brown Derby	= Monaraine	× Theodore Takiguchi	= Snow Elf
× Grace Goo	= Mata'aho		

GRACE GOO†‡ | **gouldii × Shibata** | **Lum Goo 1951**

× gouldii = Mata'aho

gracillimum‡ | **species**

× delicatum = Sun Sprite | × kingianum = Penny Ann

GREEN HORNET | **Meala × Hina Haina** | **T. Kazumura 1967**

× Golden Boy = Lime Twist

GREEN VALLEY | **May Neal × tokai** | **T. Kazumura 1967**

× May Neal = Ruveni Weerasekera

GUADALCANAL†‡ | **gouldii × Hawaii** | **Foster Bot. Gdn. 1949**

× Ismail Trengganu = Fiery Gold

GWEN HIGGINS | **Hawaiian Beauty × Lady Dorothy** | **Roy K. Hall 1975**

GWEN SLADE | **Nellie Slade × rhodostictum** | **Slade 1971**

HAGOROMO | **Sagimusume × White Pearl** | **J. Yamamoto 1971**

HALAWA BEAUTY | **Calvin Morioka × Dora Zane** | **Tanimoto 1968**

× Jaquelyn Thomas = Rayanne Nakamoto | × superbiens = Pee Oh

HALIMAH MOCHTAR LUBIS | **Pakarena × schulleri** | **Bundt 1971**

HALO | **Mini Girl × williamsianum** | **McFarlane 1975**

HAMBÜHREN GOLD | **Oborozuki × Golden Talisman** | **Elle & Co. 1975 (Elle)**

HAM SARJANA | **Louisae × affine** | **Kolopaking 1974**

HAMZY SALMAN | **Pompadour × Jaquelyn Concert** | **Mak Chin On 1975**

HAPPINESS | **Kobayashi × Misstomopink** | **J. Yamamoto 1970**

× Sagimony = Angel Wings

HAPPY RED | **Duo × nobile** | **Yonezawa 1975**

HARLEQUIN | **Tanglin × taurinum** | **S.B.G. 1958**

× Noor Aishah = Sarasvathi Giri

HARTLEY'S BLUE | **Kila Blue × phalaenopsis** | **Limberlost 1971**

HARUKO | **schulleri × Bangkhen** | **T. Yamaoka 1972 (Originator unknown)**

HATUHARU | **Misstomopink × Aurora Heart** | **J. Yamamoto 1975**

× Oborozuki = Yodogimi

HATUYUKI | **Agnusbelle × Sagimony** | **J. Yamamoto 1975**
× Pinocchio = Panda

HAUNANI GAY HO‡ | **Sunset × Janice Tanaka** | **A. C. Chang 1957 (A. C. Ho)**
× Golden Pixie = Pixie Nani
× Linda = Charal Mabe

HAWAII*†‡ | **phalaenopsis × tokai** | **Ellen Williams 1938**
× canaliculatum = Mini Charm

HAWAIIAN BEAUTY†‡ | **phalaenopsis × Lady Hamilton** | **Matsumoto 1957**
× Chao Phya River = Surisi
× Helen Fukumura = Kibi
× Lady Dorothy = Gwen Higgins
× Lady Hamilton = Sangsuriya

HAWAIIAN CHARM | **Maui Charm × Queen Emma** | **Kushima 1975**

HAWAIIAN GLORY | **American Beauty × Garden** | **R. K. Mizuta 1972**

HEARTHROB | **Betty Hecht × Juddhill** | **Teruo Oka 1973**

HELEN FUKUMURA†‡ | **Lady Constance × phalaenopsis** | **Fukumura 1952**
× Dee Lynn = Billie Wilson
× Hawaiian Beauty = Kibi
× Lady Hay = Frank Simpson
× veratrifolium = Tunku Najihah
× Waikiki Beauty = Sirimavo Bandaranaike

HELEN HESSE | **Kaneohe Velvet × Kaneohe Princess** | **Hesse 1974**

HELEN IZUTA‡ | **Caesar × Shibata** | **E. S. Kondo 1957 (Hung Ung Young)**
× May Neal = Ooi Leng Sun

HELEN OKA‡ | **American Beauty × Vera Patterson** | **K. Oka 1966**
× Bonnie = Deann Oi
× Elaine = Shirley Suzuki
× gouldii = Kellie Tamashiro
× Juddhill = Contempo

HERBERT ONG | **Ursula × Curlylocks** | **Ong Soon Lim 1958**
× ostrinoglossum = Sirima Bandaranaike

HERCULES‡ | **Prince Arthur × Thwaitesiae** | **Colman 1925**
× Sunrise = Elli Karsten

HERMONT | **Montrose × Kobayashi** | **J. Yamamoto 1969**
× Oborozuki = Yumeji

HICKAM DEB‡ | **American Beauty × Lady Fay** | **Lyle Thomas 1961 (Kushima)**
× Althea Hausermann = Amy Hausermann
× Barbara Ann Bishop = Princess April
× Black Light = Mem. George Ozment
× Carole Curry = Kam Au
× compactum = First Love
× Dee Lynn = James Dick
× Dorado = Dorado Deb
× Elaine = Midnight Dream
× Geoffrey = Lady Lisa
× Juliet = Kristen Ann
× Lady Carole = Sandra Russell
× Lady Hay = Marianne Bates
× Lily Doo = Barbara Jardine
× Margaret Joan Fell = Lunar Rose

HINANO | **May Neal × Aries Gold** | **T. Kazumura 1972**

HISAKO OKA | **Deann Oi × Steven Ai** | **Robt. Oka 1975 (K. Oka)**

HOJUN | **Snowflake × Merry Christmas** | **Yonezawa 1975**

HO KING | **Indonesia × taurinum** | **Ho King 1972 (Ah Lai)**

HOON CHEONG SAN | **Medusa × Rose Chong** | **Gem Nursery 1964**
× Buddy Shepler = Lakliya

HOPE | **Akatuki × Charm Star** | **J. Yamamoto 1975**

DENDROBIUM

HOWARD HARTING	**Carl Ludwig Bundt × williamsianum**		**Fort Caroline 1973 (Wallbrunn)**
HULA GIRL†‡	**Hawaii × undulatum**		**Goo 1945**
× Caesar	= Loo Meow Lan	× Mem. Kumajiro Nitta	= Kaneohe Velvet
× Lillian Izumo	= Jomo		
HUMIE TANAKA	**Princess Sharon × Steven Ai**		**L. Suzuki 1974 (K. Oka)**
IBU PAULA SIWABESSY	**Pakarena × Lynn Takiguchi**		**Bundt 1970**
× Pakarena	= We Bungawaliè		
ILIMA	**Nanette Leilani Todd × Bronze Queen**		**T. Kazumura 1972**
IMPACT	**Fiftieth State × phalaenopsis**		**McFarlane 1970**
× Ultimatum	= Approval		
IMPARA BEAUTY	**Top Hat × Maui Beauty**		**Limberlost 1970**
× Kibi	= Asahi	× Sybil Jones	= Warpaint
IMUA	**Isami Doi × taurinum**		**Jack Ching 1972**
INDIRA GHANDI	**Euroka Beauty × Alice Lim**		**Garth 1974**
INDONESIA†‡ (syn. Arcuatum)	**phalaenopsis × violaceo-flavens**		**van Brero 1930**
× taurinum	= Ho King		
INDOYO*	**Felicity × nobile**		**Shimadzu 1929**
× Winter Star	= Miyajima		
INTAN DELIMA	**Anouk × Constance**		**Alsagoff 1965 (M.O.N.)**
× taurinum	= Rita Lim		

ionoglossum‡ **species**

(*ionoglossum* and *toftii**†‡ are treated for registration purposes as specifically distinct from each other, though ranked as conspecific by some authorities within the species *Den. nindii.*)

× Bellflower	= Wei-lin	× Prince Akihito	= Brenda Mowe
× Blue Bonnet	= Blue Pacific	× Princess Sharon	= Flarepath
× Kimi Itagaki	= Cheryl Itagaki	× Theodore Takiguchi	= Lavender Witch
IRENE CHEONG	**Cheong Fook Sum × Lady Fay**		**Cheong Chee Yon 1970**
× Dunhill	= Lakravi	× Johore Beauty	= Laksathuta
× Jaquelyn Concert	= Tay Swee Keng		
ISABEL SANDER‡	**dearei × sanderae**		**S. 1937**
× bellatulum	= White Ibis		
ISAMI DOI	**gouldii × Jaquelyn Thomas**		**Sakamoto 1967 (Otake)**
× taurinum	= Imua		
ISE	**moniliforme × tosaense**		**Dr. H. Nishimura 1972**
× Glace	= Isuzugawa		
ISMAIL TRENGGANU	**Tumphal × schulleri**		**S.B.G. 1965**
× Guadalcanal	= Fiery Gold	× schulleri	= Dusky Gold
ISOCHIDORI	**Red Star × Oborozuki**		**J. Yamamoto 1975**
ISUZUGAWA	**Ise × Glace**		**I. Nishimura 1974**
JAMES DICK	**Hickam Deb × Dee Lynn**		**Fyfe 1973 (Thornton's)**

DENDROBIUM

JANICE TANAKA†‡ — **aries × taurinum** — **R. Tanaka 1949**

× Cathy = Cathy-Jan | × Sunset Hill = Tanya Ito

JAQ-HAWAII — **Neo-Hawaii × Jaquelyn Thomas** — **Mrs. Jack Ching 1967**

× Lim Chong Min = Bodhi Ngern | × Sunset Flush = Lim Chu Ang
× Princess Sharon = Barry Fujimoto | × Valley King = Bodhi Kaew

JAQUELYN CONCERT‡ — **Concert × Jaquelyn Thomas** — **K. Kamemoto 1966**

× Cheong Chee Yon = Dunhill | × Princess Sharon = Dorothy Oka
× Irene Cheong = Tay Swee Keng | × Pupukea Beauty = Concerto
× Nanae = Eileen Foo | × Waikiki Beauty = Singapore
× Pompadour = Hamzy Salman |

JAQUELYN THOMAS†‡ — **gouldii × phalaenopsis** — **R. K. Thomas 1949**

× Alice Spalding = Ng Eng Cheow | × Halawa Beauty = Rayanne Nakamoto
× compactum = Allyn Gem | × Seashore = Seagull
× d'albertisii = Uniwai Profusion | × Yoshie = Lillian Chong

JASON YAMASHITA — **Dale Takiguchi × phalaenopsis** — **Takiguchi 1974**

JEAN TAN — **Helen Khoo × Janice Tanaka** — **Khoo Kay Ann 1962 (A. C. Chang)**

× Caesar = Pearl See-Thoe |

JENNIFER ANNE JANSEN — **Kwa Siew Tee × Peggy Shaw** — **Jansen 1972**

JISOO SANJUME — **Princess Sharon × canaliculatum** — **Perreira 1975**

JOEJAY‡ — **May Neal × toftii** — **J. M. Jay 1956 (Hung Ung Young)**

× Gold Flush = Ahiahi |

johannis‡ — **species**

× Salak = Cape Bedford | × Tangold = Alwyn Hill

JOHN JONES — **Limberlost Beauty × Sybil Jones** — **Limberlost 1975**

JOHORE BEAUTY — **Cheong Fook Sum × Dan O'Brien** — **Cheong Chee Yon 1973**

× Irene Cheong = Laksathuta |

JOMO — **Hula Girl × Lillian Izumo** — **K. Oka 1973**

JON — **New Horizon × bigibbum** — **K. Oka 1971**

JOYCE UEHARA — **Marie Beebe × Rose Chong** — **Uehara 1964 (W. K. Nakamoto)**

× canaliculatum = Mariner's Gold | × Linda = Clarice Fujimoto

JOYCE WEERASEKERA — **Sirimavo Bandaranaike × Lady Constance** — **Quyn 1972 (Weerasekera)**

× Pompadour = Brinsly Quyn |

JUDDHILL†‡ — **Neo-Hawaii × Lady Constance** — **T. Kazumura 1956**

× Betty Hecht = Hearthrob | × Patricia Ward = Michael Sado
× Helen Oka = Contempo | × Vera Patterson = Tawnya Muramoto

JULIET — **Lady Cleo × Fay** — **Kushima 1963**

× Hickam Deb = Kristen Ann | × Lady Hamilton = Roy Bauer

JUNE BENNETT — **New Guinea × williamsianum** — **McFarlane 1972**

KAGUYAHIME — **Oborozuki × Madoromi** — **J. Yamamoto 1971**

KAHULUI RED — **Dark Victory × Glenn Young** — **Furumizo 1974**

KALANAI — **Blue Jay × Tenmujin** — **K. Oka 1971**

× Princess Sharon = Vanguard |

DENDROBIUM

KAM AU — Hickam Deb × Carole Curry — Rod McLellan Co. 1974
KAMERUNGA BEAUTY — Maui Beauty × Ale Ale Kai — Limberlost 1971
KAM HEIGHTS† — Sunda Islands × gouldii — A. C. Chang 1954
× Bluecolor = Blue Hills |

KAMOI — Brown Derby × Liholiho — T. Kazumura 1972
KAMOLVAN — Lily Yang × Spellbound — Kamol 1972 (R. T. Fukumura)

KANEALII — Liholiho × Bronze Queen — T. Kazumura 1972
KANEOHE PRINCESS — Lynn Takiguchi × Lady Fay — Hesse 1974 (Originator unknown)
× Kaneohe Velvet = Helen Hesse |

KANEOHE VELVET — Hula Girl × Mem. Kumajiro Nitta — Hesse 1974 (Originator unknown)
× Kaneohe Princess = Helen Hesse |

KAREN SNIDER — Princess Sharon × May Neal — Perreira 1975
KATHLEEN NAOMI KAGAWA†‡ — Neo-Hawaii × taurinum — H. Kagawa 1954 (T. Kazumura)
× Teri Higa = Christine Harada |

KATHLEEN OKA — Princess Sharon × Vera Patterson — K. Oka 1969
× Steven Ai = Nancy Itagaki |

KATHRYN ITAGAKI — Claire × Steven Ai — Itagaki 1975 (K. Oka)

KATHY ROOKS — Dorado × Dee Lynn — Rooks 1973
KEAHI — Prince Akihito × Meala — T. Kazumura 1972
KEIKI BELLE — Concert × compactum — Perreira 1971
KELLIE TAMASHIRO — Helen Oka × gouldii — K. Oka 1972
KHAW YEONG HONG‡ — Valerie × Lady Hamilton — Khoo Boo Hin 1958 (Kirch)
× American Beauty = Scarlet Flame |

KHEMPUNHYA — Theodore Takiguchi × farmeri — Khempunhya 1975
KIBI — Hawaiian Beauty × Helen Fukumura — Takatsuka 1971
× Impara Beauty = Asahi | × Louis Bleriot = Seto

KILA BLUE — toftii × williamsianum — Limberlost 1967
× phalaenopsis = Hartley's Blue |

KIMI ITAGAKI — Blue Jay × compactum — Itagaki 1975 (K. Oka)
× ionoglossum = Cheryl Itagaki |

kingianum*‡ — species
× gracillimum = Penny Ann |

KING LAKE — Cassiope × Lady Colman — Yonezawa 1975
KIRIL SIEBERT — Yellow Curls × Englan Blue — Lim Swee Aun 1975 (Mrs. Lim Swee Aun)

KITIPORN — Siamese Pretty × formosum — Veerabhongs 1975
KIT MUN — May Neal × T. Shioi — Tan Kit Mun 1970
× Amin = Monawen |

KOBAYASHI‡ — nobile × Merlin — J. Yamamoto 1968
× Agnusbelle = Berimont |

DENDROBIUM

KONAN‡ — **Yamazaki × Kobayashi** — **J. Yamamoto 1968**
× Angel Flower = Console | × Glorious Rainbow = Cherry Glow

KORAT — **phalaenopsis × chrysotoxum** — **Chitpimolwat 1973 (Charanasri)**

KRISTEN ANN — **Juliet × Hickam Deb** — **Levi 1973 (Miyamoto)**

KU-RING-GAI — **tetragonum × delicatum** — **Friend 1971**
KURNYA — **Meta Sari Mustika × stratiotes** — **Kolopaking 1975**
KWA SIEW TEE‡ — **Morgenster × schulleri** — **T.M.A. 1956**
× Lum Goo = Lukitasari | × Peggy Shaw = Jennifer Anne Jansen

LADY CAROLE — **Carole Curry × Lady Hay** — **M. J. Bates 1973**
× Hickam Deb = Sandra Russell

LADY CHARM‡ — **Lady Hamilton × Waikiki Beauty** — **Kushima 1958**
× Busaba = Srisomboon | × Chao Phya River = New Bangkok

LADY COLMAN*†‡ — **findlayanum × The Gem** — **Colman 1909**
× Cassiope = King Lake | × Permos = Geory

LADY CONSTANCE†‡ — **Orchidwood × phalaenopsis** — **Weber 1947**
× Sirimavo Bandaranaike = Joyce Weerasekera

LADY DOROTHY — **Lady Hamilton × Lady Hay** — **H. Y. Young 1965 (Takiguchi)**
× Hawaiian Beauty = Gwen Higgins

LADY FAY†‡ — **Lady Hamilton × Lady Constance** — **M. Yoshimura 1957 (Kushima)**
× Liholiho = Lunalilo | × Pearl = Mem. Emma Van-den-Driesen
× Lynn Takiguchi = Kaneohe Princess |
× Meng Eng = Younghua Lim | × Umphorn = Bertha Weisenbach
× Malee-Kanya = Dimbulah |

LADY HAMILTON†‡ — **Diamond Head Beauty × phalaenopsis** — **Y. Inouye 1953**
× Chao Phya River = Bee Lian Beauty | × Juliet = Roy Bauer
× Claire = Purple Beauty | × Pamela Wheeler = Maud Barfield
× compactum = Midnight Prince | × Paul Iwanaga = Lady Paul
× Hawaiian Beauty = Sangsuriya |

LADY HAY‡ — **Lady Fay × Lady Hamilton** — **Kushima 1960**
× Carole Curry = Lady Carole | × Hickam Deb = Marianne Bates
× Helen Fukumura = Frank Simpson |

LADY LISA — **Geoffrey × Hickam Deb** — **Sainsbury 1975 (George Black)**

LADY PAUL — **Lady Hamilton × Paul Iwanaga** — **L. M. McKenzie 1975 (Mackinney's)**
× bigibbum = Redcliffe Beauty

LADY SMITHERS — **regium × Tamagawa** — **Robertson 1973 (Smithers)**

LAKBIMA — **Purple Wings × Buddy Shepler** — **R. B. G. Peradeniya 1975**
LAKLIYA — **Hoon Cheong San × Buddy Shepler** — **R. B. G. Peradeniya 1975**
LAKMAL — **Buddy Shepler × Cheong Chee Yon** — **R. B. G. Peradeniya 1975**
LAKMALWATTA — **Cheryl Cummins × Cheong Chee Yon** — **R. B. G. Peradeniya 1975**
LAKMINI — **Dunhill × Anouk** — **R. B. G. Peradeniya 1975**

LAKMUTHU — **Ng Eng Cheow × Cheong Chee Yon** — **R. B. G. Peradeniya 1975**
LAKRAN — **Beach Girl × Cheong Chee Yon** — **R. B. G. Peradeniya 1975**
LAKRAVI — **Dunhill × Irene Cheong** — **R. B. G. Peradeniya 1975**
LAKSATHUTA — **Johore Beauty × Irene Cheong** — **R. B. G. Peradeniya 1975**
LATIMODJONG‡ — **Clara Bundt × Sophia Bundt** — **Bundt 1966**

× Clara Bundt = Malino

LAVENDER BEAUTY — **Bailys Blue × williamsianum** — **Limberlost 1966**

× schulleri = Wyn Lobley | × strebloceras = Modish

LAVENDER WITCH — **Theodore Takiguchi × ionoglossum** — **R. K. Mizuta 1975**
LAWRENCE SUZUKI — **Elaine × Vera Patterson** — **L. Suzuki 1974 (K. Oka)**

LEONIE JANE — **adae × falcorostrum** — **Fetherston 1973**
LIHOLIHO‡ — **May Neal × Ethel Kawamoto** — **Fukunaga 1956 (McCoy)**

× Alice Chong = Yellow Stone | × Gold Crest = Nandi
× Bronze Queen = Kanealii | × Lady Fay = Lunalilo
× Brown Derby = Kamoi | × Moonbeam = Robsan
× Charles Tanaka = Golden Giant | × Valley King = Goh Gin Hua
× Concert = Garnet Beauty

LIHOWAII — **Hawaii × Liholiho** — **Shigaki 1970 (Takemoto)**

× Golden Prince = Shigaki Neil

LILA GERA‡ — **Lady Fay × Khaw Yeong Hong** — **Gera 1966**

× Margie Thomas = Edith Howell

LILLIAN CHONG — **Yoshie × Jaquelyn Thomas** — **Takiguchi 1975**
LILLIAN IZUMO‡ — **Takami Kodama × May Neal** — **Uedoi 1955 (Otake)**

× Hula Girl = Jomo

LILY DOO† — **macrophyllum × phalaenopsis** — **D. C. Doo 1950**

× Hickam Deb = Barbara Jardine | × phalaenopsis = Fuang Fah

LILY YANG — **Theodore Takiguchi × Rose Chong** — **Zain 1966 (Fukumura)**

× Spellbound = Kamolvan

LIMBERLOST BEAUTY — **Maui Beauty × Black Mountain** — **Limberlost 1965**

× Sybil Jones = John Jones

LIM CHONG MIN†‡ — **Caesar × phalaenopsis** — **S.B.G. 1951**

× Drake Kubo = Debi Debra | × Theodore Takiguchi = Mermaid
× Jaq-Hawaii = Bodhi Ngern

LIM CHU ANG — **Jaq-Hawaii × Sunset Flush** — **Goh Gin Hwa 1975**
LIME TWIST — **Green Hornet × Golden Boy** — **Norwood 1975 (T. Kazumura)**

LIM TAR FANG‡ — **schulleri × phalaenopsis** — **Lee Kim Hong 1952**

× Cheong Chee Yon = Gordy's Girl

LIM TEE HOOI — **undulatum × strebloceras** — **Lim Swee Aun 1975 (Muir)**

LINDA — **Gold Flush × Emma Enberg** — **Aoki 1964 (Hung Ung Young)**

× Haunani Gay Ho = Charal Mabe | × Valley Gold = Bobbie Aisaka
× Joyce Uehara = Clarice Fujimoto

DENDROBIUM

LINDA JONES	**Maui Beauty × phalaenopsis**		**Limberlost 1965**
× Maui Beauty	= Mount Molloy		
lineale (see *gouldii*†‡)	**species**		
LIPSTICK	**Edythe Pung × Aiko Tengan**		**Matsumoto 1967**
× Mini Girl	= Summit	× Violaceoflush	= Meadie
LIPSTICK MAY	**Beni × May Neal**		**Shigaki 1973**
LITTLE APRIL	**Barbara Ann Bishop × compactum**		**Bishop 1975**
LITTLE DIAMOND	**Diamond Head Beauty × compactum**		**Perreira 1974**
LITTLE ELIZA‡	**Momi Cummins × undulatum**		**A. C. Chang 1958**
× Concert	= Tammy Rita		
LITTLE LULU	**New Horizon × canaliculatum**		**J. Milton Warne 1972**
× Little Profusion	= Starlet Beauty		
LITTLE PROFUSION	**Cheryl Cummins × compactum**		**Perreira 1972 (Herbert Ho)**
× bigibbum	= Vivian Snider	× Little Lulu	= Starlet Beauty
LOBBURI	**Paula Ann × Brown Derby**		**Madhyamachandra 1972 (Rojanavicha)**
LOMPOBATANG	**Anouk × Artur Elle**		**Bundt 1964**
× Pakarena	= Mochtar Lubis		
LOO MEOW LAN	**Caesar × Hula Girl**		**Chow Yee Wah 1971**
LORNA DE FONSEKA	**Maui Beauty × Lorraine Lim**		**Garth 1975**
LORRAINE LIM	**Louis Bleriot × American Beauty**		**Lim Teik Ee 1963 (Charles Lim)**
× Maui Beauty	= Lorna de Fonseka		
LOUISAE*†‡	**schroederanum × veratrifolium**		**Chevalier 1935**
× affine	= Ham Sarjana	× veratrifolium	= Lukito Husodo
× ostrinoglossum	= Gazelle		
LOUIS BLERIOT*†‡	**schroederanum × superbiens**		**V. 1929**
× Chao Phya River	= Yaowamal	× Kibi	= Seto
× Ethel Kawamoto	= Boonroje		
LOUISE HILL	**White Egret × mirbellianum**		**Tom Tucker 1973**
LOWANA BICOLOR	**Hawaii Nui × Pale Face**		**Limberlost 1967**
× Margaret Joan Fell	= Cool Waters		
LUCKY LADY	**Angel Flower × Orion**		**J. Yamamoto 1971**
LUKITASARI	**Kwa Siew Tee × Lum Goo**		**Koh Keng Hoe 1975**
LUKITO HUSODO	**Louisae × veratrifolium**		**Kolopaking 1974**
LUM GOO†‡	**gouldii × stratiotes**		**Goo 1949**
× Kwa Siew Tee	= Lukitasari		
LUNALILO	**Liholiho × Lady Fay**		**Kushima 1973**
LUNAR ECLIPSE	**Black Mountain × Margie Thomas**		**Limberlost 1969**
× Black Mountain	= Midnight Magic		
LUNAR ROSE	**Hickam Deb × Margaret Joan Fell**		**Limberlost 1975**

DENDROBIUM

LYNNE KITSUKI — **Rose Chong × Aiko Tengan** — **R. T. Fukumura 1968**
× Gold Flush = Atakit

LYNN TAKIGUCHI‡ — **Lady Hamilton × Louis Bleriot** — **Takiguchi 1957 (Otake)**
× Lady Fay = Kaneohe Princess

macrophyllum*†‡ — **species**
× Anita = Meta Sari Mustika

MADAME CHULI — **Spellbound × May Neal** — **Rujirawongse 1970 (Jayaratna)**
× May Neal = Madame Uraiwan

MADAME URAIWAN — **Madame Chuli × May Neal** — **T. T. Ploypanich 1975**
MADOROMI — **Thwaitesiae × Sagimusume** — **J. Yamamoto 1971**
× Glonmery = Elves | × Oborozuki = Kaguyahime

MAE-KLONG RIVER — **Srisomboon × Yaowamal** — **Semachai 1975**
MAEMAE — **Alice Chong × Aries Gold** — **T. Kazumura 1972**
MAILAMAI — **Ali Baba × May Neal** — **Mailamai 1975 (Paripoonanonda)**
MAILE — **Goldenhill × Gold Flush** — **T. Kazumura 1972**
MALEE-KANYA‡ — **Amethyst × Louis Bleriot** — **Sagarik 1960**
× Chao Phya River = Diamond King's | × Lady Fay = Dimbulah

MALINO — **Clara Bundt × Latimodjong** — **Bundt 1972**
MALONES — **Akatuki × Glorious Rainbow** — **J. Yamamoto 1973**
MANAD — **Rose Chong × Meala** — **Koh Keng Hoe 1975**
MANDAI CHEER — **Caesar × Tengku Abdul Rahman** — **S'pore Orchids 1972**
MANDAI FORTUNE — **Manon Mocatta × Tengku Abdul Rahman** — **S'pore Orchids 1972**
MANDAI PRIDE — **Old Gold × Tengku Abdul Rahman** — **S'pore Orchids 1972**
MANICHOTE — **Faye × Maui Beauty** — **Intachote 1975**
× Damnern Sadouk = Boonchu | × Srisomboon = Nakornpathom

MANON MOCATTA — **Carol Ann × schulleri** — **S'pore Orchids 1965**
× Tengku Abdul Rahman = Mandai Fortune

MARGARET JOAN FELL — **phalaenopsis × Pale Face** — **Chow Ah Wing 1965**
× Hickam Deb = Lunar Rose | × White Gem = Bright Eyes
× Lowana Bicolor = Cool Waters

MARGIE THOMAS‡ — **Lady Fay × Anouk** — **Lyle Thomas 1961 (Kushima)**
× American Beauty = Pirates Moon | × Dorado = Black Light
× Betty Hecht = Sandra Kurakake | × Elmer Hausermann = Better Times
× Bonnie = Patricia Ward | × Lila Gera = Edith Howell

MARIANNE BATES — **Lady Hay × Hickam Deb** — **M. J. Bates 1973**
MARIMOS — **Permos × Anne Marie** — **J. Yamamoto 1969**
× Bizen = Yayoifuji | × Utopia = Carmen

MARINER'S GOLD — **Joyce Uehara × canaliculatum** — **Hanaoka 1972 (W. K. Nakamoto)**

MARTEN HAUSERMANN — **Tim Tam × Pompadour** — **Hausermann 1968**
× Althea Hausermann = Eric Stromsland

DENDROBIUM

MARY ARIES‡ **Mary Trowse × aries** **T. Kazamura 1965**
× Rose Chong = Mary Rose

MARY KATHERINE†‡ **Pompadour × Lady Constance** **Y. Inouye 1955**
× Vera Patterson = Mecito Solis

MARY NOLA May Neal × **williamsianum** **Bibus 1973 (Kirch)**

MARY ROSE **Rose Chong × Mary Aries** **T. Kazumura 1972**
MATA'AHO **Grace Goo × gouldii** **S.B.G. 1972**
MAUD BARFIELD **Lady Hamilton × Pamela Wheeler** **Coastal Gdns. 1973**
MAUI BEAUTY‡ **Lady Hamilton × Helen Fukumura** **Fukumura 1958**
× Ale Ale Kai = Kamerunga Beauty
× Cho-Cho San = Donald Ira Wijewrdene
× Euroka Beauty = Mem. Paul Harris
× Faye = Manichote
× Frank Simpson = Colin Simpson
× Linda Jones = Mount Molloy
× Lorraine Lim = Lorna de Fonseka
× superbiens = Soh Khong Leng

MAUI CHARM **Lady Fay × Helen Fukumura** **Kushima 1964**
× Crimson Belle = Crimson Charm
× Queen Emma = Hawaiian Charm

MAY NEAL†‡ **Hawaii × schulleri** **O. Kirsch 1949**
× Ali Baba = Mailamai
× Aries Gold = Hinano
× Beni = Lipstick May
× Dhonburi = Sukontha
× Green Valley = Ruveni Weerasekera
× Helen Izuta = Ooi Leng Sun
× Madame Chuli = Madame Uraiwan
× Orange Delight = Neil's Delight
× Pikul = Anocha
× Prince Akihito = Golden Blaze
× Princess Sharon = Karen Snider
× Roy = O'Beattie Shupe
× Sunset Flush = Tunku Naquyuddin
× Valley King = Natee Phon
× williamsianum = Mary Nola

MAYNOUK‡ **Anouk × May Neal** **Miyamoto 1967**
× Misty Green = Betty Ho

MEADIE **Lipstick × Violaceoflush** **McFarlane 1975**
MEALA‡ **Strattokai × schulleri** **Gordon Lee 1956**
× Anom = Menom
× Prince Akihito = Keahi
× Rose Chong = Manad

MECITO SOLIS **Mary Katherine × Vera Patterson** **L. Suzuki 1974 (K. Oka)**

MEGAWATI **Pakarena × Pompadour** **Bundt 1965**
× rumphianum = Udjungpandang

MEI LIN‡ **Guadalcanal × Sunset** **Khoo Kay Ann 1961**
× Peggy Shaw = Anthony Jansen

MELANODISCUS*† **Ainsworthii × findlayanum** **Lawrence 1877**
× Gatton Prince = Zuiko

MELODY OF SPRING **Charm Blossom × Ailing** **J. Yamamoto 1971**
MEMORIA EMMA VAN-DEN-DRIESEN **Pearl × Lady Fay** **Garth 1973**
MEMORIA GEORGE OZMENT **Hickam Deb × Black Light** **Rainbow 1975**
MEMORIA KUMAJIRO NITTA **Clarence Tani × Lady Hamilton** **H. K. Nitta 1970**
× Hula Girl = Kaneohe Velvet

MEMORIA PAT DURUTY **Soh Swee Ying × Sunset Glow** **George Black 1974 (Duruty)**

MEMORIA PAUL HARRIS **Euroka Beauty × Maui Beauty** **R.C.K. 1974 (Garth)**

DENDROBIUM

MEMORIA PROFESSOR KNUDSON — **superbiens × formosum** — **Vajrabhaya 1973**

MEMORIA WALTER SOULÉ‡ — **Maui Beauty × Ewa** — **R. T. Fukumura 1965**
- × Betty Hecht = Sari-Janine

MENG ENG — **Lady Fay × Maui Beauty** — **Lim Swee Aun 1963 (Ooi Teng Kwee)**
- × Lady Fay = Younghua Lim | × Merza Le = Vada Kinsey

MENOM — **Meala × Anom** — **T. Kazumura 1972**

MERCEDES RABAGO — **Lady Fay × Old Wine** — **Rabago 1962 (Kushima)**
- × Crimson Charm = Crimson Bow | × Merza Le = Chew Poh Khim

MERMAID — **Lim Chong Min × Theodore Takiguchi** — **Chaisomboon 1973 (Hornvichai)**
- × formosum = Prapoothabat

MERRY CHRISTMAS — **nobile × Winter Star** — **Yonezawa 1975**
- × Snowflake = Hojun

MERZA LE — **Elaine × Ewa** — **Hawkins 1967 (Fukumura)**
- × Meng Eng = Vada Kinsey | × Mercedes Rabago = Chew Poh Khim

META SARI MUSTIKA — **Anita × macrophyllum** — **Kolopaking 1974**
- × stratiotes = Kurnya | × superbum = Eddy Djaya Remadja

MHAIRI ROBERTSON — **Bartelsianum × Murrhiniacum** — **Robertson 1973**

MICHAEL SADO — **Juddhill × Patricia Ward** — **Larry's 1975 (Teruo Oka)**

MIDNIGHT‡ — **Gracia Lewis × atroviolaceum** — **Woodlawn 1958**
- × canaliculatum = Purple Charm

MIDNIGHT DREAM — **Elaine × Hickam Deb** — **J. & S. 1974**

MIDNIGHT MAGIC — **Black Mountain × Lunar Eclipse** — **Limberlost 1973**

MIDNIGHT PRINCE — **Lady Hamilton × compactum** — **R. K. Mizuta 1972**

MIEKO UEHARA — **Theodore Takiguchi × Dale Takiguchi** — **Takiguchi 1973**

MILDRED KAZUMURA†‡ — **Hawaii × stratiotes** — **T. Kazumura 1949**
- × taurinum = Saleh Alsagoff

MILKY WAY — **Oborozuki × Angel Flower** — **J. Yamamoto 1974**

MINALYNN — **Minapac × Dee Lynn** — **Voo Doo Orchids 1974**

MINAPAC — **minax × compactum** — **Voo Doo Orchids 1974**
- × Dee Lynn = Minalynn

minax — **species**
- × compactum = Minapac

MINI CHARM — **Hawaii × canaliculatum** — **Perreira 1974**

MINI GIRL — **Edythe Pung × Red Breast** — **Matsumoto 1968**
- × Fiftieth State Beauty = Summit Gold | × williamsianum = Halo
- × Lipstick = Summit

MINI PEARL — **canaliculatum × compactum** — **Yagi 1974**

MINORI — **Valamissko × Permissko** — **J. Yamamoto 1975**
- × Akatuki = Odeon

mirbellianum*†‡ — **species**
- × White Egret = Louise Hill

DENDROBIUM

MISAKO — **Rose Yoshida × Ellen Takiguchi** — **Takiguchi 1974**

MISSTOMOPINK‡ — **Kobayashi × Taketane** — **J. Yamamoto 1968**
× Aurora Heart = Hatuharu

MISTY GREEN — **Green Curls × Ethel Kawamoto** — **Miyamoto 1967**
× Maynouk = Betty Ho

MITCHELL SADO — **Shirley Suzuki × Claire** — **L. Suzuki 1973 (K. Oka)**

MIYAJIMA — **Winter Star × Indoyo** — **Yonezawa 1975**
MOCHTAR LUBIS — **Pakarena × Lompobatang** — **Bundt 1971**
MODISH — **strebloceras × Lavender Beauty** — **McFarlane 1975**
MOLLISA — **Chao Phya River × Elaine** — **Loha-Udom 1973**
MOLLY BOND — **superbiens × Ursula** — **Alfred Bond 1971 (K. MacPherson)**

MOMOZONO — **Angel Flower × Glorious Rainbow** — **J. Yamamoto 1972**
MONARAINE — **Brown Derby × gouldii** — **Phoon Yoon Seng 1974**
MONAWEN — **Amin × Kit Mun** — **Phoon Yoon Seng 1974 (Alsagoff)**

MONIKA RENFRO — **Karen Ono × Lady Hay** — **Takiguchi 1965**
× Ellen Takiguchi = Roadrunner

monile (see *moniliforme**‡) — **species**
moniliforme*‡ — **species**
(This is retained as the horticulturally recommended name for registration purposes, even though *Dendrobium monile* is the botanically correct name for this species.)
× tosaense = Ise

MONT BLANC‡ — **Wiganiae × Gatton Beau** — **J. Yamamoto 1968 (Yamaoka)**
× Gatton Prince = White King | × Golden Wave = Golden Eagle

MONTROSE*†‡ — Ainsworthii × Thwaitesiae — **L. 1927**
× nobile = Nobirose

MOONBEAM‡ — **Roy × phalaenopsis** — **Perreira 1969 (Otake)**
× Bronze Queen = Florence Sukita | × Liholiho = Robsan

MOTOR MOUTH — **phalaenopsis × Barbara Ann Bishop** — **Bishop 1975**
MOUNT FUJI — **Sagimusume × Berimont** — **J. Yamamoto 1973**
MOUNT MOLLOY — **Maui Beauty × Linda Jones** — **Limberlost 1971**
MURRHINIACUM* — **nobile × wardianum** — R. H. Measures 1888
× Bartelsianum = Mhairi Robertson

MUSTARD‡ — **Ursula × Champagne** — **S.B.G. 1956**
× Noor Aishah = Elizabeth

MYOJO — **Glorious Rainbow × Zakimos** — **J. Yamamoto 1971**
× Charm Star = Sunshine

NAKORNPATHOM — **Srisomboon × Manichote** — **Semachai 1975**
NANAE — **Theodore Takiguchi × Neo-Hawaii** — **K. Oka 1965**
× Jaquelyn Concert = Eileen Foo

NANCY ITAGAKI — **Kathleen Oka × Steven Ai** — **Itagaki 1975 (K. Oka)**

NANDI — **Gold Crest × Liholiho** — **K. Oka 1972**

× Roberta = Baja

NANETTE LEILANI TODD†‡ — **gouldii × Louis Bleriot** — **Joseph 1952**

× Bronze Queen = Ilima

NATEE PHON — **Valley King × May Neal** — **Leelasiri 1972**

NEIL'S DELIGHT — **May Neal × Orange Delight** — **Shigaki 1975**

NELL HOADLEY — **American Beauty × Dale Takiguchi** — **George Black 1974 (Hoadley)**

NELLIE SLADE‡ — **atroviolaceum × forbesii** — **Persson & Slade 1958**

× rhodostictum = Gwen Slade

NEW BANGKOK — **Lady Charm × Chao Phya River** — **Mrs. T. Rosjanavichai 1973**

NEW GUINEA†‡ — **macrophyllum × atroviolaceum** — **Y. Inouye 1956**

× williamsianum = June Bennett

NEW HORIZON — **canaliculatum × Joanne Sawyers** — **G. B. Miwa 1958**

× bigibbum = Jon
× canaliculatum = Little Lulu

NG ENG CHEOW — **Alice Spalding × Jaquelyn Thomas** — **Koh Keng Hoe 1973**

× Cheong Chee Yon = Lakmuthu

NICOLE DE VERTEUIL — **Sunset Hill × Carol Ann** — **George Black 1974**

nindii (see *ionoglossum*‡ and *toftii**†‡) — **species**

nobile*†‡ — **species**

× Anne Marie = Dancing Waters
× Duo = Happy Red
× Montrose = Nobirose
× Winter Star = Merry Christmas

NOBIROSE — **Montrose × nobile** — **J. Yamamoto 1971**

× Valadeva = Evening Glow

NOEL — **Golden Bell × Golden Queen** — **R. K. Mizuta 1975**

NOEL'S COMPACT — **Black Moon × phalaenopsis** — **N. E. Noble 1973**

NOEL'S ULTIMATE — **Sybil Jones × Black Moon** — **N. E. Noble 1973**

NOOR AISHAH‡ — **capra × Champagne** — **S.B.G. 1961**

× Constance = Evelyn Foo
× Harlequin = Sarasvathi Giri
× Mustard = Elizabeth
× Peggy Shaw = Rahah
× schulleri = Tien Soeharto

NUUANU — **Shibata × Aina Haina** — **Yoshida 1972**

O'BEATTIE SHUPE — **May Neal × Roy** — **Perreira 1975**

OBOROZUKI — **Aurora Heart × September Moon** — **J. Yamamoto 1969**

× Angel Flower = Milky Way
× Aurora Heart = Bright Star
× Evening Glow = Oriental Paradise
× Glorious Rainbow = Otohime
× Golden Talisman = Hambühren Gold
× Hatuharu = Yodogimi
× Hermont = Yumeji
× Madoromi = Kaguyahime
× Orion = Star Carnival
× Red Star = Isochidori

ODEON — **Minori × Akatuki** — **J. Yamamoto 1975**

OOI LENG SUN — **Helen Izuta × May Neal** — **Ooi Leng Sun 1973**

OLD GOLD — **Curlylocks × Ash Brown** — **S'pore Orchids 1963**

× Tengku Abdul Rahman = Mandai Pride

OLIVE†‡ — **schulleri × mirbellianum** — **O. Kirsch 1955**

× Salome = Chang Ah Song

OLYMPIA — **Andemos × Glorious Rainbow** — **J. Yamamoto 1975**

DENDROBIUM

ONG GEOK KHIM	**Neo-Hawaii × mirbellianum**		**Wong 1969**
× Rose Chong	= Tham Choy Yin		
OOI GUAT IM	**Alice Chong × Rose Chong**		**Ooi Boon Huat 1971 (Ooi Leng Sun)**
ORANGE BLOSSOM	**Golden Wave × Dream**		**J. Yamamoto 1971**
ORANGE DELIGHT	**Winifred Morley × Goldenhill**		**Shigaki 1970 (Hung Ung Young)**
× May Neal	= Neil's Delight		
ORIENTAL PARADISE	**Evening Glow × Oborozuki**		**J. Yamamoto 1971**
ORIHIME	**Orion × Permissko**		**J. Yamamoto 1971**
ORION	**Permos × Valamissko**		**J. Yamamoto 1968**
× Ailing	= Sao Paulo	× Glorious Rainbow	= Utopia
× Angel Flower	= Lucky Lady	× Oborozuki	= Star Carnival
× Aurora Heart	= Shinonome	× Permissko	= Orihime
× Evening Glow	= Reimei	× Utopia	= Oritopia
ORITOPIA	**Orion × Utopia**		**J. Yamamoto 1975**
ostrinoglossum‡	**species**		
× Herbert Ong	= Sirima Bandaranaike	× schulleri	= Amin
× Louisae	= Gazelle	× Taurus	= Red Antlers
× Pauline	= Bougainville Beauty	× Tumphal	= Dzemal Bijedic
OTOHIME	**Oborozuki × Glorious Rainbow**		**J. Yamamoto 1972**
PAINTED DOLL	**Judy Leroy × phalaenopsis**		**Limberlost 1966**
× phalaenopsis	= Startling		
PAKARENA‡	**Simson × Lynn Takiguchi**		**Bundt 1964**
× Ibu Paula Siwabessy	= We Bungawaliè	× schulleri	= Halimah Mochtar Lubis
× Lompobatang	= Mochtar Lubis		
PALE FACE‡	**Lim Chong Min × phalaenopsis**		**S.B.G. 1958**
× Caesar	= Tinaroo Falls	× Crystal Cascades	= Sand Cay
PAMELA WHEELER‡	**Lady Nui × Lady Hamilton**		**Toogood 1962 (Kirch)**
× Lady Hamilton	= Maud Barfield		
PANDA	**Hatuyuki × Pinocchio**		**J. Yamamoto 1975**
PATRICIA WARD	**Bonnie × Margie Thomas**		**K. Oka 1971**
× Juddhill	= Michael Sado		
PAULA ANN‡	**Caesar × Anouk**		**Okubo 1954**
× Brown Derby	= Lobburi		
PAULINE†‡ (syn. Puppchen)	**phalaenopsis × undulatum**		**L. 1932**
× ostrinoglossum	= Bougainville Beauty		
PAUL IWANAGA	**Anouk × Ann**		**Kirch 1969**
× Lady Hamilton	= Lady Paul		
PAUL SUZUKI	**Vera Patterson × Claire**		**L. Suzuki 1974 (K. Oka)**
PEACE	**Perning × Akatuki**		**J. Yamamoto 1975**
PEARL†	**Owen × Hawaii Nui**		**Takiguchi 1959 (Otake)**
× Lady Fay	= Mem. Emma Van-den-Driesen		

PEARL OF SIAM — **Siam × phalaenopsis** — **Thongbai Rojanavichai 1973 (Tanad Rojanavichai)**

PEARL SEE-THOE — **Jean Tan × Caesar** — **Koh Keng Hoe 1975**

PEARL YAGI — **compactum × Betty Hecht** — **Yagi 1974 (Tomiyasu)**

PEARLY SNOW — **Walter Oumae × canaliculatum** — **R. K. Mizuta 1975**

PEE OH — **superbiens × Halawa Beauty** — **Vajrabhaya 1975**

PEGGY SHAW — **Lava × Lim Chong Min** — **Braga 1964**

× Kwa Siew Tee = Jennifer Anne Jansen
× Mei Lin = Anthony Jansen
× Noor Aishah = Rahah

PENNY ANN — **gracillimum × kingianum** — **W. T. Upton 1974**

PERFECTION*‡ — **Euryalus × nobile** — **Colman 1913**

× Fort Noble = Tammany

PERMISSKO‡ — **Permos × Kobayashi** — **J. Yamamoto 1968**

× Glorious Rainbow = Red Fairy
× Orion = Orihime
× Valamissko = Minori

PERMOS‡ — **Permer × Valadeva** — **J. Yamamoto 1968 (Hiroyuki Yamamoto)**

× Evening Glow = Perning
× Lady Colman = Geory
× Sakuragari = Saotome

PERNING — **Permos × Evening Glow** — **J. Yamamoto 1975**

× Akatuki = Peace

PETER — **fleckeri × falcorostrum** — **Bedford 1972**

PETER HOADLEY — **Golden Derby × Sunset Glow** — **George Black 1974 (Hoadley)**

phalaenopsis*†‡ (syn. *schroederanum**†) — **species**

× Barbara Ann Bishop = Motor Mouth
× Black Moon = Noel's Compact
× chrysotoxum = Korat
× Dale Takiguchi = Jason Yamashita
× Dalliance = Fond Lover
× Doreen = Anna Bibus
× formosum = Achara
× Kila Blue = Hartley's Blue
× Lily Doo = Fuang Fah
× Painted Doll = Startling
× Siam = Pearl of Siam
× Troy Mikami = Atsushi
× Waipahu = Yukiko

PHYLLIS‡ — **violaceo-flavens × superbiens** — **S.B.G. 1949**

× Blue Beauty = Fiona Dunlop

PHYLLIS CHONG — **Darcie Mikami × Akemi** — **Takiguchi 1975**

PIKUL‡ — **Indonesia × schulleri** — **Tancharoen 1959**

× May Neal = Anocha

PINOCCHIO — **Ainsworthii × Agnusbelle** — **J. Yamamoto 1973**

× Cassiope = Fubuki
× Hatuyuki = Panda
× Red Star = Santa Claus
× Shiranami = Yukidaruma
× Valamissko = Swallow

PIRATES MOON — **American Beauty × Margie Thomas** — **Bolt 1975 (A. & M.)**

PIXIE NANI — **Golden Pixie × Haunani Gay Ho** — **Shigaki 1975 (Miyamoto)**

POLESTAR — **Glorious Rainbow × Fujimusume** — **J. Yamamoto 1975**

POMPADOUR*†‡ — **Louis Bleriot × phalaenopsis** — **V. 1934**

× Jaquelyn Concert = Hamzy Salman
× Joyce Weerasekera = Brinsly Quyn

DENDROBIUM

Hybrid	Parentage	Registrant
PRANEET	**superbiens × Ruth Thomas**	**Juanyen 1974**
PRAPOOTHABAT	**Mermaid × formosum**	**Keesa-nga 1975 (Panthong)**
PRINCE AKIHITO‡	**gouldii × May Neal**	**R. Tanaka 1953**

×	=	×	=
× ionoglossum	= Brenda Mowe	× Meala	= Keahi
× May Neal	= Golden Blaze	× Taurus	= Chocolate Gold

Hybrid	Parentage	Registrant
PRINCESS APRIL	**Hickam Deb × Barbara Ann Bishop**	**Bishop 1975**
PRINCESS SHARON‡	**Lady Hamilton × Momi Cummins**	**Hudson 1966 (Edward Wong)**

×	=	×	=
× canaliculatum	= Jisoo Sanjume	× Kalanai	= Vanguard
× gouldii	= Edwin Oka	× May Neal	= Karen Snider
× ionoglossum	= Flarepath	× Steven Ai	= Humie Tanaka
× Jaq-Hawaii	= Barry Fujimoto	× Tenmujin	= Dorothy Joyce
× Jaquelyn Concert	= Dorothy Oka	× undulatum	= Alpenglow

Hybrid	Parentage	Registrant
PROFUSION	**phalaenopsis × ionoglossum**	**Woodlawn 1968 (E. Iwanaga)**

× Tomie = Tiny Mitchell

pulchellum*†‡ (syn. *dalhousieanum*†*) **species**

× C. K. Ai = Bangkok Yellow

PUPPCHEN (see Pauline†‡)

Hybrid	Parentage	Registrant
PUPUKEA BEAUTY	**Lady Cleo × Ewa**	**Kushima 1966**

× Jaquelyn Concert = Concerto

Hybrid	Parentage	Registrant
PURPLE BEAUTY	**Claire × Lady Hamilton**	**R. K. Mizuta 1975**
PURPLE CHARM	**Midnight × canaliculatum**	**R. K. Mizuta 1973**
PURPLE WINGS	**Joanne Sawers × Pompadour**	**R. B. G. Peradeniya 1961**

× Buddy Shepler = Lakbima

Hybrid	Parentage	Registrant
QUEEN EMMA‡	**Ewa × Lady Fay**	**Kushima 1964**

× Maui Charm = Hawaiian Charm

Hybrid	Parentage	Registrant
RAHAH	**Noor Aishah × Peggy Shaw**	**S.B.G. 1974**
RANI‡	**Prince Akihito × Cluny**	**Khoo Kay Ann 1962**

× williamsianum = Rouna Blue

Hybrid	Parentage	Registrant
RAYANNE NAKAMOTO	**Halawa Beauty × Jaquelyn Thomas**	**Takiguchi 1974**
RED ANTLERS	**Taurus × ostrinoglossum**	**Limberlost 1973**
REDCLIFFE BEAUTY	**Lady Paul × bigibbum**	**L. M. McKenzie 1975**
RED FAIRY	**Permissko × Glorious Rainbow**	**J. Yamamoto 1971**
RED STAR	**Zakimos × Morning Hill**	**J. Yamamoto 1970**

×	=	×	=
× Ailing	= Christmas Chime	× Glorious Rainbow	= Spring Wind
× Akatuki	= Damsel	× Oborozuki	= Isochidori
× Anglow	= White Pony	× Pinocchio	= Santa Claus
× Anne Marie	= Baron		

regium*‡ **species**

× Tamagawa = Lady Smithers

Hybrid	Parentage	Registrant
REIMEI	**Evening Glow × Orion**	**J. Yamamoto 1972**
RENEE NAKAMOTO	**Waipahu × Theodore Takiguchi**	**Takiguchi 1974**
rhodostictum‡	**species**	

× Nellie Slade = Gwen Slade

DENDROBIUM

RICKIE CORNETTI veratrifolium × toftii W. W. G. Moir 1955

× stratiotes = Thelma Keith

RITA LIM Intan Delima × taurinum Rodney Lim 1975 (Alsagoff)

RITSUKO TAKIGUCHI Yoshie × Tomie Takiguchi 1974

ROADRUNNER Monika Renfro × Ellen Takiguchi Bishop 1973 (Originator unknown)

× Anouk = Barbara Ann Bishop

ROBERTA Goldenhill × May Neal Robt. Oka 1966 (Tomiyasu)

× Nandi = Baja

ROBSAN Moonbeam × Liholiho Perreira 1973

ROSE CHONG†‡ May Neal × Janice Tanaka A. J. S. Chong 1954 (T. Kazumura)

× Alice Chong = Ooi Guat Im
× Mary Aries = Mary Rose
× Meala = Manad
× Ong Geok Khim = Tham Choy Yin

ROSEMARY JUPP striolatum × teretifolium V. & N. Jupp 1975

ROSE YOSHIDA‡ Lady Fay × Ellen Takiguchi Takiguchi 1965

× Ellen Takiguchi = Misako

ROUNA BLUE Rani × williamsianum Limberlost 1972

ROY‡ May Neal × Aina Haina A. C. Chang 1957

× May Neal = O'Beattie Shupe

ROYAL SNOW Bluecolor × williamsianum Limberlost 1971

ROY BAUER Juliet × Lady Hamilton Kushima 1973

rumphianum species

× Megawati = Udjungpandang

RUSSELL HEADS Takami Kodama × toftii Limberlost 1973 (Originator unknown)

× Salak = Bone Gold

RUTH THOMAS† schroderanum × schulleri R. K. Thomas 1950

× superbiens = Praneet

RUVENI WEERASEKERA Green Valley × May Neal Weerasakera 1972

SAGIMONY Sagimusume × Kobayashi J. Yamamoto 1969

× Agnusbelle = Hatuyuki
× Happiness = Angel Wings
× Sagimusume = Shiranami
× Shiranami = Cupid

SAGIMUSUME‡ Kaga × Agnus J. Yamamoto 1968 (K. Gotoh)

× Agnusbelle = Yukimusume
× Berimont = Mount Fuji
× Sagimony = Shiranami
× Thwaitesiae = Madoromi
× White Pearl = Hagoromo
× Yukimusume = Sasameyuki

SAKURAGARI Kaga × Gatton Belle J. Yamamoto 1968 (K. Gotoh)

× Permos = Saotome

SALAK†‡ stratiotes × undulatum Nagrok (Pre-1946)

× johannis = Cape Bedford
× Russell Heads = Bone Gold
× vestigiiferum = Ann Newton

DENDROBIUM

SALEH ALSAGOFF	Mildred Kazumura × taurinum	Alsagoff 1975
SALOME†	**Diamond Head Beauty × Louis Bleriot**	**Y. Inouye 1955**
× Olive	= Chang Ah Song	
SAND CAY	**Crystal Cascades × Pale Face**	**Limberlost 1975**
SANDRA KURAKAKE	**Margie Thomas × Betty Hecht**	**K. Oka 1971**
SANDRA RUSSELL	**Lady Carole × Hickam Deb**	**M. J. Bates 1973**
SANDY AHU	**Betty Hecht × Bonnie**	**Itagaki 1975** (Teruo Oka)
SANGSURIYA	**Lady Hamilton × Hawaiian Beauty**	**Madhyamachandra 1973**
× Siamese Pretty	= Duang Tawan	
SANTA CLAUS	**Red Star × Pinocchio**	**J. Yamamoto 1975**
SAO PAULO	**Ailing × Orion**	**J. Yamamoto 1972**
SAOTOME	**Permos × Sakuragari**	**J. Yamamoto 1972**
SARASVATHI GIRI	**Harlequin × Noor Aishah**	**S.B.G. 1972**
SARI-JANINE	**Mem. Walter Soulé × Betty Hecht**	**R. T. Fukumura 1975**
SASAMEYUKI	**Sagimusume × Yukimusume**	**J. Yamamoto 1975**
SCARLET FLAME	**American Beauty × Khaw Yeong Hong**	**Chaisomboon 1973**
schroederanum*† (see *phalaenopsis**†‡)	**species**	
schulleri†‡	**species**	

× Bangkhen	= Haruko	× Noor Aishah	= Tien Soeharto
× Beach Girl	= Sunny	× ostrinoglossum	= Amin
× Ismail Trengganu	= Dusky Gold	× Pakarena	= Halimah Mochtar Lubis
× Lavender Beauty	= Wyn Lobley		

SEAGULL	**Seashore × Jaquelyn Thomas**	**Kushima 1975**
SEAN OSHIRO	**Dale Takiguchi × Tomie**	**Takiguchi 1974**
SEASHORE	**Pearly Shells × phalaenopsis**	**Kushima 1967**
× Jaquelyn Thomas	= Seagull	
SEPIK BLUE	**Blue Toro × stratiotes**	**Limberlost 1971**
SETO	**Kibi × Louis Bleriot**	**Takatsuka 1973**
× Asahi	= Akane	
SHELLEY MAURINE THOMAS	**Margie Thomas × Hickam Deb**	**Lyle Thomas 1966**
× Elaine	= West Indian	
SHELLI‡	**Lady Ess × Lady Fay**	**Marugami 1965 (Kushima)**
× Elaine	= Yuriko	
SHEPHERD'S DELIGHT	**Carol Ann × bigibbum**	**S'pore Orchids 1964**
× Ursula	= Sim Kimhorn	
SHIBATA†‡	**taurinum × tokai**	**R. Tanaka 1947**
× Aina Haina	= Nuuanu	× Cathy-Jan = Frances Walter
SHIGAKI NEIL	Lihowaii × Golden Prince	**Shigaki 1975**
SHINONOME	**Aurora Heart × Orion**	**J. Yamamoto 1975**
SHIRANAMI	**Sagimusume × Sagimony**	**J. Yamamoto 1972**
× Pinocchio	= Yukidaruma	× Sagimony = Cupid
SHIRLEY SUZUKI	**Helen Oka × Elaine**	L. Suzuki 1973 **(K. Oka)**
× Claire	= Mitchell Sado	

SIAM‡ — **Paula Ann × May Neal** — **Siriswadi 1967**
× phalaenopsis = Pearl of Siam

SIAMESE PRETTY — **Bangkok Star × Kasetsart** — **Panjup 1967**
× formosum = Kitiporn | × Sangsuriya = Duang Tawan

SIDABUTAR — **affine × veratrifolium** — **Kolopaking 1974**
SIM KIMHORN — **Ursula × Shepherd's Delight** — **Kimhorn 1972**
SINGAPORE — **Jaquelyn Concert × Waikiki Beauty** — **George Chan 1972**
SIRIMA BANDARANAIKE — **Herbert Ong × ostrinoglossum** — **S.B.G. 1971**
SIRIMAVO BANDARANAIKE — **Helen Fukumura × Waikiki Beauty** — **Quyn 1972 (Weerasekera)**
× Lady Constance = Joyce Weerasekera

SNOWDRIFT‡ — **Caesar × johnsoniae** — **W. W. G. Moir 1963**
× formosum = Snow Queen

SNOW ELF — **Theodore Takiguchi × gouldii** — **R. K. Mizuta 1975**
SNOWFLAKE* — **Cassiope × nobile** — **Colman 1904**
× Merry Christmas = Hojun

SNOW QUEEN — **Snowdrift × formosum** — **McFarlane 1971**
SOH KHONG LENG — **superbiens × Maui Beauty** — **Adam 1975**
SOH SEW ENG — **Valley King × Doreen** — **Teoh Seng Aun 1973 (Ooi Leng Sun)**
SOH SWEE YING — **May Neal × ostrinoglossum** — **Tham Tuck Onn 1964 (Kirch)**
× Sunset Glow = Mem. Pat Duruty

SOMTHAWIL — **Caesar × Bangkhen** — **P. Chuanyen 1975**
SPELLBOUND‡ — **Valley King × Pakanu** — **K. Kamemoto 1968 (W. K. Nakamoto)**
× Lily Yang = Kamolvan

SPRING WIND — **Glorious Rainbow × Red Star** — **J. Yamamoto 1975**
SRISOMBOON — **Lady Charm × Busaba** — **Sinsook 1973**
× Manichote = Nakornpathom | × Yaowamal = Mae-Klong River

STAR CARNIVAL — **Orion × Oborozuki** — **J. Yamamoto 1973**
STARLET BEAUTY — **Little Lulu × Little Profusion** — **Perreira 1972**
STARTLING — **Painted Doll × phalaenopsis** — **Limberlost 1971**
STAR OF GOLD — **falcorostrum × tetragonum** — **V. & N. Jupp 1973**
STEPHEN MATATICS — **Tammy Wakasugi × Bertha Weisenbach** — **Matatics 1972**
STEVEN AI — **Jaquelyn Thomas × Hula Girl** — **Ai 1956 (Miyamoto)**
× Claire = Kathryn Itagaki | × Kathleen Oka = Nancy Itagaki
× Dark Crown = Blaze | × Princess Sharon = Humie Tanaka
× Deann Oi = Hisako Oka

stratiotes*†‡ — **species**
× Blue Toro = Sepik Blue | × Rickie Cornetti = Thelma Keith
× Meta Sari Mustika = Kurnya

strebloceras*‡ — **species**
× canaliculatum = Autumn Lace | × Lavender Beauty = Modish
× Fiftieth State = Flair | × undulatum = Lim Tee Hooi

striolatum **species**
× teretifolium = Rosemary Jupp |

SUEO SAKAMOTO **Elaine × compactum** **Hager 1974 (Tomiyasu)**

SUKONTHA **Dhonburi × May Neal** **Srisangkaew 1971**
SUMMIT **Mini Girl × Lipstick** **McFarlane 1975**
SUMMIT GOLD **Mini Girl × Fiftieth State Beauty** **McFarlane 1975**
SUNNY **Beach Girl × schulleri** **S.F.E.S. 1975**
SUNRISE **June Bride × Thwaitesiae** **W. W. G. Moir 1963**
× Hercules = Elli Karsten |

SUNSET FLUSH **Gold Flush × May Neal** **Matsumoto 1961**
× Jaq-Hawaii = Lim Chu Ang | × May Neal = Tunku Naquyuddin

SUNSET GLOW **Brown Derby × schulleri** **T. Kazumura 1967**
× Golden Derby = Peter Hoadley | × Soh Swee Ying = Mem. Pat Duruty

SUNSET HILL **Gloucester Crimson × schulleri** **T. Kazumura 1967**
× Carol Ann = Nicole De Verteuil | × Janice Tanaka = Tanya Ito

SUNSHINE **Myojo × Charm Star** **J. Yamamoto 1975**
SUN SPRITE **gracillimum × delicatum** **V. & N. Jupp 1975**
superbiens*†‡ (syn. *goldiei*) **species**
× formosum = Mem. Professor Knudson | × Maui Beauty = Soh Khong Leng
| × Ruth Thomas = Praneet
× Halawa Beauty = Pee Oh | × Ursula = Molly Bond

superbum*†‡ **species**
(This is retained as the horticulturally recommended name, for registration purposes, even though *anosmum* is the botanically correct name for this species.)
× Meta Sari Mustika = Eddy Djaya Remadja |

SURISI **Chao Phya River × Hawaiian Beauty** **Madhyamachandra 1973**
SURPRISE **Thwaitesiae × Tamagawa** **R. K. Mizuto 1964**
× Forty Niner = Edsa Loo |

SWALLOW **Valamissko × Pinocchio** **J. Yamamoto 1973**
SYBIL JONES **Black Mountain × Hickam Deb** **Limberlost 1969**
× Black Moon = Noel's Ultimate | × Limberlost Beauty = John Jones
× Impara Beauty = Warpaint |

TAKAMI KODAMA† **Taurus × taurinum** **Kodama 1949**
× toftii = Russell Heads |

TAMAGAWA†‡ **Cybele × Lady Colman** **G. B. Miwa 1949**
× regium = Lady Smithers |

TAMMANY **Fort Noble × Perfection** **W. W. Wilson 1975**
TAMMY RITA **Concert × Little Eliza** **Tellio 1972 (Matsumoto)**

TAMMY WAKASUGI **Margie Thomas × Lady Carmen** **Wakasugi 1966**
× Bertha Weisenbach = Stephen Matatics |

TANGOLD‡ **Pauline × Constance** **Limberlost 1962 (Tan Chee Seng)**
× johannis = Alwyn Hill |

TANYA ITO — **Sunset Hill × Janice Tanaka** — **H. Ito 1972 (R. T. Fukumura)**

taurinum*†‡ — **species**

× Alice Chong	= Ching Chee	× Isami Doi	= Imua
× Indonesia	= Ho King	× Mildred Kazumura	= Saleh Alsagoff
× Intan Delima	= Rita Lim		

TAURUS*†‡ — **taurinum × undulatum** — **Ellen Williams 1941**

× ostrinoglossum	= Red Antlers	× Prince Akihito	= Chocolate Gold

TAWNYA MURAMOTO — **Vera Patterson × Juddhill** — **Kaneshiro 1975 (Teruo Oka)**

TAY SWEE KENG — **Jaquelyn Concert × Irene Cheong** — **Koh Keng Hoe 1975**

TENGKU ABDUL RAHMAN‡ — **Hawaiian Beauty × Ale Ale Kai** — **Tie 1963**

× Caesar	= Mandai Cheer	× Old Gold	= Mandai Pride
× Manon Mocatta	= Mandai Fortune		

TENMUJIN — **Alice Chong × stratiotes** — **K. Oka 1970**

× Blue Jay	= Kalanai	× Vera Patterson	= Fire Ball
× Princess Sharon	= Dorothy Joyce		

teretifolium‡ — **species**

× striolatum	= Rosemary Jupp		

TERI HIGA — **Blue Jay × phalaenopsis** — **Higa 1969 (K. Oka)**

× Kathleen Naomi Kagawa	= Christine Harada		

tetragonum*‡ — **species**

× delicatum	= Ku-Ring-Gai	× falcorostrum	= Star of Gold

THAM CHOY YIN — **Ong Geok Khim × Rose Chong** — **C. Y. Mok 1973**

THELMA KEITH — **Rickie Cornetti × stratiotes** — **Keith 1971 (Burleigh Pk.)**

THEODORE TAKIGUCHI*†‡ — **Valley King × phalaenopsis** — **Takiguchi 1957 (T. Enomoto)**

× Dale Takiguchi	= Mieko Uehara	× ionoglossum	= Lavender Witch
× Elaine	= Tunku Irinah	× Lim Chong Min	= Mermaid
× farmeri	= Khempunhya	× Waipahu	= Renee Nakamoto
× gouldii	= Snow Elf		

THWAITESIAE*†‡ — **Ainsworthii × Wiganiae** — **Thwaites 1903**

× Glace	= Golden Dream	× Sagimusume	= Madoromi

thyrsiflorum* — **species**

(This is retained as the horticulturally recommended name for registration purposes, even though *Dendrobium densiflorum* is the botanically correct name for this species.)

× farmeri	= farmeri-thyrsiflorum (Nat. hyb.) / Farmeri-thyrsiflorum (Reg'd. grex)		

TIEN SOEHARTO — **Noor Aishah × schulleri** — **S.B.G. 1974**

TINAROO FALLS — **Pale Face × Caesar** — **Limberlost 1971**

TINY MITCHELL — **Tomie × Profusion** — **L. Suzuki 1974 (Perreira)**

toftii*†‡ — **species**

(*toftii* and *ionoglossum*‡ are treated for registration purposes as specifically distinct from each other though ranked as conspecific by some authorities within the species *Den. nindii.*)

× Takami Kodama = Russell Heads

TOMIE‡ — **Theodore Takiguchi × Jaquelyn Thomas** — **Takiguchi 1960**

× Dale Takiguchi = Sean Oshiro | × Profusion = Tiny Mitchell
× Darcie Mikami = Alma Chong | × Yoshie = Ritsuko Takiguchi

TOM JUPP — **delicatum × Andrew Persson** — **V. & N. Jupp 1974**

TONI AHU — **Chios × bigibbum** — **Itagaki 1975 (K. Oka)**

tosaense — **species**

× moniliforme = Ise

TROY MIKAMI — **Dale Takiguchi × Jaquelyn Thomas** — Takiguchi 1970

× phalaenopsis = Atsushi

TUMPHAL†‡ — **Indonesia × phalaenopsis** — **S.B.G. 1957**

× ostrinoglossum = Dzemal Bijedic

TUNKU IRINAH — **Theodore Takiguchi × Elaine** — **Trevor 1974 (Lum Choon)**

TUNKU NAJIHAH — **veratrifolium × Helen Fukumura** — **Trevor 1973 (Lum Chin)**

TUNKU NAQUYUDDIN — **May Neal × Sunset Flush** — **Trevor 1974 (Lum Choon)**

UDJUNGPANDANG — **Megawati × rumphianum** — **Bundt 1973**

ULTIMATUM — **Sensation × Maui Beauty** — **McFarlane 1970**

× Impact = Approval

UMPHORN‡ — **Cleopatra × Lady Constance** — **Vichiencharoen 1961**

× Lady Fay = Bertha Weisenbach

undulatum*†‡ — **species**

(This is retained as the horticulturally recommended name for registration purposes even though *discolor* is the botanically correct name for this species.)

× bifalce = Gold Stripe | × Princess Sharon = Alpenglow
× Fiftieth State = Copperfield | × strebloceras = Lim Tee Hooi

UNIWAI PROFUSION — **Jaquelyn Thomas × d'albertisii** — **U. of H. 1974**

URSULA†‡ — **undulatum × veratrifolium** — **S.B.G. —**

× Shepherd's Delight = Sim Kimhorn | × superbiens = Molly Bond

UTOPIA — Glorious **Rainbow × Orion** — **J. Yamamoto 1971**

× Marimos = Carmen | × Orion = Oritopia

VADA KINSEY — **Merza Le × Meng Eng** — **Hawkins 1974**

VALADEMOS‡ — **Valadeva × Permos** — **J. Yamamoto 1968**

× Anne Marie = Andemos

VALADEVA‡ — **Merlin × Lady Colman** — Peter Smithers 1959 **(M. & H.)**

× Nobirose = Evening Glow

VALAMISSKO‡ — **Kobayashi × Valadeva** — **J. Yamamoto 1968**

× Ainsmerlin = Charm Blossom | × Pinocchio = Swallow
× Permissko = Minori

VALLEY GOLD — **May Neal × Manoa Gold** — **K. Kamemoto 1967**

× Linda = Bobbie Aisaka

VALLEY KING†‡ — **Mildred Kazumura × phalaenopsis** — **T. Kazumura 1953**

× Doreen = Soh Sew Eng
× Jaq-Hawaii = Bodhi Kaew
× Liholiho = Goh Gin Hua
× May Neal = Natee Phon
× violaceo-flavens = Chic

VANGUARD — **Princess Sharon × Kalanai** — **Teruo Oka 1974**

VERA PATTERSON‡ — **Anouk × Norvelle Gillespie** — **Sakamoto 1958 (Miyata)**

× Claire = Paul Suzuki
× Elaine = Lawrence Suzuki
× Juddhill = Tawnya Muramoto
× Mary Katherine = Mecito Solis
× Tenmujin = Fire Ball

veratrifolium*†‡ — **species**

(This and *Den. gouldii* are treated for registration purposes as specifically distinct though ranked as conspecific by some authorities.)

× affine = Sidabutar
× Helen Fukumura = Tunku Najihah
× Louisae = Lukito Husodo

VERNINHA‡ — **undulatum × d'albertisii** — **McAdam 1961 (Muir)**

× Gold Flush = Canary Gold

vestigiiferum‡ — **species**

× Salak = Ann Newton

violaceo-flavens*†‡ — **species**

× Gold Flush = Violaceoflush
× Valley King = Chic

VIOLACEOFLUSH — **violaceo-flavens × Gold Flush** — **Ramu 1974**

× Lipstick = Meadie

VIVIAN SNIDER — **Little Profusion × bigibbum** — **Perreira 1975**

WAIKIKI BEAUTY†‡ — **Diamond Head Beauty × Anouk** — **McCoy 1955**

× Helen Fukumura = Sirimavo Bandaranaike
× Jaquelyn Concert = Singapore

WAIPAHU — **Valley King × stratiotes** — **Takiguchi 1968**

× phalaenopsis = Yukiko
× Theodore Takiguchi = Renee Nakamoto

WALTER OUMAE — **Theodore Takiguchi × grantii** — **Oumae 1963**

× canaliculatum = Pearly Snow

WARPAINT — **Sybil Jones × Impara Beauty** — **Limberlost 1975**

WE BUNGAWALIÈ — **Pakarena × Ibu Paula Siwabessy** — **Bundt 1972**

WEE WILLIE — **Blue Jay × canaliculatum** — **Teruo Oka 1974**

WEI-LIN — **Bellflower × ionoglossum** — **K. F. Yap 1975**

WEST INDIAN — **Elaine × Shelley Maurine Thomas** — **J. & S. 1974**

WHITE EGRET — **Sea Foam × phalaenopsis** — **Redlinger 1966**

× mirbellianum = Louise Hill

WHITE GEM — **dicuphum × phalaenopsis** — **S. 1956**

× Margaret Joan Fell = Bright Eyes

WHITE IBIS — **Isabel Sander × bellatulum** — **Crestwood 1973**

DENDROBIUM

WHITE KING — **Gatton Prince × Mont Blanc** — **Yonezawa 1975**
WHITE PEARL — **Agnus × Sagimusume** — **J. Yamamoto 1970**
× Sagimusume = Hagoromo

WHITE PONY — **Anglow × Red Star** — **J. Yamamoto 1975**
williamsianum†‡ — **species**
× Bluecolor = Royal Snow
× Carl Ludwig Bundt = Howard Harting
× May Neal = Mary Nola
× Mini Girl = Halo
× New Guinea = June Bennett
× Rani = Rouna Blue

WINIFRED FORTESCUE†‡ — **Gatton Monarch × Lady Colman** — **Strauss 1950**
× Golden Wave = Erika Reuter

WINIFRED JACKSON‡ — **Cartwheel × schulleri** — **D. C. Jackson 1961 (Kirch)**
× Euroka Beauty = Barbara Cartland

WINTER STAR — **Royal Sovereign × moniliforme** — **Gauda 1968**
× Indoyo = Miyajima
× nobile = Merry Christmas

WYN LOBLEY — **Lavender Beauty × schulleri** — **McFarlane 1972**
YAMATO — **Charm Star × Glorious Rainbow** — **J. Yamamoto 1974**
YAOWAMAL — **Louis Bleriot × Chao Phya River** — **Loha-Udom 1972**
× Srisomboon = Mae-Klong River

YAYOIFUJI — Marimos × Bizen — **J. Yamamoto 1974**
YELLOW CURLS‡ — **Champagne × undulatum** — **S.B.G. 1956**
× Englan Blue = Kiril Siebert

YELLOW STONE — **Liholiho × Alice Chong** — **Chaisomboon 1971**
YODOGIMI — **Hatuharu × Oborozuki** — **J. Yamamoto 1975**
YOSHIE — **Lim Chong Min × Akemi** — **Takiguchi 1970**
× Akemi = Doreen Eto
× Jaquelyn Thomas = Lillian Chong
× Tomie = Ritsuko Takiguchi

YOUNGHUA LIM — **Lady Fay × Meng Eng** — **Lim Swee Aun 1974 (Mrs. Lim Swee Aun)**

YUKIDARUMA — **Shiranami × Pinocchio** — **J. Yamamoto 1973**
YUKIKO — **Waipahu × phalaenopsis** — **Takiguchi 1974**
YUKIMUSUME — **Sagimusume × Agnusbelle** — **J. Yamamoto 1975**
× Sagimusume = Sasameyuki

YUMEJI — Hermont × Oborozuki — **J. Yamamoto 1973**
YURIKO — **Elaine × Shelli** — **N. Tomita 1971 (Flowers)**

YUZUKI — **Angel Flower × Dream** — **J. Yamamoto 1974**
ZAKIMOS‡ — **Yamazaki × Permos** — J. Yamamoto 1968
× Glorious Rainbow = Myojo

ZUIKO — **Gatton Prince × Melanodiscus** — **Yonezawa 1975**

DEVEREUXARA

ELLA FREED — Ascda. Meda Arnold × Phal. stuartiana — **Freed 1973**
MARJORIE WREFORD — **Phal. Zada × Ascda. Meda Arnold** — **Thornton's 1972** (Fredk. L. Thornton)
SUSANNE MARY COUTTS — **Ascda. Ophelia × Phal. serpentilingua** — **Koh Keng Hoe 1971**

DIABROUGHTONIA

ALICE HART‡ — **Diacm. bicornutum × Bro. sanguinea** — **W. W. G. Moir 1956**

× C. O'brieniana = Bwna. Robert

NEWCASTLE — **Bro. sanguinea × Alice Hart** — **W. W. G. Moir 1966**

× Ctpsta. Leona = Nash. George

DIACATTLEYA

LIN TOY	**C. walkerana × Diacm. bicornutum**	**Magin 1973**
MEFFORDS FORT	C. forbesii × Pink Glory	**Robt. Smith 1973**
PINK GLORY	**C. amethystoglossa × Diacm. bicornutum**	**E. Iwanaga 1961**

× C. forbesii = Meffords Fort

DIACRIUM

bicornutum*†‡ — **species**

(This is retained as the horticulturally recommended name for registration purposes, even though *Caularthron bicornutum* is the botanically correct name for this species.)

× C. walkerana = Diaca. Lin Toy
× Epi. ibaguense = Epdcm. Doctor Hilary Moore
× Eplc. Envy = Alna. Ocean Spray

DILLONARA

BRONZE KAHILI — **Smbl. Maunalani × Epi. diurnum** — **O. Kirsch 1966**

× Lc. Mem. Masa Matsumoto = Nrna. Rebecca

MAHOGANY BEAUTY — Epi. stamfordianum × Smbl. Garnet — Osment 1972

DORICENTRUM

PULCHERRIMIN — **Dor. pulcherrima × Asctm. miniatum** — U. of H. 1971

DORIELLA

GEORGETOWN	**Penang Gardens × Dor. pulcherrima**	**W. W. G. Moir 1973**
PENANG GARDENS	Dor. pulcherrima × King. taenialis	**W. W. G. Moir 1968**

× Dor. pulcherrima = Georgetown

DORIFINETIA

PILIALOHA — **Dor. pulcherrima × Neof. falcata** — **H. R. Starke 1975 (Sagawa)**

DORITAENOPSIS

ADAIR — **Pink Jewel × Phal. William Boyd** — **Beard 1969**

× Phal. Zada = Bonnie

AMERICAN HERITAGE	**Mem. Clarence Schubert × Phal. James Hausermann**	**Hausermann 1975**
ANNE DE BRUYNE	**Dor. pulcherrima × Phal. Palmsnow**	Hiews' 1971
BARBARA HILL	**Jerry Vande Weghe × Phal. Barbara Beard**	**Beard 1975**
BARBARA WINKELMANN	**Susan Ann Schubert × Phal. York**	**Hausermann 1971**

DORITAENOPSIS

Name	Parentage	Registrant
BEVERLY HILLS	**Herman Pigors × Phal. sumatrana**	**Hager 1974**
BICENTENNIAL	**Susan Ann Schubert × Phal. Blushing Pink**	**Hausermann 1975**
BONNIE	**Phal. Zada × Adair**	**Voo Doo Orchids 1974**
BRYAN WHEELER	**Phal. Zada × Jerri Sue King**	**Hausermann 1971**
CARDINAL	**Red Coral × Phal. Mistinguett**	**Pff. V. & L. 1972**
CHERUB	**Kenneth Schubert × Phal. Miami Maid**	**Hausermann 1974**
CHIQUITA	**Red Coral × Phal. Spica**	**Beard 1971**
CHRISTMAS	**Red Coral × Phal. fasciata**	**Beard 1969**
× Phal. violacea	= Kathy Bove	
CLARELEN‡	**Red Coral × Phal. Zada**	Clarelen 1963
× Phal. Ann Lovelace	= Malibu Pink	
CORAL GLEAM	**Red Coral × Rose Gleam**	**Hager 1966**
× Mem. Clarence Schubert	= Kyoto	
× Dor. pulcherrima	= Fuchsia Princess	
× Phal. Lavender Lady	= Coral Lady	
× Phal. Raycraft	= Ray Coral	
× Phal. Zada	= Liliane Van Heijningen	
CORAL LADY	**Coral Gleam × Phal. Lavender Lady**	**C. & I. Keyes 1974**
CORAL SEA	**Red Coral × Phal. New Horizon**	**Hager 1972**
CORCATA	**Red Coral × Phal. fuscata**	**Beard 1969**
× Phal. Melba Burnett	= Melcata	
DEBBIE LAWRENCE	**Red Lip × Phal. Red Eye**	**Beard 1973**
DELICADO	**Red Coral × Phal. White Magic**	**Hager 1974**
DRESDEN	**Mem. Clarence Schubert × Phal. mariae**	**Wichmann 1972**
ECLATANT	**Dor. pulcherrima × Phal. Ghisoni**	**Marcel Lecoufle 1974**
ELLEN SATTERWHITE	**Mem. Clarence Schubert × Phal. Ann Marie Beard**	**John H. Miller 1972**
ELMHURST CORAL	**Mem. Clarence Schubert × Phal. Shaffer's Pinkie**	**Hausermann 1974**
ENGLESIDE	**Red Coral × Red Lip**	**Beard 1973**
ERFŬRT	**Mem. Clarence Schubert × Phal. fasciata**	**Wichmann 1972**
EVA JONES	**Lake Worth × Phal. Vicki Sue Lockhart**	**Lockhart 1974**
FATIMAH	**Dor. pulcherrima × Phal. Butterfly Sim**	**Alsagoff 1971**
FIRE CRACKER	**Red Coral × Dor. pulcherrima**	**Beard 1966**
× Dor. pulcherrima	= Freed's Beautiful Girl	
FIRE OPAL	**Red Coral × Phal. Luedde-violacea**	**D. R. Sellon 1972 (Beall)**
FORTY-NINER	**Phal. Doris × Kenneth Schubert**	**Shaffer's 1973**
FOWLER'S DREAM	**Mem. Clarence Schubert × Phal. Ramona**	**Dr. J. G. Martin 1975**
FREED'S BEAUTIFUL GIRL	**Fire Cracker × Dor. pulcherrima**	**Freed 1975**
FUCHSIA PRINCESS	**Coral Gleam × Dor. pulcherrima**	**Perreira 1971**
GARY GREENLY	**Pueblo Jewel × Phal. intermedia**	**Beard 1973**
GREG COMPTON	**Mem. Clarence Schubert × Phal. Nancy Carlson**	**Hausermann 1971**
GROOVY PINK	**Phal. Groovy × Mem. Clarence Schubert**	**R. K. Mizuta 1975**
GROSSE POINT	Jerry Vande Weghe × Phal. Ruby Zada	**Beard 1973**
HAHNWALD	Dor. pulcherrima × Phal. Lippezauber	**Frese 1975**
HAPPY DAY	**Red Lip × Phal. Lois Jansen**	**Beard 1972**
HAUSERMANN'S EL TORO	**Mem. Clarence Schubert × Phal. Judith Hausermann**	**Hausermann 1972**
HAWAIIAN SNOW	Red Coral × Phal. Doris	**R. K. Mizuta 1971 (McCoy)**
HERMAN PIGORS	**Mem. Clarence Schubert × Phal. lueddemanniana**	**Hausermann 1969**
× Phal. Denise Richardson	= John Arterberry	
× Phal. sumatrana	= Beverly Hills	

HIMMELSLEITER	**Dor. pulcherrima × Phal. Lipperose**	**Röhl 1974**
ILLINOIS	**Pueblo Jewel × Phal. fuscata**	**Beard 1973**
JASON BEARD	**Pueblo Jewel × Phal. Mad Hatter**	**Beard 1972**
JEFFRY HALL	**Kristine Teoh × Phal. Lois Jansen**	**Beard 1975**
JERRI SUE KING	**Phal. Summit Snow × Dor. pulcherrima**	**King 1965 (Small)**

× Mem. Clarence Schubert = Pretty Nice
× Dor. pulcherrima = Red Velvet
× Phal. Best Girl = Vendetta
× Phal. fuscata = Suecata
× Phal. lueddemanniana = Voo Doo
× Phal. Princess Kaiulani = Princess Sue
× Phal. violacea = King Camay
× Phal. Willowbrook = Yale
× Phal. Zada = Bryan Wheeler

JERRY VANDE WEGHE	**Red Coral × Phal. Therese Frackowiak**	**Beard 1966**

× Phal. Barbara Beard = Barbara Hill
× Phal. Frances Roberts = Teoh Phaik Khuan
× Phal. Linda Winters = Susan Odom
× Phal. Ruby Zada = Grosse Point

JIM CHAN	**Phal. amboinensis × Dor. pulcherrima**	**Fort Caroline 1973 (Wallbrunn)**
JIM HAFER	**Pueblo Jewel × Phal. Red Eye**	**Beard 1974**
JOANNA JANES	**Mem. Clarence Schubert × Phal. Arpege**	**Janes 1974**
JOHN ARTERBERRY	**Herman Pigors × Phal. Denise Richardson**	**W. J. Sanders 1974 (Hager)**
KAY DROWNE	**Violet × Lake Worth**	**Lockhart 1973**
KATHY BOVE	**Christmas × Phal. violacea**	**Beard 1975**
KENNETH SCHUBERT	**Dor. pulcherrima × Phal. violacea**	**Clarelen 1963**

× Red Coral = Red Sea
× Phal. Doris = Forty-Niner
× Phal. Miami Maid = Cherub
× Phal. Ondine = Melina
× Phal. Willowbrook = Kimberly Hausermann

KIMBERLY HAUSERMANN	**Kenneth Schubert × Phal. Willowbrook**	**Hausermann 1972**
KING CAMAY	**Jerri Sue King × Phal. violacea**	**Dobkin 1971**
KRISTINE TEOH	**Pueblo Jewel × Phal. Fiery Girl**	**Beard 1971**

× Phal. Lois Jansen = Jeffry Hall

KYOTO	**Mem. Clarence Schubert × Coral Gleam**	Hattori 1975
LADY JEWEL	**Pueblo Jewel × Phal. Mildred Karleen**	**Rod McLellan Co. 1971 (Beard)**

× Phal. Mildred Karleen = Rote Funken
× Phal. Renate Frese = Michaela

LAKE WORTH	**Phal. Barbara Beard × Pink Jewel**	**Beard 1968**

× Violet = Kay Drowne
× Phal. Polar Bear = Wonder Mountain
× Phal. Vicki Sue Lockhart = Eva Jones

LEE SOO KEOW	**Dor. pulcherrima × Phal. Best Girl**	**M. K. Tan 1973**
LILIANE VAN HEIJNINGEN	**Coral Gleam × Phal. Zada**	**Koh Keng Hoe 1975**
LORI THORNTON	**Phal. Princess Kaiulani × Dor. pulcherrima**	**Fredk. L. Thornton 1972**
MALASOU	**Malaysian Beauty × Phal. Sourire**	**Janes 1974**
MALAYSIAN BEAUTY‡	**Dor. pulcherrima × Phal. Orchid Acres**	**Hiews' 1967**

× Phal. Sourire = Malasou

MALIBU PINK	**Phal. Ann Lovelace × Clarelen**	**Freed 1971**
MARTHA NEWTON	**Phal. Ruby Stripes × Red Lip**	Bachner 1974
MARY CEFALU	**Pueblo Jewel × Phal. Ruby Zada**	**Beard 1973**
MELANIE BEARD	**Red Lip × Pueblo Jewel**	**Beard 1973**
MELCATA	**Corcata × Phal. Melba Burnett**	**Lockhart 1974**

DORITAENOPSIS

MELINA	**Phal. Ondine × Kenneth Schubert**	**Shaffer's 1973**
MEMORIA ARTHUR FREED	**Mem. Clarence Schubert × Phal. sanderana**	**Freed 1975**
MEMORIA CLARENCE SCHUBERT†	**Dor. pulcherrima × Phal. Zada**	**Fields Orchids 1965 (Clarelen)**

× Coral Gleam = Kyoto
× Jerri Sue King = Pretty Nice
× Ascda. Meda Arnold = Vwga. Jerry Vande Weghe
× Asctm. miniatum = Bdra. Melrose
× Phal. Ann Marie Beard = Ellen Satterwhite
× Phal. Arpege = Joanna Janes
× Phal. Best Girl = Roberta Arnold
× Phal. fasciata = Erfürt
× Phal. Freed's Temptation = Sander's Joy
× Phal. Groovy = Groovy Pink
× Phal. James Hausermann = American Heritage
× Phal. Judith Hausermann = Hausermann's El Toro
× Phal. Lipperose = Renate Frese
× Phal. mariae = Dresden
× Phal. Marmouset = Ultra Pink
× Phal. Nancy Carlson = Greg Compton
× Phal. Pink Glamor = Red Bonanza
× Phal. Ramona = Fowler's Dream
× Phal. sanderana = Mem. Arthur Freed
× Phal. Shaffer's Pinkie = Elmhurst Coral
× Phal. Willowbrook = Paula Hausermann
× Vdnps. Henrietta Fujiwara = Hgra. Herb
× Vdps. parishii = Haus. Lucie Hausermann

MICHAELA	**Lady Jewel × Phal. Renate Frese**	**Frese 1975**
NINETEEN FOURTEEN CLASS	**Phal. Jack McQuerry × Redkar**	**Beard 1973**
PAULA HAUSERMANN	**Mem. Clarence Schubert × Phal. Willowbrook**	**Hausermann 1971**
PINKIE	**Phal. Ann Lovelace × Dor. pulcherrima**	**Freed 1971**
PINK JEWEL‡	**Dor. pulcherrima × Phal. Pink Princess**	**Markell 1964**

× Phal. Ann Lovelace = Pink Love
× Phal. lindenii = Yellow Jewel

PINK LOVE	**Pink Jewel × Phal. Ann Lovelace**	**Dobkin 1971**
PINTO LAKE	**Red Coral × Phal. Alice Gloria**	**Shaffer's 1973**
PRETTY NICE	**Mem. Clarence Schubert × Jerri Sue King**	**Hausermann 1973**
PRINCESS SUE	**Jerri Sue King × Phal. Princess Kaiulani**	**Dobkin 1971**
PUEBLO JEWEL	**Phal. Dos Pueblos × Pink Jewel**	**Beard 1968**

× Red Lip = Melanie Beard
× Phal. Fiery Girl = Kristine Teoh
× Phal. fuscata = Illinois
× Phal. intermedia = Gary Greenly
× Phal. Lois Jansen = Welcome
× Phal. Mad Hatter = Jason Beard
× Phal. Mildred Karleen = Lady Jewel
× Phal. Red Eye = Jim Hafer
× Phal. Redfan = Youthful
× Phal. Ruby Zada = Mary Cefalu

PURPLE GEM‡	**Dor. pulcherrima × Phal. equestris**	**E. Iwanaga 1963**

× Phal. Barbara Beard = Red River

RAY CORAL	**Phal. Raycraft × Coral Gleam**	**Inada 1974**
RED BONANZA	**Mem. Clarence Schubert × Phal. Pink Glamor**	**Hausermann 1975**
RED CHARLES	**Red Lip × Phal. Charles Shaffer**	**Bachner 1974**
RED CORAL‡ (formerly under *Phalaenopsis*)	**Dor. pulcherrima × Phal. Doris**	**Clarelen 1959**

× Kenneth Schubert = Red Sea
× Red Lip = Engleside
× Violet = Truly Scrumptious
× Phal. Alice Gloria = Pinto Lake
× Phal. Donnie Brandt = Snowdrift
× Phal. Doris = Hawaiian Snow
× Phal. Luedde-violacea = Fire Opal
× Phal. Mistinguett = Cardinal
× Phal. New Horizon = Coral Sea
× Phal. Redwing = Udal
× Phal. Spica = Chiquita
× Phal. White Magic = Delicado
× V. spathulata = Hgra. Yellow Coral

RED CRICKET	**Susan Ann Schubert × Phal. fasciata**	**Hausermann 1973**
RED EVE	**Phal. Evening Rose × Red Lip**	**Bachner 1974**
RED JOE	**Red Lip × Phal. Joseph Hampton**	**Bachner 1974**

DORITAENOPSIS

RED JUDY	**Phal. Judy Karleen × Red Lip**	**Bachner 1974**
REDKAR	**Red Coral × Phal. Judy Karleen**	**Beard 1968**

× Phal. Jack McQuerry = Nineteen Fourteen Class

RED LIP	**Pink Jewel × Phal. Suemid**	**Beard 1968**

× Pueblo Jewel = Melanie Beard
× Red Coral = Engleside
× Phal. Charles Shaffer = Red Charles
× Phal. Evening Rose = Red Eve
× Phal. Joseph Hampton = Red Joe
× Phal. Judy Karleen = Red Judy
× Phal. Lois Jansen = Happy Day
× Phal. Red Eye = Debbie Lawrence
× Phal. Ruby Stripes = Martha Newton
× Phal. Suemid = Solitude

RED RIVER	**Purple Gem × Phal. Barbara Beard**	**Fredk. L. Thornton 1972**
RED SEA	**Red Coral × Kenneth Schubert**	**Shaffer's 1973**
RED VELVET	**Jerri Sue King × Dor. pulcherrima**	**Dobkin 1971**
RENATE FRESE	**Mem. Clarence Schubert × Phal. Lipperose**	**Wichmann 1972 (Frese)**
ROBERTA ARNOLD	**Mem. Clarence Schubert × Phal. Best Girl**	**J. Y. Arnold 1971 (J. Y. Arnold III)**
ROBERT WINKELMANN	**Susan Ann Schubert × Phal. Edythe Wood**	**Hausermann 1971**
ROTE FUNKEN	Phal. Mildred Karleen × Lady Jewel	**Frese 1975**
SANDER'S JOY	**Mem. Clarence Schubert × Phal. Freed's Temptation**	**Dr. J. G. Martin 1975**
SHIRLEY JANES	**Dor. pulcherrima × Phal. Sourire**	Janes 1974
SNOWDRIFT	**Red Coral × Phal. Donnie Brandt**	**A. & M. 1975**
SOLITUDE	**Phal. Suemid × Red Lip**	**Beard 1973**
STEPHEN SALTZMAN	**Phal. Peppermint × Dor. pulcherrima**	**Freed 1974**
SUECATA	**Jerri Sue King × Phal. fuscata**	**Dobkin 1971**
SUSAN ANN SCHUBERT‡	**Dor. pulcherrima × Phal. Palm Beach**	**Clarelen 1963**

× Phal. Blushing Pink = Bicentennial
× Phal. Edythe Wood = Robert Winkelmann
× Phal. fasciata = Red Cricket
× Phal. York = Barbara Winkelmann

SUSAN ODOM	**Jerry Vande Weghe × Phal. Linda Winters**	**Beard 1975**
TAN SWEE ENG	**Dor. pulcherrima × Phal. gigantea**	Teoh Eng Soon 1973 (Twins Teo)
TEOH PHAIK KHUAN	**Jerry Vande Weghe × Phal. Frances Roberts**	**Beard 1974**
TRULY SCRUMPTIOUS	Violet × Red Coral	**Hager 1975**
UDAL	**Red Coral × Phal. Redwing**	**Beard 1974**
ULTRA PINK	**Mem. Clarence Schubert × Phal. Marmouset**	**Richella 1975**
UTOPIA	**Phal. Rosy Charm × Dor. pulcherrima**	**Dobkin 1971**
VENDETTA	**Jerri Sue King × Phal. Best Girl**	**Dobkin 1971**
VIOLET	**Red Coral × Phal. violacea**	**Beard 1963**

× Lake Worth = Kay Drowne
× Red Coral = Truly Scrumptious

VIRGINIA JENKINS	**Phal. Anna Tham × Dor. pulcherrima**	**Dewey 1973**
VOO DOO	**Jerri Sue King × Phal. lueddemanniana**	**Dobkin 1971**
WAR HOOP	**Phal. Samba × Dor. pulcherrima**	**Dobkin 1971**
WELCOME	**Pueblo Jewel × Phal. Lois Jansen**	**Beard 1972**
WONDER MOUNTAIN	**Lake Worth × Phal. Polar Bear**	**Beall 1974**
YALE	**Jerri Sue King × Phal. Willowbrook**	**Hausermann 1974**
YELLOW JEWEL	**Phal. lindenii × Pink Jewel**	**Bachner 1973**
YOUTHFUL	**Pueblo Jewel × Phal. Redfan**	**Beard 1971**

DORITIS

buyssoniana (see *pulcherrima*†‡) **species**
esmeralda (see *pulcherrima*†‡) **species**
pulcherrima†‡ **species**
(syn: *Doritis esmeralda; Doritis buyssoniana; Phalaenopsis esmeralda; Phalaenopsis buyssoniana.*)

× Aër. fieldingii = Aërdts. Hermon Slade
× Aër. japonica = Aërdts. Mem. Arthur Freed
× Ascda. Ophelia = Asvts. John Miller
× Asctm. miniatum = Dctm. Pulcherrimin
× Drlla. Penang Gardens = Drlla. Georgetown
× Dtps. Coral Gleam = Dtps. Fuchsia Princess
× Dtps. Fire Cracker = Dtps. Freed's Beautiful Girl
× Dtps. Jerri Sue King = Dtps. Red Velvet
× Neof. falcata = Dfta. Pilialoha
× Phal. amboinensis = Dtps. Jim Chan
× Phal. Anna Tham = Dtps. Virginia Jenkins
× Phal. Ann Lovelace = Dtps. Pinkie
× Phal. Best Girl = Dtps. Lee Soo Keow
× Phal. Butterfly Sim = Dtps. Fatimah
× Phal. Ghisoni = Dtps. Eclatant
× Phal. gigantea = Dtps. Tan Swee Eng
× Phal. Lipperose = Dtps. Himmelsleiter
× Phal. Lippezauber = Dtps. Hahnwald
× Phal. Palmsnow = Dtps. Anne de Bruyne
× Phal. Peppermint = Dtps. Stephen Saltzman
× Phal. Princess Kaiulani = Dtps. Lori Thornton
× Phal. Rosy Charm = Dtps. Utopia
× Phal. Samba = Dtps. War Hoop
× Phal. Sourire = Dtps. Shirley Janes
× Ren. philippinensis = Dtha. Yen

DORTHERA

YEN	**Dor. pulcherrima × Ren. philippinensis**	**Yen Orchid 1975**

DOWNSARA

PSYTHENIS	**Plmra. Raymond Palmer × Agn. cyanea**	**George Black 1975**

EASTONARA

ADVANCEMENT	**Gchls. monticolus × Ascda. Mem. Jim Wilkins**	**Rod McLellan Co. 1975**

ENCYCLIA

alata (see *Epidendrum alatum*†‡) species
atro-purpurea (see *Epidendrum atropurpureum**†‡) species
bifida (see *Epidendrum bifidum*‡) **species**
citrina (see *Cattleya citrina**‡) **species**
mariae (see *Epidendrum mariae*†‡) **species**
phoenicea (see *Epidendrum phoeniceum*†‡) **species**
tampensis (see *Epidendrum tampense*†‡) **species**

EPICATTLEYA

ADIN BURTON	**C. Interglossa × Epi. atropurpureum**	**Burton's 1973 (A. F. Burton)**
ALFRED BLAUMANN	**Epi. leucochilum × C. granulosa**	**Satori 1975 (Blaumann)**
ANGELA RAGAN	**Epi. adenocarpon × C. Little Angel**	**M. A. J. Orchids 1973 (Vickers)**
ANNA KESSLER	**C. Margaret Stewart × Epi. gracile**	**Fort Caroline 1971 (Wallbrunn)**

EPICATTLEYA

ANNE ANDERSON	Susan Naomi × C. Leona Bloom	Wilkins 1975 (J. A. Roth)
ANZA LODE	C. loddigesii × Epi. Anza	Rod McLellan Co. 1973
AROMA GRANDE	C. aclandiae × Epi. atropurpureum	W. W. G. Moir 1971
BACKTRACK	Fred J. Fuchs Jr. × Epi. tampense	Jesup 1975
BICHRON	C. bicolor × Epi. dichromum	Osment 1974
BLUE STAR	C. Intermediette × Epi. plicatum	Osment 1971
BRIAN DAVID	Epi. conopseum × C. Bow Bells	Beckenbach 1973
CHARLIE BROWN	C. bowringiana × Epi. gracile	Hawkins 1971 (W. W. G. Moir)
CHIQUITA BONITA	C. Gigi × Epi. Santander	Stewart Inc. 1971 (De Garmo)
DADELAND	C. Penang × Night Hawk	Wilkins 1974
DOLL BABY	C. Louise Georgianna × Epi. ionocentrum	Stevenson 1975
DOROTHY ISEMONGER	C. schillerana × Epi. Tampico	Osment 1974
DOUG BURKE	Peach Glow × Epi. cinnabarinum	W. D. Burke 1975 (Kirch)
FLORENCE BURTON	C. forbesii × Epi. atropurpureum	Burton's (A. F. Burton)
FRED J. FUCHS Jr.‡	Epi. tampense × C. dowiana	Fuchs Jr. 1958
× Epi. tampense	= Backtrack	
GEORGIA MARIAE	C. Louise Georgianna × Epi. mariae	Stevenson 1964 (Fields Orchids)
× C. Intermediette	= Icecream Frosting	
GREEN CHIFFON	C. Intermediette × Epi. mariae	Fort Caroline 1973
GREEN GEM	Epi. mariae × C. walkerana	Ilgenfritz 1973
GREEN GODDESS	C. Graniris × Epi. mariae	Rainbow 1974 (Timmons)
GREEN MARIE	Epi. mariae × C. Albatross	Redlinger 1971
HARALD	C. Kerchoveana × Epi. atropurpureum	Baggeler 1973
HAWAIIAN GEM	Epi. Brownie × C. violacea	W. W. G. Moir 1962
× Pot. Gordon Siu	= Roth. Anne	
HELLO DOLLY	C. Henrietta Japhet × Epi. obesum	Stevenson 1973
ICECREAM FROSTING	Georgia Mariae × C. Intermediette	Stevenson 1973
ICY PARFAIT	C. forbesii × Epi. umbellatum	Stevenson 1973
JESSE FERREIRA	C. mossiae × Epi. atropurpureum	Burton's 1974 (A. F. Burton)
JOSEPH RILEY	C. bicolor × Epi. tampense	Beckenbach 1973
JOYITA	Epi. conopseum × C. Claesiana	MAJ Orchids 1973 (Vickers)
KAY BOYLE	C. Intermediette × Epi. phoeniceum	Boyle 1973 (Weeki Wachee)
LEON GLICENSTEIN	Epi. atropurpureum × C. intermedia	Withner 1972
LILY MOODY	Epi. phoeniceum × C. Marie Ferriera	Osment 1962
× Bc. Daffodil	= Vnra. Ressie Toy	
LIME SHERBET	C. forbesii × Epi. mariae	W. W. G. Moir 1968
× C. Bow Bells	= Mem. Ruth Hoyt	
LITTLE BEGINNING	C. Magbarola × Epi. tampense	Stevenson 1973
LITTLE O'THAT	C. Kitchen Delight × Epi. tampense	Stevenson 1973

EPICATTLEYA

LUIS ARIZA JULIA	**C. bowringiana × Epi. eggersii**	**W. W. G. Moir 1973**
MARION RUFF SHEEHAN	**Epi. conopseum × C. mossiae**	**Beckenbach 1975**
MAYAN ROSE	**C. intermedia × Purple Glory**	**W. W. G. Moir 1973**
MEMORIA FLORENCE POOLE	**Ruben's Gold × C. Angelwalker**	**LeBuff 1975**
MEMORIA RUTH HOYT	**Lime Sherbet × C. Bow Bells**	**Simanton 1973**
MOYNETTE	**C. Little Bit × Epi. atropurpureum**	**Osment 1972**
MYRIAM-DE-VILANOVA	**C. Mrs. Mahler × Epi. plicatum**	**Osment 1974**
NIGHT HAWK	**Epi. atropurpureum × C. violacea**	**Wilkins 1974 (Originator unknown)**

× C. Penang = Dadeland

PEACH GLOW	**C. Henrietta Japhet × Epi. cinnabarinum**	**W. W. G. Moir 1963**

× Epi. cinnabarinum = Doug Burke

PLIANNA	**Epi. plicatum × C. Louise Georgianna**	**Withner 1974**
POOPSIE	**C. Bee Beament × Epi. tampense**	**Stevenson 1975**
PURPLE GLORY	**Epi. nemorale × C. violacea**	**W. W. G. Moir 1962**

× C. intermedia = Mayan Rose

ROSIANA	**C. schillerana × Rosita**	**Osment 1974**
ROSITA‡	**Epi. phoeniceum × C. bowringiana**	**Osment 1962**

× C. schillerana = Rosiana

RUBEN'S GOLD	**Epi. mariae × C. aurantiaca**	**Ruben 1966**

× C. Angelwalker = Mem. Florence Poole

SILVESTER	**C. skinneri × Epi. atropurpureum**	**W. W. G. Moir 1975**
SUSAN NAOMI	**C. Revel × Epi. atropurpureum**	**W. W. G. Moir 1964 (F. Tanaka)**

× C. Leona Bloom = Anne Anderson

TELL	**C. labiata × Epi. vitellinum**	**Munz 1972**
VICKY	**Epi. plicatum × C. Meadii**	**M. J. Bates 1973 (E. Glasgow)**

EPIDELLA

RUMRILL	**Epi. conopseum × Ngl. purpurea**	**Rumrill 1973**

EPIDENDRUM

abbreviatum **species**

× conopseum = Lemonade

adenocarpon‡ **species**

× C. Little Angel = Epc. Angela Ragan

alatum†‡ **species**

(This is retained as the horticulturally recommended name for registration purposes, even though *Encyclia alata* is the botanically correct name for this species.)

× cochleatum = He'e Pali
× radiatum = Santander
× Lc. Eva = Eplc. Elizabeth Howell
× Lc. Jean-ne Lorraine = Eplc. Rastus
× Lc. Rojo = Eplc. Fiesta

anceps† **species**

× moyobambae = Seminole
× pseudepidendrum = Suean

EPIDENDRUM

ANZA — **aromaticum × atropurpureum** — **Rod McLellan Co. 1960**

× C. loddigesii = Epc. Anza Lode

aromaticum†‡ — **species**

× replicatum = Golden Jewell

ATRONICEUM — **atropurpureum × phoeniceum** — **J. & S. 1960**

× Lc. Twinkle Star = Eplc. John Pelot

atropurpureum*†‡ — **species**

(This continues to be treated as *Epidendrum* for horticultural, including registration, purposes, though botanically reclassified as *Encyclia atropurpurea.*)

× Bumble Bee = Deanna Lynn
× ghiesbreghtianum = Steve Wakulich
× C. aclandiae = Epc. Aroma Grande
× C. forbesii = Epc. Florence Burton
× C. Interglossa = Epc. Adin Burton
× C. intermedia = Epc. Leon Glicenstein
× C. Kerchoveana = Epc. Harald
× C. Little Bit = Epc. Moynette
× C. mossiae = Epc. Jesse Ferreira
× C. skinneri = Epc. Silvester
× C. violacea = Epc. Night Hawk
× L. flava = Epl. Rio Verde
× Lc. Luminosa = Eplc. Maria Luisa
× Lc. Peggy Huffman = Eplc. Roxanne
× Yam. Fantasy = Yam. Astronaut

belizense‡ — **species**

× L. milleri = Epl. Connie

bifidum‡ — **species**

(This continues to be treated as *Epidendrum* for horticultural, including registration, purposes, though botanically reclassified as *Encyclia bifida.*)

× B. nodosa = Bepi. Bifidosa
× L. rubescens = Epl. Izobel Reid

bracteatum (see *pabstii*) — **species**

BRIGHT EYES — **Phillips Jesup × gladiatum** — **W. W. G. Moir 1974**

BUMBLE BEE — **alatum × Brownie** — **J. & S. 1962**

× atropurpureum = Deanna Lynn

CATHERINE WILSON — **pseudepidendrum × verrucosum** — **W. W. G. Moir 1968**

× schumannianum = Las Cruces

cinnabarinum*†‡ — **species**

× Costa Rica = Costabarinum
× Epc. Peach Glow = Epc. Doug Burke

cochleatum*†‡ — **species**

× alatum = He'e Pali

conopseum‡ — **species**

× abbreviatum = Lemonade
× pseudepidendrum = Rudolph
× B. cucullata = Bepi. Mini-Cu
× C. Bow Bells = Epc. Brian David
× C. Claesiana = Epc. Joyita
× C. mossiae = Epc. Marion Ruff Sheehan
× Lc. Florence Machle = Eplc. James Joseph
× Lc. Twinkle Star = Eplc. Susan Margaret Wehlburg
× Ngl. purpurea = Epdla. Rumrill
× Schom. lyonsii = Smbep. Freckles
× Schom. tibicinis = Smbep. Red Monsterette
× Soph. cernua = Ephs. Concern

COSTABARINUM — **Costa Rica × cinnabarinum** — **W. W. G. Moir 1971**

COSTA RICA — **schumannianum × pseudowallisii** — **W. W. G. Moir 1968**

× cinnabarinum = Costabarinum
× pseudowallisii = Sarapiqui
× schumannianum = Harry Szmant

DEANNA LYNN — **Bumble Bee × atropurpureum** — **Bramblett 1974**

dichromum†‡ — **species**

× C. bicolor = Epc. Bichron

EPIDENDRUM

difforme† (see *umbellatum*†‡) — **species**

eburneum* — **species**

× myrianthum = San Vito
× pfavii = Paleface

eggersii†‡ — **species**

× C. bowringiana = Epc. Luis Ariza Julia

FLORIDA PRIDE — **stamfordianum × Pride of Florida** — **Osment 1972**

ghiesbreghtianum — **species**

× atropurpureum = Steve Wakulich

gladiatum — **species**

× Phillips Jesup = Bright Eyes
× pseudoschumannianum = Panama

GOLDEN JEWELL — **aromaticum × replicatum** — **Osment 1974**

gracile‡ — **species**

× Blc. Cinnamon Peak = Yam. Midnight Magenta
× Blc. Sunkist = Yam. Hawk's Nest
× C. bowringiana = Epc. Charlie Brown
× C. Margaret Stewart = Epc. Anna Kessler
× L. flava = Epl. Alan Sues
× Lc. Sunrise Peak = Eplc. Mem. Astor Clarke
× Sc. Cleopatra = Stac. Sam

guatemalense — **species**

× Blc. Orange Sherbet = Yam. Offbeat
× Eplc. Atrocanham = Eplc. Joe Johnson

HARRY SZMANT — **schumannianum × Costa Rica** — **Szmant 1973 (W. W. G. Moir)**

HE'E PALI — **cochleatum × alatum** — **Otaguro 1972**

HELEN TROY — **nemorale × selligerum** — **Slade 1963**

× nemorale = Justine Slade

HIGHLAND MIST‡ — **schumannianum × verrucosum** — **W. W. G. Moir 1963**

× schumannianum = Zamarano

ibaguense*†‡ — **species**

(This is treated for registration purposes as specifically distinct from both *Epi. pristes* and *Epi. radicans* though the latter are ranked by some authorities as forms of *Epi. ibaguense*.)

× Diacm. bicornutum = Epdcm. Doctor Hilary Moore

ionocentrum — **species**

(Considered by some authorities to be a variety of *Epi. prismatocarpum* but treated as specifically distinct as a parent for registration purposes.)

× C. Louise Georgianna = Epc. Doll Baby

JEAN — **nutans × pseudepidendrum** — **Osment 1974**

JUSTINE SLADE — **Helen Troy × nemorale** — **Slade 1974**

KINICH AHAU — **pseudepidendrum × tampense** — **Withers 1972**

LAS CRUCES — **Catherine Wilson × schumannianum** — **W. W. G. Moir 1971**

LEMONADE — **conopseum × abbreviatum** — **Rumrill 1973**

LEMON LIME — **mariae × radiatum** — **Osment 1971**

leucochilum — **species**

× pseudepidendrum = Marcia
× C. granulosa = Epc. Alfred Blaumann

MARCIA — **pseudepidendrum × leucochilum** — **Withner 1972**

mariae†‡ — **species**

(This continues to be treated as *Epidendrum* for horticultural, including registration, purposes, though botanically reclassified as *Encyclia mariae*.)

× radiatum = Lemon Lime
× Bro. sanguinea = Eptn. Calypso

mariae†‡ (*continued*)

× C. Albatross	= Epc. Green Marie	× C. walkerana	= Epc. Green Gem
× C. Graniris	= Epc. Green Goddess	× L. cinnabarina	= Epl. Cinderella
× C. Intermediette	= Epc. Green Chiffon	× L. flava	= Epl. Marie Louise

mooreanum — **species**

× Soph. coccinea = Ephs. Crushed Raspberry

moyobambae‡ — **species**

× anceps	= Seminole	× pseudowallisii	= Sunspot
× pseudepidendrum	= Silvestre		

myrianthum‡ — **species**

× eburneum = San Vito

nemorale*†‡ — **species**

× Helen Troy = Justine Slade

nutans‡ — **species**

× pseudepidendrum = Jean

obesum — **species**

× C. Henrietta Japhet = Epc. Hello Dolly

pabstii (syn. *bracteatum*) — **species**

× B. cordata = Bepi. Surprise

PALEFACE	**eburneum × pfavii**	**Withner 1974**
PANAMA	**gladiatum × pseudoschumannianum**	**W. W. G. Moir 1975**

pfavii†‡ — **species**

× eburneum = Paleface

PHILLIPS JESUP	**schumannianum × endresii**	**W. W. G. Moir 1967**

× gladiatum	= Bright Eyes	× pseudowallisii	= Poas

phoeniceum†‡ — **species**

(This continues to be treated as *Epidendrum* for horticultural, incl. registration purposes, though botanically reclassified as *Encyclia phoenicea.*)

× C. Intermediette	= Epc. Kay Boyle	× Lc. Pleiades	= Eplc. Edna Blum
× L. cinnabarina	= Epl. Firie Gem		

plicatum*†‡ — **species**

× B. nodosa	= Bepi. Plidosa	× C. Mrs. Mahler	= Epc. Myriam-de-Vilanova
× C. Intermediette	= Epc. Blue Star	× Lc. Lee Langford	= Eplc. Douglas Allen
× C. Louise Georgianna	= Epc. Plianna		
× C. Meadii	= Epc. Vicky		

POAS	**Phillips Jesup × pseudowallisii**	**W. W. G. Moir 1973**
PRIDE OF FLORIDA	**radicans × nocturnum**	**Osment 1964**

× stamfordianum = Florida Pride

pseudepidendrum*†‡ — **species**

× anceps	= Suean	× tampense	= Kinich Ahau
× conopseum	= Rudolph	× B. glauca	= Bepi. Peggy Ann
× leucochilum	= Marcia	× B. nodosa	= Bepi. Pseudosa
× moyobambae	= Silvestre	× Lc. Florence Machle	= Eplc. Mem. Marie Osment
× nutans	= Jean		

pseudoschumannianum	**species**	

× gladiatum	= Panama		

pseudowallisii‡	**species**	

× Costa Rica	= Sarapiqui	× Phillips Jesup	= Poas
× moyobambae	= Sunspot		

radiatum*†‡	**species**	

× alatum	= Santander	× B. nodosa	= Bepi. Moon Mist
× mariae	= Lemon Lime		

radicans*†‡ **species**

(Treated for horticultural, including registration, purposes as a separate species from *Epi. ibaguense*, but considered by some botanists to be no more than a form of *ibaguense*.)

replicatum	**species**	

× aromaticum	= Golden Jewell		

RUDOLPH	**conopseum × pseudepidendrum**	**Rumrill 1973**
SANTANDER	**radiatum × alatum**	**Stewart Inc. 1971 (Originator unknown)**

× C. Gigi	= Epc. Chiquita Bonita		

SAN VITO	**myrianthum × eburneum**	**W. W. G. Moir 1973**
SARAH JESUP	**xipheres × tampense**	**W. W. G. Moir 1961**

× Sl. Psyche	= Sfdra. Sarah's Psyche		

SARAPIQUI	**Costa Rica × pseudowallisii**	**W. W. G. Moir 1971**
schumannianum†‡	**species**	

× Catherine Wilson	= Las Cruces	× Highland Mist	= Zamarano
× Costa Rica	= Harry Szmant		

SEMINOLE	**moyobambae × anceps**	**Fort Caroline 1971 (Burkhalter)**
SILVESTRE	**pseudepidendrum × moyobambae**	**W. W. G. Moir 1971**
stamfordianum*†‡	**species**	

× Pride of Florida	= Florida Pride	× Smbl. Garnet	= Dill. Mahogany Beauty
× Bro. sanguinea	= Eptn. Bohio		

STEVE WAKULICH	**atropurpureum × ghiesbreghtianum**	**Wakulich 1974**
SUEAN	**pseudepidendrum × anceps**	**W. W. G. Moir 1971**
SUNSPOT	**pseudowallisii × moyobambae**	**Withner 1972**
tampense†‡	**species**	

(This continues to be treated as *Epidendrum* for horticultural, including registration, purposes, though botanically reclassified as *Encyclia tampensis*.)

× pseudepidendrum	= Kinich Ahau	× Epc. Fred J. Fuchs Jr.	= Epc. Backtrack
× C. Bee Beament	= Epc. Poopsie	× L. grandis	= Epl. Christopher John
× C. bicolor	= Epc. Joseph Riley	× Lc. Antonica Fredrick	= Eplc. Gilbert
× C. Kitchen Delight	= Epc. Little O'that	× Lc. G. S. Ball	= Eplc. Baltimore
× C. Magbarola	= Epc. Little Beginning	× Lc. Jane Warne	= Eplc. Joseph Cornelia

TAMPICO	**phoeniceum × howardii**	**O. Kirsch 1962**

× C. schillerana	= Epc. Dorothy Isemonger		

umbellatum†‡ **species**

(This is retained as the horticulturally recommended name for registration purposes, even though *Epidendrum difforme* is the botanically correct name for this species.)

× C. forbesii	= Epc. Icy Parfait		

EPIDENDRUM

vitellinum*†‡	species	
× C. labiata	= Epc. Tell	
ZAMARANO	Highland Mist × schumannianum	W. W. G. Moir 1973

EPIDIACRIUM

DOCTOR HILARY MOORE	Diacm. bicornutum × Epi. ibaguense	F. O. Bingham 1972 (H. B. Moore)

EPILAELIA

ALAN SUES	L. flava × Epi. gracile	Fort Caroline 1973 (Wallbrunn)
CHRISTOPHER JOHN	L. grandis × Epi. tampense	Beckenbach 1973
CINDERELLA	L. cinnabarina × Epi. mariae	Wyld Court 1972
CONNIE	Epi. belizense × L. milleri	Dr. B. C. Berliner 1975
FIRIE GEM	L. cinnabarina × Epi. phoeniceum	Osment 1974
IZOBEL REID	L. rubescens × Epi. bifidum	Julia 1975
MARIE LOUISE	Epi. mariae × L. flava	Fort Caroline 1973 (Wallbrunn)
RIO VERDE	L. flava × Epi. atropurpureum	Ruben 1972

EPILAELIOCATTLEYA

ATROCANHAM	Epi. atropurpureum × Lc. Canhamiana	J. & S. 1964
× Epi. guatemalense	= Joe Johnson	
BALTIMORE	Epi. tampense × Lc. G. S. Ball	Gerbig 1972
DOUGLAS ALLEN	Lc. Lee Langford × Epi. plicatum	Fort Caroline 1971
EDNA BLUM	Lc. Pleiades × Epi. phoeniceum	Fields Orchids 1972
ELIZABETH HOWELL	Lc. Eva × Epi. alatum	Howell 1972
ENVY	Lc. Isotta × Epi. alatum	W. W. G. Moir 1966
× Diacm. bicornutum	= Alna. Ocean Spray	
FIESTA	Lc. Rojo × Epi. alatum	Voo Doo Orchids 1974
GILBERT	Lc. Antonica Fredrick × Epi. tampense	Fort Caroline 1975
JAMES JOSEPH	Epi. conopseum × Lc. Florence Machle	Beckenbach 1973
JOE JOHNSON	Atrocanham × Epi. guatemalense	Stevenson 1975
JOHN PELOT	Lc. Twinkle Star × Epi. Atroniceum	Pelot 1974
JOSEPH CORNELIA	Lc. Jane Warne × Epi. tampense	Beckenbach 1973
MARIA LUISA	Lc. Luminosa × Epi. atropurpureum	Julia 1975
MEMORIA ASTOR CLARKE	Lc. Sunrise Peak × Epi. gracile	Mrs. W. F. White 1975 (Astor Clarke)
MEMORIA MARIE OSMENT	Lc. Florence Machle × Epi. pseudepidendrum	Osment 1974
RASTUS	Lc. Jean-ne Lorraine × Epi. alatum	Stevenson 1975
ROXANNE	Lc. Peggy Huffman × Epi. atropurpureum	Tom Tucker 1973 (J. S. McKenzie)
SUSAN MARGARET WEHLBURG	Epi. conopseum × Lc. Twinkle Star	Beckenbach 1975

EPIPHRONITIS

CONCERN	Epi. conopseum × Soph. cernua	Jesup 1975
CRUSHED RASPBERRY	Epi. mooreanum × Soph. coccinea	Jesup 1975

EPITONIA

ALICE PANCOAST	**Epi. eggersii × Bro. sanguinea**	**Osment 1965**
× Bro. sanguinea	= Fort Lauderdale	
BOHIO	**Bro. sanguinea × Epi. stamfordianum**	**Osment 1974**
CALYPSO	**Epi. mariae × Bro. sanguinea**	**Osment 1974**
FORT LAUDERDALE	**Alice Pancoast × Bro. sanguinea**	**W. W. G. Moir 1973**

ESMERALDA

cathcartii (see *Arachnis cathcartii*) **species**

EUANTHE

sanderana (see *Vanda sanderana**†‡) **species**

FORGETARA

MEXICO	**Brap. Serene × Milt. Fortaleza**	**W. W. G. Moir 1972**

FUJIOARA

GEM	**Trgl. brachiata × Ascda. Meda Arnold**	**Fujio 1974**

GASTROCHILUS

formosanus **species**

× Sarco. falcatus = Gsarco. Rumrill

monticolus **species**

× Ascda. Mem. Jim Wilkins = Eas. Advancement

GASTROSARCOCHILUS

RUMRILL	**Gchls. formosanus × Sarco. falcatus**	**Rumrill 1975**

GOFFARA

EVA GOFF	**Lsnd. Uniwai × Rhy. coelestis**	**E. K. Goff 1973**

GOMESA

recurva‡ **species**

× Onc. Lovely	= Oncsa. Rosy Gold	× Wils. Insignis	= Bbra. João Rodrigues
× Rdtta. Henry Teuscher	= Brade. Brasil		

GOODALEARA

STELLA MIZUTA	**Bllra. Tahoma Glacier × Onc. Elegance**	**W. W. G. Moir 1975**

HAGERARA

HERB	Dtps. Mem. Clarence Schubert × Vdnps. Henrietta Fujiwara	W. W. G. Moir 1973
YELLOW CORAL	Dtps. Red Coral × V. spathulata	June Fowler 1973 (Vande Weghe)

HAUSERMANNARA

LUCIE HAUSERMANN	Dtps. Mem. Clarence Schubert × Vdps. parishii	Hausermann 1974

HAWAIIARA

HARVEST QUEEN	V. Oriole × Rnps. Lena Rowold	S'pore Orchids 1973

HERBERTARA

ANTIGUAZAC	Smbc. Antigua × Slc. Anzac	Ruben 1974
HERB	Schom. thomsoniana × Slc. Naomi Kerns	W. W. G. Moir 1973

HILDAARA

CHRISTIAN HILDA	Lpna. Kingston × Schom. thomsoniana	Julia 1975

HOLCOGLOSSUM

falcatum (see *Neofinetia falcata*†‡) species

(*Holcoglossum falcatum* is botanically correct but *Neofinetia falcata* is retained as the horticulturally recommended name for registration purposes.)

HOLTTUMARA

ANDROMEDA	Aranda Chia Shui Keng × Arnth. Beatrice Ng	George Black 1973
BRIGHT EYES	Arnth. Lilleput × V. tricolor	S'pore Orchids 1972
PATRICIA POSTLETHWAITE	Arnth. Bloodshot × V. limbata	Choo Yeok Koon 1972

HUEYLIHARA

HUEYLIH JANE	Rnet. Sunrise × Rhy. gigantea	Hong Sih Chen (Hueylih Jane)

HYGROCHILUS

parishii (see *Vandopsis parishii*†‡) species

IONOCIDIUM

MADELYN SCHOEPPLER	Inps. paniculata × Onc. triquetrum	Howell 1975
RAINBOW	Onc. Hopewell × Ressie Toy	Osment 1971
RESSIE TOY	Inps. paniculata × Onc. pulchellum	Osment 1968

× Onc. Hopewell = Rainbow

IONOPSIS

paniculata‡ **species**

(This is treated for registration purposes as specifically distinct from *Ionopsis utricularioides*, though ranked by some authorities as conspecific.)

× Onc. triquetrum = Incdm. Madelyn Schoeppler |

utricularioides‡ **species**

(This is treated for registration purposes as specifically distinct from *Ionopsis paniculata,* though ranked by some authorities as conspecific.)

× Rdza. decora = Rodps. Ressie Toy |

JIMENEZARA

JOSE	L. autumnalis × Lpna. Kingston	W. W. G. Moir 1973

JOANNARA

FLIRT	Ren. storiei × Rhv. Busakorn	Eikarat 1974
IVAN ANG	Rhv. Blue Angel × Rntda. Gold Nugget	Corbett 1975
JETSTAR	Rntda. Violet × Rhv. Blue Angel	R. K. Mizuta 1973
RUNGTIVAR	Rhv. Wong Yoke Sim × Ren. storiei	Sawang Somboonpol 1975
SILA-ARD	Rhv. Sagarik Wine × Ren. storiei	Sulyapong 1974 (Sagarik)

KAGAWARA

BOON RUBB	Ascda. Yip Sum Wah × Ren. storiei	Sombuntham 1972
DOUNGDEE	Ascda. Priyavadee × Ren. storiei	Sawang Somboonpol 1975
INFERNO	Ren. John Tew × Ascda. Yip Sum Wah	R. K. Mizuta 1974
JUNE	Ren. philippinensis × Ascda. Meda Arnold	Muttamara 1973
KANITH	Ascda. Honwichai × Ren. storiei	Sawang Somboonpol 1974
MADAME YIP KHEW-YING	Ren. philippinensis × Ascda. Peggy Foo	Yoon Pooi-Kong 1974
MEMORIA THEP SATREE	Ascda. Haad Ravai × Ren. storiei	Palm Orchids 1975
NELL CARLSON	Ren. imschootiana × Ascda. Sunkist	Miyamoto 1975
RED ELF	Ascda. Ophelia × Ren. imschootiana	M. Miyao 1971
RED LAVA	Ascda. Meda Arnold × Ren. imschootiana	Miyao 1972
SHUMOON ABDULALI	Ren. Brookie Chandler × Ascda. Red Gem	Wallbrunn 1974
TEO BOON HIAN	Ren. storiei × Ascda. Medasand	Teo Boon Hian 1974
VIROONCHAN RUBY	Ren. storiei × Ascda. Seechang	H. K. Lau 1975
YOON WENG-LOW	Ren. philippinensis × Ascda. Yip Sum Wah	Yoon Pooi-Kong 1974
YUTHAYONG BEAUTY	Rntda. Lyn Andrade × Ascda. Meda Arnold	Pisalsithivat 1975

KINGIDIUM

deliciosum **species**

(see *Kingiella philippinensis‡*; syn *Kingiella decumbens*)

KINGIELLA

(This generic name has been botanically changed to *Kingidium* for nomenclatural (homonymy) reasons, but *Kingiella* is retained as the horticulturally recommended generic name for registration use.)

deliciosa (*Kingidium deliciosum*) **species**

(see *Kingiella philippinensis‡*)

KINGIELLA

philippinensis‡ **species**

(This is retained as the horticulturally recommended name for registration purposes even though *Kingidium (Kingiella) deliciosum* is the botanically correct name for this species. It has also been (incorrectly) called *Kingiella decumbens.*)

× Phal. cornu-cervi	= Phlla. Speck O'Gold	× Phal. Janet Kuhn	= Phlla. Sunburst
× Phal. equestris	= Phlla. New Horizon	× Phal. mariae	= Phlla. Freckles

decumbens (see *philippinensis*‡) **species**

KOMKRISARA

THONBURI **Rnst. Queen Emma × Asctm. curvifolium** **Weerowathanamas 1974 (Komkris)**

LAELIA

acuminata* (see *rubescens*†‡) **species**

anceps*†‡ **species**

× Bc. André Guttin	= Blc. Charles Hagan	× C. Porcia	= Lc. Stepladder
× C. Bob Betts	= Lc. Small Talk	× C. Rita Renee	= Lc. Garden Delight
× C. Edithiae	= Lc. Mem. Kurazo Ogata	× C. walkerana	= Lc. Twilight Song
× C. Okami	= Lc. Kamokila		

ANCIBARINA† **anceps × cinnabarina** **Colman 1914**

× Lc. Joan Matthews	= Lc. Lola Schloat		

autumnalis*†‡ **species**

× Lpna. Kingston	= Jmzra. Jose		

cinnabarina*†‡ **species**

× C. Browniae	= Lc. Peggy Lynn Grezaffi	× Epi. phoeniceum	= Epl. Firie Gem
		× Lc. Amelia	= Lc. Kagaribi
× C. Iris	= Lc. Flaemmchen	× Lc. Easter Bonnet	= Lc. Sam
× C. Margaret Stewart	= Lc. Freshie	× Lc. Queen Alexandra	= Lc. Bit of Orange
× C. Pavlova	= Lc. Dorothy Baxter	× Schom. crispa	= Smbl. Cinnamon Crisp
× Epi. mariae	= Epl. Cinderella	× Slc. Lindores	= Slc. Torch

CORONET*†‡ **cinnabarina × harpophylla** **C. 1902**

× Blc. Pacific Gold	= Blc. Pacific Coronet	× Lc. Pacific Sun	= Lc. Sunoret
× Blc. Richard Nixon	= Blc. Ruby Lantern	× Slc. Anzac	= Slc. Corozac
× Lc. Amelia	= Lc. Amelinet		

flava*†‡ **species**

× C. Blanche	= Lc. Blanchflava	× Epi. atropurpureum	= Epl. Rio Verde
× C. Bob Betts	= Lc. Loony Goon	× Epi. gracile	= Epl. Alan Sues
× C. Highburiensis	= Lc. Midnight Street	× Epi. mariae	= Epl. Marie Louise
× C. Loddiaca	= Lc. Heidi	× Lc. Helen B. Lawrence	= Lc. Mem. Sophia Cox
× C. Southern Belle	= Lc. Small Paul	× Sl. Psyche	= Sl. Flava-Psyche

gloedeniana **species**

× C. dowiana	= Lc. War Dance		

GOLD STAR‡ **flava × harpophylla** **Rod McLellan Co. 1963**

× Blc. Ruth Cline McDade	= Blc. Crowders Mountain	× C. Henrietta Japhet	= Lc. Henrietta Gold

gouldiana*† **species**

× C. Claesiana	= Lc. Pink Panty		

grandiflora* — **species**

× Lc. Song of Norway = Lc. Ballet Folklorico

grandis*†‡ — **species**

× Bc. Brazil = Blc. Day and Night
× C. dowiana = Lc. Helena Baraya
× Epi. tampense = Epl. Christopher John

harpophylla*†‡ — **species**

× B. nodosa = Bl. Harposa
× C. Edgewood Pearl = Lc. Beverly Perry
× Lc. Crepe Suzette = Lc. Harposuzette
× Lc. Excellency = Lc. Remmel von Gritsch
× Slc. Anzac = Slc. Fiesta Gold

ICARUS‡ — **cinnabarina × flava** — **Veitch 1902**

× Lc. Chit Chat = Lc. Trick or Treat

jongheana* — **species**

× C. warneri = Lc. Jonghewar

longipes* — **species**

× Sl. Marriottiana = Sl. Creamer

lundii†‡ (syn. *regnellii†*) — **species**

× Soph. coccinea = Sl. Minuet

milleri‡ (syn. *muelleri*) — **species**

× B. cordata = Bl. Cordy Miller
× Blc. Buttercup = Blc. California Sunset
× C. bicolor = Lc. Mrs. Red
× C. elongata = Lc. Cherry Torte
× C. granulosa = Lc. Alachua
× C. guttata = Lc. Jalapa
× C. schroderae = Lc. Ben Bracey
× C. velutina = Lc. Chester Goddard
× Epi. belizense = Epl. Connie
× Lc. Ann Follis = Lc. June Gow
× Lc. Remula = Lc. Glowing Embers
× Slc. Brandywine = Slc. Spirit of 'Seventysix

muelleri (see *milleri‡*) — **species**

peduncularis (see *rubescens†‡*) — **species**

pumila*†‡ — **species**

× C. mossiae = Lc. Lorna Dene Whitlow
× Lc. Abe Montague = Lc. Luiz Ernesto Ramos
× Lc. José Dias Castro = Lc. Zuki Josemila
× Lpt. bicolor = Lptl. Leprechaun

purpurata*†‡ — **species**

× Bc. Evelyn Zuck = Blc. Romania Woolley
× Lc. Parysatis = Lc. Brazilian Sky

regnellii† (see *lundii†‡*) — **species**

rubescens†‡ — **species**

(syn. *acuminata**; syn. *peduncularis*)

× C. Claesiana = Lc. Mem. Francis Knaebel
× C. luteola = Lc. Rubescent Luteus
× Epi. bifidum = Epl. Izobel Reid

rupestris* — **species**

× Blc. Mem. Ruth Gessner = Blc. Little Boy Blue
× C. Clay O'Brien = Lc. Clay O'Pestris
× Lc. Joan Matthews = Lc. Candy
× Sl. Psyche = Sl. Tinkerbelle
× Slc. Anzac = Slc. Rupanzac

SUNOL — **xanthina × milleri** — **Rod McLellan Co. 1968**

× C. gaskelliana = Lc. Summer Sun

superbiens* (see *Schomburgkia superbiens†‡*) — **species**

tenebrosa*†‡ — **species**

× Blc. Orange Glory = Blc. Kelly Brooks
× Lc. Bonanza = Lc. Tenebon
× Lc. First Star = Lc. Walter Larrabee
× Lc. Nuuana = Lc. Guaicaipuro
× Sl. Psyche = Sl. Betty Jean Scott
× Slc. Jewel Box = Slc. Ten-e-Jewel

LAELIA

ZIP — **tenebrosa × milleri** — **Rod McLellan Co. 1965**

× Bc. Calypso = Blc. Calyzip
× Blc. Fortune = Blc. Saracen
× C. dowiana = Lc. Zippity Doodow
× C. Nuclear Age = Lc. Nuclear Zip
× Lc. Christopher Gubler = Lc. Orange Fire
× Lc. Issy = Lc. Cinders
× Lc. Mem. Albert Heinecke = Lc. Copper Glo
× Lc. Orange Gem = Lc. Zem
× Lc. Susana Tafolla = Lc. Danau Toba Idyl
× Lc. Waianae Sunset = Lc. Red Rooster
× Slc. Anzac = Slc. Zana
× Slc. Carla Carter = Slc. Potpourri

LAELIOCATONIA

ROY FIELDS — **Lc. Mattie Shave × Ctna. Keith Roth** — **Rives 1975**

LAELIOCATTLEYA

ABE MONTAGUE‡ — **Hertha × Princess Margaret** — **H. Patterson 1958**

× Luiz Martinelli = Mercedes Lisbôa Seng
× L. pumila = Luiz Ernesto Ramos

ACLANDOR — **L. dormaniana × C. aclandiae** — **Stewart Inc. 1970**

× Soph. coccinea = Slc. Twinkle Toes

ACONCAGUA*†‡ — **Schroderae × C. Maggie Raphael** — **Schroder 1926**

× Pegi Mayne = Something Special
× C. Kittiwake = Preferment

ADDISON FRIENDSHIP — **Norman Gray × Joseph Hampton** — **E.E.G. Orchids 1974**

ADELAIDE WALTMAN — **C. guttata × Elstead Gem** — **Hoyt 1964**

× C. luteola = Luteous Gem
× Slc. Paprika = Slc. Lynn Yayoi Tsuji

ADELE GODDARD — **Bonanza × C. intermedia** — **Fort Caroline 1975**

ADINA*†‡ — **General Maude × Pyramus** — **C. 1929**

× C. Titrianae = Yukiko Hironaka

ADMIRAL STOKES — **C. Joyce Hannington × Lorraine Shirai** — **Blauvelt 1972**

ADOLPH HECKER‡ — **C. Porcia × Bonanza** — **Hecker 1959**

× Bonanza = Pelot's Pride
× Bc. Daffodil = Blc. Renee Nicolson
× Blc. Herons Ghyll = Blc. Sandy Robinson
× Blc. Mem. Crispin Rosales = Blc. Jane Fleming
× C. Penang = Aquarius

ADOLPHO MENEZES — **Jośe Dias Castro × Walter Slagle** — **Altenburg 1973**

ADONIS* — **Lustrissima × Morryth** — **A. 1930**

× Gitche Manito = Mem. Takeshi Kido

AENEID†‡ — **Britannia × C. Fabianid** — **A. & M. 1947**

× Robin Hood = National Geographic

AHMAD SHEIKHI — **C. Kittiwake × Mem. Maggie Hood** — **A. & R. 1973**

AÏDA†‡ — **Britannia × C. labiata** — **V. 1948**

× Lucie Hausermann = Sophia
× C. Bob Betts = Stacey Bull

AK SAR BEN — **C. Tethys × Atlantis** — **Rod McLellan Co. 1959**

× George Cutler = Reuben Metz

AKUHEAD PUPULE — **Princess Margaret × Kismet Queen** — **Otaguro 1973**

ALACHUA — **C. granulosa × L. milleri** — **Fort Caroline 1975 (Brooks)**

ALBERT CULVER — **Matilija × Cantabile** — **Rod McLellan Co. 1971**

LAELIOCATTLEYA

ALBERT HOLLINGSWORTH — **Bonanza × Pirate King** — **Gubler 1971**

ALFREDO MARTINELLI‡ — **Léviathan × Hertha** — **Altenburg 1964 (A. F. Martinelli)**

× Hertha	= Sans Atout		

ALICE LANI CHUN — **Balkis × Seattle** — **Otaguro 1971**

ALICIA — **C. bowringiana × Roitelet** — **Marcel Lecoufle 1974**

ALICE OTAGURO — **Mysedo × Lee Langford** — **Otaguro 1974**

ALI REZA PAHLAVI — **Bonanza × Castanabid** — **A. & R. 1973**

ALISAL‡ — **Governor Gore × C. labiata** — **Rod McLellan Co. 1960 (E. W. McLellan)**

× Paradisio	= Commander	× Princess Woodstar	= Wateree

ALLAN-A-DALE‡ — **Integrity × Savitar** — **A. & R. 1975**

× Mem. Walter Armacost	= Californian Beauty		

ALMA†‡ — **Appam × Helius** — **M. 1931**

× Blc. Cheah Bean-Kee	= Blc. Alma Kee	× Slc. Rosemary Clooney	= Slc. Stacy Miyamoto

ALMA WICHMANN — **Golden Joy × Edgard van Belle** — **Wichmann 1965**

× Blc. Emerald Meadow	= Blc. Table Mountain	× Blc. Fortune	= Blc. Klondike Creek

ALOHA KOJI OTA — **Penmarth × Fedora** — **K. Ota 1975 (Otaguro)**

ALOPE‡ — **Princess Margaret × Joseph Hampton** — **Bracey 1960**

× Umatilla Reef	= Van Norman Lake		

ALRIGHT — **Cuesta × Ishtar** — **Rayridge 1975 (F. J. Bergman)**

ALTEN†‡ — **Altesse × C. Enid** — **Patterson 1945**

× C. mossiae	= Hausermann's Nocturne		

ALTESSE*†‡ — **Britannia × C. Remy Chollet** — **V. 1936**

× C. mendelii	= Tom Braverman		

AMBER CARDINAL — **Amber Glow × Cardinal** — **A. & M. 1973**

AMBER GLOW†‡ — **Derna × Anne Walker** — **McDade 1952**

× Bright Night	= Mem. Bill Mayfield	× Blc. Buttercup	= Blc. Dandy Lion
× Cardinal	= Amber Cardinal	× Blc. Jane Helton	= Blc. Golden Forest
× Chine	= Orcade	× Blc. Jewel Higdon	= Blc. Warren Wever
× Danaé	= Tango	× Blc. Lleblanche	= Blc. Faye Miyamoto
× Mary Alma Kurtz	= Elizabeth Chang	× Blc. Pamela Farrell	= Blc. Port Sherry
× Meri Segars	= Ruth McDade	× Blc. Walter Abe	= Blc. Walter's Glow
× South Esk	= Golden Fire	× C. intermedia	= Solitude
× Bc. Mount Hood	= Blc. Sunwapta Peak	× Pot. Glowing Beauty	= Pot. Ceezie Guest
× Blc. Acapana	= Blc. Jitra	× Slc. Madge Fordyce	= Slc. Sue Fordyce

AMELIA*‡ — **C. intermedia × L. cinnabarina** — **Gratrix 1898**

× Luminosa	= Niji	× L. cinnabarina	= Kagaribi
× Oriental Splendor	= September Moon	× L. Coronet	= Amelinet

AMELINET — **Amelia × L. Coronet** — Hattori 1975

ANA MARIA DUVEEN — Lee Langford × **Pacific Sun** — **R. M. Hamilton 1974 (Ilsley)**

ANDRE BAUMANN — **Saadia × Edgard van Belle** — **Marcel Lecoufle 1972**

ANDREW HAUSERMANN — **Irene Finney × Mira** — **Hausermann 1974**

LAELIOCATTLEYA

ANITA KING — **C. guttata × George Cutler** — **Owen King 1972 (M. J. Bates)**

ANNE WALKER†‡ — **Carmencita × Goldfish** — **S. 1937**

× Blc. Jewel Higdon	= Blc. Yellow Jewell		

ANN FOLLIS‡ — **C. granulosa × Ethel Merman** — **Rod McLellan Co. 1963 (E. W. McLellan)**

× Excellency	= Brilliant Splendor	× C. Fascelis	= Seminole Meadows
× Lee Langford	= Green Heritage	× C. Granfort	= Gwin
× Blc. Fortune	= Blc. Ann Fortune	× C. luteola	= Cuiseag
× Blc. Golden Llewellyn	= Blc. Heavenly Valley	× L. milleri	= June Gow
× Blc. Pimola	= Blc. Perko McAllister	× Slc. Anzac	= Slc. Plum Brandy

ANTONICA FREDRICK‡ — **C. bicolor × Charlesworthii** — **von Paulsen 1965**

× Murrie Fitch	= Lynn Richard	× C. aclandiae	= Leigh Ann Blackmore
× B. glauca	= Blc. Lothlorien	× C. aurantiaca	= Tim's Fire
× B. nodosa	= Blc. Binnie Foster	× C. bicolor	= Hot Chili Pepper
× Bc. Bill Worsley	= Blc. Merry	× C. Wolteriana	= Gimli
× Bc. Daffodil	= Blc. Voo Doo	× Epi. tampense	= Eplc. Gilbert
× Blc. Jewel-Glo	= Blc. Jane Sherouse	× Pot. Jo Ann Crouch	= Pot. Bettycake
× Blc. Jewel Higdon	= Blc. Gene McKenzie	× Sl. Gratrixiae	= Slc. Marion Stevens
× Blc. Malvern	= Blc. Malrick	× Soph. coccinea	= Slc. Ftatateeta

ANVIL PEAK — **Fabled City × Murano** — **Beall 1975**

APPLAUSE — **Bonanza × Firebon** — **Rex Foster's 1974 (Gripp)**

AQUARIUS — **C. Penang × Adolph Hecker** — **Wilkins 1972**

AQUI-FINN — **C. Suavior × Irene Finney** — **Hausermann 1974**

ARECA*†‡ — **General Maude × C. Enid** — **L. 1922**

× Cavalese	= Berkeley	× Blc. Etta K. Kinley	= Blc. Kinare

ARIEL* — **Cowanii × C. dowiana** — **H. 1907**

× Schulzeana	= Tombstone Mountain		

ARMARIS — **R. J. Chrisman × Mem. Walter Armacost** — **A. & R. 1969**

× C. Dark Emperor	= Ganado		

ARNY FREEMAN‡ — **Cassandra × Oliver Lines** — **H. Patterson 1952**

× C. Dinah	= Resolution Mountain		

ARTHUR E. MILES‡ — **Sagana × C. mossiae** — **A. E. Miles 1944**

× Titriva	= Titiles		

ARTHUR McKEE — **Doctor G. T. Moore × Saint Louis** — **Fairburn 1974**

ARTIE CARLISLE SCHWEER — **C. Probity × Grandee** — **Bracey 1963**

× Slc. Helen Veliz	= Slc. Sunflare		

ASHGROVE — **General Maude × Valencia** — **Harveyson 1961**

× Blc. Mernia	= Blc. Mem. Kevin Watford		

AT DUSK — **Elegans × C. walkerana** — **Stewart Inc. 1974**

AUGUSTA FREUND LITTMANN — **White Queen × Easter Belle** — **Mo. Bot. Gdn. 1972**

AUTUMN SYMPHONY‡ — **Medon × Cardinal** — **A. & M. 1955**

× Blc. Herons Ghyll	= Blc. Autumn Ghyll		

AVALON — **Elizabeth Off × C. labiata** — **Starke & Son 1975 (W. H. Starke)**

LAELIOCATTLEYA

AZURE HILL — **Blue Boy × C. luteola** — **Rod McLellan Co. 1975**
BABE BERGIN — **C. Portia × Schillerana** — **Kersey 1971**
BABY NUUANU — **Mercia × C. Guatemalensis** — **J. Milton Warne 1972**
BACH-AGA†‡ — **Crowborough × C. Remy Chollet** — **V. 1937**
× Hernani = Bachani

BACHANI — **Bach-Aga × Hernani** — **Marcel Lecoufle 1974**
BALDUR† — **Sargon × Spalatro** — **A. 1930**
× Ishtar = Mem. Toyo Sakumoto

BALKIS*†‡ — **Queen Mary × C. Peetersii** — **A. 1934**
× Ludgate = Sorry | × Seattle = Alice Lani Chun

BALLET FOLKLORICO — Song of Norway × L. grandiflora — **Stewart Inc. 1975**
BALLYHOO — **C. loddigesii × Jonáral** — **Rod McLellan Co. 1972**
BARBARA TSUBAKI — Faith Dee Fanchaly × Nigrescent — **Tsubaki 1972 (Rivermont)**

BARTON†‡ — **C. granulosa × Canhamiana** — **Clarelen 1947**
× C. Hybrida = Buffalo Trace

BELLE OF CELLE‡ — **Edgard van Belle × C. Nigrella** — **Wichmann 1965**
× Kilauea Iki = Kilauea Belle | × C. Irgatta = William of Woodlawn
× Lee Langford = Carmel Cone | × C. Tango = Color Plus
× Waianae Sunset = Waianae Belle

BELLE OF HILO — **Edgard van Belle × Waianae Sunset** — Haw. Mt. O. 1973 **(Hernlund)**

BELLES FLANDRES — **Musset × Ronsard** — **Pff. V. & L. 1956**
× Harold J. Patterson = Tampon

BELL O'BRONZE — **C. bicolor × Edgard van Belle** — **Rod McLellan Co. 1974**
BEN BRACEY — **L. milleri × C. schroderae** — **W. W. G. Moir 1971 (Ben Bracey)**

BENJAMIN HARRIS — C. Hardyana × South Esk — **F. L. Harris 1971 (B. Harris)**

BERGAMOTE — **Firefly × L. cinnabarina** — **F. 1970**
× Blc. Canari = Blc. Zafaran

BERKELEY — **Cavalese × Areca** — **Altenburg 1971 (A. & R.)**

BERNICE DODSON — **Hurricane × C. Peace** — **Mrs. L. Wilson 1974**
BEST REGARDS — **Bonanza × C. Dubiosa** — **Stewart Inc. 1972**
BETTY VON PAULSEN — **Hazel Abel × C. aurantiaca** — Rod McLellan Co. 1971
BEVERLY PERRY — C. Edgewood Pearl × L. harpophylla — **Kersey 1972**
BILL SHAVE — **C. Catherine Patterson × Pegi Mayne** — Trade Winds 1972
BIMUR† — **Gold Mohur × C. bicolor** — **S. 1946**
× C. luteola = Entwood

BIT OF ORANGE — Queen Alexandra × L. cinnabarina — **Stevenson 1975**
BLANCHFLAVA — **C. Blanche × L. flava** — **Lenette 1974 (Rivermont)**
× Bc. Seafoam = Blc. Yellow Sea

BLUE BOY‡ — **C. Ariel × Elegans** — **Bracey 1960**
× Twinkle Star = Night Twinkle | × C. mossiae = Clear Blue Sky
× Bc. Déesse = Blc. Rosemary Hayden | × C. walkerana = Blue Dynasty
× Blc. Mem. Ruth Gessner = Blc. Biscayne Skies | × C. warneri = Blue Ribbon
× C. luteola = Azure Hill

BLUE DYNASTY — Blue Boy × C. walkerana — Stewart Inc. 1974

BLUE PACIFIC — Mariner × C. labiata — Beall 1973

BLUE RIBBON — Blue Boy × C. warneri — Stewart Inc. 1974

BOB GORE‡ — South Esk × Boadicea — Gore 1954

× Pot. Medea = Pot. Bill

BOB'S LOVE — Guerrero × C. Portisoniae — Rod McLellan Co. 1972

BONANZA†‡ — Cavalese × C. Prospector — Bracey 1949

× Adolph Hecker = Pelot's Pride
× Bush River = Kingstree
× Castanabid = Ali Reza Pahlavi
× De Loris Ziegfeld = Ziegfeld's Bonanza
× Firebon = Applause
× Helen Street = Mildred Benis
× Hypellency = Uncle Sheu Wan
× José Dias Castro = Bonin
× Kyoko Takeda = Mitsuko Takeda
× Luiz Martinelli = José Walter Seng
× Oakland = Kalono
× Pirate King = Albert Hollingsworth
× Pirate's Gold = Deming
× Poussin = Foxfire
× Princess Esk = Bonesk
× Prophesy = Bonanza Queen
× Rojo = Claude Timmons
× Sagapyle = Patricia Hewlett
× Sangrita = Cass Hough
× Suprême = Celler Rühm
× Waianae Sunset = Bonanza Sunset
× Bc. Anton = Blc. Bonton
× Bc. Déesse = Blc. Cherry Paradise
× Bc. Doris = Blc. Dorbon
× Bc. Mount Anderson = Blc. Teng
× Bc. Mount Hood = Blc. Cannes Festival
× Blc. Amy Wakasugi = Blc. Fall Splendor
× Blc. Dark Waters = Blc. Bondark
× Blc. Eva Patterson = Blc. Norma Komiko Heen
× Blc. First Nighter = Blc. Ivan Coll
× Blc. Lucky = Blc. Lucky Bonanza
× Blc. Magenta Intense = Blc. Incandescent
× Blc. Mem. Bill Fouraker = Blc. Mark Zeug
× Blc. Momercia = Blc. Bomercia
× C. Bob Betts = Bonbetts
× C. Charybdis = Mary Kawena Pukui
× C. Dubiosa = Best Regards
× C. Esbetts = Moochie
× C. Henrietta Japhet = Bonphet
× C. intermedia = Adele Goddard
× C. Karae Lyn Sugiyama = Mary Jean Warren
× C. Moscombe = Chiou-Jye Chen
× C. Mrs. J. W. Whiteley = Mabel Carr Thornton
× C. Peanuts = Victor Canavese
× C. Portisoniae = Joe Osorio
× C. Sedlesscombe = Hong-Sie Chen
× C. Thetis = Thebon
× L. tenebrosa = Tenebon
× Pot. Patna = Pot. Shigeko Takeda
× Pot. Red Friar = Pot. Bon-Friar
× Pot. Welson Gasparini = Pot. Yamasee
× Slc. Autumn Delight = Slc. Bonlight
× Slc. Dizac = Slc. Bondizac
× Slc. Ormona = Slc. Ormanza

BONANZA QUEEN — Prophesy × Bonanza — Stewart Inc. 1974

BONANZA SUNSET — Bonanza × Waianae Sunset — Otaguro 1973

BONBETTS — C. Bob Betts × Bonanza — Miskimens 1974

BONESK — Bonanza × Princess Esk — Ruben 1972

BONIN — José Dias Castro × Bonanza — Altenburg 1972

BONPHET — C. Henrietta Japhet × Bonanza — Katsuura 1973

BOSSA NOVA — Mary Rose × Nigrescent — E. W. McLellan 1973

BOWRI-ALBIDA — C. bowringiana × L. albida — Thayer 1901

× C. bowringiana = Smile

BRAZILIAN SKY — Parysatis × L. purpurata — W. W. G. Moir 1975

BRAZORIA — Sagana × C. Enid — Proebstle 1960

× Junto = Martha Evelyn Bean
× Blc. Wake Island = Blc. Terri Hoover

BRENDA JANE — C. trianae × Tartan — Bosco 1952

× Joseph Baker = Dora Zuck

BRIDE'S BOUQUET — Easter Bonnet × C. Irene — Rivermont 1961

× C. Irene = Louise Alexander
× C. Snow White = Mem. Ronnie Endsley
× C. White Belle = White Gull

BRIGHT BIRD — Pacific Sun × Golden Wren — Rod McLellan Co. 1975

BRIGHT NIGHT‡ — C. Pittiana × L. Cinnabrosa — Rivermont 1958

× Amber Glow = Mem. Bill Mayfield
× Meri Segars = Merry and Bright
× Waianae Sunset = Hawaiian Warrior
× C. Iris = Simone Kim-Cuc Bauer
× Pot. Glowing Beauty = Pot. Breezy Dohlberg

LAELIOCATTLEYA

BRILIANT ORANGE — **Orange Ann × Orange Beauty** — **Rod McLellan Co. 1964**

× Mercia = Liebling
× Blc. Gold City = Blc. Sun Crest
× C. aurantiaca = Oroyum
× C. Guatemalensis = Orange Aurea
× Pot. Fortune Teller = Pot. Brilliant Fortune

BRILLIANT SPLENDOR — **Excellency × Ann Follis** — **Fort Caroline 1975**

BRITANSUN — **Britannia × Sunburst** — **S.A. 1951**

× Cocarde = Syvil Marquit

BROWN BEAR PASS — **Waianae Sunset × Orebus** — **Beall 1973**

BROWN DERBY‡ — **Glenferness × L. tenebrosa** — **H. D. Wright 1957**

× C. Florence Patterson = Good Try

BUCCANEER†‡ — **Cavalese × C. Dinah** — **A. 1943**

× Quadroon = Charles Plaxico
× Blc. Norman's Bay = Blc. Mem. Roy Garrity
× Pot. Gordon Siu = Pot. Lucinda Park

BUFFALO TRACE — **C. Hybrida × Barton** — **Robt. Smith 1973**

BURMA QUEEN — **C. Ardentissima × Lee Langford** — **Stewart Inc. 1972**

BUSH RIVER — **Margate × Derrynane** — **C. & H. 1968**

× Bonanza = Kingstree

BUTTERSCOTCH — **C. Leila Aronson × Golden Concolor** — **Stewart Inc. 1962**

× Elinor = Guaicamacuto

CABAZON†‡ — **Marie Dobrott × Titymoma** — **A. & R. 1941**

× Blc. Crown Prince Akihito = Blc. Yoshie Evelyn Sawai

CALANDAL — **Chantecler × C. Fabianid** — **V. 1946**

× Marceau = Marchenoir

CALIFORNIA† — **Conquistador × C. Gay Gordon** — **A. & R. 1941**

× Bc. Hartland = Blc. Hartcal

CALIFORNIAN BEAUTY — **Mem. Walter Armacost × Allan-a-Dale** — **Altenburg 1971**

CAMELOT — **Dr. G. T. Moore × C. Firebird** — **Freed 1965**

× Lorraine Shirai = William Miles

CAMILLA* — **Soulange × C. Dionysius** — **Cowan 1927**

× Mem. Albert Heinecke = Spanish Spice

CANBERRA*†‡ — **Litana × C. Venus** — **Cowan 1927**

× Golden Glow = Canberra Glow
× Blc. Joyance = Blc. Road To Rio

CANBERRA GLOW — **Canberra × Golden Glow** — **Otaguro 1973 (Originator unknown)**

× Blc. Jane Helton = Blc. Yoshiko Asato

CANDY — **Joan Matthews × L. rupestris** — **Pabst 1975**

CANHAMIANA*†‡ — **C. mossiae × L. purpurata** — **S. 1902**

× C. Fabulous = Florence Harris
× C. Princess Bells = Ricke Kaname Fujino
× C. skinneri = Florence Dawson

CANTABILE†‡ — **Fascinator-mossiae × C. warscewiczii** — **A. & R. 1946**

× Jane Warne = Helen Bowden
× Matilija = Albert Culver
× Robin Hood = Mem. Dale Hutchison
× C. Enid = Clown's Nose
× Slc. Vallezac = Slc. Cantazac

LAELIOCATTLEYA

CANTALOUPE	**C. Estelle × Golden Charm**		**Rod McLellan Co. 1965**
× Charlesworthii	= Kumquat		
CARA NOME	**C. Enid × Fedora**		**Crothers 1971**
CARDINAL†‡	**C. Serenity × Eminence**		**Bracey 1951**
× Amber Glow	= Amber Cardinal		
CARLOS RELVAS	**C. percivaliana × Ormesby**		**Altenburg 1971**
CARMEL CONE	**Belle of Celle × Lee Langford**		**Cone 1974 (E. Iwanaga)**
CARMEN ESCOBAR	**C. Porcia × Picardy**		**J. Escobar 1975**
CAROL FRET	**Dixie × Ivy Merkel**		**Pelc 1972**
CAROLYN HURTT	**C. labiata × Molly Tyler**		**Hurtt 1972 (Creve Coeur)**
CAROLYN REID	**C. aurantiaca × Twinkle Star**		**Reid 1972 (Crocker)**
CARRIE ESTELLE†‡	**Prospero × C. trianaei**		**L. 1931**
× Bc. Star Ruby	= Blc. Star Topaz	× C. Revel	= Carvel
CARROT TOP	**Cougar Gold × C. Venosa**		**Beall 1966**
× Pot. Fortune Teller	= Pot. River Range	× Pot. Tapestry Peak	= Pot. Paula Marabella
CARVEL	**Carrie Estelle × C. Revel**		**W. W. G. Moir 1971**
CASSANDRA*†‡	**Gladiator × Sargon**		**A. 1928**
× Molly Tyler	= Cassa Tyler	× Blc. Norman's Bay	= Blc. Chief Osceola
CASSA TYLER	**Molly Tyler × Cassandra**		**Thornton's 1975**
CASS HOUGH	**Sangrita × Bonanza**		**Fugedy 1974**
CASTANABID	**C. Fabianid × Fred Castator**		**A. & R. 1967**
× Bonanza	= Ali Reza Pahlavi		
CATHERINE HOOD	**C. Catherine Patterson × Mem. Maggie Hood**		**Spencer 1975 (Originator unknown)**
CAVALESE*†‡	**Lustre × C. Fabia**		**L. 1924**
× Areca	= Berkeley		
CELLER RŬHM	**Bonanza × Suprême**		**Wichmann 1972**
CHAMBERLAIN ISOTTA	**C. Chamberlainiana × Isotta**		**Otaguro 1973**
CHARLES PLAXICO	**Quadroon × Buccaneer**		**Rod McLellan Co. 1972**
CHARLESWORTHII*†‡	**C. dowiana × L. cinnabarina**		**C. 1900**
× Cantaloupe	= Kumquat	× Blc. Kong-Urai Gold	= Blc. Goldworth
× Flirtie	= Hanky-panky	× C. David Sweet	= Princess Orange
× Florence Machle	= Star Bright	× Pot. Glowing Beauty	= Pot. Mem. Kerry Turner
× Issy	= Stephen Sue	× Pot. Hidden Peak	= Pot. Starmaker
× Blc. Jane Helton	= Blc. Betty Borer	× Pot. Red Friar	= Pot. Cinnamon Stick
CHARLIE STEM	**Elissa × C. Nigritian**		**Stem 1962 (Bracey)**
× Dee Dee	= Sandy Gibson	× Blc. Mem. Crispin Rosales	= Blc. Bonnie Warren
× Pacific Rose	= Kimberly Sovereign		
CHELMO	**C. mossiae × Georgette**		**Kensington 1974**
CHEN'S BEAUTY	**C. Sedlescombe × Princess Esk**		**Hong-Sie Chen 1975** (Chung-Chweng Chen)
CHERRY TORTE	**L. milleri × C. elongata**		**Fort Caroline 1972 (Wallbrunn)**

LAELIOCATTLEYA

CHESTER GODDARD — **C. velutina × L. milleri** — **Fort Caroline 1973 (Wallbrunn)**

CHEVERNY — **Hernani × Hertha** — **Pff. V. & L. 1971**

CHICANERY — **Goldcrest × C. aurantiaca** — **Miskimens 1973**

CHIC BONNET — **Easter Bonnet × Chickamauga** — **Rivermont 1960**
× Shenandoah = Mem. Laura Brabham

CHINE‡ — **Omphale × Edgard van Belle** — **Pff. V. & L. 1962**
× Amber Glow = Orcade | × Waianae Sunset = Red Cedar Canyon

CHIOU-JYE CHEN — **C. Moscombe × Bonanza** — **Hong-Sie Chen 1975 (Chung-Chweng Chen)**

CHIRPY — **Rojo × Red Gold** — **Wilkins 1974**

CHIT CHAT — **C. aurantiaca × L. Coronet** — **Stewart Inc. 1965**
× Rojo = Ding-a-Ling | × L. Icarus = Trick or Treat

CHOLLETIANA — **C. mossiae × L. superbiens** — **Dallemagne 1902**
× Slc. Anzac = Slc. Westercelle

CHOTON† — **Mrs. Medo × ?** — **C. Takeda 1956 (Yamaoka)**
× Blc. Midas = Blc. Midaton

CHRISTMAS FAIRY‡ — **Jane Dane × Abnaki** — **Rivermont 1958**
× Stephen Oliver Fouraker = David Cole

CHRISTOPHER GUBLER — **Mem. Albert Heinecke × C. aclandiae** — **Gubler 1964 (Hanes)**
× Waianae Sunset = Indian Mountain | × L. Zip = Orange Fire

CINDERS — **Issy × L. Zip** — **Rod McLellan Co. 1974 (Fordyce)**

CINNALO‡ — **C. loddigesii × L. Cinnabrosa** — **Rivermont 1960**
× C. intermedia = Color Collage

CLARA SCHRIEVER‡ — **C. Raphaellaura × Jane Dane** — **J. & S. 1953 (Kwr.)**
× C. Catherine Patterson = Ruth Williams | × C. intermedia = Guadeloupe

CLAUDE TIMMONS — **Rojo × Bonanza** — **Voo Doo Orchids 1974**

CLAY O'PESTRIS — C. Clay O'Brien × L. rupestris — **Pabst 1975**

CLEAR BLUE SKY — **Blue Boy × C. mossiae** — **Stewart Inc. 1971**

CLIFTON DOWN — **Princess Margaret × C. mossiae** — **A. & B. 1952**
× C. Bob Betts = Freda Miskimens

CLOTH OF GOLD†‡ — **Firminii × Verviers** — **S. 1938**
× C. Iris = Mem. Garrison Ainsworth

CLOWN'S NOSE — **C. Enid × Cantabile** — **Rod McLellan Co. 1972**

COCARDE‡ — **Britannia × C. Maggie Raphael** — **V. 1937**
× Britansun = Syvil Marquit

COLONEL‡ — **Avignon × C. Amabilis** — **Gore 1954**
× Harold Carlson = Kameyo Sato

COLORAMA — C. Arctic Snow × Peggy Huffman — **Introini 1962 (Gamble)**
× Blc. Iliad = Blc. Color Equation | × C. Horace = Prism Palette
× C. Francis T. C. Au = Patinum Sun | × C. intermedia = Mime

LAELIOCATTLEYA

COLOR COLLAGE — Cinnalo × C. intermedia — Stevenson 1973
COLOR PLUS — C. Tango × Belle of Celle — Bloom's Nursery 1974
COMMANDER — Paradisio × Alisal — Rod McLellan Co. 1974
CONGO — C. Nigritian × Golden Gate — Rod McLellan Co. 1965
× Bc. Mount Anderson = Blc. Congo Mountain

COPPER GLO — Mem. Albert Heinecke × L. Zip — Rod McLellan Co. 1973 (Fordyce)

COPPERWICK‡ — Copperopolis × Golden Gate — Rod McLellan Co. 1966 (E. W. McLellan)
× Western Sunset = Sunwick | × Blc. Goldfield = Blc. Impression

CORA WILLIAMS — Quadroon × George Cutler — Rod McLellan Co. 1974
COSTA RICA†‡ — Canberra × Carmencita — B. 1942
× Slc. Naomi Kerns = Slc. Spectrum Range

CREPE SUZETTE — Charlesworthii × Bright Night — Dunn 1966 (Rivermont)
× L. harpophylla = Harposuzette

CRINOLINE — Dyver × Tyl — F. 1972
CROWBOROUGH SUNSHINE‡ — C. dowiana × Apricot Gleam — L. 1956
× Blc. Norman's Bay = Blc. Sunshine Bay | × C. Leila Aronson = Siamese Cat

CUESTA†‡ — Cavalese × Marie Dobrott — A. & R. 1941
× Ishtar = Alright | × Blc. Blanche Carter = Blc. Kona Reef
× Ludgate = Cuestagate

CUESTAGATE — Ludgate × Cuesta — Rayridge 1975 (F. J. Bergman)

CUISEAG — C. luteola × Ann Follis — Rod McLellan Co. 1975
CULMINANT — Ile de France × Gaillard — Maurice Vacherot 1957
× Ethel D. Giddings = Duchesse

CURTIS HANSARD — Chickadee × Aristocrat — Rivermont 1968
× Blc. Rising Sun = Blc. Flo

CYRANO† — Crowborough × C. Maggie Raphael — V. 1934
× Edgard van Belle = Jeremie

DAHLIA — President Wilson × C. Etta — B. 1932
× Blc. Mem. Crispin Rosales = Blc. Dahros | × C. Remy Chollet = Dahllet

DAHLLET — Dahlia × C. Remy Chollet — Katsuura 1973
DANAÉ†‡ — Francois Coppe × Jocelyn — V. 1943
× Amber Glow = Tango

DANAU TOBA IDYL — Susana Tafolla × L. Zip — Stewart Inc. 1973 (Thomdel)

DARK DOLL — Frank Lind × Land of Enchantment — Stevenson 1973
DARK EYES‡ — C. Nigritian × Princess Margaret — Altenburg 1964
× Blc. Dark Waters = Blc. Dark Smoke

DAVID COLE — Christmas Fairy × Stephen Oliver Fouraker — Jack Cole 1972 (Lines)

DAVID LOZOYA‡ — Joseph Hampton × Bonanza — Westernberger 1959 (Hecker)
× Hyperion = Mem. Chozo Takahashi | × C. Ardentissima = Davitissima

DAVITISSIMA — **David Lozoya × C. Ardentissima** — **Gauda 1973**
DEBBIE BROWN — **C. guttata × Derna** — **J. O. Brown 1973**
DECKER McALLISTER — **Pacific Sun × Yolo** — **McAllister 1974**
DEE DEE — **Quadroon × Bonanza** — **Vallemar 1960 (Dittmer)**

× Charlie Stem = Sandy Gibson
× Blc. Mem. Crispin Rosales = Blc. Mem. Richard Black
× C. Carl Hausermann = Hausermann's Pride
× C. Madeleine Knowlton = Hausermann's Rhapsody
× Pot. Diane = Pot. Barbara Fraser

DE LORIS ZIEGFELD — **Princess Margaret × C. R. Cadwalader** — **H. Patterson 1941**

× Bonanza = Ziegfeld's Bonanza

DEMING — **Bonanza × Pirate's Gold** — **H. W. Earl 1975 (Westenberger)**

DERNA†‡ — **Nugget × C. dowiana** — **B. 1941**

× C. guttata = Debbie Brown

DERRYNANE†‡ — **Balkis × Princess Margaret** — **Broughton 1943**

× C. loddigesii = Midi

DESIR — **Lykas × Hertha** — **Pff. V. & L. 1972**
DEWSBURY†‡ — **Druid × Windermere** — **L. 1949**

× Blc. Mem. Crispin Rosales = Blc. Fall Festival

DING-A-LING — **Rojo × Chit Chat** — **Wilkins 1974**
DIXIE — **Florida × Miami** — **A. & M. 1955**

× Ivy Merkel = Carol Fret

DIXIE PIXIE — **Pixie Gold × Red Gold** — **Gavelek 1973**
DOCTOR G. T. MOORE‡ — **Elissa × Ishtar** — **Mo. Bot. Gdn. 1950**

× Saint Louis = Arthur McKee

DOLORES HOYT‡ — **C. Bow Bells × Beaufighter** — **B. 1958**

× Bc. Déesse = Blc. Cheeri-Lee
× Slc. Rainbow Hill = Slc. Dolores Rainbow

DOÑA JOSEFA — **C. Rubencito × Mem. Maria Miranda** — **Ruben 1975**
DONNA'S SUNSET — **Tom Braverman × C. aurantiaca** — **Braverman 1972 (Fennell)**

DORA ZUCK — **Brenda Jane × Joseph Baker** — **Zuck 1971**
dormaniana / **DORMANIANA** — **? × ?** — **Nat. hyb.** / **hort.**

(Formerly recorded as a parent both as *L. dormaniana*†‡ and *C. dormaniana**‡, but treated from 1972 as a natural hybrid, as above, when cited as a parent in new registrations.)

× Meg Mabbs = Mini Meg
× Orange Gem = Harvest Moon
× Blc. Golden Slippers = Blc. California Fantasy
× Soph. coccinea = Slc. Wynkin and Blynkin

DOROTHY BAXTER — **C. Pavlova × L. cinnabarina** — **R. Dean 1972**
DOROTHY FRIED†‡ — **Princess Margaret × C. Dinah** — **A. & R. 1943**

× Vallandina = Litorne
× Blc. Crown Prince Akihito = Blc. Whiskey Girl
× Blc. Mem. Crispin Rosales = Blc. George Risch

DOROTHY SHIELDS — **C. Geriant × F. O. Thompson** — **R. M. Hamilton 1974 (Le Nobel)**

DOROTHY WARNE — **C. Milton Warne × Jane Warne** — **J. Milton Warne 1974**
DOTTIE KONE — **Summerland Girl × C. Tango** — **Kone 1973 (Takemoto)**

DOUBLOON — **Twinkle × C. guttata** — **J. Milton Warne 1962**

× Blc. Jane Helton = Blc. Nuuanu Sunshine

DUCHESSE — **Ethel D. Giddings × Culminant** — **Pff. V. & L. 1972**

DULHARD — **Dulzura × C. Hardyana** — **Kensington 1973**

DULZURA†‡ — **Canhamiana × C. Harold** — **A. & R. 1938**

× C. Hardyana = Dulhard

DURBIN — **Medon × Bonanza** — **Hager 1963**

× Valleybird = Harriet Breuer

DUSKY MAID — **Medon × Golden Gate** — **Hager 1963**

× Roitelet	= Stradivarius	× C. Niger	= Farandole

DYNASTIE — **Dyver × Hircho** — **F. 1972**

DYVER‡ — **Van Der Weyden × C. Ambassador** — **F. 1955**

× Hircho	= Dynastie	× Tyl	= Crinoline

EASTER BELLE†‡ — **Jacquinetta × C. mossiae** — **L. 1938**

× White Queen = Augusta Freund Littmann

EASTER BONNET†‡ — **Georgette × Mossiana** — **Rivermont 1954**

× L. cinnabarina = Sam

EDGARD van BELLE†‡ — **Cloth of Gold × Gallipoli** — **S. 1952**

× Cyrano	= Jeremie	× Blc. Circus	= Blc. Circus Belle
× Golden Charm	= Jersey	× Blc. Green-heart	= Blc. Green Belle
× Golden Halo	= Zuki Belle	× Blc. Herons Ghyll	= Blc. Herons van Belle
× Hyperion	= Mem. Jacinto Miranda	× Blc. Otomayim	= Blc. Kay Heron
× Princess Margaret	= Vulcan's Pride	× Blc. Pacific Gold	= Blc. Vanci
× Saadia	= Andre Baumann	× Blc. Pimola	= Blc. Splash Belle
× Waianae Sunset	= Belle of Hilo	× Blc. Simoun	= Blc. Parador
× Blc. Acapana	= Blc. Aspen Inlet	× C. bicolor	= Bell O'Bronze

EDGAR OMURA†‡ — **Albula × Thalia** — **Tsunoda 1949**

× Blc. Hanako M. Miyamoto	= Blc. Hanako Omura	× C. Catherine Patterson	= Kaguyama

EDMUND ROTHWELL — **C. guttata × L. cinnabarina** — **Rothwell 1902**

× Mem. Albert Heinecke	= Limerick	× Slc. Beverly Salmon	= Slc. Fire Mist
× C. Quinquecolor	= Take Five		

EL CERRITO — **L. flava × C. aurantiaca** — **Rod McLellan Co. 1962**

× C. amethystoglossa = Little Ben

elegans / **ELEGANS*†‡** — **C. leopoldii × L. purpurata** — **Nat. hyb.** / **hort.**

× C. walkerana = At Dusk

ELINOR*†‡ — **C. schroderae × L. Coronet** — **C. 1908**

× Butterscotch	= Guaicamacuto	× Blc. Xanthette	= Blc. Elinette
× Blc. Golden Myth	= Blc. Lemon Lass	× Slc. Anzac	= Slc. Gloria Jesurún Leyba

ELISSA*†‡ — **Ishtar × C. Dinah** — **A. 1934**

× Windermere = Elissamere

ELLISAMERE — **Elissa × Windermere** — **Rayridge 1975 (F. J. Bergman)**

LAELIOCATTLEYA

ELIZABETH CHANG — **Amber Glow × Mary Alma Kurtz** — **Kawabata 1972 (W. A. Chang)**

ELIZABETH OFF†‡ — **Dinard × C. Fred Sander** — **Off 1947**

× Bc. Hartland = Blc. Cherokee Chief
× Blc. Mary Battle = Blc. Hangover
× C. Bow Bells = Great Tellico
× C. labiata = Avalon
× Pot. Jo Ann Crouch = Pot. Ronald Pallister

ELLA ESK‡ — **South Esk × C. Nigrella** — **Friedel 1963 (Gore)**

× José Dias Castro = João Antonio Nicoli
× C. Maracangalha = Southe Nigra

ELSTEAD GEM*‡ — **C. bicolor × L. xanthina** — **Ingram 1895**

× Thurderniana = Robert Kane
× B. digbyana = Blc. Catnip
× Blc. Rain Forest = Blc. Little Meadow Mountain
× Slc. Carla Carter = Slc. Carla Gem

ENCHANTED JUNGLE — **Land of Enchantment × C. Nigrella** — **Redlinger 1970**

× Ishtar = Zuki Enchantar
× Pot. Medea = Pot. Meda Pretto

ENCHANTED LOU — **Land of Enchantment × Mary Lou Hauck** — **Thornton's 1975**

ENNERDALE†‡ — **Elissa × Hyperion** — **L. 1949**

× José Dias Castro = Zuki Ennerdias
× Blc. Mem. Crispin Rosales = Blc. Mem. Henry Morikubo
× Slc. Kao Hsiung = Slc. Warren Moki Sakuma

ENOREE — **Quadroon × C. Dark Emperor** — **G. Crocker 1974**

ENTWOOD — **Bimur × C. luteola** — **Voo Doo Orchids 1974**

ERMINE ROBE — **C. Enid × Peggy Huffman** — **Beall 1973**

ERNIE PYLE†‡ — **Altesse × C. mossiae** — **H. Patterson 1945**

× Georgette = Pylette
× Sagana = Sagapyle
× Wyatt Earp = Thunder River

ESTHER ANDERSON — **Quadroon × C. Nigritian** — **W. T. Anderson 1969 (Dos Pueblos)**

× Slc. Anzac = Slc. Mem. George Jacroux

ETHEL D. GIDDINGS‡ — **Sargon × Georgette** — **Rivermont 1958**

× Culminant = Duchesse
× Blc. Midas Charm = Blc. Shirley Raps

EUNICE*† — **C. chocoensis × L. anceps** — **M. 1917**

× C. Bow Bells = Lc. Mem. Zannie Melton

EVA‡ — **C. aurantiaca × L. cinnabarina** — **Veitch 1907**

× C. bicolor = Randy Redhot
× Epi. alatum = Eplc. Elizabeth Howell
× Slc. Autumn Delight = Slc. Royal Scepter

EVANGELINE FLYNN‡ — **Van Der Weyden × Flandria** — **F. 1955**

× Nelly Corradi = Myosotie
× Spinola = Ultraviolet

EVELYN MOUNTAIN†‡ — **Canberra × Golden Sunset** — **C. 1936**

× C. guttata = Sunset Flare

EVENSONG — **Snowdrift × Fedora** — **Crothers 1973**

EXCELLENCY†‡ — **Lustre × C. Suavior** — **L. 1932**

× Ann Follis = Brilliant Splendor
× Bc. Mount Hood = Blc. Brilliant Wings
× Blc. Coronet Bay = Blc. Mystic Whaler
× Blc. Norman's Bay = Blc. Tom Tom
× C. Okami = Sawtooth Mountain
× L. harpophylla = Remmel von Gritsch
× Slc. Anzac = Slc. Fantasy

LAELIOCATTLEYA

FABIADALE — **Ennerdale × C. Fabia** — **Altenburg 1970**

× Hyperion = Zuki Hyperdale | × C. Nigritian = King Ennerbia

FABLED CITY — **Sun Lakes × Kuakini** — **Beall 1968**

× Murano = Anvil Peak |

FAITH DEE FANCHALY‡ — **Canberra × Mem. Albert Heinecke** — **Bracey 1958**

× Golden Gate = Ooi Boon Huat | × Blc. Golden Slippers = Blc. Mount Mitchell
× Nigrescent = Barbara Tsubaki |

FARANDOLE — **C. Niger × Dusky Maid** — **Pff. V. & L. 1974**

FEDORA†‡ — **Laguna × C. Hardyana** — **C. 1931**

× Louella O. Parsons = Mount Pilchuck | × Snowdrift = Evensong
× Matilija = Pride of Seville | × Bc. Déesse = Blc. Meditation
× Pegi Mayne = Rose Crystal | × Blc. Kong-Urai Gold = Blc. Pimas Crown
× Penmarth = Aloha Koji Ota | × C. Enid = Cara Nome

FIERY — **Charlesworthii × L. milleri** — **Wilkins 1970 (Redlinger)**

× Bc. Bill Worsley = Blc. Magic | × C. forbesii = Sparkler

FIREBON‡ — **Bonanza × C. Firebird** — **Vallemar 1958**

× Bonanza = Applause |

FIRES OF SPRING — **Eva × Sun Lakes** — **Beall 1968**

× Blc. Secret Cove = Blc. Red Owl Mountain | × Pot. Tapestry Peak = Pot. Yukon Crossing

FIRST STAR — **Twinkle Star × C. Iris** — **McKeral 1965 (F. Fuchs Sr.)**

× L. tenebrosa = Lc. Walter Larrabee |

FLAEMMCHEN — **C. Iris × L. cinnabarina** — **Röhl 1974**

FLAVIUS — **G. S. Ball × L. flava** — **B. 1914**

× Golden Concolor = Little Canary Peaks | × Blc. Klondike Belle = Blc. Big Canary Peaks

FLIRTATIOUS OKAMI — **Flirtie × C. Okami** — **Otaguro 1972**

FLIRTIE‡ — **C. forbesii × L. flava** — **Dr. T. Fujiwara 1961 (Miyamoto)**

× Charlesworthii = Hanky-panky | × C. Okami = Flirtatious Okami
× Omphale = Rainbow Falls | × Slc. Kao Hsiung = Slc. Kaohsiung Flirt
× Bc. Daffodil = Blc. Lorrito |

FLORENCE DAWSON — **Canhamiana × C. skinneri** — **Youngkin 1971**

FLORENCE HARRIS — **Canhamiana × C. Fabulous** — **F. L. Harris 1971 (B. F. Harris)**

FLORENCE MACHLE‡ — **C. Henrietta Japhet × L. harpophylla** — **A. & M. 1962 (Machle)**

× Charlesworthii = Star Bright | × Epi. conopseum = Eplc. James Joseph
× Robon = Florescent | × Epi. pseudepidendrum = Eplc. Mem. Marie Osment
× Blc. Golden Fleece = Blc. Flo Fleece |

FLORESCENT — **Florence Machle × Robon** — **Fort Caroline 1975**

FORT LAUDERDALE‡ — **C. Nigritian × South Esk** — **Altenburg 1964 (Gore)**

× Blc. Dark Waters = Blc. Takanao Seki | × Blc. Norman's Bay = Blc. Nubia Nicoli Cabral
× Blc. Nortela = Blc. Shinsei | × Pot. Hugo Porto = Pot. Porto Feliz

FORT ORO — **Western Sunset × Mem. Albert Heinecke** — **Rod McLellan Co. 1975**

LAELIOCATTLEYA

F. O. THOMPSON	**Canejo × C. Tityus**		**A. & R. 1951**
× C. Geriant	= Dorothy Shields		
FOXFIRE	**Bonanza × Poussin**		**Fouquette 1975 (Brough)**
FRANK LIND†‡	**Helen Wilmer × Windermere**		**H. Patterson 1945**
× Land of Enchantment	= Dark Doll	× C. J. A. Carbone	= Marti Lind
× Twinkle Star	= Mem. Motomu Otaguro		
FRANK MANTUA	**Mamie Eisenhower × C. mossiae**		**Rod McLellan Co. 1971**
FRANK WILSON	**Stephen Oliver Fouraker × Lillian Wilson**		**Mrs. L. Wilson 1975**
FREDA MISKIMENS	**Clifton Down × C. Bob Betts**		**Miskimens 1972 (Originator unknown)**
FRED CASTATOR‡	**Dorothy Fried × C. Ardentissima**		**A. & R. 1955**
× Telstar	= Tribal Fair		
FRESHIE	**C. Margaret Stewart × L. cinnabarina**		**Fresh 1971**
FUSILIER	**Vallechollet × C. Nigritian**		**Stewart Inc. 1972**
GAILLARD†‡	**Mermoz × C. Trimos**		**V. 1945**
× Lykas	= Montmartre	× Bc. Thalie	= Blc. Georges Morel
× Segond-Weber	= Jane Seymour		
GANADO	**Armaris × C. Dark Emperor**		**A. & R. 1973**
GARCIA'S GOLD	**C. Helene Garcia × Henrietta Gold**		**Lenette 1974 (Rivermont)**
GARDEN DELIGHT	**L. anceps × C. Rita Renee**		**Stewart Inc. 1974 (Loren Johnson)**
GATTON GLORY†‡	**Canberra × C. Mimosa**		**Colman 1907**
× Blc. Summer Shades	= Blc. Autumn Glory		
GEMOLA	**Orange Gem × C. luteola**		**Pabst 1975**
GENA	**Georgette × C. Athena**		**Kensington 1973**
GEORGEAN	**Shenandoah × Georgette**		**Kensington 1973**
GEORGE BALDWIN†‡	**Princess Margaret × C. Enid**		**Baldwin 1941**
× Snowdrift	= Virginia Royal	× Pot. Rebecca Merkel	= Pot. Red Cardinal
× Blc. James Hausermann	= Blc. Bold Ruler		
GEORGE CUTLER‡	**Mary Rose × Manila**		**Rod McLellan Co. 1961**
× Ak Sar Ben	= Reuben Metz	× C. guttata	= Anita King
× Quadroon	= Cora Williams	× C. mossiae	= Spring Reward
× Blc. Norman's Bay	= Blc. Cutler Bay		
GEORGE MacDONELL†‡	**Helen Wilmer × Molly Tyler**		**Patterson 1952**
× Blc. Mem. Crispin Rosales	= Blc. Robert Kamiyama		
GEORGES COUDROUX	**C. Dante × Saadia**		**Marcel Lecoufle 1974**
GEORGE THOMAS	**Record × Bonanza**		**Gubler 1968**
× Princess Margaret	= Louisiana Purchase		
GEORGETTE†‡	**San Juan × Serbia**		**C. 1932**
× Ernie Pyle	= Pylette	× C. Athena	= Gena
× Lady Arrow	= Ladyette	× C. mossiae	= Chelmo
× Shenandoah	= Georgean		
GEORGE WOODHAMS*†‡	**C. Hardyana × L. purpurata**		**A. & B. 1907**
× C. Catherine Patterson	= Stela Marcia		

GILA WILDERNESS	**Kevin Green × Red Empress**	**A. & R. 1975**
GIMLI	**C. Wolteriana × Antonica Fredrick**	**Voo Doo Orchids 1974**
GITANA	**Hernani × C. Niger**	**Pff. V. & L. 1971**
GITCHE MANITO†‡	**Morvyth × C. Gay Gordon**	**A. & R. 1941**

× Adonis = Mem. Takeshi Kido

GLADYS — **C. loddigesii × L. cinnabarina** — **Fournier 1901**

× Slc. Anzac = Slc. Fujimusume

GLADYS MILLNER‡ — **C. Barbara Billingsley × L. harpophylla** — **Fouraker 1957 (Snyder Bros.)**

× Bc. Green Dawn = Blc. Kaena | × C. Mrs. Pitt = Pitcairn
× Blc. Betty Moe = Blc. Winnie The Pooh

GLADYS SANCHEZ — **C. bowringiana × Copper Charm** — **J. Milton Warne 1960**

× Magneri = Hana Noka Oi

GLENEYRIE — **C. bowringiana × Charles Futterman** — **Fort Caroline 1969**

× B. glauca = Blc. Avon Kotae

GLOWING AMBER	**C. Mrs. Pitt × Lee Langford**	**Rod McLellan Co. 1972**
GLOWING EMBERS	**Remula × L. milleri**	**Thomdel 1972**
GODIVA	**Ishtar × C. Hentschelii**	**A. 1943**

× C. Titrianae = Titriva

GOLDCREST* — **C. schroderae × L. cowanii** — **H. 1909**

× C. aurantiaca = Chicanery

GOLD DIGGER	**Red Gold × C. Warpaint**	**O'Dell 1974**
GOLDEN CHARM†‡	**Orange Blossom × L. Coronet**	**A. 1931**

× Edgard van Belle = Jersey | × C. Mary Lynn McKenzie = Joanne Sullivan
× Tangerine Beauty = Golden Tangerine

GOLDEN CONCOLOR†‡ — **Golden Jewell × C. dowiana** — **Crothers 1959 (H. Patterson)**

× Flavius = Little Canary Peaks

GOLDEN FIRE	**Amber Glow × South Esk**	**Crestwood 1973**
GOLDEN GATE†‡	**S. J. Bracey × Isotta**	**Rod McLellan Co. 1954**

× Faith Dee Fanchaly = Ooi Boon Huat | × Blc. Pimola = Blc. Gola
× Twinkle Star = Twinkle Gold

GOLDEN GIRL — **Orange Ann × C. aurantiaca** — **Rod McLellan Co. 1964**

× Slc. Naomi Kerns = Slc. Naomi Girl

GOLDEN GLOW — **Sunrise × C. Venus** — **Schroder 1921**

× Canberra = Canberra Glow | × Silva-Sugi = Mem. Toraji Murakami

GOLDEN HALO — **Edgard van Belle × C. dowiana** — **Altenburg 1966**

× Edgard van Belle = Zuki Belle

GOLDEN NYMPH — **C. aurantiaca × Luminosa** — **Small 1962**

× C. Tango = Paul Joseph Weber

GOLDEN PASSAGE — **Sun Lakes × C. Costa Rica** — **Beall 1967**

× Pot. Tapestry Peak = Pot. Golden Peak

LAELIOCATTLEYA

GOLDEN RAY†‡ Golden Gleam × C. Fulvescens A. 1946
× Blc. Xanthedo = Blc. Rusty Zeigler

GOLDEN RHAPSODY C. Tango × S. J. Bracey Bloom's Nursery 1974
GOLDEN SPRING Henrietta J. Dane × Luminosa A. & M. 1960
× B. nodosa = Blc. Rio's Spring

GOLDEN TANGERINE Golden Charm × Tangerine Beauty Sullivan 1973 (Freed)

GOLDEN WREN* Thyone × C. Iridescens A. & B. 1916
× Pacific Sun = Bright Bird

GOOD TRY C. Florence Patterson × Brown Derby Stevenson 1973
GRANDEE*†‡ Mrs. Medo × C. Aeneas A. & R. 1937
× Blc. Nugget = Blc. Lemon Light

GRANITE MOUNTAIN Parysatis × C. labiata Beall 1975
GREAT TELLICO C. Bow Bells × Elizabeth Off C. & H. 1975
GREEN HERITAGE Lee Langford × Ann Follis Spencer 1975
GRODSKE'S GOLD L. flava × C. Empress Bells Grodske 1964 (Bracey)
× Martha Chandler = Martha's Gold | × C. Peanuts = Patty Lynn Smith

GRUBDEL Grub Stake × Rondel Kensington 1973
GRUB STAKE†‡ Orosi × C. Prospector Bracey 1949
× Irving Dietsche = Splash | × Blc. Momercia = Blc. Distinction
× Rondel = Grubdel | × C. Rita Renee = Melecio Huerta

G. S. BALL*†‡ C. schroderae × L. cinnabarina Veitch 1900
× C. December Snow = Mike Shaw | × Sl. Marriottiana = Slc. Sunshine Gold
× Epi. tampense = Eplc. Baltimore

GUADELOUPE Clara Schriever × C. intermedia J. & S. 1971
GUAICAIPURO L. tenebrosa × Nuuanu Jesurún 1972
GUAICAMACUTO Butterscotch × Elinor Jesurún 1972
GUERRERO C. Portia × Bacchante Rod McLellan Co. 1960
× C. Portisoniae = Bob's Love

GWIN C. Granfort × Ann Follis Rod McLellan Co. 1975
HANA NOKA OI Gladys Sanchez × Magneri McAllister 1974
HANKY-PANKY Charlesworthii × Flirtie Wilkins 1975 (Miyamoto)

HAROLD CARLSON Irving Dietsche × C. Enid H. Patterson 1964
× Colonel = Kameyo Sato | × Kismet Queen = Haruyo Tamura

HAROLDIANA*†‡ C. Hardyana × L. tenebrosa C. 1901
× Blc. Midenette = Blc. Mildred Tucker

HAROLD J. PATTERSON‡ Princess Margaret × C. Charybdis H. Patterson 1952
× Belles Flandres = Tampon | × C. Bonanza = Hausermann's Melody
× Lee Langford = Lisa Bath | × C. Damoiseau = Roseval

HARPOSUZETTE L. harpophylla × Crepe Suzette Hattori 1975
HARRIET BREUER Durbin × Valleybird Lazetera 1974 (Hager)

HARUYO TAMURA Kismet Queen × Harold Carlson Otaguro 1972
HARVEST MOON Dormaniana × Orange Gem Pabst 1975
HASSALLII*†‡ Britannia × C. warscewiczii Hassall 1921
× C. Thebes = Joyce Pickell

HATTIE GRAHAM — **Lillian Wilson × Mem. Maggie Hood** — **Muse's 1971**

HAUSERMANN'S MELODY — **Harold J. Patterson × C. Bonanza** — **Hausermann 1972**

HAUSERMANN'S NOCTURNE — **Alten × C. mossiae** — **Hausermann 1972**

HAUSERMANN'S PRIDE — **C. Carl Hausermann × Dee Dee** — **Hausermann 1972**

HAUSERMANN'S RHAPSODY — **Dee Dee × C. Madeleine Knowlton** — **Hausermann 1972**

HAWAIIAN SUNSET†‡ — **C. bicolor × Calizona** — **Woodlawn 1953**

× S. J. Bracey = Tennessee Sunset

HAWAIIAN WARRIOR — **Bright Night × Waianae Sunset** — **Rod McLellan Co. 1975 (Originator unknown)**

HAZEL ABEL — **C. Atherton × L. flava** — **Abel 1969**

× Orange Bow = Winter's Gold | × C. aurantiaca = Betty von Paulsen

HEIDI — **C. Loddiaca × L. flava** — **Stevenson 1973**

HELENA BARAYA — **L. grandis × C. dowiana** — **Ospina 1971**

HELEN BACHNER — **Wine Festival × Oriental Splendor** — **Bachner 1974 (Kirch)**

HELEN B. LAWRENCE — **C. Barbara Billingsley × L. cinnabarina** — **H. Lawrence 1955 (Snyder Bros.)**

× L. flava = Mem. Sophia Cox

HELEN BOWDEN — **Jane Warne × Cantabile** — **J. Milton Warne 1974**

HELEN MIZUTA†‡ — **Lindhard × Princess Shimadzu** — **R. K. Mizuta 1950**

× B. nodosa = Blc. Joan Bramwell

HELEN STREET — **Margaret Keaton × C. Dark Emperor** — **Fields Orchids 1965**

× Bonanza = Mildred Benis

HELEN WILMER*†‡ — **General Maude × Wellsiana** — **F. E. Dixon 1934**

× H. G. Alexander = Wilex | × Ludgate = So So
× Lomita Park = Spring Park

HENRIETTA GOLD — **C. Henrietta Japhet × L. Gold Star** — **Lenette 1974 (Rivermont)**

× C. Helene Garcia = Garcia's Gold

HERGATE — **Ludgate × Hertha** — **Rayridge 1975 (F. J. Bergman)**

HERNALIA‡ — **Hernani × Coppelia** — **Pff. V. & L. 1959**

× Marceau = Massilia

HERNANI†‡ — **Musset × C. Admiration** — **V. 1947**

× Bach-Aga = Bachani | × C. Niger = Gitana
× Hertha = Cheverny

HERTERSIANA — **Hertha × C. Woltersiana** — **Hisazaki 1972**

HERTHA*†‡ — **Momus × C. Monarch** — **C. 1931**

× Alfredo Martinelli = Sans Atout | × Ludgate = Hergate
× Hernani = Cheverny | × Lykas = Desir
× José Dias Castro = Kamenosuke Suzuki | × Bc. Déesse = Blc. Hertéesse
× Lomita Park = Spring Tonic | × C. Woltersiana = Hertersiana

H. G. ALEXANDER†‡ — **Moloch × Momus** — **A. 1942**

× Helen Wilmer = Wilex | × Mary Carrico = Mem. Marilyn Barry

HIRCHO†‡ — **Hirella × C. Remy Chollet** — **F. 1947**

× Dyver = Dynastie

HONG-SIE CHEN — **C. Sedlescombe × Bonanza** — **Hong-Sie Chen 1975 (Chung-Chweng Chen)**

HOT CHILI PEPPER — **C. bicolor × Antonica Fredrick** — **Fort Caroline 1975**

HURRICANE — **Maya Daubon × Bonanza** — **Trade Winds 1962**

× Bc. Hartland = Blc. Lara
× C. Peace = Bernice Dodson

HUSSARD — **Lucien Pauwels × C. mendelii** — **F. 1972**

HYPELLENCY — **Excellency × Hyperion** — **Chung-Chweng Chen 1960**

× Bonanza = Uncle Sheu Wan

HYPERION*†‡ — **General Maud × C. Leda** — **L. 1933**

× David Lozoya = Mem. Chozo Takahashi
× Edgard van Belle = Mem. Jacinto Miranda
× Fabiadale = Zuki Hyperdale
× José Dias Castro = Mem. Francisco Pimentel
× Blc. Mem. Crispin Rosales = Blc. Toshikazu Takahashi

IBBIE*†‡ — **D. S. Brown × Mrs. W. N. Elkins** — **F. E. Dixon 1929**

× Blc. Herons Ghyll = Blc. Heron's Nest

IMPERIAL PALACE — **Quadroon × Walter Slagle** — **Rod McLellan Co. 1975**

IMPERIAL TORCH — **Pirate King × Waianae Sunset** — **Rod McLellan Co. 1974 (Fordyce)**

IMP OF GOLD — **Puppet × C. Venosa** — **Beall 1973**

INDIAN MOUNTAIN — **Christopher Gubler × Waianae Sunset** — **Beall 1975**

INTERMEDIO-FLAVA* — **C. intermedia × L. flava** — **Fournier 1896**

× Soph. coccinea = Slc. Martha Withner

IRA FUMIKO FIELD — **Princess Margaret × Prophesy** — **Stewart Inc. 1975 (R. M. Field)**

IRENE FINNEY‡ — **Bruno Alberts × C. J. A. Carbone** — **Hausermann 1964**

× Kari Lynn = Lake Chabaneau
× Mira = Andrew Hausermann
× Blc. Ann = Blc. Terrie
× Blc. James Hausermann = Blc. Mem. Grant Eichler
× Blc. John Beville = Blc. Lisa Irene
× C. Califlora = John MacArthur
× C. mossiae = Time-Life
× C. Suavior = Aqui-Finn

IRVING DIETSCHE‡ — **Raphaelcita × C. mossiae** — **H. Patterson 1960**

× Grub Stake = Splash
× Rondel = Rondi

ISHTAR*†‡ — **Sargon × C. Fabia** — **H. 1925**

× Baldur = Mem. Toyo Sakumoto
× Cuesta = Alright
× Enchanted Jungle = Zuki Enchantar
× C. Nigritian = Tia Maria
× C. Portia = Ishtia

ISHTIA — **Ishtar × C. Portia** — **Rayridge 1975 (F. J. Bergman)**

ISOTTA†‡ — **Sargon × C. bicolor** — **A. 1941**

× C. Chamberlainiana = Chamberlain Isotta

ISSY*†‡ — **C. guttata × L. tenebrosa** — **C. 1901**

× Charlesworthii = Stephen Sue
× Blc. Mem. Crispin Rosales = Blc. Chic Jardine
× C. bicolor = San Pablo
× L. Zip = Cinders
× Slc. Jewel Box = Slc. Prissy Red

IVY MERKEL‡ — **Titrianae × Miami** — **A. & M. 1956**

× Dixie = Carol Fret

JALAPA — **C. guttata × L. milleri** — **W. W. G. Moir 1972**

JAMES BELL — **C. Bob Betts × Suprême** — **S. Bell 1973**

JANE FROMAN‡ — **C. Alwynii × Hassallii** — **Gore 1954**
× C. Eleanore = Summer Sand

JANE SEYMOUR — **Segond-Weber × Gaillard** — **Pff. V. & L. 1973**
JANET BROWN — **C. Little Angel × Red Empress** — **J. O. Brown 1971 (Burnett)**

JANET FUJIKAWA — **Mysedo × C. Nigrella** — **Otaguro 1975**
JANE WARNE‡ — **Fedora × Priscilla** — **J. Milton Warne 1947**
× Cantabile = Helen Bowden
× C. Milton Warne = Dorothy Warne
× Epi. tampense = Eplc. Joseph Cornelia

JAY JAY — **Red Gold × C. Mary Lou** — **Mid-Florida Orch. 1973**
JEAN-NE LORRAINE — **C. forbesii × Beaufighter** — **Carmichael 1961 (J. & S.)**
× Epi. alatum = Eplc. Rastus
× Slc. Anzac = Slc. Bob Poole

JEREMIE — **Cyrano × Edgard van Belle** — **Pff. V. & L. 1971**
JERSEY — **Edgard van Belle × Golden Charm** — **E. E. Young 1975**
JOAN MATTHEWS — **C. aurantiaca × Lee Langford** — **M. C. Matthews 1962 (Ozzella)**
× L. Ancibarina = Lola Schloat
× L. rupestris = Candy

JOANNE SULLIVAN — **Golden Charm × C. Mary Lynn McKenzie** — **Sullivan 1973 (Freed)**

JOÃO ANTONIO NICOLI — **Ella Esk × José Dias Castro** — **Altenburg 1972**
JOE OSORIO — **Bonanza × C. Portisoniae** — **Rod McLellan Co. 1971**
JOHN LAYCOCK‡ — **Cloth of Gold × Goldfish** — **S. 1954**
× Yellow Skin = Yellow Shades

JOHN MacARTHUR — **C. Califlora × Irene Finney** — **Hausermann 1974**
JONÁRAL — **Pacific × Quadroon** — **Rod McLellan Co. 1964**
× C. loddigesii = Ballyhoo

JONGHEWAR — **L. jongheana × C. warneri** — **Santos 1974 (de Paula)**

JOSÉ DIAS CASTRO‡ — **C. labiata × Sam W. Soysa** — **Altenburg 1966**
× Bonanza = Bonin
× Ella Esk = João Antonio Nicoli
× Ennerdale = Zuki Ennerdias
× Hertha = Kamenosuke Suzuki
× Hyperion = Mem. Francisco Pimentel
× Paradisio = Zuki Disio
× Walter Slagle = Adolpho Menezes
× Bc. Hartland = Blc. Helena Tricca
× Blc. Norman's Bay = Blc. Mem. Beniamino Gigli
× C. Nigritian = Perle Noir
× L. pumila = Zuki Josemila
× Slc. Anzac = Slc. Zuki Josezac

JOSÉ NOÉ‡ — **L. tenebrosa × Pacific Sun** — **Rod McLellan Co. 1961**
× Pot. Rosette Savorgnan = Pot. Verinovel

JOSEPH BAKER‡ — **Asbury × C. Enid** — **Baldwin 1943**
× Brenda Jane = Dora Zuck

JOSEPH HAMPTON†‡ — **Hilary × Marie Dobrott** — **Urmston 1948**
× Norman Gray = Addison Friendship
× Bc. Dr. A. Kosky = Blc. Morris Gunderson

JOSÉ WALTER SENG — **Luiz Martinelli × Bonanza** — **Ramos 1973**
JOYCE PICKELL — **C. Thebes × Hassallii** — **Pickell 1973 (Originator unknown)**

JULIA KERSEY — **Red Gold × C. Barbara Kirch** — **Kersey 1972**
JUNE GOW — L. milleri × Ann Follis — **Fort Caroline 1972**

LAELIOCATTLEYA

JUNTO‡ Manila × Grub Stake — Fordyce 1963 (Bracey)
× Brazoria = Martha Evelyn Bean

JYLA SHEIKHI C. J. A. Carbone × Sargarno — A. & R. 1973 (Chase)

KAGARIBI Amelia × L. cinnabarina — Katsuura 1975
KAGUYAMA Edgar Omura × C. Catherine Patterson — Karasawa 1971
KALANI CASTRO Schillerana × C. Karae Lyn Sugiyama — McAllister 1972
KALONO Bonanza × Oakland — Rod McLellan Co. 1975 (Hanes)
× Seattle = Midnight Royale

KAMENOSUKE SUZUKI José Dias Castro × Hertha — N. Suzuki 1972
KAMEYO SATO Colonel × Harold Carlson — Otaguro 1973
KAMOKILA L. anceps × C. Okami — O. Kirsch 1972
KANNAPOLIS Whitewings × C. Enid — Lenette 1973
KARI LYNN Harold J. Patterson × Irving Dietsche — Hausermann 1967
× Irene Finney = Lake Chabaneau

KATHLEEN JEAL‡ Bacchante × Lustre — Jeal 1957
× Blc. Nigiana = Blc. Freda Cooke

KATREENA HOWARD C. Dindoer × Molly Tyler — F. H. Williams 1974 (Originator unknown)

KEN BATTLE L. flava × C. Confetti — Tavares 1961 (W. Schawaker)
× Blc. Mellowglow = Blc. Hofsommer's Gold

KENCOLOR‡ Kenosha × C. bicolor — Clarelen 1962
× Blc. Lester McDonald = Blc. Green Jewel

KENSELLA C. Nigrella × Bonanza — Kensington 1965
× C. Barbara Kirch = Tibouchina

KERI C. Batalinii × Semaphore — Luxen 1975 (Altenburg)

KEVIN GREEN C. Nancy Harte × Excellency — Ted Green 1960 (L.)
× Red Empress = Gila Wilderness

KILAUEA BELLE Belle of Celle × Kilauea Iki — Kirch 1974
KILAUEA IKI‡ C. Bob Betts × Mysedo — Tomiyasu 1960
× Belle of Celle = Kilauea Belle | × Blc. Mem. Crispin Rosales = Blc. Masayuki Echigo

KILIWEHI Rosa Kirsch × C. Baby Jane — O. Kirsch 1971
KIMBERLY SOVEREIGN Pacific Rose × Charlie Stem — Warren 1974
KIM MILLER C. Auranti-media × Ozark — Fort Caroline 1972
KINDEE Parysatis × C. Interglossa — Cannons 1973
KING ENNERBIA Fabiadale × C. Nigritian — Suzuki 1971
KINGSTREE Bush River × Bonanza — C. & H. 1975
KISMET QUEEN‡ Princess Ishtar × Kismet — Gore 1953
× Harold Carlson = Haruyo Tamura | × Princess Margaret = Akuhead Pupule

KODIAK ISLAND Mem. Albert Heinecke × Waianae Sunset — Beall 1972
KUMQUAT Charlesworthii × Cantaloupe — Redlinger 1975

LAELIOCATTLEYA

KYOKO TAKEDA — **Ishtar × Ennerdale** — **C. Takeda 1964**

× Bonanza = Mitsuko Takeda

LADY ARROW‡ — **Rincon Hill × Eva Robinson** — **Tomlinson 1963 (Bracey)**

× Georgette = Ladyette

LADYBUG — **Rojo × C. aurantiaca** — **Wilkins 1973**

LADYETTE — **Lady Arrow × Georgette** — **Kensington 1973**

LAGOON — **L. xanthina × C. guttata** — **Stewart Inc. 1964**

× B. digbyana = Blc. Trio
× Blc. Xanthette = Blc. Jungle River
× C. guttata = Leafwood Lane

LAKE CHABANEAU — **Irene Finney × Kari Lynn** — **Hausermann 1974**

LAND OF ENCHANTMENT‡ — **Mollie Tyler × Ibbie** — **Rivermont 1960**

× Frank Lind = Dark Doll
× Mary Lou Hauck = Enchanted Lou
× Blc. Herons Ghyll = Blc. Herons Enchantment
× Blc. Molflora = Blc. Lyda Bell Howe

LAURIE LYNN‡ — **Cuesta × Bonanza** — **Westenberger 1959 (Hecker)**

× Sausalito = Saucy Lynn
× Bc. Dr. A. Kosky = Blc. Stanton Berman
× Blc. Molflora = Blc. Candee

LAVENDER GATE — **Mary Rose × Seattle** — **Rod McLellan Co. 1975 (J. F. Hughes)**

LAWRENCE VANCE — **San Mateo Times × Quadroon** — **Rod McLellan Co. 1971**

LEAFWOOD LANE — **Lagoon × C. guttata** — **Stewart Inc. 1973**

LEE LANGFORD†‡ — **Calizona × S. J. Bracey** — **Ozzella 1948**

× Ann Follis = Green Heritage
× Belle of Celle = Carmel Cone
× Harold J. Patterson = Lisa Bath
× Mysedo = Alice Otaguro
× Pacific Sun = Ana Maria Duveen
× Ravenglass = Raven Beauty
× Wine Festival = Mem. Francesca Santoro
× B. digbyana = Blc. Sally Staggs
× B. nodosa = Blc. Enigma Variations
× Blc. Fortune = Blc. Marita
× Blc. Francis Y. Hoshino = Blc. Harriett Kawakami
× Blc. Glozan = Blc. Zanleeglo
× Blc. Malvern = Blc. Orange Gold
× Blc. Normans Bay = Blc. Dorcille Little
× Blc. Pamela Farrell = Blc. Iroquois Trail
× Blc. Summer Shades = Blc. Titian Queen
× C. Ardentissima = Burma Queen
× C. Michael Sander = Takeshi Doc Yatabe
× C. Mrs. Pitt = Glowing Amber
× C. Nellie Roberts = MeLing Ho
× Epi. plicatum = Eplc. Douglas Allen
× Slc. Brandywine = Slc. Night Song
× Slc. Kao Hsiung = Slc. Kao Lee

LEIGH ANN BLACKMORE — **C. aclandiae × Antonica Fredrick** — **J. D. Blackmore 1971 (Vagner)**

LENALANI — **Mem. Masa Matsumoto × Little Sunbeam** — **O. Kirsch 1971**

LENN FOLLETT‡ — **South Seas × Mermoz** — **J. Milton Warne 1954**

× Blc. Crown Prince Akihito = Blc. Sadao Yamamoto
× Blc. Norman's Bay = Blc. Tomoko Kubo
× C. President Wilson = Mamoru Ogata

LEONOR LISBÔA CALDAS — **C. loddigesii × Luiz Martinelli** — **Ramos 1973**

LIEBLING — **Mercia × Brilliant Orange** — **Rod McLellan Co. 1973**

LILLIAN WILSON — **C. Suavior × Regal Lady** — **Mrs. L. Wilson 1964 (Gore)**

× Mem. Maggie Hood = Hattie Graham
× Stephen Oliver Fouraker = Frank Wilson

LIMERICK — **Edmund Rothwell × Mem. Albert Heinecke** — **Stewart Inc. 1972 (Sell)**

LINDY LEE — **C. Mrs. Mahler × Luminosa** — **Marshall Orchids 1975 (Small)**

LISA BATH	**Harold J. Patterson × Lee Langford**	**Bath 1974 (Betts)**
LITORNE	**Vallandina × Dorothy Fried**	**F. 1972**
LITTLE BEN	**El Cerrito × C. amethystoglossa**	**A. & R. 1971**
LITTLE CANARY PEAKS	**Flavius × Golden Concolor**	**Beall 1975**
LITTLE GIRL	**C. Priscilla Ward × Mercia**	**J. Milton Warne 1971**
LITTLE SUNBEAM‡	**L. flava × Alma**	**Perry 1958 (T. Kazumura)**

× Mem. Masa Matsumoto	= Lenalani	× Soph. coccinea	= Slc. Sassy Sofia
× Bl. Ilima	= Blc. Mokihana		

LITTLE SUSIE‡	**C. Porcia × Molly Tyler**	**A. & R. 1959**

× Pot. Dark Eyes	= Pot. Congaree	× Slc. Anzac	= Slc. Suzac

LOGE	**Rojo × C. Wolteriana**	**Voo Doo Orchids 1974**
LOLA SCHLOAT	**L. Ancibarina × Joan Matthews**	**Schloat 1972**
LOLLYPOP	**Nuuanu × Mercia**	**J. Milton Warne 1961**

× Blc. Agnes McWilliams	= Blc. Agnes Haynes		

LOMITA PARK‡	**Derrynane × C. Remy Chollet**	**Rod McLellan Co. 1956 (E. W. McLellan)**

× Helen Wilmer	= Spring Park	× Blc. Natoma	= Blc. Medellin
× Hertha	= Spring Tonic	× C. Metapan	= Spring Arrival
× Blc. Momercia	= Blc. Spring Acres	× C. Winnietha	= Spring Romance

LONGWOOD GARDENS	**Shenandoah × C. Sohma**	**Kensington 1973**
LOONY GOON	**C. Bob Betts × L. flava**	**Stevenson 1973**
LORNA DENE WHITLOW	**C. mossiae × L. pumila**	**Stewart Inc. 1974 (Whitlow)**
LORRAINE SHIRAI†‡	**Derna × Luminosa**	**Shirai 1952**

× Camelot	= William Miles	× Blc. Malworth	= Blc. Lorraine Malworth
× B. nodosa	= Blc. Keowee	× Blc. Nanette	= Blc. Kristin
× Blc. Gold Coast	= Blc. Dana Thomas	× Blc. Polka Dot	= Blc. Billye
× Blc. Iliad	= Blc. Virgin Gold	× Blc. Spun Gold	= Blc. Formosan Gold
× Blc. Jewel-Glo	= Blc. Dinh Thuy Yen	× C. Joyce Hannington	= Admiral Stokes

LOST WEEKEND	**Mem. Buddy Clark × C. Nigritian**	**Ilsley Orchids 1972**
LOUELLA O. PARSONS†‡	**Jane Dane × C. warscewiczii**	**H. Patterson 1948**

× Fedora	= Mount Pilchuck	× Souvenir de Bonita	= Mount Tahoma

LOUIS DORP‡	**Hertha × C. mossiae**	**H. Patterson 1952**

× C. Mossmist	= Spring Fancy		

LOUISE ALEXANDER	**C. Irene × Bride's Bouquet**	**Rivermont 1971**
LOUISIANA PURCHASE	**Princess Margaret × George Thomas**	**Stewart Inc. 1975 (Roy Fields)**
LOURDES FALABELLA	**Pink Pearl × C. trianaei**	**Santos 1974**
LUCIE HAUSERMANN‡	**C. Alesia × Pegi Mayne**	**Patterson 1965**

× Aïda	= Sophia	× C. Alice Pearce	= Lupe

LUCIEN PAUWELS	**Floralies × C. mossiae**	**F. 1947**

× President de Brouwer	= Parabole	× C. mendelii	= Hussard

LUDGATE†‡	**Princess Margaret × Queen Mary**	**B. 1943**

× Balkis	= Sorry	× Hertha	= Hergate
× Cuesta	= Cuestagate	× C. Bow Bells	= Mem. Irwin DeLong
× Helen Wilmer	= So So		

LUIZ ERNESTO RAMOS — **L. pumila × Abe Montague** — **Ramos 1973**
LUIZ MARTINELLI‡ — **Paradisio × Frank Lind** — **A. F. Martinelli 1960**
× Abe Montague = Mercedes Lisbôa Seng | × C. loddigesii = Leonor Lisbôa Caldas
× Bonanza = José Walter Seng

LUMINOSA*†‡ — **C. dowiana × L. tenebrosa** — **C. 1901**
× Amelia = Niji | × C. Mrs. Mahler = Lindy Lee
× Blc. Gladys Lines = Blc. Cindita | × Epi. atropurpureum = Eplc. Maria Luisa

LUPE — **Lucie Hausermann × C. Alice Pearce** — **Ruben 1974**
LUTEOUS GEM — **Adelaide Waltman × C. luteola** — **Otaguro 1971**
LYDIA HUBBELL — **C. Nellie Roberts × Pacific Sun** — **Trout 1963 (Rod McLellan Co.)**
× Western Sunset = Sunshine Fire | × Blc. Pacific Gold = Blc. Frances Campbell DeGear
× Blc. Golden Myth = Blc. Primrose Path | × Blc. Setting Sun = Blc. Golden Hue

LYKAS‡ — **C. Luron × Gaillard** — **V. 1956**
× Gaillard = Montmartre | × Hertha = Desir

LYNDEL WORTHMAN — **Princess Margaret × C. warneri** — **A. & M. 1971**
LYNN RICHARD — **Murrie Fitch × Antonica Fredrick** — **Banka 1972 (Small)**

MABEL CARR THORNTON — **Bonanza × C. Mrs. J. W. Whiteley** — **Thornton's 1975**
MAGADHA† — **Momus × C. Dupreana** — **C. 1937**
× Bc. Mount Anderson = Blc. Floradora |

MAGGIE HURST — **C. Maggie Raphael × Penshurst** — **Fields Orchids 1965**
× Blc. Jewel Higdon = Blc. Jewelled Gold |

MAGNERI — **C. granulosa × L. tenebrosa** — **Peeters 1900**
× Gladys Sanchez = Hana Noka Oi |

MAILI BEAUTY — **Chitose Kodama × Twinkle Star** — **Higuchi 1968 (Miyamoto)**
× Quadroon = Maili Quadroon |

MAILI QUADROON — **Maili Beauty × Quadroon** — **Otaguro 1973**
MAMIE EISENHOWER†‡ — **Chevalier × Britannia** — **Rod McLellan Co. 1953 (E. W. McLellan)**
× C. mossiae = Frank Mantua |

MAMORU OGATA — **C. President Wilson × Lenn Follett** — **Otaguro 1973**
MANILA†‡ — **Cuesta × Joseph Hampton** — **Urmston 1950**
× Vallechollet = Manilavale | × Blc. Momercia = Blc. Art Banta
× Blc. Herons Ghyll = Blc. Manila Ghyll |

MANILAVALE — **Vallechollet × Manila** — **J. Escobar 1975**
MANOA SUNBURST — **S. J. Bracey × Waianae Sunset** — **Elroy Haynes 1974 (Miyamoto)**

MANU — **Rosa Kirsch × C. New Era** — **Kirsch 1971**
MARCEAU‡ — **Cocarde × C. Fred Sander** — **V. 1948**
× Calandal = Marchenoir | × Miami = Mem. Ladd Pelc
× Hernalia = Massilia |

MARCHENOIR — **Calandal × Marceau** — **Pff. V. & L. 1973**
MARIA OZZELLA‡ — **Lee Langford × C. Nigrella** — **Ozzella 1958 (J. Ozzella)**
× Blc. Mem. Crispin Rosales = Blc. Ruby Mesa | × Slc. Anzac = Slc. Catherine Wilfret

LAELIOCATTLEYA

MARIE STOCKING Thurderniana × C. bicolor Hoyt 1962
× Blc. Nugget = Blc. Nankeen Gold

MARINER‡ C. Ariel × L. purpurata Bracey 1961
× Blc. Victoria = Blc. Crater Lake
× C. Big Splash = Taco
× C. labiata = Blue Pacific
× Pot. Tapestry Peak = Pat. Mount Toil

MARK KURAO HOSHINO‡ S. J. Bracey × Princess Margaret Hoshino 1959
× Slc. Anzac = Slc. McCully Beauty

MARLACE†‡ Kitty Wallace × Princess Margaret Ogawa 1959 (S.A.)
× Miami = Mem. Pauline Pelc

MARSANDER Princess Margaret × C. Michael Sander Rod McLellan Co. 1975

MARTHA CHANDLER Recousant × Carrie Estelle E. Iwanaga 1965
× Grodske's Gold = Martha's Gold

MARTHA EVELYN BEAN Junto × Brazoria Coastal Gdns. 1974

MARTHA'S GOLD Martha Chandler × Grodske's Gold Lenette 1974 (Kirch)

MARTI LIND Frank Lind × C. J. A. Carbone A. & R. 1975

MARY ALMA KURTZ C. dowiana × Alma Takiguchi 1963 (Otake)
× Amber Glow = Elizabeth Chang

MARY CARRICO‡ C. G. P. Walker × Woltencia Gore 1951
× H. G. Alexander = Mem. Marilyn Barry

MARY JEAN WARREN C. Karae Lyn Sugiyama × Bonanza Warren 1974

MARY JO NELSON L. cinnabarina × C. Bob Betts Bracey 1958
× Blc. Summer Shades = Blc. Gold Torch

MARY KAWENA PUKUI C. Charybdis × Bonanza Otaguro 1973

MARY LITTLEFIELD Wine Festival × Sunset Flare Bachner 1974 (Kirch)

MARY LOU HAUCK‡ Karen × Princess Woodstar Thornton's 1961 (Gore)
× Land of Enchantment = Enchanted Lou

MARY ROSE†‡ Queen Mary × Rosalind A. 1938
× Nigrescent = Bossa Nova
× Seattle = Lavender Gate
× Blc. Wake Island = Blc. Mary Island

MARY WEAVER Bonanza × Kismet Trade Winds 1962 (Ken Little)
× C. Dark Emperor = Mem. Katie Muse

MASSILIA Hernalia × Marceau Pff. V. & L. 1972

MATILIJA‡ Dulzura × C. Brussels A. & R. 1948
× Cantabile = Albert Culver
× Fedora = Pride of Seville
× Blc. Lester McDonald = Blc. Gambol on Green

MATTIE SHAVE Zada Fields × C. Dark Emperor Fields Orchids 1968
× Ctna. Keith Roth = Lctna. Roy Fields

MAZARINE Tussor × Ostende F. 1972

MEDON†‡ Mrs. Medo × Sargarno A. & M. 1946
× Momus = Momus Medon
× Waianae Sunset = Wanpen
× Blc. Bobby Ward = Blc. Bobbydon

LAELIOCATTLEYA

MEG MABBS — **Golden Gate × C. forbesii** — **Stevenson 1968 (von Paulsen)**

× Dormaniana	= Mini Meg

MELECIO HUERTA — **C. Rita Renee × Grub Stake** — **Stewart Inc. 1972**

MELING HO — **C. Nellie Roberts × Lee Langford** — **Stewart Inc. 1974**

MELISSA — **Wine Festival × C. Dayana** — **Kirch 1973**

MEMORIA ALBERT HEINECKE†‡ — **Grandee × S. J. Bracey** — **Bracey 1949**

× Camilla	= Spanish Spice	× Blc. Mellowglow	= Blc. San Juan Sunset
× Edmund Rothwell	= Limerick	× Blc. Norman's Bay	= Blc. Mem. Ralph Placentia
× Nugget	= Washington Slopes	× Blc. Richard Nixon	= Blc. Frances Miles
× Waianae Sunset	= Kodiak Island	× Blc. Zeecrabbe	= Blc. Engraved
× Western Sunset	= Fort Oro	× C. Ardentissima	= Pride of Texas
× Blc. Aprica	= Blc. Oro Rico	× C. Mrs. Pitt	= Priya Rana
× Blc. Canari	= Blc. Yap Eng Hoe	× L. Zip	= Copper Glo
× Blc. Citron Pass	= Blc. Sunset Gorge	× Low. Trinket	= Pot. Marionette
× Blc. Edwin Chong	= Blc. Northern Lights	× Pot. Hidden Range	= Pot. Mountaineer Creek
× Blc. Fortune	= Blc. Thunder Mountain	× Pot. Tapestry Peak	= Pot. Halfway Mountain
× Blc. Golden Dome	= Blc. Penn State	× Sc. Cleopatra	= Slc. Arabic
× Blc. Green-heart	= Blc. Leslie Hoffman	× Slc. Beacon Hill	= Slc. Skagway
× Blc. Joyance	= Blc. Sumatra Safari	× Slc. Indian Springs	= Slc. Rugged Ridge
× Blc. Lester McDonald	= Blc. Green Empire		
× Blc. Lonesome Cove	= Blc. Grayback Mountain		

MEMORIA ALFREDO URPÍA — **C. bowringiana × Princess Cooper** — **Urpía 1974**

MEMORIA BILL MAYFIELD — **Amber Glow × Bright Night** — **Bishop 1973**

MEMORIA BUDDY CLARK — **George MacDonell × Ibbie** — **A. & R. 1963**

× C. Nigritian	= Lost Weekend

MEMORIA CHOZO TAKAHASHI — **David Lozoya × Hyperion** — **Takahashi 1971**

MEMORIA DALE HUTCHISON — **Robin Hood × Cantabile** — **Bush 1975 (Rod McLellan Co.)**

MEMORIA FRANCESCA SANTORO — **Wine Festival × Lee Langford** — **Kersey 1972**

MEMORIA FRANCISCO PIMENTEL — **Hyperion × José Dias Castro** — **Altenburg 1971**

MEMORIA FRANCIS KNAEBEL — **L. rubescens × C. Claesiana** — **Gutierrez 1974**

MEMORIA FUJIO NISHIKAWA — **Twinkle Star × Windermere** — **Otaguro 1972**

MEMORIA GARRISON AINSWORTH — **C. Iris × Cloth of Gold** — **Coastal Gdns. 1971**

MEMORIA GORDON VICKERS — C. dowiana × Michele Hege Lys — MAJ Orchids 1973 **(Vickers)**

MEMORIA IRWIN DeLONG — **C. Bow Bells × Ludgate** — **Tancig 1974 (E.F.G. Orchids)**

MEMORIA JACINTO MIRANDA — **Edgard van Belle × Hyperion** — **Ruben 1975**

MEMORIA KATIE MUSE — **Mary Weaver × C. Dark Emperor** — **Muse's 1971**

MEMORIA KURAZO OGATA — **C. Edithiae × L. anceps** — **Otaguro 1971**

MEMORIA LADD PELC — **Marceau × Miami** — **K. L. Pelc 1972 (Pelc)**

MEMORIA LAURA BRABHAM — **Chic Bonnet × Shenandoah** — **Howe 1973 (N. McDade)**

MEMORIA MAGGIE HOOD‡ — **Aconcagua × C. Enid** — **Beville 1960**

× Lillian Wilson	= Hattie Graham	× Pegi Mayne	= Tato Sheikhi
× Nevada	= Nevada Memories	× Bc. Heatonensis	= Blc. Florence Lockhart

MEMORIA MAGGIE HOOD‡ *(continued)*

× Blc. Kong-Urai Gold = Blc. Yellow Butterfly
× C. Catherine Patterson = Catherine Hood
× C. Graniris = Pilot Mountain
× C. Kittiwake = Ahmad Sheikhi
× C. Rita Renee = Nippon
× Slc. Naomi Kerns = Slc. Frances Mary

MEMORIA MARIA MIRANDA **C. trianaei × Fashionable Theo** **Ruben 1970**

× B. nodosa = Blc. Mem. Josefa Martinez
× C. Rubencito = Doña Josefa

MEMORIA MARILYN BARRY **H. G. Alexander × Mary Carrico** **Gaine 1975 (Redlinger)**

MEMORIA MASA MATSUMOTO **C. loddigesii × Dark Delight** **O. Kirsch 1967 (Hirose)**

× Little Sunbeam = Lenalani
× C. Priscilla Ward = Okana
× Dill. Bronze Kahili = Nrna. Rebecca

MEMORIA MOTOMU OTAGURO **Frank Lind × Twinkle Star** **Otaguro 1971**

MEMORIA PAULINE PELC **Marlace × Miami** **Pelc 1972**

MEMORIA RONNIE ENDSLEY **C. Snow White × Bride's Bouquet** **Howe 1974 (R. C. McDade)**

MEMORIA SOPHIA COX **Helen B. Lawrence × L. flava** **Rosen 1972**

MEMORIA TAKESBI KID **Adonis × Gitche Manito** **Kido 1972**

MEMORIA TORAJI MURAKAMI **Golden Glow × Silva-Sugi** **Murakami 1973**

MEMORIA TOYO SAKUMOTO **Ishtar × Baldur** **Kido 1973**

MEMORIA WALTER ARMACOST†‡ **Cuesta × C. Tityus** **A. & R. 1951**

× Allan-a-Dale = Californian Beauty

MEMORIA ZANNIE MELTON **Eunice × C. Bow Bells** **Lenette 1973**

MERCEDES LISBÔA SENG **Luiz Martinelli × Abe Montague** **Ramos 1973**

MERCIA*‡ **C. schroderae × L. flava** **C. 1903**

× Brilliant Orange = Liebling
× Blc. Rising Sun = Blc. Amenity
× C. aurantiaca = Snippet
× C. Guatemalensis = Baby Nuuanu
× C. Priscilla Ward = Little Girl

MERI SEGARS‡ **C. Bow Bells × Amber Glow** **Rivermont 1960**

× Amber Glow = Ruth McDade
× Bright Night = Merry and Bright

MERRY AND BRIGHT **Bright Night × Meri Segars** **Rivermont 1971**

MIAMI†‡ **Runah × Sargon** **A. & M. 1947**

× Marceau = Mem. Ladd Pelc
× Marlace = Mem. Pauline Pelc

MICHELE HEGE LYS‡ **Penmarth × C. aclandiae** **Fouraker 1965**

× C. dowiana = Mem. Gordon Vickers

MICHIO OKAYAWA **Princess Margaret × Momus** **Otaguro 1974**

MIDI **Derrynane × C. loddigesii** **Pff. V. & L. 1972**

MIDNIGHT ROYALE **Kalono × Seattle** **Rod McLellan Co. 1975 (J. F. Hughes)**

MIDNIGHT STREET **L. flava × C. Highburiensis** **Katsuura 1973**

LAELIOCATTLEYA

MIKE SHAW — **G. S. Ball × C. December Snow** — **Pickell 1973 (Originator unknown)**
× Slc. Rainbow Hill = Slc. Nick Pickell

MILDRED BENIS — **Bonanza × Helen Street** — **Benis 1972**
MIME — **Colorama × C. intermedia** — **Rod McLellan Co. 1974**
MINI MEG — **Meg Mabbs × Dormaniana** — **Stevenson 1975**
MIRA‡ — **Tegucigalpa × Winter Belle** — **Rivermont 1953**
× Irene Finney = Andrew Hausermann

MIRIAM MARKS — **Princess Margaret × Princess Frolic** — **Sieff 1954 (Ratcliffe)**
× Blc. J. H. Robinson = Blc. Eve

MITSUKO TAKEDA — **Bonanza × Kyoko Takeda** — **C. Takeda 1973**
MOLFIC — **Molly Tyler × Pacific** — **Pff. V. & L. 1972**
MOLLY TYLER*†‡ — **Mrs. W. N. Elkins × C. Leda** — **F. E. Dixon 1930**
× Cassandra = Cassa Tyler | × C. Dindoer = Katreena Howard
× Pacific = Molfic | × C. labiata = Carolyn Hurtt

MOMUS*†‡ — **Rubens × C. Octave Doin** — **C. 1916**
× Medon = Momus Medon | × Blc. Norman's Bay = Blc. Louis Palacio
× Princess Margaret = Michio Okayawa

MOMUS MEDON — **Momus × Medon** — **Gauda 1971**
MONTMARTRE — **Lykas × Gaillard** — **Pff. V. & L. 1975**
MOOCHIE — **C. Esbetts × Bonanza** — **Vic Sumner 1971**
MOUNT CHILKO — **Zada Fields × My Fancy** — **Beall 1975**
MOUNT PILCHUCK — **Fedora × Louella O. Parsons** — **Beall 1973**
MOUNT TAHOMA — **Louella O. Parsons × Souvenir de Bonita** — **Beall 1973**
MRS. MEDO*†‡ — **Luminosa × C. Venus** — **L. 1922**
× Blc. Amanda Gibson = Blc. Dream Queen

MRS. RED — **L. milleri × C. bicolor** — **Cassella 1975**
MURANO — **Areca × Bonanza** — **Hecker 1960**
× Fabled City = Anvil Peak

MURIELLE LARRABEE — **Queen Kate × C. Angel Bells** — **Mrs. W. E. Larrabee 1975**
MURRIE FITCH — **L. cinnabarina × C. Lucille Small** — **Fitch 1966 (Small)**
× Antonica Fredrick = Lynn Richard

MY FANCY — **Molly Tyler × Camolty** — **Rivermont 1960**
× Zada Fields = Mount Chilko

MYOSOTIE — **Evangeline Flynn × Nelly Corradi** — **F. 1972**
MYSEDO†‡ — **Mrs. Medo × Mysia** — **C. 1946**
× Lee Langford = Alice Otaguro | × C. Nigrella = Janet Fujikawa

NAQUI — **Souvenir de Bonita × Pegi Mayne** — **Rod McLellan Co. 1975**
NATIONAL GEOGRAPHIC — **Aeneid × Robin Hood** — **Rod McLellan Co. 1971**
NELLY CORRADI‡ — **Suprême × Manitoba** — **F. 1958**
× Evangeline Flynn = Myosotie | × Blc. Carly Hausermann = Blc. Gale Nigro

NEVADA‡ — **Peter the Great × C. Enid** — **A. & R. 1950**
× Mem. Maggie Hood = Nevada Memories

NEVADA MEMORIES — **Nevada × Mem. Maggie Hood** — **A. & R. 1973**

NEW WORLD‡ — **Costa Rica × Plymouth** — Rod McLellan Co. 1969
× Blc. Xanthette = Blc. Moon Halo

NIGEL CALDER — **Princess Margaret × Plymouth** — **B. 1974**
NIGHT TWINKLE — **Blue Boy × Twinkle Star** — **McAllister 1975**
NIGRESCENT‡ — **Bonanza × C. Nigritian** — **Abbott 1959**

× Faith Dee Fanchaly	= Barbara Tsubaki	× Blc. Carmen Cestero	= Blc. Ruby Watanabe
× Mary Rose	= Bossa Nova	× Blc. Norman's Bay	= Blc. Paul Shodo Yempuku
× Pacific	= Pacific Night		
× Bc. Hartland	= Blc. Rio Tampa	× Sl. Psyche	= Slc. Mem. Bill Eckles

NIJI — **Amelia × Luminosa** — **Katsuura 1973**
NIPPON — **C. Rita Renee × Mem. Maggie Hood** — **T. Hisazaki 1971**
NORMAN GRAY — **Ernie Pyle × C. Enid** — **H. Patterson 1968**
× Joseph Hampton = Addison Friendship

NORTH CAROLINA — C. Jacqueline Kennedy × Whitewings — **Lenette 1973**
NUCLEAR ZIP — **C. Nuclear Age × L. Zip** — **Pabst 1975**
NUGGET*†‡ — **Canberra × Mrs. Medo** — **S. 1935**
× Mem. Albert Heinecke = Washington Slopes

NUUANU†‡ — Penshurst × C. Nutley — **J. Milton Warne 1944**
× L. tenebrosa = Guaicaipuro

OAKLAND‡ — **Buccaneer × Mary Rose** — **Rod McLellan Co. 1957 (E. W. McLellan)**
× Bonanza = Kalono

ODESSA†‡ — **Canberra × Ruth** — **B. 1941**
× Blc. Fortune = Blc. Gold Range

OKANA — C. Priscilla Ward × Mem. Masa Matsumoto — **O. Kirsch 1975**
OMPHALE‡ — **Caid × C. Judah** — **V. 1951**
× Flirtie = Rainbow Falls

OOI BOON HUAT — **Golden Gate × Faith Dee Fanchaly** — **Stewart Inc. 1971**
ORANGE ANN‡ — **C. Ann Roberts × Orange Beauty** — Rod McLellan Co. 1956 **(E. W. McLellan)**
× Blc. Pacific Gold = Blc. Daystar

ORANGE AUREA — **Brilliant Orange × C. Guatemalensis** — **A. & R. 1973**
ORANGE BOW — **Orange Beauty × C. Bow Bells** — **Rod McLellan Co. 1964**
× Hazel Abel = Winter's Gold

ORANGE CHARM — **Orange Ann × Golden Charm** — Rod McLellan Co. 1964
× Blc. Rising Sun = Blc. Mandarin Bay

ORANGE FIRE — Christopher Gubler × L. Zip — **Beall 1973**
ORANGE GEM*†‡ — **Elinor × G. S. Ball** — **A. 1929**

× Dormaniana	= Harvest Moon	× L. Zip	= Zem
× Wheal Rose	= Peacock Gem	× Sc. Doris	= Slc. Summerville
× Blc. Mamie Fouraker	= Blc. Samarkand	× Sl. Jinn	= Slc. Jinn Gem
× Blc. Mellow Vista	= Blc. Glo Helin	× Slc. California Apricot	= Slc. California Delight
× C. luteola	= Gemola	× Slc. Lindores	= Slc. Gabby Gibson

ORCADE — **Chine × Amber Glow** — **Pff. V. & L. 1975**

LAELIOCATTLEYA

OREBUS*†‡ | **Appam × C. Venus** | **C. 1925**

× Waianae Sunset = Brown Bear Pass

ORIENTAL SPLENDOR‡ | **Amber Glow × C. Nellie Roberts** | **Bracey 1966**

× Amelia = September Moon
× Schillerana = Schillendor
× Wine Festival = Helen Bachner

ORMESBY‡ | **Hyperion × C. Fred Sander** | **L. 1948**

× C. percivaliana = Carlos Relvas

OROYUM | **Brilliant Orange × C. aurantiaca** | **Rod McLellan Co. 1975**

OSTENDE | **Vallandina × Van Der Weyden** | **F. 1957**

× Tussor = Mazarine

OZARK‡ | **Valstar × Isotta** | **Gore 1959**

× C. Auranti-media = Kim Miller
× Soph. coccinea = Slc. Nancy Bellows

PACIFIC†‡ | **Medon × Atlantis** | **Rod McLellan Co. 1954**

× Molly Tyler = Molfic
× Nigrescent = Pacific Night

PACIFIC NIGHT | **Pacific × Nigrescent** | **E. W. McLellan 1973**

PACIFIC ROSE | **Pacific × Mary Rose** | **Rod McLellan Co. 1964**

× Charlie Stem = Kimberly Sovereign

PACIFIC SUN†‡ | **Golden Charm × Medon** | **Rod McLellan Co. 1955 (E. W. McLellan)**

× Golden Wren = Bright Bird
× Lee Langford = Ana Maria Duveen
× Yolo = Decker McAllister
× Blc. Rising Sun = Blc. Sunshine Meadow
× Blc. Summer Shades = Blc. Golden Reward
× C. Bactia = Royal Pacific
× L. Coronet = Sunoret

PARABOLE | **Lucien Pauwels × President de Brouwer** | **F. 1972**

PARADISIO†‡ | **Robertiana × C. Remy Chollet** | **Sladden 1946**

× Alisal = Commander
× José Dias Castro = Zuki Disio
× White Queen = Spring Fashion
× Bc. Pastoral = Blc. Oswaldo Paulino Santos
× Blc. Dinsmore = Blc. Dindisio
× C. Metapan = Spring Tradition

PARYSATIS‡ | **C. bowringiana × L. pumila** | **Veitch 1893**

× C. Interglossa = Kindee
× C. labiata = Granite Mountain
× L. purpurata = Brazilian Sky

PATRICIA HEWLETT | **Bonanza × Sagapyle** | **Casa Luna 1974 (Lind)**

PATRICIA KELLY | **Peggy Huffman × C. Guatemalensis** | **Kelly 1971**

PATTY LYNN SMITH | **Grodske's Gold × C. Peanuts** | **Mrs. Paul L. Smith 1972**

PAUL JOSEPH WEBER | **C. Tango × Golden Nymph** | **Mrs. W. H. Boyd 1973 (Blauvelt)**

PEACOCK GEM | **Wheal Rose × Orange Gem** | **Crothers 1971**

PEGGY ANNA | **C. Claesiana × Peggy Huffman** | **Muse's 1971**

PEGGY HUFFMAN‡ | **Princess Margaret × C. intermedia** | **Gamble 1956**

× South Pacific = Stuart Bance
× Blc. Coronet Bay = Blc. Mount John Jay
× Blc. Holiday Gem = Blc. Ruben's Gem
× C. Claesiana = Peggy Anna
× C. Enid = Ermine Robe
× C. Guatemalensis = Patricia Kelly
× C. Sudan = Theresa Rose
× Epi. atropurpureum = Eplc. Roxanne

PEGGY LYNN GREZAFFI | **C. Browniae × L. cinnabarina** | **Grezaffi 1971**

PEGGY MOIR | **L. flava × C. Triumphans** | **W. W. G. Moir 1951**

× Slc. Radians = Slc. Gold Reward

PEGI MAYNE‡ — **Eugenie × C. May Merkel** — **H. Patterson 1956**

× Aconcagua = Something Special | × Souvenir de Bonita = Naqui
× Fedora = Rose Crystal | × C. Catherine Patterson = Bill Shave
× Mem. Maggie Hood = Tato Sheikhi | × C. Kittiwake = Persepolis

PELOT'S PRIDE — **Adolph Hecker × Bonanza** — **Pelot 1975**
PENMARTH‡ — **Poynings × Rudgwick** — **L. 1948**

× Fedora = Aloha Koji Ota

PERLE NOIR — **José Dias Castro × C. Nigritian** — **Altenburg 1971**
PERSEPOLIS — **C. Kittiwake × Pegi Mayne** — **A. & R. 1973**
PERSIMMON ROYALE — **S. J. Bracey × Wayndora** — **J. & S. 1975 (Miyamoto)**

PICARDY — **C. labiata × Dorothy Fried** — **Ilsley 1958 (Ozzella)**

× C. Porcia = Carmen Escobar

PILOT MOUNTAIN — **C. Graniris × Mem. Maggie Hood** — **Lenette 1974**
PINK PANTY — **L. gouldiana × C. Claesiana** — **Edelbrock 1973**
PINK PEARL† — **Princess Margaret × C. Etteleanore** — **Rideout 1944**

× C. trianaei = Lourdes Falabella

PIPPIN — **C. luteola × Ronselensis** — **Voo Doo Orchids 1974**
PIRATE KING‡ — **Lee Langford × Quadroon** — **Stewart Inc. 1962**

× Bonanza = Albert Hollingsworth | × Blc. Helen Morita = Blc. Guaymas
× Waianae Sunset = Imperial Torch | × Blc. Pinkie = Blc. Whitney Lawler

PIRATE'S GOLD — **C. Priscilla Ward × Little Sunbeam** — **O. Kirsch 1970**

× Bonanza = Derning

PITCAIRN — **Gladys Millner × C. Mrs. Pitt** — **O. Kirsch 1971**
PIXIE GOLD — **L. flava × C. luteola** — **Rod McLellan Co. 1964**

× Red Gold = Dixie Pixie | × Blc. Bouton D'Or = Blc. Yellow Buttons
× Bc. Daffodil = Blc. Daffy Pixie

PLATINUM SUN — **C. Francis T. C. Au × Colorama** — **Rex Foster's 1973 (Fordyce)**

PLEIADES — **C. bowringiana × Twinkle Star** — **C. & H. 1964**

× Epi. phoeniceum = Eplc. Edna Blum

PLYMOUTH†‡ — **Ruth × C. King George** — **B. 1942**

× Princess Margaret = Nigel Calder

PORTRAIT — **C. Portisoniae × Quadroon** — **Rod McLellan Co. 1975**
POTOMAC — S. J. Bracey × C. Maggie Raphael — **Kensington 1971 (Originator unknown)**

POUSSIN†‡ — **Capitaine × C. Fabia** — **V. 1940**

× Bonanza = Foxfire

PREFERMENT — **Aconcagua × C. Kittiwake** — **J. & S. 1975**
PRESIDENT DE BROUWER‡ — **C. Furnes × Gwen Sander** — **F. 1955**

× Lucien Pauwels = Parabole | × Blc. Dusk = Blc. Paonneau

PRIDE OF SEVILLE — **Matilija × Fedora** — **Stewart Inc. 1975 (Rehfield)**

PRIDE OF TEXAS — **C. Ardentissima × Mem. Albert Heinecke** — **Stewart Inc. 1973**
PRINCE GORDON — **Queen Kate × C. intermedia** — **Mrs. W. E. Larrabee 1975**
PRINCESS — **Princess Esk × South Esk** — **Muse 1966**

× Bc. Taquin = Blc. Opal Wilde

LAELIOCATTLEYA

PRINCESS COOPER | **Princess Margaret × Ruth Ley Cooper** | **J. & S. 1963**
× C. bowringiana = Mem. Alfredo Urpía

PRINCESS ESK‡ | **South Esk × Princess Ishtar** | **Gore 1953**
× Bonanza = Bonesk
× C. Sedlescombe = Chen's Beauty
× Slc. Anzac = Slc. Prinzac

PRINCESS ISHTAR†‡ | **Ishtar × Princess Margaret** | **B. 1942**
× C. Maggie Raphael = Princess Raphael

PRINCESS MARGARET*†‡ | **Profusion × C. Clotho** | **M. 1930**
× Edgard van Belle = Vulcan's Pride
× George Thomas = Louisiana Purchase
× Kismet Queen = Akuhead Pupule
× Momus = Michio Okayawa
× Plymouth = Nigel Calder
× Prophesy = Ira Fumiko Field
× Blc. Dark Waters = Blc. Dark Prince
× C. Corflambo = Summer Sunset
× C. Michael Sander = Marsander
× C. warneri = Lyndel Worthman
× Pot. Gordon Siu = Pot. Katsumi Wakatake

PRINCESS ORANGE | **C. David Sweet × Charlesworthii** | **Muse's 1971**
PRINCESS RAPHAEL | **Princess Ishtar × C. Maggie Raphael** | **Kensington 1973**
PRINCESS WOODSTAR†‡ | **Elissa × Princess Margaret** | **Gore 1948**
× Alisal = Wateree

PRISM PALETTE | **Colorama × C. Horace** | **Kay Francis 1973**
PRIYA RANA | **C. Mrs. Pitt × Mem. Albert Heinecke** | **Gubler 1971**
PROPHESY | **C. Horace × Hyperion** | **Stewart Inc. 1966**
× Bonanza = Bonanza Queen
× Princess Margaret = Ira Fumiko Field

PUPPET‡ | **L. Coronet × C. Minucia** | **Crothers 1966**
× C. Venosa = Imp of Gold

PURPLE HEART | **Morro Rock × George MacDonell** | **A. & R. 1966**
× Blc. Mem. Crispin Rosales = Blc. Heart Peaks

PURPLE MAJESTY | **Velvet Spring × C. mossiae** | Hausermann 1972
PYLETTE | **Ernie Pyle × Georgette** | **Kensington 1973**
QUADROON†‡ | **Susan × C. Nigritian** | **Bracey 1954**
× Buccaneer = Charles Plaxico
× George Cutler = Cora Williams
× Maili Beauty = Maili Quadroon
× San Mateo Times = Lawrence Vance
× Volcano = Voldroon
× Walter Slagle = Imperial Palace
× Blc. Mem. Bill Fouraker = Blc. Rose Chiyoko Kakazu
× C. Dark Emperor = Enoree
× C. Portisoniae = Portrait
× Pot. Gordon Siu = Pot. Vibrant

QUEEN ALEXANDRA*†‡ | **Bella × C. trianaei** | **Veitch 1902**
× L. cinnabarina = Bit of Orange

QUEEN KATE | **Richmond × British Queen** | **Larrabee 1969**
× C. Angel Bells = Murielle Larrabee
× C. intermedia = Prince Gordon

RAINBOW FALLS | **Flirtie × Omphale** | Hernlund 1972
RAINBOW INLETS‡ | Kuakini × Navajo Ruby | **Beall 1955**
× Blc. Emerald Meadow = Blc. Fern Grotto

RANDY REDHOT | **Eva × C. bicolor** | **Birk 1971**
RAVEN BEAUTY | Ravenglass × Lee Langford | **Funston 1975 (Rivermont)**

LAELIOCATTLEYA

RAVENGLASS†‡ — **Lucifer × Mrs. Medo** — **Broughton 1943**
× Lee Langford = Raven Beauty

RED CEDAR CANYON — **Chine × Waianae Sunset** — **Beall 1974**
RED EMPRESS — **Bonanza × Excellency** — **J. & S. 1964 (Redlinger)**
× Kevin Green = Gila Wilderness
× Bc. Bill Worsley = Blc. Empress Worsley
× C. Little Angel = Janet Brown

RED GOLD — **C. aurantiaca × Charlesworthii** — **A. & M. 1964**
× Pixie Gold = Dixie Pixie
× Rojo = Chirpy
× Blc. Bouton D'Or = Blc. Debba-Doo
× C. aurantiaca = Red Imp
× C. Barbara Kirch = Julia Kersey
× C. Mary Lou = Jay Jay
× C. Warpaint = Gold Digger

RED IMP — **Red Gold × C. aurantiaca** — **Osment 1971**
RED ROOSTER — **Waianae Sunset × L. Zip** — **Beall 1973**
REMMEL VON GRITSCH — **Excellency × L. harpophylla** — **Fort Caroline 1974**
REMULA‡ — **C. aclandiae × L. tenebrosa** — **Veitch 1900**
× L. milleri = Glowing Embers

RESOLUTION MOUNTAIN — **Arny Freeman × C. Dinah** — **Beall 1975**
× Bc. Mount Juneau = Blc. Redoubt Mountain

REUBEN METZ — **George Cutler × Ak Sar Ben** — **Rod McLellan Co. 1971**
RHONDA FISHER — **C. Venosa × Sunburst** — **Nevins 1974**
RICKE KANAME FUJINO — **Canhamiana × C. Princess Bells** — **Otaguro 1972**
RIPPLE ROCK — **Elizabeth Lind × George MacDonell** — **Beall 1957**
× Pot. Edward Rowold = Pot. Jimi Hendrix

ROBERT KANE — **Elstead Gem × Thurderniana** — **Hoyt 1971**
ROBERTSONIAE*† — **Luminosa × C. Maggie Raphael** — **S. 1915**
× Blc. Morning Sun = Blc. Sun-Son

ROBIN HOOD†‡ — **Aconcagua × Cynthia** — **McDade 1951**
× Aeneid = National Geographic
× Cantabile = Mem. Dale Hutchison

ROBON — **Robert Doig × Bonanza** — **Ilsley 1964**
× Florence Machle = Florescent

RODCO'S PLEASURE — **St. Helena × C. Mrs. Frederick Knollys** — **Rod McLellan Co. 1971**
ROITELET†‡ — **Jocelyn × Sunburst** — **V. 1949**
× Dusky Maid = Stradivarius
× C. bowringiana = Alicia

ROJO — **C. aurantiaca × L. milleri** — **Rod McLellan Co. 1965**
× Bonanza = Claude Timmons
× Chit Chat = Ding-a-Ling
× Red Gold = Chirpy
× Blc. Bouton D'Or = Blc. Bit-of-Gold
× C. aurantiaca = Ladybug
× C. Wolteriana = Loge
× Epi. alatum = Eplc. Fiesta
× Slc. Anzac = Slc. Judy Ann Cowart
× Slc. Tropic Dawn = Slc. Rojo Dawn

RONDEL†‡ — **Cuesta × Braceyana** — **Ozzella 1953**
× Grub Stake = Grubdel
× Irving Dietsche = Rondi

RONDI — **Irving Dietsche × Rondel** — **Kensington 1973**
RONSELENSIS* — **C. forbesii × L. cinnabarina** — **Wavrin 1904**
× Bc. Maikai = Blc. Royal Harbor
× C. luteola = Pippin

LAELIOCATTLEYA

ROSA KIRSCH†‡ — **Pasadena × C. Rembrandt** — **O. Kirsch 1950**
× Bc. Green Dawn = Blc. Kalakoa | × C. Baby Jane = Kiliwehi
× Blc. Frank Tatsumura = Blc. Waikane | × C. New Era = Manu

ROSE CRYSTAL — **Pegi Mayne × Fedora** — **Rod McLellan Co. 1975 (Spencer)**

ROSEVAL — **Harold J. Patterson × C. Damoiseau** — **Marcel Lecoufle 1974**
ROYAL PACIFIC — **C. Bactia × Pacific Sun** — **McAllister 1973**
ROYAL RUBY — **C. Tango × Twinkle Star** — **Bloom's Nursery 1974**
× Sargon = Summer Rhapsody |

RUBESCENT LUTEUS — **L. rubescens × C. luteola** — **Otaguro 1971**
RUTH McDADE — **Amber Glow × Meri Segars** — **Rivermont 1972**
RUTH WILLIAMS — **Clara Schriever × C. Catherine Patterson** — **J. & S. 1971**
SAADIA — **C. Nonoska × Mireille** — **Maurice Vacherot 1957**
× Edgard van Belle = Andre Baumann | × C. Dante = Georges Coudroux

SACRAMENTO‡ — **C. Prospector × Mary Rose** — **Rod McLellan Co. 1957 (E. W. McLellan)**
× Blc. Norman's Bay = Blc. Koinaba |

SAGANA*† — **San Juan × C. Hentschellii** — **C. 1931**
× Ernie Pyle = Sagapyle |

SAGAPYLE — **Sagana × Ernie Pyle** — **Casa Luna 1974 (Lind)**
× Bonanza = Patricia Hewlett |

SAINT HELENA‡ — **Snowdrift × Florence Pickard** — **Rod McLellan Co. 1959 (E. W. McLellan)**
× C. Mrs. Frederick Knollys = Rodco's Pleasure |

SAINT LOUIS‡ — **Spring Triumph × C. lueddemanniana** — **Mo. Bot. Gdn. 1950**
× Dr. G. T. Moore = Arthur McKee |

SAM — Easter Bonnet × L. cinnabarina — Fresh 1971
SANDY GIBSON — **Charlie Stem × Dee Dee** — George Black 1973
SANGRITA — Gertrude Hampton × C. labiata — **Tayama 1962**
× Bonanza = Cass Hough |

SAN MATEO TIMES — **Haidee × Griselda** — **Rod McLellan Co. 1958 (E. W. McLellan)**
× Quadroon = Lawrence Vance |

SAN PABLO — **Issy × C. bicolor** — **Fort Caroline 1971** (Wallbrunn)

SANS ATOUT — **Alfredo Martinelli × Hertha** — **Altenburg 1972**
SARGARNO†‡ — **Locarno × Sargon** — A. & M. 1946
× C. J. A. Carbone = Jyla Sheikhi |

SARGON*†‡ — **Lustre × C. Hardyana** — **H. 1915**
× Royal Ruby = Summer Rhapsody |

SAUCY LYNN — **Laurie Lynn × Sausalito** — **D. E. Herman 1971**
SAUSALITO‡ — **Susan × Altura** — **Rod McLellan Co. 1955 (E. W. McLellan)**
× Laurie Lynn = Saucy Lynn |

LAELIOCATTLEYA

SAWTOOTH MOUNTAIN — **Excellency × C. Okami** — **Beall 1975**

SCHILLENDOR — **Schillerana × Oriental Splendor** — **Katsuura 1973**

schillerana
SCHILLERANA*†‡ } — **C. intermedia × L. purpurata** — { **Nat. hyb.** / **hort.**

× Oriental Splendor = Schillendor
× C. Karae Lyn Sugiyama = Kalani Castro
× C. Portia = Babe Bergin

SCHULZEANA — **Elegans × C. labiata** — **Linden 1895**

× Ariel = Tombstone Mountain

SEATTLE‡ — **Elissa × South Esk** — **B. 1951**

× Balkis = Alice Lani Chun
× Kalono = Midnight Royale
× Mary Rose = Lavender Gate

SECURITY GATE — **American Security × Margate** — **E. F. Patterson 1967 (R. K. Fields)**

× Blc. Norman's Bay = Blc. Norman's Gate

SEGOND-WEBER† — **Altesse × C. Mrs. Robert Jewell** — **V. 1947**

× Gaillard = Jane Seymour

SEMAPHORE‡ — **Sevigne × C. Bembridge** — **V. 1953**

× C. Batalinii = Keri

SEMINOLE MEADOWS — **Ann Follis × C. Fascelis** — **Marshall Orchids 1975 (Seminole Gdns.)**

SEMINOLE SUNSET — **Constance Wigan × C. Iris** — **Beall 1967 (Ryerson)**

× Blc. Emerald Meadow = Blc. Paradise Caves

SEPTEMBER MOON — **Amelia × Oriental Splendor** — **Katsuura 1973**

SERENITY — **Amecia × Serbia** — **L. 1931**

× Slc. Anzac = Slc. Liz Cameron

SHENANDOAH†‡ — **C. Sohma × Georgette** — **Rivermont 1954**

× Chic Bonnet = Mem. Laura Brabham
× Georgette = Georgean
× C. Sohma = Longwood Gardens

SIAMESE CAT — **Crowborough Sunshine × C. Leila Aronson** — **Crothers 1973**

SILVA-SUGI — **C. Triumphans × Nugget** — **Sugiyama 1955**

× Golden Glow = Mem. Toraji Murakami

SIMONE KIM-CUC BAUER — **C. Iris × Bright Night** — **Fort Caroline 1973 (Wallbrunn)**

S. J. BRACEY†‡ — **Mrs. Medo × C. Thebes** — **A. & R. 1940**

× Hawaiian Sunset = Tennessee Sunset
× Waianae Sunset = Manoa Sunburst
× Wayndora = Persimmon Royale
× Blc. Goldenette = Blc. Golden Lyre
× Blc. Kahaopea Beauty = Blc. Yuka Miyajima
× Blc. Malvern = Blc. Gold Dune
× Blc. Naomi M. Yahiro = Blc. Hisayo Hironaka
× C. Maggie Raphael = Potomac
× C. Tango = Golden Rhapsody

SMALL PAUL — **L. flava × C. Southern Belle** — **Rayridge 1974**

SMALL TALK — **L. anceps × C. Bob Betts** — **A. & R. 1971**

SMILE — **Bowri-albida × C. bowringiana** — **Katsuura 1973**

SNIPPET — **Mercia × C. aurantiaca** — **Rod McLellan Co. 1973**

SNOWDRIFT†‡ — **Cynthia × C. Annette** — **L. 1939**

× Fedora = Evensong
× George Baldwin = Virginia Royal

LAELIOCATTLEYA

SOLITUDE	**Amber Glow × C. intermedia**	**Rex Foster's 1974 (Fordyce)**
SOMETHING SPECIAL	**Pegi Mayne × Aconcagua**	**J. & S. 1975**
SONG OF NORWAY	**Matilija × C. Ardmore**	**Stewart Inc. 1968**
× L. grandiflora = Ballet Folklorico		
SOPHIA	**Aïda × Lucie Hausermann**	**Hausermann 1971**
SORRY	**Ludgate × Balkis**	**Rayridge 1974**
SO SO	**Ludgate × Helen Wilmer**	**Rayridge 1975 (F. J. Bergman)**
SOUTHE NIGRA	**C. Maracangalha × Ella Esk**	**N. Suzuki 1971**
SOUTH ESK†‡	**Elissa × Profusion**	**B. 1943**
× Amber Glow = Golden Fire; × Blc. Molflora = Blc. Molly Esk	× C. Hardyana = Benjamin Harris	
SOUTH PACIFIC	**Samite × C. Enid**	**A. M. Thompson 1964**
× Peggy Huffman = Stuart Bance		
SOUVENIR de BONITA†	**Albula × C. Bembridge**	**Urmston 1950**
× Louella O. Parsons = Mount Tahoma	× Pegi Mayne = Naqui	
SPANISH SPICE	**Mem. Albert Heinecke × Camilla**	**Rod McLellan Co. 1974 (Fordyce)**
SPARKLER	**C. forbesii × Fiery**	**Voo Doo Orchids 1974**
SPINOLA	**Flandria × Tafal**	**F. 1948**
× Evangeline Flynn = Ultraviolet		
SPLASH	**Irving Dietsche × Grub Stake**	**Kensington 1973**
SPRING ARRIVAL	**C. Metapan × Lomita Park**	**Rod McLellan Co. 1972**
SPRING FANCY	**C. Mossmist × Louis Dorp**	**Rod McLellan Co. 1975**
SPRING FASHION	**White Queen × Paradisio**	**Rod McLellan Co. 1971**
SPRING PARK	**Helen Wilmer × Lomita Park**	**Rod McLellan Co. 1975**
SPRING REWARD	**C. mossiae × George Cutler**	**Rod McLellan Co. 1971**
SPRING ROMANCE	**C. Winnietha × Lomita Park**	**Rod McLellan Co. 1972**
SPRING TONIC	**Hertha × Lomita Park**	**Rod McLellan Co. 1972**
SPRING TRADITION	C. Metapan × Paradisio	**Rod McLellan Co. 1975**
STACEY BULL	**Aïda × C. Bob Betts**	**F. H. Williams 1974 (Originator unknown)**
STAR BRIGHT	**Florence Machle × Charlesworthii**	**Muse's 1971**
STEB TEAL	**Atlantis × Hertha**	**Rod McLellan Co. 1956 (E. W. McLellan)**
× Blc. Nacouchee = Blc. North Wind		
STELA MARCIA	**George Woodhams × C. Catherine Patterson**	**Santos 1974**
STEPHEN OLIVER FOURAKER‡	**Pagi Mayne × C. Enid**	**Fouraker 1961 (Lines)**
× Christmas Fairy = David Cole; × Lillian Wilson = Frank Wilson	× Sl. Psyche = Slc. Excella	
STEPHEN SUE	**Issy × Charlesworthii**	**Das 1971** (Redlinger)
STEPLADDER	**L. anceps × C. Porcia**	**Thornton's 1975**
STRADIVARIUS	**Dusky Maid × Roitelet**	**Pff. V. & L. 1974**
STUART BANCE	**South Pacific × Peggy Huffman**	**Bance 1973**

LAELIOCATTLEYA

SUMMERLAND GIRL C. guttata × Grandee J. & S. 1967 (Bracey)

× Blc. Jane Helton = Blc. Jane Summerland | × C. Tango = Dottie Kone
× Blc. Patrick Mizuta = Blc. Somthawil | × Slc. Estella Jewell = Slc. Manoa Jewel

SUMMER RHAPSODY Sargon × Royal Ruby Lenette 1975
SUMMER SAND C. Eleanore × Jane Froman Lenette 1974 (Originator unknown)

× C. Party Girl = Summer Symphony |

SUMMER SUN L. Sunol × C. gaskelliana Lenette 1974
SUMMER SUNSET C. Corflambo × Princess Margaret Lenette 1974
SUMMER SYMPHONY Summer Sand × C. Party Girl Lenette 1974
SUNBURN†‡ Golden Sunset × Mrs. Medo C. 1935

× Bc. Hula Girl = Blc. Sunny Sands | × Blc. Zanget = Blc. Sunshine Narrows

SUNBURST*†‡ Carmencita × C. dowiana C. 1927

× C. Venosa = Rhonda Fisher |

SUNORET Pacific Sun × L. Coronet Rod McLellan Co. 1975
SUNRISE PEAK‡ C. Sara Cohn × L. tenebrosa Beall 1957

× Epi. gracile = Eplc. Mem. Astor Clarke |

SUNSET FLARE Evelyn Mountain × C. guttata Kirch 1974

× Wine Festival = Mary Littlefield |

SUNSHINE FIRE Western Sunset × Lydia Hubbell Rod McLellan Co. 1975
SUNWICK Western Sunset × Copperwick Rod McLellan Co. 1975
SUPRÊME†‡ St. George × C. Remy Chollet F. 1948

× Bonanza = Celler Rühm | × C. Bob Betts = James Bell

SUSANA TAFOLLA C. Iris × Amber Glow Bracey 1966

× L. Zip = Danau Toba Idyl |

SUZANNE FULLERTON Bacchante × Walter Winchell Rod McLellan Co. 1960

× Blc. Edwin Chong = Blc. Sweet Sue |

SYVIL MARQUIT Cocarde × Britansun Marquit 1975
TACO C. Big Splash × Mariner Bishop 1974 (Originator unknown)

TAKE FIVE C. Quinquecolor × Edmund Rothwell Rod McLellan Co. 1974
TAKESHI DOC YATABE C. Michael Sander × Lee Langford Rod McLellan Co. 1972
TAMPON Harold J. Patterson × Belles Flandres Marcel Lecoufle 1974
TANGERINE BEAUTY‡ Mimi Koehler × C. aurantiaca Mo. Bot. Gdn. 1961

× Golden Charm = Golden Tangerine |

TANGO Danaé × Amber Glow Pff. V. & L. 1973
TATO SHEIKHI Pegi Mayne × Mem. Maggie Hood A. & R. 1973
TELSTAR Mem. Walter Armacost × Fred Castator A. & R. 1964

× Fred Castator = Tribal Fair |

TENEBON Bonanza × L. tenebrosa Katsuura 1973
TENNESSEE SUNSET Hawaiian Sunset × S. J. Bracey Lenette 1974 (Rivermont)

TERRY WAYNE‡ Blanchette × Tirlemont E. Iwanaga 1950

× Blc. Hanako Omura = Blc. Neal Blaisdell |

LAELIOCATTLEYA

THEBON	**Bonanza × C. Thetis**	**Kensington 1973**
THERESA ROSE	**C. Sudan × Peggy Huffman**	**Bance 1972 (Spencer)**
THUNDER RIVER	**Ernie Pyle × Wyatt Earp**	**Beall 1973**
THURDERNIANA†‡	**Derna × Thurgoodiana**	**McDade 1952**

× Elstead Gem	= Robert Kane	× Soph. coccinea	= Slc. Sally Dickinson
× Blc. Buttercup	= Blc. Donna Gillis	× Slc. Valentine	= Slc. Red Reason

TIA MARIA	**Ishtar × C. Nigritian**	**J. & S. 1974**
TIBOUCHINA	**C. Barbara Kirch × Kensella**	**Mrs. L. Wilson 1974**
TIME-LIFE	**C. mossiae × Irene Finney**	**Hausermann 1972**
TIM'S FIRE	**Antonica Fredrick × C. aurantiaca**	**Voo Doo Orchids 1974**
TITILES	**Arthur E. Miles × Titriva**	**Rayridge 1975 (Originator unknown)**
TITRIVA	**Godiva × C. Titrianae**	**Rayridge 1975 (Originator unknown)**

× Arthur E. Miles	= Titiles

TOFLAM	**Tokyo Rose × C. Corflambo**	**Clark Day Jr. 1973 (Originator unknown)**

× Pot. Lillie Rose	= Pot. Mount Peleé

TOKYO ROSE†‡	**Cavalese × C. Tityus**	**Urmston 1950**

× C. Corflambo	= Toflam

TOM BRAVERMAN	**Altesse × C. mendelii**	**Braverman 1972 (Fennell)**

× C. aurantiaca	= Donna's Sunset

TOMBSTONE MOUNTAIN	**Ariel × Schulzeana**	**Beall 1975**
TRIBAL FAIR	**Fred Castator × Telstar**	**A. & R. 1973**
TRICK OR TREAT	**L. Icarus × Chit Chat**	**Stewart Inc. 1973**
TUSSOR	**Jordaens × St. George**	**F. 1970**

× Ostende	= Mazarine

TWILIGHT SONG	**C. walkerana × L. anceps**	**Stewart Inc. 1974**
TWINKLE CHOLLET	**C. Remy Chollet × Twinkle Star**	**Gauda 1973**
TWINKLE GOLD	**Golden Gate × Twinkle Star**	**McAllister 1973**
TWINKLE STAR‡	**Avignon × C. Empress Frederick**	**Gore 1954**

× Blue Boy	= Night Twinkle	× Blc. Mem. Crispin Rosales	= Blc. Twinkle Rosales
× Frank Lind	= Mem. Motomu Otaguro	× C. aurantiaca	= Carolyn Reid
× Golden Gate	= Twinkle Gold	× C. Remy Chollet	= Twinkle Chollet
× Western Sunset	= Western Star	× C. Tango	= Royal Ruby
× Windermere	= Mem. Fujio Nishikawa	× Epi. Atroniceum	= Eplc. John Pelot
× Bc. Hartland	= Blc. Starland	× Epi. conopseum	= Eplc. Susan Margaret Wehlburg
× Blc. Armida	= Blc. Twilight Time	× Slc. Tropic Dawn	= Slc. Lillian Chiyoko Ito
× Blc. Matriarch	= Blc. Twinkle Mater		

TYDEA*	**C. trianaei × L. pumila**	**Veitch 1894**

× Slc. Lindores	= Slc. Helen Oyakawa

TYL	**C. Horace × Van Dyck**	**F. 1955**

× Dyver	= Crinoline

ULTRAVIOLET	**Evangeline Flynn × Spinola**	**F. 1972**
UMATILLA REEF	**Seattle × Morro Rock**	**Beall 1965**

× Alope	= Van Norman Lake

LAELIOCATTLEYA

UNCLE SHEU WAN — **Hypellency × Bonanza** — **Hong-Sie Chen 1975 (Chung-Chweng Chen)**

VALLANDINA†‡ — **Profusion × C. Dinah** — **M. 1929**
- × Dorothy Fried = Litorne

VALLECHOLLET‡ — **Bonanza × C. Remy Chollet** — **Vallemar 1960**
- × Manila = Manilavale
- × C. Nigritian = Fusilier

VALLEYBIRD‡ — **C. Firebird × Candidate** — **Vallemar 1960**
- × Durbin = Harriet Breuer

VALOR‡ — **Helen Wilmer × C. Palatine** — **Rivermont 1952**
- × Bc. Cornelius = Blc. Brandon

VAN NORMAN LAKE — **Umatilla Reef × Alope** — **Miskimens 1975**

VELVET SPRING — **Arthur E. Miles × C. mossiae** — **Hausermann 1967**
- × C. mossiae = Purple Majesty

VICTOR CANAVESE — **C. Peanuts × Bonanza** — **Rod McLellan Co. 1972**

VIRGINIA ROYAL — **Snowdrift × George Baldwin** — **O. G. Marsh 1971**

VOLCANO‡ — **Detta × C. Fabia** — **Bracey 1953**
- × Quadroon = Voldroon

VOLDROON — **Volcano × Quadroon** — **Miskimens 1975**

VULCAN'S PRIDE — **Princess Margaret × Edgard van Belle** — **W. Nielsen 1974 (Pff. V. & L.)**

WAIANAE BELLE — **Belle of Celle × Waianae Sunset** — **Kirch 1974**

WAIANAE SUNSET‡ — **Dorothy Fried × Mysedo** — **Miyamoto 1963**
- × Belle of Celle = Waianae Belle
- × Bonanza = Bonanza Sunset
- × Bright Night = Hawaiian Warrior
- × Chine = Red Cedar Canyon
- × Christopher Gubler = Indian Mountain
- × Edgard van Belle = Belle of Hilo
- × Medon = Wanpen
- × Mem. Albert Heinecke = Kodiak Island
- × Orebus = Brown Bear Pass
- × Pirate King = Imperial Torch
- × S. J. Bracey = Manoa Sunburst
- × Blc. Acapana = Blc. Mount Garibaldi
- × Blc. Nancy Wittorf = Blc. Makaha Glolight
- × Blc. Norman's Bay = Blc. War Chant
- × Blc. Zanget = Blc. Rampart Ridge
- × L. Zip = Red Rooster

WALTER LARRABEE — **First Star × L. tenebrosa** — **Mrs. W. E. Larrabee 1972**

WALTER SLAGLE‡ — **Mary Rose × Walter Winchell** — **Rod McLellan Co. 1960**
- × José Dias Castro = Adolpho Menezes
- × Quadroon = Imperial Palace
- × Bc. Mount Hood = Blc. Beauford Fisher
- × Blc. Norman's Bay = Blc. Florence Dickinson

WANPEN — **Medon × Waianae Sunset** — **Tanmukayakul 1974 (Kirch)**

WAR DANCE — **L. gloedeniana × C. dowiana** — **J. & S. 1971**

WASHINGTON SLOPES — **Nugget × Mem. Albert Heinecke** — **Beall 1973**

WATEREE — **Princess Woodstar × Alisal** — **C. & H. 1975**

WAYNDORA‡ — **Terry Wayne × Fedora** — **E. Iwanaga 1962**
- × S. J. Bracey = Persimmon Royale

WENDY TAYLER — **Golden Ray × Gatton Glory** — **Rod McLellan Co. 1966**
- × Blc. Otomayim = Blc. Otango

WESTERN STAR — **Twinkle Star × Western Sunset** — **Thornton's 1975**

WESTERN SUNSET‡ — **Golden Gate × Pacific Sun** — **Rod McLellan Co. 1963**
- × Copperwick = Sunwick
- × Lydia Hubbell = Sunshine Fire
- × Mem. Albert Heinecke = Fort Oro
- × Twinkle Star = Western Star
- × Blc. Bobby Ward = Blc. Corcoran Sunset
- × Blc. Mamie Fouraker = Blc. Caldron

WESTERN SUNSET‡ *(continued)*

× Blc. Otomayim = Blc. Kohoutek
× Blc. Setting Sun = Blc. Briteside
× Blc. Sylvia Reilly = Blc. Marigold Meadows
× Blc. Xanthette = Blc. Pacemaker
× Pot. Tapestry Peak = Pot. Western Peak
× Slc. Anzac = Slc. Rodco's Jewel

WHEAL ROSE†‡ — **Jubilee × C. Biboule** — **L. 1949**

× Orange Gem = Peacock Gem
× Blc. Jewel Higdon = Blc. Colonial Jewel

WHITE GULL — **C. White Belle × Bride's Bouquet** — **Howe 1974 (R. C. McDade)**

WHITE QUEEN†‡ — **Britannia × C. mossiae** — **F. E. Dixon 1936**

× Easter Belle = Augusta Freund Littmann
× Paradisio = Spring Fashion

WHITEWINGS‡ — **Cynthia × C. Enid** — **L. 1940**

× C. Enid = Kannapolis
× C. Jacqueline Kennedy = North Carolina

WILEX — **H. G. Alexander × Helen Wilmer** — **Kensington 1973**
WILLIAM MILES — **Lorraine Shirai × Camelot** — **Miles 1971**
WILLIAM OF WOODLAWN — **Belle of Celle × C. Irgatta** — **Kirch 1974**
WINDERMERE*†‡ — **Momus × C. trianaei** — **L. 1931**

× Elissa = Elissamere
× Twinkle Star = Mem. Fujio Nishikawa

WINE FESTIVAL‡ — **Edgard van Belle × C. guttata** — **E. Iwanaga 1962**

× Lee Langford = Mem. Francesca Santoro
× Oriental Splendor = Helen Bachner
× Sunset Flare = Mary Littlefield
× C. Dayana = Melissa
× Slc. Brandywine = Slc. Firehouse Blues
× Soph. coccinea = Slc. Chili Pepper Red

WINTER'S GOLD — **Hazel Abel × Orange Bow** — **Rod McLellan Co. 1971**
WINYAH — **C. Sand Island × Zada Fields** — **C. & H. 1975**
WYATT EARP‡ — **Paradisio × C. Prospector** — **A. & R. 1956**

× Ernie Pyle = Thunder River

YELLOWLAKE — **Mem. Albert Heinecke × C. dowiana** — **Rod McLellan Co. 1966 (Hanes)**

× Blc. Jane Helton = Blc. Diatom

YELLOW SHADES — **John Laycock × Yellow Skin** — **Altenburg 1972**
YELLOW SKIN — **C. Bow Bells × Edgard van Belle** — **Altenburg 1968**

× John Laycock = Yellow Shades

YOLO — **Pacific × Carrie Goldfarb** — **Rod McLellan Co. 1960**

× Pacific Sun = Decker McAllister
× Bc. Mount Hood = Blc. Yolo Hood

YUKIKO HIRONAKA — **Adina × C. Titrianae** — **Hironaka 1973 (Gore)**

× Blc. Mem. Crispin Rosales = Blc. Mem. Giichi Otaguro

YVETTE ANN — **Ennerdale × Seattle** — **Abbot 1962**

× Blc. Mem. Crispin Rosales = Blc. Rounder

ZADA FIELDS‡ — **C. Dark Emperor × Bonanza** — **Fields Orchids 1963**

× My Fancy = Mount Chilko
× B. nodosa = Blc. Naples Night
× Blc. Norman's Bay = Blc. Iron Cap Mountain
× C. Sand Island = Winyah

LAELIOCATTLEYA

ZEM	Orange Gem × L. Zip	Pabst 1975
ZIEGFELD'S BONANZA	De Loris Ziegfeld × Bonanza	Otaguro 1971
ZIPPITY DOODOW	L. Zip × C. dowiana	Stewart Inc. 1974
ZUKI BELLE	Golden Halo × Edgard van Belle	N. Suzuki 1971
ZUKI DISIO	Paradisio × José Dias Castro	N. Suzuki 1975
ZUKI ENCHANTAR	Ishtar × Enchanted Jungle	N. Suzuki 1972
ZUKI ENNERDIAS	Ennerdale × José Dias Castro	N. Suzuki 1971
ZUKI HYPERDALE	Fabiadale × Hyperion	N. Suzuki 1971
ZUKI JOSEMILA	L. pumila × José Dias Castro	N. Suzuki 1975

LAELONIA

JIM BLOOM	Ruby × Bro. sanguinea	W. W. G. Moir 1972
RUBY	Bro. sanguinea × L. autumnalis	W. W. G. Moir 1960

× Bro. sanguinea = Jim Bloom

LAGERARA

PRINTAW	Asp. principissa × Oda. Taw	Scardefield 1972

LEEARA

LISSOM LUCY	Aranda Lucy Laycock × Vdps. lissochiloides	S'pore Orchids 1972
MEMORIA JEAN BLACK	Aranda Chia Shui Keng × Vdps. lissochiloides	George Black 1973

LEOCHILUS

labiatus

× Onc. onustum = Lcdm. Florence Grice
× Onc. pulchellum = Lcdm. Anne Borden

species

× Onc. triquetrum = Lcdm. Red Hill

LEOCIDIUM

ANNE BORDEN	Onc. pulchellum × Lchs. labiatus	Burgun 1972
FLORENCE GRICE	Lchs. labiatus × Onc. onustum	Hawkins 1974
RED HILL	Onc. triquetrum × Lchs. labiatus	W. W. G. Moir 1973

LEPANTHES

byfieldii — **species**

× pulchella = Red Stripe

pulchella — **species**

× byfieldii = Red Stripe

RED STRIPE	pulchella × byfieldii	Kindlmann 1974

LEPTOLAELIA

LEPRECHAUN	Lpt. bicolor × L. pumila	Withner 1972

LEPTOTES

bicolor* — **species**

× L. pumila = Lptl. Leprechaun |

LEWISARA

CHITTIVAN	**Aërdns. Bogor × Ascda. Blue Boy**	**Ratanapeanchai 1975**

LIMARA

MANDAI MAJESTY	**Arach. flos-aëris × Rnps. Lena Rowold**	**S'pore Orchids 1973**

LIOPONIA

KINGSTON‡	**Bro. sanguinea × Lps. domingensis**	**W. W. G. Moir 1959**

× L. autumnalis = Jmzra. Jose | × Schom. thomsoniana = Hdra. Christian Hilda

LOWARA

PETER WHYTE	**Sl. Betty Jean Scott × B. nodosa**	**Fort Caroline 1974**
SPITFIRE	**Sl. Gratrixiae × Trinket**	**Stewart Inc. 1970**

× Blc. Golden Galleon = Pot. Tiger Tears |

TRINKET‡	**Sl. Psyche × B. digbyana**	**Stewart Inc. 1950**

× Lc. Mem. Albert Heinecke = Pot. Marionette |

LUASCOTIA

RUMRILL	**Ascf. Peaches × Lsa. teres**	**Rumrill 1974**

LUINETIA

RUMRILL	**Neof. falcata × Lsa. teres**	**Rumrill 1975**

LUINOPSIS

SOETAN MAHMOED LATIF	**Lsa. teretifolia × Phal. laycockii**	**Kolopaking 1973**

LUISANDA

DOCTOR TJINYOE TAN	V. teres × Lsa. teretifolia	**Keen 1972** (Liem Khe Wie)
RUMRILL	**V. coerulescens × Lsa. teretifolia**	**Rumrill 1973**
UNIWAI	**Lsa. teretifolia × V. Miss Joaquim**	**U. of H. 1952**

× Rhy. coelestis = Gfa. Eva Goff |

LUISIA

jonesii‡ — **species**

× Ascda. Ophelia = Dbra. Victoria de Bruyne |

megasepala (see *teres*) — **species**

LUISIA

teres (syn. *megasepala*) **species**

× Aër. japonica	= Aërsa. Rumrill	× Ascf. Peaches	= Lscta. Rumrill
× Aër. multiflora	= Aërsa. Towaco	× Neof. falcata	= Lnta. Rumrill

teretifolia† **species**

× Phal. laycockii	= Lnps. Soetan Mahmoed Latif	× V. coerulescens	= Lsnd. Rumrill
× Pmcpa. latifolia	= Pmtsa. Rumrill	× V. teres	= Lsnd. Doctor Tjinyoe Tan

LUTHERARA

RUTH TAKEMOTO — **Rnthps. Jan Goo × Rhy. gigantea** — **Takemoto 1973**

LYCASTE

AQUILA — **Brugensis × Jason** — **Wyld Court 1975**
BRUGENSIS†‡ — **longipetala × skinneri** — **S. 1921**

× Jason	= Aquila	× locusta	= Gusto

crinata **species**

× Max. cucullata	= Mxcst. Luton Gold		

cruenta*†‡ **species**

× Jason	= Chiltern Hundreds		

CHILTERN HUNDREDS — **cruenta × Jason** — **Royden 1973**
GUSTO — **Brugensis × locusta** — **W. W. Wilson 1974**
JASON — **macrobulbon × lasioglossa** — **Wyld Court 1964**

× Brugensis	= Aquila	× cruenta	= Chiltern Hundreds

lasioglossa*‡ **species**

× skinneri	= lucianii (Nat. hyb.) = Lucianii (Reg'd. grex)	× Ang. ruckeri	= Angcst. Mildred Zaìman

locusta*‡ **species**

× Brugensis	= Gusto		

lucianii / **LUCIANII‡** — **lasioglossa × skinneri** — **Nat. hyb.** / **Sparrow 1972**

macrobulbon*†‡ **species**

× Angcst. Jupiter	= Angcst. Scorpio		

macrophylla*‡ (syn. *plana**) **species**

× Angcst. Georgius Rex	= Angcst. Mem. Abbott Robinson		

plana* (see *macrophylla*‡*) **species**

skinneri*†‡ **species**

(This is retained as the horticulturally recommended name for registration purposes even though *Lyc. virginalis* is the botanically correct name for this species.)

× lasioglossa	= lucianii (Nat. hyb.) = Lucianii (Reg'd. grex)	Max. sanderana	= Mxcst. Heinz Michael Pinkepank

SUNRISE†‡ — **Imschootiana × skinneri** — **Cooke 1941**

× Angcst. Olympus	= Angcst. Highland Peak		

virginalis (see *skinneri*†‡*) species

LYCASTE

xytriophora*‡ — **species**

× Angcst. Apollo = Angcst. Gemini |

LYMANARA

FRANKFURT FIREWORKS	**Aërdns. Mandai × Ren. Brookie Chandler**	**Bannochie 1975 (S'pore Orchids)**
MANDAI GRACE	Aërdns. Rosy Dawn × Ren. storiei	S'pore Orchids 1973

MACCOYARA

HAZEL	**Vdpsd. Apple Blossom × V. sanderana**	**O. Kirsch 1972**

MACRADENIA

multiflora — **species**

× Onc. triquetrum = Oncna. Ladies Pride |

MASDEVALLIA

coriacea* — **species**

× peristeria = Periacea |

PERIACEA	**coriacea × peristeria**	**Kuhn 1975**

peristeria* — **species**

× coriacea = Periacea |

MAXILLACASTE

HEINZ MICHAEL PINKEPANK	**Max. sanderana × Lyc. skinneri**	**Pinkepank 1974**
LUTON GOLD	**Max. cucullata × Lyc. crinata**	**Royden 1974** (Hey)

MAXILLARIA

cucullata — **species**

× Lyc. crinata = Mxcst. Luton Gold |

sanderana* — **species**

× Lyc. skinneri = Mxcst. Heinz Michael Pinkepank |

MENADENIUM

labiosum (see *Zygosepalum labiosum*‡) — **species**

MENDONCELLA

grandiflora — **species**

(syn. *Zygopetalum grandiflorum*)

× Cnths. discolor = Chla. Little Turtle |

MILPASIA

BUFF BALL	**Asp. variegata × Milt. regnellii**	**George Black 1973**

MILTASSIA

BILL BURKE | **Milt. Ka Moi × Brs. Rex** | **W. D. Burke 1973 (Kirch)**

BOLD‡ | **Milt. flavescens × Brs. maculata** | **W. W. G. Moir 1961**
× Mtdm. Cleopatra = Alcra. Chiyo

BRAZILIA | **Harry Dunn × Milt. Santos** | **W. W. G. Moir 1975**
CARTAGENA‡ | **Brs. verrucosa × Milt. Anne Warne** | **W. W. G. Moir 1965**
× Mtdm. Carioca = Alcra. Don Richardson | × Onc. varicosum = Alcra. Monte Cristo

CHARLES M. FITCH‡ | **Brs. verrucosa × Milt. spectabilis** | **Fitch 1961 (Gamble)**
× Odm. Jackie Gleason = Dgmra. Admiralty Islands | × Odm. Mount Baker = Dgmra. Orcus Island
× Onc. varicosum = Alcra. Surprise Creek

COPAN | **Brs. Rex × Milt. Cogniauxiae** | **W. W. G. Moir 1972**
FORT GEORGE BEAUTY | **Milt. spectabilis × Brs. maculata** | **George Black 1973 (Kirch)**
× Milt. cuneata = J'ouvert

HARRY DUNN‡ | **Premier × Milt. Goodale Moir** | **W. W. G. Moir 1965**
× Milt. Santos = Brazilia | × Mtdm. Lee Hirsch = Alcra. Bandeira

JET SETTER | **Milt. Crimson Crest × Brs. gireoudiana** | **R. K. Mizuta 1971**
J'OUVERT | **Fort George Beauty × Milt. cuneata** | **George Black 1973**
OLMEC | **Brs. Rex × Milt. Minas Gerais** | **W. W. G. Moir 1975**
VINO | **Brs. Edvah Loo × Milt. regnellii** | **W. W. G. Moir 1967**
× Oda. Apricot Meadows = Bllra. Carnival | × Onc. marshallianum = Alcra. Maury Island

MILTONIA

ALDERWOOD‡ | **Solfatari × Wych Cross** | **Hoyt 1957**
× Cindy Kane = Melissa Baker | × Robert Rankin = Gary Baker

ALESIA | **Etendard × Piccadilly** | **Pff. V. & L. 1957**
× vexillaria = Saint Denis

ALGER‡ | **Pandora × Etendard** | **Pff. V. & L. 1957**
× Piccadilly = Sherpa

AMBRE‡ | **Nyasa × Emotion** | **Marcel Lecoufle 1962**
× vexillaria = Versailles

ANDREA BAKER | **Cindy Kane × Snohomish** | **G. R. Baker 1975**
ANJOU | **Hoggar × Piccadilly** | **Pff. V. & L. 1957**
× Armanda = Koichi Yonezawa

ANNE WARNE‡ | **Bluntii × spectabilis** | **J. Milton Warne 1949**
× Castanea = Connie Warne | × Gayety = Honolulu

APRIL BAY | **Herbert Johnson × Woodlands** | **Beall 1973**
ARMANDA*† | **Pulchra × William Pitt** | **Mercer 1933**
× Anjou = Koichi Yonezawa

BEETHOVEN†‡ | **Lycaena × Mrs. J. B. Crum** | **Strauss 1949**
× Mrs. J. B. Crum = Mrs. Anneli Loeb

MILTONIA

BELLINGHAM‡ — **Wych Cross × Woodlands** — **Hoyt 1959**

× Meadowdale	= Rose Bay	× Robert Rankin	= Everett Church
× regnellii	= Norma MacRae		

BIRCH BAY — **Rose Bay × roezlii** — **Beall 1974**

bluntii / **BLUNTII†‡** — **spectabilis × clowesii** — **Nat. hyb.** / **hort.**

× candida	= Kismet

BOTHELL‡ — **Solfatari × Ninety One** — **Hoyt 1957**

× Violet	= Gretchen Hoyt McDevitt

BREMEN — **Limelight × Herrenhausen** — **Wichmann 1967**

× Sumas	= Vanity

candida*†‡ — **species**

× Bluntii	= Kismet

CARTHAME — **Madame Revillon × Lady Veitch** — **Marcel Lecoufle 1962**

× vexillaria	= Cilaos

castanea / **CASTANEA** — **clowesii × regnellii** — **Nat. hyb.** / **hort.**

× Anne Warne	= Connie Warne	× William Kirch	= Golden Fleece

CILAOS — **Carthame × vexillaria** — **Marcel Lecoufle 1974**

CINDY KANE — **Violet × Woodlands** — **Hoyt 1968**

× Alderwood	= Melissa Baker	× Woodlands	= Waterfall Bay
× Snohomish	= Andrea Baker		

clowesii*†‡ — **species**

× Onc. papilio	= Mtdm. Rio's Star

cogniauxiae / **COGNIAUXIAE‡** — **regnellii × spectabilis** — **Nat. hyb.** / **hort.**

× May Moir	= Gold Beach	× Odcdm. Dainty	= Colm. Purple Gem
× Minas Gerais	= Tropic Dawn	× Odm. Rich Cove	= Odtna. Mauna Loa
× Brs. Rex	= Mtssa. Copan		

CONNIE WARNE — **Castanea × Anne Warne** — **J. Milton Warne 1971**

CRIMSON CREST‡ — **Purple Queen × warscewiczii** — **W. W. G. Moir 1961**

× Brs. gireoudiana	= Mtssa. Jet Setter	× Odcdm. Tiger Butter	= Colm. Ferguson Beall

cuneata — **species**

× William Kirch	= Lucille Gibson	× Mtssa. Fort George Beauty	= Mtssa. J'ouvert

DIADEME — **Emoi × Etendard** — **V. 1945**

× Edwidge Sabourin	= Seine

EDWIDGE SABOURIN‡ — **Emotion × vexillaria** — **Pff. V. & L. 1956**

× Diademe	= Seine	× vexillaria	= Oise
× Emoi	= Loire		

EMOI† — **Etendard × vexillaria** — **Pff. V. & L. 1939**

× Edwidge Sabourin	= Loire

EMOTION†‡ — **Emoi × Nyasa** — **Pff. V. & L. 1945**

× Escarboucle	= Marie Riopelle

MILTONIA

Name	Parentage	Registrant
ENDEAVOUR	**warscewiczii × Alderwood**	**E. Iwanaga 1963**
× Onc. leucochilum = Mtdm. Kendrick Williams		
ESCARBOUCLE*‡	**Belgica × Etendard**	**V. 1938**
× Emotion = Marie Riopelle		
ETENDARD*†‡	**Reine Elizabeth × Rubens**	**V. 1933**
× Sherpa = Fascination		
EVERETT CHURCH	**Bellingham × Robert Rankin**	**Hoyt 1971**
FARANDOLE	**Murcia × Piccadilly**	**Pff. V. & L. 1968**
× vexillaria = Marne		
FASCINATION	**Sherpa × Etendard**	**Pff. V. & L. 1974**
flavescens*†‡	**species**	
× roezlii = Point Galera	× Odm. Chimène = Odtna. Golden Wand	
FORTALEZA	**Rio × Anne Warne**	**W. W. G. Moir 1966**
× Brap. Serene = Fgtra. Mexico		
GARY BAKER	**Alderwood × Robert Rankin**	**Hoyt 1975**
GATTONENSIS*	**Bleuana × Jules Hye de Crom**	**Colman 1922**
× Woodlands = Gatwood		
GATWOOD	**Woodlands × Gattonensis**	**C. 1971**
GAYETY‡	**Festiva × spectabilis**	**Woodlawn 1955**
× Anne Warne = Honolulu		
GOLD BEACH	**Cogniauxiae × May Moir**	**Beall 1973 (W. W. G. Moir)**
GOLDEN FLEECE	**Castanea × William Kirch**	**J. Milton Warne 1971**
GRETCHEN HOYT McDEVITT	**Bothell × Violet**	**Hoyt 1972**
HERBERT JOHNSON	**Solfatari × Alderwood**	**Hoyt 1967**
× Woodlands = April Bay		
HONOLULU	**Gayety × Anne Warne**	**J. Milton Warne 1971**
KA MOI	**warscewiczii × regnellii**	**W. W. G. Moir 1962**
× Brs. Rex = Mtssa. Bill Burke		
KISMET	**Bluntii × candida**	**Redlinger 1973**
KOICHI YONEZAWA	**Anjou × Armanda**	**Yonezawa 1975**
lambeauiana (see *vexillaria**†‡)	**species**	
LIMELIGHT†‡	**Armstrongii × Lycaena**	**Paterson 1933**
× Mount Vernon = White Bay		
LOIRE	**Emoi × Edwidge Sabourin**	**Marcel Lecoufle 1974**
LUCILLE GIBSON	**William Kirch × cuneata**	**George Black 1973**
MARIE RIOPELLE	**Emotion × Escarboucle**	**McElderry 1974**
MARNE	**Farandole × vexillaria**	**Marcel Lecoufle 1974**
MATTO GROSSO	**Minas Gerais × May Moir**	**W. W. G. Moir 1972**
MAY MOIR‡	**spectabilis × Goodale Moir**	**W. W. G. Moir 1959**
× Cogniauxiae = Gold Beach × Minas Gerais = Matto Grosso	× Onc. zebrinum = Mtdm. El Hatillo	
MEADOWDALE‡	**Etendard × Woodlands**	**Hoyt 1962**
× Bellingham = Rose Bay		

MELISSA BAKER — **Cindy Kane × Alderwood** — **G. R. Baker 1975**

MINAS GERAIS‡ — **Anne Warne × candida** — **W. W. G. Moir 1965**

- × Cogniauxiae = Tropic Dawn
- × May Moir = Matto Grosso
- × Brs. Rex = Mtssa. Olmec
- × Mtdm. Royal Hawaiian = Mtdm. Ecuador
- × Odm. Baranof Island = Odtna. Ice Caves
- × Odm. crispum = Odtna. Johannesburg Mine
- × Vuyl. Princess Kaiulani = Vuyl. Barbacena

MOUNT MAZAMA — **roezlii × Peggy Fuller** — **R. A. Sellon 1972 (Beall)**

MOUNT VERNON — **roezlii × Edmonds** — **Hoyt 1968**

- × Limelight = White Bay

MRS. ANNELI LOEB — **Beethoven × Mrs. J. B. Crum** — **Berman 1973 (Stonehurst)**

MRS. J. B. CRUM*†‡ — **Lycaena × Princess Mary** — **Paterson 1931**

- × Beethoven = Mrs. Anneli Loeb

NORMA MacRAE — **regnellii × Bellingham** — **Hoyt 1971**

OISE — **Edwidge Sabourin × vexillaria** — **Marcel Lecoufle 1974**

PEGGY FULLER‡ — **J. M. Black × Mrs. J. B. Crum** — **Hoyt 1965**

- × roezlii = Mount Mazama

PERU — **warscewiczii × Crimson Crest** — **W. W. G. Moir 1966**

- × Odcdm. Carrykylum = Colm. Desdamona
- × Onc. Burgundy = Mtdm. Quito
- × Vuyl. Sunset Bay = Vuyl. Summit Lake

PETROPOLIS — **Royal × spectabilis** — **W. W. G. Moir 1967**

- × Oda. Swamp Fire = Vuyl. Crimson Lake
- × Onc. powellii = Mtdm. Gatum Lake

PICCADILLY†‡ — **Peony × Mrs. J. B. Crum** — **B. 1940**

- × Alger = Sherpa

POINT GALERA — **flavescens × roezlii** — **George Black 1975**

regnellii*†‡ — **species**

- × Bellingham = Norma MacRae
- × Asp. variegata = Mpsa. Buff Ball
- × Odtna. Santos = Odtna. Rose Glow
- × Onc. orthostates = Mtdm. Sunset Sky

ROBERT RANKIN — **Alderwood × Woodlands** — **Hoyt 1966**

- × Alderwood = Gary Baker
- × Bellingham = Everett Church

roezlii*‡ — **species**

- × flavescens = Point Galera
- × Peggy Fuller = Mount Mazama
- × Rose Bay = Birch Bay

ROSE BAY — **Bellingham × Meadowdale** — **Beall 1974 (Hoyt)**

- × roezlii = Birch Bay

ROYAL‡ — **warscewiczii × spectabilis** — **W. W. G. Moir 1961**

- × Onc. Elegance = Mtdm. Jupiter

SAINT DENIS — **Alesia × vexillaria** — **Marcel Lecoufle 1974**

SAINT MARTINS — **Bluntii × Pulchra** — **Hoyt 1964**

- × Odtna. Santos = Odtna. Glass Creek

SANTOS — **Campos × Sunset** — **W. W. G. Moir 1967**

- × Mtssa. Harry Dunn = Mtssa. Brazilia

SEINE — **Diademe × Edwidge Sabourin** — **Marcel Lecoufle 1974**

MILTONIA

SHERPA — **Alger × Piccadilly** — **Pff. V. & L. 1974**

× Etendard = Fascination

SNOHOMISH — **Solfatari × Bellingham** — **Hoyt 1968**

× Cindy Kane = Andrea Baker

spectabilis*†‡ — **species**

× Brs. maculata = Mtssa. Fort George Beauty
× Oda. Bohème = Vuyl. Sao Francisco
× Odm. bictoniense = Odtna. Marie Elle
× Odtna. Debutante = Odtna. John Fancher
× Onc. barbatum = Mtdm. Katrina
× Onc. Nona = Mtdm. Richard Peterson

SUMAS‡ — **Lynnwood × Woodlands** — **Hoyt 1960**

× Bremen = Vanity

TROPIC DAWN — **Cogniauxiae × Minas Gerais** — **W. W. G. Moir 1971**
VANITY — **Sumas × Bremen** — **Rod McLellan Co. 1971**
VERSAILLES — **Ambre × vexillaria** — **Marcel Lecoufle 1974**
vexillaria*†‡ (syn. *lambeauiana*) — **species**

× Alesia = Saint Denis
× Ambre = Versailles
× Carthame = Cilaos
× Edwidge Sabourin = Oise
× Farandole = Marne

VIOLET‡ — **Lypatia × Lingwood** — **Hoyt 1964**

× Bothell = Gretchen Hoyt McDevitt

warscewiczii*†‡ — **species**

× Onc. hastatum = Mtdm. Talofa

WATERFALL BAY — **Woodlands × Cindy Kane** — **Beall 1973**
WHITE BAY — **Mount Vernon × Limelight** — **Beall 1973**
WILLIAM KIRCH‡ — **Bluntii × regnellii** — **W. W. G. Moir 1958**

× Castanea = Golden Fleece
× cuneata = Lucille Gibson
× Odtna. Santos = Odtna. Sangre Grande

WOODLANDS†‡ — **Swinburn × Armanda** — **L. 1949**

× Cindy Kane = Waterfall Bay
× Gattonensis = Gatwood
× Herbert Johnson = April Bay

MILTONIDIUM

ARISTOCRAT‡ — **Milt. schroderana × Onc. leucochilum** — **M. & H. 1940**

× Cleopatra = Robert Dugger
× Lustre = Juno
× Surprise = Fortin

AUTUMN GLOW — **Milt. warscewiczii × Onc. aloisii** — **W. W. G. Moir 1961**

× Odm. Yukon Harbor = Colm. Hawaii Nei

AZTEC GOLD — **Onc. powellii × Aristocrat** — **W. W. G. Moir 1967**

× Oda. Isabella = Burr. Sambu River
× Odm. Mount Baker = Colm. Cauca Valley
× Odm. Yukon Harbor = Colm. Moon Gold

CARIOCA — **Milt. Sergipe × Onc. varicosum** — **W. W. G. Moir 1966**

× Mtssa. Cartagena = Alcra. Don Richardson

CLEOPATRA — **Onc. Moir × Aristocrat** — **W. W. G. Moir 1965**

× Aristocrat = Robert Dugger
× Mtssa. Bold = Alcra. Chiyo
× Odm. Mount Baker = Colm. Bogota
× Vuyl. Sunset Bay = Burr. Sanguine

MILTONIDIUM

ECUADOR	Royal Hawaiian × Milt. Minas Gerais	W. W. G. Moir 1973
EL HATILLO	Milt. May Moir × Onc. zebrinum	W. W. G. Moir 1974
FORTIN	Surprise × Aristocrat	W. W. G. Moir 1972
GATUM LAKE	Milt. Petropolis × Onc. powellii	W. W. G. Moir 1973
HAPAHAOLE‡	Milt. Festiva × Onc. leucochilum	W. W. G. Moir 1961
× Oda. Apricot Meadows	= Burr. Akala	
JUNO	Lustre × Aristocrat	W. W. G. Moir 1971
JUPITER	Milt. Royal × Onc. Elegance	W. W. G. Moir 1974
KATRINA	Milt. spectabilis × Onc. barbatum	Osment 1972
KENDRICK WILLIAMS	Milt. Endeavour × Onc. leucochilum	Dugger 1972
LEE HIRSCH†‡	Onc. varicosum × Milt. spectabilis	Gamble 1952
× Mtssa. Harry Dunn	= Alcra. Bandeira	
LUSTRE	Onc. powellii × Milt. warscewiczii	W. W. G. Moir 1958
× Aristocrat	= Juno	
QUITO	Milt. Peru × Onc. Burgundy	W. W. G. Moir 1974
RICHARD PETERSON	Onc. Nona × Milt. spectabilis	Rod McLellan Co. 1974
RIO'S STAR	Milt. clowesii × Onc. papilio	Ruben 1973
ROBERT DUGGER	Cleopatra × Aristocrat	W. W. G. Moir 1972
ROYAL HAWAIIAN	Milt. spectabilis × Onc. macranthum	W. W. G. Moir 1964
× Milt. Minas Gerais	= Ecuador	
SUMMER FANTASY‡	Onc. El Vulcan Barru × Milt. warscewiczii	W. W. G. Moir 1965
× Odtna. Debutante	= Colm. Shower of Gold	
SUNSET SKY	Onc. orthostates × Milt. regnellii	George Black 1973
SURPRISE‡	Milt. warscewiczii × Onc. sawyeri	W. W. G. Moir 1967
× Aristocrat	= Fortin	× Odm. Mount Baker = Colm. Puget Sound
TALOFA	Milt. warscewiczii × Onc. hastatum	R. K. Mizuta 1971

MOIRARA

TRISTAR	Vdnps. Hong Trevor × Ren. storiei	S'pore Orchids 1972

MOKARA

BOVORN	Arach. hookerana × Ascda. Buddy Choo	Prayoonratana 1975
DEAR HEART	Arach. Maggie Oei × Ascda. Yip Sum Wah	R. K. Mizuta 1972
ENA LING	Arach. hookerana × Ascda. Yip Sum Wah	Charles Lim 1973 (Wong Loong Fatt)
HARRIET LIM	Arach. Ishbel × Ascda. Yip Sum Wah	Charles Lim 1973 (Wong Loong Fatt)
KELVIN	Arach. hookerana × Ascda. Habanananda	Kranji 1974
LIM SIN KIAW	Arach. Ishbel × Ascda. Wilas	Charles Lim 1973 (Wong Loong Fatt)
MADAME YIP KHEW-YING	Arach. hookerana × Ascda. Coppertone	Yoon Pooi-Kong 1974
MAGMEDA	Arach. Maggie Oei × Ascda. Meda Arnold	Prayoonratana 1975 (Kasetsart Univ.)
× Ascda. Stephen Sng	= Oil	
MONIQUE	Aranda Lily Chong × Ascda. Yee Peng	How Yee Peng 1975
OIL	Magmeda × Ascda. Stephen Sng	Prayoonratana 1975

MOKARA

SALLY LIM	**Arach. hookerana × Ascda. Meda Arnold**	**Charles Lim 1973 (Wong Loong Fatt)**
SAYAN	**Ascda. Medasand × Arach. hookerana**	**Sombuntham 1974**
SOON KHIM	**Aranda Lucy Laycock × Ascda. Medasand**	**Lim Soon Khim 1973**
VIROONCHAN	**Arach. hookerana × Ascda. Mangkiatkul**	**H. K. Lau 1975**
VIROONCHAN BLUE	**Arach. hookerana × Ascda. Navy Blue**	**H. K. Lau 1975**
WINNIE LING	**Arach. hookerana × Ascda. Wilas**	**Charles Lim 1973 (Wong Loong Fatt)**
YOON WENG-LOW	**Arach. hookerana × Ascda. Koh Man**	**Yoon Pooi-Kong 1974**

NAGELIELLA

purpurea — **species**

× Epi. conopseum = Epdla. Rumrill

NAKAMOTOARA

SIEM REAP	**Wendy × V. Blue Button**	**W. W. G. Moir 1973**
WENDY‡	**Neof. falcata × Ascda. Meda Arnold**	**W. K. Nakamoto 1964**

× Blue Button = Siem Reap

NASHARA

GEORGE	**Diab. Newcastle × Ctpsta. Leona**	**W. W. G. Moir 1973**

NEOFINETIA

falcata†‡ — **species**

(This is retained as the horticulturally recommended name for registration purposes, although *Holcoglossum falcatum* is the botanically correct name for this species.)

× Dor. pulcherrima = Dfta. Piliahoa
× Lsa. teres = Lnta. Rumrill
× Phal. equestris Phnta. Irene

NOBLEARA

WELLSIAN BEAUTY	**V. tricolor × Rnds. Mahani**	**George Black 1973**

NORTHENARA

REBECCA	**Lc. Mem. Masa Matsumoto × Dill. Bronze Kahili**	**O. Kirsch 1973**

ODONTIODA

ADMIRAL ALOETTE	**Aloette × Blue Admiral**	**M. & H. 1975**
ALBEAM‡	**Odm. Alorcus × Sunbeam**	**M. & H. 1966**

× Ann Dore = Oreal
× Drumory = Drumbeat
× Phoenix = Carisette
× Odm. Aglina = Albina

ALBINA	**Albeam × Odm. Aglina**	**M. & H. 1972**
ALLIANCE‡	**Charlotte × Odm. Clomador**	**Hoyt 1964**

× Lautrix = Imperial Red

ALOETTE	**Marie Antoinette × Odm. Pescalo**	**Mrs. Kay Rinaman 1963 (C.)**

× Blue Admiral = Admiral Aloette
× Florence Stirling = Alstir
× Phoenix = Mem. Eijire Sugimoto
× Odm. crispum = White Heron
× Odm. Quisto = Mem. Ernesto Alvarez

ODONTIODA

ALSTIR — **Aloette × Florence Stirling** — **Dugger 1973**
ANN DORE‡ — **Cora × Odm. Alorcus** — **Marsden 1962 (M. & H.)**

× Albeam	= Oreal	× Odm. crispum	= Ispann
× Matanda	= Matador		

ANN JOHNSON — **Fremar × Ray Buckman** — **Dugger 1975**
ANTON — **Ann Dore × Odm. Halton** — **M. & H. 1967**

× Oncda. Crowborough = Wils. Rocksley

APRICOT MEADOWS — **Lautrix × Odm. Yukon Harbor** — **Beall 1969**

× Mtdm. Hapahaole	= Burr. Akala	× Odcdm. Crowborough	= Wils. Tiger Mountain
× Mtssa. Vino	= Bllra. Carnival		

ARAGON — **Sirias × Florence Stirling** — **Pff. V. & L. 1972**

ARIITEA†‡ — **Odm. Adrien Lefebvre × Minos** — **V. 1950**

× Cda. noezliana = Picasso

AVIEMORE — **Memory × Toriava** — **M. & H. 1972**
BALEK†‡ — **Brackenhurst × Petit Prince** — **V. 1954**

× Henriette Lecoufle	= Esterel	× Vuyl. Rutilant	= Vuyl. Conquistador

BELLA BELLA — **Echanson × Pygmalion** — **Beall 1972**
BIARRITZ — **Odm. Deference × Ithaque** — **Pff. V. & L. 1975**
BICTAW — **Odm. bictoniense × Taw** — **Scardefield 1972**
BLUE ADMIRAL — **Apoda × Odm. Patrina** — **Collett 1964**

× Aloette = Admiral Aloette

BOGOTÁ — **Odm. Stropheon × Elpheon** — **Schmidt-Mumm 1973**
BOHÈME‡ — **Franchita × Ithaque** — **Pff. V. & L. 1958**

× Milt. spectabilis = Vuyl. Sao Francisco

BROCADE — **Fred Bradley × Ingera** — **C. 1965**

× Odm. crispum = Lippstadt

CARISETTE — **Albeam × Phoenix** — **M. & H. 1973**
CARL KEYES — **Grenadier × Lautrix** — **Liebman 1974 (Originator unknown)**

× Odm. crispum = Mem. Harry Seigel

CARMINE†‡ — **Chanticleer × Colinge** — **L. 1942**

× Odm. harryanum	= Red Knight	× Onc. Goldiana	= Wils. Red Galaxy
× Onc. concolor	= Wils. Accolade	× Onc. ventilabrum	= Wils. Rock Island

CARNAVAL — **Petit Prince × Florence Stirling** — **Pff. V. & L. 1973**
CHARLETTE† — **Charlesworthii × Marie Antoinette** — **C. 1945**

× Odm. crispum = Crislette

CHARLOTTE BUCKMAN — **Dalmar × Ray Buckman** — **Dugger 1974**
CHERRY CREEK — **Bradshawiae × Carmine** — **Beall 1967**

× Swamp Fire = Crimson Glory

CLIFTON — Odm. Edalva × Marzorka — **K. Andrew 1971 (Zool. Soc. Bristol)**

COLWELL‡ — **Argia × Aysha** — **C. 1957**

× Memory = Joyful

ODONTIODA

CORNOSA — **Cornelia × Odm. Mimosa** — **C. 1960**

× Odm. Pacific	= Pacific Gold		

COTA — **Odm. triumphans × Ingera** — **Schmidt-Mumm 1974**

CRIMSON GLORY — **Cherry Creek × Swamp Fire** — **Beall 1973**

CRISLETTE — **Charlette × Odm. crispum** — **C. & I. Keyes 1975 (C.)**

CRISPHEON — **Odm. crispum × Phoenix** — **Liebman 1974**

CROWN JEWEL‡ — **Olegia × Odm. crispum** — **L. 1958**

× Odm. Stropheon	= Medellin		

DALESK — **Odm. Esk × Dalmar** — **M. & H. 1972**

DALMAR‡ — **Odm. Mandalum × Margia** — **C. 1957**

× Ray Buckman	= Charlotte Buckman	× Odm. Esk	= Dalesk
× Odcdm. Tiger Butter	= Wils. Cardiff	× Odm. Mystery	= Terymar
× Odm. Connero	= Mem. Len Page	× Odm. Opheon	= Little Lady

DANILO — **Odm. Stropheon × Lippestern** — **Hark 1973**

DARK VELVET — **Dolcoath × Nutley** — **M. W. Miller 1972 (L.)**

DOLCOATH — **Castalia × Cheer** — **L. 1948**

× Nutley	= Dark Velvet		

DORANTE — **Balek × Odm. Francoeur** — **Pff. V. & L. 1966**

× Picador	= Rantador		

DORIC‡ — **Rosamond × Odm. Patnina** — **Ferrer 1963 (M. & H.)**

× Odm. Lord Harold	= Dorold	× Onc. tigrinum	= Wils. Tigerwood
× Odm. Mystery	= Mystic		

DOROLD — **Doric × Odm. Lord Harold** — **M. & H. 1972**

DRUMBEAT — **Albeam × Drumory** — **M. & H. 1975**

DRUMORY — **Drumsuie × Memory** — **M. & H. 1970**

× Albeam	= Drumbeat		

ECHANSON — **Balek × Odm. Petit Ami** — **Pff. V. & L. 1961**

× Pygmalion	= Bella Bella	× Odm. Yukon Harbor	= Grouse Mountain
× Odm. Grand Tetons	= White Rock		

ELAC — **Actia × Elpheon** — **C. 1962**

× Florence Stirling	= Feu Rouge	× Odm. crispum	= Sherry

ELPHEON‡ — **A. G. Ellwood × Odm. Opheon** — **C. 1951**

× Topa	= Ruth Berman	× Odm. Phioman	= Philomel
× Odm. Alimo	= Jack Greatwood	× Odm. Stropheon	= Bogotá
× Odm. Hyrastro	= Hilary Greatwood		

ESTEREL — **Balek × Henriette Lecoufle** — **Pff. V. & L. 1973**

FEDORA — **Odm. Pheonel × Lippestern** — **Hark 1973**

FEUERBALL — **Marzorka × Lautrix** — **Wichmann 1967**

× Feuerschein	= Feuerglut	× Odtna. Debutante	= Vuyl. Feuerzauber
× Plezeta	= Nueva Granada		

FEUERGLUT — **Feuerball × Feuerschein** — **Elle & Co. 1974 (Elle)**

FEUERSCHEIN — **Marzorka × Jessmia** — **Wichmann 1967**

× Feuerball	= Feuerglut	× Odm. rossii	= Hambühren
× Odm. bictoniense	= Ryoko Miyamoto		

ODONTIODA

FEU ROUGE — **Florence Stirling × Elac** — **Frese 1975**

FLOMAR — **Astomar × Florence Stirling** — **C. 1970**

× Odm. Alimo = Irene Williams

FLORENCE STIRLING†‡ — **Astoria × Melina** — **Stirling 1948**

× Aloette = Alstir
× Elac = Feu Rouge
× Fremar = Glenn Pollard
× Niragia = Roter Lampion
× Petit Prince = Carnaval
× Sirias = Aragon
× Odm. Chatoyant = Kaino
× Onc. incurvum = Wils. Widecombe Fair
× Onc. tigrinum = Wils. Morelia

FRANZ WICHMANN‡ — **Odm. Tordonia × Ingera** — **Wichmann 1967**

× Lippestern = Zsupan

FRED BRADLEY‡ — **Pola × A. G. Ellwood** — **C. 1954**

× Red Flame = Michie Donning

FREMAR — **Fred Bradley × Dalmar** — **C. 1964**

× Florence Stirling = Glenn Pollard
× Ray Buckman = Ann Johnson
× Odm. Quisto = Marquis

GERAGIA†‡ — **Argia × Gera** — **C. 1944**

× Niobe = Niragia

GIASTO‡ — **Geragia × Astoria** — **C. 1953**

× Odm. Connero = Taunton

GLENN POLLARD — **Fremar × Florence Stirling** — **Dugger 1973**

GRENADIER* — **Chanticleer × Sanderae** — **S. 1921**

× Lautrix = Carl Keyes

GROUSE MOUNTAIN — **Odm. Yukon Harbor × Echanson** — **Beall 1972**

HAMBÜHREN — **Odm. rossii × Feuerschein** — **Elle & Co. 1974 (Elle)**

HELEN BROUGH — **Odm. Quisto × Lautrix** — **Dugger 1974**

HENRIETTE LECOUFLE‡ — **Balek × Odm. Pacha** — **Pff. V. & L. 1959**

× Balek = Esterel

HILARY GREATWOOD — **Elpheon × Odm. Hyrastro** — **Dugger 1974**

HONFLEUR — **Sirias × Odm. Golden Grove** — **Pff. V. & L. 1975**

IMPERIAL RED — **Lautrix × Alliance** — **Beall 1973**

INGERA‡ — **Odm. Incana × Gera** — **C. 1956**

× Odm. bictoniense = Robert Stolz
× Odm. Gledroy = Raroy
× Odm. triumphans = Cota

IRENE WILLIAMS — **Odm. Alimo × Flomar** — **Dugger 1974**

ISABELLA* — **Chanticleer × Odm. crispum** — **C. 1920**

× Mtdm. Aztec Gold = Burr. Sambu River

ISPANN — **Odm. crispum × Ann Dore** — **M. & H. 1975**

ITHAQUE†‡ — **Petit Prince × Odm. Adrien Lefebvre** — **V. 1952**

× Sirias = Sing Sing
× Odm. Deference = Biarritz

JACK GREATWOOD — **Odm. Alimo × Elpheon** — **Dugger 1973**

JOYFUL — **Colwell × Memory** — **M. & H. 1975**

KAINO — **Odm. Chatoyant × Florence Stirling** — **Pff. V. & L. 1972**

KARL HEINZ HANISCH — **Lippestern × Odm. Pescalo** — **Krieger 1975**

KEITH GASKELL — **Odm. Ardentissimum × Toriava** — **M. & H. 1973**

ODONTIODA

LAUTRIX‡ **Beatrix × Laurette** **C. 1953**

× Alliance	= Imperial Red	× Odm. Quisto	= Helen Brough
× Grenadier	= Carl Keyes	× Odm. Stropheon	= Ray Buckman
× Minel	= San Elijo Gem	× Odm. Sunfly	= Suntrix
× Taw	= Scarlet Point	× Odm. Tordonia	= Torridon
× Odm. Golden Ransom	= Rantrix	× Wils. Autumn	= Wils. Mem. Austin Carlton
× Odm. Hyrastro	= Rixro	× Wils. Jean Du Pont	= Wils. Rixpont
× Odm. Perolia	= Pentland		

LIANGERA **Astliana × Ingera** **C. 1968**

× Wils. Jean Du Pont = Wils. Harry Brough

LIPPESTERN **Odm. Connero × Fred Bradley** **Hark 1968**

× Franz Wichmann	= Zsupan	× Odm. Pheonel	= Fedora
× Odm. Gavotte	= Schwerte	× Odm. Stropheon	= Danilo
× Odm. Pescalo	= Karl Heinz Hanisch	× Odtna. Andraena	= Vuyl. Eleganz

LIPPSTADT **Brocade × Odm. crispum** **Hark 1971**

× Odm. crispum = Micheltorina

LITTLE LADY **Odm. Opheon × Dalmar** **F. Johnson 1973 (C.)**

MARCRIS **Odm. crispum × Margia** **C. 1970**

× Onc. tigrinum = Wils. Kurt Rinne

MARGIA†‡ **Argia × Marie Antoinette** **C. 1944**

× Odm. Brimstone Butterfly = Sheila Hands †

MARQUIS **Odm. Quisto × Fremar** **Dugger 1975**

MARZORKA‡ **Margia × Zorka** **C. 1957**

× Nicola	= Zorkola	× Odm. Edalva	= Clifton
× Phoenix	= Toorak		

MATADOR **Matanda × Ann Dore** **M. & H. 1975**

MATANDA **Matrona × Pumanda** **C. 1964**

× Ann Dore	= Matador	× Wils. Jean Du Pont	= Wils. Lillian May
× Onc. sphacelatum	= Wils. Acemanda		

MEDELLIN **Odm. Stropheon × Crown Jewel** **Schmidt-Mumm 1974**

MEMORIA EIJIRE SUGIMOTO **Aloette × Phoenix** **Sugimoto 1972**

MEMORIA ERNESTO ALVAREZ **Aloette × Odm. Quisto** **Dugger 1973**

MEMORIA HARRY SEIGEL **Carl Keyes × Odm. crispum** **Liebman 1974**

MEMORIA LEN PAGE **Odm. Connero × Dalmar** **R. J. Elliott 1975 (Page)**

MEMORY‡ **Florence Stirling × Odm. Adonia** **Stirling 1957**

× Colwell	= Joyful	× Odm. Gledroy	= Rachel Gaskell
× Toriava	= Aviemore		

MICHELTORINA **Odm. crispum × Lippstadt** **Liebman 1974**

MICHIE DONNING **Red Flame × Fred Bradley** **Donning 1972 (A. & B.)**

MINEL **Elpheon × Minosha** **C. 1965**

× Lautrix	= San Elijo Gem	× Onc. tigrinum	= Wils. Solana Surprise
× Odtna. Debutante	= Vuyl. Royal Velvet		

MYSTIC **Doric × Odm. Mystery** **M. & H. 1972**

NICOLA† **Geisha × Cda. noezliana** **C. 1937**

× Marzorka = Zorkola

ODONTIODA

NIOBE*†‡ — **Bradshawiae × Odm. Jasper** — **A. & B. 1916**
× Geragia = Niragia

NIRAGIA — **Niobe × Geragia** — **Frese 1975 (C.)**
× Florence Stirling = Roter Lampion

NUEVA GRANADA — **Plezeta × Feuerball** — **Schmidt-Mumm 1974**

NUTLEY — **Jennifer × Goya** — **L. 1958**
× Dolcoath = Dark Velvet

OREAL — **Albeam × Ann Dore** — **M. & H. 1975**

PACIFIC GOLD — **Cornosa × Odm. Pacific** — **C. C. 1974 (C.)**

PENTLAND — **Lautrix × Odm. Perolia** — **Andrew Orchids 1972**

PETIT PRINCE†‡ — **Ferrieres × Odm. Watteau** — **V. 1945**
× Florence Stirling = Carnaval

PHILOMEL — **Elpheon × Odm. Phioman** — **A. & B. 1973**

PHOENIX — **Lautrix × Odm. Opheon** — **C. 1961**
× Albeam = Carisette
× Aloette = Mem. Eijire Sugimoto
× Marzorka = Toorak
× Odm. crispum = Crispheon
× Odm. Gledroy = Royen

PICADOR — **Balek × Bohème** — **Pff. V. & L. 1964**
× Dorante = Rantador
× Sirias = Picarias

PICARIAS — **Sirias × Picador** — **Pff. V. & L. 1975**

PICASSO — **Ariitea × Cda. noezliana** — **Pff. V. & L. 1973**

PLEZETA — **Zeta × Odm. Pleiades** — **C. 1959**
× Feuerball = Nueva Granada

PYGMALION — **Odm. Ismène × Balek** — **Pff. V. & L. 1968**
× Echanson = Bella Bella

RACHEL GASKELL — **Odm. Gledroy × Memory** — **M. & H. 1973**

RANTADOR — **Dorante × Picador** — **Pff. V. & L. 1975**

RANTRIX — **Odm. Golden Ransom × Lautrix** — **Dugger 1973**

RAROY — **Ingera × Odm. Gledroy** — **M. & H. 1975**

RAVA — **Toriava × Odm. Eider** — **M. & H. 1975**

RAY BUCKMAN — **Odm. Stropheon × Lautrix** — **Dugger 1972 (C.)**
× Dalmar = Charlotte Buckman
× Fremar = Ann Johnson
× Odcdm. Incali = Wils. Mem. Tom Lyles
× Odcdm. Tiger Butter = Wils. Tigerman
× Odtna. Tango = Vuyl. Tanman
× Onc. sphacelatum = Wils. Spaceman
× Wils. Jean Du Pont = Wils. Comitan

RED FLAME — **Grenadier × Lambeauiana** — **A. & B. 1937**
× Fred Bradley = Michie Donning

RED KNIGHT — **Odm. harryanum × Carmine** — **Beall 1973**

RIXRO — **Odm. Hyrastro × Lautrix** — **Dugger 1975**

ROBERT STOLZ — **Odm. bictoniense × Ingera** — **Elle & Co. 1974 (Elle)**

ROTER LAMPION — **Niragia × Florence Stirling** — **Frese 1975**

ROYEN — **Phoenix × Odm. Gledroy** — **M. & H. 1975**

RUTH BERMAN — **Topa × Elpheon** — **Berman 1974 (Stonehurst)**

ODONTIODA

RYOKO MIYAMOTO	**Odm. bictoniense × Oda. Feuerschein**	**Elle & Co. 1975**
SAN ELIJO GEM	**Minel × Lautrix**	**Dugger 1974**
SCARLET POINT	**Lautrix × Taw**	**Beall 1973**
SCHWERTE	**Lippestern × Odm. Gavotte**	**Schottler 1975**
SHEILA HANDS	**Odm. Brimstone Butterfly × Margia**	**Hands 1971 (C.)**
SHERRY	**Elac × Odm. crispum**	**Frese 1975**
SING SING	**Ithaque × Sirias**	**Pff. V. & L. 1975**
SIRIAS†‡	**Petit Prince × Mrs. F. M. Ogilvie**	**V. 1953**

× Florence Stirling = Aragon | × Odm. Golden Grove = Honfleur
× Ithaque = Sing Sing | × Odtna. Salam = Vuyl. Medellin
× Picador = Picarias

SUNSET WEST	**Odm. Baranof Island × Swamp Fire**	**Beall 1973**
SUNTRIX	**Lautrix × Odm. Sunfly**	**C. 1971**
SWAMP FIRE‡	**Victory × Chanticleer**	**Beall 1963**

× Cherry Creek = Crimson Glory | × Odm. Baranof Island = Sunset West
× Milt. Petropolis = Vuyl. Crimson Lake | × Odm. Jackie Gleason = Tiger Mountain

TAUNTON	**Giasto × Odm. Connero**	**Pedlar 1971 (A. & B.)**
TAW‡	**Sebastia × Valeria**	**L. 1952**

× Lautrix = Scarlet Point | × Odm. bictoniense = Bictaw
× Asp. principissa = Lgra. Printaw | × Onc. tigrinum = Wils. Tiger Talk

TERYMAR	**Odm. Mystery × Dalmar**	**M. & H. 1975**
TIGER MOUNTAIN	**Odm. Jackie Gleason × Swamp Fire**	**Beall 1973**
TOORAK	**Phoenix × Marzorka**	**Hubbard 1973**
TOPA†	**Laura × Marie Antoinette**	**C. 1938**

× Elpheon = Ruth Berman |

TORIAVA	**Astoria × Avala**	**C. 1957**

× Memory = Aviemore | × Odm. Eider = Rava
× Odm. Ardentissimum = Keith Gaskell |

TORRIDON	**Lautrix × Odm. Tordonia**	**Andrew Orchids 1972**
WHITE HERON	**Aloette × Odm. crispum**	**I. D. James 1975**
WHITE ROCK	**Echanson × Odm. Grand Tetons**	**Beall 1973**
ZORKOLA	**Nicola × Marzorka**	**C.C. 1974 (C.)**
ZSUPAN	Lippestern × Franz Wichmann	**Hark 1973**

ODONTOBRASSIA

INCA	**Brs. antherotes × Odm. wyattianum**	**Kuhn 1975**

ODONTOCIDIUM

AUTUMN GLOW	**Odm. bictoniense × Onc. olivaceum**	**H. Winter 1975**
AZTEC TIGER	**Onc. tigrinum × Odm. Omega**	**Don Richardson 1971**
BIG MAC	**Onc. maculatum × Odm. hallii**	**Kuhn 1975**
BITI	**Odm. bictoniense × Onc. tigrinum**	**H. Winter 1974**
CARRYKYLUM	**Odm. cariniferum × Onc. leucochilum**	**Kirch 1969**

× Milt. Peru = Colm. Desdamona |

ODONTOCIDIUM

CROWBOROUGH — **Onc. leucochilum × Odm. Golden Guinea** — **L. 1965**

× Oda. Apricot Meadows = Wils. Tiger Mountain | × Odm. Yukon Harbor = Gold Bluffs
× Odm. Yellowstone Basin = Golden Dawn

CYRTOMAC — **Odm. maculatum × Onc. macranthum** — **Kuhn 1975**
DAINTY — **Odm. pulchellum × Onc. montanum** — **George Black 1973 (Kirch)**

× Milt. Cogniauxiae = Colm. Purple Gem

DON RICHARDSON — **Onc. tigrinum × Odm. Crowborough Sunrise** — **J. & L. 1972**
ENCINITAS — **Tiger Butter × Odm. Moselle** — **Dugger 1975**
GOLD BAR MOUNTAIN — **Odm. Yukon Harbor × Onc. oblongatum** — **Beall 1974**
GOLD BEACH — **Pauline × Odm. Grand Tetons** — **Beall 1975**
GOLD BLUFFS — **Crowborough × Odm. Yukon Harbor** — **Beall 1975**
GOLDEN DAWN — **Crowborough × Odm. Yellowstone Basin** — **Beall 1973**
GOLDEN TIGER — **Tiger Butter × Odm. Panise** — **Kuhn 1975**
GOODALE MOIR — **Onc. Moir × Odm. Hyrastro** — **Dugger 1974**
HALGRIN — **Onc. tigrinum × Odm. hallii** — **Dugger 1973**
HANS NEUENHAUS — **Onc. tigrinum × Odm. Moselle** — **Röllke 1975**
INCALI — **Onc. incurvum × Odm. Alimo** — **Dugger 1972**

× Oda. Ray Buckman = Wils. Mem. Tom Lyles

JACOBERT — **Tiger Butter × Odm. Toralis** — **J. A. Young 1974 (Rod McLellan Co.)**
JANE ELLEN — **Odm. York × Onc. Kulee** — **Scardefield 1972**
MacKENZIE MOUNTAINS — **Onc. altissimum × Odm. Jeanne-Marie** — **Beall 1972**
MARY ANN — **Onc. oblongatum × Odm. Kopan** — **Scardefield 1972**
MEMORIA HERMAN von DRATELN‡ — **Onc. incurvum × Odm. crispum** — **Trade Winds 1959 (von Drateln)**

× Odm. Jackie Gleason = Raymond McCullough

MEMORIA NORMAN GAUNT — **Onc. incurvum × Odm. Lumesca** — **Dugger 1973**
MYLÈNE — **Odm. bictoniense × Onc. Kunawaii** — **M. Paul 1974**
PAULINE — **Odm. Golden Emblem × Onc. tigrinum** — **L. 1948**

× Odm. Grand Tetons = Gold Beach

PEGGY MAC — **Onc. maculatum × Odm. Peggy Richardson** — **Kuhn 1975**
RAYMOND McCULLOUGH — **Odm. Jackie Gleason × Mem. Herman von Drateln** — **Dugger 1975**
SIERRA GOLD — **Tiger Butter × Onc. marshallianum** — **Rod McLellan Co. 1974**
SOLANA — **Onc. wentworthianum × Odm. Moselle** — **Dugger 1973**
TIGER BUTTER — **Onc. tigrinum × Odm. Golden Avalanche** — **Rod McLellan Co. 1962**

× Milt. Crimson Crest = Colm. Ferguson Beall | × Odm. Panise = Golden Tiger
× Oda. Dalmar = Wils. Cardiff | × Odm. Peggy Richardson = White Tiger
× Oda. Ray Buckman = Wils. Tigerman | × Odm. Toralis = Jacobert
× Odm. Moselle = Encinitas | × Onc. marshallianum = Sierra Gold

UNIWAI — **Onc. maculatum × Odm. cariniferum** — **W. W. G. Moir 1975 (V. of H.)**

WHITE TIGER — **Tiger Butter × Odm. Peggy Richardson** — **Kuhn 1975**
WINTERGOLD — **Odm. bictoniense × Onc. onustum** — **H. Winter 1974**

ODONTOGLOSSUM

AGLINA — **Aglaon × Patnina** — **M. & H. 1966**

× Oda. Albeam = Oda. Albina

ODONTOGLOSSUM

ALDONIA‡ — **Alperor × Tordonia** — **C. 1946**

× Pheonel = Blue Boy

ALIMO — **Molyneux × Alispum** — **C. 1964**

× Oda. Elpheon = Oda. Jack Greatwood
× Oda. Flomar = Oda. Irene Williams
× Onc. incurvum = Odcdm. Incali

ANNELIESE ROTHENBERGER — **bictoniense × Goldrausch** — **Elle & Co. 1975 (Elle)**

ARDENTISSIMUM*†‡ — **crispum × pescatorei** — **E. de R. 1898**

× Oda. Toriava = Oda. Keith Gaskell

BARANOF ISLAND — **Yukon Harbor × Manade** — **Beall 1967**

× Milt. Minas Gerais = Odtna. Ice Caves
× Oda. Swamp Fire = Oda. Sunset West

BARONESS LEITHNER — **Tolcarne × Chiddingfold** — **L. 1956**

× Crystal Orb = Crystess

BASSANIO†‡ — **Bure × Lawrenceanum** — **L. 1937**

× Crowborough Sunrise = Inca Gold

bictoniense*‡ — **species**

× Goldrausch = Anneliese Rothenberger
× Moselle = Paradiese
× Comp. falcata = Odrta. Violetta
× Comp. macroplectron = Odrta. Dümmerbrand
× Comp. speciosa = Odrta. Mandarine
× Milt. spectabilis = Odtna. Marie Elle
× Oda. Feuerschein = Oda. Ryoko Miyamoto
× Oda. Ingera = Oda. Robert Stolz
× Oda. Taw = Oda. Bictaw
× Onc. Kunawaii = Odcdm. Mylène
× Onc. olivaceum = Odcdm. Autumn Glow
× Onc. onustum = Odcdm. Wintergold
× Onc. tigrinum = Odcdm. Biti
× Rdza. strobellii = Rdgm. Dolly

BLUE BOY — **Aldonia × Pheonel** — **Stonehurst 1974**

BRIMSTONE BUTTERFLY*†‡ — **Armstrongii × crispum** — **A. & B. 1933**

× Oda. Margia = Oda. Sheila Hands

BUTTERCUP PASS — **hallii × Mirum** — **Beall 1973**

CADMIUM‡ — **Golden Emblem × Mirum** — **L. 1942**

× Golden Guinea = Goldrausch

cariniferum†‡ — **species**

× Onc. maculatum = Odcdm. Uniwai

CHATOYANT†‡ — **Adrien Lefebvre × Horace Vernet** — **V. 1953**

× Oda. Florence Stirling = Oda. Kaino

CHIMÈNE‡ — **Miramar × Chilgrove** — **Pff. V. & L. 1959**

× Milt. flavescens = Odtna. Golden Wand

CONCORDE — **Dominant Concord × Kopan** — **M. & H. 1975**

CONNERO‡ — **Nerophion × Claricon** — **C. 1957**

× Stropheon = Costro
× Oda. Dalmar = Oda. Mem. Len Page
× Oda. Giasto = Oda. Taunton
× Wils. Autumn = Wils. San Dieguito

COSTRO — **Stropheon × Connero** — **C. 1971**

CRAGGWOOD — **uro-skinneri × Helstone** — **M. & H. 1973**

CRISPANIA†‡ — **Ascania × crispum** — **C. 1943**

× Golden Guinea = Many Waters

CRISPANN — **crispum × Katherine Ann** — **Scardefield 1974**

crispum*†‡ — **species**

× Crystal Orb = Snowball
× Grand Tetons = Ocean Falls

crispum*†‡ *(continued)*

× Katherine Ann = Crispann
× Milt. Minas Gerais = Odtna. Johannesburg Mine
× Oda. Aloette = Oda. White Heron
× Oda. Ann Dore = Oda. Ispann
× Oda. Brocade = Oda. Lippstadt
× Oda. Carl Keyes = Oda. Mem. Harry Seigel
× Oda. Charlette = Oda. Crislette
× Oda. Elac = Oda. Sherry
× Oda. Lippstadt = Oda. Micheltorina
× Oda. Phoenix = Oda. Crispheon
× Odtna. Zizette = Odtna. Crispette

CRISTOR‡ **crispum × Tordonia** **C. 1948**

× harryanum = Fusa

CROWBOROUGH SUNRISE‡ **Waveney × Chilgrove** **L. 1955**

× Bassanio = Inca Gold
× Onc. tigrinum = Odcdm. Don Richardson

CRYSTAL ORB **Tolcarne × crispum** **L. 1956**

× Baroness Leithner = Crystess
× crispum = Snowball

CRYSTESS **Baroness Leithner × Crystal Orb** **M. & H. 1973**

DAUPHIN†‡ **crispum × L'Empereur** **C. 1927**

× Victory = Trafalgar

DEFERENCE **Trophée × Connétable** **Pff. V. & L. 1960**

× Oda. Ithaque = Oda. Biarritz

DOMINANT CONCORD **Brimstone Butterfly × crispum** **Stirling 1963 (A. & B.)**

× Kopan = Concorde

EDALVA‡ **Edwarcus × Alvarloo** **C. 1959**

× Oda. Marzorka = Oda. Clifton

EDWARCUS†‡ **Alorcus × Prince Edward** **C. 1940**

× Odtna. Andraena = Odtna. Frances Stott

EIDER‡ **Berwick × Thella** **L. 1955**

× Oda. Toriava = Oda. Rava

ESK† **Assuan × Espoir** **L. 1949**

× Oda. Dalmar = Oda. Dalesk

FANFARE **Patnoll × Queen Carroll** **M. & H. 1972**

FERNHILL **Talor × Gledhow** **M. & H. 1973**

FUSA **Cristor × harryanum** **Schmidt-Mumm 1974**

GAVOTTE†‡ **Nabab × Alorcus** **V. 1953**

× Oda. Lippestern = Oda. Schwerte

GENE CASEY **Mimosa × Moselle** **Dugger 1973**

GLEDHOW‡ **Crystal × Mary Seville** **M. & H. 1952**

× Talor = Fernhill

GLEDROY **Viceroy × Gledhow** **M. & H. 1970**

× Oda. Ingera = Oda. Raroy
× Oda. Memory = Oda. Rachel Gaskell
× Oda. Phoenix = Oda. Royen

GOLD BASIN **Yellowstone Basin × Jeanne-Marie** **Beall 1973**

GOLDEN GLACIER **Yellowstone Basin × Wilckeanum** **Beall 1972**

GOLDEN GROVE **Chilgrove × Golden Belle** **L. 1954**

× Oda. Sirias = Oda. Honfleur

ODONTOGLOSSUM

GOLDEN GUINEA‡	**Apelles × Chilgrove**		**L. 1955**
× Cadmium	= Goldrausch	× hallii	= Golden Halls
× Crispania	= Many Waters		
GOLDEN HALLS	**hallii × Golden Guinea**		**Kuhn 1975**
GOLDEN RANSOM	**Yukon Harbor × Golden Butterfly**		**Beall 1967**
× Oda. Lautrix	= Oda. Rantrix		
GOLDRAUSCH	**Golden Guinea × Cadmium**		**Elle & Co. 1975 (L.)**
× bictoniense	= Anneliese Rothenberger		
grande*†	**species**		
× Odtna. Wonder	= Odtna. Tiger Cub		
GRAND TETONS‡	**crispum × Almee**		**Beall 1964**
× crispum	= Ocean Falls	× Oda. Echanson	= Oda. White Rock
× Mount Baker	= Snowshoe Rapids	× Odcdm. Pauline	= Odcdm. Gold Beach
× Asp. epidendroides	= Aspgm. Coyote Rocks	× Vuyl. Rainbow Falls	= Vuyl. Soleduck Falls
hallii*‡	**species**		
× Golden Guinea	= Golden Halls	× Odtna. Debutante	= Odtna. Red Breast
× Mirum	= Buttercup Pass	× Onc. maculatum	= Odcdm. Big Mac
× Peggy Richardson	= Hallipeg	× Onc. tigrinum	= Odcdm. Halgrin
HALLIPEG	**hallii × Peggy Richardson**		**Kuhn 1975**
harryanum*†	**species**		
× Cristor	= Fusa	× Oda. Carmine	= Oda. Red Knight
× Sedlescombe	= Queen Charlotte Straits		
HELSTONE	**Hellemense × Brimstone Butterfly**		**M. & H. 1970**
× uro-skinneri	= Craggwood		
HYRASTRO	**Stropheon × Ophyras**		**C. 1966**
× Oda. Elpheon	= Oda. Hilary Greatwood	× Onc. Moir	= Odcdm. Goodale Moir
× Oda. Lautrix	= Oda. Rixro		
INCA GOLD	**Crowborough Sunrise × Bassanio**		**M. & H. 1972**
JACKIE GLEASON	**Mount McKinley × Ismène**		**Beall 1964**
× Mount Constance	= Monarch Mountain	× Oda. Swamp Fire	= Oda. Tiger Mountain
× Mtssa. Charles M. Fitch	= Dgmra. Admiralty Islands	× Odcdm. Mem. Herman von Drateln	= Odcdm. Raymond McCullough
JEANNE-MARIE	**Goldhurst × crispum**		**A. N. Rowland 1953**
× Yellowstone Basin	= Gold Basin	× Onc. altissimum	= Odcdm. Mackenzie Mountains
KATHERINE ANN	**Elise × Alispum**		**Don Richardson 1959**
× crispum	= Crispann		
KOMARY	**Mary × Kopan**		**C. 1971**
KOPAN	**Konia × Pancho**		**C. 1958**
× Dominant Concord	= Concorde	× Onc. oblongatum	= Odcdm. Mary Ann
× Mary	= Komary		
LADY MARY	**Lord Harold × Mary**		**M. & H. 1975**
LORD HAROLD‡	**Aristocrat × York**		**Ferrer 1965 (M. & H.)**
× Mary	= Lady Mary	× Oda. Doric	= Oda. Dorold

LUMESCA — **pescatorei × Petulum** — **C. 1960**

× Onc. incurvum = Odcdm. Mem. Norman Gaunt

maculatum* — **species**

× Onc. macranthum = Odcdm. Cyrtomac

MANY WATERS — **Crispania × Golden Guinea** — **Stonehurst 1974**

MARY — **Brimstone Butterfly × triumphans** — **C. 1946**

× Kopan = Komary
× Lord Harold = Lady Mary

MIMOSA†‡ — **Ascanense × Ascania** — **C. 1947**

× Moselle = Gene Casey

MIRUM*† — **crispum × Wilckeanum** — **Crawshay 1900**

× hallii = Buttercup Pass

MONARCH MOUNTAIN — **Mount Constance × Jackie Gleason** — **Beall 1972**

MOSELLE — **Elise × Mimosa** — **C. 1965**

× bictoniense = Paradiese
× Mimosa = Gene Casey
× Odcdm. Tiger Butter = Odcdm. Encinitas
× Onc. tigrinum = Odcdm. Hans Neuenhaus
× Onc. wentworthianum = Odcdm. Solana

MOUNT BAKER‡ — **Goeland × crispum** — **Beall 1960**

× Grand Tetons = Snowshoe Rapids
× Mtssa. Charles M. Fitch = Dgmra. Orcus Island
× Mtdm. Aztec Gold = Colm. Cauca Valley
× Mtdm. Cleopatra = Colm. Bogota
× Mtdm. Surprise = Colm. Puget Sound

MOUNT CONSTANCE — **Mendenhall × Crispania** — **Beall 1964**

× Jackie Gleason = Monarch Mountain

MYSTERY — **Pearlmist × Victory** — **M. & H. 1967**

× Relton = Myston
× Oda. Dalmar = Oda. Terymar
× Oda. Doric = Oda. Mystic

MYSTON — **Mystery × Relton** — **M. & H. 1972**

NICKY STRAUSS — **Theron × pescatorei** — **Stonehurst 1972**

OCEAN FALLS — **crispum × Grand Tetons** — **Beall 1972**

OMEGA*† — **Aglaon × St. James** — **C. 1924**

× Onc. tigrinum = Odcdm. Aztec Tiger

OPHEON†‡ — **Neron × Ophelia** — **C. 1939**

× Oda. Dalmar = Oda. Little Lady

PACIFIC‡ — **Crispinum × Ascania** — **C. 1958**

× Oda. Cornosa = Oda. Pacific Gold

PANISE — **Elise × Pancho** — **C. 1946**

× Odcdm. Tiger Butter = Odcdm. Golden Tiger

PARADIESE — **bictoniense × Moselle** — **Röhl 1975**

PATNOLL‡ — **Patnina × Carroll** — **M. & H. 1966**

× Queen Carroll = Fanfare

PEGGY RICHARDSON‡ — **Alispum × Perrytonia** — **Don Richardson 1959**

× hallii = Hallipeg
× Rich Cove = Rich Peggy
× Asp. principissa = Aspgm. Peggy Richardson
× Odcdm. Tiger Butter = Odcdm. White Tiger
× Onc. maculatum = Odcdm. Peggy Mac

PEROLIA **Perryanum × Mongolia** **C. 1957**
× Oda. Lautrix = Oda. Pentland

PESCADERO **Pescalo × pescatorei** **McElderry 1974 (C.)**

PESCALO‡ **Alorcus × pescatorei** **C. 1953**
× pescatorei = Pescadero
× Oda. Lippestern = Oda. Karl Heinz Hanisch

pescatorei*†‡ **species**
× Pescalo = Pescadero
× Theron = Nicky Strauss

PHEONEL‡ **Clommel × Opheon** **C. 1953**
× Aldonia = Blue Boy
× Oda. Lippestern = Oda. Fedora

PHIOMAN **Nerophion × Manperor** **C. 1959**
× Oda. Elpheon = Oda. Philomel

pulchellum*‡ **species**
(This is retained as the horticulturally recommended name for registration purposes, even though *Osmoglossum pulchellum* is the botanically correct name for this species.)
× Onc. montanum = Odcdm. Dainty

QUEEN CARROLL **Carroll × Virgin Queen** **M. & H. 1966**
× Patnoll = Fanfare

QUEEN CHARLOTTE STRAITS **Sedlescombe × harryanum** **Beall 1972**

QUISTO **Opheon × Quistrum** **C. 1968**
× Oda. Aloette = Oda. Mem. Ernesto Alvarez
× Oda. Fremar = Oda. Marquis
× Oda. Lautrix = Oda. Helen Brough
× Wils. Autumn = Wils. Granados

RELTON **Redskin × Halton** **M. & H. 1966**
× Mystery = Myston
× Varanum = Valton

RICH COVE **Mount McKinley × Manade** **Beall 1967**
× Peggy Richardson = Rich Peggy
× Milt. Cogniauxiae = Odtna. Mauna Loa

RICH PEGGY **Rich Cove × Peggy Richardson** **Kuhn 1975**

rossii*‡ **species**
× Oda. Feuerschein = Oda. Hambühren

SEDLESCOMBE†‡ **Angmering × crispum** **L. 1950**
× harryanum = Queen Charlotte Straits

SNOWBALL **Crystal Orb × crispum** **M. & H. 1972**

SNOWSHOE RAPIDS **Grand Tetons × Mount Baker** **Beall 1972**

STROPHEON‡ **Opheon × Robert Strauss** **C. 1957**
× Connero = Costro
× Oda. Crown Jewel = Oda. Medellin
× Oda. Elpheon = Oda. Bogotá
× Oda. Lautrix = Oda. Ray Buckman
× Oda. Lippestern = Oda. Danilo

SUNFLY‡ **Brimstone Butterfly × Sunglow** **C. 1943**
× Oda. Lautrix = Oda. Suntrix

TALOR **Toreador × Talulah** **M. & H. 1970**
× Gledhow = Fernhill

THERON*†‡ **crispum × Erzerum** **C. 1929**
× pescatorei = Nicky Strauss

ODONTOGLOSSUM

TORALIS — **Alispum × Cristor** — **C. 1961**
× Odcdm. Tiger Butter = Odcdm. Jacobert

TORDONIA*†‡ — **Clydonia × Toreador** — **C. 1935**
× Oda. Lautrix = Oda. Torridon

TRAFALGAR — **Victory × Dauphin** — **Andrew Orchids 1972**

triumphans*†‡ — **species**
× Oda. Ingera = Oda. Cota | × Odtna. Debutante = Odtna. Superdeb

uro-skinneri*‡ — **species**
× Helstone = Craggwood

VALTON — **Relton × Varanum** — **M. & H. 1975**

VARANUM — **Perryanum × Nervara** — **C. 1959**
× Relton = Valton

VICTORY*‡ — **crispum × h. ign.** — **A. & B. 1915**
× Dauphin = Trafalgar

wilckeanum / **WILCKEANUM*†‡** — **crispum × luteopurpureum** — **Nat. hyb.** / **hort.**
× Yellowstone Basin = Golden Glacier

wyattianum — **species**
× Brs. antherotes = Odbrs. Inca | × Odtna. Maunakea = Odtna. Clinton Tooley

YELLOWSTONE BASIN‡ — **Midas × Golden Harvest** — **Beall 1959**
× Jeanne-Marie = Gold Basin | × Asp. epidendroides = Aspgm. Copper Butte
× Wilckeanum = Golden Glacier | × Odcdm. Crowborough = Odcdm. Golden Dawn

YORK‡ — **Hellemense × Mary Seville** — **M. & H. 1952**
× Onc. Kulee = Odcdm. Jane Ellen

YUKON HARBOR‡ — **Crispania × Natrium** — **Beall 1959**
× Mtdm. Autumn Glow = Colm. Hawaii Nei | × Odcdm. Crowborough = Odcdm. Gold Bluffs
× Mtdm. Aztec Gold = Colm. Moon Gold | × Onc. oblongatum = Odcdm. Gold Bar Mountain
× Oda. Echanson = Oda. Grouse Mountain

ODONTONIA

ANDRAENA†‡ — **Andromeda × Milt. Lycaena** — **C. 1946**
× Oda. Lippestern = Vuyl. Eleganz | × Odm. Edwarcus = Frances Stott

CLINTON TOOLEY — **Maunakea × Odm. wyattianum** — **Kuhn 1975**

CRISPETTE — **Zizette × Odm. crispum** — **Askin 1973**

DEBUTANTE‡ — **Milt. warscewiczii × Odm. cariniferum** — **E. Iwanaga 1960**
× Milt. spectabilis = John Fancher | × Oda. Minel = Vuyl. Royal Velvet
× Mtdm. Summer Fantasy = Colm. Shower of Gold | × Odm. hallii = Red Breast
× Oda. Feuerball = Vuyl. Feuerzauber | × Odm. triumphans = Superdeb

FRANCES STOTT — **Andraena × Odm. Edwarcus** — **Stott 1971 (Stonehurst)**

GLASS CREEK — Santos × Milt. Saint Martins — **Beall 1974**

GOLDEN WAND — **Milt. flavescens × Odm. Chimène** — **Crestwood 1973**

ICE CAVES — **Odm. Baranof Island × Milt. Minas Gerais** — **Beall 1974**

JOHANNESBURG MINE — **Milt. Minas Gerais × Odm. crispum** — **Beall 1973**

JOHN FANCHER — **Debutante × Milt. spectabilis** — **Fort Caroline 1972**

ODONTONIA

MARIE ELLE	**Odm. bictoniense × Milt. spectabilis**	**Elle & Co. 1975 (Elle)**
MAUNAKEA	**Milt. spectabilis × Odm. Serene**	**W. W. G. Moir 1964**
× Odm. wyattianum	= Clinton Tooley	
MAUNA LOA	**Milt. Cogniauxiae × Odm. Rich Cove**	**W. W. G. Moir 1973**
RED BREAST	**Debutante × Odm. hallii**	**Kuhn 1975**
ROSE GLOW	**Milt. regnellii × Santos**	**George Black 1975**
SALAM‡	**Lulli × Odm. Rembrandt**	**V. 1953**
× Oda. Sirias	= Vuyl. Medellin	
SANGRE GRANDE	**Milt. William Kirch × Santos**	**George Black 1975**
SANTOS	**Milt. Anne Warne × Wonder**	**W. W. G. Moir 1966**
× Milt. regnellii	= Rose Glow	× Milt. William Kirch = Sangre Grande
× Milt. Saint Martins	= Glass Creek	
SUPERDEB	**Debutante × Odm. triumphans**	**Kuhn 1975**
TANGO	**Debutante × Odm. Yellowstone Basin**	**E. Iwanaga 1968**
× Oda. Ray Buckman	= Vuyl. Tanman	
TIGER CUB	**Odm. grande × Wonder**	**Rod McLellan Co. 1973**
WONDER‡	**Odm. grande × Milt. regnellii**	**M. Yamada 1956**
× Odm. grande	= Tiger Cub	
ZIZETTE	**Rosemary × Odm. Espoir**	**L. 1948**
× Odm. crispum	= Crispette	

ODONTORETTIA

DÜMMERBRAND	**Odm. bictoniense × Comp. macroplectron**	**Lemförder Orch. 1975**
MANDARINE	**Odm. bictoniense × Comp. speciosa**	**H. Winter 1975 (B. Holm)**
VIOLETTA	**Odm. bictoniense × Comp. falcata**	**H. Winter 1975 (B. Holm)**

ONCIDENIA

LADIES PRIDE	**Onc. triquetrum × Mcdn. multiflora**	**Osment 1974**

ONCIDESA

ROSY GOLD	**Onc. Lovely × Gom. recurva**	**W. W. G. Moir 1973**

ONCIDETTIA

COLOMBIA	**Ecuador × Comp. macroplectron**	**W. W. G. Moir 1971**
ECUADOR	**Onc. desertorum × Comp. speciosa**	**W. W. G. Moir 1966**
× Comp. macroplectron	= Colombia	
RUBEN'S TWINKLE	**Onc. leitzii × Comp. macroplectron**	**Ruben 1975**
SUNFLAKE	**Onc. Tiny Tim × Comp. speciosa**	**Crawford 1975**

ONCIDIODA

BEATRICE RAMIREZ	**Cda. sanguinea × Onc. ornithorhynchum**	**Withner 1972**

ONCIDIODA

CROWBOROUGH — **Cooksoniae × Onc. auriferum** — **L. 1950**
× Oda. Anton = Wils. Rocksley

ROBIN — **Onc. incurvum × Cda. sanguinea** — **Withner 1972**

ONCIDIUM

AFTERGLOW — **Mem. Pepita de Restrepo × Miami Beach** — **Wallbrunn 1972**
ALEXANDRIA‡ — **Lovely × pulchellum** — **W. W. G. Moir 1967**
× Calypso Queen = Castleton | × Savanna La Mar = Savanna Sunset
× Mixto = Blue Mountains

ALICE TOWN — **Claremont × Bimini** — **W. W. G. Moir 1973**
ALLYN GOLD — **Gardneri × Waiomao Gold** — **V. & N. Jupp 1974**
altissimum*†‡ — **species**
× wentworthianum = Clyde Des Sain | × Odm. Jeanne-Marie = Odcdm. Mackenzie Mountains

ampliatum*‡ — **species**
× lankesteri = Towaco

AMY — **Java × desertorum** — **Beard 1974**
ann-hadderiae (see grex *Onc.* Les Cayes) — **variegatum × haitiense** — **Nat. hyb. 1972** / **W. W. G. Moir 1964**
(Registered hybrids from either *ann-hadderiae* or Les Cayes will be listed under Les Cayes.)
ANNIE CLARE PRINTER — **Sundance × Lava Flow** — **V. & N. Jupp 1974**
ANNONDALE — **Port Royal × Calypso Queen** — **W. W. G. Moir 1971**
ANSE ROUGE — **Robert Warne × Tiny Tim** — **W. W. G. Moir 1967**
× Tiny Tim = Haitian Red

ansiferum† — **species**
× maculatum = Panther

anthocrene*†‡ — **species**
× leucochilum = Anthroclus

ANTHROCLUS — **anthocrene × leucochilum** — **Kirsch 1972**

ANTIGUA‡ — **urophyllum × variegatum** — **W. W. G. Moir 1967**
× Skipper Kilbourne = Lizzer Belle

ANTILLES — **prionochilum × triquetrum** — **W. W. G. Moir 1975**
arizajulianum — **species**
× Luis Ariza Julia = Bao River

AUTUMN GOLD — **Farandole × Goldflakes** — **Kirsch 1971**
AUTUMN GLOW — **Golden Glow × Red Belt** — **Ruben 1975**
AZULEJO — **Osmentii × Jamie Sutton** — **Osment 1974**
BABALU — **Red Belt × Juanita** — **Ruben 1972**
BALLERINA — **Catherine Wilson × Pink Sherbet** — **Ruben 1975**
BALLET — **maculatum × stenotis** — **Rod McLellan Co. 1975**
BAO RIVER — **Luis Ariza Julia × arizajulianum** — **W. W. G. Moir 1972**
barbatum‡ — **species**
× Discovery Bay = Orange Bay | × sphacelatum = Mariposa Manchada
× lanceanum = Mem. Henry Ammarell | × Milt. spectabilis = Mtdm. Katrina

BERRY ISLES — **triquetrum × Bimini** — **W. W. G. Moir 1973**
bicallosum‡ — **species**
× Faye = Green Gold

ONCIDIUM

BIG GOLD — **Mirebalais × desertorum** — **W. W. G. Moir 1974**

BIMINI — **triquetrum × lucayanum** — **W. W. G. Moir 1966**

× Claremont	= Alice Town	× Tiny Tim	= Masque
× pulchellum	= Chapelton	× triquetrum	= Berry Isles

BLUE MOUNTAINS — **Mixto × Alexandria** — **W. W. G. Moir 1974**

BOG WALK — **Port Royal × pulchellum** — **W. W. G. Moir 1973**

BONANZA — **Red Velvet × Calypso Queen** — **W. W. G. Moir 1971**

BONITA — **triquetrum × La Citadelle** — **Howell 1973**

BORINQUEN — **Ochos Rios × prionochilum** — **V. Daubón 1970**

× triquetrum	= Florida Beauty

BROWNIE — **Florida Gold × lindenii** — **Osment 1972**

BURGEFFIANUM* — **marshallianum × varicosum** — **Burgeff 1921**

× varicosum	= Sancho

BURGUNDY — **ornithorhynchum × leucochilum** — **W. W. G. Moir 1962**

× Milt. Peru	= Mtdm. Quito

BUTTERFLY SUNSET — **sphacelatum × macranthum** — **Osment 1972**

CALICO GAL — **Red Velvet × Mixto** — **W. W. G. Moir 1973**

calochilum — **species**

× Red Belt	= Ole'Ressie

CALYPSO QUEEN‡ — **Golden Glow × pulchellum** — **W. W. G. Moir 1965**

× Alexandria	= Castleton	× Stanley Smith	= Queen's Best
× Port Royal	= Annondale	× Waikiki Sunset	= Kensington
× Red Velvet	= Bonanza		

CAMBRIDGE — **Red Velvet × Freckles** — **W. W. G. Moir 1973**

CANDY BARRS — **Puerto Plata × pulchellum** — **W. W. G. Moir 1971**

CARIBBE‡ — **pulchellum × Isabella** — **W. W. G. Moir 1967**

× Tiny Tim	= Red Shield

CARIBBEAN CHOICE — **Haitian Red × moirianum** — **F. E. Little 1975 (W. W. G. Moir)**

carthagenense*‡ — **species**

× leucochilum	= John Germaske	× Mem. Pepita de Restrepo	= Russet Dawn Surprise

CASTLETON — **Calypso Queen × Alexandria** — **W. W. G. Moir 1973**

CATHERINE WILSON‡ — **triquetrum × pulchellum** — **W. W. G. Moir 1959**

× Caymanas	= Pink Sherbet	× pulchellum	= Fort Myers
× Gardneri	= Mem. Darrell Walker	× Red Velvet	= Colorful
× Golden Glow	= Muñequita	× Waikiki Sunset	= Sunset Luau
× Hopewell	= Mem. Harry Howell	× Rdtta. Hawaii	= Wnra. Pinkie
× leitzii	= Mancha Verde	× Rdza. secunda	= Rdcm. Rojo
× Pink Sherbet	= Ballerina		

CAYMANAS‡ — **Anna Rosa × pulchellum** — **W. W. G. Moir 1964**

× Catherine Wilson	= Pink Sherbet	× Jamaica	= Jamanas

cebolleta†‡ — **species**

(Treated for registration purposes as specifically distinct from *Onc. sprucei*, although they are considered as conspecific by some authorities.)

× Mem. Pepita de Restrepo	= Richard Saporita

CHAPELTON — **Bimini × pulchellum** — **W. W. G. Moir 1973**

ONCIDIUM

CHARLES YASUDA — **triquetrum × Henri Christophe** — **W. W. G. Moir 1971**

chrysornis‡ — **species**

× Brs. gireoudiana = Brsdm. Golden Delicious

CLAREMONT‡ — **Catherine Wilson × Rosalani** — **W. W. G. Moir 1967**

× Bimini = Alice Town | × triquetrum = Malvern

CLARENDON — **Valverde × Stanley Smith** — **W. W. G. Moir 1973**

CLAUDE — **Delight × desertorum** — **Voo Doo Orchids 1974**

CLYDE DES SAIN — **altissimum × wentworthianum** — **Rod McLellan Co. 1971**

COLORFUL — **Red Velvet × Catherine Wilson** — **Perreira 1973**

concavum — **species**

× pulchellum = {hartii (Nat. hyb.) / Hartii (hort.)}

concolor*‡ — **species**

× Kuwon = Rex Alstyne | × Oda. Carmine = Wils. Accolade

× sphacelatum = Goldfinch

CONNIE KU — **Farandole × Ronaele** — **Kugust 1971**

crispum*†‡ — **species**

× Gardneri = Lava Flow | × Colm. Goodale = Colm. Winter Sunshine

× Kultane = Kernel Ku

cubense / **CUBENSE** — **variegatum × leiboldii** — **Nat. hyb. 1972** / **hort.**

× triquetrum = Habana

cucullatum (see *olivaceum*) — **species**

cuneilabium — **species**

× desertorum = Jaminican | × triquetrum = Vera's Friend

curtum* — **species**

× Kenny Ku = Easton

dasystyle*†‡ — **species**

× Hopewell = Pink Vanity

DAVID LITTLE — **lindenii × nanum** — **Mrs. J. P. Little 1973**

DELIGHT†‡ — **pulchellum × henekenii** — **W. W. G. Moir 1958**

× desertorum = Claude | × Lovely = Marion Liberty

desertorum*†‡ — **species**

(syn. *intermedium* auctt., not *intermedium* Bertero 1826)

× cuneilabium = Jaminican | × La Citadelle = Rojo

× Delight = Claude | × Mirebalais = Big Gold

× Hopewell = Red Dot | × Port Royal = Portland Point

× Java = Amy | × Royal Claret = Grandma Dingee

DESPERATION — **Red Velvet × Red Belt** — **Howell 1975**

DESSALINES — **Petionville × Tiny Tim** — **W. W. G. Moir 1973**

DISCOVERY BAY — **Robert Warne × Sweetheart** — **W. W. G. Moir 1969**

× barbatum = Orange Bay

DOCTOR SCHRAGEN‡ — **lanceanum × splendidum** — **S.A. 1949**

(syn. Luzon)

× lanceanum = Noorah

DOROTHY ISEMONGER — **nanum × sprucei** — **Osment 1973**

ONCIDIUM

EASTER — **Lovely × Osmentii** — **W. W. G. Moir 1972**

EASTON — **Kenny Ku × curtum** — **Kuhn 1975**

ELEGANCE — **hastatum × leucochilum** — **W. W. G. Moir 1966**

× Bllra. Tahoma Glacier = Gdlra. Stella Mizuta | × Milt. Royal = Mtdm. Jupiter

ERMA WARNE‡ — **urophyllum × pulchellum** — **W. W. G. Moir 1957**

× Waikiki Sunset = Pink Ears

EVAN FRANCES CHAMBERS — **triquetrum × lindenii** — **Chambers 1973 (Rootstein)**

FARANDOLE*† — **Comtesse de Bretonne × mantinii** — **V. 1935**

× Goldflakes = Autumn Gold | × Ronaele = Connie Ku

FASCINATION — **hastatum × obryzatum** — **Perreira 1973**

FAYE‡ — **Maureen × lanceanum** — **Miyamoto 1951**

× bicallosum = Green Gold

FLEXOEL — **flexuosum × pulchellum** — **Ruben 1969**

× triquetrum = Rio's Valentine

flexuosum*†‡ — **species**

× triquetrum = Triflex

FLORIDA BEAUTY — **Borinquen × triquetrum** — **Howell 1975**

FLORIDA GOLD — **splendidum × bicallosum** — **A. & M. 1964**

× lanceanum = Maui Gold | × lindenii = Brownie

forbesii*†‡ — **species**

× Kultane = Katherine Tompkins | × Asp. epidendroides = Aspsm. Cherry-Pie
× oblongatum = Gold Coin Butte | × Brsdm. Gemini = Brsdm. Aloha
× Varimyre = Goldrausch

FORT MYERS — **pulchellum × Catherine Wilson** — **Howell 1973**

FRECKLES‡ — **Tiny Tim × triquetrum** — **W. W. G. Moir 1965**

× Red Velvet = Cambridge

FREEPORT — **Tiger Wong × Grand Bahama** — **W. W. G. Moir 1973**

furcyense (see grex *Onc.* Jeremie) — **variegatum × scandens** — **Nat. hyb. 1969 / W. W. G. Moir 1966**

(Registered hybrids from either *furcyense* or Jeremie will be listed under Jeremie.)

gardneri / GARDNERI*†‡ — **forbesii × dasystyle** — **Nat. hyb. / hort.**

× Catherine Wilson = Mem. Darrell Walker | × varicosum = Sundance
× crispum = Lava Flow | × Waiomao Gold = Allyn Gold
× Sultane = Raiatean Ballet

gauntlettii‡ — **species**

× triquetrum = Rose de Mask

GAYLE — **Tiny Tim × Rose Hall** — **W. W. G. Moir 1973**

GOLD COIN BUTTE — **oblongatum × forbesii** — **Beall 1975**

GOLDEN BINOT — **marshallianum × ottonis** — **Withner 1972**

GOLDEN EMBER — **Waiomao Gold × Lava Flow** — **V. & N. Jupp 1973**

GOLDEN GLOW‡ — **triquetrum × urophyllum** — **W. W. G. Moir 1957**

× Catherine Wilson = Muñequita | × Tiny Tim = Thief Neck Island
× Mini-skirt = Mini Glow | × Rdza. secunda = Rdcm. Maria
× Red Belt = Autumn Glow

GOLDEN LURE — **Summit Gold × luridum** — **Fort Caroline 1975**

GOLDEN STATE — **Sarcatum × Nona** — **Rod McLellan Co. 1975**

GOLDEN SUNSET — **Stanley Smith × Tiny Tim** — **Aisaka 1975 (Perreira)**

GOLDFINCH — **concolor × sphacelatum** — **Crestwood 1974**

GOLDFLAKES — **flexuosum × hyphaematicum** — **O. Kirsch 1959**

× Farandole = Autumn Gold

GOLDIANA‡ — **flexuosum × sphacelatum** — **Atherton 1940**

× lanceanum = Jeu Kang
× maculatum = Mago
× Oda. Carmine = Wils. Red Galaxy

GOLDRAUSCH — **forbesii × Varimyre** — **Herbert Bernhart 1975**

GONAIVES — **Mixto × Petionville** — **W. W. G. Moir 1973**

GORDON JUPP — **Phyllis Wells × Nona** — **V. & N. Jupp 1975**

GRAND BAHAMA — **lucayanum × desertorum** — **W. W. G. Moir 1967**

× Tiger Wong = Freeport

GRANDMA DINGEE — **Royal Claret × desertorum** — **Howell 1974**

GREEN GOLD — **Faye × bicallosum** — **Perreira 1971**

HABANA — **triquetrum × Cubense** — **W. W. G. Moir 1973**

HAITIAN RED — **Tiny Tim × Anse Rouge** — **W. W. G. Moir 1972**

× moirianum = Caribbean Choice

haitiense‡ — **species**

× henekenii = Palenke
× variegatum = ann-hadderiae (Nat. hyb. 1972); Les Cayes (reg'd. grex 1964)

harrisonianum — **species**

× lindenii = Queen Bee

hartii / **HARTII** — **pulchellum × concavum** — **Nat. hyb.** / **hort.**

× pulchellum = Kingston

HARVEST MOON — **Jeremie × Red Belt** — **W. W. G. Moir 1973**

hastatum‡ — **species**

× obryzatum = Fascination
× Milt. warscewiczii = Mtdm. Talofa

henekenii†‡ — **species**

× haitiense = Palenke
× onustum = Yellow Charm

HENRI CHRISTOPHE — **velutinum × haitiense** — **W. W. G. Moir 1965**

× triquetrum = Charles Yasuda

HOPEWELL — **Red Velvet × pulchellum** — **W. W. G. Moir 1970**

× Catherine Wilson = Mem. Harry Howell
× dasystyle = Pink Vanity
× desertorum = Red Dot
× Jamaica = Pelucha
× Juanita = Spanish Wells
× Incdm. Ressie Toy = Incdm. Rainbow

incurvum*†‡ — **species**

× Cda. sanguinea = Oncda. Robin
× Oda. Florence Stirling = Wils. Widecombe Fair
× Odm. Alimo = Odcdm. Incali
× Odm. Lumesca = Odcdm. Mem. Norman Gaunt
× Rdza. secunda = Rdcm. Camp

intermedium auctt. — **species**

(see *desertorum**†‡, including vars. *alborubrum, album,* and *aureorubrum*) (NOT *intermedium* Bertero 1826)

IRENE VAN ALSTYNE — **Savanna La Mar × Isabella** — **W. W. G. Moir 1971**

ISABELLA‡ — **Agnes Ann × henekenii** — **W. W. G. Moir 1964**

× Red Velvet	= Midnight Red	× Tiny Tim	= Maria Luisa Leschhorn
× Savanna La Mar	= Irene Van Alstyne		

JAMAICA‡ — **pulchellum × tetrapetalum** — **W. W. G. Moir 1956**

× Caymanas	= Jamanas	× pulchellum	= Little Chickadee
× Hopewell	= Pelucha	× Stanley Smith	= Moshi Moshi

JAMANAS — **Jamaica × Caymanas** — **R. K. Mizuta 1972**

JAMIE SUTTON — **ornithorhynchum × powellii** — **Osment 1969**

× Osmentii = Azulejo

JAMINICAN — **cuneilabium × desertorum** — **Howell 1974**

JAVA†‡ — **flexuosum × varicosum** — **Nagrok 1936**

× desertorum	= Amy	× microchilum	= Vanaman

JEREMIE — **variegatum × scandens** — **W. W. G. Moir 1966**

(Also described as a Nat. hyb. *Onc.* × *furcyense* in 1969. Future registered hybrids from either *furcyense* or Jeremie will be listed under Jeremie.)

× Red Belt = Harvest Moon

JEU KANG — **Goldiana × lanceanum** — **Lim Ming Kwei 1971**

JOHN GERMASKE — **leucochilum × carthagenense** — **Rod McLellan Co. 1974**

JUANITA — **Lovely × Tiny Tim** — **W. W. G. Moir 1968**

× Hopewell	= Spanish Wells	× Red Belt	= Babalu
× pulchellum	= Mambo	× varicosum	= Juanita Gold

JUANITA GOLD — **Juanita × varicosum** — **Osment 1974**

KALIHI — **krameranum × papilio** — **Kihara 1945**

× papilio = Mariposa

KATHERINE TOMPKINS — **forbesii × Kultane** — **P. W. Johnston 1973 (Tompkins)**

× Kultane = Tiffany Renee Colborne

KAYTEE — **Kingston × triquetrum** — **W. W. G. Moir 1975**

KENNY KU — **anthocrene × crispum** — **Kugust 1969**

× curtum = Easton

KENSINGTON — **Calypso Queen × Waikiki Sunset** — **W. W. G. Moir 1971**

KERNEL KU — **Kultane × crispum** — **Kugust 1971**

KINGSTON — **Hartii × pulchellum** — **W. W. G. Moir 1974**

× triquetrum = Kaytee

KULEE — **tigrinum × Ronaele** — **Kugust 1962**

× Odm. York = Odcdm. Jane Ellen

KULTANE‡ — **Sultane × Saladin** — **Kugust 1959**

× crispum	= Kernel Ku	× Ronaele	= Phyllis Ku
× forbesii	= Katherine Tompkins	× varicosum	= Rachel Lee
× Katherine Tompkins	= Tiffany Renee Colborne		

KUNAWAII — **flexuosum × forbesii** — **T. Kazumura 1950**

× Odm. bictoniense = Odcdm. Mylène

KUTOO — **ornithorhynchum × variegatum** — **Kugust 1958**

× pulchellum = Slip Showed

KUWON — **Java × forbesii** — **Kugust 1957**

× concolor = Rex Alstyne

ONCIDIUM

LA CITADELLE‡ — **Red Velvet × desertorum** — **W. W. G. Moir 1967**

× desertorum	= Rojo	× triquetrum	= Bonita

lanceanum*†‡ — **species**

× barbatum	= Mem. Henry Ammarell	× Mem. Pepita de Restrepo	= Noel Schoenrock
× Dr. Schragen	= Noorah	× stramineum	= Mary Saporita
× Florida Gold	= Maui Gold	× Trctm. pfavii	= Trcdm. Peter Allen
× Goldiana	= Jeu Kang		
× Mahogany Beauty	= Mahogany Lance		

lankesteri — **species**

× ampliatum	= Towaco		

LAVA FLOW — **Gardneri × crispum** — **Slade 1973**

× Sundance	= Annie Clare Printer	× Waiomao Gold	= Golden Ember

leiboldii‡ — **species**

× variegatum	= cubense (Nat. hyb.) / Cubense (hort.)		

leitzii‡ — **species**

× Catherine Wilson	= Mancha Verde	× Comp. macroplectron	= Onctta. Ruben's Twinkle

LES CAYES — **variegatum × haitiense** — **W. W. G. Moir 1964**

(Also described as a Nat. hyb. *Onc.* × *ann-hadderiae* in 1972. Future registered hybrids from either *ann-hadderiae* or Les Cayes will be listed under Les Cayes.)

leucochilum*†‡ — **species**

× anthocrene	= Anthroclus	× Milt. Endeavour	= Mtdm. Kendrick Williams
× carthagenense	= John Germaske		

LIBBY HAWLEY — **Raiatean Ballet × Waiomao Gold** — **V. & N. Jupp 1973**

LINDA LITTLE — **lindenii × stramineum** — **Mrs. J. P. Little 1975**

lindenii‡ (syn. *retemeyeranum*) — **species**

× Florida Gold	= Brownie	× stramineum	= Linda Little
× harrisonianum	= Queen Bee	× triquetrum	= Evan Frances Chambers
× nanum	= David Little	× Trctm. tigrinum	= Trcdm. Teddy Bear

LITTLE CHICKADEE — **pulchellum × Jamaica** — **R. K. Mizuta 1971**

LIZZER BELLE — **Skipper Kilbourne × Antigua** — **Chambers 1974**

LOVELY‡ — **Delight × triquetrum** — **W. W. G. Moir 1960**

× Delight	= Marion Liberty	× Port Antonio	= Pink Beauty
× Osmentii	= Easter	× Gom. recurva	= Oncsa. Rosy Gold

LUIS ARIZA JULIA‡ — **calochilum × henekenii** — **W. W. G. Moir 1963**

× arizajulianum	= Bao River		

luridum*†‡ — **species**

(This and *Onc. guttatum* are treated as specifically distinct for registration purposes although regarded as conspecific by some authorities.)

× microchilum	= Mahogany Beauty	× Summit Gold	= Golden Lure

LUZON (see Doctor Schragen‡)

macranthum*†‡ — **species**

(This is retained as the horticulturally recommended name for registration purposes, even though *Cyrtochilum macranthum* is the botanically correct name for this species.)

× sphacelatum	= Butterfly Sunset	× Odm. maculatum	= Odcdm. Cyrtomac

maculatum*‡ — **species**

× ansiferum	= Panther	× Goldiana	= Mago

maculatum*‡ *(continued)*

× stenotis	= Ballet	× Odm. hallii	= Odcdm. Big Mac
× Brs. longissima	= Brsdm. Fiesta	× Odm. Peggy Richardson	= Odcdm. Peggy Mac
× Odm. cariniferum	= Odcdm. Uniwai		

MAGO	**Goldiana × maculatum**	**Ruben 1975**
MAHOGANY BEAUTY	**microchilum × luridum**	**R. D. Saporita 1975 (Originator unknown)**

× lanceanum	= Mahogany Lance	× Russet Dawn Surprise	= Red Devil Star

MAHOGANY LANCE	**Mahogany Beauty × lanceanum**	**R. D. Saporita 1975**
MALVERN	**Claremont × triquetrum**	**W. W. G. Moir 1973**
MAMBO	**Juanita × pulchellum**	**Ruben 1975**
MANCHA VERDE	**leitzii × Catherine Wilson**	**Osment 1971**
MARGIE CRAWFORD	**triquetrum × Stanley Smith**	**Crawford 1974**
MARIA LUISA LESCHHORN	**Tiny Tim × Isabella**	**W. W. G. Moir 1973**
MARION LIBERTY	**Lovely × Delight**	**Nicholson 1974**
MARIPOSA	**papilio × Kalihi**	**Ruben 1972**
MARIPOSA MANCHADA	**sphacelatum × barbatum**	**Osment 1972**
MARJORIE JUPP	**Waiomao Gold × Nona**	**V. & N. Jupp 1974**
marshallianum*†‡	**species**	

× ottonis	= Golden Binot	× sarcodes	= Summer Gold
× Palmyre	= Mem. Ron Gerard	× Mtssa. Vino	= Alcra. Maury Island
× Sarcatum	= Winter Glow	× Odcdm. Tiger Butter	= Odcdm. Sierra Gold

MARY SAPORITA	**lanceanum × stramineum**	**R. D. Saporita 1975**
MASQUE	**Bimini × Tiny Tim**	**Howell 1974**
MAUI GOLD	**Florida Gold × lanceanum**	**Mrs. T. Takakura 1974 (Takakura)**
MAY PEN	**Port Royal × Tiny Tim**	**W. W. G. Moir 1974**
MEMORIA DARRELL WALKER	**Catherine Wilson × Gardneri**	**Dunkelberger 1974 (Kirch)**
MEMORIA HARRY HOWELL	**Hopewell × Catherine Wilson**	**Howell 1975**
MEMORIA HENRY AMMARELL	**lanceanum × barbatum**	**Kugust 1971**
MEMORIA PEPITA DE RESTREPO	**luridum × splendidum**	**De Saram 1949**

× carthagenense	= Russet Dawn Surprise	× lanceanum	= Noel Schoenrock
× cebolleta	= Richard Saporita	× Miami Beach	= Afterglow

MEMORIA RON GERARD	**Palmyre × marshallianum**	**Gerard 1975**
MEMORIA VERA HOWELL	**withneranum × triquetrum**	**Howell 1973**
MIAMI BEACH	**Doctor Schragen × aurisasinorum**	**J. & S. 1962**

× Mem. Pepita de Restrepo	= Afterglow		

MICHAEL JUPP	**Splinter × sarcodes**	V. & N. Jupp 1975
microchilum†‡	**species**	

× Java	= Vanaman	× luridum	= Mahogany Beauty

MIDAS	**Red Belt × onustum**	**W. W. G. Moir 1974**
MIDNIGHT RED	**Red Velvet × Isabella**	**W. W. G. Moir 1973**
MINI DOLL	**pulchellum × Mini-skirt**	**Ruben 1975**
MINI GLOW	**Golden Glow × Mini-skirt**	**Ruben 1975**
MINI-SKIRT	**bahamense × urophyllum**	**Ruben 1970**

× Golden Glow	= Mini Glow	× triquetrum	= Trimini
× pulchellum	= Mini Doll		

Name	Parentage	Registrant
MIREBALAIS	**Lovely × desertorum**	**W. W. G. Moir 1966**

× desertorum	= Big Gold	× triquetrum	= Palomita

Name	Parentage	Registrant
MISSY	**Stanley Smith × William Thurston**	**R. K. Mizuta 1974**
MIXTO‡	**Lovely × Golden Glow**	**W. W. G. Moir 1965**

× Alexandria	= Blue Mountains	× Red Velvet	= Calico Gal
× Petionville	= Gonaives		

Name	Parentage	Registrant
MOIR‡	**altissimum × leucochilum**	**W. W. G. Moir 1959**

× Odm. Hyrastro	= Odcdm. Goodale Moir		

Name	Parentage	Registrant
moirianum	**species**	

× Haitian Red	= Caribbean Choice		

Name	Parentage	Registrant
montanum	**species**	

× varicosum	= Waiomao Gold	× Odm. pulchellum	= Odcdm. Dainty

Name	Parentage	Registrant
MOSHI MOSHI	**Stanley Smith × Jamaica**	**R. K. Mizuta 1974**
MUÑEQUITA	**Golden Glow × Catherine Wilson**	**Ruben 1975**
nanum‡	**species**	

× lindenii	= David Little	× sprucei	= Dorothy Isemonger
× splendidum	= Splendid Nan		

Name	Parentage	Registrant
NAPLES	**pulchellum × quadrilobum**	**Voo Doo Orchids 1974**
NOEL SCHOENROCK	**Mem. Pepita de Restrepo × lanceanum**	**Fort Caroline 1972 (Wallbrunn)**
NONA‡	**crispum × varicosum**	**Orchidwood 1938**

× Phyllis Wells	= Gordon Jupp	× Waiomao Gold	= Marjorie Jupp
× Sarcatum	= Golden State	× Milt. spectabilis	= Mtdm. Richard Peterson

Name	Parentage	Registrant
NOORAH	**lanceanum × Dr. Schragen**	**Alsagoff 1972**
oblongatum‡	**species**	

× forbesii	= Gold Coin Butte	× Odm. Yukon Harbor	= Odcdm. Gold Bar Mountain
× Odm. Kopan	= Odcdm. Mary Ann		

Name	Parentage	Registrant
obryzatum‡	**species**	

× hastatum	= Fascination	× sphacelatum	= Sunspot

Name	Parentage	Registrant
OLE'RESSIE	**Red Belt × calochilum**	**Howell 1975**
olivaceum (syn. *cucullatum*)	**species**	

× Odm. bictoniense	= Odcdm. Autumn Glow		

Name	Parentage	Registrant
onustum‡	**species**	

× henekenii	= Yellow Charm	× Odm. bictoniense	= Odcdm. Wintergold
× Red Belt	= Midas	× Rdtta. Henry Teuscher	= Wnra. Stanley Taba
× Lchs. labiatus	= Lcdm. Florence Grice		

Name	Parentage	Registrant
ORANGE BAY	**Discovery Bay × barbatum**	**W. W. G. Moir 1973**
ornithorhynchum*†‡	**species**	

× sphacelatum	= Patrapara Charusorn	× Cda. sanguinea	= Oncda. Beatrice Ramirez

Name	Parentage	Registrant
orthostates	**species**	

× Colm. Sir Jeremiah	= Colm. Mustard Pot	× Milt. regnellii	= Mtdm. Sunset Sky

Name	Parentage	Registrant
OSCAR HOWELL	**Spanish Wells × triquetrum**	**Howell 1975**
osmentii / **OSMENTII‡**	**quadrilobum × haitiense**	**Nat. hyb.** / **hort.**

× Jamie Sutton	= Azulejo	× triquetrum	= Samana Santa
× Lovely	= Easter	× velutinum	= Selle

ONCIDIUM

ottonis‡ — **species**

× marshallianum = Golden Binot

PALENKE — **haitiense × henekenii** — **Osment 1974**

PALMYRE†‡ — **Saladin × varicosum** — **V. 1951**

× marshallianum = Mem. Ron Gerard

PALOMITA — **triquetrum × Mirebalais** — **Ruben 1975**

PANTHER — **ansiferum × maculatum** — **Korasawa 1971**

papilio*†‡ — **species**

× Kalihi = Mariposa | × Milt. clowesii = Mtdm. Rio's Star

× Asp. lunata = Aspsm. Rio Luna

PARADISE ISLAND — **Tiger Wong × Red Belt** — **W. W. G. Moir 1973**

PATRAPARA CHARUSORN — **sphacelatum × ornithorhynchum** — **Charusorn 1975 (Alsagoff)**

PEGGY RICHARDSON — **Delight × Rosalani** — **W. W. G. Moir 1967**

× Port Antonio = Trelawny

PELUCHA — **Jamaica × Hopewell** — **Ruben 1972**

PETIONVILLE — **Helen Brown × velutinum** — **W. W. G. Moir 1966**

× Mixto = Gonaives | × Tiny Tim = Dessalines

PHYLLIS KU — **Kultane × Ronaele** — **Kugust 1971**

PHYLLIS WELLS — **Kuron × Gardneri** — **Slade 1964**

× Nona = Gordon Jupp

PINK BEAUTY — **Lovely × Port Antonio** — **W. W. G. Moir 1973**

PINK EARS — **Erma Warne × Waikiki Sunset** — **Ruben 1975**

PINK GLORY — **Red Velvet × variegatum** — **Osment 1974**

PINK SHERBET — **Catherine Wilson × Caymanas** — **Ruben 1975**

× Catherine Wilson = Ballerina | × Red Belt = Rio's Spot

PINK VANITY — **Hopewell × dasystyle** — **Osment 1971**

PORT ANTONIO‡ — **Delight × pulchellum** — **W. W. G. Moir 1966**

× Lovely = Pink Beauty | × pulchellum = Royal Purple

× Peggy Richardson = Trelawny

PORTLAND POINT — **Port Royal × desertorum** — **W. W. G. Moir 1973**

PORT ROYAL — **Catherine Wilson × Lovely** — **W. W. G. Moir 1966**

× Calypso Queen = Annondale | × Tiny Tim = May Pen

× desertorum = Portland Point | × triquetrum = Port Wine

× pulchellum = Bog Walk

PORT WINE — **Port Royal × triquetrum** — **W. W. G. Moir 1972**

powellii†‡ — **species**

× Milt. Petropolis = Mtdm. Gatum Lake

prionochilum‡ — **species**

× triquetrum = Antilles

PUERTO PLATA — **Yellow Jacket × pulchellum** — **W. W. G. Moir 1967**

× pulchellum = Candy Barrs

pulchellum†‡ — **species**

× Bimini = Chapelton | × Jamaica = Little Chickadee

× Catherine Wilson = Fort Myers | × Juanita = Mambo

× concavum = {hartii (Nat. hyb.), Hartii (hort.)} | × Kutoo = Slip Showed

× Hartii = Kingston | × Mini-skirt = Mini Doll

pulchellum†‡ *(continued)*

× Port Antonio = Royal Purple
× Port Royal = Bog Walk
× Puerto Plata = Candy Barrs
× quadrilobum = Naples
× Royal Purple = Roselle
× Tiny Tim = Rainbow
× Brs. maculata = Brsdm. Lady in Red
× Lchs. labiatus = Lcdm. Anne Borden
× Rdza. Burgundy = Rdcm. Beauty Spots

quadrilobum‡	**species**	

× pulchellum = Naples

QUEEN BEE	**lindenii × harrisonianum**	**Osment 1971**
QUEEN'S BEST	**Stanley Smith × Calypso Queen**	**W. W. G. Moir 1973**
RACHEL LEE	**Kultane × varicosum**	**Scandefield 1974**
RAINBOW	**pulchellum × Tiny Tim**	**R. K. Mizuta 1972**
RAIATEAN BALLET	**Gardneri × Sultane**	**Slade 1973**

× Waiomao Gold = Libby Hawley

RANDALL McLAUGHLIN‡	**Dr. Schragen × lindenii**	**McLaughlin 1964**

× splendidum = Red Lip

RED BELT‡	**Golden Glow × triquetrum**	**W. W. G. Moir 1963**

× calochilum = Ole'Ressie
× Golden Glow = Autumn Glow
× Jeremie = Harvest Moon
× Juanita = Babalu
× onustum = Midas
× Pink Sherbet = Rio's Spot
× Red Velvet = Desperation
× Tiger Wong = Paradise Island
× Rdza. secunda = Rdcm. Freckles

RED DEVIL STAR	**Mahogany Beauty × Russet Dawn Surprise**	**R. D. Saporita 1975**
RED DOT	**desertorum × Hopewell**	**Osment 1974**
RED LIP	**Randall McLaughlin × splendidum**	**Ruben 1971**
RED SHIELD	**Tiny Tim × Caribbe**	**W. W. G. Moir 1972**
RED VELVET‡	**triquetrum × henekenii**	**W. W. G. Moir 1962**

× Calypso Queen = Bonanza
× Catherine Wilson = Colorful
× Freckles = Cambridge
× Isabella = Midnight Red
× Mixto = Calico Gal
× Red Belt = Desperation
× triquetrum = Shada
× variegatum = Pink Glory

retemeyerauum (see *lindenii‡*)	**species**	
REX ALSTYNE	**Kuwon × concolor**	**A. & M. 1971**
RICHARD SAPORITA	**Mem. Pepita de Restrepo × cebolleta**	**Wallbrunn 1971**
RIO'S SPOT	**Pink Sherbet × Red Belt**	**Ruben 1975**
RIO'S VALENTINE	**Flexoel × triquetrum**	**Ruben 1974**
ROJO	**La Citadelle × desertorum**	**Osment 1974**
RONAELE†‡	**crispum × forbesii**	**Lager 1954**

× Farandole = Connie Ku
× Kultane = Phyllis Ku

ROSE DE MASK	**triquetrum × gauntlettii**	**Jesup 1975**
ROSE HALL	**Tower Isle × Tiny Tim**	**W. W. G. Moir 1968**

× Tiny Tim = Gayle

ROSELLE	**pulchellum × Royal Purple**	**W. W. G. Moir 1975**
ROYAL CLARET	**Rosy Glow × Tiny Tim**	**W. W. G. Moir 1970**

× desertorum = Grandma Dingee

ROYAL PURPLE	**pulchellum × Port Antonio**	**W. W. G. Moir 1973**

× pulchellum = Roselle

RUSSET DAWN SURPRISE — **Mem. Pepita de Restrepo × carthagenense** — **R. D. Saporita 1975**

× Mahogany Beauty = Red Devil Star

SAINT THOMAS — **Walter Isle × Tiny Tim** — **W. W. G. Moir 1973**

SAMANA SANTA — **triquetrum × Osmentii** — **W. W. G. Moir 1972**

SANCHO — **Burgeffianum × varicosum** — **Pff. V. & L. 1974**

SAN JUAN — **triquetrum × leiboldii** — **W. W. G. Moir 1964**

× triquetrum = San-Tri

SAN-TRI — **San Juan × triquetrum** — **Howell 1974**

SARCATUM — **sphacelatum × sarcodes** — **A. & M. 1962**

× marshallianum = Winter Glow
× Nona = Golden State

sarcodes*‡ — **species**

× marshallianum = Summer Gold
× Splinter = Michael Jupp

SAVANNA LA MAR — **Red Belt × Catherine Wilson** — **W. W. G. Moir 1967**

× Alexandria = Savanna Sunset
× Isabella = Irene Van Alstyne
× Stanley Smith = Thelma Beaumont

SAVANNA SUNSET — **Savanna La Mar × Alexandria** — **W. W. G. Moir 1973**

SELLE — **velutinum × Osmentii** — **W. W. G. Moir 1974**

SHADA — **Red Velvet × triquetrum** — **W. W. G. Moir 1972**

SKIPPER KILBOURNE — **pulchellum × variegatum** — **W. W. G. Moir 1963**

× Antigua = Lizzer Belle

SLIP SHOWED — **Kutoo × pulchellum** — **Jesup 1975**

SPANISH WELLS — **Juanita × Hopewell** — **Ruben 1971**

× triquetrum = Oscar Howell

sphacelatum*†‡ — **species**

× barbatum = Mariposa Manchada
× concolor = Goldfinch
× macranthum = Butterfly Sunset
× obryzatum = Sunspot
× ornithorhynchum = Patrapara Charusorn
× Brs. caudata = Brsdm. Moonbeam
× Oda. Matanda = Wils. Acemanda
× Oda. Ray Buckman = Wils. Spaceman

SPLENDID NAN — **splendidum × nanum** — **Wallbrunn 1971**

SPLINTER‡ — **sphacelatum × leucochilum** — **W. W. G. Moir 1959**

× sarcodes = Michael Jupp

splendidum*†‡ — **species**

× nanum = Splendid Nan
× Randall McLaughlin = Red Lip
× Brs. maculata = Brsdm. Mayan Dancer

sprucei‡ — **species**

(Treated for registration purposes as specifically distinct from *Onc. cebolleta,* although they are considered conspecific by some authorities.)

× nanum = Dorothy Isemonger

STANLEY SMITH‡ — **Red Belt × pulchellum** — **W. W. G. Moir 1967**

× Calypso Queen = Queen's Best
× Jamaica = Moshi Moshi
× Savanna La Mar = Thelma Beaumont
× Tiny Tim = Golden Sunset
× triquetrum = Margie Crawford
× Valverde = Clarendon
× William Thurston = Missy

stenotis†‡ — **species**

× maculatum = Ballet

ONCIDIUM

stramineum‡	**species**		
× lanceanum	= Mary Saporita	× lindenii	= Linda Little
SULTAMYRE‡	**Sultane × Palmyre**		**Pff. V. & L. 1959**
× Colm. Sir Jeremiah	= Colm. Martin Orenstein		
SULTANE†	**Boissiense × Farandole**		**V. 1943**
× Gardneri	= Raiatean Ballet		
SUMMER GOLD	**marshallianum × sarcodes**		**V. & N. Jupp 1975 (Slade)**
SUMMIT GOLD†‡	**Ronaele × Boissiense**		**L. & H. 1954**
× luridum	= Golden Lure		
SUNDANCE	**Gardneri × varicosum**		**Slade 1973**
× Lava Flow	= Annie Clare Printer		
SUNSET LUAU	**Waikiki Sunset × Catherine Wilson**		**Ruben 1975**
SUNSPOT	**sphacelatum × obryzatum**		**Rod McLellan Co. 1975**
THELMA BEAUMONT	**Savanna La Mar × Stanley Smith**		**W. W. G. Moir 1972**
THELMA LEIVES	**Tiny Tim × Tiger Wong**		**W. W. G. Moir 1972**
THIEF NECK ISLAND	**Golden Glow × Tiny Tim**		**Barron 1975**
TIFFANY RENEE COLBORNE	**Kultane × Katherine Tompkins**		**Colborne 1975 (Tompkins)**
TIGER WONG	**Red Belt × triquetrum**		**W. W. G. Moir 1968**
× Grand Bahama	= Freeport	× Tiny Tim	= Thelma Leives
× Red Belt	= Paradise Island		
tigrinum*†‡	**species**		
× Oda. Doric	= Wils. Tigerwood	× Odm. Crowborough Sunrise	= Odcdm. Don Richardson
× Oda. Florence Stirling	= Wils. Morelia	× Odm. Moselle	= Odcdm. Hans Neuenhaus
× Oda. Marcris	= Wils. Kurt Rinne	× Odm. hallii	= Odcdm. Halgrin
× Oda. Minel	= Wils. Solana Surprise	× Odm. Omega	= Odcdm. Aztec Tiger
× Oda. Taw	= Wils. Tiger Talk		
× Odm. bictoniense	= Odcdm. Biti		
TINY TIM‡	**triquetrum × desertorum**		**W. W. G. Moir 1957**
× Anse Rouge	= Haitian Red	× pulchellum	= Rainbow
× Bimini	= Masque	× Rose Hall	= Gayle
× Caribbe	= Red Shield	× Stanley Smith	= Golden Sunset
× Golden Glow	= Thief Neck Island	× Tiger Wong	= Thelma Leives
× Isabella	= Maria Luisa Leschhorn	× Walter Isle	= Saint Thomas
× Petionville	= Dessalines	× Comp. speciosa	= Onctta. Sunflake
× Port Royal	= May Pen		
TOWACO	**lankesteri × ampliatum**		**Rumrill 1973**
TRELAWNY	**Peggy Richardson × Port Antonio**		**W. W. G. Moir 1973**
TRIFLEX	**triquetrum × flexuosum**		**Ruben 1975**
TRIMINI	**Mini-skirt × triquetrum**		**Ruben 1974**
triquetrum†‡	**species**		
× Bimini	= Berry Isles	× Kingston	= Kaytee
× Borinquen	= Florida Beauty	× La Citadelle	= Bonita
× Claremont	= Malvern	× lindenii	= Evan Frances Chambers
× Cubense	= Habana	× Mini-skirt	= Trimini
× cuneilabium	= Vera's Friend	× Mirebalais	= Palomita
× Flexoel	= Rio's Valentine	× Osmentii	= Samana Santa
× flexuosum	= Triflex	× Port Royal	= Port Wine
× gauntlettii	= Rose de Mask	× prionochilum	= Antilles
× Henri Christophe	= Charles Yasuda	× Red Velvet	= Shada

triquetrum†‡ *(continued)*

× San Juan	= San-Tri	× Inps. paniculata	= Incdm. Madelyn Schoeppler
× Spanish Wells	= Oscar Howell	× Lchs. labiatus	= Lcdm. Red Hill
× Stanley Smith	= Margie Crawford	× Mcdn. multiflora	= Oncna. Ladies Pride
× withneranum	= Mem. Vera Howell	× Rdza. secunda	= Rdcm. Rio's Red Robin

VALVERDE — **Yellow Jacket × Red Belt** — **W. W. G. Moir 1967**

× Stanley Smith	= Clarendon		

VANAMAN — **Java × microchilum** — **Beard 1974**

varicosum*†‡ — **species**

× Burgeffianum	= Sancho	× Alcra. Pacesetter	= Alcra. Palolo
× Gardneri	= Sundance	× Mtssa. Cartagena	= Alcra. Monte Cristo
× Juanita	= Juanita Gold	× Mtssa. Charles M. Fitch	= Alcra. Surprise Creek
× Kultane	= Rachel Lee	× Rdcm. Norma Faye	= Rdcm. Rio
× montanum	= Waiomao Gold		

variegatum†‡ — **species**

× haitiense	= ann-hadderae (Nat. hyb. 1972); Les Cayes (reg'd. grex 1964)	× Red Velvet	= Pink Glory
× leiboldii	= cubense (Nat. hyb.); Cubense (hort.)	× velutinum	= varvelum (Nat. hyb. 1972); Varvel (reg'd. grex 1971)

VARIMYRE‡ — **Sultamyre × varicosum** — **E. Iwanaga 1963**

× forbesii	= Goldrausch		

VARVEL — **variegatum × velutinum** — **W. W. G. Moir 1971**

(Also described as a Nat. hyb. *Onc.* × *varvelum* in 1972. Future registered hybrids from either Varvel or *varvelum* will be listed under Varvel.)

varvelum (see grex *Onc.* Varvel) — **variegatum × velutinum** — **Nat. hyb. 1972; W. W. G. Moir 1971**

(Hybrids from either *varvelum* or Varvel will be listed under Varvel.)

velutinum‡ — **species**

× Osmentii	= Selle	× variegatum	= varvelum (Nat. hyb. 1972); Varvel (reg'd grex 1971)

ventilabrum — **species**

× Oda. Carmine	= Wils. Rock Island		

VERA'S FRIEND — **triquetrum × cuneilabium** — **Howell 1974**

WAIKIKI SUNSET‡ — **pulchellum × desertorum** — **Okubo 1957 (W. W. G. Moir)**

× Calypso Queen	= Kensington	× Erma Warne	= Pink Ears
× Catherine Wilson	= Sunset Luau		

WAIOMAO GOLD — **montanum × varicosum** — **V. & N. Jupp 1973 (Kirch)**

× Gardneri	= Allyn Gold	× Nona	= Marjorie Jupp
× Lava Flow	= Golden Ember	× Raiatean Ballet	= Libby Hawley

WALTER ISLE — **prionochilum × pulchellum** — **W. W. G. Moir 1968**

× Tiny Tim	= Saint Thomas		

wentworthianum*†‡ — **species**

× altissimum	= Clyde Des Sain	× Dam. Moselle	= Odcdm. Solana
× Brs. longissima	= Brsdm. Gilded Urchin		

ONCIDIUM

WILLIAM THURSTON	**Red Belt × Tiny Tim**	**W. W. G. Moir 1969**
× Stanley Smith	= Missy	
WINTER GLOW	**marshallianum × Sarcatum**	**George Black 1973**
withneranum	**species**	
× triquetrum	= Mem. Vera Howell	
YELLOW CHARM	**onustum × henekenii**	**R. F. Fuchs 1975 (Originator unknown)**
zebrinum	**species**	
× Milt. May Moir	= Mtdm. El Hatillo	

OPSISANDA

BEATRICE BURNS	**Vdps. gigantea × V. Eisenhower**	**Orchid Pacifica 1974**
CONSTELLATION	**V. Mem. T. Iwasaki × Vdps. gigantea**	**S'pore Orchids 1973**
DENIPAR	**V. denisoniana × Vdps. parishii**	**Kasetsart Univ. 1975**
FASCINATION	**V. Josephine van Brero × May M. Kawanishi**	**S'pore Orchids 1964**
× V. sanderana	= Opulence	
GINO OOI	**Vdps. parishii × V. Wongse**	**Ooi Leng Sun 1975**
MOONGLEAM	**V. dearei × Vdps. gigantea**	**S'pore Orchids 1973**
OPULENCE	**Fascination × V. sanderana**	**S'pore Orchids 1973**
RUMRILL	**Vdps. parishii × V. Rothschildiana**	**Rumrill 1975**
THIN THAI NGAM	**V. brunnea × Vdps. parishii**	**Banluesin 1974 (Thanchitt)**

OPSISTYLIS

MEMORIA MARY NATTRASS	**Vdps. gigantea × Rhy. gigantea**	**Redlinger 1972**

OSMOGLOSSUM

pulchellum (see Odontoglossum pulchellum*‡)	**species**	

PALMERARA

RAYMOND PALMER	**Btst. Silver Star × Zspm. labiosum**	**George Black 1973**
× Agn. cyanea	= Dwsa. Psythenis	

PAPHIOPEDILUM

ACAPULCO GOLD	**McLaren Park × San Carlos**	**Hawley 1973 (Rod McLellan Co.)**
ACCORDANCE	**Cadence × Luna**	**Ratcliffe 1972**
ACE HIGH	**Betty Wilson × Winston Churchill**	**Hanes 1975**
ACOLYTE	**sukhakulii × spiceranum**	**Thomdel 1974**
ACTAEUS*†‡ (syn. Actaeus Bianca)	**insigne × Leeanum**	**Veitch 1895**
× Hellas	= Betty Bell	
ACTAEUS BIANCA (see Actaeus*†‡)		
ADAMS APPLE	**chamberlainianum × appletonianum**	**Cryder 1974**
A. DIMMOCK*	**Godseffianum × druryi**	**S. 1902**
× Paeony	= King Alfred	

PAPHIOPEDILUM

ADORNABLE — **Paeony × F. C. Puddle** — **Ratcliffe 1972**
ADORNMENT — **Harbur × Burleigh Mohur** — **Rod McLellan Co. 1972**
ADULATION — **Littledean × Rimalang** — **Rod McLellan Co. 1973**
ADVANCEMENT — **Blagrose × Mecca** — **Hanes 1969 (Sherman)**

× Betty Wilson = Progression | × Farnmoore = Farmingdale
× Bourneva = Serendipity | × Wendbourn = Wendfall
× Carl Keyes = Redwave |

ADVENTURE — **victoria-regina × stonei** — **Rod McLellan Co. 1975**
AGNES DE BURC†‡ — **Dickler × Gwen Hannen** — **Jensen 1940**

× Caddiana = Sheila Hanes | × insigne = Halle
× Derdene = Candle Light | × Mariano Martin = Fran Rothman

AIKO YAMAMOTO‡ — **Finetta × Yumedono** — **Hiroyuki Yamamoto 1957**

× Langtye = May Green | × Moreton Bay = Aloha Wakami Toyota

AIR DE BALLET†‡ — **Akeley × Chatwode** — **B. 1947**

× Kismet = Circlet |

AKELEY*† — **Grace Darling × Josette** — **B. 1937**

× Caddiana = Caddley | × Euryostom = Akstom

AKSTOM — **Euryostom × Akeley** — **Kensington 1973**
ALABASTER BROOK — **Hellas × Huddle** — **G. A. Wright 1974**
ALBACON — **Albion × concolor** — **Cryder 1975**
ALBION*†‡ — **Astarte × niveum** — **L. 1922**

× concolor = Albacon | × Gorse = Columba
× Doramasan = Trouvere | × Lemon Hart = Heart of England

ALBULA — **Trismegistris × Rosalie** — **Gunzenhauser 1969 (Cosanka)**

× Monte Generoso = Monte Rosso |

ALDEN‡ — **Recruit × Blendia** — **Ratcliffe 1968**

× Hollywood = Alderwood | × Small World = World Cruise

ALDERGROVE‡ — **Beaufort × Ophelia** — **L. 1950**

× Trigal = Meijō |

ALDERWOOD — **Alden × Hollywood** — **Ratcliffe 1971**
ALENCON — **Fugue × Rollright** — **Pff. V. & L. 1975**
ALETSCH — **Mississippi × Fred Cosanka** — **Gunzenhauser 1975**
ALICE GRIPP — **Honey Dew × San Carlos** — **Santa Barbara 1974**
ALICE PINK — **F. C. Puddle × Lockinge** — **Ratcliffe 1972**
ALIESCUM — **Floralies × Cullum** — **Sieff 1957**

× Baroque = Bravura | × Mildred Hunter = Westfalen
× Botan = Flamelet | × Winston Churchill = Lybra

ALISAL — **callosum × robinsonii** — **Cryder 1974**
ALLENDALE†‡ — **Gold Mohur × Thias** — **C. Cookson 1936**

× Golden Orb = Limagold | × Miriam Sacher = Merry Andrew

ALLRIGHT — **Allure × Rollright** — **Pff. V. & L. 1975**
ALLURE†‡ — **Nesta II × Robert Paterson** — **Cooke 1938**

× Raïta = Volpone | × Rollright = Allright

ALOHA WAKAMI TOYOTA — **Moreton Bay × Aiko Yamamoto** — **Toyota 1975**

PAPHIOPEDILUM

ALTELS — **Wildstrubel × Fred Cosanka** — **Gunzenhauser 1975**

ALTHEA — **Hestred × Noyo** — **Tonkin 1967 (Rod McLellan Co.)**

× Winston Churchill	= Varina Vaughn		

amabile (Hallier 1897) — **species**

(See *bullenianum**. The epithet Amabile was used for the grex *hookerae* × Sementa by Bleu in 1890, which precludes the later use of the epithet *amabile* for a species; the earliest synonym *bullenianum* is therefore used for this species for registration purposes as a parent.)

AMANDA — **Radley × Paeony** — **Sieff 1965**

× Baroque	= Merrythought	× Izalco	= Zalamanda
× Canasta	= Play-Girl	× Jamaycus	= Comely Ann
× Chenille	= Armilla	× Loganna	= Ringarose
× Compton	= Veritilario	× Lucid	= Mandy-lu
× Dusty Miller	= Rosy Prospect	× Lyric	= Song-bird
× Flamenco	= Jolliday	× Qantas	= Joy-ride
× Fred Cosanka	= Selun	× Rampion	= Cardinal Polish
× Geelong	= City Lark	× Samantha	= Amaranthea
× Gitana	= Romany Gay	× Startler	= Some Lady
× Hazel Hankey	= Vibrance	× Wendbourn	= Wandrian
× Heather Bell	= Rapturist	× Winston Churchill	= Amandahill
× Impeyan	= Impetuous Lass		

AMANDAHILL — **Winston Churchill × Amanda** — **McElderry 1975**

AMARANTHEA — **Samantha × Amanda** — **Ratcliffe 1974**

AMARILLO — **Hellas × Bromohur** — **Hanes 1972**

AMBELLINA — **Hellas × Challow** — **Ratcliffe 1972**

AMBERDALE — **Restdale × Amber Star** — **Ratcliffe 1969**

× Heather Bell	= Another Round		

AMBER-GLOW — **Hellas × Reezy** — **Hanes 1973**

AMBER STAR‡ — **Blendia × Beauté** — **Ratcliffe 1965**

× Audrey Sacher	= Pirouette	× Inferno	= Blazing Comet
× Beauté	= Star Cluster	× Qantas	= Star Spree
× Botan	= Star Turn	× Small World	= Starry World
× Cholsey	= Carfax	× World Venture	= Dream World

AMBIENCE — **Chilton × Honey Dew** — **Ratcliffe 1962**

× Sunland	= Goldmantle		

AMBROSIA — **Minster Lovell × Bradford** — **Ratcliffe 1965**

× Celadon	= Belinda Green	× Sunwillow	= Dewy Green
× Sungrove	= Petalon		

ANACONDA — **Brailes × Aldergrove** — **Stirling 1961**

× Roger Coulson	= Pumblechook		

ANENA — **Nena × Ayot St. Lawrence** — **Hanes 1962 (Sherman)**

× Gwenpur	= Gwenann	× Milmoore	= Milnena

ANGELA WILSON — **glaucophyllum × Cymatodes** — **Voelker 1972**

ANIMO — **Clementine H. Churchill × Solferino** — **Hark 1973**

ANITA*† — **Actaeus × Sanacderae** — **Adamson 1927**

× Avine	= Tom Thumb	× glaucophyllum	= Betty Nichols Powell

ANNA-NUTKIN — **Beechmast × Loganna** — **Ratcliffe 1975**

PAPHIOPEDILUM

ANNA PAVLOVA†‡ — **Gwen Dixon × Sumurun** — **S. 1943**
× Gwen Hannen = Squamish

ANN BARLOW†‡ — **Anthony Eden × Warrior** — **Barlow 1935**
× Mildred Hunter = Grand March

ANN BELINDA — **Olinda × Botan** — **Ratcliffe 1973**
ANNE DAVIES — **Cardinal Mercier × Nitens-Leeanum** — **King 1932**
× Milnetta = Mildavies

ANNE GRIPP — **Desire × Margaret Brands** — **Santa Barbara 1973**
ANNETTA HANES — **Crescent Meadow × Caddiana** — **Hanes 1975**
ANN HARPER†‡ — **Diana Broughton × Grace Darling** — **Jensen 1945**
× Glasnevin = Minquas
× Hellas = Honeybrook
× Rosy Dawn = Crystal Brook

ANOTHER ROUND — **Amberdale × Heather Bell** — **Ratcliffe 1975**
ANOTHER WORLD — **Geelong × Small World** — **Ratcliffe 1972**
ANOVATION — **Captivation × Loganna** — **Ratcliffe 1975**
APACHE — **Winston Churchill × Red Angel** — **W. W. Wilson 1974**
APPLE HONEY — **Sunol × Oscar Sherman** — **Santa Barbara 1974**
appletonianum‡ — **species**
× chamberlainianum = Adams Apple
× Cymatodes = Salinas
× sukhakulii = Nisqually
× venustum = Mem. Heinie Christ

APRIL‡ — **Dervish × Diana Broughton** — **Cooke 1945**
× Brailes = Colin Aislabie
× Minster Lovell = Larkfield
× Sunrise = April Sun

APRIL SUN — **Sunrise × April** — **Lodge 1973**
APROPO — **Diversion × Brownly** — **Rod McLellan Co. 1973**
AQUARELLA — **Giallo × F. C. Puddle** — **Ratcliffe 1971**
ARAMINGO — **Wallur × McLaren Park** — **W. W. Wilson 1975**
ARAPAHO — **Great Mogul × Burpham** — **W. W. WIlson 1973**
argus* — **species**
× glaucophyllum = Mascotte
× venustum = Christmas Cheer

ARGYLL — **Bagley × Bailson** — **M. 1974 (C.)**

ARISTOCRATIC BEAUTY — **Wendover × Chardmoore** — **Rod McLellan Co. 1971**
ARISTOTE — **Calvi × Blendia** — **Pff. V. & L. 1975**
ARLINA — **Atlantis × Tearlath** — **A. & B. 1954**
× Milionette = Eminence
× Perilise = Boston Tea Party

ARMILLA — **Chenille × Amanda** — **Ratcliffe 1973**
ARNE HONI — **Wendbourn × fairieanum** — **Holm Nielsen 1975**
ARTSHADES — **Bagshot × Bonheure** — **Hanes 1975**
ASMAR — **Aspac × Martinique** — **Pff. V. & L. 1974**
ASPAC — **Blendia × Rollright** — **Yamato-Noen 1969**
× Exelmans = Davout
× Martinique = Asmar
× Regent = Natacha

ASSELINE — **Velizy × Marie-Galante** — **Pff. V. & L. 1975**
ASSINIBOINE — **glaucophyllum × Hellas** — **W. W. Wilson 1974**
ASTARTE*† — **insigne × Psyche** — **St. Quintin 1914**
× Hymettus = Stardora

PAPHIOPEDILUM

ASTERIA	**F. C. Puddle × Celadon**	**Ratcliffe 1973**
ATLANTIS*†‡	**Cardinal Mercier × Chloris**	**B. 1927**

× Leven	= Lelantis	× Pinkridge	= Pink Panties
× Menthule	= Thulantis	× Vallarrow	= Vallantis

AUDREY SACHER	**Gold Mohur × Beauté**	**Sieff 1966 (Ratcliffe)**

× Amber Star	= Pirouette

AUNINA	**Solferino × Bingleyense**	**Hark 1973**
AVINE‡	**Grace Darling × Margaret MacCaull**	**Basson 1960 (E. C. Wilcox)**

× Anita	= Tom Thumb	× McLaren Park	= Carillon
× Crescent Meadow	= Silver Dollar	× Radar	= Joe Johnson
× Golden Moon	= Royal Flush	× Yerba Buena	= Via Angel Verde
× Greenhorn	= Via Victoria		

AYJAY	**Maginot × Paeony**	**A. J. Bell 1974**
AYLESBURY*†‡	**Euryostom × Everest**	**B. 1937**

× Ayot St. Lawrence	= Aylesyot	× Redstart	= Sylvan Glade
× Bell Ringer	= Merrybells	× Winston Churchill	= Normandy

AYLESYOT	**Ayot St. Lawrence × Aylesbury**	**Hanes 1973**
AYOT SAINT LAWRENCE†‡	**Cardinal Mercier × Roundhead**	**S. 1937**

× Aylesbury	= Aylesyot

BAGSHOT†‡	**Euryostom × Rosemary Waithman**	**B. 1944**

× Bonheure	= Artshades	× Omar	= Lillian Pitta
× Mildrington	= King Lear	× Wendwater	= Wendshot

BAGLEY	**Langley Pride × Bagshot**	**B. 1958**

× Bailson	= Argyll

BAHRAM*†‡	**Anita × Grace Darling**	**Cooke 1935**

× Renton	= Baton

BAILSON	**Banchory × Betty Wilson**	**C. 1961**

× Bagley	= Argyll

BALACLAVA*†‡	**Gwen Hannen × Warrior**	**L. de R. 1933**

× Challow	= Conjola	× Shagreen	= Green Turban
× Dalla	= Talladale	× Small World	= Mad Hatter
× Resominster	= Saxony		

BALLET GIRL*†‡	**(almost certainly a Leeanum 'Clinkerberryanum' hybrid)**	**H. pre-1930**

× chamberlainianum	= Tip Top	× haynaldianum	= Bob Cryder
× Decameron	= Choreography	× Olivia	= West Virginia
× fairieanum	= Fairy Slipper		

BALMBERG	**Frieda Gunzenhauser × Miriam Sacher**	**Gunzenhauser 1975**
BALMHORN	**Princess Diana × Silberhorn**	**Gunzenhauser 1975**
BANDARILLA	**Danella × Blondel**	**Ratcliffe 1973**
BANDIT KING	**Baroque × Botan**	**Ratcliffe 1975**
BANNER MAN	**Robert Paterson × Cadence**	**Ratcliffe 1972**
BARBARITA	**Barbarrosa × Raïta**	**Pff. V. & L. 1967**

× Milchurch	= Bunker Hill

PAPHIOPEDILUM

BARBARROSA†‡ — **Wendwater × Fulminster** — **B. 1952**

× Regent = Capdepera
× Warrior = Campaigner

BARBARY‡ — **Barbarrosa × Petronella** — **Ratcliffe 1963**

× Botan = Enameline

barbatum*†‡ — **species**

× chamberlainianum = Carmel
× linii = Barlina
× Paeony = Royalet
× Papyrus = Primitive

BARLINA — **linii × barbatum** — **Ratcliffe 1974 (Rands)**

BARNABY BRIGHT — **Chipmunk × Botan** — **Ratcliffe 1973**

BAROQUE — **Tapestry × Peter Adam** — **Ratcliffe 1965**

× Aliescum = Bravura
× Amanda = Merrythought
× Botan = Bandit King
× Clemency = Tristana
× Danella = Dartington
× Floramond = Roquette
× Grove = Woodcrest
× Highlight = High Perfection
× Lockinge = Kilverstone
× Lombardy = Barytone
× Magrose = Cherry Plum
× Tombola = Royal Gamble

BARYTA — **Blagrose × Compton** — **Ratcliffe 1971**

BARYTONE — **Lombardy × Baroque** — **Ratcliffe 1973**

BATON — **Renton × Bahram** — **Herbert Bernhart 1973 (Originator unknown)**

BATTERSEA — **Whitemoor × Bradford** — **Morgenstern 1956**

× Dusty Miller = Olney Mill
× Sheerline = Sealine

BATTLE OF EGYPT — **Miracle × Redstart** — **S. 1942**

× Chickadee = Redbrook

BAVARIA — **Hickstead × Huntsman** — **Stewart Inc. 1974 (Wichmann)**

BEACON POINT — **Compass × Loganna** — **Ratcliffe 1973**

BEATRICE ERNST — **Evansrose × Winston Churchill** — **Ernst 1973**

BEAUBOROUGH‡ — **Beaufort × Bidborough** — **L. 1957**

× Langtye = Rica Gold

BEAUTÉ†‡ — **Great Mogul × Warrior** — **A. E. Dale 1933**

× Amber Star = Star Cluster
× Bell Ringer = Bell Beauté
× Buccaneer = High Seas
× Chardmoore = Kingsize
× Milmoore = Mem. Franz Wichmann
× Nowara = Octave
× Vallarrow = Red Flame

BEAUTY GOSHIMA — **Cavalcade × Goshima** — **Ishikawa 1973 (Ikeda)**

BEECHMAST — **Blagrose × Dalla** — **Ratcliffe 1965**

× Crimbourne = Monte Brione
× Loganna = Anna-nutkin

BEEDON‡ — **Dalla × Minster Lovell** — **Ratcliffe 1958**

× Yellow Crest = Cresdon

BELACCOYLE — **Clemency × Tapestry** — **Ratcliffe 1972**

BEL AIR‡ — **Pilgrim × Abaran** — **E. C. Wilcox 1955**

× Margaret MacCaull = Belcaull

BELAMY — **Blagrose × Lockinge** — **Ratcliffe 1972**

BELCAULL — **Bel Air × Margaret MacCaull** — **Craig's 1974**

PAPHIOPEDILUM

BELINDA GREEN	**Ambrosia × Celadon**	**Ratcliffe 1973**
BELLADENE	**Denehurst × bellatulum**	**Clark Day Jr. 1975**
BELLALBA	**bellatulum × King of Sweden**	**McElderry 1975**
bellatulum*†‡	**species**	

× Denehurst	= Belladene	× McLaren Park	= Belodi
× F. C. Puddle	= Weissenstein	× Matchless	= Coranta
× Harbur	= Harbell	× Menthule	= Myzantha
× King of Sweden	= Bellalba	× Wendbourn	= Wendbell

BELL BEAUTÉ	**Beauté × Bell Ringer**	**Hanes 1972**
BELL CLIFF	**Bell Ringer × Sea Cliff**	**Hanes 1971**
BELL RINGER‡	**Chardmoore × Woodburn**	**E. C. Wilcox 1949**

× Aylesbury	= Merrybells	× Sea Cliff	= Bell Cliff
× Beauté	= Bell Beauté	× W. N. Evans	= Red Creek

BELODI	**bellatulum × McLaren Park**	**McElderry 1975**
BENENDEN†‡	**Chrysostom × Mem. J. H. Walker**	**L. 1936**

× Hestred	= Maroon Beauty	× Montecito	= Yahagi

BENGAL LANCERS	**haynaldianum × parishii**	**Thomdel 1974**
BENHURST	**Happy Ben × Evanhurst**	**Cryder 1974 (E. C. Wilcox)**

× haynaldianum	= Redbud		

BENLOMOND	**Royale × Tombola**	**Ratcliffe 1971**
BENTE HONI	**Desire × Buckhurst**	**Holm Nielsen 1975**
BERNADETTE*	**Chloris × Robert Paterson**	**B. 1931**

× Sparsholt	= Spardetta		

BERNSTEIN	**San-Actaeus × Chilton**	**Wichmann 1966**

× Turmalin	= Turmastein		

BESNOW	**Yerba Buena × niveum**	**Rod McLellan Co. 1973**
BESTCREST	**Betty Bracey × Crescent Meadow**	**Hanes 1973**
BETSY ROSS	**Ukiah × Floralies**	**Stewart Inc. 1974**
BETTY ANDERSON	**Tommie Hanes × Kay Rinaman**	**Hanes 1975**
BETTY-ANNA	**Betty Bracey × Caddiana**	**Hanes 1973**
BETTY BELL	**Actaeus × Hellas**	**A. J. Bell 1974**
BETTY BRACEY	**Gwenpur × Actaeus**	**Bracey 1956**

× Caddiana	= Betty-Anna	× Julia Mash	= Brett Hughes
× Crescent Meadow	= Bestcrest	× Michael Stewart	= Emerald Isle
× La Honda	= Spring Morning		

BETTY NICHOLS POWELL	**glaucophyllum × Anita**	**The Orchid House 1974**
BETTY WILSON‡	**Portsmouth × Maginot**	**B. 1951**

× Advancement	= Progression	× Winston Churchill	= Ace High

BEVIS	**Christopher × Blendia**	**Ratcliffe 1974**

× Wendbourn	= Wood Magic		

BIBURY†	**Chardmoore × Gee Saxon**	**L. W. Brummitt 1940**

× Maudiae	= Mount Vernon		

BINGLEYENSE*†‡	**charlesworthii × Harrisianum**	**K. 1899**

× F. C. Puddle	= Spotted Puddle	× Solferino	= Aunina

PAPHIOPEDILUM

BIT-O'-SUNSHINE | **McLaren Park × Diversion** | **Rod McLellan Co. 1965**

× Van Ness = Mem. Arthur Falk

BITTER LEMON | **Selina × Lemon Hart** | **Ratcliffe 1971**

BIRDSONG | **Impeyan × Cadence** | **Ratcliffe 1971**

BLACK MOORE | **Black Thorpe × Farnmoore** | **S.A. 1960**

× Chardmoore = Torquay

BLACK THORPE†‡ | **Dixon Thorpe × J. M. Black** | **S.A. 1946**

× fairieanum = Wichita
× Winston Churchill = Duncan York

BLAGROSE*†‡ | **Cardinal Mercier × Eurybiades** | **Cooke 1939**

× Canasta = Polaris
× Clementine H. Churchill = Elizabeth Steen
× Compton = Baryta
× Culmo = Calimosa
× Floralies = Florosa
× Floramond = Chillipink
× Harbur = Hargrose
× Lockinge = Belamy
× Milionette = Khartoum
× Milmoore = Chance Medley
× Momag = Magrose
× Neil McKerral = Rose Kerral
× Pittsburg = Roseburg
× Questover = Questox
× Ravenswing = Pavo

BLANCHE SAWYER | **F. C. Puddle × Gwen Hannen** | **Clark Day Jr. 1962**

× niveum = Pearlesant
× Paeony = Mem. Tom Brown
× Yerba Buena = Frosty Glow

BLAZING COMET | **Amber Star × Inferno** | **Ratcliffe 1972**

BLENDIA*†‡ | **Lucarola × Mem. F. M. Ogilvie** | **Cooke 1938**

× Cadence = Quartette
× Calvi = Aristote
× Christopher = Bevis
× Exelmans = Calvi
× Geelong = Broché
× Nowara = Mergola
× Sharnden = Parry Gripp

BLENHEIM PALACE | **Winston Churchill × Floralies** | **Stewart Inc. 1971 (J. E. Wilson)**

BLIND MAN'S BUFF | **Canasta × Masked Light** | **Ratcliffe 1974**

BLONDEL | **Gorse × Inca** | **Ratcliffe 1962**

× Copperware = Jolly Copper
× Danella = Bandarilla
× F. C. Puddle = Watersprite
× Sarella = Tangold
× Sharon = Lady Honey
× Tafel Rose = Gaystone

BOB CRYDER | **haynaldianum × Ballet Girl** | **Stewart Inc. 1975 (Cryder)**

BOB GUNTHER | **Fairburn × Mildred Hunter** | **R. K. Meredith 1974**

BOLERO | **Dramatic × Graceful** | **A. & B. 1963**

× Sussex Gold = Golden Jacket

BONHEURE‡ | **Gayhurst × Hillesden** | **B. 1947**

× Bagshot = Artshades
× Floralies = Roughhewn
× Orchilla = Plumly
× Sandra Mary = California Queen

BONIFACIO | **Rollright × Calvi** | **Pff. V. & L. 1975**

BORBURN†‡ | **Bordube × Chardmoore** | **A. & B. 1937**

× F. C. Puddle = Botan-Yuki
× Mariano Martin = Green Heart
× Mildred Hunter = Portelet Bay
× Swiftdene = Bouley Bay

BORDENE | **Bordube × Denehurst** | **W. W. Wilson 1972 (Wyld Court)**

× Glasnevin = Huron

BORDUBE*†‡	**Florence Spencer × Viridissimum**	**Miss Moore 1928**

× Denehurst	= Bordene	× Dianita	= Margie Pitta

BORDURE†‡	**Bordube × Diana Broughton**	**Lawson 1943**

× Gowerianum	= Dolores Carrion		

BORN FREE	**Pudsana × Golden Acres**	**Rod McLellan Co. 1971**
BOSTON TEA PARTY	**Perilise × Arlina**	**Stewart Inc. 1974**
BOTAN	**Paeony × Wendbourn**	**Kimura 1963 (Ratcliffe)**

× Aliescum	= Flamelet	× Jamaycus	= Crimson Whirl
× Amber Star	= Star Turn	× Lockinge	= Rosy Dusk
× Barbary	= Enameline	× Lyric	= Tenorino
× Baroque	= Bandit King	× Momag	= Jasperite
× Canasta	= Rouelle	× Olinda	= Ann Belinda
× Chipmunk	= Barnaby Bright	× Radley	= Jentique
× Dalla	= Santalin	× Redstart	= Gay Bunting
× Dusty Miller	= Show Boat	× Royale	= Tudoresque
× Flamenco	= Valeta	× Samantha	= Manchette
× Floramond	= Kildary	× Startler	= Startan Ruby
× Florosa	= Major Rose	× Sunland	= Cimarine
× Geelong	= Capital Red	× Tapestry	= Fine Arts
× Grove	= Ventora	× Timbrel	= Manifesto
× Heather Bell	= Rederica	× Tombola	= Cloverica

BOTAN-YUKI	**Borburn × F. C. Puddle**	**Tokugawa 1971**
bouganvilleanum	**species**	

× chamberlainianum	= South Pacific	× sukhakulii	= Helen Milton

BOULEY BAY	**Borburn × Swiftdene**	**E. E. Young 1973**
BOURNDILLY‡	**Santa Claus × Wendbourn**	**W. W. Wilson 1959**

× Winston Churchill	= Emistesigo		

BOURNETTE	**Milionette × Bourneva**	**Stewart Inc. 1971**
BOURNEVA	**Wendbourn × W. N. Evans**	**C. 1959**

× Advancement	= Serendipity	× Milionette	= Bournette

BOXFORD†‡	**Euryostom × Welcome**	**B. 1941**

× Winston Churchill	= Marlborough		

BRADFORD†‡	**Bahram × Grace Darling**	**K. 1950**

× Jocelyn	= Mount Fuji	× Sunland	= Whimsey Green

BRAILES†‡	**Doris Black × Gold Mohur**	**L. W. Brummitt 1940**

× April	= Colin Aislabie	× Gwenpur	= Lou Sasso

BRAVURA	**Aliescum × Baroque**	**Ratcliffe 1973**
BRENNER PASS	**Festive Hunter × Winston Churchill**	**Stewart Inc. 1973**
BRENO	**Hillthorpe × Schneeflocke**	**Gunzenhauser 1975**
BRETT HUGHES	**Julia Mash × Betty Bracey**	**Lambert Day 1975**
BRIGHT ALARY	**Startler × Floramond**	**Ratcliffe 1971**
BROADWATER‡	**King George VI × Angel Luscombe**	**A. & B. 1953**

× Mecca	= Monmouth Gem		

BROADWAY	**Great Mogul × Perseus**	**Duveen 1939**

× Gitana	= Lipperland		

BROCHÉ	**Blendia × Geelong**	**Ratcliffe 1973**

PAPHIOPEDILUM

BROMFIELD — **Bromohur × Burleigh Mohur** — **Rod McLellan Co. 1957 (E. W. McLellan)**

× Pittsburg	= Marty		

BROMOHUR†‡ — **Diana Broughton × Gold Mohur** — **S.A. 1946**

× Hellas	= Amarillo		

BROWN GLEN — **Glenpit × Bromka** — **Rod McLellan Co. 1965**

× Omar	= Gingersnap		

BROWNLY — **Burleigh Mohur × Littledean** — **Rod McLellan Co. 1966**

× Diversion	= Apropo	× Haroun	= Cashmere

BROWN OUSEL† — **Chrysostom × Elidia** — **W. G. Berry 1950**

× Rockland	= Passwang		

BRULMOORE — **Doris Brummitt × Milmoore** — **E. C. Wilcox 1970**

× Winston Churchill	= Everett Wilcox		

BRUNELLA — **Petronella × Floramond** — **Ratcliffe 1971**

BRUNSWICK — **Hickstead × Minster Lovell** — **Stewart Inc. 1974 (Wichmann)**

BUCCANEER† — **Chloris × Warrior** — **B. 1928**

× Beauté	= High Seas	× Winston Churchill	= Wineer

BUCHBERG — **Fred Cosanka × Shooting Star** — **Gunzenhauser 1975**

BUCK EYE — **Pittsburg × Neil McKerral** — **Thomdel 1975**

BUCKHURST — **Spring Vigil × Greenville** — **L. 1964**

× Desire	= Bente Honi		

bullenianum* (syn. *amabile*, Hallier 1897) — **species**

× curtisii	= Gentle Breeze	× spiceranum	= Small Fry
× fairieanum	= Mary-Irene	× sukhakulii	= Quinault
× philippinense	= Oriental Magic		

BUNKER HILL — **Barbarita × Milchurch** — **Stewart Inc. 1975**

BURLEIGH MOHUR†‡ — **Burleigh Brae × Gold Mohur** — **S.A. 1946**

× Harbur	= Adornment		

BURNHAM† — **Senator × Warrior** — **B. 1928**

× Showoff	= Criterion Creek		

BURPHAM — **Finesse × Winston Churchill** — **L. 1967**

× City	= Red Eagle	× Olympic Forest	= Santee
× Great Mogul	= Arapaho	× Redezelle	= Pima
× Matchless	= Conshohocken	× Winston Churchill	= Tree of Legend

B. WHITE — **Edenbridge × Susan Mercier** — **Hankey 1948**

× Desert Sun	= Mervyn Grant	× Letitzia	= Levity

CABALLEROS — **Neil McKerral × Wendwater** — **Hanes 1971**

CADDIANA — **Golden Diana × Cadia** — **Rod McLellan Co. 1963**

× Agnes de Burc	= Sheila Hanes	× Denehurst	= Verde Oro
× Akeley	= Caddley	× Golden Acres	= Cherokee
× Betty Bracey	= Betty-Anna	× Gwenpur	= Leah Hanes
× Crescent Meadow	= Annetta Hanes	× Halo	= Green Jade

CADDIANA *(continued)*

× Lemon Slipper	= French Creek	× Reezy	= Little Irene
× Malibu	= Fredrico	× Yerba Buena	= Via Muchos Ninos
× Mariano Martin	= Lambert Day		

CADDLEY	**Akeley × Caddiana**	**Hanes 1973**
CADENCE	**Allure × Paeony**	**Ratcliffe 1963**

× Blendia	= Quartette	× Mildred Hunter	= Choco
× Canberra	= Town Festival	× Qantas	= Wings of Song
× Dazzler	= Melodist	× Regent	= Royal Trill
× Geelong	= Musicality	× Robert Paterson	= Banner Man
× Highlight	= Sonnetta	× Rollright	= Glamour Spot
× Impeyan	= Birdsong	× Small World	= World Song
× Ingcar	= Mishawaka	× Sparsholt	= Catrillo
× Lombardy	= Doremy	× Testmatch	= Catch-song
× Luna	= Accordance	× Timbrel	= Flying Colours
× Mendocino	= Zuni		

CAJTO	**Cameo × Winston Churchill**	**W. W. Wilson 1972**
CALIFORNIA QUEEN	**Sandra Mary × Bonheure**	**Rod McLellan Co. 1971**
CALIMOSA	**Culmo × Blagrose**	**Ratcliffe 1975**
CALLOSO-BARBATUM*† (syn. Mirabile)	**barbatum × callosum**	**Jolibois 1890**

× sukhakulii	= Wedding Bells		

callosum*†‡	**species**	

× glaucophyllum	= James Fisher	× Sanacderae	= Ravensberg
× linii	= Spook	× sukhakulii	= Montagnard
× robinsonii	= Alisal		

CALVERLEY‡	**Mrs. William Pickup × Windrush**	**A. & B. 1952**

× Winston Churchill	= Motoo Kimura		

CALVI	**Exelmans × Blendia**	**Pff. V. & L. 1973**

× Blendia	= Aristote	× Rollright	= Bonifacio

CALYX	**Onyx × callosum**	**V. 1953**

× Gaël	= Lyxel		

CAMBERWICK	**Sunland × Lemora**	**Ratcliffe 1972**
CAMEO*†‡	**Etta × Nesta II**	**Cooke 1937**

× Dahmoy	= Seeker	× Nowara	= Newcomer
× Dilys	= Campanero	× Winston Churchill	= Cajto
× Langley Pride	= Mem. Charles Sladden		

CAMPAIGNER	**Barbarrosa × Warrior**	**Ratcliffe 1974 (Sieff)**
CAMPANERO	**Dilys × Cameo**	**Ratcliffe 1971**

× Sparsholt	= Max Mann		

CAMPION	**niveum × Lucid**	**Ratcliffe 1963**

× Silvara	= Her Grace		

CANASTA‡	**Floralies × Peter Adam**	**Ratcliffe 1967**

× Amanda	= Play-Girl	× Loganna	= Playtime
× Blagrose	= Polaris	× Lyric	= Glee Singer
× Botan	= Rouelle	× Masked Light	= Blind Man's Buff
× Challow	= Country Dance	× Orchilla	= Orcadian
× Cholsey	= Merriment	× Rosewood	= Teryrose
× Lockinge	= Peacemaker	× Small World	= World Cup

PAPHIOPEDILUM

CANBERRA‡ | **Cameo × Robert Paterson** | **B. 1942**

× Cadence = Town Festival
× Challow = Town Major
× Compton = Jamboree
× Farnmoore = Farnberra
× Heather Bell = Cittadella
× Strawberry Fair = Fair City
× Winston Churchill = Canbhill

CANBHILL | **Canberra × Winston Churchill** | **McElderry 1975**
CANDLE LIGHT | **Agnes de Burc × Derdene** | **Stewart Inc. 1973 (E. C. Wilcox)**
CANDLE-TREE | **Grove × Clemency** | **Ratcliffe 1973**
CANDY | **Gorse × Chardmoore** | **L. W. Brummitt 1968**

× Dalla = Chadalla
× F. C. Puddle = Shareba
× Lombardy = Lombard Sweet

CANDY PINK | **Balgrose × niveum** | **Ratcliffe 1959**

× Sarella = Palm Court
× Snowberry = Maid of Honour

CAPDEPERA | **Barbarrosa × Regent** | **Pff. V. & L. 1973**
CAPITAL RED | **Botan × Geelong** | **Ratcliffe 1974**
CAPITOL | **glaucophyllum × Cardinal Mercier** | **Hark 1973**
CAPITOLIAN | **Challow × Geelong** | **Ratcliffe 1972**
CAPRISSA | **Olinda × Timbrel** | **Ratcliffe 1972**
CAPTIVATION | **Allure × Lucid** | **Cooke 1953**

× Floramond = Fancy Day
× Loganna = Anovation
× Tapestry = Captress

CAPTRESS | **Captivation × Tapestry** | **Ratcliffe 1973**
CARAT GOLD | **Sunwillow × Sungrove** | **Ratcliffe 1971**
CARAVELLE | **Martinique × Paeony** | **Pff. V. & L. 1974**
CARDINAL MERCIER*†‡ | **Lathamianum × ?** | **Crombleholme 1921**

× Enoshima = Sakayatama
× glaucophyllum = Capitol
× Mem. H. J. Elwes = Hanamizu
× Radley = Nassarah
× Sohma = Shigitatsusawa
× Wendover = Nichien
× Weser = Grünberg

CARDINAL POLISH | **Rampion × Amanda** | **Ratcliffe 1972**
CAREFREE | **Thumbelisa × Farnmoore** | **Stewart Inc. 1975**
CARFAX | **Amber Star × Cholsey** | **Ratcliffe 1971**
CARILLON | **Avine × McLaren Park** | **Rod McLellan Co. 1973**
CARIMO | **Carl Keyes × John Dovan** | **C. & I. Keyes 1975**
CARL KEYES | **W. N. Evans × Firebrand** | **Keyes 1968 (Bracey)**

× Advancement = Redwave
× John Dovan = Carimo
× Lady Moxham = Red Radiance
× Monge = Redflash
× Polka Dot = Philippe E'Loy
× Winston Churchill = Keyeshill

CARMEL | **chamberlainianum × barbatum** | **Cryder 1973**
CARMENTA | **Olinda × Lockinge** | **Ratcliffe 1974**
CARNIVAL‡ | **Masked Light × Floralies** | **R. K. Fields 1967 (Ratcliffe)**

× Wendbourn = Fornax

CAROLTIME | **Sungrove × Whitemoor** | **Ratcliffe 1971**
CASHMERE | **Brownly × Haroun** | **Rod McLellan Co. 1972**
CASTILLO | **Ravenhunter × Martinique** | **Pff. V. & L. 1974**
CATCH-SONG | **Testmatch × Cadence** | **Ratcliffe 1975**
CATHAY† | **Desdemona × Moonlight** | **A. 1939**

× Jocelyn = Cathyn

PAPHIOPEDILUM

CATHYN	**Jocelyn × Cathay**	**Ratcliffe 1975 (Florentia)**
CATRILLO	**Sparsholt × Cadence**	**Ratcliffe 1972**
CAVALCADE	**Gertrude West × Nena**	**B. 1939**

× Goshima	= Beauty Goshima	× Winston Churchill	= Wincade

CELADON	**Lemon Hart × Gorse**	**Ratcliffe 1965**

× Ambrosia	= Belinda Green	× F. C. Puddle	= Asteria

CELANDINE‡	**Divert × Gold Rush**	**Stirling 1949**

× Denehurst	= La Collette		

CERRITOS	**Golden Acres × Denehurst**	**Clark Day Jr. 1975**
CHADALLA	**Candy × Dalla**	**Hark 1972**
CHAFFYN	**F. C. Puddle × Chantal**	**Ratcliffe 1971**
CHALCEDONY	**Rosewood × Challow**	**Ratcliffe 1971**
CHALEMELLE	**Sharon × Sarella**	**Ratcliffe 1973**
CHALLOW‡	**Radley × Viking**	**Ratcliffe 1957**

× Balaclava	= Conjola	× Geelong	= Capitolian
× Canasta	= Country Dance	× Hellas	= Ambellina
× Canberra	= Town Major	× Lockinge	= Rosemary Leigh
× Chipmunk	= Cherissant	× Robert Paterson	= Tree of Ikegawa
× Ferox	= Saint Aubins Bay	× Rosewood	= Chalcedony

chamberlainianum*† — **species**

(This and *glaucophyllum**†‡ continue to be treated as distinct species for parental purposes in registration, although botanically treated by some authorities as sub-species of *victoria-regina**.)

× appletonianum	= Adams Apple	× bouganvilleanum	= South Pacific
× Ballet Girl	= Tip Top	× Hellas	= Hell's Chamber
× barbatum	= Carmel	× lowii	= Mem. Arthur Freed

CHANCE MEDLEY	**Milmoore × Blagrose**	**Thomdel 1975**
CHANTAL	**Bradford × Chilton**	**Ratcliffe 1962**

× Dusty Miller	= Miller's Daughter	× Snowberry	= Glaciator
× F. C. Puddle	= Chaffyn	× Whitemoor	= May Song
× Miriam Sacher	= New Blend	× Wintersweet	= Sweet Chant

CHARDMOORE*†‡	**Christopher × Lena**	**Moore 1927**

× Beauté	= Kingsize	× Lemon Hart	= Hapless
× Black Moore	= Torquay	× Milnetta	= Hayama
× Crescent Meadow	= Copper Penny	× Pittsburg	= Fair Start
× Gitana	= Roman Umber	× Wendover	= Aristocratic Beauty
× Gwenpur	= Chargwen	× Yerba Buena	= White Ice
× Jack Tonkin	= Wendy Wilson		

CHARGWEN	**Gwenpur × Chardmoore**	**Hanes 1975**
CHARHILL	**Charjan × Winston Churchill**	**Hanes 1975**
CHARJAN	**Trojan × Charmaine**	**Casamajor 1954 (A.)**

× Winston Churchill	= Charhill		

CHARLES DAVID	**Emil Vacin × Maudiae**	**Craig's 1973**
charlesworthii*†	**species**	

× Dover Bridge	= Joanne	× Maudiae	= Schaetzchen
× glaucophyllum	= Prelude	× sukhakulii	= Sue Worth
× lowii	= Quadriga	× victoria-regina	= Old Spice

CHARMWOOD	**Happy Landing × Grove**	**Ratcliffe 1975**
CHASSERAL	**Fred Cosanka × Santa Margarita**	**Gunzenhauser 1975**

PAPHIOPEDILUM

Grex	Parentage	Registrant
CHATTAHOOCHEE	Redstart × Milionette	W. W. Wilson 1973
CHAUMONT	Ernst Gunzenhauser × Monge	Gunzenhauser 1975
CHECKMATE	Divisadero × Denehurst	Rod McLellan Co. 1973
CHEER LEADER	Lombardy × Lemon Hart	Ratcliffe 1975
CHEESOHEHA	Hellas × Judith Dance	W. W. Wilson 1973
CHEHALIS	sukhakulii × linii	M. E. Powers 1973 (Rands)
CHENILLE	Lucid × Culmo	Ratcliffe 1965

× Amanda = Armilla | × Loganna = Filoselle

Grex	Parentage	Registrant
CHÈQUE	Karacorum × Ralph	Maggi Ponti 1975
CHERIMOYA	Rampion × Loganna	Ratcliffe 1973
CHERISSANT	Chipmunk × Challow	Ratcliffe 1974
CHEROKEE	Caddiana × Golden Acres	David Blue 1975 (Hanes)
CHERRY PLUM	Magrose × Baroque	Ratcliffe 1972
CHERYL ANN BOYD	Winston Churchill × Roseling	Gene Boyd 1971 (P. Ilsley)
CHEVALIER NOIR	Rodin × Ravenhunter	Pff. V. & L. 1973
CHEYENNE	Sitting Bull × Sioux	W. W. Wilson 1975
CHIANTI‡	Gorse × Chilton	Ratcliffe 1962

× F. C. Puddle = Wynnetta | × Sunland = Mosella
× Honda Gold = Golden Chianti |

Grex	Parentage	Registrant
CHICKADEE	John Dovan × W. N. Evans	Hoyt 1968

× Battle of Egypt = Redbrook | × Red Creek = Roaring Creek

Grex	Parentage	Registrant
CHICOPEE	concolor × Golden Slipper	W. W. Wilson 1971
CHILLIPINK	Blagrose × Floramond	Ratcliffe 1972
CHILTON†‡	Culver × Grace Darling	Ratcliffe 1952

× Kay Rinaman = Statuesque |

Grex	Parentage	Registrant
CHILTON BAY	Moreton Bay × Chilton	Itoh 1968

× Schneegloeckchen = Mischabel |

Grex	Parentage	Registrant
CHIPMUNK	Gitana × Dalla	Ratcliffe 1965

× Botan = Barnaby Bright | × Lockinge = Pintado
× Challow = Cherissant | × Loganna = Tamirose
× Impeyan = High Feather | × Sunwillow = Chipwillow

Grex	Parentage	Registrant
CHIPWILLOW	Chipmunk × Sunwillow	Ratcliffe 1973
CHOCO	Mildred Hunter × Cadence	W. W. Wilson 1975
CHOCOLATE ROUGE	Floramond × Royale	Ratcliffe 1973
CHOLSEY‡ (h. ign.)	? × ?	Ratcliffe 1967

× Amber Star = Carfax | × Canasta = Merriment

Grex	Parentage	Registrant
CHOREOGRAPHY	Ballet Girl × Decameron	Lodge 1973
CHORLEY	Adela × Leonora	L. 1950

× Pauline Cosanka = Jolimont |

Grex	Parentage	Registrant
CHRISTINE E'LOY	Langley Pride × Louis V. Dorp	The Orchid House 1975
CHRISTMAS CHEER	argus × venustum	D'Lin 1975 (Rands)
CHRISTOPHER*†	Aureum × Leeanum	Thompson 1902

× Blendia = Bevis |

PAPHIOPEDILUM

Name	Parentage	Registrant
CHRYSOSTOM*†‡	**Christopher × Pyramus**	**Moore 1922**
× Glosan = Sansostom	× Yumedono = Heathy Hill	
CHUBBY†	**Alcibiades × Mowgli**	**Cussons 1937**
× Lady Kitty Laura = Chubby Landy		
CHUBBY LANDY	**Chubby × Lady Kitty Laura**	**A. J. Bell 1974**
CIMARINE	**Sunland × Botan**	**Ratcliffe 1974**
CIPRIANO FABUNAN	**Walter Moore × Greenwick**	**Rod McLellan Co. 1974**
CIRCLET	**Air de Ballet × Kismet**	**B. 1971**
CITTADELLA	**Canberra × Heather Bell**	**Ratcliffe 1971**
CITY†	**Cardinal Mercier × Londinam**	**S. 1942**
× Burpham = Red Eagle		
CITY BAND	**Timbrel × Geelong**	**Ratcliffe 1974**
CITY CREST	**Impeyan × Geelong**	**Ratcliffe 1972**
CITY GLOW	**Culmo × Geelong**	**Ratcliffe 1974**
CITY LARK	**Amanda × Geelong**	**Ratcliffe 1974**
CITY WEAVER	**Tapestry × Geelong**	**Ratcliffe 1974**
CLAIR DE LUNE*†‡	**Emerald × Alma Gavaert**	**S. 1927**
× sukhakulii = Green Goddess		
CLAIRVOYANCE	**Sweet Harmony × Sarella**	**Ratcliffe 1972**
CLARET TREE	**John Dovan × Winston Churchill**	**Kimura 1973**
CLEAR PEARL	**Lemora × Silvara**	**Ratcliffe 1972**
CLEMENCY	**Happy Landing × Hellas**	**Ratcliffe 1965**
× Baroque = Tristana × Grove = Candle-tree	× Tapestry = Belaccoyle	
CLEMENTINE H. CHURCHILL†‡	**Festivity × Lewis Crampton**	**S.A. 1946**
× Blagrose = Elizabeth Steen × Solferino = Animo	× Winston Churchill = Punxsutawney	
CLOVERICA	**Tombola × Botan**	**Ratcliffe 1971**
COHOCKSINK	**Ingcar × Inca**	**W. W. Wilson 1973**
COLIN AISLABIE	**April × Brailes**	**Sasso 1974**
COLLEGEGROVE	**Radley × Grove**	**Ratcliffe 1974 (Sieff)**
COLLEVANS	**Paeony × John Dovan**	**A. J. Bell 1974**
COLORKULII	**sukhakulii × concolor**	**Andrews Orchids 1973 (L. Miller)**
COLUMBA	**Albion × Gorse**	**Ratcliffe 1971**
COLUMBARY	**Compton × Jamaycus**	**Ratcliffe 1973**
COMELY ANN	**Jamaycus × Amanda**	**Ratcliffe 1973**
COMMODORE*	**Alcibiades × Memoria Jerninghamiae**	**Worsley 1916**
× Marsha White = Marshadore		
COMPASS	**Blendia × Cholsey**	**Ratcliffe 1967**
× Loganna = Beacon Point		
COMPLIMENT	**Rampion × Floramond**	**Ratcliffe 1973**
COMPTON‡	**Lucid × Gitana**	**Ratcliffe 1967**
× Amanda = Veritilario × Blagrose = Baryta × Canberra = Jamboree	× Dalla = John Peel × Jamaycus = Columbary	
CONCINNITY	**Heather Bell × Geelong**	**Ratcliffe 1973**

PAPHIOPEDILUM

Grex	Parentage	Registrant
concolor*‡	**species**	

× Albion = Albacon
× delenatii = Pisar
× glaucophyllum = Tinicum
× godefroyae = {wellesleyanum (Nat. hyb.) / Wellesleyanum (Reg'd. grex)}
× Golden Slipper = Chicopee
× niveum = Doctor Jack
× sukhakulii = Colorkulii
× Van Ness = Meadow Sprite

Grex	Parentage	Registrant
CONJOLA	**Challow × Balaclava**	**Ratcliffe 1971**
CONSHOHOCKEN	**Matchless × Burpham**	**W. W. Wilson 1972**
CONTRALTO	**Glowyn × Lyric**	**Ratcliffe 1972**
COOL AFFAIR	**Jocelyn × Zephyr**	**Ratcliffe 1975**
COPPER PENNY	**Crescent Meadow × Chardmoore**	**E. C. Wilcox 1972**
COPPERWARE	**Sharon × Hellas**	**Ratcliffe 1968**

× Blondel = Jolly Copper

Grex	Parentage	Registrant
CORANTA	**Matchless × bellatulum**	**Ratcliffe 1971**
COTTON CANDY	**Wendover × delenatii**	**D'Lin 1975 (B.)**
COULISSE	**Culmo × Floralies**	**Ratcliffe 1973 (Sieff)**
COUNTERPOINT	**Floramond × Needlepoint**	**Ratcliffe 1972**
COUNTRY DANCE	**Challow × Canasta**	**Ratcliffe 1975**
COUNTY FAIR	**London Wall × Elizabeth Keeley**	**E. C. Wilcox 1972**
COURT JESTER‡	**Allure × Blendia**	**Ratcliffe 1968**

× Matchless = Testmatch
× Myzantha = Little Clown

Grex	Parentage	Registrant
CRADILLON	**Cramore × Lady Dillon**	**C. 1945**

× Winston Churchill = Poquessing

Grex	Parentage	Registrant
CRAMOISY	**Flamenco × Loganna**	**Ratcliffe 1972**
CRASTIA†‡	**Astarte × Mrs. Carl Holmes**	**Aberconway 1936**

× Pudston = Crystal Creek

Grex	Parentage	Registrant
CRAZY WORLD	**Tantrum × Small World**	**Ratcliffe 1973**
CRESCENT MEADOW†‡	**Agnes de Burc × Margaret MacCaull**	**A. & R. 1949**

× Avine = Silver Dollar
× Betty Bracey = Bestcrest
× Caddiana = Annetta Hanes
× Chardmoore = Copper Penny
× Diversion = Meadow Crest
× hirsutissimum = Fiddle Faddle
× La Honda = Lacrescent
× McLaren Park = Oasis
× Yerba Bueno = Polar Cap

Grex	Parentage	Registrant
CRESDON	**Beedon × Yellow Crest**	**Mann 1975**
CRIMBOURNE	**Domby × Overstrand**	**L. 1952**

× Beechmast = Monte Brione
× Monte Generoso = Monte Tamaro

Grex	Parentage	Registrant
CRIMSONTIDE	**Startler × Lockinge**	**Ratcliffe 1971**
CRIMSON WHIRL	**Jamaycus × Botan**	**Ratcliffe 1972**
CRITERION CREEK	**Showoff × Burnham**	**Beall 1975**
CRONULLA	**Keelat × Lady Kitty Laura**	**Sasso 1975**
CROSS-BOW	**Tantrum × Sparsholt**	**Ratcliffe 1973**
CROSS-STITCH	**Tapestry × Lockinge**	**Ratcliffe 1972**
CROW CREEK	**Evanhurst × Winston Churchill**	**Beall 1975 (E. C. Wilcox)**
CRUSADER*†	**Julian × Lucifer**	**H. 1922**

× Floralies = Crusalies

Grex	Parentage	Registrant
CRUSALIES	**Crusader × Floralies**	**Mann 1974**

CRYSTAL BROOK	**Ann Harper × Rosy Dawn**	**G. A. Wright 1974**
CRYSTAL CREEK	**Pudston × Crastia**	**Beall 1975**
CULLUM†‡	**Luna × Mem. F. M. Ogilvie**	**Cooke 1942**

× Grove = Martelet
× Lyric = Recital
× Paeony = Flush Royal

CULMAVINA	**Culmo × Wendbourn**	**Ratcliffe 1973**
CULMO‡	**Great Mogul × Cullum**	**A. & B. 1954**

× Blagrose = Calimosa
× Floralies = Coulisse
× Geelong = City Glow
× Wendbourn = Culmavina

CURFEW-TIME	**Repose × Heather Bell**	**Ratcliffe 1972**
curtisii*‡	**species**	

× bullenianum = Gentle Breeze

CUYAHOGA	**Red Angel × Milionette**	**W. W. Wilson 1975**
CYCLOPS*†‡	**Actaeus × Fulshawense**	**H. 1913**

× Garibaldi = Winter's Imp

CYMATODES*	**curtisii × superbiens**	**R. H. Measures 1893**

× appletonianum = Salinas
× glaucophyllum = Angela Wilson
× sukhakulii = Jurgen Netzer

DAHMOY	**Chrysostom × Regent**	**Heaton 1945**

× Cameo = Seeker

DAIGO	**Maudiae × Lemon Hart**	**Hattori 1975**
DAINTY LASS	**Orpheus × fairieanum**	**Thomdel 1973 (Van Delden)**
DAKAR†	**Blagrose × Luna**	**C. 1945**

× Hanney = Far Hills
× Paeony = Domina

DALLA†‡	**Luna × The Gurka**	**Cooke 1943**

× Balaclava = Talladale
× Botan = Santalin
× Candy = Chadalla
× Compton = John Peel
× Heide = Marlene
× Moongrove = Shirleydale
× Redstart = Dear John
× Royale = Philopena
× William Stirling = Fatiha

DANELLA	**Hellas × Dalla**	**Ratcliffe 1968**

× Baroque = Dartington
× Blondel = Bandarilla

DARTINGTON	**Danella × Baroque**	**Ratcliffe 1974**
DAVOUT	**Exelmans × Aspac**	**Pff. V. & L. 1975**
DAWN CHORUS	**Ranleigh × Spring Vigil**	**Ratcliffe 1973 (Sieff)**
DAWN FAIRY	**Rosy Dawn × fairieanum**	**Rod McLellan Co. 1972**
dayanum*‡	**species**	

× glaucophyllum = Navigator

DAZZLER	**Inferno × Rollright**	**Ratcliffe 1967**

× Cadence = Melodist

DEANHILL	**Winston Churchill × Littledean**	**McElderry 1975**
DEAR HEART	**La Honda × Mariano Martin**	**Hanes 1973**
DEAR JOHN	**Dalla × Redstart**	**Ratcliffe 1972**
DECAMERON*†‡	**Garibaldi × Muriel II**	**A. 1932**

× Ballet Girl = Choreography
× Milionette = Iberia

delenatii*†‡ — **species**

- × concolor = Pisar
- × sukhakulii = Quasimodo
- × Wendover = Cotton Candy

DEMOFAIR — **Zephyr × F. C. Puddle** — **Ratcliffe 1971**

DEMURA — **Blendia × bellatulum** — **Ratcliffe 1966**

- × Geelong = Star-raker
- × Loganna = Taslet

DENEHURST†‡ — **Dervish × Lady Mona** — **Cooke 1943**

- × bellatulum = Belladene
- × Bordube = Bordene
- × Caddiana = Verde Oro
- × Celandine = La Collette
- × Divisadero = Checkmate
- × Golden Acres = Cerritos
- × Golden Diana = King of Sweden
- × La Honda = Stan Bachman's Choice
- × McLaren Park = Parkhurst
- × Mariano Martin = Dene Martin
- × Norella = Nordene
- × Stoke Poges = Stokehurst
- × Vestalia = Pequot

DENE MARTIN — **Denehurst × Mariano Martin** — **A. & R. 1973**

DERDENE — **Dervish × Denehurst** — **Stewart Inc. 1961**

- × Agnes de Burc = Candle Light
- × F. C. Puddle = Sévres

DEROCLES — **Pericles × Divisadero** — **McElderry 1971**

DERVISH*†‡ — **Bordube × Grace Darling** — **Cooke 1938**

- × Snowberry = Miss Prim

DESERT SUN† — **Golden Emblem × Mrs. Geoffrey Webb** — **Farnes 1944**

- × B. White = Mervyn Grant

DESIRAMA — **Dorama × Desire** — **Pff. V. & L. 1975**

DESIRE*†‡ — **Golden Wren × Luna** — **Cooke 1939**

- × Buckhurst = Bente Honi
- × Dorama = Desirama
- × Margaret Brands = Anne Gripp

DEWY GREEN — **Ambrosia × Sunwillow** — **Ratcliffe 1973**

DIAMORA — **Dimity × Silvara** — **Ratcliffe 1972**

DIANITA† — **Anita × Diana Broughton** — **Stirling 1944**

- × Bordube = Margie Pitta

DICKLER*†‡ — **Dick × Golden Eagle** — **Miss Moore 1930**

- × Dicksum = Wild Duck

DICKSUM — **Ansum × Dickler** — **A. & R. 1959**

- × Dickler = Wild Duck

DILYS — **Adorn × Etta** — **Cooke 1945**

- × Cameo = Campanero

DIMITY — **F. C. Puddle × Gorse** — **Ratcliffe 1964**

- × Silvara = Diamora

DIVERSION†‡ — **Alpha × Aussie** — **B. 1947**

- × Brownly = Apropo
- × Crescent Meadow = Meadow Crest
- × Golden Acres = Erma Shulda
- × Greenstede = Saint Helier
- × Majorling = Mayvirsion
- × Wallur = Via Rio Verde

DIVISADERO‡ — **Diversion × Golden Diana** — **Rod McLellan Co. 1962**

- × Denehurst = Checkmate
- × Hellas = Helladero
- × Pericles = Derocles
- × Wallur = Engraved
- × Yerba Buena = Shirley Holloway

DOCTEUR KNOCK — **Procrustes × Maudiae** — **Pff. V. & L. 1973**

DOCTOR JACK — concolor × niveum — Cryder 1975
DOLLY BIRD — Floramond × Impeyan — Ratcliffe 1973
DOLORES CARRION — Gowerianum × Bordure — Ted Fischer 1974
DOLORES WEBER — Julia Mash × McLaren Park — Mrs. Kay Rinaman 1975
DOMINA — Dakar × Paeony — Ratcliffe 1972
DONZEL — Olinda × Loganna — Ratcliffe 1972
DORAMA†‡ — Alma × Dora — V. 1941
× Desire = Desirama

DORAMASAN — San-Actaeus × Dorama — V. 1950
× Albion = Trouvere

DOREMY — Lombardy × Cadence — Ratcliffe 1974
DORIS HUNTER†‡ — Doris Stanton × Mildred Hunter — S.A. 1949
× Ecrennes = Montoz

DOVER BRIDGE — Edenbridge × Wendover — D. 1953
× charlesworthii = Joanne

DOWNEND — Harry Endersby × J. M. Black — Cooke 1945
× Exelmans = Manacor

DRAGOON — Mildred Hunter × Mildrington — Stewart Inc. 1972
DRAMA GIRL — Sharon × Dramatic — Ratcliffe 1973 (Sieff)

DRAMATIC†‡ — Grace Darling × Desire — Cooke 1951
× Elaine Blond = Fair Play | × Orryon = Marin
× Jocelyn = Lippesonne | × Sharon = Drama Girl

DREAM WORLD — Amber Star × World Venture — Ratcliffe 1974
DRIFTING STORM — Milmoore × Dunscott — Stewart Inc. 1974
DULCIANA — Royale × Loganna — Ratcliffe 1972
DUNCAN YORK — Winston Churchill × Black Thorpe — Riopelle 1971 (Duncan York)

DUNSCOTT — Scotia × Dunvegan — S.A. 1953
× Milmoore = Drifting Storm | × Trojan = Thunder Squall

DUNSTAN† — Wendron × Brailes — L. 1950
× Lemon Hart = Higashiyama

DUSKY MAIDEN — Sophomore × Susan Tucker — Hanes 1973

DUSTY MILLER — F. C. Puddle × Chardmoore — Ratcliffe 1959
× Amanda = Rosy Prospect | × Silvara = Miller's Luck
× Battersea = Olney Mill | × Snowberry = Snowy Miller
× Botan = Show Boat | × Sunland = Miller's Boy
× Chantal = Miller's Daughter | × Whitemoor = Miller's Pride
× F. C. Puddle = Jolly Miller | × Wintersweet = Winter's Mill
× Lemora = Mavourneen

DUSTY ROSE — Wendwater × F. C. Puddle — Stewart Inc. 1972
ECRENNES‡ — L'Yser × Blendia — Pff. V. & L. 1961
× Doris Hunter = Montoz

EDITH SASSO — Lady Moxham × Keelat — Sasso 1975
EIGHTH — Chardburn × Hestia — S. 1943
× Winston Churchill = Muriel Day

ELAINE BLOND — **Minster Lovell × Bordure** — **Sieff 1966 (Ratcliffe)**
× Dramatic = Fair Play

ELEGY — **Stoke Poges × London Wall** — **McElderry 1973**
ELIZABETH KEELEY†‡ — **Cranfield × Emmer Green** — **B. 1950**
× London Wall = County Fair | × Wallur = Green Ruffles

ELIZABETH STEEN — **Clementine H. Churchill × Blagrose** — **Steen 1975 (Robert Craig)**

ELLORA — **Miriam Sacher × Sarella** — **Ratcliffe 1975**
EMBA — **Challow × Gorse** — **Ratcliffe 1965**
× Lockinge = Emberings | × Sarella = Glenalla

EMBERINGS — **Emba × Lockinge** — **Ratcliffe 1975**
EMERALD ISLE — **Michael Stewart × Betty Bracey** — **Hanes 1973**
EMIL VACIN‡ — **Margaret MacCaull × Actaeus** — **E. C. Wilcox 1952**
× Maudiae = Charles David | × Reezy = Que Sera

EMINENCE — **Milionette × Arlina** — **Stewart Inc. 1972**
EMISTESIGO — **Bourndilly × Winston Churchill** — **W. W. Wilson 1974**
ENAMELINE — **Barbary × Botan** — **Ratcliffe 1972**
ENGRAVED — **Divisadero × Wallur** — **Rod McLellan Co. 1971**
ENHANCED — **Golden Acres × Gwenpur** — **Rod McLellan Co. 1973**
ENOSHIMA — **Maisham × Mrs. Rickards** — **Karasawa 1972 (Ikeda)**
× Cardinal Mercier = Sakayatama | × Kanchanjunga = Sazareishi
× Finetta = Zushi | × Mulatto = Kohraisan
× Gold Mohur = Golden Jagur | × Nena = Koiso

ERIDGE†‡ — **Doris Stanton × Rosalie** — **L. 1942**
× Santa Margarita = Excitement

ERIE — **Jim Dandy × Olympic Forest** — **W. W. Wilson 1974**
ERMA SHULDA — **Diversion × Golden Acres** — **Rod McLellan Co. 1974**
ERNEST BIRTLE — **Ann Coventry × Mrs. Eley** — **K. 1944**
× Gertrude West = Hearty

ERNST GUNZENHAUSER — **Amwell × Clavaham** — **Cosanka 1963**
× Fred Cosanka = Grand Combin | × Noyo = Grammont
× Monge = Chaumont

ESPRESSO — **Gitana × Solferino** — **Hark 1974**
ESSYLINE — **Hellas × Sandra Mary** — **Alberts 1974**
ETHEL MORAN — **Sea Cliff × Pacific Ocean** — **Moran 1975**
ETTA*†‡ — **Chardwar × Mrs. Rickards** — **Rickards 1922**
× John Keeling = Keelat

EUGENE NOEL — **Santa Margarita × Langley Pride** — **Rod McLellan Co. 1973**
EURYOSTOM*†‡ — **Chrysostom × Eurybiades** — **B. 1930**
× Akeley = Akstom | × Main Oiso = Oisostom

EVANHURST†‡ — **Gayhurst × W. N. Evans** — **B. 1949**
× Happy Ben = Benhurst | × Winston Churchill = Crow Creek

EVANSROSE‡ — **Rosemary Waithman × W. N. Evans** — **B. 1950**
× Hellas = Zealandia | × Matcheck = Rosecheck

EVANSROSE‡ *(continued)*

× Omar Hill = Rosehill
× Peter Adam = Rose-apple
× Radley = Rosie Ley
× Stoke Poges = Stokes Rose
× Tearlath = Welsh Rose
× Wendwater = Red Model
× Winston Churchill = Beatrice Ernst

EVEREST*†‡	**Gertrude West × Robert Paterson**	**Paterson 1932**

× Johnbourn = Leo Organo

EVERETT WILCOX	**Brulmoore × Winston Churchill**	**Stewart Inc. 1975**
EXCITEMENT	**Eridge × Santa Margarita**	**Rod McLellan Co. 1971**
EXELMANS†‡	**Atlantis × Sully**	**V. 1941**

× Aspac = Davout
× Blendia = Calvi
× Downend = Manacor
× Gitana = Madame Sans Gene
× Rollright = Fugue

EXOLICA	**Loganna × Rollright**	**Ratcliffe 1971**
exul*†	**species**	

× glaucophyllum = Sun Pebbles

FAIRBURN	**London Wall × Chardmoore**	**E. C. Wilcox 1961**

× Mildred Hunter = Bob Gunther

FAIR CITY	**Strawberry Fair × Canberra**	**Ratcliffe 1971**
fairieanum*†‡	**species**	

× Ballet Girl = Fairy Slipper
× Black Thorpe = Wichita
× bullenianum = Mary-Irene
× F. C. Puddle = Mem. Bill Bourgoin
× hirsutissimum = Wissinoming
× Inca = Osage
× Inez = Jan Honi
× javanicum = Octoberfest
× John Keeling = Jaunty Fairy
× linii = Green Elf
× lowii = Zingano
× Orpheus = Dainty Lass
× Rosy Dawn = Dawn Fairy
× Sheba = Fairy Princess
× sukhakulii = Papa Röhl
× venustum = Pandion
× Wendbourn = Arne Honi

FAIR PLAY	**Dramatic × Elaine Blond**	**Ratcliffe 1974 (Sieff)**
FAIR START	**Pittsburg × Chardmoore**	**Stewart Inc. 1975**
FAIRY PRINCESS	**Sheba × fairieanum**	**Stewart Inc. 1972**
FAIRY SLIPPER	**Ballet Girl × fairieanum**	**Stewart Inc. 1972**
FALL BROOK	**Rositza × W. N. Evans**	**G. A. Wright 1974 (Hoyt)**
FAMILY CIRCLE	**Paeony × Lockinge**	**Ratcliffe 1975**
FANCIFUL	**glaucophyllum × insigne**	**Thomdel 1975**
FANCY DAY	**Captivation × Floramond**	**Ratcliffe 1973**
FANCY FAIR	**Strawberry Fair × Startler**	**Ratcliffe 1973**
FANTASTICO	**Flamenco × Lockinge**	**Ratcliffe 1973**
FAR HILLS	**Hanney × Dakar**	**Ratcliffe 1971**
FARMINGDALE	**Farnmoore × Advancement**	**Sakell 1974 (A. & R.)**
FARNBERRA	**Farnmoore × Canberra**	**Hanes 1975**
FARNCHECK	**Matcheck × Farnmoore**	**McElderry 1975**
FARNMOORE†‡	**Chardmoore × Farnley**	**S.A. 1946**

× Advancement = Farmingdale
× Canberra = Farnberra
× Matcheck = Farncheck
× Noyo = Farnoyo
× Sea Cliff = Oceanid
× Thumbelisa = Carefree
× Winston Churchill = Winmoore

FARNOYO	**Farnmoore × Noyo**	**McElderry 1975**

PAPHIOPEDILUM

Grex	Parentage	Registrant
FAST COLOUR	**Startler × Paeony**	**Ratcliffe 1973**
FATIHA	**William Stirling × Dalla**	**Stewart Inc. 1975**
F. C. PUDDLE*†‡	**Actaeus × Astarte**	**McLaren 1932**

×	=	×	=
× bellatulum	= Weissenstein	× Golden Acres	= Golden Puddle
× Bingleyense	= Spotted Puddle	× Lemon Slipper	= Snow Creek
× Blondel	= Watersprite	× Lockinge	= Alice Pink
× Borburn	= Botan-Yuki	× Loganna	= Lady Virtuous
× Candy	= Shareba	× Miriam Sacher	= Quiet Green
× Celadon	= Asteria	× Nowara	= Rosepoint
× Chantal	= Chaffyn	× Paeony	= Adornable
× Chianti	= Wynnetta	× Sandman	= Land of Nod
× Derdene	= Sévres	× Sheerline	= Rockaway
× Dusty Miller	= Jolly Miller	× Stuart Wilcox	= Memory Rosina Pitta
× fairieanum	= Mem. Bill Bourgoin	× Sunwillow	= Willowpool
× Fidelity	= Luminance	× Sweet Harmony	= Swan Gold
× Finetta	= Gan	× Wendwater	= Dusty Rose
× Giallo	= Aquarella	× Zephyr	= Demofair

Grex	Parentage	Registrant
FERN CANYON	**lowii × tonsum**	**Thomdel 1974**
FEROX‡	**Greenville × Aldergrove**	**L. 1963**

×	=	×	=
× Challow	= Saint Aubins Bay	× Renby	= Renox
× Lemon Hart	= Mount Bingham		

Grex	Parentage	Registrant
FESTIVE HUNTER‡	**Festivity × Mildred Hunter**	**S.A. 1952**

×	=	×	=
× Milionette	= Odyssey	× Winston Churchill	= Brenner Pass

Grex	Parentage	Registrant
FIDDLE FADDLE	**hirsutissimum × Crescent Meadow**	**Santa Barbara 1975**
FIDELITY	**Gorse × Brixton**	**Ratcliffe 1967**

×	=	×	=
× F. C. Puddle	= Luminance		

Grex	Parentage	Registrant
FILOSELLE	**Chenille × Loganna**	**Ratcliffe 1973**
FINE ARTS	**Botan × Tapestry**	**Ratcliffe 1971**
FINETTA*†‡	**Christopher × Chrysostom**	**A. E. Dale 1930**

×	=	×	=
× Enoshima	= Zushi	× Major Hanbury Carlile	= Goshima
× F. C. Puddle	= Gan	× Maudiae	= Halve
× Golden Fleece	= Golnetta	× Mildred	= Milnetta
× Lemon Hart	= Lemonetta	× Wallur	= Kan-Ichi Torizawa

Grex	Parentage	Registrant
FIREBRAND†‡	**Balaclava × Cardinal Mercier**	**Farnes 1945**

×	=	×	=
× Winston Churchill	= Ojibway		

Grex	Parentage	Registrant
FIRE GIRL†‡	**Atlantis × Joyce Winifred**	**Hankey 1945**

×	=	×	=
× W. N. Evans	= Romage		

Grex	Parentage	Registrant
FLAME-CAP	**Startler × Geelong**	**Ratcliffe 1973**
FLAMELET	**Aliescum × Botan**	**Ratcliffe 1973**
FLAMENCO	**Gitana × Redstart**	**Ratcliffe 1963**

×	=	×	=
× Amanda	= Jolliday	× Loganna	= Cramoisy
× Botan	= Valeta	× Paeony	= Gaudy-night
× Lockinge	= Fantastico	× Small World	= World Fandango

Grex	Parentage	Registrant
FLIGHT PATH	**Sparsholt × Qantas**	**Ratcliffe 1972**
FLORALIES*†‡	**Atlantis × Meigle**	**B. 1933**

×	=	×	=
× Blagrose	= Florosa	× Roaqua	= Quarles
× Bonheure	= Roughhewn	× Tendresse	= Manana
× Crusader	= Crusalies	× Ukiah	= Betsy Ross
× Culmo	= Coulisse	× Winston Churchill	= Blenheim Palace
× Jamaycus	= Vivo		

Grex	Parentage	Registrant
FLORAMOND	**Telmond × Floralies**	**Ratcliffe 1963**

×	=	×	=
× Baroque	= Roquette	× Blagrose	= Chillipink

FLORAMOND *(continued)*

× Botan	= Kildary	× Olinda	= Olivine
× Captivation	= Fancy Day	× Paeony	= Royal Revel
× Happy Landing	= Loveday	× Petronella	= Brunella
× Heather Bell	= Mountain Glow	× Rampion	= Compliment
× Impeyan	= Dolly Bird	× Royale	= Chocolate Rouge
× Leeanum	= Westfalengruss	× Samantha	= Vanadia
× Lockinge	= Kayenda	× Solferino	= Ruby Sparkler
× Loganna	= Rayande	× Startler	= Bright Alary
× Lyric	= Flower Song	× Stromboli	= Flower Power
× Meigle	= Hamburg Harbour	× Tantrum	= Floritura
× Needlepoint	= Counterpoint		

FLORIN-HANCAR	**Florina × Hancar**	**Umaki 1958**

× Julia Mash	= Wendy Sue

FLORITURA	**Floramond × Tantrum**	**Ratcliffe 1975**
FLOROSA	**Blagrose × Floralies**	**Ratcliffe 1974**

× Botan	= Major Rose

FLOSS-SILK	**Tapestry × Startler**	**Ratcliffe 1973**
FLOWER POWER	**Stromboli × Floramond**	**Ratcliffe 1975**
FLOWER SONG	**Floramond × Lyric**	**Ratcliffe 1974**
FLUSH ROYAL	**Paeony × Cullum**	**Ratcliffe 1971**
FLYING COLOURS	**Timbrel × Cadence**	**Ratcliffe 1972**
FLYING WORLD	**Orestes × Small World**	**Ratcliffe 1974**
FOREST KING (see Thias*†‡)		
FORNAX	**Carnival × Wendbourn**	**Hark 1974**
FORT WEST	**Gertrude West × Maginot**	**Stirling 1965 (B.)**

× Fred Cosanka	= Monte Forno

FRANK PEARCE	**Winston Churchill × Paeony**	**McElderry 1973**

× Noyo	= Jim Riopelle

FRAN ROTHMAN	**Agnes de Burc × Mariano Martin**	**Hanes 1973**
FRED COSANKA	**Chrysostom × Pauline Cosanka**	**Gunzenhauser 1964 (Cosanka)**

× Amanda	= Selun	× Monte Generoso	= Monte Cervino
× Ernst Gunzenhauser	= Grand Combin	× Rimrock	= Wasserfalle
× Fort West	= Monte Forno	× San Bernardino	= Mesocco
× Frieda Gunzenhauser	= Romont	× Santa Margarita	= Chasseral
× Hans Bloch	= Frohburg	× Shooting Star	= Buchberg
× Mississippi	= Aletsch	× Wildstrubel	= Altels

FREDRICO	**Caddiana × Malibu**	**Alberts 1973**
FRENCH CREEK	**Caddiana × Lemon Slipper**	**Beall 1975**
FRIEDA GUNZENHAUSER	**Chrysostom × Mere**	**Gunzenhauser 1969 (Cosanka)**

× Fred Cosanka	= Romont	× Miriam Sacher	= Balmberg

FROHBURG	**Hans Bloch × Fred Cosanka**	**Gunzenhauser 1975**
FRORY GOLD	**H. Rushton × Gorse**	**Ratcliffe 1972**
FROSTLIGHT	**Stoke Poges × Gigi**	**Hanes 1975**
FROSTY GLOW	**Yerba Buena × Blanche Sawyer**	**Rod McLellan Co. 1971**
FUGUE	**Exelmans × Rollright**	**Pff. V. & L. 1975**

× Rollright	= Alencon

FULKING — **Catalina × Dolcoath** — **L. 1953**
× Whybourne = Noble Tree

GAËL† — **Alma Gavaert × Goultenianum** — **V. 1947**
× Calyx = Lyxel

GAMBOLA — **Paeony × Geelong** — **Ratcliffe 1973**
GAN — **F. C. Puddle × Finetta** — **Kubo 1973**
GARIBALDI*‡ — **Bronzino × Earl of Tankerville** — **H. 1918**
× Cyclops = Winter's Imp

GATES OF SPAIN — **Perilise × Huntava** — **Stewart Inc. 1975**
GAUDY-NIGHT — **Flamenco × Paeony** — **Ratcliffe 1972**
GAYBOURN — **Lambourn × Gayhurst** — **B. 1951**
× Matcheck = Gaycheck

GAY BUNTING — **Redstart × Botan** — **Ratcliffe 1972**
GAYCHECK — **Gaybourn × Matcheck** — **McElderry 1971**
× Winston Churchill = Redcheck

GAY SARA — **Happy Landing × Sarella** — **Ratcliffe 1973**
GAYSTONE — **Blondel × Tafel Rose** — **Ratcliffe 1975**
GEELONG — **Rollright × Canberra** — **Ratcliffe 1966**

× Amanda	= City Lark	× Lyric	= Sing-along
× Blendia	= Broché	× Miriam Sacher	= Merry Cascade
× Botan	= Capital Red	× Qantas	= Sky High
× Cadence	= Musicality	× Paeony	= Gambola
× Challow	= Capitolian	× Small World	= Another World
× Culmo	= City Glow	× Sparsholt	= Happy Dandy
× Demura	= Star-raker	× Startler	= Flame-Cap
× Heather Bell	= Concinnity	× Tantrum	= Tempean Spot
× Highlight	= High-Jinks	× Tapestry	= City Weaver
× Impeyan	= City Crest	× Timbrel	= City Band

GENIALITY — **Rubella × Paeony** — **Ratcliffe 1974**
GENTLE BREEZE — **bullenianum × curtisii** — **Thomdel 1974**
GERALDINE‡ — **Gertrude West × Mem. F. M. Ogilvie** — **L. 1939**
× Langley Pride = Our Creation

GERTRUDE WEST*†‡ — **Lady Phulmoni × Robert Paterson** — **B. 1929**
× Ernest Birtle = Hearty | × Gorse = Tree of Wonder

G. F. MOORE*† (see Lady Dillon*†‡)
GIALLO — **Dramatic × Lemon Hart** — **Ratcliffe 1964**
× F. C. Puddle = Aquarella | × Sunland = Grangiallo

GIANT SIMON‡ — **Christopher × Cameo** — **Sieff 1957**
× Radley = Simplesse

GIGI‡ — **Sheba × Momag** — **Freed 1958 (A.)**

× Harbur	= Via Luna Este	× Sandra Mary	= Sparkling Wine
× Harrow	= Girow	× Stoke Poges	= Frostlight
× Hellas	= Helgi	× Wendover	= Quintessence
× Lelantis	= Gilantis		

GILANTIS — **Lelantis × Gigi** — **Hanes 1972**
GINGERSNAP — **Brown Glen × Omar** — **Rod McLellan Co. 1974**
GIPSY MOTH — **Gitana × Royale** — **Ratcliffe 1972**
GIROW — **Gigi × Harrow** — **Hanes 1971**

GITANA‡	**Blagrose × Cullum**	**Cooke 1953**

× Amanda	= Romany Gay	× Lemanii Ducis	= Lematana
× Broadway	= Lipperland	× Royale	= Gipsy Moth
× Chardmoore	= Roman Umber	× Solferino	= Espresso
× Exelmans	= Madame Sans Gene	× Winston Churchill	= Wintana

GLACIATOR	**Snowberry × Chantal**	**Ratcliffe 1971**
GLAMOUR SPOT	**Rollright × Cadence**	**Ratcliffe 1973**
GLASNEVIN	**Southampton × Roger Coulson**	**D.S.O. 1963 (S.)**

× Ann Harper	= Minquas	× Golden Slipper	= Wapiti
× Bordene	= Huron	× Greenella	= Kingsessing

glaucophyllum*†‡	**species**	

(This and *chamberlainianum**† continue to be treated as distinct species for parental purposes in registration, although botanically treated by some authorities as sub-species of *victoria-regina**.)

× Anita	= Betty Nichols Powell	× hirsutissimum	= Mishtawayawininiwak
× argus	= Mascotte	× insigne	= Fanciful
× callosum	= James Fisher	× lawrenceanum	= Lawrencifillum
× Cardinal Mercier	= Capitol	× Maudiae	= Song of Mississippi
× charlesworthii	= Prelude	× purpuratum	= Pigmy
× concolor	= Tinicum	× spiceranum	= Mazurka
× Cymatodes	= Angela Wilson	× stonei	= Stone Ground
× dayanum	= Navigator	× sukhakulii	= Santa Cruz
× exul	= Sun Pebbles	× superbiens	= Mem. Rolf Bolin
× Hellas	= Assiniboine	× victoria-regina	= Vedanta

GLEE SINGER	**Lyric × Canasta**	**Ratcliffe 1973**
GLENALLA	**Sarella × Emba**	**Ratcliffe 1973**
GLENCANE†‡	**Glenshea × Hurricane**	**B. 1947**

× New Zealand	= Glenland	× Thunder Bay	= Thunderglen

GLENLAND	**Glencane × New Zealand**	**Rod McLellan Co. 1973**
GLEN MILL	**Glencane × Mill Valley**	**Rod McLellan Co. 1963**

× Hickstead	= Magic Garden		

GLOSAN‡	**Glorita × insigne**	**Nagano 1963 (Ikeda)**

× Chrysostom	= Sansostom	× Megantic	= Sakamachi

GLOWYN	**Culmo × Paeony**	**Ratcliffe 1964**

× Lockinge	= Westering	× Lyric	= Contralto

godefroyae*‡	**species**	

× concolor	= wellesleyanum (Nat. hyb.) Wellesleyanum (Reg'd. grex)	× philippinense	= Jennifer Stage
		× Santa Margarita	= Pinwheel
		× William Mathews	= Milestone

GOLDAMMER	**Sanacderae × Sweet Harmony**	**Hark 1971**
GOLD CREEK	**Pittsburg × Hellas**	**G. A. Wright 1974**
GOLDELATION	**Gorse × Lemora**	**Ratcliffe 1972**
GOLDEN ACRES‡	**Golden Diana × McLaren Park**	**Rod McLellan Co. 1963**

× Caddiana	= Cherokee	× Many Waters	= West Park
× Denehurst	= Cerritos	× Mariano Martin	= Gold Heart
× Diversion	= Erma Shulda	× Pudsana	= Born Free
× F. C. Puddle	= Golden Puddle	× Sheerline	= Rod McLellan
× Gwenpur	= Enhanced		

PAPHIOPEDILUM

Grex	Parentage	Registrant
GOLDEN CHIANTI	**Honda Gold × Chianti**	**Ratcliffe 1975 (Florentia)**
GOLDEN DIANA‡	**Dianalus × Golden Hind**	**Rod McLellan Co. 1955 (E. W. McLellan)**

× Denehurst	= King of Sweden	× Redezelle	= Goldenelle
× Gwenpur	= Robert Jones	× Rob-Ann	= LaVonne Meredith
× Pinkridge	= Vivian Sears		

Grex	Parentage	Registrant
GOLDENELLE	**Golden Diana × Redezelle**	**R. K. Meredith 1975**
GOLDEN FLEECE*†	**insigne × Antinous**	**H. 1915**

× Finetta	= Golnetta		

Grex	Parentage	Registrant
GOLDEN FROST	**H. Rushton × Sungrove**	**Ratcliffe 1971**
GOLDEN JACKET	**Bolero × Sussex Gold**	**Dunning 1973**
GOLDEN JAGUR	**Gold Mohur × Enoshima**	**Ishikawa 1973 (Ikeda)**
GOLDEN MOON*†‡	**Gold Mohur × Hancar**	**Hanbury 1937**

× Avine	= Royal Flush	× Spring Verdure	= Spring Moonlight

Grex	Parentage	Registrant
GOLDEN ORB†	**Ballyhandy × Gold Mohur**	**Cooke 1940**

× Allendale	= Limagold	× Shagreen	= Valency

Grex	Parentage	Registrant
GOLDEN PUDDLE	**F. C. Puddle × Golden Acres**	**R. K. Meredith 1974**
GOLDEN SLIPPER	**Minster Lovell × Golden Radiance**	**Freed 1961**

× concolor	= Chicopee	× Glasnevin	= Wapiti

Grex	Parentage	Registrant
GOLDEN TREASURY	**Sunwillow × Lemora**	**Ratcliffe 1972**
GOLD HEART	**Golden Acres × Mariano Martin**	**Hanes 1973**
GOLDMANTLE	**Sunland × Ambience**	**Ratcliffe 1974**
GOLD MOHUR*†‡	**Goliath × Lady Dillon**	**Moore 1922**

× Enoshima	= Golden Jagur	× Marsha White	= Marsha Gold
× Kanchanjunga	= Kanchan Mohur	× villosum	= Villos Mohur

Grex	Parentage	Registrant
GOLNETTA	**Golden Fleece × Finetta**	**Kubo 1973**
GORSE†‡	**Lady Mona × Ann Harper**	**Ratcliffe 1954**

× Albion	= Columba	× Lemora	= Goldelation
× Gertrude West	= Tree of Wonder	× Selina	= Katarina
× H. Rushton	= Frory Gold	× White Hart	= Wavey

Grex	Parentage	Registrant
GOSHIMA	**Major Hanbury Carlile × Finetta**	**Ishikawa 1973 (Ikeda)**

× Cavalcade	= Beauty Goshima	× Marsha White	= Hachizaemon

Grex	Parentage	Registrant
GOULTENIANUM*†	**callosum × curtisii**	**Goulton 1894**

× Madame Martinet	= Josephine		

Grex	Parentage	Registrant
GOWERIANUM*†‡	**curtisii × lawrenceanum**	**S. 1893**

× Bordure	= Dolores Carrion	× philippinense	= Yesteryear

Grex	Parentage	Registrant
GRACE BAY	**Moreton Bay × Grace Darling**	**Ozawa 1975**
GRACE DARLING*†‡	**Gwen Hannen × Fantasy**	**B. 1931**

× Jocelyn	= Zitronenfalter	× Moreton Bay	= Grace Bay

Grex	Parentage	Registrant
GRAMMONT	**Noyo × Ernst Gunzenhauser**	**Gunzenhauser 1975**
GRAND CANYON	**Minotaur × Farnmoore**	**Rod McLellan Co. 1963**

× Milionette	= William Milliken		

PAPHIOPEDILUM

GRAND COMBIN	Ernst Gunzenhauser × Fred Cosanka	Gunzenhauser 1975
GRAND MARCH	Mildred Hunter × Ann Barlow	Rod McLellan Co. 1973
GRANGIALLO	Sunland × Giallo	Ratcliffe 1975 (Florentia)
GREAT MOGUL*†‡	King Nicholas × Lady Dillon	Miss Moore 1929
× Burpham	= Arapaho	
GREAT PACIFIC	Pacific Ocean × Winston Churchill	McElderry 1975
GREAT WALL	London Wall × Thumbelisa	Hanes 1973
GREEN ELF	fairieanum × linii	Thomdel 1973 (Van Delden)
GREENELLA	Mimosa × Norella	Corban 1964 (M. & H.)
× Glasnevin	= Kingsessing	
GREEN GABLE‡	Beaufort × Sophelia	L. 1955
× Langtye	= Tenpaku	
GREEN GODDESS	Clair de Lune × sukhakulii	Lambert Day 1975
GREEN HEART	Borburn × Mariano Martin	Hanes 1973
GREENHORN‡	Diversion × Roger Coulson	Vallemar 1956
× Avine	= Via Victoria	
GREEN JADE	Halo × Caddiana	Hanes 1975
GREEN JEWEL	Greentippe × Halo	Rod McLellan Co. 1972
GREEN MINSTER	Bordube × Minster Lovell	Ratcliffe 1958
× Lemora	= Icegreen	
GREEN MINT	Van Ness × Gwenpur	Rod McLellan Co. 1974
GREEN MOON	La Honda × San Carlos	Rod McLellan Co. 1972
GREEN RUFFLES	Elizabeth Keeley × Wallur	D'Lin 1975 (Santa Barbara)
GREENSHANK	Beauté × Luna	Ratcliffe 1965
× Nowara	= Moleyne	× Sarella = Kiltie
GREEN SHEEN	Sunland × Zephyr	Ratcliffe 1975
GREENSTEDE†‡	Golden Moon × Dickler	Strauss 1960 (Farnes)
× Diversion	= Saint Helier	
GREENTIPPE‡	Xantippe × Green Dragon	E. C. Wilcox 1955
× Halo	= Green Jewel	
GREEN TURBAN	Shagreen × Balaclava	Ratcliffe 1974
GREENVILLE‡	Bodiam × Bahram	L. 1954
× Lemon Hart	= Hand Ball	
GREENWICK	Agnes de Burc × Yerba Buena	Rod McLellan Co. 1966 (Hanes)
× Walter Moore	= Cipriano Fabunan	
GRETNA GREEN	Sunland × Lombardy	Ratcliffe 1973
GROSVENOR	Broadwater × Calverley	A. & B. 1963
× Polpier	= Polgrove	
GROVE‡	Radley × Dalla	Ratcliffe 1967
× Baroque	= Woodcrest	× Clemency = Candle-tree
× Botan	= Ventora	× Cullum = Martelet

GROVE‡ *(continued)*

× Happy Landing	= Charmwood	× Professor Burgeff	= Libelle
× Luna	= Jozanda	× Radley	= Collegegrove
× Paeony	= Norroy	× Sarella	= Wood-hue

GRÜNBERG — **Weser × Cardinal Mercier** — **Hark 1974**
GWENANN — **Anena × Gwenpur** — **Hanes 1972**
GWEN HANNEN*†‡ — **Christopher × Florence Spencer** — **Moore 1922**

× Anna Pavlova	= Squamish	× Quarmby	= Kishacaquillas

GWENMAR — **Mariano Martin × Gwenpur** — **Hanes 1973**
GWENPUR*†‡ — **Gwen Hannen × Purity** — **Stevens Perry 1935**

× Anena	= Gwenann	× Halo	= Halgwen
× Brailes	= Lou Sasso	× McLaren Park	= Sue Brogan
× Caddiana	= Leah Hanes	× Mariano Martin	= Gwenmar
× Chardmoore	= Chargwen	× Smith Hepworth	= Laelia Aislabie
× Golden Acres	= Enhanced	× Van Ness	= Green Mint
× Golden Diana	= Robert Jones	× Yerba Buena	= Henrietta Hanes

HABITANT — **Stamperland × Yumedono** — **Hattori 1975**
HACHIZAEMON — **Goshima × Marsha White** — **Goshima 1975**
HALGWEN — **Halo × Gwenpur** — **Hanes 1973**
HALLE — **insigne × Agnes de Burc** — **Bernhart 1971**
HALO — **La Honda × Littledean** — **Rod McLellan Co. 1966**

× Caddiana	= Green Jade	× Gwenpur	= Halgwen
× Greentippe	= Green Jewel	× McLaren Park	= Lodi Spring

HALVE — **Maudiae × Finetta** — **Hattori 1975**
HAMBURG HARBOUR — **Floramond × Meigle** — **Stewart Inc. 1974 (Wichmann)**
HANAMIZU — **Cardinal Mercier × Mem. H. J. Elwes** — **Ishikawa 1973 (Ikeda)**
HAND BALL — **Greenville × Lemon Hart** — **Hattori 1975**
HANNEY — **Peter Adam × Masked Light** — **Ratcliffe 1969**

× Dakar	= Far Hills	× Wendbourn	= Solferino

HANS BLOCH — **Festive Hunter × Pauline Cosanka** — **Gunzenhauser 1969 (Cosanka)**

× Fred Cosanka	= Frohburg		

HAPLESS — **Chardmoore × Lemon Hart** — **Hattori 1975**
HAPPY BEN — **Baldovan × Ranleigh** — **Hankey 1939**

× Evanhurst	= Benhurst		

HAPPY DANDY — **Sparsholt × Geelong** — **Ratcliffe 1974**
HAPPY LANDING†‡ — **Blagrose × Great Mogul** — **Cooke 1945**

× Floramond	= Loveday	× Petronella	= Truepenny
× Grove	= Charmwood	× Sarella	= Gay Sara
× Lockinge	= Overture		

HARBELL — **Harbur × bellatulum** — **Hanes 1973**
HARBEST — **Harbur × Harrow** — **Hanes 1973**
HARBUR‡ — **Burleigh Mohur × Haroun** — **Rod McLellan Co. 1958**

× bellatulum	= Harbell	× Gigi	= Via Luna Este
× Blagrose	= Hargrose	× Harrow	= Harbest
× Burleigh Mohur	= Adornment		

HARGROSE — **Harbur × Blagrose** — **Hanes 1973**
HARMOTOME — **Lemora × Sweet Harmony** — **Ratcliffe 1971**

PAPHIOPEDILUM

HAROUN†‡ — **Lawrence of Arabia × Lucarola** — **A. 1939**

× Brownly = Cashmere

HARRI-LEEANUM*† — **Harrisianum × Leeanum** — **W. C. Clark 1893**

× Memphis = Harriphis

HARRIPHIS — **Harri-Leeanum × Memphis** — **Hattori 1975**

HARROW†‡ — **Wendwater × W. N. Evans** — **B. 1945**

×	=	×	=
× Gigi	= Girow	× Matchless	= Matrow
× Harbur	= Harbest	× Mildred Hunter	= Milrow

HAYAMA — **Milnetta × Chardmoore** — **Karasawa 1971 (Ikeda)**

haynaldianum*‡ — **species**

×	=	×	=
× Ballet Girl	= Bob Cryder	× parishii	= Bengal Lancers
× Benhurst	= Redbud	× victoria-regina	= Quirola

HAZEL HANKEY† — **Hesketh × Mrs. Marling** — **Hankey 1939**

× Amanda = Vibrance

HAZELLA — **Honey Plume × Sarella** — **Ratcliffe 1974**

HEADWATERS — **Whitehall × Qualala** — **Rod McLellan Co. 1971**

HEART OF ENGLAND — **Albion × Lemon Hart** — **Ratcliffe 1971**

HEARTY — **Ernest Birtle × Gertrude West** — **Hattori 1975**

HEATHER BELL‡ — **Wendbourn × Drayton** — **Ratcliffe 1963**

×	=	×	=
× Amanda	= Rapturist	× Geelong	= Concinnity
× Amberdale	= Another Round	× Lockinge	= Meridian Glory
× Botan	= Rederica	× Orchilla	= Orchestra
× Canberra	= Cittadella	× Repose	= Curfew-time
× Floramond	= Mountain Glow	× Wildstrubel	= Lohner

HEATHY HILL — **Chrysostom × Yumedono** — **Hattori 1975**

HEIDE‡ — **Moonrays × Sanacderae** — **Hennis 1963**

× Dalla = Marlene

HELEN MICHEL — **niveum × Matcheck** — **McElderry 1975**

HELEN MILTON — **sukhakulii × bouganvilleanum** — **M. E. Powers 1973 (Rands)**

HELGI — **Hellas × Gigi** — **Pitta 1975 (Hanes)**

HELLADERO — **Hellas × Divisadero** — **Rod McLellan Co. 1973**

HELLAMOORE — **Hellas × Milmoore** — **Nagai 1974 (Santa Barbara)**

HELLAS†‡ — **Desdemona × Tania** — **A. 1940**

×	=	×	=
× Actaeus	= Betty Bell	× La Honda	= Spring Tree
× Ann Harper	= Honeybrook	× Milmoore	= Hellamoore
× Bromohur	= Amarillo	× Paeony	= Tama
× Challow	= Ambellina	× Pittsburg	= Gold Creek
× chamberlainianum	= Hell's Chamber	× Reezy	= Amber-Glow
× Divisadero	= Helladero	× Revelstoke	= Ruth Wright
× Evansrose	= Zealandia	× San Carlos	= Via Oro
× Gigi	= Helgi	× Sandra Mary	= Essyline
× glaucophyllum	= Assiniboine	× Sunset	= Wissahickon
× Huddle	= Alabaster Brook	× Swallow	= Swahellas
× Judith Dance	= Cheesoheha	× Whitemoor	= Miniconjou

HELL'S CHAMBER — **Hellas × chamberlainianum** — **Cryder 1973**

HENRIETTA HANES — **Yerba Buena × Gwenpur** — **Hanes 1974**

HER GRACE — **Campion × Silvara** — **Ratcliffe 1975**

HESTRED†‡ | **Hestia × Mildred Hunter** | **S.A. 1948**

× Benenden = Maroon Beauty | × Wendbourn = Kimberley
× Vallarrow = Our Love

H. G. VANDER SLUIS | **Happy Landing × Lucid** | **A. & R. 1957**

× Lucid = Monterey Bay

HICKSTEAD‡ | **Beaufort × Selina** | **L. 1955**

× Glen Mill = Magic Garden | × Minster Lovell = Brunswick
× Huntsman = Bavaria

HIGASHIYAMA | **Dunstan × Lemon Hart** | **Hattori 1975**
HIGH FEATHER | **Chipmunk × Impeyan** | **Ratcliffe 1972**
HIGH-JINKS | **Highlight × Geelong** | **Ratcliffe 1975**
HIGHLIGHT | **Menthule × Cholsey** | **Ratcliffe 1967**

× Baroque = High Perfection | × Geelong = High-Jinks
× Cadence = Sonnetta

HIGH PERFECTION | **Highlight × Baroque** | **Ratcliffe 1974**
HIGH SEAS | **Buccaneer × Beauté** | **Hanes 1973**
HIGHWAYMAN | **Robin I. Hall × Sancho** | **Ratcliffe 1974**
HILDREUS | **Hildesheim × Doraeus** | **Hark 1966**

× Jocelyn = Thussi

HILLTHORPE | **Clementine H. Churchill × Oakthorpe** | **S.A. 1960**

× Schneeflocke = Breno

hirsutissimum*† | **species**

× Crescent Meadow = Fiddle Faddle | × glaucophyllum = Mishtawayawininiwak
× fairieanum = Wissinoming

HISTORIC WILLIAMSBURG | **Santa Margarita × Pacific Ocean** | **Stewart Inc. 1974**
HOLLYWOOD | **Wendover × Wooburn** | **Hankey 1945**

× Alden = Alderwood

HONDA GOLD | **Golden Diana × La Honda** | **Rod McLellan Co. 1963**

× Chianti = Golden Chianti | × Showoff = Salmonberry Creek

HONEYBROOK | **Hellas × Ann Harper** | **G. A. Wright 1974**
HONEY DEW†‡ | **Ansum × Lady Mona** | **Ratcliffe 1952**

× San Carlos = Alice Gripp

HONEY GORSE‡ | **Gorse × Honey Dew** | **Ratcliffe 1960**

× Lemora = Standon Green

HONEY PLUME | **Hellas × Honey Dew** | **Ratcliffe 1960**

× Sarella = Hazella

H. RUSHTON‡ | **Chilton × Whitemoore** | **Ratcliffe 1960**

× Gorse = Frory Gold | × Sungrove = Golden Frost

HUDDLE | **Hellas × F. C. Puddle** | **W. W. Wilson 1963 (Greendyke)**

× Hellas = Alabaster Brook

HUNKPAPA | **Inca × mastersianum** | **W. W. Wilson 1974**

HUNSTON | **Huntava × Winston Churchill** | **Hanes 1971**

PAPHIOPEDILUM

HUNTAVA†‡ — **Balaclava × Mildred Hunter** — **B. 1947**

× Matcheck = Via Sol Rojo
× Perilise = Gates of Spain
× Vallarrow = Valhunt
× Winston Churchill = Hunston

HUNTSMAN — **Joyce Winifred × Santa Claus** — **Farnes 1947**

× Hickstead = Bavaria

HURON — **Bordene × Glasnevin** — **W. W. Wilson 1972**

HYMETTUS‡ — **Minster Lovell × Honey Dew** — **Ratcliffe 1958**

× Astarte = Stardora

IANTHA STAGE — **sukhakulii × rothschildianum** — **Stage 1973 (Rands)**

IBERIA — **Decameron × Milionette** — **Stewart Inc. 1973**

ICEGREEN — **Green Minster × Lemora** — **Ratcliffe 1971**

IKEDA RED — **Shigitatsusawa × Narikatsu Ikeda** — **Ishikawa 1973 (Ikeda)**

IMOGENE KEYES — **Milionette × W. N. Evans** — **C. & I. Keyes 1975**

IMPETUOUS LASS — **Amanda × Impeyan** — **Ratcliffe 1973**

IMPEYAN — **Wendbourn × Regent** — **Ratcliffe 1965**

× Amanda = Impetuous Lass
× Cadence = Birdsong
× Chipmunk = High Feather
× Floramond = Dolly Bird
× Geelong = City Crest
× Samantha = Roseworthy
× Small World = World Flight

INCA‡ — **Chardmoore × Hellas** — **A. 1948**

× fairieanum = Osage
× Ingcar = Cohocksink
× Judith Dance = Kwakiutis
× Littledean = Incadean
× mastersianum = Hunkpapa
× Mendocino = Yakima
× Winston Churchill = Shawnee
× Yerba Buena = Incabuena

INCABUENA — **Inca × Yerba Buena** — **McElderry 1975**

INCADEAN — **Inca × Littledean** — **McElderry 1975**

INDIAN SUNSET — **Sheba × Santa Margarita** — **Stewart Inc. 1973**

INEZ‡ — **Chardmoore × Greenville** — **L. 1969**

× fairieanum = Jan Honi

INFERNO‡ — **Wendover × Fire Girl** — **D. 1952**

× Amber Star = Blazing Comet
× Small World = World Prix

INGCAR — **Trismegistris × Hancar** — **S.A. 1951**

× Cadence = Mishawaka
× Inca = Cohocksink

insigne*†‡ — **species**

× Agnes de Burc = Halle
× glaucophyllum = Fanciful

ISHAWOOA — **Susan Tucker × Whitemoor** — **W. W. Wilson 1974**

ISLAND SONG — **Jamaycus × Lyric** — **Ratcliffe 1975**

IZALCO — **Barbarrosa × Volcano** — **Sieff 1962**

× Amanda = Zalamanda

JACANA — **Floralies × David Sampson** — **Ratcliffe 1969**

× Small World = World Fantasy

JACKANORY — **Happy Grace × Tingay** — **Ratcliffe 1968**

× Small World = Jack's World

JACK'S WORLD — **Small World × Jackanory** — **Ratcliffe 1975**

PAPHIOPEDILUM

JACK TONKIN — **McLaren Park × F. C. Puddle** — **Rod McLellan Co. 1966**
× Chardmoore = Wendy Wilson

JACQUELINE KRANZ — **Barbarrosa × Floralies** — **B. 1961**
× Loganna = Ring-time

JAMAYCUS — **Radley × Drayton** — **Ratcliffe 1962**
× Amanda = Comely Ann
× Botan = Crimson Whirl
× Compton = Columbary
× Floralies = Vivo
× Lockinge = Jayking
× Lyric = Island Song
× Paeony = Royal Spice
× Samantha = Syncopation

JAMBOREE — **Compton × Canberra** — **Ratcliffe 1973**

JAMES FISHER — **callosum × glaucophyllum** — **V. Moffet 1974 (Rands)**

JAN HONI — **fairieanum × Inez** — **Holm Nielsen 1975**

JASMINE†‡ — **Golden Beauty × Florence Spencer** — **A. 1938**
× Whitemoor = Jasmoor

JASMOOR — **Whitemoor × Jasmine** — **W. W. Wilson 1971 (Greendyke)**

JASPERITE — **Momag × Botan** — **Ratcliffe 1971**

JAUNTY FAIRY — **John Keeling × fairieanum** — **Stewart Inc. 1971 (J. E. Wilson)**

javanicum*‡ — **species**
× fairieanum = Octoberfest

JAYKING — **Jamaycus × Lockinge** — **Ratcliffe 1974**

JENNIFER STAGE — **godefroyae × philippinense** — **Stage 1975 (Rands)**

JENTIQUE — **Botan × Radley** — **Ratcliffe 1972**

JIM DANDY — **Mem. F. M. Ogilvie × Blackamoor** — **E. C. Wilcox 1956**
× Olympic Forest = Erie

JIM RIOPELLE — **Noyo × Frank Pearce** — **McElderry 1975**

JOAN McLELLAN TAYLER — **Noyo × Winston Churchill** — **McElderry 1974**

JOANNE — **Dover Bridge × charlesworthii** — **Ratcliffe 1973 (Robinson)**

JOCELYN — **Minster Lovell × Desire** — **Ratcliffe 1967**
× Bradford = Mount Fuji
× Cathay = Cathyn
× Dramatic = Lippesonne
× Grace Darling = Zitronenfalter
× Hildreus = Thussi
× Lemon Grove = Major Green
× Zephyr = Cool Affair

JOCOSE — **Josette × Welcome** — **B. 1947**
× Mendocino = Tree ot Jester

JOE JOHNSON — **Radar × Avine** — **Pitta 1975 (The Orchid House)**

JOHNBOURN — **Wendbourn × Aylesbury** — **Rod McLellan Co. 1967 (Hanes)**
× Everest = Leo Organo

JOHN DOVAN†‡ — **Baldovan × John Henry** — **Jensen 1937**
× Carl Keyes = Carimo
× Paeony = Collevans
× Portland = Portovan
× Ravenswater = Rusty Rinaman

JOHN DOVAN†‡ *(continued)*

× Sunniside = Sunny Day
× Vallarrow = Mildred Munday
× Wendover = Supered
× Windrush = Windhover
× Winston Churchill = Claret Tree

JOHN HANES‡ — **Wendbourn × Gigi** — **Rod McLellan Co. 1966 (Hanes)**

× Nubian = Nairobi

JOHN KEELING*†‡ — **Mrs. Eley × Warrior** — **K. 1936**

× Etta = Keelat
× fairieanum = Jaunty Fairy

JOHN PEEL — **Dalla × Compton** — **Ratcliffe 1971**

JOHN PITTS — **Great Mogul × Noble** — **Cooke 1945**

× Startler = Star-Stone

JOLIMONT — **Chorley × Pauline Cosanka** — **Gunzenhauser 1975**

JOLLIDAY — **Flamenco × Amanda** — **Ratcliffe 1971**

JOLLY COPPER — **Copperware × Blondel** — **Ratcliffe 1972**

JOLLY MILLER — **F. C. Puddle × Dusty Miller** — **Ratcliffe 1971**

JOSEPHINE — **Madame Martinet × Goultenianum** — **Pff. V. & L. 1974**

JOY-RIDE — **Qantas × Amanda** — **Ratcliffe 1972**

JOZANDA — **Grove × Luna** — **Ratcliffe 1971**

JUDITH DANCE‡ — **Hassallii × Hestia** — **Branch 1940**

× Hellas = Cheesoheha
× Inca = Kwakiutis
× Winston Churchill = Maconaquah

JULIA MASH — **Maginot × Ann Harper** — **B. 1955**

× Betty Bracey = Brett Hughes
× Florin-Hancar = Wendy Sue
× McLaren Park = Dolores Weber
× Winston Churchill = Winnepesaukee

JURGEN NETZER — **Cymatodes × sukhakulii** — **Senghas 1973 (Netzer)**

KALANG — **Sparsholt × Kiandra** — **Ratcliffe 1974**

KANCHANJUNGA† — **The Princess × Warrior** — **Paterson 1932**

× Enoshima = Sazareishi
× Gold Mohur = Kanchan Mohur
× Milnetta = Shiraiwa

KANCHAN MOHUR — **Kanchanjunga × Gold Mohur** — **Ishikawa 1973 (Ikeda)**

KAN-ICHI TORIZAWA — **Wallur × Finetta** — **Kimura 1974**

KAPRICCIO — **Rossetti × sukhakulii** — **Röhl 1974**

KARACORUM — **Capablanca × Quadroon** — **Maggi Ponti 1955**

× Ralph = Chèque

KAREN OLSON — **Sandra Mary × Ravenswater** — **Mrs. Kay Rinaman 1975**

KATARINA — **Selina × Gorse** — **Ratcliffe 1972**

KATHERINE JASON‡ — **Milvara × Langley Pride** — **Rod McLellan Co. 1967**

× Littledean = Pacific Pride

KAYENDA — **Floramond × Lockinge** — **Ratcliffe 1972**

KAY RINAMAN — **Yerba Buena × Diversion** — **Rod McLellan Co. 1967**

× Chilton = Statuesque
× Tommie Hanes = Betty Anderson

KEELAT — **Etta × John Keeling** — **Sasso 1975 (Originator unknown)**

× Lady Kitty Laura = Cronulla
× Lady Moxham = Edith Sasso

KEYESHILL	**Carl Keyes × Winston Churchill**	**McElderry 1974**
KEYSTONE	**Marie Monday × Milionette**	**Stewart Inc. 1973**
KHARTOUM	**Blagrose × Milionette**	**Stewart Inc. 1973**
KIANDRA	**Court Jester × Canberra**	**Ratcliffe 1968**
× Sparsholt = Kalang	× Tantrum = Stampede	
KILDARY	**Floramond × Botan**	**Ratcliffe 1973**
KILTIE	**Greenshank × Sarella**	**Ratcliffe 1973**
KILVERSTONE	**Baroque × Lockinge**	**Ratcliffe 1972**
KIMBERLEY	**Hestred × Wendbourn**	**John E. Wilson 1972**
KING ALFRED	**A. Dimmock × Paeony**	**Ratcliffe 1974**
KING ARTHUR*†‡	**Bingleyense × Monsieur de Curte**	**Crombleholme 1915**
× Sandra Mary = King Sandra		
KING LEAR	**Bagshot × Mildrington**	**Stewart Inc. 1973**
KING OF SWEDEN	**Golden Diana × Denehurst**	**Rod McLellan Co. 1971**
× bellatulum = Bellalba		
KING SANDRA	**King Arthur × Sandra Mary**	**Cryder 1973**
KINGSESSING	**Glasnevin × Greenella**	**W. W. Wilson 1973**
KINGSIZE	**Chardmoore × Beauté**	**Ratcliffe 1971**
× Sweet Lute = Princess Charming		
KISHACAQUILLAS	**Gwen Hannen × Quarmby**	**W. W. Wilson 1971**
KISMET	**Aussie × Wendwater**	**B. 1955**
× Air de Ballet = Circlet		
KISO	**Wolsey × Lancaster**	**Kojima 1971 (L.)**
KOHRAISAN	**Mulatto × Enoshima**	**Ishikawa 1973 (Ikeda)**
KOISO	**Enoshima × Nena**	**Ishikawa 1973 (Ikeda)**
KOYURUGI	**Villos Mohur × Marsha White**	**Ishikawa 1973 (Ikeda)**
KWAKIUTIS	**Judith Dance × Inca**	**W. W. Wilson 1974**
LACE-WING	**Timbrel × Needlepoint**	**Ratcliffe 1973**
LA COLLETTE	**Denehurst × Celandine**	**E. E. Young 1975**
LACRESCENT	**La Honda × Crescent Meadow**	**Hanes 1972**
LADY CANARY	**Lemora × Sungrove**	**Ratcliffe 1972**
LADY DILLON*†‡ (syn. G. F. Moore*†)	**Mrs. William Mostyn × Nitens**	**Moore 1904**
× Moureen = Moudillon	× Thias = Sohma	
LADY HONEY	**Blondel × Sharon**	**Ratcliffe 1973**
LADY KITTY LAURA	**Openshaw × Resolute**	**Wiggins 1943**
× Chubby = Chubby Landy	× Keelat = Cronulla	
LADY MOXHAM	**Aylesbury × Gayhurst**	**Sasso 1950**
× Carl Keyes = Red Radiance	× Keelat = Edith Sasso	
LADY VIRTUOUS	**F. C. Puddle × Loganna**	**Ratcliffe 1972**
LAELIA AISLABIE	**Smith Hepworth × Gwenpur**	**Sasso 1974**
LA HONDA‡	**Dianalus × Cadina**	**Rod McLellan Co. 1956 (E. W. McLellan)**
× Betty Bracey = Spring Morning	× Crescent Meadow = Lacrescent	

LA HONDA‡ *(continued)*

× Denehurst = Stan Bachman's Choice
× Hellas = Spring Tree
× Mariano Martin = Dear Heart
× San Carlos = Green Moon

LAILA EMAMI	**Marbon × Winston Churchill**	**Clark Day Jr. 1972**
LAMBERT DAY	**Mariano Martin × Caddiana**	**A. & R. 1972**
LANCASTER†	**Cardinal Mercier × Grace Darling**	**Kuni 1949**

× Wolsey = Kiso

LAND OF NOD	**Sandman × F. C. Puddle**	**Ratcliffe 1971**
LANGLEY PRIDE†‡	**Euryostom × Maginot**	**B. 1947**

× Cameo = Mem. Charles Sladden
× Geraldine = Our Creation
× Louis V. Dorp = Christine E'Loy
× Milmoore = Langmoore
× Omar = Veribest
× Oxus = Xavier
× Roseland = Selspride
× Santa Margarita = Eugene Noel
× Sea Cliff = Trenchant
× Van Ness = Rodco's Pride

LANGMOORE	**Langley Pride × Milmoore**	**Stewart Inc. 1973**
LANGTYE‡	**Mongolia × Ophelia**	**L. 1949**

× Aiko Yamamoto = May Green
× Beauborough = Rica Gold
× Green Gable = Tenpaku

LANKERRAL	**Lelantis × Neil McKerral**	**Hanes 1972**
LAPPAWINZE	**Redstart × Winston Churchill**	**W. W. Wilson 1972**
LARKFIELD	**Minster Lovell × April**	**Ratcliffe 1971**
LaVONNE MEREDITH	**Rob-Ann × Golden Diana**	**R. K. Meredith 1972**
lawrenceanum*†‡	**species**	

× glaucophyllum = Lawrencifillum

LAWRENCIFILLUM	**glaucophyllum × lawrenceanum**	**Cryder 1973**
LEAH HANES	**Gwenpur × Caddiana**	**Hanes 1971**
LEEANUM*†‡	**insigne × spiceranum**	**Lawrence 1884**

× Floramond = Westfalengruss

LELANTIS	**Leven × Atlantis**	**Hanes 1971 (Rod McLellan Co.)**

× Gigi = Gilantis
× Mem. Percy Bannerman = Pink Fantasy
× Neil McKerral = Lankerral
× Perseus = Perlantis
× Winston Churchill = Winlantis

LEMANII DUCIS*†‡	**Alcibiades × Curtmannii**	**Lambeau 1918**

× Gitana = Lematana

LEMATANA	**Lemanii Ducis × Gitana**	**Pff. V. & L. 1975**
LEMONETTA	**Finetta × Lemon Hart**	**Hattori 1975**
LEMON GROVE	**Lemon Hart × Sungrove**	**Ratcliffe 1967**

× Jocelyn = Major Green

LEMON HART†‡	**Ann Harper × Desire**	**Ratcliffe 1956**

× Albion = Heart of England
× Chardmoore = Hapless
× Dunstan = Higashiyama
× Ferox = Mount Bingham
× Finetta = Lemonetta
× Greenville = Hand Ball
× Lemora = Linota
× Lombardy = Cheer Leader
× Maudiae = Daigo
× Minster Lovell = Saint Clement
× Moreton Bay = Mizuho
× Selina = Bitter Lemon
× Sunland = Lemon Sun

LEMONORA	**Lemon Silk × Lemora**	**Ratcliffe 1972**
LEMON SILK‡	**Minster Lovell × Dramatic**	**Ratcliffe 1963**

× Lemora = Lemonora

LEMON SLIPPER	**Diana Broughton × Golden Diana**	**Rod McLellan Co. 1963**

× Caddiana	= French Creek	× Revelstoke	= Otter Creek
× F. C. Puddle	= Snow Creek		

LEMON SUN	**Sunland × Lemon Hart**	**Ratcliffe 1974**
LEMORA‡	**Lemon Hart × Chilton**	**Ratcliffe 1962**

× Dusty Miller	= Mavourneen	× Silvara	= Clear Pearl
× Gorse	= Goldelation	× Sungrove	= Lady Canary
× Green Minster	= Icegreen	× Sunland	= Camberwick
× Honey Gorse	= Standon Green	× Sunwillow	= Golden Treasury
× Lemon Hart	= Linota	× Sweet Harmony	= Harmotome
× Lemon Silk	= Lemonora	× Whitemoor	= White Topper
× Sharon	= Minty-tint		

LEO ORGANO	**Johnbourn × Everest**	**Rod McLellan Co. 1973**
LETITZIA	**Happy Landing × Floralies**	**Sieff 1962**

× B. White	= Levity	× Paeony	= Letty Regal
× Oak Rose	= Letozia		

LETOZIA	**Letitzia × Oak Rose**	**Ratcliffe 1973 (Sieff)**
LETTY REGAL	**Letitzia × Paeony**	**Ratcliffe 1973 (Sieff)**
LEVEN*†	**Dickler × Floralies**	**B. 1939**

× Atlantis	= Lelantis		

LEVITY	**Letitzia × B. White**	**Ratcliffe 1973 (Sieff)**
LIBELLE	**Grove × Professor Burgeff**	**Hark 1971**
LILLIAN PITTA	**Bagshot × Omar**	**Pitta 1974 (The Orchid House)**
LIMAGOLD	**Allendale × Golden Orb**	**Ratcliffe 1971**
LINDA VASQUEZ	**Winston Churchill × Ravenswater**	**Freed 1972**
linii	**species**	

× barbatum	= Barlina	× fairieanum	= Green Elf
× callosum	= Spook	× sukhakulii	= Chehalis

LINOTA	**Lemon Hart × Lemora**	**Ratcliffe 1972**
LIPPEPERLE	**Sweet Harmony × Solferino**	**Hark 1971**
LIPPERLAND	**Broadway × Gitana**	**Hark 1971**
LIPPESONNE	**Jocelyn × Dramatic**	**Hark 1971**
LIPPETAL	**Tafel Rose × Solferino**	**Hark 1971**
LITTLE CLOWN	**Court Jester × Myzantha**	**Ratcliffe 1971**
LITTLEDEAN†‡	**Akeley × Leven**	**B. 1945**

× Inca	= Incadean	× Wallur	= Mount Tamalpias
× Katherine Jason	= Pacific Pride	× Winston Churchill	= Deanhill
× Rimalang	= Adulation		

LITTLE IRENE	**Reezy × Caddiana**	**A. & R. 1973**
LITTLE PEARL	**Rosy Dawn × niveum**	**D'Lin 1975 (Hanes)**
LOCKINGE	**Paeony × Drayton**	**Ratcliffe 1959**

× Baroque	= Kilverstone	× Canasta	= Peacemaker
× Blagrose	= Belamy	× Challow	= Rosemary Leigh
× Botan	= Rosy Dusk	× Chipmunk	= Pintado

LOCKINGE *(continued)*

× Emba	= Emberings	× Olinda	= Carmenta
× F. C. Puddle	= Alice Pink	× Paeony	= Family Circle
× Flamenco	= Fantastico	× Petronella	= Notch-wing
× Floramond	= Kayenda	× Picture	= Tempera
× Glowyn	= Westering	× Radley	= Luxury Red
× Happy Landing	= Overture	× Rampion	= Rollicker
× Heather Bell	= Meridian Glory	× Rosewood	= Rosier Red
× Jamaycus	= Jayking	× Startler	= Crimsontide
× Lyric	= Neranie	× Tapestry	= Cross-stitch

LODI SPRING — **McLaren Park × Halo** — **Rod McLellan Co. 1974**

LOGANNA — **Paeony × W. N. Evans** — **Ratcliffe 1964**

× Amanda	= Ringarose	× Lyric	= March-Fire
× Beechmast	= Anna-nutkin	× Maccoboy	= Matadora
× Canasta	= Playtime	× Olinda	= Donzel
× Captivation	= Anovation	× Paeony	= Queenanna
× Chenille	= Filoselle	× Radley	= Palestra
× Chipmunk	= Tamirose	× Rampion	= Cherimoya
× Compass	= Beacon Point	× Rollright	= Exolica
× Demura	= Taslet	× Royale	= Dulciana
× F. C. Puddle	= Lady Virtuous	× Solferino	= Pinkanaline
× Flamenco	= Cramoisy	× Startler	= Loganstone
× Floramond	= Rayande	× Tapestry	= Magic Carpet
× Jacqueline Kranz	= Ring-time	× Tombola	= Loyola

LOGANSTONE — **Startler × Loganna** — **Ratcliffe 1972**

LOHNER — **Wildstrubel × Heather Bell** — **Gunzenhauser 1975**

LOMBARD SWEET — **Candy × Lombardy** — **Ratcliffe 1973**

LOMBARDY — **Beauté × Desire** — **Ratcliffe 1964**

× Baroque	= Barytone	× Lemon Hart	= Cheer Leader
× Cadence	= Doremy	× Sunland	= Gretna Green
× Candy	= Lombard Sweet		

LONDON WALL†‡ — **Akeley × Commander Howard Wethy** — **B. 1947**

× Elizabeth Keeley	= County Fair	× Stoke Poges	= Elegy
× Pittsburg	= Scatter Creek	× Thumbelisa	= Great Wall

LORENA GORE — **Governor Robert Gore × Mem. F. M. Ogilvie** — **Siegwart 1953**

× Shooting Star	= Ruschberg		

LOUDWATER*† — **Cardinal Mercier × John Henry** — **B. 1935**

× Wendbourn	= Motoo Shimizu	× Winston Churchill	= Tree Village

LOUIS V. DORP — **Leah × Governor Robert Gore** — **Lines 1956 (Dorp)**

× Langley Pride	= Christine E'Loy		

LOU SASSO — **Brailes × Gwenpur** — **Sasso 1974**

LOVEDAY — **Happy Landing × Floramond** — **Ratcliffe 1972**

LOVENITY — **Serenity × Minster Lovell** — **Ratcliffe 1973 (Sieff)**

lowii*† — **species**

× chamberlainianum	= Mem. Arthur Freed	× fairieanum	= Zingano
× charlesworthii	= Quadriga	× tonsum	= Fern Canyon

LOYOLA — **Loganna × Tombola** — **Ratcliffe 1972**

LUCID*†‡ — **Cardinal Mercier × Lucarolo** — **Cooke 1936**

× Amanda	= Mandy-lu	× Wendover	= Superlative
× H. G. Vander Sluis	= Monterey Bay		

PAPHIOPEDILUM

LUMINANCE — **Fidelity × F. C. Puddle** — **Ratcliffe 1973**

LUNA*†‡ — **Desdemona × Mrs. Carey Batten** — **A. & B. 1923**

× Cadence = Accordance
× Grove = Jozanda
× Paeony = Regency Gold
× Windrush = Lunabrook

LUNABROOK — **Luna × Windrush** — **Ratcliffe 1974 (Sieff)**

LUNAR ORBIT‡ — **Luna × Hestia** — **Rod McLellan Co. 1964**

× Mildred Hunter = Tall Girl

LUTANIST — **Radley × Lyric** — **Ratcliffe 1971**

LUXURY RED — **Lockinge × Radley** — **Ratcliffe 1972**

LYBRA — **Aliescum × Winston Churchill** — **Hark 1974**

LYRELLO — **Rampion × Lyric** — **Ratcliffe 1973**

LYRIC — **Paeony × Lucid** — **Ratcliffe 1964**

× Amanda = Song-bird
× Botan = Tenorino
× Canasta = Glee Singer
× Cullum = Recital
× Floramond = Flower Song
× Geelong = Sing-along
× Glowyn = Contralto
× Jamaycus = Island Song
× Lockinge = Neranie
× Loganna = March-Fire
× Martelet = Plain-Song
× Radley = Lutanist
× Rampion = Lyrello
× Solferino = Solveig's Song
× Startler = Singing Star
× Tombola = Tantara

LYXEL — **Calyx × Gaël** — **Pff. V. & L. 1974**

MACCOBOY — **Wendbourn × Luna** — **Ratcliffe 1970**

× Loganna = Matadora

McLAREN PARK‡ — **Diversion × Bordube** — **Rod McLellan Co. 1957 (E. W. McLellan)**

× Avine = Carillon
× bellatulum = Belodi
× Crescent Meadow = Oasis
× Denehurst = Parkhurst
× Gwenpur = Sue Brogan
× Halo = Lodi Spring
× Julia Mash = Dolores Weber
× San Carlos = Acapulco Gold
× Snow Bunting = White Pinnacle
× Wallur = Aramingo

MACONAQUAH — **Judith Dance × Winston Churchill** — **W. W. Wilson 1975**

MADAME MARTINET*†‡ — **callosum × delenatii** — **V. 1932**

× Goultenianum = Josephine

MADAME SANS GENE — **Gitana × Exelmans** — **Pff. V. & L. 1975**

MAD HATTER — **Balaclava × Small World** — **Ratcliffe 1971**

MAGIC CARPET — **Loganna × Tapestry** — **Ratcliffe 1972**

MAGIC GARDEN — **Glen Mill × Hickstead** — **Stewart Inc. 1974 (Wichmann)**

MAGIC WORLD — **Wood Magic × Small World** — **Ratcliffe 1975**

MAGINOT*†‡ — **Chloristopher × Lady Chesham** — **B. 1940**

× Mooreheart = Moorenot
× Omar = Verinew
× Pacific Ocean = Veronique E'Loy
× Paeony = Ayjay

MAGROSE — **Momag × Blagrose** — **Ratcliffe 1972**

× Baroque = Cherry Plum

MAID OF HONOUR — **Candy Pink × Snowberry** — **Ratcliffe 1973**

MAIN OISO — **Viridissimum × Yokohama** — **Ishikawa 1973 (Ikeda)**

× Euryostom = Oisostom

PAPHIOPEDILUM

MAISHAM†	**Bisham × Maisie**	**M. Moore 1950**
× Mrs. Rickards = Enoshima		
MAJOR GREEN	**Jocelyn × Lemon Grove**	**Ratcliffe 1975**
MAJOR HANBURY CARLILE*†‡	**Troilus × Smaragdinum**	**Hanbury 1919**
× Finetta = Goshima		
MAJORLING‡	**Robert Casamajor × Grace Darling**	**E. C. Wilcox 1955**
× Diversion = Mayvirsion		
MAJOR ROSE	**Florosa × Botan**	**Ratcliffe 1974**
MAKULI	**Maudiae × sukhakulii**	**Andrew Orchids 1974**
MALIBU‡	**Ruskington × Bettina**	**Freed 1957**
× Caddiana = Fredrico		
MANACOR	**Downend × Exelmans**	**Pff. V. & L. 1973**
MANANA	**Tendresse × Floralies**	**Rod McLellan Co. 1971**
MANCHETTE	**Botan × Samantha**	**Ratcliffe 1975**
MANDY-LU	**Lucid × Amanda**	**Ratcliffe 1974**
MANIFESTO	**Timbrel × Botan**	**Ratcliffe 1972**
MANY WATERS	**Golden Moon × Commander Howard Wethey**	**Strauss 1951**
× Golden Acres = West Park		
MARBLEHEAD	**Milmoore × Vallarrow**	**Thomdel 1974**
MARBON	**Bonita × Margaret Brands**	**Clark Day Jr. 1970 (Originator unknown)**
× Winston Churchill = Laila Emami		
MARCH-FIRE	**Loganna × Lyric**	**Ratcliffe 1972**
MARGARET BRANDS*†‡	**Great Mogul × Luna**	**Jensen 1940**
× Desire = Anne Gripp		
MARGARET MacCAULL†‡	**Chesham × Doris Black**	**A & R. 1943**
× Bel Air = Belcaull		
MARGIE PITTA	**Dianita × Bordube**	**M. Pitta 1974**
MARIANO MARTIN	**Crescent Meadow × Denehurst**	**A. & R. 1959**
× Agnes de Burc = Fran Rothman	× Golden Acres = Gold Heart	
× Borburn = Green Heart	× Gwenpur = Gwenmar	
× Caddiana = Lambert Day	× La Honda = Dear Heart	
× Denehurst = Dene Martin	× Puddleham = White Mist	
MARIE-GALANTE	**Blendia × Regent**	**Pff. V. & L. 1968**
× Velizy = Asseline		
MARIE MONDAY‡	**Woodburn × Maginot**	**E. C. Wilcox 1970 (Originator unknown)**
× Milionette = Keystone	× Sandra Mary = Outrigger	
MARIN	**Orryon × Dramatic**	**Gunzenhauser 1975**
MARION FISCHER	**Sunol × San Carlos**	**Ted Fischer 1972 (Santa Barbara)**
MARLBOROUGH	Boxford × Winston Churchill	Stewart Inc. 1972
MARLENE	**Heide × Dalla**	**Herbert Bernhart 1972 (Wulfert)**
MAROON BEAUTY	**Hestred × Benenden**	**Rod McLellan Co. 1971**
MARSHADORE	**Commodore × Marsha White**	**Ishikawa 1973 (Ikeda)**

MARSHA GOLD — **Marsha White × Gold Mohur** — **Ishikawa 1973 (Ikeda)**

MARSHA WHITE‡ — **Diana Broughton × Langley Pride** — **B. 1955**

× Commodore	= Marshadore	× Goshima	= Hachizaemon
× Gold Mohur	= Marsha Gold	× Villos Mohur	= Koyurugi

MARTELET — **Cullum × Grove** — **Ratcliffe 1971**

× Lyric	= Plain-Song

MARTINIQUE — **Raïta × Blendia** — **Pff. V. & L. 1968**

× Aspac	= Asmar	× Ravenhunter	= Castillo
× Paeony	= Caravelle		

MARTY — **Pittsburg × Bromfield** — **R. K. Meredith 1975**

MARY-IRENE — **bullenianum × fairieanum** — **D'Lin 1975 (Rands)**

MARY MATCH — **Matchless × Sandra Mary** — **Cryder 1973**

MASCOTTE — **glaucophyllum × argus** — **Thomdel 1973 (Van Delden)**

MASKED LIGHT†‡ — **Cardinal Mercier × Cullum** — **Cooke 1950**

× Canasta	= Blind Man's Buff

mastersianum* — **species**

× Inca	= Hunkpapa

MATADORA — **Maccoboy × Loganna** — **Ratcliffe 1975**

MATCHECK — **Checkendon × Matchless** — **McElderry 1966 (B.)**

× Evansrose	= Rosecheck	× Redezelle	= Xclnt
× Farnmoore	= Farncheck	× Santa Margarita	= Santacheck
× Gaybourn	= Gaycheck	× Telesis	= Telecheck
× Huntava	= Via Sol Rojo	× Winston Churchill	= Wincheck
× niveum	= Helen Michel		

MATCHLESS*†‡ — **Festivity × Wargrave** — **B. 1943**

× bellatulum	= Coranta	× Harrow	= Matrow
× Burpham	= Conshohocken	× Olympic Forest	= Micmac
× Court Jester	= Testmatch	× Sandra Mary	= Mary Match

MATROW — **Matchless × Harrow** — **Hanes 1973**

MAUDIAE*†‡ — **callosum × lawrenceanum** — **C. 1900**

× Bibury	= Mount Vernon	× Lemon Hart	= Daigo
× charlesworthii	= Schaetzchen	× Mildred Hunter	= Plateau
× Emil Vacin	= Charles David	× philippinense	= Weather Vane
× Finetta	= Halve	× Procrustes	= Docteur Knock
× glaucophyllum	= Song of Mississippi	× sukhakulii	= Makuli

MAVOURNEEN — **Lemora × Dusty Miller** — **Ratcliffe 1973**

MAX MANN — **Sparsholt × Campanero** — **Gerd Röllke 1971 (Ratcliffe)**

MAY GREEN — **Aiko Yamamoto × Langtye** — **Hiroyuki Yamamoto 1973**

MAY SONG — **Whitemoor × Chantal** — **Ratcliffe 1971**

MAYVIRSION — **Mayorling × Diversion** — **Cryder 1974**

MAZURKA — **spiceranum × glaucophyllum** — **Stewart Inc. 1973 (Cryder)**

MEADOW CREST — **Diversion × Crescent Meadow** — **Hanes 1975**

MEADOW SPRITE — **concolor × Van Ness** — **Rod McLellan Co. 1974**

MECCA*†‡ — **Cardinal Mercier × Prince Albert** — **Miss Moore 1930**

× Broadwater	= Monmouth Gem

PAPHIOPEDILUM

MEGANTIC*†‡	Chrysostom × Sir H. Rawlinson	C. Moore 1929
× Glosan = Sakamachi		
MEIGLE*	Perseus × Robert Paterson	B. 1932
× Floramond = Hamburg Harbour		
MEIJŌ	Trigal × Aldergrove	K. Kojima 1973 (L.)
MELODIST	Dazzler × Cadence	Ratcliffe 1975
MEMORIA ARTHUR FALK	Bit-O'-Sunshine × Van Ness	Rod McLellan Co. 1972
MEMORIA ARTHUR FREED	lowii × chamberlainianum	Freed 1974 (Rands)
MEMORIA BILL BOURGOIN	F. C. Puddle × fairieanum	Rod McLellan Co. 1971
MEMORIA CHARLES SLADDEN	Cameo × Langley Pride	The Orchid House 1975
MEMORIA FRANZ WICHMANN	Beauté × Milmoore	Stewart Inc. 1974 (Wichmann)
MEMORIA HEINIE CHRIST	appletonianum × venustum	Cryder 1973
MEMORIA H. J. ELWES*†	Christopher × Satyr	Moore 1922
× Cardinal Mercier = Hanamizu		
MEMORIA PERCY BANNERMAN	Evanhurst × niveum	R. O. Wagner 1958 (Hager)
× Lelantis = Pink Fantasy		
MEMORIA ROLF BOLIN	glaucophyllum × superbiens	Cryder 1974
MEMORIA TOM BROWN	Paeony × Blanche Sawyer	Mrs. T. Brown 1974 (Clark Day Jr.)
MEMORY LANE	Whitemoor × Snowshine	Ratcliffe 1972
MEMORY MARGARET SPORER	Xantippe × Mrs. Carl Holmes	Pitta 1975 (E. C. Wilcox)
MEMORY ROSINA PITTA	F. C. Puddle × Stuart Wilcox	Pitta 1975 (E. C. Wilcox)
MEMPHIS*†	Cardinal Mercier × Chrysostom	C. Moore 1929
× Harri-Leeanum = Harriphis		
MENDOCINO‡	Margaret × Farnmoore	Rod McLellan Co. 1957
× Cadence = Zuni	× Jocose = Tree of Jester	
× Inca = Yakima	× Noyo = Noyocino	
MENTHULE†‡	Thule × Windrush	M. 1943
× Atlantis = Thulantis	× bellatulum = Myzantha	
MERE‡	Helem × Mayfair	L. 1950
× Whitehall = Whitemere		
MERGOLA	Nowara × Blendia	Ratcliffe 1975
MERIDIAN GLORY	Heather Bell × Lockinge	Ratcliffe 1972
MERRIMENT	Canasta × Cholsey	Ratcliffe 1971
MERRY ANDREW	Miriam Sacher × Allendale	Ratcliffe 1971
MERRYBELLS	Aylesbury × Bell Ringer	Hanes 1972
MERRY CASCADE	Geelong × Miriam Sacher	Ratcliffe 1974
MERRYTHOUGHT	Baroque × Amanda	Ratcliffe 1974
MERVYN GRANT	Desert Sun × B. White	Berman 1974 (Stonehurst)
MESOCCO	San Bernardino × Fred Cosanka	Gunzenhauser 1975

MICHAEL STEWART‡ — **William Kirch × Cathay** — **Stewart Inc. 1955**

× Betty Bracey	= Emerald Isle

MICMAC — **Matchless × Olympic Forest** — **W. W. Wilson 1973**

MILCHURCH — **Mildred Hunter × Clementine H. Churchill** — **S.A. 1960**

× Barbarita	= Bunker Hill

MILDAVIES — **Anne Davies × Milnetta** — **Ishikawa 1973 (Ikeda)**

MILDLAND — **Mildred Hunter × Portland** — **Hark 1971**

MILDRED*†‡ — **Bourtonense × Christopher** — **L. 1942**

× Finetta	= Milnetta

MILDRED HUNTER*†‡ — **Atlantis × Everest** — **B. 1937**

× Aliescum	= Westfalen	× Lunar Orbit	= Tall Girl
× Ann Barlow	= Grand March	× Maudiae	= Plateau
× Borburn	= Portelet Bay	× Mildrington	= Dragoon
× Cadence	= Choco	× Polka Dot	= Tryit Yulelikit
× Fairburn	= Bob Gunther	× Portland	= Mildland
× Harrow	= Milrow	× Winston Churchill	= Uncas

MILDRED MUNDAY — **Vallarrow × John Dovan** — **Mrs. Kay Rinaman 1975**

MILDRINGTON — **Sherrington × Mildred Hunter** — **S.A. 1952**

× Bagshot	= King Lear	× Mildred Hunter	= Dragoon

MILESTONE — **William Mathews × godefroyae** — **Rod McLellan Co. 1974**

MILIONETTE‡ — **Clarionette × Mildred Hunter** — **S.A. 1953**

× Arlina	= Eminence	× Paeony	= Sun Dance
× Blagrose	= Khartoum	× Red Angel	= Cuyahoga
× Bourneva	= Bournette	× Redstart	= Chattahoochee
× Decameron	= Iberia	× Vallarrow	= Sovereign
× Festive Hunter	= Odyssey	× Winston Churchill	= Omdurman
× Grand Canyon	= William Milliken	× W. N. Evans	= Imogene Keyes
× Marie Monday	= Keystone		

MILLER'S BOY — **Sunland × Dusty Miller** — **Ratcliffe 1973**

MILLER'S DAUGHTER — **Chantal × Dusty Miller** — **Ratcliffe 1971**

MILLER'S LUCK — **Dusty Miller × Silvara** — **Ratcliffe 1975**

MILLER'S PRIDE — **Dusty Miller × Whitemoor** — **Ratcliffe 1973**

MILL VALLEY‡ — **Clementine H. Churchill × Milvara** — **Rod McLellan Co. 1963 (E. W. McLellan)**

× Winston Churchill	= Western World

MILMOORE†‡ — **Mildred Hunter × Farnmoore** — **S.A. 1953**

× Anena	= Milnena	× Hellas	= Hellamoore
× Beauté	= Mem. Franz Wichmann	× Langley Pride	= Langmoore
× Blagrose	= Chance Medley	× Vallarrow	= Marblehead
× Dunscott	= Drifting Storm	× Winston Churchill	= Quiberon Bay

MILNENA — **Anena × Milmoore** — **Gene Boyd 1974**

MILNETTA — **Mildred × Finetta** — **Karasawa 1971**

× Anne Davies	= Mildavies	× Kanchanjunga	= Shiraiwa
× Chardmoore	= Hayama	× Ysolde	= Milsolde

MILROW — **Mildred Hunter × Harrow** — **Hanes 1972**

MILSOLDE — **Ysolde × Milnetta** — **Ishikawa 1973 (Ikeda)**

MINICONJOU — **Whitemoor × Hellas** — **W. W. Wilson 1974**

MINQUAS — **Ann Harper × Glasnevin** — **W. W. Wilson 1973**

MINSTER LOVELL†‡ **Grace Broughton × Lady Mona** **Ratcliffe 1952**

× April = Larkfield
× Hickstead = Brunswick
× Lemon Hart = Saint Clement
× Serenity = Lovenity

MINTY-TINT **Sharon × Lemora** **Ratcliffe 1973**

MIRABILE (see Calloso-barbatum*†)

MIRIAM SACHER **Hunters Moon × Bradford** **Sieff 1965 (Ratcliffe)**

× Allendale = Merry Andrew
× Chantal = New Blend
× F. C. Puddle = Quiet Green
× Frieda Gunzenhauser = Balmberg
× Geelong = Merry Cascade
× Sarella = Ellora
× Sunwillow = Willowsheen

MISCHABEL **Chilton Bay × Schneegloeckchen** **Gunzenhauser 1975**

MISHAWAKA **Ingcar × Cadence** **W. W. Wilson 1973**

MISSISSIPPI **St. Lawrence × Missouri** **Stirling 1955 (Horridge)**

× Fred Cosanka = Aletsch

MISS PRIM **Dervish × Snowberry** **Ratcliffe 1971**

MISHTAWAYAWININIWAK **glaucophyllum × hirsutissimum** **W. W. Wilson 1975**

MIZUHO **Moreton Bay × Lemon Hart** **Itoh 1973**

MOLEYNE **Nowara × Greenshank** **Ratcliffe 1974**

MOMAG†‡ **Cappamagna × Great Mogul** **A. & B. 1936**

× Blagrose = Magrose
× Botan = Jasperite

MONGE†‡ **Alain Gerbault × Richelieu** **V. 1942**

× Carl Keyes = Redflash
× Ernst Gunzenhauser = Chaumont

MONMOUTH GEM **Mecca × Broadwater** **Collett 1972 (A. & B.)**

MONTAGNARD **callosum × sukhakulii** **Thomdel 1975**

MONTE BRIONE **Crimbourne × Beechmast** **Gunzenhauser 1975**

MONTE CERVINO **Fred Cosanka × Monte Generoso** **Gunzenhauser 1975**

MONTECITO† **Bingleyense × Euryostom** **L. 1940**

× Benenden = Yahagi

MONTE FORNO **Fred Cosanka × Fort West** **Gunzenhauser 1975**

MONTE GENEROSO **Wroxham × Pauline Cosanka** **Gunzenhauser 1969 (Cosanka)**

× Albula = Monte Rosso
× Crimbourne = Monte Tamaro
× Fred Cosanka = Monte Cervino
× Piz Bernina = Monte Spluga

MONTEREY BAY **H. G. Vander Sluis × Lucid** **Cryder 1973 (Santa Barbara)**

MONTE ROSSO **Albula × Monte Generoso** **Gunzenhauser 1975**

MONTE SPLUGA **Piz Bernina × Monte Generoso** **Gunzenhauser 1975**

MONTE TAMARO **Monte Generoso × Crimbourne** **Gunzenhauser 1975**

MONTOZ **Doris Hunter × Ecrennes** **Gunzenhauser 1975**

MOONGROVE‡ **Lady Mona × Bordure** **Ratcliffe 1956**

× Dalla = Shirleydale

MOOREHEART‡ **Greatheart × Farnmoore** **Rod McLellan Co. 1957 (E. W. McLellan)**

× Maginot = Moorenot

MOORENOT **Mooreheart × Maginot** **McElderry 1975**

PAPHIOPEDILUM

Name	Parentage	Registrant
MORETON BAY†‡	**Spring Verdure × Whitehall**	**L. 1950**
× Aiko Yamamoto = Aloha Wakami Toyota	× Lemon Hart = Mizuho	
× Grace Darling = Grace Bay	× Sir Trevor = Tenryu	
MOSSO	**Sanacderae × Rampion**	**Hark 1973**
MOSELLA	**Sunland × Chianti**	**Ratcliffe 1974**
MOTOO KIMURA	**Winston Churchill × Calverley**	**B. 1974 (Kimura)**
MOTOO SHIMIZU	**Loudwater × Wendbourn**	**Kimura 1975**
MOUDILLON	**Moureen × Lady Dillon**	**Ishikawa 1973 (Ikeda)**
MOUNTAIN GLOW	**Heather Bell × Floramond**	**Ratcliffe 1972**
MOUNT BINGHAM	**Lemon Hart × Ferox**	**E. E. Young 1973**
MOUNT FUJI	**Jocelyn × Bradford**	**Goshima 1973**
MOUNT TAMALPIAS	**Wallur × Littledean**	**Rod McLellan Co. 1972**
MOUNT VERNON	**Maudiae × Bibury**	**Stewart Inc. 1974**
MOUREEN	**Chrysostom × Nesta**	**M. 1936**
× Lady Dillon = Moudillon		
MRS. CARL HOLMES*†‡	**Gwen Hannen × Moonlight**	**B. 1928**
× Xantippe = Memory Margaret Sporer		
MRS. RICKARDS*	**Earl of Tankerville × Monsieur de Curte**	**Rickards 1915**
× Maisham = Enoshima		
MUDCREEK	**Revelstoke × Pittsburg**	**G. A. Wright 1974**
MULATTO*†	**Demeter × Shogun**	**H. 1920**
× Enoshima = Kohraisan	× Worsleyi = Takatori	
MURIEL DAY	**Winston Churchill × Eighth**	**Lambert Day 1975**
MUSICALITY	**Geelong × Cadence**	**Ratcliffe 1972**
MYZANTHA	**Menthule × bellatulum**	**Ratcliffe 1971**
× Court Jester = Little Clown		
NAGARA	**Sussex Gold × Sir Trevor**	**Kojima 1971**
NAIROBI	**John Hanes × Nubian**	**Rex Foster's 1975 (Originator unknown)**
NARIKATSU IKEDA	**Betsy Raper × Carola**	**Ikeda 1968**
× Shigitatsusawa = Ikeda Red		
NASSARAH	**Cardinal Mercier × Radley**	**Ratcliffe 1972**
NATACHA	**Regent × Aspac**	**Pff. V. & L. 1974**
NAVIGATOR	**glaucophyllum × dayanum**	**Thomdel 1974**
NEEDLEPOINT	**Atlantis × Beauté**	**Ratcliffe 1965**
× Floramond = Counterpoint	× Timbrel = Lace-wing	
NEIL McKERRAL‡	**Sheba × Atlantis**	**Stewart Inc. 1960**
× Blagrose = Rose Kerral	× Pittsburg = Buck Eye	
× Lelantis = Lankerral	× Wendwater = Caballeros	
NENA*†‡	**Christopher × Senator**	**B. 1929**
× Enoshima = Koiso		
NERANIE	**Lockinge × Lyric**	**Ratcliffe 1973**
NEW BLEND	**Miriam Sacher × Chantal**	**Ratcliffe 1972**

PAPHIOPEDILUM

NEWCOMER — **Cameo × Nowara** — **Ratcliffe 1973**

NEW ZEALAND† — **Maori × Quadroon** — **S. 1947**

× Glencane = Glenland

NICHIEN — **Cardinal Mercier × Wendover** — **Ishikawa 1973 (Ikeda)**

NISQUALLY — **appletonianum × sukhakulii** — **M. E. Powers 1973 (Rands)**

niveum*†‡ — **species**

× Blanche Sawyer	= Pearlesant	× Rosy Dawn	= Little Pearl
× concolor	= Doctor Jack	× Snowberry	= Spindrift
× Matcheck	= Helen Michel	× Yerba Buena	= Besnow
× Oliviana	= Orvin		

NOBLE*† — **Garland × Redstar** — **Cooke 1937**

× Wendbourn = Wenoble

NOBLE TREE — **Whybourne × Fulking** — **Kimura 1971**

NONO — **Pinkridge × Noyo** — **R. K. Meredith 1975**

NORDENE — **Norella × Denehurst** — **Ratcliffe 1973 (Sieff)**

NORELLA‡ — **Resolute × Norina** — **M. 1953**

× Denehurst = Nordene

NORMANDY — **Aylesbury × Winston Churchill** — **Stewart Inc. 1972**

NORROY — **Grove × Paeony** — **Ratcliffe 1971**

NOTCH-WING — **Petronella × Lockinge** — **Ratcliffe 1971**

NOVENKA — **Sparsholt × Nowara** — **Ratcliffe 1973**

NOVISPHERE — **Nowara × Small World** — **Ratcliffe 1972**

NOWARA — **Bagshot × Boxford** — **B. 1969**

× Beauté	= Octave	× Greenshank	= Moleyne
× Blendia	= Mergola	× Small World	= Novisphere
× Cameo	= Newcomer	× Sparsholt	= Novenka
× F. C. Puddle	= Rosepoint		

NOYO‡ — **Paterglen × Haroun** — **Rod McLellan Co. 1963 (E. W. McLellan)**

× Ernst Gunzenhauser	= Grammont	× Pinkridge	= Nono
× Farnmoore	= Farnoyo	× Port Meadow	= Portnoyo
× Frank Pearce	= Jim Riopelle	× Revaneh	= Tossup
× Mendocino	= Noyocino	× Winston Churchill	= Joan McLellan Tayler
× Parsenn	= Silvretta		

NOYOCINO — **Noyo × Mendocino** — **McElderry 1975**

NUBIAN*†‡ — **(h. ign.—probably a Bingleyense cross)** — **— pre-1935**

× John Hanes	= Nairobi	× Redvale	= Obsidian
× Ravenhunter	= Red Beauty		

OAK ROSE — **Oakham × Evansrose** — **Sieff 1962**

× Letitzia = Letozia

OASIS — **McLaren Park × Crescent Meadow** — **Stewart Inc. 1973**

OBSIDIAN — **Redvale × Nubian** — **Rod McLellan Co. 1975**

OCEANID — **Farnmoore × Sea Cliff** — **Stewart Inc. 1973**

OCTAVE — **Nowara × Beauté** — **Hark 1973**

OCTOBERFEST — **javanicum × fairieanum** — **D'Lin 1974 (Rands)**

ODYSSEY — **Festive Hunter × Milionette** — **Stewart Inc. 1972**

PAPHIOPEDILUM

OISOSTOM — Euryostom × Main Oiso — Ishikawa 1973 (Ikeda)

OJIBWAY — Firebrand × Winston Churchill — W. W. Wilson 1973

OLD SPICE — victoria-regina × charlesworthii — Thomdel 1973 (Van Delden)

OLINDA — Cullum × Luna — Ratcliffe 1964

- × Botan = Ann Belinda
- × Floramond = Olivine
- × Lockinge = Carmenta
- × Loganna = Donzel
- × Timbrel = Caprissa

OLIVINE — Floramond × Olinda — Ratcliffe 1971

OLIVIA* — niveum × tonsum — O. Ames 1898

- × Ballet Girl = West Virginia

OLIVIANA‡ — Olivette × Diana Broughton — S.A. 1952

- × niveum = Orvin

OLNEY MILL — Dusty Miller × Battersea — Ratcliffe 1974

OLYMPIC FOREST‡ — Menthule × Milmoore — Beall 1960

- × Burpham = Santee
- × Jim Dandy = Erie
- × Matchless = Micmac

OMAR*†‡ — Hestia × Puffin — A. 1931

- × Bagshot = Lillian Pitta
- × Brown Glen = Gingersnap
- × Langley Pride = Veribest
- × Maginot = Verinew

OMAR HILL — Clementine H. Churchill × Omar — S.A. 1960

- × Evansrose = Rosehill

OMDURMAN — Winston Churchill × Milionette — Stewart Inc. 1972 (John E. Wilson)

ORCADIAN — Orchilla × Canasta — Ratcliffe 1972

ORCHESTRA — Orchilla × Heather Bell — Ratcliffe 1975

ORCHILLA — Paeony × Redstart — Ratcliffe 1962

- × Bonheure = Plumly
- × Canasta = Orcadian
- × Heather Bell = Orchestra
- × Winston Churchill = Winchilla

ORESTES† — Blendia × Conigar — Cooke 1944

- × Small World = Flying World

ORIENTAL MAGIC — bullenianum × philippinense — Thomdel 1974

ORPHEUS* — callosum × venustum — S. 1891

- × fairieanum = Dainty Lass

ORRYON‡ — Princess Marie × Avis — Kasky 1962 (Cosanka)

- × Dramatic = Marin

ORVIN — Oliviana × niveum — Gunzenhauser 1975

OSAGE — fairieanum × Inca — W. W. Wilson 1974

OSCAR SHERMAN‡ — Jasmine × Walter Moore — Sherman 1956

- × Sunol = Apple Honey

OTTER CREEK — Revelstoke × Lemon Slipper — Beall 1975 (G. A. Wright)

OUR CREATION — Geraldine × Langley Pride — Rod McLellan Co. 1971

OUR LOVE — Vallarrow × Hestred — Rod McLellan Co. 1972

OUTRIGGER — Marie Monday × Sandra Mary — Stewart Inc. 1973

OVERTURE | **Happy Landing × Lockinge** | **Ratcliffe 1972**

OXUS†‡ | **Clovis × Hestia** | **S. 1947**

× Langley Pride	= Xavier		

PACIFIC OCEAN‡ | **Farnmoore × Langley Pride** | **Vallemar 1956**

× Maginot	= Veronique E'Loy	× Sea Cliff	= Ethel Moran
× Santa Margarita	= Historic Williamsburg	× Winston Churchill	= Great Pacific

PACIFIC PRIDE | **Katherine Jason × Littledean** | **McElderry 1974**

PAEONY†‡ | **Noble × Belisaire** | **Ratcliffe 1956**

× A. Dimmock	= King Alfred	× Loganna	= Queenanna
× barbatum	= Royalet	× Luna	= Regency Gold
× Blanche Sawyer	= Mem. Tom Brown	× Maginot	= Ayjay
× Cullum	= Flush Royal	× Martinique	= Caravelle
× Dakar	= Domina	× Milionette	= Sun Dance
× F. C. Puddle	= Adornable	× Petronella	= Royal Vandyke
× Flamenco	= Gaudy-night	× Rampion	= Proud Tudor
× Floramond	= Royal Revel	× Robert Paterson	= Robertny
× Geelong	= Gambola	× Rubella	= Geniality
× Grove	= Norroy	× Sarella	= Saronia
× Hellas	= Tama	× Small World	= Regal World
× Jamaycus	= Royal Spice	× Startler	= Fast Colour
× John Dovan	= Collevans	× Whitemoor	= White Royal
× Letitzia	= Letty Regal	× Winston Churchill	= Frank Pearce
× Lockinge	= Family Circle		

PALESTRA | **Loganna × Radley** | **Ratcliffe 1973**

PALM COURT | **Candy Pink × Sarella** | **Ratcliffe 1975**

PANDION | **venustum × fairieanum** | **Wyld Court 1972**

PAPA RÖHL | **sukhakulii × fairieanum** | **Röhl 1972**

PAPYRUS*† | **charlesworthii × Earl of Tankerville** | **Mrs. Gratrix 1923**

× barbatum	= Primitive		

parishii*† | **species**

× haynaldianum	= Bengal Lancers		

PARKHURST | **Denehurst × McLaren Park** | **Rod McLellan Co. 1972**

PARRY GRIPP | **Sharnden × Blendia** | **Santa Barbara 1974**

PARSENN | **Trismegistris × Whitehall** | **Gunzenhauser 1969 (Cosanka)**

× Noyo	= Silvretta		

PASSWANG | **Brown Ousel × Rockland** | **Gunzenhauser 1975**

PAULINE COSANKA‡ | **Chrysostom × Finesse** | **Cosanka 1963**

× Chorley	= Jolimont		

PAVO | **Ravenswing × Blagrose** | **Hark 1974**

PEACEMAKER | **Canasta × Lockinge** | **Ratcliffe 1973**

PEARLESANT | **Blanche Sawyer × niveum** | **Clark Day Jr. 1975**

PEQUOT | **Vestalia × Denehurst** | **W. W. Wilson 1973**

PERFECT HARMONY | **Sweet Harmony × Sungrove** | **Ratcliffe 1973**

PERICLES‡ | **Petrel × Worsleyi** | **A. 1937**

× Divisadero	= Derocles		

PERILISE | **Pericles × Elise II** | **Stewart Inc. 1969**

× Arlina	= Boston Tea Party	× Huntava	= Gates of Spain

PERLANTIS | **Perseus × Lelantis** | **Hanes 1972**

Name	Parentage	Registrant
PERSEUS*†‡	**Alcibiades × Lady Dillon**	**W. R. Lee 1917**

× Lelantis = Perlantis

Name	Parentage	Registrant
PETALON	**Ambrosia × Sungrove**	**Ratcliffe 1971**
PETER ADAM‡	**Cullum × Lucid**	**Sieff 1957**

× Evansrose = Rose-apple | × Radley = Qunita

Name	Parentage	Registrant
PETER BLACK	**Littledean × Hellas**	**Hoyt 1960**

× Sarella = Robert McElderry

Name	Parentage	Registrant
PETRONELLA‡	**Ravenswing × Wendover**	**D. 1953**

× Floramond = Brunella
× Happy Landing = Truepenny
× Lockinge = Notch-wing
× Paeony = Royal Vandyke
× Samantha = Vivante

Name	Parentage	Registrant
PHILIPPE E'LOY	**Polka Dot × Carl Keyes**	**The Orchid House 1975**
philippinense*‡ (syn. *roebelinii*)	**species**	

× bullenianum = Oriental Magic
× godefroyae = Jennifer Stage
× Gowerianum = Yesteryear
× Maudiae = Weather Vane
× sukhakulii = Recovery

Name	Parentage	Registrant
PHILOPENA	**Dalla × Royale**	**Ratcliffe 1971**
PICTURE	**Canasta × Paeony**	**Ratcliffe 1967**

× Lockinge = Tempera

Name	Parentage	Registrant
PIGMY	**glaucophyllum × purpuratum**	**Thomdel 1973 (Van Delden)**
PIMA	**Burpham × Redezelle**	**W. W. Wilson 1975**
PINKANALINE	**Loganna × Solferino**	**Ratcliffe 1974**
PINK FANTASY	**Lelantis × Mem. Percy Bannerman**	**Rod McLellan Co. 1972**
PINK PANTIES	**Atlantis × Pinkridge**	**R. K. Meredith 1975**
PINKRIDGE	**Mildred Hunter × Mojave**	**Rod McLellan Co. 1967**

× Atlantis = Pink Panties
× Golden Diana = Vivian Sears
× Noyo = Nono

Name	Parentage	Registrant
PINTADO	**Chipmunk × Lockinge**	**Ratcliffe 1973**
PINWHEEL	**Santa Margarita × godefroyae**	**Rod McLellan Co. 1971**
PIROUETTE	**Audrey Sacher × Amber Star**	**Ratcliffe 1974**
PISAR	**concolor × delenatii**	**Birk 1973**
PITTLANDS†‡	**Brownlands × H. T. Pitt**	**S.A. 1948**

× Sandra Mary = Spellbinder

Name	Parentage	Registrant
PITTSBURG‡	**Pittlands × Gurkley**	**Rod McLellan Co. 1960 (E. W. McLellan)**

× Blagrose = Roseburg
× Bromfield = Marty
× Chardmoore = Fair Start
× Hellas = Gold Creek
× London Wall = Scatter Creek
× Neil McKerral = Buck Eye
× Revelstoke = Mudcreek
× Roble Hall = Shifting Sands

Name	Parentage	Registrant
PIZ BERNINA	**Mersey × Missouri**	**Gunzenhauser 1970 (Cosanka)**

× Monte Generoso = Monte Spluga

Name	Parentage	Registrant
PLAIN-SONG	**Martelet × Lyric**	**Ratcliffe 1971**
PLATEAU	**Mildred Hunter × Maudiae**	**Rod McLellan Co. 1971**
PLAY-GIRL	**Amanda × Canasta**	**Ratcliffe 1972**
PLAYTIME	**Canasta × Loganna**	**Ratcliffe 1972**
PLUMLY	**Bonheure × Orchilla**	**Rod McLellan Co. 1974**

POLAR CAP	**Yerba Bueno × Crescent Meadow**	**Rod McLellan Co. 1973**
POLARIS	**Blagrose × Canasta**	**Stewart Inc. 1973 (Wichmann)**
POLGROVE	**Polpier × Grosvenor**	**A. & B. 1971**
POLKA DOT	**Farnmoore × Milvara**	**Rod McLellan Co. 1963**

× Carl Keyes = Philippe E'Loy | × Mildred Hunter = Tryit Yulelikit

POLPIER	**Nancie Gamble × Edenbridge**	**Strauss 1951**

× Grosvenor = Polgrove

POQUESSING	**Cradillon × Winston Churchill**	**W. W. Wilson 1974**
PORTELET BAY	**Mildred Hunter × Borburn**	**E. E. Young 1973**
PORTLAND	**Weymouth × Ravenswing**	**D. 1952**

× John Dovan = Portovan | × Mildred Hunter = Mildland

PORT MEADOW	**Tombola × Rampion**	**Ratcliffe 1971**

× Noyo = Portnoyo

PORTNOYO	**Noyo × Port Meadow**	**McElderry 1975**
PORTOVAN	**Portland × John Dovan**	**Stewart Inc. 1975**
PRELUDE	**glaucophyllum × charlesworthii**	**Thomdel 1974**
PRIMITIVE	**Papyrus × barbatum**	**Rod McLellan Co. 1972**
PRINCESS CHARMING	**Sweet Lute × Kingsize**	**Ratcliffe 1975**
PRINCESS DIANA‡	**Diana Broughton × Princess Marie**	**C. 1961**

× Silberhorn = Balmhorn

PROCRUSTES	**Gowerianum × Maudiae**	**A. & R. 1948**

× Maudiae = Docteur Knock

PROFESSOR BURGEFF	**Hildesheim × Dammtor**	**Hennis 1964**

× Grove = Libelle | × Weser = Teutoburg

PROGRESS	**John Dovan × Decameron**	**Hanes 1969**

× Vallarrow = Telesis

PROGRESSION	**Betty Wilson × Advancement**	**Hanes 1973**
PROUD TUDOR	**Rampion × Paeony**	**Ratcliffe 1975**
PUDDLEHAM	**F. C. Puddle × Golden Diana**	**Rod McLellan Co. 1966**

× Mariano Martin = White Mist

PUDSANA‡	**Sanacderae × F. C. Puddle**	**Rod McLellan Co. 1968**

× Golden Acres = Born Free

PUDSTON	**Luston × Pudsana**	**Rod McLellan Co. 1968**

× Crastia = Crystal Creek

PUMBLECHOOK	**Roger Coulson × Anaconda**	**G. J. A. Brown 1972 (A. & B.)**
PUNXSUTAWNEY	**Clementine H. Churchill × Winston Churchill**	**W. W. Wilson 1972**
purpuratum*‡	**species**	

× glaucophyllum = Pigmy

QANTAS	**Canberra × Blendia**	**Ratcliffe 1964**

× Amanda = Joy-ride | × Robert Paterson = Skymaster
× Amber Star = Star Spree | × Small World = World Quest
× Cadence = Wings of Song | × Sparsholt = Flight Path
× Geelong = Sky High | × World Venture = Queenslander

QUADRIGA	**lowii × charlesworthii**	**Thomdel 1974**
QUALALA‡	**Selma × Clementine H. Churchill**	**Rod McLellan Co. 1957 (E. W. McLellan)**

× Whitehall = Headwaters

QUARLES	**Roaqua × Floralies**	**Stewart Inc. 1973**
QUARMBY	**Aldergrove × F. C. Puddle**	**Eastwood 1963 (M. & H.)**

× Gwen Hannen = Kishacaquillas

QUARTETTE	**Blendia × Cadence**	**Ratcliffe 1973**
QUASIMODO	**delenatii × sukhakulii**	**Birk 1974**
QUEENANNA	**Loganna × Paeony**	**Ratcliffe 1975**
QUEENSLANDER	**Qantas × World Venture**	**Ratcliffe 1974**
QUE SERA	**Emil Vacin × Reezy**	**Stewart Inc. 1973**
QUESTOVER‡	**Pocahontas × Mazeppa**	**Nell Howard 1962 (A.)**

× Blagrose = Questox

QUESTOX	**Questover × Blagrose**	**Stewart Inc. 1972**
QUIBERON BAY	**Milmoore × Winston Churchill**	**Stewart Inc. 1973**
QUIET GREEN	**Miriam Sacher × F. C. Puddle**	**Ratcliffe 1972**
QUINAULT	**sukhakulii × Quinault**	**M. E. Powers 1973 (Rands)**
QUINTESSENCE	**Gigi × Wendover**	**Rod McLellan Co. 1973**
QUIROLA	**haynaldianum × victoria-regina**	**Thomdel 1975**
QUNITA	**Peter Adam × Radley**	**Ratcliffe 1971**
RADAR	**Radina × Grace Darling**	**B. 1951**

× Avine = Joe Johnson

RADLEY†‡ — **Lucid × Blagrose** — **Ratcliffe 1954**

× Botan = Jentique
× Cardinal Mercier = Nassarah
× Evansrose = Rosie Ley
× Giant Simon = Simplesse
× Grove = Collegegrove
× Lockinge = Luxury Red
× Loganna = Palestra
× Lyric = Lutanist
× Peter Adam = Qunita
× Royale = Red Majesty

RAÏTA‡ — **Cappamagna × Regent** — **V. 1955**

× Allure = Volpone

RALPH — **Olympus × Sundown** — **Maggi Ponti 1955**

× Karacorum = Chèque

RAMPAGE	**Tigerina × Rampion**	**Ratcliffe 1973**
RAMPION	**Drayton × Telmond**	**Ratcliffe 1964**

× Amanda = Cardinal Polish
× Floramond = Compliment
× Lockinge = Rollicker
× Loganna = Cherimoya
× Lyric = Lyrello
× Paeony = Proud Tudor
× Sanacderae = Mosso
× Tigerina = Rampage
× Tombola = Port Meadow

RANLEIGH*† — **Actaeus × Christopher** — **Bromilow 1927**

× Spring Vigil = Dawn Chorus

RAPTURIST	**Heather Bell × Amanda**	**Ratcliffe 1973**
RAVENHUNTER†‡	**Mildred Hunter × Ravenswing**	**S.A. 1948**

× Martinique = Castillo
× Nubian = Red Beauty
× Rodin = Chevalier Noir

RAVENSBERG Sanacderae × callosum Herbert Bernhart 1973
RAVENSWATER Ravenswing × Wendwater B. 1958
× John Dovan = Rusty Rinaman | × Winston Churchill = Linda Vasquez
× Sandra Mary = Karen Olson

RAVENSWING†‡ Ethel H. du Pont × Floralies Hankey 1938
× Blagrose = Pavo

RAYANDE Floramond × Loganna Ratcliffe 1971
RECITAL Cullum × Lyric Ratcliffe 1973
RECOVERY sukhakulii × philippinense D'Lin 1974 (Rands)
RED ANGEL Mandalay × Angel Luscombe W. W. Wilson 1968 (M. & H.)
× Milionette = Cuyahoga | × Winston Churchill = Apache

RED BEAUTY Nubian × Ravenhunter Hanes 1974
REDBROOK Battle of Egypt × Chickadee G. A. Wright 1974
REDBUD Benhurst × haynaldianum Cryder 1974
REDCHECK Winston Churchill × Gaycheck McElderry 1975
RED CREEK Bell Ringer × W. N. Evans G. A. Wright 1974 (Hoyt)
× Chickadee = Roaring Creek

RED EAGLE Burpham × City W. W. Wilson 1975 (L.)
REDERICA Heather Bell × Botan Ratcliffe 1972
REDEZELLE‡ Robert Paterson × Doris Hunter E. C. Wilcox 1970
× Burpham = Pima | × Red Hunter = Strawberry Blond
× Golden Diana = Goldenelle | × Robin I. Hall = Red Robin
× Matcheck = Xclnt

RED FLAME Beauté × Vallarrow Hanes 1974
REDFLASH Monge × Carl Keyes Hanes 1975
RED GALETTE Solferino × Sparsholt Ratcliffe 1971
RED HUNTER Mildred Hunter × Hestred S.A. 1960
× Redezelle = Strawberry Blond

RED MAJESTY Radley × Royale Ratcliffe 1974
RED MODEL Evansrose × Wendwater Hager 1973
RED RADIANCE Carl Keyes × Lady Moxham Hanes 1975
RED ROBIN Redezelle × Robin I. Hall Rod McLellan Co. 1973
REDRUSH†‡ Red Admiral × Windrush V. 1942
× Winston Churchill = Sea Lord

REDSAND Wendwater × Sandra Mary Hanes 1972
REDSTART*†‡ Bingleyense × ? — pre-1938
× Aylesbury = Sylvan Glade | × Milionette = Chattahoochee
× Botan = Gay Bunting | × Winston Churchill = Lappawinze
× Dalla = Dear John

REDVALE Redezelle × Bonheure Rod McLellan Co. 1969
× Nubian = Obsidian

REDWAVE Advancement × Carl Keyes Hanes 1975

PAPHIOPEDILUM

REEZY — Agnes de Burc × Denehurst — Casamajor 1958 (Bracey)

× Caddiana = Little Irene
× Emil Vacin = Que Sera
× Hellas = Amber-Glow

REGAL WORLD — Paeony × Small World — Ratcliffe 1971

REGENCY GOLD — Luna × Paeony — Ratcliffe 1971

REGENT*†‡ — Eureka × Marne — Cooke 1938

× Aspac = Natacha
× Barbarrosa = Capdepera
× Cadence = Royal Trill

RENBY — Selena × Moreton Bay — L. 1964

× Ferox = Renox

RENOX — Renby × Ferox — Dunning 1973

RENTON‡ — Blagrose × Renute — M. 1954

× Bahram = Baton

REPOSE — Paeony × Blagrose — Ratcliffe 1964

× Heather Bell = Curfew-time

RESOMINSTER† — Fulminster × Resolute — M. 1943

× Balaclava = Saxony

REVANEH — Regent × Pervaneh — Stewart Inc. 1961

× Noyo = Tossup

REVELSTOKE — Ingenuense × Hellas — Hoyt 1966

× Hellas = Ruth Wright
× Lemon Slipper = Otter Creek
× Pittsburg = Mudcreek

RICA GOLD — Langtye × Beauborough — Kubo 1973 (Karasawa)

RIMALANG†‡ — Maori × Maginot — B. 1947

× Littledean = Adulation

RIMROCK† — Odin × Doris Stanton — Beall 1952

× Fred Cosanka = Wasserfalle

RINGAROSE — Amanda × Loganna — Ratcliffe 1974

RING-TIME — Jacqueline Kranz × Loganna — Ratcliffe 1972

ROAQUA — Quadroon × Roactaeus — S.A. 1946

× Floralies = Quarles

ROARING CREEK — Chickadee × Red Creek — Beall 1975 (G. A. Wright)

ROB-ANN — Shooting Star × Margaret MacCaull — Craig's 1962 (E. C. Wilcox)

× Golden Diana = LaVonne Meredith

ROBERT JONES — Golden Diana × Gwenpur — Rod McLellan Co. 1973

ROBERT McELDERRY — Peter Black × Sarella — Mrs. Kay Rinaman 1975

ROBERTNY — Robert Paterson × Paeony — Itoh 1973

ROBERT PATERSON*† — Eurybiades × Mem. F. M. Ogilvie — B. 1925

× Cadence = Banner Man
× Challow = Tree of Ikegawa
× Paeony = Robertny
× Qantas = Skymaster

ROBIN I. HALL‡ — **Momag × Floralies** — **Ratcliffe 1960**
× Redezelle = Red Robin | × Tapestry = Tapdancer
× Sancho = Highwayman |

robinsonii — **species**
× callosum = Alisal |

ROBLE HALL‡ — **Diversion × Dianalus** — **Rod McLellan Co. 1956 (E. W. McLellan)**
× Pittsburg = Shifting Sands |

ROCKAWAY — **Sheerline × F. C. Puddle** — **Ratcliffe 1971**
ROCKLAND — **Bordube × Trismegistris** — **L. 1951**
× Brown Ousel = Passwang |

RODCO'S PRIDE — **Langley Pride × Van Ness** — **Rod McLellan Co. 1971**
RODIN — **Ingres × L'Yser** — **V. 1945**
× Ravenhunter = Chevalier Noir |

ROD McLELLAN — **Sheerline × Golden Acres** — **Rod McLellan Co. 1975**
roebelinii (see philippinense*‡) — **species**
ROGER COULSON†‡ — **Emerald × Walter Moore** — **Farnes 1944**
× Anaconda = Pumblechook |

ROLLICKER — **Rampion × Lockinge** — **Ratcliffe 1973**
RÒLLRIGHT†‡ — **Mem. F. M. Ogilvie × Regent** — **Ratcliffe 1952**
× Allure = Allright | × Exelmans = Fugue
× Cadence = Glamour Spot | × Fugue = Alencon
× Calvi = Bonifacio | × Loganna = Exolica

ROMAGE — **W. N. Evans × Fire Girl** — **Pitta 1975 (The Orchid House)**
ROMAN UMBER — **Gitana × Chardmoore** — **Stewart Inc. 1975 (Van Delden)**
ROMANY GAY — **Gitana × Amanda** — **Ratcliffe 1974**
ROMONT — **Frieda Gunzenhauser × Fred Cosanka** — **Gunzenhauser 1975**
RONA‡ — **Radina × Lady Mona** — **B. 1954**
× Wellesley = Wellaron |

RON HAWLEY — **rothschildianum × Telesis** — **McElderry 1975**
ROQUETTE — **Floramond × Baroque** — **Ratcliffe 1974**
ROSANALINE — **Solferino × Tombola** — **Ratcliffe 1971**
ROSE-APPLE — **Peter Adam × Evansrose** — **Ratcliffe 1973 (Sieff)**
ROSEBURG — **Blagrose × Pittsburg** — **Stewart Inc. 1975**
ROSECHECK — **Matcheck × Evansrose** — **McElderry 1971**
ROSE FRECKLES — **Susan Tucker × Wendwater** — **Stewart Inc. 1973 (Lerchenmuller)**
ROSEHILL — **Omar Hill × Evansrose** — **Gene Boyd 1971 (Ilsley)**
ROSE KERRAL — **Neil McKerral × Blagrose** — **Hanes 1971**
ROSELAND‡ — **Mecca × Atlantis** — **A. N. Rowland 1954 (A. & B.)**
× Langley Pride = Selspride |

ROSELING‡ — **Blagrose × Gantling** — **E. C. Wilcox 1955**
× Winston Churchill = Cheryl Ann Boyd |

ROSEMARY LEIGH — **Lockinge × Challow** — **Ratcliffe 1972**

ROSEPOINT	**F. C. Puddle × Nowara**	**Ratcliffe 1972**
ROSE TAMBOUR	**Solferino × Timbrel**	**Ratcliffe 1973**
ROSEWOOD	**Paeony × Gitana**	**Ratcliffe 1963**

× Canasta = Teryrose | × Lockinge = Rosier Red
× Challow = Chalcedony |

ROSEWORTHY	**Samantha × Impeyan**	**Ratcliffe 1972**
ROSIE LEY	**Evansrose × Radley**	**Ratcliffe 1973 (Sieff)**
ROSIER RED	**Lockinge × Rosewood**	**Ratcliffe 1975**
ROSITZA‡	**Rosemary Waithman × Koritza**	**B. 1947**

× W. N. Evans = Fall Brook |

ROSSETTI*†	**insigne × Maudiae**	**H. 1908**

× sukhakulii = Kapriccio |

ROSY DAWN*†‡	**Astarte × Gwen Hannen**	**Aberconway 1935**

× Ann Harper = Crystal Brook | × niveum = Little Pearl
× fairieanum = Dawn Fairy |

ROSY DUSK	**Lockinge × Botan**	**Ratcliffe 1974**
ROSY PROSPECT	**Dusty Miller × Amanda**	**Ratcliffe 1974**
ROSY VALLEY	**Wheal Rose × Vale**	**Ratcliffe 1973 (Sieff)**
rothschildianum*‡	**species**	

× sukhakulii = Iantha Stage | × Telesis = Ron Hawley

ROUELLE	**Botan × Canasta**	**Ratcliffe 1972**
ROUGHHEWN	**Bonheure × Floralies**	**Rod McLellan Co. 1971**
ROUSSILLON	**Startler × Royale**	**Ratcliffe 1972**
ROYALE	**Paeony × Tapestry**	**Ratcliffe 1965**

× Botan = Tudoresque | × Loganna = Dulciana
× Dalla = Philopena | × Radley = Red Majesty
× Floramond = Chocolate Rouge | × Startler = Roussillon
× Gitana = Gipsy Moth | × Tombola = Benlomond

ROYALET	**barbatum × Paeony**	**Ratcliffe 1971**
ROYAL FLUSH	**Golden Moon × Avine**	**E. C. Wilcox 1972**
ROYAL GAMBLE	**Tombola × Baroque**	**Ratcliffe 1972**
ROYAL REVEL	**Floramond × Paeony**	**Ratcliffe 1973**
ROYAL SPICE	**Paeony × Jamaycus**	**Ratcliffe 1972**
ROYAL TRILL	**Regent × Cadence**	**Ratcliffe 1973**
ROYAL VANDYKE	**Petronella × Paeony**	**Ratcliffe 1973**
RUBELLA	**Barbarrosa × Blagrose**	**Ratcliffe 1964**

× Paeony = Geniality |

RUBY SPARKLER	**Solferino × Floramond**	**Ratcliffe 1971**
RUSCHBERG	**Lorena Gore × Shooting Star**	**Gunzenhauser 1975**
RUSTY RINAMAN	**John Dovan × Ravenswater**	**Mrs. Kay Rinaman 1975**
RUTH WRIGHT	**Hellas × Revelstoke**	**G. A. Wright 1974**
SAINT AUBINS BAY	**Ferox × Challow**	**E. E. Young 1973**
SAINT CLEMENT	**Lemon Hart × Minster Lovell**	**Lodge 1973**
SAINT HELIER	**Diversion × Greenstede**	**E. E. Young 1973**
SAKAMACHI	**Glosan × Megantic**	**Hattori 1975**
SAKAYATAMA	**Cardinal Mercier × Enoshima**	**Ishikawa 1973 (Ikeda)**

SALINAS	**Cymatodes × appletonianum**	**Cryder 1972**
SALMONBERRY CREEK	**Honda Gold × Showoff**	**Beal 1975**
SAMANTHA	**Lucid × Redstart**	**Ratcliffe 1962**

× Amanda	= Amaranthea	× Impeyan	= Roseworthy
× Botan	= Manchette	× Jamaycus	= Syncopation
× Floramond	= Vanadia	× Petronella	= Vivante

SANACDERAE*†‡	**insigne × San-Actaeus**	**N. C. Cookson 1905**

× callosum	= Ravensberg	× Sweet Harmony	= Goldammer
× Rampion	= Mosso		

SAN BERNARDINO	**Lady Beckton × Clementine H. Churchill**	**Gunzenhauser 1969 (Cosanka)**

× Fred Cosanka	= Mesocco		

SANBOURN	**Wendbourn × Santa Margarita**	**Hanes 1975**
SAN CARLOS‡	**Diversion × Cadina**	**Rod McLellan Co. 1959**

× Hellas	= Via Oro	× McLaren Park	= Acapulco Gold
× Honey Dew	= Alice Gripp	× Sunol	= Marion Fischer
× La Honda	= Green Moon		

SANCHO‡	**Great Mogul × Drayton**	**Ratcliffe 1961**

× Robin I. Hall	= Highwayman		

SAND HILL	**Winston Churchill × Sandra Mary**	**Lambert Day 1975**
SANDMAN	**Bradford × Dena**	**Ratcliffe 1963**

× F. C. Puddle	= Land of Nod		

SANDRA MARY‡	**Noyo × Santa Margarita**	**Rod McLellan Co. 1963**

× Bonheure	= California Queen	× Pittlands	= Spellbinder
× Gigi	= Sparkling Wine	× Ravenswater	= Karen Olson
× Hellas	= Essyline	× Wendover	= Tree of Glory
× King Arthur	= King Sandra	× Wendwater	= Redsand
× Marie Monday	= Outrigger	× Winston Churchill	= Sand Hill
× Matchless	= Mary Match		

SANSOSTOM	**Glosan × Chrysostom**	**Hattori 1975**
SANTACHECK	**Matcheck × Santa Margarita**	**McElderry 1975**
SANTA CRUZ	**glaucophyllum × sukhakulii**	**Cryder 1973**
SANTALIN	**Dalla × Botan**	**Ratcliffe 1973**
SANTA MARGARITA‡	**Margaret × Paterglen**	**Rod McLellan Co. 1957 (E. W. McLellan)**

× Eridge	= Excitement	× Pacific Ocean	= Historic Williamsburg
× Fred Cosanka	= Chasseral	× Sea Cliff	= Ziganka
× godefroyae	= Pinwheel	× Sheba	= Indian Sunset
× Langley Pride	= Eugene Noel	× Wendbourn	= Sanbourn
× Matcheck	= Santacheck		

SANTEE	**Olympic Forest × Burpham**	**W. W. Wilson 1975**
SARALINDA	**Sunland × Snowberry**	**Ratcliffe 1971**
SARELLA	**Hellas × Lady Sara**	**Morgenstern 1966**

× Blondel	= Tangold	× Miriam Sacher	= Ellora
× Candy Pink	= Palm Court	× Paeony	= Saronia
× Emba	= Glenalla	× Peter Black	= Robert McElderry
× Greenshank	= Kiltie	× Tafel Rose	= Tawny Blush
× Grove	= Wood-hue	× Sharon	= Chalemelle
× Happy Landing	= Gay Sara	× Sweet Harmony	= Clairvoyance
× Honey Plume	= Hazella		

SARONIA	**Paeony × Sarella**	**Ratcliffe 1974**
SAXONY	**Resominster × Balaclava**	**Stewart Inc. 1974 (Wichmann)**

SAZAREISHI		**Kanchanjunga × Enoshima**	**Ishikawa 1973 (Ikeda)**
SCATTER CREEK		**Pittsburg × London Wall**	**G. A. Wright 1974**
SCHAETZCHEN		**Maudiae × charlesworthii**	**Röhl 1974**
SCHNEEFLOCKE		**White Emblem × Sumurun**	**Cosanka 1963**
× Hillthorpe	= Breno		
SCHNEEGLOECKCHEN		**Sumurun × F. C. Puddle**	**Cosanka 1963**
× Chilton Bay	= Mischabel		
SEA CLIFF‡		**Littledean × Farnmoore**	**Vallemar 1956**
× Bell Ringer	= Bell Cliff	× Pacific Ocean	= Ethel Moran
× Farnmoore	= Oceanid	× Santa Margarita	= Ziganka
× Langley Pride	= Trenchant	× Warrior	= Seawar
SEALINE		**Battersea × Sheerline**	**Ratcliffe 1974**
SEA LORD		**Winston Churchill × Redrush**	**John E. Wilson 1975**
SEAWAR		**Warrior × Sea Cliff**	**Hanes 1972**
SEEKER		**Cameo × Dahmoy**	**M. W. Wood 1972 (Ratcliffe)**
× Sparsholt	= Sentinel		
SELINA		**Anita × Selene**	**M. 1936**
× Gorse	= Katarina	× Lemon Hart	= Bitter Lemon
SELSPRIDE		**Langley Pride × Roseland**	**A. J. Bell 1974**
SELUN		**Amanda × Fred Cosanka**	**Gunzenhauser 1975**
SENTINEL		**Seeker × Sparsholt**	**M. W. Wood 1972 (Ratcliffe)**
SERENDIPITY		**Advancement × Bourneva**	**Hanes 1972**
SERENITY		**Desire × April**	**Ratcliffe 1966**
× Minster Lovell	= Lovenity		
SÉVRES		**F. C. Puddle × Derdene**	**Thomdel 1975**
SHAGREEN		**Beauté × Allendale**	**Ratcliffe 1967**
× Balaclava	= Green Turban	× Golden Orb	= Valency
SHAREBA		**Candy × F. C. Puddle**	**Ratcliffe 1971**
SHARNDEN‡		**Balaclava × Otome**	**L. 1949**
× Blendia	= Parry Gripp		
SHARON‡		**Bonanza × Chilton**	**M. Ratcliffe 1959 (Ratcliffe)**
× Blondel	= Lady Honey	× Lemora	= Minty-tint
× Dramatic	= Drama Girl	× Sarella	= Chalemelle
SHAWNEE		**Winston Churchill × Inca**	**W. W. Wilson 1972**
SHEBA*†		**Decameron × Mem. J. H. Walker**	**A. 1941**
× fairieanum	= Fairy Princess	× Stoke Poges	= Spring Blush
× Santa Margarita	= Indian Sunset		
SHEERLINE		**Bradford × Lemon Hart**	**Ratcliffe 1962**
× Battersea	= Sealine	× Golden Acres	= Rod McLellan
× F. C. Puddle	= Rockaway		
SHEILA HANES		**Agnes de Burc × Caddiana**	**Hanes 1972**
SHIFTING SANDS		**Roble Hall × Pittsburg**	**Stewart Inc. 1975**

SHIGITATSUSAWA — **Cardinal Mercier × Sohma** — **Ishikawa 1973 (Ikeda)**

× Narikatsu Ikeda = Ikeda Red

SHIRAIWA — **Kanchanjunga × Milnetta** — **Ishikawa 1973 (Ikeda)**

SHIRLEYDALE — **Moongrove × Dalla** — **Ratcliffe 1971**

SHIRLEY HOLLOWAY — **Divisadero × Yerba Buena** — **McElderry 1975**

SHOOTING STAR†‡ — **Camelot × Walter Moore** — **Stirling 1948**

× Fred Cosanka = Buchberg | × Lorena Gore = Ruschberg

SHOW BOAT — **Dusty Miller × Botan** — **Ratcliffe 1973**

SHOWOFF — **Golden Diana × Gurkley** — **Rod McLellan Co. 1965**

× Burnham = Criterion Creek | × Honda Gold = Salmonberry Creek

SILBERHORN — **Renee Dupont × F. C. Puddle** — **Gunzenhauser 1969 (Cosanka)**

× Princess Diana = Balmhorn

SILVARA — **Sungrove × F. C. Puddle** — **Ratcliffe 1964**

× Campion = Her Grace | × Lemora = Clear Pearl
× Dimity = Diamora | × Snowberry = Silverberry
× Dusty Miller = Miller's Luck | × Whitemoor = Sylmar

SILVERBERRY — **Silvara × Snowberry** — **Ratcliffe 1973**

SILVER DOLLAR — **Crescent Meadow × Avine** — **E. C. Wilcox 1972**

SILVRETTA — **Parsenn × Noyo** — **Gunzenhauser 1975**

SIMPLESSE — **Radley × Giant Simon** — **Ratcliffe 1974 (Sieff)**

SING-ALONG — **Lyric × Geelong** — **Ratcliffe 1973**

SINGING STAR — **Startler × Lyric** — **Ratcliffe 1972**

SIOUX — **Winston Churchill × Gigi** — **W. W. Wilson 1969**

× Sitting Bull = Cheyenne

SIR TREVOR* — **Christopher × Casella** — **Moore 1926**

× Moreton Bay = Tenryu | × Sussex Gold = Nagara

SITTING BULL — **Great Mogul × Winston Churchill** — **W. W. Wilson 1965**

× Sioux = Cheyenne

SKY HIGH — **Geelong × Qantas** — **Ratcliffe 1973**

SKYMASTER — **Robert Paterson × Qantas** — **Ratcliffe 1972**

SMALL FRY — **bullenianum × spiceranum** — **Thomdel 1974**

SMALL WORLD‡ — **Maori × Beauté** — **Ratcliffe 1959**

× Alden = World Cruise | × Jacana = World Fantasy
× Amber Star = Starry World | × Jackanory = Jack's World
× Balaclava = Mad Hatter | × Nowara = Novisphere
× Cadence = World Song | × Orestes = Flying World
× Canasta = World Cup | × Paeony = Regal World
× Flamenco = World Fandango | × Qantas = World Quest
× Geelong = Another World | × Tantrum = Crazy World
× Impeyan = World Flight | × Wood Magic = Magic World
× Inferno = World Prix | × Woodruff = World Special

SMITH HEPWORTH — **Camelot × Princess Marie** — **K. 1944**

× Gwenpur = Laelia Aislabie

SNOWBERRY | **F. C. Puddle × Lemon Hart** | **Ratcliffe 1960**

× Candy Pink = Maid of Honour
× Chantal = Glaciator
× Dervish = Miss Prim
× Dusty Miller = Snowy Miller
× niveum = Spindrift
× Silvara = Silverberry
× Sunland = Saralinda

SNOW BUNTING†‡ | **F. C. Puddle × Florence Spencer** | **Aberconway 1942**

× McLaren Park = White Pinnacle

SNOW CREEK | **F. C. Puddle × Lemon Slipper** | **G. A. Wright 1974**

SNOWSHINE | **Moongrove × F. C. Puddle** | **Ratcliffe 1966**

× Whitemoor = Memory Lane

SNOWY MILLER | **Dusty Miller × Snowberry** | **Ratcliffe 1973**

SOHMA | **Lady Dillon × Thias** | **Ishikawa 1973 (Ikeda)**

× Cardinal Mercier = Shigitatsusawa

SOLFERINO | **Hanney × Wendbourn** | **Ratcliffe 1971**

× Bingleyense = Aunina
× Clementine H. Churchill = Animo
× Floramond = Ruby Sparkler
× Gitana = Espresso
× Loganna = Pinkanaline
× Lyric = Solveig's Song
× Sparsholt = Red Galette
× Sweet Harmony = Lippeperle
× Tafel Rose = Lippetal
× Timbrel = Rose Tambour
× Tombola = Rosanaline

SOLVEIG'S SONG | **Solferino × Lyric** | **Ratcliffe 1974**

SOME LADY | **Startler × Amanda** | **Ratcliffe 1973**

SONG-BIRD | **Lyric × Amanda** | **Ratcliffe 1973**

SONG OF MISSISSIPPI | **Maudiae × glaucophyllum** | **Dickey 1975 (Rands)**

SONNETTA | **Highlight × Cadence** | **Ratcliffe 1973**

SOPHOMORE | **fairieanum × Chardmoore** | **E. C. Wilcox 1956**

× Susan Tucker = Dusky Maiden

SOUTH PACIFIC | **chamberlainianum × bouganvilleanum** | **Cryder 1974**

SOVEREIGN | **Milionette × Vallarrow** | **Stewart Inc. 1973**

SPARDETTA | **Bernadette × Sparsholt** | **Ratcliffe 1973 (Sieff)**

SPARKLING WINE | **Sandra Mary × Gigi** | **Rod McLellan Co. 1972**

SPARSHOLT‡ | **Ernest E. Platt × Blendia** | **Ratcliffe 1959**

× Bernadette = Spardetta
× Cadence = Catrillo
× Campanero = Max Mann
× Geelong = Happy Dandy
× Kiandra = Kalang
× Nowara = Novenka
× Qantas = Flight Path
× Seeker = Sentinel
× Solferino = Red Galette
× Tantrum = Cross-bow
× Timbrel = Timoneer
× Wood Magic = Sparticus

SPARTICUS | **Sparsholt × Wood Magic** | **Ratcliffe 1974**

SPELLBINDER | **Sandra Mary × Pittlands** | **Rod McLellan Co. 1973**

spiceranum*†‡ | **species**

× bullenianum = Small Fry
× glaucophyllum = Mazurka
× sukhakulii = Acolyte

SPINDRIFT | **Snowberry × niveum** | **Ratcliffe 1971**

SPOOK | **callosum × linii** | **Feairheller 1973**

SPOTTED PUDDLE | **Bingleyense × F. C. Puddle** | **Cryder 1973 (A. & R.)**

SPRING BLUSH | **Stoke Poges × Sheba** | **Hanes 1975**

PAPHIOPEDILUM

SPRING MOONLIGHT	Spring Verdure × Golden Moon	Ratcliffe 1973 (Sieff)
SPRING MORNING	Betty Bracey × La Honda	Hanes 1975
SPRING TREE	La Honda × Hellas	Kimura 1973
SPRING VERDURE†‡	Elaine × Minnow	L. 1946

× Golden Moon	= Spring Moonlight		

SPRING VIGIL‡	Spring Verdure × Vigilant	L. 1957

× Ranleigh	= Dawn Chorus		

SQUAMISH	Gwen Hannen × Anna Pavlova	W. W. Wilson 1974
STAMPEDE	Tantrum × Kiandra	Ratcliffe 1975
STAMPERLAND*†	Christopher × Glorita	Paterson 1924

× Yumedono	= Habitant		

STAN BACHMAN'S CHOICE	La Honda × Denehurst	Rod McLellan Co. 1971
STANDON GREEN	Honey Gorse × Lemora	Ratcliffe 1972
STAR CLUSTER	Beauté × Amber Star	Ratcliffe 1973
STARDORA	Hymettus × Astarte	Ratcliffe 1971
STAR-RAKER	Demura × Geelong	Ratcliffe 1973
STARRY WORLD	Amber Star × Small World	Ratcliffe 1973
STAR SPREE	Amber Star × Qantas	Ratcliffe 1973
STAR-STONE	John Pitts × Startler	Ratcliffe 1975
STARTAN RUBY	Startler × Botan	Ratcliffe 1973
STARTLER	Masked Light × Redstart	Ratcliffe 1962

× Amanda	= Some Lady	× Loganna	= Loganstone
× Botan	= Startan Ruby	× Lyric	= Singing Star
× Floramond	= Bright Alary	× Paeony	= Fast Colour
× Geelong	= Flame-Cap	× Royale	= Roussillon
× John Pitts	= Star-Stone	× Strawberry Fair	= Fancy Fair
× Lockinge	= Crimsontide	× Tapestry	= Floss-silk

STAR TURN	Botan × Amber Star	Ratcliffe 1972
STATUESQUE	Chilton × Kay Rinaman	Rod McLellan Co. 1973
STOKEHURST	Denehurst × Stoke Poges	Gesler 1973 (N. Powell)
STOKE POGES‡	Woodnote × Emmer Green	B. 1951

× Denehurst	= Stokehurst	× London Wall	= Elegy
× Evansrose	= Stokes Rose	× Sheba	= Spring Blush
× Gigi	= Frostlight		

STOKES ROSE	Evansrose × Stoke Poges	McElderry 1974
STONE GROUND	stonei × glaucophyllum	Cryder 1975
stonei*	species	

× glaucophyllum	= Stone Ground	× victoria-regina	= Adventure

STRAWBERRY BLOND	Red Hunter × Redezelle	Cryder 1975
STRAWBERRY FAIR	Rollright × bellatulum	Ratcliffe 1960

× Canberra	= Fair City	× Startler	= Fancy Fair

STROMBOLI	Nubia × Gaston Bultel	Schroder 1929

× Floramond	= Flower Power		

STUART WILCOX	Blagrose × Evanhurst	E. C. Wilcox 1960

× F. C. Puddle	= Memory Rosina Pitta		

SUE BROGAN | **McLaren Park × Gwenpur** | **Fischer 1975 (Santa Barbara)**

SUE WORTH | **sukhakulii × charlesworthii** | **Waskow 1974**

sukhakulii‡ | **species**

× appletonianum	= Nisqually	× fairieanum	= Papa Röhl
× bouganvilleanum	= Helen Milton	× glaucophyllum	= Santa Cruz
× bullenianum	= Quinault	× linii	= Chehalis
× Calloso-barbatum	= Wedding Bells	× Maudiae	= Makuli
× callosum	= Montagnard	× philippinense	= Recovery
× charlesworthii	= Sue Worth	× Rossetti	= Kapriccio
× Clair de Lune	= Green Goddess	× rothschildianum	= Iantha Stage
× concolor	= Colorkulii	× spiceranum	= Acolyte
× Cymatodes	= Jurgen Netzer	× William Mathews	= Supersuk
× delenatii	= Quasimodo		

SUMMER-TIME | **Sunland × Sunwillow** | **Ratcliffe 1972**

SUN DANCE | **Milionette × Paeony** | **John E. Wilson 1975**

SUNGROVE‡ | **Minster Lovell × Chilton** | **Ratcliffe 1957**

× Ambrosia	= Petalon	× Sunwillow	= Carat Gold
× H. Rushton	= Golden Frost	× Sweet Harmony	= Perfect Harmony
× Lemora	= Lady Canary	× Whitemoor	= Caroltime
× Sunland	= Suntana		

SUNLAND | **Sungrove × Gorse** | **Ratcliffe 1963**

× Ambience	= Goldmantle	× Lemora	= Camberwick
× Botan	= Cimarine	× Lombardy	= Gretna Green
× Bradford	= Whimsey Green	× Snowberry	= Saralinda
× Chianti	= Mosella	× Sungrove	= Suntana
× Dusty Miller	= Miller's Boy	× Sunwillow	= Summer-time
× Giallo	= Grangiallo	× Sweet Harmony	= Sweet Land
× Lemon Hart	= Lemon Sun	× Zephyr	= Green Sheen

SUNNISIDE† | **Chrysostom × Our Prince** | **C. Cookson 1935**

× John Dovan	= Sunny Day		

SUNNY DAY | **Sunniside × John Dovan** | **Sasso 1975 (Originator unknown)**

× Tearlath	= Sunny Tears		

SUNNY TEARS | **Sunny Day × Tearlath** | **Sasso 1975 (Originator unknown)**

SUNOL | **Gantling × Bromohur** | **Rod McLellan Co. 1956 (E. W. McLellan)**

× Oscar Sherman	= Apple Honey	× San Carlos	= Marion Fischer

SUN PEBBLES | **exul × glaucophyllum** | **Stewart Inc. 1975 (A. Ferguson)**

SUNRISE | **Mrs. Carey Batten × Gold Mohur** | **Lodge 1967**

× April	= April Sun		

SUNSET†‡ | **Earl of Chester × Maudiae** | **S. 1935**

× Hellas	= Wissahickon		

SUNTANA | **Sunland × Sungrove** | **Ratcliffe 1971**

SUNWILLOW | **Sharon × Gorse** | **Ratcliffe 1964**

× Ambrosia	= Dewy Green	× Miriam Sacher	= Willowsheen
× Chipmunk	= Chipwillow	× Sungrove	= Carat Gold
× F. C. Puddle	= Willowpool	× Sunland	= Summer-time
× Lemora	= Golden Treasury		

superbiens*	**species**		
× glaucophyllum	= Mem. Rolf Bolin		
SUPERED	**Wendover × John Dovan**		**Rod McLellan Co. 1973**
SUPERLATIVE	**Lucid × Wendover**		**Rod McLellan Co. 1973**
SUPERSUK	**William Mathews × sukhakulii**		**Rod McLellan Co. 1973**
SUSAN TUCKER‡	**Shalimar × F. C. Puddle**		**A. 1954 (Atkinson)**
× Sophomore	= Dusky Maiden	× Whitemoor	= Ishawooa
× Wendwater	= Rose Freckles		
SUSSEX GOLD‡	**Beaufort × Langtye**		**L. 1964**
× Bolero	= Golden Jacket	× Sir Trevor	= Nagara
SWAHELLAS	**Hellas × Swallow**		**Cryder 1973**
SWALLOW*†	**Satyr × Swallowtail**		**H. 1921**
× Hellas	= Swahellas		
SWAN GOLD	**F. C. Puddle × Sweet Harmony**		**Ratcliffe 1974**
SWEET CHANT	**Wintersweet × Chantal**		**Ratcliffe 1974**
SWEET HARMONY	**Gorse × Desire**		**Stirling 1962 (Ratcliffe)**
× F. C. Puddle	= Swan Gold	× Solferino	= Lippeperle
× Lemora	= Harmotome	× Sungrove	= Perfect Harmony
× Sanacderae	= Goldammer	× Sunland	= Sweet Land
× Sarella	= Clairvoyance		
SWEET LAND	**Sweet Harmony × Sunland**		**Ratcliffe 1974**
SWEET LUTE	**Lucid × Beauté**		**Ratcliffe 1969**
× Kingsize	= Princess Charming	Wood Magic	= Sweet Magic
SWEET MAGIC	**Sweet Lute × Wood Magic**		**Ratcliffe 1974**
SWIFTDENE	**Gad × Mayfair**		**L. 1951**
× Borburn	= Bouley Bay		
SYLMAR	**Whitemoor × Sylvara**		**Ratcliffe 1973**
SYLVAN GLADE	**Aylesbury × Redstart**		**Scriven 1975 (Adelaide)**
SYNCOPATION	**Samantha × Jamaycus**		**Ratcliffe 1973**
TAFEL ROSE	**Hellas × Nubian**		**Ratcliffe 1965**
× Blondel	= Gaystone	× Solferino	= Lippetal
× Sarella	= Tawny Blush		
TAKATORI	**Mulatto × Worsleyi**		**Ishikawa 1973 (Ikeda)**
TALLADALE	**Balaclava × Dalla**		**Ratcliffe 1972**
TALL GIRL	**Mildred Hunter × Lunar Orbit**		Rod McLellan Co. **1971**
TAMA	**Hellas × Paeony**		**W. W. Wilson 1971**
TAMIROSE	**Chipmunk × Loganna**		**Ratcliffe 1974**
TANGOLD	**Sarella × Blondel**		**Ratcliffe 1971**
TANTARA	**Lyric × Tombola**		**Ratcliffe 1971**
TANTRUM	**Blendia × Castley**		**Ratcliffe 1965**
× Floramond	= Floritura	× Small World	= Crazy World
× Geelong	= Tempean Spot	× Sparsholt	= Cross-bow
× Kiandra	= Stampede		
TAP DANCER	**Tapestry × Robin I. Hall**		**Ratcliffe 1971**

TAPESTRY‡ — **Conrad × Gitana** — **Ratcliffe 1965**

× Botan = Fine Arts | × Lockinge = Cross-stitch
× Captivation = Captress | × Loganna = Magic Carpet
× Clemency = Belaccoyle | × Robin I. Hall = Tapdancer
× Geelong = City Weaver | × Startler = Floss-silk

TASLET — **Demura × Loganna** — **Ratcliffe 1973**
TAWNY BLUSH — **Tafel Rose × Sarella** — **Ratcliffe 1975**
TEARLATH†‡ — **Balaclava × Nancie Gamble** — **Jensen 1940**

× Evansrose = Welsh Rose | Sunny Day = Sunny Tears

TELECHECK — **Matcheck × Telesis** — **McElderry 1975**
TELESIS — **Vallarrow × Progress** — **Hanes 1972**

× Matcheck = Telecheck | × rothschildianum = Ron Hawley

TEMPEAN SPOT — **Geelong × Tantrum** — **Ratcliffe 1975**
TEMPERA — **Picture × Lockinge** — **Ratcliffe 1973**
TENDRESSE† — **Mildred Hunter × Wendover** — **B. 1947**

× Floralies = Manana |

TENORINO — **Botan × Lyric** — **Ratcliffe 1972**
TENPAKU — **Green Gable × Langtye** — **K. Kojima 1975 (L.)**
TENRYU — **Moreton Bay × Sir Trevor** — **K. Kojima 1971 (L.)**
TERYROSE — **Rosewood × Canasta** — **Ratcliffe 1973**
TESTMATCH — **Matchless × Court Jester** — **Ratcliffe 1971**

× Cadence = Catch-song |

TEUTOBURG — **Weser × Professor Burgeff** — **Herbert Bernhart 1974**
THIAS*†‡ (syn. Forest King) — **Beeckmanii × Desdemona** — **C. 1919**

× Lady Dillon = Sohma |

THULANTIS — **Menthule × Atlantis** — **A. J. Bell 1974**
THUMBELISA† — **Luna × Warrior** — **Jensen 1938**

× Farnmoore = Carefree | × London Wall = Great Wall

THUNDER BAY — **Blagrose × Blue Order** — **Beall 1960**

× Glencane = Thunderglen |

THUNDERGLEN — **Glencane × Thunder Bay** — **Hanes 1975**
THUNDER SQUALL — **Trojan × Dunscott** — **Stewart Inc. 1975**
THUSSI — **Hildreus × Jocelyn** — **Hark 1973**
TIGERINA — **Allure × Drayton** — **Ratcliffe 1967**

× Rampion = Rampage |

TIMBREL — **Blagrose × Regent** — **Ratcliffe 1964**

× Botan = Manifesto | × Olinda = Caprissa
× Cadence = Flying Colours | × Solferino = Rose Tambour
× Geelong = City Band | × Sparsholt = Timoneer
× Needlepoint = Lace-wing |

TIMONEER — **Timbrel × Sparsholt** — **Ratcliffe 1974**
TINICUM — **glaucophyllum × concolor** — **W. W. Wilson 1971**
TIP TOP — **chamberlainianum × Ballet Girl** — **Cryder 1973**

TOMBOLA Blagrose × Wendbourn Ratcliffe 1962
× Baroque = Royal Gamble
× Botan = Cloverica
× Loganna = Loyola
× Lyric = Tantara
× Rampion = Port Meadow
× Royale = Benlomond
× Solferino = Rosanaline

TOMMIE HANES Gwenpur × Greensleeves Rod McLellan Co. 1967 (Hanes)
× Kay Rinaman = Betty Anderson

TOM THUMB Anita × Avine E. C. Wilcox 1974
tonsum* species
× lowii = Fern Canyon

TORQUAY Black Moore × Chardmoore Thomdel 1975
TOSSUP Revaneh × Noyo Stewart Inc. 1975
TOWN FESTIVAL Canberra × Cadence Ratcliffe 1975
TOWN MAJOR Canberra × Challow Ratcliffe 1971
TREE OF GLORY Sandra Mary × Wendover Kimura 1973 (Rod McLellan Co.)
TREE OF IKEGAWA Robert Paterson × Challow Kimura 1974
TREE OF JESTER Jocose × Mendocino Kimura 1975 (Rod McLellan Co.)
TREE OF LEGEND Winston Churchill × Burpham Kimura 1973 (L.)
TREE OF WONDER Gertrude West × Gorse Kimura 1975
TREE VILLAGE Loudwater × Winston Churchill Kimura 1973
TRENCHANT Sea Cliff × Langley Pride Stewart Inc. 1973
TRIGAL† Conference × Sir William Chance M. 1937
× Aldergrove = Meijō

TRISTANA Clemency × Baroque Ratcliffe 1973
TROJAN†‡ Cardinal Mercier × Gerda A. 1937
× Dunscott = Thunder Squall

TROUVERE Doramasan × Albion Pff. V. & L. 1973
TRUEPENNY Happy Landing × Petronella Ratcliffe 1971
TRYIT YULELIKIT Polka Dot × Mildred Hunter Rod McLellan Co. 1972
TUDORESQUE Botan × Royale Ratcliffe 1973
TURMALIN Gitana × Cardinal Mercier Wichmann 1966
× Bernstein = Turmastein

TURMASTEIN Bernstein × Turmalin Hark 1971
UKIAH Balafine × Haroun Rod McLellan Co. 1957 (E. W. McLellan)
× Floralies = Betsy Ross

UNCAS Winston Churchill × Mildred Hunter W. W. Wilson 1972
VALE‡ Hestia × Eridge L. 1952
× Wheal Rose = Rosy Valley

VALENCY Golden Orb × Shagreen Ratcliffe 1973
VALETA Flamenco × Botan Ratcliffe 1972
VALHUNT Huntava × Vallarrow Hanes 1975
VALLANTIS Atlantis × Vallarrow Thomdel 1975

VALLARROW‡	**Rosemary Waithman × Harrow**		**Vallemar 1959**
× Atlantis	= Vallantis	× Milionette	= Sovereign
× Beauté	= Red Flame	× Milmoore	= Marblehead
× Hestred	= Our Love	× Progress	= Telesis
× Huntava	= Valhunt	× Wendbourn	= Wendarrow
× John Dovan	= Mildred Munday	× Winston Churchill	= Valwin
VALWIN	**Winston Churchill × Vallarrow**		**Hanes 1975**
VANADIA	**Samantha × Floramond**		**Ratcliffe 1972**
VAN NESS‡	**Golden Diana × Burleigh Mohur**		**Rod McLellan Co. 1962**
× Bit-O'-Sunshine	= Mem. Arthur Falk	× Gwenpur	= Green Mint
× concolor	= Meadow Sprite	× Langley Pride	= Rodco's Pride
VARINA VAUGHN	**Althea × Winston Churchill**		**McElderry 1975**
VEDANTA	**glaucophyllum × victoria-regina**		**Thomdel 1975**
VELIZY	**Exelmans × Regent**		**Pff. V. & L. 1968**
× Marie-Galante	= Asseline		
VENTORA	**Grove × Botan**		**Ratcliffe 1973**
venustum*†‡	**species**		
× appletonianum	= Mem. Heinie Christ	× fairieanum	= Pandion
× argus	= Christmas Cheer		
VERDE ORO	**Denehurst × Caddiana**		**Hanes 1972**
VERIBEST	**Omar × Langley Pride**		**Rod McLellan Co. 1972**
VERINEW	**Omar × Maginot**		**Rod McLellan Co. 1973**
VERITILARIO	**Compton × Amanda**		**Ratcliffe 1973**
VERONIQUE E'LOY	**Maginot × Pacific Ocean**		**The Orchid House 1975**
VESTALIA*†‡	**Doris Black × F. C. Puddle**		**Aberconway 1938**
× Denehurst	= Pequot		
VIA ANGEL VERDE	**Avine × Yerba Buena**		**G. & S. 1974**
VIA LUNA ESTE	**Harbur × Gigi**		**G. & S. 1974**
VIA MUCHOS NINOS	**Yerba Buena × Caddiana**		**G. & S. Int. 1975**
VIA ORO	**Hellas × San Carlos**		**G. & S. 1974**
VIA RIO VERDE	**Diversion × Wallur**		**G. & S. Int. 1975**
VIA SOL ROJO	**Huntava × Matcheck**		**G. & S. 1974**
VIA VICTORIA	**Greenhorn × Avine**		**G. & S. 1974**
VIBRANCE	**Hazel Hankey × Amanda**		**Ratcliffe 1973**
victoria-mariae* (see victoria-regina*)	**species**		
victoria-regina*	**species**		

(syn. *victoria-mariae**. *Paph. chamberlainianum**† and *Paph. glaucophyllum**†‡ continue to be treated as distinct species for horticultural, including registration, purposes, although treated as sub-species of *victoria-regina** by some authorities.)

× charlesworthii	= Old Spice	× haynaldianum	= Quirola
× glaucophyllum	= Vedanta	× stonei	= Adventure
VILLOS MOHUR	**Gold Mohur × villosum**		**Ishikawa 1973 (Ikeda)**
× Marsha White	= Koyurugi		
villosum*†‡	**species**		

(This and *Paph. boxallii**† are treated as specifically distinct for registration purposes, although regarded as conspecific by some authorities.)

× Gold Mohur	= Villos Mohur		
VIRIDISSIMUM*	**aureum × villosum**		**Shackleton 1911**
× Yokohama	= Main Oiso		

VISTAMOOR — **Chardmoore × Vista** — **L. 1952**

× Wildstrubel = Wildhorn

VIVANTE — **Samantha × Petronella** — **Ratcliffe 1973**
VIVIAN SEARS — **Golden Diana × Pinkridge** — **R. K. Meredith 1972**
VIVO — **Jamaycus × Floralies** — **Hark 1973**
VOLPONE — **Raïta × Allure** — **Pff. V. & L. 1973**
WALLUR‡ — **London Wall × Bromohur** — **Rod McLellan Co. 1958 (E. W. McLellan)**

× Diversion = Via Rio Verde
× Divisadero = Engraved
× Elizabeth Keeley = Green Ruffles
× Finetta = Kan-Ichi Torizawa
× Littledean = Mount Tamalpias
× McLaren Park = Aramingo

WALTER MOORE*†‡ — **Gwea Hannen × Mrs. Eley** — **Miss Moore 1931**

× Greenwick = Cipriano Fabunan

WANDRIAN — **Amanda × Wendbourn** — **Ratcliffe 1974 (Sieff)**

WAPITI — **Glasnevin × Golden Slipper** — **W. W. Wilson 1974**
WARHILL — **Warrior × Winston Churchill** — **Hanes 1975**
WARRIOR*† — **Alcibiades × Lord Wolmer** — **S. 1920**

× Barbarrosa = Campaigner
× Sea Cliff = Seawar
× Winston Churchill = Warhill

WASSERFALLE — **Rimrock × Fred Cosanka** — **Gunzenhauser 1975**
WATERSPRITE — **F. C. Puddle × Blondel** — **Ratcliffe 1975**
WAVEY — **Gorse × White Hart** — **Ratcliffe 1971**
WEATHER VANE — **Maudiae × philippinense** — **Thomdel 1975**
WEDDING BELLS — **sukhakulii × Calloso-barbatum** — **Andrew Orchids 1974**
WEISSENSTEIN — **bellatulum × F. C. Puddle** — **Gunzenhauser 1975**
WELLARON — **Wellesley × Rona** — **Stewart Inc. 1973 (Hoyt)**

WELLESLEY*† — **Grace Darling × Ranger** — **S.A. 1937**

× Rona = Wellaron

wellesleyanum / **WELLESLEYANUM** — **godefroyae × concolor** — **Nat. hyb.** / **Alberts 1975**
WELSH ROSE — **Evansrose × Tearlath** — **Lodge 1973**
WENDARROW — **Vallarrow × Wendbourn** — **Hanes 1973**
WENDBELL — **Wendbourn × bellatulum** — **Hanes 1973**
WENDBOURN†‡ — **Lambourn × Wendwater** — **B. 1949**

× Advancement = Wendfall
× Amanda = Wandrian
× bellatulum = Wendbell
× Bevis = Wood Magic
× Carnival = Fornax
×. Culmo = Culmavina
× fairieanum = Arne Honi
× Hanney = Solferino
× Hestred = Kimberley
× Loudwater = Motoo Shimizu
× Noble = Wenoble
× Santa Margarita = Sanbourn
× Vallarrow = Wendarrow

WENDFALL — **Wendbourn × Advancement** — **Hanes 1973**
WENDHILL — **Wendwater × Winston Churchill** — **Hanes 1972**
WENDOVER*†‡ — **Atlantis × John Henry** — **B. 1936**

× Cardinal Mercier = Nichien
× Chardmoore = Aristocratic Beauty
× delenatii = Cotton Candy
× Gigi = Quintessence
× John Dovan = Supered
× Lucid = Superlative
× Sandra Mary = Tree of Glory

WENDSHOT — **Wendwater × Bagshot** — **Hanes 1975**
WENDWATER*†‡ — **Loudwater × Wendover** — **B. 1943**

× Bagshot = Wendshot
× Evansrose = Red Model
× F. C. Puddle = Dusty Rose
× Neil McKerral = Caballeros
× Sandra Mary = Redsand
× Susan Tucker = Rose Freckles
× Winston Churchill = Wendhill

WENDY SUE — **Julia Mash × Florin-Hancar** — **Lambert Day 1975**
WENDY WILSON — **Jack Tonkin × Chardmoore** — **John E. Wilson 1975**
WENOBLE — **Wendbourn × Noble** — **Hanes 1975**
WESER‡ — **Scarlet Prince × Cardeba** — **Hennis 1959**

× Cardinal Mercier = Grünberg
× Professor Burgeff = Teutoburg

WESTERING — **Lockinge × Glowyn** — **Ratcliffe 1974**
WESTERN WORLD — **Mill Valley × Winston Churchill** — **McElderry 1974**
WESTFALEN — **Aliescum × Mildred Hunter** — **Hark 1971**
WESTFALENGRUSS — **Leeanum × Floramond** — **Hark 1971**
WEST PARK — **Golden Acres × Many Waters** — **E. E. Young 1973**
WEST VIRGINIA — **Ballet Girl × Olivia** — **Cryder 1974**
WHEAL ROSE† — **Carandra × Doris Stanton** — **L. 1946**

× Vale = Rosy Valley

WHIMSEY GREEN — **Sunland × Bradford** — **Ratcliffe 1971**
WHITEHALL†‡ — **Conference × A. K. Berry** — **S. 1942**

× Mere = Whitemere
× Qualala = Headwaters

WHITE HART — **Whitemoor × Lemon Hart** — **Ratcliffe 1960**

× Gorse = Wavey

WHITE ICE — **Chardmoore × Yerba Buena** — **Hanes 1975**
WHITEMERE — **Mere × Whitehall** — **W. W. Wilson 1971**
WHITE MIST — **Mariano Martin × Puddleham** — **Hanes 1973**
WHITEMOOR†‡ — **Dervish × F. C. Puddle** — **Cooke 1947**

× Chantal = May Song
× Dusty Miller = Miller's Pride
× Hellas = Miniconjou
× Jasmine = Jasmoor
× Lemora = White Topper
× Paeony = White Royal
× Silvara = Sylmar
× Snowshine = Memory Lane
× Sungrove = Caroltime
× Susan Tucker = Ishawooa

WHITE PINNACLE — **Snow Bunting × McLaren Park** — **Rod McLellan Co. 1971**
WHITE ROYAL — **Whitemoor × Paeony** — **Ratcliffe 1972**
WHITE TOPPER — **Whitemoor × Lemora** — **Ratcliffe 1971**
WHYBOURNE‡ — **Georgetta × Vista** — **L. 1951**

× Fulking = Noble Tree

WICHITA — **Black Thorpe × fairieanum** — **W. W. Wilson 1974**
WILD DUCK — **Dickler × Dicksum** — **Jo Johnstone 1975 (Clark Day Jr.)**
WILDHORN — **Wildstrubel × Vistamoor** — **Gunzenhauser 1975**
WILDSTRUBEL — **Hickling × Pauline Cosanka** — **Gunzenhauser 1969 (Cosanka)**

× Fred Cosanka = Altels
× Heather Bell = Lohner
× Vistamoor = Wildhorn

WILLIAM MATHEWS* — **lawrenceanum × mastersianum** — **C. 1899**

× godefroyae = Milestone
× sukhakulii = Supersuk

WILLIAM MILLIKEN	**Milionette × Grand Canyon**	**Rod McLellan Co. 1973**
WILLIAM STIRLING†	**Juliet × Lucifer**	**S. 1940**

× Dalla = Fatiha

WILLOWPOOL	**F. C. Puddle × Sunwillow**	**Ratcliffe 1971**
WILLOWSHEEN	**Miriam Sacher × Sunwillow**	**Ratcliffe 1975**
WINCADE	**Cavalcade × Winston Churchill**	**Hanes 1972**
WINCHECK	**Winston Churchill × Matcheck**	**Hanes 1975**
WINCHILLA	**Winston Churchill × Orchilla**	**McElderry 1975**
WINDHOVER	**John Dovan × Windrush**	**Ratcliffe 1973 (Sieff)**
WINDRUSH*†‡	**Christopher × Radiosum**	**Miss Moore—**

× John Dovan = Windhover
× Luna = Lunabrook

WINEER	**Buccaneer × Winston Churchill**	**Hanes 1975**
WINGS OF SONG	**Qantas × Cadence**	**Ratcliffe 1972**
WINLANTIS	**Winston Churchill × Lelantis**	**Hanes 1972**
WINMOORE	**Winston Churchill × Farnmoore**	**Kensington 1974**
WINNEPESAUKEE	**Julia Mash × Winston Churchill**	**W. W. Wilson 1975**
WINSTON CHURCHILL†‡	**Eridge × Hampden**	**L. 1951**

× Aliescum = Lybra
× Althea = Varina Vaughn
× Amanda = Amandahill
× Aylesbury = Normandy
× Betty Wilson = Ace High
× Black Thorpe = Duncan York
× Bourndilly = Emistesigo
× Boxford = Marlborough
× Brulmoore = Everett Wilcox
× Buccaneer = Wineer
× Burpham = Tree of Legend
× Calverley = Motoo Kimura
× Cameo = Cajto
× Canberra = Canbhill
× Carl Keyes = Keyeshill
× Cavalcade = Wincade
× Charjan = Charhill
× Clementine H. Churchill = Punxsutawney
× Cradillon = Poquessing
× Eighth = Muriel Day
× Evanhurst = Crow Creek
× Evansrose = Beatrice Ernst
× Farnmoore = Winmoore
× Festive Hunter = Brenner Pass
× Firebrand = Ojibway
× Floralies = Blenheim Palace
× Gaycheck = Redcheck
× Gitana = Wintana
× Huntava = Hunston
× Inca = Shawnee
× John Dovan = Claret Tree
× Judith Dance = Maconaquah
× Julia Mash = Winnepesaukee
× Lelantis = Winlantis
× Littledean = Deanhill
× Loudwater = Tree Village
× Marbon = Laila Emami
× Matcheck = Wincheck
× Mildred Hunter = Uncas
× Milionette = Omdurman
× Mill Valley = Western World
× Milmoore = Quiberon Bay
× Noyo = Joan McLellan Tayler
× Orchilla = Winchilla
× Pacific Ocean = Great Pacific
× Paeony = Frank Pearce
× Ravenswater = Linda Vasquez
× Red Angel = Apache
× Redrush = Sea Lord
× Redstart = Lappawinze
× Roseling = Cheryl Ann Boyd
× Sandra Mary = Sand Hill
× Vallarrow = Valwin
× Warrior = Warhill
× Wendwater = Wendhill

WINTANA	**Gitana × Winston Churchill**	**Hanes 1975**
WINTER'S IMP	**Cyclops × Garibaldi**	**Rod McLellan Co. 1972**
WINTER'S MILL	**Dusty Miller × Wintersweet**	**Ratcliffe 1975**
WINTERSWEET	**Sungrove × Brixton**	**Ratcliffe 1967**

× Chantal = Sweet Chant
× Dusty Miller = Winter's Mill

WISSAHICKON	**Sunset × Hellas**	**W. W. Wilson 1975**
WISSINOMING	**fairieanum × hirsutissimum**	**W. W. Wilson 1974**
W. N. EVANS*†‡	**Floralies × Kay Kay**	**B. 1941**

× Bell Ringer = Red Creek
× Fire Girl = Romage
× Milionette = Imogene Keyes
× Rositza = Fall Brook

PAPHIOPEDILUM

Hybrid	Parentage	Registrant
WOLSEY‡	**Cardinal Mercier × Perseus**	**A. E. Dale 1930**
× Lancaster	= Kiso	
WOODCREST	**Baroque × Grove**	**Ratcliffe 1975**
WOOD-HUE	**Grove × Sarella**	**Ratcliffe 1975**
WOOD MAGIC	**Wendbourn × Bevis**	**Ratcliffe 1974**
× Small World	= Magic World	× Sweet Lute = Sweet Magic
× Sparsholt	= Sparticus	
WOODRUFF	**Blendia × Small World**	**Ratcliffe 1967**
× Small World	= World Special	
WORLD CRUISE	**Alden × Small World**	**Ratcliffe 1973**
WORLD CUP	**Canasta × Small World**	**Ratcliffe 1973**
WORLD FANDANGO	**Flamenco × Small World**	**Ratcliffe 1971**
WORLD FANTASY	**Jacana × Small World**	**Ratcliffe 1973**
WORLD FLIGHT	**Impeyan × Small World**	**Ratcliffe 1971**
WORLD PRIX	**Small World × Inferno**	**Ratcliffe 1971**
WORLD QUEST	**Qantas × Small World**	**Ratcliffe 1974**
WORLD SONG	**Cadence × Small World**	**Ratcliffe 1971**
WORLD SPECIAL	**Woodruff × Small World**	**Ratcliffe 1975**
WORLD VENTURE	**Small World × Sparsholt**	**Ratcliffe 1968**
× Amber Star	= Dream World	× Qantas = Queenslander
WORSLEYI*†	**Hestia × Lady Dillon**	**H. Worsley 1925**
× Mulatto	= Takatori	
WYNNETTA	**F. C. Puddle × Chianti**	**Ratcliffe 1974**
XANTIPPE*†‡	**Gwen Hannen × Sir Trevor**	**A. & B. 1936**
× Mrs. Carl Holmes	= Memory Margaret Sporer	
XAVIER	**Langley Pride × Oxus**	**Stewart Inc. 1973**
XCLNT	**Redezelle × Matcheck**	**Rod McLellan Co. 1972**
YAHAGI	**Montecito × Benenden**	**Kojima 1971**
YAKIMA	**Inca × Mendocino**	**W. W. Wilson 1974**
YELLOW CREST	**Gleaming × Bradford**	**Ratcliffe 1956**
× Beedon	= Cresdon	
YERBA BUENA†	**Sanacderae × Diversion**	**Rod McLellan Co. 1955 (E. W. McLellan)**
× Avine	= Via Angel Verde	× Divisadero = Shirley Holloway
× Blanche Sawyer	= Frosty Glow	× Gwenpur = Henrietta Hanes
× Caddiana	= Via Muchos Ninos	× Inca = Incabuena
× Chardmoore	= White Ice	× niveum = Besnow
× Crescent Meadow	= Polar Cap	
YESTERYEAR	**Gowerianum × philippinense**	**Stewart Inc. 1973**
YOKOHAMA†	**Gertrude West × Ilium**	**C. Takeda 1956 (Yokohama Nursery)**
× Viridissimum	= Main Oiso	
YSOLDE*†	**Florence Spencer × Gwen Hannen**	**King 1930**
× Milnetta	= Milsolde	
YUMEDONO†‡	**Midas × Yokohama**	**C. Takeda 1956 (Kaga)**
× Chrysostom	= Heathy Hill	× Stamperland = Habitant

PAPHIOPEDILUM

ZALAMANDA	Amanda × Izalco	Ratcliffe 1974 (Sieff)
ZEALANDIA	Hellas × Evansrose	Corban 1972
ZEPHYR‡	Dramatic × Goldbar	Ratcliffe 1969

× F. C. Puddle = Demofair
× Jocelyn = Cool Affair
× Sunland = Green Sheen

ZIGANKA	Santa Margarita × Sea Cliff	Stewart Inc. 1973
ZINGANO	lowii × fairieanum	Thomdel 1973 (Van Delden)
ZITRONENFALTER	Jocelyn × Grace Darling	Hark 1974
ZUNI	Mendocino × Cadence	W. W. Wilson 1974
ZUSHI	Enoshima × Finetta	Karasawa 1972

PAPILIONANTHE

hookerana (see *Vanda hookerana**†‡) species
teres (see *Vanda teres**†‡) species

PARACHILUS

PERKY	Sarco. hartmannii × Psarco. spathulatus	I. A. Butler 1972

PARASARCOCHILUS

spathulatus species
× Sarco. hartmannii = Prcls. Perky

PAULSENARA

MEDELLIN	Trgl. fasciata × Aërdns Colombia	von Paulsen 1972 (B. von Paulsen)

PELACENTRUM

SUEBSANGUAN	Pthia. ctenoglossa × Asctm. Sagarik Gold	Suebsanguan 1974

PELATANTHERIA

ctenoglossa species
× Asctm. Sagarik Gold = Plctm. Suebsanguan

PHALAENOPSIS

AALBANE	Gertrude Homsher × Mantilla	Beard 1973
AALIA ABDULALI	Hi Boy × violacea	Wallbrunn 1974
AALSMEER ROSE†‡	Ruby × Marmouset	Shaffer 1960 (de Jong)

× Aitkenvale = Ted Reilly
× Lipperose = Rosenrot
× Samba = Tango

AARON COMPTON	Capitola × amboinensis	Hausermann 1973
ABENDROT	Lippezauber × Lippstadt	Hark 1974
ABONDANCE	Sourire × Barbara Beard	Pff. V. & L. 1974

PHALAENOPSIS

ABRAM McANDLESS	**Redport × Percy Porter**	**Hausermann 1974**
ABSOLUM	**Mad Lips × Ruby Zada**	**Rod McLellan Co. 1974**
ACHAT	**Sigrid × Lipperose**	**Gart. Seidel 1973 (K. Seidel)**
ADAGIO	**Grace Palm × Mildred Karleen**	**Gart. Seidel 1974 (Alfred Seidel)**
ADELAIDE	**Cindy Brandt × Terri Cook**	**June Fowler 1973 (Vande Weghe)**

× Scotti Maguire = Ixion

ADELHEIT	**Doris Wells × amboinensis**	**Hark 1973**
ADELIE	**Eva × Alice Gloria**	**Pff. V. & L. 1974**
ADORNO	**lindenii × Intermedia**	**Ozaki 1975**
ADRIAN HAUSERMANN	**Theresa Hausermann × Grace Palm**	**Elmhurst 1972**
AGLOW	**Jubilee × Zada**	**Hager 1970**

× Brasilia = Brazilian Glow
× Percy Porter = Wendel George

AILEEN STOOPS	**lueddemanniana × Coral Isles**	**Stoops 1974**
AITKENVALE	**Dos Pueblos × Pink Vision**	**Waddell 1964 (Kirch)**

× Aalsmeer Rose = Ted Reilly

AJO DESERT	**Mrs. J. H. Veitch × Bruce Shaffer**	**Shaffer's 1972**
ALICE BOWEN†‡	**Dark Hawaii × Pink Cloud**	**McCoy 1955**

× lueddemanniana = Valeria

ALICE CAROL	**New Hope × lueddemanniana**	**R. C. Turner 1972 (Small)**
ALICE GLORIA‡	**Ramona × Grace Palm**	**Rayola 1961**

× Allegria = Candida
× Ambodoris = Ambo-Gloria
× Ambomanniana = Golden West
× Apollo = Sonnet Glory
× Aristocrat = Tobruk
× Arpege = Ferveur
× Boynton = Anna Merkel
× Cast Iron Monarch = Freed's Devilish
× Cathrine Pillsbury = Parilee Bourgoin
× Celie = Courchevel
× Christopher Lynn = Spring Fever
× Concorde = Alicorne
× Dos Pueblos = Dolores Buchanan
× Edythe Wood = Malibu White
× Eva = Adelie
× Fairway Park = Fair Alice
× fasciata = Saffron Elizanne
× Federal Monarch = Federal Glo
× Francine = Melissa Dawn
× fuscata = Summer Sun
× gigantea = Fort Caroline
× Golden Sands = Rhonda Dunn
× Henriette Lecoufle = Splendeur
× Hermosa = Verle
× Hi Boy = Hi Glow
× Hoosumi = Zuki Gloria
× Intermedia = Harold Borer
× Irma Rath = Malibu Carnival
× Joseph Hampton = Criswell Gonzales
× Keith Shaffer = Schooner
× Louis Merkel = Lois Partin
× lueddemanniana = Sioux Maize
× Mantilla = Mem. Anton Smith
× Martha Jane = Martha Gloria
× Mem. Harold Shaffer = Patricia Rose
× Mem. William Shaban = Leslie Ann
× Ministripes = Seventh Heaven
× Monarch of Venus = Clifford Richards
× Mrs. J. H. Veitch = Ruth Gee
× Norman Peterson = Milkmaid
× Opaline = Demoiselle
× Palmsnow = Patrick Jon
× Patrick Jon = White Bird
× Polka = Mazurka
× Princess Susan = Mem. Ray Thornton
× Ramona = Candeur
× Reinaldo = Mem. Arnold Remmert
× Schöne von Celle = Schöne Gloria
× Sid = Linda Hunter
× Sonja = Pepperdine University
× Stuartiano-mannii = Dan Dickey
× sumatrana = Annette Wichmann
× Susan Merkel = Lorraine Thornton
× Terri Cook = Ivy Armour
× Thordale = Glory Dale
× Treasure Island = Petie Demma
× Unna = Zaubergloria
× Vallehigh = Schneewittchen
× violacea = Viogloria
× Wanda Williams = Sylvia Tiedtke
× White Magic = Evangeline
× Dtps. Red Coral = Dtps. Pinto Lake
× Ren. Brookie Chandler = Rnthps. Renee

PHALAENOPSIS

ALICE JEAN	**Doris × Alice Gloria**	**Shaffer's 1967**

× Little Worrall	= Gidget White	× White Sails	= Little Durward

ALICE MILLARD	**stuartiana × amboinensis**	**Fort Caroline 1969 (Wallbrunn)**

× Doris	= Aureola		

ALICE MUNSON	**Darleen × Mildred Karleen**	**Shaffer's 1975**
ALICE SHELLEY	**Ruby Stripes × Taffy**	**Lockhart 1972**

× Jimmy Arnold	= Dale Lockhart	× Lois Jansen	= Martha Odum

ALICORNE	**Alice Gloria × Concorde**	**Pff. V. & L. 1974**
ALIGHT	**Phylis-Kay × Bandleader**	**Hager 1970**

× Glamour Girl	= Crimson Heart	× Kathy Marie	= Pat Reinke

ALII‡	**Rosa B. Kirsch × lueddemanniana**	**W. W. G. Moir 1962**

× Anne Cavaco	= San Carlos	× gigantea	= Aliitea
× De Haro	= Kumuokalani		

ALIITEA	**Alii × gigantea**	**W. W. G. Moir 1975**
ALLEGRETTO	**Allegria × Capitola**	**Pff. V. & L. 1974**
ALLEGRIA	**Wilma Hughes × Alice Gloria**	**Pff. V. & L. 1970**

× Alice Gloria	= Candida	× Wilma Hughes	= Wilmagria
× Capitola	= Allegretto		

ALLSPICE	**Spica × amboinensis**	**Hager 1973**
ALTA GOODMAN	**Red Eye × Mad Hatter**	**Beard 1974**
amabilis*†‡	**species**	

(syn. *aphrodite**†; *formosa; grandiflora; rimestadiana**†)

× Gladys Read	= Juan Escobar	× Mambo	= Happy
× Makaha Surf	= Professor Derra		

AMADO VAZQUEZ	**Hawaiian Sunshine × Pin Up Girl**	**Freed 1974**
AMARGOSA DESERT	**Ondine × Nemesio Mendiola**	**Shaffer's 1971**
AMBER SANDS	**Susan Merkel × fasciata**	**Beard 1969**

× Ambomanniana	= Pagan Love Song	× Quality Belle	= Jane Le Noir
× Gertrude Beard	= Golden Dream	× Bdra. Charles Beard	= Bdra. Gertrude Beard

AMBERSOL	**cornu-cervi × Schillambo**	**Shaffer's 1973**
AMBLEARIS	**amboinensis × cochlearis**	**Wallbrunn 1972**
AMBODORIS	**Doris × amboinensis**	**E. Iwanaga 1965**

× Alice Gloria	= Ambo-Gloria	× micholitzii	= Emerald Star
× lueddemanniana	= Tropic Lightning		

AMBO-GLORIA	**Ambodoris × Alice Gloria**	**Carlson 1974**
amboinensis*†‡	**species**	

× Ann Marie Beard	= Golden Diana	× gigantea	= David Lim
× Barbara Kirch	= Ritzy	× Gladys Read	= Antigua
× Best Girl	= Zoom	× Hermina Ford	= Caravan
× Capitola	= Aaron Compton	× Honey Dew	= Bamboo Baby
× Clyde	= Artienne	× Inspiration	= Crazy Ambo
× cochlearis	= Amblearis	× Joseph Hampton	= Yellow Ice
× cornu-cervi	= Corona	× Linda Schumpert	= Spenge
× Delightful	= Golden Zebra	× Lipperose	= Liambo
× Doris Wells	= Adelheit	× maculata	= Good Cheer
× Elaine-Liem	= Raka Sumichan	× Mary Andrews	= Bravo
× fasciata	= Golden Pride	× Miami Maid	= Lemon Queen
× fimbriata	= Elaine-Liem	× Muriel Turner	= Ice Age

amboinensis*†‡ *(continued)*

× Nedra = South Coast
× Painted Desert = Desert Dawn
× pantherina = Doris Blomquist
× Peach Glow = Micronesia
× Rosy Charm = Penang
× Satin Rouge = Dorothy Venéy
× Show Girl = Temple Dancer
× Spica = Allspice
× White Monarch = Crestwood Ivory
× Zada = Lorraine Kenny
× Dor. pulcherrima = Dtps. Jim Chan
× Rnthps. Dana = Rnthps. Shangri-La

AMBOMANNIANA‡ — **amboinensis × lueddemanniana** — **Fredk. L. Thornton 1965**

× Alice Gloria = Golden West
× Amber Sands = Pagan Love Song
× Ann Hatter = Jungle Queen
× Erick Hansen = Freed's Cupid
× Estrellita = Ana Roja
× Luedde-violacea = Manitoba
× Mannicata = Freed's Distinction
× Satin Rouge = Dusky Rouge
× Wilma Hughes = Golden State

AMIGO — **Sunbeam × lueddemanniana** — **Dobkin 1971**
AMNUEY PORN — **Sonja × Gladys Read** — **Sathirasut 1974**
AMREETA — **Ann Lovelace × Samba** — **Dobkin 1971**
AMY HOWARD — **Redwing × Irene van Alstyne** — **Beard 1974**
AMY MAGUIRE — **Jennie Swank × Redfan** — **Beard 1972**
ANA ROJA — **Ambomanniana × Estrellita** — **Shaffer's 1975**
ANDREA — **Vallehigh × Star of Diamond Head** — **Hans Koch 1974**
ANGELA ANGELIDIS — **Spice Islands × Dos Pueblos** — **Fort Caroline 1972 (Wallbrunn)**

ANGELA DUMAS‡ — **Wilma Hughes × Doris** — **J. F. Hughes 1967**

× Bruce Shaffer = James Dick
× Capitola = Sheri Bohnett
× Richard Shaffer = Eureka Canyon

ANGELS FLIGHT — **Wilma Hughes × Gladys Read** — **Rod McLellan Co. 1973**
ANGEL WINGS — **Palm Beach × Susan Merkel** — **A. & M. 1975**
ANITA YOUNG — **Helen Miller × Daryl Beard** — **Beard 1972**

× Kimberly Odum = Quaker

ANNA GOLETA — **Anna Tham × Goleta** — **M. J. Bates 1973**
ANNA MERKEL — **Alice Gloria × Boynton** — **A. & M. 1975**
ANNA THAM‡ — **Dos Pueblos × Doreen** — **Tham Tuck Onn 1962 (Kirch)**

× Goleta = Anna Goleta
× Grace Palm = Mount Fuji
× Mambo = Marg Knowles
× Ruth Roesler = Gadis Singapura
× Dor. pulcherrima = Dtps. Virginia Jenkins

ANN BEAL — **Rising Sun × Ruby Lips** — **Beard 1975**
ANN CHOVY — **Ann Lovelace × Doris** — **Dobkin 1971**
ANNE — **Vallemar × Snowbird** — **Nonaka 1963 (Kodama)**

× Dos Pueblos = Pueblo Anne

ANNE CAVACO‡ — **Jane L. Kingsbury × San Marino** — **A. S. Cavaco 1960 (Kodama)**

× Alii = San Carlos
× Betty Conroy = Jean Dunn
× Bruce Shaffer = Calawaii
× Gladys Read = Ironside

ANNE GURKE — **Quality Belle × Cindy Sue** — **D. B. White 1974**
ANNE HAMILTON — **Chieftain × Dorval** — **R. M. Hamilton 1974 (Ilsley)**

ANNEMARIE PINKEPANK — **Lipperose × Mistinguett** — **Pinkepank 1972**
ANNETTE WICHMANN — **Alice Gloria × sumatrana** — **Wichmann 1972**

ANN HATTER‡ — **Juanita × New Era** — **J. F. Hughes 1962**

×	=	×	=
× Ambomanniana	= Jungle Queen	× Red Lip	= Chestnut Vale
× Cher Ann	= Lip Frost	× Sugar 'n Spice	= Norma Marion
× Erick Hansen	= Antique	× Viroonchan	= Freed's Dazzler
× Judy Karleen	= Pottstown		

ANNIE HOFFMAN — **Doris × stuartiana** — **Swearingen 1948**

×	=	×	=
× Francine	= Kruemel		

ANN LINDEN — **Ann Lovelace × lindenii** — **Freed 1972**

ANN LOVELACE‡ — **Radiant Glow × Sunrise** — **McCoy 1962**

×	=	×	=
× Ann Marie Beard	= Freed's Temptation	× Pink Chiffon	= Pink Formal
× Autumn Glow	= Vampire	× Raycraft	= Freed's Delectable
× Barbara Beard	= Pink Horizon	× Rosy Charm	= Love Charm
× Doris	= Ann Chovy	× Samba	= Amreeta
× Eventide	= Love Tide	× sanderana	= Freed's Celebrity
× Fanfare	= Charming	× Summit Snow	= Frosty Pink
× gigantea	= Bold Queen	× violacea	= Rose Petal
× lindenii	= Ann Linden	× Dtps. Clarelen	= Dtps. Malibu Pink
× Margaret Bean	= Fairy Pink	× Dtps. Pink Jewel	= Dtps. Pink Love
× Palmyra	= Lovely Ann	× Dor. pulcherrima	= Dtps. Pinkie
× Peppermint	= Baby Doll		

ANN MARIE BEARD‡ — **Palm Beach Rouge × Rosada** — **Beard 1966**

×	=	×	=
× amboinensis	= Golden Diana	× Jimmy Mize	= Iberia
× Ann Lovelace	= Freed's Temptation	× Kathryn Leahey	= Tyr
× Bardor	= Cabala	× Lois Jansen	= Fancy Girl
× Bariana	= Quadrille	× Naughty Pink	= Portrait
× Betty Beard	= Winnie Boyd	× Pink Formal	= Rhoda Fredricks
× Clara Birk	= Elaine Kilpatrick	× Redwing	= William Beard
× Clay Miller	= Azurite	× Satin Rouge	= Ruby Lorenzen
× Daryl Beard	= Kay Thomas	× sumatrana	= Sumarie
× Frances Roberts	= Gabbardine	× Dtps. Mem. Clarence Schubert	= Dtps. Ellen Satterwhite
× Hedy Maerkl	= Mab		
× Jean Johnston	= Wacke		

ANN SNOOK — **Elinor Shaffer × Fiery** — **R. F. Fuchs 1971**

ANN WADE — **Cast Iron Monarch × Bonita Linda** — **Ridgeway 1967**

×	=	×	=
× Pacific Princess	= Dora Jean Fox	× William Boyd	= Oubrey McCarter

ANOUCHE‡ — **Fanchette × Isis** — **Pff. V. & L. 1970**

×	=	×	=
× Eva	= Bauge	× Karleen's Wendy	= Minouche
× Francine	= Mouchette	× Rapture	= Vitrail

ANTARCTIC — **Celie × Henriette Lecoufle** — **Pff. V. & L. 1974**

ANTIGUA — **amboinensis × Gladys Read** — **Shaffer's 1975**

ANTIQUE — **Erick Hansen × Ann Hatter** — **Rex Foster's 1974**

APACHE — **Pink Ice × Satin Rouge** — **Ridgeway 1973**

APFELBLÜTE — **Unna × Vallehigh** — **Hans Koch 1974**

aphrodite*† (see *amabilis**†‡) — **species**

APOLLO — **Luna Bianca × Via Lactea** — **Altenburg 1969**

×	=	×	=
× Alice Gloria	= Sonnet Glory	× Via Lactea	= Hoosumi

APOLLO FIFTEEN — **Grace Palm × Mambo** — **Fredk. L. Thornton 1973**

APOLLO FOURTEEN — **Princess Susan × Mambo** — **Fredk. L. Thornton 1973**

APOLLO TEN — **Aristocrat × Mambo** — **Thornton's 1970 (Fredk. L. Thornton)**

×	=	×	=
× Ella Freed	= Karlyne		

APPARITION*† — amabilis × Jeanne d'Arc — V. 1935
× Intermedia = Leora Hewlett

APPLAUSE — Norman Peterson × Persistent — Rod McLellan Co. 1973
APREMONT — Margaret Bean × Latone — Marcel Lecoufle 1974
APRICOT NECTAR — fuscata × Palmsnow — J. & S. 1971
ARCADIA†‡ — Grace Palm × Chieftain — Browne 1956 (Bean)
× Bruce Shaffer = Sensation
× Grace Palm = White Lady
× Irma Rath = Arcama
× Long Life = Nordpol
× lueddemanniana = Sternstaub
× Palm Beach = Orlando
× Ren. storiei = Rnthps. Apricot Gold

ARCADO — Doris × Arcadia — Rivermont 1963
× Snow Chief = Ruth Dean

ARCAMA — Irma Rath × Arcadia — Kensington 1973
ARCTIC BELLE — Barbetta Bell × Polar Bear — Beall 1974
ARCTIC FOX — Bridesmaid × Dos Pueblos — Beall 1973
ARIETTE — Arpege × Henriette Lecoufle — Pff. V. & L. 1974
ARISTOCRAT‡ — Snowbird × Grace Palm — McCoy 1960
× Alice Gloria = Tobruk
× Bleeding Heart = James Arnold
× Daryl Beard = Donna O'Neal
× Hollywood = Marion Furst
× Margaret Bean = Yellow Lip
× Serenity = White Aristocrat
× sumatrana = Aristrana
× Wendy Beard = Elportal
× Ren. Brookie Chandler = Rnthps. Glory

ARISTRANA — Aristocrat × sumatrana — Fort Caroline 1975 (Wallbrunn)

ARLENE MARIE FINNEY — Elinor Shaffer × Fairway Park — Hausermann 1969
× Marten Hausermann = White Pearl

ARPEGE — Wilma Hughes × Henriette Lecoufle — Pff. V. & L. 1970
× Alice Gloria = Ferveur
× Henriette Lecoufle = Ariette
× Dtps. Mem. Clarence Schubert = Dtps. Joanna Janes

ARTHUR FREED — Show Girl × Painted Princess — Freed 1970
× Darleen = Chad Mizuta

ARTHUR PAYNTER — Madelon Kasten × Louis Merkel — Lockhart 1971
ARTIENNE — Clyde × amboinensis — Hager 1972
ARTIGNY — Exquis × Eva — Pff. V. & L. 1971
ART MILLER — Donnie Brandt × Daryl Beard — Beard 1972
ARTUR ELLE — Mad Hatter × mariae — Wichmann 1971
AUDREY PORTER — Nuel N. Songer × lindenii — Crestwood 1973
AUREOLA — Alice Millard × Aureola — Ozaki 1975
AUTUMN GLOW‡ — Golden Louis × sanderana — Fantastic Gdns. 1962
× Ann Lovelace = Vampire
× Best Girl = Unique

AUTUMN GOLD — fasciata × Barcelona — Shaffer's 1973
AUTUNITE — Scotti Maguire × fasciata — Beard 1972
AVILA — Wilma Hughes × Juanita — Shaffer's 1964
× Keith Shaffer = Lauralin

AZTEC — Pink Ice × Zada — Ridgeway 1973
AZURITE — Clay Miller × Ann Marie Beard — Beard 1973
BAALIST — Key Lime × Sulip — Beard 1973

PHALAENOPSIS

BABY DOLL	**Ann Lovelace × Peppermint**	**Freed 1971**
BABY SHOE PASS	**Fiji × Esther Edris**	**Beall 1975**
BAGATTELE	**Denise Richardson × Baguio**	**A. & M. 1975**
BAGUIO‡	**schillerana × lindenii**	**W. W. G. Moir 1966**

× Caroline Oberling	= Ethel Shreffler	× Harlequin	= Pink Zebra
× Denise Richardson	= Bagattele	× Mahinhin	= Gem Stone
× Doris	= Pink Stripes		

BALLERINA	**Lolita × Silver Cloud**	**McCoy 1966 (Hieda)**

× lueddemanniana	= Ochrarina	× sumatrana	= Leprechaun

BAMBOO BABY	**Honey Dew × amboinensis**	**J. & S. 1971**
BANDLEADER‡	**Sara Jane × Capitola**	**Hager 1967**

× Breathless	= Bright Lights	× Mad Lips	= Lorelei
× equestris	= Larry Oberhaus	× New Horizon	= Dorothy Ordway
× Far Horizon	= Georgia Seaman		

BARBARA BEARD‡	**Virginia × Zada**	**Beard 1962**

× Ann Lovelace	= Pink Horizon	× Naughty Pink	= Shangri-La
× Bardor	= Doctor George Morris	× Misty Rose	= Pinkridge
		× Redwing	= Lyrical
× Clara Birk	= Nabob	× Satin Rouge	= Patti Logan
× Doris	= Davao	× Sourire	= Abondance
× Frances Roberts	= Jean Marshall	× Dtps. Jerry Vande Weghe	= Dtps. Barbara Hill
× Jean Johnston	= Fable		
× Jimmy Mize	= Oak Ridge	× Dtps. Purple Gem	= Dtps. Red River
× Mary Wieler	= Zulu	× V. Janet Tagawa	= Vdnps. Phyllis Sumner

BARBARA BOHMER	**Golden Sands × sumatrana**	**Bachner 1973**
BARBARA FREED SALTZMAN	**Show Girl × Pin Up Girl**	**Freed 1972**

× Jennifer Beard	= Music

BARBARA KAY‡	**Katherine Siegwart × Barbara Kirch**	**Lorenzen 1963**

× Ren. Brookie Chandler	= Rnthps. Memoria Beverly Fontenot

BARBARA KIRCH‡	**Jane L. Kingsbury × Monique**	**Kirch 1961**

× amboinensis	= Ritzy

BARBARA MOLER	**Donnie Brandt × Spica**	**Beard 1971**

× Lois Jansen	= Virginia Anderson	× Rising Sun	= Edith Scoville
× Moon Probe	= Carol Owens		

BARBETTA BELL	**Palm Beach × Dos Pueblos**	**Ryerson 1966**

× Polar Bear	= Arctic Belle

BARCELONA‡	**Dos Pueblos × Ramona**	**Shaffer's 1964**

× Capitola	= Marie Boner	× Keith Shaffer	= George Woodward
× Cast Iron Monarch	= Castelona	× Princess Grace	= Netta Shepherd
× fasciata	= Autumn Gold	× Richard Shaffer	= Robert Stephan
× Hermosa	= Marylou Woodward		

BARDOR	**Barbara Beard × Dorrose**	**Beard 1968**

× Ann Marie Beard	= Cabala	× Bariana	= System
× Barbara Beard	= Doctor George Morris	× Mary Wieler	= Evernia

PHALAENOPSIS

BARIANA — Barbara Beard × sanderana — Beard 1968

× Ann Marie Beard = Quadrille
× Bardor = System
× Betty Beard = Kyack
× Jimmy Mize = Hyssop
× Mary Wieler = Queenie
× Texas Pink = Ryot

BARRY EAMER‡ — Zada × Judith — Beard 1962

× Frances Roberts = Futurist

BASTOGNE — Lillian Germaske × New Era — Thornton's 1962

× Cathrine Pillsbury = Lisa Marie

BAUGE — Anouche × Eva — Pff. V. & L. 1971

BEATIE GREENLY — William Boyd × Virginia Beard — Beard 1968

× Irene van Alstyne = Yacht
× Kathy Maguire = Newport
× Melba Burnett = Imperial Valley
× Teena = Teresa Lykins

BEAUGENCY — Roswell × Mistinguett — Pff. V. & L. 1971

BEAUREGARD — Nuel N. Songer × Ramona — Pff. V. & L. 1971

BEDLAM — Princess Grace × Mildred Karleen — James 1972

BEEHIVE PASS — Maria Vasquez × Polar Bear — Beall 1975

BELINDA‡ — Doris × Aristocrat — Jenkins 1964

× White Medallion = David Addy Bishop

BERTIE DE MARTINI — Linda Mia × Bruce Shaffer — Rod McLellan Co. 1973 (McElderry)

BERT SHELLEY — Fiery × Suemid — Lockhart 1971

BESSMANN — Bess Wells × lueddemanniana — Tsukagoshi 1974

BESS WELLS†‡ — amabilis × Rothschildiana — de Jong 1954

× lueddemanniana = Bessmann

BEST GIRL‡ — Pink Vision × Sunrise — McCoy 1961

× amboinensis = Zoom
× Autumn Glow = Unique
× Denise Richardson = Theresa Hirsch
× fuscata = Gloria Turner
× gigantea = Esma
× Jimmy Mize = Florence Rose
× mariae = Caressa
× Mildred Karleen = Tres Jolie
× Nedra = Christina
× Ondine = Dear Heart
× Samba = Red Sun
× sanderana = Hobe Sound
× sumatrana = Crusader
× Therese Frackowiak = War Paint
× Dtps. Jerri Sue King = Dtps. Vendetta
× Dtps. Mem. Clarence Schubert = Dtps. Roberta Arnold
× Dor. pulcherrima = Dtps. Lee Soo Keow

BETSY RUE — Madrid × Sonja — Gubler 1973

BETSY TURNER — Tyler Carlson × lueddemanniana — R. C. Turner 1975

BETTY BEARD‡ — Alice Bowen × Virjudy — Beard 1966

× Ann Marie Beard = Winnie Boyd
× Bariana = Kyack
× Clara Birk = Uzbek
× Evening Rose = Dottie Hemming
× Mary McLane = Fiery Ball
× Melba Burnett = Tillie
× Ruby Zada = Haaf

BETTY CONROY — Gladys Read × Bruce Shaffer — Shaffer's 1970

× Anne Cavaco = Jean Dunn
× Gladys Read = Ward Munson
× Terri Cook = Rosemary Shaffer

BETTYLEE BURKE — Zada × violacea — W. D. Burke 1971 (Lynn Dewey)

BETTY SISTRUNK — Gertrude Homsher × Spica — Lockhart 1974

BETTY SOARS — Daryl Beard × Mantilla — Lockhart 1973

BEWITCHED — Kathleen Edris × Queen Emma — Lorenzen 1975

BIG CHIEF†‡ — Chieftain × Louise Georgianna — Rod McLellan Co. 1958

× Boynton = Spirit of Seventysix
× Dos Pueblos = Madelon Kasten

PHALAENOPSIS

BILLET-DOUX	**Redfan × Spitfire**	**Rod McLellan Co. 1971**
BILLIE PICKELL	**Gemini × Terri Cook**	**Pickell 1972 (Thornton Labs.)**
BILL LOCKHART	**Cindy Brandt × Daryl Beard**	**Beard 1972**
BILL'S YELLOW	**Jane Shaffer × fuscata**	**W. J. Shaban 1974**
BIMINI	**gigantea × Red Lip**	**J. & S. 1971**
BLACK ROCK DESERT	**Doris × Nemesio Mendiola**	**Shaffer's 1971**
BLEEDING HEART	**Sally Lowrey × Roswell**	**Shaffer's 1966**

× Aristocrat = James Arnold

BLITHE SPIRIT	**Native Girl × Sillouette**	**Hager 1971**
BLOSSOMWOOD SNOW	**Keith Shaffer × Dazzling Snowcloud**	**Funston 1975 (Rivermont)**
BLUSHING PINK	**Willowbrook × Zada**	**Hausermann 1969**

× Lipperose = Pink Parfait
× Dtps. Susan Ann Schubert = Dtps. Bicentennial

BOBBIE GAYE LISTA	**Hermosa × Spica**	**Peter E. Lista 1975**
BOB TURNER	**Golden Sands × Ruby Zada**	**Beard 1973**
BOEDIARDJO	**denevei × laycockii**	**Kolopaking 1972**
BOLD ADVENTURE	**Texas Star × mariae**	**Dobkin 1973**
BOLD QUEEN	**Ann Lovelace × gigantea**	**Dobkin 1973**
BONANZA	**Snowbird × Princess Grace**	**McCoy 1967**

× Doris = Citation
× gigantea = Daisy Mae
× Richard Shaffer = White Halo

BON NUIT BAY	**Redfan × Pin Up Girl**	**E. E. Young 1975**
BONNY DOON	**Overglow × Jean Stephan**	**Shaffer's 1974**
BOO KOLSHAK	**Utopia × fasciata**	**Lockhart 1975**
BOUTONNIERE	**Yap Wee Hiong × equestris**	**Osgood 1973**
boxallii (see *mannii**†‡)	**species**	
BOYNTON‡	**Joanna Magale × Doris**	**A. & M. 1961**

× Alice Gloria = Anna Merkel
× Big Chief = Spirit of Seventysix
× fasciata = Spots of Gold
× fuscata = Gold Charm
× Hymen = Sun King
× Louis Merkel = Patience Benjamin
× Susan Merkel = Mae Carper

BRANDENBURG	**Bruce Shaffer × fasciata**	**Wichmann 1972**
BRASILIA	**Sparkle × Harlequin**	**Hager 1970**

× Aglow = Brazilian Glow
× Harlequin = Gentle Rain
× Jennifer Beard = Ellen Murk
× Polynesian Sunset = Brazilian Sunset
× Samba = Carnival Ball

BRAVO	**Mary Andrews × amboinensis**	**Dobkin 1973**
BRAZILIAN GLOW	**Aglow × Brasilia**	**Hager 1974**
BRAZILIAN SUNSET	**Polynesian Sunset × Brasilia**	**Hager 1973**
BREATHLESS	**Sillouette × Vercors**	**Hager 1971**

× Bandleader = Bright Lights
× Far Horizon = Priscilla Pyfrom
× Mad Lips = Infatuation

BRIDESMAID‡	**Juanita × Thomas Tucker**	**Santa Cruz 1961**

× Dos Pueblos = Arctic Fox
× fasciata = Golden Maiden
× gigantea = Schamott
× Hermosa = Formal
× Mrs. J. H. Veitch = Desert Morn
× Nuel N. Songer = Fiji
× Zada = Esther Edris

BRIGHT ANGEL	**Irma Rath × Gladys Read**	**Rod McLellan Co. 1972**
BRIGHT LIGHTS	**Bandleader × Breathless**	**Hager 1974**

PHALAENOPSIS

BRIGHT SPOT — **Red Eye × Redfan** — **Rod McLellan Co. 1971 (Beard)**

× Eva Lou = Pamela Wolf
× Port Mayaka = Cathy Funstum

BRIGHT STRIPES — **Rouge × Ruby Zada** — **Beard 1969**

× Ruby Zada = Xray

BRONZE BEAUTY — **Bronze Maiden × Zada** — **John H. Miller 1972**

BRONZE KING — **Florence Perera × mannii** — **Fernando 1974**

× Rose Parade = Red Gem

BRONZE MAIDEN — **schillerana × mannii** — **McCoy 1964**

× Zada = Bronze Beauty

BRONZE QUEEN — **Les Hedge × Mambo** — **R. K. Mizuta 1975**

BRUCE LEBARON — **Peter Wallbrunn × fuscata** — **Wallbrunn 1973**

BRUCE SHAFFER‡ — **Gladys Read × Elinor Shaffer** — **Shaffer's 1964**

× Angela Dumas = James Dick
× Anne Cavaco = Calawaii
× Arcadia = Sensation
× Capitola = Mary Carolyn
× Cathrine Pillsbury = Dorothy Von Belding
× equestris = Magdeburg
× fasciata = Brandenburg
× Grace Palm = Heidi Hausermann
× Hebe = Lois Jean Lilly
× Kahala Queen = John Rose
× Keith Shaffer = Genevieve Saunders
× Linda Mia = Bertie De Martini
× Louis Merkel = White Viking
× Luedde-violacea = Greifswald
× Mrs. J. H. Veitch = Ajo Desert
× Princess Grace = Mem. Anna Ventosa
× Ramona = Pearlie
× Theresa Hausermann = Joyce White
× Trials = Quiescence
× William Shaffer = White Cap

BUENA VISTA — **Pink Melallion × Makaha Surf** — **Schöttler 1975**

BURGUTEA — **Rose of Burgundy × gigantea** — **W. W. G. Moir 1975**

BUTTERBALL — **Golden Sands × stuartiana** — **Redlinger 1974**

BUTTERFLY SIM — **Pamela Martin × San Marino** — **Tan Gim Hoon 1970 (Alsagoff)**

× Dor. pulcherrima = Dtps. Fatimah

buyssoniana (see *Doritis pulcherrima*†‡) — **species**

BYZANTINE — **Melba Burnett × Jimmy Mize** — **Beard 1973**

CABALA — **Bardor × Ann Marie Beard** — **Beard 1973**

CABRILLO STAR‡ — **Ramona × lueddemanniana** — **Santa Cruz 1961**

× Mad Lips = Dandee

CADI ANN — **Cadifa × Cher Ann** — **Hans Koch 1975**

CADIFA — **White Lady × Francine** — **Röhl 1975**

× Cher Ann = Cadi Ann
× fasciata = Sterntaler
× Francisca = Franka
× Renate Frese = Cadirena
× violacea = Vicadi
× Westfalica = Wecadifa

CADIRENA — **Cadifa × Renate Frese** — **Hans Koch 1975**

CÀIRNS CENTENARY — **Karen Ann McFarlane × Robyn Stone** — **McFarlane 1975**

CALAWAII — **Bruce Shaffer × Anne Cavaco** — **Shaffer's 1972**

× Ernst Haussermann = Royal Diadem
× Kenneth Stromsland = Kazuko Fujii

CALLIE FLYNN — **Zada × sanderana** — **Noble Mason 1964**

× Esther Edris = Widow Pass
× Fairway Park = Eileen's Pink
× Satin Rouge = Culmination
× White Medallion = Pink Cheeks
× Zada = Calza
× Zadian = Indonesia

CALZA — **Callie Flynn × Zada** — **Redlinger 1974**

PHALAENOPSIS

CANASTA — **Ramona × Concorde** — **Pff. V. & L. 1974**

CANDEUR — **Ramona × Alice Gloria** — **Pff. V. & L. 1972**

× Henriette Lecoufle = Marie-Noel

CANDIDA — **Alice Gloria × Allegria** — **Pff. V. & L. 1974**

CANDYLAND — **Cher Ann × fimbriata** — **Rod McLellan Co. 1974**

CANDY WAKASUGI — **Texas Star × Ruby Lips** — **Dale Shaffer 1962 (Beard)**

× Ruby Zada = Eden Rock

CAPE CANAVERAL‡ — **Myra Wright × Satellite** — **H. D. Wright 1960**

× Lolita = Wendell Sawyer

CAPITOLA‡ — **Winged Victory × Ramona** — **Santa Cruz 1962**

× Allegria = Allegretto
× amboinensis = Aaron Compton
× Angela Dumas = Sheri Bohnett
× Barcelona = Marie Boner
× Bruce Shaffer = Mary Carolyn
× Celie = Isola
× Charles Shaffer = Melanie
× Clyde = Pajaro Blanco
× Dolores = Frank Gottburg
× Fairway Park = Hausermann's Glacier
× Golden Sands = Poppee
× Goldiana = Fair Maiden
× Hermosa = Empire Snow
× Keith Shaffer = Susan Shipley
× Miami Maid = Cele Young
× Norman Peterson = Cordial
× Orchid Acres = White Gull
× Sonja = Ed Lista
× violacea = Linda Lista

CAPITOLA ROSE — **Jean Stephan × Doris** — **Shaffer's 1973**

CAPRICE — **Mary Lou Stoddard × Palm Beach** — **J. & S. 1967 (Stoddard)**

× Fancy Quest = Reinaldo

CARAVAN — **Hermina Ford × amboinensis** — **Hager 1975**

CAREER GIRL — **Show Girl × Mad Hatter** — **Freed 1971**

× Ella Freed = Freed's Danseuse

CARESSA — **Best Girl × mariae** — **R. K. Mizuta 1974**

CARIOCA — **Clyde × Star of Florida** — **Hager 1972**

CARL HAUSERMANN — **Edythe Wood × Angela Dumas** — **Hausermann 1969**

× Edythe Wood = Westwood

CARLOTTA — **Love Tide × lueddemanniana** — **Dobkin 1975**

CARMEN COLL — **violacea × Ella Freed** — **Freed 1973**

CARNIVAL — **White Medallion × lueddemanniana** — **Woodlawn 1969**

× Winter Dawn = Winter Carnival
× Zada = Shinonome

CARNIVAL BALL — **Samba × Brasilia** — **Hager 1974**

CAROL — **Hobe Sound × Hedy Maerkl** — **Lockhart 1975**

CAROLINE OBERLING — **Mattie Shave × Aristocrat** — **Price 1967**

× Baguio = Ethel Shreffler

CAROL OWENS — **Moon Probe × Barbara Moler** — **Beard 1975**

CAROLYN GRANDY — **Mildred Karleen × Sharon Karleen** — **Hager 1964**

× Show Girl = Show Oaks

CAROLYN KRAUS — **Sarah Pusey × Sparkle Toe** — **H. Webb 1972**

CAROLYN WILKES — **Spotted Moon × Pin Up Girl** — **Beard 1972**

× Ruby Lips = Jane Kulka

CAROUSEL — **Cathrine Pillsbury × sumatrana** — **Hager 1971**

CARTER SHENK	**Lois Jansen × Suemid**	**Beard 1972**
CARUSO‡	**Hi Ho × Doris**	**Hiew Kim Sang 1962 (Kirch)**

× Juanita	= Nina		

CASSANDRA‡	**equestris × stuartiana**	**Veitch 1896**

× David Herbert	= Mini Moth	× Marmouset	= Poco Pink
× Doris	= Little Pink Doris	× schillerana	= Palm Coast
× Ice Palace	= Ice Cube		

CASTELONA	**Barcelona × Cast Iron Monarch**	**E. F. Patterson 1973**
CAST IRON MONARCH†‡	**Louise Georgianna × Doris**	**Kwr. 1957**

× Alice Gloria	= Freed's Devilish	× Richard Shaffer	= Tropical Knight
× Barcelona	= Castelona	× Sally Lowrey	= Freed's Broadway Rhythm
× Edythe Wood	= Page Oates	× Sonja	= Patricia Neal
× gigantea	= China Doll	× Summit Snow	= Snow Monarch
× Gladys Read	= Peggy O'Neill	× White Virgin	= White Cast
× Kauai	= Kauai Monarch	× Wilma Hughes	= Malibu Queen
× Madrid	= Freed's Criterion	× V. sanderana	= Vdnps. Nell Miller
× Princess Grace	= Monaco Monarch		

CATHEDRAL BELLS	**Daryl Beard × Cathrine Pillsbury**	**Rod McLellan Co. 1973**
CATHERINE ADAMS	**Mem. Elva Hamric × Zada**	**Ted Fischer 1975**
CATHRINE PILLSBURY‡	**Ramona × Fairway Park**	**Peterson Bros. 1966**

× Alice Gloria	= Parilee Bourgoin	× Little Worrall	= Frances White
× Bastogne	= Lisa Marie	× Long Life	= Frosting
× Bruce Shaffer	= Dorothy Von Belding	× Norman Peterson	= Cotillion
× Daryl Beard	= Cathedral Bells	× Quality Belle	= Durward Belmont White
× Fairway Park	= Robert Green	× sumatrana	= Carousel
× Irma Rath	= Mooncrest		

CATHY FUNSTUM	**Bright Spot × Port Mayaka**	**Beard 1975**
CATHY OWENS	**Lois Jansen × Spica**	**Beard 1970**
CELEBRATION	**Judy Karleen × New Horizon**	**Hager 1966**

× Lillian Hozaki	= Cherry Lips		

CELE YOUNG	**Miami Maid × Capitola**	**Hausermann 1972**
CELIE	**Dos Pueblos × Dampierre**	**Pff. V. & L. 1968**

× Alice Gloria	= Courchevel	× Concorde	= Intimité
× Capitola	= Isola	× Henriette Lecoufle	= Antarctic

CHAD MIZUTA	**Darleen × Arthur Freed**	**R. K. Mizuta 1974**
CHAMPAGNE LADY	**Gertrude Beard × Wilma Hughes**	**Rod McLellan Co. 1971 (Beard)**
CHANG CHAO-TANG	**Sea Mist × Ella Freed**	**Chang Chao-Tang 1975**
CHANTELOIRE	**Mildred Karleen × Lachésis**	**Pff. V. & L. 1974**
CHARLES McKAY	**James Hausermann × Denise Richardson**	**W. J. Shaban 1974**
CHARLES SHAFFER	**Gladys Read × Ramona**	**Shaffer's 1965**

× Capitola	= Melanie	× fasciata	= Harrison Kennicott
× Coral Isles	= Chris	× Grace Palm	= John Martin
× Ernst Haussermann	= Kenneth Benjamin	× Miami Maid	= Villa Park
× Fairway Park	= Hausermann's Moonbeam	× Theresa Hausermann	= Springfield
		× Dtps. Red Lip	= Dtps. Red Charles

CHARMEUR	**Morzine × Redfan**	**Pff. V. & L. 1974**
CHARMING	**Fanfare × Ann Lovelace**	**Lorenzen 1971 (Small)**
CHER ANN	**Karleen's Wendy × Ann Hatter**	**J. F. Hughes 1969**

× Ann Hatter	= Lip Frost	× Delightful	= Hetty Modaff
× Cadifa	= Cadi Ann	× Ernst Haussermann	= Jim Toskey

CHER ANN *(continued)*

× fimbriata	= Candyland	× Samba	= Lombard
× Irene Finney	= Toy Clown	× Theresa Hausermann	= Jole
× Mad Lips	= Shigeharu Fujii	× violacea	= Peter Lista
× Redfan	= Kerlu		

CHER LEE	**Lipstick × Mad Lips**	**Hausermann 1973**
CHERRY LIPS	**Celebration × Lillian Hozaki**	**Takase 1975**
CHERRY PINK	**Doris × Sunrise**	**Takemoto 1975**
CHERRY SUNDAE	**Mem. William Shaban × Mad Lips**	**W. J. Shaban 1973**
CHESTNUT VALE	**Ann Hatter × Red Lip**	**Osgood 1975 (Kuhn)**
CHIEFTAIN†‡	**Doris × La Canada**	**Curson 1949**

× Dorval	= Anne Hamilton	× Samba	= Mary Fairburn
× fuscata	= Mabel Allard	× Springtime	= Spring Chief

CHINA DOLL	**gigantea × Cast Iron Monarch**	**J. & S. 1971**
CHIYE TOYAMA	**Zada Kaala × Zada**	**Y. Toyama 1974**
CHRIS	**Charles Shaffer × Coral Isles**	**Hausermann 1974**
CHRISTI FLOYD	**Chuck's Red Lip × Maria Vasquez**	**W. J. Shaban 1974**
CHRISTINA	**Nedra × Best Girl**	**Hager 1971**
CHRISTINE ANN	**Hymen × fuscata**	**Merlo 1971 (Hager)**
CHRISTMAS CANDY	**Ministripes × Keith Shaffer**	**J. & S. 1974**
CHRISTOPHER LYNN	**Ministripes × Timbo**	**J. & S. 1971**

× Alice Gloria	= Spring Fever	× Percy Porter	= Playmate
× Jiminy Cricket	= Stephen Douglas		

CHRISTOPHER WINKELMANN	**Mad Lips × Theresa Ann**	**Hausermann 1973**
CHUCK'S RED LIP	**Red Lip × Pacesetter**	**Fort Caroline 1972 (Originator unknown)**

× Debbie Wallace	= Freed's Chieftain	× Maria Vasquez	= Christi Floyd
× Gold Coin	= Gold Bar	× Star of Diamond Head	= Star Lip
× Lipstick	= Freed's Adventure	× violacea	= Freed's Choice
× lueddemanniana	= Henry Wallbrunn		

CINDY BOTHE	**Sally Lowrey × Cindy Brandt**	**Beard 1972**
CINDY BRANDT‡	**Goleta × Palm Beach**	**Beard 1963**

× Daryl Beard	= Bill Lockhart	× Quality Belle	= White Waters
× fasciata	= Suzanne Wenzel	× Sally Lowrey	= Cindy Bothe
× Masu Hamacher	= Dos Amarillos	× Terri Cook	= Adelaide
× Moon Probe	= Yellow Ace	× Utopia	= Ronnie Hollyman
× New Moon	= Lagoon Moon	× violacea	= Linda Henry
× Palette	= Xyster		

CINDY LU	**Cindy Sue × lueddemanniana**	**Lockhart 1973**
CINDY SUE	**Cindy Brandt × Susan Merkel**	**Beard 1966**

× Daryl Beard	= Susan Sherrill	× Masu Hamacher	= Daisy Arnold
× lueddemanniana	= Cindy Lu	× Quality Belle	= Anne Gurke

CINDY TSAI	**Red Lip × Jiminy Cricket**	**Dobkin 1975**
CINNAMON CANDY	**Zada × Painted Desert**	**J. Ewing 1973**
CINNAMON STICK	**Mrs. J. H. Veitch × mannii**	**Wallbrunn 1966**

× Luedde-violacea	= Claudia Creasy	× Ondine	= Masquerade

CIRRUS	**Dolores × stuartiana**	**Andrew Orchids 1972**
CITATION	**Doris × Bonanza**	**Dobkin 1973**

CLARA BIRK	**Clara I. Knight × Aalsmeer Rose**		**Beard 1968**
× Ann Marie Beard	= Elaine Kilpatrick	× Frances Roberts	= Ruth Stout
× Barbara Beard	= Nabob	× Redwing	= Dorothy Brock
× Betty Beard	= Uzbek		
CLARENCE RUSSELL	**Zada × sumatrana**		**A. & M. 1973**
CLASSIC	**Dos Pueblos × Snow White**		**Lorenzen 1972**
CLAUDIA CREASY	**Cinnamon Stick × Luedde-violacea**		**McQuerry 1971**
CLAY MILLER	**Aalsmeer Rose × Barbara Beard**		**Clay Miller 1967**
× Ann Marie Beard	= Azurite		
CLEOPATRA	**Sunbeam × Zada**		**J. & S. 1974**
CLIFFORD RICHARDS	**Monarch of Venus × Alice Gloria**		**Fredk. L. Thornton 1975**
CLOWN'S MASK	**Dos Pueblos × cornu-cervi**		**Rod McLellan Co. 1972**
CLYDE	**Grace Palm × Elinor Shaffer**		**Enright 1965**
× amboinensis	= Artienne	× Norman Peterson	= Norman Clyde
× Capitola	= Pajaro Blanco	× Show Girl	= Snow Rose
× Dee Haberlitz	= Mattie Mae Chambers	× Star of Florida	= Carioca
× Inspiration	= Kim Cuc Bauer	× Ren. monachica	= Rnthps. Billie Dotte Voelker
× Keith Shaffer	= Jasper Ayers		
cochlearis‡	**species**		
× amboinensis	= Amblearis	× Golden Sands	= Island Sands
× Daryl Beard	= Zephyr	× Janet Kuhn	= Scotch Mist
× fasciata	= Golden Jubilee	× Luedde-violacea	= Jac-Qui
COMTESSE BETTINA	**Lipperose × Fischers Liebling**		**Hans Koch 1975**
CONCORDE	**Gladys Read × Capitola**		**Shaffer's 1969**
× Alice Gloria	= Alicorne	× Keith Shaffer	= Portland Bill
× Celie	= Intimité	× Norman Peterson	= Mayday
× Henriette Lecoufle	= Conquete	× Ramona	= Canasta
× Juanita	= Mem. Paul Deutschberger	× Wilma Hughes	= Jumbo
CONFLAGRATION	**Dorisellita × sumatrana**		**Hager 1975**
CONQUETE	**Concorde × Henriette Lecoufle**		**Pff. V. & L. 1974**
CORAL ISLES	**Princess Kaiulani × lueddemanniana**		**Fredk. L. Thornton 1967**
× Charles Shaffer	= Chris	× lueddemanniana	= Aileen Stoops
× Judith Hausermann	= Lynn Diane		
CORAL PINK	**Percy Porter × Pin Up Girl**		**R. K. Mizuta 1975**
CORDIAL	**Norman Peterson × Capitola**		**Rod McLellan Co. 1974**
corningiana	**species**		
× Doris	= Twenty Grand	× sumatrana	= Double Eagle
× Inspiration	= My Fancy	× Violet Glow	= Dots Violet
× Samba	= Electra		
cornu-cervi*†‡	**species**		
× amboinensis	= Corona	× mariae	= Little Leopard
× Dos Pueblos	= Clown's Mask	× Schillambo	= Ambersol
× Elinor Shaffer	= Elcornu	× sumatrana	= Tiger Cub
× fasciata	= Little Girl	× King. philippinensis	= Phlla. Speck O'Gold
CORONA	**cornu-cervi × amboinensis**		**Shaffer's 1973**
COTABATA	**fasciata × De Haro**		**W. W. G. Moir 1969**
× fuscata	= Freckled Gold		
COTILLION	**Norman Peterson × Cathrine Pillsbury**		**Rod McLellan Co. 1973**

PHALAENOPSIS

Grex	Parentage	Originator
COURCHEVEL	Celie × Alice Gloria	Pff. V. & L. 1974
COVER GIRL‡	Sally Lowrey × Doris	Hager 1958

× Show Girl	= Glamour Girl

Grex	Parentage	Originator
CRAZY AMBO	Inspiration × amboinensis	Peter E. Lista 1972
CREAM PUFF	Golden Sands × Donnie Brandt	Beard 1969

× Jack McQuerry	= Hugh Wells	× Wendy Beard	= Czarina
× Jean Johnston	= Fyke		

Grex	Parentage	Originator
CRESCENDO	Mildred Karleen × Pin Up Girl	Osgood 1975
CRESTWOOD IVORY	White Monarch × amboinensis	Crestwood 1975
CRIMSON HEART	Alight × Glamour Girl	Lorenzen 1975
CRISWELL GONZALES	Alice Gloria × Joseph Hampton	Starke & Son 1975
CRUSADER	Best Girl × sumatrana	Hager 1971
CRY BABY	Hermosa × Doris	Naugle 1975
CULMINATION	Callie Flynn × Satin Rouge	Rod McLellan Co. 1973
CZARINA	Cream Puff × Wendy Beard	Beard 1973
DABBLED	Gloriosa × Sunset Glow	Beard 1973
DAINTY GIRL	Texas Pink × Mistinguett	Lorenzen 1971
DAISY ARNOLD	Masu Hamacher × Cindy Sue	Lockhart 1973
DAISY MAE	Bonanza × gigantea	Dobkin 1973
DALE LOCKHART	Jimmy Arnold × Alice Shelley	Lockhart 1974
DAMPIERRE‡	Lachésis × Blizzard	Pff. V. & L. 1960

× Ramona	= Dampira

Grex	Parentage	Originator
DAMPIRA	Dampierre × Ramona	Pff. V. & L. 1972
DANDEE	Cabrillo Star × Mad Lips	Hausermann 1973
DAN DICKEY	Stuartiano-mannii × Alice Gloria	John H. Miller 1972
DARLEEN	Doris × Mildred Karleen	Shaffer's 1969

× Arthur Freed	= Chad Mizuta	× Hugo Freed	= Spinner
× Doris	= Monton	× Mildred Karleen	= Alice Munson

Grex	Parentage	Originator
DARLENE MOORE	Tulip Time × Phylis-Kay	John H. Miller 1971
DARYL BEARD‡	Dos Pueblos × Cindy Brandt	Beard 1966

× Ann Marie Beard	= Kay Thomas	× Kathleen Arnold	= David Lockhart
× Aristocrat	= Donna O'Neal	× Long Life	= Vera Henderson
× Cathrine Pillsbury	= Cathedral Bells	× Madelon Kasten	= Everett Soars
× Cindy Brandt	= Bill Lockhart	× Mannicata	= Oneda Kansman
× Cindy Sue	= Susan Sherrill	× Mantilla	= Betty Soars
× cochlearis	= Zephyr	× Nemesio Mendiola	= Lulu McQuerry
× Donnie Brandt	= Art Miller	× Norman	= Gladys Burkey
× Erick Hansen	= Scotty	× Norman Peterson	= Quotient
× Fairway Park	= Iago	× Quality Belle	= Oasis
× fasciata	= Winnie Brecht	× Scotti Maguire	= Jimmy Hall
× fuscata	= Jeniffer Hall	× Spica	= Nancy Lockhart
× Gertrude Beard	= Zirconia	× sumatrana	= Vacation
× Helen Miller	= Anita Young	× Utopia	= Joe Feirer
× Hymen	= Hydar	× White Plains	= Rabbit
× Irma Rath	= Platonic	× Ren. imschootiana	= Rnthps. Rio's Star

Grex	Parentage	Originator
DARYL LOCKHART	Suemid × Spica	Lockhart 1975
DAVA ALYSON BISHOP	Juanita May × Winifred Prahl	David Bishop 1971 (Bluegrass)
DAVAO	Doris × Barbara Beard	W. W. G. Moir 1973
DAVID ADDY BISHOP	White Medallion × Belinda	Bishop 1972 (Mrs. E. Iwanaga)

DAVID HERBERT‡ | **Marmouset × equestris** | **Fredk. L. Thornton 1965**

× Cassandra = Mini Moth
× Doris = Winafred Hirsch
× Go-Go Girl = Royal Stripe
× Mad Hatter = Vixen
× Princess Kaiulani = David's Princess
× Queen Emma = Pink Rays

DAVID LIM | **amboinensis × gigantea** | **David Lim 1974 (Alsagoff)**

DAVID LOCKHART | **Daryl Beard × Kathleen Arnold** | **Lockhart 1971**

DAVID'S PRINCESS | **David Herbert × Princess Kaiulani** | **Fredk. L. Thornton 1973**

DAZZLER†‡ | **Margaret Bean × Thomas Tucker** | **H. D. Wright 1957**

× Snow Cloud = Dazzling Snowcloud

DAZZLING SNOWCLOUD | **Snow Cloud × Dazzler** | **Funston 1975 (Originator unknown)**

× Keith Shaffer = Blossomwood Snow

DEAR HEART | **Best Girl × Ondine** | **Hager 1971**

DEAR ONE | **My Fair Lady × Susie Darlin** | **J. & S. 1971 (McCoy)**

× gigantea = Little David
× Malibu Pink = Freed's Aristocrat

DEBBIE MARTIAN | **Sea Mist × Juanita** | **D. Tom 1971 (Miyamoto)**

× Juanita = Mildred Tom
× Leilehua = Winter Dawn

DEBBIE WALLACE | **Mad Hatter × Terri Cook** | **Gubler 1973 (Wallace)**

× Chuck's Red Lip = Freed's Chieftain
× Ella Freed = Freed's Dashing
× Samba = Freed's Beguiled
× Viroonchan = Shu King

DEBONAIR | **Natasha × sumatrana** | **Dobkin 1975**

decumbens (see *parishii*†‡) | **species**

DEE HABERLITZ‡ | **Fairway Park × Margaret Bean** | **Peterson Bros. 1966**

× Clyde = Mattie Mae Chambers
× Norman Peterson = Moonsilk

DE HARO‡ | **Dr. Henry O. Eversole × Margaret Bean** | **Rod McLellan Co. 1961**

× Alii = Kumuokalani
× Juanita = Mauna Kea

DELICATE LADY | **Dos Pueblos × Gladys Read** | **Rod McLellan Co. 1973**

DELIGHTFUL | **Show Girl × Lipstick** | **Freed 1973**

× amboinensis = Golden Zebra
× Cher Ann = Hetty Modaff

DELLA BEL KRAUSE | **Zada × Luedde-Wave** | **Peter E. Lista 1974**

DEMOISELLE | **Opaline × Alice Gloria** | **Pff. V. & L. 1974**

denevei*†‡ | **species**

× laycockii = Boediardjo
× Ren. monachica = Rnthps. Osceola
× Ren. philippinensis = Rnthps. Margaret
× V. Siti Zain = Vdnps. Hashim Idros

DENISE RICHARDSON‡ | **Doris × Zada** | **Fields Orchids 1961**

× Baguio = Bagattele
× Best Girl = Theresa Hirsch
× fuscata = Maria Vasquez
× Go-Go Girl = Pink Circus
× James Hausermann = Charles McKay
× Nuel N. Songer = Mem. Bob Hack
× Peppermint = Joseph Masse
× Zada = Diane Rigg
× Dtps. Herman Pigors = Dtps. John Arterberry

DEPUTY | **Elizabeth Marshall × Zondine** | **Shaffer's 1975**

DESERT DAWN | **Painted Desert × amboinensis** | **J. Ewing 1975**

DESERT FLAME | **Painted Desert × lueddemanniana** | **J. Ewing 1975**

PHALAENOPSIS

Name	Parentage	Registrant
DESERT GLOW	Painted Desert × sumatrana	J. Ewing 1975
DESERT GOLD	Painted Desert × fasciata	Shaffer's 1973
DESERT MORN	Mrs. J. H. Veitch × Bridesmaid	Shaffer's 1973
DESERT SANDS	Painted Desert × Zondine	Carlson 1974
DESIRE	Rosy Charm × Lipperose	Schöttler 1975
DESTINY	Star of Santa Cruz × sumatrana	Hager 1972
DEW DROPS	Robin × fuscata	R. K. Mizuta 1973
DIAMOND LIL	Ella Freed × Renee Freed	Dobkin 1975
DIAMOND PASS	Polar Bear × Grace Heartfield	Beall 1975
DIAMOND PINK	Pink Shadow × Zada	Petch Aporn 1975

× William Boyd = Madame Surin

Name	Parentage	Registrant
DIANA HAUSERMANN	Theresa Hausermann × Keith Shaffer	E. F. G. Orchids 1972
DIANE RIGG	Denise Richardson × Zada	Bachner 1971

× lueddemanniana = Mem. Mary Lista | × Ruby Stripes = Mem. Irene Mallory

Name	Parentage	Registrant
DICK MUNSON	Elisa × Estrellita	Shaffer's 1974
DICK WHEELER	Miami Maid × lueddemanniana	Hausermann's 1971
DIPANG-BEAUTY	Dipang Ruby Lips × gigantea	Cheah Kheng Cheong 1974
DIPANG RUBY LIPS	Terri Cook × Fiery	Cheah Kheng Cheong 1974

× Fiery = Monarick | × gigantea = Dipang-Beauty

Name	Parentage	Registrant
DOC CANN	Gertrude Homsher × Donnie Brandt	Beard 1973
DOCTOR GEORGE MORRIS	Bardor × Barbara Beard	Beard 1972
DOCTOR HENRY O. EVERSOLE†‡	Altadena × Winged Victory	Orchid Research 1950

× V. spathulata = Vdnps. Henrietta Fujiwara

Name	Parentage	Registrant
DOCTOR TEOH	Miami Maid × Jimmy Hall	Teoh Phaik Khuan 1974
DOLORES‡	Chief Tucker × Mem. Nasu Tomoguchi	Shaffer's 1957

× Capitola = Frank Gottburg | × stuartiana = Cirrus

Name	Parentage	Registrant
DOLORES BUCHANAN	Alice Gloria × Dos Pueblos	Fort Caroline 1972 (Wallbrunn)
DONALD PERRY	Nemesio Mendiola × Orchid Acres	Fort Caroline 1973
DON BURKE	Madelon Kasten × Gertrude Beard	Lockhart 1971
DONNA LOU ASKEW	Zada × Tropicana	Vaughn 1971
DONNA O'NEAL	Daryl Beard × Aristocrat	Mrs. W. H. Boyd 1971
DONNIE BRANDT‡	Big Chief × Susan Merkel	Beard 1964

× Daryl Beard = Art Miller | × Mantilla = Yukon Ice
× Gertrude Homsher = Doc Cann | × Spica = Barbara Moler
× Madrid = Jennifer Gaine | × Dtps. Red Coral = Dtps. Snowdrift

Name	Parentage	Registrant
DORA JEAN FOX	Pacific Princess × Ann Wade	Fouquette 1975 (Bertsch)
DORA McCARTY	Miami Maid × White Sails	D. B. White 1974
DOREEN‡	Barbara Kirch × San Marino	Cavaco 1961 (Kodama)

× Irene Stephens = Mount Rokko | × Terri Cook = Terdoreen
× Sea Mist = Kurt Nagel | × Vallemar = Dorval
× Sigrid = Paul Lippold | × Ren. Kilauea = Rnthps. Limberlost

Name	Parentage	Registrant
DORIS†‡	Elisabethae × Katherine Siegwart	Duke Farms 1940

× Alice Millard = Aureola | × Baguio = Pink Stripes
× Ann Lovelace = Ann Chovy | × Barbara Beard = Davao

DORIS†‡ (*continued*)

× Bonanza = Citation
× Cassandra = Little Pink Doris
× corningiana = Twenty Grand
× Darleen = Monton
× David Herbert = Winafred Hirsch
× Dorisellita = Pleasure Point
× Elizabeth Marshall = Pink Coach
× Fiery = Royal Pattern
× fuscata = Sun Spots
× Hebe = Elaine Christine
× Hermosa = Cry Baby
× Jane Almquist = Rosera
× Jean Stephan = Capitola Rose
× Jewel = Shoulé
× Lipperose = Dorli
× Luedde-violacea = Easter Parade
× Mad Hatter = Schwerte
× Margaret J. Degenhardt = Fanfare
× Nemesio Mendiola = Black Rock Desert
× Ondine = Paula Hallenbeck
× Paula Hallenbeck = Mem. Florentino Ventosa
× Princess Kaiulani = Princess Doris
× Richard Shaffer = Granada
× Rosy Charm = Speckles
× Spica = Nadine
× sumatrana = Stellular
× Sunrise = Cherry Pink
× Sunset Glow = Torch Song
× Vallehigh = Valledor
× Vosa = Pink Surrey
× Dtps. Kenneth Schubert = Dtps. Forty-Niner
× Dtps. Red Coral = Hawaiian Snow
× V. Rothschildiana = Vdnps. Lee Fennell

DORIS BLOMQUIST — **pantherina × amboinensis** — **Kolopaking 1975**

DORISELLITA — **Estrellita × Doris** — **Shaffer's 1968**

× Doris = Pleasure Point
× Lipperose = Plum Beauty
× Ondine = Phyllis-Jean
× Satin Rouge = Wyn Seaman
× Shaffer's Pinkie = Rosemarie Lindsay
× sumatrana = Conflagration
× Zada = Sonoma

DORISSTAR — **Star of Diamond Head × Doris Wells** — **Hans Koch 1974**

DORIS WELLS‡ — **Doris × Ruby Wells** — **Hark 1969**

× amboinensis = Adelheit
× Lipperose = Lippstadt
× Lippezauber = Sesam
× Ruby Wells = Lippia
× Star of Diamond Head = Dorisstar

DORLI — **Doris × Lipperose** — **Röhl 1974**

DOROTHY BROCK — **Clara Birk × Redwing** — **Beard 1975**

DOROTHYLITA — **Estrellita × Dorothy Miller** — **Shaffer's 1972**

DOROTHY MILLER — **Elisa × Barbara Beard** — **Fredk. L. Thornton 1967**

× Estrellita = Dorothylita
× Ondine = Roja

DOROTHY ORDWAY — **Bandleader × New Horizon** — **W. J. Sanders 1973 (Hager)**

DOROTHY VENÉY — **amboinensis × Satin Rouge** — **Carlson 1975**

DOROTHY VON BELDING — **Cathrine Pillsbury × Bruce Shaffer** — **Hager 1972**

DORVAL — **Vallemar × Doreen** — **R. M. Hamilton 1973 (B. Kodama)**

× Chieftain = Anne Hamilton

DOS AMARILLOS — **Masu Hamacher × Cindy Brandt** — **Beard 1972**

DOS-AMBO — **Dos Pueblos × amboinensis** — **E. Iwanaga 1967**

× lueddemanniana = Yellow Jewel
× Sonja = Freed's Dignitary
× Star of Florida = Mystic Land
× Sulawesi = Fantasia

DOS PUEBLOS†‡ — **Doris × Grace Palm** — **Bean 1956**

× Alice Gloria = Dolores Buchanan
× Anne = Pueblo Anne
× Big Chief = Madelon Kasten
× Bridesmaid = Arctic Fox
× cornu-cervi = Clown's Mask
× Gladys Read = Delicate Lady
× Gracia = Grazioso
× Joanna Magale = Virginia MacBride
× Mahinhin = Malahini Missy
× Margaret Bean = Sri Lanka
× Scotti Maguire = Zachariah
× Snow White = Classic
× Spice Islands = Angela Angelidis
× Wilma Hughes = Snow Flower
× Ascps. Irene Dobkin = Ascps. Rayna Wallbrunn
× Ren. Brookie Chandler = Rnthps. Sun Dance
× Ren. coccinea = Rnthps. Na'imah
× Ren. imschootiana = Rnthps. Cat Island

Name	Parentage	Originator
DOTS VIOLET	Violet Glow × corningiana	C. & I. Keyes 1974
DOTTIE BUCHECK	Quality Belle × Spica	Lockhart 1974
DOTTIE HEMMING	Betty Beard × Evening Rose	Beard 1975
DOUBLE EAGLE	corningiana × sumatrana	Dobkin 1974
DOUGLAS ALLEN	Intermedia × parishii	Wallbrunn 1973
DUPAGE	Shaffer's Pinkie × Lipperose	Hausermann 1974
DURABLE PINK	Clara I. Knight × Fairway Park	Rod McLellan Co. 1966

× Esther Edris = Shell Canyon

Name	Parentage	Originator
DURWARD BELMONT WHITE	Quality Belle × Cathrine Pillsbury	D. B. White 1975
DUSKY ROUGE	Satin Rouge × Ambomanniana	C. & I. Keyes 1974
DYNAMO	Mary Wieler × Frances Roberts	Beard 1973
EAGER	Intermedia × Evening Rose	Beard 1974
EAGLE	Kathryn Leahey × Irene van Alstyne	Beard 1973
EARL HEMMING	Linda Winters × Jimmy Mize	Beard 1975
EARL STEWART	Gertrude Beard × Yellow Lip	Beard 1973
EARLY SPRING	Tyler Carlson × violacea	Hager 1973
EASTER PARADE	Luedde-violacea × Doris	Shaffer's 1974
EDEN ROCK	Candy Wakasugi × Ruby Zada	Beard 1971
EDITH SCOVILLE	Rising Sun × Barbara Moler	Beard 1975
ED LISTA	Capitola × Sonja	Peter E. Lista 1975
EDYTHE WOOD‡	Grace Palm × Princess Grace	Bernie Wood 1961

× Alice Gloria = Malibu White
× Carl Hausermann = Westwood
× Cast Iron Monarch = Page Oates
× Ernst Haussermann = Jamaica Sunshine
× fuscata = Yellow Albatross
× Keith Shaffer = Paula Kramer
× Miami Maid = Marten Hausermann
× Wilma Hughes = Marilyn Freed Browning
× Dtps. Susan Ann Schubert = Dtps. Robert Winkelmann

Name	Parentage	Originator
EILEEN ASHBURN	Princess Michiko × Jane Shaffer	Gemenis 1971
EILEEN'S PINK	Callie Flynn × Fairway Park	Rod McLellan Co. 1974
ELAINE CHRISTINE	Hebe × Doris	Thornton's 1975
ELAINE KILPATRICK	Clara Birk × Ann Marie Beard	Lockhart 1972
ELAINE-LIEM	fimbriata × amboinensis	Kolopaking 1972

× amboinensis = Raka Sumichan
× Professor Asmino = Sri Rejeki

Name	Parentage	Originator
ELCORNU	cornu-cervi × Elinor Shaffer	C. A. Russell 1973 (J. & L.)
ELDORA†‡	Doris × Elinor	M. Ryerson 1957

× Robert W. Miller = Linesides

Name	Parentage	Originator
ELECTRA	Samba × corningiana	Dobkin 1974
ELIANA	Elinor × schillerana	Rumrill 1973 (Originator unknown)

× Zada = Joy Jost

Name	Parentage	Originator
ELINOR†	Gyp × Rothschildiana	S. A. 1938

× schillerana = Eliana

Name	Parentage	Originator
ELINOR SHAFFER‡	Juanita × Doris	Shaffer's 1960

× cornu-cervi = Elcornu
× Fiery = Ann Snook
× Holiday Eggnog = Kiwi
× Irma Rath = Prodigious
× Kauai = Malibu River
× Nicol Jean Orear = Ski Patrol
× Norman Peterson = Virtuoso
× Palm Beach = Malibu Wedding
× Polar Bear = White Bear Pass
× Princess Grace = Gay Senorita
× Redfan = Jane Seymour
× R. H. Montgomery = White Virgin
× Snow White = June Bride
× Susan Merkel = Richard Kimbrel
× Terri Cook = Lillie Wooldridge
× Ren. Brookie Chandler = Rnthps. Red Flash

ELISA‡	**Grace Palm × Aalsmeer Rose**	**Shaffer's 1959**

×	=	×	=
× Estrellita	= Dick Munson	× Mistinguett	= Mistellisa
× Golden Sands	= Ruth Shaban	× Phieng-rudi Pink	= Freed's Daredevil
× Karen Rosea	= Olga Malek	× Pink Vogue	= Vosa

ELIZABETH MARSHALL	**Gladys Read × Roswell**	**Shaffer's 1966**

×	=	×	=
× Doris	= Pink Coach	× Overglow	= Tiger Rose
× Mistinguett	= Reshana	× Zondine	= Deputy
× Ondine	= Modine		

ELLA FREED	**Show Girl × Samba**	**Freed 1970**

×	=	×	=
× Apollo Ten	= Karlyne	× Pin Up Girl	= Malibu Optimists
× Career Girl	= Freed's Danseuse	× Renee Freed	= Diamond Lil
× Debbie Wallace	= Freed's Dashing	× Ruby Stripes	= Lucky Stripes
× gigantea	= May Lee	× Ruby Zada	= Freed's Curvaceous
× Hawaiian Sunshine	= Freed's Darling	× Sea Mist	= Chang Chao-Tang
× Jiminy Cricket	= Johanna	× Show Girl	= Freed's Cherub
× Mad Lips	= Hugo Freed	× violacea	= Carmen Coll
× Mahinhin	= Ruby Gem	× Viroonchan	= Liang Fong King
× Natasha	= Sherluch		

ELLA MAE GEORGE	**Taffy × Viroonchan**	**Peter E. Lista 1973**
ELLEN MURK	**Jennifer Beard × Brasilia**	**W. J. Sanders 1975 (Hager)**
ELOQUENCE	**My Fair Lady × Sunbeam**	**Dobkin 1974**
ELPORTAL	**Aristocrat × Wendy Beard**	**Fields Orchids 1973**

×	=	×	=
× Redkar	= Redport	× Ruby Zada	= Norma Cole

EMERALD STAR	**Ambodoris × micholitzii**	**John H. Miller 1974**
EMPIRE SNOW	**Hermosa × Capitola**	**Shaffer's 1974**
ENCHANTER	**Satin Rouge × sumatrana**	**Rod McLellan Co. 1973**
ENG LAN	**Cast Iron Monarch × Jane L. Kingsbury**	**Lim Swee Aun 1964 (Ooi Teng Kwee)**

×	=	×	=
× Fong Cheong Mooi	= Youngaun Lim		

equestris*†‡ (syn. *rosea**†)	**species**	

×	=	×	=
× Bandleader	= Larry Oberhaus	× Mildred Karleen	= Swiss Miss
× Bruce Shaffer	= Magdeburg	× Percy Porter	= Paradise Pink
× Freed's Broadway Rhythm	= Freed's Destiny	× Rosy Charm	= Junior Miss
× Keith Shaffer	= Halle	× Sparkle	= Wee One
× Lady Doreen	= Pink Snow	× Yap Wee Hiong	= Boutonniere
× maculata	= Little Sister	× Asctm. Sagarik Gold	= Ascps. Vivacious Vixen
× Mem. William Shaban	= Robin Floyd	× King. philippinensis	= Phlla. New Horizon
		× Neof. falcata	= Phnta. Irene

ERICK HANSEN	**Alice Gloria × Grace Palm**	**Gubler 1965 (Hansen)**

×	=	×	=
× Ambomanniana	= Freed's Cupid	× lueddemanniana	= Freed's Damsel
× Ann Hatter	= Antique	× Nicol Jean Orear	= Vera Miller
× Daryl Beard	= Scotty	× Verle	= Wollochet

ERNST HAUSSERMANN	**Fairway Park × Miami Maid**	**Hausermann 1969**

×	=	×	=
× Calawaii	= Royal Diadem	× Edythe Wood	= Jamaica Sunshine
× Charles Shaffer	= Kenneth Benjamin	× Kenneth Stromsland	= White Gem
× Cher Ann	= Jim Toskey	× Marten Hausermann	= Gladys Wright

ESMA	**Best Girl × gigantea**	**Dobkin 1973**
esmeralda (see *Doritis pulcherrima*†‡)	**species**	
ESTABLO	**Pueblo Anne × Estrellita**	**Y. Toyama 1975**
ESTELLA	**Love Tide × Ruby Stripes**	**Dobkin 1975**

Name	Parentage	Registrant
ESTHER EDRIS	**Zada × Bridesmaid**	**Beall 1974 (Edris)**

× Callie Flynn	= Widow Pass	× Hedy Maerkl	= Rosy Ridge
× Durable Pink	= Shell Canyon	× Strawberry Meadows	= Wild Rose Ridge
× Fiji	= Baby Shoe Pass		

Name	Parentage	Registrant
ESTRELLITA‡	**Ruby Wells × lueddemanniana**	**Shaffer's 1963**

× Ambomanniana	= Ana Roja	× Ondine	= Nitzan
× Dorothy Miller	= Dorothylita	× Pink Jewel	= Jewelita
× Elisa	= Dick Munson	× Pueblo Anne	= Establo
× lueddemanniana	= Redwine	× Sourire	= Turkish Delight
× Luedde-violacea	= Little Rose	× Zondine	= Zealous

Name	Parentage	Registrant
ETHEL SHREFFLER	**Baguio × Caroline Oberling**	**MAJ Orchids 1973 (Ragan)**
ETHYL SANDERS	**Jubilee × Harlequin**	**W. J. Sanders 1973**
EUREKA CANYON	**Richard Shaffer × Angela Dumas**	**Frank Hughes 1974**
EVA	**Damas × Diva**	**Pff. V. & L. 1966**

× Alice Gloria	= Adelie	× Exquis	= Artigny
× Anouche	= Bauge	× Henriette Lecoufle	= Fantac

Name	Parentage	Registrant
EVA LOU	**Suemid × Redfan**	**Beard 1971**

× Bright Spot	= Pamela Wolf		

Name	Parentage	Registrant
EVANGELINE	**Alice Gloria × White Magic**	**Hager 1972**
EVA WELLS	**Nicol Jean Orear × Quality Belle**	**Beard 1974**
EVELYN WEAVER	**Helen Miller × Spica**	**Lockhart 1974**
EVENING ROSE	**Ann Marie Beard × Best Girl**	**Beard 1970**

× Betty Beard	= Dottie Hemming	× Melba Burnett	= Xenia
× Intermedia	= Eager	× Redwing	= Youngs Town
× Jimmy Mize	= Rigby	× Dtps. Red Lip	= Dtps. Red Eve

Name	Parentage	Registrant
EVENING SKY	**Pink Ice × Valentinii**	**Rod McLellan Co. 1974**
EVENTIDE‡	**Pink Beauty × Marmouset**	**McCoy 1956**

× Ann Lovelace	= Love Tide	× gigantea	= High Tide

Name	Parentage	Registrant
EVERETT SOARS	**Madelon Kasten × Daryl Beard**	**Lockhart 1973**
EVERNIA	**Mary Wieler × Bardor**	**Beard 1974**
EXQUIS	**Diva × Fanchette**	**Pff. V. & L. 1970**

× Eva	= Artigny		

Name	Parentage	Registrant
EYE DEE	**Star of Rio × gigantea**	**Dobkin 1972**
EZRA	**Jimmy Mize × Jean Johnston**	**Beard 1973**
FABLE	**Barbara Beard × Jean Johnston**	**Beard 1973**
FAIR ALICE	**Fairway Park × Alice Gloria**	**Freed 1972**

× Gelinotte	= Freed's Devoted		

Name	Parentage	Registrant
FAIR MAIDEN	**Capitola × Goldiana**	**Hausermann 1973**
FAIRVALE	**Fairway Park × Pink Chief**	**Rod McLellan Co. 1969**

× V. cristata	= Vdnps. Revelation		

Name	Parentage	Registrant
FAIRWAY PARK‡	**Thomas Tucker × Winged Victory**	**Vallemar 1957**

× Alice Gloria	= Fair Alice	× Daryl Beard	= Iago
× Callie Flynn	= Eileen's Pink	× Intermedia	= Jamboree
× Capitola	= Hausermann's Glacier	× Venus	= Modest Beauty
× Cathrine Pillsbury	= Robert Green	× White Gull	= Ternate Princess
× Charles Shaffer	= Hausermann's Moonbeam		

FAIRYFLOSS	**Zadian × Lavender Lady**	**Valley Orchids 1974**
FAIRY PINK	**Margaret Bean × Ann Lovelace**	**Lorenzen 1971 (Small)**

× mannii	= Mandeville Sunset

FAITH LEEBELL COWDEN	**lueddemanniana × Luedde-violacea**	**Freed 1973 (Cowden)**
FANCY GIRL	**Ann Marie Beard × Lois Jansen**	**Beard 1974**
FANCY QUEST	**Cast Iron Monarch × Pasadena**	**J. & S. 1967 (Stoddard)**

× Caprice	= Reinaldo

FANFARE	**Margaret J. Degenhardt × Doris**	**Lorenzen 1971 (Small)**

× Ann Lovelace	= Charming

FANNIE MAE	**Masu Hamacher × Ruby Zada**	**Beard 1972**
FANTAC	**Eva × Henriette Lecoufle**	**Pff. V. & L. 1974**
FANTASIA	**Dos-Ambo × Sulawesi**	**Lorenzen 1975**
FAR HORIZON	**New Horizon × Vercors**	**Hager 1970**

× Bandleader	= Georgia Seaman	× Hugo Freed	= Heathercliff
× Breathless	= Priscilla Pyfrom		

fasciata‡ **species**

(syn. *reichenbachiana*) (*Phal. fasciata* and *Phal. lueddemanniana* are treated as specifically distinct for registration purposes, although regarded as conspecific by some authorities.)

× Alice Gloria	= Saffron Elizanne	× Miami Maid	= Lynn Hausermann
× amboinensis	= Golden Pride	× Miss Muffitt	= Golden Triangle
× Barcelona	= Autumn Gold	× Nancy Carlson	= New Penny
× Boynton	= Spots of Gold	× Painted Desert	= Desert Gold
× Bridesmaid	= Golden Maiden	× Ramona	= Yellow Bird
× Bruce Shaffer	= Brandenburg	× Scotti Maguire	= Autunite
× Cadifa	= Sterntaler	× Snow Chief	= Goldie
× Charles Shaffer	= Harrison Kennicott	× Star Fire	= Starfas
× Cindy Brandt	= Suzanne Wenzel	× Suemid	= Yellow Warbler
× cochlearis	= Golden Jubilee	× sumatrana	= Kathy Kornahrens
× cornu-cervi	= Little Girl	× Utopia	= Boo Kolshak
× Daryl Beard	= Winnie Brecht	× Wilma Hughes	= Golden Cloud
× Gertrude Homsher	= Rosa Lee Pittman	× Dtps. Mem. Clarence Schubert	= Dtps. Erfürt
× gigantea	= Reichentea		
× Gladys Read	= Tyler	× Dtps. Susan Ann Schubert	= Dtps. Red Cricket
× Golden Beach	= Golden Queen		
× Hymen	= Hymenata		

FASCINATION	**sumatrana × Federal Monarch**	**Dobkin 1974**
FATIMA	**sumatrana × Ivy Merkel**	**Dobkin 1973**
FAYE WHITE	**White Sails × White Falcon**	**D. B. White 1971**
FEDERAL GLO	**Federal Monarch × Alice Gloria**	**Kensington 1973**
FEDERAL MONARCH‡	**Joanna Magale × Palm Beach**	**A. & M. 1961**

× Alice Gloria	= Federal Glo	× sumatrana	= Fascination

FERVEUR	**Arpege × Alice Gloria**	**Pff. V. & L. 1974**
FIERY‡	**Firefly × New Era**	**Small 1965**

× Dipang Ruby Lips	= Monarick	× Ministripes	= Tinkerbell
× Doris	= Royal Pattern	× Pacesetter	= Sugar 'n Spice
× Elinor Shaffer	= Ann Snook	× Suemid	= Bert Shelley
× Go-Go Girl	= Fiery Girl	× Terri Cook	= Dipang Ruby Lips
× Keith Shaffer	= Tropic Snow	× Texas Star	= Flagler
× Louis Merkel	= Trudy		

FIERY BALL	**Mary McLane × Betty Beard**	**Beard 1973**

FIERY GIRL | **Go-Go Girl × Fiery** | **A. & M. 1971**

- × Jennie Swank = Mary Overby
- × Red Eye = Ginny McConville
- × Suemid = Robbie Vanaman
- × Dtps. Pueblo Jewel = Dtps. Kristine Teoh

FIESTA | **Mardi Gras × Aalsmeer Rose** | **John H. Miller 1970**

- × Overglow = Fiesta Glow
- × Zada = Louisiana Lady

FIESTA GLOW | **Fiesta × Overglow** | **John H. Miller 1974**

FIFI | **Minouche × Redfan** | **Pff. V. & L. 1974**

FIJI | **Nuel N. Songer × Bridesmaid** | **Beall 1974 (Edris)**

- × Esther Edris = Baby Shoe Pass

fimbriata‡ | **species**

- × amboinensis = Elaine-Liem
- × Cher Ann = Candyland
- × Mad Hatter = Harpoon
- × micholitzii = Green Valley
- × Mildred Karleen = Mayleen
- × parishii = Green Imp

FIRST LIGHT | **Ruth Wallbrunn × Princess Kaiulani** | **Hager 1975**

FISCHERS ICE | **Fischers Liebling × Pink Ice** | **Hans Koch 1975**

FISCHERS LIEBLING | **Zada × Pollux** | **Hans Koch 1975**

- × Gabizada = Gabis Liebling
- × Lipperose = Comtesse Bettina
- × Pink Ice = Fischers Ice
- × Unna = Morgensonne
- × Zada = Liezada

FLAGLER | **Texas Star × Fiery** | **J. & S. 1971**

FLIRTATION | **Intermedia × Juanita** | **Andrew Orchids 1972**

FLOR DE MATO | **Zada × Satin Rouge** | **Hager 1972**

FLORENCE KROECK | **Texas Pink × Hedy Maerkl** | **Beard 1975**

FLORENCE PERERA | **Mrs. J. H. Veitch × Mistinguett** | **Fernando 1974 (H. E. Perera)**

- × mannii = Bronze King

FLORENCE ROSE | **Jimmy Mize × Best Girl** | **C. R. Rose 1972**

FLORENCE THORNTON‡ | **Summer Monarch × Fenton Davis Avant** | **Fredk. L. Thornton 1967 (Fields)**

- × Mambo = Mem. Pat Peeler
- × Tenaya = Sheba

FLORENTINE | **New Horizon × Star of Florida** | **Hager 1975**

FONG CHEONG MOOI | **Hermione × Pinkie** | **Lim Swee Aun 1966 (Ooi Teng Kwee)**

- × Eng Lan = Youngaun Lim

FORMAL | **Hermosa × Bridesmaid** | **Shaffer's 1975**

formosa (see *amabilis**†‡) | **species**

FORT CAROLINE | **gigantea × Alice Gloria** | **Wallbrunn 1971**

FRANCES ROBERTS | **Ann Marie Beard × Barry Eamer** | **Beard 1969**

- × Ann Marie Beard = Gabbardine
- × Barbara Beard = Jean Marshall
- × Barry Eamer = Futurist
- × Clara Birk = Ruth Stout
- × Jimmy Mize = Zwingli
- × Kathryn Leahey = Wyandot
- × Linda Winters = Key Largo
- × Mary Wieler = Dynamo
- × Texas Pink = Helen Farlow
- × Theodosia Gibson = Quarterly
- × Dtps. Jerry Vande Weghe = Dtps. Teoh Phaik Khuan

FRANCES WHITE | **Little Worrall × Cathrine Pillsbury** | **D. B. White 1974**

FRANCINE	**Domremy × Damas**	**Pff. V. & L. 1966**

× Alice Gloria = Melissa Dawn | × Lipperose = Hokuspokus
× Annie Hoffman = Kruemel | × Rapture = Scherzo
× Anouche = Mouchette | × White Lady = Cadifa
× Kruemel = Kruemeline | × Zada = Zacine

FRANCISCA‡	**Grace Palm × equestris**	**Shaffer's 1959**

× Cadifa = Franka | × Vallehigh = Francishigh

FRANCISHIGH	**Vallehigh × Francisca**	**Hans Koch 1974**
FRANKA	**Cadifa × Francisca**	**Hans Koch 1975**
FRANK GOTTBURG	**Dolores × Capitola**	**J. F. Hughes 1973**
FRANK PEARCE	**Linda Mia × Mantilla**	**Rod McLellan Co. 1973 (McElderry)**
FRECKLED GOLD	**Cotabata × fuscata**	**W. W. G. Moir 1973**
FREED'S ADMIRATION	**Show Girl × Phylis-Kay**	**Freed 1974**
FREED'S ADORABLE	**Show Girl × Luora**	**Freed 1974**
FREED'S ADVENTURE	**Lipstick × Chuck's Red Lip**	**Freed 1975**
FREED'S AMIGO	**gigantea × Sonja**	**Freed 1975**
FREED'S ANGEL	**Show Girl × Ruby Zada**	**Freed 1975**
FREED'S ARISTOCRAT	**Dear One × Malibu Pink**	**Freed 1975**
FREED'S BEDEVILLED	**Kauai × Norman Peterson**	**Freed 1975**
FREED'S BEGUILED	**Samba × Debbie Wallace**	**Freed 1975**
FREED'S BROADWAY MELODY	**Lipstick × Ruby Lips**	**Freed 1975**
FREED'S BROADWAY RHYTHM	**Cast Iron Monarch × Sally Lowrey**	**Freed 1975**

× equestris = Freed's Destiny | × Show Girl = Painted Doll Wedding

FREED'S CELEBRITY	**Ann Lovelace × sanderana**	**Freed 1975**
FREED'S CHERUB	**Show Girl × Ella Freed**	**Freed 1975**
FREED'S CHIEFTAIN	**Debbie Wallace × Chuck's Red Lip**	**Freed 1975**
FREED'S CHOICE	**Chuck's Red Lip × violacea**	**Freed 1975**
FREED'S CONNOISSEUR	**Redfan × Lipstick**	**Freed 1975**
FREED'S COQUETTE	**Sonja × violacea**	**Freed 1975**
FREED'S CRITERION	**Madrid × Cast Iron Monarch**	**Freed 1975**
FREED'S CUPID	**Ambomanniana × Erick Hansen**	**Freed 1975**
FREED'S CURTAIN CALL	**Golden Chief × Princess Michiko**	**Freed 1975**
FREED'S CURVACEOUS	**Ruby Zada × Ella Freed**	**Freed 1975**
FREED'S DAMSEL	**Erick Hansen × lueddemanniana**	**Freed 1975**
FREED'S DANSEUSE	**Ella Freed × Career Girl**	**Freed 1975**
FREED'S DAREDEVIL	**Phieng-rudi Pink × Elisa**	**Freed 1975**
FREED'S DARLING	**Hawaiian Sunshine × Ella Freed**	**Freed 1975**
FREED'S DASHING	**Debbie Wallace × Ella Freed**	**Freed 1975**
FREED'S DAZZLER	**Viroonchan × Ann Hatter**	**Freed 1975**
FREED'S DEBONAIR	**Martha's Gem × sanderana**	**Freed 1975**
FREED'S DELECTABLE	**Raycraft × Ann Lovelace**	**Freed 1975**
FREED'S DELICIOUS	**Mrs. J. H. Veitch × Luedde-violacea**	**Freed 1975**
FREED'S DESTINY	**Freed's Broadway Rhythm × equestris**	**Freed 1975**
FREED'S DEVILISH	**Cast Iron Monarch × Alice Gloria**	**Freed 1975**
FREED'S DEVOTED	**Fair Alice × Gelinotte**	**Freed 1975**
FREED'S DIGNITARY	**Dos-Ambo × Sonja**	**Freed 1975**

FREED'S DIMPLE	**Norman × sanderana**	**Freed 1975**
FREED'S DISTINCTION	**Ambomanniana × Mannicata**	**Freed 1975**
FREED'S DIVINE	**Ruby Lips × Viroonchan**	**Freed 1975**
FREED'S LUCKY STAR	**Sonja × lueddemanniana**	**Freed 1975**
FREED'S PRIDE	**Norman Peterson × Sonja**	**Freed 1974**
FREED'S TEMPTATION	**Ann Lovelace × Ann Marie Beard**	**Freed 1975**

× Dtps. Mem. Clarence Schubert	= Dtps. Sander's Joy		

FRENCH BEAUTY	**Mistinguett × Ghisoni**	**Shaffer's 1972**
FRETEVAL	**Ramona × Mistinguett**	**Pff. V. & L. 1974**
FROST FIRE	**Frosty Lip × Lip Rouge**	**Rod McLellan Co. 1973**
FROSTING	**Cathrine Pillsbury × Long Life**	**Rod McLellan Co. 1973**
FROSTY LIP‡	**Goleta × Spitfire**	**Rod McLellan Co. 1964**

× Lip Rouge	= Frost Fire	× Redfan	= Snow Ruby
× Mad Hatter	= Serenata		

FROSTY PINK	**Summit Snow × Ann Lovelace**	**Lorenzen 1971 (Small)**
FULL PINK	**Pink Wow × Zada**	**Shaffer's 1975**
fuscata‡	**species**	

× Alice Gloria	= Summer Sun	× Louis Merkel	= Goldilocks
× Best Girl	= Gloria Turner	× mariae	= Golden Jewel
× Boynton	= Gold Charm	× Palmsnow	= Apricot Nectar
× Chieftain	= Mabel Allard	× Peter Wallbrunn	= Bruce LeBaron
× Cotabata	= Freckled Gold	× Red Lip	= Polka Dot
× Daryl Beard	= Jeniffer Hall	× Robert Pigors	= Northwoods
× Denise Richardson	= Maria Vasquez	× Robin	= Dew Drops
× Doris	= Sun Spots	× Samba	= Justine LeBaron
× Edythe Wood	= Yellow Albatross	× Sea Mist	= Kinta Gold
× Gladys Read	= Oak Flame	× Tenaya	= Golden Sunset
× Golden Sands	= Marcia Leigh	× Wilma Hughes	= Gingo
× Hymen	= Christine Ann	× Dtps. Jerri Sue King	= Dtps. Suecata
× Irma Rath	= Midnight Sun	× Dtps. Pueblo Jewel	= Dtps. Illinois
× Jane Shaffer	= Bill's Yellow		

FUTURIST	**Frances Roberts × Barry Eamer**	**Beard 1974**
FYKE	**Cream Puff × Jean Johnston**	**Beard 1973**
GABBARDINE	**Ann Marie Beard × Frances Roberts**	**Beard 1973**
GABI KOCH	**Pollux × Mistinguett**	**Koch 1971**

× Zada	= Gabizada		

GABIS LIEBLING	**Gabizada × Fischers Liebling**	**Hans Koch 1975**
GABIZADA	**Gabi Koch × Zada**	**Recker-Koch 1971 (Hans Koch)**

× Fischers Liebling	= Gabis Liebling		

GADIS SINGAPURA	**Anna Tham × Ruth Roesler**	**Peh Eng Kee & Peh Eng Khim 1971**
GAIL LYNNE	**Golden Sands × Queen Emma**	**W. J. Shaban 1972**
GAY HEART	**Red Lip × Luedde-violacea**	**J. & S. 1971**
GAY PAREE	**Trancas × Marmouset**	**Freed 1964**

× Zada	= Norm's Fantasy		

GAY SENORITA	**Elinor Shaffer × Princess Grace**	**Lorenzen 1973**

GEDWO — **Kenneth Stromsland × Redport** — **Plewka 1975**

GELINOTTE — **Wilma Hughes × Capitola** — **Pff. V. & L. 1970**

×	=
× Fair Alice	= Freed's Devoted

GEMINI — **Dazzler × Myra Wright** — **Plaxico 1965 (Wright)**

×	=
× Terri Cook	= Billie Pickell

GEM STONE — **Mahinhin × Baguio** — **Osgood 1973**

GENEVIEVE ELAM — **Linda Mia × Wilma Hughes** — **McElderry 1971**

GENEVIEVE SAUNDERS — **Keith Shaffer × Bruce Shaffer** — **Shaffer's 1971**

GENTLE RAIN — **Brasilia × Harlequin** — **Hager 1975**

GEORGE VASQUEZ — **violacea × Luedde-violacea** — **Freed 1974**

GEORGE WOODWARD — **Barcelona × Keith Shaffer** — **Shaffer's 1972**

GEORGIA SEAMAN — **Bandleader × Far Horizon** — **Hager 1975**

GERTRUDE BEARD‡ — **Susan Merkel × Dos Pueblos** — **Beard 1964**

×	=
× Amber Sands	= Golden Dream
× Daryl Beard	= Zirconia
× Gertrude Homsher	= Kaaba
× Madelon Kasten	= Don Burke
× Mantilla	= Vince Cefalu
× micholitzii	= Snowdrift
× Ruby Zada	= Jungle King
× Spica	= Joan Hall
× Utopia	= Jean Girardeau
× Wilma Hughes	= Champagne Lady
× Yellow Lip	= Earl Stewart

GERTRUDE CAMPBELL — **Mildred Karleen × Mad Lips** — **Hager 1972**

GERTRUDE HOMSHER — **Dos Pueblos × Louis Merkel** — **Beard 1966**

×	=
× Donnie Brandt	= Doc Cann
× fasciata	= Rosa Lee Pittman
× Gertrude Beard	= Kaaba
× Intermedia	= Vulgate
× Mantilla	= Aalbane
× Scotti Maguire	= Zara Spook
× Spica	= Betty Sistrunk
× Utopia	= Ozone
× White Plains	= Pat Colton

GHISONI‡ — **Mistinguett × Guignol Rose** — **Marcel Lecoufle 1962**

×	=
× Juanita	= Pink Dove
× Mistinguett	= French Beauty
× Painted Desert	= Painted Dolly
× Dor. pulcherrima	= Dtps. Eclatant

GIANT — **Grace Palm × Hermosa** — **Shaffer's 1967**

×	=
× Keith Shaffer	= Jolly Odin

GIATGONG — **Sonja × Kauai** — **Giatgong 1973 (Euyprayoonwong)**

GIDGET WHITE — **Alice Jean × Little Worrall** — **D. B. White 1974**

gigantea*‡ — **species**

×	=
× Alice Gloria	= Fort Caroline
× Alii	= Aliitea
× amboinensis	= David Lim
× Ann Lovelace	= Bold Queen
× Best Girl	= Esma
× Bonanza	= Daisy Mae
× Bridesmaid	= Schamott
× Cast Iron Monarch	= China Doll
× Dear One	= Little David
× Dipang Ruby Lips	= Dipang-Beauty
× Ella Freed	= May Lee
× Eventide	= High Tide
× fasciata	= Reichentea
× Golden Beach	= Golden Touch
× Hermione	= Yip
× Jackie	= Lulu
× lueddemanniana	= Joey
× mannii	= Rosie Clouse
× My Fair Lady	= Kim
× Painted Desert	= Rainbow Sherbet
× Red Lip	= Bimini
× Rose of Burgundy	= Burgutea
× Samba	= Natasha
× Sonja	= Freed's Amigo
× Star of Florida	= Mosaic
× Star of Rio	= Eye Dee
× Terri Cook	= Mem. Jim Knowles
× Texas Star	= Texas Pride
× Winter Jewel	= Varina Vaughn
× Zada	= Marion Fowler
× Dor. pulcherrima	= Dtps. Tan Swee Eng

GIGI‡	**Pink Sunset × Diamond Head**	**McCoy 1959**

× Zada	= Mrs. Lester McCoy		

GINGO	**Wilma Hughes × fuscata**	**Dobkin 1972**
GINNY McCONVILLE	**Fiery Girl × Red Eye**	**Lockhart 1975**
GLADYS BURKEY	**Norman × Daryl Beard**	**Beard 1975**
GLADYS READ‡	**Juanita × Grace Palm**	**Santa Cruz 1961**

× amabilis	= Juan Escobar	× Joseph Hampton	= Green Meadows
× amboinensis	= Antigua	× Keith Shaffer	= Snow Lady
× Anne Cavaco	= Ironside	× Princess Grace	= Mem. Marian Baker
× Betty Conroy	= Ward Munson	× Sharon Karleen	= Jungle Belle
× Cast Iron Monarch	= Peggy O'Neill	× Sonja	= Amnuey Porn
× Dos Pueblos	= Delicate Lady	× violacea	= Vioqueen
× fasciata	= Tyler	× Virginia MacBride	= June Starke
× fuscata	= Oak Flame	× White Summit	= Pat Strothmann
× Ice Palace	= Peggy Nagel	× Wilma Hughes	= Angels Flight
× Irma Rath	= Bright Angel		

GLADYS WRIGHT	**Marten Hausermann × Ernst Haussermann**	**Hausermann 1974**
GLAMOUR GIRL	**Show Girl × Cover Girl**	**Peter E. Lista 1974 (Originator unknown)**

× Alight	= Crimson Heart		

GLENBARD	**Lipperose × Zawell**	**Hausermann 1974**
GLEN MARSHALL	**Ministripes × Orlando**	**J. & S. 1974**
GLORIA TURNER	**Best Girl × fuscata**	**A. & M. 1975**
GLORIOSA†‡	**Pink Glory × stuartiana**	**A. & M. 1948**

× Sunset Glow	= Dabbled		

GLORY DALE	**Thordale × Alice Gloria**	**Fredk. L. Thornton 1973**
GO-GO GIRL‡	**Lipstick × Grace Palm**	**Dodge 1970 (Freed)**

× David Herbert	= Royal Stripe	× Fiery	= Fiery Girl
× Denise Richardson	= Pink Circus		

GOLD BAR	**Gold Coin × Chuck's Red Lip**	**Dobkin 1975**
GOLD CHARM	**Boynton × fuscata**	**A. & M. 1975**
GOLD COIN	**Samba × mariae**	**Dobkin 1972**

× Chuck's Red Lip	= Gold Bar		

GOLDEN BEACH	**Fenton Davis Avant × mannii**	**Fields Orchids 1963**

× fasciata	= Golden Queen	× gigantea	= Golden Touch

GOLDEN CHIEF‡	**Chieftain × mannii**	**Vaughn 1958**

× Princess Michiko	= Freed's Curtain Call		

GOLDEN CLOUD	**fasciata × Wilma Hughes**	**Shaffer's 1973**
GOLDEN DIANA	**Ann Marie Beard × amboinensis**	**Beard 1975**
GOLDEN DREAM	**Amber Sands × Gertrude Beard**	**Beard 1975**
GOLDEN GLOW	**Mrs. J. H. Veitch × Hymen**	**Crestwood 1963**

× Mistinguett	= Gran Desierto	× Sunrise	= Misty Pink
× Ramona	= Yuma Desert		

GOLDEN JEWEL	**mariae × fuscata**	**Dobkin 1973**
GOLDEN JUBILEE	**cochlearis × fasciata**	**Dobkin 1975**
GOLDEN MAIDEN	**fasciata × Bridesmaid**	**Shaffer's 1975**
GOLDEN MANNII	**mannii × Goldenrod**	**Lemförder Orch. 1973 (Christ)**

GOLDEN MARINO	**mannii × San Marino**	**Gauda 1975**
GOLDEN MIST	**mannii × Golden Palm**	**McCoy 1965**

× Juanita	= Green Gold		

GOLDEN PEACE	**Peace × lueddemanniana**	**John H. Miller 1974**
GOLDEN PIXIE	**Tyler Carlson × mariae**	**Dobkin 1975**
GOLDEN PRIDE	**amboinensis × fasciata**	**Dobkin 1975**
GOLDEN QUEEN	**Golden Beach × fasciata**	**Dobkin 1973**
GOLDENROD	**Helen Richards × mannii**	**McCoy 1961**

× mannii	= Golden Manii		

GOLDEN SANDS‡	**Fenton Davis Avant × lueddemanniana**	**Fields Orchids 1964**

× Alice Gloria	= Rhonda Dunn	× Mem. William Shaban	= Mem. Knox Daniel
× Capitola	= Poppee	× Polar Bear	= Lemon Point
× cochlearis	= Island Sands	× Queen Emma	= Gail Lynne
× Elisa	= Ruth Shaban	× Ruby Zada	= Bob Turner
× fuscata	= Marcia Leigh	× stuartiana	= Butterball
× Judith Hausermann	= Shellie Lynn	× sumatrana	= Barbara Bohmer
× lueddemanniana	= Goldiana	× Yellow Lip	= Green Center

GOLDEN STATE	**Wilma Hughes × Ambomanniana**	**John H. Miller 1974**
GOLDEN SUNSET	**fuscata × Tenaya**	**W. W. G. Moir 1973**
GOLDEN TOUCH	**gigantea × Golden Beach**	**Dobkin 1975**
GOLDEN TRIANGLE	**Miss Muffitt × fasciata**	**Osgood 1974**
GOLDEN WEST	**Ambomanniana × Alice Gloria**	**John H. Miller 1972**
GOLDEN ZEBRA	**Delightful × amboinensis**	**Osgood 1975**
GOLDIANA	**Golden Sands × lueddemanniana**	**Fields Orchids 1973 (Wm. A. Miles)**

× Capitola	= Fair Maiden	× Miami Maid	= Jan Grove

GOLDIE	**Snow Chief × fasciata**	**Nicholson 1971**
GOLDILOCKS	**Louis Merkel × fuscata**	**Dobkin 1972**
GOLD NUGGET‡	**Big Chief × mannii**	**Beard 1968**

× Mary	= Mary Ann Bogaert		

GOLETA‡	**Doris × Margaret Bean**	**Bean 1956**

× Anna Tham	= Anna Goleta	× Ren. Brookie Chandler	= Rnthps. Mem. Edward Allen
× Terri Cook	= Margaret Harrison		

GOOD CHEER	**maculata × amboinensis**	**Hager 1973**
GRACE HEARTFIELD	**Barcelona × Alice Gloria**	**Shaffer's 1970**

× Polar Bear	= Diamond Pass		

GRACE PALM†‡	**Doris × Winged Victory**	**Ryerson 1950**

× Anna Tham	= Mount Fuji	× Mildred Karleen	= Adagio
× Arcadia	= White Lady	× New Luora	= Overthorpe
× Bruce Shaffer	= Heidi Hausermann	× Raycraft	= Otohime
× Charles Shaffer	= John Martin	× Sunrise	= Sakura
× Ice Palace	= Malibu Holiday	× Theresa Hausermann	= Adrian Hausermann
× Irene Stephens	= Mount Shigi	× violacea	= Malibu Violet
× Island Sunshine	= Theresa Ann	× Ren. storiei	= Rnthps. Malibu Beach
× Kauai	= Kauai Palm	× V. tessellata	= Vdnps. Pink Blush
× Mambo	= Apollo Fifteen		

GRACE PIERCE	**Spice Islands × Kay Star**	**Fort Caroline 1972 (Wallbrunn)**

GRACIA | **Grace Palm × mariae** | **O. Kirsch 1962**

× Dos Pueblos = Grazioso

GRACIOUS LADY	**Princess Grace × Lady Gladys**	**Trymwood 1974**
GRANADA	**Richard Shaffer × Doris**	**Shaffer's 1972**
GRAN DESIERTO	**Mistinguett × Golden Glow**	**Shaffer's 1972**
grandiflora (see *amabilis**†‡)	**species**	
GRAZIOSA	**Gracia × Dos Pueblos**	**Wallbrunn 1971**
GREEN CENTER	**Golden Sands × Yellow Lip**	**Beard 1975**
GREEN GOLD	**Golden Mist × Juanita**	**W. W. G. Moir 1973**
GREEN IMP	**fimbriata × parishii**	**Fredk L. Thornton 1973**
GREEN MEADOWS	**Gladys Read × Joseph Hampton**	**W. H. Starke 1973**
GREEN VALLEY	**fimbriata × micholitzii**	**Fredk. L. Thornton 1972**
GREIFSWALD	**Bruce Shaffer × Luedde-violacea**	**Wichmann 1972**
GROOVY	**Robin × lueddemanniana**	**R. K. Mizuta 1970**

× Dtps. Mem. Clarence Schubert = Dtps. Groovy Pink

GYROSE	**Rising Sun × Yellow Lip**	**Beard 1973**
HAAF	**Betty Beard × Ruby Zada**	**Beard 1973**
HALLE	**equestris × Keith Shaffer**	**Wichmann 1972**
HAMAOKA	**Pueblo Anne × Mount Kaala**	**Y. Toyama 1975**
HAPPY	**amabilis × Mambo**	**R. K. Mizuta 1974 (McCoy)**
HARLEQUIN‡	**Rosita × Grace Palm**	**O. Kirsch 1959**

× Baguio = Pink Zebra | × Inspiration = Lovely Stripes
× Brasilia = Gentle Rain | × Jubilee = Ethyl Sanders

HAROLD BORER	**Alice Gloria × Intermedia**	**Fort Caroline 1972 (Wallbrunn)**
HAROLDS HATTER	**Mad Hatter × Mem. Harold Shaffer**	**C. A. Russell 1973**
HARPOON	**Mad Hatter × fimbriata**	**Rod McLellan Co. 1974**
HARRISON KENNICOTT	**Charles Shaffer × fasciata**	**Hausermann 1972**
HATSUHI	**Intermedia × Mount Kaala**	**Karasawa 1971**
HAUSERMANN'S AQUARIUS	**Miami Maid × violacea**	**Hausermann 1972**
HAUSERMANN'S ARTISTRY	**Sharon Karleen × Ruby Lips**	**Hausermann 1974**
HAUSERMANN'S ATHENA	**Lipstick × violacea**	**Hausermann 1972**
HAUSERMANN'S GLACIER	**Fairway Park × Capitola**	**Hausermann 1972**
HAUSERMANN'S HOT LIPS	**Mad Lips × Ruby Lips**	**Hausermann 1972**
HAUSERMANN'S MOONBEAM	**Charles Shaffer × Fairway Park**	**Hausermann 1972**
HAUSERMANN'S VENUS	**Nancy Carlson × lueddemanniana**	**Hausermann 1972**
HAWAIIAN MAID	**Rosy Charm × lueddemanniana**	**R. K. Mizuta 1973**
HAWAIIAN SUNSET	**Ondine × Jane Almquist**	**Shaffer's 1974**
HAWAIIAN SUNSHINE	**Snowbird × lueddemanniana**	**McCoy 1963**

× Ella Freed = Freed's Darling | × Zada = Sunshine Pink
× Pin Up Girl = Amado Vazquez

HAWAIIAN WELCOME | **Sunburst × Zada** | **J. & S. 1969 (McCoy)**

× Hedy Maerkl = Willamette Pass | × Mistinguett = Strawberry Meadows

HAZEL McQUERRY — **Gertrude Beard × Helen Miller** — **Beard 1968**

× Wilma Hughes = Kimberly Odum

HEATHERCLIFF — **Far Horizon × Hugo Freed** — **J. Ewing 1975**

HEBE†‡ — **equestris × sanderana** — **Veitch 1897**

× Bruce Shaffer = Lois Jean Lilly
× Doris = Elaine Christine

HEDY MAERKL — **Barbara Beard × Barry Eamer** — **Beard 1968**

× Ann Marie Beard = Mab
× Esther Edris = Rosy Ridge
× Hawaiian Welcome = Willamette Pass
× Hobe Sound = Carol
× Linda Winters = Paul Stauffer
× Texas Pink = Florence Kroeck

HEIDI HAUSERMANN — **Bruce Shaffer × Grace Palm** — **Elmhurst 1972**

HEIDEPERLE‡ — **Aalsmeer Rose × Pasadena** — **Wichmann 1965**

× Mem. Emil Richter = Walter Richter

HELEN BACHMAN — **Barbara Beard × Palm Beach Rouge** — **Beard 1966**

× Helen Kuhn = Undine

HELEN BACHNER — **Cabrillo Star × Mad Hatter** — **Chester Hills 1970 (Bachner)**

× Joseph Hampton = JoAnn Bachner

HELEN FARLOW — **Texas Pink × Frances Roberts** — **Beard 1974**

HELEN KUHN‡ — **Zada × fuscata** — **Beard 1966 (Kuhn)**

× Helen Bachman = Undine

HELEN MILLER‡ — **Susan Merkel × Fairway Park** — **Beard 1964**

× Daryl Beard = Anita Young
× Irma Rath = Radiant Moon
× Redfan = Oak Creek
× Spica = Evelyn Weaver

HELEN STAUFFER — **Inca Gold × Ruby Lips** — **Beard 1975**

HELEN WEBB — **Utopia × Ronald Prairie** — **Beard 1975**

HELLO DOLLY — **Rosy Charm × Sunburst** — **McCoy 1966**

× Lipperose = Tampico

HELMA PINKEPANK (see Zauberrose)

HENRIETTE LECOUFLE‡ — **Lachésis × Ramona** — **Pff. V. & L. 1967**

× Alice Gloria = Splendeur
× Arpege = Ariette
× Candeur = Marie-Noel
× Celie = Antarctic
× Concorde = Conquete
× Eva = Fantac
× Lachésis = Larzac
× Lipperose = Rosa bonheur
× Opaline = Opalescence
× Ramona = Polka
× Redfan = Petit Prince
× White Lady = Silbermond

HENRY WALLBRUNN — **Chuck's Red Lip × lueddemanniana** — **Fort Caroline 1972**

HERBERT BOONE — **Grace Palm × Martha Daniels** — **R. K. Mizuta 1968**

× Lady Doreen = Mische

HERMINA FORD — **Alice Gloria × Hong Trevor** — **Hager 1969**

× amboinensis = Caravan

HERMIONE†‡ — **lueddemanniana × stuartiana** — **Veitch 1899**

× gigantea = Yip

HERMOSA‡ — **Cast Iron Monarch × Ramona** — **Shaffer's 1963**

× Alice Gloria = Verle
× Barcelona = Marylou Woodward
× Bridesmaid = Formal
× Capitola = Empire Snow

HERMOSA‡ (*continued*)

× Doris	= Cry Baby	× Spica	= Bobbie Gaye Lista
× Kauai Monarch	= Limona	× Terri Cook	= Tahoe Belle
× Keith Shaffer	= Mem. Truman Green	× violacea	= Laurie Lista
× Richard Shaffer	= Seville		

HETTY MODAFF — **Cher Ann × Delightful** — **Peter E. Lista 1974**

HI BOY — **Hymen × amboinensis** — **Wallbrunn 1966**

× Alice Gloria	= Hi Glow	× violacea	= Aalia Abdulali

hieroglyphica (see *lueddemanniana**†‡) — **species**

HIGH TIDE — **gigantea × Eventide** — **Dobkin 1975**

HI GLOW — **Alice Gloria × Hi Boy** — **Fort Caroline 1975 (Wallbrunn)**

HOBE SOUND — **Best Girl × sanderana** — **Lockhart 1975 (Vande Weghe)**

× Hedy Maerkl	= Carol	× Irene van Alstyne	= Marie Posten

HOKUSPOKUS — **Lipperose × Francine** — **Röhl 1974**

HOLIDAY EGGNOG — **Palmsnow × fasciata** — **Phalaenoptimists 1969**

× Elinor Shaffer	= Kiwi

HOLLYWOOD†‡ — **Grace Palm × Thomas Tucker** — **Bean 1956**

× Aristocrat	= Marion Furst

HONEY DEW — **Moon Monarch × Sunbeam** — **J. & S. 1967**

× amboinensis	= Bamboo Baby

HONEY GOLD — **Serenity Beach × Hymen** — **A. & M. 1975**

HONG KONG — **Hymen × lueddemanniana** — **J. & S. 1971**

HOOSUMI — **Via Lactea × Apollo** — **N. Suzuki 1972**

× Alice Gloria	= Zuki Gloria

HOT DROPS — **Mad Hatter × Mad Lips** — **Rod McLellan Co. 1973**

× Princess Ruby	= Ruby Drops	× Renate Frese	= Lollipop

HOT LIPS — **Fiery × Red Lip** — **Matatics 1967**

× Mad Hatter	= Mary Augusta Secrist

HUGH WELLS — **Cream Puff × Jack McQuerry** — **Beard 1975**

HUGO FREED — **Ella Freed × Mad Lips** — **Freed 1973**

× Darleen	= Spinner	× Far Horizon	= Heathercliff

HYDAR — **Daryl Beard × Hymen** — **Beard 1971**

HYMEN†‡ — **lueddemanniana × mannii** — **Veitch 1900**

× Boynton	= Sun King	× Sarah Wilder	= Hysara
× Daryl Beard	= Hydar	× Schillerano-stuartiana	= Pagliaccio
× fasciata	= Hymenata	× Serenity Beach	= Honey Gold
× fuscata	= Christine Ann	× violacea	= Magic Fire
× lueddemanniana	= Hong Kong		

HYMENATA — **Hymen × fasciata** — **A. & M. 1975**

HYSARA — **Sarah Wilder × Hymen** — **R. K. Mizuta 1973**

HYSSOP — **Jimmy Mize × Bariana** — **Beard 1973**

IAGO — **Fairway Park × Daryl Beard** — **Beard 1973**

IBERIA — **Jimmy Mize × Ann Marie Beard** — **Beard 1974**

ICE AGE — **amboinensis × Muriel Turner** — **Hager 1973**

ICE CUBE | **Ice Palace × Cassandra** | **Nell C. Roberts 1971**
ICE PALACE‡ | **Winged Anna × Joanna Magale** | **Rivermont 1963**
× Cassandra = Ice Cube | × Grace Palm = Malibu Holiday
× Gladys Read = Peggy Nagel | × Margaret Bean = Snow Maiden

IMPERIAL VALLEY | **Beatie Greenly × Melba Burnett** | **Beard 1974**
INCA GOLD | **Gertrude Beard × fasciata** | **Beard 1970**
× Ruby Lips = Helen Stauffer

INDONESIA | **Zadian × Callie Flynn** | **J. & S. 1974**
INES DANKMEYER | **Mad Hatter × Initial** | **Wichmann 1972**
INFATUATION | **Mad Lips × Breathless** | **Hager 1974**
INGRID HAUSERMANN | **Theresa Hausermann × Miami Maid** | **E.F.G. Orchids 1974**
INITIAL | **Fairway Park × violacea** | **Rod McLellan Co. 1967**
× Mad Hatter = Ines Dankmeyer

INSPIRATION‡ | **Juanita × lueddemanniana** | **Santa Cruz 1961**
× amboinensis = Crazy Ambo | × lueddemanniana = Touch of Lemon
× Clyde = Kim Cuc Bauer | × Mildred Karleen = Target
× corningiana = My Fancy | × violacea = Intensity
× Harlequin = Lovely Stripes

INTENSITY | **Inspiration × violacea** | **C. & I. Keyes 1974**
intermedia / **INTERMEDIA*†‡** | **aphrodite × equestris** | **Nat. hyb.** / **Veitch 1886**
× Alice Gloria = Harold Borer | × Keith Shaffer = Mark Twain
× Apparition = Leora Hewlett | × lindenii = Adorno
× Evening Rose = Eager | × Mount Kaala = Hatsuhi
× Fairway Park = Jamboree | × parishii = Douglas Allen
× Gertrude Homsher = Vulgate | × Dtps. Pueblo Jewel = Dtps. Gary Greenly
× Juanita = Flirtation

INTIMITÉ | **Celie × Concorde** | **Pff. V. & L. 1974**
IRENE FINNEY | **Edythe Wood × fasciata** | **Hausermann 1970**
× Cher Ann = Toy Clown

IRENE STEPHENS‡ | **Shirley Temple × Juanita** | **Stephens 1964 (Kirch)**
× Doreen × Mount Rokko | × Grace Palm = Mount Shigi

IRENE VAN ALSTYNE‡ | **Carol Brandt × Barbara Beard** | **Beard 1967**
× Beatie Greenly = Yacht | × Kathryn Leahey = Eagle
× Hobe Sound = Marie Posten | × Redwing = Amy Howard
× Jack McQuerry = Twin Cities | × Ruby Zada = Terry-Beth Ballard
× Jimmy Mize = Jabiru

IRMA RATH‡ | **Grace Palm × Palm Beach** | **Freed 1967**
× Alice Gloria = Malibu Carnival | × Elinor Shaffer = Prodigious
× Arcadia = Arcama | × fuscata = Midnight Sun
× Cathrine Pillsbury = Mooncrest | × Gladys Read = Bright Angel
× Daryl Beard = Platonic | × Helen Miller = Radiant Moon

IRONSIDE | **Gladys Read × Anne Cavaco** | **Shaffer's 1971**
ISIS†‡ | **Chérubin × Cendrillon** | **V. 1955**
× Ramona = Ismona

ISLAND SANDS | **Golden Sands × cochlearis** | **Beard 1971**

ISLAND SUNSHINE — Sparkle × Queen Emma — Hager 1968
× Grace Palm = Theresa Ann

ISMONA — Isis × Ramona — Pff. V. & L. 1972
ISOLA — Capitola × Celie — Pff. V. & L. 1974
IVY ARMOUR — Terri Cook × Alice Gloria — Armour 1972
IVY MERKEL — Mary Lou Stoddard × La Fleur Blanche — A. & M. 1961
× sumatrana = Fatima

IXION — Scotti Maguire × Adelaide — Beard 1973
JABIRU — Jimmy Mize × Irene van Alstyne — Beard 1973
JACK HAGGARD — Jack McQuerry × Ruby Zada — Beard 1974
JACKIE — Susie Darlin × lueddemanniana — McCoy 1962
× gigantea = Lulu

JACK McQUERRY — Suemid × Ruby Lips — Beard 1970
× Cream Puff = Hugh Wells
× Irene van Alstyne = Twin Cities
× Lois Jansen = Teoh Phaik Khuan
× Ruby Zada = Jack Haggard
× Dtps. Redkar = Dtps. Nineteen Fourteen Class

JACQUELINE BASSETTA — Susan Merkel × sumatrana — A. & M. 1975
JAC-QUI — cochlearis × Luedde-violacea — Dobkin 1975
JAMAICA SUNSHINE — Edythe Wood × Ernst Haussermann — Hausermann 1974
JAMBOREE — Fairway Park × Intermedia — Rod McLellan Co. 1971
JAMES ARNOLD — Aristocrat × Bleeding Heart — J. Y. Arnold 1973
JAMES DICK — Angela Dumas × Bruce Shaffer — Thornton's 1973
JAMES HAUSERMANN — Samba × Edythe Wood — Hausermann 1970
× Denise Richardson = Charles McKay
× Dtps. Mem. Clarence Schubert = Dtps. American Heritage

JANE ALMQUIST — Estrellita × Zada — Shaffer's 1969
× Doris = Rosera
× Ondine = Hawaiian Sunset

JANE KULKA — Carolyn Wilkes × Ruby Lips — Beard 1975
JANE LE NOIR — Amber Sands × Quality Belle — Beard 1974
JANE SEYMOUR — Redfan × Elinor Shaffer — E. E. Young 1973
JANE SHAFFER — Mary Lou Stoddard × lueddemanniana — Fields Orchids 1962
× fuscata = Bill's Yellow
× Princess Michiko = Eileen Ashburn

JANET KUHN‡ — Dos Pueblos × fuscata — Beard 1965
× cochlearis = Scotch Mist
× Valfas = Valjan
× King. philippinensis = Phlla. Sunburst

JAN GROVE — Miami Maid × Goldiana — Fields Orchids 1973
JANICE HALL — Wendy Beard × Jimmy Arnold — Beard 1975
JAPET — Fanchette × stuartiana — Marcel Lecoufle 1958
× Lipperose = Wintermärchen

JASPER AYERS — Keith Shaffer × Clyde — J. F. Hughes 1975 (Ayers)

JEAN DUNN — Betty Conroy × Anne Cavaco — Valley Orchids 1974
JEAN GIRARDEAU — Utopia × Gertrude Beard — Beard 1975
JEAN JOHNSTON — Virginia Beard × Ann Marie Beard — Beard 1969
× Ann Marie Beard = Wacke
× Barbara Beard = Fable
× Cream Puff = Fyke
× Jimmy Mize = Ezra
× Mary Wieler = Kristi Vanaman
× Redwing = Paca

JEAN MARSHALL	**Barbara Beard × Frances Roberts**		**Beard 1974**
JEANNETTE	**Saint Petersburg × mariae**		**Fennell 1972**
JEAN STEPHAN	**Elisa × Rouge**		**Shaffer's 1969**
× Doris	= Capitola Rose	× Overglow	= Bonny Doon
JEFFREY	**Patty Turner × Keith Shaffer**		**R. C. Turner 1975**
JENIFFER HALL	**Daryl Beard × fuscata**		**Beard 1974**
JENNIE SWANK‡	**Serenity × Colomba**		**Beard 1962**
× Fiery Girl	= Mary Overby	× Redfan	= Amy Maguire
JENNIFER BEARD	**Ruby Zada × Wendy Beard**		**Beard 1972**
× Barbara Freed Saltzman	= Music	× Brasilia	= Ellen Murk
JENNIFER GAINE	**Donnie Brandt × Madrid**		**Gaine 1973 (Noble Mason)**
JERSEY	**Norman Peterson × Redfan**		**E. E. Young 1973**
JESSICA McDONALD	**Ann Hatter × Mildred Karleen**		**Minne 1968 (J. & L.)**
× Princess Ruby	= Princess Jessica	× Schillerano-stuartiana	= Towaco
JESTER	**Mad Hatter × Ruby Zada**		**Rod McLellan Co. 1973**
JEWEL‡	**Dolores × Rosy Pam**		**Santa Cruz 1961**
× Doris	= Shoulé		
JEWELITA	**Pink Jewel × Estrellita**		**Shaffer's 1972**
JEWEL LIPS	**Jewel × Mildred Karleen**		**Shaffer's 1969**
× Overglow	= Tiger Stripe		
JIMINY CRICKET	**Ministripes × Red Lip**		**J. & S. 1971**
× Christopher Lynn	= Stephen Douglas	× Red Lip	= Cindy Tsai
× Ella Freed	= Johanna		
JIMMY	**Jimmy Arnold × Therese Frackowiak**		**Lockhart 1975**
JIMMY ARNOLD	**Ruby Lips × Rosada**		**J. Y. Arnold 1967**
× Alice Shelley	= Dale Lockhart	× Ruby Zada	= Margaret Hardy
× Lois Jansen	= Toni Featherstone	× Therese Frackowiak	= Jimmy
× Ruby Stripes	= Joan Gates	× Wendy Beard	= Janice Hall
JIMMY HALL	**Scotti Maguire × Daryl Beard**		**Beard 1971**
× Miami Maid	= Doctor Teoh		
JIMMY MIZE‡	**Virjudy × Barbara Beard**		**Beard 1966**
× Ann Marie Beard	= Iberia	× Kathryn Leahey	= Yuman
× Barbara Beard	= Oak Ridge	× Lewis Barber	= Pyxis
× Bariana	= Hyssop	× Linda Winters	= Earl Hemming
× Best Girl	= Florence Rose	× Mary Wieler	= Optimist
× Evening Rose	= Rigby	× Melba Burnett	= Byzantine
× Frances Roberts	= Zwingli	× Redwing	= Labarum
× Irene van Alstyne	= Jabiru	× Suemid	= Jim Sue
× Jean Johnston	= Ezra		
JIM SUE	**Jimmy Mize × Suemid**		**Beard 1972**
JIM TOSKEY	**Ernst Haussermann × Cher Ann**		**Hausermann 1974**
JOAN GATES	**Jimmy Arnold × Ruby Stripes**		**Lockhart 1972**
JOAN HALL	**Gertrude Beard × Spica**		**Beard 1972**

JOANNA MAGALE‡ — **Chieftain × Cast Iron Monarch** — **Kwr. 1957**

× Dos Pueblos = Virginia MacBride | × Mary Lou Stoddard = Mem. Elaine Thornton
× Margaret J. Degenhardt = Snow King

JOANN BACHNER — **Helen Bachner × Joseph Hampton** — **Bachner 1974**
JOE FEIRER — **Daryl Beard × Utopia** — **Lockhart 1973**
JOEY — **gigantea × lueddemanniana** — **Fort Caroline 1973 (Wallbrunn)**

JOHANNA — **Ella Freed × Jiminy Cricket** — **Dobkin 1975**
JOHN — **Terri Cook × Pasadena** — **M. J. Bates 1973**
JOHN GIRARDEAU — **Wendy Beard × Lois Jansen** — **Beard 1975**
JOHN MARTIN — **Charles Shaffer × Grace Palm** — **Bachner 1971**
JOHN ROSE — **Bruce Shaffer × Kahala Queen** — **C. R. Rose 1973**
JOHN TEOH — **Scotti Maguire × Wilma Hughes** — **Beard 1972**
JOKESI — **Keith Shaffer × Peppermint** — **Janes 1974**
JOLE — **Cher Ann × Theresa Hausermann** — **Hausermann 1973**
JOLLY ODIN — **Keith Shaffer × Giant** — **Manor Orchids 1974**
JOSEPH HAMPTON‡ — **Monarch Glen × Doris** — **Dos Pueblos 1966**

× Alice Gloria = Criswell Gonzales | × sumatrana = Katherine Kimbrel
× amboinensis = Yellow Ice | × Terri Cook = Mimi Starke
× Gladys Read = Green Meadows | × violacea = Joviola
× Helen Bachner = JoAnn Bachner | × Dtps. Red Lip = Dtps. Red Joe
× Mariposa = Penelope Williams

JOSEPH MASSE — **Peppermint × Denise Richardson** — **W. J. Shaban 1973**
JOVIOLA — **Joseph Hampton × violacea** — **Bachner 1973**
JOYCE WHITE — **Theresa Hausermann × Bruce Shaffer** — **Elmhurst 1971**
JOY JOST — **Eliana × Zada** — **Rumrill 1973 (R. P. Jost)**

JUAN ESCOBAR — **Gladys Read × amabilis** — **C. A. Escobar 1975 (J. Escobar)**

JUANITA†‡ — **Chief Tucker × Grace Palm** — **Shaffer's 1957**

× Caruso = Nina | × Golden Mist = Green Gold
× Concorde = Mem. Paul Deutschberger | × Intermedia = Flirtation
× Debbie Martian = Mildred Tom | × Leilehua = Leinita
× De Haro = Mauna Kea | × Margaret Bean = Saint Petersburg
× Ghisoni = Pink Dove | × Sea Mist = Debbie Martian

JUANITA MAY‡ — **Winifred Prahl × Iron Man** — **H. D. Wright 1960**

× lueddemanniana = Old Ivory | × Winifred Prahl = Dava Alyson Bishop

JUBILEE‡ — **Clara I. Knight × New Horizon** — **Hager 1966**

× Harlequin = Ethyl Sanders | × Rnthps. James Herbert Boone = Rnthps. Bali Ha'i
× Judy Karleen = Port Mayaka
× violacea = Think Pink

JUDITH HAUSERMANN — **lueddemanniana × Mariposa** — **Hausermann 1969**

× Coral Isles = Lynn Diane | × Dtps. Mem. Clarence Schubert = Dtps. Hausermann's El Toro
× Golden Sands = Shellie Lynn
× mariae = Just Me

JUDITH MERKEL — **Spring Chief × Susan Merkel** — **A. & M. 1975**
JUDY KARLEEN†‡ — **Chieftain × Sally Lowrey** — **Karleen 1957**

× Ann Hatter = Pottstown | × Dtps. Red Lip = Dtps. Red Judy
× Jubilee = Port Mayaka

Grex	Parentage	Registrant
JUMBO	Concorde × Wilma Hughes	Pff. V. & L. 1974
JUNE BRIDE	Elinor Shaffer × Snow White	Lorenzen 1972
JUNE STARKE	Virginia MacBride × Gladys Read	W. H. Starke 1973
JUNE TAKASE	Percy Porter × Tomi	Takase 1975
JUNGLE BELLE	Gladys Read × Sharon Karleen	Fairburn 1974
JUNGLE KING	Gertrude Beard × Ruby Zada	Fairburn 1974
JUNGLE QUEEN	Ann Hatter × Ambomanniana	Rod McLellan Co. 1974
JUNIOR MISS	Rosy Charm × equestris	Hager 1975
JUSTINE LeBARON	Samba × fuscata	Wallbrunn 1972
JUST ME	Judith Hausermann × mariae	Hausermann 1973
JUVENILE	Two Grand × Yankee Town	Beard 1973
KAABA	Gertrude Homsher × Gertrude Beard	Beard 1973
KAALA HATTER	Mount Kaala × Mad Hatter	Y. Toyama 1971
KADIROSE	Kadith × Aalsmeer Rose	Chung-Chweng Chen 1970
× schillerana = Sheu Shou-Pao Chen		
KAHALA QUEEN	Hala × Queen Emma	O. Kirsch 1969
× Bruce Shaffer = John Rose		
KAREN ANN McFARLANE	Robyn Stone × Mad Hatter	McFarlane 1972
× Robyn Stone = Cairns Centenary		
KAREN ROSEA	equestris × Karen	E. Iwanaga 1967
× Elisa = Olga Malek		
KARFUNKEL	Regnier × Zada	Röhl 1974
KARLEEN OAKS	Mildred Karleen × Thousand Oaks	Millington 1971
KARLEEN'S WENDY‡	Mildred Karleen × Judy Karleen	Hager 1964
× Anouche = Minouche	× Redfan = Vivaldi	
× Morzine = Lampion		
KARLYNE	Apollo Ten × Ella Freed	Dobkin 1975
KATHERINE KIMBREL	Joseph Hampton × sumatrana	Bachner 1973
KATHERYN MALIA OSGOOD	Mahinhin × White Knight	Osgood 1973
KATHLEEN ARNOLD	Cindy Brandt × Serenity Beach	J. Y. Arnold Sr. 1966
× Daryl Beard = David Lockhart		
KATHLEEN EDRIS	Terri Cook × violacea	Edris 1970
× Queen Emma = Bewitched		
KATHLEEN FLAHERTY	Red Eye × Robbie Vanaman	Beard 1975
KATHLEEN VOELKER	Rosalind × Mistinguett	Voelker 1972
KATHRYN LEAHEY	Kathy Maguire × Betty Beard	Beard 1969
× Ann Marie Beard = Tyr	× Jimmy Mize = Yuman	
× Frances Roberts = Wyandot	× Redwing = Zenith	
× Irene van Alstyne = Eagle		
KATHRYN SALTZMAN	Pin Up Girl × Midlip	Freed 1974
KATHY KORNAHRENS	sumatrana × fasciata	Fort Caroline 1973 (Wallbrunn)
KATHY LYKINS	Mad Hatter × Midlip	Beard 1972
KATHY MAGUIRE‡	Gloriosa × Zada	Beard 1964
× Beatie Greenly = Newport		

KATHY MARIE — **Laniloa × Phylis-Kay** — **Takase 1973**

× Alight = Pat Reinke
× Lillian Hozaki = Pat Darby
× Luciana = Linda Kathleen

KATHY REYES — **Queen Emma × Zada** — **Reyes 1973**

KAUAI‡ — **Dos Pueblos × Barbara Kirch** — **Freed 1965 (B. Kodama)**

× Cast Iron Monarch = Kauai Monarch
× Elinor Shaffer = Malibu River
× Grace Palm = Kauai Palm
× Mem. Loke Sokeen = Tan Chin Keat
× Norman Peterson = Freed's Bedevilled
× Sonja = Giatgong
× Terri Cook = Veronica
× Winged Victory = Malibu Victory

KAUAI MONARCH — **Cast Iron Monarch × Kauai** — **Freed 1972**

× Hermosa = Limona
× Sonja = Mimi Coertze

KAUAI PALM — **Kauai × Grace Palm** — **Freed 1972**

KAY STAR — **Phylis-Kay × Lucky Star** — **Hager 1967**

× Spice Islands = Grace Pierce
× Rnthps. Native Dancer = Rnthps. Star Dancer

KAY THOMAS — **Daryl Beard × Ann Marie Beard** — **Lockhart 1972**

KAZUKO FUJII — **Kenneth Stromsland × Calawaii** — **Hausermann 1974**

KEITH SHAFFER — **Grace Palm × Gladys Read** — **Shaffer's 1965**

× Alice Gloria = Schooner
× Avila = Lauralin
× Barcelona = George Woodward
× Bruce Shaffer = Genevieve Saunders
× Capitola = Susan Shipley
× Clyde = Jasper Ayers
× Concorde = Portland Bill
× Dazzling Snowcloud = Blossomwood Snow
× Edythe Wood = Paula Kramer
× equestris = Halle
× Fiery = Tropic Snow
× Giant = Jolly Odin
× Gladys Read = Snow Lady
× Hermosa = Mem. Truman Green
× Intermedia = Mark Twain
× lueddemanniana = Lenora Turner
× Ministripes = Christmas Candy
× Opaline = Temple Cloud
× Patrick Jon = Paulette André
× Patty Turner = Jeffrey
× Peppermint = Jokesi
× Princess of Denmark = Prince Charles
× Richard Shaffer = Mem. Jonathan Williams
× Theresa Hausermann = Diana Hausermann
× White Sails = Mildred White
× Zada = Thornhill

KEKUALANI SNOW WHITE — **Makua Shore × Pokai Bay** — **Mrs. Ethel Jones 1974 (Kodama)**

KENNETH BENJAMIN — **Charles Shaffer × Ernst Haussermann** — **Hausermann 1973**

KENNETH STROMSLAND — **Fairway Park × Edythe Wood** — **Hausermann 1970**

× Calawaii = Kazuko Fujii
× Ernst Haussermann = White Gem
× Redport = Gedwo

KERLU — **Redfan × Cher Ann** — **Rod McLellan Co. 1974**

KEY LARGO — **Frances Roberts × Linda Winters** — **Beard 1974**

KEY LIME — **Texas Star × Susan Merkel** — **Beard 1966**

× Sulip = Baalist

KIM — **gigantea × My Fair Lady** — **Dobkin 1975**

KIMBERLY ODUM — **Hazel McQuerry × Wilma Hughes** — **Beard 1972**

× Anita Young = Quaker

KIM CUC BAUER — **Inspiration × Clyde** — **Stewart Inc. 1974**

KINTA GOLD — **Sea Mist × fuscata** — **Teoh Eng Soon 1974 (Cheah Kheng Cheong)**

KITTY TAYLOR	**Palette × Spica**	**Lockhart 1974**
KIWI	**Holiday Eggnog × Elinor Shaffer**	**J. & S. 1974**
KOLIBRI	**Star of Diamond Head × lueddemanniana**	**Gart. Seidel 1975 (Ottens)**
KOLOPAKING	**laycockii × serpentilingua**	**Ilgenfritz 1969 (Liem Khe Wie)**

× V. Miss Joaquim = Vdnps. Handoyoharjo

KOSHER PINK	**Rosalind × Zada**	**R. K. Mizuta 1973**
KRISTI VANAMAN	**Jean Johnston × Mary Wieler**	**Beard 1973**
KRUEMEL	**Annie Hoffman × Francine**	**Röhl 1974**

× Francine = Kruemeline

KRUEMELINE	**Kruemel × Francine**	**Röhl 1974**
KUCHIBENI	**White Virgin × Queen Emma**	**Ozaki 1973**
KUMUOKALANI	**Alii × De Haro**	**W. W. G. Moir 1971**
KURT HAUSERMANN	**Mad Lips × violacea**	**Hausermann 1972**
KURT NAGEL	**Sea Mist × Doreen**	**Gart. Seidel 1974 (K. Seidel)**
KWAN YIN	**Princess Grace × mannii**	**Casa Luna 1971**
KYACK	**Bariana × Betty Beard**	**Beard 1969**
LABARUM	**Redwing × Jimmy Mize**	**Beard 1973**
LACHÉSIS†‡	**Fanchette × Cendrillon**	**V. 1955**

× Henriette Lecoufle = Larzac
× Madrid = Spring Valley
× Mildred Karleen = Chanteloire

LADY DOREEN	**Aristocrat × Doreen**	**E. Iwanaga 1964**

× equestris = Pink Snow
× Herbert Boone = Mische
× Millie Rodrigues = Witchcraft
× sumatrana = Mem. Julian Aherrera
× Valley Queen = Queen Doreen
× violacea = Pale Beauty
× Ascps. Irene Dobkin = Ascps. Sirena

LADY FLORENCE	**Redfan × Mad Hatter**	**Rod McLellan Co. 1971**
LADY GLADYS	**Kauai × Princess Grace**	**Trymwood 1969**

× Princess Grace = Gracious Lady
× violacea = Lady Violet

LADY LORRAINE	**Progress × Redfan**	**Rod McLellan Co. 1972**
LADY MORZINE	**Rodco's Lady × Morzine**	**Pff. V. & L. 1974**
LADY RUBY	**Ruby Zada × Midlip**	**Rod McLellan Co. 1971 (Beard)**

× Redfan = Marquise

LADY VIOLET	**Lady Gladys × violacea**	**Trymwood 1973**
LAGOON MOON	**New Moon × Cindy Brandt**	**Beard 1972**
LAMPION	**Morzine × Karleen's Wendy**	**Elsner 1975**
LANILOA	**Doris × Anna Tham**	**Takase 1965**

× Leilehua = Leilani
× Phylis-Kay = Kathy Marie

LARA AY-LAN	**Sunny × laycockii**	**Kolopaking 1974**
LARRY OBERHAUS	**Bandleader × equestris**	**W. J. Sanders 1974 (Hager)**
LARZAC	**Lachésis × Henriette Lecoufle**	**Pff. V. & L. 1974**
LATONE†‡	**Blizzard × San Marino**	**V. 1953**

× Margaret Bean = Apremont

LAURALIN	**Avila × Keith Shaffer**	**V. & M. Anderson 1975**

LAURIE LISTA	Hermosa × violacea	Peter E. Lista 1975
LAVENDER LADY	Zada × Best Girl	Hager 1967

× Madrid = Monchito | × Rosy Charm = Thoroughbred
× Penang = Shady Lady | × Zadian = Fairyfloss
× Percy Porter = Lei | × Dtps. Coral Gleam = Dtps. Coral Lady

laycockii‡	species	

× denevei = Boediardjo | × Lsa. teretifolia = Lnps. Soetan Mahmoed Latif
× Sunny = Lara Ay-Lan

LAYLA BEARD	Lois Jansen × Pin Up Girl	Beard 1973
LEI	Lavender Lady × Percy Porter	G. M. Fukumara 1973 (Takase)
LEILANI	Laniloa × Leilehua	Takase 1973
LEILEHUA‡	Gladys Read × Anna Tham	Takase 1965

× Debbie Martian = Winter Dawn | × Lillian Hozaki = Luciana
× Juanita = Leinita | × Queen Emma = Tomi
× Laniloa = Leilani

LEINITA	Leilehua × Juanita	Takase 1973
LEMON MERINGUE	Palette × Red Eye	Beard 1975
LEMON POINT	Golden Sands × Polar Bear	Beall 1974
LEMON QUEEN	Miami Maid × amboinensis	Hausermann 1975
LENA BATES	Terdoreen × Norman Peterson	M. J. Bates 1973
LENORA TURNER	Keith Shaffer × lueddemanniana	R. C. Turner 1975
LEORA HEWLETT	Apparition × Intermedia	Casa Luna 1971
LEPRECHAUN	Ballerina × sumatrana	R. K. Mizuta 1975
LES HEDGE	Robin × Kon Fah	R. K. Mizuta 1968

× Mambo = Bronze Queen |

LESLIE ANN	Mem. William Shaban × Alice Gloria	Shaban 1971
LEWIS BARBER	Barbara Beard × Hylam	Beard 1969

× Jimmy Mize = Pyxis |

LIAMBO	Lipperose × amboinensis	Röhl 1974
LIANG FONG KING	Viroonchan × Ella Freed	Freed 1975
LIEZADA	Fischers Liebling × Zada	Hans Koch 1975
LILI-MARLEN	Renate Frese × sumatrana	Frese 1975
LILLIAN HOZAKI	Queen Emma × Juanita	Hozaki 1968 (Tomiyasu)

× Celebration = Cherry Lips | × Leilehua = Luciana
× Kathy Marie = Pat Darby

LILLIE WOOLDRIDGE	Terri Cook × Elinor Shaffer	Wooldridge 1975
LIMONA	Kauai Monarch × Hermosa	Naugle 1975
LINDA HENRY	Cindy Brandt × violacea	Beard 1975
LINDA HUNTER	Sid × Alice Gloria	McFarlane 1975
LINDA KATHLEEN	Luciana × Kathy Marie	Takase 1975
LINDA LISTA	Capitola × violacea	Peter E. Lista 1975
LINDA MIA‡	Ramona × Thomas Tucker	Shaffer's 1963

× Bruce Shaffer = Bertie De Martini | × Wilma Hughes = Genevieve Elam
× Mantilla = Frank Pearce

LINDA MOLER	Sally Lowrey × Suemid	Beard 1971
LINDA SCHUMPERT	Marguerite W. Stephens × Dos Pueblos	Stephens 1964 (E. Iwanaga)

× amboinensis = Spenge |

PHALAENOPSIS

LINDA WINTERS — **Rosada × Ann Marie Beard** — **Beard 1969**

- × Frances Roberts = Key Largo
- × Hedy Maerkl = Paul Stauffer
- × Jimmy Mize = Earl Hemming
- × Dtps. Jerry Vande Weghe = Dtps. Susan Odom

lindenii*†‡ — **species**

- × Ann Lovelace = Ann Linden
- × Intermedia = Adorno
- × mariae = Marie Linden
- × Nuel N. Songer = Audrey Porter
- × Terri Cook = Prissy
- × Dtps. Pink Jewel = Dtps. Yellow Jewel

LINESIDES — **Eldora × Robert W. Miller** — **John H. Miller 1974**

LIPANDA GLOW — **Violet Glow × Pink Success** — **Lipanda 1975**

LIP FROST — **Ann Hatter × Cher Ann** — **Rod McLellan Co. 1974**

LIPPEGLUT — **Lippstadt × Zauberrose** — **Hark 1975**

LIPPEROSE‡ — **Ruby Wells × Zada** — **Hark 1968**

- × Aalsmeer Rose = Rosenrot
- × amboinensis = Liambo
- × Blushing Pink = Pink Parfait
- × Doris = Dorli
- × Dorisellita = Plum Beauty
- × Doris Wells = Lippstadt
- × Fischers Liebling = Comtesse Bettina
- × Francine = Hokuspokus
- × Hello Dolly = Tampico
- × Henriette Lecoufle = Rosa Bonheur
- × Japet = Wintermärchen
- × Lippstadt = Morgenrot
- × Lippezauber = Zauberrose
- × lueddemanniana = Stattsbad Salzuflen
- × mannii = Pastella
- × Mistinguett = Annemarie Pinkepank
- × Pink Ice = Rosa Ice
- × Red Rock = Red Rose
- × Rosalind = Tiffany
- × Rosy Charm = Desire
- × Shaffer's Pinkie = DuPage
- × Sigrid = Achat
- × Sourire = Romance
- × Unna = Unnarose
- × Vallehigh = Vallerose
- × Westfalica = Westfalenrose
- × Zauberrose = Lipperot
- × Zawell = Glenbard
- × Dtps. Mem. Clarence Schubert = Dtps. Renate Frese
- × Dor. pulcherrima = Dtps. Himmelsleiter

LIPPEROT — **Lipperose × Zauberrose** — **Hark 1975**

LIPPESEE — **Vallehigh × Long Life** — **Hark 1975**

LIPPEZAUBER — **Doris Wells × Zada** — **Hark 1969**

- × Doris Wells = Sesam
- × Lipperose = Zauberrose
- × Lippstadt = Abendrot
- × Ruby Wells = Zauberwells
- × Westfalica = Westfalenzauber
- × Zauberrose = Zauberrot
- × Dor. pulcherrima = Dtps. Hahnwald

LIPPIA — **Ruby Wells × Doris Wells** — **Hark 1975**

LIPPSTADT — **Doris Wells × Lipperose** — **Hark 1971**

- × Lipperose = Morgenrot
- × Lippezauber = Abendrot
- × Zauberrose = Lippeglut

LIP ROUGE — **Pink Cherub × Ann Hatter** — **Rod McLellan Co. 1968**

- × Frosty Lip = Frost Fire

LIPSTICK‡ — **Palm Beach × Star of Rio** — **Freed 1960 (Kwr.)**

- × Chuck's Red Lip = Freed's Adventure
- × Mad Lips = Cher Lee
- × Redfan = Freed's Connoisseur
- × Ruby Lips = Freed's Broadway Melody
- × Show Girl = Delightful
- × violacea = Hausermann's Athena

LISA MARIE — **Bastogne × Cathrine Pillsbury** — **Thornton's 1975**

LITTLE DAVID — **gigantea × Dear One** — **J. & S. 1971**

LITTLE DURWARD — **Alice Jean × White Sails** — **D. B. White 1975**

LITTLE ECLIPSE — **Norman Peterson × violacea** — **Hausermann 1973**

LITTLE GIRL — **fasciata × cornu-cervi** — **H. Webb 1974 (Fredk. L. Thornton)**

× Yellow Lip = Palm Trail

LITTLE LEOPARD — **cornu-cervi × mariae** — **Wallbrunn 1973**
LITTLE PINK DORIS — **Doris × Cassandra** — **Carlson 1975**
LITTLE ROSE — **Luedde-violacea × Estrellita** — **Shaffer's 1975**
LITTLE SISTER — **maculata × equestris** — **Hager 1973**
LITTLE WORRALL — **Snow Cloud × Elinor Shaffer** — **P. W. Johnston 1965**

× Alice Jean = Gidget White
× Cathrine Pillsbury = Frances White

LOIS JANSEN — **Barbara Beard × Ruby Lips** — **Beard 1969**

× Alice Shelley = Martha Odum
× Ann Marie Beard = Fancy Girl
× Barbara Moler = Virginia Anderson
× Jack McQuerry = Teoh Phaik Khuan
× Jimmy Arnold = Toni Featherstone
× Pin Up Girl = Layla Beard
× Ruby Zada = Xylophone
× Spica = Cathy Owens
× Suemid = Carter Shenk
× Wendy Beard = John Girardeau
× Dtps. Kristine Teoh = Dtps. Jeffry Hall
× Dtps. Pueblo Jewel = Dtps. Welcome
× Dtps. Red Lip = Dtps. Happy Day

LOIS JEAN LILLY — **Hebe × Bruce Shaffer** — **Thornton's 1975**
LOIS PARTIN — **Louis Merkel × Alice Gloria** — **A. & M. 1975**
LOLITA‡ — **Pink Vision × lueddemanniana** — **McCoy 1963**

× Cape Canaveral = Wendell Sawyer
× Wendell Sawyer = Mistique
× Zada = Royal Pink

LOLLIPOP — **Renate Frese × Hot Drops** — **Frese 1975**
LOMBARD — **Samba × Cher Ann** — **Hausermann 1973**
LONG LIFE — **Orchid Acres × Fairway Park** — **Rod McLellan Co. 1967**

× Arcadia = Nordpol
× Cathrine Pillsbury = Frosting
× Daryl Beard = Vera Henderson
× Vallehigh = Lippesee
× White Plains = Sable

LORELEI — **Bandleader × Mad Lips** — **Hager 1972**
LOREN BOHNETT — **Sonja × Princess of Denmark** — **Steindorf 1974**
LORRAINE KENNY — **Zada × amboinensis** — **Fredk. L. Thornton 1972**
LORRAINE THORNTON — **Susan Merkel × Alice Gloria** — **Fredk. L. Thornton 1975**
LOUISIANA LADY — **Fiesta × Zada** — **John H. Miller 1974**
LOUIS MERKEL‡ — **Mary Lou Stoddard × Doris** — **A. & M. 1961**

× Alice Gloria = Lois Partin
× Boynton = Patience Benjamin
× Bruce Shaffer = White Viking
× Fiery = Trudy
× fuscata = Goldilocks
× Madelon Kasten = Arthur Paynter
× Martha Jane = Walrus
× Serenity Beach = Sincerity
× Susan Merkel = Thelma Weaver

LOVE CHARM — **Ann Lovelace × Rosy Charm** — **Dobkin 1971**
LOVELY ANN — **Palmyra × Ann Lovelace** — **Dobkin 1971**
LOVELY STRIPES — **Inspiration × Harlequin** — **Shaffer's 1972**
LOVE TIDE — **Ann Lovelace × Eventide** — **Dobkin 1971**

× lueddemanniana = Carlotta
× Ruby Stripes = Estella

LOWANA GOLDLIP‡ — **Grace Palm × stuartiana** — **Limberlost 1962 (Freed)**

× Ruby Lips = Malibu Gold Lip

LUCATA — **lueddemanniana × fuscata** — **Fredk. L. Thornton 1967**

× Terri Cook = Terricata

LUCIANA	**Leilehua × Lillian Hozaki**	**Takase 1974**

× Kathy Marie = Linda Kathleen

LUCIFER	**Mahinhin × violacea**	**O. Kirsch 1973**
LUCKY STRIPES	**Ella Freed × Ruby Stripes**	**Dobkin 1975**
lueddemanniana*†‡	**species**	

(syn. *hieroglyphica, pallens, pulchra*) (*Phal. lueddemanniana* and *Phal. fasciata* are treated as specifically distinct for registration purposes, although regarded as conspecific by some authorities.)

×	=	×	=
× Alice Bowen	= Valeria	× mariae	= Tigerette
× Alice Gloria	= Sioux Maize	× Miami Maid	= Dick Wheeler
× Ambodoris	= Tropic Lightning	× Nancy Carlson	= Hausermann's Venus
× Arcadia	= Sternstaub	× Natasha	= Missirene
× Ballerina	= Ochrarina	× New Hope	= Alice Carol
× Bess Wells	= Bessmann	× Norman Peterson	= Mary McEdwards
× Chuck's Red Lip	= Henry Wallbrunn	× Nuel N. Songer	= Pay Dirt
× Cindy Sue	= Cindy Lu	× Painted Desert	= Desert Flame
× Coral Isles	= Aileen Stoops	× Peace	= Golden Peace
× Diane Rigg	= Mem. Mary Lista	× Rhapsody	= Shalimar
× Dos-Ambo	= Yellow Jewel	× Rosy Charm	= Hawaiian Maid
× Erick Hansen	= Freed's Damsel	× Samba	= Walter Beville
× Estrellita	= Redwine	× Sonja	= Freed's Lucky Star
× gigantea	= Joey	× Star of Diamond Head	= Kolibri
× Golden Sands	= Goldiana	× Sunbeam	= Amigo
× Hymen	= Hong Kong	× Tyler Carlson	= Betsy Turner
× Inspiration	= Touch of Lemon	× Utopia	= Onyx
× Juanita May	= Old Ivory	× White Lady	= Zitronenfalter
× Keith Shaffer	= Lenora Turner	× Ascps. Irene Dobkin	= Ascps. Feetz Cornwell
× Lipperose	= Staatsbad Salzuflen	× Dtps. Jerri Sue King	= Dtps. Voo Doo
× Love Tide	= Carlotta	× Rnthps. Dana	= Rnthps. Lotus Land
× Luedde-violacea	= Faith Leebell Cowden		

LUEDDE-VIOLACEA*‡	**lueddemanniana × violacea**	**Veitch—**

×	=	×	=
× Ambomanniana	= Manitoba	× Mistinguett	= Red Mist
× Bruce Shaffer	= Greifswald	× Mrs. J. H. Veitch	= Freed's Delicious
× Cinnamon Stick	= Claudia Creasy	× Princess Kaiulani	= Prima
× cochlearis	= Jac-Qui	× Red Lip	= Gay Heart
× Doris	= Easter Parade	× sumatrana	= Mayaimi
× Estrellita	= Little Rose	× violacea	= George Vasquez
× lueddemanniana	= Faith Leebell Cowden	× Dtps. Red Coral	= Dtps. Fire Opal

LUEDDE-WAVE‡	**Pink Wave × lueddemanniana**	**Osgood 1966**

× Zada = Della Bel Krause

LULU	**Jackie × gigantea**	**Dobkin 1973**
LULU McQUERRY	**Nemesio Mendiola × Daryl Beard**	**McQuerry 1974**
LUORA‡	**Hollywood × Mildred Karleen**	**Hager 1966**

× Muriel Turner = Snow Job | × Show Girl = Freed's Adorable

LUZON (see Mrs. J. H. Veitch‡; see also special note under Luzon in Sander's List of Orchid Hybrids; Addendum 1961/70).

LYNN DIANE	**Coral Isles × Judith Hausermann**	**Hausermann 1974**
LYNN HAUSERMANN	**Miami Maid × fasciata**	**Hausermann 1971**
LYRICAL	**Barbara Beard × Redwing**	**Beard 1973**
MAB	**Hedy Maerkl × Ann Marie Beard**	**Beard 1973**
MABEL ALLARD	**Chieftain × fuscata**	**A. & M. 1975**
maculata‡	**species**	

× amboinensis = Good Cheer | × violacea = Spring Rain
× equestris = Little Sister

MADALENE FOBERT	**Sonja × Ramona**	**Freed 1973**
MADAME SURIN	**Diamond Pink × William Boyd**	**Petch Aporn 1975**

PHALAENOPSIS

MADELINE EDLING — **lueddemanniana × Summit Queen** — **Schaffner 1957**

× mannii	= Wounded Knee		

MADELON KASTEN — **Big Chief × Dos Pueblos** — **Kasten 1971 (Lockhart)**

× Daryl Beard	= Everett Soars	× Louis Merkel	= Arthur Paynter
× Gertrude Beard	= Don Burke		

MAD HATTER‡ — **Spitfire × Ann Hatter** — **Rod McLellan Co. 1965**

× David Herbert	= Vixen	× Red Eye	= Alta Goodman
× Doris	= Schwerte	× Redfan	= Lady Florence
× fimbriata	= Harpoon	× Renate Frese	= Stemshorn
× Frosty Lip	= Serenata	× Robyn Stone	= Karen Ann McFarlane
× Hot Lips	= Mary Augusta Secrist	× Roselle	= Rosy Hat
× Initial	= Ines Dankmeyer	× Ruby Zada	= Jester
× Mad Lips	= Hot Drops	× Show Girl	= Career Girl
× mannii	= Mad Man	× Suemid	= Opal Mountain
× mariae	= Artur Elle	× Terri Cook	= Debbie Wallace
× Mem. Harold Shaffer	= Harolds Hatter	× Vallehigh	= White Spring
× Midlip	= Kathy Lykins	× Dtps. Pueblo Jewel	= Dtps. Jason Beard
× Mount Kaala	= Kaala Hatter		

MAD LIPS — **Ann Hatter × Mad Hatter** — **Rod McLellan Co. 1969**

× Bandleader	= Lorelei	× Percy Porter	= Wilma Schoppe
× Breathless	= Infatuation	× Pin Up Girl	= Streaker
× Cabrillo Star	= Dandee	× Redport	= Sheer Delight
× Cher Ann	= Shigeharu Fujii	× Ruby Lips	= Hausermann's Hot Lips
× Ella Freed	= Hugo Freed	× Ruby Zada	= Absolum
× Lipstick	= Cher Lee	× Theresa Ann	= Christopher Winkelmann
× Mad Hatter	= Hot Drops		
× Mem. William Shaban	= Cherry Sundae	× violacea	= Kurt Hausermann
× Mildred Karleen	= Gertrude Campbell		

MAD MAN — **Mad Hatter × mannii** — **Rod McLellan Co. 1972**

MADRID — **Dos Pueblos × Juanita** — **Shaffer's 1965**

× Cast Iron Monarch	= Freed's Criterion	× Lavender Lady	= Monchito
× Donnie Brandt	= Jennifer Gaine	× Sonja	= Betsy Rue
× Lachesis	= Spring Valley		

MAE CARPER — **Boynton × Susan Merkel** — **A. & M. 1975**

MAGDEBURG — **Bruce Shaffer × equestris** — **Wichmann 1972**

MAGIC FIRE — **Hymen × violacea** — **A. & M. 1975**

MAHINHIN‡ — **equestris × lueddemanniana** — **John H. Miller 1958**

× Baguio	= Gem Stone	× Pink Sunset	= Pink Gold
× Dos Pueblos	= Malahini Missy	× Snowbird	= Redbird
× Ella Freed	= Ruby Gem	× violacea	= Lucifer
× Mildred Karleen	= Redstone	× White Knight	= Katheryn Malia Osgood

MAKAHA SURF — **Chieftain × San Marino** — **Kodama 1965**

× amabilis	= Professor Derra	× Pink Melallion	= Buena Vista

MAKUA SHORE — **Juanita × Doreen** — **Kodama 1968**

× Pokai Bay	= Kekualani Snow White		

MALAHINI MISSY — **Mahinhin × Dos Pueblos** — **Mrs. N. Pattison 1973 (Osgood)**

MALIBU CARNIVAL — **Irma Rath × Alice Gloria** — **Freed 1974**

MALIBU GOLD LIP — **Lowana Goldlip × Ruby Lips** — **Freed 1972**

MALIBU HOLIDAY — **Ice Palace × Grace Palm** — **Freed 1974**

MALIBU LIPSTICK — **Show Girl × Redfan** — **Freed 1974**

MALIBU OPTIMISTS — **Pin Up Girl × Ella Freed** — **Freed 1973**

PHALAENOPSIS

MALIBU PINK	**Ann Lovelace × Zada**		**Freed 1968**
× Dear One	= Freed's Aristocrat	× Samba	= Sonia Clark

MALIBU QUEEN	**Wilma Hughes × Cast Iron Monarch**	**Freed 1971**
MALIBU RIVER	**Kauai × Elinor Shaffer**	**Freed 1974**
MALIBU SUNSET	**Oneohone × Zada**	**Freed 1974**
MALIBU VICTORY	**Winged Victory × Kauai**	**Freed 1974**
MALIBU VIOLET	**Grace Palm × violacea**	**Freed 1971**
MALIBU WEDDING	**Palm Beach × Elinor Shaffer**	**Freed 1974**
MALIBU WHITE	**Alice Gloria × Edythe Wood**	**Freed 1972**

MAMBO‡	**amboinensis × mannii**		**Fredk. L. Thornton 1965**
× amabilis	= Happy	× Les Hedge	= Bronze Queen
× Anna Tham	= Marg Knowles	× Miami Maid	= Mambo Maid
× Grace Palm	= Apollo Fifteen	× Princess Susan	= Apollo Fourteen
× Florence Thornton	= Mem. Pat Peeler		

MAMBO MAID	**Miami Maid × Mambo**	**Fields Orchids 1973**
MANDEVILLE SUNSET	**Fairy Pink × mannii**	**Breckinridge 1975**
MANITOBA	**Luedde-violacea × Ambomanniana**	**Shaffer's 1973**

MANNICATA‡	**mannii × fuscata**		**Kuhn 1966**
× Ambomanniana	= Freed's Distinction	× Daryl Beard	= Oneda Kansman

mannii*†‡ (syn. *boxallii*)	**species**		
× Fairy Pink	= Mandeville Sunset	× Mad Hatter	= Mad Man
× Florence Perera	= Bronze King	× parishii	= Parma
× gigantea	= Rosie Clouse	× Patricia Lea	= Patricia Goff
× Goldenrod	= Golden Mannii	× Princess Grace	= Kwan Yin
× Lipperose	= Pastella	× San Marino	= Golden Marino
× Madeline Edling	= Wounded Knee		

MANTILLA‡	**Juanita × Fairway Park**		**J. F. Hughes 1956**
× Alice Gloria	= Mem. Anton Smith	× Gertrude Beard	= Vince Cefalu
× Daryl Beard	= Betty Soars	× Gertrude Homsher	= Aalbane
× Donnie Brandt	= Yukon Ice	× Linda Mia	= Frank Pearce

MARCIA LEIGH	**Golden Sands × fuscata**		**W. J. Shaban 1972**
MARDI GRAS‡	**Rothschildiana × lueddemanniana**		**John H. Miller 1961**
× Sparkle	= Radiant Impact		

MARGARET BEAN†‡	**Doris × Altadena**		**Bean 1953**
× Ann Lovelace	= Fairy Pink	× Juanita	= Saint Petersburg
× Aristocrat	= Yellow Lip	× Latone	= Apremónt
× Dos Pueblos	= Sri Lanka	× Terri Cook	= Margaret Cook
× Ice Palace	= Snow Maiden		

MARGARET COOK	**Margaret Bean × Terri Cook**		**M. J. Bates 1973**
MARGARET HARDY	**Jimmy Arnold × Ruby Zada**		**Lockhart 1974**
MARGARET HARRISON	**Terri Cook × Goleta**		**M. J. Bates 1973**
MARGARET J. DEGENHARDT‡	**Winged Victory × Margaret Bean**		**Degenhardt 1959 (Rivermont)**
× Doris	= Fanfare	× Joanna Magale	= Snow King

MARGARET MIZUTA	**Pink Vision × Lakmé**		**Richella 1968**
× Rosy Charm	= Marguerite Stone		

MARG KNOWLES	**Mambo × Anna Tham**	**Knowles 1971 (Lynn Dewey)**

MARGUERITE STONE	**Rosy Charm × Margaret Mizuta**	**R. K. Mizuta 1971**
mariae‡	**species**	

× Best Girl	= Caressa	× Salamonca	= Weimar
× cornu-cervi	= Little Leopard	× Samba	= Gold Coin
× fuscata	= Golden Jewel	× Star of Santa Cruz	= Mischief
× Judith Hausermann	= Just Me	× Texas Star	= Bold Adventure
× lindenii	= Marie Linden	× Tyler Carlson	= Golden Pixie
× lueddemanniana	= Tigerette	× violacea	= Violet Charm
× Mad Hatter	= Artur Elle	× Dtps. Mem. Clarence Schubert	= Dtps. Dresden
× Robin	= Terry Teruko Robertson		
× Saint Petersburg	= Jeannette	× King. philippinensis	= Phlla. Freckles

MARIA VASQUEZ	**Denise Richardson × fuscata**	**Freed 1973 (R. K. Fields)**

× Chuck's Red Lip	= Christi Floyd	× Polar Bear	= Beehive Pass

MARIE BONER	**Capitola × Barcelona**	**Frank Hughes 1974**
MARIE LINDEN	**mariae × lindenii**	**W. W. G. Moir 1975**
MARIE-NOEL	**Candeur × Henriette Lecoufle**	**Pff. V. & L. 1974**
MARIE POSTEN	**Hobe Sound × Irene van Alstyne**	**Lockhart 1975**
MARILYN FREED BROWNING	**Edythe Wood × Wilma Hughes**	**Freed 1973**
MARION COLE	**Painted Desert × Overglow**	**Shaffer's 1973**
MARION FOWLER	**gigantea × Zada**	**Freed 1973**
MARION FURST	**Hollywood × Aristocrat**	**Furst 1971 (E. Iwanaga)**
MARIPOSA‡	**Goleta × Grace Palm**	**Faitel 1964**

× Joseph Hampton	= Penelope Williams		

MARK TWAIN	**Intermedia × Keith Shaffer**	**R. C. Turner 1975**
MARMIST‡	**Dawn Mist × Marmouset**	**Rod McLellan Co. 1955 (E. W. McLellan)**

× Zada	= Red Lightning		

MARMOUSET†‡	**Ninon × schillerana**	**V. 1943**

× Cassandra	= Poco Pink	× Dtps. Mem. Clarence Schubert	= Dtps. Ultra Pink

MARQUISE	**Redfan × Lady Ruby**	**Pff. V. & L. 1975**
MARTEN HAUSERMANN	**Miami Maid × Edythe Wood**	**Hausermann 1971**

× Arlene Marie Finney	= White Pearl	× Norman Peterson	= White Diamond
× Ernst Haussermann	= Gladys Wright		

MARTHA†‡	**Doris × Elisabethae**	**A. & M. 1954**

× Sharon Karleen	= Vero Beach		

MARTHA DANIELS‡	**R. H. Montgomery × Fairway Park**	**E. Iwanaga 1963**

× Ren. Brookie Chandler	= Rnthps. Richella's Delight		

MARTHA GLORIA	**Martha Jane × Alice Gloria**	**Dobkin 1971**
MARTHA JANE	**Doris × White Monarch**	**Small 1960**

× Alice Gloria	= Martha Gloria	× Louis Merkel	= Walrus

MARTHA ODUM	**Lois Jansen × Alice Shelley**	**Beard 1975**
MARTHA'S GEM	**Martha Daniels × equestris**	**E. Iwanaga 1967**

× sanderana	= Freed's Debonair		

MARVIN RAGAN	**Michael Oberling × Norman**	**MAJ Orchids 1973 (Ragan)**

MARY	Texas Star × Palm Beach	Beard 1965
× Gold Nugget = Mary Ann Bogaert		
MARY ANDREWS	Dos Pueblos × violacea	Raymond Palmer 1967 (Bracey)
× amboinensis = Bravo		
MARY ANN BOGAERT	Gold Nugget × Mary	Beard 1974
MARY AUGUSTA SECRIST	Hot Lips × Mad Hatter	D. B. White 1975
MARY BETH WEBER	Red Lip × Show Girl	Mrs. W. H. Boyd 1975 (McClain)
MARY CAROLYN	Bruce Shaffer × Capitola	Shaffer's 1973
MARY FAIRBURN	Chieftain × Samba	Fairburn 1974
MARY LOU STODDARD‡	Cast Iron Monarch × Louise Georgianna	Stoddard 1960 (Kwr.)
× Joanna Magale = Mem. Elaine Thornton		
MARY LOU WOODWARD	Barcelona × Hermosa	Shaffer's 1972
MARY McEDWARDS	Norman Peterson × lueddemanniana	W. J. Sanders 1973
MARY McLANE	Clara I. Knight × Barbara Beard	Beard 1966
× Betty Beard = Fiery Ball		
MARY OVERBY	Jennie Swank × Fiery Girl	Beard 1972
MARY WIELER	Virjudy × Virginia Beard	Beard 1968
× Barbara Beard = Zulu × Bardor = Evernia × Bariana = Queenie	× Frances Roberts = Dynamo × Jean Johnston = Kristi Vanaman × Jimmy Mize = Optimist	
MASQUERADE	Cinnamon Stick × Ondine	Andrew Orchids 1974
MASU HAMACHER‡	Hymen × Dos Pueblos	Wallbrunn 1963
× Cindy Brandt = Dos Amarillos × Cindy Sue = Daisy Arnold	× Ruby Zada = Fannie Mae	
MATTIE MAE CHAMBERS	Dee Haberlitz × Clyde	Freed 1973
MAUNA KEA	De Haro × Juanita	W. W. G. Moir 1973
MAXINE HEATH	Wanda Williams × violacea	Wallbrunn 1975
MAYAIMI	Luedde-violacea × sumatrana	J. & S. 1971
MAYDAY	Norman Peterson × Concorde	Rod McLellan Co. 1974
MAY LEE	gigantea × Ella Freed	Dobkin 1975
MAYLEEN	fimbriata × Mildred Karleen	Shaffer's 1974
MAZEL	Samba × Rosalind	Dobkin 1974
MAZURKA	Polka × Alice Gloria	Pff. V. & L. 1974
MELANIE	Charles Shaffer × Capitola	Hausermann 1973
MELBA BURNETT	Kathy Maguire × Palm Beach Rouge	Beard 1969
× Beatie Greenly = Imperial Valley × Betty Beard = Tillie × Evening Rose = Xenia	× Jimmy Mize = Byzantine × Dtps. Corcata = Dtps. Melcata	
MELISSA DAWN	Alice Gloria × Francine	Ernst 1973
MEMORIA ANNA VENTOSA	Bruce Shaffer × Princess Grace	Carlson 1973
MEMORIA ANTON SMITH	Alice Gloria × Mantilla	Universal 1972
MEMORIA ARNOLD REMMERT	Alice Gloria × Reinaldo	J. & S. 1975
MEMORIA BOB HACK	Denise Richardson × Nuel N. Songer	Hack 1971
MEMORIA ELAINE THORNTON	Joanna Magale × Mary Lou Stoddard	Fredk. L. Thornton 1972 (Fields Orchids)

MEMORIA ELVA HAMRIC | **Dawn Mist × Calpine** | **Ted Fischer 1969**

× Zada = Catherine Adams

MEMORIA EMIL RICHTER | **sanderana × Yoshino** | **Richter 1966**

× Heideperle = Walter Richter

MEMORIA FLORENTINO VENTOSA | **Doris × Paula Hallenbeck** | **Carlson 1975**

MEMORIA HAROLD SHAFFER | **Juanita × Gladys Read** | **Shaffer's 1965**

× Alice Gloria	= Patricia Rose	× Mad Hatter	= Harolds Hatter

MEMORIA IRENE MALLORY | **Ruby Stripes × Diane Rigg** | **Bachner 1974**

MEMORIA JIM KNOWLES | **gigantea × Terri Cook** | **Wilkins 1975 (Mitterer)**

MEMORIA JONATHAN WILLIAMS | **Richard Shaffer × Keith Shaffer** | **Shaffer's 1971**

MEMORIA JULIAN AHERRERA | **Lady Doreen × sumatrana** | **Richella 1975**

MEMORIA KNOX DANIEL | **Golden Sands × Mem. William Shaban** | **Shaban 1971**

MEMORIA LOKE SOKEEN‡ | **Chieftain × Jane L. Kingsbury** | **Chow 1959 (Kirch)**

× Kauai = Tan Chin Keat

MEMORIA MARIAN BAKER | **Princess Grace × Gladys Read** | **E. F. Patterson 1973**

MEMORIA MARY LISTA | **Diane Rigg × lueddemanniana** | **Peter E. Lista 1975**

MEMORIA PAT PEELER | **Florence Thornton × Mambo** | **Eureka 1971**

MEMORIA PAUL DEUTSCHBERGER | **Concorde × Juanita** | **Bolt 1974**

MEMORIA RAY THORNTON | **Princess Susan × Alice Gloria** | **Fredk. L. Thornton 1973**

MEMORIA REVEREND PARISH | **Princess Kaiulani × parishii** | **Fredk. L. Thornton 1973**

MEMORIA TRUMAN GREEN | **Hermosa × Keith Shaffer** | **Shaffer's 1971**

MEMORIA WILLIAM SHABAN | **Grace Palm × Fandango** | **W. J. Shaban 1967**

× Alice Gloria	= Leslie Ann	× Mad Lips	= Cherry Sundae
× equestris	= Robin Floyd	× Princess Grace	= Thea
× Golden Sands	= Mem. Knox Daniel	× Queen Emma	= Renā Dunn

MERCY DRILON | **Rose Parade × stuartiana** | **Valmayor 1974**

MEXACALI ROSE | **Pottstown × Zada** | **Osgood 1975**

MIAMI MAID‡ | **Mattie Shave × Winifred Prahl** | **Fields Orchids 1968**

× amboinensis	= Lemon Queen	× Mambo	= Mambo Maid
× Capitola	= Cele Young	× Norman Peterson	= Vista
× Charles Shaffer	= Villa Park	× Theresa Hausermann	= Ingrid Hausermann
× Edythe Wood	= Marten Hausermann	× violacea	= Hausermann's Aquarius
× fasciata	= Lynn Hausermann	× White Gull	= Winter Maiden
× Goldiana	= Jan Grove	× White Sails	= Dora McCarty
× Jimmy Hall	= Doctor Teoh	× Dtps. Kenneth Schubert	= Dtps. Cherub
× lueddemanniana	= Dick Wheeler		

MICHAEL OBERLING	**Aristocrat × Boynton**	**Price 1968**

× Norman	= Marvin Ragan		

micholitzii‡	**species**	

× Ambodoris	= Emerald Star	× Princess Grace	= Snowfall
× fimbriata	= Green Valley	× sumatrana	= Sumitz
× Gertrude Beard	= Snowdrift		

MICRONESIA	**Peach Glow × amboinensis**	**Hager 1975**
MIDLIP‡	**Ruby Lips × Elwyn Middleton**	**Beard 1966**

× Mad Hatter	= Kathy Lykins	× Ruby Zada	= Lady Ruby
× Pin Up Girl	= Kathryn Saltzman		

MIDNIGHT SUN	**fuscata × Irma Rath**	**Rod McLellan Co. 1974**
MILDRED KARLEEN‡	**Judy Karleen × Sharon Karleen**	**Hager 1960**

× Best Girl	= Tres Jolie	× Pin Up Girl	= Crescendo
× Darleen	= Alice Munson	× Princess Grace	= Bedlam
× equestris	= Swiss Miss	× Redfan	= Rodco's Lady
× fimbriata	= Mayleen	× Rosamont	= Rosa Karleen
× Grace Palm	= Adagio	× Samba	= Tempest
× Inspiration	= Target	× stuartiana	= Stuart Karleen
× Lachésis	= Chanteloire	× Thousand Oaks	= Karleen Oaks
× Mad Lips	= Gertrude Campbell	× Dtps. Lady Jewel	= Dtps. Rote Funken
× Mahinhin	= Redstone	× Dtps. Pueblo Jewel	= Dtps. Lady Jewel

MILDRED TOM	**Debbie Martian × Juanita**	**D. Tom 1971**
MILDRED WHITE	**Keith Shaffer × White Sails**	**D. B. White 1974**
MILKMAID	**Norman Peterson × Alice Gloria**	**Rod McLellan Co. 1974**
MILLIE RODRIGUES	**Queen Emma × lueddemanniana**	**Rodrigues 1970 (Kikuchi)**

× Lady Doreen	= Witchcraft		

MIMI COERTZE	**Kauai Monarch × Sonja**	**Freed 1974**
MIMI STARKE	**Terri Cook × Joseph Hampton**	**Starke & Son 1975**
MINI MOTH	**Cassandra × David Herbert**	**Fairburn 1974**
MINISTRIPES	**Rosy Charm × Pinocchio**	**J. & S. 1968 (Stoddard)**

× Alice Gloria	= Seventh Heaven	× Percy Porter	= Thrill
× Fiery	= Tinkerbell	× Red Lip	= Jiminy Cricket
× Keith Shaffer	= Christmas Candy	× Timbo	= Christopher Lynn
× Orlando	= Glen Marshall		

MINOUCHE	**Karleen's Wendy × Anouche**	**Pff. V. & L. 1971**

× Morzine	= Montevran	× Redfan	= Fifi

MISCHE	**Lady Doreen × Herbert Boone**	**R. K. Mizuta 1974**
MISCHIEF	**Star of Santa Cruz × mariae**	**Hager 1975**
MISSIRENE	**Natasha × lueddemanniana**	**Dobkin 1975**
MISS MUFFITT†	**San Marina × La Canada**	**Curson 1951**

× fasciata	= Golden Triangle		

MISTELLISA	**Elisa × Mistinguett**	**Pff. V. & L. 1973**
MISTINGUETT†‡	**Rothomago × Hellé**	**Marcel Lecoufle 1956**

× Elisa	= Mistellisa	× Pollux	= Gabi Koch
× Elizabeth Marshall	= Reshana	× Ramona	= Freteval
× Ghisoni	= French Beauty	× Rosalind	= Kathleen Voelker
× Golden Glow	= Gran Desierto	× Rose Parade	= Pink Imp
× Hawaiian Welcome	= Strawberry Meadows	× Roswell	= Beaugency
× Lipperose	= Annemarie Pinkepank	× Texas Pink	= Dainty Girl
× Luedde-violacea	= Red Mist	× Zada	= Zaguett
× Mrs. J. H. Veitch	= Florence Perera	× Dtps. Red Coral	= Dtps. Cardinal
× Nemesio Mendiola	= Smoke Creek Desert	× Ren. Brookie Chandler	= Rnthps. Ruby Jewell
× Ondine	= Ondinette		

PHALAENOPSIS

MISTIQUE	**Wendell Sawyer × Lolita**	**R. K. Mizuta 1975**
MISTY PINK	**Sunrise × Golden Glow**	**R. K. Mizuta 1975**
MISTY ROSE‡	**Marmist × Aalsmeer Rose**	**Rod McLellan Co. 1964**

× Barbara Beard = Pinkridge

MIXED BLESSING	**Zada × Star of Florida**	**Hager 1973**
MODEST BEAUTY	**Fairway Park × Venus**	**Rod McLellan Co. 1972**
MODINE	**Ondine × Elizabeth Marshall**	**Shaffer's 1974**
MOLINEUF	**Teena × Redfan**	**Pff. V. & L. 1974**
MONACO MONARCH	**Princess Grace × Cast Iron Monarch**	**E. F. Patterson 1973**
MONARCH OF VENUS	**Venusta × Cast Iron Monarch**	**Stoddard 1960 (Kwr.)**

× Alice Gloria = Clifford Richards

MONARICK	**Dipang Ruby Lips × Fiery**	**Phoon Yoon Seng 1974 (Cheah Kheng Cheong)**
MONCHITO	**Lavender Lady × Madrid**	**Gubler 1974**
MONTEVRAN	**Morzine × Minouche**	**Pff. V. & L. 1974**
MONTON	**Doris × Darleen**	**Shaffer's 1975**
MOONCREST	**Irma Rath × Cathrine Pillsbury**	**Rod McLellan Co. 1973**
MOON PROBE	**fuscata × Cindy Brandt**	**Beard 1968**

× Barbara Moler = Carol Owens
× Cindy Brandt = Yellow Ace
× Wendy Beard = Urban

MOON RIVER	**Mrs. J. H. Veitch × Susan Merkel**	**Thornton's 1972 (Fredk. L. Thornton)**
MOONSILK	**Dee Haberlitz × Norman Peterson**	**Rod McLellan Co. 1974**
MORGENROT	**Lipperose × Lippstadt**	**Hark 1974**
MORGENSONNE	**Fischers Liebling × Unna**	**Hans Koch 1975**
MORNING CLOUD	**Renate Frese × violacea**	**Frese 1975**
MORZINE	**Sandrina × Karleen's Wendy**	**Pff. V. & L. 1970**

× Karleen's Wendy = Lampion
× Minouche = Montevran
× Redfan = Charmeur
× Rodco's Lady = Lady Morzine

MOSAIC	**gigantea × Star of Florida**	**Hager 1975**
MOUCHETTE	**Francine × Anouche**	**Pff. V. & L. 1972**
MOUNT FUJI	**Anna Tham × Grace Palm**	**Karasawa 1971**
MOUNT KAALA	**Doreen × Elinor Shaffer**	**Kodama 1966**

× Intermedia = Hatsuhi
× Mad Hatter = Kaala Hatter
× Pueblo Anne = Hamaoka
× Zada = Zada Kaala

MOUNT ROKKO	**Doreen × Irene Stephens**	**Karasawa 1971**
MOUNT SHIGI	**Irene Stephens × Grace Palm**	**Karasawa 1971**
MRS. J. H. VEITCH‡ (syn. Luzon)	**sanderana × lueddemanniana**	**Veitch —**

× Alice Gloria = Ruth Gee
× Bridesmaid = Desert Morn
× Bruce Shaffer = Ajo Desert
× Luedde-violacea = Freed's Delicious
× Mistinguett = Florence Perera
× Pasadena = Nedra
× Princess Kaiulani = Princess Luzon
× Susan Merkel = Moon River
× Vallemar = Peach Parfait

MRS. LESTER McCOY	**Gigi × Zada**	**R. K. Mizuta 1975**
MURIEL TURNER	**Bruce Shaffer × Alice Gloria**	**Shaffer's 1970**

× amboinensis = Ice Age
× Luora = Snow Job

MUSIC	**Jennifer Beard × Barbara Freed Saltzman**	**Shaffer's 1975**

MY FAIR LADY‡ — **Aalsmeer Rose × Radiant Glow** — **McCoy 1961**

× gigantea = Kim | × Sunbeam = Eloquence
× schillerana = Patty Turner | × Susie Darlin = Dear One

MY FANCY — **Inspiration × corningiana** — **C. & I. Keyes 1974**
MYRA WRIGHT†‡ — **Elisabethae × Thomas Tucker** — **H. D. Wright 1957**

× violacea = Purple Star

MYSTIC LAND — **Dos-Ambo × Star of Florida** — **Lorenzen 1975**
MYTH — **Red Eye × Taffy Sue** — **Beard 1973**
NABOB — **Clara Birk × Barbara Beard** — **Beard 1973**
NADINE — **Doris × Spica** — **Lockhart 1975**
NANCY CARLSON‡ — **Grace Palm × Roswell** — **Shaffer's 1965**

× fasciata = New Penny | × Dtps. Mem. Clarence Schubert = Dtps. Greg Compton
× lueddemanniana = Hausermann's Venus
× Ondine = Shaffer's Pinkie

NANCY LOCKHART — **Spica × Daryl Beard** — **Lockhart 1972**
NAN KNOX — **Terri Cook × White Sails** — **D. B. White 1974**
NATASHA — **gigantea × Samba** — **Dobkin 1971**

× Ella Freed = Sherluch | × sumatrana = Debonair
× lueddemanniana = Missirene

NATIVE GIRL — **Judy Karleen × amboinensis** — **Hager 1963**

× Sillouette = Blithe Spirit

NAUGHTY PINK — **Elisa × Pink Chief** — **Rod McLellan Co. 1966**

× Ann Marie Beard = Portrait | × Barbara Beard = Shangri-La

NEDRA — **Mrs. J. H. Veitch × Pasadena** — **Hager 1971**

× amboinensis = South Coast | × Spica = Penny Clark
× Best Girl = Christina | × violacea = Nedra's Violets

NEDRA'S VIOLETS — **Nedra × violacea** — **Hager 1973**

NEMESIO MENDIOLA‡ — **Mrs. J. H. Veitch × lueddemanniana** — **Crestwood 1969**

× Daryl Beard = Lulu McQuerry | × Ondine = Amargosa Desert
× Doris = Black Rock Desert | × Orchid Acres = Donald Perry
× Mistinguett = Smoke Creek Desert

NETTA SHEPHERD — **Princess Grace × Barcelona** — **George Black 1974**
NEW HOPE‡ — **Doris × Firefly** — **Small 1965**

× lueddemanniana = Alice Carol

NEW HORIZON‡ — **Mildred Karleen × Sparkle** — **Hager 1964**

× Bandleader = Dorothy Ordway | × Dtps. Red Coral = Dtps. Coral Sea
× Star of Florida = Florentine

NEW LUORA — **Luora × New Horizon** — **Hager 1968**

× Grace Palm = Overthorpe

NEW MOON — **Dos Pueblos × fasciata** — **Beard 1969**

× Cindy Brandt = Lagoon Moon

NEW PENNY — **Nancy Carlson × fasciata** — **Hausermann 1973**
NEWPORT — **Kathy Maguire × Beatie Greenly** — **Beard 1972**
NICOL JEAN OREAR — **Elinor Shaffer × Dos Pueblos** — **Orear 1965**

× Elinor Shaffer = Ski Patrol | × Quality Belle = Eva Wells
× Erick Hansen = Vera Miller

NIMBUS — **Ruby Wells × stuartiana** — **Andrew Orchids 1972**

× Rose Parade	= Polly

NINA — **Caruso × Juanita** — **McFarlane 1972**

× Spring Showers	= Sid

NITZAN — **Estrellita × Ondine** — **Shaffer's 1971**

NORDPOL — **Arcadia × Long Life** — **Hark 1974**

NORMA COLE — **Elportal × Ruby Zada** — **Fields Orchids 1973**

NORMA MARION — **Ann Hatter × Sugar 'n Spice** — **Mrs. H. Marion 1973 (Dewey)**

NORMAN — **fasciata × violacea** — **Beard 1969**

× Daryl Beard	= Gladys Burkey	× sanderana	= Freed's Dimple
× Michael Oberling	= Marvin Ragan		

NORMAN CLYDE — **Norman Peterson × Clyde** — **Miskimens 1975**

NORMAN PETERSON‡ — **Fairway Park × Grace Palm** — **Peterson Bros. 1964**

× Alice Gloria	= Milkmaid	× Marten Hausermann	= White Diamond
× Capitola	= Cordial	× Miami Maid	= Vista
× Cathrine Pillsbury	= Cotillion	× Persistent	= Applause
× Clyde	= Norman Clyde	× Princess Grace	= White Rabbit
× Concorde	= Mayday	× Redfan	= Jersey
× Daryl Beard	= Quotient	× Roswell	= Pleased Pink
× Dee Haberlitz	= Moonsilk	× Sonja	= Freed's Pride
× Elinor Shaffer	= Virtuoso	× Terdoreen	= Lena Bates
× Kauai	= Freed's Bedevilled	× violacea	= Little Eclipse
× lueddemanniana	= Mary McEdwards	× Ren. monachica	= Rnthps. Bernice Voelker

NORM'S FANTASY — **Gay Paree × Zada** — **Normoyle 1972**

NORTHWOODS — **Robert Pigors × fuscata** — **Hausermann 1974**

NUEL N. SONGER‡ — **Doris × lueddemanniana** — **H. D. Wright 1952**

× Bridesmaid	= Fiji	× lueddemanniana	= Pay Dirt
× Denise Richardson	= Mem. Bob Hack	× Ramona	= Beauregard
× lindenii	= Audrey Porter		

NYMPH — **Rising Sun × Suemid** — **Beard 1973**

OAK CREEK — **Helen Miller × Redfan** — **Beard 1971**

OAK FLAME — **fuscata × Gladys Read** — **Shaffer's 1973**

OAK RIDGE — **Jimmy Mize × Barbara Beard** — **Beard 1973**

OASIS — **Quality Belle × Daryl Beard** — **Beard 1973**

OCHRARINA — **Ballerina × lueddemanniana** — **R. K. Mizuta 1973**

OLD IVORY — **Juanita May × lueddemanniana** — **Fields Orchids 1971**

OLGA MALEK — **Karen Rosea × Elisa** — **W. J. Shaban 1972**

ONDINE‡ — **Mistinguett × sanderana** — **Pff. V. & L. 1964**

× Best Girl	= Dear Heart	× Jane Almquist	= Hawaiian Sunset
× Cinnamon Stick	= Masquerade	× Mistinguett	= Ondinette
× Doris	= Paula Hallenbeck	× Nancy Carlson	= Shaffer's Pinkie
× Dorisellita	= Phyllis-Jean	× Nemesio Mendiola	= Amargosa Desert
× Dorothy Miller	= Roja	× Princess Kaiulani	= Princess Ondine
× Elizabeth Marshall	= Modine	× Zada	= Zondine
× Estrellita	= Nitzan	× Dtps. Kenneth Schubert	= Dtps. Melina

ONDINETTE — **Ondine × Mistinguett** — **Pff. V. & L. 1971**

ONEDA KANSMAN — **Mannicata × Daryl Beard** — **Beard 1975**

ONEOHONE — **Rose-Bowl × San Songer** — **Freed 1974 (Originator unknown)**

× Zada	= Malibu Sunset

ONYX — **Utopia × lueddemanniana** — **Beard 1974**

OPALESCENCE — **Opaline × Henriette Lecoufle** — **Pff. V. & L. 1974**

OPALINE — **Henriette Lecoufle × Capitola** — **Pff. V. & L. 1970**

× Alice Gloria	= Demoiselle	× Keith Shaffer	= Temple Cloud
× Henriette Lecoufle	= Opalescence	× stuartiana	= Schneeball

PHALAENOPSIS

OPAL MOUNTAIN	**Suemid × Mad Hatter**	**Rod McLellan Co. 1974**
OPTIMIST	**Jimmy Mize × Mary Wieler**	**Beard 1972**
ORCHID ACRES‡	**Dawn Mist × Doris**	**Rod McLellan Co. 1959**

× Capitola = White Gull | × Nemesio Mendiola = Donald Perry
× Polar Bear = Polar Pass

ORCHID ALLEY	**Wilma Hughes × Princess of Denmark**	**Steindorf 1974**
ORLANDO	**Arcadia × Palm Beach**	**J. & S. 1974 (Sparks)**

× Ministripes = Glen Marshall

OTOHIME	**Grace Palm × Raycraft**	**Watanabe 1973**
OUBREY McCARTER	**Ann Wade × William Boyd**	**Fouquette 1975 (Bertsch)**
OUR LOVE AFFAIR	**Viroonchan × Ruby Zada**	**Freed 1974**

× violacea = Robbie Turner

OVERGLOW	**Overture × Radiant Glow**	**John H. Miller 1967**

× Elizabeth Marshall = Tiger Rose | × Jewel Lips = Tiger Stripe
× Fiesta = Fiesta Glow | × Painted Desert = Marion Cole
× Jean Stephan = Bonny Doon

OVERTHORPE	**Grace Palm × New Luora**	**Baitson 1973**
OZONE	**Gertrude Homsher × Utopia**	**Beard 1973**
PACA	**Jean Johnston × Redwing**	**Beard 1973**
PACESETTER	**Sharon Karleen × Serenity**	**Lorenzen 1972**

× Fiery = Sugar 'n Spice | × Red Lip = Chuck's Red Lip

PACIFIC PRINCESS‡	**Doris × Chieftain**	**Rod McLellan Co. 1954 (E. W. McLellan)**

× Ann Wade = Dora Jean Fox

PAGAN LOVE SONG	**Ambomanniana × Amber Sands**	**Freed 1974**
PAGE OATES	**Edythe Wood × Cast Iron Monarch**	**E. F. Patterson 1973**
PAGLIACCIO	**Schillerano-stuartiana × Hymen**	**Rumrill 1973 (Jost & Rumrill)**
PAINTED DESERT‡	**Mrs. J. H. Veitch × Juanita**	**Shaffer's 1966**

× amboinensis = Desert Dawn | × Overglow = Marion Cole
× fasciata = Desert Gold | × sumatrana = Desert Glow
× Ghisoni = Painted Dolly | × violacea = Peachy Keen
× gigantea = Rainbow Sherbet | × Zada = Cinnamon Candy
× lueddemanniana = Desert Flame | × Zondine = Desert Sands

PAINTED DOLL WEDDING	**Freed's Broadway Rhythm × Show Girl**	**Freed 1974**
PAINTED DOLLY	**Painted Desert × Ghisoni**	**Shaffer's 1971**
PAINTED PRINCESS‡	**Princess Grace × Ruby Lips**	**Markell 1966**

× Ruby Zada = Princess Ruby

PAJARO BLANCO	**Clyde × Capitola**	**J. F. Hughes 1975**
PALE BEAUTY	**Lady Doreen × violacea**	**Freed 1972 (E. Iwanaga)**
PALETTE	**Cindy Brandt × lueddemanniana**	**Beard 1969**

× Cindy Brandt = Xyster | × Spica = Kitty Taylor
× Red Eye = Lemon Meringue | × Wendy Beard = Uban
× Ruby Lips = Qualified

pallens (see *lueddemanniana**†‡) **species**

PALM BEACH†‡ **Doris × Cast Iron Monarch** **Beard 1958 (Kwr.)**

× Arcadia	= Orlando	× Susan Merkel	= Angel Wings
× Elinor Shaffer	= Malibu Wedding		

PALM COAST **Cassandra × schillerana** **Thornton's 1972 (Fredk. L. Thornton)**

PALMSNOW‡ **Palm Beach × Snowbird** **J. & S. 1962**

× Alice Gloria	= Patrick Jon	× Dor. pulcherrima	= Dtps. Anne de Bruyne
× fuscata	= Apricot Nectar		

PALM TRAIL **Little Girl × Yellow Lip** **H. Webb 1974**

PALMYRA‡ **Grace Palm × amboinensis** **O. Kirsch 1968**

× Ann Lovelace	= Lovely Ann		

PAMELA WOLF **Eva Lou × Bright Spot** **Beard 1975**

pantherina **species**

× amboinensis	= Doris Blomquist	× Star of Rio	= Professor Asmino

PARADISE PINK **Percy Porter × equestris** **R. K. Mizuta 1975**

PARILEE BOURGOIN **Alice Gloria × Cathrine Pillsbury** **Graham 1973 (Hager)**

parishii†‡ **species**

(This is retained as the horticulturally recommended name for registration purposes even though *Phal. decumbens* is the botanically correct name for this species.)

× fimbriata	= Green Imp	× mannii	= Parma
× Intermedia	= Douglas Allen	× Princess Kaiulani	= Mem. Reverend Parish

PARKER **Terri Cook × White Falcon** **M. J. Bates 1973**

PARMA **mannii × parishii** **Norrsell 1971**

PASADENA†‡ **Grace Palm × Margaret Bean** **Bean 1956**

× Mrs. J. H. Veitch	= Nedra	× violacea	= Pasadena Violet
× Terri Cook	= John		

PASADENA VIOLET **Pasadena × violacea** **Miskimens 1972 (Originator unknown)**

PASTELLA **Lipperose × mannii** **Röhl 1974**

PAT COLTON **Gertrude Homsher × White Plains** **Beard 1975**

PAT DARBY **Kathy Marie × Lillian Hozaki** **Takase 1975**

PATIENCE BENJAMIN **Boynton × Louis Merkel** **A. & M. 1975**

PAT REINKE **Kathy Marie × Alight** **Takase 1975**

PATRICIA GOFF **Patricia Lea × mannii** **E. K. Goff 1973**

PATRICIA LEA†‡ **amabilis × Doris** **Romanoff 1951**

× mannii	= Patricia Goff		

PATRICIA NEAL **Sonja × Cast Iron Monarch** **Freed 1973**

PATRICIA OAKS **Thousand Oaks × sumatrana** **Millington 1974**

PATRICIA ROSE **Alice Gloria × Mem. Harold Shaffer** **C. R. Rose 1973**

PATRICK JON **Palmsnow × Alice Gloria** **J. & S. 1971**

× Alice Gloria	= White Bird	× Keith Shaffer	= Paulette André

PAT STROTHMANN **White Summit × Gladys Read** **Furrow 1972**

PATTI LOGAN **Satin Rouge × Barbara Beard** **Universal 1972**

PATTY TURNER **My Fair Lady × schillerana** **R. C. Turner 1975 (Kirch)**

× Keith Shaffer	= Jeffrey		

PAULA HALLENBECK — **Doris × Ondine** — **Shaffer's 1971**

× Doris = Mem. Florentino Ventosa

PAULA KRAMER — **Edythe Wood × Keith Shaffer** — **E.F.G. Orchids 1972**
PAULETTE ANDRÉ — **Keith Shaffer × Patrick Jon** — **J. & S. 1974**
PAUL LIPPOLD — **Sigrid × Doreen** — **Gart. Seidel 1974 (K. Seidel)**
PAUL STAUFFER — **Linda Winters × Hedy Maerkl** — **Beard 1975**
PAY DIRT — **lueddemanniana × Nuel N. Songer** — **Kirch 1974**
PEACE — **Serenity × Grace Palm** — **Vaughn 1962**

× lueddemanniana = Golden Peace

PEACH GLOW — **Elinor Shaffer × lueddemanniana** — **Kuhn 1970**

× amboinensis = Micronesia

PEACH PARFAIT — **Vallemar × Mrs. J. H. Veitch** — **Peter E. Lista 1972 (L. C. Riley)**

× Zada = Raspberry Sherbert

PEACHY KEEN — **Painted Desert × violacea** — **J. Ewing 1975**
PEARLIE — **Ramona × Bruce Shaffer** — **Dr. J. G. Martin 1975**
PEGGY NAGEL — **Gladys Read × Ice Palace** — **Nagel 1971**
PEGGY O'NEILL — **Gladys Read × Cast Iron Monarch** — **E. F. Patterson 1973**
PENANG — **Rosy Charm × amboinensis** — **Hager 1972**

× Lavender Lady = Shady Lady | × Star of Florida = Star Bright

PENELOPE WILLIAMS — **Joseph Hampton × Mariposa** — **Fischer 1971**
PENNY CLARK — **Nedra × Spica** — **Hager 1973**
PEPPERDINE UNIVERSITY — **Alice Gloria × Sonja** — **Freed 1973**
PEPPERMINT — **lindenii × Pink Profusion** — **Freed 1964**

× Ann Lovelace = Baby Doll | × Pin Up Girl = Shirley Marie
× Denise Richardson = Joseph Masse | × Renate Frese = Toxi
× Keith Shaffer = Jokesi | × Dor. pulcherrima = Dtps. Stephen Saltzman

PEPPERMINT STICK — **Rosy Charm × Suemid** — **June Fowler 1973 (Vande Weghe)**
PERCY PORTER — **Harlequin × Mildred Karleen** — **Rodrigues 1970 (A. S. Cavaco)**

× Aglow = Wendel George | × Ministripes = Thrill
× Christopher Lynn = Playmate | × Pin Up Girl = Coral Pink
× equestris = Paradise Pink | × Queen Emma = Tony Cavaco
× Lavender Lady = Lei | × Redport = Abram McAndless
× Mad Lips = Wilma Schoppe | × Tomi = June Takase

PERSISTENT — **Dos Pueblos × Fairway Park** — **Rod McLellan Co. 1967**

× Norman Peterson = Applause

PETER LISTA — **Cher Ann × violacea** — **Peter E. Lista 1975**
PETER WALLBRUNN — **Hymen × stuartiana** — **Wallbrunn 1964**

× fuscata = Bruce LeBaron

PETIE DEMMA — **Treasure Island × Alice Gloria** — **Hager 1971 (Rinaman)**
PETIT PRINCE — **Henriette Lecoufle × Redfan** — **Pff. V. & L. 1972**

PHIENG-RUDI PINK	**Hannah Nair × Best Girl**		**B'kok Gdng. Supplies 1970 (Freed)**
× Elisa	= Freed's Daredevil		
PHYLIS-KAY‡	**Judy Karleen × Sparkle**		**Hager 1966**
× Laniloa	= Kathy Marie	× Tulip Time	= Darlene Moore
× Show Girl	= Freed's Admiration		
PHYLLIS-JEAN	**Dorisellita × Ondine**		**Shaffer's 1973**
PINK BALL‡	**Zada × Pink Hawaii**		**Beard 1964**
× Ruby Zada	= Universe		
PINK CHEEKS	**Callie Flynn × White Medallion**		**Saucier 1975**
PINK CHIFFON‡	**Pink Hawaii × Doris**		**A. & M. 1958**
× Ann Lovelace	= Pink Formal		
PINK CIRCUS	**Denise Richardson × Go-Go Girl**		**A. & M. 1975**
PINK COACH	**Doris × Elizabeth Marshall**		**Shaffer's 1974**
PINK DOVE	**Juanita × Ghisoni**		**Andrew Orchids 1972**
PINK FORMAL	**Pink Chiffon × Ann Lovelace**		**Freed 1972**
× Ann Marie Beard	= Rhoda Fredricks		
PINK FROST	**Ronnie Wilson × Star of Rio**		**C. & I. Keyes 1974**
PINK GIN	**amabilis × Arisan**		**S'pore Orchids 1968**
× violacea	= Sapphire		
PINK GLAMOR	**Nancy Carlson × Zada**		**Hausermann 1970**
× Shaffer's Pinkie	= Red Desire	× Dtps. Mem. Clarence Schubert	= Dtps. Red Bonanza
PINK GOLD	**Pink Sunset × Mahinhin**		**John H. Miller 1971**
PINK HORIZON	**Barbara Beard × Ann Lovelace**		**Freed 1972**
PINK ICE	**Fairway Park × Blushing Girl**		**Rod McLellan Co. 1968**
× Fischers Liebling	= Fischers Ice	× Valentinii	= Evening Sky
× Lipperose	= Rosa Ice	× Zada	= Aztec
× Satin Rouge	= Apache		
PINK IMP	**Mistinguett × Rose Parade**		**Andrew Orchids 1975**
PINK JEWEL	**Jewel × Valencia**		**Shaffer's 1969**
× Estrellita	= Jewelita		
PINK LEMONADE	**Zadian × Zada**		**J. & S. 1975**
PINK MELALLION	**Lakmé × Pink Symphony**		**E. Iwanaga 1967**
× Makaha Surf	= Buena Vista	× Zada	= Zadallion
PINK PARFAIT	**Blushing Pink × Lipperose**		**Hausermann 1974**
PINK PUFF	**Blushing Girl × Zada**		**Rod McLellan Co. 1970**
× Satin Rouge	= Risque		
PINK RAYS	**David Herbert × Queen Emma**		**A. & M. 1975**
PINKRIDGE	**Misty Rose × Barbara Beard**		**Universal 1972**
PINK SHADOW	**Aalsmeer Rose × Judith**		**Kodama 1965**
× Zada	= Diamond Pink		
PINK SNOW	**Lady Doreen × equestris**		**Richella 1975**
PINK STRIPES	**Doris × Baguio**		**Shaffer's 1971**
PINK SUCCESS	**Pink Symphony × Elisa**		**Kirch 1969 (E. Iwanaga)**
× Violet Glow	= Lipanda Glow		

PINK SUNRISE — **Sunset Glow × Zada** — **A. & M. 1965**
× South Pacific = Plum Blossom

PINK SUNSET†‡ — **Rêve Rose × Pamela** — **McCoy 1951**
× Mahinhin = Pink Gold
× Rnthps. Jan Goo = Rnthps. Dana

PINK SUPREME — **Pink Veil × Sunrise** — **Ozaki 1973**
PINK SURREY — **Vosa × Doris** — **Shaffer's 1974**
PINK VEIL — **schillerana × Sunrise** — **Ozaki 1973 (Takemoto)**
× Sunrise = Pink Supreme

PINK VOGUE — **Diamond Head × lueddemanniana** — **E. Iwanaga 1961**
× Elisa = Vosa

PINK WOW — **Valencia × Roswell** — **Shaffer's 1969**
× Zada = Full Pink

PINK ZEBRA — **Baguio × Harlequin** — **Frank Hughes 1974**
PINOCCHIO‡ — **White Foam × equestris** — **O. Kirsch 1959**
× Summer Monarch = Sarah Pusey

PIN UP GIRL — **Show Girl × Ruby Lips** — **Freed 1967**
× Ella Freed = Malibu Optimists
× Hawaiian Sunshine = Amado Vazquez
× Lois Jansen = Layla Beard
× Mad Lips = Streaker
× Midlip = Kathryn Saltzman
× Mildred Karleen = Crescendo
× Peppermint = Shirley Marie
× Percy Porter = Coral Pink
× Queen Emma = Rae Rae
× Redfan = Bon Nuit Bay
× Ruby Zada = Whimsey
× Shari = Rosetta Wittorf
× Show Girl = Barbara Freed Saltzman
× Spotted Moon = Carolyn Wilkes

PLATONIC — **Irma Rath × Daryl Beard** — **Rod McLellan Co. 1973**
PLAYMATE — **Christopher Lynn × Percy Porter** — **J. & S. 1974**
PLEASED PINK — **Norman Peterson × Roswell** — **Voelker 1974**
PLEASURE POINT — **Doris × Dorisellita** — **Shaffer's 1973**
PLUM BEAUTY — **Dorisellita × Lipperose** — **Hausermann 1974**
PLUM BLOSSOM — **South Pacific × Pink Sunrise** — **W. W. G. Moir 1973**
POCO PINK — **Cassandra × Marmouset** — **R. K. Mizuta 1974**
POKAI BAY — **Doreen × Surfrider** — **Kodama 1968**
× Makua Shore = Kekualani Snow White

POLAR BEAR — **Elinor Shaffer × Cast Iron Monarch** — **Beall 1969**
× Barbetta Bell = Arctic Belle
× Elinor Shaffer = White Bear Pass
× Golden Sands = Lemon Point
× Grace Heartfield = Diamond Pass
× Maria Vasquez = Beehive Pass
× Orchid Acres = Polar Pass
× Zadian = Rose Quartz Ridge
× Dtps. Lake Worth = Dtps. Wonder Mountain

POLAR PASS — **Polar Bear × Orchid Acres** — **Beall 1974**
POLKA — **Ramona × Henriette Lecoufle** — **Pff. V. & L. 1972**
× Alice Gloria = Mazurka

POLKA DOT — **Red Lip × fuscata** — **J. & S. 1971**
POLLUX — **Rêve Rose × stuartiana** — **Munz 1971 (Hans Koch)**
× Mistinguett = Gabi Koch
× Zada = Fischers Liebling

POLLY — **Rose Parade × Nimbus** — **Andrew Orchids 1975**
POLYNESIAN SUNSET — **Samba × New Horizon** — **Hager 1966**
× Brasilia = Brazilian Sunset

PHALAENOPSIS

Name	Parentage	Registrant
POPPEE	**Golden Sands × Capitola**	**Pff. V. & L. 1972**
PORTLAND BILL	**Concorde × Keith Shaffer**	**Andrew Orchids 1974**
PORT MAYAKA	**Judy Karleen × Jubilee**	**Beard 1974 (Kuhn)**

× Bright Spot	= Cathy Funstum

Name	Parentage	Registrant
PORTRAIT	**Ann Marie Beard × Naughty Pink**	**Rod McLellan Co. 1974**
POTTSTOWN	**Judy Karleen × Ann Hatter**	**Osgood 1975 (Kuhn)**

× Zada	= Mexacali Rose

Name	Parentage	Registrant
POWDERY ROSE	**Robert Pigors × violacea**	**Hausermann 1975**
PRIMA	**Luedde-violacea × Princess Kaiulani**	**Shaffer's 1975**
PRINCE CHARLES	**Princess of Denmark × Keith Shaffer**	**Manor Orchids 1974**
PRINCESS DORIS	**Doris × Princess Kaiulani**	**Fredk. L. Thornton 1973**
PRINCESS GRACE‡	**Cast Iron Monarch × Grace Palm**	**Freed 1959 (Kwr.)**

× Barcelona	= Netta Shepherd	× mannii	= Kwan Yin
× Bruce Shaffer	= Mem. Anna Ventosa	× Mem. William Shaban	= Thea
× Cast Iron Monarch	= Monaco Monarch	× micholitzii	= Snowfall
× Elinor Shaffer	= Gay Senorita	× Mildred Karleen	= Bedlam
× Gladys Read	= Mem.Marian Baker	× Norman Peterson	= White Rabbit
× Lady Gladys	= Gracious Lady	× Wilma Hughes	= Princess Wilma

Name	Parentage	Registrant
PRINCESS JESSICA	**Jessica McDonald × Princess Ruby**	**Frese 1975**
PRINCESS KAIULANI‡	**violacea × amboinensis**	**O. Kirsch 1961**

× David Herbert	= David's Princess	× Ruth Wallbrunn	= First Light
× Doris	= Princess Doris	× Samba	= Princess Samba
× Luedde-violacea	= Prima	× Star of Florida	= Star of Kaiulani
× Mrs. J. H. Veitch	= Princess Luzon	× violacea	= Princess Violet
× Ondine	= Princess Ondine	× Dtps. Jerri Sue King	= Dtps. Princess Sue
× parishii	= Mem. Reverend Parish	× Dor. pulcherrima	= Dtps. Lori Thornton

Name	Parentage	Registrant
PRINCESS LUZON	**Mrs. J. H. Veitch × Princess Kaiulani**	**Wallbrunn 1972**
PRINCESS MICHIKO‡	**Aalsmeer Rose × Sunrise**	**Alsagoff 1964**

× Golden Chief	= Freed's Curtain Call	× Jane Shaffer	= Eileen Ashburn

Name	Parentage	Registrant
PRINCESS OF DENMARK	**Gladys Read × Alice Gloria**	**Shaffer's 1967**

× Keith Shaffer	= Prince Charles	× Sonja	= Loren Bohnett
× Show Time	= Show Princess	× Wilma Hughes	= Orchid Alley

Name	Parentage	Registrant
PRINCESS ONDINE	**Princess Kaiulani × Ondine**	**Shaffer's 1974**
PRINCESS RUBY	**Painted Princess × Ruby Zada**	**Freed 1972**

× Hot Drops	= Ruby Drops	× Jessica McDonald	= Princess Jessica

Name	Parentage	Registrant
PRINCESS SAMBA	**Samba × Princess Kaiulani**	**Dobkin 1971**
PRINCESS SUSAN	**Pacific Princess × Susan Merkel**	**Beard 1965**

× Alice Gloria	= Memoria Ray Thornton	× Mambo	= Apollo Fourteen

Name	Parentage	Registrant
PRINCESS VIOLET	**Princess Kaiulani × violacea**	**Wallbrunn 1973**
PRINCESS WILMA	**Princess Grace × Wilma Hughes**	**Freed 1972**
PRISCILLA PYFROM	**Breathless × Far Horizon**	**W. J. Sanders 1975 (Hager)**
PRISSY	**Terri Cook × lindenii**	**Fort Caroline 1975**
PRODIGIOUS	**Irma Rath × Elinor Shaffer**	**Rod McLellan Co. 1973**
PROFESSOR ASMINO	**pantherina × Star of Rio**	**Wallbrunn 1972 (Liem Khe Wie)**

× Elaine-Liem	= Sri Rejeki

PHALAENOPSIS

PROFESSOR DERRA	**Makaha Surf × amabilis**	**Schöttler 1975**
PROGRESS‡	**Dos Pueblos × Francisca**	**Rod McLellan Co. 1966**

× Redfan = Lady Lorraine | × Spitfire = Progress Maid

PROGRESS MAID	**Progress × Spitfire**	**Rod McLellan Co. 1971**
PUEBLO ANNE	**Dos Pueblos × Anne**	**Y. Toyama 1975**

× Estrellita = Establo | × Mount Kaala = Hamaoka

pulchra (see *lueddemanniana**†‡)	**species**	
PURPLE STAR	**Myra Wright × violacea**	**Crestwood 1975**
PYXIS	**Lewis Barber × Jimmy Mize**	**Beard 1973**
QUADRILLE	**Bariana × Ann Marie Beard**	**Beard 1973**
QUAKER	**Anita Young × Kimberly Odum**	**Beard 1975**
QUALIFIED	**Palette × Ruby Lips**	**Beard 1972**
QUALITY BELLE‡	**Dos Pueblos × Terri Cook**	**Beard 1968**

× Amber Sands = Jane Le Noir
× Cathrine Pillsbury = Durward Belmont White
× Cindy Brandt = White Waters
× Cindy Sue = Anne Gurke
× Daryl Beard = Oasis
× Nicol Jean Orear = Eva Wells
× Scotti Maguire = Ronald Prairie
× Spica = Dottie Bucheck

QUARTERLY	**Theodosia Gibson × Frances Roberts**	**Beard 1974**
QUEEN DOREEN	**Lady Doreen × Valley Queen**	**R. K. Mizuta 1972**
QUEEN EMMA‡	**Doris × Ruby Lips**	**McCoy 1960 (Donald Chow)**

× David Herbert = Pink Rays
× Golden Sands = Gail Lynne
× Kathleen Edris = Bewitched
× Leilehua = Tomi
× Mem. William Shaban = Renā Dunn
× Percy Porter = Tony Cavaco
× Pin Up Girl = Rae Rae
× Roselle = Tateyama
× Ruby Lips = Striped Velvet
× Samba = Silver Piece
× White Virgin = Kuchibeni
× Zada = Kathy Reyes

QUEENIE	**Mary Wieler × Bariana**	**Beard 1972**
QUEEN OF HEARTS	**Rosy Charm × sumatrana**	**Hager 1975**
QUIESCENCE	**Trials × Bruce Shaffer**	**Stewart Inc. 1974 (Van Delden)**
QUOTIENT	**Daryl Beard × Norman Peterson**	**Beard 1973**
RABBIT	**Daryl Beard × White Plains**	**Beard 1974**
RADIANT IMPACT	**Mardi Gras × Sparkle**	**John H. Miller 1974**
RADIANT MOON	**Helen Miller × Irma Rath**	**Rod McLellan Co. 1972 (Beard)**
RAE RAE	**Pin Up Girl × Queen Emma**	**R. K. Mizuta 1974**
RAINBOW SHERBET	**gigantea × Painted Desert**	**J. Ewing 1975**
RAINBOW STRIPES	**Sunbeam × Samba**	**Dobkin 1971**
RAKA SUMICHAN	**Elaine-Liem × amboinensis**	**Kolopaking 1975**
RAMONA‡	**Thomas Tucker × Mem. Nasu Tomoguchi**	**Shaffer's 1957**

× Alice Gloria = Candeur
× Bruce Shaffer = Pearlie
× Concorde = Canasta
× Dampierre = Dampira
× fasciata = Yellow Bird
× Golden Glow = Yuma Desert
× Henriette Lecoufle = Polka
× Isis = Ismona
× Mistinguett = Freteval
× Nuel N. Songer = Beauregard
× Sonja = Madalene Fobert
× Dtps. Mem. Clarence Schubert = Dtps. Fowler's Dream

RAPTURE	**Anouche × Isis**	**Pff. V. & L. 1970**

× Anouche = Vitrail | × Francine = Scherzo

RASPBERRY SHERBERT	**Peach Parfait × Zada**	**Peter E. Lista 1972**

RAUHREIF	**Renate Frese × stuartiana**	**Frese 1975**
RAYCRAFT‡	**Doris × Aalsmeer Rose**	**Ernst 1962 (Santa Cruz)**

× Ann Lovelace	= Freed's Delectable	× Dtps. Coral Gleam	= Dtps. Ray Coral
× Grace Palm	= Otohime		

REDBIRD	**Mahinhin × Snowbird**	**Osgood 1974**
RED DESIRE	**Pink Glamor × Shaffer's Pinkie**	**Hausermann 1975**
RED EYE	**Fred Thomson × Suemid**	**Beard 1968**

× Fiery Girl	= Ginny McConville	× Robbie Vanaman	= Kathleen Flaherty
× Mad Hatter	= Alta Goodman	× Taffy Sue	= Myth
× Palette	= Lemon Meringue	× Dtps. Pueblo Jewel	= Dtps. Jim Hafer
× Redfan	= Bright Spot	× Dtps. Red Lip	Dtps. Debbie Lawrence

REDFAN	**Goleta × Ann Hatter**	**Rod McLellan Co. 1967**

× Cher Ann	= Kerlu	× Morzine	= Charmeur
× Elinor Shaffer	= Jane Seymour	× Norman Peterson	= Jersey
× Frosty Lip	= Snow Ruby	× Pin Up Girl	= Bon Nuit Bay
× Helen Miller	= Oak Creek	× Progress	= Lady Lorraine
× Henriette Lecoufle	= Petit Prince	× Red Eye	= Bright Spot
× Jennie Swank	= Amy Maguire	× Show Girl	= Malibu Lipstick
× Karleen's Wendy	= Vivaldi	× Spitfire	= Billet-doux
× Lady Ruby	= Marquise	× Suemid	= Eva Lou
× Lipstick	= Freed's Connoisseur	× Teena	= Molineuf
× Mad Hatter	= Lady Florence	× Zaguett	= Romantic
× Mildred Karleen	= Rodco's Lady	× Dtps. Pueblo Jewel	= Dtps. Youthful
× Minouche	= Fifi		

RED GEM	**Bronze King × Rose Parade**	**Fernando 1974**

REDKAR	**Red Lip × Sharon Karleen**	**Fields Orchids 1974**

× Elportal	= Redport		

RED LIGHTNING	**Marmist × Zada**	**Rod McLellan Co. 1974**
RED LIP‡	**New Hope × New Era**	**Small 1965**

× Ann Hatter	= Chestnut Vale	× Ministripes	= Jiminy Cricket
× fuscata	= Polka Dot	× Pacesetter	= Chuck's Red Lip
× gigantea	= Bimini	× Sharon Karleen	= Redkar
× Jiminy Cricket	= Cindy Tsai	× Show Girl	= Mary Beth Weber
× Luedde-violacea	= Gay Heart		

RED MIST	**Luedde-violacea × Mistinguett**	**Shaffer's 1974**
REDPORT	**Redkar × Elportal**	**Fields Orchids 1974**

× Kenneth Stromsland	= Gedwo	× Percy Porter	= Abram McAndless
× Mad Lips	= Sheer Delight		

RED ROCK	**Lucie Hausermann × violacea**	**Hausermann 1970**

× Lipperose	= Red Rose		

RED ROSE	**Red Rock × Lipperose**	**Hausermann 1974**
REDSTONE	**Mahinhin × Mildred Karleen**	**Osgood 1974**
RED SUN	**Best Girl × Samba**	**Dobkin 1971**
REDWINE	**Estrellita × lueddemanniana**	**Fennell 1972**

× Zada	= Vintage Wine		

REDWING	**Barbara Beard × Betty Beard**	**Beard 1969**

× Ann Marie Beard	= William Beard	× Jean Johnston	= Paca
× Barbara Beard	= Lyrical	× Jimmy Mize	= Labarum
× Clara Birk	= Dorothy Brock	× Kathryn Leahey	= Zenith
× Evening Rose	= Youngs Town	× Dtps. Red Coral	= Dtps. Udal
× Irene van Alstyne	= Amy Howard		

PHALAENOPSIS

Name	Parentage	Registrant
REGNIER†‡	lueddemanniana × schillerana	Regnier 1922

× Zada = Karfunkel

Name	Parentage	Registrant
reichenbachiana (see *fasciata*‡)	species	
REICHENTEA	fasciata × gigantea	W. W. G. Moir 1975
REINALDO	Fancy Quest × Caprice	J. & S. 1971

× Alice Gloria = Mem. Arnold Remmert

Name	Parentage	Registrant
RENĀ DUNN	Queen Emma × Mem. William Shaban	W. J. Shaban 1973
RENATE FRESE	Pasaris Celle × Mad Hatter	Wichmann 1969

× Cadifa = Cadirena
× Hot Drops = Lollipop
× Mad Hatter = Stemshorn
× Peppermint = Toxi
× stuartiana = Rauhreif
× sumatrana = Lili-Marlen
× violacea = Morning Cloud
× Dtps. Lady Jewel = Dtps. Michaela

Name	Parentage	Registrant
RENEE FREED	Show Girl × violacea	Freed 1970

× Ella Freed = Diamond Lil

Name	Parentage	Registrant
RESHANA	Mistinguett × Elizabeth Marshall	Shaffer's 1975
RÊVE ROSE*†‡	Alger × schillerana	V. 1932

× stuartiana = Pollux

Name	Parentage	Registrant
RHAPSODY‡	Princess Grace × lueddemanniana	Markell 1966

× lueddemanniana = Shalimar

Name	Parentage	Registrant
R. H. MONTGOMERY†‡	Doris × Gilles Gratiot	Jordahn 1950

× Elinor Shaffer = White Virgin

Name	Parentage	Registrant
RHODA FREDRICKS	Ann Marie Beard × Pink Formal	Freed 1973
RHONDA DUNN	Golden Sands × Alice Gloria	W. J. Shaban 1973
RICHARD KIMBREL	Susan Merkel × Elinor Shaffer	Bachner 1973 (Kuhn)
RICHARD SHAFFER‡	Ramona × Elinor Shaffer	Shaffer's 1964

× Angela Dumas = Eureka Canyon
× Barcelona = Robert Stephan
× Bonanza = White Halo
× Cast Iron Monarch = Tropical Knight
× Doris = Granada
× Hermosa = Seville
× Keith Shaffer = Mem. Jonathan Williams

Name	Parentage	Registrant
RIGBY	Jimmy Mize × Evening Rose	Beard 1975
rimestadiana*† (see *amabilis**†‡)	species	
RISING SUN	Susan Merkel × lueddemanniana	Beard 1969

× Barbara Moler = Edith Scoville
× Ruby Lips = Ann Beal
× Spica = Spotted Sun
× Suemid = Nymph
× Yellow Lip = Gyrose

Name	Parentage	Registrant
RISQUE	Satin Rouge × Pink Puff	Rod McLellan Co. 1973
RITZY	Barbara Kirch × amboinensis	Lorenzen 1972
ROBBIE TURNER	Our Love Affair × violacea	R. C. Turner 1975
ROBBIE VANAMAN	Suemid × Fiery Girl	Beard 1972

× Red Eye = Kathleen Flaherty

Name	Parentage	Registrant
ROBERT GREEN	Cathrine Pillsbury × Fairway Park	Rod McLellan Co. 1973
ROBERT PIGORS	Salamonca × Edythe Wood	Hausermann 1969

× fuscata = Northwoods
× violacea = Powdery Rose

Name	Parentage	Registrant
ROBERT STEPHAN	Richard Shaffer × Barcelona	Shaffer's 1973

ROBERT W. MILLER‡ — **lindenii × sanderana** — **John H. Miller 1960**
- × Eldora = Linesides

ROBIN‡ — **Pink Vision × Ramona** — **Stella Mizuta 1963**
- × fuscata = Dew Drops
- × mariae = Terry Teruko Robertson

ROBIN FLOYD — **Mem. William Shaban × equestris** — **W. J. Shaban 1974**

ROBYN STONE — **Cover Girl × Doreen** — **Nevins 1967**
- × Karen Ann McFarlane = Cairns Centenary
- × Mad Hatter = Karen Ann McFarlane

RODCO'S LADY — **Redfan × Mildred Karleen** — **Rod McLellan Co. 1971**
- × Morzine = Lady Morzine

ROJA — **Ondine × Dorothy Miller** — **Shaffer's 1973**

ROMANCE — **Sourire × Lipperose** — **Pff. V. & L. 1974**

ROMANTIC — **Zaguett × Redfan** — **Pff. V. & L. 1974**

RONALD PRAIRIE — **Quality Belle × Scotti Maguire** — **Beard 1972**
- × Utopia = Helen Webb

RONNIE HOLLYMAN — **Cindy Brandt × Utopia** — **Beard 1974**

RONNIE WILSON — **Dr. Henry O. Eversole × Rêve Rose** — **J. J. Wilson 1956**
- × Star of Rio = Pink Frost

ROSA BONHEUR — **Lipperose × Henriette Lecoufle** — **Pff. V. & L. 1975**

ROSA ICE — **Lipperose × Pink Ice** — **Hans Koch 1974**

ROSA KARLEEN — **Rosamont × Mildred Karleen** — **Frese 1975**

ROSA LEE PITTMAN — **Gertrude Homsher × fasciata** — **Beard 1973**

ROSALIND‡ — **Rosy Charm × Radiant Glow** — **McCoy 1965**
- × Lipperose = Tiffany
- × Mistinguett = Kathleen Voelker
- × Samba = Mazel
- × Zada = Kosher Pink

ROSAMONT‡ — **R. H. Montgomery × equestris** — **Vaughn 1962**
- × Mildred Karleen = Rosa Karleen

rosea*† (see *equestris*†‡*) — **species**

ROSE-BOWL — **Raritan × sanderana** — **Bean 1957**
- × San Songer = Oneohone

ROSEGAY — **Zada × Veitchiana** — **Hausermann 1971**

ROSELLE†‡ — **Elisabethae × equestris** — **Atherton 1942**
- × Mad Hatter = Rosy Hat
- × Queen Emma = Tateyama

ROSEMARIE LINDSAY — **Dorisellita × Shaffer's Pinkie** — **Hausermann 1974**

ROSEMARY SHAFFER — **Betty Conroy × Terri Cook** — **Shaffer's 1975**

ROSENROT — **Lipperose × Aalsmeer Rose** — **Frese 1975**

ROSE OAKS — **Thousand Oaks × Rose Parade** — **Millington 1971**

ROSE OF BURGUNDY — **Doris × fasciata** — **W. W. G. Moir 1965**
- × gigantea = Burgutea

ROSE PARADE‡ — **Doris × sanderana** — **Bean 1957**
- × Bronze King = Red Gem
- × Mistinguett = Pink Imp
- × Nimbus = Polly
- × stuartiana = Mercy Drilon
- × Thousand Oaks = Rose Oaks

ROSE PETAL — **Ann Lovelace × violacea** — **Dobkin 1971**

ROSE QUARTZ RIDGE — **Zadian × Polar Bear** — **Beall 1975**

ROSERA — **Jane Almquist × Doris** — **Shaffer's 1973**

ROSETTA WITTORF — **Pin Up Girl × Shari** — **R. K. Mizuta 1973 (S. Kagawa)**

ROSIE CLOUSE — **gigantea × mannii** — **Fort Caroline 1971 (Wallbrunn)**

ROSWELL‡ — **Ruby Wells × Aalsmeer Rose** — **Shaffer's 1960**

× Mistinguett = Beaugency
× Norman Peterson = Pleased Pink
× Satin Rouge = Roswell Rouge
× Texas Pink = Texas Rose
× Zada = Zawell

ROSWELL ROUGE — **Roswell × Satin Rouge** — **Carlson 1973**

ROSY CHARM‡ — **Hermione × Pink Wave** — **E. Iwanaga 1962**

× amboinensis = Penang
× Ann Lovelace = Love Charm
× Doris = Speckles
× equestris = Junior Miss
× Lavender Lady = Thoroughbred
× Lipperose = Desire
× lueddemanniana = Hawaiian Maid
× Margaret Mizuta = Marguerite Stone
× stuartiana = Virtue
× Suemid = Peppermint Stick
× sumatrana = Queen of Hearts
× violacea = Tahan
× Dor. pulcherrima = Dtps. Utopia

ROSY HAT — **Roselle × Mad Hatter** — **Toyama 1974**

ROSY RIDGE — **Esther Edris × Hedy Maerkl** — **Beall 1975**

ROYAL DIADEM — **Calawaii × Ernst Haussermann** — **Hausermann 1974**

ROYAL PATTERN — **Doris × Fiery** — **A. & M. 1971**

ROYAL PINK — **Lolita × Zada** — **R. K. Mizuta 1975**

ROYAL STRIPE — **David Herbert × Go-Go Girl** — **A. & M. 1975**

ROZELLA — **Zada × Windy City** — **Hausermann 1971**

RUBY DROPS — **Hot Drops × Princess Ruby** — **Frese 1975**

RUBY GEM — **Mahinhin × Ella Freed** — **Osgood 1974**

RUBY LIPS†‡ — **Roselle × Doris** — **McCoy 1955**

× Carolyn Wilkes = Jane Kulka
× Inca Gold = Helen Stauffer
× Lipstick = Freed's Broadway Melody
× Lowana Goldlip = Malibu Gold Lip
× Mad Lips = Hausermann's Hot Lips
× Palette = Qualified
× Queen Emma = Striped Velvet
× Rising Sun = Ann Beal
× Sharon Karleen = Hausermann's Artistry
× Virooncham = Freed's Divine

RUBY LORENZEN — **Satin Rouge × Ann Marie Beard** — **John H. Miller 1974**

RUBY STRIPES — **Harlequin × Fiery** — **Chester Hills 1970 (Small)**

× Diane Rigg = Mem. Irene Mallory
× Ella Freed = Lucky Stripes
× Jimmy Arnold = Joan Gates
× Love Tide = Estella
× Taffy = Alice Shelley
× Dtps. Red Lip = Dtps. Martha Newton

RUBY WELLS†‡ — **Ruby × Bess Wells** — **Shaffer's 1960 (de Jong)**

× Doris Wells = Lippia
× Lippezauber = Zauberwells
× stuartiana = Nimbus

RUBY ZADA‡ — **Zada × Ruby Lips** — **Beard 1965**

× Betty Beard = Haaf
× Bright Stripes = Xray
× Candy Wakasugi = Eden Rock
× Ella Freed = Freed's Curvaceous
× Elportal = Norma Cole
× Gertrude Beard = Jungle King
× Golden Sands = Bob Turner
× Irene van Alstyne = Terry-Beth Ballard
× Jack McQuerry = Jack Haggard
× Jimmy Arnold = Margaret Hardy
× Lois Jansen = Xylophone
× Mad Hatter = Jester
× Mad Lips = Absolum
× Masu Hamacher = Fannie Mae
× Midlip = Lady Ruby
× Painted Princess = Princess Ruby
× Pink Ball = Universe
× Pin Up Girl = Whimsey
× Show Girl = Freed's Angel
× Virooncham = Our Love Affair
× Wendy Beard = Jennifer Beard
× Dtps. Jerry Vande Weghe = Dtps. Grosse Point
× Dtps. Pueblo Jewel = Dtps. Mary Cetalu

RUTH DEAN — **Arcado × Snow Chief** — **R. Dean 1971**
RUTH GEE — **Mrs. J. H. Veitch × Alice Gloria** — **Shaffer's 1973**
RUTH ROESLER‡ — **Pink Dawn × Marmouset** — **E. Iwanaga 1963**
× Anna Tham = Gadis Singapura

RUTH SHABAN — **Golden Sands × Elisa** — **W. J. Shaban 1971**
RUTH STOUT — **Clara Birk × Frances Roberts** — **Beard 1973**
RUTH WALLBRUNN — **Dos Pueblos × sumatrana** — **Wallbrunn 1967**
× Princess Kaiulani = First Light

RYOT — **Texas Pink × Bariana** — **Beard 1973**
SABLE — **White Plains × Long Life** — **Beard 1974**
SAFARI — **Sparkle × Star of Florida** — **Hager 1973**
SAFFRON ELIZANNE — **fasciata × Alice Gloria** — **Terry 1973 (Shaffer's)**

SAINT PETERSBURG — **Margaret Bean × Juanita** — **Fennell 1972 (Small)**
× mariae = Jeannette

SAKURA — **Sunrise × Grace Palm** — **Takemoto 1975**
SALAMONCA‡ — **Wilma Hughes × Ramona** — **Shaffer's 1964**
× mariae = Weimar

SALLY LOWREY†‡ — **Pua Kea × equestris** — **O. Kirsch 1954**

× Cast Iron Monarch	= Freed's Broadway Rhythm	× Cindy Brandt	= Cindy Bothe
		× Suemid	= Linda Moler

SALLY PRICE — **Sri Lanka × Sharon Karleen** — **Fernando 1974**
SAMBA‡ — **Star of Rio × amboinensis** — **Wm. J. Sanders 1963 (Bracey)**

× Aalsmeer Rose	= Tango	× lueddemanniana	= Walter Beville
× Ann Lovelace	= Amreeta	× Malibu Pink	= Sonia Clark
× Best Girl	= Red Sun	× mariae	= Gold Coin
× Brasilia	= Carnival Ball	× Mildred Karleen	= Tempest
× Cher Ann	= Lombard	× Princess Kaiulani	= Princess Samba
× Chieftain	= Mary Fairburn	× Queen Emma	= Silver Piece
× corningiana	= Electra	× Rosalind	= Mazel
× Debbie Wallace	= Freed's Beguiled	× sumatrana	= Summer Samba
× fuscata	= Justine LeBaron	× Sunbeam	= Rainbow Stripes
× gigantea	= Natasha	× Dor. pulcherrima	= Dtps. War Hoop

SAN CARLOS — **Alii × Anne Cavaco** — **W. W. G. Moir 1973**
sanderana*†‡ — **species**

× Ann Lovelace	= Freed's Celebrity	× Norman	= Freed's Dimple
× Best Girl	= Hobe Sound	× Dtps. Mem. Clarence Schubert	= Dtps. Mem. Arthur Freed
× Martha's Gem	= Freed's Debonair		

SAN MARINO†‡ — **Gilles Gratiot × Katherine Siegwart** — **Orchid Research 1946**
× mannii = Golden Marino

SAN SONGER†‡ — **Rêve Rose × Marmouset** — **Songer 1954**
× Rose-Bowl = Oneohone

SAPPHIRE — **Pink Gin × violacea** — **S'pore Orchids 1973**
SARAH PUSEY — **Pinocchio × Summer Monarch** — **Stoddard 1972**
× Sparkle Toe = Carolyn Kraus

SARAH WILDER‡ — **Pink Dawn × Dark Hawaii** — **McCoy 1961**
× Hymen = Hysara

SATIN ROUGE — **Pink Chief × Riley** — **Rod McClellan Co. 1967 (J. F. Hughes)**

× amboinensis	= Dorothy Venéy	× Pink Ice	= Apache
× Ambomanniana	= Dusky Rouge	× Pink Puff	= Risque
× Ann Marie Beard	= Ruby Lorenzen	× Roswell	= Roswell Rouge
× Barbara Beard	= Patti Logan	× sumatrana	= Enchanter
× Callie Flynn	= Culmination	× Zada	= Flor de Mato
× Dorisellita	= Wyn Seaman		

SCHAMOTT — **gigantea × Bridesmaid** — **Shaffer's 1975**

SCHERZO — **Francine × Rapture** — **Pff. V. & L. 1974**

SCHILLAMBO — **schillerana × amboinensis** — **Fredk. L. Thornton 1968**

× cornu-cervi	= Ambersol		

schillerana*†‡ — **species**

× Cassandra	= Palm Coast	× My Fair Lady	= Patty Turner
× Elinor	= Eliana	× Sunrise	= Pink Veil
× Kadirose	= Sheu Shou-Pao Chen	× Ren. Brookie Chandler	= Rnthps. Plum Red

schillerano-stuartiana / **SCHILLERANO-STUARTIANA*** — **schillerana × stuartiana** — **Nat. hyb. / hort.**

× Hymen	= Pagliaccio	× Jessica McDonald	= Towaco

SCHNEEBALL — **Opaline × stuartiana** — **Frese 1975**

SCHNEEWITTCHEN — **Vallehigh × Alice Gloria** — **Hark 1973**

SCHÖNE GLORIA — **Alice Gloria × Schöne von Celle** — **Hans Koch 1974**

SCHÖNE VON CELLE — **Alice Gloria × Elinor Shaffer** — **Wichmann 1969**

× Alice Gloria	= Schöne Gloria	× Vallehigh	= Schöne von Unna

SCHÖNE VON UNNA — **Schöne von Celle × Vallehigh** — **Hans Koch 1974**

SCHOONER — **Alice Gloria × Keith Shaffer** — **J. & S. 1974**

SCHWERTE — **Doris × Mad Hatter** — **Schöttler 1975**

SCOTCH MIST — **Janet Kuhn × cochlearis** — **Beard 1972**

SCOTTI MAGUIRE — **Princess Leta × Susan Merkel** — **Beard 1966**

× Adelaide	= Ixion	× Gertrude Homsher	= Zara Spook
× Daryl Beard	= Jimmy Hall	× Quality Belle	= Ronald Prairie
× Dos Pueblos	= Zachariah	× Utopia	= Yolande Scott
× fasciata	= Autunite	× Wilma Hughes	= John Teoh

SCOTTY — **Erick Hansen × Daryl Beard** — **Orchids unLtd. 1975 (Scott)**

SEA MIST — **Doris × Dos Pueblos** — **Kodama 1965**

× Doreen	= Kurt Nagel	× Juanita	= Debbie Martian
× Ella Freed	= Chang Chao-Tang	× Sigrid	= Toni Seidel
× fuscata	= Kinta Gold		

SENSATION — **Arcadia × Bruce Shaffer** — **Hans Koch 1974**

SERENATA — **Mad Hatter × Frosty Lip** — **Rod McLellan Co. 1973**

SERENITY‡ — **Doris × Thomas Tucker** — **Vaughn 1957**

× Aristocrat	= White Aristocrat	× Vallehigh	= Servalle
× Sharon Karleen	= Pacesetter		

SERENITY BEACH‡ — **Palm Beach × Serenity** — **Beard 1962**

× Hymen	= Honey Gold	× Louis Merkel	= Sincerity

serpentilingua‡ — **species**

× Ascda. Ophelia	= Dvra. Susanne Mary Coutts	× Ren. philippinensis	= Rnthps. Steven Lim
		× V. coerulea	= Vdnps. Frail Fancy
× Ren. matutina	= Rnthps. Heng-yee	× V. tessellata	= Vdnps. Quietude

SERVALLE — Vallehigh × Serenity — Hans Koch 1974
SESAM — Lippezauber × Doris Wells — Hark 1973
SEVENTH HEAVEN — Ministripes × Alice Gloria — J. & S. 1974
SEVILLE — Richard Shaffer × Hermosa — Shaffer's 1972
SHADY LADY — Penang × Lavender Lady — Hager 1974
SHAFFER'S PINKIE — Ondine × Nancy Carlson — Hausermann 1974 (Shaffer's)

× Dorisellita = Rosemarie Lindsay
× Lipperose = DuPage
× Pink Glamor = Red Desire
× Zada = Uvaldo
× Dtps. Mem. Clarence Schubert = Dtps. Elmhurst Coral

SHALIMAR — lueddemanniana × Rhapsody — Dobkin 1974
SHANGRI-LA — Barbara Beard × Naughty Pink — Rod McLellan Co. 1973
SHARI — Doris × Queen Emma — K. Oka 1965 (McCoy)

× Pin Up Girl = Rosetta Wittorf

SHARON KARLEEN†‡ — Sally Lowrey × Thomas Tucker — Karleen 1957

× Gladys Read = Jungle Belle
× Martha = Vero Beach
× Red Lip = Redkar
× Ruby Lips = Hausermann's Artistry
× Serenity = Pacesetter
× Sri Lanka = Sally Price

SHEBA — Tenaya × Florence Thornton — Eureka 1971
SHEER DELIGHT — Mad Lips × Redport — Hausermann 1974
SHELL CANYON — Esther Edris × Durable Pink — Beall 1975
SHELLIE LYNN — Golden Sands × Judith Hausermann — Hausermann 1975
SHEU SHOU-PAO CHEN — schillerana × Kadirose — Hong-Sie Chen 1975 (Chung-Chweng Chen)
SHERI BOHNETT — Capitola × Angela Dumas — Steindorf 1973 (Frank Hughes)
SHERLUCH — Natasha × Ella Freed — Dobkin 1975
SHIGEHARU FUJII — Cher Ann × Mad Lips — Hausermann 1973
SHINONOME — Carnival × Zada — Y. Toyama 1974
SHIRLEY MARIE — Peppermint × Pin Up Girl — W. J. Shaban 1973
SHOULÉ — Doris × Jewel — Shaffer's 1971
SHOW GIRL‡ — Doris × Lipstick — Freed 1964

× amboinensis = Temple Dancer
× Carolyn Grandy = Show Oaks
× Clyde = Snow Rose
× Cover Girl = Glamour Girl
× Ella Freed = Freed's Cherub
× Freed's Broadway Rhythm = Painted Doll Wedding
× Lipstick = Delightful
× Luora = Freed's Adorable
× Mad Hatter = Career Girl
× Phylis-Kay = Freed's Admiration
× Pin Up Girl = Barbara Freed Saltzman
× Redfan = Malibu Lipstick
× Red Lip = Mary Beth Weber
× Ruby Zada = Freed's Angel

SHOW OAKS — Carolyn Grandy × Show Girl — Millington 1973
SHOW PRINCESS — Show Time × Princess of Denmark — Manor Orchids 1974
SHOW TIME — Gladys Read × Linda Mia — Shaffer's 1967

× Princess of Denmark = Show Princess

SHU KING — Viroonchan × Debbie Wallace — Freed 1975
SID — Nina × Spring Showers — McFarlane 1975

× Alice Gloria = Linda Hunter

SIGRID — Juanita × Polar Gull — Frank Hughes 1969

× Doreen = Paul Lippold
× Lipperose = Achat
× Sea Mist = Toni Seidel

SILBERMOND — White Lady × Henriette Lecoufle — Röhl 1974

SILLOUETTE‡ — Juanita × Mildred Karleen — Hager 1966
× Native Girl = Blithe Spirit | × Vercors = Breathless

SILVER PIECE — Samba × Queen Emma — Dobkin 1975
SINCERITY — Serenity Beach × Louis Merkel — A. & M. 1975
SIOUX MAIZE — lueddemanniana × Alice Gloria — Shaffer's 1973
SIROCCO — Tyler Carlson × Spica — Hager 1974
SKI PATROL — Nicol Jean Orear × Elinor Shaffer — Gubler 1973
SMALL WONDER — Swiss Miss × stuartiana — Hager 1975
SMOKE CREEK DESERT — Mistinguett × Nemesio Mendiola — Shaffer's 1972
SNOWBIRD†‡ — Doris × Atala — McCoy 1955
× Mahinhin = Redbird

SNOW CHIEF — Fenton Davis Avant × Big Chief — Weeki Wachee 1965
× Arcado = Ruth Dean | × fasciata = Goldie

SNOW CLOUD‡ — Arcadia × Joanna Magale — Rivermont 1963
× Dazzler = Dazzling Snowcloud

SNOWDRIFT — Gertrude Beard × micholitzii — John H. Miller 1972
SNOWFALL — Princess Grace × micholitzii — John H. Miller 1974
SNOW FLOWER — Wilma Hughes × Dos Pueblos — Rod McLellan Co. 1971
SNOW JOB — Luora × Muriel Turner — Hager 1975
SNOW KING — Margaret J. Degenhardt × Joanna Magale — Crestwood 1973
SNOW LADY — Gladys Read × Keith Shaffer — Shaffer's 1975
SNOW MAIDEN — Margaret Bean × Ice Palace — Rod McLellan Co. 1971
SNOW MONARCH — Summit Snow × Cast Iron Monarch — Casa Luna 1973
SNOW ROSE — Show Girl × Clyde — Voelker 1972
SNOW RUBY — Redfan × Frosty Lip — Rod McLellan Co. 1973
SNOW WHITE‡ — Winged Victory × Barbara Kirch — Lorenzen 1964
× Dos Pueblos = Classic | × Elinor Shaffer = June Bride

SONIA CLARK — Malibu Pink × Samba — Dobkin 1975
SONJA — Elinor Shaffer × Wilma Hughes — J. F. Hughes 1968
× Alice Gloria = Pepperdine University | × Kauai Monarch = Mimi Coertze
× Capitola = Ed Lista | × lueddemanniana = Freed's Lucky Star
× Cast Iron Monarch = Patricia Neal | × Madrid = Betsy Rue
× Dos-Ambo = Freed's Dignitary | × Norman Peterson = Freed's Pride
× gigantea = Freed's Amigo | × Princess of Denmark = Loren Bohnett
× Gladys Read = Amnuey Porn | × Ramona = Madalene Fobert
× Kauai = Giatgong | × violacea = Freed's Coquette

SONNET GLORY — Apollo × Alice Gloria — Jesurún 1974 (Correa)

SONOMA — Dorisellita × Zada — Shaffer's 1974
SOURIRE — Henriette Lecoufle × Mistinguett — Pff. V. & L. 1970
× Barbara Beard = Abondance | × Dtps. Malaysian Beauty = Dtps. Malasou
× Estrellita = Turkish Delight | × Dor. pulcherrima = Dtps. Shirley Janes
× Lipperose = Romance

SOUTH COAST — Nedra × amboinensis — Hager 1974
SOUTH PACIFIC — Hanalei × Hollywood — W. W. G. Moir 1963
× Pink Sunrise = Plum Blossom

SPARKLE‡ — Judy Karleen × Ruby Lips — Hager 1960
× equestris = Wee One | × Star of Florida = Safari
× Mardi Gras = Radiant Impact

SPARKLE TOE	**Sparkle × Angel Toe**		**Beard 1965**
× Sarah Pusey	= Carolyn Kraus		
SPECKLES	**Rosy Charm × Doris**		**Kirch 1975**
SPENGE	**Linda Schumpert × amboinensis**		**Juergens 1974**
			(Originator unknown)
SPICA (syn. Yardstick)	**fasciata × lueddemanniana**		**Osgood 1969**
			(Kuhn)

× amboinensis	= Allspice	× Lois Jansen	= Cathy Owens
× Daryl Beard	= Nancy Lockhart	× Nedra	= Penny Clark
× Donnie Brandt	= Barbara Moler	× Palette	= Kitty Taylor
× Doris	= Nadine	× Quality Belle	= Dottie Bucheck
× Gertrude Beard	= Joan Hall	× Rising Sun	= Spotted Sun
× Gertrude Homsher	= Betty Sistrunk	× Suemid	= Daryl Lockhart
× Helen Miller	= Evelyn Weaver	× Tyler Carlson	= Sirocco
× Hermosa	= Bobbie Gaye Lista	× Dtps. Red Coral	= Dtps. Chiquita

SPICE ISLANDS‡	**Mrs. J. H. Veitch × Dos Pueblos**		**Wallbrunn 1963**
× Dos Pueblos	= Angela Angelidis	× Kay Star	= Grace Pierce
SPINNER	**Darleen × Hugo Freed**		**Shaffer's 1975**
SPIRIT OF SEVENTYSIX	**Big Chief × Boynton**		**A. & M. 1972**
SPITFIRE‡	**Margaret Bean × Roselle**		**Rod McLellan Co. 1960**
× Progress	= Progress Maid	× Redfan	= Billet-doux
SPLENDEUR	**Alice Gloria × Henriette Lecoufle**		**Pff. V. & L. 1974**
SPOTS OF GOLD	**Boynton × fasciata**		**A. & M. 1975**
SPOTTED MOON	**Gertrude Beard × lueddemanniana**		**Beard 1969**
× Pin Up Girl	= Carolyn Wilkes		
SPOTTED SUN	**Rising Sun × Spica**		**Beard 1975**
SPRING CHIEF	**Springtime × Chieftain**		**A. & M. 1975**
× Susan Merkel	= Judith Merkel		
SPRING FEVER	**Alice Gloria × Christopher Lynn**		**J. & S. 1975**
SPRINGFIELD	**Charles Shaffer × Theresa Hausermann**		**Hausermann 1973**
SPRING RAIN	**maculata × violacea**		**Hager 1974**
SPRING SHOWERS‡	**Doreen × Doris**		**Kodama 1965**
× Nina	= Sid	× Ren. Brookie Chandler	= Rnthps. Joan Nevins
SPRINGTIME†‡	**Summer Cloud × Doris**		**A. & M. 1954**
× Chieftain	= Spring Chief		
SPRING VALLEY	**Madrid × Lachésis**		**Limberlost 1972**
SRI LANKA	**Dos Pueblos × Margaret Bean**		**Fernando 1974**
			(H. E. Perera)
× Sharon Karleen	= Sally Price		
SRI REJEKI	**Elaine-Liem × Professor Asmino**		**Kolopaking 1975**
STAATSBAD SALZUFLEN	**Lipperose × lueddemanniana**		**Bernhart 1974**
STAR BRIGHT	**Penang × Star of Florida**		**Hager 1974**
STARFAS	**Starfire × fasciata**		
STARFIRE‡	**Eglantine × Star of Sao Paulo**		
× fasciata	= Starfas		
STAR LIP	**Star of Diamond Head × Chuck's Red Lip**		**Hans Koch 1974**
STAR OF CAMAY	**Star of Rio × violacea**		**Dobkin 1971**

STAR OF DIAMOND HEAD — **Grace Palm × lueddemanniana** — **McCoy 1961**

× Chuck's Red Lip = Star Lip
× Doris Wells = Dorisstar
× lueddemanniana = Kolibri
× Vallehigh = Andrea

STAR OF FLORIDA — **Princess Kaiulani × Ambotrana** — **Fredk. L. Thornton 1967**

× Clyde = Carioca
× Dos-Ambo = Mystic Land
× gigantea = Mosaic
× New Horizon = Florentine
× Penang = Star Bright
× Princess Kaiulani = Star of Kaiulani
× Sparkle = Safari
× sumatrana = Tropic Sunset
× Tyler Carlson = Summertime
× Zada = Mixed Blessing
× Rnthps. Salute = Rnthps. Florida Salute

STAR OF KAIULANI — **Star of Florida × Princess Kaiulani** — **W. J. Shaban 1973**

STAR OF RIO†‡ — **Bataan × lueddemanniana** — **Morgenstern 1956 (Burgeff)**

× gigantea = Eye Dee
× pantherina = Professor Asmino
× Ronnie Wilson = Pink Frost
× violacea = Star of Camay

STAR OF SANTA CRUZ‡ — **Mem. Nasu Tomoguchi × lueddemanniana** — **Shaffer 1959**

× mariae = Mischief
× sumatrana = Destiny

STELLULAR — **sumatrana × Doris** — **Shaffer's 1974**

STEMSHORN — **Mad Hatter × Renate Frese** — **Lemförder Orch. 1975**

STEPHEN DOUGLAS — **Christopher Lynn × Jiminy Cricket** — **J. & S. 1974**

STERNSTAUB — **Arcadia × lueddemanniana** — **Hans Koch 1974**

STERNTALER — **Cadifa × fasciata** — **Röhl 1975**

STRAWBERRY MEADOWS — **Mistinguett × Hawaiian Welcome** — **Beall 1974**

× Esther Edris = Wild Rose Ridge

STREAKER — **Mad Lips × Pin Up Girl** — **Rod McLellan Co. 1974**

STRIPED VELVET — **Queen Emma × Ruby Lips** — **Dobkin 1974**

stuartiana*†‡ — **species**

× Dolores = Cirrus
× Golden Sands = Butterball
× Mildred Karleen = Stuart Karleen
× Opaline = Schneeball
× Renate Frese = Rauhreif
× Rêve Rose = Pollux
× Rose Parade = Mercy Drilon
× Rosy Charm = Virtue
× Ruby Wells = Nimbus
× sumatrana = Susanti
× Swiss Miss = Small Wonder
× Vallehigh = Vallestuart
× Ascda. Meda Arnold = Dvra. Ella Freed

STUARTIANO-MANNII — **mannii × stuartiana** — **Veitch 1898**

× Alice Gloria = Dan Dickey

STUART KARLEEN — **stuartiana × Mildred Karleen** — **Hager 1974**

SUEMID‡ — **Susan Merkel × Elwyn Middleton** — **Beard 1965**

× fasciata = Yellow Warbler
× Fiery = Bert Shelley
× Fiery Girl = Robbie Vanaman
× Jimmy Mize = Jim Sue
× Lois Jansen = Carter Shenk
× Mad Hatter = Opal Mountain
× Redfan = Eva Lou
× Rising Sun = Nymph
× Rosy Charm = Peppermint Stick
× Sally Lowrey = Linda Moler
× Spica = Daryl Lockhart
× Dtps. Red Lip = Dtps. Solitude

SUGAR 'N SPICE — **Fiery × Pacesetter** — **Lorenzen 1972**

× Ann Hatter = Norma Marion

SULACEOUS — **sumatrana × violacea** — **Fort Caroline 1975 (Wallbrunn)**

SULAWESI — **Princess Kaiulani × fimbriata** — **Fredk. L. Thornton 1967**

× Dos-Ambo = Fantasia

SULIP | **Susan Merkel × Ruby Lips** | **Beard 1966**

× Key Lime = Baalist

SULOCHANA | **Kauai × Best Girl** | **Kanniah 1967 (Chow Yee Wah)**

× Aranda Queen of Purples = Trev. Wong Sew Lan

SUMA CHIEF | **Wilma Hughes × sumatrana** | **Rod McLellan Co. 1973**

SUMARIE | **Ann Marie Beard × sumatrana** | **Bachner 1974**

sumatrana*†‡ | **species**

× Alice Gloria = Annette Wichmann
× Ann Marie Beard = Sumarie
× Aristocrat = Aristrana
× Ballerina = Leprechaun
× Best Girl = Crusader
× Cathrine Pillsbury = Carousel
× corningiana = Double Eagle
× cornu-cervi = Tiger Cub
× Daryl Beard = Vacation
× Doris = Stellular
× Dorisellita = Conflagration
× fasciata = Kathy Kornahrens
× Federal Monarch = Fascination
× Golden Sands = Barbara Bohmer
× Ivy Merkel = Fatima
× Joseph Hampton = Katherine Kimbrel
× Lady Doreen = Mem. Julian Aherrera
× Luedde-violacea = Mayaimi
× micholitzii = Sumitz
× Natasha = Debonair
× Painted Desert = Desert Glow
× Renate Frese = Lili-Marlen
× Rosy Charm = Queen of Hearts
× Samba = Summer Samba
× Satin Rouge = Enchanter
× Star of Florida = Tropic Sunset
× Star of Santa Cruz = Destiny
× stuartiana = Susanti
× Susan Merkel = Jacqueline Bassetta
× Thousand Oaks = Patricia Oaks
× Tyler Carlson = Tyler's Travels
× violacea = Sulaceous
× Wilma Hughes = Suma Chief
× Zada = Clarence Russell
× Dtps. Herman Pigors = Dtps. Beverly Hills

SUMITZ | **sumatrana × micholitzii** | **Wallbrunn 1973**

SUMMER MONARCH†‡ | **Cast Iron Monarch × Summer Cloud** | **J. & S. 1950 (Kwr.)**

× Pinocchio = Sarah Pusey

SUMMER SAMBA | **sumatrana × Samba** | **Hager 1973**

SUMMER SUN | **fuscata × Alice Gloria** | **Shaffer's 1973**

SUMMERTIME | **Tyler Carlson × Star of Florida** | **Hager 1973**

SUMMIT SNOW†‡ | **Confirmation × Doris** | **Lager 1950**

× Ann Lovelace = Frosty Pink
× Cast Iron Monarch = Snow Monarch

SUNBEAM‡ | **Gigi × Sunrise** | **McCoy 1963**

× My Fair Lady = Eloquence
× lueddemanniana = Amigo
× Samba = Rainbow Stripes
× Zada = Cleopatra

SUN KING | **Boynton × Hymen** | **A. & M. 1975**

SUNNY | **serpentilingua × denevei** | **Mrs. Gracia Lewis 1964**

(Also described as a nat. hyb. *Phal.* × *thorntonii* in 1966. Future registered hybrids from either will be listed under Sunny.)

× laycockii = Lara Ay-Lan

SUNRISE†‡ | **Lively Susan × Roselle** | **McCoy 1956**

× Doris = Cherry Pink
× Golden Glow = Misty Pink
× Grace Palm = Sakura
× Pink Veil = Pink Supreme
× schillerana = Pink Veil

SUNSET GLOW‡ | **Hymen × Gloriosa** | **Beard 1962**

× Doris = Torch Song
× Gloriosa = Dabbled

SUNSHINE PINK | **Hawaiian Sunshine × Zada** | **Richella 1975**

SUN SPOTS | **Doris × fuscata** | **A. & M. 1973**

SUSAN MERKEL‡ — **Chieftain × Palm Beach** — **A. & M. 1960**

× Alice Gloria = Lorraine Thornton
× Boynton = Mae Carper
× Elinor Shaffer = Richard Kimbrel
× Louis Merkel = Thelma Weaver
× Mrs. J. H. Veitch = Moon River
× Palm Beach = Angel Wings
× Spring Chief = Judith Merkel
× sumatrana = Jacqueline Bassetta

SUSAN SHERRILL — **Cindy Sue × Daryl Beard** — **Lockhart 1972**
SUSAN SHIPLEY — **Capitola × Keith Shaffer** — **Shaffer's 1973**
SUSANTI — **sumatrana × stuartiana** — **Kolopaking 1975**
SUSIE DARLIN‡ — **Doris × Pink Sunset** — **McCoy 1959**

× My Fair Lady = Dear One

SUZANNE WENZEL — **Cindy Brandt × fasciata** — **Beard 1974**
SWISS MISS — **Mildred Karleen × equestris** — **Hager 1974**

× stuartiana = Small Wonder

SYLVIA TIEDTKE — **Wanda Williams × Alice Gloria** — **Fort Caroline 1973 (Wallbrunn)**

SYSTEM — **Bardor × Bariana** — **Beard 1974**
TAFFY‡ — **Sparkle × Ruby Lips** — **Wilkins 1965 (Beard)**

× Ruby Stripes = Alice Shelley
× Viroonchan = Ella Mae George

TAFFY SUE — **Suemid × Taffy** — **Beard 1969**

× Red Eye = Myth

TAHAN — **Rosy Charm × violacea** — **Hager 1972**
TAHOE BELLE — **Terri Cook × Hermosa** — **Shaffer's 1974**
TAMPICO — **Hello Dolly × Lipperose** — **Schöttler 1975**
TAN CHIN KEAT — **Mem. Loke Sokeen × Kauai** — **Andrew Tan 1973**
TANGO — **Samba × Aalsmeer Rose** — **John H. Miller 1972**
TARGET — **Inspiration × Mildred Karleen** — **Shaffer's 1973**
TATEYAMA — **Roselle × Queen Emma** — **Ozaki 1973 (E. Iwanaga)**

TED REILLY — **Aitkenvale × Aalsmeer Rose** — **Waddell 1972**
TEENA — **Virginia Beard × Barbara Beard** — **Beard 1968**

× Beatie Greenly = Teresa Lykins
× Redfan = Molineuf

TEMPEST — **Samba × Mildred Karleen** — **Dobkin 1974**
TEMPLE CLOUD — **Opaline × Keith Shaffer** — **Andrew Orchids 1974**
TEMPLE DANCER — **Show Girl × amboinensis** — **John H. Miller 1974**
TENAYA — **Hollywood × Margaret Bean** — **Rod McLellan Co. 1960**

× Florence Thornton = Sheba
× fuscata = Golden Sunset

TEOH PHAIK KHUAN — **Jack McQuerry × Lois Jansen** — **Beard 1974**
TERDOREEN — **Terri Cook × Doreen** — **M. J. Bates 1973**

× Norman Peterson = Lena Bates

TERESA LYKINS — **Teena × Beatie Greenly** — **Beard 1972**
TERNATE PRINCESS — **Fairway Park × White Gull** — **Hausermann 1974**
TERRICATA — **Terri Cook × Lucata** — **Fort Caroline 1973**
TERRI COOK‡ — **Doris × Ramona** — **Spencer 1962 (Daniel M. Hill)**

× Alice Gloria = Ivy Armour
× Betty Conroy = Rosemary Shaffer
× Cindy Brandt = Adelaide
× Doreen = Terdoreen
× Elinor Shaffer = Lillie Wooldridge
× Fiery = Dipang Ruby Lips
× Gemini = Billie Pickell
× gigantea = Mem. Jim Knowles
× Goleta = Margaret Harrison
× Hermosa = Tahoe Belle

TERRI COOK‡ *(continued)*

× Joseph Hampton = Mimi Starke
× Kauai = Veronica
× lindenii = Prissy
× Lucata = Terricata
× Mad Hatter = Debbie Wallace
× Margaret Bean = Margaret Cook
× Pasadena = John
× White Falcon = Parker
× White Sails = Nan Knox
× Ren. Brookie Chandler = Rnthps. Terri Gem

TERRY-BETH BALLARD — **Irene van Alstyne × Ruby Zada** — **Beard 1972**

TERRY TERUKO ROBERTSON — **Robin × mariae** — **R. K. Mizuta 1972**

TEXAS PINK‡ — **Doris × Pink Birthday** — **Small 1961**

× Bariana = Ryot
× Frances Roberts = Helen Farlow
× Hedy Maerkl = Florence Kroeck
× Mistinguett = Dainty Girl
× Roswell = Texas Rose

TEXAS PRIDE — **gigantea × Texas Star** — **Dobkin 1975**

TEXAS ROSE — **Roswell × Texas Pink** — **Wallbrunn 1971**

× Fiery = Flagler

TEXAS STAR‡ — **Evening Star × lueddemanniana** — **H. Lawrence 1958 (Rivermont)**

× gigantea = Texas Pride
× mariae = Bold Adventure

THEA — **Mem. William Shaban × Princess Grace** — **W. J. Shaban 1973**

THELMA WEAVER — **Louis Merkel × Susan Merkel** — **A. & M. 1975**

THEODOSIA GIBSON — **Barbara Beard × Ann Marie Beard** — **Beard 1969**

× Frances Roberts = Quarterly

THERESA ANN — **Grace Palm × Island Sunshine** — **Hausermann 1971**

× Mad Lips = Christopher Winkelmann

THERESA HAUSERMANN‡ — **Princess Grace × Goleta** — **Hausermann 1966**

× Bruce Shaffer = Joyce White
× Charles Shaffer = Springfield
× Cher Ann = Jole
× Grace Palm = Adrian Hausermann
× Keith Shaffer = Diana Hausermann
× Miami Maid = Ingrid Hausermann

THERESA HIRSCH — **Best Girl × Denise Richardson** — **A. & M. 1975**

THERESE FRACKOWIAK‡ — **Doris × violacea** — **Frackowiak 1961**

× Jimmy Arnold = Jimmy

THINK PINK — **Jubilee × violacea** — **Hager 1971**

THORDALE‡ — **Margaret J. Degenhardt × Serenity** — **Thornton's 1962**

× Alice Gloria = Glory Dale

THORNHILL — **Keith Shaffer × Zada** — **Baitson 1973**

thorntonii (see grex *Phal.* Sunny) — **serpentilingua × denevei** — **Nat. hyb. 1966** / **Mrs. Gracia Lewis 1964**

(Registered hybrids from either *thorntonii* or Sunny will be listed under Sunny).

THOROUGHBRED — **Rosy Charm × Lavender Lady** — **Hager 1974**

THOUSAND OAKS‡ — **Dorleta × Ramona** — **Millington 1969**

× Mildred Karleen = Karleen Oaks
× Rose Parade = Rose Oaks
× sumatrana = Patricia Oaks
× violacea = Violet Oaks

THRILL — **Ministripes × Percy Porter** — **J. & S. 1974**

TIFFANY — **Rosalind × Lipperose** — **Schöttler 1975**

TIGER CUB — **cornu-cervi × sumatrana** — **Wallbrunn 1972**

TIGERETTE — **lueddemanniana × mariae** — **Hausermann 1974**

Name	Parentage	Registrant
TIGER ROSE	Overglow × Elizabeth Marshall	Shaffer's 1973
TIGER STRIPE	Overglow × Jewel Lips	Shaffer's 1973
TILLIE	Betty Beard × Melba Burnett	Beard 1975
TIMBO	Bobby Boy × Snowbird	J. & S. 1962
× Ministripes	= Christopher Lynn	
TINKERBELL	Ministripes × Fiery	J. & S. 1975
TOBRUK	Aristocrat × Alice Gloria	Fredk. L. Thornton 1975
TOMI	Queen Emma × Leilehua	Takase 1975 (Tomiyasu)
× Percy Porter	= June Takase	
TONI FEATHERSTONE	Lois Jansen × Jimmy Arnold	Beard 1973
TONY SEIDEL	Sigrid × Sea Mist	Gart. Seidel 1974 (K. Seidel)
TONY CAVACO	Queen Emma × Percy Porter	Osgood 1974
TORCH SONG	Sunset Glow × Doris	A. & M. 1975
TOUCH OF LEMON	Inspiration × lueddemanniana	Peter E. Lista 1973
TOWACO	Schillerano-stuartiana × Jessica McDonald	Rumrill 1973
TOXI	Renate Frese × Peppermint	Frese 1975
TOY CLOWN	Irene Finney × Cher Ann	Hausermann 1975
TREASURE ISLAND	Mrs. J. H. Veitch × Gladys Read	Shaffer's 1966
× Alice Gloria	= Petie Demma	
TRES JOLIE	Best Girl × Mildred Karleen	R. K. Mizuta 1971
TRIALS	Alice Gloria × Judy Karleen	Hager 1969
× Bruce Shaffer	= Quiescence	
TROPICAL KNIGHT	Richard Shaffer × Cast Iron Monarch	E. F. Patterson 1973
TROPICANA	Star of Sao Paulo × sanderana	Vaughn 1963
× Zada	= Donna Lou Askew	
TROPIC LIGHTNING	lueddemanniana × Ambodoris	J. T. Carlson 1975
TROPIC SNOW	Keith Shaffer × Fiery	J. & S. 1974
TROPIC SUNSET	Star of Florida × sumatrana	Hager 1974
TRUDY	Louis Merkel × Fiery	Lockhart 1972
TULIP TIME	Roseglow × Aalsmeer Rose	John H. Miller 1970
× Phylis-Kay	= Darlene Moore	
TURKISH DELIGHT	Estrellita × Sourire	Andrew Orchids 1974
TWENTY GRAND	Doris × corningiana	Dobkin 1975
TWIN CITIES	Irene van Alstyne × Jack McQuerry	Beard 1975
TWO GRAND	Barbara Beard × Donnie Brandt	Beard 1969
× Yankee Town	= Juvenile	
TYLER	Gladys Read × fasciata	Carlson 1975
TYLER CARLSON	Gladys Read × lueddemanniana	Shaffer's 1965
× lueddemanniana	= Betsy Turner	
× mariae	= Golden Pixie	
× Spica	= Sirocco	
× Star of Florida	= Summertime	
× sumatrana	= Tyler's Travels	
× violacea	= Early Spring	
TYLER'S TRAVELS	Tyler Carlson × sumatrana	Hager 1975
TYR	Ann Marie Beard × Kathryn Leahey	Beard 1974
UBAN	Palette × Wendy Beard	Beard 1973
UNDINE	Helen Bachman × Helen Kuhn	Beard 1971
UNIQUE	Autumn Glow × Best Girl	Dobkin 1971
UNIVERSE	Pink Ball × Ruby Zada	Beard 1972

UNNA | **R. H. Montgomery × Mistinguett** | **Hans Koch 1970**

× Alice Gloria = Zaubergloria
× Fischers Liebling = Morgensonne
× Lipperose = Unnarose
× Vallehigh = Apfelblüte
× Zada = Westfalica

UNNAROSE | **Lipperose × Unna** | **Hans Koch 1974**

URBAN | **Moon Probe × Wendy Beard** | **Beard 1972**

UTOPIA | **Helen Miller × Cindy Brandt** | **Beard 1969**

× Cindy Brandt = Ronnie Hollyman
× Daryl Beard = Joe Feirer
× fasciata = Boo Kolshak
× Gertrude Beard = Jean Girardeau
× Gertrude Homsher = Ozone
× lueddemanniana = Onyx
× Ronald Prairie = Helen Webb
× Scotti Maguire = Yolande Scott

UVALDO | **Shaffer's Pinkie × Zada** | **Hausermann 1974**

UZBEK | **Betty Beard × Clara Birk** | **Beard 1973**

VACATION | **Daryl Beard × sumatrana** | **Beard 1973**

valentinii / **VALENTINII‡** | **cornu-cervi × violacea** | **Nat. hyb.** / **hort.**

× Pink Ice = Evening Sky

VALERIA | **Alice Bowen × lueddemanniana** | **Beard 1972**

VALFAS‡ | **Valkyrie × fasciata** | **Beard 1964**

× Janet Kuhn = Valjan

VALJAN | **Valfas × Janet Kuhn** | **Beard 1971**

VALLEDOR | **Doris × Vallehigh** | **Hark 1972**

VALLEHIGH | **Dos Pueblos × Grace Palm** | **Vallemar 1959**

× Alice Gloria = Schneewittchen
× Doris = Valledor
× Francisca = Francishigh
× Lipperose = Vallerose
× Long Life = Lippesee
× Mad Hatter = White Spring
× Schöne von Celle = Schöne von Unna
× Serenity = Servalle
× Star of Diamond Head = Andrea
× stuartiana = Vallestuart
× Unna = Apfelblüte

VALLEMAR†‡ | **Grace Palm × Atlanta** | **Vallemar 1957**

× Doreen = Dorval
× Mrs. J. H. Veitch = Peach Parfait

VALLEROSE | **Lipperose × Vallehigh** | **Hark 1972**

VALLESTUART | **Vallehigh × stuartiana** | **Hans Koch 1974**

VALLEY QUEEN | **Royal Veil × Recoverer** | **R. K. Mizuta 1968 (H. Kagawa)**

× Lady Doreen = Queen Doreen

VAMPIRE | **Autumn Glow × Ann Lovelace** | **Dobkin 1971**

VARINA VAUGHN | **gigantea × Winter Jewel** | **Vaughn 1973**

veitchiana / **VEITCHIANA‡** | **equestris × schillerana** | **Nat. hyb.** / **hort.**

× Zada = Rosegay

VENUS | **lindenii × equestris** | **Mitsumi 1923**

× Fairway Park = Modest Beauty
× violacea = Viovenus

VERA HENDERSON | **Daryl Beard × Long Life** | **Beard 1974**

VERA MILLER | **Erick Hansen × Nicol Jean Orear** | **John F. Miller 1973**

VERCORS‡ | **Lachésis × Domremy** | **Pff. V. & L. 1968**

× Sillouette = Breathless
× violacea = Verlacea

VERLACEA | **Vercors × violacea** | **Hager 1971**

VERLE | **Alice Gloria × Hermosa** | **Orchids unLtd. 1975 (Originator unknown)**

× Erick Hansen = Wollochet

VERO BEACH	**Martha × Sharon Karleen**	**Fairburn 1974**
VERONICA	**Kauai × Terri Cook**	**R. Seidel 1973**
VIA LACTEA‡	**Lachésis × Latone**	**Altenburg 1960**

× Apollo = Hoosumi

VICADI	**Cadifa × violacea**	**Röhl 1975**
VICKI SUE LOCKHART	**Ann Marie Beard × Irene van Alstyne**	**Lockhart 1970**

× Dtps. Lake Worth = Dtps. Eva Jones

VILLA PARK	**Charles Shaffer × Miami Maid**	**Hausermann 1973**
VINCE CEFALU	**Gertrude Beard × Mantilla**	**Beard 1973**
VINTAGE WINE	**Redwine × Zada**	**Hager 1974**
VIOGLORIA	**Alice Gloria × violacea**	**Shaffer's 1972**
violacea*†‡	**species**	

× Alice Gloria = Viogloria
× Ann Lovelace = Rose Petal
× Cadifa = Vicadi
× Capitola = Linda Lista
× Cher Ann = Peter Lista
× Chuck's Red Lip = Freed's Choice
× Cindy Brandt = Linda Henry
× Ella Freed = Carmen Coll
× Gladys Read = Vioqueen
× Grace Palm = Malibu Violet
× Hermosa = Laurie Lista
× Hi Boy = Aalia Abdulali
× Hymen = Magic Fire
× Inspiration = Intensity
× Joseph Hampton = Joviola
× Jubilee = Think Pink
× Lady Doreen = Pale Beauty
× Lady Gladys = Lady Violet
× Lipstick = Hausermann's Athena
× Luedde-violacea = George Vasquez
× maculata = Spring Rain
× Mad Lips = Kurt Hausermann
× Mahinhin = Lucifer
× mariae = Violet Charm
× Miami Maid = Hausermann's Aquarius
× Myra Wright = Purple Star
× Nedra = Nedra's Violets
× Norman Peterson = Little Eclipse
× Our Love Affair = Robbie Turner
× Painted Desert = Peachy Keen
× Pasadena = Pasadena Violet
× Pink Gin = Sapphire
× Princess Kaiulani = Princess Violet
× Renate Frese = Morning Cloud
× Robert Pigors = Powdery Rose
× Rosy Charm = Tahan
× Sonja = Freed's Coquette
× Star of Rio = Star of Camay
× sumatrana = Sulaceous
× Thousand Oaks = Violet Oaks
× Tyler Carlson = Early Spring
× Venus = Viovenus
× Vercors = Verlacea
× Wanda Williams = Maxine Heath
× Zada = Bettylee Burke
× Dtps. Christmas = Dtps. Kathy Bove
× Dtps. Jerri Sue King = Dtps. King Camay
× Rnthps. Dana = Rnthps. Thai Silk

VIOLET CHARM	**violacea × mariae**	**Freed 1971**
VIOLET GLOW‡	**Hermione × Susie Darlin**	**E. Iwanaga 1963**

× corningiana = Dots Violet
× Pink Success = Lipanda Glow

VIOLET OAKS	**violacea × Thousand Oaks**	**Millington 1974**
VIOQUEEN	**violacea × Gladys Read**	**Shaffer's 1972**
VIOVENUS	**Venus × violacea**	**C. A. Russell 1973 (Thornton's)**
VIRGINIA ANDERSON	**Barbara Moler × Lois Jansen**	**Beard 1975**
VIRGINIA MacBRIDE	**Dos Pueblos × Joanna Magale**	**W. H. Starke 1973**

× Gladys Read = June Starke

VIROONCHAN	**Snowbird × Queen Emma**	**B'kok Gdng. Supplies 1970 (McCoy)**

× Ann Hatter = Freed's Dazzler
× Debbie Wallace = Shu King
× Ella Freed = Liang Fong King
× Ruby Lips = Freed's Divine
× Ruby Zada = Our Love Affair
× Taffy = Ella Mae George

VIRTUE	**Rosy Charm × stuartiana**	**Hager 1975**
VIRTUOSO	**Elinor Shaffer × Norman Peterson**	**Rod McLellan Co. 1973**
VISTA	**Miami Maid × Norman Peterson**	**Hausermann 1973**
VITRAIL	**Rapture × Anouche**	**Pff. V. & L. 1975**

PHALAENOPSIS

VIVALDI	**Redfan × Karleen's Wendy**		**Pff. V. & L. 1975**
VIXEN	**Mad Hatter × David Herbert**		**Ridgeway 1974**
VOSA	**Elisa × Pink Vogue**		**Shaffer's 1974 (Originator unknown)**
× Doris	= Pink Surrey		
VULGATE	**Intermedia × Gertrude Homsher**		**Beard 1974**
WACKE	**Jean Johnston × Ann Marie Beard**		**Beard 1974**
WALRUS	**Martha Jane × Louis Merkel**		**Dobkin 1971**
WALTER BEVILLE	**Samba × lueddemanniana**		**Dobkin 1971**
WALTER RICHTER	**Heideperle × Mem. Emil Richter**		**Pinkepank 1971**
WANDA WILLIAMS	**lindenii × amboinensis**		**Wallbrunn 1967**
× Alice Gloria	= Sylvia Tiedtke	× violacea	= Maxine Heath
WARD MUNSON	**Betty Conroy × Gladys Read**		**Shaffer's 1975**
WAR PAINT	**Therese Frackowiak × Best Girl**		**Dobkin 1971**
WECADIFA	**Westfalica × Cadifa**		**Hans Koch 1975**
WEE ONE	**Sparkle × equestris**		**Dobkin 1971**
WEIMAR	**Salamonca × mariae**		**Wichmann 1972**
WENDEL GEORGE	**Percy Porter × Aglow**		**Takase 1975**
WENDELL SAWYER	**Lolita × Cape Canaveral**		**R. K. Mizuta 1971 (McCoy)**
× Lolita	= Mistique		
WENDY BEARD‡	**Louise Georgianna × Ruby Lips**		**Beard 1962**
× Aristocrat	= Elportal	× Moon Probe	= Urban
× Cream Puff	= Czarina	× Palette	= Uban
× Jimmy Arnold	= Janice Hall	× Ruby Zada	= Jennifer Beard
× Lois Jansen	= John Girardeau		
WESTFALENROSE	**Westfalica × Lipperose**		**Hans Koch 1975**
WESTFALENZAUBER	**Westfalica × Lippezauber**		**Hans Koch 1975**
WESTFALICA	**Zada × Unna**		**Hans Koch 1974**
× Cadifa	= Wecadifa	× Lippezauber	= Westfalenzauber
× Lipperose	= Westfalenrose		
WESTWOOD	**Edythe Wood × Carl Hausermann**		**Hausermann 1973**
WHIMSEY	**Ruby Zada × Pin Up Girl**		**Rod McLellan Co. 1973**
WHITE ARISTOCRAT	**Serenity × Aristocrat**		**Dobkin 1971**
WHITE BEAR PASS	**Elinor Shaffer × Polar Bear**		**Beall 1974**
WHITE BIRD	**Alice Gloria × Patrick Jon**		**J. & S. 1974**
WHITE CAP	**William Shaffer × Bruce Shaffer**		**Ridgeway 1974**
WHITE CAST	**White Virgin × Cast Iron Monarch**		**Ozaki 1975**
WHITE DIAMOND	**Norman Peterson × Marten Hausermann**		**Hausermann 1975**
WHITE FALCON	**Doreen × Grace Palm**		**Lyle Thomas 1962**
× Terri Cook	= Parker	× White Sails	= Faye White
WHITE GEM	**Kenneth Stromsland × Ernst Haussermann**		**Hausermann 1975**
WHITE GULL	**Orchid Acres × Capitola**		**Beall 1973**
× Fairway Park	= Ternate Princess	× Miami Maid	= Winter Maiden
WHITE HALO	**Bonanza × Richard Shaffer**		**Dobkin 1971**
WHITE KNIGHT	**Snowbird × Cast Iron Monarch**		**McCoy 1965**
× Mahinhin	= Katheryn Malia Osgood		
WHITE LADY	**Arcadia × Grace Palm**		**Röhl 1974**
× Francine	= Cadifa	× lueddemanniana	= Zitronenfalter
× Henriette Lecoufle	= Silbermond		

PHALAENOPSIS

Name	Parentage			Registrant
WHITE MAGIC	**Capitola × Grace Palm**			**Hager 1966**
× Alice Gloria	= Evangeline	× Dtps. Red Coral	= Dtps. Delicado	
WHITE MEDALLION‡	**Doris × White Rhythm**			**E. Iwanaga 1963**
× Belinda	= David Addy Bishop	× Callie Flynn	= Pink Cheeks	
WHITE MONARCH†	**Katherine Siegwart × Cast Iron Monarch**			**Small 1960**
× amboinensis	= Crestwood Ivory			
WHITE PEARL	**Marten Hausermann × Arlene Marie Finney**			**Hausermann 1975**
WHITE PLAINS	**Cindy Brandt × Gertrude Beard**			**Beard 1968**
× Daryl Beard	= Rabbit	× Long Life	= Sable	
× Gertrude Homsher	= Pat Colton			
WHITE RABBIT	**Norman Peterson × Princess Grace**			**Rod McLellan Co. 1974**
WHITE SAILS	**Susan Merkel × Gertrude Beard**			**Beard 1968**
× Alice Jean	= Little Durward	× Terri Cook	= Nan Knox	
× Keith Shaffer	= Mildred White	× White Falcon	= Faye White	
× Miami Maid	= Dora McCarty			
WHITE SPRING	**Mad Hatter × Vallehigh**			**Lemförder Orch. 1975**
WHITE SUMMIT‡	**Princess Grace × Summit Snow**			**Hausermann 1968**
× Gladys Read	= Pat Strothmann			
WHITE VIKING	**Louis Merkel × Bruce Shaffer**			**Dobkin 1971**
WHITE VIRGIN	**R. H. Montgomery × Elinor Shaffer**			**Ozaki 1973 (E. Iwanaga)**
× Cast Iron Monarch	= White Cast	× Queen Emma	= Kuchibeni	
WHITE WATERS	**Quality Belle × Cindy Brandt**			**Beard 1972**
WIDOW PASS	**Esther Edris × Callie Flynn**			**Beall 1975**
WILD ROSE RIDGE	**Esther Edris × Strawberry Meadows**			**Beall 1975**
WILLAMETTE PASS	**Hedy Maerkl × Hawaiian Welcome**			**Beall 1975**
WILLIAM BEARD	**Ann Marie Beard × Redwing**			**Beard 1973**
WILLIAM BOYD‡	**Zada × Aalsmeer Rose**			**Beard 1964**
× Ann Wade	= Oubrey McCarter	× Diamond Pink	= Madame Surin	
WILLIAM SHAFFER	**Elinor Shaffer × Juanita**			**Shaffer's 1964**
× Bruce Shaffer	= White Cap			
WILLOWBROOK‡	**White Summit × Zada**			**Hausermann 1968**
× Dtps. Jerri Sue King	= Dtps. Yale	× Dtps. Mem. Clarence Schubert	= Dtps. Paula Hausermann	
× Dtps. Kenneth Schubert	= Dtps. Kimberly Hausermann			
WILMAGRIA	**Wilma Hughes × Allegria**			**Pff. V. & L. 1974**
WILMA HUGHES‡	**Juanita × Ramona**			**J. F. Hughes 1962**
× Allegria	= Wilmagria	× Gertrude Beard	= Champagne Lady	
× Ambomanniana	= Golden State	× Gladys Read	= Angels Flight	
× Cast Iron Monarch	= Malibu Queen	× Hazel McQuerry	= Kimberly Odum	
× Concorde	= Jumbo	× Linda Mia	= Genevieve Elam	
× Dos Pueblos	= Snow Flower	× Princess Grace	= Princess Wilma	
× Edythe Wood	= Marilyn Freed Browning	× Princess of Denmark	= Orchid Alley	
× fasciata	= Golden Cloud	× Scotti Maguire	= John Teoh	
× fuscata	= Gingo	× sumatrana	= Suma Chief	
WILMA SCHOPPE	**Mad Lips × Percy Porter**			**Hausermann 1974**
WINAFRED HIRSCH	**David Herbert × Doris**			**A. & M. 1975**
WINDY CITY‡	**Zada × Elisa**			**Hausermann 1966**
× Zada	= Rozella			
WINGED VICTORY†‡	**Elisabethae × La Canada**			**Orchid Research 1946**
× Kauai	= Malibu Victory			

Name	Parentage	Registrant
WINIFRED PRAHL†‡	**Harry Prahl × Thomas Tucker**	**H. D. Wright 1957**
× Juanita May	= Dava Alyson Bishop	
WINNIE BOYD	**Ann Marie Beard × Betty Beard**	**Beard 1971**
WINNIE BRECHT	**Daryl Beard × fasciata**	**Lockhart 1974**
WINTER CARNIVAL	**Winter Dawn × Carnival**	**Takase 1975**
WINTER DAWN	**Leilehua × Debbie Martian**	**Takase 1973**
× Carnival	= Winter Carnival	
WINTER JEWEL	**Snowbird × Marguerite W. Stephens**	**Vaughn 1963**
× gigantea	= Varina Vaughn	
WINTER MAIDEN	**Miami Maid × White Gull**	**Hausermann 1973**
WINTERMÄRCHEN	**Japet × Lipperose**	**Herbert Bernhart 1974**
WITCHCRAFT	**Millie Rodrigues × Lady Doreen**	**R. K. Mizuta 1975**
WOLLOCHET	**Verle × Erick Hansen**	**Orchids unLtd. 1975**
WOUNDED KNEE	**Madeline Edling × mannii**	**W. W. Wilson 1975**
WYANDOT	**Frances Roberts × Kathryn Leahey**	**Beard 1973**
WYN SEAMAN	**Dorisellita × Satin Rouge**	**Hager 1974**
XENIA	**Melba Burnett × Evening Rose**	**Beard 1973**
XRAY	**Ruby Zada × Bright Stripes**	**Beard 1972**
XYLOPHONE	**Ruby Zada × Lois Jansen**	**Beard 1973**
XYSTER	**Palette × Cindy Brandt**	**Beard 1973**
YACHT	**Beatie Greenly × Irene van Alstyne**	**Beard 1973**
YANKEE TOWN	**Palm Beach Rouge × Donnie Brandt**	**Beard 1969**
× Two Grand	= Juvenile	
YAP WEE HIONG‡	**Dos Pueblos × schillerana**	**Yap Wee Chee 1964 (Kirch)**
× equestris	= Boutonniere	
YARDSTICK (see Spica)		
YELLOW ACE	**Moon Probe × Cindy Brandt**	**Beard 1972**
YELLOW ALBATROSS	**Edythe Wood × fuscata**	**Hausermann 1975**
YELLOW BIRD	**fasciata × Ramona**	**Shaffer's 1971**
YELLOW ICE	**amboinensis × Joseph Hampton**	**Bachner 1974**
YELLOW JEWEL	**Dos-Ambo × lueddemanniana**	**Lorenzen 1971**
YELLOW LIP	**Aristocrat × Margaret Bean**	**June Fowler 1973 (Vande Weghe)**
× Gertrude Beard	= Earl Stewart	
× Golden Sands	= Green Center	
× Little Girl	= Palm Trail	
× Rising Sun	= Gyrose	
YELLOW WARBLER	**Suemid × fasciata**	**Beard 1974**
YIP	**gigantea × Hermione**	**Dobkin 1975**
YOLANDE SCOTT	**Utopia × Scotti Maguire**	**Beard 1975**
YORK‡	**Grace Palm × Zada**	**Hausermann 1967**
× Dtps. Susan Ann Schubert	= Dtps. Barbara Winkelmann	
YOUNGAUN LIM	**Eng Lan × Fong Cheong Mooi**	**Lim Swee Aun 1975 (Mrs. Lim Swee Aun)**
YOUNGS TOWN	**Redwing × Evening Rose**	**Beard 1974**
YUKON ICE	**Donnie Brandt × Mantilla**	**Beard 1973**
YUMA DESERT	**Ramona × Golden Glow**	**Shaffer's 1971**
YUMAN	**Jimmy Mize × Kathryn Leahey**	**Beard 1973**
ZACHARIAH	**Dos Pueblos × Scotti Maguire**	**Beard 1973**

ZACINE — **Zada × Francine** — **Röhl 1974**

ZADA‡ — **Sam Songer × Doris** — **Fields Orchids 1958**

× amboinensis = Lorraine Kenny
× Bridesmaid = Esther Edris
× Bronze Maiden = Bronze Beauty
× Callie Flynn = Calza
× Carnival = Shinonome
× Denise Richardson = Diane Rigg
× Dorisellita = Sonoma
× Eliana = Joy Jost
× Fiesta = Louisiana Lady
× Fischers Liebling = Liezada
× Francine = Zacine
× Gabi Koch = Gabizada
× Gay Paree = Norm's Fantasy
× gigantea = Marion Fowler
× Gigi = Mrs. Lester McCoy
× Hawaiian Sunshine = Sunshine Pink
× Keith Shaffer = Thornhill
× Lolita = Royal Pink
× Luedde-Wave = Della Bel Krause
× Marmist = Red Lightning
× Mem. Elva Hamric = Catherine Adams
× Mistinguett = Zaguett
× Mount Kaala = Zada Kaala
× Ondine = Zondine
× Oneohone = Malibu Sunset
× Painted Desert = Cinnamon Candy
× Peach Parfait = Raspberry Sherbert
× Pink Ice = Aztec
× Pink Melallion = Zadallion
× Pink Shadow = Diamond Pink
× Pink Wow = Full Pink
× Pollux = Fischers Liebling
× Pottstown = Mexacali Rose
× Queen Emma = Kathy Reyes
× Redwine = Vintage Wine
× Regnier = Karfunkel
× Rosalind = Kosher Pink
× Roswell = Zawell
× Satin Rouge = Flor de Mato
× Shaffer's Pinkie = Uvaldo
× Star of Florida = Mixed Blessing
× sumatrana = Clarence Russell
× Sunbeam = Cleopatra
× Tropicana = Donna Lou Askew
× Unna = Westfalica
× Veitchiana = Rosegay
× violacea = Bettylee Burke
× Windy City = Rozella
× Zada Kaala = Chiye Toyama
× Zadian = Pink Lemonade
× Ascda. Meda Arnold = Dvra. Marjorie Wreford
× Dtps. Adair = Dtps. Bonnie
× Dtps. Coral Gleam = Dtps. Liliane Van Heijningen
× Dtps. Jerri Sue King = Dtps. Bryan Wheeler
× Ren. John Tew = Rnthps. Futura
× Rnthps. Dana = Rnthps. Shalimar

ZADA KAALA — **Zada × Mount Kaala** — **Y. Toyama 1974**

× Zada = Chiye Toyama

ZADALLION — **Pink Melallion × Zada** — **Y. Toyama 1974**

ZADIAN — **lueddemanniana × Zada** — **J. & S. 1967**

× Callie Flynn = Indonesia
× Lavender Lady = Fairyfloss
× Polar Bear = Rose Quartz Ridge
× Zada = Pink Lemonade

ZAGUETT — **Zada × Mistinguett** — **Pff. V. & L. 1971**

× Redfan = Romantic

ZARA SPOOK — **Scotti Maguire × Gertrude Homsher** — **Beard 1972**

ZAUBERGLORIA — **Unna × Alice Gloria** — **Hans Koch 1974**

ZAUBERROSE — **Lipperose × Lippezauber** — **Hark 1972**

(syn. Helma Pinkepank)

× Lipperose = Lipperot
× Lippezauber = Zauberrot
× Lippstadt = Lippeglut

ZAUBERROT — **Lippezauber × Zauberrose** — **Hark 1975**

ZAUBERWELLS — **Lippezauber × Ruby Wells** — **Hark 1975**

ZAWELL — **Zada × Roswell** — **Shaffer's 1971**

× Lipperose = Glenbard

ZEALOUS — **Zondine × Estrellita** — **Shaffer's 1975**

ZENITH — **Kathryn Leahey × Redwing** — **Beard 1975**

ZEPHYR — **Daryl Beard × cochlearis** — **Beard 1971**

ZIRCONIA — **Daryl Beard × Gertrude Beard** — **Beard 1974**

ZITRONENFALTER — **White Lady × lueddemanniana** — **Röhl 1974**

ZONDINE — **Zada × Ondine** — **Shaffer's 1971**

× Elizabeth Marshall = Deputy
× Estrellita = Zealous
× Painted Desert = Desert Sands

PHALAENOPSIS

ZOOM	Best Girl × amboinensis	Dobkin 1971
ZUKI GLORIA	Hoosumi × Alice Gloria	N. Suzuki 1975
ZULU	Mary Wieler × Barbara Beard	Beard 1972
ZWINGLI	Frances Roberts × Jimmy Mize	Beard 1972

PHALANETIA

IRENE	Neof. falcata × Phal. equestris	Sagawa 1975

PHALIELLA

FRECKLES	Phal. mariae × King. philippinensis	Fredk. L. Thornton 1972
NEW HORIZON	Phal. equestris × King. philippinensis	Fredk. L. Thornton 1972
SPECK O'GOLD	Phal. cornu-cervi × King. philippinensis	Fredk. L. Thornton 1972
SUNBURST	Phal. Janet Kuhn × King. philippinensis	Fredk. L. Thornton 1972

PHRAGMIPEDIUM

boissieranum* species
× longifolium = Praying Mantis |

longifolium* species
× boissieranum = Praying Mantis |

PRAYING MANTIS	longifolium × boissieranum	Stewart Inc. 1975

POMATISIA

RUMRILL	Pmcpa. latifolia × Lsa. teretifolia	Rumrill 1973

POMATOCALPA

latifolia species
× Lsa. teretifolia = Pmtsa. Rumrill |

POTINARA

APOCALYPSE	Gordon Siu × Slc. Tropic Flare	Rex Foster's 1973 (Fordyce)
AYANO-MIYA FUMIHITO	Blc. Crown Prince Akihito × Slc. Tropic Dawn	Otaguro 1973
BARBARA FRASER	Diane × Lc. Dee Dee	George Black 1973
BARBARA WICHMANN	Blc. Sylvia Reilly × Slc. Anzac	Wichmann 1972
BAYZAC	Sunset Bay × Slc. Anzac	Ruben 1974
BETTYCAKE	Jo Ann Crouch × Lc. Antonica Fredrick	Fields Orchids 1973
BETTY WATSON	C. bowringiana × Judy Lynn King	Ainsworth 1973 (L. H. Williamson)
BICENTENNIAL	Blc. Piney Patterson × Rebecca Merkel	Hausermann 1975
BILL	Lc. Bob Gore × Medea	Tsukagoshi 1974
BON-FRIAR	Lc. Bonanza × Red Friar	Sierke 1971 (Originator unknown)

POTINARA

Name	Parentage	Registrant
BREEZY DOHLBERG	Glowing Beauty × Lc. Bright Night	Fort Caroline 1973 (Wallbrunn)
BRILLIANT FORTUNE	Fortune Teller × Lc. Brilliant Orange	Rex Foster's 1974
CANYON SANDS	Slc. Fort Caroline × Blc. Fortune	Trymwood 1971
CEEZIE GUEST	Lc. Amber Glow × Glowing Beauty	Fort Caroline 1974 (Wallbrunn)
CHENILLE	Slc. Sunburst × Gordon Siu	Crothers 1971
CHERRY BLOSSOM	Bc. Déesse × Slc. Brandywine	A. G. Tharp 1973 (A. & R.)
CHIMNEY ROCKS	Slc. Brandywine × Tapestry Peak	Beall 1973
CINNAMON STICK	Lc. Charlesworthii × Red Friar	Furrow 1971
CLEO BAY	Sc. Cleopatra × Blc. Norman's Bay	Muse's 1971
CLOWN	Slc. Naomi Kerns × Blc. Malworth	J. & S. 1975
CONGAREE	Dark Eyes × Lc. Little Susie	C. & H. 1973 (E. Iwanaga)
CORAL QUEEN	Soph. coccinea × Gordon Siu	Gauda 1974 (Ilsley)
CRIMSON GLORY	Dark Beam × Slc. Anzac	Altenburg 1971
CUMBERLAND SUNSET	Sunset Bay × Blc. Jane Helton	Ruben 1974
DARK BEAM‡	Creole × Slc. Lindores	Altenburg 1966
× Slc. Anzac	= Crimson Glory	
DARK EYES‡	Lc. Mirabelle × Medea	Zuck 1957
× Lc. Little Susie	= Congaree	
DARLENE	Slc. Radians × Blc. Leila	Voo Doo Orchids 1974 (Originator unknown)
DIANE‡	Red Friar × Lc. Princess Margaret	B. 1955
× Lc. Dee Dee	= Barbara Fraser	× Slc. Meulange = Diane Meulange
DIANE MEULANGE	Slc. Meulange × Diane	Gauda 1974
DOROTHY L. ADAIR	Slc. Comuse × B. digbyana	Fuchs Jr. 1960
× Bc. Mrs. J. Leemann	= Memoria Arthur Armbrister	
EDITH HANCOCK	Slc. Brandywine × Blc. Setting Sun	Hancock 1973
EDWARD ROWOLD	Slc. Rainbow Hill × Blc. Cynde Fujino	Miyamoto 1967
× Lc. Ripple Rock	= Jimi Hendrix	× Slc. Ramona = Florence Honda
EMIKO TOGASHI	Blc. Landscape × Gordon Siu	Haw. Mt. O. 1973 (Miyamoto)
ESPERANZA DELA CRUZ	Slc. Mossiabella × Blc. Oriental Gem	Otaguro 1973
ESTELLE SMITH‡	Jo Ann Crouch × Blc. Mellowglow	Fields Orchids 1967
× Sl. Betty Jean Scott	= Isle of Palms	
ESTHER COSTA	Blc. Jane Helton × Gordon Siu	Miyamoto 1975
EVENING GLOW	Blc. Mem. Crispin Rosales × Slc. Marion Black	Rex Foster's 1973 (Fordyce)
FLORENCE BRADY	Slc. Estella Jewell × Blc. Mem. Crispin Rosales	Fort Caroline 1972
FLORENCE HONDA	Edward Rowold × Slc. Ramona	Otaguro 1975

POTINARA

FLORENCE POWELL‡	**Blc. Xanthea × Slc. Ramona**		**Dane 1940**
× Blc. Primate	= Soraya		
FORTUNE TELLER	**Blc. Xanthette × Slc. Tropic Flare**		**Stewart Inc. 1966**
× Lc. Brilliant Orange	= Brilliant Fortune	× Lc. Carrot Top	= River Range
GLOWING BEAUTY‡	**Blc. Zanturano × Red Friar**		**Rivermont 1960**
× C. Fascelis	= Stella Maris	× Lc. Bright Night	= Breezy Dohlberg
× Lc. Amber Glow	= Ceezie Guest	× Lc. Charlesworthii	= Mem. Kerry Turner
GOLDEN PEAK	**Tapestry Peak × Lc. Golden Passage**		**Beall 1974**
GOLDEN SANDS	**Bc. Déesse × Lemon Tree**		**Stewart Inc. 1975**
GOLD PIECE	**Slc. Emberglow × Blc. Malvern**		**Rod McLellan Co. 1974 (Fordyce)**
GORDON SIU‡	**Slc. Radians × Bc. Hartland**		**Siu 1951**
× Blc. Acapana	= Troublesome Creek	× Epc. Hawaiian Gem	= Roth. Anne
× Blc. Fortune	= Spice Islands	× Lc. Buccaneer	= Lucinda Park
× Blc. Golden Slippers	= Siu Slippers	× Lc. Quadroon	= Vibrant
× Blc. Jane Helton	= Esther Costa	× Lc. Princess Margaret	= Katsumi Wakatake
× Blc. Landscape	= Emiko Togashi	× Slc. Sunburst	= Chenille
× Blc. Norman's Bay	= Norman's Glory	× Slc. Tropic Flare	= Apocalypse
× C. Helene Garcia	= Petite	× Soph. coccinea	= Coral Queen
GRINDAL SHOALS	**Slc. Naomi Kerns × Bc. Hartland**		**C. & H. 1975 (Kirch)**
HALFWAY MOUNTAIN	**Lc. Mem. Albert Heinecke × Tapestry Peak**		**Beall 1975**
HAYSTACK MOUNTAINS	**Blc. Sylvia Reilly × Tapestry Peak**		**Beall 1974**
HEIDI GUBLER	**Blc. Golden Dome × Slc. Vallezac**		**Gubler 1973**
HICEE	**Blc. Malvern × Slc. Ramona**		**Ichijyo 1974**
HIDDEN CHASM	**Hidden Peak × Bc. Reflection Lake**		**Beall 1973**
HIDDEN PEAK	**Sl. Gratrixiae × Bc. Déesse**		**Beall 1966**
× Bc. Reflection Lake	= Hidden Chasm	× Lc. Charlesworthii	= Starmaker
HIDDEN RANGE	**Bc. Déesse × Slc. Lindores**		**Beall 1966**
× Lc. Mem. Albert Heinecke	= Mountaineer Creek		
HUGO PORTO	**Jorge Verboonen × Blc. Norman's Bay**		**Altenburg 1964 (Verboonen)**
× Blc. Osiris	= Palmetto	× Lc. Fort Lauderdale	= Porto Feliz
IRENE BROUARD	**Slc. Rainbow Hill × Blc. Jane Helton**		**Mrs. W. H. Boyd 1971 (Miyamoto)**
ISLE OF PALMS	**Estelle Smith × Sl. Betty Jean Scott**		**Fort Caroline 1975**
JACK WEAVER	**Blc. Molflora × Slc. Anzac**		**Fort Caroline 1972**
JACQUIE AWANA	**Blc. Jane Helton × Slc. Kao Hsiung**		**Otaguro 1975**
JIMI HENDRIX	**Lc. Ripple Rock × Edward Rowold**		**Kyle 1971**
JO ANN CROUCH‡	**Yvonne Pearson × Bc. Hartland**		**Fields Orchids 1961**
× Lc. Antonica Fredrick	= Bettycake	× Lc. Elizabeth Off	= Ronald Pallister
JUDY LYNN KING	**Lc. George Baldwin × Red Friar**		**Lois D. King 1961 (Fields Orchids)**
× C. bowringiana	= Betty Watson		
KATSUMI WAKATAKE	**Lc. Princess Margaret × Gordon Siu**		**Otaguro 1973**
KISKA VOLCANO	**Slc. California Apricot × Tapestry Peak**		**Beall 1975**

POTINARA

Name	Parentage	Registrant
LAFAYETTE NERY	Creole × Blc. Norman's Bay	Altenburg 1968
× Blc. Dark Waters	= Tutomu Suzuki	
LAVA GLOW	Blc. Mellowglow × Red Lava	Trymwood 1973
LEMON TREE	Blc. Jane Helton × Slc. Paprika	Stewart Inc. 1970
× Bc. Déesse	= Golden Sands	
LILLIE ROSE‡	Gordon Siu × Lc. Mem. Albert Heinecke	Wooldridge 1966 (Roy Fields)
× Lc. Toflam	= Mount Peleé	
LIM THENG HIN	Slc. Rainbow Hill × Blc. Parade	Ng & Tan 1956 (Kirch)
× C. Nellie Roberts	= Tun Abdul Razak	
LITTLE SUZIE	B. fragrans × Slc. Anzac	Kubo 1972
LUCINDA PARK	Gordon Siu × Lc. Buccaneer	Bush 1972 (Park)
MANAGUA	Bc. Golden Sunshine × Sl. Psyche	W. W. G. Moir 1973
MARIONETTE	Lc. Mem. Albert Heinecke × Low. Trinket	Stewart Inc. 1973
MARGARET SADOYAMA	Blc. Ruth Witbeck × Slc. Langleyensis	Otaguro 1973
MARIE PALLISTER	Yamockul × Blc. Mem. Roselyn Reisman	Pallister 1974
MEDA PRETTO	Medea × Lc. Enchanted Jungle	N. Suzuki 1972
MEDEA†‡	Blc. Beatrice × Slc. Cleopatra	A. 1946
× Blc. Golden Galleon	= Wanda Mayo	
× C. Nigrella	= Potomac	
× Lc. Bob Gore	= Bill	
× Lc. Enchanted Jungle	= Meda Pretto	
MELISANDE	B. nodosa × Slc. Anzac	Voo Doo Orchids 1974
MEMORIA ARTHUR ARMBRISTER	Dorothy L. Adair × Bc. Mrs. J. Leemann	Ruben 1974
MEMORIA BILL WHITE	Soph. coccinea × Blc. Manatee Gold	Mrs. W. F. White 1975 (William F. White)
MEMORIA GRACE SOKOLOWSKI	Blc. Acapana × Spanish Banks	Repasky 1975 (Beall)
MEMORIA KERRY TURNER	Glowing Beauty × Lc. Charlesworthii	Bishop 1974 (Originator unknown)
MEMORIA SEICHI IWASAKI	Slc. Naomi Kerns × Blc. Waikiki Sunset	Tomita 1971 (Miyamoto)
MENEZAC	Blc. Mene × Slc. Anzac	Ruben 1974
METAL CREEK	Blc. Nacouchee × Slc. Helen Veliz	A. & R. 1975
MOUNTAINEER CREEK	Lc. Mem. Albert Heinecke × Hidden Range	Beall 1973
MOUNT PELEÉ	Lc. Toflam × Lillie Rose	Clark Day Jr. 1973 (Rietkerk)
MOUNT TOIL	Lc. Mariner × Tapestry Peak	Beall 1975
NEVER RED	Slc. East Mona × Red Friar	Rayridge 1975 (F. J. Bergman)
NORMAN'S GLORY	Blc. Norman's Bay × Gordon Siu	Miyamoto 1975
PACIFIC WARRIOR	Blc. Pacific Gold × Slc. Anzac	Roccaforte 1974
PALMETTO	Blc. Osiris × Hugo Porto	J. & S. 1974
PATNA	Bc. Princess Patricia × Slc. Ramona	C. Takeda 1961
× Lc. Bonanza	= Shigeko Takeda	
PAULA MARABELLA	Lc. Carrot Top × Tapestry Peak	Marabella 1974 (Beall)

POTINARA

Name	Parentage	Originator
PERSIAN BAY	Slc. Persian Garden × Blc. Norman's Bay	Glen Brown 1975 (Originator unknown)
PETER HAYNES	Blc. Norman's Bay × Slc. Naomi Kerns	Elroy Haynes 1972 (B. Kodama)
PETITE	C. Helene Garcia × Gordon Siu	J. & S. 1974
PORTO FELIZ	Hugo Porto × Lc. Fort Lauderdale	N. Suzuki 1971
POTOMAC	C. Nigrella × Medea	Kensington 1973
PRECIOUS	Blc. Jane Russell × Slc. Anzac	Ted Green 1975 (Miyamoto)
REBECCA MERKEL	Blc. Lyranda × Slc. Anzac	A. & M. 1969
× Blc. Piney Patterson	= Bicentennial	× Lc. George Baldwin = Red Cardinal
RED CARDINAL	Lc. George Baldwin × Rebecca Merkel	Hausermann 1975
RED DAWN‡	Blc. Dawn Angela × Red Friar	Fields Orchids 1957
× C. Iris	= Shawnee Hills	
RED FRIAR†‡	Blc. The Friar × Slc. Vulcan	B. 1942
× Lc. Bonanza	= Bon-Friar	× Slc. East Mona = Never Red
× Lc. Charlesworthii	= Cinnamon Stick	
RED LAVA‡	Slc. Lindores × Belgravia	Fujio 1961 (Gore)
× Blc. Mellowglow	= Lava Glow	
RIVER RANGE	Lc. Carrot Top × Fortune Teller	Beall 1973
RONALD PALLISTER	Jo Ann Crouch × Lc. Elizabeth Off	Lines 1971
ROSETTE SAVORGNAN	Blc. Momercia × Slc. Anzac	Rod McLellan Co. 1966
× Lc. José Noé	= Verinovel	
ROUGE	Blc. Circus × Slc. Anzac	Rod McLellan Co. 1973
RUBEN'S SUNSET	Sunset Bay × Blc. Acapana	Ruben 1974
RUTH RETTIG	Blc. Marjorie Frey × Slc. Anzac	Wallbrunn 1974
SANTA RITA	Slc. Helen Veliz × Tripoli	A. & R. 1975
SCOTT HOLGUIN	Slc. Helen Veliz × Blc. Norman's Bay	A. & R. 1975
SHAWNEE HILLS	C. Iris × Red Dawn	Robt. Smith 1973
SHIGEKO TAKEDA	Patna × Lc. Bonanza	C. Takeda 1971
SIU SLIPPERS	Blc. Golden Slippers × Gordon Siu	J. & S. 1975
SORAYA	Florence Powell × Blc. Primate	Crothers 1971
SPANISH BANKS	Blc. Jane Helton × Slc. Lindores	Beall 1965
× Blc. Acapana	= Mem. Grace Sokolowski	
SPECIZAC	Bc. Speciosa × Slc. Anzac	Gauda 1973
SPICE ISLANDS	Gordon Siu × Blc. Fortune	Stewart Inc. 1972 (J. Rikel)
SPICEY	Blc. Goldfield × Slc. Anzac	Rod McLellan Co. 1971
STARMAKER	Hidden Peak × Lc. Charlesworthii	Rod McLellan Co. 1974
STELLA MARIS	C. Fascelis × Glowing Beauty	Fort Caroline 1973 (Wallbrunn)
SUNDANCE	Blc. Mellowglow × Soph. coccinea	Stewart Inc. 1973
SUNNY'S FAVORITE	Blc. Mem. Crispin Rosales × Slc. Pearl Spencer	Zeramby 1971 (Spencer)
SUNRAY	Blc. Ruth Witbeck × Sc. Cleopatra	Roccaforte 1973 (Gamble)
SUNSET BAY	Yvonne Pearson × Blc. Jane Helton	Fields Orchids 1968
× Blc. Acapana	= Ruben's Sunset	× Slc. Anzac = Bayzac
× Blc. Jane Helton	= Cumberland Sunset	

POTINARA

SUNSET BUTTE — **Slc. Charlotte K. Hodsdon × Tripoli** — **Beall 1975**
SUSAN WANNER — **Blc. Flo Fleece × Sc. Cleopatra** — **Yocom 1975**
TABO — **Blc. Malvern × Slc. Hermes** — **Robt. Smith 1972 (Ryerson Orchids)**

TAPESTRY PEAK — **Bc. Déesse × Gordon Siu** — **Beall 1966**

× Blc. Sylvia Reilly = Haystack Mountains
× Lc. Carrot Top = Paula Marabella
× Lc. Fires of Spring = Yukon Crossing
× Lc. Golden Passage = Golden Peak
× Lc. Mariner = Mount Toil
× Lc. Mem. Albert Heinecke = Halfway Mountain
× Lc. Western Sunset = Western Peak
× Slc. Brandywine = Chimney Rocks
× Slc. California Apricot = Kiska Volcano

TIGER TEARS — **Low. Spitfire × Blc. Golden Galleon** — **Stewart Inc. 1975**
TREASURE GLOW — **Blc. Golden Spires × Slc. Paprika** — **Rod McLellan Co. 1973 (Fordyce)**

TRIPOLI†‡ — **Blc. Ishbel × Slc. Ramona** — **B. 1943**

× Slc. Charlotte K. Hodsdon = Sunset Butte
× Slc. Helen Veliz = Santa Rita

TROUBLESOME CREEK — **Gordon Siu × Blc. Acapana** — **Beall 1973 (Bracey)**
TUN ABDUL RAZAK — **Lim Theng Hin × C. Nellie Roberts** — **Ng & Tan 1973**
TUTOMU SUZUKI — **Lafayette Nery × Blc. Dark Waters** — **N. Suzuki 1971**
VALLESPIN — **Blc. Mem. Crispin Rosales × Slc. Vallezac** — **Takihashi 1971**
VERINOVEL — **Lc. José Noé × Rosette Savorgnan** — **Rod McLellan Co. 1972**
VIBRANT — **Lc. Quadroon × Gordon Siu** — **J. & S. 1971**
WANDA MAYO — **Medea × Blc. Golden Galleon** — **Stewart Inc. 1972**
WAR DANCE — **Blc. Hazel Dell × Slc. Brandywine** — **Beall 1973**
WELSON GASPARINI — **Belgravia × Lc. Ishtar** — **Wenzel 1967 (Gore)**

× Lc. Bonanza = Yamasee

WESTERN PEAK — **Lc. Western Sunset × Tapestry Peak** — **Beall 1975**
YAMASEE — **Lc. Bonanza × Welson Gasparini** — **C. & H. 1975**
YAMOCKUL — **Slc. Brandywine × Blc. Golden Myth** — **Yamockul 1968 (A. & R.)**

× Blc. Mem. Roselyn Reisman = Marie Pallister

YUKON CROSSING — **Tapestry Peak × Lc. Fires of Spring** — **Beall 1975**
YURIKO HANANOKI — **Blc. Mem. Crispin Rosales × Slc. Anzac** — **Otaguro 1972**

RECCHARA

DOCTOR HARRY ARNOLD — **Smbl. Maunalani × Bc. Cornelius** — **O. Kirsch 1974**
EGLON SCOTT — **Blc. Marjorie Frey × Smbc. Perfection** — **Fort Caroline 1972**
ZAMBOANGA — **Blc. Fortune × Schom. thomsoniana** — **Stewart Inc. 1974**

RENADES

EVA JEAN — **Aër. multiflora × Ren. Tom Thumb** — **Gutierrez 1974**
HONEYMOON — **Aër. odorata × Ren. Tom Thumb** — **Gutierrez 1974**
HOULSTORIA — **Aër. houlletiana × Ren. storiei** — **Bachner 1974 (Redlinger)**
MAHANI — **Ren. storiei × Aër lawrenceae** — **Perlstein 1957 (McCoy)**

× Rhy. retusa = Chew. Ruth Wong
× V. tricolor = Nlra. Wellsian Beauty

RENADES

MEMORIA JOHN DONNELLY	Aër. crassifolia × Ren. coccinea	Muse's 1971 (Donnelly)
RED JEWEL	Aër. lawrenceae × Ren. Brookie Chandler	E. Iwanaga 1961
× Ascda. Meda Arnold	= Rbnra. Kosher Red	
ROSETTE	Ren. Brookie Chandler × Aër. multiflora	Mrs. R. Porlick 1975
SPRING JOY	Ren. Brookie Chandler × Aër. quinquevulnerum	Jack Ching 1972
SUMMER LIGHT	Ren. Brookie Chandler × Aër. odorata	Friend 1973

RENAGLOTTIS

CLARENCE RUSSELL	Ren. monachica × Trgl. fasciata	Fort Caroline 1971

RENANCENTRUM

VORAVUT	Ren. storiei × Asctm. miniatum	Prayoonrat 1974

RENANETIA

SUNRISE	Neof. falcata × Ren. imschootiana	S. Takagi 1967
× Rhy. gigantea	= Hylra. Hueylih Jane	

RENANOPSIS

GORDON SNOOK	Vdps. gigantea × Ren. Brookie Chandler		R. F. Fuchs 1975
HIIAKA	Lena Rowold × Ren. imschootiana		O. Kirsch 1972
LENA ROWOLD†‡	Ren. storiei × Vdps. lissochiloides		O. Kirsch 1948
× Arach. flos-aëris	= Lim. Mandai Majesty	× Rhy. gigantea	= Ynra. Hadrian
× Ren. imschootiana	= Hiiaka	× V. Oriole	= Haw. Harvest Queen
YENCHIT	Ren. coccinea × Vdps. parishii		Chuanyen 1975

RENANSTYLIS

BALLERINA	Ren. imschootiana × Rhy. gigantea	Wilkins 1971 (Redlinger)
FABULOSA	Ren. Brookie Chandler × Rhy. gigantea	R. K. Mizuta 1972
GEISHA	Ren. Kilauea × Rhy. gigantea	Wilkins 1973
GLENEYRIE	Ren. monachica × Rhy. gigantea	Fort Caroline 1971 (Wallbrunn)
QUEEN EMMA	Ren. storiei × Rhy. gigantea	O. Kirsch 1961
× Asctm. curvifolium	= Kom. Thonburi	

RENANTANDA

ANDROMEDA	V. T.M.A. × Ren. coccinea	S'pore Orchids 1975
ANNA KUBYSHKINA	V. Muthiya × Ren. coccinea	Choo Yeok Koon 1972
BANGKAE BEAUTY	V. Charlesworthii × Ren. storiei	Ratanapeanchai 1975
CHANG MIN-TAT	V. lamellata × Ren. histrionica	Thong 1973
COPPERTONE	V. Mem. T. Iwasaki × Ren. storiei	S'pore Orchids 1972
EL TIGRE	Ren. Brookie Chandler × V. tessellata	O. Kirsch 1970
× Ren. storiei	= Hon Kim San	
GOLD NUGGET†‡	Ren. storiei × V. spathulata	R. E. Warne 1947
× Rhv. Blue Angel	= Jnna. Ivan Ang	

RENANTANDA

HARNPONGTHAM	Ren. storiei × V. bensonii	S. Harnpongtham 1974
HERB HAGER	Violet × V. spathulata	Roccaforte 1974 (Hager)
HON KIM SAN	El Tigre × Ren. storiei	Hon San 1973
IOLANI LUAHINE	Ren. Brookie Chandler × V. Iolani	O. Kirsch 1973
ITSUKUSHIMA	Ren. imschootiana × V. James Harding	Ichijyo 1973
KIM ALMAS	Ren. imschootiana × V. cristata	MAJ Orchids 1973 (Ragan)
LEAN YIN	V. Harvest Time × Ren. storiei	Lim Swee Guan 1975 (Chow Yee Wah)
LOH BOON SIEW	V. Mrs. Margaret Meyer × Ren. Brookie Chandler	Ng & Tan 1974 (Ho Kean Keat)
LONGCHEN	Ren. coccinea × V. denisoniana	Vatanamas 1972
LORNA WURTZBURG	V. Chimey Walker × Ren. storiei	Choo Yeok Choon 1972
LYN ANDRADE	Ren. storiei × V. merrillii	Andrade 1950

× Ascda. Meda Arnold = Kgw. Yuthayong Beauty

MAHIOLE	V. limbata × Ren. monachica	O. Kirsch 1975
MANDAI	V. Julia Sideris × Ren. storiei	S'pore Orchids 1973
MEMORIA ARTHUR FREED	Ren. Cheok Thiam Huat × V. coerulea	Freed 1975 (Originator unknown)
ONG JIN KAR	V. Princess Blue × Ren. storiei	Ong Aye Ho 1975 (Loke Luen She)
PATCHAREE	V. Mok Sau Lan × Ren. coccinea	C. Y. Mok 1972
RUMRILL	V. coerulescens × Ren. monachica	Rumrill 1973
SALYAPHONGSE	V. brunnea × Ren. storiei	Salyaphongse 1974
SANGVICHIAN	V. coerulescens × Ren. coccinea	Laddaland 1975 (Pramwuet)
SUNSET STORY	V. Sunset × Ren. storiei	Muse's 1972
TEO BOON HIAN	V. Diane Ogawa × Ren. storiei	Teo Boon Hian 1974
THAILAND	V. brunnea × Ren. coccinea	Silpaprasert 1975 (Chaisomboon)
TOWACO	V. cristata × Ren. monachica	Rumrill 1974
TUMIRA SKINNER	Ren. storiei × V. James Toogood	Skinner 1971 (Teoline)
VIOLET	Ren. storiei × V. amoena	Kodama 1954

× Rhv. Blue Angel = Jnna. Jetstar | × V. spathulata = Herb Hager

WONG YIN FON	V. sumatrana × Ren. philippinensis	Wong Hi Yet 1971 (Wong Yin Khoon)
WUNNA JAIDES	V. Rothschildiana × Ren. coccinea	N. P. R. Thong 1974

RENANTHERA

ALEX HAWKES	coccinea × storiei	W. W. G. Moir 1954 (Woodlawn)

× storiei = George Radcliffe

BANGKOK FLAME	coccinea × Red Feathers	Laksanaphuk 1973
BROOKIE CHANDLER†‡	monachica × storiei	J. P. Russell 1950

× Aërdns. Mandai	= Lymra. Frankfurt Fireworks	× Arach. cathcartii	= Arnth. Sauleda
× Aër. multiflora	= Rnds. Rosette	× Arnth. Lilleput	= Arnth. Lillibrook
× Aër. quinquevulnerum	= Rnds. Spring Joy	× Ascda. Red Gem	= Kgw. Shumoon Abdulali
× Aër. odorata	= Rnds. Summer Light	× Phal. Alice Gloria	= Rnthps. Renee
		× Phal. Aristocrat	= Rnthps. Glory

BROOKIE CHANDLER†‡ *(continued)*

× Phal. Barbara Kay = Rnthps. Mem. Beverly Fontenot
× Phal. Dos Pueblos = Rnthps. Sun Dance
× Phal. Elinor Shaffer = Rnthps. Red Flash
× Phal. Goleta = Rnthps. Mem. Edward Allen
× Phal. Martha Daniels = Rnthps. Richella's Delight
× Phal. Mistinguett = Rnthps. Ruby Jewell
× Phal. schillerana = Rnthps. Plum Red
× Phal. Spring Showers = Rnthps. Joan Nevins
× Phal. Terri Cook = Rnthps. Terri Gem
× Rhy. gigantea = Rnst. Fabulosa
× V. Iolani = Rntda. Iolani Luahine
× V. Mrs. Margaret Meyer = Rntda. Loh Boon Siew
× Vdps. gigantea = Rnps. Gordon Snook

CHEOK THIAM HUAT — **monachica × Brookie Chandler** — **Cheok Jiak Kim 1964 (Kirch)**

× V. coerulea = Rntda. Mem. Arthur Freed

coccinea*†‡ — **species**

× Red Feathers = Bangkok Flame
× Aër. crassifolia = Rnds. Mem. John Donnelly
× Phal. Dos Pueblos = Rnthps. Na'imah
× V. brunnea = Rntda. Thailand
× V. coerulescens = Rntda. Sangvichian
× V. denisoniana = Rntda. Longchen
× V. Mok Sau Lan = Rntda. Patcharee
× V. Muthiya = Rntda. Anna Kubyshkina
× V. Rothschildiana = Rntda. Wunna Jaides
× V. T.M.A. = Rntda. Andromeda
× Vdps. parishii = Rnps. Yenchit

GEORGE RADCLIFFE — **storiei × Alex Hawkes** — **G. Radcliffe 1975**

histrionica‡ — **species**

(This species is classified by some botanists under the generic name of *Renantherella*, but for horticultural (including registration) purposes, the generic name *Renanthera* is being retained.)

× storiei = Ratha
× V. lamellata = Rntda. Chang Min-Tat

hookerana (see *Arachnis hookerana**†‡) — **species**

imschootiana*†‡ — **species**

× Arach. cathcartii = Arnth. Ruben
× Ascda. Meda Arnold = Kgw. Red Lava
× Ascda. Ophelia = Kgw. Red Elf
× Ascda. Sunkist = Kgw. Nell Carlson
× Phal. Daryl Beard = Rnthps. Rio's Star
× Phal. Dos Pueblos = Rnthps. Cat Island
× Rnps. Lena Rowold = Rnps. Hiiaka
× Rhy. gigantea = Rnst. Ballerina
× V. cristata = Rntda. Kim Almas
× V. James Harding = Rntda. Itsukushima

isosepala — **species**

× Arach. Maggie Oei = Arnth. Ubol

JESSIE LOKE — **matutina × storiei** — **Loke Che Sung 1967 (Weeks)**

× storiei = Koo Wek Chai

JOHN TEW — **Brookie Chandler × Nancy Chandler** — **R. K. Mizuta 1967**

× Ascda. Yip Sum Wah = Kgw. Inferno
× Phal. Zada = Rnthps. Futura

KILAUEA‡ — **imschootiana × storiei** — **Nuuanu 1942**

× monachica = Kilauea Iki
× Phal. Doreen = Rnthps. Limberlost
× Rhy. gigantea = Rnst. Geisha

KILAUEA IKI — **Kilauea × monachica** — **O. Kirsch 1975**

KOO WEK CHAI — **Jessie Loke × storiei** — **Lum Chin Orchids 1973**

matutina†‡ — **species**

× Arach. Ishbel = Arnth. Alice Fuss
× Phal. serpentilingua = Rnthps. Heng-yee

monachica*†‡ — **species**

× Kilauea = Kilauea Iki
× Ascf. Peaches = Rskra. Liliput

RENANTHERA

monachica*†‡ (*continued*)

× Ascgm. calopterum	= Rngm. Rumrill	× Rhy. gigantea	= Rnst. Gleneyrie
× Phal. Clyde	= Rnthps. Billie Dotte Voelker	× Trgl. fasciata	= Rngl. Clarence Russell
		× V. coerulescens	= Rntda. Rumrill
× Phal. denevei	= Rnthps. Osceola	× V. cristata	= Rntda. Towaco
× Phal. Norman Peterson	= Rnthps. Bernice Voelker	× V. limbata	= Rntda. Mahiole

philippinensis‡ — **species**

× Arach. Ishbel	= Arnth. Yee Peng	× Ascda. Yip Sum Wah	= Kgw. Yoon Weng-Low
× Arach. Maggie Oei	= Arnth. Tanewan	× Dor. pulcherrima	= Dtha. Yen
× Ascda. Meda Arnold	= Kgw. June	× Phal. denevei	= Rnthps. Margaret
× Ascda. Peggy Foo	= Kgw. Madame Yip Khew-Ying	× Phal. serpentilingua	= Rnthps. Steven Lim
		× V. sumatrana	= Rntda. Wong Yin Fon

RED FEATHERS‡ — **coccinea × imschootiana** — **W. W. G. Moir 1964**

× coccinea	= Bangkok Flame		

RATHA — **storiei × histrionica** — **Gnanasuntharam 1972**

storiei*†‡ — **species**

× Alex Hawkes	= George Radcliffe	× Rnthps. Moon Walk	= Rnthps. Taibah
× histrionica	= Ratha	× Rhv. Busakorn	= Jnna. Flirt
× Jessie Loke	= Koo Wek Chai	× Rhv. Sagarik Wine	= Jnna. Sila-ard
× Aërdns. Rosy Dawn	= Lymra. Mandai Grace	× Rhv. Wong Yoke Sim	= Jnna. Rungtivar
× Aër. houlletiana	= Rnds. Houlstoria	× V. bensonii	= Rntda. Harnpongtham
× Arach. breviscapa	= Arnth. Mandai Clarion	× V. brunnea	= Rntda. Salyaphongse
× Ascda. Haad Ravai	= Kgw. Mem. Thep Satree	× V. Charlesworthii	= Rntda. Bangkae Beauty
× Ascda. Honwichai	= Kgw. Kanith	× V. Chimey Walker	= Rntda. Lorna Wurtzburg
× Ascda. Medasand	= Kgw. Teo Boon Hian	× V. Diane Ogawa	= Rntda. Teo Boon Hian
× Ascda. Priyavadee	= Kgw. Doungdee	× V. Harvest Time	= Rntda. Lean Yin
× Ascda. Seechang	= Kgw. Viroonchan Ruby	× V. James Toogood	= Rntda. Tumira Skinner
× Ascda. Yip Sum Wah	= Kgw. Boon Rubb	× V. Julia Sideris	= Rntda. Mandai
× Asctm. miniatum	= Rnctm. Voravut	× V. Mem. T. Iwasaki	= Rntda. Coppertone
× Phal. Arcadia	= Rnthps. Apricot Gold	× V. Princess Blue	= Rntda. Ong Jin Kar
× Phal. Grace Palm	= Rnthps. Malibu Beach	× V. Sunset	= Rntda. Sunset Story
× Rntda. El Tigre	= Rntda. Hon Kim San	× Vdnps. Hong Trevor	= Moir. Tristar

TOM THUMB‡ — **monachica × imschootiana** — **E. Iwanaga 1957 (W. W. G. Moir)**

× Aër. multiflora	= Rnds. Eva Jean	× Aër. odorata	= Rnds. Honeymoon

RENANTHERELLA

histrionica (see *Renanthera histrionica*‡) — **species**

RENANTHOGLOSSUM

RED DELIGHT‡ — **Ren. storiei × Ascgm. calopterum** — **E. Iwanaga 1963**

× Ascda. Ophelia	= Shgra. Tangerine Beauty		

RUMRILL — **Ren. monachica × Ascgm. calopterum** — **Rumrill 1974**

RENANTHOPSIS

AMY RUSSELL‡ — **Ren. Brookie Chandler × Phal. denevei** — **J. E. Russell 1961**

× Ascda. Ophelia	= Stmra. Rayna		

APRICOT GOLD — **Ren. storiei × Phal. Arcadia** — **Freed 1971 (Originator unknown)**

RENANTHOPSIS

BALI HA'I	**James Herbert Boone × Phal. Jubilee**	**Hager 1972**
BERNICE VOELKER	**Ren. monachica × Phal. Norman Peterson**	**Voelker 1972**
BILLIE DOTTE VOELKER	**Ren. monachica × Phal. Clyde**	**Voelker 1975**
CAT ISLAND	**Ren. imschootiana × Phal. Dos Pueblos**	**Fort Caroline 1973 (Wallbrunn)**
DANA	**Jan Goo × Phal. Pink Sunset**	**Hager 1971**

× Phal. amboinensis = Shangri-La | × Phal. violacea = Thai Silk
× Phal. lueddemanniana = Lotus Land | × Phal. Zada = Shalimar

FLORIDA SALUTE	**Salute × Phal. Star of Florida**	**Hager 1973**
FUTURA	**Ren. John Tew × Phal. Zada**	**R. K. Mizuta 1975**
GLORY	**Ren. Brookie Chandler × Phal. Aristocrat**	**Nell C. Roberts 1971**
HENG YEE	**Ren. matutina × Phal. serpentilingua**	**K. F. Yap 1973**
JAMES HERBERT BOONE	**Jan Goo × Phal. Pink Vision**	**Richella 1965**

× Phal. Jubilee = Bali Ha'i |

JAN GOO‡	**Phal. sanderana × Ren. monachica**	**Goo 1950**

× Phal. Pink Sunset = Dana | × Rhy. gigantea = Luth. Ruth Takemoto

JOAN NEVINS	**Ren. Brookie Chandler × Phal. Spring Showers**	**R. Nevins 1972**
LIMBERLOST	**Ren. Kilauea × Phal. Doreen**	**Limberlost 1973**
LOTUS LAND	**Dana × Phal. lueddemanniana**	**Hager 1974**
MALIBU BEACH	**Phal. Grace Palm × Ren. storiei**	**Freed 1972**
MARGARET	**Phal. denevei × Ren. philippinensis**	**S.B.G. 1973**
MEMORIA BEVERLY FONTENOT	**Ren. Brookie Chandler × Phal. Barbara Kay**	**Peter E. Lista 1973**
MEMORIA EDWARD ALLEN	**Ren. Brookie Chandler × Phal. Goleta**	**Peter E. Lista 1971 (Nell Roberts)**
MOON WALK	**Phal. serpentilingua × Ren. Brookie Chandler**	**Weeki Wachee 1970 (Redlinger)**

× Ascda. Meda Arnold = Stmra. Noel | × Ren. storiei = Taibah

NA'IMAH	**Phal. Dos Pueblos × Ren. coccinea**	**S. A. Bakar 1971**
NATIVE DANCER	**Ren. storiei × Phal. amabilis**	**McCoy 1965**

× Phal. Kay Star = Star Dancer |

OSCEOLA	**Ren. monachica × Phal. denevei**	**J. & S. 1971**
PLUM RED	**Ren. Brookie Chandler × Phal. schillerana**	**Fort Caroline 1973 (Wallbrunn)**
RED FLASH	**Ren. Brookie Chandler × Phal. Elinor Shaffer**	**Shaffer's 1973**
RENEE	**Ren. Brookie Chandler × Phal. Alice Gloria**	**Shaffer's 1973**
RICHELLA'S DELIGHT	**Ren. Brookie Chandler × Phal. Martha Daniels**	**R. K. Mizuta 1971**
RIO'S STAR	**Ren. imschootiana × Phal. Daryl Beard**	**Ruben 1975**
RUBY JEWELL	**Ren. Brookie Chandler × Phal. Mistinguett**	**Peter E. Lista 1973**
SALUTE	**Ren. imschootiana × Phal. Judy Karleen**	**Dobkin 1967**

× Phal. Star of Florida = Florida Salute |

SHALIMAR	**Dana × Phal. Zada**	**Hager 1973**
SHANGRI-LA	**Dana × Phal. amboinensis**	**Hager 1971**
STAR DANCER	**Native Dancer × Phal. Kay Star**	**Fort Caroline 1975 (Wallbrunn)**
STEVEN LIM	**Phal. serpentilingua × Ren. philippinensis**	**Koh Keng Hoe 1975**

RENANTHOPSIS

SUN DANCE	Ren. Brookie Chandler × Phal. Dos Pueblos	Fort Caroline 1972 (Wallbrunn)
TAIBAH	Moon Walk × Ren. storiei	Alsagoff 1972 (M.O.N.)
TERRI GEM	Ren. Brookie Chandler × Phal. Terri Cook	E. C. Marshall 1974 (Redlinger)
THAI SILK	Dana × Phal. violacea	Hager 1973

RHYNCHOCENTRUM

BAMRUNG	Sagarik × Asctm. ampullaceum	Thaisrisuthi 1971
BANGKAE	Sagarik × Asctm. miniatum	Thaisrisuthi 1971
BUMROONGSOONTHORN	Asctm. miniatum × Rhy. gigantea	Bumroongsoonthorn 1975 (Veerabhongs)
LADDA GOLD	Asctm. miniatum × Rhy. coelestis	Laddaland 1975 (Pantapa)
PETCHBURI GOLD	Rhy. coelestis × Asctm. Sagarik Gold	M. S. Tang 1973
SAGARIK	Rhy. coelestis × Asctm. curvifolium	Sagarik 1963

× Asctm. ampullaceum = Bamrung
× Asctm. curvifolium = Siriporn
× Asctm. miniatum = Bangkae
× V. Rothschildiana = Vasco. Rojanadara

SIRIPORN	Sagarik × Asctm. curvifolium	Siriyakorn 1973

RHYNCHOLAELIA

digbyana (see *Brassavola digbyana**†‡) **species**

glauca (see *Brassavola glauca**†‡) **species**

RHYNCHORIDES

CHOLRATANAKUL	Rhy. coelestis × Aër. multiflora	Cholratanakul 1972
KORAT	Aër. crassifolia × Rhy. gigantea	Watanarojrueng 1975
THAI NOI	Rhy. coelestis × Aër. flabellata	Suddhipaca 1973

RHYNCHOSTYLIS

coelestis‡ **species**

× Aër. flabellata = Rhrds. Thai Noi
× Aër. multiflora = Rhrds. Cholratanakul
× Arach. Maggie Oei = Arnst. Choompoo
× Ascda. Elieen Beauty = Vasco. Dreamy Blue
× Ascda. Ophelia = Vasco. Mem. Charles Blauvelt
× Asctm. miniatum = Rhctm. Ladda Gold
× Asctm. Sagarik Gold = Rhctm. Petchburi Gold
× Lsnd. Uniwai = Gfa. Eva Goff
× Rhv. Busakorn = Rhv. Thiansiri
× Rhv. Yayee = Rhv. Little Star
× V. Bonnie Blue Fukumura = Rhv. Ewe Lean Im
× V. Carolyn Koshiro = Rhv. Falling Sky
× V. Charlesworthii = Rhv. Bangwag
× V. coerulea = Rhv. Thailand
× V. Laurel Yap = Rhv. Sea Breeze
× V. Mary Catherine Bowman = Rhv. Cabaret
× V. Thai = Rhv. Chiengmai
× V. Trisher = Rhv. Merlene Nitta
× V. Winifred Kurihara = Rhv. Herbert Kurihara

gigantea†‡ **species**

× Aërdns. Bogor = Sgka. Siam
× Aër. crassifolia = Rhrds. Korat
× Ascda. Blue Boy = Vasco. Karavek
× Asctm. miniatum = Rhctm. Bumroongsoonthorn
× Rnet. Sunrise = Hylra. Hueylih Jane
× Rnps. Lena Rowold = Ynra. Hadrian
× Ren. Brookie Chandler = Rnst. Fabulosa
× Ren. Kilauea = Rnst. Geisha
× Ren. imschootiana = Rnst. Ballerina

gigantea†‡ (*continued*)

× Ren. monachica	= Rnst. Gleneyrie	× V. Janet Tagawa	= Rhv. Louise Boyd
× Rnthps. Jan Goo	= Luth. Ruth Takemoto	× V. Mem. Madame Pranerm	= Rhv. Natee Day
× Rhv. Sagarik Wine	= Rhv. Prinya Phornprapha	× V. teres	= Rhv. Kauhana
× V. bensonii	= Rhv. Tha Yang	× Vdps. gigantea	= Opst. Mem. Mary Nattrass
× V. coerulea	= Rhv. Azure		
× V. coerulescens	= Rhv. Ladda		

retusa†‡

× Rnds. Mahani	= Chew. Ruth Wong

species

× Sarco. hartmannii	= Srts. Blue Knob

RHYNCHOVANDA

AZURE	**Rhy. gigantea × V. coerulea**	**Redlinger 1972**
BANGKOK SKY	**V. sanderana × Rhy. coelestis**	**Sagarik 1967**

× Ascda. Meda Arnold	= Vasco. Tukta	× Asctm. miniatum	= Vasco. Nutmeg Dolly
× Ascda. Red Gem	= Vasco. Pranee	× Vasco. Blue Fairy	= Vasco. Chin
× Ascda. Yip Sum Wah	= Vasco. Somboonpol		

BANGWAG	**V. Charlesworthii × Rhy. coelestis**	**Chuanyen 1975**
BLUE ANGEL‡	**V. Rothschildiana × Rhy. coelestis**	**Takakura 1961**

× Ascda. Yip Sum Wah	= Vasco. Bluebird	× Rntda. Violet	= Jnna. Jetstar
× Rntda. Gold Nugget	= Jnna. Ivan Ang		

BUSAKORN	**Rhy. coelestis × V. Bill Sutton**	**Triswasdi 1967**

× Ascda. Yip Sum Wah	= Vasco. Chitswang	× Rhy. coelestis	= Thiansiri
× Ren. storiei	= Jnna. Flirt	× V. Rothschildiana	= Juthatip

CABARET	**V. Mary Catherine Bowman × Rhy. coelestis**	**R. K. Mizuta 1973**
CHIENGMAI	**V. Thai × Rhy. coelestis**	**W. W. G. Moir 1974**
EWE LEAN IM	**V. Bonnie Blue Fukumura × Rhy. coelestis**	**Foo Hock Lee 1973 (Fukumura Orchids)**
FALLING SKY	**V. Carolyn Koshiro × Rhy. coelestis**	**Vipar 1972**
HERBERT KURIHARA	**V. Winifred Kurihara × Rhy. coelestis**	**H. K. Nitta 1973**
GALEN KANAYAMA	**V. Hilo Blue × Blue Angel**	**Kanayama 1968 (Miyamoto)**

× Ascda. Meda Arnold	= Vasco. Janice Kanayama

JUTHATIP	**V. Rothschildiana × Busakorn**	**T. Orchids 1973 (Lim-im)**
KAUHANA	**V. teres × Rhy. gigantea**	**H. K. Nitta 1975**
LADDA	**V. coerulescens × Rhy. gigantea**	**Laddaland 1975 (Pantapa)**
LITTLE STAR	**Yayee × Rhy. coelestis**	**Vipar 1972**
LOUISE BOYD	**Rhy. gigantea × V. Janet Tagawa**	**Mrs. W. H. Boyd 1973 (Goff)**
MERLENE NITTA	**V. Trisher × Rhy. coelestis**	**H. K. Nitta 1975**
NATEE DAY	**V. Mem. Madame Pranerm × Rhy. gigantea**	**Leelasiri 1973**
PRINYA PHORNPRAPHA	**Sagarik Wine × Rhy. gigantea**	**Phornprapha 1973 (Sagarik)**
SAGARIK WINE	**V. denisoniana × Rhy. gigantea**	**W. P. Orchid 1970**

× Ascda. Meda Arnold	= Vasco. Prasarn	× Rhy. gigantea	= Prinya Phornprapha
× Ren. storiei	= Jnna. Sila-ard		

RHYNCHOVANDA

SEA BREEZE	**V. Laurel Yap × Rhy. coelestis**	**Wilkins 1975**
TAN GEAT LENG‡	**Rhy. coelestis × V. coerulescens**	**Tan Geat Leng 1962 (W. W. G. Moir)**

× V. Hilo Blue = Telaga Biru |

TELAGA BIRU	**Tan Geat Leng × V. Hilo Blue**	**K. F. Yap 1974**
THAILAND	**Rhy. coelestis × V. coerulea**	**T. Orchids 1974**
THA YANG	**V. bensonii × Rhy. gigantea**	**Suebsanguan 1975**
THIANSIRI	**Busakorn × Rhy. coelestis**	**Thiansiri 1975**
WONG YOKE SIM	**V. Rothschildiana × Blue Angel**	**Wong Chong Kew 1967**

× Ascda. Meda Arnold = Vasco. Apricot Gleam | × Ascda. Tan Chai Beng = Vasco. Blue Kahili
× Ascda. Priyavadee = Vasco. Jairak | × Ren. storiei = Jnna. Rungtivar

YAYEE	**V. Boonya × Rhy. coelestis**	**Darunee 1969 (Honwichai)**

× Rhy. coelestis = Little Star |

ROBINARA

KOSHER RED	**Rnds. Red Jewel × Ascda. Meda Arnold**	**R. K. Mizuta 1972**

RODRETTIA

HAWAII‡	**Comp. falcata × Rdza. secunda**	**Okubo 1958 (W. W. G. Moir)**

× Onc. Catherine Wilson = Wnra. Pinkie |

HENRY TEUSCHER	**Rdza. teuscheri × Comp. falcata**	**W. W. G. Moir 1967**

× Gom. recurva = Brade. Brasil | × Onc. onustum = Wnra. Stanley Taba

RODRICIDIUM

BEAUTY SPOTS	**Onc. pulchellum × Rdza. Burgundy**	**Perreira 1975**
ÇAMP	**Onc. incurvum × Rdza. secunda**	**Withner 1972**
FRECKLES	**Onc. Red Belt × Rdza. secunda**	**Ruben 1973**
MARIA	**Onc. Golden Glow × Rdza. secunda**	**Ruben 1974**
NORMA FAYE	**Onc. Brazil × Rdza. secunda**	**Richella 1961**

× Onc. varicosum = Rio |

PRIMI	**Onc. sarcodes × Rdza. secunda**	**Ruben 1970**

× Comp. macroplectron = Wnra. Ruben |

RIO	**Norma Faye × Onc. varicosum**	**W. W. G. Moir 1973**
RIO'S RED ROBIN	**Onc. triquetrum × Rdza. secunda**	**Ruben 1975**
ROJO	**Onc. Catherine Wilson × Rdza. secunda**	**Ruben 1975**

RODRIGLOSSUM

DOLLY	**Odm. bictoniense × Rdza. strobellii**	**Wyld Court 1973**

RODRIGUEZIA

BURGUNDY	**secunda × venusta**	**Elliott Flynn 1965**

× Onc. pulchellum = Rdcm. Beauty Spots |

RODRIGUEZIA

decora‡ — species
- × Inps. utricularioides = Rodps. Ressie Toy

secunda†‡ — species
- × Onc. Catherine Wilson = Rdcm. Rojo
- × Onc. Golden Glow = Rdcm. Maria
- × Onc. incurvum = Rdcm. Camp
- × Onc. Red Belt = Rdcm. Freckles
- × Onc. triquetrum = Rdcm. Rio's Red Robin

strobellii — species
- × Odm. bictoniense = Rdgm. Dolly

RODRIOPSIS

RESSIE TOY	**Rdza. decora × Inps. utricularioides**	**Osment 1971**

ROLFEARA

LITTLE MOUNTAIN	**Soph. coccinea × Bc. Daffodil**	**C. & H. 1975**

ROSAKIRSCHARA

LILIPUT	**Ren. monachica × Ascf. Peaches**	**O. Kirsch 1972**

ROTHARA

ANNE	**Epc. Hawaiian Gem × Pot. Gordon Siu**	**Gene Boyd 1975**

SAGARIKARA

SIAM	**Aërdns. Bogor × Rhy. gigantea**	**Uathawikul 1975**

SARCOCHILUS

australis — species
- × hartmannii = Southern Cross

ceciliae‡ — species
- × hillii = Confetti

CONFETTI	**ceciliae × hillii**	**I. A. Butler 1972**

falcatus‡ — species
- × Gchls. formosanus = Gsarco. Rumrill

hartmannii‡ — species
- × australis = Southern Cross
- × Psarco. spathulatus = Prcls. Perky
- × Rhy. retusa = Srts. Blue Knob

hillii‡ — species
- × ceciliae = Confetti

SOUTHERN CROSS	**hartmannii × australis**	**I. A. Butler 1972**

SARTYLIS

BLUE KNOB	**Sarco. hartmannii × Rhy. retusa**	**Cannons 1973 (Chick)**

SCHOMBAVOLA

DIPSY DOODLE	**Schom. superbiens × B. digbyana**	**Crothers 1973**

SCHOMBOCATTLEYA

ANTIGUA	**Schom. Kahili × C. Guatemalensis**	**W. W. G. Moir 1962**
× Slc. Anzac	= Hbtr. Antiguazac	
BILLIE PICKELL	**Schom. tibicinis × C. guttata**	**Pickell 1975 (Fields Orchids)**
DING BAT	**Snow White × C. loddigesii**	**Bishop 1975**
ELEGANCE	**C. schillerana × Schom. thomsoniana**	**Osment 1974**
GEE WILLIKERS	**C. guttata × Schom. thomsoniana**	**Stewart Inc. 1974**
HARRY DUNN†‡	**C. R. Prowe × Schom. lueddemanniana**	**Osment 1958**
× C. Empress Bells	= Yaquina	
MERINGUE	**Snow White × C. walkerana**	**J. & S. 1971**
PERFECTION	**Schom. tibicinis × C. loddigesii**	**Fort Caroline 1972 (Originator unknown)**
× Blc. Marjorie Frey	= Recc. Eglon Scott	
SNOW WHITE	**C. R. Prowe × Schom. lyonsii**	**W. W. G. Moir 1962**
× C. loddigesii	= Ding Bat	× C. walkerana = Meringue
URIMARE	**Schom. crispa × C. Gigi**	**Jesurún 1971**
YAQUINA	**Harry Dunn × C. Empress Bells**	**Bonniewood 1971**

SCHOMBOEPIDENDRUM

FRECKLES	**Epi. conopseum × Schom. lyonsii**	**Beckenbach 1975**
RED MONSTERETTE	**Epi. conopseum × Schom. tibicinis**	**Beckenbach 1975**

SCHOMBOLAELIA

CINNAMON CRISP	**Schom. crispa × L. cinnabarina**	**Withner 1972**
GARNET	**Schom. undulata × L. rubescens**	**W. W. G. Moir 1958**
× Epi. stamfordianum	= Dill. Mahogany Beauty	
MAUNALANI‡	**L. anceps × Schom. undulata**	**W. W. G. Moir 1952**
× Bc. Cornelius	= Recc. Dr. Harry Arnold	

SCHOMBURGKIA

brysiana (see *thomsoniana*†‡)		**species**
crispa‡		**species**
× C. Gigi	= Smbc. Urimare	× L. cinnabarina = Smbl. Cinnamon Crisp
lyonsii‡		**species**
× Epi. conopseum	= Smbep. Freckles	
superbiens†‡ (syn. *Laelia superbiens**)		**species**
× B. digbyana	= Smbv. Dipsy Doodle	

SCHOMBURGKIA

thomsoniana†‡ **species**

(The botanically correct name is *brysiana* (var *minor*) but *thomsoniana* continues to be used as the horticulturally recommended name for all *Schom. brysiana*.)

× Blc. Fortune	= Recc. Zamboanga	× Lpna. Kingston	= Hdra. Christian Hilda
× C. guttata	= Smbc. Gee Willikers	× Slc. Naomi Kerns	= Hbtr. Herb
× C. schillerana	= Smbc. Elegance		

tibicinis*†‡ **species**

× C. guttata	= Smbc. Billie Pickell	× Epi. conopseum	= Smbep. Red Monsterette
× C. loddigesii	= Smbc. Perfection		

SEDIREA

japonica (see *Aërides japonica**‡) **species**

SEIDENFADENIA

mitrata (see *Aërides mitrata*‡) **species**

SHIGEURAARA

TANGERINE BEAUTY **Rngm. Red Delight × Ascda. Ophelia** **R. K. Mizuta 1972**

SOPHROCATTLEYA

BONFIRE **Cleopatra × C. guttata** **Rex Foster's 1973 (Fordyce)**

CHAMBERLAINIANA* **C. harrisoniana × Soph. coccinea** **Chamberlain 1898**

× C. intermedia	= Petitpoint Pink

CLEOPATRA*‡ **C. guttata × Soph. coccinea** **C. 1898**

× Blc. Flo Fleece	= Pot. Susan Wanner	× Lc. Mem. Albert Heinecke	= Slc. Arabic
× Blc. Norman's Bay	= Pot. Cleo Bay	× Slc. Lindores	= Slc. Romance
× Blc. Ruth Witbeck	= Pot. Sunray	× Slc. My Choice	= Slc. Ginger Gibson
× C. Barbara Kirch	= Nubbin	× Slc. Ramona	= Slc. Fire Wagon
× C. Bow Bells	= Nile Queen	× Slc. Vallezac	= Slc. Vallepatra
× C. guttata	= Bonfire		
× Epi. gracile	= Stac. Sam		

DORIS*†‡ **C. dowiana × Soph. coccinea** **Bull 1904**

× Lc. Orange Gem	= Slc. Summerville	× Slc. Jewel Box	= Slc. Madge Fordyce

ELLEN ESTHER HOOD **C. Auranti-media × Soph. coccinea** **Fort Caroline 1971 (G. C. West)**

FRUDO **C. luteola × Soph. cernua** **Voo Doo Orchids 1974**

LITTLE BIGRED **Luton Charm × C. guttata** **Kirch 1973**

LUTON CHARM **C. forbesii × Soph. coccinea** **Hey 1966**

× C. guttata	= Little Bigred

MARIONETTE **C. Bow Bells × Soph. coccinea** **Crestwood 1974**

NILE QUEEN **Cleopatra × C. Bow Bells** **Roccaforte 1973 (Gamble)**

NUBBIN **C. Barbara Kirch × Cleopatra** **Rod McLellan Co. 1974**

PEARLOUIS **C. bicolor × Soph. coccinea** **L. C. Muller 1975**

PETITE CLAIRE **C. Claris × Petite Fleur** **Roccaforte 1973 (Gamble)**

PETITE FLEUR‡ **Soph. coccinea × C. Arctic Snow** **Kern 1962 (Gamble)**

× C. Claris	= Petite Claire

SOPHROCATTLEYA

PETITPOINT PINK	**Chamberlainiana × C. intermedia**		**Fort Caroline 1975**
RETHA	**C. Fitz Eugene Dixon × Soph. coccinea**		**Fort Caroline 1973**
ROSE PIXIE	**C. Bob Betts × Soph. coccinea**		**Stewart Inc. 1974**
YONE ARAI	**Soph. coccinea × C. George Eastman**		**Arai 1974**

SOPHROLAELIA

AFFRIC	**L. Coronet × Soph. coccinea**		**L. de R. 1933**
× Slc. Shasta Gold	= Slc. Mem. Philip Fehlandt		
BETTY JEAN SCOTT	**L. tenebrosa × Psyche**		**Fort Caroline 1972**
× B. nodosa	= Low. Peter Whyte	× Pot. Estelle Smith	= Pot. Isle of Palms
CREAMER	**Marriottiana × L. longipes**		**Jesup 1975**
FLAVA-PSYCHE	**L. flava × Psyche**		**Otaguro 1974 (W. K. Nakamoto)**
× Slc. Anzac	= Slc. Anzac Darling		
GRATRIXIAE*‡	**L. tenebrosa × Soph. coccinea**		**C. 1901**
× C. Iris	= Slc. Painted Savage	× Slc. Caroline Scott	= Slc. Red Rich
× Lc. Antonica Fredrick	= Slc. Marion Stevens	× Slc. Persian Fantasy	= Slc. Burns Triumph
GUSTAVE VINCKE‡	**L. perrinii × Soph. coccinea**		**Vincke 1928**
× C. Celia	= Slc. Maxine Hudson	× C. Portia	= Slc. Marie King
× C. Fulvescens	= Slc. Linda Jones		
JINN	**Soph. coccinea × L. milleri**		**Spencer 1966**
× C. intermedia	= Slc. Lilliput	× Soph. cernua	= Sparklet
× Lc. Orange Gem	= Slc. Jinn Gem		
MARRIOTTIANA*†‡	**L. flava × Soph. coccinea**		**Marriott 1896**
× L. longipes	= Creamer	× Lc. G. S. Ball	= Slc. Sunshine Gold
MINUET	**L. lundii × Soph. coccinea**		**Stewart Inc. 1972**
PSYCHE*†‡	**L. cinnabarina × Soph. coccinea**		**C. 1902**
× Bc. Golden Sunshine	= Pot. Managua	× L. rupestris	= Tinkerbelle
× C. aclandiae	= Slc. Precious Stones	× L. tenebrosa	= Betty Jean Scott
× C. Baby Kay	= Slc. Ginny Champion	× Lc. Nigrescent	= Slc. Mem. Bill Eckles
× C. percivaliana	= Slc. Psychedelic Virgin	× Lc. Stephen Oliver Fouraker	= Slc. Excella
× C. Princess Bells	= Slc. Henry Severin		
× Epi. Sarah Jesup	= Sfdra. Sarah's Psyche	× Slc. Helen Veliz	= Slc. Colorific
× L. flava	= Flava-Psyche	× Slc. Phena	= Slc. Tiger Eye
SPARKLET	**Jinn × Soph. cernua**		**Pabst 1975**
TINKERBELLE	**Psyche × L. rupestris**		**Jesup 1975**

SOPHROLAELIOCATTLEYA

AGUILINO PICHE	**C. Barbara Kirch × Anzac**		**Rod McLellan Co. 1973**
ALETHEA	**Kao Hsiung × C. aurantiaca**		**Bertram 1973**
AMSELWEG	**Bellicent × Atoll**		**Baggeler 1973**
ANZAC*†‡	**Marathon × Lc. Dominiana**		**C. 1972[1]**
× Beau Alex	= Cazan	× Honolulu	= Perkle
× Charlotte K. Hodsdon	= James McWilliams	× B. fragrans	= Pot. Little Suzie
× Estella Jewell	= So Sad	× B. nodosa	= Pot. Melisande
× Fort Caroline	= Birch Seville	× Bc. Speciosa	= Pot. Specizac

ANZAC*†‡ *(continued)*

× Blc. Circus = Pot. Rouge
× Blc. Goldfield = Pot. Spicey
× Blc. Jane Russell = Pot. Precious
× Blc. Marjorie Frey = Pot. Ruth Rettig
× Blc. Mem. Crispin Rosales = Pot. Yuriko Hananoki
× Blc. Mene = Pot. Menezac
× Blc. Molflora = Pot. Jack Weaver
× Blc. Pacific Gold = Pot Pacific Warrior
× Blc. Sylvia Reilly = Pot. Barbara Wichmann
× C. Barbara Kirch = Aguilino Piche
× C. Fabingiana = Fabinzac
× C. Moscombe = Yeong-Huei Chen
× C. Mrs. Pitt = Penza
× C. Nigrella = Primi
× C. Sedlescombe = Grace Chen
× L. Coronet = Corozac
× L. harpophylla = Fiesta Gold
× L. rupestris = Rupanzac
× L. Zip = Zana
× Lc. Ann Follis = Plum Brandy
× Lc. Cholletiana = Westercelle
× Lc. Elinor = Gloria Jesurún Leyba
× Lc. Esther Anderson = Mem. George Jacroux
× Lc. Excellency = Fantasy
× Lc. Gladys = Fujimusume
× Lc. Jean-ne Lorraine = Bob Poole
× Lc. José Dias Castro = Zuki Josezac
× Little Susie = Suzac
× Lc. Maria Ozzella = Catherine Wilfret
× Lc. Mark Kurao Hoshino = McCully Beauty
× Lc. Princess Esk = Prinzac
× Lc. Rojo = Judy Ann Cowart
× Lc. Serenity = Liz Cameron
× Lc. Western Sunset = Rodco's Jewel
× Pot. Dark Beam = Pot. Crimson Glory
× Pot. Sunset Bay = Pot. Bayzac
× Smbc. Antigua = Hbtr. Antiguazac
× Sl. Flava-Psyche = Anzac Darling

ANZAC DARLING — **Sl. Flava-Psyche × Anzac** — **Otaguro 1974**

ARABIC — **Sc. Cleopatra × Lc. Mem. Albert Heinecke** — **Stewart Inc. 1972 (Sell)**

ATOLL — **Lc. Paradisio × Meuna** — **Sladden 1950**

× Bellicent = Amselweg

AUTUMN DELIGHT‡ — **Lc. S. J. Bracey × Anzac** — **A. & B. 1955**

× Lc. Bonanza = Bonlight
× Lc. Eva = Royal Scepter

BEACON HILL — **Lc. Sunrise Peak × Hermes** — **Beall 1962**

× C. aurantiaca = Sangre de Dios
× Lc. Mem. Albert Heinecke = Skagway

BEAU ALEX — **Fall Beauty × Lc. H. G. Alexander** — **Rivermont 1962**

× Anzac = Cazan

BELLICENT — **Lc. Bonanza × Soph. coccinea** — **Paul Miller 1967**

× Atoll = Amselweg

BEVERLY SALMON — **Anzac × Lc. Cuesta** — **Kwr. 1954**

× Lc. Edmund Rothwell = Fire Mist

BILL'S RED — **Naomi Kerns × C. Batalinii** — **Kirch 1974**

BIRCH SEVILLE — **Fort Caroline × Anzac** — **Fort Caroline 1972**

BOB POOLE — **Lc. Jean-ne Lorraine × Anzac** — **Fresh 1972**

BONDIZAC — **Lc. Bonanza × Dizac** — **C. Takeda 1972**

BONLIGHT — **Lc. Bonanza × Autumn Delight** — **Katsuura 1973**

BRANDYWINE‡ — **Anzac × Lindores** — **Gore 1959**

× Lindores = Nancy Cassella
× Naomi Kerns = Cascade Sunset
× Bc. Déesse = Pot. Cherry Blossom
× Blc. Hazel Dell = Pot. War Dance
× Blc. Setting Sun = Pot. Edith Hancock
× C. aurantiaca = Titillate
× C. Mrs. Mahler = Castle Mountain
× L. milleri = Spirit of 'Seventysix
× Lc. Lee Langford = Night Song
× Lc. Wine Festival = Firehouse Blues
× Pot. Tapestry Peak = Pot. Chimney Rocks

BURNS TRIUMPH — **Persian Fantasy × Sl. Gratrixiae** — **W. T. Burns 1975**

CALIFORNIA APRICOT — **Lc. Pacific Sun × Soph. coccinea** — **Rod McLellan Co. 1964**

× Jewel Box = Hazel Boyd
× Lc. Orange Gem = California Delight
× Pot. Tapestry Peak = Pot. Kiska Volcano

CALIFORNIA DELIGHT California Apricot × Lc. Orange Gem — Pabst 1975
CANTAZAC Vallezac × Lc. Cantabile — J. Milton Warne 1974
CANZAC†‡ Anzac × Lc. Canberra — B. 1949
× C. Nigritian = Fred King |

CARLA CARTER†‡ Anzac × Ramona — Carter 1948
× L. Zip = Potpourri | × Lc. Elstead Gem = Carla Gem

CARLA GEM Lc. Elstead Gem × Carla Carter — Rod McLellan Co. 1975
CAROLINE SCOTT‡ Lc. Derna × Anzac — Rivermont 1960
× Sl. Gratrixiae = Red Rich |

CASCADE C. Melody × Naomi Kerns — Elroy Haynes 1974 (Kodama)

CASCADE SUNSET Naomi Kerns × Brandywine — Beall 1974
CASTLE MOUNTAIN Brandywine × C. Mrs. Mahler — Beall 1975
CATHERINE WILFRET Lc. Maria Ozzella × Anzac — Wilfret 1973 (Ilsley Orchids)

CAZAN Beau Alex × Anzac — Rod McLellan Co. 1975
CHARLOTTE K. HODSDON Marion Black × Anzac — Rivermont 1958
× Anzac = James McWilliams | × Pot. Tripoli = Pot. Sunset Butte

CHILI PEPPER RED Lc. Wine Festival × Soph. coccinea — Redlinger 1973 (Beall)

COLORIFIC Sl. Psyche × Helen Veliz — Keyes 1971
COMET SEEKER Sunburst × Ramona — Kay Francis 1974
COROZAC L. Coronet × Anzac — Gauda 1971
DIZAC C. Dinah × Anzac — C. Takeda 1963
× Lc. Bonanza = Bondizac |

DOLORES RAINBOW Lc. Dolores Hoyt × Rainbow Hill — Gauda 1971
DR. VERNE ECHOLS Radians × Lindores — Oakley 1971
EAST MONA C. George Eastman × Ramona — Hiroyuki Yamamoto 1953
× Pot. Red Friar = Pot. Never Red |

EMBERGLOW Sc. Doris × Lc. Amber Glow — Fordyce 1968
× Blc. Malvern = Pot. Gold Piece |

ESTELLA JEWELL†‡ Radians × C. trianaei — Orchidwood 1938
× Anzac = So Sad | × C. Mrs. Mahler = Fiesta
× Blc. Mem. Crispin Rosales = Pot. Florence Brady | × Lc. Summerland Girl = Manoa Jewel

EXCELLA Sl. Psyche × Lc. Stephen Oliver Fouraker — Hausermann 1973
FABINZAC C. Fabingiana × Anzac — Gauda 1971
FANTASY Lc. Excellency × Anzac — Fort Caroline 1975
FIESTA C. Mrs. Mahler × Estella Jewell — H. A. Hill 1972
FIESTA GOLD L. harpophylla × Anzac — Lorenzen 1973
FIREFLY†‡ Marathon × Lc. Empress Frederick — S. 1924
× C. Barbara Kirch = Orange Psyche |

FIREHOUSE BLUES Lc. Wine Festival × Brandywine — Beall 1973
FIRE MIST Lc. Edmund Rothwell × Beverly Salmon — Beall 1972
FIRE WAGON Sc. Cleopatra × Ramona — Rod McLellan Co. 1973
FORT CAROLINE Fire Queen × Lc. Lee Langford — Fouraker 1961 (Stewart Inc.)
× Anzac = Birch Seville | × Blc. Fortune = Pot. Canyon Sands

SOPHROLAELIOCATTLEYA

Name	Parentage	Registrant
FRANCES MARY	Naomi Kerns × Lc. Mem. Maggie Hood	Fort Caroline 1974 (Brooks)
FRED KING	Canzac × C. Nigritian	Suzuki 1971
FROUFROU	C. Barbara Kirch × Sunburst	Rod McLellan Co. 1973
FTATATEETA	Lc. Antonica Fredrick × Soph. coccinea	Fort Caroline 1971
FUJIMUSUME	Lc. Gladys × Anzac	Gauda 1971
GABBY GIBSON	Lc. Orange Gem × Lindores	R. A. Gibson 1975 (Stewart Inc.)
GINGER GIBSON	Sc. Cleopatra × My Choice	Fort Caroline 1971 (Wallbrunn)
GINNY CHAMPION	C. Baby Kay × Sl. Psyche	Champion 1974
GLORIA JESURÚN LEYBA	Lc. Elinor × Anzac	Jesurún 1973
GOLD REWARD	Lc. Peggy Moir × Radians	W. W. G. Moir 1975
GRACE CHEN	C. Sedlescombe × Anzac	Hong-Sie Chen 1975 (Chung-Chweng Chen)
HAZEL BOYD	California Apricot × Jewel Box	Rod McLellan Co. 1975
HELEN OYAKAWA	Lindores × Lc. Tydea	Otaguro 1975
HELEN VELIZ‡	Rainbow Hill × Sc. Eleanor	A. & R. 1960

× Blc. Nacouchee	= Pot. Metal Creek	× Pot. Tripoli	= Pot. Santa Rita
× Blc. Norman's Bay	= Pot. Scott Holguin	× Sl. Psyche	= Colorific
× Lc. Artie Carlisle Schweer	= Sunflare		

Name	Parentage	Registrant
HENRY SEVERIN	C. Princess Bells × Sl. Psyche	Severin 1973
HERMES*†‡	Isabella × Lc. St. Gothard	C. 1928

× Blc. Malvern	= Pot. Tabo		

Name	Parentage	Registrant
HONG KONG	C. bicolor × Indian Springs	J. & S. 1974
HONOLULU‡	Lc. Joseph Hampton × Radians	Y. Abe 1958 (Kwr.)

× Anzac	= Perkle		

Name	Parentage	Registrant
INDIAN SPRINGS	Lindores × Lc. Grandee	Beall 1964

× C. bicolor	= Hong Kong	× Lc. Mem. Albert Heinecke	= Rugged Ridge

Name	Parentage	Registrant
JAMES McWILLIAMS	Charlotte K. Hodsdon × Anzac	Rod McLellan Co. 1971
JEWEL BOX‡	C. aurantiaca × Anzac	Stewart Inc. 1962

× California Apricot	= Hazel Body	× Lc. Issy	= Prissy Red
× L. tenebrosa	= Ten-e-Jewel	× Sc. Doris	= Madge Fordyce

Name	Parentage	Registrant
JINN GEM	Sl. Jinn × Lc. Orange Gem	Stewart Inc. 1975
JUDY ANN COWART	Lc. Rojo × Anzac	Cowart 1973
KAO HSIUNG	Lc. General Maude × Rainbow Hill	Li Chin-sheng 1959

× Tropic Dawn	= Kobe	× Lc. Ennerdale	= Warren Moki Sakuma
× Blc. Jane Helton	= Pot. Jacquie Awana	× Lc. Flirtie	= Kaohsiung Flirt
× C. aurantiaca	= Alethea	× Lc. Lee Langford	= Kao Lee

Name	Parentage	Registrant
KAOHSIUNG FLIRT	Lc. Flirtie × Kao Hsiung	Otaguro 1973
KAO LEE	Kao Hsiung × Lc. Lee Langford	Otaguro 1973
KAY GAVIN	Little Barbara × Naomi Kerns	Bachner 1974 (Kirch)
KIAORA RED	Phena × Dorothy Watkins	Schultz 1964 (Arvida)

× C. aurantiaca	= Swizzle		

Name	Parentage	Registrant
KOBE	Kao Hsiung × Tropic Dawn	C. Takeda 1973

SOPHROLAELIOCATTLEYA

Name	Parentage	Originator
LANGLEYENSIS*	**Marathon × C. dowiana**	**B. 1921**
× Blc. Ruth Witbeck	= Pot. Margaret Sadoyama	
LILLIAN CHIYOKO ITO	**Lc. Twinkle Star × Tropic Dawn**	**Otaguro 1975**
LILLIPUT	**Sl. Jinn × C. intermedia**	**Fort Caroline 1974**
LINDA JONES	**Sl. Gustave Vincke × C. Fulvescens**	**Limberlost 1974**
LINDORES†‡	**Anzac × Lc. Ishtar**	**B. 1943**
× Brandywine	= Nancy Cassella	
× Radians	= Dr. Verne Echols	
× C. aurantiaca	= Thrill	
× C. Dubiosa	= Saucy One	
× C. Edith Aurum	= Ohelohelo	
× L. cinnabarina	= Torch	
× Lc. Orange Gem	= Gabby Gibson	
× Lc. Tydea	= Helen Oyakawa	
× Sc. Cleopatra	= Romance	
LITTLE BARBARA	**C. Barbara Kirch × Sl. Psyche**	**Kirch 1968 (E. Iwanaga)**
× Naomi Kerns	= Kay Gavin	
LIZ CAMERON	**Lc. Serenity × Anzac**	**W. T. McBroom 1975 (Originator unknown)**
LYNN YAYOI TSUJI	**Lc. Adelaide Waltman × Paprika**	**Otaguro 1973**
MABEL GOERTH	**Pacific Gem × C. Wolteriana**	**Mid-Florida Orch. 1973**
McCULLY BEAUTY	**Lc. Mark Kurao Hoshino × Anzac**	**Hironaka 1973**
MADGE FORDYCE	**Sc. Doris × Jewel Box**	**Fordyce 1971**
× Lc. Amber Glow	= Sue Fordyce	
MANOA JEWEL	**Lc. Summerland Girl × Estella Jewell**	**Elroy Haynes 1973 (Takemoto)**
MARIE KING	**C. Portia × Sl. Gustave Vincke**	**Limberlost 1973**
MARION BLACK†‡	**Ramona × Windsor**	**Kirkwood 1949**
× Blc. Mem. Crispin Rosales	= Pot. Evening Glow	
MARION STEVENS	**Lc. Antonica Fredrick × Sl. Gratrixiae**	**G. Crocker 1973**
MARTHA WITHNER	**Soph. coccinea × Lc. Intermedio-flava**	**Withner 1972**
MAXINE HUDSON	**C. Celia × Sl. Gustave Vincke**	**Limberlost 1971**
MEMORIA BILL ECKLES	**Sl. Psyche × Lc. Nigrescent**	**Ted Green 1972 (Landamar)**
MEMORIA GEORGE JACROUX	**Lc. Esther Anderson × Anzac**	**Otaguro 1973**
MEMORIA PHILIP FEHLANDT	**Sl. Affric × Shasta Gold**	**Orchids unLtd. 1975 (Fehlandt)**
MEULANGE	**Meuse × Lc. Soulange**	**M. 1928**
× Pot. Diane	= Pot. Diane Meulange	
MEUZAC†‡	**Anzac × Meuse**	**A. & B. 1936**
× C. Fabia	= National City	
MOSSIABELLA‡	**Isabella × C. mossiae**	**C. 1942**
× Blc. Oriental Gem	= Pot. Esperanza dela Cruz	
MY CHOICE‡	**Lc. Thurderniana × Anzac**	**Rivermont 1960**
× Sc. Cleopatra	= Ginger Gibson	
NANCY BELLOWS	**Lc. Ozark × Soph. coccinea**	**Fort Caroline 1972**
NANCY CASSELLA	**Brandywine × Lindores**	**Withner 1973 (A. & R.)**
NAOMI GIRL	**Lc. Golden Girl × Naomi Kerns**	**J. & S. 1975**

SOPHROLAELIOCATTLEYA

NAOMI KERNS‡ — **Lc. S. J. Bracy × Rainbow Hill** — **T. Kazumura 1956**

× Brandywine	= Cascade Sunset	× C. Batalinii	= Bill's Red
× Little Barbara	= Kay Gavin	× C. Melody	= Cascade
× Bc. Hartland	= Pot. Grindal Shoals	× Lc. Costa Rica	= Spectrum Range
× Blc. Norman's Bay	= Pot. Peter Haynes	× Lc. Golden Girl	= Naomi Girl
× Blc. Malworth	= Pot. Clown	× Lc. Mem. Maggie Hood	= Frances Mary
× Blc. Waikiki Sunset	= Pot. Mem. Seichi Iwasaki	× Schom. thomsoniana	= Hbtr. Herb

NATIONAL CITY — **Meuzac × C. Fabia** — **J. E. Bell 1971 (F. Fordyce)**

NICK PICKELL — **Lc. Mike Shaw × Rainbow Hill** — **Pickell 1973 (Miyamoto)**

NIGHT SONG — **Lc. Lee Langford × Brandywine** — **Rex Foster's 1973 (Fordyce)**

OHELOHELO — **C. Edith Aurum × Lindores** — **Otaguro 1972**

ORANGE PSYCHE — **C. Barbara Kirch × Firefly** — **W. W. G. Moir 1973**

ORMANZA — **Ormona × Lc. Bonanza** — **C. Takeda 1973**

ORMONA — **Lc. Orebus × Ramona** — **Hiroyuki Yamamoto 1962**

× Lc. Bonanza = Ormanza

PACIFIC GEM‡ — **L. flava × Sunburst** — **Gronwall 1958 (Kirch)**

× C. Wolteriana = Mabel Goerth

PAINTED SAVAGE — **Sl. Gratrixiae × C. Iris** — **Robt. Smith 1973**

PAPRIKA‡ — **Lc. Orange Gem × Anzac** — **Stewart Inc. 1960**

× Sugar Plum	= Paprika Plum	× Lc. Adelaide Waltman	= Lynn Yayoi Tsuji
× Blc. Golden Spires	= Pot. Treasure Glow		

PAPRIKA PLUM — **Sugar Plum × Paprika** — **Otaguro 1973**

PEARL SPENCER — **C. Heydey × Meuzac** — **Genevieve Toy 1961 (Louie Y. Toy)**

× Blc. Mem. Crispin Rosales = Pot. Sunny's Favorite

PENZA — **C. Mrs. Pitt × Anzac** — **Rod McLellan Co. 1975**

PERKLE — **Anzac × Honolulu** — **Bingham 1971 (E. F. Lawrence)**

PERSIAN FANTASY‡ — **Persian Garden × Anzac** — **Rivermont 1962**

× Sl. Gratrixiae = Burns Triumph

PERSIAN GARDEN‡ — **Lc. Mrs. Medo × Anzac** — **Rivermont 1946**

× Blc. Norman's Bay = Pot. Persian Bay

PHENA‡ — **Meuse × Rainbow** — **M. 1930**

× C. General Patton	= Shigedonia	× Sl. Psyche	= Tiger Eye

PLUM BRANDY — **Lc. Ann Follis × Anzac** — **Fort Caroline 1975**

POTPOURRI — **L. Zip × Carla Carter** — **Rod McLellan Co. 1972**

PRECIOUS STONES — **Sl. Psyche × C. aclandiae** — **Stewart Inc. 1971**

PRIMI — **C. Nigrella × Anzac** — **Ruben 1972**

PRINZAC — **Lc. Princess Esk × Anzac** — **Ruben 1971**

PRISSY RED — **Jewel Box × Lc. Issy** — **Trymwood 1973**

PSYCHEDELIC VIRGIN — **Sl. Psyche × C. percivaliana** — **Doan 1972**

RADIANS*†‡ — **Isabella × C. Princess Royal** — **C. 1925**

× Lindores	= Dr. Verne Echols	× Lc. Peggy Moir	= Gold Reward
× Blc. Leila	= Pot. Darlene		

SOPHROLAELIOCATTLEYA

RAINBOW HILL†‡ — **Ramona × Lc. Alma** — **G. B. Miwa 1949**

× Blc. Jane Helton = Pot. Irene Brouard | × Lc. Mike Shaw = Nick Pickell
× Lc. Dolores Hoyt = Dolores Rainbow |

RAMONA*†‡ — **Meuse × Lc. Linda** — **M. 1928**

× Sunburst = Comet Seeker | × C. General Patton = Yuko Shiono
× Blc. Malvern = Pot. Hicee | × Pot. Edward Rowold = Pot. Florence Honda
× C. Chocolate Drop = Redhead | × Sc. Cleopatra = Fire Wagon

REDHEAD — **C. Chocolate Drop × Ramona** — **Rex Foster's 1974 (Fordyce)**

RED REASON — **Lc. Thurderniana × Valentine** — **Dos Pueblos 1975**
RED RICH — **Sl. Gratrixiae × Caroline Scott** — **Crestwood 1974**
RODCO'S JEWEL — **Lc. Western Sunset × Anzac** — **Rod McLellan Co. 1972**
ROJO DAWN — **Lc. Rojo × Tropic Dawn** — **Otaguro 1975**
ROMANCE — **Sc. Cleopatra × Lindores** — **H. A. Hill 1972**
ROSEMARY CLOONEY — **Rainbow Hill × L. flava** — **Peters 1963 (M. Yamada)**

× Lc. Alma = Stacy Miyamoto |

ROYAL SCEPTER — **Lc. Eva × Autumn Delight** — **Beall 1974**
RUGGED RIDGE — **Indian Springs × Lc. Mem. Albert Heinecke** — **Beall 1973**
RUPANZAC — **L. rupestris × Anzac** — **Pabst 1975**
SALLY DICKINSON — **Lc. Thurderniana × Soph. coccinea** — **Wallbrunn 1974**
SANGRE DE DIOS — **Beacon Hill × C. aurantiaca** — **Osment 1974**
SASSY SOFIA — **Soph. coccinea × Lc. Little Sunbeam** — **J. A. Young 1974 (Polacheck)**

SAUCY ONE — **C. Dubiosa × Lindores** — **J. & S. 1971**
SHASTA GOLD‡ — **C. Mount Shasta × Firefly** — **W. W. G. Moir 1965**

× Sl. Affric = Mem. Philip Fehlandt |

SHIGEDONIA — **Phena × C. General Patton** — **C. Takeda 1971**
SKAGWAY — **Lc. Mem. Albert Heinecke × Beacon Hill** — **Beall 1972**
SO SAD — **Estella Jewell × Anzac** — **Rayridge 1974**
SPECTRUM RANGE — **Lc. Costa Rica × Naomi Kerns** — **Beall 1975**
SPIRIT OF 'SEVENTYSIX — **L. milleri × Brandywine** — **Stewart Inc. 1974**
STACY MIYAMOTO — **Rosemary Clooney × Lc. Alma** — **Miyamoto 1975**
SUE FORDYCE — **Lc. Amber Glow × Madge Fordyce** — **Rod McLellan Co. 1973 (Fordyce)**

SUGAR PLUM — **Lc. Tenebrule × Diablito** — **Stewart Inc. 1967**

× Paprika = Paprika Plum |

SUMMERVILLE — **Sc. Doris × Lc. Orange Gem** — **Crothers 1971**
SUNBURST†‡ — **Lc. Sunburst × Soph. coccinea** — **S. 1936**

× Ramona = Comet Seeker | × C. Barbara Kirch = Froufrou
× Tropic Flare = Tahitian Sunset | × Pot. Gordon Siu = Pot. Chenille

SUNFLARE — **Lc. Artie Carlisle Schweer × Helen Veliz** — **Rex Foster's 1974 (Fordyce)**

SUNSHINE GOLD — **Sl. Mariottiana × Lc. G. S. Ball** — **W. W. G. Moir 1971**
SUZAC — **Lc. Little Susie × Anzac** — **Ruben 1971**
SWIZZLE — **Kiaora Red × C. aurantiaca** — **J. & S. 1974 (Mrs. L. Wilson)**

TAHITIAN SUNSET — **Sunburst × Tropic Flare** — **Rod McLellan Co. 1974 (Fordyce)**

TEN-E-JEWEL — **L. tenebrosa × Jewel Box** — **Trymwood 1973**

SOPHROLAELIOCATTLEYA

THRILL	**Lindores × C. aurantiaca**	**J. & S. 1974**
TIGER EYE	**Sl. Psyche × Phena**	**Beall 1973**
TITILLATE	**Brandywine × C. aurantiaca**	**Rod McLellan Co. 1973**
TORCH	**L. cinnabarina × Lindores**	**J. & S. 1971**
TROPIC DAWN‡	**Canzac × Anzac**	**B. 1965**

× Kao Hsiung	= Kobe	× Lc. Rojo	= Rojo Dawn
× Blc. Crown Prince Akihito	= Pot. Ayano-Miya Fumihito	× Lc. Twinkle Star	= Lillian Chiyoko Ito

TROPIC FLARE‡	**Lc. Miami × Ramona**	**A. & M. 1962**

× Sunburst	= Tahitian Sunset	× Pot. Gordon Siu	= Pot. Apocalypse

TWINKLE TOES	**Lc. Aclandor × Soph. coccinea**	**Stewart Inc. 1974**
VALENTINE‡	**Cicily Watson × Anzac**	**Rivermont 1954**

× Lc. Thurderniana	= Red Reason		

VALLEPATRA	**Sc. Cleopatra × Vallezac**	**Stewart Inc. 1972 (Sell)**
VALLEZAC‡	**C. Golden Gate × Anzac**	**Vallemar 1960**

× Blc. Golden Dome	= Pot. Heidi Gubler	× Lc. Cantabile	= Cantazac
× Blc. Mem. Crispin Rosales	= Pot. Vallespin	× Sc. Cleopatra	= Vallepatra

WARREN MOKI SAKUMA	**Lc. Ennerdale × Kao Hsiung**	**Otaguro 1975**
WESTERCELLE	**Lc. Cholletiana × Anzac**	**Wichmann 1973**
WYNKIN AND BLYNKIN	**Lc. Dormaniana × Soph. coccinea**	**Stewart Inc. 1975**
YEONG-HUEI CHEN	**C. Moscombe × Anzac**	**Hong-Sie Chen 1975 (Chung-Chweng Chen)**
YUKO SHIONO	**C. General Patton × Ramona**	**C. Takeda 1972**
ZANA	**L. Zip × Anzac**	**Rod McLellan Co. 1975**
ZUKI JOSEZAC	**Lc. José Dias Castro × Anzac**	**N. Suzuki 1975**

SOPHRONITIS

cernua‡ **species**

× C. luteola	= Sc. Frudo	× Sl. Jinn	= Sl. Sparklet
× Epi. conopseum	= Ephs. Concern		

coccinea*†‡ (syn. *grandiflora*†*) **species**

× B. glauca	= Bnts. Claire Beaumont	× L. lundii	= Sl. Minuet
× Bc. Daffodil	= Rolf. Little Mountain	× Lc. Aclandor	= Slc. Twinkle Toes
× Blc. Manatee Gold	= Pot. Mem. Bill White	× Lc. Antonica Fredrick	= Slc. Ftatateeta
× Blc. Mellowglow	= Pot. Sundance	× Lc. Dormaniana	= Slc. Wynkin and Blynkin
× C. Auranti-media	= Sc. Ellen Esther Hood	× Lc. Intermedio-flava	= Slc. Martha Withner
× C. bicolor	= Sc. Pearlouis	× Lc. Little Sunbeam	= Slc. Sassy Sofia
× C. Bob Betts	= Sc. Rose Pixie	× Lc. Ozark	= Slc. Nancy Bellows
× C. Bow Bells	= Sc. Marionette	× Lc. Thurderniana	= Slc. Sally Dickinson
× C. Fitz Eugene Dixon	= Sc. Retha	× Lc. Wine Festival	= Slc. Chili Pepper Red
× C. George Eastman	= Sc. Yone Arai	× Pot. Gordon Siu	= Pot. Coral Queen
× Epi. mooreanum	= Ephs. Crushed Raspberry		

grandiflora*† (see *coccinea*†‡*) **species**

STACYARA

SAM	**Epi. gracile × Sc. Cleopatra**	**Stacy 1973**

STAMARIAARA

NOEL	Rnthps. Moon Walk × Ascda. Meda Arnold	K. F. Yap 1974 (Sta Maria)
RAYNA	Rnthps. Amy Russell × Ascda. Ophelia	Fort Caroline 1975 (Wallbrunn)

STANFIELDARA

SARAH'S PSYCHE	Epi. Sarah Jesup × Sl. Psyche	Jesup 1971

SYMPHOGLOSSUM

sanguineum (see *Cochlioda sanguinea**†) — species

TREVORARA

WONG SEW LAN	Aranda Queen of Purples × Phal. Sulochana	Hon San 1972

TRICHOCENTRUM

pfavii — species
× Onc. lanceanum = Trcdm. Peter Allen

tigrinum†‡ — species
× Onc. lindenii = Trcdm. Teddy Bear

TRICHOCIDIUM

PETER ALLEN	Trctm. pfavii × Onc. lanceanum	Chambers 1973 (Rootstein)
TEDDY BEAR	Trctm. tigrinum × Onc. lindenii	Das 1974 (Vagner)

TRICHOGLOTTIS

brachiata†‡ — species
× Ascda. Meda Arnold = Fjo. Gem | × V. Fair Queen = Trcv. Dark Star

fasciata†‡ — species
× Aërdns. Colombia = Plsra. Medellin | × Ren. monachica = Rngl. Clarence Russell

TRICHOVANDA

DARK STAR	Trgl. brachiata × V. Fair Queen	Wilkins 1973 (R. Baker)
DEAR ULAULA	V. dearei × Ulaula	Otaguro 1974
ULAULA	Trgl. brachiata × V. sanderana	Foster Bot. Gdn. 1948
× V. dearei	= Dear Ulaula	

VANDA

ADORABLE	Lenavat × Judy Miyamoto	Ooi Leng Sun 1975 (Phairot's)

AFTERGLOW†‡ — **insignis × sanderana** — **R. E. Warne 1952**
× Mimi Palmer = Polly Woo

AGNES JOAQUIM (see Miss Joaquim*†‡)
ALICE CHAN‡ — **Ernest Fujinaga × Waipuna** — **Chan 1960**
× tessellata = Susie Whitesell

ALICIA ONO‡ — **Jennie Hashimoto × sanderana** — **Ono 1960 (E. Y. Hashimoto)**
× Waimea = Honuapo Dream | × Aranda Lily Chong = Aranda Singapura

AMARA — **Sinard × Patou** — **Chavalit 1975**
AMBERA — **Mem. Madame Pranerm × Aurawan** — **Vipar 1974**
amesiana†‡ — **species**
× coerulea = Martha Ragan | × lamellata = Kevin Almas

AMIGO FRITZ — **Charm × sanderana** — **Garth 1971**
AMPHAI — **Thananchai × Onomea** — **Satirasut 1973 (Soonthonwana)**
ANDRE YEE — **Colorsan × Sarojini** — **M.O.N. 1973**
APHIRADEE — **Rose Davis × Thananchai** — **Chantramontol 1974**
ARNOTHAI — **Lenavat × Onomea** — **Lenavat 1974**
ASMARA — **Kohala × Carolyn Koshiro** — **Ooi Leng Sun 1974**
AURAWAN — **Eisensander × sanderana** — **Vipar 1969**
× Boonchoke = Praneet | × Thananchai = Seeprai
× Mem. Madame Pranerm = Ambera | × Ascda. Meda Arnold = Ascda. Kitiga
× Satta = Samsuk | × Ascda. Medasand = Ascda. Ployphommas

BABY FACE — **Kekaseh × merrillii** — **S'pore Orchids 1975**
BANDON — **Sinard × Hilo Queen** — **Chavalit 1973**
BANGCHANG BEAUTY — **Pikul × Eisenhower** — **Lim Kim Yoo 1971**
BANGKAPI — **James Toogood × Hilo Queen** — **Chavalit 1974**
BANGKHEN — **sanderana × Wongse** — **Chindavanic 1973 (T. Kono)**
BANGKHUNSRI — **Thananchai × Mem. Madame Pranerm** — **Niamnuamtham 1974**
BANGKOK BLUE — **Diane Ogawa × coerulea** — **B.G.S. Orchids 1972**
× Laurel Yap = Blue Empress

BANGKRABUE — **laotica × teres** — **Bangkrabue 1974**
BANG NARA — **Prachark Chit × Sinard** — **Riewthong 1974**
BANGPAI — **Rothschildiana × Charlesworthii** — **Chuanyen 1975**
BANGPHA — **Sathupradit × coerulea** — **Muttamara 1974**
BANG RUK — **Thananchai × Jennie Hashimoto** — **Sathirasut 1974**
BANGSAN — **Iolani × sanderana** — **Gesmaris 1970**
× Betsy Sumner = Lumpini

BANGYIKHAN — **Rothschildiana × Karen Ono** — **Sathirasut 1974**
BANLARD VITHYA — **Tan Chin Tuan × Jennie Hashimoto** — **Vipar 1973**
batemannii (see *Vandopsis lissochiloides*†‡) — **species**
BEEBE SUMNER‡ — **Onomea × Clara Shipman Fisher** — **G. W. Sumner 1955 (Nishimura)**
× Boonchoke = Sahanawin | × Aër. crassifolia = Aërdv. Sumalee
× Mem. Madame Pranerm = Madame Sivaporn | × Arach. Maggie Oei = Aranda Phuket
× sanderana = Sun Tan

BEE LIAN — **Onomea × Satta** — **Bee Lian 1975**

BELL RINGER | **Laurel Yap × Jennie Hashimoto** | **Wilkins 1974**

bensonii* | **species**

× Diane Ogawa	= Madame Supit	× Ascda. Medasand	= Ascda. Sam Muang
× Pikul	= Chantram	× Asctm. curvifolium	= Ascda. Sarasiri
× Arach. Maggie Oei	= Aranda Sansai	× Ren. storiei	= Rntda. Harnpongtham
× Ascda. Elieen Beauty	= Ascda. Maneetarn	× Rhy. gigantea	= Rhv. Tha Yang
× Ascda. Meda Arnold	= Ascda. Jim Lim		

BETSY SUMNER†‡ | **Faustii × sanderana** | **O. Kirsch 1949**

× Bangsan	= Lumpini	× Ellen Noa	= Sayang

BHIMAYOTHIN | **Lenavat × Jennie Hashimoto** | **Bhimayothin 1974**

BILL HENDERSON | **Iliwai × Tom Ritter** | **Thomas Ritter 1974**

BILL SUTTON†‡ | **Manila × sanderana** | **O. Kirsch 1951**

× Eisensander	= Hilo Glory	× Aër. odorata	= Aërdv. Kalya
× Helen Adams	= Brava August	× Ascda. Yip Sum Wah	= Ascda. Pink Doll
× Kuniko Sugihara	= Teoh Chee Keat		

BLUE BUTTON | **coerulescens × lamellata** | **W. W. G. Moir 1963**

× Nak. Wendy	= Nak. Siem Reap

BLUE EMPRESS | **Bangkok Blue × Laurel Yap** | **Palm Orchids 1975 (Vipar)**

BLUE FANTASY‡ | **Charlesworthii × coerulescens** | **Mrs. Gracia Lewis 1968**

× Aërdns. Bogor	= Burk. Fancy Free

BLUE SAPPHIRE | **Maurice Restrepo × coerulea** | **Fernando 1974**

× tessellata	= Dick Johnston

BLUET | **Gilbert Triboulet × Flammerolle** | **Marcel Lecoufle 1972**

BOECIEN | **Pink Blush × Rothschildiana** | **Marcel Lecoufle 1974**

BONNIE BLUE FUKUMURA‡ | **Pukele × coerulea** | **R. T. Fukumura 1967**

× Joan Rothsand	= Chin Teohlim	× Ascda. Blue Boy	= Ascda. Lorene Beauty
× Rothschildiana	= Suvitcha	× Ascda. Yip Sum Wah	= Ascda. Tiny Bubble
× sanderana	= Bukit Beauty	× Rhy. coelestis	= Rhv. Ewe Lean Im

BOONCHOKE | **Waimea × denisoniana** | **Tancharoen 1969 (Tubtimtep)**

× Aurawan	= Praneet	× Satta	= Golden Bangphra
× Beebe Sumner	= Sahanawin	× Ascda. Meda Arnold	= Ascda. Ring Lyman
× denisoniana	= Kampirananda	× Ascda. Medasand	= Ascda. Malini
× Eisensander	= Toh-chirakul	× Ascda. Tropicana	= Ascda. Kanokwon
× Jennie Hashimoto	= Sumana	× Ascda. Yip Sum Wah	= Ascda. Madame Kenny
× Mem. Madame Pranerm	= Panitta		

BOONPRAME | **Onomea × Tubtimtepya** | **Potisuk 1973 (Praimanee)**

BOONYA‡ | **sanderana × Bill Sutton** | **Boonyakanchana 1961**

× coerulea	= Sini

B. P. MOK‡ | **Sumarie × Miss van Deun** | **B. P. Mok 1962**

× Yukum Braga	= Ma Siau Kee	× Ascda. Yip Sum Wah	= Ascda. Sam Ang

BRAVA AUGUST | **Bill Sutton × Helen Adams** | **Doubrava 1973 (Augustyniak)**

BROWNIE‡ | **merrillii × Miss Joaquim** | **Foster Bot. Gdn. 1947**

(syn. Wong Peng Soon)

× Hilo Blue	= Leslie Yee

brunnea‡ — **species**

× Rose Davis = Hiranburana
× sanderana = Krajib
× teres = Panid
× Aër. falcata = Aërdv. Suebsanguan
× Arach. Maggie Oei = Aranda Sulyaphongse
× Asctm. miniatum = Ascda. Kitival
× Ren. coccinea = Rntda. Thailand
× Ren. storiei = Rntda. Salyaphongse
× Vdps. parishii = Opsis. Thin Thai Ngam

BUKIT BEAUTY — **Bonnie Blue Fukumura × sanderana** — **Tang Tee Heng 1973 (R. T. Fukumura)**

CAROLE HIRANO†‡ — **Gilbert Triboulet × sanderana** — **Hirano 1950**

× Jennie Hashimoto = Rara
× Onomea = Evelyn Williams

CAROLYN KOSHIRO‡ — **Walter F. Dillingham × sanderana** — **Shimamoto 1956**

× Diane Ogawa = Haad Song-Khla
× Jennie Hashimoto = Chartniyom
× Kohala = Asmara
× Lenavat = Rotchanai
× Shane Sugihara = Lim Jet Thien
× Rhy. coelestis = Rhv. Falling Sky

CHAIFA — **Patou × coerulea** — **Yen Orchid 1974**
CHAIKIT BLUE — **Diane Ogawa × Mimi Palmer** — **Tatiyawanitkul 1974**
CHAIYA — **Thananchai × Eisensander** — **Lim-im 1975**
CHALERMSUKE — **James Toogood × Karen Ono** — **Chindavanic 1974**
CHANENAM RAPHAEL — **Eisenhower × Sunray** — **Chantramontol 1975**
CHANTEK — **Kohala × Ellen Noa** — **Ooi Leng Sun 1974**
CHANTRAM — **Pikul × bensonii** — **Pengboonma 1974 (Ueprayoonvong)**

CHANTRAMONTOL — **Varavan × sanderana** — **Chantramontol 1973 (Sunthonwon)**

CHANUD PIYAOUI — **Saeng Pra-Artitya × Jennie Hashimoto** — **Chantramontol 1974**
CHARLES CAMPBELL — **Eisenhower × insignis** — **John H. Miller 1972**
charlesworthii / **CHARLESWORTHII*†‡** — **bensonii × coerulea** — **Nat. hyb.** / **hort.**

× Rothschildiana = Bangpai
× Ascda. Ophelia = Ascda. One Blue
× Ascda. Yip Sum Wah = Ascda. Chao Khun Yarn
× Ren. storiei = Rntda. Bangkae Beauty
× Rhy. coelestis = Rhv. Bangwag

CHARM‡ — **coerulescens × sanderana** — **W. W. G. Moir 1960**

× sanderana = Amigo Fritz

CHAROENRAT — **Chawee × Lenavat** — **Phatanadom 1973**
CHARTNIYOM — **Jennie Hashimoto × Carolyn Koshiro** — **Chartniyom 1974**
CHAVANANAND — **Jennie Hashimoto × Joan Rothsand** — **Piswong 1974**
CHAWEE — **Oscar M. Kirsch × sanderana** — **Rojanadara 1967 (T. Kono)**

× Lenavat = Charoenrat

CHERRY GLOW — **Cherry Ripe × sanderana** — **S'pore Orchids 1975**
CHERRY RIPE — **Norbert Alphonso × insignis** — **S'pore Orchids 1964**

× sanderana = Cherry Glow

CHEU MING SHUAN — **Honolii × Onomea** — **Cheu Ming Shuan 1975**
CHIA KAY HENG — **Josephine van Brero × Dawn Nishimura** — **Chia Kay Heng 1972**
CHIMEY WALKER‡ — **Flammerole × sanderana** — **Walker 1952**

× Mabelmae Kamahele = Kiliwehi Ciotti
× Ren. storiei = Rntda. Lorna Wurtzburg

CHINDA — **Onomea × Patou** — **Weerawathanamas 1975**
CHIN TEOHLIM — **Bonnie Blue Fukumura × Joan Rothsand** — **Ooi Leng Sun 1975 (Phairot's)**

CHONG CHEE YON — **Teo Koon Hwa × coerulea** — **C. Y. Mok 1971**

CHUSRI NARATTRUGSA	**Jennie Hashimoto × Mem. Madame Pranerm**	**Narattrugsa 1973**
CITRON BEAUTY	**Eisensander × Eisenhower**	**Bloom's Nursery 1974**
CLAIRE LUI	**Judy Miyamoto × Diane Ogawa**	**Lui 1975 (H. Kagawa)**
CLARA SHIPMAN FISHER†‡	**sanderana × Tatzeri**	**Shipman 1940**

× Waimea = Suvat

CLAUDIE LUI	**Pukele × Diane Ogawa**	**Lui 1975 (H. Kagawa)**

coerulea*†‡ — **species**

× amesiana = Martha Ragan
× Boonya = Sini
× Diane Ogawa = Bangkok Blue
× Hilo Queen = Sonthaya
× James Toogood = Nok
× Jeffrey = Patsy Leuterio
× Karen Ono = Nakorn Sawan
× Lenavat = Varavuth
× Maurice Restrepo = Blue Sapphire
× Patou = Chaifa
× Princess Blue = Ploenchit
× Sathupradit = Bangpha
× Sinard = Prasarn
× Sivanart Palm = Sukonth'sithi Blue
× Suvat = Pornchai
× Teo Koon Hwa = Chong Chee Yon
× Thananchai = Thanpuying Chongkol
× Aër. jarckiana = Aërdv. Blue Chips
× Ascda. Bonanza = Ascda. Leontine Ho
× Ascda. Erika Reuter = Ascda. Navy Blue
× Ascda. Medasand = Ascda. Rakpaibulsombat
× Ascda. Pensom = Ascda. Tud Tou
× Ascda. Sunkist = Ascda. Srisupa
× Ascda. Tan Chai Beng = Ascda. Pudtan
× Ascda. Yip Sum Wah = Ascda. Karen Ono
× Asctm. curvifolium = Ascda. Sara
× Phal. serpentilingua = Vdnps. Frail Fancy
× Ren. Cheok Thiam Huat = Rntda. Mem. Arthur Freed
× Rhy. coelestis = Rhv. Thailand
× Rhy. gigantea = Rhv. Azure

coerulescens*†‡ — **species**

× Miss Joaquim = Towaco
× Ascda. Elieen Beauty = Ascda. Louise Boyd
× Lsa. teretifolia = Lsnd. Rumrill
× Ren. coccinea = Rntda. Sangvichian
× Ren. monachica = Rntda. Rumrill
× Rhy. gigantea = Rhv. Ladda

COLORFUL†‡	**insignis × Miss Joaquim**	**C. & H. 1948**

× Ascda. Meda Arnold = Ascda. Lulu

COLORSAN†‡	**Colorful × sanderana**	**E. Iwanaga 1956**

× Sarojini = Andre Yee

COOPERI†‡ (syn. White Wings)	**hookerana × Miss Joaquim**	**— (Pre-1946)**

× Arach. Ishbel = Aranda Easter Joy

CRIMSON GLORY	**Onomea × Sun Tan**	**Sathirasut 1974**

cristata*†‡ — **species**

× merrillii = Mellow Days
× Rothschildiana = Razz
× Ascda. Yip Sum Wah = Ascda. Mem. Arthur Freed
× Asctm. curvifolium = Ascda. Rumrill
× Phal. Fairvale = Vdnps. Revelation
× Ren. imschootiana = Rntda. Kim Almas
× Ren. monachica = Rntda. Towaco

DARLENE ONO	**Jeffrey × sanderana**	**Ono 1972**
DAWN NISHIMURA‡	**Rothschildiana × Hilo Blue**	**Dr. H. Nishimura 1966**

× Josephine van Brero = Chia Kay Heng
× Aërdns. Bogor = Burk. Ong Thye Chiew
× Arach. hookerana = Aranda Noorah Alsagoff
× Arach. Maggie Oei = Aranda Neo Hoe Kiat
× Arach. Maroon Maggie = Aranda Ang Hee Seng
× Aranda Lily Chong = Aranda Wong Bee Yeok
× Aranda Tay Theng Suan = Aranda How Yee Peng

dearei*†‡ — **species**

× Ruby Prince = Gordon Dunlop
× Trcv. Ulaula = Trcv. Dear Ulaula
× Vdnps. Emily Yong = Vdnps. Tiger Cub
× Vdps. gigantea = Opsis. Moongleam

DENISE SUGIHARA | **Kuniko Sugihara × Mabelmae Kamahele** | **Sugihara 1975**

denisoniana*†‡ | **species**

× Boonchoke	= Kampirananda	× Aër. flabellata	= Aërdv. Vieng Ping
× Eisensander	= Homchuen	× Ascda. Meda Arnold	= Ascda. Tavivat
× Kekaseh	= Pierre Lardin	× Ascda. Medasand	= Ascda. Nibha
× Mem. Madame Pranerm	= Petchburi	× Ascda. Ophelia	= Ascda. Philoden
× merrillii	= Somthawil	× Ascda. Sunkist	= Ascda. Theptong
× Thananchai	= Rachadaporn	× Asctm. miniatum	= Ascda. Chaisiri
× Aër. crassifolia	= Aërdv. Pranin	× Ren. coccinea	= Rntda. Longchen
× Aër. falcata	= Aërdv. Photisan	× Vdps. parishii	= Opsis. Denipar

DENIZONICA†‡ | **denisoniana × luzonica** | **Shipman 1948**

× Ascda. Ophelia = Ascda. No Ka Oi

DENNISAND | **Denizonica × sanderana** | **Bowman 1955**

× Eisenhower = Dennisandhower

DENNISANDHOWER | **Dennisand × Eisenhower** | **Mrs. H. W. Fox 1975 (T. Ogawa Orchids)**

DIANA (see Poepoe†‡)

DIANE OGAWA‡ | **Hilo Blue × sanderana** | **Ogawa 1964**

× bensonii	= Madame Supit	× Pukele	= Claudie Lui
× Carolyn Koshiro	= Haad Song-Khla	× Satta	= Doctor Kanai
× coerulea	= Bangkok Blue	× Sun Tan	= Mem. Madame Liab
× Eisenhower	= Viroonchan	× Thananchai	= Sunkakul
× Hilo Queen	= Hilo Deb	× Varavan	= Issop Dinar
× Jennie Hashimoto	= Thonglor	× Aër. jarckiana	= Aërdv. Deechai
× Joan Rothsand	= Viraya	× Arach. hookerana	= Aranda Suharto
× Judy Miyamoto	= Claire Lui	× Ascda. Elieen Beauty	= Ascda. Polly Adams
× Kapiolani	= Major Suvicha	× Ascda. Mangkiatkul	= Ascda. Cholnapha
× Mem. Madame Pranerm	= Siam	× Ascda. Medasand	= Ascda. Suthisan
× Mimi Palmer	= Chaikit Blue	× Ascda. Tan Chai Beng	= Ascda. Savita
× Nancy Rodillas	= Teoline Crimson	× Ascda. Yip Sum Wah	= Ascda. Hawaiian Delight
× Onomea	= Wanajutha	× Ren. storiei	= Rntda. Teo Boon Hian
× Pikul	= Mem. Adolphus McLeod	× Vasco. Susan	= Vasco. Jim Snider

DICK JOHNSTON | **Blue Sapphire × tessellata** | **Fernando 1974**

DOCTOR JIM CHAN | **Thananchai × Sunray** | **Chantramontol 1975**

DOCTOR KANAI | **Satta × Diane Ogawa** | **Chavalit 1974**

DOCTOR NANDHIKA | **Kapiolani × Patou** | **Chavalit 1974**

DOLORES-ANNE‡ | **Ruby × tessellata** | **Braga 1959**

× luzonica = Louis von Planta

DONJADEE | **Pikul × Jennie Hashimoto** | **W. P. Orchid 1974**

DORIS ROYAL | **Rothschildiana × Jennie Hashimoto** | **E. L. Royal 1964 (Dr. H. Nishimura)**

× Ohuohu	= Pastel Lady	× Rothschildiana	= Teoline Sapphire

DOROTHEA | **T.M.A. × tessellata** | **Garth 1971**

D. S. SENANAYAKE | **coerulea × Cooperi** | **de Saram 1948**

× tessellata = Hemamali

EISENHOWER†‡ | **Ellen Noa × sanderana** | **Y. Fujinaga 1953 (Kodama)**

× Dennisand	= Dennisandhower	× Mem. Madame Pranerm	= Pranerm Haze
× Diane Ogawa	= Viroonchan	× Pikul	= Bangchang Beauty
× Eisensander	= Citron Beauty	× Pukele	= Teoline Summer
× Hukilau	= Teoline Haze	× Sunray	= Chanenam Raphael
× insignis	= Charles Campbell	× Aër. flabellata	= Aërdv. Bronze Triumph
× James Toogood	= Teoline Sunrise	× Ascda. Elieen Beauty	= Ascda. Eisen Beauty
× Joyce Lynne Chong	= Keoni Noa	× Ascda. Lani Bird	= Ascda. Paradise Queen
× Mary Foster	= Georgia Brown	× Ascda. Meda Arnold	= Ascda. Capricorn

EISENHOWER†‡ *(continued)*

× Ascda. Red Gem = Ascda. Robert Berryman
× Ascda. Yip Sum Wah = Ascda. Korb Fah
× Asctm. curvifolium = Ascda. Darcey Starr
× Asctm. miniatum = Ascda. Maui Gold
× Vdps. gigantea = Opsis. Beatrice Burns

EISENSANDER‡ **Eisenhower × sanderana** **J. & S. 1962**

× Bill Sutton = Hilo Glory
× Boonchoke = Toh-chirakul
× denisoniana = Homchuen
× Eisenhower = Citron Beauty
× Frank Crook = Kona Sunset
× Harvest Time = Wong Yoot Gnoh
× Helen Paoa = Wong Weng Hoong
× Hilo Blue = Hilo Dawn
× Hilo Queen = Hilo Gem
× James Toogood = Teoline Sunset
× Jennie Hashimoto = Teoline Queen
× Judith Y. Nishimura = Wong Kok Peng
× Laurel Yap = Francin Yap
× Mem. Madame Pranerm = Pranerm Violet
× Ohuohu = Sauvanee
× Onomea = Roy Dome
× Rothschildiana = Hilo Princess
× Satta = Pusdee
× Thananchai = Chaiya
× Ascda. Meda Arnold = Ascda. Mittaparb Rama
× Ascda. Yip Sum Wah = Ascda. Madame Vanida

ELLEN NOA†‡ **dearei × sanderana** **J. K. Noa 1946**

× Betsy Sumner = Sayang
× Green Gold = Stuart Furumizo
× James Toogood = Teoline Sunny
× Kohala = Chantek
× lamellata = Yellowstone
× Ascda. Portia Doolittle = Ascda. Laureen Ono

EMMA VAN DEVENTER†‡ **teres × tricolor** **van Deventer 1926**

× Hilo Queen = Hilo Moon
× Judy Miyamoto = Pasha
× Ascda. Meda Arnold = Ascda. Ching Mook Choon
× Ascda. Mem. Choo Laikeun = Ascda. Carolaine
× Ascda. Yip Sum Wah = Ascda. Little Pasha

ERIC GARTH **Ruby Garth × sanderana** **Garth 1973**

EVE **sanderana × Manisaki** **Garth 1968**

× Ascda. Tropicana = Ascda. Marlene Sundermier

EVELYN RITTER **Nellie Morley × Tom Ritter** **Thomas Ritter 1974**

EVELYN WILLIAMS **Carole Hirano × Onomea** **F. H. Williams 1974**

EVENING TIDE **Princess Blue × Rothschildiana** **Wilkins 1974**

FAIR QUEEN‡ **Clara Shipman Fisher × Rothschildiana** **Shimamoto 1950**

× Rothschildiana = Gladys Sellers
× sanderana = Teoline Fairqueen
× Aranda Hilda Galistan = Aranda Sweet Honey
× Ascda. Ophelia = Ascda. Palm Beach Maid
× Trgl. brachiata = Trcv. Dark Star

FARAH PAHLAVI **Ling × tessellata** **S.B.G. 1974**

FLAMMEROLLE†‡ **coerulea × luzonica** **V. 1945**

× Gilbert Triboulet = Bluet

FRANCIN YAP **Laurel Yap × Eisensander** **Leo Yap 1972**

FRANCIS CHEONG **Rothschildiana × Rose Davis** **Cheong Chee Yon 1973**

FRANCIS RODILLAS **Nancy Rodillas × Onomea** **Rodillas 1974**

FRANK CROOK‡ **Honolulu × sanderana** **R. E. Warne 1956**

× Eisensander = Kona Sunset
× Hilo Queen = Papaaloa Queen
× Laurel Yap = Mem. Joseph Mitterer
× Lenavat = Mem. Mowchita
× Mabelmae Kamahele = Sapan Kwai
× Mem. Madame Pranerm = Queen Thonburi
× Pikul = Saeng Pra-Artitya
× sanderana = Pacific Sunset
× Ascda. Medasand = Ascda. Prayoon
× Ascda. Yip Sum Wah = Ascda. Flora Yap

FRED THORNTON **Lester McCoy × insignis** **John H. Miller 1971**

GEORGIA BROWN **Mary Foster × Eisenhower** **Ruben 1974**

GERTRUDE MIYAMOTO†‡ **Mem. G. Tanaka × sanderana** **E. Iwanaga 1951**

× Patricia Lee = Sundance

VANDA

GILBERT TRIBOULET*†‡ | **coerulea × tricolor** | **Gratiot 1919**

× Flammerolle = Bluet
× Aranda Lucy Laycock = Aranda Danny Boy

GILLIAN TREVOR‡ | **Josephine van Brero × Eisenhower** | **Trevor 1962 (Chow Yee Wah)**

× Jennie Hashimoto = Jennifer
× Laurel Yap = Shadow
× Ascda. Meda Arnold = Ascda. Aries

GLADYS SELLERS | **Fair Queen × Rothschildiana** | **Mese 1974**

GOLDEN BANGPHRA | **Boonchoke × Satta** | **Muttamara 1974**

GORDON DUNLOP | **Ruby Prince × dearei** | **Lazaroo 1972 (S.B.G.)**

GREEN GOLD‡ | **Venus × sanderana** | **Takakura 1965**

× Ellen Noa = Stuart Furumizo

HAAD SONG-KHLA | **Diane Ogawa × Carolyn Koshiro** | **Palm Orchids 1972**

HAIHAI | **coerulea × Eisenhower** | **Miyao 1966**

× Ascda. Meda Arnold = Ascda. Ooi Boon Huat

HARRIET MIYAO‡ | **Nellie Morley × coerulea** | **Miyao 1958**

× Rothschildiana = Issei
× Ascda. Meda Arnold = Ascda. Hawaiian Blue

HARRY WILLIAMS | **Jennie Hashimoto × Tom Ritter** | **H. G. Williams 1974**

HARVEST TIME‡ | **dearei × Ellen Noa** | **Woodlawn 1954**

× Eisensander = Wong Yoot Gnoh
× Arach. flos-aëris = Aranda Toh Chong Boon
× Ren. storiei = Rntda. Lean Yin

HELEN ADAMS† | **dearei × suavis** | **De Saram 1944**

× Bill Sutton = Brava August

HELEN MARTINO | **Yolanda × Rothschildiana** | **Martino 1974**

HELEN PAOA†‡ | **Emily Notley × sanderana** | **R. Tanaka 1950**

× Eisensander = Wong Weng Hoong

helvola‡ | **species**

× Ascda. Yip Sum Wah = Ascda. Constance de Bruyne

HEMAMALI | **D. S. Senanayake × tessellata** | **Piyasena 1973**

HILO BLUE‡ | **Bill Sutton × coerulea** | **Miyao 1960**

× Brownie = Leslie Yee
× Eisensander = Hilo Dawn
× Hilo Queen = Hilo Song
× Joan Rothsand = Sky Raider
× Kiliwehi Kono = Taiping
× Mem. Madame Pranerm = Khuen Petch
× Takeji Ogawa = Princess Punalu'u
× Waianae Blue = Pokai Bay
× Waimea = Pahala
× Aër. lawrenceae = Aërdv. Moonface
× Arach. Ishbel = Aranda Johore Beauty
× Aranda Golden Sands = Aranda Beach Belle
× Ascda. Yip Sum Wah = Ascda. Madame Nok
× Rhv. Tan Geat Leng = Rhv. Telaga Biru

HILO CHARM | **Hilo Blue × Frank Crook** | **Miyao 1969**

× Hilo Queen = Pasu
× Ascda. Yip Sum Wah = Ascda. Major Chamnien

HILO DAWN | **Eisensander × Hilo Blue** | **Miyao 1973**

HILO DEB | **Hilo Queen × Diane Ogawa** | **Miyao 1973**

HILO GEM | **Eisensander × Hilo Queen** | **Miyao 1973**

HILO GLORY | **Eisensander × Bill Sutton** | **Miyao 1975**

HILO MOON | **Emma van Deventer × Hilo Queen** | **Miyao 1973**

HILO PRINCESS | **Rothschildiana × Eisensander** | **Miyao 1973**

HILO QUEEN	**Eisenhower × Jennie Hashimoto**	**Miyao 1963**

× coerulea	= Sonthaya	× Patou	= Ratchada
× Diane Ogawa	= Hilo Deb	× Rothschildiana	= Lore Paul
× Eisensander	= Hilo Gem	× sanderana	= Hilo Sand
× Emma van Deventer	= Hilo Moon	× Satta	= Supatra
× Frank Crook	= Papaaloa Queen	× Sinard	= Bandon
× Hilo Blue	= Hilo Song	× Ascda. Mangkiatkul	= Ascda. Lady Arunee
× Hilo Charm	= Pasu	× Ascda. Meda Arnold	= Ascda. Hilo Rose
× James Toogood	= Bangkapi	× Ascda. Medasand	= Ascda. Mem. Verawan
× Jennie Hashimoto	= Pechkire	× Ascda. Ophelia	= Ascda. Hilo Sunset
× Lenavat	= Patricia		

HILO SAND	**Hilo Queen × sanderana**	**Chindavanic 1972 (Chavalit)**
HILO SONG	**Hilo Queen × Hilo Blue**	**Miyao 1973**
HIRANBURANA	**Rose Davis × brunnea**	**Hiranburana 1975**
HO KING	**Karen Ogawa × Puainako**	**Ah Lai 1971**
HOMCHUEN	**Eisensander × denisoniana**	**Vipar 1973**
HONOLII†‡	**Herziana × sanderana**	**Tanabe 1951**

× Mem. Madame Pranerm	= Segamat	× Ascda. Meda Arnold	= Ascda. Sunny Day
× Onomea	= Cheu Ming Shuan	× Asctm. curvifolium	= Ascda. Miami

HONOLULU†‡	**Frank Scudder × sauderana**	**R. Tanaka 1948**

× Aranda Lily Chong	= Aranda Tan Seng Beng	× Ascda. Sunkist	= Ascda. Lulukist

HONOMU	**Ohuohu × Ellen Noa**	**Fujimoto 1954 (Yamada)**

× Pukele	= Mae-Joe	× Rothschildiana	= Lim Eang Kim

HONUAPO DREAM	**Alicia Ono × Waimea**	**Nishiguchi 1973**

hookerana*†‡	**species**	

(This name is retained for horticultural, including registration, purposes, although this species is classified within the genus *Papilionanthe* by some authorities.)

× Mem. Marie Osment	= Osment

HUKILAU	**Hilo Blue × Jennie Hashimoto**	**Miyao 1967**

× Eisenhower	= Teoline Haze	× sanderana	= Teoline Royal
× Onomea	= Teoline Blush	× Ascda. Meda Arnold	= Ascda. Teoline Fiery
× Rothschildiana	= Teoline Rosieblue		

ILIWAI‡	**Eisenhower × Mabelmae Kamahele**	**Ono 1966**

× Tom Ritter	= Bill Henderson

IMELDA ROMUALDEZ MARCOS	**Yuet Yeng Lim × Richard Warne**	**Schaffner 1973**

insignis*†‡	**species**	

× Eisenhower	= Charles Campbell	× Lester McCoy	= Fred Thornton
× Josephine van Brero	= Sunbrero		

INTAN	**Pikul × Miss Joaquim**	**Ooi Leng Sun 1975**
IOLANI†‡	**Clara Shipman Fisher × merrillii**	**Lau 1950**

× Ren. Brookie Chandler	= Rntda. Iolani Luahine

ISSEI	**Harriet Miyao × Rothschildiana**	**R. K. Mizuta 1972**
ISSOP DINAR	**Varavan × Diane Ogawa**	**Chantramontol 1975**
IWALANI‡	**Ellen Noa × coerulea**	**Takeya 1952**

× Rothschildiana	= Lido Sunset

JAMES HARDING — **Bill Sutton × Rothschildiana** — **Harding 1963 (Takakura)**

× Ascda. Tan Chai Beng	= Ascda. Paidee Madee	× Ren. imschootiana	= Rntda. Itsukushima

JAMES TOOGOOD‡ — **Waipuna × sanderana** — **Toogood 1963 (Limberlost)**

× coerulea	= Nok	× Onomea	= Kamanit
× Eisenhower	= Teoline Sunrise	× Pukele	= Teoline Aster
× Eisensander	= Teoline Sunset	× Rothschildiana	= Jiranuwat
× Ellen Noa	= Teoline Sunny	× Teoline Rosieglow	= Teoline Harvest
× Hilo Queen	= Bangkapi	× Ascda. Meda Arnold	= Ascda. Lieutenant Chor
× Jennie Hashimoto	= Vimol	× Ascda. Yip Sum Wah	= Ascda. Leng
× Karen Ono	= Chalermsuke	× Ren. storiei	= Rntda. Tumira Skinner

JANET TAGAWA‡ — **Kalihi Beauty × luzonica** — **Tagawa 1951**

× Phal. Barbara Beard	= Vdnps. Phyllis Sumner	× Rhy. gigantea	= Rhv. Louise Boyd

JAROYPON — **Ohuohu × Karen Ono** — **Chavalit 1974**

JEAN FUKUDO — **merrillii × Manila** — **Fukudo 1953**

× Asctm. curvifolium	= Ascda. Kathy Erne		

JEFFREY‡ — **Eisenhower × Rothschildiana** — **K. Miyamoto 1962**

× coerulea	= Patsy Leuterio	× Ascda. Meda Arnold	= Ascda. Joanna Ono
× sanderana	= Darlene Ono	× Asctm. curvifolium	= Ascda. Florida Sunset
× Takeji Ogawa	= Joel Aherrera		

JENNIE HASHIMOTO†‡ — **sanderana × Onomea** — **E. Y. Hashimoto 1954 (E. Iwanaga)**

× Boonchoke	= Sumana	× Pukele	= Teoline Winsome
× Carole Hirano	= Rara	× Rose Davis	= Teoline Honour
× Carolyn Koshiro	= Chartniyom	× Saeng Pra-Artitya	= Chanud Piyaoui
× Diane Ogawa	= Thonglor	× Tan Chin Tuan	= Banlard Vithya
× Eisensander	= Teoline Queen	× tessellata	= Piyasena
× Gillian Trevor	= Jennifer	× Thananchai	= Bang Ruk
× Hilo Queen	= Pechkire	× Tom Ritter	= Harry Williams
× James Toogood	= Vimol	× Waimea	= Phimpong
× Joan Rothsand	= Chavananand	× Ascda. Darcey Starr	= Ascda. Phrapinit
× Laurel Yap	= Bell Ringer	× Ascda. Medasand	= Ascda. South East Star
× Lenavat	= Bhimayothin	× Ascda. Priyavadee	= Ascda. Nongkham
× Mamo	= Lucy Pang	× Ascda. Tan Chai Beng	= Ascda. Pim Siri
× Manisaki	= Mem. Lennie	× Ascda. Tropicana	= Ascda. Taratikun
× Mem. Madame Pranerm	= Chusri Narattrugsa	× Ascda. Yip Sum Wah	= Ascda. Sauvanee
× Nancy Rodillas	= Teoline Pinksworth		
× Pikul	= Donjadee		

JENNIFER — **Gillian Trevor × Jennie Hashimoto** — **Wilkins 1973**

JIRANUVAT — **Rothschildiana × James Toogood** — **Jiranuvat 1971**

JOAN ROTHSAND‡ — **Joan Swearingen × Onomea** — **Lenavat 1964**

× Bonnie Blue Fukumura	= Chin Teohlim	× Mem. Madame Pranerm	= Supan-Buri
× Diane Ogawa	= Viraya	× Onomea	= Opha
× Hilo Blue	= Sky Raider	× Sarojini	= Varai
× Jennie Hashimoto	= Chavananand	× Varavan	= Madame Somboon
× Mabelmae Kamahele	= Lone Star	× Asctm. curvifolium	= Ascda. Captain Chor

JOEL AHERRERA — **Jeffrey × Takeji Ogawa** — **Ono 1973**

JOHN'S HO — **Ohuohu × Sunray** — **Chantramontol 1975**

JOSEPHINE (see Miss Joaquim*†‡)

JOSEPHINE van BRERO†‡ — **insignis × teres** — **van Brero 1936**

× Dawn Nishimura	= Chia Kay Heng	× Puainako	= Margaret Foster
× insignis	= Sunbrero	× Aër. lawrenceae	= Aërdv. Aristocrat
× Kekaseh	= Nona Manis	× Aërctm. Luke Nok	= Chtra. Malibu Gold

JOSEPHINE van BRERO†‡ *(continued)*

× Ascda. Hilo Rose = Ascda. Heah Hock Heng
× Ascda. Mem. Choo Laikeun = Ascda. Karen Codling
× Ascda. Red Gem = Ascda. Yeap Eng Sim
× Ascda. Yip Sum Wah = Ascda. Chaiyot

JOYCE LYNNE CHONG — **Henrietta Ho × Ellen Noa** — **Kam In Chong 1954 (J. K. Noa)**

× Eisenhower = Keoni Noa
× Ascda. Ophelia = Ascda. Kay Yoshida

JUDITH Y. NISHIMURA — **Frank Scudder × dearei** — **Kodama 1951**

× Eisensander = Wong Kok Peng

JUDY MIYAMOTO‡ — **Mabelmae Kamahele × Rothschildiana** — **K. Miyamoto 1962**

× Diane Ogawa = Claire Lui
× Emma van Deventer = Pasha
× Lenavat = Adorable
× Rothschildiana = Richella Blue
× sanderana = Teoline Chieftain
× Ascda. Elieen Beauty = Ascda. Dr. Shinso Kagawa
× Ascda. Meda Arnold = Ascda. Agnes Kagawa

JULIA SIDERIS†‡ — **Rothschildiana × tricolor** — **O. Kirsch 1949**

× Ren. storiei = Rntda. Mandai

KALAMA MAUI — **Pukele × Mabelmae Kamahele** — **Furumizo 1970**

× Ascda. Meda Arnold = Ascda. Mildred Furumizo
× Ascda. Tan Chai Beng = Ascda. Dawn Fukumura
× Ascda. Yip Sum Wah = Ascda. Maui Kaimana

KAMANA BLUE — **Sarojini × Rothschildiana** — **Rodillas 1974**

KAMANIT — **James Toogood × Onomea** — **Jiranuvat 1975**

KAMPIRANANDA — **Boonchoke × denisoniana** — **Ratananda 1973**

KAPIOLANI‡ — **Ohuohu × Onomea** — **Ogawa 1956**

× Diane Ogawa = Major Suvicha
× Patou = Doctor Nandhika
× Pukele = Sithaman
× Ascda. Elieen Beauty = Ascda. Paratee
× Ascda. Meda Arnold = Ascda. Chumpol
× Ascda. Yip Sum Wah = Ascda. Luk Jeap

KAREN OGAWA — **Mabelmae Kamahele × sanderana** — **Ogawa 1961**

× Puainako = Ho King

KAREN ONO — **Rothschildiana × Frank Crook** — **Ono 1967**

× coerulea = Nakorn Sawan
× James Toogood = Chalermsuke
× Mem. Fumiko Omoto = Viroonchan Blue
× Ohuohu = Jaroypon
× Rothschildiana = Bangyikhan
× sanderana = Khong Swee Wah
× Sinard = Lumpoon
× Thananchai = Sakchai
× Ascda. Tan Chai Beng = Ascda. Vuthichai
× Ascda. Yip Sum Wah = Ascda. Santisuk

KASET BANGPRA — **Rothschildiana × Patou** — **Prombutra 1974 (Tongdee)**

KATHY OLYPHANT‡ — **Manila × Jennie Hashimoto** — **Ono 1969**

× Ascda. Elieen Beauty = Ascda. Lois Kashiwada
× Ascda. Meda Arnold = Ascda. Mary Strann

KEKASEH — **insignis × cristata** — **S'pore Orchids 1968 (Mrs. Gracia Lewis)**

× denisoniana = Pierre Lardin
× Josephine van Brero = Nona Manis
× merrillii = Baby Face

KEONI NOA — **Joyce Lynne Chong × Eisenhower** — **John Noa 1972**

× Ascda. Yip Sum Wah = Ascda. Hawaiian Monarch

KEVIN ALMAS — **amesiana × lamellata** — **MAJ Orchids 1975**

KHONG SWEE WAH — **Karen Ono × sanderana** — **Lum Chin Orchids 1974**
KHUEN PETCH — **Hilo Blue × Mem. Madame Pranerm** — **Vipar 1971**
KHUN KLANG — **Onomea × Kiliwehi Kono** — **N. P. R. Thong 1974**
KILIWEHI CIOTTI — **Mabelmae Kamahele × Chimey Walker** — **T. Kono 1973**
KILIWEHI KONO — **Onomea × Trisher** — **T. Kono 1971**

× Hilo Blue	= Taiping	× Onomea	= Khun Klang

KIYOKO FURUMIZO — **Mary Foster × Mabelmae Kamahele** — **Furumizo 1974**
KOHALA — **sanderana × Carole Hirano** — **H. N. Kawamoto 1954**

× Carolyn Koshiro	= Asmara	× Ellen Noa	= Chantek

KOH PHAIK LEAN — **Mem. Frieda Hantober × Rothschildiana** — **Wong Weng Hoong 1973**
KONA SUNSET — **Eisensander × Frank Crook** — **Miyao 1972**
KO SOOM — **Thananchai × Poepoe** — **Sombuntham 1974**
KRAJIB — **brunnea × sanderana** — **Wechsawarn 1975**
KUNIKO SUGIHARA — **Piihonua × Jennie Hashimoto** — **Sugihara 1968**

× Bill Sutton	= Teoh Chee Keat	× Mabelmae Kamahele	= Denise Sugihara

LADDA — **Thananchai × Pikul** — **T. Orchids 1975**
LAMDUAN — **Pikul × Pukele** — **Kanpai 1973**
lamellata*†‡ — **species**

× amesiana	= Kevin Almas	× Ascda. Yip Sum Wah	= Ascda. Dittagone
× Ellen Noa	= Yellowstone	× Ren. histrionica	= Rntda. Chang Min-Tat
× Ascda. Red Gem	= Ascda. Nicky Ng		

laotica‡ — **species**

× teres	= Bangkrabue	× Ascda. Yip Sum Wah	= Ascda. Pradit

LAUREL YAP — **Frank Crook × coerulea** — **Leo Yap 1965 (Miyao)**

× Bangkok Blue	= Blue Empress	× Arach. hookerana	= Aranda Anne Khoo
× Eisensander	= Francin Yap	× Ascda. Meda Arnold	= Ascda. Hilo Belle
× Frank Crook	= Mem. Joseph Mitterer	× Ascda. Sunkist	= Ascda. Goulds Glow
× Gillian Trevor	= Shadow	× Ascda. Tan Chai Beng	= Ascda. Wasana
× Jennie Hashimoto	= Bell Ringer	× Ascda. Tropicana	= Ascda. Hollis Yap
× Rothschildiana	= Sai Wan Loo	× Asctm. curvifolium	= Ascda. Violet Yap
× sanderana	= Renton Hutchison	× Rhy. coelestis	= Rhy. Sea Breeze
× Sun Tan	= Prakypetch		

LENAVAT — **Joan Rothsand × sanderana** — **Lenavat 1969**

× Carolyn Koshiro	= Rotchanai	× Satta	= Yanawa
× Chawee	= Charoenrat	× Serene	= Namprasert
× coerulea	= Varavuth	× Thananchai	= Urbchitr
× Frank Crook	= Mem. Mowchita	× Ascda. Buddy Choo	= Ascda. Toh Chin Soo
× Hilo Queen	= Patricia	× Ascda. Cholburi	= Ascda. Thai Ruby
× Jennie Hashimoto	= Bhimayothin	× Ascda. Mangkiatkul	= Ascda. Ann
× Judy Miyamoto	= Adorable	× Ascda. Meda Arnold	= Ascda. Djaja
× Mem. Madame Pranerm	= Yongyuth	× Ascda. Medasand	= Ascda. Phairot
× Onomea	= Arnothai	× Ascda. Tan Chai Beng	= Ascda. Yachitr
× Patou	= Pimsai	× Ascda. Yip Sum Wah	= Ascda. Sthaporn
× Rothschildiana	= Thospol		

LESLIE H. KAGAWA‡ — **Iolani × Miss Joaquim** — **H. Kagawa 1959**

× Asctm. curvifolium	= Ascda. Kathleen Kagawa

LESLIE YEE — **Brownie × Hilo Blue** — **M.O.N. 1974**
LESTER McCOY†‡ — **coerulea × dearei** — **J. A. Cummins 1945**

× insignis	= Fred Thornton

LIDO SUNSET — **Rothschildiana × Iwalani** — **Cheong Chee Yon 1973**
limbata†‡ — **species**

× Arnth. Bloodshot	= Holtt. Patricia Postlethwaite	× Ren. monachica	= Rntda. Mahiole

Hybrid	Parentage	Registrant (Originator)
LIM EANG KIM	**Rothschildiana × Honomu**	**Tatichalearn 1975 (Pinvatanapruk)**
LIM JET THIEN	**Shane Sugihara × Carolyn Koshiro**	**Lim Jet Thien 1974 (Pang Keng How)**
LING	**Kapoho × insignis**	**K. C. Lim 1966 (S.B.G.)**
× tessellata	= Farah Pahlavi	
LONE STAR	**Mabelmae Kamahele × Joan Rothsand**	**Panczak 1975 (Sakdi Sri)**
LOPBURI	**Sapan Kwai × Rose Davis**	**T. Orchids 1975 (Sakuldejtana)**
LORE PAUL	**Hilo Queen × Rothschildiana**	**H. Paul 1974 (Murakami)**
LOUIS VON PLANTA	**Dolores-Anne × luzonica**	**A. G. Alphonso 1973 (S.B.G.)**
LOW KEE SING	**Bill Sutton × Ohuohu**	**Low Kee Sing 1962 (Ogawa)**
× Asctm. curvifolium	= Ascda. Aurora	
LUCY PANG	**Mamo × Jennie Hashimoto**	**Lim Jet Thien 1974 (Originator unknown)**
LUMPINI	**Bangsan × Betsy Sumner**	**Lenavat 1972**
× Ascda. Meda Arnold	= Ascda. Cholburi	
LUMPOON	**Karen Ono × Sinard**	**Chindavanic 1975**
luzonica*†‡	**species**	
× Dolores-Anne	= Louis von Planta	
LYNNE SUGIHARA‡	**Piihonua × sanderana**	**Sugihara 1952**
× Asctm. curvifolium	= Ascda. Lani Girl	
MABELMAE KAMAHELE†‡	**Ohuohu × sanderana**	**Harvest 1953 (Ogawa)**
× Chimey Walker	= Kiliwehi Ciotti	
× Frank Crook	= Sapan Kwai	
× Joan Rothsand	= Lone Star	
× Kuniko Sugihara	= Denise Sugihara	
× Mary Foster	= Kiyoko Furumizo	
× Rose Davis	= Madam Foong Khum	
× Ascda. Yip Sum Wah	= Ascda. Gisele Martin	
MADAME RATTANA	**Sun Tan × Mem. Madame Pranerm**	**Chunhopakorn 1974 (Thephasdin)**
MADAME SIVAPORN	**Beebe Sumner × Mem. Madame Pranerm**	**Charoen-ngam 1974**
MADAME SOMBOON	**Varavan × Joan Rothsand**	**Lim-im 1972**
MADAME SUPIT	**Diane Ogawa × bensonii**	**Tonganant 1974 (Pechpaisit)**
MADAM FOONG KHUM	**Mabelmae Kamahele × Rose Davis**	**S. S. H. Cheong 1974**
MAE-JOE	**Pukele × Honomu**	**Thornton's 1975**
MAJOR SUVICHA	**Kapiolani × Diane Ogawa**	**Sukontasup 1975 (Chavalit)**
MAMO‡	**hookerana × Tatzeri**	**Miyao 1957**
× Jennie Hashimoto	= Lucy Pang	
MANILA†‡	**luzonica × sanderana**	**Rapella 1943**
× Pikul	= Mary Fermin	
MANISAKI‡	**Mem. T. Iwasaki × Manila**	**Dr. W. Carter 1953**
× Jennie Hashimoto	= Mem. Lennie	
× Aër. lawrenceae	= Aërdv. Janice Choo	
MARGARET CHEONG	**Soo Hor Weng × Mem. Frieda Hantober**	**Cheong Pak Yik 1972 (Hiews')**

MARGARET FOSTER — **Josephine van Brero × Puainako** — **Trevor 1972 (Chow Yee Wah)**

MARGUERITE RICE‡ — **Honolulu × Manila** — **Rice 1956 (Pimental)**

× Ascda. Ophelia	= Ascda. Palm Beach Delight

MARTHA RAGAN — **coerulea × amesiana** — **M.A.J. Orchids 1975**

MARY CATHERINE BOWMAN‡ — **Onomea × Rothschildiana** — **Bowman 1957**

× Mem. Madame Pranerm	= Pranerm Crimson	× Ascda. Meda Arnold	= Ascda. Gracious Lady
× Rothschildiana	= Nell Allan	× Ascda. Yip Sum Wah	= Ascda. Mem. Vivian Fuse
× Varavan	= Rangsri Pearl	× Rhy. coelestis	= Rhv. Cabaret

MARY FERMIN — **Pikul × Manila** — **T. Orchids 1975 (Originator unknown)**

× Asctm. curvifolium	= Ascda. Chum Long

MARY FOSTER†‡ — **merrillii × sanderana** — **Foster Bot. Gdn. 1945**

× Eisenhower	= Georgia Brown	× Ascda. Meda Arnold	= Ascda. Lady Fay
× Mabelmae Kamahele	= Kiyoko Furumizo	× Asctm. curvifolium	= Ascda. Tiny June

MA SIAU KEE — **B. P. Mok × Yukum Braga** — **Choo Yeok Koon 1972**

MAURICE RESTREPO†‡ — **sanderana × teres** — **de Saram 1945**

× coerulea	= Blue Sapphire

MELLOW DAYS — **merrillii × cristata** — **S'pore Orchids 1972 (Mrs. Gracia Lewis)**

MEMORIA ADOLPHUS McLEOD — **Pikul × Diane Ogawa** — **Laurent 1975 (T. Orchids)**

MEMORIA FRIEDA HANTOBER‡ — **Rose Davis × sanderana** — **Hackett 1963 (Kirch)**

× Rothschildiana	= Koh Phaik Lean	× Ascda. Ophelia	= Ascda. To Soon
× Soo Hor Weng	= Margaret Cheong	× Ascda. Red Gem	= Ascda. Lee Yoke Sum

MEMORIA FUMIKO OMOTO‡ — **Onomea × coerulea** — **R. Yahiro 1958 (T. Kono)**

× Karen Ono	= Viroonchan Blue

MEMORIA HIROKADZU GAUDA — **Punchbowl × Rothschildiana** — **Gauda 1973**

MEMORIA JOSEPH MITTERER — **Laurel Yap × Frank Crook** — **Wilkins 1974**

MEMORIA LENNIE — **Manisaki × Jennie Hashimoto** — **Garth 1971**

MEMORIA MADAME LIAB — **Diane Ogawa × Sun Tan** — **Louboonmee 1975 (Pongplab)**

MEMORIA MADAME PRANERM‡ — **Waipuna × Eisenhower** — **Palm Orchids 1962**

× Aurawan	= Ambera	× Jennie Hashimoto	= Chusri Narattrugsa
× Beebe Sumner	= Madame Sivaporn	× Joan Rothsand	= Supan-Buri
× Boonchoke	= Panitta	× Lenavat	= Yongyuth
× denisoniana	= Petchburi	× Mary Catherine Bowman	= Pranerm Crimson
× Diane Ogawa	= Siam	× Neva H. Mitchell	= Pranerm Fanfare
× Eisenhower	= Pranerm Haze	× Onomea	= South-East Gold
× Eisensander	= Pranerm Violet	× Pikul	= Pranerm Flame
× Frank Crook	= Queen Thonburi	× Pukele	= Phong-aksorn
× Hilo Blue	= Khuen Petch	× Rothschildiana	= Pranerm Cloud
× Honolii	= Segamat	× sanderana	= Pranerm Ornete

MEMORIA MADAME PRANERM‡ *(continued)*

× Satta = Pontip
× Sun Tan = Madame Rattana
× Suvat = Wilai
× Thananchai = Bangkhunsri
× Wongse = Tawee
× Aër. flabellata = Aërdv. Natee Gold
× Ascda. Medasand = Ascda. Haad Ravai
× Rhy. gigantea = Rhv. Natee Day

MEMORIA MARIE OSMENT — **Sunset × hookerana** — **Osment 1963**

× hookerana = Osment

MEMORIA MOWCHITA — **Frank Crook × Lenavat** — **Napasab 1974**

MEMORIA PERCY VAN-DEN-DRIESEN — **teres × T.M.A.** — **Garth 1973**

MEMORIA TADAICHI DOI‡ — **Trisher × sanderana** — **C. M. Matsuo 1956 (T. Doi)**

× Ascda. Pearly = Ascda. Ruth Levin

MEMORIA T. IWASAKI*†‡ — **dearei × tricolor** — **Shimadzu 1934**

× Ren. storiei = Rntda. Coppertone
× Vdps. gigantea = Opsis. Constellation

merrillii*†‡ — **species**

× cristata = Mellow Days
× denisoniana = Somthawil
× Kekaseh = Baby Face
× Arach. Maggie Oei = Aranda Merry Maggie
× Aranda Chia Shui Keng = Aranda Iris Bannochie
× Ascda. Yip Sum Wah = Ascda. Merrill Sum Wah

MICHAEL OOI — **Rothschildiana × Pukele** — **Ooi Leng Sun 1974**

MIMI PALMER — **Tan Chay Yan × tessellata** — **Gem Nursery 1963**

× Afterglow = Polly Woo
× Diane Ogawa = Chaikit Blue
× Rothschildiana = Soo Kwong Man

MISS JOAQUIM*†‡ — **hookerana × teres** — **Ridley 1893 (Joaquim)**
(syn. Agnes Joaquim; syn. Josephine)

× coerulescens = Towaco
× Pikul = Intan
× Phal. Kolopaking = Vdnps. Handoyoharjo

MISS van DEUN*†‡ — **Miss Joaquim × teres** — **van Brero—**

× teres = Snowdon

MOK SAU LAN‡ — **Gertrude Miyamoto × Clara Shipman Fisher** — **C. Y. Mok 1963**

× Ren. coccinea = Rntda. Patcharee

MONACENSIS†‡ — **Burgeffii × Gilbert Triboulet** — **Munich Bot. Gdns 1933**

× Aër. lawrenceae = Aërdv. Stanley Smith

MRS. MARGARET MEYER — **Joan Swearingen × sanderana** — **Sekimura 1954**

× Ren. Brookie Chandler = Rntda. Loh Boon Siew

MUTHIYA‡ — **luzonica × Kapoho** — **Mackenzie 1964 (S.B.G.)**

× Ren. coccinea = Rntda. Anna Kubyshkina

NAKORN SAWAN — **coerulea × Karen Ono** — **Tiew 1974 (Baramee)**

NAMPRASERT — **Serene × Lenavat** — **Rotchanai 1975**

NANCY RODILLAS — **Mabelmae Kamahele × Jennie Hashimoto** — **Rodillas 1963**

× Diane Ogawa = Teoline Crimson
× Jennie Hashimoto = Teoline Pinksworth
× Onomea = Francis Rodillas
× sanderana = Nancysander
× Sarojini = Sukhum
× Ascda. Meda Arnold = Ascda. Teoline Festival
× Ascda. Ophelia = Ascda. Kristi Nakatsu
× Asctm. curvifolium = Ascda. Sisom

NANCYSANDER	**Nancy Rodillas × sanderana**	**Lenavat 1974**
NELL ALLAN	**Mary Catherine Bowman × Rothschildiana**	**H. L. Allan 1975**
NELLIE MORLEY†‡	**Emma van Deventer × sanderana**	**Morley 1952**

× Tom Ritter	= Evelyn Ritter		

NEVA H. MITCHELL‡	**Ellen Noa × Onomea**	**Hawaii V.N. 1956**

× Mem. Madame Pranerm	= Pranerm Fanfare	× sanderana	= Queensland Suntan

NOK	**James Toogood × coerulea**	**T. Rakpaiboonsombat 1972 (S. Rakpaiboonsombat)**
NONA MANIS	**Josephine van Brero × Kekaseh**	**K. F. Yap 1974**
NUUANU SKIES	**Oscar M. Kirsch × Rothschildiana**	**J. Milton Warne 1973**
OHUOHU†‡	**Clara Shipman Fisher × sanderana**	**Hirose 1947**

× Doris Royal	= Pastel Lady	× Thananchai	= Vasittee
× Eisensander	= Sauvanee	× Ascda. Darcey Starr	= Ascda. Pakawadee
× Karen Ono	= Jaroypon	× Ascda. Ophelia	= Ascda. Palm Beach Holiday
× Pikul	= Pong Tong		
× Sunray	= John's Ho		

ONOMEA†‡	**Rothschildiana × sanderana**	**Tani 1948**

× Carole Hirano	= Evelyn Williams	× Tellee	= Rainbow Trail
× Diane Ogawa	= Wanajutha	× Thananchai	= Amphai
× Eisensander	= Roy Dome	× Trisher	= Kiliwehi Kono
× Honolii	= Cheu Ming Shuan	× Tubtimtepya	= Boonprame
× Hukilau	= Teoline Blush	× Aër. falcata	= Aërdv. Permmit
× James Toogood	= Kamanit	× Aër. multiflora	= Aërdv. Gaine
× Joan Rothsand	= Opha	× Arach. Ishbel	= Aranda Blue Star
× Kiliwehi Kono	= Khun Klang	× Ascda. Anjo Mitterer	= Ascda. Anjomea
× Lenavat	= Arnothai	× Ascda. Mem. Choo Laikeun	= Ascda. Goodhope
× Mem. Madame Pranerm	= South-East Gold	× Ascda. Sunkist	= Ascda. Onokist
× Nancy Rodillas	= Francis Rodillas	× Ascda. Tan Chai Beng	= Ascda. Venus
× Patou	= Chinda	× Asctm. miniatum	= Ascda. Ella Freed
× Rose Davis	= Satitayapong	× Asctm. Sagarik Gold	= Ascda. Sagarik Shine
× Satta	= Bee Lian		
× Sun Tan	= Crimson Glory		

OPHA	**Onomea × Joan Rothsand**	**Lenavat 1972**
ORIOLE‡	**dearei × merrillii**	**S'pore Orchids 1962**

× Rnps. Lena Rowold	= Haw. Harvest Queen		

OSCAR M. KIRSCH‡	**Monacensis × sanderana**	**R. B. Kirsch 1954**

× Rothschildiana	= Nuuano Skies	× Ascda. Tropicana	= Ascda. Lil

OSMENT	**Memoria Marie Osment × hookerana**	**Osment 1974**
PACIFIC SUNSET	**Frank Crook × sanderana**	**Miyao 1972**
PAHALA	**Hilo Blue × Waimea**	**Nishiguchi 1973**
PANID	**teres × brunnea**	**Paireepairit 1974**
PANITTA	**Boonchoke × Mem. Madame Pranerm**	**Toh-chirakul 1974**
PAPAALOA QUEEN	**Hilo Queen × Frank Crook**	**Leo Yap 1972 (Murakami)**
parviflora*†‡	**species**	

× Asctm. curvifolium	= Ascda. Piyada		

PASHA	**Emma van Deventer × Judy Miyamoto**	**R. K. Mizuta 1971**
PASTEL LADY	**Doris Royal × Ohuohu**	**Bloom's Nursery 1974**
PASU	**Hilo Charm × Hilo Queen**	**Chavalit 1974**
PATOU	**James Toogood × Diane Ogawa**	**Chavalit 1970**

× coerulea	= Chaifa	× Onomea	= Chinda
× Hilo Queen	= Ratchada	× Rothschildiana	= Kaset Bangpra
× Kapiolani	= Doctor Nandhika	× Sinard	= Amara
× Lenavat	= Pimsai		

VANDA

PATRICIA | **Hilo Queen × Lenavat** | **Marugame 1975 (H. Kagawa)**

PATRICIA LEE | **Gertrude Miyamoto × Ellen Noa** | **K. C. Lee 1959 (Kirch)**

× Gertrude Miyamoto	= Sundance	× Asctm. curvifolium	= Ascda. Pacalarann
× Aranda Chia Shui Keng	= Aranda Nicole Kong		

PATRICIA LOW | **Josephine van Brero × Jennie Hashimoto** | **T.M.A. 1961**

× Ascda. Meda Arnold	= Ascda. Lollipop	× Ascda. Yip Sum Wah	= Ascda. Grace Callard

PATSY LEUTERIO | **Jeffrey × coerulea** | **Ono 1972**

PAUAHI | **Betsy Sumner × Mary Foster** | **O. Kirsch 1964**

× tessellata	= Tessie	× Ascda. Ophelia	= Ascda. Ahuimanu

PECHKIRE | **Jennie Hashimoto × Hilo Queen** | **Kareboon 1974 (Pechpaisit)**

PETCHBURI | **Mem. Madame Pranerm × denisoniana** | **Snimthong 1975**

PHIMPONG | **Waimea × Jennie Hashimoto** | **Phimpong 1974 (Pechpaisit)**

PHONG-AKSORN | **Pukele × Mem. Madame Pranerm** | **Phong-aksorn 1975 (Kanpai)**

PIERRE LARDIN | **Kekaseh × denisoniana** | **K. F. Yap 1975**

PIHA MOON‡ | **Ohuohu × Manila** | **Ogawa 1954**

× Aranda Bintang	= Aranda Lovely Bird	× Ascda. Meda Arnold	= Ascda. Teoline Blaze
× Aranda Lucy Laycock	= Aranda De Zon Singapura		

PIKUL‡ | **Faye × Waipuna** | **Tancharoen 1966 (Shimamoto)**

× bensonii	= Chantram	× Mem. Madame Pranerm	= Pranerm Flame
× Diane Ogawa	= Mem. Adolphus McLeod	× Miss Joaquim	= Intan
× Eisenhower	= Bangchang Beauty	× Ohuohu	= Pong Tong
× Frank Crook	= Saeng Pra-Artitya	× Pukele	= Lamduan
× Jennie Hashimoto	= Donjadee	× Thananchai	= Ladda
× Manila	= Mary Fermin	× Ascda. Red Gem	= Ascda. Chom Yong

PIMSAI | **Lenavat × Patou** | **Weerawathanamas 1975**

PINK BLUSH | **Rothschildiana × Herziana** | **Andrade 1951**

× Rothschildiana	= Boecien		

PIYASENA | **Jennie Hashimoto × tessellata** | **Piyasena 1973**

PLOENCHIT | **Princess Blue × coerulea** | **Bangyikun 1974**

POEPOE†‡ (syn. Diana) | **Cooperi × teres** | **Shipman 1948**

× Thananchai	= Ko Soom	× Aërdns. Rosy Dawn	= Burk. Fancy Flight
× Aërdns. Bogor	= Burk. Coy Maiden		

POKAI BAY | **Hilo Blue × Waianae Blue** | **Redlinger 1974 (Miyamoto)**

POLLY WOO | **Mimi Palmer × Afterglow** | **C. T. Woo 1971 (Dr. P. S. Bun)**

PONG TONG | **Pikul × Ohuohu** | **Mangkiatkul 1973 (Narattrugsa)**

PONTIP | **Satta × Mem. Madame Pranerm** | **Siriyakorn 1975**

PORNCHAI | **Suvat × coerulea** | **T. Orchids 1974 (Ratana)**

PRACHARK CHIT	**Joan Rothsand × Rothschildiana**	**Chit 1969 (Vipar)**

× Sinard	= Bang Nara	× Asctm. curvifolium	= Ascda. Ladavan

PRAIMANEE	**Tubtimtepya × Rothschildiana**	**Praimanee 1971**
PRAKYPETCH	**Sun Tan × Laurel Yap**	**Raksa 1974**
PRANEET	**Boonchoke × Aurawan**	**Toh-chirakul 1974**
PRANERM CLOUD	**Rothschildiana × Mem. Madame Pranerm**	**Vipar 1971**
PRANERM CRIMSON	**Mary Catherine Bowman × Mem. Madame Pranerm**	**Vipar 1972**
PRANERM FANFARE	**Neva H. Mitchell × Mem. Madame Pranerm**	**Vipar 1971**
PRANERM FLAME	**Pikul × Mem. Madame Pranerm**	**Vipar 1971**
PRANERM HAZE	**Eisenhower × Mem. Madame Pranerm**	**Vipar 1971**
PRANERM ORNETE	**Mem. Madame Pranerm × sanderana**	**Vipar 1971**

× Thananchai	= Rasri		

PRANERM VIOLET	**Eisensander × Mem. Madame Pranerm**	**Vipar 1971**

× Ascda. Honwichai	= Ascda. Ponpen		

PRASARN	**Sinard × coerulea**	**Chavalit 1974**
PRINCESS BLUE	**Jennie Hashimoto × coerulea**	**Miyao 1963**

× coerulea	= Ploenchit	× Ascda. Erika Reuter	= Ascda. Pramote
× Rose Davis	= Teoline Imperial	× Ascda. Meda Arnold	= Ascda. Humdinger
× Rothschildiana	= Evening Tide	× Ren. storiei	= Rntda. Ong Jin Kar
× sanderana	= Teoline Princess		

PRINCESS PUNALU'U	**Takeji Ogawa × Hilo Blue**	**Nishiguchi 1973**
PUAINAKO‡	**Onomea × Eisenhower**	**Ogawa 1960**

× Josephine van Brero	= Margaret Foster	× Karen Ogawa	= Ho King

PUKELE‡	**Betsy Sumner × sanderana**	**O. Kirsch 1957**

× Diane Ogawa	= Claudie Lui	× Pikul	= Lamduan
× Eisenhower	= Teoline Summer	× Rothschildiana	= Michael Ooi
× Honomu	= Mae-Joe	× sanderana	= Teoline Supreme
× James Toogood	= Teoline Aster	× Ascda. Elieen Beauty	= Ascda. Weeravan
× Jennie Hashimoto	= Teoline Winsome	× Ascda. Koh Man	= Ascda. Susan Mae
× Kapiolani	= Sithaman	× Ascda. Ophelia	= Ascda. Pata
× Mem. Madame Pranerm	= Phong-aksorn	× Ascda. Yip Sum Wah	= Ascda. Darunee

PUNCHBOWL‡	**Rothschildiana × teres**	**G. B. Miwa 1952**

× Rothschildiana	= Mem. Hirokadzu Gauda		

PUSDEE	**Satta × Eisensander**	**Chavalit 1974**
QUEEN OF THAILAND	**Suvat × Sun Tan**	**Sophonsiri 1974 (Thephasdin)**
QUEENSLAND SUNTAN	**Neva H. Mitchell × sanderana**	**M. Kelley 1975 (Ilsley Orchids)**
QUEEN THONBURI	**Mem. Madame Pranerm × Frank Crook**	**Narattrugsa 1973**
RACHADAPORN	**Thananchai × denisoniana**	**Mrs. R. Harnpongtham 1974**
RAINBOW TRAIL	**Onomea × Tellee**	**Muse's 1971**
RANGSRI PEARL	**Mary Catherine Bowman × Varavan**	**Vipar 1973**
RARA	**Carole Hirano × Jennie Hashimoto**	**Cochran 1971 (Dr. H. Nishimura)**
RASRI	**Thananchai × Pranerm Ornete**	**Satirasut 1975**
RATCHADA	**Hilo Queen × Patou**	**Yen Orchid 1975**
RAZZ	**cristata × Rothschildiana**	**Rumrill 1975**
RENTON HUTCHISON	**sanderana × Laurel Yap**	**Hutchison 1973 (Leo Yap)**

RICHARD WARNE — **Princess Elizabeth × sanderana** — **Nuuanu O.G. 1960**

× Yuet Yeng Lim	= Imelda Romualdez Marcos

RICHELLA BLUE — **Judy Miyamoto × Rothschildiana** — **R. K. Mizuta 1973**

ROSE DAVIS‡ — **Rothschildiana × coerulea** — **R. Tanaka 1951**

× brunnea	= Hiranburana	× Sinard	= Suratana
× Jennie Hashimoto	= Teoline Honour	× Thananchai	= Aphiradee
× Mabelmae Kamahele	= Madam Foong Khum	× Waimea	= Teoline Violet
× Onomea	= Satitayapong	× Arach. Maggie Oei	= Aranda Er Cheng Meng
× Princess Blue	= Teoline Imperial	× Ascda. Medasand	= Ascda. Morakot
× Rothschildiana	= Francis Cheong	× Ascda. Yip Sum Wah	= Ascda. Dechjun
× Sapan Kwai	= Lopburi	× Vasco. Blue Fairy	= Vasco. Rose Fairy

ROTCHANAI — **Carolyn Koshiro × Lenavat** — **Rotchanai 1975**

ROTHSCHILDIANA*†‡ — **coerulea × sanderana** — **Chassaing 1931**

× Bonnie Blue Fukumura	= Suvitcha	× Tubtimtepya	= Praimanee
× Charlesworthii	= Bangpai	× Waimea	= Shizu Kanno
× cristata	= Razz	× Yolanda	= Helen Martino
× Doris Royal	= Teoline Sapphire	× Aërdns. Bogor	= Burk. Tidarma Suling
× Eisensander	= Hilo Princess	× Aër. flabellata	= Aërdv. Wittaya
× Fair Queen	= Gladys Sellers	× Aër. jarckiana	= Aërdv. Siam Orchids
× Harriet Miyao	= Issei	× Aër. multiflora	= Aërdv. Suraprabha
× Hilo Queen	= Lore Paul	× Arach. cathcartii	= Aranda Primi
× Honomu	= Lim Eang Kim	× Arach. flos-aëris	= Aranda Mem. Lilian Garth
× Hukilau	= Teoline Rosyblue		
× Iwalani	= Lido Sunset	× Aranda Lily Chong	= Aranda Mas
× James Toogood	= Jiranuvat	× Ascda. Aroonsri Beauty	= Ascda. Silpaprasert
× Judy Miyamoto	= Richella Blue	× Ascda. Chris Miles	= Ascda. Rio's Sapphire
× Karen Ono	= Bangyikhan	× Ascda. Honwichai	= Ascda. Ruby Belle
× Laurel Yap	= Sai Wan Loo	× Ascda. Mangkiatkul	= Ascda. Thidaratana
× Lenavat	= Thospol	× Ascda. Medasand	= Ascda. Queen Florist
× Mary Catherine Bowman	= Nell Allan	× Ascda. Mem. Jim Wilkins	= Ascda. Spellbound
× Mem. Frieda Hantober	= Koh Phaik Lean	× Ascda. Red Gem	= Ascda. Priyavadee
× Mem. Madame Pranerm	= Pranerm Cloud	× Ascda. Seechang	= Ascda. Seedee
× Mimi Palmer	= Soo Kwong Man	× Ascda. Sunkist	= Ascda. Rothkist
× Oscar M. Kirsch	= Nuuanu Skies	× Ascda. Tan Chai Beng	= Ascda. Prima Belle
× Patou	= Kaset Bangpra	× Asctm. aurantiacum	= Ascda. Bill Fox
× Pink Blush	= Boecien	× Asctm. miniatum	= Ascda. Pong
× Princess Blue	= Evening Tide	× Asctm. Sagarik Gold	= Ascda. Kasetsart Beauty
× Pukele	= Michael Ooi	× Phal. Doris	= Vdnps. Lee Fennell
× Punchbowl	= Mem. Hirokadzu Gauda	× Ren. coccinea	= Rntda. Wunna Jaides
× Rose Davis	= Francis Cheong	× Rhctm. Sagarik	= Vasco. Rojanadara
× Sarojini	= Kamana Blue	× Rhv. Busakorn	= Rhv. Juthatip
× Thananchai	= Thananroths	× Vdps. parishii	= Opsis. Rumrill
× Tom Ritter	= Teresa Williams		

roxburghii*† (see *tessellata**†‡) — **species**

ROYAL BLUE — **Rothschildiana × Janice** — **R. K. Mizuta 1968**

× Ascda. Blue Boy	= Ascda. Harry Blauvelt

ROY DOME — **Onomea × Eisensander** — **Suphatamakit 1974**

RUBY GARTH‡ — **La Coquette × Rothschildiana** — **Garth 1962**

× sanderana	= Eric Garth

RUBY PRINCE†‡ — **Ruby × Cooperi** — **S.B.G. 1951**

× dearei	= Gordon Dunlop

SAENG PRA-ARTITYA — **Frank Crook × Pikul** — **Satirasut 1972 (Raksa)**

× Jennie Hashimoto	= Chanud Piyaoui

SAHANAWIN — **Beebe Sumner × Boonchoke** — **Sahanawin 1974 (Kenny)**

SAI WAN LOO	**Laurel Yap × Rothschildiana**	**Leo Yap 1973**
SAKCHAI	**Thananchai × Karen Ono**	**N. P. R. Thong 1974**
SAMSUK	**Satta × Aurawan**	**Prachak 1973**
SANDAMO‡	**Amoena × sanderana**	**E. Iwanaga 1952**

× Aër. odorata	= Aërdv. Hideichi Nitta	× Asctm. curvifolium	= Ascda. Steere Noda
× Ascda. Meda Arnold	= Ascda. Ronald Nitta		
× Ascda. Ophelia	= Ascda. Malibu Oneohtwo		

sanderana*†‡ **species**

(This is retained as the horticulturally recommended name for registration purposes even though *Euanthe sanderana* is the botanically correct name for this species.)

× Beebe Sumner	= Sun Tan	× Teoline Rosieglow	= Teoline Rosiecharm
× Bonnie Blue Fukumura	= Bukit Beauty	× Thananchai	= Thananchaisand
× brunnea	= Krajib	× Varavan	= Chantramontol
× Charm	= Amigo Fritz	× Wongse	= Bangkhen
× Cherry Ripe	= Cherry Glow	× Aërdns. Bogor	= Burk. Sanderling
× Fair Queen	= Teoline Fairqueen	× Aranda Ruby Pestana	= Aranda Naomi
× Frank Crook	= Pacific Sunset	× Ascda. Bonanza	= Ascda. Hong Kok Hoo
× Hilo Queen	= Hilo Sand	× Ascda. Erika Reuter	= Ascda. Christine Ang
× Hukilau	= Teoline Royal	× Ascda. Mem. Choo Laikeun	= Ascda. Happy Beauty
× Jeffrey	= Darlene Ono	× Ascda. Medasand	= Ascda. Thonglor
× Judy Miyamoto	= Teoline Chieftain	× Ascda. Peggy Foo	= Ascda. Tan Chin Heong
× Karen Ono	= Khong Swee Wah	× Ascda. Sagarik	= Ascda. Noparat
× Laurel Yap	= Renton Hutchison	× Ascda. Seechang	= Ascda. Sethtee
× Mem. Madame Pranerm	= Pranerm Ornete	× Ascda. Sunkist	= Ascda. Sandkist
× Nancy Rodillas	= Nancysander	× Ascda. Tan Chai Beng	= Ascda. Chomnard
× Neva H. Mitchell	= Queensland Suntan	× Opsis. Fascination	= Opsis. Opulence
× Princess Blue	= Teoline Princess	× Phal. Cast Iron Monarch	= Vdnps. Nell Miller
× Pukele	= Teoline Supreme	× Vdnps. Pang Nyuk Yin	= Vdnps. Linden Beauty
× Ruby Garth	= Eric Garth	× Vdpsd. Apple Blossom	= Mcyra. Hazel
× Sarojini	= Teoline Fairway		

SAPAN KWAI	**Frank Crook × Mabelmae Kamahele**	**T. Orchids 1975**

× Rose Davis	= Lopburi

SAROJINI‡	**coerulea × Mabelmae Kamahele**	**Thiagarajan 1965 (Ogawa)**

× Colorsan	= Andre Yee	× Sun Tan	= Sunray
× Joan Rothsand	= Varai	× Aër. flabellata	= Aërdv. Rungsit
× Nancy Rodillas	= Sukhum	× Ascda. Blue Boy	= Ascda. Fermilliana Calma
× Rothschildiana	= Kamana Blue		
× sanderana	= Teoline Fairway	× Ascda. Erika Reuter	= Ascda. Jessie May

SATHUPRADIT	**James Toogood × Joan Rothsand**	**Lenavat 1969**

× coerulea	= Bangpha	× Ascda. Piswong	= Ascda. Ayer Itam Beauty

SATITAYAPONG	**Onomea × Rose Davis**	**Chavalit 1973**
SATTA	**James Toogood × Ohuohu**	**Chavalit 1969**

× Aurawan	= Samsuk	× Lenavat	= Yanawa
× Boonchoke	= Golden Bangphra	× Mem. Madame Pranerm	= Pontip
× Diane Ogawa	= Doctor Kanai	× Onomea	= Bee Lian
× Eisensander	= Pusdee	× Ascda. Meda Arnold	= Ascda. Busadee
× Hilo Queen	= Supatra	× Ascda. Medasand	= Ascda. Panthong

SAUVANEE	**Eisensander × Ohuohu**	**Chindavanic 1975**
SAYANG	**Betsy Sumner × Ellen Noa**	**Ooi Leng Sun 1974**
SEEPRAI	**Thananchai × Aurawan**	**Lenavat 1974**
SEGAMAT	**Honolii × Mem. Madame Pranerm**	**Vipar 1972**
SERENE	**Hilo Blue × coerulea**	**Miyao 1969**

× Lenavat	= Namprasert

VANDA

SHADOW	**Gillian Trevor × Laurel Yap**	**Wilkins 1974**
SHANE SUGIHARA	**Jennie Hashimoto × Betsy Sumner**	**Sugihara 1969**

× Carolyn Koshiro = Lim Jet Thien

SHIZU KANNO	**Rothschildiana × Waimea**	**M. Miyao 1971**
SIAM	**Diane Ogawa × Mem. Madame Pranerm**	**W. P. Orchid 1972**
SINARD	**James Toogood × sanderana**	**Chavalit 1969**

× coerulea	= Prasarn	× Rose Davis	= Suratana
× Hilo Queen	= Bandon	× Thananchai	= Vivan
× Karen Ono	= Lumpoon	× Ascda. Elieen Beauty	= Ascda. Daeng Siam
× Patou	= Amara	× Ascda. Mangkiatkul	= Ascda. Busaraporn
× Prachark Chit	= Bang Nara	× Ascda. Medasand	= Ascda. Vilawan

SINI	**Boonya × coerulea**	**Muttamara 1975**
SITHAMAN	**Pukele × Kapiolani**	**Muttamara 1973**
SITI ZAIN	**dearei × Carousel**	**Alsagoff 1963 (Choo Yeok Koon)**

× Phal. denevei = Vdnps. Hashim Idros

SIVANART PALM	**Laukapu × Rothschildiana**	**Palm Orchids 1963**

× coerulea	= Sukonth'sithi Blue	× Ascda. Yip Sum Wah	= Ascda. Puang Lada

SKY RAIDER	**Hilo Blue × Joan Rothsand**	**Vipar 1971**
SNOWDON	**Miss van Deun × teres**	**S. P. Bell 1975**
SOMTHAWIL	**merrillii × denisoniana**	**Chuanyen 1975**
SONTHAYA	**Hilo Queen × coerulea**	**Chindavanic 1975**
SOO HOR WENG	**Faye × sanderana**	**Hiew Kim Sang 1964 (T. Kono)**

× Mem. Frieda Hantober	= Margaret Cheong	× Asctm. curvifolium	= Ascda. Hugo Freed

SOO KWONG MAN	**Mimi Palmer × Rothschildiana**	**Soo Kwong Man 1974**
SOUTH-EAST GOLD	**Mem. Madame Pranerm × Onomea**	**Cha-om 1972**
spathulata*†‡	**species**	

× Dtps. Red Coral	= Hgra. Yellow Coral	× Rntda. Violet	= Rntda. Herb Hager
× Phal. Dr. Henry O. Eversole	= Vdnps. Henrietta Fujiwara		

STUART FURUMIZO	**Green Gold × Ellen Noa**	**H. Furumizo 1971**
suavis*† (see *tricolor**†‡)	**species**	
SUE SAITO	**Queenie Pei × sanderana**	**H. Kagawa 1966**

× Ascda. Meda Arnold = Ascda. Mitsy Shinsato

SUKHUM	**Sarojini × Nancy Rodillas**	**Niamnuamtham 1974**
SUKONTH'SITHI BLUE	**Sivanart Palm × coerulea**	**Sukonth'sithi 1972 (Raksa)**
SUMANA	**Jennie Hashimoto × Boonchoke**	**Vardhanabhuti 1974 (Asdornithee)**
sumatrana*†‡	**species**	

× Ren. philippinensis = Rntda. Wong Yin Fon

SUNBRERO	**Josephine van Brero × insignis**	**S'pore Orchids 1973**
SUNDANCE	**Patricia Lee × Gertrude Miyamoto**	**Wilkins 1974**
SUNKAKUL	**Diane Ogawa × Thananchai**	**P. Sunkakul 1973 (T. Sunkakul)**

VANDA

SUNRAY **Sarojini × Sun Tan** **Thephasdin 1973**

× Eisenhower = Chanenam Raphael | × Thananchai = Doctor Jim Chan
× Ohuohu = John's Ho |

SUNSET‡ **sanderana × spathulata** **R. E. Warne 1946**

× Ren. storiei = Rntda. Sunset Story |

SUN TAN **Beebe Sumner × sanderana** **Lenavat 1972**
(Raksa)

× Diane Ogawa = Mem. Madame Liab | × Onomea = Crimson Glory
× Laurel Yap = Prakypetch | × Sarojini = Sunray
× Mem. Madame Pranerm = Madame Rattana | × Suvat = Queen of Thailand

SUPAN-BURI **Joan Rothsand × Mem. Madame Pranerm** **Vipar 1971**
SUPATRA **Satta × Hilo Queen** **Chavalit 1973**
SURATANA **Sinard × Rose Davis** **Chavalit 1975**
SUSAN LYNN‡ **Jennie Hashimoto × Bill Sutton** **Houston 1962**
(Kodama)

× Asctm. curvifolium = Ascda. Honor First |

SUSIE WHITESELL **tessellata × Alice Chan** **Whitesell 1974**
SUVAT **Clara Shipman Fisher × Waimea** **Ratana 1972**

× coerulea = Pornchai | × Sun Tan = Queen of Thailand
× Mem. Madame Pranerm = Wilai |

SUVITCHA **Rothschildiana × Bonnie Blue Fukumura** **Napasab 1974**
SUWANNA **Thananchai × Varavan** **P. Chantramontol 1974**
TAIPING **Kiliwehi Kono × Hilo Blue** **Ng Hoe Hai 1975**
(Ooi Leng Sun)
TAKEJI OGAWA‡ **Ohuohu × Jennie Hashimoto** **Ogawa 1960**

× Hilo Blue = Princess Punalu'u | × Ascda. Meda Arnold = Ascda. Iliwai
× Jeffrey = Joel Aherrera | × Ascda. Yip Sum Wah = Ascda. Karen McCloskey
× Aranda Lily Chong = Aranda Yeap Hong Ghee | × Asctm. curvifolium = Ascda. Alicia Ono

TAN CHAY YAN†‡ **dearei × Josephine van Brero** **Tan 1952**

× Tatzeri = Yeoh Bok Choon |

TAN CHIN TUAN‡ **Josephine van Brero × Rothschildiana** **T.M.A. 1958**

× Jennie Hashimoto = Banlard Vithya | × Ascda. Yip Sum Wah = Ascda. Picharn

TATZERI*†‡ **sanderana × tricolor** **Prague Bot. Gdns. 1919**

× Tan Chay Yan = Yeoh Bok Choon |

TAWEE **Wongse × Mem. Madame Pranerm** **T. Orchids 1975**
TELLEE **Jack Walker × Sissie Boyd** **Mrs. D. D. Reed 1967**
(R. Fields)

× Onomea = Rainbow Trail |

TEOH CHEE KEAT **Bill Sutton × Kuniko Sugihara** **Teoh Chee Keat 1973**
(R. T. Fukumura)
TEO KOON HWA‡ **Trimerrill × sanderana** **Teo Koon Hong 1964**
(C. Y. Mok)

× coerulea = Chong Chee Yon |

TEOLINE ASTER **Pukele × James Toogood** **Teo Boon Hian 1974**
TEOLINE BLUSH **Onomea × Hukilau** **Teo Boon Hian 1974**
TEOLINE CHIEFTAIN **Judy Miyamoto × sanderana** **Teo Boon Hian 1974**
TEOLINE CRIMSON **Nancy Rodillas × Diane Ogawa** **Teo Boon Hian 1974**

TEOLINE FAIRQUEEN	**sanderana × Fair Queen**	**Teo Boon Hian 1974**
TEOLINE FAIRWAY	**sanderana × Sarojini**	**Teo Boon Hian 1974**
TEOLINE HARVEST	**James Toogood × Teoline Rosieglow**	**Teo Boon Hian 1974**
TEOLINE HAZE	**Eisenhower × Hukilau**	**Teo Boon Hian 1974**
TEOLINE HONOUR	**Jennie Hashimoto × Rose Davis**	**Teo Boon Hian 1974**
TEOLINE IMPERIAL	**Princess Blue × Rose Davis**	**Teo Boon Hian 1974**
TEOLINE PINKSWORTH	**Nancy Rodillas × Jennie Hashimoto**	**Teo Boon Hian 1974**
TEOLINE PRINCESS	**sanderana × Princess Blue**	**Teo Boon Hian 1974**
TEOLINE QUEEN	**Eisensander × Jennie Hashimoto**	**Teo Boon Hian 1974**
TEOLINE ROSIEBLUE	**Rothschildiana × Hukilau**	**Teo Boon Hian 1974**
TEOLINE ROSIECHARM	**sanderana × Teoline Rosieglow**	**Teo Boon Hian 1974**
TEOLINE ROSIEGLOW	**sanderana × Diane Ogawa**	**Teo Boon Hian 1970**

× James Toogood = Teoline Harvest
× sanderana = Teoline Rosiecharm
× Ascda. Meda Arnold = Ascda. Teoline Celebration

TEOLINE ROYAL	**Hukilau × sanderana**	**Teo Boon Hian 1974**
TEOLINE SAPPHIRE	**Doris Royal × Rothschildiana**	**Teo Boon Hian 1974**
TEOLINE SUMMER	**Eisenhower × Pukele**	**Teo Boon Hian 1974**
TEOLINE SUNNY	**Ellen Noa × James Toogood**	**Teo Boon Hian 1974**
TEOLINE SUNRISE	**James Toogood × Eisenhower**	**Teo Boon Hian 1974**
TEOLINE SUNSET	**James Toogood × Eisensander**	**Teo Boon Hian 1974**
TEOLINE SUPREME	**sanderana × Pukele**	**Teo Boon Hian 1974**
TEOLINE VIOLET	**Waimea × Rose Davis**	**Teo Boon Hian 1974**
TEOLINE WINSOME	**Jennie Hashimoto × Pukele**	**Teo Boon Hian 1974**
teres*†‡	**species**	

(This is retained as the horticulturally recommended name for registration purposes, although this species is classified within the genus *Papilionanthe* by some authorities.)

× brunnea = Panid
× laotica = Bangkrabue
× Miss van Deun = Snowdon
× T.M.A. = Mem. Percy Van-den-Driesen
× Ascda. Ophelia = Ascda. Peacock Flower
× Lsa. teretifolia = Lsnd. Doctor Tjinyoe Tan
× Rhy. gigantea = Rhv. Kauhana

TERESA WILLIAMS	**Rothschildiana × Tom Ritter**	**Thomas Ritter 1974**
tessellata*†‡ (syn. *roxburghii**†)	**species**	

× Alice Chan = Susie Whitesell
× Blue Sapphire = Dick Johnston
× D. S. Senanayake = Hemamali
× Jennie Hashimoto = Piyasena
× Ling = Farah Pahlavi
× Pauahi = Tessie
× T.M.A. = Dorothea
× Arach. flos-aëris = Aranda Bussaracum
× Aranda Tay Theng Suan = Aranda Lee York Sim
× Ascda. Medasand = Ascda. Lim Kim Yoo
× Ascda. Tropicana = Ascda. Mem. Lovell Garth
× Ascda. Yip Sum Wah = Ascda. Flambeau
× Asctm. curvifolium = Ascda. Carnival
× Phal. Grace Palm = Vdnps. Pink Blush
× Phal. serpentilingua = Vdnps. Quietude

TESSIE	**Pauahi × tessellata**	**O. Kirsch 1975**
THAI‡	**lamellata × parviflora**	**W. W. G. Moir 1962**

× Asctm. curvifolium = Ascda. Khem Thai
× Rhy. coelestis = Rhv. Chiengmai

THANANCHAI	**Mem. Madame Pranerm × Tubtimtepya**	**Sunthonwan 1968**

× Aurawan = Seeprai
× coerulea = Thanpuying Chongkol
× denisoniana = Rachadaporn
× Diane Ogawa = Sunkakul
× Eisensander = Chaiya
× Jennie Hashimoto = Bang Ruk
× Karen Ono = Sakchai
× Lenavat = Urbchitr
× Mem. Madame Pranerm = Bangkhunsri
× Ohuohu = Vasittee
× Onomea = Amphai
× Pikul = Ladda
× Poepoe = Ko Soom
× Pranerm Ornete = Rasri
× Rose Davis = Aphiradee
× Rothschildiana = Thananroths
× sanderana = Thananchaisand
× Sinard = Vivan
× Sunray = Doctor Jim Chan
× Varavan = Suwanna

THANANCHAI *(continued)*

× Arach. hookerana = Aranda Adilah
× Ascda. Buddy Choo = Ascda. Kasetsilp
× Ascda. Captain Chor = Ascda. Yellow Captain
× Ascda. Elieen Beauty = Ascda. Impossible Star
× Ascda. Erika Reuter = Ascda. Royal Flight
× Ascda. Guo Chia Long = Ascda. Udomsuk
× Ascda. Lady Boonkua = Ascda. Swangaroon
× Ascda. Laikeun = Ascda. Pasana
× Ascda. Meda Arnold = Ascda. Took-Ta
× Ascda. Medasand = Ascda. Aribarg
× Ascda. Ophelia = Ascda. Teoline Bewitch
× Ascda. Seechang = Ascda. Seelom
× Ascda. Sunkist = Ascda. Sunee
× Ascda. Tan Chai Beng = Ascda. Darakam
× Ascda. Wilas = Ascda. South East Light
× Ascda. Yip Sum Wah = Ascda. Duang Porn

THANANCHAISAND — **Thananchai × sanderana** — **Praimanee 1974**
THANANROTHS — **Thananchai × Rothschildiana** — **Sunthonwan 1974**
THANPUYING CHONGKOL — **Thananchai × coerulea** — **Khunawat 1973 (Fuglerk)**

THONGLOR — **Jennie Hashimoto × Diane Ogawa** — **T. Orchids 1974**
THOSPOL — **Lenavat × Rothschildiana** — **Bhimayothin 1973**
T.M.A.‡ — **sanderana × Josephine van Brero** — **T.M.A. 1957**

× teres = Mem. Percy Van-den-Driesen
× tessellata = Dorothea
× Ren. coccinea = Rntda. Andromeda

TOH-CHIRAKUL — **Boonchoke × Eisensander** — **Toh-chirakul 1974**
TOM RITTER — **Onomea × Kilohana** — **Thomas Ritter 1965 (Ogawa)**

× Iliwai = Bill Henderson
× Jennie Hashimoto = Harry Williams
× Nellie Morley = Evelyn Ritter
× Rothschildiana = Teresa Williams
× Ascda. Ruth Shave = Ascda. Tammy Wakasugi

TOWACO — **coerulescens × Miss Joaquim** — **Rumrill 1973**

tricolor*†‡ (syn. *suavis**†)

(*V. tricolor* and *V. hindsii* are treated as specifically distinct for registration purposes, although regarded as conspecific by some authorities.)

× Aërdns. Mandai = Burk. August Rose
× Arnth. Lilleput = Holtt. Bright Eyes
× Rnds. Mahani = Nlra. Wellsian Beauty

TRIMERRILL†‡ — **merrillii × tricolor** — **Shipman 1948**

× Ascda. Sunkist = Ascda. Trikist
× Asctm. curvifolium = Ascda. Red Glow

TRISHER†‡ — **Clara Shipman Fisher × tricolor** — **E. Iwanaga 1951**

× Onomea = Kiliwehi Kono
× Ascda. Meda Arnold = Ascda. Kazuto Nitta
× Rhy. coelestis = Rhv. Merlene Nitta

TROTS (see Josephine van Brero†‡)

TUBTIMTEPYA‡ — **sanderana × Gertrude Miyamoto** — **Tubtimtepya 1961**

× Onomea = Boonprame
× Rothschildiana = Praimanee
× Ascda. Meda Arnold = Ascda. Daisy May
× Ascda. Yip Sum Wah = Ascda. Ram Indra
× Asctm. curvifolium = Ascda. Athit-Uthai
× Asctm. miniatum = Ascda. Prachit Gold

URBCHITR — **Thananchai × Lenavat** — **Napasab 1973**
VARAI — **Sarojini × Joan Rothsand** — **Napasab 1971 (Soonthonwana)**

VARAVAN‡ — **Hilo Blue × Onomea** — **Holvichai 1961**

× Diane Ogawa = Issop Dinar
× Joan Rothsand = Madame Somboon
× Mary Catherine Bowman = Rangsri Pearl
× sanderana = Chantramontol
× Thananchai = Suwanna
× Ascda. Tan Chai Beng = Ascda. Maeklong

VARAVUTH — **Lenavat × coerulea** — **Napasab 1973 (Phit)**

VASITTEE — **Thananchai × Ohuohu** — **Jiranuvat 1974**
VIMOL — **James Toogood × Jennie Hashimoto** — **Chindavanic 1974**

VANDA

Name	Parentage	Originator
VIRAYA	**Diane Ogawa × Joan Rothsand**	**Tancharoen 1973**
VIROONCHAN	**Diane Ogawa × Eisenhower**	**B.G.S. Orchids 1972**
VIROONCHAN BLUE	**Mem. Fumiko Omoto × Karen Ono**	**H. K. Lau 1975**
VIVAN	**Sinard × Thananchai**	**Yuktanonda 1975 (Lenavat)**
WAIANAE BLUE	**Rothschildiana × Helen Paoa**	**Miyamoto 1965 (M. Yamada)**

× Hilo Blue = Pokai Bay

Name	Parentage	Originator
WAIMEA‡	**Ohuohu × Rothschildiana**	**Ogawa 1954**

× Alicia Ono = Honuapo Dream
× Clara Shipman Fisher = Suvat
× Hilo Blue = Pahala
× Jennie Hashimoto = Phimpong
× Rose Davis = Teoline Violet
× Rothschildiana = Shizu Kanno

Name	Parentage	Originator
WAIPUNA†‡	**Ellen Noa × Rothschildiana**	**Y. Fujinaga 1952**

× Ascda. Yip Sum Wah = Ascda. Teoline Worth

Name	Parentage	Originator
WANAJUTHA	**Onomea × Diane Ogawa**	**Chavalit 1974**
WHITE WINGS (see Cooperi†‡)		
WILAI	**Suvat × Mem. Madame Pranerm**	**Suppachatwong 1975 (Lorpongpanich)**
WINIFRED KURIHARA	**Nellie Morley × Miss Joaquim**	**H. K. Nitta 1963**

× Ascda. Meda Arnold = Ascda. Mem. Jutaro Nitta
× Asctm. curvifolium = Ascda. Winifred Hamamoto
× Rhy. coelestis = Rhv. Herbert Kurihara

Name	Parentage	Originator
WONG KOK PENG	**Eisensander × Judith Y. Nishimura**	**Wong Weng Hoong 1973**
WONG PENG SOON (see Brownie‡)		
WONGSE	**Jennie Hashimoto × Onomea**	**Rojanadara 1967 (Shimamoto)**

× Mem. Madame Pranerm = Tawee
× sanderana = Bangkhen
× Ascda. Meda Arnold = Ascda. Teoline Apron
× Ascda. Tan Chai Beng = Ascda. Itthipol
× Vdps. parishii = Opsis. Gino Ooi

Name	Parentage	Originator
WONG WENG HOONG	**Helen Paoa × Eisensander**	**Wong Weng Hoong 1973**
WONG YOOT GNOH	**Harvest Time × Eisensander**	**Wong Yoot Gnoh 1973**
YANAWA	**Satta × Lenavat**	**Lenavat 1974**
YELLOWSTONE	**Ellen Noa × lamellata**	**Church 1974 (Originator unknown)**

× Asctm. curvifolium = Ascda. Ham Reilly

Name	Parentage	Originator
YEOH BOK CHOON	**Tan Chay Yan × Tatzeri**	**Choo Yeok Koon 1972**
YOLANDA	**Clara Shipman Fisher × Manila**	**Kodama 1953**

× Rothschildiana = Helen Martino

Name	Parentage	Originator
YONGYUTH	**Mem. Madame Pranerm × Lenavat**	**Napasab 1973**
YUET YENG LIM‡	**Maurice Restrepo × sanderana**	**Lim Chooi Seng 1959**

× Richard Warne = Imelda Romualdez Marcos

Name	Parentage	Originator
YUKUM BRAGA‡	**dearei × Gilbert Triboulet**	**Braga 1958**

× B. P. Mok = Ma Siau Kee
× Arach. Maroon Maggie = Aranda Yeok Koon

VANDACHNIS

Name	Parentage	Originator
SOMTHAWIL	**Arach. Maggie Oei × Vdps. parishii**	**Juanyen 1974 (Kasetsart Univ.)**

VANDAENOPSIS

EMILY YONG‡	**V. lamellata × Phal. serpentilingua**	**Yong Swee Kee 1963**
× V. dearei	= Tiger Cub	
FRAIL FANCY	**Phal. serpentilingua × V. coerulea**	**S'pore Orchids 1971**
HANDOYOHARJO	**Phal. Kolopaking × V. Miss Joaquim**	**Kolopaking 1975**
HASHIM IDROS	**V. Siti Zain × Phal. denevei**	**Alsagoff 1971**
HENRIETTA FUJIWARA	**V. spathulata × Phal. Dr. Henry O. Eversole**	**W. W. G. Moir 1973 (Mrs. T. F. Fujiwara)**
× Dtps. Mem. Clarence Schubert	= Hgra. Herb	
HONG TREVOR	**V. Denizonica × Phal. serpentilingua**	**Trevor 1962**
× Ren. storiei	= Moir. Tristar	
LEE FENNELL	**V. Rothschildiana × Phal. Doris**	**Fennell 1972 (T. A. Fennell)**
LINDEN BEAUTY	**Pang Nyuk Yin × V. sanderana**	**Cheong Chee Yon 1972 (Chong Chok Chye)**
NELL MILLER	**V. sanderana × Phal. Cast Iron Monarch**	**Miller Coll. 1975**
PANG NYUK YIN‡	**V. Ellen Noa × Phal. denevei**	**Yap 1959**
× V. sanderana	= Linden Beauty	
PHYLLIS SUMNER	**V. Janet Tagawa × Phal. Barbara Beard**	**R. D. Sumner 1972 (Dewey)**
PINK BLUSH	**Phal. Grace Palm × V. tessellata**	**Richards 1975**
QUIETUDE	**Phal. serpentilingua × V. tessellata**	**S'pore Orchids 1972 (Mrs. Gracia Lewis)**
REVELATION	**V. cristata × Phal. Fairvale**	**Rod McLellan Co. 1975**
TIGER CUB	**V. dearei × Emily Yong**	**S'pore Orchids 1973**

VANDEWEGHEARA

JERRY VANDE WEGHE	**Dtps. Mem. Clarence Schubert × Ascda. Meda Arnold**	**June Fowler 1975 (Vande Weghe)**

VANDOFINETIA

PREMIER‡	**Neof. falcata × V. lamellata**	**M. Yamada 1960**
× Aër. mitrata	= Vfds. Rumrill	

VANDOFINIDES

RUMRILL	**Vf. Premier × Aër. mitrata**	**Rumrill 1974**

VANDOPSIDES

APPLE BLOSSOM	**Aër. lawrenceae × Vdps. lissochiloides**	**McCoy 1958**
× V. sanderana	= Mcyra. Hazel	

VANDOPSIS

gigantea†‡ **species**

× parishii	= Sagarik	× V. dearei	= Opsis. Moongleam
× Ren. Brookie Chandler	= Rnps. Gordon Snook	× V. Eisenhower	= Opsis. Beatrice Burns
× Rhy. gigantea	= Opst. Mem. Mary Nattrass	× V. Mem. T. Iwasaki	= Opsis. Constellation

VANDOPSIS

lissochiloides†‡ (syn. *Vanda batemannii*) **species**

× Aranda Chia Shui Keng	= Leeara Memoria Jean Black	× Aranda Lucy Laycock	= Leeara Lissom Lucy

parishii†‡ **species**

(This is retained as the horticulturally recommended name for registration purposes, even though *Hygrochilus parishii* is the botanically correct name for this species.)

× gigantea	= Sugarik	× Dtps. Mem. Clarence Schubert	= Haus. Lucie Hausermann
× Arach. Maggie Oei	= Vchns. Somthawil	× Ren. coccinea	= Rnps. Yenchit
× Ascda. Honwichai	= Wknsra. Samphan	× V. brunnea	= Opsis. Thin Thai Ngam
× Ascda. Medasand	= Wknsra. Thanasuwat	× V. denisoniana	= Opsis. Denipar
× Ascda. Red Gem	= Wknsra. Gemini	× V. Rothschildiana	= Opsis. Rumrill
× Ascda. Yip Sum Wah	= Wknsra. Lopburi	× V. Wongse	= Opsis. Gino Ooi
× Asctm. curvifolium	= Ascdps. Scarlet Flame		

SAGARIK	**parishii × gigantea**	**Sagarik 1973**

VASCOSTYLIS

APRICOT GLEAM	**Rhv. Wong Yoke Sim × Ascda. Meda Arnold**	**Hershy 1975 (Miyamoto)**
ASDORNITHEE	**Blue Fairy × Ascda. Yip Sum Wah**	**Asdornithee 1972**
BANGKOK BALL	**Ascda. Ophelia × Susan**	**Sagarik 1972**
BLUEBIRD	**Ascda. Yip Sum Wah × Rhv. Blue Angel**	**Stacy 1972**
BLUE FAIRY‡	**Ascda. Meda Arnold × Rhy. coelestis**	**Takakura 1963**

× Arach. hookerana	= Bov. Bovorn Beauty	× Ascda. Yip Sum Wah	= Asdornithee
× Ascda. Meda Arnold	= Mem. Arthur Freed	× Rhv. Bangkok Sky	= Chin
× Ascda. Tan Chai Beng	= Kled Kaew	× V. Rose Davis	= Rose Fairy

BLUE KAHILI	**Rhv. Wong Yoke Sim × Ascda. Tan Chai Beng**	**Perreira 1973**
CHIN	**Blue Fairy × Rhv. Bangkok Sky**	**Akranithi 1975**
CHITSWANG	**Rhv. Busakorn × Ascda. Yip Sum Wah**	**Chitswang 1975 (Maneetarn)**
DREAMY BLUE	**Rhy. coelestis × Ascda. Elieen Beauty**	**R. K. Mizuta 1971**
FLIRTASIA	**Susan × Ascda. Yip Sum Wah**	**R. K. Mizuta 1973**
JAIRAK	**Rhv. Wong Yoke Sim × Ascda. Priyavadee**	**Sawang Somboonpol 1975**
JANICE KANAYAMA	**Rhv. Galen Kanayama × Ascda. Meda Arnold**	**Kanayama 1973**
JIM SNIDER	**Susan × V. Diane Ogawa**	**Perreira 1975**
KARAVEK	**Ascda. Blue Boy × Rhy. gigantea**	**Tunprayoon 1974**
KIAT SILP	**Susan × Ascda. Laikeun**	**Sulyapong 1974 (Sagarik)**
KLED KAEW	**Ascda. Tan Chai Beng × Blue Fairy**	**Muttamara 1973**
MEMORIA ARTHUR FREED	**Ascda. Meda Arnold × Blue Fairy**	**Freed 1974**
MEMORIA CHARLES BLAUVELT	**Ascda. Ophelia × Rhy. coelestis**	Mrs. W. H. Boyd 1972 **(Richella)**
NUTMEG DOLLY	Rhv. Bangkok Sky × Asctm. miniatum	Breckinridge 1975 (Originator unknown)
PRANEE	Rhv. Bangkok Sky × Ascda. Red Gem	Phunthonglor 1974
PRASARN	Rhv. Sagarik Wine × Ascda. Meda Arnold	Tavivatana 1975 (Sagarik)
ROJANADARA	Rhctm. Sagarik × V. Rothschildiana	Rojanadara 1972
ROSE FAIRY	V. Rose Davis × Blue Fairy	Kasem 1975

VASCOSTYLIS

SOMBOONPOL — Rhv. Bangkok Sky × Ascda. Yip Sum Wah — Sawang Somboonpol 1975

SUSAN — Rhv. Blue Angel × Ascda. Meda Arnold — Perreira 1966

× Ascda. Laikeun = Kiat Silp | × Ascda. Yip Sum Wah = Flirtasia
× Ascda. Ophelia = Bangkok Ball | × V. Diane Ogawa = Jim Snider

TUKTA — Rhv. Bangkok Sky × Ascda. Meda Arnold — Sawang Somboonpol 1975

VAUGHNARA

RESSIE TOY — Epc. Lily Moody × Bc. Daffodil — Osment 1973

VUYLSTEKEARA

BARBACENA	Princess Kaiulani × Milt. Minas Gerais	W. W. G. Moir 1973
CONQUISTADOR	Oda. Balek × Rutilant	Pff. V. & L. 1974
CRIMSON LAKE	Milt. Petropolis × Oda. Swamp Fire	W. W. G. Moir 1973
ELEGANZ	Odtna. Andraena × Oda. Lippestern	Hark 1973
FEUERZAUBER	Odtna. Debutante × Oda. Feuerball	Elle & Co. 1975 (Elle)
MEDELLIN	Oda. Sirias × Odtna. Salam	Pff. V. & L. 1973
PRINCESS KAIULANI	Milt. candida × Oda. Astomar	W. W. G. Moir 1969

× Milt. Minas Gerais = Barbacena

RAINBOW FALLS	Oda. Cloud Cap × Odtna. Catana	Beall 1969

× Odm. Grand Tetons = Soleduck Falls

ROYAL VELVET	Odtna. Debutante × Oda. Minel	Dugger 1975
RUTILANT	Fragonard × Oda. Corail	V. 1941

× Oda. Balek = Conquistador

SAO FRANCISCO	Milt. spectabilis × Oda. Bohème	W. W. G. Moir 1973
SOLEDUCK FALLS	Rainbow Falls × Odm. Grand Tetons	Beall 1972
SUMMIT LAKE	Milt. Peru × Sunset Bay	Beall 1972 (W. W. G. Moir)
SUNSET BAY	Oda. Balek × Odtna. Ophelia	Beall 1967

× Milt. Peru = Summit Lake | × Mtdm. Cleopatra = Burr. Sanguine

TANMAN — Odtna. Tango × Oda. Ray Buckman — Dugger 1975

WARNEARA

PINKIE	Onc. Catherine Wilson × Rdtta. Hawaii	W. W. G. Moir 1972
RUBEN	Rdcm. Primi × Comp. macroplectron	Ruben 1975
STANLEY TABA	Rdtta. Henry Teuscher × Onc. onustum	W. W. G. Moir 1973

WARSCEWICZELLA

discolor (see *Cochleanthes discolor*†‡) species

WILKINSARA

GEMINI	Vdps. parishii × Ascda. Red Gem	Wilkins 1973
LOPBURI	Vdps. parishii × Ascda. Yip Sum Wah	Saengswang 1974
SAMPHAN	Ascda. Honwichai × Vdps. parishii	Tunprayoon 1975
THANASUWAT	Ascda. Medasand × Vdps. parishii	Thanasuwat 1975

WILSONARA

Grex	Parentage	Registrant
ACCOLADE	Oda. Carmine × Onc. concolor	Rod McLe[illegible]n Co. 1975
ACEMANDA	Onc. sphacelatum × Oda. Matanda	D[illegible]gger 1974
AUTUMN	Onc. tigrinum × Oda. Carmine	Rod McLellan [illegible]o. 1968
× Oda. Lautrix = Mem. Austin Carlton	× Odm. Quisto = Granados	
× Odm. Connero = San Dieguito		
CARDIFF	Odcdm. Tiger Butter × Oda. Dalmar	Dugger 1[illegible]
COMITAN	Jean Du Pont × Oda. Ray Buckman	Dugger 19[illegible]
GRANADOS	Autumn × Odm. Quisto	Dugger 1975
HARRY BROUGH	Oda. Liangera × Jean Du Pont	Dugger 1974
INSIGNIS	Odm. illustrissimum × Oncda. Charlesworthii	C. 1916
× Gom. recurva = Bbra. João Rodrigues		
JEAN DU PONT	Oda. Carmine × Onc. leucochilum	Rod McLellan Co. 1969
× Oda. Lautrix = Rixpont	× Oda. Matanda = Lillian May	
× Oda. Liangera = Harry Brough	× Oda. Ray Buckman = Comitan	
KURT RINNE	Onc. tigrinum × Oda. Marcris	Röllke 1975
LILLIAN MAY	Jean Du Pont × Oda. Matanda	Dugger 1975
MEMORIA AUSTIN CARLTON	Autumn × Oda. Lautrix	Dugger 1975
MEMORIA TOM LYLES	Odcdm. Incali × Oda. Ray Buckman	Dugger 1975
MORELIA	Onc. tigrinum × Oda. Florence Stirling	Dugger 1975
RED GALAXY	Onc. Goldiana × Oda. Carmine	Ruben 1974
RIXPONT	Jean Du Pont × Oda. Lautrix	Dugger 1975
ROCK ISLAND	Oda. Carmine × Onc. ventilabrum	Beall 1972
ROCKSLEY	Oncda. Crowborough × Oda. Anton	Mrs. D. V. Dickinson 1975 (Brian Smith)
SAN DIEGUITO	Autumn × Odm. Connero	Dugger 1975
SOLANA SURPRISE	Onc. tigrinum × Oda. Minel	Dugger 1975
SPACEMAN	Onc. sphacelatum × Oda. Ray Buckman	Dugger 1975
TIGERMAN	Odcdm. Tiger Butter × Oda. Ray Buckman	Dugger 1975
TIGER MOUNTAIN	Odcdm. Crowborough × Oda. Apricot Meadows	Beall 1972
TIGER TALK	Oda. Taw × Onc. tigrinum	Rod McLellan Co. 1974
TIGERWOOD	Onc. tigrinum × Oda. Doric	M. & H. 1973
WIDECOMBE FAIR	Oda. Florence Stirling × Onc. incurvum	Burnham 1973

YAMADARA

Grex	Parentage	Registrant
ASTRONAUT	Fantasy × Epi. atropurpureum	Muse's 1971
FANTASY	Blc. Freckles × Epi. phoeniceum	Small 1961
× Epi. atropurpureum = Astronaut		
HAWK'S NEST	Blc. Sunkist × Epi. gracile	Fort Caroline 1973 (Wallbrunn)
MIDNIGHT MAGENTA	Blc. Cinnamon Peak × Epi. gracile	Edelbrock 1972
OFFBEAT	Epi. guatemalense × Blc. Orange Sherbet	Stevenson 1973

YONEOARA

Grex	Parentage	Registrant
HADRIAN	Rnps. Lena Rowold × Rhy. gigantea	O. Kirsch 1972

YUSOFARA

Grex	Parentage	Registrant
NONG	Arnth. Anne Black × Ascda. Meda Arnold	Alsagoff 1972

ZYGOPETALUM

BLACKII†‡ — **crinitum × Perrenoudii** — **B. 1914**
× crinitum = John Banks

crinitum — **species**
× Bl[illegible] = John Banks

gr[illegible]nifolium — **species**
× intermedium = Skippy Ku

[illegible]andiflorum — **species**
(see *Mendoncella grandiflora*)

intermedium* — **species**
× graminifolium = Skippy Ku

JOHN BANKS — **Blackii × crinitum** — **Wyld Court 1975**

rostratum — **species**
(see *Zygosepalum labiosum‡*)

SKIPPY KU — **graminifolium × intermedium** — **Dr. B. C. Berliner 1975 (Kugust)**

ZYGOSEPALUM

labiosum‡ — **species**
(Syn. *Zygopetalum rostratum*; *Menadenium labiosum*)
× Btst. Silver Star = Plmra. Raymond Palmer